ACCOUNTING

FINANCIAL AND ORGANISATIONAL DECISION MAKING

CARNEGIE

JONES

NORRIS

WIGG

WILLIAMS

The McGraw-Hill Companies, Inc.

Sydney New York San Francisco Auckland
Bangkok Bogotá Caracas Hong Kong
Kuala Lumpur Lisbon London Madrid
Mexico City Milan New Delhi San Juan
Seoul Singapore Taipei Toronto

Irwin/McGraw-Hill

A Division of The McGraw-Hill Companies

Disclaimer

With respect to the use of case studies in this book, the authors and publisher have gone to considerable effort to ensure the practical authenticity of the accounting issues raised. The authors and publisher have refrained, however, from making judgements on any element or circumstance of any case study based on actual events and companies. The authors and publisher do not intend that anything written in the text should reflect on the legality or propriety of the events described in any case study, or on the business judgement shown by those individuals involved. Instead, the authors and publisher conclude that all such individuals acted appropriately and properly in the circumstances. It is fair and proper, however, to prompt readers of this book to consider how various individuals did act and the reason for their actions, based on the information available. Except in those case studies when a specific source is acknowledged, it is not intended that the names, dates, places and events in the case studies be identified with real persons or events.

Reprinted 1999

Text, illustrations & design © 1999 McGraw-Hill Book Company Australia Pty Limited

Additional owners of copyright material are credited in on-page credits.

National Library of Australia Cataloguing-in-Publication data:

Accounting: financial and organisational decision making

Includes index
ISBN 007 470 654 3.

1. Accounting—Decision making. I. Carnegie, Garry D.

657

Published in Australia by
McGraw-Hill Book Company Australia Pty Limited
4 Barcoo Street, Roseville NSW 2069, Australia
Acquisitions Editor: Julie McNab
Production Editors: Caroline Hunter and Felicity Shea
Permissions Editor: Leanne Peters
Indexer: Diane Harriman
Designed, illustrated and typeset by The Modern Art Production Group, Melbourne
Printed in Hong Kong by Best Tri Color Printing & Packaging co

Contents

Foreword

I am very pleased to express some introductory comments in relation to *Accounting: Financial and Organisational Decision Making* by the Deakin University author team comprising Carnegie, Jones, Norris, Wigg and Williams. It is several years now since the publication of the book on which this is based—Carrick Martin's *An Introduction to Accounting,* fourth edition. During the intervening years there have been many developments in the accounting profession and accounting education and, of course, in business and society in general. It is therefore gratifying to note the publication of this book and, in particular, the directions observed to have been taken.

Recent inquiries into accounting education in Australia and elsewhere have all called for accounting education to keep pace with the changes occurring in the business world. Enabling students to understand the role of accounting in decision making and its related impacts on organisations and society in general, while providing an introduction to accounting systems, is a key feature of this book. The structural organisation of this text allows educators maximum flexibility in combining or separating the teaching of theoretical and practical aspects of accounting.

Among the skills set required of today's accounting graduate, critical and analytical thinking, communication and interpersonal and negotiation skills are paramount. It is pleasing to observe that another key aim of this text is to develop and hone such skills by incorporating a case-based emphasis. The effective use of case studies, often drawn from real-life situations and organisations, enables students to become aware of the contentious nature of accounting and improves their ability to research, analyse and make decisions about a wide range of issues. It is also important for students to become aware of the ethical dimensions of the accounting profession and the types of situations they will almost inevitably encounter later in their professional life. The various ethical case studies and questions raised throughout the text are excellent tools for the achievement of this goal.

Finally, and perhaps most significantly, the impact of the ever-increasing globalisation of business activities provides an additional challenge for today's generation of accounting students. It is satisfying to note the commitment made in this text to an appreciation of the movement towards global harmonisation of accounting standards. Reproduction of the IASC *Framework* statement, as well as treatment of IAS standards alongside current Australian pronouncements, provides students with the opportunity to appreciate accounting as a truly cross-national profession.

This text is expected to provide students with a solid and well-rounded understanding of the complex and dynamic nature of accounting and assist in developing a range of skills that will prepare them well for the challenges that lie ahead.

David Boymal
National Director, Accounting and Auditing Standards
Ernst and Young
October 1998

A note on the origin of this book

This book is based upon *An Introduction to Accounting* fourth edition by Carrick Martin, Graeme Harrison, Jill McKinnon and Sue Wright. Their support and encouragement of this edition is greatly appreciated.

Preface

Accounting pervades all organisations in all countries. Its study solely within a national or local context is incompatible with the forces of globalisation and related moves for a single set of international accounting standards. This book places the study of accounting in an international context. It is based on Martin's *An Introduction to Accounting*, fourth edition, and enhances the conceptual focus of that book through the introduction of a case study emphasis.

The case studies featured in this book are drawn from real life situations or have been constructed to closely reflect practices and conditions in actual organisational contexts. Teaching accounting through the use of case studies does more than just place learning in its organisational and social contexts. It provides an effective way for students to research and analyse contemporary issues in accounting, as well as to solve problems and make decisions. Through a case-based emphasis, students come to understand the contentious nature of accounting and the role of assumptions and judgement in accounting decision making. Indeed, accounting turns out to be a controversial field of endeavour and is, perhaps to many, surprisingly intriguing.

We have sought to provide a solid theoretical foundation for understanding accounting. Since accounting practices in most countries are based on the same underlying principles, the theoretical framework enables the text to transcend national borders. We also provide an understanding of the fundamental processes of accounting. However, in today's competitive environment, accounting is not simply a numerical calculation exercise. In this book, accounting is considered in terms of its important role in organisational and social functioning. Students today are expected to learn more than just a set of accounting techniques and rules. They should come to understand accounting's central role in financial and organisational decision making. We attempt to make students aware of the impact of decision-making processes involving the use of accounting information on the structure and shape of organisations and also society in general. Rather than being a neutral, benign, technical practice, accounting is being increasingly regarded as social and organisational practice as its pervasiveness and consequences are subjected to closer examination.

The accounting profession's push for international harmonisation of accounting standards is a key consideration throughout this book. To this end, the International Accounting Standards Committee (IASC) conceptual framework and the International Accounting Standards (IAS) of that committee are addressed alongside the relevant Australian pronouncements where applicable. In our view, the use of international accounting pronouncements is a necessary pre-condition to locating and understanding accounting in an international context. We also place a concentration on management accounting which further extends the book's cross-national orientation.

The book comprises six parts: (1) Accounting in an international context; (2) The recording and external reporting focus; (3) Financial management; 4) The conceptual framework applied; (5) Accounting information systems; and (6) Accounting for management decisions. These parts need not be studied in sequence. The structure has been designed to foster considerable flexibility across the institutions using this book particularly in the structuring or restructuring of their first year accounting programs.

Various reviewers of the manuscript during the preparation phase of this work provided helpful and constructive comments. Nevertheless, it is impossible to please all tastes and preferences. Just as accounting is contested, so too is the subject of the structure and content of the 'ideal' first year accounting book. We have endeavoured to produce a book for the times—a modern work—yet based on its successful past which, in any case, must persist as a strong influence in this first rewrite. We trust the book is influential in expanding the horizons of students who are afforded the opportunity to use it in achieving their learning objectives. This book has been designed to develop and improve their analytical and critical thinking skills, communication skills and interpersonal and negotiation skills as well as their technical skills. All of these qualities are demanded today and will surely be demanded, even more strongly, in the next generation of accountants.

Enjoy the experience of accounting about to unfold!

Garry Carnegie
Stewart Jones
Gweneth Norris
Roy Wigg
Brian Williams
School of Accounting and Finance
Deakin University
October 1998

Acknowledgements

The authors are grateful to many people who contributed to this project in a variety of ways. Special thanks are extended to our colleague, Graeme Wines, who prepared Chapters 18 and 19 in this volume. Other academic colleagues in the School of Accounting and Finance are thanked for their preparedness to support the project in many different ways. The feedback provided by external reviewers was very much appreciated: Brian West (University of Ballarat), Barbara Burns (RMIT) and Len Therry (Edith Cowan University). Tom Lee of the University of Alabama also provided helpful comments in the early stages of this project on chapters dealing with historic cost and alternative accounting systems. Kym Brown, Jan Greenhill, Allison Oemcke, Denise Patterson and Zlatica Kovac provided valuable secretarial assistance in preparing manuscript for this book. The project became possible through the efforts of Julie McNab, Acquisitions Editor, McGraw-Hill, who placed her trust in the Deakin University author team and managed the project with good grace and enthusiasm. Caroline Hunter competently performed the role as editor with enthusiasm under tight timelines. Appreciation is also expressed to all other members of the McGraw-Hill production team. Finally, Carrick Martin, Graeme Harrison, Jill McKinnon and Sue Wright are thanked for providing the Deakin team with the opportunity to further develop and improve a text of long-standing prominence in its field.

Additional website resources

A dedicated web page has been set up for this textbook within McGraw-Hill's Accounting Supersite at **http://www.mcgraw-hill.com.au/mhhe/acc**. This site will provide lecturers with additional resources for teaching their course such as solutions to the text questions, PowerPoint™ slides for lectures, and computerised testing questions. Students will be able to access the PowerPoint™ slides for self study along with updates for the book and other useful websites.

PART 1

Accounting in an international context

CHAPTER 1
The accounting environment

Introduction

This chapter introduces the reader to the 'world of accounting'. It examines the meaning of accounting, and how this meaning has changed over time. The chapter also examines the roles and functions of accounting information in a number of social, economic and business contexts and settings. It will be seen that accounting information is not only an essential decision-making tool for business organisations, but also has great significance to the functioning of society itself. The wider social significance of accounting can best be understood and explained by reference to the diverse and sometimes complex environment in which accounting exists. Accounting both influences and is influenced by the environment in which it operates. Environmental factors that have shaped the development of accounting include: (1) the regulatory environment, (2) the economic decision-making environment, and (3) the international environment. Each of these aspects of the accounting environment has important implications for society. Together, they explain the relevance and pervasiveness of accounting in society.

Accounting defined

Accounting has been traditionally defined as the process of 'recording, classifying and reporting' the financial activities and transactions of a business enterprise.[1] The process of recording and classifying business transactions is commonly referred to as *bookkeeping*. The bookkeeping function of accounting still forms the foundation of much accounting activity and the early part of this textbook presents a broad outline of the traditional manual recording process. An accountant is usually defined as 'one who is skilled in accounting'.[2] At the beginning of the twentieth century, however, the role of the accountant did not extend much beyond a bookkeeping function, that is, the keeping of records according to a set of well-defined rules and procedures. At this time, accountants were generally referred to as 'bookkeepers'. In the business world of the late 1990s, the activities and responsibilities of accountants extend far beyond mere bookkeeping and the keeping of records. They include the interpretation and analysis of accounting reports, the design and operation of computer-based systems, the planning and conduct of business activities, and the understanding of complex accounting regulations that have accumulated over many years. This broad range of service is provided by accountants for both private sector enterprises and public sector organisations.

Accountants serve a potentially wide variety of user groups. The many different users of accounting information include the owners or shareholders of a business entity, the people who have lent money to the entity, the entity's employees, government regulatory agencies and other social and political interest groups, such as environmental groups and trade unions. In addition, internal users will need information to assist with managerial decisions regarding the discharge of accountability and the maintenance of competitive strategy. In providing information for these users, accountants frequently need to consider more than just financial factors. For example, in recent years ethical and environmental considerations have become particularly important. Accounting has a wide-ranging function and hence a broad definition of the field of accounting is needed, one that embraces the variety of professional activities engaged in by accountants.

Several years ago a committee of the American Accounting Association (an influential body whose members include the leading academics and practitioners in accounting) defined accounting beyond its mere traditional definition (the 'recording, classification and

---

[1] See W. W. Cooper and Y. Ijiri (eds), *Kohler's Dictionary for Accountants*, 6th edn, Prentice-Hill, Englewood Cliffs, NJ, 1983, p. 8.

[2] See definition of accounting in *Kohler's Dictionary for Accountants*, ibid.

reporting' of transactions). This committee defined accounting in a broader and more modern context as 'the process of identifying, measuring and communicating economic information to permit informed judgements and decisions by users of the information'.[3] This definition has won widespread acceptance because it covers the essential facets of accounting.

Primarily, accountants are concerned with 'communicating economic information'. As providers of information, they are similar to the newspaper or television reporter, the editor of a technical journal or the teacher. All must be skilful in conveying information concisely and accurately to their chosen audiences. As communicators, accountants are mainly interested in conveying 'economic information', by which is meant the results of financial transactions and events involving a firm. Using *financial statements*, accountants are capable of summarising the effects of a mass of seemingly unrelated financial events on an individual or an organisation. Further, internal users such as managers, require information about financial and non-financial aspects of operating activities.

Classification and summarisation are essential whenever it is desired to communicate information, since the human brain is incapable of comprehending masses of data in a short space of time. On television, a 30-minute news telecast summarises events in distant places, each consisting of many minor events that would take hours to relate in full. In communicating economic data through financial reports, the accountant acts in the same way to summarise the available information. The approach adopted is discussed in the first chapters of this book, which consider how relevant events are identified, measured and communicated to users in summary form.

The second aspect to the American Accounting Association's definition of accounting gives direction on what to communicate. The purpose of the information is to 'permit informed judgements and decisions by users of the information'. Just as the publisher of a technical journal selects articles relevant to the interests of subscribers, and the teacher, it is hoped, restricts the discussion to facts or concepts relevant to the assigned topic, the accountant must report on events that are useful to those who receive accounting reports.

To be useful, the information must be relevant for some decision the user is to make and it must assist in the choice between alternative courses of action. For example, to be told that it is raining in a neighbouring country is not useful unless, perhaps, one intends to fly there and suitable clothing must be selected. The accountant's purpose may therefore be found in the decisions the users of accounting information must make.

Key financial statements

The key financial statements are the *profit and loss statement*, the *balance sheet* and the *cash flow statement*. Only the profit and loss statement and balance sheet will be introduced in this chapter. A more detailed discussion of the financial statements is provided in Chapter 2 and also in Chapters 9 and 10.

The profit and loss statement reports the revenues, expenses and profit (or the surplus of revenues over expenses) that have been made during a given period. The statement shows how an entity's revenues were obtained and how the expenses were incurred. The profit and loss statement provides an important indication of the financial performance of the entity. The balance sheet lists the *assets* or resources of value controlled by the enterprise, its debts, and the owner's claim on the entity. The balance sheet provides an indication of the financial position of an entity at any given point in time. Some sample statements are shown on page 6. A sole trader has been chosen for illustrative purposes in this chapter.

---

[3] American Accounting Association, *A Statement of Basic Accounting Theory*, Florida, 1966, p. 1.

Reading the financial statements

The assets in our example begin with the bank balance of $1000. This is the most liquid of the assets but, since balances in bank accounts usually earn low interest, entities are not inclined to hold surplus cash beyond that required to meet immediate commitments. Accordingly, the Firstup Store has invested $3000 in shares in a company, Beep Ltd. These shares may be sold for cash and therefore are assets of Firstup Store.

PROFIT AND LOSS STATEMENT: FIRSTUP STORE
for the year ended 31 December 20X9

Sales revenue		$100 000
less Cost of goods sold		40 000
Gross profit		60 000
less Other expenses:		
Advertising	$ 9 000	
Wages	26 000	
Depreciation expense	2 000	
Interest on loans	5 000	42 000
Net profit		$ 18 000

BALANCE SHEET: FIRSTUP STORE
as at 31 December 20X9

Assets			Liabilities		
Cash at bank	$ 1 000		Accounts payable		$ 20 000
Shares in Beep Ltd	3 000		Mortgage loan		33 000
					53 000
Accounts receivable	8 000				
Inventory	25 000		**Owners' equity**		
Furniture & fittings			Capital	$61 000	
(*less* Depreciation)	30 000		*plus* Profit	18 000	
Land & buildings	60 000		*less* Withdrawals	5 000	74 000
	$127 000				$127 000

The balance owing on accounts receivable is an asset because it represents credit sales to customers against whom enforceable claims amounting to $8000 have been created. The amount for inventory represents the goods both in stock and unsold at the end of the year.

The furniture and fittings of $30 000 represent the various shop fittings and office furniture to be found in the retail store. This amount has been reduced by depreciation, a reduction for the gradual using up of the asset. The land and buildings are the most valuable resources held by the retail store and they benefit the trading activities of the store. All of these assets represent resources that the enterprise may use to earn revenue from sales, or which will produce cash for the enterprise to use.

The other side of the balance sheet acknowledges that each of these assets must be claimed by someone. The first claim on the assets belongs to those who have lent money or extended credit to the enterprise. These claims are known as *liabilities*. In the example, Firstup Store owes $20 000 to various accounts payable. These mainly represent the unpaid balance for purchases made on credit. It also owes $33 000 on a mortgage loan, presumably an amount borrowed when the land and the buildings were acquired.

The difference between the assets and the liabilities is called the *net assets*. Net assets represent the claim the owners of the enterprise have on the assets and is a residual claim to all assets not claimed by the liabilities. The term *owners' equity* will be used to describe this claim. For information purposes, the claim is shown in the balance sheet at $61 000 of contributed capital plus $13 000 of retained profits for the current year, which have been reinvested in the enterprise by its owner.

The balance sheet presents its information in conformity with the following identity:

$$assets = liabilities + owners' equity$$

The equation is true by definition since it has been stipulated that the assets remaining after settling claims by liabilities belong to the owners. To reflect this relationship, the equation may be rearranged to read:

$$assets - liabilities = owners' equity$$

The profit is what remains after the expenses of operations have been deducted from the revenue earned.

Revenue represents amounts earned during a period, usually by selling goods or performing services. Expenses consist of the outflows of resources that were necessary in order to earn the revenue for the period. The *net profit* is the difference between revenues and expenses and is the net surplus from business activities during the period. This surplus increases the net assets of the entity and it therefore increases the owners' stake in the enterprise.

The owner may decide to withdraw some or all of the profit for 'personal' use. This is known as a *withdrawal* and, in the balance sheet, it is deducted from the sum of the capital plus the profit to yield the capital remaining in the enterprise. In the present example, $13 000 of the profit has been retained in the enterprise to increase the capital.

In Firstup Store, the enterprise has earned revenue of $100 000 entirely from the sale of goods. These goods originally cost $40 000. It is useful to calculate a gross profit at this point. The selling price is often set as a mark-up on the cost of the goods and it is useful in such cases to determine what mark-up was actually obtained. Firstup Store achieved a gross margin of 60 per cent ($60 000/$100 000) and the mark-up on cost was 150 per cent ($60 000/$40 000).

The gross profit has to cover all of the other expenses, sometimes known as overhead, as well as to provide a profit for the proprietor of Firstup Store. In the example, the major expense was for wages, although a reasonable amount of advertising was undertaken. The depreciation expense consists of an amount by which the furniture and fittings were reduced as their benefits expired.

Published annual reports in many countries, including Australia, generally do not disclose the detailed information about revenues and expenses that appears in this example. Only limited disclosure of information is required by law and companies are reluctant to go beyond their legal requirements, possibly because they do not wish to disclose their detailed financial results to competitors. This means, unfortunately, that frequently the public is not given sufficient information to enable a full review of the company's trading activities to be conducted. Balance sheets, however, are more fully reported.

What are accounting entities?

This section examines the types of organisation (or accounting entities) for which accounting information, in the form of financial statements, is prepared. It also examines the information needs of those *external* to the entity who use these financial statements.

Chapter 2 introduces the role of the internal user and related information requirements. Part 6 covers this aspect of accounting in more detail. The external users include owners, lenders, government authorities and a wide range of other interested parties.

In accounting, the reporting (or accounting) entity is considered to be *separate* from its owners, who are therefore regarded as external parties. An accounting entity is the area of activity in which users of accounting information have an interest. Accounting entities may include an individual, a company, a company branch office, a professional practice, a club, a government department or a small business enterprise. The owners are variously called shareholders, partners or proprietors, depending on the form of legal organisation they adopt. The emergence of greater interest in government enterprises and in the public sector generally has revealed that these entities have broadly similar information needs to private sector entities.

Sole proprietorships

The simplest form of ownership is the sole proprietor. Many small businesses are owned by one person. No particular legal formalities are required to commence operations, although it is common practice to set up a business bank account and operate under a business name, which must, in certain circumstances, be registered. Amounts contributed to the business by the owner are called capital.

As noted above, for accounting purposes the business is considered separate from the owner, although in law the two are one and the owner remains liable for all business debts. The sole trader form of ownership is designed for the small business.

Most businesses exist to make profits. Owners may withdraw funds obtained from profitable trading for their personal use, or may choose to reinvest them in the business. If desired, they may also withdraw previous contributions of capital.

The owner usually manages the business and the decisions to be made therefore include those to be discussed later for management. The owner typically must decide:

- whether to invest more capital or to withdraw capital from the business
- how much profit to withdraw
- whether to expand the business, sell out or cease operations
- whether the business is financially stable.

These decisions overlap; for example, the owner might decide to invest more capital by leaving the profit in the business.

Partnerships

As with sole proprietorships, partnerships are not separate legal entities from their owners and in law they remain 'unincorporated'. The partners are personally liable for any debts contracted by the partnership and, if necessary, may follow the partnership into bankruptcy. The partners are the partnership and should a partner die the partnership is normally dissolved.

The decisions of partners are similar to those of the sole trader, with one important added responsibility. The partners must be able to assess their respective claims on the partnership. The partners may agree on how much capital each will contribute and how much each may withdraw as salaries, interest, or as a share of the profit. In the absence of a formal agreement, a Partnership Act normally applies that requires the partners to share all profits equally. For most partnerships, no more than 20 partners may be admitted.

The desire to safeguard the individual claims of each partner creates an important need for accounting information. Records must be maintained of capital contributions, withdrawals and the sharing of profits so that the partners can decide how much they may withdraw or, alternatively, will need to contribute as additional capital to maintain the partnership.

Shareholders in companies

In this section a brief introduction is given to some of the terminology that will be used throughout the book. Almost all larger businesses are incorporated as companies, limited by share capital. Their shareholders enjoy limited liability status. Capital is contributed by making payment for *shares* in the company. The company is created as a separate legal entity from its owners who, in most cases, are not personally liable for the debts of the company beyond amounts unpaid on their shares. The term *limited* (Ltd) after a company's name acknowledges that the liability of the shareholder is limited. *Unlimited liability* companies exist but are rare. Since companies are independent legal entities, their existence is not affected by the death of a shareholder or a change in ownership.

Proprietary Limited (Pty Ltd) companies abound, and they are generally small, privately owned companies or companies owned by other companies. There must be at least one but no more than 50 shareholders. The transfer of ownership shares is restricted and proprietary companies are generally not permitted to advertise for the contribution of funds, either by way of share capital or through loans.

Companies that are not proprietary companies are known as public companies. They must have at least one member, but there is no maximum number. They may advertise for funds and ownership shares may be bought and sold freely. The prices at which a company's shares are traded will fluctuate according to investors' beliefs about the value of each share. Many public companies are listed on stock exchanges, which are organised markets for the trading of shares and other securities.

What decisions must investors or shareholders make? In valuing shares, investors need to evaluate the progress of the company. This task is difficult, because most investors in modern companies are remote from the day-to-day operations. A large company might have thousands of shareholders spread across the globe. Obviously, they cannot all manage the company and, accordingly, the shareholders elect a board of directors to act for them. The directors, in turn, appoint managers to supervise the day-to-day operations of the company. However, the directors retain the responsibility to ensure that shareholders' interests are always prominent when decisions are being made.

The directors are required each year to call an *annual general meeting* of shareholders. The decisions to be made at this meeting include:

- the election of directors for the coming year
- the appointment of an auditor to examine the profit and loss statement and balance sheet
- determination of the *dividend*, which is the proportion of the profit to be paid out to shareholders as a return for their investment.

In making these decisions, the investors require an account of the *directors' stewardship*, meaning their activities as custodians of the funds entrusted to them by the shareholders. This is contained in an *annual report*, which includes statements by the directors on the progress of the company and their expectations for the future. Also included in the annual report is the profit and loss statement and the balance sheet.

Public companies, and those proprietary companies owned by other companies, must make their reports available to the public. Other proprietary companies, which are called *small proprietary companies*, need not reveal their results to the public.

The company's accountant prepares the financial statements for the annual report. It is the directors' responsibility to ensure that these reports give a 'true and fair' representation of the company's activities. However, since the company's accountants, as employees, are responsible to the directors, and since the report will be used to evaluate the directors, a further step is taken to ensure that the reports are 'true and fair' and not disguised to mislead the shareholders as to the achievements of the directors. In all public companies and in some proprietary companies an *auditor* must be appointed by the shareholders to make an independent examination of the financial statements. The auditor is usually a firm of public accountants. A report by the auditor is included in the annual report.

As owners, shareholders must make some important decisions, including the following:

1. Should the directors be reappointed? In making this decision, shareholders require an account of the year's financial performance. This can be compared with performance in previous years or with the results of other companies.
2. What dividend should be paid? The dividend is the amount a shareholder receives in a distribution of the profits. Dividends may not be paid unless the company has profits available for distribution. Otherwise, the dividend would amount to a return of capital. In practice, the full profit is rarely distributed. Profits are retained in the company to cope with unexpected future commitments, to cope with higher costs due to inflation, or to allow the company to grow. Reinvested profits are a major source of funds for expanding businesses.

   In deciding how much dividend to pay, shareholders normally vote to endorse an amount recommended by the directors. In approving a recommended dividend, a shareholder must know how much profit was available for distribution and, if profits are to be retained, what purposes are to be served by the retained profits. Again, the shareholder is in need of financial information that accounting reports are intended to provide.
3. If the management desires either to close down or to 'liquidate', the shareholder would want to know what cash is likely to be received before agreeing to the liquidation.

These decisions, made at meetings of shareholders, are often left to those with major shareholdings in the company. When shares are traded on a stock exchange, the shareholder has a simpler way of expressing dissatisfaction with the company, that of selling the shares and allowing the new shareholder to contend with the poor management or meagre dividends. The decision to sell shares, or to buy them if the prospects are good, is probably the only decision many shareholders will consider.

Public sector proprietorships

The public sector in Australia refers to federal and state governments, local councils and all associated structures that they own or control such as departments, statutory authorities, boards and commissions, and business enterprises such as certain transportation services.

Many public sector business enterprises have broadly similar organisational structures to the private sector, and therefore have similar financial reports. Nevertheless it should be remembered that they are unique for a number of reasons. First, public sector proprietorship is ownership on behalf of constituents, that is, taxpayers. Public sector entities manage the resources available to them on the public's behalf. Second, the objective of the enterprise is not focused solely on making profits. Unlike private sector organisations, which have in common the profit motive, public sector business enterprises are generally set up to provide a service that, for a variety of reasons, would not be provided at an acceptable price, quantity or quality without government intervention. Public sector business enterprises are not ultimately dependent on the profit motive for their existence, and profit generation is only one of many considerations for public sector entities. Some of their other objectives may include efficiency, effectiveness, equality, growth, stability, or the promotion of social welfare, culture, defence, history, education or environmental considerations. These are complex matters on which to report.

In former times it was commonly believed that a fairly simple form of accounting would suffice for public sector organisations. A statement of cash receipts and payments was often all that was available. However, as governments have become increasingly accountable for their stewardship of community resources, and as more sophisticated management has been adopted within public sector entities, the requirements for accounting information to support decisions are now as demanding as those of the private sector.

While many of the accounting concepts in later chapters are developed within a framework of private sector entities, it should be borne in mind that the principles are equally applicable in the public sector.

The environment of accounting

So far we have briefly introduced the meaning of accounting, the nature of financial statements and the types of accounting entities that prepare financial statements. In this section we discuss how accounting influences, and is influenced by, the environment that surrounds it. There are many features and dimensions to the environment of accounting. These dimensions provide much of the richness and diversity of the accounting discipline, as well as explaining its importance in society. As mentioned in the introduction to this chapter, the environment of accounting includes the regulatory environment, the economic decision-making environment and the international environment. All of these facets of the accounting environment are, to some extent at least, interdependent. Furthermore, all three environmental influences on accounting impact on society more generally. These interdependencies are summarised in Figure 1.1.

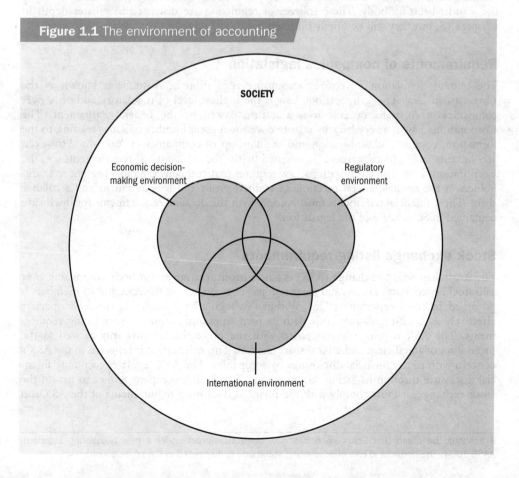

Figure 1.1 The environment of accounting

We will first discuss each of the 'inner circles' of Figure 1.1, the regulatory, economic decision-making and international environments of accounting. We will then examine how each of these 'inner circles' impact on the 'outer circle' (society) in Figure 1.1.

The regulatory environment

The work of the practising accountant is governed by a wide range of accounting regulations, some of which have already been alluded to earlier in the discussion on accounting entities. Accounting regulations form the rules and principles that govern the structure, content, audit and disclosure of financial information. The ethical responsibilities of accountants in performing their professional accounting duties are also governed by a number of regulations.

Accounting regulations are principally designed to protect investors, creditors and other users from potential financial losses associated with fraudulent, misleading or poor-quality financial statements. High-quality financial statements, which are deemed to reflect a 'true and fair' view of an entity's performance and financial position, are not only essential for protecting individual investors against potential losses, but they play an important role in maintaining credibility and confidence in our financial systems and institutions, and the business community more generally.

Regulations must be followed by professional accountants or they risk punitive measures which can be imposed by the law and/or by the disciplinary processes of the accounting profession. In Australia, for instance, there are essentially three main sources of accounting regulation: (1) the requirements of companies legislation, (2) the Australian Stock Exchange listing requirements for public companies, and (3) accounting standards issued by the standard-setting body. These sources of regulation are discussed in greater depth in Chapter 13, but they will be briefly outlined here.

Requirements of companies legislation

The relevant legislation governing accounting regulation in Australia is known as the *Corporations Law*. The Corporations Law is the highest level of regulatory authority over companies in Australia because it is a statute passed by the Federal Parliament. The Corporations Law is a very lengthy statute covering a great number of issues relating to the formation, conduct, administration and winding-up of companies in Australia. However, accountants are generally more concerned with the accounting requirements of the Corporations Law. The Corporations Law requires that company directors present to shareholders at the annual general meeting an audited profit and loss statement and a balance sheet. These financial statements must comply with the detailed requirements for disclosure contained in Schedule 5 of the legislation.[4]

Stock exchange listing requirements

The Australian Stock Exchange (ASX) is a non-profit, private sector body comprising over 100 stockbroker corporations and partnerships. The conduct of the ASX and its members is governed by the Corporations Law. Within this legislative framework, the ASX operates effectively as a self-regulatory body with its own strict and comprehensive listing requirements. The ASX is primarily concerned with the protection of investors as well as the promotion of an efficient and ethical share-market. This orientation is reflected in the ASX's concern with timely financial disclosures by companies. The ASX regulates corporate financial disclosure through its listing requirements. That is, if a company wishes to list on the stock exchange, it must comply with the financial disclosure requirements of the ASX and

---

[4] It should be noted that Schedule 5 has now been subsumed under a new accounting standard, AASB 1034. The nature and role of accounting standards is discussed in the next section.

other listing requirements. These requirements, like those of the Corporations Law, have traditionally been concerned with disclosure rather than with technical accounting issues such as the different ways to measure and classify transactions in the financial statements. Australian accounting standards provide the detailed rules for measuring and classifying accounting transactions.

Accounting standards

Accounting standards provide detailed rules on how particular types of financial transactions and other events should be dealt with in an entity's accounting records. Accounting standards, for example, explain how different types of assets should be valued and how they should be set out and disclosed in the financial statements. Accounting standards help to ensure that an entity's profit and loss statement and balance sheet represent a 'true and fair' representation of its performance and financial position. Many countries in the world, including Australia, prepare accounting standards. Accounting standards are also set at the international level by the International Accounting Standards Committee (IASC). As we will see in a later section, a major objective of the IASC is to develop an internationally compatible set of accounting standards which, hopefully, all countries can readily adopt. At present, accounting standards around the world tend to differ from country to country, and have varying degrees of enforceability.

Accounting standards in Australia are issued by the Australian Accounting Standards Board (AASB) and the Public Sector Accounting Standards Board (PSASB). Accounting standards issued by the AASB are know as *Approved Australian Accounting Standards*. The AASB is given authority under the Corporations Law to issue accounting standards that are legally binding on all publicly listed companies in Australia. In other words, all listed companies must comply with the provisions and requirements of Approved Australian Accounting Standards. Company directors and professional accountants who do not comply with these standards risk a variety of punitive measures which can be imposed under the law, such as fines and imprisonment.

Accounting standards issued by the PSASB are known as professional accounting standards, or 'AAS' standards. These standards apply to public sector entities and not-for-profit entities in the private sector. Although compliance with these standards does not have the force of law under the Corporations Law, they are required to be adopted by public sector entities in various public sector regulations, such as in the State of Victoria the *Victorian Financial Reporting Act 1989*.

Because accounting standards deal with the detailed aspects of disclosure and measurement in the financial statements, the release of a new accounting standard can have important consequences for an entity. For example, accounting standards often impact on the profitability and financial position of companies, which in turn influences the economic decisions of users such as investors and lenders. Consider an accounting standard that increases a company's debt levels or reduces company profit. Such a standard is likely to be opposed by managers who may want, for example, to negotiate with bankers for a significant loan advancement. The banker in question may be prompted to increase the interest rate on the loan or request greater security for the loan. Furthermore, managers may be concerned about the adverse effects of such a standard on perceptions of their own performance in the marketplace or on the share price of the company.

Because accounting standards can have important economic consequences for companies, it is common for powerful business groups to lobby against the AASB, either to prevent an 'unpopular' accounting standard from being released or to have it significantly amended. These lobbying activities against the AASB by business interests have greatly increased the politicisation of the process of setting accounting standards in Australia, an issue which is explored in greater deal in Chapter 13.

The economic decision-making environment

It was mentioned earlier in this chapter that the function of accounting is to communicate 'economic information to permit informed judgements and decisions by users of the information'. The relationship between financial statements, economic decisions and users is summarised in Figure 1.2.

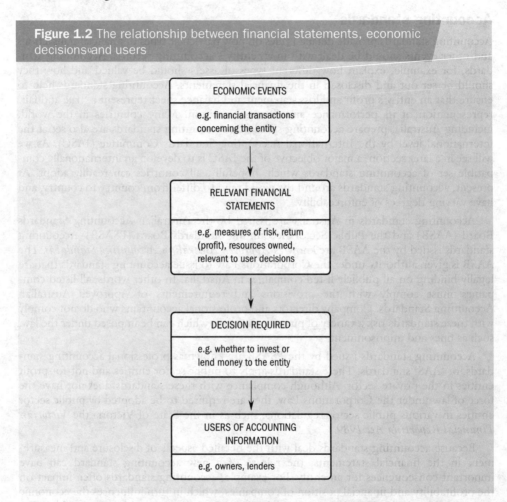

Figure 1.2 The relationship between financial statements, economic decisions and users

ECONOMIC EVENTS

e.g. financial transactions concerning the entity

RELEVANT FINANCIAL STATEMENTS

e.g. measures of risk, return (profit), resources owned, relevant to user decisions

DECISION REQUIRED

e.g. whether to invest or lend money to the entity

USERS OF ACCOUNTING INFORMATION

e.g. owners, lenders

Who then are the users of financial statements, and what kinds of economic decisions do they make? There are several categories of users, and they make a variety of economic decisions based on company financial statements. The users of the financial statements include investors, lenders and others.

Investors

Investors are usually the shareholders or owners of a company. Shareholders purchase a company's share capital with the expectation of receiving a satisfactory return on their investment. Shareholders usually look for return on their investment in two forms: *dividend payments* and *capital gain* (increases in the share price). The return on investment needs to be commensurate with the level of risk. The higher the perceived risk of an investment, the higher will be the expected return required by investors, and vice versa. Shareholders need accounting information to help them (1) determine whether they should buy, hold or sell their share investments, and (2) to assess the ability of an entity to pay dividends.

Lenders

Lenders are of various types and are usually termed *creditors*. They may be long-term or short-term and their loans may or may not carry a fixed rate of interest. Lenders have priority over investors for repayment when an entity is wound up. Lenders need accounting information in order to assess the risk of their loans, that is, the likelihood that the borrower will be able to meet the interest and principal repayment terms of the loan. Lenders may require a higher interest and/or greater security from a borrower who is perceived to possess higher risk.

Short-term lenders

Suppliers of inventory commonly demand payment within 30 days. Normally, no interest is charged and a discount may be offered for early payment. Other short-term debts might be for electricity, telephone, other utilities and various services.

Short-term lenders need to assess whether the enterprise will remain stable for the period of the loan and whether future cash flows from earnings will be sufficient to cover repayments of the loan plus interest.

Long-term lenders

Any entity may attempt to borrow long-term funds by offering its assets as security for the loan. Land and buildings may be purchased, for example, by giving the seller, or a bank or finance company, a mortgage over the property in return for a loan. If repayments are not made, the property is forfeited.

Companies generally have greater borrowing opportunities than other forms of organisation. They may issue *debentures*, which are secured either by specific assets (mortgage debentures), or by a general floating charge over the company's assets. Public companies may offer debentures for sale to the general public.

Debenture certificates normally carry a fixed rate of interest. Debentures of large companies are listed on the stock exchange and may be traded at the going price.

Companies may also issue unsecured notes, which are effectively debentures without security. They may also issue notes that are convertible into shares at some later date, known as convertible notes.

Long-term lenders have a longer-term perspective. They must determine the likelihood that the entity will collapse prior to repayment of the loan. They also must form an opinion about whether the future expected cash flows from trading activities will cover interest commitments. These concerns are close to those of the shareholder. Both parties are concerned with returns, but the lender is concerned solely that the return should be sufficient to meet repayments, whereas the shareholder wishes to maximise future returns. Both are concerned with the risk of failure.

Other external users

Accounting information is also used as the basis of taxation returns. These reports are prepared in accordance with taxation law, which differs in certain respects from the principles of valuation to be discussed in this book. Accounting is concerned with a measure of profit useful for decision making, whereas taxation law is concerned with such principles as obtaining a fair distribution of the tax burden according to the taxpayer's ability to pay. In many cases, therefore, taxable income differs substantially from accounting profit.

Taxpayers, ratepayers and social interest groups, such as those concerned with environmental protection or the welfare of disadvantaged groups, are also important users of accounting information. Ratepayers, for example, may wish to ascertain whether a special levy earmarked for a particular community project has been used for that purpose and in an efficient manner.

Other users of accounting information include employees, who are interested in knowing whether the organisation is able to continue, or perhaps whether it can sustain higher wage payments without incurring losses. Accounting information is also used in assessing tariffs and customs duties and in the deliberations of investigatory commissions established to determine whether particular industries require assistance from the government. Further, accounting information provides a host of statistical data for economic analysis, including calculation of the national income. These are but some of the uses of accounting information.

The international accounting environment

The world's business and commercial environment of the late 1990s is, in many respects, very different from earlier decades. The rapid globalisation of the world's finance and consumer markets, the increasing internationalisation of business activities, particularly the proliferation of multinational corporations, has created numerous financial and economic interdependencies in international commerce. Features of today's international business environment have been captured as follows:

> We approach the 21st Century knowing that global events will increasingly affect our lives. New nations and new economic powers are emerging. As a result, old alliances are changing, and there are shifts in the well-worn patterns of trade and international commerce. The dismantling of the former Soviet Union, the fast-growing economies of South-East Asia, the integration of the European Community, and the implementation of the North American Free Trade Agreement all illustrate the dramatic changes that are under way. Advances in computer and communications technology are also having their impact. For example, currency markets are open continuously, 24 hours a day, as they move around the world from New York to Tokyo to London to New York. Foreign exchange trading now stands at $1 trillion per day. Information can travel long distances quickly, and it is increasingly easier and cheaper to get. Indeed, new technology makes the internationalisation of product and finance markets possible. Corporations, too, are making themselves over to adapt to the global economy. Flexibility is the key as more and more of them reorganise as networks and stress interdependent alliances and strategic partnerships with other companies, rather than self-sufficiency in all areas. Information, including accounting information, is a critical resource in these makeovers, supporting the linkages both internally and with the outside world.[5]

These are at least some of the prominent reasons why the international environment of accounting has now become more important than ever. In the same manner that countries around the world have different cultural, political, economic and legal systems, so too do they have different accounting regulations and practices. No two countries have produced a completely identical approach to accounting regulation and practice. For example, companies in Australia are permitted under existing regulations to report changes in the value of certain assets such as land and buildings and plant and equipment. In the United States companies are not permitted to report changes in the value of such assets in their financial statements.

At least four factors can contribute to differences in accounting regulations and practices in different countries. These factors include:

- *State of economic development.* National economies around the world vary in terms of the extent of their economic development.
- *State of business complexity.* National economies vary in terms of their technological and industrial know-how, creating differences in their business needs as well as their business output. This can also influence accounting diversity.
- *Shade of political persuasion.* National economies vary in terms of their political systems, from the centrally controlled economy to the market-oriented economy.

---

5 See G. Mueller, H. Gernon and G. Meek, *Accounting: An International Perspective*, Irwin, 3rd edn, 1994, p. vii.

- *Reliance on some particular system of law.* National economies vary in terms of their supporting legal system. They may rely on either a common-law system or a code-law system; they may have protective legislation and unfair trade and competition laws, for example.[6]

Notwithstanding that no one country has exactly the same accounting standards, regulations and practices as another, it is possible to group the different countries of the world under different accounting approaches. Mueller, Gernon and Meek (1994, pp. 8–13) use at least four different models to classify the accounting approaches of different nations around the world. These models include (1) the British–American model, (2) the Continental model, (3) the South American model, and (4) the mixed economy model. Figure 1.3 shows how these authors grouped the nations of the world.

Figure 1.3 Four major accounting models and selected countries

British–American model

Australia	India	Panama
Bahamas	Indonesia	Papua New Guinea
Barbados	Ireland	Philippines
Benin	Israel	Puerto Rico
Bermuda	Jamaica	Singapore
Botswana	Kenya	South Africa
Canada	Liberia	Tanzania
Cayman Islands	Malawi	Trinidad & Tobago
Central America	Malaysia	Uganda
Colombia	Mexico	United Kingdom
Cyprus	Netherlands	United States
Dominican Republic	New Zealand	Venezuela
Fiji	Nigeria	Zambia
Ghana	Pakistan	Zimbabwe
Hong Kong		

Continental model

Algeria	Germany	Norway
Angola	Greece	Portugal
Austria	Guinea	Senegal
Belgium	Italy	Sierra Leone
Burkina	Ivory Coast	Spain
Cameroon	Japan	Sweden
Denmark	Luxembourg	Switzerland
Egypt	Mali	Togo
Finland	Morocco	Zaire
France		

South American model

Argentina	Chile	Paraguay
Bolivia	Ecuador	Peru
Brazil	Guyana	Uruguay

continues

[6] See also A. R. Belkaoui and S. Jones, *Accounting Theory*, Harcourt Brace, Sydney, 1996, p. 581. Taken from G. G. Mueller, H. Gernon and G. K. Meek, *Accounting: An International Perspective*, Irwin, New York, 1986, pp. 92–3.

Figure 1.3 continued

Mixed economy model		
Armenia	Hungary	Russia
Azerbaidzhan	Kazakhstan	Serbia
Belorussia	Kirgizia	Slovak Republic
Bosnia-Herzegovina	Latvia	Slovenia
Bulgaria	Lithuania	Tadzhikstan
Croatia	Moldavia	Turkmenistan
Czech Republic	Poland	Ukraine
Estonia	Romania	Uzbekistan
Georgia		

Mueller et al. (1994, pp. 8–12) also identified the accounting characteristics of each of the four models. The following description of the models has been reproduced or paraphrased (where appropriate) from Mueller's work:

British–American model

- Accounting is orientated to the economic decision-making needs of user groups, such as investors and creditors.
- Accounting education levels are high, and users of financial statements tend to be sophisticated.
- These countries typically have well-developed accounting standards.
- These countries also possess many large, multinational corporations.

Continental model

- Nations in this grouping include most of continental Europe and Japan.
- Companies in this jurisdiction tend to have very close ties to their banks, which supply most of their capital needs.
- Financial accounting is more legalistic in its orientation, and accounting practices tend to be quite conservative.
- Accounting is not primarily oriented towards the economic decision-making needs of users.
- Accounting information is often designed to satisfy government-imposed requirements, such as computing income taxes or demonstrating levels of compliance with the national government's macroeconomic plan.
- Generally, French-speaking African countries follow the Continental financial accounting model.

South American model

- Nations in this model include most countries in South America. With the exception of Brazil, the citizens of which speak Portuguese, these nations share a common language—Spanish. They also share a common cultural heritage.
- What distinguishes the South American model from the British–American and Continental models is the persistent use of accounting adjustments for inflation. These countries have necessarily gained a great deal of experience in coping with inflation, and in dealing with the associated accounting ramifications.
- Generally speaking, accounting is oriented towards the needs of government planners, and uniform practices are imposed on accounting entities.

Mixed economy model

- The political upheavals in Eastern Europe and the former Soviet Union, between 1989 and 1991 in particular, have resulted in a model that incorporates elements of tight central economic planning and control as well as market-oriented enterprise activities.
- Where this form of model applies, enterprises typically operate dual accounting systems. One system typically produces information for managers who are used to the former system, which is oriented towards a command economy. This system relies heavily on uniform charts of accounts and budgeted rather than actual financial information. The other system has a capitalist market orientation, and attempts to emulate the British–American accounting model. The focus is to provide information primarily for investors, bankers and corporate financial analysts from capitalist countries.
- Reconciling these two very different conceptual approaches to financial accounting has proven to be a difficult if not impossible task.

The different systems or models identified above are likely to affect the development of accounting regulation, and to explain the diversity of accounting practices used from one country to another.

Harmonisation of accounting standards

It can be seen from Figure 1.3 that there is a wide diversity in accounting standards and principles in countries around the world. To combat international diversity, there have been many calls to harmonise the accounting standards of the world. Harmonisation entails developing internationally compatible accounting standards that every country can adopt. If successful, harmonisation of accounting standards will result in business entities in different countries preparing financial statements on the same or a similar basis of accounting. Harmonisation would produce a number of benefits. For instance, some countries, particularly developing nations, have not fully developed their own set of accounting standards and principles. An internationally accepted set of accounting standards would allow developing nations to immediately become part of the mainstream of accepted international accounting standards. Another benefit of harmonisation is that companies which need to raise finance in foreign markets may find this process easier if their financial statements are consistent and comparable with a commonly accepted set of international accounting standards. In the case of Australia, it would enable foreign investors to more readily evaluate the performance and financial position of Australian companies relative to other companies in the international business arena.

However, there are limitations to harmonisation as well. As can be seen in Figure 1.3, many countries around the world adopt different approaches to accounting regulation and practice. Such wide differences could render international harmonisation a difficult if not impossible task. Chapter 13 reviews in greater detail the pros and cons of the international harmonisation effort, and particularly the role Australia is playing in these initiatives.

Accounting and society

As indicated by Figure 1.1, accounting has the potential to have a very pervasive influence on society itself. The relationships expressed in Figure 1.1 indicate that society is affected by accounting through the regulatory environment, the economic decision-making environment and the international environment of accounting. Let us now briefly consider the impact of each of these factors on society.

The regulatory environment and society

The pervasiveness and influence of accounting in society can be explained, at least in part, by the observation that the modern business corporation has become an increasingly integrated part of the social fabric. Companies provide much of the world's employment, consumer products/services and technology. The economic progress and standards of living of the industrialised world have depended to a significant extent on business enterprise. Companies are also a major source of government revenue, through company income tax and other taxes. This revenue is used to fund, among other things, social welfare and economic programs, and to maintain a satisfactory standard of living.

On the negative side, companies are a major contributor to pollution and environmental damage in the world. Furthermore, companies that fail (whether due to fraudulent or culpable managerial behaviour, mismanagement or poor business dealings) can cause incalculable damage to local communities and economies and, in some circumstances, the national and international economies. For instance, as was demonstrated in recent corporate history in Australia, the failure of companies can cause significant social distress and dislocation, through loss of employment to workers, loss of revenue for the government, loss of investment by shareholders and creditors and loss of products/services for consumers. The collapse of many corporations all at once, as occurred in Australia and other countries after the international stock-market crash in October 1987, can cause deep economic recession.

These are some of the reasons why companies have become more tightly regulated and closely monitored by government regulatory agencies in recent years. Just as the business corporation has become more embedded in the social fabric, so too has accounting. This is partly because accounting information is often likened to the 'road map' of the corporation. The linkages here between accounting and cartography are well founded. Accounting is widely recognised as the only viable information source that can display where an organisation is going in a financial sense, how well it is achieving its profit-making objectives and whether managers are using resources in a manner consistent with organisational objectives.

Accounting information can display whether the performance of managers has been superlative or otherwise, and it can also signal warnings of impending business distress and ultimately collapse. The most visible signal of impending company collapse is when the cash-flow position of a company can no longer sustain the cost of operations, particularly fixed commitments such as interest payments on loans. It is mainly accounting records that are capable of communicating such precise and crucial financial details to managers and users.

As mentioned earlier in this chapter, the importance of accounting information to users has been recognised in companies legislation and other forms of accounting regulation. Regulation imposes considerable responsibilities on accounting entities and professional accountants to produce relevant and reliable financial statements for economic decision-making and accountability purposes. Considered historically, the purpose behind accounting regulation is to afford a framework of protection to society, particularly against the production of potentially fraudulent, misleading or poor-quality financial statements which, among other things, can mask the true financial position of a company.

Accounting in its regulatory context impacts on society in other important ways. We discussed above the users who rely on financial information for economic decision making. These users collectively represent the 'stakeholders' of a company. Many of these stakeholders participate, directly or indirectly, in an entity's revenue or profit. Investors or shareholders obtain their share of the profit in terms of dividends. Lenders obtain their share of the profit in terms of interest and principal payments. Government obtains its share of the profit in terms of tax collection. Suppliers and other trade creditors obtain their share of the profit in terms of payment of invoices. Managers and employees obtain their share in terms of wages, bonuses and other remuneration. Each of the user groups is assumed to have a vested economic interest in maximising their share of an entity's 'revenue pie'. This can lead to conflicts of self-interest among the users, and perhaps even attempts by some parties (such as managers) to manipulate profit information in order to achieve more of the 'revenue pie' at the expense of other parties (such as the shareholders). Hence, accounting regulations and principles that guide the determination of an entity's profit figure could have an important role in the process of establishing social equity and equanimity among potentially competing and conflicting interests in the business arena.[7]

Accounting information can serve numerous other social equity functions. Consider the following examples:

- Accounting information, particularly profit information, is often an important factor in conflicts between trade unions and employers in battles for wage increases and improvements in working conditions. Employer groups may support, resist or amend demands for wage increases by unions on the basis of an entity's profitability information.
- Many large corporations provide essential services to the community, such as in the banking, communications and transportation industries. Governments can, from time to time, exert influence over such organisations because of the essential nature of the services. The financial position of large companies such as the National Australia Bank and Telstra, in the case of Australia, are often under public scrunity. If these industries disclose high sustained profits in the financial statements, the government can put these industries under pressure not to increase the prices of their services, among other things. For example, the Australian government has been known to pressurise banks from time to time not to increase bank fees or interest rates at times when the industry has recorded record profits.
- Governments can subsidise struggling industries such as farming and agriculture in times of drought or banks and financial institutions in times of financial crisis and panic. Again, accounting records are the basis for determining the degree of financial distress.
- Many government services are provided on a 'user pays' basis, such as public health, transportation and education. The price charged for essential services to the community is often based on the financial cost of providing the service. Detailed cost information is invariably provided by accounting records, notwithstanding that the assumptions in determining such costs are often contentious.
- Accounting information has an important role in the redistribution of wealth throughout the community. Companies must legally pay income tax on their net profit figures. The taxation of company profit provides a significant source of income to government to fund crucial social and economic programs in the community, such as social security distributions, health care, education and development and maintenance of infrastructure assets (such as roads and bridges). Determination of an entity's net profit is ascertainable only from the relevant accounting records.

Economic decision-making environment and society

We have seen that accounting's regulatory environment impacts on society in many ways. The economic decision-making environment also pervades society in a number of ways. Accounting's decision-making environment is concerned with the efficient allocation of scarce economic resources. The end goal of efficient resource allocation is growth of the economy. As was discussed above, all users of accounting information are concerned with the allocation of scarce economic resources. Needless to say, all users, assuming they are rational decision makers, are concerned about allocating their scarce resources as efficiently as possible.

The *Oxford Dictionary* defines 'efficiency' in terms of the 'ratio of useful work performed to energy expended'. This is an input to output relationship, or, in other words, what you get in return (output) for what is sacrificed or expended (input). To an investor, this is translated into the following: What return do I get on my investment? Is the return satisfactory, given the relative riskiness of the investment? To a lender, the question may be: Is the interest rate I get a sufficient return on the funds advanced, given the risk of the loan? Suppliers and other trade creditors are concerned with whether amounts owing to them will be paid on a timely basis. Their question might be: Should I extend credit terms to

---

[7] See A. C. Littleton, *Structure of Accounting Theory*, American Accounting Association, New York, 1953.

Company A or Company B? From which of the two companies am I most likely to get timely repayment?

Accounting information is an important guide to users in making efficient resource allocations. Accounting information discloses vital information about the financial condition and future prospects of a company. A rational decision emphasis would suggest that investors, lenders and other users are more likely to expend resources on companies with better financial conditions and prospects than other companies, because they have a better chance of getting a higher return with less risk. Accounting information is relied on in making these assessments.

In the absence of fraud or error, accounting information can be used to identify the prosperous, high-performing companies over the more mediocre or struggling companies. Stock-market analysts and funds managers depend heavily on accounting information to make decisions to buy, sell or hold a company's securities. Loan officers and managers also depend heavily on accounting information in decisions about whether to extend loans to companies and in assessing the relative riskiness of the loan. Poor-quality accounting information could result in an investor making a potentially disastrous investment in a company, or a lending officer granting an equally disastrous loan. Hence, accounting plays an important role in the allocation of scarce resources throughout the economy.

The efficient allocation of resources in an economy has great importance to society in general. An efficient well-functioning economy can deliver, among other things, higher standards of living for members of the community, including better technologies, higher employment levels, better health care and education, and a host of other social and economic services and programs for the community.

The international environment and society

The international environment of accounting also impacts on society, particularly through the influence of foreign investment on the national economy. In Australia, for instance, it has long been recognised that it is in the country's economic interests to encourage a strong regulatory accounting framework that will promote the production of high-quality company financial statements. Many companies in Australia need to raise capital on overseas markets in order to grow their businesses or expand their operations. Financial statements that are perceived by foreign investors to be of high quality, and internationally comparable with other leading industrialised nations, is likely to assist in this process. The social, economic and political implications of Australia's involvement in the international harmonisation of accounting standards is discussed in greater detail in Chapter 13.

Accounting and society: a case illustration

An example of the impact of accounting on economic decision making and society can be seen in the following article, 'Heritage hangs in the balance'. The writers of this article challenge recent attempts by the standard-setting body in Australia to require government departments to report on the financial value of the nation's heritage assets, which include collections held in not-for-profit public museums, including galleries and also libraries. The authors argue that placing financial values on heritage assets of this kind can result in some unfavourable social and economic consequences.

(a) Read the article carefully and identify the reasons the authors give for opposing the requirements for government departments to report the financial (monetary) value of heritage assets.

(b) In what ways do the authors believe that the requirement to value heritage assets might adversely impact on society? Do you agree with their views?

Heritage hangs in the balance

Putting a monetary value on museum collections is a futile exercise and may endanger priceless cultural records, write Garry Carnegie and Peter Wolnizer.

The following scene should be recorded for posterity as an example of late 20th Century accounting nonsense. Right now, scores of accountants and valuers are combing through the back vaults of Australia's not-for-profit museums, libraries and public record offices trying to put dollar signs on collections of stuffed animals, indigenous relics, fossils, specimens, and artistic and literary works.

These taxpayer-funded valuations are required for financial reporting purposes under Australian Accounting Standard AAS 29, 'Financial Reporting by Government Departments', which became operative for 'difficult to measure' assets from July 1.

Accountants and valuers may be buoyed by the opportunity to 'value' public collections, but most Australian museum managers do not welcome this intrusion into their job of preserving and enhancing the cultural, heritage, scientific, educative and other non-financial values of these public assets.

Rightly, most museum managers are not convinced that the accounting information will be useful. Instead, they are concerned that advocates of financial valuation have little understanding of the primary function of their collections, which is 'to be' and 'to hold'.

The objectives or mission statements of many Australian and overseas public museums exclude references to income generation, wealth creation, profitability and surplus distribution. Indeed, museum managers are not allowed, under the statutes which govern their organisations, to do so.

Collections of public museums are held in trust for the national and the international community. John Carman writes in *Valuing Ancient Things: Archaeology and Law* that heritage laws are important morally and culturally, elevating museum objects out of the everyday world into the higher realms of the 'public domain'. The financial valuation of collections effectively miscategorises them. It places collections in an economic realm where they have no place.

This miscategorisation has important implications, particularly for 'reserve' (or not on display) collections which may be seen as 'excessive' by some accountants and government policy-makers, even though they are an integral part of the museum's complete collection. Collections can only be regarded as excessive if they are regarded as 'stock'.

Thus, the financial valuation of collections may have unexpected counter-productive or even destructive consequences. For instance, it may lead to government-imposed charges on museums, such as an annual capital charge based on the financial valuation of assets, which could destroy the integrity of publicly owned collections. Saleable items may have to be liquidated just to pay the charges.

Collections, of themselves, do not generate net cash inflows either through normal museum operations or by commercial exchanges. Financial valuation is appropriate only where items have been de-accessioned (that is, removed from the public domain) and a resale market exists for them.

It is an empirical impossibility to reliably quantify in monetary terms the values of collections, such as their cultural, heritage, scientific and educative values. How can the 'value' of Phar Lap to the community be quantified in money terms—or the value of indigenous artefacts to the people whose ancestors made them?

The valuation of collections for financial reporting purposes is not required outside of Australia and New Zealand. Such ideas were aired in the United States in the early 1990s. The US Financial Accounting Standards Board eventually withdrew its mandatory valuation proposal, acknowledging widespread concerns about the excessive costs of obtaining reliable estimates of value and the difficulties of assigning values to collection items in the absence of objective commercial evidence. More recently, the Accounting Standards Board in Canada stated it was 'unaware of any significant demand' for dollar-value information about collections.

The Australian proposals for valuing museum collections come from a 'limited-scope' financial accountability focus adopted by the accounting standard-setters as part of a shift to 'commercial accounting' for public sector management. But, for public museums, a more functional notion of accountability is needed. We suggest that a wider range of factual 'indicators' be developed to strengthen accountability while maintaining the integrity of their organisational missions.

While terms such as 'efficiency' and 'effectiveness' are in vogue, our approach emphasises the 'vitality' and 'viability' of museums. It provides a framework for a wide range of financial and non-financial quantitative data and qualitative data to explain the actions of museum managers and enable informed assessment of their performance in meeting the aims of their museums.

If the maintenance of accurate and up-to-date records of the existence, use and condition of collection items is the real aim of those who advocate the financial valuation of collections, then we agree with this objective. However, we remain unconvinced that financial values placed on public collections have any commercial meaning or can indicate the effectiveness with which museum managers discharge their responsibilities. Placing of financial values on things of this kind may lead to misrepresentation that could damage the proper management and integrity of collections that ought to be preserved for the advancement of knowledge and understanding by this and future generations.

- *Professor Garry D. Carnegie is head of the School of Accounting and Finance at Deakin University, and Professor Peter W. Wolnizer is Dean of the Faculty of Business and Law at Deakin University*

Australian Financial Review,
10 July 1997, p. 16

Ethical issues

As members of professional societies, accountants regard themselves as professionals, just as doctors or lawyers are members of their own professional bodies.

Membership of a profession is a status to which many individuals aspire, including many readers of this book! It provides a recognition of scholastic achievement and the importance of the profession's role in society. However, to be rewarded with such status a professional must also accept significant responsibilities towards the community, which are reinforced by the professional societies. Members of professional societies must possess knowledge and expertise appropriate to their professional standing and must maintain that knowledge.

The most important obligation, however, is to act with integrity on all occasions, whether dealing with clients or with the general public. Clients should be entitled to expect complete honesty and discretion from their accountant. Just as we would not condone the actions of a medical practitioner who deliberately gave a false diagnosis or who disclosed confidential information about a patient's condition, so we would expect the same degree of integrity from an accountant.

The professional societies have established codes of ethical conduct to which members must adhere or else face disciplinary action. These standards prescribe good conduct between the accountant, clients, other members of the profession and the general public.

Unfortunately, directors, managers and accountants do not always act honestly and with proper regard for the rights of those to whom they have a responsibility. The consequence has been heavy losses of funds entrusted to the enterprises concerned, often by those in the community least able to sustain a loss. Apart from these personal tragedies, there has been a loss of confidence in business activities and a large cost to the community in replenishing losses suffered by banks, insurance companies and government instrumentalities. Of course, poor management decisions, adverse economic conditions or other factors beyond management control might also contribute to company collapses. In some past cases, however, factors such as greed, dishonesty and rampant self-interest appear to have been prominent.

It is therefore important for students to become aware of the ethical dimension to accounting practice. Accordingly, various questions are included in this book inviting students and their tutors to identify and resolve, through discussion, some of the ethical dilemmas encountered in the professional life of an accountant.

Summary

Accounting is a communication system designed to provide economic information useful for decision making by users of the information. A primary user is the owner. Forms of ownership vary and consequently the needs for information vary. In general, however, owners must make decisions about whether to continue or to expand their investments in the entity. They must decide how much profit to withdraw as drawings or dividends, or how much revenue to allocate to the entity in the future (as in the case of government departments). They must know the size of the ownership claim on the entity's assets.

In companies, where the owners' interests are represented by a board of directors, shareholders require information enabling them to evaluate the stewardship and performance of the directors. Apart from these ownership interests, the shareholder may take the viewpoint of an investor, with the option of selling the shares if the selling price exceeds the value the investor places on the shares.

All ownership groups have a general need for information about the performance of the enterprise and its present financial state. Accounting reports are designed to supply some, though not all, of the information an owner requires. Public sector proprietorship has emerged in recent years as a special type of ownership.

Creditors, whether short- or long-term, must decide whether their loans will be repaid. They therefore must assess whether future returns will be adequate to meet repayment commitments and whether the entity will remain financially sound. These information needs are not fundamentally different from those of the investor.

Accounting's response to these information requirements is, at least in part, to prepare two major financial statements: a profit and loss statement and a balance sheet. It will be seen in Chapter 2 that the basis of valuation adopted is mainly the original or historical cost. Whether these statements are adequate for decision making is an issue that will be taken up when the conventional basis of accounting has been thoroughly understood. Only then can the alternatives be evaluated.

It was also shown in this chapter that accounting both influences and is influenced by its environment. There are principally three environmental factors that affect accounting: the regulatory environment, the economic decision-making environment and the international environment. All three environments are to some extent interdependent, and all have a profound affect on society in general. With respect to the regulatory environment, financial statements prepared by companies in Australia must be in accordance with Schedule 5 of the Corporations Law, the AASB series of accounting standards, and Australian Stock Exchange listing requirements. The preparation of financial statements by non-corporate entities is guided by the requirements of the AAS series of accounting standards. Public sector entities must also comply with the disclosure requirements of specific government legislation. The purpose behind accounting regulation is to provide a measure of financial protection to the various user groups, and society itself, against the potentially detrimental impacts of fraudulent, misleading or poor-quality financial statements. Financial statements can be used to either display or mask the true financial position of a company. Company insolvencies can cause significant financial losses to individual investors, and dislocation and social distress to local communities. In the case of widespread corporate collapses, they can even bring recession to national and international economies. It was shown that accounting information can play a key role in a number of other social-equity-related functions, such as providing financial mechanisms to assist the redistribution of wealth in the community. Furthermore, regulations and guidelines that guide the determination of profit can assist in the reconciliation of potential conflicts between competing economic interests in the business arena.

The economic decision-making environment stresses the importance of accounting information in assisting in the efficient allocation of scarce resources in the economy. All user groups are concerned with allocating their scarce resources efficiently, and accounting information is a key ingredient in such decisions. Here again, accounting information impacts on society in a profound way, in the sense that an efficient, well-functioning economy is the basis for economic growth, including better living standards for the community. Finally, the implications of the international accounting environment on society was considered, particularly in relation to the harmonisation of accounting standards and the impact of foreign investment on the economy.

 **Review exercises**

Discussion questions

1.1 'If resources were not scarce, there would be no need for accounting.' Discuss.

1.2 Explain why, in your opinion, extensive resources are expended to produce accounting reports.

1.3 It has been suggested that accounting information fulfils many functions. What are the functions of accounting information and which function do you consider to be the most important? Explain your answer.

1.4 Explain the purpose of financial reporting and accounting information.

1.5 In the chapter it is stated that investment decisions should take into account the prospective risk and return associated with each alternative action. Identify the major factors that might be considered when deciding:

(a) whether to purchase a fishing boat to commence a fishing business
(b) whether to purchase and operate a neighbourhood grocery store
(c) whether to cease employment and commence a full-time study program.

1.6 In what ways does the need for accounting information change when a sole trader takes in a partner?

1.7 'An accounting entity may be, but is not necessarily, a legal entity.' Discuss in relation to the various types of business enterprise.

1.8 Discuss the different forms of public sector enterprise and provide examples of each form.

1.9 There are three major forms of private sector business enterprise. What are they? Compare and contrast the main features of each one.

1.10 Compare the rights and obligations of:

(a) holders of shares in limited companies
(b) holders of debentures in limited companies
(c) partners in a partnership
(d) sole traders

1.11 In what broad ways might public sector entities differ from private sector entities? In what ways are they similar?

1.12 Make a list of the various people or external parties who may be interested in receiving financial information about a government department or a government trading enterprise. What might these parties want this information for?

1.13 As a ratepayer, what financial (and non-financial) information would you like to have disclosed in the annual report of your local council?

1.14 Think of two different public sector entities. What are the main sources of revenue for each entity?

1.15 Outline the main sources of authority for the rules of accounting.

1.16 Discuss the role of the ethical accountant.

1.17 Provide an example of an ethical dilemma that an accountant may be faced with in her or his everyday work.

1.18 Two years ago B. Cheerful purchased 5000 $1 shares in Running Pty Ltd, which was 20 per cent of its issued capital. She contributed 40 cents per share, with the remainder being uncalled. The company is presently being liquidated and the available assets have been distributed to creditors. Insufficient assets are available, however, to repay debts of $700 000.

(a) How much could B. Cheerful be required to contribute towards the repayment of creditors?
(b) Would your answer be different if this had been a partnership?

1.19 In deciding whether to make the following investment decisions, what factors would you take into consideration?

(a) Buying debentures in a publicly listed company.

(b) Investing in a bank term deposit with a fixed interest rate.

1.20 What is a limited company? Discuss the major features of the three most common forms of limited companies.

1.21 Explain the major features of company formation. What are the advantages and disadvantages of company formation?

1.22 What is a company's annual general meeting and what is its purpose?

1.23 What is the role of an external auditor of a public company?

1.24 Make a list of the various people or external parties that might be interested in receiving financial information about a publicly listed company and suggest what those interests might be.

1.25 Accounting information is used by internal as well as external users. List as many different groups of users as you can and identify the type of accounting information that would be the most useful to each group.

1.26 What useful information do the profit and loss statement and balance sheet provide to assist an external user's investment decision? What other non-financial information might also be important in such a decision?

1.27 (a) C. Lutch recently opened a motor-cycle repair shop, using the back garden as his place of business.

   (i) Assuming he buys parts for cash and renders services for cash, what accounting data would be required?

   (ii) Assume alternatively that he buys parts on credit and extends credit to some customers. What accounting data would he then require?

   (iii) He wonders how business is progressing this month versus last month. What data would you collect to answer this question?

   (b) After five successful years, C. Lutch now owns a shop that sells and services motor cycles. He wants to stock a new line of cycle that will retail for $3000. What data would be required to help decide whether to stock the new line?

   (c) To finance his expanding business, C. Lutch approaches the bank for an overdraft. What information might the bank require?

1.28 Betty Bungle recently won $25 000 from the Hillsdale Country Club poker machines. Betty decided to invest her winnings. A close friend, Cathy Crompton, advised her to invest in a gold-mining company, Lustre Ltd, as the company was expecting to find a significant gold deposit at Birch Gap. After due consideration Betty felt that this investment was too risky and decided instead to use the money to purchase debentures in a recently established finance company, Addnas Finance Ltd.

   What financial and non-financial information do you think Betty would have considered was important to her investment decision?

1.29 What are the purposes of accounting regulation?

1.30 Explain how the regulatory environment of accounting impacts on society.

1.31 What do you understand by the meaning of *efficient* resource allocation?

1.32 Explain how the economic decision-making environment impacts on society.

1.33   Why has the international accounting environment become so important in recent years?

1.34   In the context of the international accounting environment, explain the differences between the British–American model, the Continental model, the South American model and the mixed economy model.

1.35   What is meant by the international harmonisation of accounting standards?

1.36   Do you believe international harmonisation is desirable? Achievable? Why?

 Problems

1.37   *Decisions involving risk*

Gwen Morgan has won $40 000 in a lottery and plans to use it in one year's time to finance her university education. In the meantime, she must decide whether to invest the amount in a fixed-interest loan for one year at an interest rate of 17 per cent or to buy shares in Bananas Ltd, a wholesaler of fruit. On investigation, she believes the resale value of the investment in Bananas Ltd after one year could be either $90 000 or $10 000, although it seems 70 per cent likely that the higher amount will be achieved.

(a) What information would have been useful in assessing:

(i) the risk of the investment project?
(ii) the likely return from the project?

(b) What other considerations might also be relevant?

1.38   *Measuring performance and financial position*

1.   Michelle Mann owns a hot-jam-donut van that she operates inside Kardinia Park football ground. The only capital she has invested in the business is an equipped van that she values at $4000 and $500 cash which she keeps in her wallet. During the first week of operations she purchased flour $20, sugar $5, raspberry jam $6, yeast $4, petrol $10 and a gas refill $8. Her takings for the week were $220 and she withdrew $150 for personal use. At the end of the week all the ingredients had been used as well as half of the petrol and gas.

How would you measure the results of Michelle's operations for the week? Quantify your answer as much as possible and list the items, if any, which you found difficult to quantify.

2.   Freddy Board has bought a mobile hot-dog van that he intends to operate at the local football ground. The only capital he has invested in the business is the van, which cost him $8000. He borrowed $500 from the bank to get the business started.

On the morning of his first Saturday trading day, Freddy bought bread rolls for $120, frankfurts $50, mustard $25, tomato sauce $35, petrol $40 and a gas refill $60. Freddy's takings during the afternoon were $450. At the end of the day he had used up all the foodstuffs but only about half the petrol and gas.

On his way home he remembered his wife's birthday and, because he felt he had had a good day's trading, decided that he would buy her a worthwhile present out of the takings. He stopped at a pub and bought her a box of chocolates for $10 from the bottle shop. While there, he decided the business could buy him a little treat as well, so he bought two bottles of malt whisky for $90.

How would you measure the results of Freddy's operations for the day? Quantify your answer as much as possible.

CHAPTER 2
Accounting reports: their nature and uses

Learning objectives

In this chapter you will be introduced to:

1. financial accounting and management accounting

2. the elements of financial statements and the criteria for their recognition

3. the structure, contents and uses of the major financial statements

4. financial ratio analysis

5. the historical cost basis of accounting

6. the nature and use of estimation and judgement in accounting.

Introduction

Accounting is often portrayed as 'the language of business'. This international language has monetary measurement as its most distinguishing feature. Like all languages, accounting has its own terminology, conventions, practices and rules. These typically constitute the knowledge base of the accounting profession. *Accounting reports,* on the other hand, are the outputs of accounting and the prime communication tools of accountants.

Today, accountants are recognised for their expertise in the identification, measurement and communication of financial and non-financial information that reflects the outcomes of economic activity or predictions of anticipated activities. Using accounting reports, accountants are capable of summarising the effects of seemingly unrelated transactions and other events on an entity. Several million of these transactions and other events might be summarised on a single page of results in, for example, an annual report. This information provides the basis of review, decision making and action throughout the private and public sectors nationally and globally.

Decisions are based on accounting and, of course, other information. The accountant's purpose may therefore be found in the decisions the users of accounting information must make. As pointed out in Chapter 1, decisions based on accounting information have effects on people and organisations and also on society in general. What information is collected and when, how it is interpreted and reported and how it is used in decision making are influential determinants in shaping the structure of organisations and society and thus people's lives. Accounting, therefore impacts on organisational and social functioning.

The first section of this chapter explains the main differences between financial accounting or external reporting and management accounting or internal reporting. The key financial statements published in the 1997 Annual Report of Coca-Cola Amatil Ltd are then discussed in outlining, in summary terms, the structure, contents and uses of these financial statements. Recognition criteria and the historical cost basis of accounting are introduced, followed by a discussion of the nature and use of estimation and judgement in accounting.

Two major forms of accounting

The two major forms of accounting are known as *financial accounting* and *management accounting*. The key sets of reports prepared by financial accountants are 'general purpose financial reports' and 'special purpose financial reports'. Figure 2.1 shows a diagrammatic representation of 'accounting'.

The differences between financial accounting and management accounting are discussed in the following sections.

Financial accounting

Financial accounting information is oriented primarily toward users of financial reports who are external to an organisation. External parties or 'outsiders' include investors, employees, lenders, suppliers and trade creditors, customers, governments and their agencies, community groups and other interested parties. It is important to recognise the key differences between general purpose and special purpose financial reports.

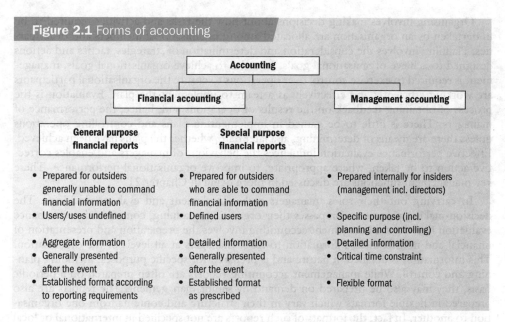

Figure 2.1 Forms of accounting

```
                              Accounting
                  ┌──────────────────┴──────────────────┐
          Financial accounting                  Management accounting
      ┌─────────────┴─────────────┐
 General purpose          Special purpose
 financial reports        financial reports
```

• Prepared for outsiders generally unable to command financial information	• Prepared for outsiders who are able to command financial information	• Prepared internally for insiders (management incl. directors)
• Users/uses undefined	• Defined users	• Specific purpose (incl. planning and controlling)
• Aggregate information	• Detailed information	• Detailed information
• Generally presented after the event	• Generally presented after the event	• Critical time constraint
• Established format according to reporting requirements	• Established format as prescribed	• Flexible format

General purpose financial reports or external financial reports are prepared for users who are unable to command the preparation of reports tailored specifically to satisfy their particular needs. They are intended to provide information useful for making and evaluating decisions about the allocation of scarce resources and for accountability purposes. *Special purpose financial reports* are prepared for users who are able to command reports tailored specifically to suit their purposes and which are prepared according to agreed timelines or on demand. Some users, such as taxation authorities, central banks and grant commissions, have specialised needs and will possess the authority to obtain information to meet those needs. Users possessing the authority to obtain the information they require may also make use of general-purpose financial reports.

General purpose and special purpose financial reports are presented at the end of an accounting period, such as a financial year, or on demand in the case of certain users who are able to command information tailored to their needs. The information contained in general purpose financial reports is aggregate in nature, whereas special purpose financial reports are often more detailed and thus more specific about certain facets of an entity's performance and financial position. General purpose financial reports are presented in prescribed formats in accordance with applicable reporting requirements such as international or local accounting standards, while special purpose financial reports are typically presented in formats that have been specified by the users of those reports. For example, taxation authorities require the income tax returns of companies and other types of entities to be in established formats.

Management accounting

Accounting information is also prepared for use by people within an organisation, or 'insiders'. Such information is used by people at all levels to help them manage the organisation as a whole, or their particular part of the organisation. The functions of business management include organising, planning, control and performance evaluation. Accounting information is needed and used in each function.

Organising involves making decisions about how the tasks and activities required to be undertaken by an organisation are allocated among organisational members and other parties. Planning involves the consideration and determination of strategies, tactics and actions designed to achieve organisational goals. In order to achieve organisational goals, management is required to exercise control over operations to ensure the organisational participants are working efficiently and effectively as a team to implement the plan. Evaluation is the process of obtaining feedback on the results of operations and, hence, the performance of managers. There is little to be gained in implementing plans and controlling operations unless there are means of determining, at a later date, whether the plans have been achieved. Effective performance evaluation influences the behaviour of managers and enables corrective action to be taken, where appropriate, to improve organisational performance. These key management functions are discussed in more detail in Chapter 21.

In carrying out their roles, managers make, implement and evaluate decisions. The decision-making process encompasses their organising, planning, control and performance evaluation functions. Management accounting involves the preparation and presentation of financial and non-financial information to assist managers at all levels of the organisation. This information is detailed in nature and is prepared for specific purposes, including planning and control. While management accounting reports are often prepared on a periodic basis, they may also be prepared on demand by senior management. The reports are also prepared in flexible formats which vary in their structure and contents from one organisation to another. In fact, the formats of such reports are not specified in international or local accounting standards that are only concerned with external reporting.

An effective management accounting system is essential for effective organisational management. In some organisations, especially large or complex ones, management accounting is a separate part of the overall accounting function. In other organisations, accountants may be jointly responsible for external reporting and management accounting. Irrespective of their specific position title, accountants dealing primarily with the internal uses of accounting information deal with the implementation and operation of accounting systems that enable reports to be prepared for management's use in decision processes. Therefore, the management accountant is required to gather timely information, analyse, organise and evaluate that information for its relevance to organisational management, and communicate it to managers on a regular or ad hoc basis by means of internal reports. Management accounting, including the wide range of reports prepared by management accountants, is the subject of Part 6 of this book.

The role of accounting information in the management of organisations is introduced at this stage for two main reasons. The first is to provide, in conjunction with Chapter 1, a general perspective on both the external and internal uses and purposes of accounting information. The second is that, although internal management is a different user group of accounting information from external parties, many of the processes and concepts that underpin the provision of accounting information for external users are relevant also to internal users. The main differences between internal and external reporting are outlined in the following section.

Internal versus external reporting

There are two major differences between reporting for internal purposes and reporting for external purposes, which should be borne in mind as you progress through this book. The first is that the external users of accounting information are many and varied. They include, as noted in Chapter 1, owners (as sole proprietors, partners or shareholders), lenders or creditors (both short-term and long-term), employees, and a range of government and regulatory agencies and bodies. These users have a variety of different needs that, except in cases where users have the authority to command specific information for their purposes, have to be satisfied eventually by a limited set of highly summarised financial reports or statements about an organisation. The statements have to be sufficiently general to satisfy a multiplicity of users, and relatively standardised so that users can make reasonable comparisons across organisations and across time, based on the accounting reports.

By contrast, no such constraint exists on the provision of accounting information for internal management purposes. Here, managers can specify the particular decision or purpose for which information is needed, and the informational content and reporting format can be tailor-made to the specific decision and dedicated to the particular purpose.

The second difference between reporting for external and internal purposes is that legal obligations are at stake in respect of external relationships. In the context of companies, the legal relationship between the directors of a company and the shareholders has meant that external financial reports have been based heavily on data that can be supported by evidence in a court of law if necessary. No such legal limitation constrains the information provided to assist internal management decisions. Here, the information can be more speculative, more subjective, more probabilistic; it can be directed to estimating the likely outcomes of management decisions under a range of hypothetical 'what-if' scenarios.

Thus, whereas the accounting information provided for external reporting is determined largely by statutory and/or professional accounting standard-setting bodies, that provided for internal reporting is determined largely by the costs of obtaining the information relative to its benefits and the information preferences of management in carrying out their management functions. Accounting standard setting is discussed in Chapter 13.

The major financial statements

Three major questions that are asked by users of financial statements are:

- How well has the entity performed?
- What is the financial position of the entity?
- What is the ability of the entity to generate cash to pay its debts?

The financial statements, or financial reports, portray the financial effects of transactions and other events on a periodic basis. Here, our main concern is with the *profit and loss statement*, *balance sheet* and *cash flow statement*.

Whereas the true profitability of a firm cannot be determined until its closure or liquidation, profitability can be periodically estimated. The profit and loss statement reports the profit (or loss) that has been made during a given period and how it was obtained. The balance sheet is prepared at the end of a period to show the assets of the entity, its debts, and the owner's claim on the entity. It gives an indication of the entity's financial position at that date. The cash flow statement reports the cash flows during a period from operating, investing and financing activities. It summarises the cash flow effects of these activities during a given period.

In the following sections, a cursory study is undertaken of the financial statements published in the 1997 Annual Report of Coca-Cola Amatil (CCA) Ltd. We stress that you are not expected at this stage to understand all the terms or information shown in these financial statements. In addition, we have calculated some financial ratios, for illustrative purposes only, based on the figures reported in the financial statements. *Financial ratio analysis* involves taking two significant figures from the financial statements and expressing their relationship in terms of a ratio or percentage. We recommend you check for yourself the ratio results we have determined, in order to better understand the form of analysis conducted. Financial statement analysis, including financial ratio analysis, is explored in greater detail in Chapter 12.

As stated in the annual report, CCA 'is an anchor bottler[1] in the Coca-Cola System. CCA operates in 18 countries throughout Australasia, South East Asia and Central and Eastern Europe'. Its prime long-term objective is 'to enhance the value of the Company to its shareholders by balancing growth, profitability and return on investment' (p. 2).

The key financial statements published in the 1997 Annual Report include comparative figures for the 1996 financial year and are reproduced in the following sections. The focus is on the 'CCA Group' results which are those of the group of entities comprising CCA Ltd and its controlled entities. The figures reported under 'CCA Entity' are of CCA Ltd only.

Profit and loss statement

The profit and loss statement, or operating statement, reports as profit (or loss) the difference between the *revenue* earned and the *expenses* incurred during a given period. Earned increases in resources are revenues; consumed resources are expenses.

The revenue from a retail store comes from its sales of goods. A bus operator derives revenue from fares, an accountant from fees charged for professional services, an estate agent from commissions on property sales and rent collections, and a financier from interest received and loan establishment fees from borrowers. The revenue might be received immediately as cash; alternatively, the customer might owe the money so that the revenue is represented initially by an account receivable or a debtor. Some transactions may involve the receipt of a portion of the transaction amount immediately in the form of cash while the balance is represented by an account receivable.

Expenses are incurred in earning revenue. In a retail store a major expense is the cost of goods sold. Other major expenses include rent, electricity, wages and salaries, advertising, and interest charges on any borrowed monies. Expenses may not be paid in cash immediately, in which case the expense is represented initially as an account payable or a creditor.

Combining revenue and expenses in the profit and loss statement results in *net profit*— the net increase in earned resources of the entity. Profitable trading increases the net assets of the entity and it therefore increases the owner's stake in the enterprise. Thus, the items that are themselves the cause of the net change in equity resulting from the operations of the entity comprise the contents of the profit and loss statement.

The profit and loss statement typically identifies the major sources of revenue and expenses as either *operating* or *extraordinary* items. Operating revenue and expenses arise from an entity's ordinary operations. Ordinary operations are regarded as those activities that are carried on regularly from one period to the next to achieve the objectives of the entity. Extraordinary items are those items of revenue and expenses not relating to the ordinary operations of the entity and which are of a non-recurring nature. Operating revenue and expenses that are regarded as *abnormal* because of their size and effect on the operating profit or loss for the period are required to be disclosed separately in the profit and loss statement. Operating and extraordinary items are examined in more detail in Chapter 9.

As shown in Figure 2.2, the CCA Group reported 'total operating revenue' of $4965.5 million for the financial year ended 31 December 1997. After deducting the expenses of operations, a 'trading profit' of $528 million was disclosed. The 'operating profit' before income-tax of $377.6 million was derived after deducting net interest expenses from the trading profit. Operating profit after income tax amounted to $245.1 million, an increase of $97.1 million over the prior year. The CCA Group did not disclose any abnormal items within operating profit or report any extraordinary items for the year.

---

[1] The annual report defines 'anchor bottlers' as 'select business partners in the worldwide Coca-Cola System whose strategic goals are aligned with those of The Coca-Cola Company, and who are distinguished by their strong financial and management resources and commitment to long-term growth' (p. 2).

Figure 2.2 Profit and loss accounts of Coca-Cola Amatil Ltd and its controlled entities, for financial year ended 31 December 1997

	Refer Note	CCA Group 1997 $M	1996 $M	CCA Entity 1997 $M	1996 $M
Sales revenue		4828.4	3704.8	–	–
Other operating revenue		137.1	75.7	1420.4	323.4
Total operating revenue	2	4965.5	3780.5	1420.4	323.4
Trading profit		528.0	316.8		
Finance expenses (other than interest)		1.0	(13.6)		
Operating profit before interest and tax		529.0	303.2		
Net interest expense	2&3	(151.4)	(106.6)		
Operating profit	3	377.6	196.6	332.5	83.9
Income tax expense applicable	4	(132.5)	(48.6)	(24.6)	(22.8)
Operating profit after income tax		245.1	148.0	307.9	61.1
Outside equity interests in operating profit after income tax		(2.9)	(8.1)		
Operating profit after income tax attributable to ordinary shareholders of Coca-Cola Amatil Limited		242.2	139.9	307.9	61.1
Retained profits at the beginning of the year		622.9	580.1	165.9	203.9
Aggregate of amounts transferred from reserves	19	14.6	2.0	–	–
Total available for appropriation		879.7	722.0	473.8	265.0
Dividends provided for or paid—					
Ordinary shares		(114.6)	(99.1)	(114.6)	(99.1)
Payable by controlled entity in lieu of dividend on suspended dividend shares	18	(18.3)	–	–	–
Retained profits at the end of the year		746.8	622.9	359.2	165.9
Earnings per share					
Basic earnings per share*		31.5¢	27.4¢		
Weighted average number of ordinary shares on issue used in the calculation of basic earnings per share (millions)†		769.6	510.5		

* Diluted earnings per share figures are unchanged from basic earnings per share.

† The weighted average number of shares used to calculate earnings per share has been notionally adjusted to include shares issued in respect of the Philippines transaction as from the effective date of acquisition, 3 April 1997.

Note 2 to the CCA financial statements is reproduced in Figure 2.3. This note shows the components of operating revenue. CCA Group sales for the year ended 31 December 1997 were $4828.4 million. This represents an increase of $1123.6 million or 30.3 per cent over sales for the same period in the previous year.

Figure 2.3 Note 2 to the CCA financial statements

	Refer Note	CCA Group 1997 $M	CCA Group 1996 $M	CCA Entity 1997 $M	CCA Entity 1996 $M
2. Operating revenue—					
Sales		4828.4	3704.8	–	–
Other operating revenue—					
Dividends—					
from controlled entities	32			530.0	65.0
Interest—					
from controlled entities	32			75.2	73.2
from non-related parties		62.0	52.1	5.0	10.1
Management and guarantee fees	32			215.3	173.6
Proceeds from the sale of non-current assets		75.1	23.6	594.9	1.5
		137.1	75.7	1420.4	323.4
Total operating revenue		4965.5	3780.5	1420.4	323.4

Balance sheet

The balance sheet, or statement of financial position, reports the resources of value controlled by the enterprise and the claims of owners and non-owners to those resources as at a given date. To be valuable, a resource must be capable of providing benefits to the enterprise either by sale or by use. These benefits are the *assets* of the enterprise. For present purposes, assets typically produce net cash inflows, especially for commercial organisations. Commercial organisations have as their prime objective the enhancement of periodic profits or the maximisation of the wealth of owners.

The financial claims of non-owners are reported in the balance sheet as the *liabilities* of the enterprise. Liabilities are typically repaid or discharged using cash, that is, through net cash outflows. In essence, *equity* represents the excess of assets over liabilities or *net assets* and constitutes the interest of the owners. The amount at which equity is recorded in the balance sheet is thus dependent on the measurement of assets and liabilities.

The balance sheet shows the financial position of an enterprise at a particular point in time. Assets are reported in balance sheets in descending order of *liquidity*. Liquidity is judged on time and intention criteria. *Time* means how quickly an asset can be converted into cash with minimum loss in value. *Intention* is management's decision to convert, or not to convert, an asset into cash during the next accounting period. Assets are thus classified as either current or non-current.

Current assets are assets that are intended to be converted to cash or consumed within the next financial year. Current assets include cash and deposits, short-term marketable securities, trade and other receivables, inventories or stock-in-trade and prepayments. *Non-current assets* are assets intended to be held for continuing use rather than exchange. Non-current assets are usually subdivided into physical resources such as plant and equipment, land and buildings, motor vehicles and non-physical resources or *intangible assets* such as goodwill, licences and patent rights.

Liabilities are also customarily classified according to the urgency with which they must be discharged. Liabilities are thus also classified into current and non-current categories. *Current liabilities* are liabilities that must be discharged within 12 months from balance date. Current liabilities include trade creditors, bank overdraft, provision for taxation, proposed dividends, and short-term borrowings payable within 12 months. *Non-current liabilities* are all other liabilities and include long-term borrowings, debentures and mortgages maturing at times beyond the next 12 months.

As shown in Figure 2.4, the total assets and net assets of the CCA Group as at 31 December 1997 were $9466.3 million and $5422.8 million respectively. Of total assets, $2247 million or 23.7 per cent were current assets. Liabilities amounted to $4043.5 million, of which $1690.2 million or 41.8 per cent were current liabilities. The proportion of current assets to current liabilities, otherwise known as the *current ratio*, was 1.33 as at 31 December 1997. This ratio, which is also known as the working capital ratio, gives an indication of the ability of an entity to repay its short-term debts.

Total shareholders' equity and net assets amounted to $5422.8 million, a $2784.9 million increase since 31 December 1996. Shareholders' equity comprises share capital, reserves and retained profits. These components of shareholders' equity will be discussed in Chapter 9. For now, *retained profits* represents the owners' claims on the entity's assets that result from profits that have not been paid out previously to owners in the form of dividends. The other component of shareholders' funds, *reserves*, comprises specific reserves of a capital and/or revenue nature.

Figure 2.4 Balance sheet of Coca-Cola Amatil Ltd and its controlled entities, as at 31 December 1997

| | Refer | CCA Group | | CCA Entity | |
| | | **1997** | 1996 | **1997** | 1996 |
	Note	**$M**	$M	**$M**	$M
Current assets					
Cash and cash equivalents	6	**435.6**	877.1	**116.0**	52.1
Receivables	7	**734.8**	645.9	**1579.1**	889.3
Cross currency swap receivables relating to borrowings		**24.0**	0.6	**11.0**	0.6
Inventories	8	**817.3**	628.8	**0.1**	0.3
Prepayments		**235.3**	170.6	**14.5**	18.6
Total current assets		**2247.0**	2323.0	**1720.7**	960.9
Non-current assets					
Receivables	7	**66.7**	13.3	**910.9**	870.2
Cross currency swap receivables relating to borrowings		**159.6**	1.1	**159.6**	–
Investments in securities	9	**15.7**	12.3	**6503.7**	3239.3
Investments in bottlers' agreements	10	**3598.7**	1376.0	–	–
Property, plant and equipment	11	**3206.6**	2247.7	**58.7**	62.6
Intangibles	12	**10.2**	10.8	–	–
Prepayments		**69.5**	30.0	–	–
Future income tax benefits	13	**92.3**	77.5	**12.4**	10.4
Total non-current assets		**7219.3**	3768.7	**7645.3**	4182.5
Total assets		**9466.3**	6091.7	**9366.0**	5143.4
Current liabilities					
Accounts payable	14	**591.2**	441.9	**922.8**	850.7
Borrowings	15	**478.1**	706.5	**329.7**	430.0
Provisions	16	**234.6**	166.1	**121.7**	88.1
Accrued charges		**386.3**	307.1	**88.1**	34.3
Total current liabilities		**1690.2**	1621.6	**1462.3**	1403.1

continues

Figure 2.4 continued

	Refer Note	CCA Group 1997 $M	CCA Group 1996 $M	CCA Entity 1997 $M	CCA Entity 1996 $M
Non-current liabilities					
Accounts payable	14	**23.1**	25.3	**342.9**	385.6
Borrowings	15	**2083.1**	1672.6	**1610.4**	1072.9
Provision for deferred income tax	17	**226.8**	113.1	**8.6**	4.5
Provision for employee entitlements		**20.3**	21.2	**5.7**	5.4
Total non-current liabilities		**2353.3**	1832.2	**1967.6**	1468.4
Total liabilities		**4043.5**	3453.8	**3429.9**	2871.5
Net assets		**5422.8**	2637.9	**5936.1**	2271.9
Shareholders' equity					
Share capital	18	**467.4**	316.7	**467.4**	316.7
Reserves	19	**4130.6**	1630.2	**5109.5**	1789.3
Retained profits	*123.9*	**746.8**	622.9	**359.2**	165.9
Shareholders' equity attributable to ordinary					
shareholders of Coca-Cola Amatil Limited		**5344.8**	2569.8	**5936.1**	2271.9
Outside equity interests in controlled entities					
Share capital		**22.5**	17.6		
Reserves		**23.9**	34.3		
Retained profits		**31.6**	16.2		
Total outside equity interests		**78.0**	68.1		
Total shareholders' equity		**5422.8**	2637.9	**5936.1**	2271.9

The *capital structure* of an entity is the mix of owners' equity and liabilities adopted in financing the entity's total assets. The term *leverage* refers to the ability to purchase assets using borrowed funds and thus to 'lever up' an entity's total assets. The use of external debt enables the entity to have command over more assets than would be otherwise possible using funds contributed by owners. As long as the assets acquired using borrowed funds provide a return greater than the cost of the debt, the 'excess returns' flow to the owners. Thus, the successful use of debt enables an entity to 'lever up' returns to shareholders and other owners. Increasing the level of debt also means that the risk of an entity defaulting on interest payments and/or loan repayments increases.

The total assets of the CCA Group increased by $3374.6 million from $6091.7 to $9466.3 million over the 12-month period. This increase in total assets was enabled in part by an increase in liabilities, which rose by $589.7 million from $3453.8 million to $4043.5 million. Of this increase in liabilities, $521.1 million was in the form of additional non-current liabilities. As indicated earlier, shareholders also contributed to the asset expansion of the group by contributing further share capital. Most of the substantial increase in share capital related to the acquisition of Coca-Cola Bottlers Philippines, Inc (CCBPI) where 275 million ordinary shares in CCA were issued as consideration in acquiring that group of entities from its original owners, effective from 3 April 1997 (see note to 'profit and loss accounts' and 'statement of cash flows'). In addition, profits retained in the group during the year, amounting to $123.9 million, also assisted in financing the increase in total assets.

The proportion of debt to equity, or total liabilities to total shareholders' equity ratio, of the CCA Group as at 31 December 1997 was 0.75 compared with 1.31 as at 31 December 1996. This indicates that a greater proportion of shareholders' equity was financing the group's assets at 31 December 1997 than was the case at the end of 1996. The extent to which an entity is financed by external debt is also ascertained by use of the debt to assets ratio. The proportion of total liabilities to total assets of the CCA Group as at 31 December 1997 was 0.43 compared with 0.57 as at 31 December 1996. This ratio moves in line with movements in the debt to equity ratio.

Profitability measures can be determined by using the information contained in the profit and loss statement and balance sheet. For the CCA Group, the return on assets, or the ratio of operating profit after income tax to total assets (at year end) for the year ended 31 December 1997, was 2.6 per cent compared with 2.4 per cent for the previous financial year. However, the return on equity, or the ratio of operating profit after income tax to total shareholders' equity (at year end), for 1997 was 4.5 per cent compared with 5.6 per cent in 1996. Based on the average number of shares on issue during the year, the return on equity for the year ended 31 December 1997 was stated by CCA to be 6.1 per cent.[2] This ratio is 0.5 per cent higher than the one calculated above on equity at year-end because a lesser number of shares, on average, were on issue throughout the whole of 1997 than was so on 31 December 1997.

A further key profitability measure is the *earnings per share* result. This ratio is designed to measure the earnings for the period on a per share basis. Figure 2.2 shows the earnings per share of the CCA Group for the 1996 and 1997 financial years. As indicated, the ratio is based on the average number of ordinary shares on issue. This ratio has shown an improvement in 1997, increasing by 4.1 cents per share to 31.5 cents per share.

Unlike the above calculated return on assets ratio and return on equity ratio, the CCA Group earnings per share results are based on average figures for the period. Average figures over a financial year are more appropriate indicators of performance where entities show substantial asset growth during the year as has occurred in this case illustration. This is because a sizeable portion of the total assets at year end of high-growth entities has been held for only parts of the financial year and thus has not contributed to operating revenue and operating profits for the full financial year. In our case, CCBPI contributed to the sales and profits of the CCA Group for a period of nine months only, from 3 April 1997 to 31 December 1997.

Entities that are diversified either by industry or geography or both are often required to disclose financial information based on their industry or geographic segments. *Segment reports* usually disclose the sales, segment result and segment assets for each identifiable segment. This information is intended to enable more comprehensive assessments of the performance of diversified entities and to assist in predicting their future prospects.

Note 5 to the CCA financial statements is shown in Figure 2.5. As indicated, the CCA group operates in the beverages industry and is thus not regarded as being diversified by industry. However, the CCA Group is diversified by geography, as shown in the figure. Using the segment result to total segment assets ratio, the most profitable segment of the four identified for the year ended 31 December 1997 was Australia, closely followed by South East Asia/Pacific. As indicated earlier, the operations of CCBPI were acquired during 1997, which explains the absence of segment information for the Philippines in 1996. Which was the most profitable segment in 1996?

---

[2] This ratio figure is taken from the 'Financial Highlights' on page 2 of the CCA annual report. The comparative ratio for the prior year was recorded at 6.2 per cent. This represents a 0.1 per cent decrease for the 1997 financial year based on the average number of shares on issue over the respective financial years.

Figure 2.5 Note 5 to the CCA financial statements

	Year ended 31 December 1997			Year ended 31 December 1996		
	Sales $M	Segment result $M	Segment assets $M	Sales $M	Segment result $M	Segment assets $M
5. Financial reporting by geographic segments						
Australia	1423.5	204.8	1710.8	1345.6	174.6	1564.5
South East Asia/Pacific	708.6	85.1	790.9	635.8	68.9	1039.7
Europe	1775.1	74.7	2914.4	1723.4	73.3	2504.2
	3907.2	364.6	5416.1	3704.8	316.8	5108.4
Philippines	921.2	163.4	3292.7	–	–	–
Total	4828.4	528.0	8708.8	3704.8	316.8	5108.4

(a) The Group operates in the beverage industry, within which it manufactures, distributes and markets carbonated soft drinks, mineral waters, fruit juices and other alcohol-free beverages.

(b) Segment result, disclosed as trading profit in the profit and loss account, is pre-tax and excludes interest income and expense and other finance expenses.

(c) Segment assets exclude future income tax benefits and assets which relate to the Group's financing activity, all of which amount to $757.5M (1996 $983.3M).

Cash flow statement

Business failure typically imposes losses on shareholders and lenders alike. It also imposes costs generally on society. Post-mortems on failed entities typically reveal a range of difficulties that came about during the last few years of their operations. In the final analysis, enterprises fail because of cash flow problems. A lack of cash flow may be caused by a variety of factors. However, it is important to be able to undertake an analysis which heightens awareness of an entity's ability to generate cash flows in order to assess its debt-paying capacity.

The cash flow statement reports the effects of all transactions involving a flow of cash into or out of the entity, whether those transactions are operational, financial or investment in nature. Thus, a cash flow statement classifies cash flows during the period from operating, investing and financing activities. The cash flow statement therefore enables the evaluation of an entity's performance in cash flow terms. Because it summarises flows for a certain period of time, the statement is similar in this respect to the profit and loss statement.

As shown in Figure 2.6, the cash flows from operating, investing and financing activities for the CCA Group during the year ended 31 December 1997 were $433.7 million, ($608.4 million) and $64.4 million respectively. The cash flows from financing activities, as shown, indicate that only $95.5 million was received in the form of cash from the issue of shares. As mentioned earlier, although the total shareholders' funds increased substantially during the 1997 financial year, most of the shares issued were in exchange for interests in the shares of other entities, especially CCBPI (see note to 'statements of cash flows'). Hence, these shares were not issued for cash and thus the transaction is excluded from the face of the cash flow statement. There was an overall decrease in cash held amounting to $110.3 million, declining to $271.9 million as at 31 December 1997 from $406.4 million at the end of the 1996 financial year. This compares with a net increase in cash held recorded for the previous financial year of $110.1 million.

Figure 2.6 Statement of cash flows of Coca-Cola Amatil Ltd and its controlled entities, for the financial year ended 31 December 1997

		CCA Group		CCA Entity	
	Refer	**1997**	1996	**1997**	1996
	Note	**$M**	$M	**$M**	$M
Inflows (outflows)					
Cash flows from operating activities					
Receipts from customers		**4745.7**	3642.5	–	–
Receipts from related parties for					
management and guarantee fees				**215.3**	173.6
Payments to suppliers and employees		**(4116.7)**	(3416.7)	**(234.5)**	(117.0)
Dividends received		–	–	**530.0**	65.0
Interest and bill discounts received		**79.3**	35.1	**80.1**	83.2
Interest and other costs of finance paid		**(187.3)**	(154.4)	**(128.6)**	(138.8)
Income tax paid		**(87.3)**	(68.1)	**(0.3)**	(13.5)
		433.7	38.4	**462.0**	52.5
Cash flows from investing activities					
Proceeds from—					
sale of property, plant and equipment		**75.1**	23.6	**13.0**	1.5
settlement of legal claim (purchase price adjustment)		–	11.6	–	–
sale of investments		–	–	**581.9**	–
Payment for—					
property, plant and equipment		**(777.9)**	(679.5)	**(12.5)**	(29.9)
investments		–	(2.4)	**(695.0)**	(1022.6)
acquisitions of entities, net of cash acquired	29	**95.0**	(126.5)	–	–
goodwill		**(0.6)**	–	–	–
		(608.4)	(773.2)	**(112.6)**	(1051.0)
Cash flows from financing activities					
Proceeds from issue of shares		**95.5**	750.0	**95.5**	750.0
Proceeds from borrowings		**656.7**	763.1	**839.6**	261.6
Borrowings repaid		**(583.6)**	(570.9)	**(275.8)**	(309.2)
Net increase in intragroup loans				**(544.0)**	(163.3)
Dividends paid		**(104.2)**	(97.3)	**(104.2)**	(94.0)
		64.4	844.9	**11.1**	445.1
Net increase (decrease) in cash held		**(110.3)**	110.1	**360.5**	(553.4)
Cash held at the beginning of the year		**406.4**	319.1	**(377.9)**	175.5
Exchange rate adjustments to cash held					
at the beginning of the year		**(24.2)**	(22.8)	–	–
Cash at the end of the year		**271.9**	406.4	**(17.4)**	(377.9)

continues

Figure 2.6 continued

	Refer Note	CCA Group 1997 $M	1996 $M	CCA Entity 1997 $M	1996 $M
Reconciliation of cash flows from operating activities to operating profit after income tax					
Operating profit after income tax		245.1	148.0	307.9	61.1
Depreciation and amounts set aside to provisions		297.6	202.4	707.7	(2.9)
Losses (profits) from disposal of non-current assets		(11.1)	4.8	(480.5)	(0.2)
(Increase) decrease in—					
interest receivable		17.3	(17.0)	(0.1)	(0.1)
other receivables		(114.6)	(140.9)	(229.1)	(824.1)
inventories		(154.9)	(145.9)	0.2	–
prepayments		15.0	(90.4)	4.1	(0.8)
Increase (decrease) in—					
interest payable		26.1	4.3	29.4	(0.4)
tax payable		45.2	(19.5)	24.3	9.3
other payables		95.6	37.8	72.4	821.2
accrued charges		(27.6)	54.8	25.7	(10.6)
Cash flows from operating activities		433.7	38.4	462.0	52.5

Changes in assets and liabilities are net of effects from purchases of entities.

Reconciliation of cash

For the purposes of the statements of cash flows, cash includes cash on hand and in banks and investments in money market instruments, net of bank overdrafts and short-term borrowings.

Cash and cash equivalents	6	435.6	877.1	116.0	52.1
Call deposits (included in loans)		(119.8)	(420.5)	(119.8)	(420.5)
Bank overdrafts		(43.9)	(50.2)	(13.6)	(9.5)
Cash at the end of the year		271.9	406.4	(17.4)	(377.9)

Non-cash financing and investing activities

During the year, the Group issued 275 million ordinary shares for the acquisition of 100% of the common shares of Coca-Cola Bottlers Philippines, Inc and 18 million ordinary shares as consideration for a non-compete agreement from the San Miguel Corporation in certain countries in Asia. These shares were issued at $11.52 each, amounting to a total of $3375.4M

Statements of cash flows typically include a reconciliation of cash flows from operating activities to the operating profit after income tax result. As Figure 2.6 shows, the operating profit after income tax of $245.1 million for the year ended 31 December 1997 is reconciled to the net cash flows from operating activities of $433.7 million. Cash flow statements are examined in greater detail in Chapter 10.

Recognition criteria

The components of financial statements (assets, liabilities, equity, revenue and expenses) discussed above are known as financial statement *elements*. Assets and expenses, revenue, and liabilities are explored in greater depth in Chapters 15, 16 and 17 respectively.

For now, it should be appreciated that decisions are required to be made in deciding when financial statement elements are *recognised* in the financial statements. That is, at what point should they be recorded in the financial statements? For example, the process of earning revenue is likely to involve various stages. In the case of a wholesaler these may include the receipt of an order from a customer, delivery of the product, invoicing the customer, and the collection of payment. Revenue is said to be recognised when it is entered in the entity's accounts as revenue and thus to be reported on the face of the profit and loss statement. A similar issue arises in connection with expenses and the other elements of financial statements.

The recognition criteria commonly applied for the elements of financial statements comprise *probability* and *measurability* tests. In the case of revenue, for example, the concept of probability relates to the degree of uncertainty that the benefits embodied in an item will flow to the entity. Something is 'probable' when the chances of it eventuating are likely (that is, a greater than 50 per cent chance). The measurement concept relates to the assignment of an amount or value to an item that can be measured reliably. Elements are therefore recognised when the tests of probability and measurement are met. Case 2.1 provides a context in which to apply the tests of probability and measurability in deciding when to recognise revenue.

Case 2.1 Windfall gains and revenue recognition

F. Brasco was overjoyed on hearing the results of an analysis of a 75 centimetre rock purchased from an old-time, outback miner for the sum of $200 000 on 30 June. The opal-bearing rock, dubbed 'Opalgold', was identified after analysis by experts on 15 July to be worth more than three times the original value Brasco placed on it when deciding to make an offer to acquire it.

It has been reliably estimated that at least 75 per cent of the rock would be cut into marketable stones of high quality. Up to 30 000 stones were expected to be cut during the six months from 15 August. Marketing of the stones would be undertaken over a period of 18 months from 15 September.

On which of the following dates, if any, do you believe Brasco should recognise revenue related to this windfall gain:

(a) 30 June (date of purchase)
(b) 15 July (date of analysis)
(c) after six months (finalisation of stone cutting)
(d) as gems are sold
(e) as cash is received from gem sales.

Valuation in accounting

As well as understanding the meaning of the various components of the financial statements, it is necessary to understand how they are valued. A block of land generally has future usefulness, which qualifies it as an asset, but it may be valued in one of several ways, including its original cost, an estimate of the price for which it could be sold (that is, net realisable value), or the price that would have to be paid to replace the land with a property capable of offering identical services (that is, current replacement cost).

It has been previously argued that the information provided in accounting reports should be that which is most useful for decision making. Accordingly, accountants should choose the value that is most appropriate for the decisions investors and others must make. It will be discovered, however, that this choice is not an easy one and that throughout the world accountants have been unable to decide on the ideal basis of valuation.

The basis that is used in practice is primarily valuation at original cost. This is known as *historical cost accounting*, because the figures stated in financial statements are obtained from the historical set of transactions engaged in by the business. At first glance original cost may seem the least relevant basis for decisions about the future. Yet the accounting profession worldwide has clung to it. It is therefore appropriate to present the historical cost system clearly and fully. Once the nature of present practice has been explained, it will be possible to compare it with alternative accounting systems. The choice of a single alternative system to historical cost accounting remains a contentious and unresolved issue in accounting.

Under the historical cost system, the assets are recorded at their original cost. Non-current assets which are subject to depreciation charges are stated in the balance sheet at their written-down historical cost. In practice, variations from the principle of stating assets at their historical cost are found. For example, in recent decades private sector companies in certain jurisdictions such as Australia have, on an ad hoc basis, revalued certain long-lived assets such as land and buildings from their historical cost to their current value. The basis of valuation adopted by CCA is stated in its 1997 annual report thus: 'The financial statements have been prepared on the basis of historical cost and, except where otherwise stated, do not account for changing money values or valuations of non-current assets'. The practice of stating assets at their current values will be discussed in later chapters.

The public sector has recently adopted a more formalised approach. The aim is to implement a policy of regular asset revaluation (probably every three or five years) of the major assets of all public sector entities, with the emphasis on stating assets at current values such as their replacement cost. Stating assets at their current replacement cost is also shown as *deprival valuation*. Deprival valuation has been adopted in various jurisdictions in reforming public sector accounting by means of the adoption of full accrual accounting systems.[3]

In Case 2.2 your present ideas on financial valuation are put to the test in contemplating the 'worth' of an established business.

---

[3] In the case of the Australian reforms see, for example, P. Boxall, 'The Revolution in Government Accounting', *Australian CPA*, April 1998, pp. 18–20, and J. Guthrie, 'Application of Accrual Accounting in the Australian Public Sector—Rhetoric or Reality?', *Financial Accountability & Management*, February 1998, pp. 1–19.

Case 2.2 Evaluating the 'worth' of a business

B. Hwok, a young university arts graduate, was considering the purchase of a long-established business which had built a reputation for caring for its customers and employees. The accountant for the vendor supplied three different sets of figures to Hwok. Hwok heard you were studying commerce at university and sought your advice on what the business was 'worth'. The figures supplied to Hwok are as follows:

	Historical cost (net where applicable) $000	Net realisable value $000	Current replacement cost $000
Assets			
Cash at bank	5	5	5
Accounts receivable	30	27	27
Inventory	40	80	50
Motor vehicles	35	28	40
Equipment	90	50	100
Land and buildings	110	200	220
	310	390	442
Liabilities			
Accounts payable	40	40	40
Short-term borrowings	80	80	80
Long-term borrowings	50	50	50
Employee entitlements	25	25	25
	195	195	195
Net assets	115	195	247

Based on these sets of figures, what is the business 'worth'? In contemplating this question, recognise that Hwok, or anyone else interested in owning this business, will usually apply hard-earned savings and also borrow monies to purchase the business.

Estimation and judgement in accounting

In preparing accounting reports, accountants are required to make a large number of accounting policy choices and also make estimates and approximations in arriving at most of the figures appearing in the financial statements. Whereas cash inflows and outflows represent 'hard' numbers in that the amounts moving into and out of the entity are definite and can be verified by another party, *accrual accounting* systems involve substantial estimation in arriving at the figures to be reported in financial statements. As will become more evident as you progress through this book, these estimates typically involve making judgements about what is likely to happen in the future.

The basis of accrual accounting is the recognition of transactions and other events as goods and services are provided or consumed during an accounting period rather than when a flow of cash occurs. Where accrual accounting is adopted, revenue and expenses are recognised in the period in which they relate rather than when cash is transferred to or from the entity. Accounting on the basis of future expectations or what is 'probable', as reflected in the commonly adopted recognition criteria discussed earlier, contributes to the contentious nature of accounting. What may seem to be a 'cut and dried' affair becomes an intriguing and controversial field of study and practice.

The application of judgement in making accounting estimates is found in the instance of Ashton Mining Ltd and its reported write-down of the Argyle underground diamond mine in Western Australia (*Age*, 31 January 1998, p. 4; *Weekend Australian*, 1 February 1998, p. 53). The press reports of this case stated that the write-down would lead to the recording of a $95 million abnormal charge against revenue in 1997. The company had decided to bring forward the mine depreciation and amortisation charges which would have been recognised as expenses after 2003 to the 1997 financial year. The *Age* report stated that the reason for the write-down was because of 'delays in finding a mining method to extend the [mine's] life'.

It should also be recognised that accounting has been practised in one form or another for centuries and that it is as 'old' as commercial life itself. Commercial people centuries ago did not 'discover' how to keep accounting records. Instead, they accounted in ways to suit their purposes. In other words, they 'invented' the accounting process. Over the years a diversity of accounting practices or treatments have arisen. Clearly, some practices are more accepted than others, which gives rise to the notion of *generally accepted accounting practice*. In this sense, traditional practice itself is a source of authority for *conventional practice*.

Accounting standard-setters and other rule-makers have endeavoured in recent decades to reduce the level of diversity in accounting practice, with the objective of improving the quality of external reporting. Although accounting standards prescribe certain practices, and thus generally limit the number of alternative choices available, it should be recognised that accounting standards require to be interpreted. Thus key terms contained in accounting standards and to be examined later, such as 'probable', 'measurable', 'beyond any reasonable doubt', 'virtually certain', 'material', 'control', 'significant influence' and 'useful life', all need to be interpreted in the specific organisational context. Such 'professional' judgements are influenced by a range of factors and are typically made once the potential impacts of certain accounting treatments on the profitability and financial position of an entity have been ascertained.

Several different profit or loss results and net assets figures may be derived for the same entity over any given accounting period. We hope this statement of fact does not cause you any consternation! Different entities may adopt different accounting policies and arrive at different interpretations and estimates in treating like transactions and other events. Therefore, the value of financial comparisons over time (*inter-temporal comparisons*) and between entities (*inter-entity comparisons*), to be examined in depth in Chapter 11, largely depends on whether the entity/entities have adopted the same, or closely similar, accounting policies and practices over the period of the analysis.

Ethical issues

Reliance would not be placed on accounting reports unless they contained relevant and reliable information. Accountants are expected to act ethically. In fact, the codes of conduct that apply to them as members of professional accounting bodies command ethical behaviour. Business and community confidence would be severely eroded if users of accounting reports were generally unable to rely on those reports because of fears about the ethical standards of the preparers.

Ethical issues assume great importance with the increasing complexity of business in a global environment where individuals are expected, or are personally driven, to achieve at high levels. Sometimes these individuals are working at a frantic pace. Pressures to succeed, combined with financial and other incentives to meet or exceed designated results, can place certain individuals in positions where their behaviour may be subject to question. In times of economic downturn and the associated business failures, directors, managers, accountants, lawyers and other groups face scrutiny from the media and, of course, the general public. The fallout of an economic downturn includes exposure of poor and unethical practices and the prosecution of certain individuals because of their behaviour. Accountants and auditors are only too well aware of the increasing litigious environment in which we live.

In the same way that few, if any, people would state publicly that they are racist, few would state in public that they are unethical. Behaviour can, however, be construed as racist and/or unethical by others. If serious misbehaviour is exposed, the consequences for the implicated individual may be harsh. Accountants who behave unethically may be dealt with by the disciplinary committees of their professional bodies. The law courts may also become involved where fraud or other charges are alleged.

Case 2.15 in the 'Review exercises' provides a context in which to address ethical issues and to form an opinion on what constitutes appropriate professional behaviour.

 ## Summary

Accounting reports are the outputs of accounting and the prime communication tools of accountants, whether they be financial accountants, management accountants or both. Financial accounting or external reporting is primarily concerned with reporting to external parties. These may be general purpose or special purpose financial statement users. Management accounting primarily involves the preparation of internal reports for organisational management. However, many of the processes and concepts that underpin the preparation of accounting information for external users are relevant also to internal users.

This chapter was primarily concerned with the major financial statements: the profit and loss statement, the balance sheet and the cash flow statement. The structure and contents of these statements were introduced and discussed in the context of a major organisation, the CCA Group. This exposition involved an introduction to the elements of financial statements and the criteria for their recognition. Financial ratios, as tools of financial analysis, were also introduced in the context of the CCA results.

The basis of historical cost accounting was outlined. However, departures from this basis of accounting are evident in practice, such as the adoption of current values for certain long-lived assets. An understanding of accounting requires an appreciation of the use of estimates and approximations in practice and the role and application of judgement in preparing accounting reports. Accounting is a contentious practice and is more intriguing and controversial than many students realise.

Accounting reports are important inputs in decision processes. Accounting information is influential at all levels in organisations and throughout society. Although accounting is sometimes portrayed in student texts as a neutral, benign, technical practice, it is actually an organisational and social practice that has increasing implications in all our lives. In this era of calculative order, accounting, the contentious nature of accounting and its impacts are beginning to be studied more broadly within the contexts in which it operates.

This formative chapter is intentionally broad in scope. Throughout the remainder of the book we examine in greater depth the terms, concepts, ratios, issues and debates introduced in this chapter.

 ## Review exercises

Discussion questions

2.1   Distinguish between general purpose financial reporting and special purpose financial reporting.

2.2   Identify five types of users who rely on special purpose financial reports.

2.3 Describe the four key functions of management introduced in the chapter.

2.4 Outline two major differences between reporting about an organisation for external users of accounting information and internal users of accounting information.

2.5 State the role of the profit and loss statement, the balance sheet and the cash flow statement.

2.6 What information would be required by an investor in deciding whether to purchase shares in a publicly listed company?

2.7 What information might a bank require in deciding whether to make a long-term loan to a small-business operator?

2.8 'A profit and loss statement is concerned with results for the past period. Decision making is concerned with what will happen in the future. Therefore, profit and loss statements are irrelevant for decision making.' State whether you agree or disagree with this statement, and give your reasons.

2.9 For each item below, state whether it will appear in the profit and loss statement or the balance sheet and whether it should be classified as revenue (R), an expense (E), an asset (A), a liability (L) or owners' equity (OE).

(a) Cash on hand
(b) Land and buildings
(c) Sales to customers
(d) Cost of goods sold
(e) Accounts receivable
(f) Accounts payable to suppliers of goods
(g) A mortgage loan on the entity's land and buildings
(h) Interest paid on the mortgage
(i) Interest earned on an investment of funds
(j) The capital contribution of the owner

2.10 W. Brown has been operating a pharmacy for five years. Brown is considering the purchase of the recently vacated shop premises next door for $200 000 in order to either expand the pharmacy by introducing a gift section or rent them to a relative who wishes to open an exclusive fashion boutique. What information, both financial and non-financial, would you consider important to Brown in making his decision?

2.11 'Accounting is concerned with precision and financial statements are always accurate.' Discuss whether you agree or disagree with this statement.

 Problems

2.12 *Statement of financial position*

D. Pinch asks you to open a set of books. From the following information prepare a statement that will show Pinch's net investment in the business:

	$
Cash on hand	200
Amounts owing to suppliers	10 000
Amounts owing by customers	7 800
Bank overdraft	6 000

	$
Inventory in stock	16 000
Mortgage payable (due in 10 years time)	10 000
Delivery equipment	5 000
Furniture and fixtures	3 000
Building	17 000
Land	8 000

2.13 *Analysing financial statements*

B. Bunker has received a legacy of $10 000 from a grandparent's estate on the condition that it is invested as capital in one of two family businesses. The following financial information is available for the last financial year:

PROFIT AND LOSS STATEMENTS
for the year ending 31 December 20X0

	Hardware Store		Supermarket	
Sales revenue	$800 000	100%	$1 200 000	100%
less Cost of goods sold	560 000	70%	960 000	80%
	240 000	30%	240 000	20%
less Expenses:				
Salespersons' salaries	80 000	10%	72 000	6%
Rent	40 000	5%	–	–
Interest	–	–	36 000	3%
Electricity	24 000	3%	48 000	4%
Advertising	64 000	8%	24 000	2%
Total expenses	208 000	26%	180 000	15%
Net profit	32 000	4%	60 000	5%
less Personal withdrawals	16 000	2%	48 000	4%
Retained profit	16 000	2%	12 000	1%

BALANCE SHEETS
as at 31 December 20X0

	Hardware Store	Supermarket
Assets		
Cash at bank	$ 30 000	–
Accounts receivable	20 000	$ 10 000
Stock of inventory	60 000	70 000
Furniture and fittings	90 000	120 000
Land	–	100 000
	200 000	300 000
Liabilities		
Accounts payable	40 000	60 000
Mortgage loan	–	80 000
	40 000	140 000

continues

BALANCE SHEETS as at 31 December 20X0	Hardware Store	Supermarket
Owners' equity		
Capital	144 000	148 000
plus Retained profit	16 000	12 000
	160 000	160 000
	200 000	300 000

(a) List the main differences between the two businesses as revealed by the financial statements.

(b) Which business should Bunker invest in? Why?

(c) What other information might have been useful in making the investment decision?

2.14 *Analysing financial statements*

R. Rebecca and P. Neal are considering whether to lend $15 000 to either their good friend K. Stefano, who owns a fashion warehouse, or to Neal's father who owns and operates a soft-drink distribution and wholesale business. Based on the following financial statements for the year ended 30 June 20X0, what would be your recommendation to Rebecca and Neal? Your answer should include a discussion of the major differences between the two businesses.

PROFIT AND LOSS STATEMENTS for the year ending 30 June 20X0	Stefano's Fashion House		Neal's Beverages	
Sales revenue	$380 000		$635 000	
less Cost of goods sold	247 000		496 000	
Gross profit	133 000	(35%)	139 000	(22%)
less Expenses:				
Wages	41 000		57 300	
Electricity	8 700		10 400	
Rent	16 000		23 000	
Interest	18 000		24 600	
Advertising	7 500		–	
Cleaning	6 500		8 300	
Repairs and maintenance	23 000		–	
Net profit	12 300	(9%)	15 400	(11%)
less Withdrawals	4 300		6 400	
Retained profit	8 000		9 000	

BALANCE SHEETS

as at 30 June 20X0

	Stefano's Fashion House	Neal's Beverages
Assets		
Cash	$ 41 000	–
Trade debtors	68 000	97 000
Inventory	53 000	45 000
Fixtures and fittings	105 000	77 000
Delivery truck	–	32 000
Plant and equipment	–	131 000
Total assets	267 000	382 000
Liabilities		
Bank loan	20 000	10 000
Trade creditors	51 000	75 000
Long-term loan	87 000	100 000
Bank overdraft	–	73 000
Total liabilities	158 000	258 000
Owners' equity		
Capital	90 000	100 000
plus Retained profit	19 000	24 000
	109 000	124 000
Total equity	267 000	382 000

Case studies

2.15 *Kim P. Jones faces an ethical dilemma*

Having been employed in a large accounting firm for about seven years, Kim P. Jones commenced practising as a sole practitioner on 1 April 20X6. With few clients and a need to provide for a young family, Kim accepted a position as auditor of the local football club. St James Football Club has enjoyed much success in recent years and has a large local following of supporters. Kim believed that the auditing role would result in an increase in the client base of the practice from people connected with the club such as players, officials, trainers, supporters and sponsors.

Although not having any prior official links with the club, Kim had attended some home games and had heard a rumour about the use of a 'silent' gate at the home ground. (A silent gate is a gate through which the paying public enter, but where the cash takings on the day are not counted for official record-keeping purposes; the takings are used to make certain cash payments, such as bonuses to players for special on-field performances.) When presented with the books, records and financial statements by the club secretary for audit, Kim enquired about the collection and banking of monies from home games. The secretary assured Kim that the books reflected whatever monies were collected. The secretary also pointed out that the club was required to report accurately the details of takings at home games to the controlling association for the purpose of determining a periodic administration and marketing levy payable by clubs to the association.

Kim conducted the audit with due care and diligence and signed an unqualified audit opinion which stated that 'the financial statements present fairly in accordance with accounting standards the financial position of the St James Football Club as at 30 June 20X6 and the results of its operations for the year then ended'. Kim subsequently returned the books, records and audited financial statements to the secretary who invited Kim to attend the Club's annual meeting to be held in two weeks time. Within one week of returning these items, the club captain visited Kim's office and asked Kim to prepare his 20X5–X6 income tax return. Kim was keen to accept this engagement and was anxious to impress the captain, hoping that it would lead to more income-tax work from other players at the club.

The captain was a partner in a nearby law practice and indicated the importance of stating all his assessable income and not overstating his allowable deductions, in order not to put at risk the public trust which came with his position in the firm. Kim understood and endorsed these views and proceeded to prepare the captain's income tax return. The captain informed Kim that included in his assessable income was $5000 he had received in cash from the money taken at the silent gate. Kim acted in accordance with the wishes of the new client but was uneasy about the revelation that a silent gate had in fact operated at the home games of the club.

After a restless night Kim decided to make a telephone call to the secretary to request that the signed audit report be returned for amendment. Kim had decided to change the report on the basis of the recently acquired knowledge about the silent gate. On arriving at the office, Kim took a telephone call from the club president who was an influential business leader with significant business interests. The president advised Kim that he wished to make an appointment to discuss the prospect of engaging Kim as his new accountant. Kim was delighted with this news but, given the overnight reflection on the contents of the audit report of the football club, was in something of a dilemma. Nevertheless, Kim rang the secretary to advise him of the decision to amend the audit opinion. The secretary became suspicious and asked Kim to outline exactly what changes were to be made. Feeling tense and uncomfortable, Kim advised him that the changes were to the wording of the opinion and were not of major consequence.

Kim spent the next three hours drafting and redrafting sentences to arrive at a tenable position in view of recent happenings. The new audit opinion stated that 'the financial statements present fairly in accordance with accounting standards the financial position of the St James Football Club for the year ended 30 June 20X6 and the results of its operations for the year then ended based on the books and records that were made available for audit'. Kim left the office that evening feeling relaxed and purchased a bottle of wine on the way home to celebrate encouraging times ahead for the practice.

Required

(a) What is the ethical dilemma facing Kim P. Jones?
(b) Provide advice to Kim on what you would consider to be appropriate professional conduct in the circumstances.

2.16 *Australian Society of Certified Practising Accountants*

The financial statements of the Australian Society of CPAs for the year ended 31 December 1997 showed a marked improvement in performance and financial position over the previous financial year. The 'consolidated' operating statement for the year and the consolidated balance sheet as at year end are reproduced below from the *Report to Members 1997*.

OPERATING STATEMENT
for the year ended 31 December 1997

	Consolidated	
	1997	1996
	$000	$000
Revenue	51 835	45 759
Expenses	(48 418)	(47 419)
Operating surplus (deficit) before abnormal items & income tax	3 417	(1 660)
Abnormal items before income tax	(455)	(1 074)
Surplus (deficit) before income tax	2 962	(2 734)
Income tax	–	–
Surplus (deficit) after income tax	2 962	(2 734)
Retained surplus at the beginning of the financial year	5 894	8 628
Retained surplus at the end of the financial year	8 856	5 894

BALANCE SHEET
as at 31 December 1997

	Consolidated	
	1997	1996
	$000	$000
Current assets		
Cash	6 369	3 402
Receivables	904	985
Inventories	266	540
Prepayments	452	949
Total current assets	7 991	5 876
Non-current assets		
Property, plant and equipment	16 419	18 515
Total non-current assets	16 419	18 515
Total assets	24 410	24 391
Current liabilities		
Creditors	5 375	5 697
Borrowings	320	–
Provisions	1 856	1 098
Subscriptions and fees in advance	6 211	7 847
Total current liabilities	13 762	14 642
Non-current liabilities		
Borrowings	610	–
Provisions	122	83
Total non-current liabilities	732	83
Total liabilities	14 494	14 725
NET ASSETS	9 916	9 666
Members' funds		
Reserves	1 060	3 772
Retained surplus	8 856	5 894
TOTAL MEMBERS' FUNDS	9 916	9 666

Required

(a) Identify the major financial changes that occurred based on the 1996 and 1997 results.

(b) Comment specifically on the current ratio position of the Society as at the end of each financial year.

2.17 *Using balance sheets to introduce an infrastructure charge*

The following article titled 'Qualified Support for Assets Charge' by Dorothy Illing appeared in the *Australian* on 14 January 1998, p. 32:

Queensland University of Technology has given in-principle support to the contentious infrastructure charge flagged in the West committee's review of higher education.

However, its response to the committee's discussion paper says this is only on the proviso that an 'appropriate and fair measure' is developed.

The West committee's discussion paper asserts that under current arrangements universities are the recipients of 'hidden' subsidies in the form of the publicly funded assets held by institutions.

It says there are no direct incentives for universities to manage these assets in a more efficient way and that an infrastructure charge based on an expected rate of return on assets would provide such incentives.

The QUT cites two main approaches—one based on the measurement of gross assets of an institution (the value of land, buildings, equipment and assets) and the other based on the measurement of asset use (gross assets as a ratio of student numbers).

It favours the second approach but points to the problem of deriving a fair performance indicator for the charge.

'In addition to the confounding factors already identified by the West Review, there would be a number of other significant issues which would make the measurement of asset utilisation difficult, including land values for city campuses, the degree to which electronic means of delivery are used, and the funding background of institutions', the response says.

It says if an appropriate measure were to be found, any revenue generated by the charge could be distributed to those institutions with better asset use.

'It would be reasonable for a phased approach to be taken to the introduction of an infrastructure charge.

'Under this proposal, a base-line could be set and then institutions could be rewarded or penalised depending on their performance in improving their asset utilisation.'

The response supports the 'theoretical model' of student-based funding (vouchers).

However, it says putting such a system into practice would be difficult and potentially costly from an administrative perspective.

It supports student-centred research funding, through scholarships, and public support for basic research and research training.

Required

(a) Discuss accounting's role in 'reforming' universities on the basis of the suggestion to introduce an assets or financing charge as outlined.

(b) Of the two approaches outlined, which is likely to provide more useful information? Justify your view.

(c) What are the possible consequences of introducing such a charging regime?

2.18 *Foster's Brewing Group Ltd*

Like Coca-Cola Amatil Ltd, Foster's Brewing Group (FBG) Ltd is in the beverages industry. The 1997 Annual Report of FBG stated that the group 'is a global beer and wine company dedicated to delivering premium branded products to consumers in more than 120 countries around the world' (p. 1). The key consolidated or group financial statements published in the 1997 Annual Report include comparative figures for the 1996 financial year and are reproduced below. FBG's financial year ends on 30 June.

PROFIT AND LOSS STATEMENT
consolidated for the year ended 30 June 1997

	Note	1997	1996
		Consolidated	
		$m	$m
Operating revenue	2	2779.9	2535.8
Operating profit before interest and abnormal items		426.8	363.5
Net interest expense	3	(90.1)	(61.3)
Operating profit before abnormal items and income tax	3	336.7	302.2
Abnormal items	4	(41.0)	(1.7)
Operating profit before income tax		295.7	300.5
Income tax attributable to operating profit	5	(47.7)	(8.5)
Operating profit after income tax		248.0	292.0
Outside equity interest in operating profit after income tax		2.5	1.3
Operating profit after income tax attributable to members of the chief entity		250.5	293.3
Retained profits/(accumulated losses) at the beginning of the financial year		89.6	(1307.9)
Adjustment resulting from capital reconstruction	17	–	1303.5
Adjustment resulting from change in accounting policy	9	(115.0)	–
Aggregate of amounts transferred from reserves	18	28.0	16.5
Total available for appropriation		253.1	305.4
Ordinary dividends	21		
—interim paid		(98.1)	(98.1)
—final payable		(102.5)	(117.7)
Retained profits at the end of the financial year		52.5	89.6

BALANCE SHEET
consolidated as at 30 June 1997

	Note	1997	1996
		Consolidated	
		$m	$m
Current assets			
Cash	6	**120.0**	147.7
Receivables	7	**279.0**	305.7
Inventories	8	**206.2**	211.0
Investments	9	**10.7**	–
Residual Lensworth assets	12	**104.0**	96.2
Other	13	**42.8**	40.1
Total current assets		**762.7**	800.7
Non-current assets			
Receivables	7	**51.7**	116.9
Inventories	8	**100.3**	78.5
Investments	9	**1028.5**	1121.3
Property, plant and equipment	10	**1699.2**	1530.3
Intangibles	11	**1013.0**	1021.3
Residual Lensworth assets	12	**218.2**	338.2
Other	13	**70.8**	48.0
Total non-current assets		**4181.7**	4254.5
Total assets		**4944.4**	5055.2
Current liabilities			
Accounts payable	14	**291.5**	367.6
Borrowings	15	**72.6**	47.1
Provisions	16	**223.4**	251.0
Total current liabilities		**587.5**	665.7
Non-current liabilities			
Accounts payable	14	**17.6**	10.3
Borrowings	15	**1182.1**	1167.5
Provisions	16	**259.6**	267.4
Total non-current liabilities		**1459.3**	1445.2
Total liabilities		**2046.8**	2110.9
Net assets		**2897.6**	2944.3
Shareholders' equity			
Share capital	17	**1963.5**	1962.2
Reserves	18	**845.2**	853.9
Retained profits		**52.5**	89.6
Shareholders' equity attributable to members of the chief entity		**2861.2**	2905.7
Outside equity interest in controlled entities	19	**36.4**	38.6
Total shareholders' equity		**2897.6**	2944.3

STATEMENT OF CASH FLOWS
consolidated for the year ended 30 June 1997

	Note	1997	1996
		Inflows/(Outflows)	
		Consolidated	
		$m	$m
Cash flows from operating activities			
Receipts from customers		3888.3	3638.0
Payments to suppliers, employees, principals		(3534.3)	(3345.0)
Dividends received		1.0	1.4
Interest received		36.7	20.9
Interest paid		(131.8)	(132.7)
Income tax paid		(18.6)	(24.1)
Funds withdrawn from Molson Breweries Partnership		14.2	62.9
Net cash flows from operating activities	28	255.5	221.4
Cash flows from investing activities			
Payments to acquire controlled entities (net of cash balances acquired)	28	(44.4)	(511.2)
Payments to acquire outside equity interest in controlled entities		(29.5)	(9.3)
Payments for property, plant and equipment		(195.8)	(190.0)
Payments for acquisition of investments and other assets		(5.3)	(6.7)
Loans made		(14.9)	(39.6)
Proceeds from repayment of loans		75.1	117.3
Proceeds from sale of property, plant and equipment		18.4	2.8
Proceeds from sale of other investments and other assets		208.3	147.6
Proceeds from sale of Courage brewing business	28	–	892.8
Net cash flows from investing activities		11.9	403.7
Cash flows from financing activities			
Proceeds from borrowings	15	1775.6	2417.8
Repayment of borrowings	15	(1870.4)	(2780.9)
Dividends paid		(215.8)	(212.5)
Equity contribution from outside equity interests		0.1	3.8
Net cash flows from financing activities		(310.5)	(571.8)
Total cash flows from activities	15	(43.1)	53.3
Cash at the beginning of the financial year		140.4	120.7
Effect of exchange rate changes on foreign currency cash flows and cash balances		13.8	(33.6)
Cash at the end of the financial year	28	111.1	140.4

Required

Examine and comment on the results of FBG relative to those reported by CCA.

PART 2

The recording and external reporting focus

CHAPTER 3
Classification and analysis of transactions

Learning objectives

In this chapter you will be introduced to:

1. transaction analysis, in terms of the effects of transactions on the accounting equation

2. net profit/loss and the profit and loss statement

3. the accounting equation and simple balance sheet

4. the difference between withdrawals and expenses

5. the difference between assets and expenses

6. which portion of costs incurred by an entity constitute expenses and which portions are assets

7. the differences between the cash-flow statement and other financial reports

8. how to expense an asset over time.

Introduction

Chapter 2 presented an outline of the end products of the accounting process, namely the profit and loss statement, the balance sheet and the cash-flow statement. Before these statements are able to be prepared, the accountant must classify and summarise all relevant business transactions in a logical and structured form.

Classification precedes summarisation

Suppose a trainee accountant was given a list of 500 transactions undertaken by an organisation in its first year of operations and asked, 'How is the company performing? What is the state of the company's financial health?' How would the trainee accountant answer those questions?

One possibility would be simply to list all of the transactions in chronological order, but this would take many pages and the manager would be no wiser than before. The art of communication, whether it be the evening television news or a financial statement, is to compress the events into a summary that gives a clear picture of the overall effect of the events.

Any attempt to summarise a large number of events requires three steps:

1. A decision about the purpose the summary is to serve.
2. Selection of the aspects of each event that are relevant to that purpose.
3. Preparation of a summary.

Any transaction or event has a number of aspects of possible interest, which will be defined as its 'attributes'. A transaction to purchase a green tractor for $2000 to use on a farm has several attributes of possible interest. At various times the owner of the farm may be interested in summarising all of the tractor purchases, or all of the purchases for one farm against other farms, or even all the purchases of green objects (but this is unlikely). Finally, the farmer may be interested in analysing cash payments. This one transaction has attributes relevant to all of those matters.

Having selected the attribute of interest (say cash payments), all transactions having the same characteristic (a cash payment) are combined and a summary is produced.

Example: *Classification and summarisation*

Transactions:

A. Contributed cash at start of $24 000.
B. Bought three red tractors for $2000 each in cash.
C. Bought two yellow tractors for $7500 each on credit.
D. Sold one red tractor for $8000 cash.
E. Sold one yellow tractor for $9000 on credit.

Different classificatory schemes will be used to extract different attributes from the transactions to suit different purposes.

1. The farmer wishes to know how many tractors are available for the harvest. To determine this, it is necessary to produce a summary of tractors on hand (see over).

   The first column presents sufficient information to answer the farmer's question. However, for more detailed questions, such as determining the availability of red tractors, the *subclassification* in the other columns would be required.

   The bottom line presents the summary in accordance with the attributes selected for analysis. Other possible attributes, such as whether the transaction was for cash or credit, have no influence on this summary. They are relevant, however, if other questions are asked.

Transaction	Change in tractors	Red	Yellow
A	nil		
B	+3	+3	
C	+2		+2
D	−1	−1	
E	−1		−1
Tractors on hand	+3	+2	+1

2. The farmer wishes to purchase more tractors, providing adequate cash is on hand.

Transaction	Effect on cash	
	$	
A	+ 24 000	
B	− 6 000	
C	nil	(credit transaction)
D	+ 8 000	
E	nil	(credit transaction)
Cash on hand	+ 26 000	

In this analysis the numbers and colours of tractors were of no interest.

Classification in accounting reports

Both types of summaries in the previous example will be found in accounting practice. However, the most basic classification used in accounting is that which produces summary financial statements in the form of the profit and loss statement and the balance sheet, as shown in Chapter 2.

The present task is to explain how a multitude of apparently unrelated transactions may be classified and summarised in the basic financial statements. The technique is known as *transaction analysis.*

The relationship between assets and claims on assets may be expressed as an ownership equation for the business:

$$assets = equities$$

Since equities consist of liabilities or owners' equity,

$$assets = liabilities + owners' equity$$

For example, an enterprise has assets totalling $50 000 and liabilities of $4000. In this case, the owner's interest is the assets after deducting liabilities, which is $46 000 (or $50 000 – $4000). This calculation is possible due to the accounting equation as follows:

$$assets = liabilities + owners' equity$$

or

$$\$50\ 000 = \$4000 + \$46\ 000$$

The equation may be rearranged to demonstrate the true nature of owners' equity as the residual after subtracting the liabilities from the assets:

$$assets - liabilities = owners' equity$$

As discussed in Chapter 2, the financial statement that presents a summary of the assets, liabilities and owners' equity of an entity is known as a *balance sheet*. All of the elements of any transaction will ultimately be classified under one of the following headings: assets, liabilities and owners' equity. These three elements require a clear definition before a balance sheet can be prepared.

Assets

Assets are resources owned or controlled by the entity for the purpose of providing benefits to that entity.

Assets may be thought of as 'bundles of future benefit'. Assets are generally thought of as physical objects. The accountant, however, views assets differently and asks whether an object offers any future benefit to the entity. If it does not, it is not an asset. Cash is nearly always an asset (unless it is counterfeit) since it may be used to finance future transactions and thus to provide future benefits to an organisation. A machine producing goods for sale is an asset until it is no longer usable, that is, until its capacity to provide future benefits has expired. A useless machine is no longer an asset. Thus, not all physical objects owned by the entity are assets.

Conversely, an asset need not be present in the form of a physical object. Rent or insurance premiums paid in advance are assets for accounting purposes because they will produce benefits (such as a use of space or insurance cover) in the future. There are many other examples of non-physical assets, such as prepaid wages, patents and rights to intellectual property.

It is also important to note that an asset may be recorded as belonging to an entity even though it has not been paid for. A vehicle purchased with the assistance of a loan is an asset because it promises future benefits to the entity and is under its control.

The primary test of an asset, then, is that it should offer future benefits to the entity. These benefits may be of two types, either as a value in use (e.g. equipment making goods for sale or a bus for carrying passengers) or as a value in exchange (e.g. inventory or merchandise in a retail store). These concepts are explored more fully in Chapter 6. When an asset's benefits are used up or consumed, it becomes an expense.

As explained in Chapter 2, assets are reported in the balance sheet in descending order of liquidity. Liquidity refers to the ability of an entity to convert assets into cash. The following list is typical of a general order of assets within a balance sheet:

1. *Cash at bank*. This is used to record deposits and withdrawals from an entity's bank account.
2. *Accounts receivable*. This is used to record amounts owed to the firm by customers. Accounts receivable may also be termed debtors.
3. *Prepayments*. This records payments made prior to a service being received, for example prepaid insurance.
4. *Inventory or stock*. This defines items held for the purpose of resale. This type of asset is generally relevant to merchandising operations.
5. *Motor vehicles*. This refers to motor vehicles owned or controlled by the entity that are used for the purpose of generating business.
6. *Plant and equipment*. This includes equipment owned or controlled by the entity for the purpose of productive output.
7. *Buildings*. This asset refers to buildings used in the normal course of business. Buildings that are not used for productive purposes may be deemed an 'investment', which in itself is a specific type of asset category.

Liabilities

Liabilities represent future obligations or sacrifices and are usually settled using cash.

Liabilities represent debts owed by the entity to outside parties. These parties may include regular suppliers, lending institutions or, in the case of a public company, the general community through a debt instrument such as a debenture issue. Issuing debentures is effectively issuing debt by inviting people or institutions from the public to lend an entity funds. Debts may also be owed to employees within an enterprise as wages payable. Liabilities are generally repaid in cash, but in some circumstances may be extinguished by the performance of a service.

Those liabilities expected to be extinguished earliest are reported first in the balance sheet. The following are common liabilities:

1. *Wages and salaries payable.* These represent wages and salaries that have been earned by employees but not yet paid by the entity.
2. *Accounts payable.* This records amounts owed by the entity generally to regular suppliers. Accounts payable may also be termed creditors.
3. *Unearned revenues.* This records funds that have been received prior to the entity providing a service. At the point of receipt they are recorded as liabilities and subsequently recognised as revenue (or income) as they are earned.
4. *Mortgage payable.* This represents funds borrowed by the entity where the lending institution has a charge over a specific asset. Should the entity fail to repay the loan, the lender may claim the asset.

Owners' equity

Owners' equity represents the owners' claim or net worth in the assets of the entity.

The most common form of owners' equity accounts are:

1. *Capital.* This records the contributions of the owner to the entity.
2. *Withdrawals.* Otherwise called drawings, these are used to record the withdrawals of assets (normally cash) by the owner from the entity.
3. *Revenue.* Revenue (or income)[1] records increases in owners' equity as a result of the activities of the entity. Examples of revenue transactions include receipts from the performance of services, sales of goods, or the earning of interest or dividends.
4. *Expenses.* This records decreases in owners' equity as a result of the consumption of assets or loss of resources. Examples of expenses include last week's rent, electricity bills, wages paid to employees and petrol consumed.

The accounting entity

Before any transactions can be analysed, a viewpoint must be established. To illustrate, suppose the owner of a business contributed $10 000 in cash as additional capital. From the owner's viewpoint, this transaction reflects a payment of cash to the entity. From the entity's viewpoint, it has received cash from its owner.

For accounting purposes, the viewpoint taken is that of the entity being accounted for.

---

[1] The IASC *Framework* for the preparation and presentation of financial statements refers to income rather than revenue.

The analysis of transactions

The process of analysis of transactions will be explained by means of the following examples.

Example 1: *Transaction analyses: J. Doff*

On 1 April 20XX J. Doff decided to open a painting business called J. Doff Painting Services. The following transactions took place during the first month of April.

1   Owner contributed $20 000 cash to commence business.
2   Billed customers for services performed, $9000.
3   Purchased painting supplies on credit for $400.
4   Received $4000 from customers from (2) above.
5   Purchased a van for $8000, paying $2000 in cash and obtaining a loan for the remainder.
6   Paid $100 off amount due for supplies from (3) above.
7   J. Doff withdrew $1000.
8   Used $100 worth of painting supplies.
9   Paid expenses in cash (advertising $300, telephone $400, electricity $300).
10 Paid $2000 off loan for van in (5) above.

Required

(a) Record the transactions in an accounting equation table.
(b) Prepare a profit and loss statement, capital statement and balance sheet for the month.

Notes

- After each transaction is complete the accounting equation must remain in balance.
- All transactions involving capital contributions, revenues, expenses or drawings in the following accounting equation analysis will always affect the owners' equity column since they reflect increases or decreases in the owners' claim on the entity.
- Before commencing each transaction the following questions should be addressed:
  - *Classification*. What elements of the equation are affected as a result of the transaction?
  - *Change*. Has that element increased or decreased as a result of the transaction?
  - *Items affected*. What specific items are affected?

Answers

(a) **Transactions**

  1. Owner input $20 000

Classification	Change	Items affected
Asset	Increase	Cash
Owners' equity—capital	Increase	Capital

Explanation: The entity has gained cash, but must acknowledge the owners' claim on the entity.

	Assets				=	Liabilities	+	Owners' equity
	Cash at bank	*Accounts receivable*	*Supplies*	*Van*		*Accounts payable*	*Loan payable*	
1	+ 20 000							+ 20 000 C*

---

* C = Capital, R = Revenue, D = Drawings, E = Expenses

2. Billed customers $9000

Classification	Change	Items affected
Asset	Increase	Accounts receivable
Owners' equity—revenue	Increase	Service revenue

Explanation: The entity has earned revenue through an increase in assets. Since the owner has the residual claim on the entity's surplus, the owners' claim has increased.

	Assets			=	Liabilities	+	Owners' equity
	Cash at bank	*Accounts receivable*	*Supplies*	*Van*	*Accounts payable*	*Loan payable*	
1	+ 20 000						+ 20 000 C*
2		+ 9 000					+ 9 000 R

3. Purchased painting supplies on credit $400

Classification	Change	Items affected
Asset	Increase	Supplies
Liability	Increase	Accounts payable

Explanation: The painting supplies will provide future benefits through use and therefore are an asset. The other effect is to record a liability to the supplier.

	Assets			=	Liabilities	+	Owners' equity
	Cash at bank	*Accounts receivable*	*Supplies*	*Van*	*Accounts payable*	*Loan payable*	
1	+ 20 000						+ 20 000 C*
2		+ 9 000					+ 9 000 R
3			+ 400		+ 400		

4. Received $4000 from customers billed in (2) above

Classification	Change	Items affected
Asset	Increase	Cash
Asset	Decrease	Accounts receivable

Explanation: Cash has been received, increasing that asset. However, the asset recording the customer's debt must be reduced by the same amount.

	Assets			=	Liabilities	+	Owners' equity
	Cash at bank	*Accounts receivable*	*Supplies*	*Van*	*Accounts payable*	*Loan payable*	
1	+ 20 000						+ 20 000 C*
2		+ 9 000					+ 9 000 R
3			+ 400		+ 400		
4	+ 4 000	− 4 000					

5. Purchased a van for $8000, paying $2000 in cash and obtaining a loan for the remainder

Classification	Change	Items affected
Asset	Increase	Van
Asset	Decrease	Cash
Liability	Increase	Loan payable

Explanation: Here there are three effects, as the increase in an asset, the van, is financed partly by decreasing the asset 'cash' and partly by an increase in the liability 'loan payable'.

	Assets				=	Liabilities	+	Owners' equity
	Cash at bank	Accounts receivable	Supplies	Van		Accounts payable	Loan payable	
1	+ 20 000							+ 20 000 C*
2		+ 9 000						+ 9 000 R
3			+ 400			+ 400		
4	+ 4 000	– 4 000						
5	– 2 000			+ 8 000			+ 6 000	

6. Paid $100 off account for supplies

Classification	**Change**	**Items affected**
Liability	Decrease	Accounts payable
Asset	Decrease	Cash

Explanation: The liability is reduced through a reduction in the asset 'cash'. The supplies item is unaffected as that asset was previously recorded under (3) above.

	Assets				=	Liabilities	+	Owners' equity
	Cash at bank	Accounts receivable	Supplies	Van		Accounts payable	Loan payable	
1	+ 20 000							+ 20 000 C*
2		+ 9 000						+ 9 000 R
3			+ 400			+ 400		
4	+ 4 000	– 4 000						
5	– 2 000			+ 8 000			+ 6 000	
6	– 100					– 100		

7. Withdrawal $1000

Classification	**Change**	**Items affected**
Owners' equity—drawings	Decrease	Drawings
Asset	Decrease	Cash

Explanation: The reduction in the entity's cash is matched by a reduction in the owners' claim, due to drawings.

	Assets				=	Liabilities	+	Owners' equity
	Cash at bank	Accounts receivable	Supplies	Van		Accounts payable	Loan payable	
1	+ 20 000							+ 20 000 C*
2		+ 9 000						+ 9 000 R
3			+ 400			+ 400		
4	+ 4 000	– 4 000						
5	– 2 000			+ 8 000			+ 6 000	
6	– 100					– 100		
7	– 1 000							– 1 000 D

8. Used $100 worth of painting supplies

Classification	**Change**	**Items affected**
Asset	Decrease	Supplies
Owners' equity—expenses	Decrease	Supplies consumed

Explanation: An asset has been used up. As the resources of the entity have decreased, the owner's claim has fallen. The decrease in owners' equity is recorded as an expense.

	Assets				=	Liabilities	+	Owners' equity
	Cash at bank	Accounts receivable	Supplies	Van		Accounts payable	Loan payable	
1	+ 20 000							+ 20 000 C*
2		+ 9 000						+ 9 000 R
3			+ 400			+ 400		
4	+ 4 000	− 4 000						
5	− 2 000			+ 8 000			+ 6 000	
6	− 100					− 100		
7	− 1 000							− 1 000 D
8			− 100					− 100 E

9. Paid expenses in cash $1000

Classification	Change	Items affected
Owners' equity—expenses	Decrease	Advertising expense
		Electricity expense
		Telephone expense
Asset	Decrease	Cash

Explanation: All of these payments are for benefits that have been consumed. Therefore, no asset arises and, instead, the owner's claim is diminished by recognition of expenses.

	Assets				=	Liabilities	+	Owners' equity
	Cash at bank	Accounts receivable	Supplies	Van		Accounts payable	Loan payable	
1	+ 20 000							+ 20 000 C*
2		+ 9 000						+ 9 000 R
3			+ 400			+ 400		
4	+ 4 000	− 4 000						
5	− 2 000			+ 8 000			+ 6 000	
6	− 100					− 100		
7	− 1 000							− 1 000 D
8			− 100					−100 E
9	− 1 000							− 1 000 E

10. Paid $2000 off loan for van

Classification	Change	Items affected
Liability	Decrease	Loan payable
Asset	Decrease	Cash

Explanation: A reduction of the assets side of the equation is matched by a reduction in liabilities. The asset of the van is unaffected. As this is the final transaction, the table will now be totalled.

	Assets				=	Liabilities	+	Owners' equity
	Cash at bank	Accounts receivable	Supplies	Van		Accounts payable	Loan payable	
1	+ 20 000							+ 20 000 C*
2		+ 9 000						+ 9 000 R
3			+ 400			+ 400		
4	+ 4 000	– 4 000						
5	– 2 000			+ 8 000			+ 6 000	
6	– 100					– 100		
7	– 1 000							– 1 000 D
8			– 100					–100 E
9	– 1 000							– 1 000 E
10	– 2 000						– 2 000	
	17 900	+ 5 000	+ 300	+ 8 000		300	+ 4 000	26 900
or	**31 200**				**=**	**4 300**	**+**	**26 900**

This summary can now be used to prepare the financial statements.

(b) **Financial statements**

The owner will want to know how this initial contribution of $20 000 grew to $26 900. The sources of change in owners' equity are of two main kinds: those resulting from profitable trading or those resulting from contributions or withdrawals of capital.

Profitable trading is revealed by a comparison of changes in owners' equity due to revenue and expense transactions. These are summarised in a profit and loss statement:

PROFIT AND LOSS STATEMENT: J. DOFF PAINTING SERVICES
for the month ended 30 April 20XX

Service revenue		$9000
less Expenses		
Supplies	$100	
Advertising	300	
Telephone	400	
Electricity	300	1100
Net profit		$7900

A further statement can now be prepared that reconciles the opening and closing amounts of capital. The 'capital statement' might appear as follows:

CAPITAL STATEMENT: J. DOFF PAINTING SERVICES
for the month ended 30 April 20XX

Owners' equity (beginning of month)	$20 000
plus Net profit	7 900
	27 900
less Drawings	1 000
Owners' equity (end of month)	$26 900

BALANCE SHEET: J. DOFF PAINTING SERVICES

as at 30 April 20XX

Assets	$	Liabilities	$
Cash at bank	17 900	Accounts payable	300
Accounts receivable	5 000	Loan payable	4 000
Supplies	300		4 300
Van	8 000	**Owners' equity**	
		Capital	26 900
	31 200		31 200

Relationship between the financial statements

The relationships stem from the basic accounting equation:

$$\text{assets} = \text{liabilities} + \text{owners' equity}$$

or $$A = L + OE$$

The changes in owners' equity are further subdivided into these categories: capital contributions (C), withdrawals or drawings (D), revenue (R) and expenses (E). The equation can then be expressed as:

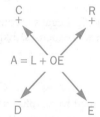

The equations for the financial statements are:

(i)   Profit and loss statement: $P = R - E$
(ii) Capital statement: $OE_{(end)} = OE_{(beg.)} + P + C - D$
(iii) Balance sheet: $A = L + OE_{(end)}$

Therefore, referring back to our example, the relationships are:

(i)
PROFIT AND LOSS STATEMENT	
Revenues	$ 9 000
less Expenses	1 100
Net profit	7 900

(ii)
CAPITAL STATEMENT	
Owners' equity (beg.)	$ 20 000
add Net profit	7 900
	27 900
less Drawings	1 000
Owners' equity (end)	$26 900

(iii)
BALANCE SHEET			
A	$31 200	L	$ 4 300
		OE	26 900
	$31 200		$31 200

Case 3.1 The accounting equation

Francis D'amico invested $50 000 in a legal firm at the commencement of 20X1. The firm is registered under the name of K. L. Legal. On 1 April he borrowed $30 000 on an interest only loan of 10 per cent per annum from the International Finance Company. At year end Francis is trying to determine his profit for the period and has asked for your assistance.

At 31 December 20X1 the business's assets and liabilities were as follows:

Current assets (including accounts receivable)	$150 000
Non-current assets	130 000
Current liabilities	140 000
Non-current liabilities (loan)	30 000

From banking records he is able to determine that receipts from legal services earned and banked totalled $110 000.

He has also kept meticulous records of cash withdrawn from the business bank account for his personal use, $7000. No capital contributions were made by him to the business during the year.

(a) From the information provided, is it possible to determine K. L. Legal's revenue for the year? Explain.
(b) Calculate K. L. Legal's profit for the year. **Hint:** Use your knowledge of the accounting equation.
(c) If you were informed that K. L. Legal's accounts receivable were $50 000, could you now estimate the business's expenses? Explain.

Example 2: *Transaction analyses: Alex Trownin*

On 1 July 20X1 Alex Trownin decided to establish a television rental business, to be known as A1-TV Hire. Her transactions for the first month were:

1. Contributed $20 000 capital in the form of a business bank account.
2. Bought 20 television sets on credit from E. W. E. Wholesalers for $300 each, a total of $6000.
3. Bought a delivery vehicle for cash $2600.
4. Paid E. W. E. Wholesalers $1500 on account.
5. Rented six television sets to customers for one month at $25 per set payable in advance (total $150).
6. Each customer paid an additional $100 per set as a refundable deposit (total $600).
7. Rented 10 television sets to Sierra Motels for a total of $250 per fortnight and sent them an invoice. Rental was due at the end of each fortnight.
8. Paid $26 for petrol used by delivery van.
9. Paid $41 for an advertisement in TV Daze.
10. One customer returned a television set at the end of the month and was refunded the $100 deposit (see transaction 6).
11. Sierra Motels paid $250 for the first fortnight's rental.
12. The proprietor took a television set which cost $300 for use as her own private set.

Required

(a) Analyse the transactions by means of an analysis table.
(b) Prepare financial statements.

Note

The previous example showed in detail the process of analysis and produced a table summarising assets and liabilities by item. It is recommended that students follow this formal process, at least until confident with the procedure. In this second example, the process is abbreviated, with the financial statements being prepared by summarising changes in each item as revealed by the analysis table.

Answers

(a) Analysis of transactions

A1-TV HIRE

Analysis of transactions

		Assets	=	Liabilities		+	Owners' equity	
		$			$			$
1.	Cash	+ 20 000					Capital	+ 20 000
2.	TV sets	+ 6 000	A/cs payable	+ 6 000				
3.	Vehicle	+ 2 600						
	Cash	− 2 600						
4.	Cash	− 1 500	A/cs payable	− 1 500				
5.	Cash	+ 150					Rental revenue	+ 150
6.	Cash	+ 600	Customer deposits	+ 600				
7.	A/cs receivable	+ 250					Rental revenue	+ 250
8.	Cash	− 26					Petrol expense	− 26
9.	Cash	− 41					Advertising expense	− 41
10.	Cash	− 100	Customer deposits	− 100				
11.	Cash	+ 250						
	A/cs receivable	− 250						
12.	TV sets	− 300					Withdrawals	− 300

Explanation of entries

1. *Contribution of capital.* To preserve the equation, it is necessary to record both the asset of cash and the proprietor's claim on the business.
2. *Purchase of television sets.* Since the sets were purchased on credit, the asset is accompanied by a liability, usually called accounts payable (abbreviated to A/cs payable) or creditors.
3. *Purchase of vehicle for cash.* This is an exchange of assets.
4. *Payment on account.* The purchase of television sets has already been recorded, so this transaction reduces the liability to accounts payable and the balance of cash.
5. *Rental for cash.* The revenue increases the owners' claim on the business. No change occurs in the asset for television sets. Although the business no longer has the sets in its office, ownership is retained. An asset need not always be in the physical possession of the entity.
6. *Deposits received.* These amounts are to be refunded when the sets are returned. They are held in trust for the customers, who have a claim on the business, which they will exercise when the sets are returned. Hence, a liability is created to record this claim.
7. *Rental on credit.* Revenue is recognised, even though cash has not been received. Instead of cash, the business has a valid claim on the motel, which it can pursue if necessary through the courts. Accounts receivable is an asset representing this claim to cash.

8. *Payment for petrol.* This use of resources creates an expense for the month. Just as revenue increases owners' equity, an expense reduces the owners' claim.
9. *Payment for advertising.* This is another expense of doing business, incurred in the hope of deriving increased revenue from customer rentals.
10. *Refund of deposit.* This entry merely reverses the effect of entry 6. The deposit liability is reduced by $100, as is cash.
11. *Rental from Sierra Motels.* The revenue was recognised previously (entry 7) and must not be counted again. Instead, the cash received is offset by the cancellation of the business claim on Sierra Motels (accounts receivable).
12. *Proprietor takes television set.* This is a withdrawal of a business asset for private use. Withdrawals need not be in cash.

(b) Profit and loss statement, capital statement and balance sheet.

PROFIT AND LOSS STATEMENT: A1-TV HIRE		
for the month ended 31 July 20X1		
Rental revenue		$400
less Expenses		
Petrol	$26	
Advertising	41	67
Net profit		$333

CAPITAL STATEMENT: A1-TV HIRE	
for the month ended 31 July 20X1	
Capital 1 July 20X1	$20 000
plus Net profit	333
	20 333
less Withdrawals	300
Capital 31 July 20X1	$20 033

BALANCE SHEET: A1-TV HIRE			
as at 31 July 20X1			
Assets		**Liabilities**	
Cash at bank	$16 733	Accounts payable	$ 4 500
TV sets	5 700	Customer deposits	500
Delivery vehicle	2 600		5 000
Accounts receivable	–		
		Owners' equity	
		Capital	$20 033
	$25 033		$25 033

Interpretation of the statements

A moment's reflection on Example 2 will strengthen the understanding of the principles. It should be apparent that each transaction has had offsetting effects on the basic equation.

The financial statements (above) summarise these transactions and are used to gain an understanding of the progress of the business. The proprietor increased her equity by $333 through profitable trading, which may seem a small amount to sustain a month's living expenses. It is evident that her personal living expenses were provided from other sources, since her withdrawals consisted merely of one television set for personal use. After the withdrawal, $33 of profit still remained in the business, which is represented somewhere in the net assets. The balance sheet shows that the initial capital, augmented by borrowing, has been invested in a variety of assets and is no longer represented simply by cash. A question the proprietor might ask is, 'How is it that I made a profit and yet the balance of cash has fallen by over $3000 during the month?' One answer is that cash was used to buy other assets and that these events did not affect profit. The earning of profits does not guarantee an increase in cash and all that may be said is that a profit will increase the net assets of a business before taking into account any withdrawals by the owner.

The relationship between the profit and loss statement and the other financial statements should be appreciated. The profit and loss statement explains those changes in the owners' equity that are attributable to revenues and expenses. The resulting net profit becomes the input for the capital statement, while the ending capital figure for the month is reported in the balance sheet.

A further observation should also be made. The basic classificatory scheme adopted has been in terms of assets, liabilities and owners' equity. It is possible, however, to subdivide changes in owners' equity into four types of change: revenue, expenses, capital contributions and withdrawals. The individual items that appear in the financial statements may then be grouped under their appropriate classes, as in Figure 3.1.

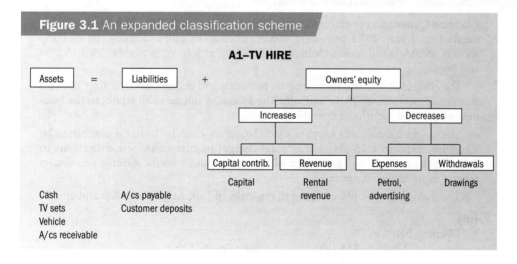

Figure 3.1 An expanded classification scheme

Cash flows

In Chapter 2 reference was made to the statement of cash flows. The purpose of the statement is to summarise the cash effects of business transactions for the period. Thus like a profit and loss statement it shows flows of cash for a period. However, unlike a profit and loss statement its aim is to show the effects of transactions upon cash. The profit and loss statement is prepared on an accrual basis; that is, the revenues are recognised when they are earned and expenses when they are incurred regardless of when the cash is received or paid.

The statement of cash flow below shows how the item Cash at Bank in A1-TV Hire was determined.

STATEMENT OF CASH FLOWS: A1-TV HIRE
for the month ended 31 July 20X1

	$	$
Cash inflows		
Capital	20 000	
Rental revenue	150	
Deposits received	600	
Receipts from accounts receivable	250	21 000
less Cash outflows		
Vehicle purchase	2 600	
Payment to accounts payable	1 500	
Payments for petrol	26	
Payments for advertising	41	
Repayment of deposits	100	4 267
Cash balance at 31 July 20X1		16 733

As discussed in Chapter 2, this statement could be classified further to indicate the cash flows from operating, investing and financing. The preparation and use of these classified cash flow statements will be considered in Chapter 10.

Case 3.2 Cash and profit

Claudine Cummaudo operates Central Cleaning Services (CCS). The business commenced on 1 July 20X1 providing home, office and factory cleaning. Its cleaning services include a full spring clean, as well as smaller jobs such as cleaning windows and ovens.

She ensures that all accounts are paid promptly and endeavours to collect all debts from customers within 30 days of sale. The following information relates to the business's first three months of operations.

Stocks of materials and supplies used (based on a similar business conducted by Claudine), represent 25 per cent of total charges to customers. She endeavours to maintain stocks equal to 25 per cent of her next month's needs. Assume actual sales reflects those expected needs.

The following took place during the months of July, August and September.

July
- Opening balances
  - Cash $15 000   Supplies $250
- Business activities for the month of July
  - CCS provided services on account for $1000 and paid wages of $500 and purchased supplies for cash, $400.

August
- Opening balances
  - Cash $14 100   Supplies $400
- Business activities for the month of August
  - During August CCS provided services on account for $1600 and paid wages of $800 and purchases supplies for cash, $600. Receivables from July customers were collected.

September
* Opening balances
>   Cash $13 700   Supplies $600
* Business activities for the month of September
>   During September CCS provided services on account for $2400 and paid wages of $1200 and purchased supplies for cash, $800. Receivables from August customers were collected.

(a) Prepare a statement showing the cash inflows and outflows for each of the three months.
(b) Prepare a statement showing the profit for each of the three months.
(c) Why has cash flow deteriorated despite profitable operations?

Expensing an asset over time

Advanced issues

(Students having difficulty with this chapter may safely defer this section until the basic concepts have been mastered.)

The analysis of transactions cannot proceed without adequate definitions of the different components of the equation. In particular, a distinction is required between assets and expenses. Assets result from transactions that provide benefits that are as yet unconsumed. Expenses arise when these benefits are consumed. Expenses may arise immediately, as with wages paid for the previous week, or slowly over time as assets expire. Assets that expire slowly include prepaid rent, vehicles and machinery.

The distinction between assets and expenses is necessary because the life of a business must be broken up into accounting periods. At any one moment, some expenditures will have given their benefit and become expenses, while others will have further services to give and will therefore be regarded as assets. The allocation of an expenditure over time in accordance with the expiration of its benefits is done so that each period bears its fair burden of the costs of operation.

Rent of $7500 paid for three years in advance may be used to illustrate the process of writing off an asset. If it is assumed that the services from the rental contract expire evenly over time, the proportion of the rent expense consumed in each year for three years would be $2500 ($7500/3). The transaction analysis is:

EXPENSING RENT OVER TIME						
	Assets		=	Liabilities	+	Owners' equity
		$		$		$
Payment at 1/1/X1	Cash	− 7500				
	Rent prepaid	+ 7500				
Expense for 20X1	Rent prepaid	− 2500			Rent expense	− 2500
Expense for 20X2	Rent prepaid	− 2500			Rent expense	− 2500
Expense for 20X3	Rent prepaid	− 2500			Rent expense	− 2500

How these items appear in the financial statements for each year is shown on the following page.

EXPENSING RENT OVER TIME			
	20X1	20X2	20X3
Profit and loss statement for the year ended 31 December			
Revenue	$	$	$
less Expenses			
Rent	2500	2500	2500
Balance sheet as at 31 December			
Assets			
Prepaid rent	5000	2500	–

Although it would be theoretically correct to recognise the rent expense daily, there is in practice no need to do so until accounting reports are to be prepared at the end of each period. As shown above, the asset account for prepaid rent will fall annually from $7500 at 1 January 20X1, reflecting the expenditure of the benefits in the asset, until at the end of 20X3 no future benefit remains.

This method of allocating a long-term expense over the period of its life is part of what is known as the *matching process*. An attempt is being made to match the expense with the revenue over the periods in which it gives its benefits. It would be inequitable and misleading to write off all of the prepaid rent of $7500 in the first year, when the other two periods will also benefit from the rented premises. A fairer assessment of annual profit is obtained if the expense is allocated over its useful life.

There are numerous examples of payments that give benefit over several periods and which therefore must be allocated or 'matched'. The major examples are the physical assets, such as machines and motor vehicles, which are used for a number of years and are then sold or scrapped. The process of expensing these assets gradually over time is called *depreciation*. It is important to note that depreciation is just one class of cost allocation and that accordingly it obeys the same rules for asset and expense measurement as were given previously. Suppose a farmer paid $10 000 for a tractor with a five-year productive life. In the simplest case, matching would be achieved by transferring $2000 each year from the tractor asset to an expense for depreciation of tractors. Apart from the terminology, the method is the same as that used in the example on prepaid rent.

Ethical issues

The proprietor of a small hardware shop often takes items for his personal use without recording them as drawings. His annual vacation is always paid for by the business as 'promotional items' and deducted for taxation. He argues that, as he owns the business, no one suffers. In any case, everybody cheats on taxation.

Are these reasons sufficient to justify his actions?

Summary

This chapter introduces the process by which an unlimited number of transactions affecting an enterprise may be summarised in four informative financial statements: a profit and loss statement, a capital statement, a balance sheet and a statement of cash flows.

Classification is the means by which apparently unlike transactions are brought together. In accounting, transactions are classified according to their effects on the basic accounting equation:

assets = liabilities + owners' equity

These summarised changes form the balance sheet. Also, because owners' equity is such an important category, it is further subdivided into four classes representing the major causes of change in owners' equity: capital contributions, withdrawals, revenue and expenses. A profit and loss statement is prepared to display the net profit or net loss, which is the difference between revenues and expenses. The profit and loss statement therefore explains that part of the change in owners' equity that is attributable to operating activities. The statement of cash flows is prepared to display the receipts and payments of cash and may be classified further to show cash from operating, investing and financing activities.

Review exercises

Discussion questions

3.1 Explain why every accounting transaction has at least two effects on the accounting equation.

3.2 Classify the following accounts as either an asset (A), liability (L), revenue (R), expense (E) or owners' equity (OE) item:

Fixtures and shelves
Land
Bank overdraft
Unearned revenue
Rent paid in advance
Interest received
Accounts payable
Insurance prepaid
Cash
J. Jones drawings
Depreciation expense
H. Smith capital
Merchandise
Accrued wages
Loan secured by mortgage

3.3 What are the four types of transactions that change owners' equity? How is it affected by each transaction?

3.4 'Withdrawals reduce owners' equity, as do expenses, hence withdrawals are expenses.' Comment on this statement.

3.5 Explain the relationship between the profit and loss statement, the balance sheet and the statement of cash flows.

3.6 Explain how and why accountants distinguish between assets and expenses.

3.7 'All wasting assets are eventually used up and become expenses, hence there is no need to distinguish between assets and expenses.' Do you agree with this statement? Explain your answer.

3.8 Explain the rationale of the matching process. Illustrate your answer with a specific example.

3.9 A student began a year of university study with savings of $3500. She received no cash during the year other than a small allowance from her parents, and by the time the year ended her savings had dwindled to $1300. Do you think that she was not as 'well off' at the end of the year as she was at the beginning? Explain your answer.

3.10 'Classification is a major part of accounting'. Explain how classification is incorporated in the accounting reports.

3.11 The manager of Ferraro Enterprises was heard to say, 'The business must have made a loss because its bank account balance has declined.' Do you agree? Explain.

Problems

3.12 *Using the accounting equation to determine profit*

1. From the following particulars, ascertain the profit for the year ended 31 December 20X1.

	Assets	Liabilities
1 January 20X1	38 000	22 000
31 December 20X1	43 000	20 000

During the year there were no drawings and no additional capital contributed by the owner.

2. From the following particulars, ascertain the profit for the year ended 31 December 20X2.

	Assets	Liabilities
1 January 20X2	80 000	20 000
31 December 20X2	150 000	60 000

During the year there were $20 000 drawings and additional capital contributed, $40 000.

3. Vintage Glass commenced business on 1 January 20X3 with assets of $160 000 and liabilities of $60 000. On December 20X3 the business had assets of $230 000 and liabilities of $140 000. During the year the owner had contributed additional capital of $50 000 and had withdrawn $40 000. During the year a fire had destroyed $10 000 of inventory. Calculate the profit or loss for 20X3.

3.13 *Using the accounting equation to prepare financial statements*

1. The following are the first week's transactions of Campus Delivery, a firm that operates a service delivering parcels between universities:

Sept. 1   Proprietor contributed $40 000 as capital.
       1   Acquired computer for cash, $3000.
       2   Purchased a motor vehicle from Rialto Ford for $30 000, paying $10 000 deposit.
       3   Filled the tank with petrol, $40. The petrol was used up during the week.
       3   Paid week's rent on office, $200.
       4   Received $120 for delivering parcels for Macquarie University.
       5   Sent a bill for $170 to the University of Sydney for parcels delivered.
       5   Paid the first week's instalment on the motor vehicle, $400.
       6   Withdrew $80 for luncheon costs to celebrate the first week's operations.
       7   The University of Sydney paid $30 on account.

(a) Analyse each transaction according to its effect on the basic accounting equation (assets = liabilities + owners' equity).
(b) Prepare a statement listing the assets, liabilities and owners' equity at the end of the first week, and a profit and loss statement for the week. Depreciation may be ignored.
(c) Did the proprietor have reason to celebrate?

2. Dec. 1   G. Gracious, a beauty consultant, commenced business at Gertie's Salon with a bank balance of $7000.
        3   Purchased hairdryer for cash, $426.
        4   Bought cash register on credit from Cobbles & Co., $220.
        5   Received $800 from P. Jane for a comprehensive treatment.
        6   Paid $140 for cosmetics, all to be used in December.
        9   Paid electricity bill, $21, to cover December.
        12   G. George lent the business $5000.
        15   Invoiced U. Dyall for a complete facial, $300.
        17   U. Dyall paid her account.
        19   Paid for cash register bought previously.
        21   Paid $300 for Christmas party for staff.
        22   Received $100 for a shampoo and set from A. Mopp.
        23   Paid for newspaper advertisement, $310.
        24   Paid office wages, $265.
        27   Paid rent for December, $700.
        28   G. Gracious contributed her own car, worth $2700, to the business.
        31   Paid dentist's account, $75.

(a) Analyse each transaction according to its effect on the basic accounting equation (assets = liabilities + owners' equity).
(b) Prepare a statement listing the assets, liabilities and owners' equity at the end of December, and a profit and loss statement for the month.
(c) Was it a profitable month for G. Gracious?

3. Fair Go Pty Ltd is an advertising agency that earns commission by planning and carrying out advertising campaigns for its clients. On 1 September 20X5 its assets and liabilities were as follows:

Cash	$6000
Accounts receivable	6500
Office supplies	1000
Accounts payable	3500

Transactions of Fair Go Pty Ltd for the month of September were as follows:

Sept.	1	Earned cash commissions, $4800.
	2	Commissions billed but not yet received, $19 000.
	3	Collected cash on accounts receivable, $13 500.
	4	Paid salaries and wages, $14 000.
	5	Incurred entertainment expenses of $1200, payable in October.
	6	Used up office supplies, $500.
	7	Paid rent, $3000.
	8	Paid cash on accounts payable, $1450.
	9	Purchased a car for $11 950, paying $80 deposit.

(a) Establish the balance sheet equation from the balances provided on 1 September 20X5.

(b) Complete a transaction analysis and from it prepare a profit and loss statement for the month of September and a balance sheet as at 30 September 20X5.

3.14 *Calculating profit and owners' equity*

Brendan Bilge conducts fishing expeditions in a boat he hires daily for $100. On Monday he set out with $200 in his business wallet. He stopped to buy bait for $180 on which he paid $30 deposit and promised to pay the rest at the end of the day. He then paid $24 for a day's supply of petrol for the boat. He had 20 customers who paid $16 each for the day's fishing. After returning to port, he paid the boat rental, paid for the bait, and stored in his freezer the left-over bait, which was half of what he had bought. He had two glasses of beer at $1 each and then returned home to his family.

(a) What profit was made on the day's trading?

(b) What was Mr Bilge's equity in the business at the end of the day?

3.15 *Calculating profit for the period*

From the following information, determine the profit for the month of April 20X1 for the Mailstrike Courier Service.

Apr.	2	Received cash for:
		Services performed in March, $9000.
		Services performed in April, $12 000.
		Services to be performed in May (in advance), $3000.
		Loan from proprietor's cousin, $20 000.
	10	Performed service in April for which customers have not yet paid, $5200.
	15	Paid rent for April, May and June totalling $3600.

22   Paid wages for March $2300; April $7100.

23   Wages owing for April and unpaid are $1000.

28   Paid $6000 of an amount owing on the company's furniture.

29   The proprietor withdrew $500 for personal expenses.

Note: Depreciation may be ignored.

3.16 *Determining total expenses for the period*

During November, Michelle Lawson, a well-respected dentist of Hamilton, incurred the following expenditure:

Purchased office stationery	$ 470
Rent for November and December for dental rooms	1500
Purchased new dental equipment, which is expected to	
have a useful life of five years	960
Received delivery of 12 boxes of anaesthetic syringes	180
Paid telephone account for September and October	140
Paid M. Wentworth, the part-time receptionist, a fortnight's wages	490
Purchased 8 boxes of amalgam pellets	160
Purchased 40 dental bibs	200
Withdrew cash for personal use	400

At the end of November unused stationery amounted to $190. Two boxes of amalgam pellets, three boxes of anaesthetic syringes and 13 dental bibs remained on hand for use next month. Ms Lawson owed the receptionist a fortnight's wages.

What are the total expenses Ms Lawson incurred for the month of November?

3.17 *Analysis of transactions that impact on the balance sheet*

List a set of four transactions that would account for the changes in the balance sheet of Underhand Ltd. (*Note:* Several combinations of transactions may be possible.)

BALANCE SHEET: UNDERHAND LTD				
		1 July 20X4		*15 July 20X4*
Assets				
Cash at bank		$10 000		$12 700
Accounts receivable		5 000		3 800
Furniture		23 000		27 000
		38 000		43 500
Liabilities				
Accounts payable		3 000		7 000
Owners' equity				
Capital	$28 000		$30 000	
plus Retained profits	7 000	35 000	6 500	36 500
		$38 000		$43 500

3.18 *Preparation of balance sheet and analysis of business type*

The following are account balances for Mystery Ltd at 31 December 20X7.

Accounts payable	$ 13 000
Accounts receivable	7 000
Building	240 000
Cash	3 900
Delivery equipment	40 000
Furniture	7 000
Inventory	29 000
Investment in bonds	5 000
Land	300 000
Mortgage payable	150 000
Owners' equity	364 000

(a) Prepare a balance sheet from these account balances. No capital contributions or withdrawals were made during the period.

(b) For each item, identify the kind of transaction from which it probably originated. Based on your analysis, what type of business do you think Mystery Ltd operates?

3.19 *Accounting equation and financial statements*

The following transactions concern a small business, the *Weekly Whisper*, set up to provide a pictorial newspaper for Sydney readers.

Aug.	1	The proprietor, Ms J. A. List, contributed $30 000 as capital to start the business.
	1	Bought fancy office equipment on credit from E. Z. Chair for $15 000.
	2	Paid a deposit of $1000 on the office equipment.
	3	Paid for a delivery van, $20 000.
	4	Paid week's wages to reporter/photographer, $1000.
	5	Sold first week's newspaper to various shops for cash, $1200.
	6	Sold first week's newspaper to Corner Stall for $300 on credit.
	7	Withdrew $80 for personal use.
	7	Corner Stall paid $140 of the amount owing.

(a) Analyse each transaction as it affects the basic ownership equation of the business.

(b) Summarise the effects in a profit and loss statement, balance sheet and cash-flow statement.

3.20 *Using the accounting equation for decision making*

I. T. Burns and Son is a family business, the members of which own 180 hectares of land at Seal Rocks adjacent to an excellent surf beach. They wish to provide camping facilities but are unsure of what fees to charge. They provide the following data:

1. They have $17 000 in a business bank account.

2. The land cost $100 000 and there is an outstanding mortgage of $13 000 on which $1000 interest is paid annually, together with a mortgage repayment of $4000.

3. The following additional costs will have to be paid during the year:

Installation of pit toilets and water tanks	$5 000
(expected to last 40 years)	
Fencing (20-year life expected)	4 000
Salary of caretaker	17 600
Rates and land tax	3 900
Advertising	1 300
Cost of pumping water into tanks	600

4. A group of fishing enthusiasts are willing to pay $2800 per year to the proprietors for stowing their boats on the property.
5. The number of camping groups per year is expected to be 1500, with an average stay of seven nights.
6. Other camping grounds in similar locations and with comparable amenities charge $8 per night per group.

(a) Assuming the camping fee is set at $5 per night, prepare a projected profit and loss statement for the year and a balance sheet at the end of the year.
(b) What percentage return will the owners receive on their initial investment?
(c) The proprietors wish to withdraw the entire profits from the business. Have they contributed sufficient capital to ensure that the business will remain liquid?
(d) Suppose a return on assets of 20 per cent was required. Approximately what camping fee should be charged? Assume that campers would not be deterred by higher fees.
(e) What other factors might be considered relevant in deciding whether to open a camping ground?

Hint: The best way to unravel this problem may be to adopt the transaction analysis procedure.

3.21 *Public sector: using the accounting equation to prepare financial statements*

1. Pentford Council has just constructed a new heated swimming pool for the local area. The area is rapidly expanding and the local schools have been asking the council to provide a heated pool for many years. The pool complex cost five million dollars to build. It was constructed on council land that was valued at one million dollars. The pool complex, the land and a cash sum of $5000 represent the council's equity (initial capital) in the swimming pool. The pool is to be self-funding. It opened on 1 September and the following transactions relate to that month.

Beginning September
1. Purchased chlorine and cleaning supplies for $2000 on credit from Allpool Supplies Ltd.
2. Rented garden equipment at a cost of $1000 per month and paid for the first two months' rent.
3. Purchased stationery for $2000 cash.

During September

4. Received $20 000 for entrance fees in cash.
5. Billed local schools for carnivals held earlier in the month, $5000.
6. Paid wages, $8000.
7. Received $2000 of amount owing from local schools for carnivals.
8. Paid heating bill, $4000.

End September

9. Chlorine and cleaning supplies on hand cost $500. Stationery on hand cost $1000.
10. Sundry bills outstanding, $1500.
11. Wages owing $4000.

Analyse the above transactions and prepare an operating statement (or a statement of profit and loss) for the month ending 30 September 20X4, and a balance sheet as at 30 September 20X4.

2. Carlinghill Council resolved to establish a public library for the local community. Three million dollars was invested in establishing the library. One million was spent on land, one million on a new building, half a million on furniture and fittings and half a million on books. On 1 February 20X3 the library opened its doors. Mel Skinner was appointed as librarian and two assistants were hired. The following transactions occurred during the first month of the library's operations.

Beginning February

1. Purchased stationery on credit for $1000 from Recycle Paper Ltd.
2. Received a monthly grant of $24 000 from Carlinghill Council. Of the grant, $16 000 was a monthly operating grant and $8000 was for capital works.
3. Rented a fax machine from Megacom and paid rent for February, March and April, $3000.
4. Ordered new books from Wisebook Ltd at a cost of $2000.

During February

5. Paid wages for first fortnight, $6000.
6. Paid $1000 on account to Recycle Paper Ltd.
7. Paid cleaners, $500.
8. Received books from Wisebook Ltd accompanied by an invoice for $2000.

End February

9. Wages for the second fortnight will not be paid until 1 March 20X3.
10. An electricity bill for $1000 was outstanding.
11. Stationery on hand cost $400.

Analyse the above transactions and prepare an operating statement (a profit and loss statement) for the month ending 28 February 20X3, and a balance sheet as at 28 February 20X3.

CHAPTER 4
The recording focus

Learning objectives

In this chapter you will be introduced to:

1. the principles of the double-entry system

2. the rules of debit and credit

3. the effect of transactions on the accounting equation and how to apply the rules of debit and credit, as appropriate, to such analyses

4. general ledger accounts in T-format and columnar format

5. the trial balance, and to why errors may exist in the accounting records even though the trial balance 'balances'

6. how to prepare a trial balance, a profit and loss statement and a balance sheet from information you have entered into the general ledger of an entity

7. basic computerised accounting (optional)

8. how to make entries in the general journal

9. how to make closing entries

10. interim reports.

Introduction

Once a scheme for classifying events has been devised, it is necessary to design a means of recording them. Increasingly, computers are taking over the recording functions associated with bookkeeping, but even computers must follow procedures designed by human beings. This chapter introduces a traditional means of recording transactions, embodying principles that remain relevant in a computer age. Certain records that were formerly kept by hand will not be emphasised, however, as they form part of the detailed data processing systems to be discussed in Part 4.

The main objective in these early chapters is to provide an overview of the financial statements that result from the classification and recording of transactions and especially the principles of valuation on which they are based. However, some knowledge of recording procedures will provide a useful framework within which to discuss profit measurement and asset valuation. In this chapter the ledger is introduced, mysteries surrounding terms such as 'double-entry', 'debits' and 'credits' are unravelled and the reader will acquire the ability to maintain a ledger for a small business and to prepare financial statements from that ledger.

Designing a simple manual recording system

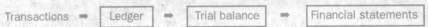

Transactions ➡ Ledger ➡ Trial balance ➡ Financial statements

Any recording system must satisfy three main requirements: efficiency, control and accessibility. An efficient system is one that processes transactions with the minimum recording procedures. Cumbersome systems cost more to maintain, and they increase the likelihood of errors by inserting more steps in the recording chain.

Control is the second important requirement. The system should provide checks against routine errors caused by faulty addition or the misclassification of transactions. The chain of recording in the following diagram begins with evidence of the original transactions, such as receipts and invoices. These events are classified and summarised in various accounting records and the final summaries appear as financial statements. Control is required to ensure that the financial statements are consistent with the original evidence records and that no interference, intentional or otherwise, has occurred in the recording process.

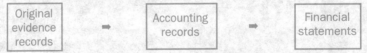

Original evidence records ➡ Accounting records ➡ Financial statements

The need for accessibility is easily overlooked but is of considerable importance. The financial statements summarise the events, but there is often a need to peruse more detailed records. Management might like to know who bought goods in the last month. The auditor certainly will need to be able to read and interpret the records so as to be satisfied that correct recording procedures were followed.

These principles will help to explain the procedures now to be outlined and they should be borne in mind during the discussion. The design of a system capable of processing thousands of transactions efficiently, and with control and accessibility, is a challenging task, regardless of whether the recording is to be done manually, on a machine or through a computer. It is very much part of the traditional art of accounting.

The basic recording system used in accounting may be summarised as follows:

Activity		Records and reports
Input/actual events	=	Source document/transactions
Recording of events	=	General journal
Classifying and summarising	=	General ledger
Verification and summarising in preparation for final output	=	Trial balance
Output	=	Financial statements

Original evidence records

In order to ensure that the financial statements are consistent with the original evidence (i.e. that they do reflect actual transactions and events), the rule is that all entries to the general journal and ledger must be traceable back to evidence. For many transactions, the evidence will be through normal business documents such as invoices to customers or from suppliers, bank records or cheque butts, formal contracts, delivery dockets and receipts. When an entry is not based on a transaction, it must be authorised in writing by an appropriate officer of the organisation.

This topic is explored in more detail in Chapter 20.

Journal entries

These are discussed below (see 'Journal entries' on page 105).

Ledger accounts

Ledger accounts are the basic storage unit for business transactions and the simplest form of account is the T-form account. (Other forms are discussed later in the chapter.)

NAME OF ACCOUNT	A/c no.
Left hand or debit side (DR)	Right hand or credit side (CR)

Notes

1. There is a separate account for each individual asset, liability, owners' equity, revenue and expense category.
2. Accounts assist in summarising all information relating to a particular item. For example, at the end of a period all information relating to cash at bank will be summarised in the cash at bank account.
3. Accounts may be referenced by either name or number.

The origins and importance of double-entry bookkeeping

As early as 1494 Luca Pacioli, a Franciscan friar, had, in his book *Summa de Arithmetica, Geometria, Proportioni et Proportionalita,* described the double-entry bookkeeping practices of Venice at the time. This method spread throughout Europe in the sixteenth and seventeenth centuries. In more recent times some economic historians have claimed that double-entry bookkeeping has been extremely important to the development or evolution of capitalism. Max Weber argued that the development of capitalistic enterprise would not have been possible without rational bookkeeping and this thesis has been expanded by Sombart, who states:

> One cannot imagine what capitalism would be without double-entry bookkeeping: the two phenomena are connected as intimately as form and content.

More recent research has debated whether double-entry did little more than provide a framework into which accounting data can be fitted and within which the data could be arranged, grouped and re-grouped. Yamey has argued that double-entry bookkeeping is not necessary for determining profit and capital and was only useful for routine tasks, whereas Winjum has provided evidence that as early as the sixteenth century profit and loss was an important facet of double-entry bookkeeping.[1]

The rules of double-entry recording

The rules for the use of debits and credits merely provide a code for recording the offsetting effects of transactions on the accounting equation. They are designed to provide control over the recording process by ensuring that the opposing effects of each transaction are recorded and that the equation remains in balance.

The test applied is that every transaction must have equal debit and credit entries. This is achieved by recording opposing effects on opposite sides of the ledger. For example, if a proprietor contributed $10 000 cash as capital, then:

Account	Change	Amount	Rule
Cash	Increase	$10 000	Debit
Capital	Increase	$10 000	Credit

In general, the rules are:

$$
\begin{array}{ccccc}
\text{DR} & & \text{CR} & & \\
+ & & + & & \\
\text{A} & = & \text{L} & + & \text{OE} \\
- & & - & & \\
\text{CR} & & \text{DR} & &
\end{array}
$$

In the examples that follow it will be found that debit entries always equal credit entries for any transaction.

---

[1] This section draws upon material from A. R. Belkaoui & S. Jones, *Accounting Theory,* First Australian Edition, Harcourt Brace and Company, Sydney, 1996, pp. 17–19.

Example 1: *The rules of double-entry recording*

Assets

ASSET	
Debit to increase	Credit to decrease

Example Purchased supplies for cash, $1000. As a result of this transaction, the supplies account increases. It is an asset, therefore apply the rule to debit this amount. The cash at bank account decreases. It is an asset, therefore apply the rule to credit the amount.

SUPPLIES		CASH	
1000			1000

Liabilities

LIABILITY	
Debit to decrease	Credit to increase

Example Purchased equipment on credit for $4000. As a result of this transaction, the equipment account increases. It is an asset, therefore apply the rule to debit the amount. The accounts payable account increases. It is a liability, therefore apply the rule to credit the amount.

EQUIPMENT		ACCOUNTS PAYABLE	
4000			4000

Owners' equity

OWNERS' EQUITY	
Debit to decrease	Credit to increase

Example Owner inputs $50 000 to commence operations. As a result of this transaction, the cash at bank account increases. It is an asset, therefore apply the rule to debit the amount. The capital account increases. It has an owners' equity classification, therefore apply the rule to credit the amount.

CASH		CAPITAL	
50 000			50 000

Revenues

REVENUE	
Debit to decrease	Credit to increase

Example Provided services on credit, $6000. As a result of this transaction, the accounts receivable account increases. It is an asset, therefore apply the rule to debit the amount. The service revenue records account increases in owners' equity. Therefore apply the rule to credit the amount.

ACCOUNTS RECEIVABLE		SERVICE REVENUE	
6000			6000

Expenses

EXPENSES	
Debit to increase	Credit to decrease

Example Received the telephone bill for the month, $600. As a result of this transaction, the telephone expense account increases. It is a decrease in owners' equity through an expense, therefore apply the rule to debit the amount. The accounts payable account increases. It is a liability, therefore apply the rule to credit the amount.

TELEPHONE EXPENSE		ACCOUNTS PAYABLE	
600			600

Note after analysing the double-entry rules:

- The accounting system is always in balance—total debits equal total credits.
- Each classification has a separate rule applying to it.

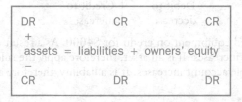

Debit and credit rules—a summary including revenues and expenses

Debit entries	increase	Assets and expenses
	decrease	Liabilities, owners' equity and revenues
Credit entries	increase	Liabilities, owners' equity and revenues
	decrease	Assets and expenses

In the following example this important set of rules for classifying transactions will be illustrated and explained further.

Example 2: *A simplified recording system*

Sydney Todd has retained Hiram Old and Mavis Trusty, accountants, to set up an accounting system for his new men's hairdressing business.

The following were Mr Todd's transactions for his first week of operations:

June 1 Established a business bank account with a capital contribution of $5000.
2 Bought haircutting equipment for cash $1200.
3 Purchased furniture on credit for $7000.
4 Paid portion of account payable on furniture purchased on 3 June, $500.
5 Received from customers for haircuts $210, and for shaves $140.
6 Paid week's rent of $100 and the electricity bill of $15.
7 Withdrew $83 for private use.

TRANSACTION ANALYSIS: TODD'S BARBER SHOPPE				
Date	Assets	= Liabilities	+	Owners' equity
	$	$		$
June 1	Cash			
	+ 5000			Capital
2	Equipment			+ 5000
	+ 1200			
	Cash			
	− 1200			
3	Furniture	A/cs payable		
	+ 7000	+ 7000		
4	Cash	A/cs payable		
	− 500	− 500		Haircutting revenue
5	Cash			+ 210
	+ 210			Shaving revenue
	Cash			+ 140
	+ 140			Rent expense
6	Cash			− 100
	− 100			Electricity expense
	Cash			− 15
	− 15			Drawings
7	Cash			− 83
	− 83			

Alternatively, the table for transaction analysis could be displayed as follows:

Date	Accounts affected	Increase/ decrease +/−	Type of account (A, L, OE, E, R)	Debit $	Credit $
June 1	Cash	+	A	5000	
	Capital	+	OE		5000
	etc.				

Note: Every entry in this table must take at least two lines since every transaction affects at least two accounts.

The ability to analyse transactions is an essential prerequisite for the next step, which is the recording of their effects in the ledger. Although an accountant would not prepare such a document, it may be helpful to prepare a transaction analysis before proceeding to the ledger (see above).

Mr Todd's accountants began by determining what the output of the accounting system should be and decided that a profit and loss statement and balance sheet would suffice. They listed the individual items that would appear in those statements and prepared a *chart of accounts*.

CHART OF ACCOUNTS: TODD'S BARBER SHOPPE

Assets	=	Liabilities	+		Owners' equity		
				Capital contributions	Withdrawals	Revenue	Expense
Cash at bank		Accounts		Capital	Drawings	Haircutting	Rent
Equipment		payable				Shaves	Electricity
Furniture							

Next, an *account* was established for each item. An account may appear as a page in a book, a card in a file, a defined storage area within a computer, or in any other convenient form. The collection of accounts is referred to as the *ledger*.

The ruling of an account also varies. The running or continuous balance form used in this example is usually similar to the following:

FORM OF LEDGER ACCOUNT

Account name: .... No.........................

Date	Particulars	Debit	Credit	Balance

Note that this is an alternative form of account to the T-form account, which was discussed earlier. Whatever the form of the account, it will contain at least two columns, or 'sides'. The left-hand column is called the *debit side* and the right-hand column the *credit side*.

The debit and credit columns are so titled simply because of tradition and perhaps to mystify the non-accountant. Debit means 'left' and credit means 'right' and the words have no other meanings in accounting. It is necessary to discard the non-specialist's notion that debits are bad and credits are good, as these meanings are not appropriate in accounting. In practice 'debit' is abbreviated to 'DR' and credit to 'CR'.

The rules for ledger recording are based on the principles of being efficient, facilitating control, and providing for accessibility. All follow logically from the principles of transaction analysis, as will now be explained.

June 1: Capital contribution of $5000

Mr Todd's first transaction was a contribution of capital, involving an increase of the asset cash and a corresponding increase in the owners' equity account for capital. The transaction is entered as follows:

Date	Particulars	Debit	Credit	Balance
Assets		**Cash at bank**		
June 1	Capital	5000		5000 DR
Owners' equity		**Capital**		
June 1	Cash at bank		5000	5000 CR

By convention, the increase in the asset, cash at bank, appears on the debit side of that account. It may be thought that the increase in the capital account should also appear as a debit. However, in order to achieve control over the recording process, the rules provide that every transaction must have its opposing effects recorded on opposite sides of the ledger. In this way, every transaction must have debit entries equalling credit entries and a check is provided to ensure that the recording procedure has chosen a feasible combination of entries. Since an increase in assets may be accompanied by an increase in owners' equity, the rule is that the increase in the asset will be recorded as a debit entry and the increase in owners' equity will appear as a credit entry in the capital account. This provides for control over the entry process.

Accessibility is provided by placing the date of the transaction in the appropriate column and by placing in the particulars column the name of the other account affected by this transaction. This enables the reader to trace the dual effects of the transaction. The balance in each account appears in the third column, with an indication of whether it is 'in debit' or 'in credit'.

June 2: Cash purchase of equipment $1200

In this transaction, the two effects are an increase in an asset for equipment and a decrease in another asset, cash at bank. On 1 June, the increase in the asset cash resulted in a debit to that account. To be consistent, it is necessary to place a debit entry in the equipment account to record the increase in that asset. The decrease in cash is then recorded by placing a credit entry in the cash at bank account. Hence, increases in assets are debits and decreases in assets are credits. After this transaction the ledger appears as follows:

Date	Particulars	Debit	Credit	Balance
Assets		**Cash at bank**		
June 1	Capital	5000		5000 DR
2	Equipment		1200	3800 DR
		Equipment		
June 2	Cash at bank	1200		1200 DR
Owners' equity		**Capital**		
June 1	Cash at bank		5000	5000 CR

The balance columns show that there is cash of $3800 and equipment of $1200 on the asset side, equalled by capital of $5000 on the equities side. Note also that the total debits equal the total credits.

June 3: Purchase of furniture on credit for $7000

So far, the following recording rules have been illustrated:

DR		?		CR
increase		increase		increase
A	=	L	+	OE
decrease		decrease		decrease
CR		?		?

This next transaction will extend the rules a little further. The purchase of furniture on credit is classified as an increase in the asset account for furniture and is matched by an increase in a liability to accounts payable. Following the above rules, a debit entry is required to increase the furniture account. Since the other entry must be a credit, accounts payable must receive a credit entry of $5000 to represent the increase in the liability. All increases in liabilities must be credits because they may be accompanied by increases in assets, which are always debits.

Only two more rules are required and they are easily derived. Because increases in liabilities are always credits, decreases in liabilities must always be debits. Similarly, because increases in owners' equity are always credits, decreases in owners' equity accounts are always debits.

Control over the recording process has been established by recording increases as debits on one side of the basic equation and as credits on the other side, thus:

$$
\begin{array}{ccc}
\text{DR} & & \text{CR} \\
+ & & + \\
\text{assets} & = & \text{equities} \\
- & & - \\
\text{CR} & & \text{DR}
\end{array}
$$

The set of recording rules showing the accounting equation is:

$$
\begin{array}{ccccc}
\text{DR} & & \text{CR} & & \text{CR} \\
+ & & + & & + \\
\text{A} & = & \text{L} & + & \text{OE} \\
- & & - & & - \\
\text{CR} & & \text{DR} & & \text{DR}
\end{array}
$$

In summary, these rules are derived from the following principles:

1. As with any equation, the accounting equation of $A = L + OE$ must remain in balance. To achieve this, each transaction must have at least two offsetting effects on the equation.
2. The offsetting effects are to appear on opposite sides of the ledger as debits and credits. This provides a check on whether the entries will preserve the equality of the accounting equation.
3. Increases in assets are recorded as debits. The reasons for this convention are obscured by time.

The control provided by this system may be seen by examining the state of the ledger accounts at 3 June for Mr Todd.

GENERAL LEDGER: TODD'S BARBER SHOPPE				
Transactions to 3 June 20X1				
Date	Particulars	Debit	Credit	Balance
Assets		**Cash at bank**		
June 1	Capital	5000		5000 DR
2	Equipment		1200	3800 DR
		Equipment		
June 2	Cash at bank	1200		1200 DR
		Furniture		
June 3	Accounts payable	7000		7000 DR
Liabilities		**Accounts payable**		
June 3	Furniture		7000	7000 CR
Owners' equity		**Capital**		
June 1	Cash at bank		5000	5000 CR

A listing of the account balances at 3 June will test whether the recording procedures have followed the rules. The listing is known as a *trial balance*.

TRIAL BALANCE: TODD'S BARBER SHOPPE
as at 3 June 20X1

	Debit	Credit
Cash at bank	$ 3 800	
Equipment	1 200	
Furniture	7 000	
Accounts payable		$ 7 000
Capital		5 000
	12 000	12 000

The equality of debits and credits indicates that each transaction has been recorded with opposing debit and credit entries and that the balances have been correctly computed. The trial balance is a list of each account and its balance at a specific point in time. It is not a financial statement but a list of all account balances after all transactions have been recorded in the ledger prior to the preparation of final reports.

Using the trial balance

If the debit and credit totals of a trial balance are not equal, it may be due to any of the following types of errors:

- errors in preparing the trial balance, such as incorrect addition of totals, incorrect recording of the amount of an account balance, or recording the account balance on the wrong side of the trial balance
- errors in recording account balances in the ledger, such as incorrect calculation of a balance, recording a balance on the wrong side of an account
- errors in recording a transaction in a ledger account, such as omitting a debit or credit entry or entering the transaction using an incorrect amount in one of these accounts.

However, if the trial balance *does* balance, the accounting records may still contain errors. For example, the following errors may not be discovered in taking out a trial balance:

- the complete omission of transactions
- debit and credit entries reversed when recording
- the recording of transactions twice
- transactions entered in the wrong account (e.g. debit in motor vehicles account for an equipment purchase)
- the wrong amounts entered in both accounts.

The remaining transactions also must follow the recording rules and are entered as shown (see page 101). Comment is required, however, on the revenue and expense entries.

Revenue and expense transactions

The dual effects of the revenue transactions on 5 June are an increase in the asset cash and an increase in owners' equity through revenue. Following the rules, the cash account is debited for the asset increase and appropriate revenue accounts are credited to record the increase in owners' equity. The increase could have been credited directly to the capital account, but this would have obscured the reason for the increase. It is preferable to establish a separate account within owners' equity to show that the increase was due to the earning of revenue.

The expense transactions on 6 June reduce the asset cash and reduce owners' equity by corresponding amounts. The asset reductions result in credits to cash and the reductions in owners' equity appear as debits. Again, it is desirable to create separate accounts for these reductions in owners' equity, known as expense accounts, so that detailed information on expenses will be available when the accounting reports are prepared.

The full rules for recording are now:

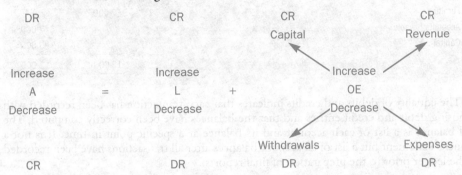

			CODING OF TRANSACTIONS: TODD'S BARBER SHOPPE		
Date	Account affected	Effect on equation		DR/CR	Amount
June 1	Cash at bank	+	Assets	Debit	5000
	Capital	+	OE	Credit	5000
2	Equipment	+	Asset	Debit	1200
	Cash at bank	−	Asset	Credit	1200
3	Furniture	+	Asset	Debit	7000
	Accounts payable	+	Liab.	Credit	7000
4	Accounts payable	−	Liab.	Debit	500
	Cash at bank	−	Asset	Credit	500
5	Cash at bank	+	Asset	Debit	210
	Haircutting revenue	+	OE	Credit	210
5	Cash at bank	+	Asset	Debit	140
	Shaving revenue	+	OE	Credit	140
6	Rent expense	−	OE	Debit	100
	Cash at bank	−	Asset	Credit	100
	Electricity expense	−	OE	Debit	15
	Cash at bank	−	Asset	Credit	15
7	Drawings	−	OE	Debit	83
	Cash at bank	−	Asset	Credit	83

GENERAL LEDGER: TODD'S BARBER SHOPPE
as at 7 June 20X1

Date		Particulars	Debit	Credit	Balance
Assets			**Cash at bank**		
June	1	Capital	5000		5000 DR
	2	Equipment		1200	3800 DR
	4	Accounts payable		500	3300 DR
	5	Haircutting revenue	210		3510 DR
	5	Shaving revenue	140		3650 DR
	6	Rent expense		100	3550 DR
	6	Electricity expense		15	3535 DR
	7	Drawings		83	3452 DR
			Equipment		
June	2	Cash at bank	1200		1200 DR
			Furniture		
June	3	Accounts payable	7000		7000 DR
Liabilities			**Accounts payable**		
June	3	Furniture		7000	7000 CR
	4	Cash	500		6500 CR
Owners' equity			**Capital**		
June	1	Cash at bank		5000	5000 CR
			Drawings		
June	7	Cash at bank	83		83 CR
			Haircutting revenue		
June	5	Cash at bank		210	210 CR
			Shaving revenue		
June	5	Cash at bank		140	140 CR
			Rent expense		
June	6	Cash at bank	100		100 DR
			Electricity expense		
June	6	Cash at bank	15		15 DR

TRIAL BALANCE: TODD'S BARBER SHOPPE
as at 7 June 20X1

	Debit	Credit
Cash at bank	$ 3 452	
Equipment	1 200	
Furniture	7 000	
Accounts payable		$ 6 500
Capital		5 000
Drawings	83	
Haircutting revenue		210
Shaving revenue		140
Rent expense	100	
Electricity expense	15	
	11 850	11 850

The trial balance at 7 June (in preceding table) was prepared after completion of the ledger entries. When a trial balance 'balances', there is reasonable certainty that all additions were correct and that each transaction was analysed into feasible combinations of changes to the equation, resulting in an equality of debits and credits. Nevertheless, the combinations may not always have been correct. A purchase of equipment may have been debited to an expense account rather than to an asset account for equipment. This type of error may be uncovered only by an examination of each transaction against the underlying original evidence records, or by an independent appraisal of the assets and liabilities that should appear in the financial statements.

Having satisfied themselves of the accuracy of their recording, the accountants of Todd's Barber Shoppe prepared some *interim* financial statements for the week (see below). Interim statements are those prepared for a period of less than one year. *Final* statements will be prepared at the conclusion of the year's trading. A comparison of the barber shop's financial statements with the trial balance reveals that the function of the profit and loss statement is to bring together the changes in owners' equity brought about by revenue and expense transactions. The difference, or net profit, then appears in the balance sheet as an addition to owners' equity. The information on page 103 shows how all the amounts in the trial balance are represented in the balance sheet, with revenues and expenses being summarised by the net profit. Thus, just as the trial balance balances, so must the balance sheet.

PROFIT AND LOSS STATEMENT: TODD'S BARBER SHOPPE		
for the week ending 7 June 20X1		
	$	$
Revenue		
Haircutting		210
Shaving		140
		350
less Expenses		
Rent	100	
Electricity	15	115
Net profit		235

CAPITAL STATEMENT: TODD'S BARBER SHOPPE	
as at 7 June 20X1	
Capital at 1 June 20X1	$5000
plus Net profit	235
	5235
less Drawings	83
Capital at 7 June 20X1	$5152

BALANCE SHEET: TODD'S BARBER SHOPPE			
as at 7 June 20X1			
Assets	$	**Liabilities**	$
Cash at bank	3 452	Accounts payable	6 500
Equipment	1 200		
Furniture	7 000	**Owners' equity**	
		Capital	5 152
	11 652		11 652

TODD'S BARBER SHOPPE

Relationship between trial balance and financial statements

Trial balance as at 7 June 20X1

	Debit	Credit
Cash at bank	$3452	
Equipment	1200	
Furniture	7000	
Accounts payable		$6500
Capital		5000
Drawings	83	
Net profit		$ 235
Haircutting revenue		210
Shaving revenue		140
Rent expense	100	
Electricity expense	15	

A system for computing applications

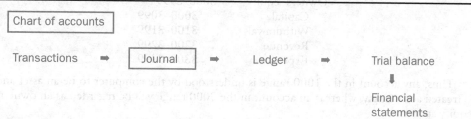

Chart of accounts

Transactions ➡ Journal ➡ Ledger ➡ Trial balance
⬇
Financial statements

Before using a basic accounting package on a computer, it will be necessary to understand more about the traditional recording process. Computers, being inanimate, require a greater degree of formality in the recording process and more careful planning is required. Whereas in a manual system an understandable entry may be made in the ledger by freehand writing, computers can accept input only in predetermined formats, and according to precise and preplanned instructions. On the other hand, computers need not be told what they already know. These differences will affect the keeping of a ledger in two main ways:

1. The chart of accounts needs to be specified in advance.
2. The procedure for making an entry needs to be specified—entries will be made through a journal rather than through the ledger.

Example: *Cotswold Tours*

On 1 July 20X9 Dale Slaughter established Cotswold Tours, offering tourist packages to the United Kingdom. The following transactions occurred in the first month.

July	1	Contributed capital in cash of $60 000.
	6	Purchased office equipment on credit for $65 000.
	8	Paid month's rent on premises, $8000.
	14	Sold tour packages for $25 000, receiving deposits totalling $2500.
	15	These tour packages were arranged with UK Travel Ltd, who charged Cotswold Tours $16 000, to be paid by the end of July.
	21	Received $20 000 from clients who had purchased packages on 14 July.
	22	Paid $3000 of the amount owing on the office equipment.
	23	Withdrew $1700 for private use.
	30	Paid UK Travel Ltd the amount owing.

Chart of accounts

The chart of accounts is the list of accounts to be maintained for the accounting entity. It has great significance not only in a manual accounting system but also in a computer-based system as it provides the foundation upon which the ledger file is established, and is the reference point for relating account numbers to account names. The first stage, then, is to design a chart of accounts suitable for the reporting needs of Cotswold Tours. This is done by considering the likely transactions and the reports within which they should be summarised.

It is strongly suggested that the accounts be listed in the order given by the accounting equation. Then, so as to avoid typing the account name each time it is to be entered, each account should be given a distinctive number. This account number is entered when transactions are recorded instead of the name. Particular sequences of numbers denote particular account types, thus providing ease of reference and offering some protection against the use of wrong account codes. For example:

Assets	1000–1999
Liabilities	2000–2999
Owners' equity	3000–3999
Capital	3000–3099
Withdrawals	3100–3199
Revenue	3200–3299
Expenses	3300–3399

Thus, any account in the 1000 range is understood by the computer to be an asset and is treated accordingly, whereas an account in the 3000 range will be regarded as an owners' equity account.

It is also quite common for revenues and expenses to be assigned a separate range of numbers distinct from other owners' equity accounts, for example revenue 4000–4999 and expenses 5000–5999.

In the case of Cotswold Tours our accountant has elected to use the following 'account codes'. Note that gaps have been left for the later possible inclusion of additional accounts.

	Code	Account
Assets		
Current	1010	Cash at bank
	1020	Accounts receivable
Non-current	1100	Office equipment
Liabilities		
Current	2010	Accounts payable
Non-current	2100	Mortgage loan
	3000	Capital
	3100	Drawings
Owners' equity	3201	Sales revenue
	3303	Rent expense
	3310	Tour package expenses

In this example, the client's name is abbreviated to 'Cotswo'.

In a manual accounting system, once the chart has been created it is necessary to draw up a ledger with accounts for each listing in the chart. In the accounting package this is unnecessary as the ledger file is created automatically in accordance with the chart.

Journal entries

In the simplified recording problems in this chapter, entries are made directly to the ledger accounts. That procedure is satisfactory for the learning of basic recording principles. In a full manual system, however, entries are *never* made directly to the ledger. All transactions and other entries are first recorded in a *journal*. The journal entries are subsequently 'posted' separately to the ledger. Thus, the full recording sequence is:

transaction ➡ journal ➡ ledger

There are various types of journal. However, for the present purpose only the most basic form of journal will be used, known as the general journal.

The form of a general journal entry is:

JOURNAL ENTRY FORMAT			
Date	Particulars	Debit	Credit
June 1	Cash at bank	5000	
	Capital		5000
	(Contribution of capital by proprietor)		

The account to be debited normally appears first, against the margin. In manual form the credit entry is indented. In some cases there may be more than one debit or credit within the journal entry. An explanation of the transaction, known as the narration, sometimes appears at the bottom. This narration also provides an opportunity to record a reference to the original source document on which the entry is based.

The general journal conveniently describes the ledger entries and provides the basis for them. In this and later chapters entries will often be shown in journal form rather than in the more cumbersome ledger format.

Note that it is possible to have *multiple* debits or credits in the one journal entry. Had the proprietor's capital contributions been cash of $2000 and a car worth $3000, then the entry would have been:

Date	Particulars	Debit	Credit
June 1	Cash at bank	2000	
	Motor vehicle	3000	
	Capital		5000
	(Contribution of capital by proprietor)		

The journal helps to ensure that all entries are kept together, so there is a sequential and complete record of all entries made in the accounting records.

The reader with access to a computer package may now wish to make up journal entries to record the transactions for Cotswold Tours. If the transactions are entered into the computer as general journal entries, the listing should appear somewhat as follows:

GENERAL JOURNAL: COTSWO
as at 30 July X1

Date		Particulars	Debit	Credit
July 1	1010	Cash at bank	60 000	
	3000	Capital		60 000
July 6	1100	Office equipment	65 000	
	2010	Accounts payable		65 000
July 8	3303	Rent expense	8 000	
	1010	Cash at bank		8 000
July 14	1020	Accounts receivable	25 000	
	3201	Sales revenue		25 000
July 14	1010	Cash at bank	2 500	
	1020	Accounts receivable		2 500
July 15	3310	Tour package expenses	16 000	
	2010	Accounts payable		16 000
July 21	1010	Cash at bank	20 000	
	1020	Accounts receivable		20 000
July 22	2010	Accounts payable	3 000	
	1010	Cash at bank		3 000
July 23	3100	Drawings	1 700	
	1010	Cash at bank		1 700
July 30	2010	Accounts payable	16 000	
	1010	Cash at bank		16 000

The computer performs the remaining tasks automatically. It is usually possible to view or print the ledger, the trial balance or simplified financial statements by choosing the relevant options from the menu. These should appear as follows:

GENERAL LEDGER
as at 30 July X1

Date	Particulars	Debit	Credit	Balance
1010—Asset	**Cash at bank**			
July 1	Capital	60 000		60 000 DR
July 8	Rent expense		8 000	52 000 DR
July 14	Accounts receivable	2 500		54 500 DR
July 21	Accounts receivable	20 000		74 500 DR
July 22	Accounts payable		3 000	71 500 DR
July 23	Drawings		1 700	69 800 DR
July 30	Accounts payable		16 000	53 800 DR
1020—Asset	**Accounts receivable**			
July 14	Sales revenue	25 000		25 000 DR
July 14	Cash at bank		2 500	22 500 DR
July 21	Cash at bank		20 000	2 500 DR
1100—Asset	**Office equipment**			
July 6	Accounts payable	65 000		65 000 DR
2010—Liability	**Accounts payable**			
July 6	Office equipment		65 000	65 000 CR
July 15	Tour package expenses		16 000	81 000 CR
July 22	Cash at bank	3 000		78 000 CR
July 30	Cash at bank	16 000		62 000 CR
3000—Owners' equity	**Capital**			
July 1	Cash at bank		60 000	60 000 CR
3100—Owners' equity	**Drawings**			
July 23	Cash at bank	1 700		1 700 DR
3201—Owners' equity	**Sales revenue**			
July 14	Accounts receivable		25 000	25 000 CR
3303—Owners' equity	**Rent expense**			
July 8	Cash at bank	8 000		8 000 DR
3310—Owners' equity	**Tour package expenses**			
July 15	Accounts payable	16 000		16 000 DR

TRIAL BALANCE
as at 30 July X1

	Debit	Credit
Cash at bank	$ 53 800	
Accounts receivable	2 500	
Office equipment	65 000	
Accounts payable		$ 62 000
Capital		60 000
Drawings	1 700	
Sales revenue		25 000
Rent expense	8 000	
Tour package expenses	16 000	
	147 000	147 000

PROFIT AND LOSS STATEMENT		
for year ending 30 July X1		
Revenue		
Sales revenue		$25 000
		25 000
less Expenses		
Rent expense	$ 8 000	
Tour package expenses	16 000	
		24 000
Net profit/loss		$ 1 000

BALANCE SHEET		
as at 30 July X1		
Assets	$	$
Current		
Cash at bank	53 800	
Accounts receivable	2 500	56 300
Non-current		
Office equipment		65 000
		121 300
Liabilities		
Current		
Accounts payable		62 000
Owners' equity		
Capital		60 000
plus Profit		1 000
less Drawings		1 700
		$121 300

In this example, the capital statement has been replaced by including its detail with the owners' equity section of the balance sheet. This is the more common form of presentation.

Final reports and closing entries

Once a year it is necessary to prepare final reports covering the entire year's operations. For most companies, these reports are required to be audited and included in an annual report to shareholders. The reports also form the basis of the annual taxation return, although certain modifications may be made to conform with the requirements of the taxation regulations.

The end of the year is also a time when the ledger is 'tidied up'. Various adjustments are made to recorded amounts, including depreciation and recognition of unpaid accounts, which are discussed in Chapter 7. Also, the temporary revenue and expense accounts are closed off so as to start the new year with a clean sheet. This *closing entry* sequence will now be described.

The term *closing the ledger* is misleading, since it implies that all accounts are closed off. In reality, the closing process describes those ledger entries made to transfer the temporary revenue and expense accounts to a profit and loss summary account in the ledger and then to the capital accounts. Drawings are also transferred against the capital balance. These entries are made once a year as at the last day of the year.

Example: *Closing entries*

Limousine Services prepares its annual statements as at 30 June. On 30 June 20X7 its trial balance was as shown below.

Classification is the key to understanding the closing process. The revenue and expense accounts are part of owners' equity. They were created temporarily, to retain information that would have been lost if expenses and revenue had been respectively deducted from and added to capital directly. They are nevertheless artificial; cash exists, but rent expense does not. At year end, these artificial accounts are transferred to a profit and loss summary account by 'closing entries'.

TRIAL BALANCE: LIMOUSINE SERVICES as at 30 June 20X7	Debit $	Credit $
Cash	1 000	
Accounts receivable	5 000	
Inventory	7 000	
Land	12 000	
Accounts payable		2 000
Bank overdraft		3 000
Capital		18 000
Drawings	1 500	
Sales revenue		28 900
Advertising expenses	12 300	
Rent expense	5 400	
Wages expense	7 700	
	51 900	51 900

The closing process may be illustrated as on pages 110–11, with the closing entries represented by arrows. After all closing entries have been made, the only accounts with open balances will be assets, liabilities and capital.

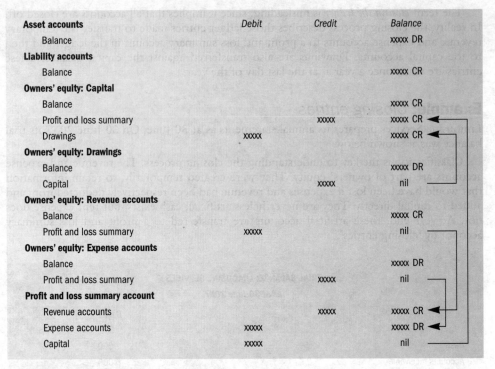

	Debit	Credit	Balance
Asset accounts			
Balance			xxxxx DR
Liability accounts			
Balance			xxxxx CR
Owners' equity: Capital			
Balance			xxxxx CR
Profit and loss summary		xxxxx	xxxxx CR
Drawings	xxxxx		xxxxx CR
Owners' equity: Drawings			
Balance			xxxxx DR
Capital		xxxxx	nil
Owners' equity: Revenue accounts			
Balance			xxxxx CR
Profit and loss summary	xxxxx		nil
Owners' equity: Expense accounts			
Balance			xxxxx DR
Profit and loss summary		xxxxx	nil
Profit and loss summary account			
Revenue accounts		xxxxx	xxxxx CR
Expense accounts	xxxxx		xxxxx DR
Capital	xxxxx		nil

The closing entries for Limousine Services will first be presented as general journal entries, thus:

GENERAL JOURNAL: LIMOUSINE SERVICES			
Date	Particulars	Debit	Credit
June 30	Sales revenue	28 900	
	Profit and loss summary		28 900
	(Transfer of revenue)		
June 30	Profit and loss summary	25 400	
	Advertising expense		12 300
	Rent expense		5 400
	Wages expense		7 700
	(Transfer of expenses)		

These are the closing entries in the ledger. Each of the revenue and expense accounts will be transferred to the profit and loss summary account in the following manner. A debit of $28 900 is placed in the sales revenue account and a corresponding credit in the profit and loss summary account. The balance in sales revenue is now nil. Similarly, the balances in advertising expense, rent expense and wages expense are transferred to the profit and loss summary and the three expense accounts are then 'closed'. After these transfers, the balance of $3500 in the profit and loss summary account represents the difference between revenue and expenses, which is the net profit.

			Debit	Credit
June 30	Profit and loss summary		3500	
	Capital			3500
	(Transfer of net profit to capital)			
June 30	Capital		1500	
	Drawings			1500
	(Transfer of drawings against capital)			

Since this business is a sole trader, all profit belongs to the owner and this is recognised by transferring the net profit from the profit and loss summary account to the capital account. This entry closes off the profit and loss summary account. The closing process is then completed by transferring the balance of $1500 in the drawings account to the capital account to reduce the balance in that account. After these entries, the only owners' equity account remaining open is capital, all the temporary accounts having been closed.

The remaining balances in the ledger consist of the assets, the liabilities and, within owners' equity, the capital account. These remaining balances will comprise the balance sheet.

The ledger accounts affected by closing entries are presented below:

PORTION OF GENERAL LEDGER: LIMOUSINE SERVICES

Date	Particulars	Debit	Credit	Balance
Owners' equity	**Capital**			
June 30	Balance			18 000 CR
	Profit and loss summary		3 500	21 500 CR
	Drawings	1 500		20 000 CR
	Drawings			
June 30	Balance			1 500 DR
	Capital		1 500	—
	Sales revenue			
June 30	Balance			28 900 CR
	Profit and loss summary	28 900		—
	Advertising expense			
June 30	Balance			12 300 DR
	Profit and loss summary		12 300	—
	Rent expense			
June 30	Balance			5 400 DR
	Profit and loss summary		5 400	—
	Wages expenses			
June 30	Balance			7 700 DR
	Profit and loss summary		7 700	—
	Profit and loss summary			
June 30	Sales revenue		28 900	28 900 CR
	Advertising expense	12 300		16 600 CR
	Rent expense	5 400		11 200 CR
	Wages expense	7 700		3 500 CR
	Capital (profit)	3 500		—

Having closed the ledger, the financial statements are prepared. The profit and loss statement presents the same information as in the ledger account for the profit and loss summary, but in a more readable form suitable for publication. The two should not be confused. The profit and loss summary account is part of the ledger, whereas the profit and loss statement is a report prepared outside the ledger and presented to interested parties. The relationship between the balance sheet and the ledger should also be noted, with the balance sheet representing the ledger accounts remaining open after the closing ledger entries have been completed.

Interim financial statements may be prepared directly from the trial balance.

Comprehensive example: *Transactions and closing entries*

The following transactions took place in the first month of trading of Clean Laundry Services.

May	1	Owner contributed $30 000 as capital.
	4	Purchased equipment for $7000, paying $1000 deposit and obtaining a long-term loan for the balance.
	5	Provided cleaning services totalling $12 000. Received $2000 with the remainder due next month.
	12	Received the following bills: • Electricity $1600 • Telephone $700
	24	Owner withdrew $600.

Required

(a) Analyse the transactions.
(b) Prepare the relevant journal entries.
(c) Post the journal entries to the ledger.
(d) Prepare a trial balance.
(e) Prepare closing entries.
(f) Prepare a profit and loss statement and balance sheet.

Answers

(a) Analysis of transactions

May	1	Cash at bank account increases: it is an asset, therefore DEBIT Capital account increases: it is owners' equity, therefore CREDIT
	4	Equipment account increases: it is an asset, therefore DEBIT Cash at bank account decreases: it is an asset, therefore CREDIT Loan payable account increases: it is a liability, therefore CREDIT
	5	Cash at bank account increases: it is an asset, therefore DEBIT Accounts receivable account increases: it is an asset, therefore DEBIT Cleaning revenue account increases: it is an increase in owners' equity, revenue, therefore CREDIT
	12	Electricity expense account increases: it is a decrease in owners' equity, expense, therefore DEBIT Telephone expense account increases: it is a decrease in owner's equity, expense, therefore DEBIT Accounts payable account increases: it is a liability, therefore CREDIT
	24	Drawings account increases, which reduces owners' equity, therefore DEBIT Cash at bank account decreases: it is an asset, therefore CREDIT

(b) Journal entries

	GENERAL JOURNAL: CLEAN LAUNDRY SERVICES		
Date	Particulars	Debit	Credit
May 1	Cash at bank	30 000	
	Capital		30 000
	(To record owner's initial contribution)		
4	Equipment	7 000	
	Cash at bank		1 000
	Loan payable		6 000
	(To record purchase of equipment)		
5	Cash at bank	2 000	
	Accounts receivable	10 000	
	Cleaning revenue		12 000
	(To record revenue earned)		
12	Electricity expense	1 600	
	Telephone expense	700	
	Accounts payable		2 300
	(To record expenses incurred)		
24	Drawings	600	
	Cash		600
	(To record owner's withdrawal from the business)		

(c) Ledger entries

	GENERAL LEDGER: CLEAN LAUNDRY SERVICES			
Date	Particulars	Debit	Credit	Balance
	Cash at bank			
May 1	Capital	30 000		30 000 DR
4	Equipment		1 000	29 000 DR
5	Cleaning revenue	2 000		31 000 DR
24	Drawings		600	30 400 DR
	Accounts receivable			
May 5	Cleaning revenue	10 000		10 000 DR
	Equipment			
May 4	Cash at bank/loan payable	7 000		7 000 DR
	Accounts payable			
May 12	Electricity expense/telephone expense		2 300	2 300 CR
	Loan payable			
May 4	Equipment		6 000	6 000 CR
	Capital			
May 1	Cash at bank		30 000	30 000 CR
				continues

GENERAL LEDGER: CLEAN LAUNDRY SERVICES

Date	Particulars	Debit	Credit	Balance
	Drawings			
May 24	Cash at bank	600		600 DR
	Cleaning revenue			
May 5	Cash at bank/accounts receivable		12 000	12 000 CR
	Electricity expense			
May 12	Accounts payable	1 600		1 600 DR
	Telephone expense			
May 12	Accounts payable	700		700 DR

(d) Trial balance

TRIAL BALANCE: CLEAN LAUNDRY SERVICES
as at 31 May 20X0

	Debit	Credit
Cash at bank	$30 400	
Accounts receivable	10 000	
Equipment	7 000	
Accounts payable		$ 2 300
Loan payable		6 000
Capital		30 000
Drawings	600	
Cleaning revenue		12 000
Electricity expense	1 600	
Telephone expense	700	
	50 300	50 300

(e) Closing entries

GENERAL JOURNAL: CLEAN LAUNDRY SERVICES

Date	Particulars	Debit	Credit
May 31	Cleaning revenue	12 000	
	Profit and loss summary		12 000
	(Transfer of revenue)		
	Profit and loss summary	2 300	
	Electricity expense		1 600
	Telephone expense		700
	(Transfer of expense)		
	Profit and loss summary	9 700	
	Capital		9 700
	(Transfer of profit to capital)		
	Capital	600	
	Drawings		600
	(Transfer of drawings against capital)		

The ledger accounts affected by closing entries are repeated in this next section to show the effects of the closing journal entries on the ledger accounts.

PORTION OF GENERAL LEDGER: CLEAN LAUNDRY SERVICES

Date	Particulars	Debit	Credit	Balance
	Capital			
May 31	Balance			30 000 CR
	Profit and loss summary		9 700	39 700 CR
	Drawings	600		39 100 CR
	Drawings			
May 31	Balance			600 DR
	Capital		600	–
	Cleaning revenue			
May 31	Balance			12 000 CR
	Profit and loss summary	12 000		–
	Electricity expense			
May 31	Balance			1 600 DR
	Profit and loss summary		1 600	–
	Telephone expense			
May 31	Balance			700 DR
	Profit and loss summary		700	–
	Profit and loss summary			
May 31	Cleaning revenue		12 000	12 000 CR
	Electricity expense	1 600		10 400 CR
	Telephone expense	700		9 700 CR
	Capital (profit)	9 700		–

(f) Financial statements

PROFIT AND LOSS STATEMENT: CLEAN LAUNDRY SERVICES
for the month ended 31 May 20X0

Cleaning revenue		$12 000
less Expenses		
Electricity expense	$1 600	
Telephone expense	700	2 300
Net profit		$ 9 700

BALANCE SHEET: CLEAN LAUNDRY SERVICES as at 31 May 20X0					
Assets	$	$	**Liabilities**	$	$
Current			Current		
Cash at bank	30 400		Accounts payable		2 300
Accounts receivable	10 000	40 400	Non-current		
Non-current			Loan payable		6 000
					8 300
Equipment		7 000			
			Owners' equity		
			Capital	30 000	
			plus Net profit	9 700	
			less Drawings	600	39 100
		$47 400			$47 400

The recording and reporting process in accounting so far

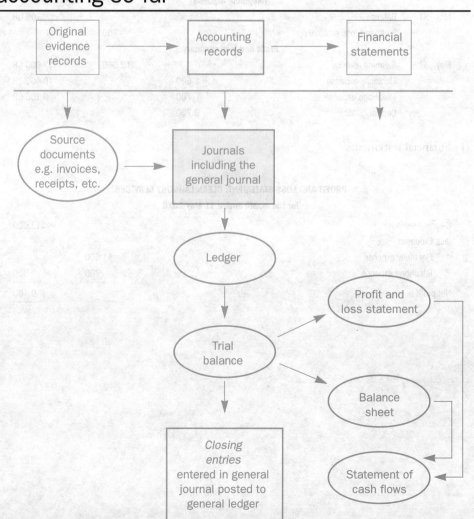

Statements of cash flows will be considered in detail in Chapter 10.

Summary

This chapter has introduced a simplified double-entry recording system, which will provide a most useful framework for the following chapters. The analysis of transactions according to their effects on the basic ownership equation provides the starting point for the recording system. The various changes are recorded in accounts, with a separate account being provided for each item that will appear in the financial statements. The collection of accounts is known as a ledger.

The ledger, with its double-entry coding into debits and credits, provides a well-controlled means of processing a large number of transactions. The requirement that every transaction must have offsetting debits and credits provides automatic protection against attempts to analyse transactions in such a way that the basic equation will become unbalanced. If, for example, it were decided that a purchase of a machine on credit led to an increase in an asset and a decrease in a liability, two debits would result, alerting the accountant to the fact that the analysis was wrong.

The terms 'debit' and 'credit' have no meanings in accounting other than 'left' or 'right' respectively. They are names which have been used in accounting for centuries.

Following the recording of transactions, a trial balance is drawn up, from which interim reports may be prepared. At the end of the year the temporary revenue and expense accounts are closed by transferring their balances to a profit and loss summary account and thence to capital. Final accounting reports are then prepared for presentation to interested parties.

As will become more evident in later chapters, decisions necessarily made in preparing accounts and reports are often discussed and debated within organisations. Such decisions, which may be controversial, impact on the numbers reported periodically such as net profit, total assets and net assets. While an impression may have been given in this chapter that precision or accuracy is the hallmark of accounting, the opposite is the case even though this may not be immediately apparent. The precision demanded in balancing accounts is not a characteristic of many of the numbers actually reported.

Review exercises

Discussion questions

4.1 What are the three important characteristics of any recording system? Discuss why each is important.

4.2 Describe how efficiency, control and accessibility are achieved in a manual accounting system.

4.3 Indicate whether you would expect each of the following accounts to have a debit or a credit balance. Give reasons for your answer.

Accounts receivable
Bank overdraft
B. McDonald drawings
Inventory on hand
Accounts payable
Motor vehicles
Supplies on hand

Interest received
B. McDonald capital
Prepaid rent
Stationery used

4.4   A friend who has just started learning accounting is rather mystified by it and asks you to explain the following points:

(a) We have been told that a credit balance in the bank account signifies an overdraft. When my bank says my account is in credit, they mean that I have money in hand. Why is this?

(b) Apparently, a correct balance sheet should always balance, although mine seldom does. Why should this collection of apparently unrelated figures necessarily give two equal totals?

(c) A debit balance is sometimes a loss, which is a bad thing, and sometimes an asset, which is a good thing. Why this paradox?

(d) The capital account seems to represent an amount owed to the proprietor of the business. Since the proprietor owns it, how can it owe the proprietor anything?

(e) Why have all of these rules instead of a simple principle that states that increases in *any* account are debits and decreases credits?

(f) If I looked in a textbook in the library and found that the balance sheets in it were the opposite way around from what we have been told, does this mean we have been wrongly taught?

4.5   If the sum of the total debits is equal to the sum of the total credits on the trial balance, no errors have been made. Do you agree? Why?

4.6   Liabilities and owners' equity both have credit balances, hence there is no difference between them. Do you agree or disagree with this statement? Explain your answer.

4.7   Give an example, if possible, of a transaction that

(a) increases assets and increases liabilities

(b) increases liabilities and decreases owners' equity

(c) decreases assets and increases owners' equity

(d) increases one asset account, increases liabilities and decreases another asset account

(e) increases assets and decreases liabilities

(f) decreases and increases different asset accounts.

4.8   Explain how classification procedures are incorporated in the double-entry recording system. Refer to journals, ledgers and other accounting records.

4.9   What are the advantages of a double-entry recording system?

4.10   'It's not possible to prepare accounting reports unless double-entry records are pre-pared'. Critically examine this statement.

4.11   'Double-entry records ensure that the information in the accounting system is reliable'. Critically examine this statement.

Problems

4.12 *Ledger accounts—introduction*

The following ledger accounts appeared in the records of Fire Equipment Services for the week ended 31 January. The business commenced operations on 24 January.

Date	Particulars	Debit	Credit	Balance
	GENERAL LEDGER: FIRE EQUIPMENT SERVICES			
	Cash at bank			
Jan. 24	Capital	5 000		5 000 DR
25	Fees	1 200		6 200 DR
26	Repairs		1 000	5 200 DR
27	Insurance		750	4 450 DR
28	Drawings		300	4150 DR
	Accounts receivable			
Jan. 28	Fees	900		900 DR
	Equipment			
Jan. 27	Loan Co.	30 000		30 000 DR
	Repairs			
Jan. 26	Bank	1 000		1 000 DR
	Insurance			
Jan. 27	Bank	750		750 DR
	Loan Co.			
Jan. 27	Equipment		30 000	30 000 CR
	Drawings			
Jan. 28	Bank	300		300 DR
	Capital—F. Blazer			
Jan. 24	Bank		5 000	5 000 CR
	Fees			
Jan. 25	Bank		1 200	1 200 CR
28	Accounts receivable		900	2 100 CR

From the above information, answer the following questions:

(a) How much capital was contributed by Blazer to commence the business?
(b) What was the total amount of cash banked for the week?
(c) What was the total amount of cash paid out for the week?
(d) What was the total of assets purchased for the week?
(e) How much did the owner withdraw for personal use?
(f) What was the total amount of revenue earned for the week?
(g) What was the total debt at the end of the week?
(h) What was the profit for the week?
(i) What is the owners' equity at the end of the week?
(j) What is the value of total assets at the end of the week?

4.13 *Preparation of financial statements using journals, ledgers and a trial balance*

1. The following are the transactions of the first fortnight of practice of N. Able, a public accountant.

July   1   N. Able began business as a public accountant with a deposit of $10 000 in a trading bank account.

         2   Bought a computer for cash, $3000.

         3   Bought office furniture and equipment on credit from Furniture Suppliers, $7000.

         4   Paid one fortnight's rent of an office, $600.

         5   Received $800 from J. Midas for accounting services rendered.

         9   Invoiced A. Trusty for accounting services, $560.

      11   Paid Furniture Suppliers $2000 on account.

      12   Paid week's wages to secretary, $500.

      13   A. Trusty paid his account.

      14   Paid $800 for annual vacation at Surfers Paradise.

(a) Enter the transactions in a transaction analysis table.

(b) Prepare journal entries for each transaction.

(c) Enter the transactions in a general ledger.

(d) Prepare a trial balance.

(e) Prepare a profit and loss statement, a capital statement and a balance sheet.

2. The Mornington Maulers football team, which plays in the Yarra League, has been taken over by Phil Forward. It was previously a social club with no material assets and no liabilities. The following were the transactions for the first month of play in 20X9.

April   1   P. Forward paid $100 000 into a bank account as capital.

         2   Paid $20 000 to the Yarra League for a lifetime licence to operate the club. The licence is transferable.

         8   Purchased new uniforms on credit for $12 500.

      12   Lost the first game, but gate receipts totalled $4200.

      13   Paid players' fees for game 1, $1200.

      17   Paid ground rental for April and May, $9000.

      18   Paid instalment due on uniforms purchased on 8 April, $3400.

      19   Game 2. Another loss, but gate proceeds were $3300.

      20   Pay players' fees for game 2, $1200.

      22   Received donation from the supporters' club, $4000.

      23   Received invoice for advertisement to be run immediately but to be paid for in May, $1500.

      24   Withdrew for private use $17 000.

      26   Game 3. A loss by twenty goals. Gate proceeds were $2600.

      27   Paid players' fees for game 3, $600. Promised to restore full payments when the team won a match.

      30   Paid second instalment on uniforms, $3400.

      30   Withdrew for private use $5000.

(a) Prepare journal entries for each of the above transactions.

(b) Post each journal entry to the appropriate ledger accounts.

(c) Prepare a trial balance.

(d) Prepare necessary closing entries.

(e) Prepare a profit and loss statement for the month and a balance sheet as at 30 April 20X9.

4.14 *Trial balance—detection of errors*

Peta Portelli, proprietor of Portelli Portable Buildings, offers for rental a range of buildings such as temporary shelters, recreation rooms, site buildings, portable toilets, etc.

An audit clerk has detected the following errors in the recording of transactions in the ledger of the business.

(a) A credit to accounts payable of $380 was omitted.

(b) A debit of $1500 to accounts receivable was entered twice.

(c) A debit of $195 to stationery was entered as $915.

(d) A transaction to debit wages expense and credit cash at bank for $700 was omitted from the ledger.

(e) A credit of $205 to accounts receivable was incorrectly entered as sales.

Consider each case individually and assuming no other errors have taken place indicate:

(a) by 'yes' or 'no' whether the trial balance would be out of balance;

(b) if your answer to (a) is 'yes', the amount by which the trial balance totals would differ;

(c) the column of the trial balance that would have the larger total.

Answers should be presented in the following form:

Error	(a) Out of balance	(b) Difference	(c) Larger total

4.15 *Preparation of financial statements given opening balances and a series of transactions*

John and Joan, a husband and wife team, registered their business under the name of 'J & J Shoe Repairs'. They opened a shoe repair shop in a shopping arcade on 1 November 20X5. On 31 December 20X5 the balances in the books were as follows:

	$?
Capital—J & J	$?
Cash at bank	6 805
Motor vehicle	7 500
Equipment	4 650
Furniture and fittings	990
Debtors	200
Creditors—General Stores Ltd	1 800
Loan from bank	10 000
Shoe repair revenue	6 000
Advertising expense	50
Shop supplies expense	225
Rent paid	1 800
Car repairs and maintenance	180
Sundry creditors (insurance)	133
Insurance expense	133

The transactions for January 20X6 were as follows:

Jan.	4	Purchased shop supplies worth $105 on credit from General Stores Ltd. All the supplies were used during the month.
	6	Banked receipts for cash repair jobs, $2120.
	10	Furniture recorded at $230 collapsed and was scrapped.
	12	Paid creditors, $850.
	16	Paid for advertising in local newspaper, $25.
	18	Banked receipts for cash repair jobs, $1120.
	24	Collected $80 from debtors.
	29	Withdrew $450 for own use.
		Paid premium of $800 for a one-year insurance policy purchased on commencement of business.
	31	Paid $600 rental to R. Ltd for shop space. Rent of $600 per month is payable in advance.

John and Joan wish to know their financial position as at 31 January 20X6 and their operating results for the past three months. As their accountant, you are required to:

(a) Design a suitable chart of accounts.
(b) Prepare journal entries for each transaction.
(c) Open a general ledger, insert opening balances and enter transactions.
(d) Draw up a profit and loss statement and a balance sheet.
(e) Comment on your client's current financial position and operating results for the three months ending 31 January 20X6.

4.16 *Designing a chart of accounts*

Nicky Nicolosi operates the Progressive Driving School. The business focuses on advanced driving skills such as skid control and defensive driving as well as advanced tuition for experienced drivers and high performance/motor racing tuition. The following chart represents a system aimed at classifying and identifying the accounts of the business in some orderly sequence. Nicky was given it by a friend who operates an electrical repairs business.

CHART OF ACCOUNTS

1.		ASSETS	3.		OWNERS' EQUITY
1.1		Current Assets	3.1		Capital
	1.1.1	Bank			
	1.1.2	Materials			
			4.		REVENUE
1.2		Non-Current Assets	4.1		Sales
	1.2.1	Equipment	4.2		Interest Revenue
	1.2.2	Furniture			
2.		LIABILITIES	5.		EXPENSES
2.1		Current Liabilities	5.1		Wages
	2.1.1	Bank Overdraft	5.2		Advertising
2.2		Non-Current Liabilities	5.3		Interest Expense
	2.2.1	Mortgage Loan	5.4		Petrol and Oil
			5.5		Rent

(a) Is this chart of accounts suitable for Nicky's business? Explain.

(b) Nicky's brother has suggested that it would be best to prepare the chart of accounts for the business 'after the business has been operating for a reasonable time' as then Nicky will know exactly what accounts are needed. Do you agree? Explain.

4.17 *Accounting equation, ledger, trial balance and financial statements*

1. The following are the first week's transactions of Heavenly Insurance Brokers, a firm that operates a service selling insurance policies from door to door for various insurance companies.

(i) Proprietor contributed $20 000 as capital.

(ii) Acquired office furniture for cash, $6000.

(iii) Purchased a motor vehicle from Canter Ford for $12 000, paying $4000 deposit.

(iv) Filled the tank with petrol, $36. All petrol used during the week.

(v) Paid week's rent on offices, $100.

(vi) Received $120 commission for insurance policies sold in West Ryde area.

(vii) Sent a bill for $70 to the L. & D. Insurance Company for commission due on policies sold on their behalf.

(viii) Paid the first week's instalment on the motor vehicle, $400.

(ix) Withdrew $160 for luncheon expenses to celebrate the first week's operations.

(x) The L. & D. Insurance Company paid $30 on account.

(a) Analyse each transaction according to its effect on the basic accounting equation (assets = liabilities + owners' equity).

(b) Enter the transaction in a general ledger.

(c) Prepare a trial balance.

(d) Prepare a profit and loss statement, a capital statement and a balance sheet.

2. Willy Ballence, a public accountant of high repute, has decided to commence his own practice. The following occurred in the first fortnight:

Nov. 1 Deposited $100 000 into a business bank account.

2 Purchased a small office building for $80 000 on credit from K. Mark Ltd. Paid a further $5000 for minor renovations. Office furniture cost $2000, paid in cash.

3 Paid $120 for a fortnight's rent of a micro-computer.

4 Office stationery cost $320. It had all been used up by 14 November.

8 Withdrew $100 for his own use. Sent out accounts for services rendered as follows:

J. Jones	$ 400
I. M. Broke	700
M. Fifi	400
L. Greensleeves	170
	$1670

(*Note:* One ledger account, 'Accounts receivable', will suffice, and it is necessary only to enter the totals.)

10 Paid for typing and photocopying services, $180. Received cash from

M. Fifi	$400
L. Greensleeves	170
	$570

(Enter the total figure only.)

14 Sent the following accounts to customers:

G. Oil	$ 350
C. Water	300
A. Capone	400
	$1050

Received $200 cash from J. Jones.
Withdrew $220 for personal use.
Paid $2000 on account to K. Mark Ltd.

(a) Analyse the transactions, showing their effects on the basic accounting equation.
(b) Record them in appropriate ledger accounts.
(c) Prepare a profit and loss statement for the period and a balance sheet as at 14 November.

4.18 *Accounting equation, ledger, trial balance, closing entries and financial statements*
Peter Dolphin established an aquarium at Coffs Harbour. The aquarium and related customer facilities cost $200 000 to construct and there is an outstanding mortgage of $50 000 on which he pays 10 per cent interest per annum, together with a six-monthly mortgage repayment of $5000. A summary of his transactions for the first half of the year is as follows:

March quarter Paid salaries to attendants, $10 000.
Purchased feed on credit, $500.
Purchased water pump and treatment plant from Aquarium Outfitters Ltd at a cost of $6000, paying $2000 cash.
Entrance receipts, $27 000 cash.
Paid electricity bill for March quarter, $300.

June quarter Paid remaining $4000 to Aquarium Outfitters Ltd.
Paid salaries to attendants, $12 000.
Withdrew $18 000 to purchase a motor vehicle for personal use.
Entrance receipts, $31 000 cash.
Paid $500 for feed purchased in the previous quarter.
Paid interest and mortgage repayment for March/June quarters.
Purchased shark feed for $600 on credit; half remained unused at the end of the quarter.
The electricity bill for the June quarter, amounting to $350, was unpaid.

(a) Analyse the transactions showing their effects on the basic accounting equation.

(b) Record them in appropriate ledger accounts.

(c) Prepare a trial balance.

(d) Make closing entries in the general ledger. Ignore depreciation.

(e) Prepare a profit and loss statement for the six months ending 30 June and a balance sheet at that date.

4.19 *Preparation of closing entries*

Given the following information that relates to AP Services, prepare relevant closing general journal entries.

AP capital	$14 000
Service revenue	75 000
Salaries expense	12 000
Insurance expense	1 400
AP drawings	790
Rental revenue	1 200
Rates expense	1 000
Interest revenue	970

4.20 *Journals, ledger, trial balance, closing entries and financial statements*

Clyde Collins decided to become self-employed. On 1 April he commenced business as C.C. Cleaning Services, providing all home and office cleaning services. He incurred the following transactions during his first month of trading.

April 1 Placed $15 000 into a business bank account.

Purchased a heavy-duty vacuum cleaner and attachments, $2200 cash.

Designed and had printed 500 leaflets advertising his newly established business and distributed them to nearby homes and offices.

Printing and delivery costs totalled $210.

2 Purchased a second-hand delivery van from J. Morgan for $4000, paying $1000 immediately, the balance to be paid by the end of May.

Filled the van with petrol, $45.

3 Signed a contract to hire a floor polisher for $100 a month. The terms of the contract stated that the hiring fees must be paid one month in advance, with an initial deposit of $300 when the contract is signed, but which is fully refundable at the termination of the contract.

Signed an insurance contract on the van with Wheels Insurance Brokers.

5 Purchased on credit cleaning equipment that included brooms, mops, buckets and cleaning cloths for $630. Purchased cleaning materials including antiseptic, biodegradable detergent, window cleaner and floor wax for $340 cash.

6 Received a call from Cedar Real Estate requesting Clyde to clean two recently vacated homes managed by the agent.

R. Wilson, a dentist, contracted Clyde to clean his surgery each fortnight.

7 Cleaned the homes for Cedar Real Estate and sent an invoice for the service, $160.

Paid the annual insurance premium on the delivery van, $720.

8　　Received an invoice from *The Field Times* for advertisements appearing on 5 and 7 April, $180.
Refilled van with petrol, $31.
Withdrew $300 from the business for personal use.

10　　Received a cheque from Cedar Real Estate for $160.
Cleaned R. Wilson's surgery and sent an invoice for the service, $90.

11　　D. Mansfield, a public accountant, contracted Clyde to clean her offices each Friday evening, commencing 16 April.

12　　Repairs to delivery van, $85 cash.
Purchased on credit additional cleaning material for $240.

15　　Paid J. Morgan $500 of the amount owing to him.
Cedar Real Estate again engaged Clyde to clean two recently vacated home units.

16　　Filled the van with petrol, $38.
Cleaned D. Mansfield's offices and sent an invoice for the service, $190.

17　　Thoroughly cleaned two home units for Cedar Real Estate and sent an invoice for $240.
Clyde's van ran over two of his steel buckets that had cost $80. The buckets were disposed of and two new ones purchased for $95 cash.

19　　Received cheque from R. Wilson for $90.
Dr H. Smith contracted Clyde to clean her surgery on a weekly basis, commencing on 23 April.

20　　Paid invoice received from *The Field Times* on 8 April.
Withdrew $200 for personal use.

23　　Cleaned D. Mansfield's offices and sent an invoice for the service, $140.
Filled van with petrol, $29, and purchased a new tyre to replace the tyre that punctured during the week, $93.

24　　Cleaned Dr Smith's surgery and sent an invoice for the service, $110.
Paid for cleaning materials purchased on 12 April.

25　　Received another invoice from *The Field Times* for advertising that appeared on 12 and 14 April, $220.
Cleaned R. Wilson's surgery and sent an invoice for the service, $90.
Received cheque from D. Mansfield in payment of invoice dated 16 April.
Received and paid an account for $78 from H. Smith's surgery. Clyde had been suffering from a virus and visited the surgery for treatment.

26　　Received cheque from Cedar Real Estate for the two home units cleaned on 17 April.
Purchased on credit, 30 litres of disinfectant and 10 tubs of cream cleanser for $130.

27　　Received cheque from Dr Smith for $110. Cleaned a recently vacated house for Cedar Real Estate and sent an invoice, $120.

30　　Cleaned surgery for Dr Smith and sent an invoice for the service, $100.
Withdrew $400 for personal use.

At the end of April, Clyde had cleaning materials that had cost $230 remaining on hand.

(a) Prepare journal entries for each transaction.
(b) Enter the transactions in a general ledger.
(c) Prepare a trial balance.
(d) Prepare closing entries.
(e) Prepare financial statements for April.

4.21 *Public sector: transaction analysis, ledgers and financial statements*

The PR Department (PRD) provides media and promotional services to other depart-ments. PRD charges market rates for its services and is completely self-funding. It is allowed to retain all profits (or surpluses) for reinvestment.

On 1 June 20X5 the computerised accounting system failed. It had not been fixed by 30 June and management was demanding draft financial statements for the year. Luckily, the accountant knew what the balances in the accounts were when the com-puter went down and had a summary of transactions for June, the last month of the financial year.

On 1 June 20X5 the balances in PRD's general ledger were as follows:

Cash	10 000 DR	Accounts payable	10 000 CR
Accounts receivable	15 000 DR	Revenue	100 000 CR
Office supplies	5 000 DR	Wages expense	60 000 DR
Computer	20 000 DR	Rent expense	20 000 DR
		Capital	20 000 CR

Transactions for the month of June were as follows:

1. Collected cash on accounts receivable, $10 000.
   Received telephone bill and paid it, $5000.
2. Paid salaries and wages, $10 000.
3. Purchased a car for $20 000, paying $5000 deposit.
4. Billed departments for services rendered, $20 000.
5. Collected cash on accounts receivable, $15 000.
6. Paid cash on accounts payable, $11 000.
7. Paid rent for the month of June, $4000.
8. Used up office supplies which had cost $4000.
9. At the end of June wages owing amounted to $8000.

(a) Open a general ledger and enter the opening balances for PRD. Record the trans-actions for June 20X5 and take out a trial balance.
(b) Prepare a profit and loss statement for the year ended 30 June 20X5 and a bal-ance sheet as at 30 June 20X5.

4.22 *Accounting equation and financial statements*

Dr S. Sever has just established a medical practice.

(a) Analyse the following transactions showing their effects on the basic accounting equation.
(b) Record them in the appropriate ledger accounts.
(c) Prepare a trial balance, profit and loss statement and balance sheet.

Mar. 1   Paid $10 000 into a separate bank account to provide capital for the business.

        1   Hired receptionist and agreed to pay $220 per week.

        2   Paid $1000 for furniture and fittings.

        3   Purchased medical equipment on credit from Medical Suppliers, $8000.

        4   Received $80 fees in cash from patients. A further $75 is due from Medibank.

        5   Received $90 in cash fees. Amount due from Medibank, $40.

        7   Paid receptionist, $220. Dr Sever withdrew $200 for personal use. Cash fees, $85.

        8   Cash fees received, $120. Amount due from Medibank, $60.

        9   Cash fees, $110. Amount due from Medibank, $30.

     10   Paid Medical Suppliers $3000 of the amount owing.

     11   Cash fees, $100.

     12   Dr Sever withdrew $40 for personal use. Cash fees, $80.

     13   Paid current fortnight's rent on surgery, $200.

     14   Paid receptionist, $220.

     15   Paid $40 telephone rental in advance.

4.23 *Accounting equation, general ledger and financial statements*

Giulietta Bertoni commenced a service centre business for Alfa Romeo cars on Monday 1 April 20X8. The following transactions occurred during the month of April.

April 1   Giulietta contributed her garage, worth $50 000, and cash of $5000 to establish the business.

        3   Borrowed $30 000 from the BAN Bank for three years at an interest rate of 17 per cent. The loan is repayable at the end of three years. Interest is payable quarterly.

        4   Purchased electronic tuning equipment for $15 000 cash. Bought a car hoist for $8000 on credit. Installation costs, also on credit, were $1000. The full $9000 is due on 1 June 20X8.

        5   Bought a variety of hand tools for $6000 cash.

        8   Purchased oils and lubricants for $1000 on credit.

     10   Hired a mechanic on a salary of $800 per week payable at the end of each fortnight, commencing 10 April.
Serviced cars for cash customers, $500.

     11   Serviced cars for cash customers, $600.

     18   Billed a customer $2500 for major work done on a GTV.

     22   Serviced cars for cash customers, $200, and credit customers, $500.

     24   Paid first fortnight's salary to mechanic. Serviced cars for cash customers, $600.

     29   Paid for oils and lubricants purchased on 8 April. Received $1500 from the GTV customer billed on 18 April.

     30   An electricity bill for $200 for the month of April has not been paid. Oils and lubricants worth $300 were on hand.

(a) Analyse the transactions for April in accordance with the accounting equation.

(b) Record the transactions for April in the general ledger for Giulietta Bertoni's business.

(c) Prepare a profit and loss statement for the month ending 30 April 20X8 and a balance sheet as at 30 April 20X8 for the business.

4.24 *General ledger, trial balance, financial statements and analysis*

Mr T. Briggs owns and operates a charter plane business that provides scenic tours on the New South Wales Central Coast. On 1 June 20X9 he had the following account balances:

Cash	$ 9 450
Aircraft	38 000
Office furniture	5 200
Unearned revenue	280
Sundry creditor	350
Accounts payable	2 400
Capital	?
Retained profit	10 070

During June 20X9 he recorded the following transactions.

June   2   Paid annual insurance premium of $1560.

Paid George's Real Estate office rent for June, $650.

3   Purchased a motor vehicle for business use, $9800. The purchase was financed by a 3-year bank loan at an interest rate of 15 per cent.

Received $240 for flights to be given on June 4 and 5.

5   Paid Jake's Mechanical Repairs $640 to service one of the aircraft.

No Frills Furniture delivered a new office desk and chair, which cost $520 and were purchased on credit.

7   Paid subscription to *Go Anywhere* travel magazine for the June and July issues, $80.

Received $210 for flights undertaken on this day.

8   Received a cheque for $1700 from Express Tours, a regular customer, for flights undertaken from 1 June to 6 June.

Drew a cheque for $350 that was sent to the *Gosford Tribune* for advertisements, which appeared during May and June. $170 related to May advertisements.

9   Mr Briggs withdrew $370 for his own use.

Received $240 for flights to be undertaken on 9 and 10 June.

10   Paid a fortnight's wages to office staff, $780. Paid E. Manual, a creditor, amount due at end of May, $1100.

12   Purchased sundry stationery items which were all used by the end of June, $245.

13   Paid No Frills Furniture $220 of the amount owing.

Received $305 for flights to be undertaken on 13, 14 and 15 June.

16   Received payment from Express Tours for flights undertaken from 9 to 15 June, $850.

17   Received and paid electricity account of $360 for period covering 1 May to 30 June 20X9.

18 Paid $270 to the *Umina Express* for advertising during the first two weeks of June.
Received $120 for flights taken on 18 and 19 June.
20 Received $770 from Express Tours for flight services performed from 16 to 19 June.
21 Paid office staff a fortnight's wages, $780.
23 Withdrew $370 for private purposes.
Received $95 for flights taken on this day.
26 Paid June interest due on bank loan.
Received $230 for flights to be undertaken on 27, 28 and 29 June.
27 Celebrated the end of the financial year with an office lunch as the Hillston Country Club, $150.
28 Received a cheque from Express Tours for flight services performed from 21 to 28 June, $1040.
29 C.C. Cleaning Services cleaned the office and invoiced Mr Briggs $185.
30 Received $120 for flights to be undertaken on 30 June and $210 for flights to be taken on 1 and 2 July.
Sent Express Tours an invoice for flights taken on 29 and 30 June, $350.

(a) Record the transactions for the month of June in the appropriate ledger accounts.
(b) Prepare a trial balance for the month of June.
(c) Prepare a suitably classified profit and loss statement and balance sheet for June.
(d) Has Mr Briggs had a profitable month? Why?

4.25 *The accounting process: An extensive analysis*

Part A

At Christmas 20X7 Peter Prince decided finally to cease work as an accountant and fulfil his dream of running an island paradise. The following were his transactions for the first three months of trading in 20X8:

April 1 Contributed $100 000 cash as capital in a business to be known as Nirvana Island Holidays.
1 Completed the purchase of Rundown Island from I. V. Hadinuff for $500 000 and renamed it Nirvana Island. The island had 10 huts valued at a total of $80 000. The purchase was financed by a loan of $460 000 from Risky Finance Ltd, the balance being paid in cash. The interest rate was 15 per cent per annum.
Hint: Record this as a loan of $500 000 and then pay $40 000 off the loan.
16 Paid wages, $9250.
30 Constructed two new units at a total cost of $55 000, paid in cash.
May 6 Paid for food and supplies, $17 000.
15 Invoiced the following travel agents for accommodation supplied:

Campus Travel	$26 300
Quick Escape	38 400
Cut-Rite Tours	6 100
Total	$70 800

Note: Enter the total only in 'Accounts receivable'. The revenue account is 'Accommodation fees'.

16	Paid for laundry and cleaning	$ 4 100
	Paid wages	9 250
	Paid for food and supplies	3 100
	Withdrew for private use	15 000

17 Made minor repairs and paid in cash, $4500.

18 Advertising account received payable to *New Image*, $4140.

20 Purchased food and supplies from Island Supplies Ltd on credit, $6400.

21 Accounts paid in full by Campus Travel and Quick Escape.

22 Arranged with bank an available overdraft, if required, of $80 000.

23 Invoiced travel agents:

Campus Travel	$32 000
Quick Escape	14 800
	46 800

30 Purchased motor vehicle for cash, $18 000.

June 4 Paid Island Supplies the due amount.

5 Campus Travel queried their 23 May account, and it was adjusted downwards by $3000 because an error had been made. They then paid the remaining amount due.

12 Payments made for:

Wages	$ 9 600
Laundry and cleaning	5 900
Minor repairs	2 700
Private use	12 000

20 Paid *New Image* amount due (see 18 May).
Received further account from *New Image* for advertising, $4500.

25 Invoiced Cut-Rite Tours for:

Account rendered on 15 May	$ 6100
June bookings	8 300
	$14 400

29 Made first repayment on loan from Risky Finance consisting of:

Interest for 3 months	$17 250
Loan repayment	20 000
	$37 250

30   Mr Prince estimated that the following amounts were owing for expenses incurred in the quarter just ended. They will be paid in July. The liability amount for both of these should be titled 'Sundry creditors'.

Wages	$4300
Telephone	970
Food supplies unused were estimated to be worth	$ 620

Depreciation may be ignored.

(a) Prepare journal entries for each of the above transactions.

(b) Open a general ledger for Mr Prince and post each journal entry to the appropriate ledger accounts.

(c) Prepare a trial balance.

(d) Prepare a profit and loss statement for June and a balance sheet as at 30 June 20X8.

Part B

It is 1 July 20X8 and Mr Prince is dismayed at the poor work his accountants have done. He demands that closing and reversing entries be made before July work is commenced. (Reversing entries are not covered formally until Chapter 7, but they may usefully be introduced at this point. They provide a technique for ensuring that minor end-of-period adjustments are not overlooked later on.)

1.   On 30 June entries were made to recognise unpaid (accrued) expenses for wages and telephone. These amounts presumably will be paid as part of some larger account in the ensuing year. To ensure that they are not forgotten, we reverse the adjusting entries as at 1 July 20X8 to eliminate their effect. Thus, the accrual of wages had been recorded as:

		Debit	*Credit*
June 30	Wages expense	$4300	
	Sundry creditors		$4300

To 'reverse' the entry, debit 'Sundry creditors' and credit 'Wages expense' with $4300.

2.   The same should be done with the telephone account due.

3.   The entry for food supplies on hand should also be reversed, since the supplies will undoubtably be used up in the ensuing year.

The following occurred in July 20X8:

July 1   The bank expressed its concern at the high level of overdraft and Mr Prince paid in $30 000 as additional capital to reduce the overdraft.

3   Cut-Rite Tours paid their account of $14 400.

5   Invoiced Campus Travel $39 000 for July bookings.

6   Paid telephone account, $1425.

8   Quick Escape paid their account of $14 800.

9   Bought and paid for food and supplies, $8230.

10 Paid wages, $9420.

12 Withdrew for private use $8000.

14 Campus Travel paid the 5 July account.

15   A cyclone struck the island, destroying every building. Mr Prince, in an endeavour to reduce costs, had carried no insurance. The buildings and motor vehicles were a complete loss, together with all food and supplies. Mr Prince ceased business immediately.

20   Travel bookings that could no longer be accommodated were valued at $23 400. As the bank would no longer honour cheques, the various travel agencies could not receive refunds.

31   The following additional amounts were due but unpaid:

Wages	$3200
Interest on loan	$5500

Mr Prince has decided to file for bankruptcy but wants a profit and loss statement for July 20X8 and a balance sheet as at 31 July 20X8 based on the above information and after a trial balance as at 31 July 20X8 has been prepared.

Part C

On 1 August an overseas investor bought the island for $950 000 cash. Mr Prince immediately paid all amounts due, including the loans. There was no penalty for early repayment; indeed, the lenders were vastly relieved.

1.   Prepare journal entries for the above transactions and post to the appropriate ledger accounts.
2.   Prepare the trial balance as at 1 August 20X8.
3.   Prepare a profit and loss statement for the period from 1 July and a balance sheet as at 1 August 20X8 to include the above.
4.   Make closing entries, following the previous procedure.
5.   There should now be just two accounts remaining open: 'Cash' and 'Capital'. Record the repayment to the delighted Mr Prince and thus end the venture.

Case study

4.26 *Accounting records*

In May 20X1 Dale Huang, a carpenter living in the suburbs, decided to invest a part of his hard-earned savings in equipment and in refitting a building which had formerly been used as a small garage. Dale had always wanted to build quality outdoor furniture from Australian hardwoods. These would be decorated by carvings of Australian flora and fauna.

By June 20X1 Dale had the workshop completely fitted and had hired two employees. Dale also found it necessary to lease a portable shed to store timber and other materials. A second-hand van was purchased to enable Dale to make deliveries. After enquiries from several customers relating to credit, Dale decided to provide credit to a select few. In that same month, in connection with a substantial order for tables requiring six to eight weeks of shop activity, Dale talked with the manager of the bank about the need for some temporary financial assistance to enable him to purchase the necessary materials and supplies. In granting the loan, the manager suggested that Dale would now need to spend more time and money on financial operating records than had been necessary when the work was almost entirely a matter of personal services. The banker suggested that Dale's recording system should be relatively simple but readily provide the financial information necessary to prepare timely reports and to keep a check on various aspects of the business so that errors in recording would be minimal and efficiency would be maintained.

A week or so after the meeting at the bank, Dale had a long and satisfactory talk with a friend, who was manager of a manufacturing business, about the need for additional records. Up to this point Dale had managed well with the stubs of cheque books, plus some notes relating to transactions which had been carefully kept for reference purposes. The friend agreed that it is easy to overdo 'this business of keeping records'.

He suggested that, as a starter, Dale might draw up a list of the assets used in operating the business and a corresponding list of the debts which had grown out of this business, together with the amounts of money that Dale had invested in it. 'With these two lists', he said, 'we can draw up a beginning financial statement of your assets and liabilities, which should be helpful in talking over your need for figures'. Dale said he now understood the need for such a statement but was still unsure about how to determine how the business was performing and what records were necessary in order to regularly update this statement of assets and liabilities.

The friend knew of experts in accounting procedures who specialised in making periodic visits to small concerns such as Dale's for the purpose of relieving their clients of much of the clerical burden of keeping operating records. But he said it would nevertheless be necessary for Dale to keep a memorandum record or daybook of transactions practically as they occurred. The manager suggested that as time went on Dale might want to give some attention to the accepted ways of keeping accounting records.

Required

(a) Why did Dale need any records? What records should have been kept by Dale?

(b) Draw up a list of Dale's assets and liabilities, as the manager suggested, making any assumptions you consider useful. (No dollar amounts required.)

(c) What would be the general format of a profit and loss statement for Dale's new business? (That is, state expenses and revenues likely to be shown.) How frequently should Dale require such a report?

(d) Dale recently made the comment that accounting is merely 'keeping records and reporting the financial activities of a business'. In what respect can it be said that accounting involves more than that described by Dale?

CHAPTER 5
Inventory transactions

Learning objectives

In this chapter you will be introduced to:

1. the difference between the measurement and reporting of profit for service and merchandising organisations

2. accounting for inventory using the perpetual system

3. accounting for inventory using the periodic system

4. the difference between the perpetual and periodic methods of recording inventory

5. the preparation of closing entries under the perpetual and periodic systems

6. a comparison of the profit and loss statement for a merchandising organisation under the perpetual and periodic systems

7. the effects of errors in inventory valuation on the reported profit.

Introduction

The transactions analysed in previous chapters are primarily concerned with those of businesses that sell services. In this chapter more focus will be placed on the accounting processes of merchandisers. These businesses, while selling a service, buy and sell goods as their primary activity. Retailers and wholesalers are merchandisers. The significant difference in the accounting processes of these businesses is the determination of cost of goods sold for the period and the inventory on hand at the end of the period.

Profit measurement: merchandiser and service enterprises

Unlike a service organisation, merchandisers buy inventory to resell at a profit. The term inventory may be defined as goods held for the purpose of resale. Other terms commonly used include merchandise, stock or merchandise inventory.

Generally merchandisers operate at the retail level. Examples include newsagencies, supermarkets and pharmacies. In some circumstances they might act as wholesalers distributing inventory to retail outlets.

Profit is determined for a service enterprise by matching revenues earned with expenses incurred for a period. The merchandiser follows the same philosophy based on the accounting equation. However, an extra category of expense must be included to record the cost of inventory sold.

Typical profit and loss statement formats for each type of enterprise are presented below. The new terms will be explained as the chapter proceeds.

MERCHANDISER	SERVICE ENTERPRISE
Profit and loss statement	**Profit and loss statement**
for the period ended XX	**for the period ended XX**
Sales revenue	Service revenue
less Sales returns	
Net sales	
less Cost of goods sold	
Gross profit	
less Expenses	*less* Expenses
Net profit	Net profit

Note

1. A merchandiser's revenue is referred to as sales revenue, not service revenue. Reductions of revenue due to inventory returned for any reason are recorded as sales returns, which is offset against sales revenue for the period.
2. Cost of goods sold accumulates all the costs associated with the inventories sold. The format of cost of goods sold may vary depending on the inventory recording approach adopted.
3. Gross profit is determined by subtracting cost of goods sold from net sales revenue. It reflects the profit margin applied to the cost of the goods when pricing them for sale.
4. The expenses sections of both profit and loss statements generally contain the same types of accounts, including items such as telephone, electricity and other general expenses.

The relative importance of inventory as a proportion of total assets

For some companies inventory represents their most valuable asset. The following companies listed on the Australian Stock Exchange show significant differences in the reported value of inventory as a proportion of total assets. For example, compare Woolworths Ltd (41.8 per cent) with Qantas Airways Ltd (1.5% per cent). Note also that some companies report that they have inventories classified as non-current assets.

Company*	Inventory ($m)		Total assets	Inventory % of
	Current	Non-current		total assets
Boral Ltd	547.8	–	6333.9	8.6
Coles Myer Ltd	2524.3	–	6696.6	37.7
Fosters Brewing Group Ltd	206.2	100.3	4944.4	6.2
Normandy Mining Ltd	139.0	29.4	2614.4	6.4
Qantas Airways Ltd	149.5	–	9912.0	1.5
Woolworths Ltd	1488.3	–	3563.5	41.8

*Results drawn from 1997 annual reports

Recording inventory for a merchandiser: perpetual and periodic systems

Two inventory systems are available for use by the merchandiser:

1. The perpetual inventory system
2. The periodic inventory system

The choice of system is determined by the characteristics of the business, including type, value and volume of inventory sold.

The perpetual inventory system

The perpetual inventory system adopts an asset approach to inventory recording. All goods purchased for sale are recorded as an asset on acquisition. As goods are sold, a decrease in the asset, inventory, and a corresponding increase in the expense, cost of goods sold, is recorded. Throughout the accounting period changes in the inventory account are recorded as they occur. At any point in the accounting period it ought to be possible to determine the cost of goods available for sale and the cost of goods sold to date. The actual position might be different, due to unrecorded movements in inventory levels attributable to spoilage, theft or clerical errors. These movements can be isolated as the perpetual system is accompanied by a physical inventory count at the end of the accounting period. The discrepancy between the actual and the recorded levels of inventory may provide management with an indication of the efficiency of inventory control. The inventory count may also draw attention to the existence of obsolete inventory. This system will be explained by the following example, dealing with the six main types of inventory events:

1. Purchase of inventory from suppliers
2. Return of inventory to suppliers
3. Sale of inventory to customers
4. Return of undamaged inventory from customers
5. Return of damaged inventory from customers
6. Theft or loss of inventory

Example: *Recording inventory transactions*

April 1   Happy Traders was established with contributed capital of $40 000 cash.
2   Bought 1000 Smiling Face Masks for $1 each on credit from D. S. Geise.
3   Returned 50 masks that were found to be scowling and received a credit note from the supplier.
4   Sold 90 masks on credit to Party Jinks Ltd for $6 each.
5   Party Jinks Ltd returned 12 masks which were no longer needed and received credit.
6   Party Jinks Ltd returned 8 masks that had arrived with broken noses and received credit. They were destroyed.
7   A stock count at the end of the week revealed 870 masks on hand.

Explanation of entries

A transaction analysis appears on page 140 and the corresponding ledger entries on pages 140–1.

April 1   This is the initial contribution of capital.
2   Purchase of inventory. An asset of inventory has been acquired, matched by an increase in liabilities to accounts payable. The inventory account is debited and accounts payable is credited.
3   Return to supplies. This entry is the reverse of the purchase entry. The asset is returned and the claim of the creditor is reduced, resulting in a debit to accounts payable and a credit to inventory.
4   Credit sale of 90 units. Four changes take place, and it is necessary to determine both the sale price (90 × $6 = $540) and the cost of the inventory sold (90 × $1 = $90).
   • The sale price of $540 is added to accounts receivable, and matched by an increase in owner's equity through sales revenue.
   • It must also be recognised that the inventory has been reduced. Since inventory is recorded at cost, the cost of $90 is taken from the inventory account and transferred to an expense account, cost of goods sold. The inventory asset has been 'used up' in gaining the revenue.
   • By deducting cost of goods sold of $90 from sales revenue of $540, the profit on the sale of $450 may be calculated.
   • The ledger entries follow this analysis (see pages 140–1). In journal form, they are:

	Debit	Credit
Accounts receivable	540	
Sales revenue		540
(Recording revenue on sale of goods)		
Cost of goods sold	90	
Inventory		90
(Recording cost of sale)		

April 5   Sales returns of undamaged inventory. This entry is in principle the reverse of the sale entry. The sale is cancelled, so revenue must be reduced, as must the claims on the customer through accounts receivable. This entry is made at sale price. The second change is that, since the goods have been returned undamaged, they must be added back to stock (the inventory asset account) and the cost of goods sold must be cancelled. This entry is made at the original cost price.
         The one unexpected entry is that instead of reducing sales revenue by a debit entry, the debit is placed in an account for sales returns. This is done to keep a

separate record of returns, since a high level of returns may indicate inferior merchandise or other problems requiring management attention. This device of subdividing an account to separate increases and decreases for information purposes is called the creation of a contra account. In journal form, the entries for the return of undamaged inventory are:

	Debit	Credit
Sales returns	72	
Accounts receivable		72
(To cancel the sale)		
Inventory	12	
Cost of goods sold		12
(To cancel the cost transfer)		

April 6   Sales return of damaged goods. The only difference between this and the previous entry is that the stock is not brought back into inventory. Instead, an expense account for stock damage losses is opened to reflect the loss of $8 which must be borne by owner's equity. The entries are:

	Debit	Credit
Sales returns	48	
Accounts receivable		48
(Cancellation of sale)		
Inventory damage losses	8	
Cost of goods sold		8
(Recording loss of damaged inventory)		

April 7   Stock count and stock loss. Refer to the inventory account on page 140. Since the inventory account has been updated for each increase or decrease in stock, the balance at 6 April represents the stock that should be on hand. The balance is $872 and a total of 872 units (at cost of $1 each) should therefore be on hand. A physical count of the stock is made to determine the actual situation and it is discovered that only 870 units are on hand at a total cost of $870. It is therefore necessary to recognise the loss of two units of inventory by means of the following entry:

	Debit	Credit
Stock shortage loss	2	
Inventory		2
(Inventory shortage)		

The financial statements for the week appear on page 141. The sales returns contra account has been deducted directly from sales revenue to produce the net sales. The cost of goods sold is then subtracted to produce the gross profit. Otherwise, the financial statements follow the same format as those previously encountered.

TRANSACTION ANALYSIS: HAPPY TRADERS

			A	=	L	+	OE
April	1	Capital	Cash				Capital
			+ 40 000				+ 40 000
	2	Credit	Inventory		A/cs payable		
		purchase	+ 1 000		+ 1 000		
	3	Purchase	Inventory		A/cs payable		
		return	−50		−50		
	4	Credit	A/cs rec.				Sales revenue
		sale	+ 540				+ 540
			Inventory				COGS
			−90				−90
	5	Sales	A/cs rec.				Sales returns
		returns	−72				−72
		(undamaged	Inventory				COGS
		stock)	+ 12				+ 12
	6	Sales	A/cs rec.				Sales returns
		returns	−48				−48
		(damaged					COGS
		stock)					+ 8
							Inventory damage losses
							−8
	7	Inventory			Inventory		Inventory shortage
		shortage			−2		−2

LEDGER ACCOUNTS: HAPPY TRADERS

Assets

Cash at bank

April	1	Capital	40 000		40 000 DR

Inventory

April	2	Accounts payable	1 000		1 000 DR
	3	Accounts payable		50	950 DR
	4	Cost of goods sold		90	860 DR
	5	Cost of goods sold	12		872 DR
	7	Stock shortage losses		2	870 DR

Accounts receivable

April	4	Sales revenue	540		540 DR
	5	Sales returns		72	468 DR
	6	Sales returns		48	420 DR

Liabilities

Accounts payable

April	2	Inventory		1 000	1 000 CR
	3	Inventory	50		950 CR

continues

LEDGER ACCOUNTS: HAPPY TRADERS

Owners' equity

Capital

April	1	Cash		40 000	40 000 CR

Sales revenue

April	4	A/cs receivable		540	540 CR

Sales returns (contra to sales)

April	5	A/cs receivable	72		72 DR
	6	A/cs receivable	48		120 DR

Cost of goods sold

April	4	Inventory	90		90 DR
	5	Inventory		12	78 DR
	6	Stock damage losses		8	70 DR

Inventory damage losses

April	6	Cost of goods sold	8		8 DR

Inventory shortage losses

April	7	Inventory	2		2 DR

FINANCIAL STATEMENTS: HAPPY TRADERS
Profit and loss statement for the week ended 7 April 20X1

Sales revenue		$540
less Sales returns		120
Net sales (70 units)		420
less Cost of goods sold (70 units)		70
Gross profit		350
less Expenses		
Inventory damage losses	$8	
Inventory shortage losses	2	10
Net profit		$340

BALANCE SHEET
as at 7 April 20X1

Assets	$	**Liabilities**	$
Cash at bank	40 000	Accounts payable	950
Accounts receivable	420		
Inventory	870	**Owners' equity**	
		Capital	40 340
	41 290		41 290

The periodic inventory system

The perpetual inventory system may not always be appropriate. Small firms, or firms dealing in low-value, high-turnover products, may find that the benefits of continuous information about inventory and cost of goods sold do not warrant the costs involved. Instead, they may adopt a simpler system, known as the periodic inventory system. This system is based on a physical count of inventory taken in successive periods and the record of purchases made during the period. Accordingly, it is sometimes known as the physical inventory system.

The periodic inventory system adopts an expense orientation. All purchases of goods for sale are recorded in a purchases (expense) account so that throughout the period the expense account becomes progressively larger. At the end of the period, the purchases are transferred to the profit and loss summary account, together with the opening balance in the inventory account. A count of inventory is then taken and the cost of inventory on hand is debited in the inventory account as an asset and shown as a deduction from inventory expenses in the profit and loss (i.e. as a credit). Cost of goods sold is determined as follows:

> inventory at beginning of period (physical count)
> + purchases (ledger records)
> = inventory available for sale
> − inventory at end of period (physical count)
> = cost of goods sold

Example: *Periodic inventory*

Endfile Ltd uses a periodic inventory system. During 20X2 the following purchases and sales were recorded (all for cash):

Purchases			Sales		
Jan.	1000 units		Jan.	1000 units	
Mar.	3000 units		Mar.	1250 units	
Oct.	2000 units		Oct.	1500 units	

Inventory counts were taken on 31 December 20X1 and 31 December 20X2. The quantities were:

31 Dec. 20X1	500 @ $1
31 Dec. 20X2	2000 @ $1

Assume all purchases were made at $1 per unit and all sales at $2 per unit.

The ledger entries are shown below and the relevant portions of the financial statements on page 143.

Periodic Inventory Method
PORTION OF GENERAL LEDGER: ENDFILE LTD

		Debit	Credit	Balance
Assets				
		Inventory on hand		
Dec. X1	Balance			$ 500 DR
Dec. X2	Profit and Loss		500	−
	Profit and Loss	2000		2000 DR
				continues

PORTION OF GENERAL LEDGER: ENDFILE LTD

		Debit	Credit	Balance
Owners' equity				
		Purchases		
Jan. X2	Cash	1000		1000 DR
Mar.	Cash	3000		4000 DR
Oct.	Cash	2000		6000 DR
Dec.	Profit and Loss		6000	–
		Sales revenue		
Mar. X2	Cash		2000	2000 CR
	Cash		2500	4500 CR
Oct.	Cash		3000	7500 CR
Dec.	Profit and loss summary	7500		–
		Profit and loss summary		
Dec. X2	Sales		7500	7500 CR
	Inventory (beginning)	500		7000 CR
	Purchases	6000		1000 CR
	Inventory (ending)		2000	3000 CR

PROFIT AND LOSS STATEMENT: ENDFILE LTD
for year ended 31 December 20X2

Sales		$7500
less Cost of goods sold:		
Opening inventory	$ 500	
plus Purchases	6000	
Inventory available for sale	6500	
less Closing inventory	2000	
Cost of goods sold		4500
Gross profit		$3000

The periodic inventory method does not provide a continuous record of the movement in inventory. There is therefore no record of the inventory that ought to be on hand that may be compared with the actual stock count. Consequently, the loss of stock through theft and wastage (amounting to $750 in the above example) cannot be identified separately. It is contained in the cost of goods sold, which should more accurately be entitled 'cost of goods that left the company'. Hence, information that may be useful for inventory control is not generated by a periodic inventory system.

A comparison of inventory methods

The following simple example will demonstrate the differences in the profit and loss statements.

Determination of cost of goods sold

1. Transactions
    All units of inventory cost $10 each.

    (a) Opening inventory   1000 units
    (b) Purchases   2250 units
    (c) Sales   650 units
    (d) Closing inventory   2460 units

2. Inventory methods

	Perpetual		Periodic	
		Expenses		Expenses
Opening inventory	$10 000		$10 000	
plus Purchases	22 500		22 500	
Available for sale	32 500		32 500	
less Cost of sales	6 500	$6500	?	
Theoretical closing inventory	26 000		?	
Actual closing inventory	24 600		24 600	
Stock loss	1 400	1400		
Cost of sales (periodic)			7 900	$7900
Total expenses on inventory		$7900		$7900

Note

1. Both systems produce the same total of expenses since both are reconciled to the closing balance.
2. The perpetual system reveals the actual cost of sales and the extent of any stock loss.

Accounting for a merchandiser: perpetual and periodic methods

The following more detailed example provides a comparative analysis of the two inventory systems.

Assume an opening inventory of 10 units at $50 each.

1. Purchased 20 items of inventory at $50 each on credit from suppliers and paid cash for freight costs of $100.[1]
2. Returned one unit of inventory to suppliers.
3. Sold 12 units on credit to customers for $200 each.
4. Customer returned one unit undamaged.
5. Customer returned two units that had arrived damaged. They were destroyed.
6. Stocktake revealed 15 units on hand at the end of the period.

---

[1] It would be preferable because of the matching principle to treat the freight costs as part of the costs of inventory. However, for simplicity all freight has been treated as an expense.

Required

(a) Prepare relevant journal entries for each inventory method.
(b) Prepare profit and loss statements for each inventory method.

General journal entries

	Perpetual				Periodic		
		Debit	*Credit*			*Debit*	*Credit*
1.	Inventory	$1000			Purchases	$1000	
	Accounts payable		$1000		Accounts payable		$1000
	(Cost price 20 × $50)				(Cost price 20 × $50)		
	Cost of goods sold[2]	100			Freight inwards	100	
	Cash at bank		100		Cash at bank		100
	(Freight charge)				(Freight charge)		
2.	Accounts payable	50			Accounts payable	50	
	Inventory		50		Purchases returns		50
	(Cost price 1 × $50)				(Cost price 1 × $50)		
3.	Accounts receivable	2400			Accounts receivable	2400	
	Sales revenue		2400		Sales revenue		2400
	(Sale price 12 × $200)				(Sale price 12 × $200)		
	Cost of goods sold	600			No entry		
	Inventory		600				
	(Cost price 12 × $50)						
4.	Sales returns	200			Sales returns	200	
	Accounts receivable		200		Accounts receivable		200
	(Sale price 1 × $200)				(Sale price 1 × $200)		
	Inventory	50			No entry		
	Cost of goods sold		50				
	(Cost price 1 × $50)						
5.	Sales returns	400			Sales returns	400	
	Accounts receivable		400		Accounts receivable		400
	(Sale price 2 × $200)				(Sale price 2 × $200)		
	Inventory damage loss	100			No entry		
	Cost of goods sold		100				
	(Cost price 2 × $50)						
6.	Inventory shortage loss	150			No entry		
	Inventory		150				
	(Cost price 3 × $50)						

Points to note from the perpetual system

1. Inventory purchases are recorded by debiting the inventory account because the asset has increased.
2. Inventory returns to the supplier are recorded by crediting the inventory account because the asset has decreased.
3. Two entries are required when inventory is sold or returned by the customer. The first is to record the sale price and the second to record the cost price.
4. When a customer returns damaged goods, an inventory damage loss account must be created.
5. If, after an inventory count, inventory records are greater than physical inventory, an inventory shortage loss account must be created.
6. The perpetual method records more relevant information than the periodic method, enabling the user to determine inventory levels and cost of goods sold at any time.

---

[2] It would be preferable because of the matching principle to treat the freight costs as part of the costs of inventory. However, for simplicity all freight has been treated as an expense.

Points to note from the periodic system

1. Inventory purchases are recorded by debiting the purchases account.
2. Inventory returns to the supplier are recorded by crediting the purchase returns account.
3. Only one entry is made when inventory is sold or returned by the customer and it is recorded at sale price.

Profit and loss statements

1. Perpetual inventory system

Sales revenue		$2400
less Sales returns		600
Net sales		1800
less Cost of goods sold (includes freight)		550
Gross profit		1250
less Expenses:		
Inventory damage loss	$100	
Inventory shortage loss	150	250
Net profit		1000

2. Periodic inventory system

Sales revenue			$2400
less Sales returns			600
Net sales revenue			1800
Cost of goods sold			
Inventory (beginning of period)		$ 500	
add Purchases	$1000		
Freight inwards	100		
	1100		
less Purchase returns	50		
Net purchases		1050	
Cost of goods available for sale		1550	
less Inventory (end of period)		750	
Cost of goods sold			800
Gross profit			1000
less Expenses			–
Net profit			$1000

Note

Both systems produce the same profit because they are reconciled to the closing stock count. However, the perpetual system discloses greater and more accurate information.

Accounting for inventory and computers

Chapter 20 discusses in detail the role of computers in management information systems and in particular principles of control. However, it is important to discuss briefly how computers enhance management's control over inventory. By being able to update inventory records instantaneously after every purchase and sale for often thousands of different stock items the computer can provide timely information for management decision making. For example, the computer assists management in ordering inventory. In managing inventory the goal is to keep the minimum amount of stock on hand, bearing in mind several factors:

- lead time for the supplier to fill your order
- supplier's payment terms
- seasonal fluctuations in demand
- customers' expectations of available product range
- inventory deterioration and obsolescence

The computer is able to determine inventory reorder points, that is the minimum permitted stock level before an order is generated. It can also determine the quantity of stock to be ordered. Thus the computer is able to implement management policies that will maximise the use of the business's resources (e.g. bank overdraft levels, shelf space and staff time).

Some computer systems enable the store to electronically place orders with a wholesaler. In these circumstances when an order is placed the computer system can generate for the wholesaler an electronic invoice containing cost and quantities of goods supplied, and printed labels may be supplied when the retail store has verified that goods have been received.

The computer can significantly contribute to sales performance in that it can be used to provide the customer with prompt information relating to availability, price and likely delivery date. For example, when a customer orders a product the salesperson can use the computer to check whether the goods are in stock, provide details about date of delivery and the unit price and total invoice price. The computer can also be used to prepare the invoice and to update not only inventory records but also records relating to sales and accounts receivable. In so doing it not only significantly contributes to control over inventory but it also provides valuable information for control of accounts receivable.

An example of the use of computers in inventory control that all students would be familiar with is the use of computers and perpetual inventory recording in large retail stores using bar codes. The bar codes on the products are read by the coding machine and the cash register not only records the sale but updates inventory records.

Case 5.1 Inventory recording systems

Carmichael-Hing Trading Co Ltd has operated for many years with an inventory system based on an annual physical stocktake. The business of the company consists of importing from Malaysia and Indonesia silks and other fabrics in addition to furniture and handicrafts. Recording was kept to a minimum and all duties and transport costs of inventory were expensed in the period the costs had been incurred. The physical stocktake did not always take place at the same time each year as sometimes inventory was in transit. If large shipments were due it was felt to be more reliable to wait a few days until they had arrived rather than estimate what might be delivered, as sometimes the number and quality differed from instructions received from the suppliers in Malaysia and Indonesia.

Late in 20X2 the company introduced a new computerised system including continuous inventory recording. Under this system goods were identified with bar code labels and transport costs and import duties were assigned to the various products.

Management was convinced that this new system would result in better matching for the period and that inventory control would be significantly improved.

At balance date, at 30 June 20X3, a physical stocktake was undertaken and soon after the financial statements for the year were made available to the chief executive officer. He was not impressed as profit was significantly less than in previous years, but inventory shortages were listed as a significant expense in the profit and loss statement.

(a) Explain the essential features of the two systems of inventory recording that were used by the company.
(b) Identify some problems that might have existed with the inventory recording system prior to the introduction of the new computerised system of recording.
(c) Identify some improvements that might be expected with the introduction of the new recording system.
(d) Would the identification of inventory shortages lead to a fall in profits? Explain.

Closing entries for a merchandiser

The procedure for closing the accounts varies slightly depending on which inventory approach is being adopted. Using the information in the previous section, closing entries are prepared under both methods.

1. Perpetual inventory system

Date	Particulars	Debit	Credit
Last day of period	Sales	$2400	
	Profit and loss summary		$2400
	(Transfer to profit and loss summary)		
	Profit and loss summary	600	
	Sales returns		600
	(Transfer to profit and loss summary)		
	Profit and loss summary	800	
	Cost of goods sold		550
	Inventory damage loss		100
	Inventory shortage loss		150
	(Transfer to profit and loss summary)		
	Profit and loss summary	1000	
	Capital		1000
	Capital		–
	Drawings		–

2. Periodic inventory system

Date	Particulars	Debit	Credit
Last day	Sales	$2400	
of period	Profit and loss summary		$2400
	(Transfer to profit and loss summary)		
	Profit and loss summary	600	
	Sales returns		600
	(Transfer to profit and loss summary)		
	Profit and loss summary	1600	
	Inventory (at beginning)		500
	Purchases		1000
	Freight in		100
	(Transfer to profit and loss summary)		
	Purchase returns	50	
	Profit and loss summary		50
	(Transfer to profit and loss summary)		
	Inventory	750	
	Profit and loss summary		750
	(Inventory as per physical stocktake)		
	Profit and loss summary	1000	
	Capital		1000
	(Transfer of net profit)		
	Capital	–	
	Drawings		–
	(Transfer of drawings to capital)		

This could be summarised as:

Date	Particulars	Debit	Credit
Last day	Profit and loss summary	$2200	
of period	Inventory (beginning)		$ 500
	Sales returns		600
	Purchases		1000
	Freight inward		100
	Sales	2400	
	Purchase returns	50	
	Inventory (ending)	750	
	Profit and loss summary		3200
	Profit and loss summary	1000	
	Capital		1000
	Capital	–	
	Drawings		–

Errors in stock valuation

The perpetual and periodic inventory systems both depend critically on an independent count of the inventory at the end of the period. Inventory counts are conducted physically. It may be necessary to count many items in different storage locations and to attempt to attach cost prices to each category of item. Errors are inevitable.

The effect is demonstrated below, showing the difference when closing inventory is overvalued by $15 000.

1. Period A

	Correct values	Incorrect values
Sales revenue	$200 000	$200 000
less Cost of sales		
Inventory (beginning)	40 000	40 000
plus Purchases	130 000	130 000
	170 000	170 000
less Inventory (end)	50 000	65 000
	120 000	105 000
Gross profit	$ 80 000	$ 95 000

2. Note that an overvaluation of closing inventory increases profit by the same amount. This should not be a surprise, since:

$$A \qquad = \quad L \quad + \qquad OE$$
$$\text{inventory} + \$15\ 000 \qquad\qquad \text{profit} + \$15\ 000$$

3. Period B
The closing inventory becomes next year's opening inventory. Now, assuming the closing inventory at the end of period B is correctly valued, the effect is reversed.

	Correct values	Incorrect values
Sales revenue	$400 000	$400 000
less Cost of sales		
Inventory (beginning)	50 000	65 000
plus Purchases	200 000	200 000
	250 000	265 000
less Inventory (end)	100 000	100 000
	150 000	165 000
Gross profit	$250 000	$235 000

Therefore, over two periods the error cancels out. However, both yearly results are incorrect and the trend in profit has been distorted.

Ethical issues

Big Estates Ltd is a real estate company that has fared poorly in recent years. It has heavy debt and must raise more capital by an issue of shares in order to stay afloat. The managing director has proposed that $40 million (20 per cent) be added to the closing inventory value. He believes this optimism should be justified when the market recovers. If this is not done, the company will fail and the shareholders and creditors will suffer.

As chief accountant, and being aware of the current market, should you be concerned? What could happen if you fail to protest?

Summary

Accounting for a merchandiser is more complex than that required for a service enterprise. Profit measurement for a merchandiser is effected by deducting cost of goods sold and expenses from net sales revenue.

The format of cost of goods sold depends on the inventory system being adopted. Two options are available to a merchandiser, the periodic and the perpetual inventory systems. The choice of method depends on the volume and value of inventory relevant to an entity. The accounting procedure required for the perpetual system is tedious in comparison to the periodic method in that it requires knowledge of the cost of every sale or return. However, more useful information is readily at hand using the perpetual inventory system. This system reveals both the actual cost of sales and the extent of any inventory loss. The process of closing the merchandiser's accounts is similar to that of the service enterprise, with slight refinements required depending on the inventory approach adopted.

Review exercises

Discussion questions

5.1 Define the term 'inventory' as it relates to a merchandiser.

5.2 Explain the periodic and perpetual inventory systems. In what situations might each be appropriately used and what are the advantages and disadvantages of each system?

5.3 'The perpetual inventory system results in a better record of events than the periodic inventory system.' Comment on this statement.

5.4 Compare and contrast the measurement of profit for merchandise and service enterprises.

5.5 When using the perpetual inventory system, are stocktakes necessary? Why or why not?

5.6 A purchases account is not used with a perpetual inventory system. Why is this so?

5.7 How is a stock shortage accounted for under:

(a) the periodic inventory system?
(b) the perpetual inventory system?

 **Problems**

5.8 *Calculating gross profit using a periodic inventory approach*

A company had inventory of $18 000 at 1 January 20X7. Sales for the year amounted to $190 000. Purchases cost $72 000. Returns to suppliers, at cost, were $6300. Returns from customers were $15 000 at sales value. A physical stocktake at 31 December 20X7 revealed $10 200 on hand at cost.

(a) Calculate gross profit using the periodic inventory approach.

(b) Provide two reasons why the cost of goods sold, as computed in (a), may not be accurate.

5.9 *Periodic versus perpetual inventory systems*

1. The Lackaday Department Store keeps as few records as possible. At 30 June 20X7 it reports the following transactions concerning inventory:

Balance on hand at 1 July 20X6	$ 35 000
Purchases for year	145 000
Sales revenue for year	420 000
Returns to suppliers	17 000
Returns from customers	48 000
Balance on hand at 30 June 20X7 as per a physical stocktake	47 000

(a) Prepare relevant ledger accounts and the gross profit section of the profit and loss statement for the year ended 30 June 20X7.

(b) An ambitious employee has calculated some further figures he believes are relevant. They are:

Cost of goods sold	$133 500
Returns from customers had a cost value of	20 000

The management thought such information redundant.

(i) How would this information affect the ledger accounts and statements in (a) above if the inventory recording method was changed?

(ii) Was the additional information useful?

2. The Trumper Bros Department Store has summarised at 30 June 20X7 the following transactions concerning inventory:

Balance on hand at 1 July 20X6	$ 72 000
Purchases for year	190 000
Sales revenue for year	840 000
Cost of sales (before returns etc.)	262 000
Returns to suppliers	6 000
Returns from customers	72 000
Cost value of returns from customers	31 000
Balance on hand at 30 June 20X7 as per a physical stocktake	21 300

(a) Prepare relevant ledger accounts and profit and loss statement entries under:

    (i) the periodic inventory approach

    (ii) the perpetual inventory approach

(b) What are the main advantages and disadvantages of each system?

5.10 *Comparison of perpetual and periodic inventory systems*

Given the following information, prepare general journal entries and a profit and loss statement using:

(i) the perpetual inventory system

(ii) the periodic inventory system

    1. Opening inventory was 35 units at $60 each.
    2. Returned seven units to suppliers.
    3. Sold 15 units on credit for $140 each.
    4. Customer returned two units undamaged.
    5. Customer returned one unit that had arrived damaged. It was destroyed.
    6. Stocktake revealed 11 units on hand at the end of the period.

5.11 *Calculating profit given a periodic inventory system*

Given the following information obtained from the records of DB Ltd, prepare a profit and loss statement.

Rent expense	$ 1 200
Insurance expense	950
Sales returns	1 390
Purchases	12 005
Selling expenses	2 150
Inventory (beginning of period)	7 900
Sales	69 000
Freight inwards	395
Inventory (end of period)	3 900
Interest expense	920

5.12 *Calculating profit given a perpetual inventory system*

Given the following information obtained from the records of CD Ltd, prepare a profit and loss statement.

Freight inwards	$ 490
Sales	75 800
Cost of goods sold	18 700
Rent expense	390
Selling expenses	470
Depreciation expense	600
Rates expense	1 200
Sales returns	1 100

5.13 *Closing entries for a periodic inventory system*

The following information is available for AP Merchandisers. Prepare relevant closing entries.

Purchases	$ 4 200
Rent expense	1 100
Sales	56 000
Sales returns	1 400
Inventory (beginning)	1 650
Inventory (end)	700
Freight inward	220
AP drawings	400
Telephone expense	110

5.14 *Closing entries for a perpetual inventory system*

The following information is available for ROOK Merchandisers. Prepare relevant closing entries.

Drawings	$ 1 100
Sales	18 300
Cost of goods sold	7 400
Freight inward	190
Sales returns	720
Administration expenses	315
Financial expenses	170

5.15 Kim's Furniture Store uses the periodic inventory method. When carrying out the physical stocktake at 30 June 20X2, the stock in one section of the warehouse was missed resulting in an understatement of inventory of $9000. What effect will this have on the net profit reported for the years ending 30 June 20X2, 20X3 and 20X4?

5.16 *Public sector: periodic inventory system*

1. The Tourist Information Centre at Macquarie National Park sells a very popular book on park fauna and flora. The books are purchased from the author, who organises the printing and publishing. The books cost $10 each and are sold to park visitors for $20. A special price of $16 is available for students and pensioners.

    At the beginning of the year, 1 July 20X1, 50 books were on hand. The opening balance in the cash account was $1000. During the year a further 1000 books were purchased for cash. Book sales amounted to $14 560. Two hundred books were returned to the supplier because the printing in that shipment of books was defective. A cash refund was received. A stock count at 30 June 20X2 revealed 40 books on hand.

    (a) Show relevant ledger accounts under the periodic inventory method including closing entries at the end of the year.
    (b) What amount of gross profit was made on the book sales?

2. The Tourist Information Centre at Macquarie National Park also has a popular range of posters depicting Australian birds, animals and flowers. The posters are purchased for cash from Postprint Pty Ltd at a cost of $1 each. The posters sell for $5 with a special price of $4 for students and pensioners.

At the beginning of the year, 1 July 20X1, 120 posters were on hand. The opening balance in the cash account was $1000. During the year a further 1500 posters were purchased for cash. One hundred posters were returned to the supplier for a cash refund because they were damaged in shipment. Poster sales amounted to $7080 cash. Ten posters were returned in good order by customers who received a cash refund of $50. A stock count on 30 June 20X2 revealed 90 posters on hand.

(a) Show relevant ledger accounts under the periodic inventory method including closing entries at the end of the year.
(b) What amount of gross profit was made on the poster sales?

5.17 *General journal, general ledger, trial balance and financial statements for a merchandiser*
C. Grass has commenced business as a wholesaler of Irish moss, which a growing number of people are consuming because of its therapeutic effects. The following are her transactions for the first week:

Aug. 1   Contributed $10 000 as capital.
    2   Bought a delivery van for $4000, paying $1800 deposit.
    3   Bought 2000 kg of Irish moss at $3 per kg for cash.
    4   Returned 50 kg that was water damaged. Received cash refund.
    5   Sold 1200 kg for cash at $17 per kg.
    5   Sold 230 kg to Offside Traders for $25 per kg on credit.
    6   Offside Traders returned 70 kg excess Irish moss and received credit.
    6   Paid wages to employee, $120.
    7   Offside Traders paid $250 on account.

A count of the stock on 7 August revealed 520 kg on hand. An amount of $100 was owing for rent.

(a) Prepare general journal entries for each of the above transactions.
(b) Present ledger entries to record the above.
(c) Prepare a trial balance.
(d) Prepare a profit and loss statement and a balance sheet.

5.18 *Analysis of the perpetual inventory system*
Cracker Computers is a specialised wholesale operation run by Rae Tube. It sells two computers only:

Model	Name	Cost ($)	Normal retail price ($)
CCS	Super Cracker	1000	3000
CCB	Basic Cracker	700	2000

On 1 June 20X9 Rae Tube had the following assets and liabilities:

Cash at bank	$ 46 000
CCS model (30 units)	30 000
CCB model (48 units)	33 600
Store fixtures	125 000
Accounts receivable	71 500
Accounts payable	39 000
Wages owing	2 400
Sales revenue	235 000

Cost of goods sold	79 000
Wages expense	87 950
Rent expense	72 000
Insurance expense	14 200
Capital	322 850
Drawings	40 000

Transactions for June were:

June 3   Purchased 12 CCS and 25 CCB models at the usual price, on credit from the supplier.

4   Sold eight CCS models for cash.

6   Returned two faulty CCS machines to the supplier and received a credit.

7   Paid wages owing for the last week in May plus those for the current week, totalling $5400 in all.

8   Customers paid amounts owing, $38 400.

10   A credit customer returned three CCB models found to be defective and was given full credit. Two of these were repaired at no cost by staff and returned to stock for sale again. The third was useless and was written off.

12   Sold on credit to The Computer Store 14 CCS models and six CCB models at a discount of 10 per cent.

14   Paid the following:

Wages	$2 740
Rent	8 000
Insurance	5 200
Accounts payable	13 000

15   A check of the bank statement reveals that the cash received from customers of 8 June was actually $34 800.

17   Rae Tube withdrew as 'wages' $5000.

21   Sold on credit to Home Sales five CCS models at the normal retail price.

24   The Computer Store returned two of the CCB models purchased on 12 June for full credit. They were returned to stock.

26   Purchased additional shelving for the storeroom for cash, $3100.

30   The manager states that the following matters require attention:

Wages owing (to be paid in July)	$ 6 350
Depreciation to be written off on fittings	13 000

30   A physical count of the stock on hand revealed the following:

Model	Number on hand
CCS	13
CCB	60

(a) Prepare journal entries for each of the above transactions.

(b) Post each journal entry to the appropriate ledger accounts.

(c) Prepare a trial balance.

(d) Prepare a profit and loss statement for the month and a balance sheet as at 30 June 20X9.

Note: You are required to maintain separate inventory accounts for each line of inventory and to use the perpetual inventory method of accounting.

5.19   *Recording transactions and the preparation of financial statements for a merchandiser*
Joe Mussel has just opened a bait shop at Brooklyn. He plans to sell two types of bait: prawns and worms. He can buy the prawns for $2 a kg and will sell them for $4 a kg, and he can buy the worms for $3 a kg and will sell them for $6 a kg. The following is a record of the first week's transactions (20X5):

April 1   Joe invested cash in the business.
He purchased a shop for $40 000 cash and spent $1000 cash on fittings (including a freezer).

2   Joe purchased 100 kg of prawns and 50 kg of worms from Fresh Bait Pty Ltd on credit.

3   10 kg of prawns smelt decidedly bad and were very promptly returned to Fresh Bait Pty Ltd. Joe was given a credit.
Joe sold 30 kg of prawns and 10 kg of worms for cash.
He paid Fresh Bait Pty Ltd $150.
He sold 25 kg of prawns to his friend Jack on credit.
At the end of the day Joe allowed Jack to return 10 kg of the bait. The prawns were still frozen so Joe returned them to the freezer for resale.

5   Joe sold 30 kg of prawns and 30 kg of worms for cash.
One customer returned 5 kg of bad worms. Joe couldn't return them to the supplier so he threw them in the Hawkesbury River.

6   Paid Fresh Bait Pty Ltd $100.

7   Bought 50 kg of prawns and 30 kg of worms for cash.
Joe counted the bait in his freezer. He had 60 kg of prawns and 40 kg of worms.

(a) Record the first week's transactions for the bait shop in the appropriate ledger accounts. Use a single merchandise account for bait and establish a set of merchandise cards to record the movements in each type of bait.

(b) Prepare a profit and loss statement for the week ending 7 April 20X5 and a balance sheet as at 7 April 20X5.

5.20   *Perpetual inventory: correction of recording errors*
The following entry was recorded in the general journal of Watts & Co. The business uses the perpetual inventory system of inventory recording.

Date	Ledger account	Debit	Credit
20X1		$	$
June 30	Accounts receivable	60	
	Sales		60
	Cost of goods sold	80	
	Inventory		80

The entry should have been recorded as cost $60 and selling price $80. If the error went undetected at balance date, explain the effects of the incorrect entry on:

(a) the profit and loss statement for the year ended 30 June 20X1

(b) the balance sheet as at 30 June 20X1

5.21   *Perpetual inventory: correction of recording errors*
Modern Motors sells vehicle accessories. The business uses the perpetual inventory method of recording inventory. The accountant of Modern Motors investigated the reasons for the inventory gain of $600 which was shown in the business's draft financial statements at 30 June 20X2. As a consequence, the accountant decided that the following two items require correction/adjustment using general journal entries before preparation of the business's annual reports.

Item 1
The sales manager took home an item of inventory which cost $200, for his own personal use. Although this withdrawal was made prior to stocktaking it was not recorded. Management of the business has decided to record the event as a sale at cost price.

Item 2
A clerk has wrongly recorded the sale of seat covers which were priced at $40 (cost $25) by making the following entries:

	Debit	Credit
Accounts receivable	$25	
Sales		$25
Cost of sales	40	
Inventory		40

(a) Prepare the general journal entries at 30 June 20X2 to record the corrections/adjustments.
(b) Explain the purpose of an inventory gain account and suggest circumstances which might have caused such a gain to be present.

5.22   *General ledger and financial statements for a merchandiser*
Bev Bennett won a large sum on the Football Pools and decided to invest $10 000 of it in a business venture on 1 July 20X4. During July the following occurred:

1. Paid $10 000 into a special bank account for business purposes.
2. Agreed to rent premises and paid $100 rent for July in advance.
3. Bought and received delivery of equipment costing $2000, paying in cash.
4. Bought goods for resale costing $8000. Ten per cent of the purchase price was paid when the goods were delivered.
5. Sold goods that had cost $2000 for $3000. Of this, $500 was received immediately in cash, the rest to be paid later.
6. Paid various small expenses in cash, $120.
7. Received $1000 of the amount owed by customers.
8. Returned to suppliers goods that had cost $300. Since the goods were faulty, this amount can be set off against the amount owed to suppliers.
9. Paid $5000 on account to suppliers of goods for resale.
10. Received balances owing by customers, except for $150.
11. The customer owing the $150 returned the goods (cost $100) and they were returned to stock. Credit was granted in full.
12. Took goods that had cost $750 for her own private use.
13. Drew $1000 from the bank for own private expenses.
14. A customer returned defective goods that cost $50 and had been sold to him for $70. A cash refund was paid.

15. Discarded other stock on hand which had cost $500 but which had perished.
16. Successfully claimed $600, received by cheque, being full cost of some equipment damaged by fire and insured against this eventuality. The equipment was not replaced.
17. Discovered that $50 cash had been stolen. This was not insured.
18. Ordered a further $1000 worth of goods for resale to be delivered when available and paid for on delivery.
19. A physical count of the stock at 31 July 20X4 revealed $4180 on hand, at cost.

   (a) Prepare ledger accounts for the above transactions.
   (b) Prepare a profit and loss statement for July 20X4 and a balance sheet as at 31 July 20X4.

5.23 *General ledger, trial balance and financial statements for a merchandiser*
1. Enter the following information into general ledger accounts and prepare a trial balance, a profit and loss statement and a balance sheet for the week ended 7 January 20X9.

Jan. 1   A. Fitt commenced business as a retailer under the name 'Jeans Galore' with an initial capital contribution of $20 000.
      2   Paid three weeks rent of store, $1800.
      2   Bought store fixtures on credit for $12 000, paying $3000 deposit.
      3   Bought merchandise from Shabby Jeans Ltd on credit for $5000.
      3   Sold merchandise on credit to T. Rendy for $950 (cost $320).
      4   Sold merchandise for cash $1700 (cost $680).
      5   T. Rendy returned merchandise worth $25 (cost $6) and received credit.
      6   T. Rendy paid the balance of his account less $12 discount.
      7   Faulty merchandise, which had cost $800, was returned to the supplier and credit was received.
      7   Paid $2000 of the amount owing on the store fixtures.
      7   Sold goods on credit to V. Peachy for $430 (cost $190).

Additional information at 7 January:
The salesperson was owed a week's wages of $160.
A count of the stock revealed $2905 on hand, at cost.

2. *Part A*
Record the following transactions in the appropriate ledger accounts and prepare a trial balance, a profit and loss statement and a balance sheet.

20XX
April 1   Brett Gearloose opened a car sales yard for pre-loved cars. He deposited $50 000 into a business bank account.
      2   Borrowed $40 000 from the bank.
           Purchased a small block of land for the yard with a small office on it for $70 000 cash.
      3   Paid $500 deposit to have electricity connected (this will be refunded when and if the service is discontinued and the account settled).
           Telephone connection fee, $120. Telephone rental for four months, paid in advance, $80.

4   Bought these cars for the following costs for resale later:

DAB-227	$1500
CPJ-110	$1200
CZT-991	$ 800
CAS-456	$1100
DAN-231	$ 700
	$5300

(*Note:* A single 'Merchandise' account may be used and it is only necessary to enter the total. Individual cars may be recorded elsewhere on stock cards.)

5   Sold CPJ-110 for $1800 cash.

7   Withdrew $100 for personal use.
Paid advertising expenses of $150.

10   Sold DAB-227 for $2000 to U. Gettit, who paid a deposit of $500. (*Note:* Use a single account for all 'Accounts receivable'.)

11   Bought ETC-921 for $750 on credit from R. N. Swell. ('Accounts payable').

15   Withdrew $80 for personal use.

17   Sold CAS-456 for $1600 cash.
Car cleaning costs, $80.

19   Bought EDA-123 for $ 200
         EAB-797 for $1000
         DOB-821 for $ 750

CAS-456 broke down one kilometre from the yard and the purchaser was refunded the money. The car was fixed easily and is now back in the sales yard.

21   Sold DAN-231 for $1000 and EDA-123 for $450. Both sales were for cash.

22   Withdrew $85 for personal use.
Sold CAS-456 for $1750 cash.

24   Paid R. N. Swell $500 on account.

28   Received $1300 from U. Gettit in full settlement of his purchase. He was allowed $200 discount for early payment.

30   Cleaning expenses of $60 were owing at the end of the month.

A check of the cars showed that CZT-991 was missing. It was then recovered and deemed worthless. The car was not insured.

Interest due on the bank loan was $20.

Part B
While attending a meeting of RAMD (Regional Association of Motor Dealers), Mr Gearloose obtained by undisclosed means the latest profit and loss statement of his fiercest competitor, Big Deal Car Sales.

Prepare a brief statement comparing the results with those of Gearloose Car Sales and indicate possible reasons for differences in performance.

PROFIT AND LOSS STATEMENT: BIG DEAL CAR SALES
for month ending 30 April

			%
Sales		$8000	100
less Cost of sales		4800	60
Gross profit		3200	40
less Expenses			
Advertising	$500		6.3
Cleaning	200		2.5
Discount	Nil		–
Interest	25		0.3
Rent	25		0.3
Telephone	140		1.8
		890	11.2
Net profit		$2310	28.8

CHAPTER 6
Underlying assumptions of the historical cost accounting system

Introduction

One of the basic difficulties we encounter in dealing with any systematic process (accounting or otherwise) is that of choosing between a number of alternatives. This chapter explains why most endeavours in life need some form of theoretical framework to guide these choices. A simple example of a systematic approach, the establishment of a new tennis magazine, is used to illustrate this point, with the development of objectives, assumptions, principles and rules forming the basis for the framework.

Attention is focused on the historical cost accounting system as a means of reporting financial information about the entity to investors and other users, as this is by far the most prevalent accounting system used in practice. This is demonstrated by Figure 6.1, which is a section from the Coca-Cola Amatil Ltd financial statements and would be typical for the large majority of companies. A theoretical framework for the historical cost accounting system is developed in this chapter, indicating the objectives, assumptions and principles underlying it, in preparation for a more detailed study of the applications of the rules of accounting in following chapters. These principles affect how the elements of financial statements (assets, liabilities, owners' equity, revenue and expenses) are defined and recognised.

Figure 6.1 A section from the 'Notes to the Financial Statements' of Coca-Cola Amatil Ltd and its controlled entities, 1997

1. Statement of Accounting Policies

The financial statements are general purpose financial reports and have been prepared in accordance with applicable Accounting Standards, Urgent Issues Group Consensus Views and the Corporations Law. A summary of the significant accounting policies adopted by the Coca-Cola Amatil Limited Group is set out below. These policies have been consistently applied.

a) Historical cost

The financial statements have been prepared on the basis of historical cost and, except where otherwise stated, do not account for changing money values or valuations of non-current assets.

The problem of choice

From the start of the recording and reporting process, choices have to be made between alternative courses of action, with different outcomes resulting from each choice. The first decision concerns whether a particular event should be recorded in the accounting system. Given that it would be impossible to capture the impact of every event that occurs and that might have some impact on the organisation, it is necessary to choose between them. The set from which we must choose is enormous, ranging from major events, such as the purchase of a new factory, through to the trivial, such as the non-arrival of the morning tea at 11.15 am. From this wide range of events, appropriate choices must be made, keeping in mind the objectives of the accounting system. It is not surprising that some guidance is necessary to ensure that the system produces an appropriate end product, namely the financial statements.

Once an event has been selected for recording in the accounting system, it is necessary to decide how the components of the accounting equation are affected by the event. The events with which accounting deals may be interpreted in various ways. A payment for the purchase of stationery, for example, may be regarded either as acquiring an asset or incurring an expense, depending on the particular circumstances. The result of this choice has an effect on the profit as shown in the profit and loss statement and the asset position as shown in the balance sheet, so it can be a very significant decision. Many similar choices exist throughout the recording and reporting processes and it is necessary to establish some principles to guide the decision on the appropriate classification in each case.

Case 6.1 Problem transactions

How would you record the following events which occurred during the year ended 20X1 and, more particularly, why would you choose that course of action?

(a) The business paid $10 000 to enable the owner to visit her sick mother in northern Scotland.
(b) The business paid $6000 to cover rent for the three years from 20X1 to 20X3.
(c) The owner lent the business $4000.
(d) Wages of $20 000 were owing at the end of 20X1 and will be paid in 20X2.

We will return to these situations later in the chapter.

Some of the basic concepts of classification have already been discussed, including those involving assets, expenses and the accounting entity. Later in the chapter these will be extended and combined within a framework of accounting principles applicable to the historical cost system of accounting.

The problem of having to make choices and the need for some form of guiding framework within which these can be made is certainly not restricted to the accounting system. The following illustration will help to 'set the scene' for the establishment of such a framework for the historical cost accounting system. As you read through it, note how the establishment of various guidelines (objectives, assumptions, principles and rules) assists in building an appropriate framework to help in the decisions that have to be made, both immediately and in the future.

An illustration of the development of a framework to aid in decision making

Chris Martinez, having retired from the tennis circuit, is looking to start a business. With a love of tennis and an extensive network of 'contacts', Chris has decided to publish a new tennis magazine, *Net Hop*. Knowing that a large number of small businesses fail, a careful plan for its establishment was developed.

Chris first decided that the *objective* of establishing the magazine was to make the largest profit possible. As with any venture, profit-making was not the only objective, but in this case it was the major one. To achieve this objective, the highest possible circulation would be required and this would require a magazine that the majority of readers would find useful for their purposes.

The readers, of course, had a number of purposes for wanting to read a tennis magazine, so a 'useful' magazine must contain articles that are *relevant* to the interests of potential readers, identified as tennis enthusiasts. Chris also knew that the information in the magazine must be *reliable* if it was to be successful. If it concentrated on reporting scandalous love matches, based only on rumours, or gave coaching tips that proved unsound, readers would eventually stop wanting to read the magazine. Hence, at the risk of omitting some articles that might be interesting and relevant for a certain number of readers, Chris decided to concentrate on *reliable* articles. Thus reliability was seen as a necessary quality of the information in the magazine if it was to succeed.

Chris then gave some thought to the broad policies that would ensure relevance. Based on past experience and some preliminary market research, the following *assumptions* were made:

- Being an international sport, readers prefer to read articles about players from a range of countries, perhaps with an emphasis on the countries where the magazine is expected to be well received.
- Most readers will take out postal subscriptions rather than purchase the magazine at stores.
- Readers prefer articles that avoid too much technical detail.

These were the explicitly identified assumptions. Others were implicit, in that they were not formally stated but they nevertheless influenced the magazine. For example, the assumption was made that the postal service would deliver the magazine. Overall, the assumptions provided important guidelines for designing the format of the magazine and its content to ensure its relevance to readers. To achieve reliability, three conditions were believed to be necessary:

- All reported facts must be supported by evidence.
- Tennis tips should be well proven.
- Neutrality must be preserved; for example, the magazine should not be biased in favour of particular players.

Based on the objectives and assumptions, Chris developed a magazine according to certain principles that would meet the requirements of readers. Each *principle* was derived from one or more of the assumptions. For example, if readers prefer an Australian viewpoint, then most space should be devoted to news from Australia, with Australian writers contributing the articles. Also, if readers prefer a postal subscription, then the magazine must conform to all postal service requirements (e.g. size and weight).

These principles were then converted into *working rules* covering all the details necessary to produce the magazine. Items such as the number of pages, whether it was to be a colour magazine, and the methods of reporting tournament results were decided within the framework of these principles.

Although the magazine was carefully planned, this does not guarantee its success. Chris may have made incorrect assumptions about readers' tastes; Chris may have overstressed reliability, or the working rules may not be consistent with the broad assumptions. It can be asserted, however, that prior planning greatly improved the chances of success.

The tennis magazine in the above illustration was designed to communicate sporting information to a specific group of readers. Similarly, an accounting system is designed to communicate financial information to a specific group of readers, so that, as a communication system, it has features in common with the tennis magazine. Thus, these two 'tools of communication' have a number of features in common and both benefit from having a framework within which decisions regarding choices have some foundation.

A general framework to aid decision making

The aim of this section is to explain some terms that will be used in the framework for historical cost accounting and will also be used elsewhere in the text. Words such as 'assumption', 'principle' and 'rule' are often used when writing about accounting to represent the same or very similar things. Thus, although the explanations given in this section are not the only meanings that these words can have, they are believed to be the most useful for our purposes.

Many activities involve planning and design to achieve a particular objective and as we have seen can benefit from having a framework in which decisions can be made. The tennis magazine illustrates one approach to this and could be represented by Figure 6.2.

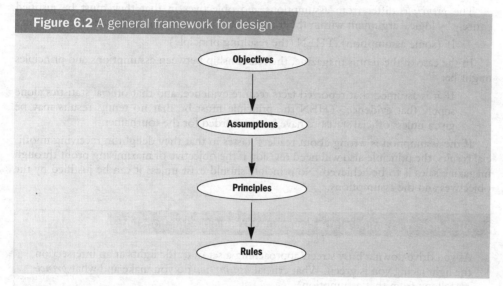

Figure 6.2 A general framework for design

The setting of *objectives* helps to guide the entire process, whether it be the design of a robot, a weekly magazine or an accounting system. Everything we design or plan is directed towards some purpose, and unless that purpose is clearly defined the final outcome is unlikely to be successful.

Having decided what the objective of the process is to be, *assumptions* are made to guide the work and decisions aimed at achieving that objective. All designs are based on assumed knowledge of the world around us. For instance, a clockmaker assumes that each day has 24 hours and expects that the purchasers of the clocks will accept this assumption or else purchase clocks made under some other assumption. These assumptions are statements accepted by the designer as self-evident facts without argument.

The sources of assumptions are many and their degree of certainty is variable. There are well-established 'facts' from scientific research, such as the melting point of various metals, that are essential assumptions for certain production processes. There are other, more tentative, assumptions that are relied on by producers, such as the results of market research about consumers' preferences for particular types of wine. In many other cases, however, the assumptions relied on may have no firm support, either because they have not been tested or because they cannot be tested. A farmer, in deciding which crops to plant and when to plant them, must make assumptions about future weather conditions which cannot be 'proved' in advance.

A most important point to remember, particularly with regard to assumptions in accounting, is that no matter how firmly they appear to be based, they are all subject to change. Assumptions based on hunches and market surveys are particularly fragile, but even scientific laws may change with new discoveries. It is wise, then, to regard all assumptions with an element of caution. Should the design fail to meet its objective, one or more of the assumptions may have to be changed.

A particular characteristic of an assumption is that it is taken as given within the design process. The planner or designer takes advantage of the work of others to set these assumptions. Ideally they should appear reasonable without any argument, perhaps even to the extent of being obvious.

In the framework of historical cost accounting discussed later in this chapter, the assumptions may appear quite obvious and trivial. However, the need for these assumptions will become apparent as the complexity of accounting increases in later chapters. This is also why it is very important that you have a sound background knowledge of them now, so that you are able to better understand what is introduced later in the text.

The *principles* differ from assumptions and objectives in that they must be justified entirely by logical argument within the framework. In general, principles take the form of:

IF (some assumption), THEN (the resulting principle).

In the case of the tennis magazine, the relationship between assumptions and principles might be:

IF it is assumed that reported facts require evidence, and that official statistics alone supply that evidence, THEN the principle must be that no tennis results may be given unless official statistics have been recorded for the tournament.

If the assumption is wrong about readers' tastes in that they delight in receiving unofficial results, the principle also will need revision if the objective of maximising profit through magazine sales is to be achieved. No principle should exist unless it can be justified by the objectives and the assumptions.

An everyday example of the assumption/principle relationship

As you drive down a busy street, approaching a set of traffic lights at an intersection, the light facing you is green. What crucial *assumption* do you make and what *principle* follows from that assumption?

As you are facing a green light, you would assume that the light facing the other street is red and it would be safe to cross the intersection. If your *assumption* is incorrect and the other light is also green (for whatever reason), the *principle* of proceeding ahead when facing a green light would need to be changed—fast!

Once the principles have been established by logical argument, the detailed applications of these principles are specified as working *rules*. There may be a hierarchy or ranking of rules, with broad rules being subdivided into special rules for different situations. Flowing from the principles, which are the broad guidelines, rules will be established to cover general situations, then more specific situations, with the rules becoming narrower as additional, very specific, situations arise. Table 6.1 illustrates this process, using the magazine example.

Table 6.1 Portion of the design framework

Objective:	To provide reliable information.
Assumption:	All reported facts require evidence.
Principle:	Results must be from official sources only.
Rule 1	For major tournaments, contact World Tennis Association and publish results without further inquiry.
Rule 2	For minor tournaments, contact the Association involved.
Rule 2A	If registered with World Tennis, publish results if verified in writing by tournament director.
Rule 2B	If not registered, do not publish results.

Various names are used to describe the overall framework of *objectives, assumptions, principles* and *rules*. For a tennis magazine, it might be described as a finished design or plan of action. The word *model* is now used widely to describe any logical process of reasoning that leads to a design, whether it be a building, a magazine, or a method of analysing transactions to produce financial statements. The word *system* is similarly used. A computer system is a good example, as it is designed with given objectives that can only be achieved if certain assumptions are made relating to the central processing unit, memory, monitor, software, printer etc. In scholarly work, the word *theory* may be used to describe the collection of assumptions and arguments that justify a proposed course of action.

The subtle differences between all of these terms are not particularly relevant at this stage. In this book, an integrated set of objectives, assumptions, principles and rules will usually be referred to as an *accounting system*. In other texts, however, they may be referred to as models or theories.

When designing something new, as in the example discussed in the sections above, it may be appropriate to use the approach of setting objectives and making assumptions, then identifying principles and rules that flow from them. The finished design or model can then be tested to see whether it achieves the objectives set for it. If it fails, a new one can be designed based on different assumptions or a more rigorous development of the rules. This method of design or reasoning is known as a *deductive* approach, since the principles and rules are *deduced* from the objectives and assumptions.

A very different approach needs to be taken when looking at a framework for a system which already exists. This is the situation we must deal with when looking at the historical cost accounting system. It has been developing for centuries, so it is logical to expect that a large number of rules already exist. These have evolved in an ad hoc, unstructured manner during this time rather than in response to some original system of objectives, assumptions and principles.

A method of research known as empirical inductive research is used in many scientific activities where, through observation of a certain set of events, certain general principles which the observer believes to be true for all such events are *induced*. The development of a framework for historical cost accounting is a task that has relied on a similar inductive approach. Observations of the rules accountants use have provided the empirical evidence from which the theoretical structure can be implied, inferring the principles underlying them. From a study of these principles, it has been possible to determine the assumptions accountants have made and hence the objectives. Using this type of research in some fields might result in a formal structure and a set of rules that everyone agrees on, but in accounting there are still very differing views about what should be inferred from the observations and what is an appropriate system for accounting in the current climate.

You should keep in mind, as you work through the following sections, that the system we are referring to is what could be called the 'pure' historical cost accounting system. Such a system probably does not exist today, as it has had to adapt to accommodate a variety of economic and social issues. It is, however, important for you to understand the framework presented here, so that you can begin to see its strengths and weaknesses and have a better appreciation of why it has changed and perhaps how it should continue to change.

In the next section we discuss the objectives, assumptions and principles of the historical cost accounting system which have been determined through an inductive approach. Some of the rules based on this framework have already been covered in earlier chapters and others will be dealt with in later chapters. This section will put them into a theoretical context and help you to appreciate the basis for *why* they are used.

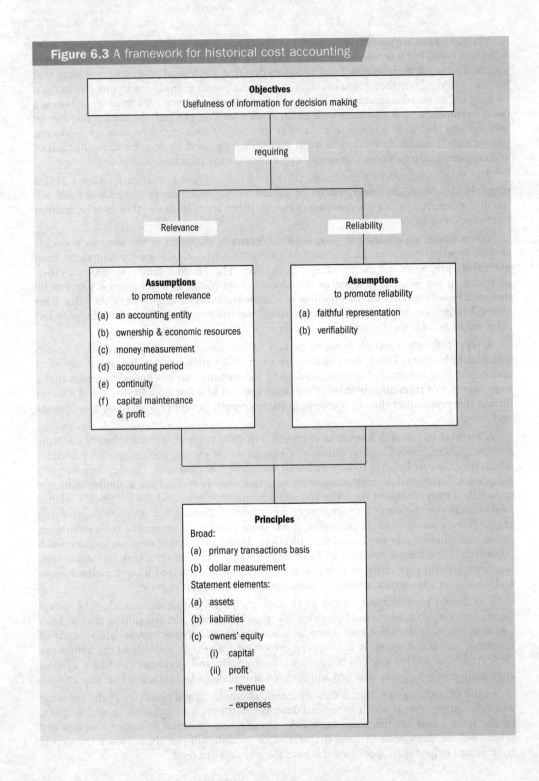

Figure 6.3 A framework for historical cost accounting

Objectives
Usefulness of information for decision making

requiring

Relevance

Reliability

Assumptions
to promote relevance

(a) an accounting entity

(b) ownership & economic resources

(c) money measurement

(d) accounting period

(e) continuity

(f) capital maintenance
    & profit

Assumptions
to promote reliability

(a) faithful representation

(b) verifiability

Principles
Broad:

(a) primary transactions basis

(b) dollar measurement

Statement elements:

(a) assets

(b) liabilities

(c) owners' equity

   (i) capital

   (ii) profit

    – revenue

    – expenses

The objectives of the historical cost accounting system

As we indicated earlier in this chapter, choice is the reason why decision making is necessary. What assists us in our decision-making process is information about the alternatives available to us. However, we do not want just any information, we want information that we can rely on to be accurate, timely and without bias. We also want our information to be relevant to the decisions we are trying to make. People who use the information produced by an accounting system are no different in that they also want information that is relevant and reliable to help them to make choices between the various alternatives available to them.

The objective of an accounting system can therefore be said to involve the production of relevant and reliable information to aid the users of this information in their decision-making process. One of the problems with this is that some of the most relevant information is highly unreliable; for example, investors would find it highly relevant to know next year's profits and dividends for each of their investment choices. However, any such assessment of the future cannot be said to be at all reliable. Another problem is that sometimes the most reliable information, for example the cost an organisation paid for equipment 10 years ago, is not at all relevant to a particular decision, for example the current price of new equipment to replace the old equipment.

As we have seen in earlier chapters, the historical cost system values its assets at the original prices established by actual transactions with other entities. The documentation representing the transactions provides verifiable evidence on which to base the original valuations. A current price system values assets at current market prices, notwithstanding that the assets have not actually been sold. Uncertainty over the sale price of assets is believed, by advocates of traditional accounting, to result in less reliable valuations since there is no proven sale value on which to base estimates.

A different, more traditional objective of accounting is to provide information on management's stewardship over resources—that is, to report on how the resources which existed at the start of a period have been used to produce profit and how the resources have changed over the same period. In this view, the purpose of accounting is merely to provide an 'account' of past historical events as reflected in transactions actually engaged in by the organisation. As changes in market prices of assets held are not historical events of the enterprise, they are not represented in the accounting reports. Similarly, under this traditional view, the likely revenue from assets developed within the company, such as oil reserves discovered by exploration, may not be recorded until the revenue is realised through external transactions. The resulting financial statements provide an account of stewardship in terms of actual transactions incurred by management. In the simpler world of yesteryear, no records other than actual transactions would have been necessary. In fact, some small businesses may survive today with no more information than statements of cash receipts and cash payments.

This simple picture is certainly not true of a large company or public sector organisation. Investors in and managers of these complex organisations are not only interested in the past transactions; their decisions also require knowledge of current prices. Information of this kind would certainly be relevant, yet it is not provided by the historical cost accounting system. The reason seems to be the belief that historical cost information is the only information that is sufficiently reliable to be useful. This view trades off relevance in favour of reliability by placing a great deal of emphasis on the provision of reliable information. Therefore, when working through the assumptions and principles of historical cost accounting, it can be presumed that reliability is of much greater importance then relevance.

The traditional view of stewardship as the objective of accounting has been overshadowed, in the more complex business world of recent times, by the objective of providing relevant and reliable information to assist the users of that information with their decisions.

Case 6.2 A difference of opinion

Two accountants were quietly discussing what they are trying to achieve when they produce financial statements. One suggested that the main objective is to report to the owners of the business how well their resources had been utilised during the period and whether they had increased during that time. The other suggested that as the statements were used by many different parties, the main objective should be to try to meet their demands for information to help them make decisions.

On overhearing this discussion, a bright new accounting graduate interrupted and suggested that the financial statements could meet both the traditional 'steward-ship' objective and also the 'decision-usefulness' objective. Justify which of these three views you agree with.

The assumptions of the historical cost accounting system

Various assumptions have been made to help shape accounting reports so that they contain relevant and reliable information for shareholders and other external parties. Many are implicit, such as an assumption that the reports should appear in a readable form. The following assumptions, however, are believed to be essential for deriving the principles of accounting.

Assumptions designed to promote relevance

Accounting entity

The accounting entity assumption has two related parts:

(a) Separation, which suggests that for accounting purposes the enterprise is separated from its owner
(b) Viewpoint, which suggests that accounting procedures are conducted from the viewpoint of the entity

The *separation* notion distinguishes between the private affairs of the owner of the business and those of the business itself. If we are trying to report information about the business, it is essential to ensure that events relating to the private transactions of the owner are not included. Consequently, any payments made from the *business bank account* relating to personal items of the owner, such as living expenses, entertainment and travel expenses, are treated as withdrawals of some of the owners' equity and not as expenses of the business.

In smaller business organisations, the boundaries between the business entity and the owner/s are sometimes difficult to identify. At law, a sole trader and his or her business are viewed as being one legal entity, however, for the purposes of accounting we must make a clear distinction between the business and the owner. This is also true of partnerships. However, a company, at law, is viewed as a separate entity, so the distinction between its activities and those of its shareholders (owners) is more clearly defined.

The *viewpoint* aspect of the entity assumption implies that, in determining how a transaction affects the business entity, it is interpreted from the viewpoint of the business. The owner is therefore viewed as an external party to the business. Without some assumption regarding the viewpoint to be taken, the contribution of an additional $20 000 by the owner could be interpreted in either of two ways. From the owner's viewpoint, cash has been given up in exchange for an increase in the asset of investment in the company. The business, however, would consider that cash of $20 000 had been received and that an external party, in this case the owner, had an increased claim on the business of $20 000.

Under the entity assumption, accounting is conducted from the viewpoint of the accounting entity so that relevant information may be presented on the affairs of the business. The accounting system does not record the owner's private transactions in which the business is not involved. Where the business is a party to a transaction with the owner, that transaction must be treated formally within the system, as if it had been with any other external person or organisation.

Ownership and economic resources

The 'wealth' of an individual may be defined very broadly as what makes the person feel 'well-off'. Individuals might boast about their wealth of ideas, memories, friendships and satisfactions of various kinds, and might even try to measure these aspects of well-offness, but they are unlikely to hire an accountant for the task. In traditional practice, the accountant is assigned the less ambitious task of measuring only those resources that have *economic value*.

There are two sources of economic value which can be measured: *value in exchange* and *value in use*. A resource has value in exchange if it can be sold or exchanged for cash or any other consideration (including the receipt of other resources or the cancellation of debts). Examples of resources that have value in exchange include inventory, land, rights to use land (such as mining claims) and shares in companies. The value in exchange of a resource is generally referred to as its market value.

Other economic resources have value in use, in that they may be used to create other economic resources which, in turn, have value in exchange or some further value in use. Examples of these resources include raw materials and productive machinery.

Accounting assumes that only information about resources which have some value in use or value in exchange will be of relevance to the users of accounting reports. Such vague resources as wisdom or 'happy memories' or others which might add to a feeling of 'well-offness' are excluded from the accounting system. More importantly, it requires the removal from the accounting system of information about resources that have lost their economic value, such as worn-out equipment, or inventory that has deteriorated and cannot be sold.

Case 6.3 The value of art and artefacts

In a 1995 article, G. Carnegie & P. Wolnizer (*Australian Accounting Review*, Vol. 5, No. 1, p. 31) argue that the collections in not-for-profit public museums and art institutions should not be valued for balance sheet purposes, even though there had been a strong push from accounting regulators to do so. One of the arguments for not valuing these items was that they had neither a value in exchange (under normal operating conditions) nor a value in use (since it is the public which gains the benefit of using the collections). Do you agree?

One further requirement for an economic resource to be reported about is that it must be scarce. Air and water from a river are certainly resources which are used by businesses and therefore have value in use. However, because they are normally plentiful, they are not economic resources. They do not have the feature of scarcity.

Once a resource becomes scarce and acquires some economic value, an entity will claim ownership of it. A person who discovers gold will stake a claim on the goldfield and an inventor will register ownership of the patent to an invention. On occasions, drought makes water in an area scarce and it is brought in and sold in limited quantities. If a river dries up and it has been used by a business in some production process, the organisation would be forced to buy-in a supply of water in order to stay in business. Someone now 'owns' that water by virtue of having gone to the trouble of collecting it from one area and delivering what has become a scarce resource to another.

This notion of scarcity is of great importance for double-entry accounting. As every scarce resource has an owner, this means all economic resources possessed by an entity have ownership rights vested in them. This leads to the duality notion underlying the basic accounting equation discussed in earlier chapters, of 'assets = equities'. If assets are defined as economic resources, there must be an ownership claim on those assets. Ownerless resources, those that are plentiful or have no value in use or in exchange, are not assets in accounting.

Accounting must meet the needs of external parties with different legal relationships to the entity, so it must provide some distinction between the claims of the major parties involved. Creditors provide economic resources for use by the entity and have a corresponding claim on the entity. A creditor who lends money to the entity no longer 'owns' that money, but certainly has a claim on the entity for that amount. The owners of the entity have a different relationship with the entity in that they have a 'residual claim' to all the resources not claimed by the liability group.

These assumptions about the nature of financial relationships in the world lead to the following statement:

$$\text{economic resources} = \text{creditors' claims} + \text{owners' claims}$$

Or, as they are defined in accounting and presented to you in earlier chapters:

$$\text{assets} = \text{liabilities} + \text{owners' equity}$$

The 'residual' nature of the owners' claim is best expressed as:

$$\text{owners' equity} = \text{assets} - \text{liabilities}$$
$$= \text{net assets}$$

The equality of economic resources and claims on resources provides a means of justifying the double-entry system of accounting. This assumption is grounded in economics and, in so far as it is a true statement about the world, it guides accounting practice towards a relevant way of viewing assets and ownership.

This assumption defines economic resources, but importantly, it does *not* determine the appropriate basis of valuation of those resources. A resource such as a piece of equipment might be valued for its value in exchange (e.g. the market price) or its value in use (e.g. the present value of the future cash flow it will generate) or its replacement cost. The choice of the basis of valuation must therefore depend on other assumptions and principles.

Money measurement

In any system that is trying to place a relevant value on the resources it is reporting, the unit of measurement it chooses for that value is obviously of extreme importance. It is also important that the resources are measured using a common unit.

The economic resources of an entity could be measured in various ways. For example:

Cash	100	dollars
Inventory	5 000	units
Equipment	2	lathes
	3	presses
Total	5 105	????

By not using a common unit, any total or aggregate of the economic resources becomes very difficult or impossible to interpret. Accountants have recognised the need to aggregate this information. By totalling the assets, it is possible to examine the change in total assets over time and to compare the size of one enterprise with another. The respective total claims of owners and creditors may also be assessed. The uses for aggregated information are many and, to achieve this end, each measurement must be standardised by the use of a common unit of measurement. In times when bartering was the means of exchange, the standard measure of value may have been pigs, sheep or bags of wheat.

Today, money is the principal medium of exchange and, since the concept of wealth includes value in exchange, money is assumed to be the unit of measurement best suited to provide relevant information. Hence, it is assumed that economic resources and claims to them will be measured in the monetary unit of the country where the measurement is being reported. It has been and will continue to be assumed in this book that the unit of measurement is the dollar.

Monetary measurement may seem an obvious assumption, but it is not without its problems. It has been argued that, through inflation and/or fluctuating exchange rates, a monetary unit is not a reliable unit for standardising measurement. In 1985, dollars had far more purchasing power than they had in 1995. This suggests that to add the dollar cost of land purchased in 1985 to the dollar cost of land purchased in 1995 is no more sensible than attempting to add inches to metres. Rather than being stable and providing us with a standardised unit of measurement, the unit has shown considerable variability over time, as the following indicates.

Figure 6.4 *Source: Australian Financial Review*, 11 and 23 June 1998 (headlines), 11 June 1998 (graph)

Nothing new in currency volatility

$A slides with yen in reverse

$A heads for record low

$A FALL AIDS FOREIGN BUYERS

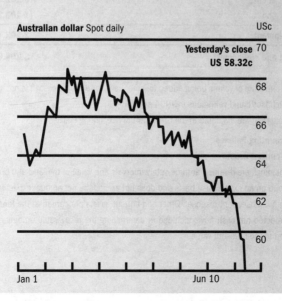

Australian dollar Spot daily

This variability in the measurement unit impacts greatly on the financial statements, both in trying to compare information over time (e.g. total assets in 1985 with those in 1995) and in adding figures recorded over a number of periods.

Within the historical cost accounting system, however, it is assumed that the dollar is the most relevant measurement unit for reporting purposes. This means that the historical cost accounting system ignores the effects of inflation. It should be noted that several alternative accounting systems, to be considered later in the book, are based on measurement in such units as *constant dollars*, that is, dollars indexed for changes in general purchasing power in an effort to overcome some of the problems with the money measurement assumption.

Figure 6.5 Extracts from the 'Notes to the Financial Statements' of Coca-Cola Amatil Ltd and its controlled entities, 1997

	CCA Group	
	1997 $M	1996 $M
11. Property, plant and equipment		
Freehold and leasehold land and buildings at cost	491.6	453.8
Provision for depreciation and amortisation	(21.2)	(31.8)
	470.4	422.0
Freehold and leasehold land and buildings at independent valuations –		
1997	625.9	–
1994	–	140.4
at Directors' valuations –		
1997	12.3	–
1994	–	120.9
	638.2	261.3
Provision for depreciation and amortisation	(4.7)	(3.4)
	633.5	257.9
Total property	1 103.9	679.9
Plant and equipment at cost	3 202.9	2 264.5
Provision for depreciation	(1 100.2)	(696.7)
Total plant and equipment	2 102.7	1 567.8
Total property, plant and equipment	3 206.6	2 247.7

Note that there is a mixture of values being added together here, for example cost (it is not known over what period these items were purchased), and valuations in 1994 and 1997.

Other bases for valuation are indicated in the Statement of Accounting Policies:

1. Statement of Accounting Policies

e) Valuation of non-current assets

Freehold land and buildings are revalued at three-yearly intervals. The value of the land and buildings is assessed on their worth to the Group on an existing use basis and does not exceed the net amount expected to be recovered from their continued use and subsequent disposal. Other non-current assets are carried at the lower of cost and recoverable amount. The expected net cash flows included in determining the recoverable amounts of non-current assets have been discounted to their present value.

> **f) Inventories**
>
> As a general principle, inventories are valued at the lower of cost (including fixed and variable factory overheads where applicable) and net realisable value. Cost is determined on the basis of first-in-first-out, average or standard, whichever is the most appropriate in each case.
>
> When the various asset categories are aggregated to give a total assets figure, what does the total figure really represent?

Accounting period

The accounting period assumption is based on the belief that owners and other interested parties require information about the entity's performance and financial position at regular intervals. This is necessary so that they can make timely and informed decisions about their interests in the entity. It is also necessary to satisfy the requirements of the appropriate taxation laws and the disclosure requirements of the corporate authorities.

Although this appears to be a necessary and appropriate assumption to make, it is responsible for many problems when put into practice within the accounting system. The business activities of any entity comprise a series of 'ventures'. They vary in length from very short, such as the purchase of some postage stamps, to very long, such as the construction of a major freeway, and all periods in between.

It is only when all of these 'ventures' are fully completed that we can, with complete certainty, assess the effect of them on the entity. The imposition of a 'cut-off' date is an artificial interruption to this process. Some ventures are started and completed within the accounting period and can be accurately reflected in the accounting reports; however, many remain incomplete at the end of the period and decisions must be made as to how these should be dealt with in the reports. For example, inventory may have been purchased, not sold and not yet paid for at the end of the period, or a freeway may be only partially completed.

At the end of the accounting period the accountant must try to evaluate the progress on these incomplete ventures by assigning values to the resources that remain on hand, such as the unsold inventory and the 'work in progress' on the freeway. This is the procedure of recognising and measuring assets for balance sheet purposes. At the same time the accountant must decide on other issues, such as what resources have been used up during the accounting period, and represent these as expenses in the reports.

In the earlier discussion of assets and expenses we indicated that the difference between them was one of timing, in that many assets can be regarded as long-term expenses—that is, resources waiting to be used up. If the accounting period was long enough, there would be no need to distinguish between assets and expenses, since all those 'wasting assets' eventually become expenses. The imposition of an artificial end to business activities at the end of an accounting period requires the accountant to allocate expenses over arbitrary periods of time and to value unused resources at that time.

The apparently obvious assumption of an accounting period therefore has some effect on many accounting activities, particularly around the end of the period, and causes many problems in accounting for economic resources represented in incomplete ventures.

Continuity or 'going concern'

This assumption suggests that in the absence of evidence to the contrary, the entity is assumed to continue in operation into the foreseeable future.

Some assumption about the future is necessary, even in an accounting system that is concerned with past transactions. The accounting period assumption raises problems with incomplete ventures and necessitates assumptions about how they will eventually be resolved. There is also the aspect of whether the business will continue in operation over the longer term. At the end of the accounting period the continuity of each of the incomplete ventures (i.e. short-term continuity) can be assessed and adjustments made as appropriate (e.g. it would not be difficult to assess whether the organisation will gain the benefit from one month's rent paid for at the end of an accounting period). An assumption about the continuity of the business in the longer term can also be made. If it is assumed to continue normally, it may be expected that inventory on hand at the end of one period will be sold in the next, projects under way will be completed and pieces of equipment will be used for their normal lives, for example. If, instead, it is expected that the business will shortly cease operations, some longer-term incomplete ventures will need to be looked at differently (e.g. where the assets will be sold at liquidation values).

Assets being carried forward in a balance sheet, valued on a basis consistent with their continued use, is consistent with an assumption of continuity of operations. For equipment, this may be one of a number of values, including original cost, cost to replace the asset, or the present value of the future cash flows to be generated by the equipment. These are often termed the 'going concern' values. By contrast, an assumption that the entity is to enter liquidation would permit the adoption of one valuation basis only, the amount to be received if the assets were sold immediately.

The choice between continuity and liquidation as an assumption about the future can therefore influence the choice of values. The evidence is that most companies do continue in operation and most accounting systems therefore assume continuity as the normal case.

Capital maintenance and profit

This assumption is a very important one and suggests that profit can only be recognised after the value of owners' equity at the beginning of the period has at least been maintained (hence the term 'capital maintenance').

Most accounting systems assume that it is relevant to identify the change in the economic resources over an accounting period and to identify whether there has been any growth in these resources as a result of profit. In order to achieve this, there must be a distinction made by the system between capital and profit.

This notion is built into the law relating to corporations. For example, the following section appears in the Australian Corporations Law:

> *Division 4—Maintenance of Capital*
> **201 (1)** No dividend shall be payable to a shareholder of a company except out of profits ...

> (Corporations Law)

We have already identified capital as being the net assets of the entity—that is, the economic resources of the entity less claims on those resources by parties other than the owners. If there has been any growth over the accounting period of these net assets it must be as a result of either additional contributions by the owner (less any withdrawals) or profit earned as a result of its operations.

To illustrate, suppose an entity had $100 000 in net assets at the start of the period and this had grown to $120 000 by the end of the period. If we establish that there had not been any additional contributions or withdrawals by the owner over this period, then the increase is assumed to be profit. It is this amount that the owners would be able to withdraw without reducing any of the interest in the entity they had at the start of the period. Simply, profit is the increase in the owners' wealth after capital has been maintained. The relationship between net assets, capital and profit is represented in Figure 6.6.

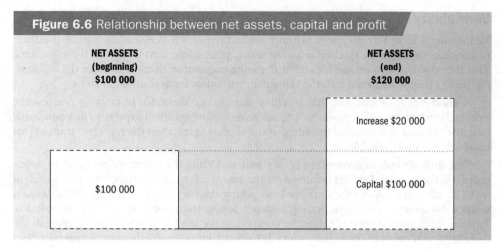

Figure 6.6 Relationship between net assets, capital and profit

This simple representation of capital maintenance is assumed under the historical cost accounting system. It is said to maintain *money capital*. That is, it maintains only the monetary value of net assets at the start of the period. No account is taken of whether the capital maintained at the end will enable the same level of activity to occur (e.g. the ability to have the same level of inventory available for sale). If there had been any decrease in the purchasing power of the currency, it would require a higher level of capital to be maintained to operate at the same level. This would then have an effect on the level of profit that could be recognised. A system of capital maintenance that takes this approach is said to be maintaining physical capital. Systems using alternate capital maintenance concepts are discussed in Chapter 19.

The capital maintenance and profit assumption used under the historical cost accounting system is however the simple maintenance of money capital as represented in the example above.

Assumptions designed to promote reliability

Information will be reliable when its users can depend on it to be an accurate representation of what it is supposed to represent. It should also not contain any bias or errors as a result of its preparation or presentation.

Faithful representation

Users of accounting information must be able to rely on the information to be a faithful representation of the transactions and events that it suggests it represents. Thus it is assumed that the financial statements faithfully represent all the transactions and events in the accounting period which have a bearing on the revenue, expenses, assets, liabilities and owners' equity shown in the statements.

The historical cost accounting system is said to do this particularly well. If an asset is purchased for $30 000 during the period and is then represented in the balance sheet at that figure under the heading of 'Assets', then the purchase transaction has certainly been faithfully represented. Even in 10 years time, the entry in the balance sheet (unless adjusted) will faithfully represent the original transaction. This is certainly appropriate if the balance sheet is used for that purpose only. If, however, it is to be assumed by users that the balance sheet represents the 'financial position' of the entity at balance date, then perhaps a different set of figures would give a more faithful representation of this situation.

Verifiability

Verifiability is linked to the above assumption and requires that essentially similar measures or conclusions would be reached if two or more qualified persons examined the same data. This means that if two people looked at the same transaction that occurred in the accounting period they would treat it in the same manner within the accounting system.

A good means of ensuring that an entry in a balance sheet, for instance, is not just the personal estimate of a biased person is to ask two or more qualified experts to independently examine the data that initiated the entry. If the experts agree, then the representation of that transaction is more reliable.

One difficult task in accounting is to count and value the inventory on hand to determine whether a stock loss has occurred. If the task is left to one person, that person might make an error in counting the items or in attaching the correct costs to them. If the work is verified by another employee, acting independently, the possibility of error is reduced. Further verification is then obtained by comparing the stock count with the balance in the merchandise account in the ledger, which is calculated independently using actual purchases and sales of stock.

Before information can be verified by two independent experts, there must be tangible evidence on which both may base their conclusions. In the case of a stock count, there are physical items of stock to be counted, invoices to confirm purchase prices and sales dockets to confirm sales to customers. If no evidence existed, it is unlikely that independent experts could agree. If experts were asked to predict the price at which a particular share would be selling in one year's time, a wide diversity of predictions would be expected, since there is no evidence to support this particular prediction.

The achievement of reliability is a most important objective of the historical cost system of accounting and the requirement that information must be verified therefore has considerable influence on accounting practice.

Case 6.1 revisited

Earlier in the chapter we presented some events and asked how you would treat each one and why you would treat them in that way. Having now looked at the assumptions behind historical cost accounting, we can more easily see what the choices would be:

(a) The business paid $10 000 to enable the owner to visit her sick mother in Scotland. This would be treated as a withdrawal, not an expense of the business, because of the accounting entity assumption. The transaction represents a withdrawal of equity from the business for private purposes.

(b) The business paid $6000 to cover rent for the three years from 20X1 to 20X3. One-third of this would be treated as an expense and two-thirds would be treated as an asset, because of the accounting period and continuity assumptions.

(c) The owner lent the business $4000. This would be recorded as a liability by the business because of the entity assumption. This is not a contribution of equity by the owner. It is a normal loan transaction.

(d) Wages of $20 000 were owing at the end of 20X1 and will be paid in 20X2. This would be recorded as a liability by the business and as an expense, because of the accounting period and continuity assumptions.

Keep these transactions in mind and see if you can justify the choice of element affected by each when we look at the definitions of the elements later in the chapter.

The broad principles of historical cost accounting

The major objectives and assumptions underlying the historical cost system of accounting have been examined. The system seeks to provide information useful for economic decisions, by ensuring that the data are both relevant and reliable, and a number of assumptions are made to ensure that this occurs. With this background, it is possible to derive some principles governing accounting practice. There appear to be two broad principles that identify the historical cost system of accounting and which underlie the various definitions of the elements of financial statements.

Primary transactions basis

No primary entry may be made in the accounting system unless it is evidenced by a past external transaction involving the entity.

The essence of a transaction is that it is an event involving more than just the entity; hence it provides independent, verifiable evidence by which independent experts may agree on the valuations to be adopted. The evidence of a transaction might include such documents as invoices, sales contracts, cancelled cheques and receipts.

We can define an external transaction as 'an external event involving the transfer of something of value (future economic benefit) between two (or more) entities'. The transaction may be an exchange in which each participant both receives and sacrifices value, such as in the sale of goods. Alternatively, it may be a non-reciprocal transfer, in which only one entity gains something of value. Non-reciprocal transfers include gifts to or by the entity, and the imposition of taxes on the entity.

All external transactions involving the entity must be recorded in the accounts and they will be defined as primary entries. They include, among others, purchases and sales of goods, payments of expenses and contributions of capital.

Secondary entries also exist. These are generally reallocations of amounts established by primary entries, such as writing off an asset as an expense. For example, a transaction involving the prepayment of rent will result in a primary entry creating an asset for prepaid rent. On expiry of the rental period, this amount will be transferred to an expense account for rent. This is a secondary reallocation entry. Other examples of secondary entries include depreciation on assets, recognition of the cost of goods sold when assets are sold, and the writing off of assets that are lost or destroyed.

Since secondary entries are essentially reallocations of amounts established by previous transactions, no current transaction is required to support them. The amount recorded as cost of goods sold, for example, is based on the price paid when the goods were acquired.

Of all events affecting an enterprise, only those based directly on transactions (primary entries) or those involving reallocations of previously established amounts (secondary entries) may be recorded in the accounts. Thus the historical cost system gives only a partial picture of the affairs of the entity, as Figure 6.7 depicts.

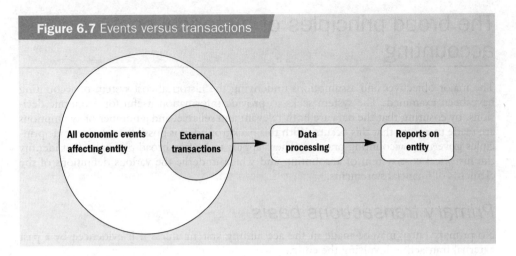

Figure 6.7 Events versus transactions

Dollar measurement

The second broad principle states that every transaction or event recorded in the accounts shall be measured in dollars. This follows from the money measurement assumption that dollars are more relevant than any other unit of measurement.

These broad principles lead to more detailed principles governing the definition and measurement of the elements of financial statements. This is the basis of our discussion in the next section.

Statement elements

Assets

We adopted a fairly simple definition of an asset for the purposes of earlier chapters, but it is appropriate to combine some of the subsequent discussions into a definition. We should also introduce some tests, consistent with the assumptions of historical cost accounting, to assist in determining when an asset should be recognised in the financial statements.

> Assets are economic resources controlled by the entity for the purpose of providing future benefits to that entity.

In deciding whether an item should be an asset, the following tests are commonly applied. The appropriate assumptions are also listed:

1. It must be an economic resource offering future benefits through use or exchange (*ownership and economic resources assumption*).
2. It must be under the control of the entity (*entity and ownership and economic resources assumptions*).
3. It must have been acquired in a past, external transaction (*primary transactions principle*).

Our earlier discussions indicated that past transactions must be faithfully represented in our financial statements if the information is to be reliable. It is necessary, therefore, to identify the property of the asset that is to be faithfully represented. The value, measured in dollar terms, is the means of achieving this representation and the only value associated with the external transaction is the original cost.

Assets partially consumed

Under the historical cost system a block of land is stated at its original cost and this, under a strict application of the system, remains stated as an asset for as long as it is held. (Certain exceptions will be discussed at a later stage.) Wasting assets, however, will not remain at original cost.

A payment of $60 000 for three years rental in advance, for example, is an asset that will expire over time. The asset should be thought of as a 'bundle of benefits', with the benefits being consumed over time. After one year, only two-thirds of these benefits remain unconsumed. Following the tests for asset recognition, the remaining value in use of the asset is only two years rental in advance. The cost of this asset is therefore $40 000, not the original cost of $60 000. Assets are valued at the cost of the remaining benefits from the use or sale of the original asset, that is, at their unexpired cost.

In summary, under historical cost accounting an asset is a future benefit under the control of the entity and acquired by a past external transaction. It is measured at its unexpired original cost expressed in dollars.

Liabilities

In general, the same questions of definition and measurement apply to liabilities. For now, a liability may be regarded as an obligation which the entity has at the present time and that meets the following tests:

1. There is a claim on the entity involving a future sacrifice of economic resources (*ownership and economic resources assumptions*).

2. The resources are to be sacrificed by the accounting entity to an external entity (*entity assumption*).

3. The liability arises out of a past external transaction (*primary transactions principle*).

It should be noted that, although the claim on the entity often involves a sacrifice of cash in the future, the claim could also be extinguished by the transfer of assets other than cash, the provision of services or the conversion of the obligation into owners' equity.

Owners' equity

Owners' equity represents the interests of shareholders or other owners in the net assets of an enterprise at any time. Once principles for the definition and measurement of assets and liabilities have been determined, the owners' equity arises automatically as the difference between them:

$$\text{owners' equity} = \text{assets} - \text{liabilities}$$

Nevertheless, owners' equity should be considered further so that it may be subdivided into the two separate components of capital and profit, as required by the capital maintenance assumption discussed earlier.

Capital

Changes in capital consist either of contributions or withdrawals by the owners. Contributions include direct contributions of capital by the owners, whether in cash, other assets or decreases of liabilities. These contributions do not form part of profit. Capital may also be contributed indirectly by allowing previous profits to remain in the business.

If a sole trader begins 20X1 with capital of $100 000, earns $45 000 during the year and withdraws only $40 000, then the capital to maintain at the beginning of 20X2 is $105 000.

Withdrawals are the opposite of contributions, in that they are reductions of owners' equity by withdrawals of resources from the entity by the owners. As with contributions, the withdrawals may be in cash, other assets or an increase of liabilities.

Profit

As we saw in earlier discussions, profit is the increase in owners' equity during the period, adjusted for contributions and withdrawals, after capital has been maintained. Assuming that no contributions or withdrawals of capital have occurred, profit for a period may be determined as:

$$\text{profit} = \text{OE}_{(end)} - \text{OE}_{(beg.)}$$

This method of calculating profit demonstrates that profit represents the growth in net assets over time. It is called the *stock approach* to profit determination because it determines profit as the difference between stocks of net assets at two points in time.

The stock approach has the difficulty that not all changes in owners' equity affect profit, especially changes due to contributions and withdrawals of capital. Also, it is not always feasible to value the assets and liabilities directly at the end of each accounting period.

The alternative is to accumulate the values of assets and liabilities by analysing and recording transactions as they occur. The values at balance date are then those appearing in the records. This is known as the *events approach*, so named because each event is analysed into its effects on the basic equation. The historical cost system takes an events approach following the transaction analysis procedures outlined in earlier chapters.

Under the events approach, two new terms are introduced: *revenues* and *expenses*. Revenues are those events that increase profit and expenses are those events that decrease profit. Profit is then defined as:

$$\text{net profit} = \text{revenues} - \text{expenses}$$

The stock and events approaches are based on the same underlying ownership equation and must lead to the same net profit.

Example: *Determining profit under stock and events approaches*

A business began the year with: Cash $10 000

                                    Liabilities   2 000

During the year the business recorded the following:

Commission was received on work performed	$ 500
Rent was paid on the buildings	300
Liabilities were paid to the extent of	1 400
Additional capital was contributed	4 000
Withdrawals amounted to	650

Profit under an events approach:

net profit	=	revenues – expenses
	=	$500 – $300
	=	**$200**

Profit under a stock approach:

$$
\begin{aligned}
\text{OE}_{\text{(beg.)}} &= \text{A}_{\text{(beg.)}} - \text{L}_{\text{(beg.)}} \\
&= \$10\ 000 - \$2\ 000 \\
&= \$8\ 000 \\
\text{OE}_{\text{(end)}} &= \text{A}_{\text{(end)}} - \text{L}_{\text{(end)}} \\
&= (\$10\ 000 + 500 - 300 - 1\ 400 + 4\ 000 - 650) - (2\ 000 - 1400) \\
&= \$12\ 150 - \$600 \\
&= \$11\ 550 \\
\text{net profit} &= \text{OE}_{\text{(end)}} - \text{OE}_{\text{(beg.)}} - \text{C} + \text{W} \\
&= \$11\ 550 - 8\ 000 - 4\ 000 + 650 \\
&= \mathbf{\$200}
\end{aligned}
$$

The stock and events approaches to profit determination are identical in result because both adhere to the notion that profit is determined after capital has been maintained.

This is more obvious with the stock approach, but is *implicit* in the events approach in that the deduction of expenses is made so that resources consumed in deriving revenue are recovered before profit is determined. In that way, capital is maintained. When a business sells goods that cost $300 for $500, it declares a profit of only $200 because the other $300 received from the sale must be retained to recover the cost of the goods sold. The charging of an expense against revenue is done so as to recover the cost of resources that have been consumed and thus to maintain capital.

The two elements, of revenue and expenses, used by the events approach must be defined carefully if the net profit is to be identical with that under the stock approach.

Revenue

Revenues:

1. are accomplishments of the earning process of a business enterprise during a period
2. usually represent cash inflows that have occurred or will probably eventuate
3. will be as a result of the enterprise's operations during the period.

This topic is discussed in greater detail later in the text. For now, it may be noted that revenue is not restricted to the sale of goods, that credit transactions may also result in revenue and that contributions of capital by the owner are not revenue.

Expenses

For now, expenses may be regarded as expired assets, as economic resources that have been consumed during the period. The tests for their recognition are derived from the tests for an asset. They are:

1. The resources consumed must have been acquired in a past external transaction (*primary transactions basis*).
2. They must represent economic resources that have expired during the period (*ownership and economic resources assumption*).
3. Withdrawals are not expenses but reductions in capital (*capital maintenance and profit assumption*).

The measurement of expenses is also consistent with assets in that resources consumed are measured at their original costs expressed in dollars.

The difficulty in measuring expenses is to decide *when* a resource has been consumed and *how much* has been consumed. Having divided the enterprise's life into arbitrary periods, under the period assumption, it becomes difficult to determine how best to write off a long-term expense over its life.

To assist in this process we can look at how the resource has been consumed. We will find that some expire upon the occurrence of a particular event (product costs), whereas others expire with the passing of time (period costs). Inventory on hand, for example, normally expires at the date of sale. Other costs, such as delivery and manufacturing costs, are similarly related to products and the expense may be recognised when the revenue for the product is recognised. Period costs include insurance on office buildings, wages paid to salespeople and rent on the showroom. In these cases, the benefits are considered to expire evenly over time and are spread accordingly.

Summary

Historical cost accounting is the basis for the large majority of accounting information systems in practice today. It has evolved to its present state over very many years without being developed within a well-defined and logical framework. In this chapter we have endeavoured to establish a theoretical framework for the historical cost accounting system.

In doing this we have shown, using a simple illustration, that planning or designing anything new can best be done by developing a framework made up of objectives, assumptions, principles and rules. Each of these sections of the framework have been explained and their interrelationships illustrated by reference to the example.

The chapter has also introduced the difference between deductive and inductive means of logical argument or development. When planning something from the start, the deductive method of development was shown to be appropriate—that is, first establishing the objectives of the project, making some assumptions, identifying related principles from those assumptions and finally establishing rules to follow in order to achieve the objectives. As the historical cost accounting system already exists, in order to establish a theoretical framework for it we used the inductive approach—that is, looking at the rules accountants use and logically working back through the principles and assumptions adopted in order to establish the objectives of the system.

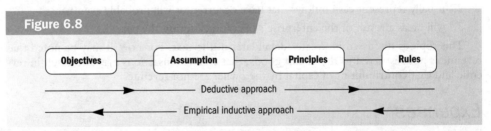

Figure 6.8

The major objective of historical cost accounting is to provide useful information to users. Useful information must be both relevant and reliable, two qualities that we saw are often in conflict. Under the historical cost system, great stress is placed on providing reliable information, with the possible sacrifice of relevance.

The various assumptions built into the historical cost system to promote relevance include the notion of an accounting equity, and assumptions that accounting is concerned with reporting on economic resources and ownership claims, measured in dollars and valued on the belief that the enterprise will normally continue in operation beyond the balance date. A further assumption is made that users are concerned to measure the profit, which represents the growth in economic resources beyond the initial capital base. The need for reliable information is assumed to be satisfied by the provision of information that is verifiable.

Two broad principles were derived from these assumptions. The primary transactions principle asserts that all entries must be based on external transactions, either as primary entries or as secondary reallocations of amounts recorded in primary entries. All other events, such as the increase in market values of assets, are omitted. Under the dollar measurement principle it is required that all measurements should be in dollars.

In the process of the development of this framework, we identified some of the practical implications of the acceptance of the objectives, assumptions and principles of the historical cost accounting system, including the effect on the definitions and recognition criteria of the elements of the profit and loss statement and balance sheet.

We saw that the change in net assets over a period is composed of changes in capital (contributions and withdrawals) and net profit and that profit may be determined in either of two ways. The *stock approach* regards profit as the increase in net assets, measured at two points in time, after writing back the effects of contributions and withdrawals, and the *events approach* measures profit as the difference between revenues and expenses. Both approaches are derived from the ownership equation, adhere to an identical concept of capital maintenance, and must therefore yield the same profit.

Now that the objective, assumptions and principles have been established for the historical cost accounting system, more of the working rules may be discussed. A sound understanding of these principles, and associated assumptions, should make the task of learning the rules more manageable and meaningful.

 **Review exercises**

Discussion questions

6.1   Outline a set of the major objectives, assumptions and principles that would guide you in establishing any one of the following businesses:

(a) a sporting goods store in an affluent suburb
(b) a luxury car dealership
(c) a Japanese food supplies shop
(d) a vegetarian restaurant

6.2   Consider the framework within which students study an accounting unit at university. List the objectives, assumptions and principles that might be appropriate for this framework.

6.3   According to the definitions given in the chapter, how do assumptions differ from principles? Give an example of some possible assumptions of accounting and of some principles related to those assumptions.

6.4   Why is it important to specify objectives before formulating a theory of accounting? How would you determine the objectives accounting should follow?

6.5   'The assumptions and principles underlying the conventional accounting system must be established by inductive reasoning.' Do you agree or disagree with this statement? Give reasons for your position.

6.6   How do the objectives of accounting aid in determining what is measured, how it is measured and how the measured material is communicated? Use an example to illustrate your answer.

6.7 Several years ago an accounting author contended that it was less important to *tell what had happened* to a firm than to provide information about *what was going to happen* to it.

(a) What limits have accountants traditionally placed on the kinds of economic information that they report about firms?

(b) Do these limitations conflict with legitimate desires of investors for information? Explain.

6.8 Why do accountants often have to make a trade-off between relevance and reliability in their preparation of information for users? Illustrate your answer with examples.

6.9 Briefly explain the meaning of each of the following accounting concepts and give at least one illustration of the effect of each concept on accounting practice.

(a) the accounting entity

(b) continuity and the accounting period

(c) capital maintenance

6.10 Identify the problems that arise from using the dollar as the measurement unit for recording transactions and indicate how these problems might be overcome.

6.11 What do accountants mean when they refer to objective information? Provide examples of information that is objective and information that is not objective.

6.12 Explain the concepts of *profit* and *financial position* used in historical cost accounting.

6.13 Explain the nature and measurement of assets and expenses under the historical cost system of accounting and illustrate your discussion by reference to particular items appearing in accounting reports.

6.14 'All assets are merely long-term expenses.' Discuss.

6.15 Explain the statement 'Expenses are expired assets'. Is this always the case?

6.16 Prepaid insurance and inventory are both classified as unexpired costs in the historical cost accounting system:

(a) What are the basic similarities between these items?

(b) What is the primary dissimilarity in an accounting sense?

 Problems

6.17 *Identifying accounting transactions*

Indicate which of the following are transactions that will be entered in the ledger and explain each answer.

(a) Inventory is purchased by a hardware store.

(b) The store manager hires a new clerk.

(c) The store delivers an order to a customer, who is purchasing the goods on credit.

(d) A customer looks at several items in the store and indicates that they intend to return tomorrow to buy one of them.

(e) The store manager calls the local newspaper and reserves a full-page advertising space in next week's Sunday edition.

(f) A week after the advertisement appears, an invoice is received for it from the newspaper.

(g) The hardware store manager tells two employees to paint the store, using paint from the store shelves that was originally intended to be sold to customers.

6.18 *Identifying assets and expenses*

The following items appear in the trial balance of Wondering Ltd at 31 December 20X1.

(a) In each case, determine whether the item at that date is an asset or an expense.
(b) If it is an asset, might it become an expense?
(c) If it is an expense, indicate whether it is a product or a period cost.

1. Stationery on hand.
2. Rent paid for January 20X2.
3. Amount paid for advertising brochures printed in September 20X1 and to be distributed in February 20X2.
4. Equipment that is of no further use to the company, but which may be sold for $1000.
5. Another obsolete piece of equipment that has no resale value.
6. Land on which mining activities are being carried out.
7. An amount paid for the right to use a sporting star's name in support of the company's products in 20X2.

6.19 *Identifying assets*

At the beginning of 20X1, XLX Ltd spent $750 000 purchasing specialised equipment for manufacturing and packaging HiPro, a high-protein snack food. The firm expected this equipment to be useful for 10 years and valueless thereafter. Simultaneously, the firm spent $1 000 000 on initial advertising for the product, expecting this campaign to have half of its impact in 20X1 and the remainder in 20X2 and 20X3.

Sales of HiPro were disastrous during 20X1. By the end of 20X1 the firm had stopped production of the product and was negotiating to sell its remaining inventories at whatever price it could obtain.

Under the historical cost accounting system, what economic resources do you think the firm has at the end of 20X1? (*Note:* A valuation of those resources is not required.)

6.20 *Applying assumptions and principles*

(a) When inventory that had cost $100 is sold for $300 cash, only $200 may be distributed to investors as a dividend despite the fact that the company now has $300 more in cash. Explain why.
(b) Each of the following events would be difficult to analyse without some basic assumptions and principles. Identify the relevant concept in each case and state how the event would be reported for the year ended 31 December 20X1.

(i) The owner has invented new technology that she believes is worth $15 million. She wishes to include it among the assets.
(ii) The business received $20 000 from a customer for a sale made in 20X0.
(iii) A company has been given free access to river water.

6.21   *Applying assumptions and principles*

The assumptions of the historical cost system determine the impact of transactions and events on the accounting equation that concern the firm. For each of the following:

(a) State the impact of the event on the accounting equation for the year ending 30 June 20X1.

(b) Identify the assumption that has most directly influenced your decision.

KWONG TRADING LTD

(i)   Paid $100 000 to cover rent for July and August 20X1.

(ii) Purchased inventory for $2000 on 1 June 20X1. The goods purchased were still on hand at 30 June 20X1, but to replace the inventory would now cost 10 per cent more.

(iii) The company uses a section of the Haw Haw River to test out boats that it sells and believes that this is worth $800 000 per year in savings on warranty costs.

SYDNEY WHOLESALERS LTD

The company is placed in receivership. The official receiver estimates that the 'forced sale' value of the company's assets is $200 000 below their historical cost book value.

ASHTOWN LTD

(i)   On 2 July 20X1 the company sold goods which cost $300 for $400 cash.

(ii) The managing director, who owns 5 per cent of Ashtown Ltd's shares, borrowed $3000 from the company.

(iii) The financial controller estimates that the company has self-developed goodwill that must be worth at least $500 000 to the company.

(iv) The company has equipment that cost $80 000 but which is no longer usable and has no resale value.

6.22   *Applying assumptions and principles*

Explain why all transactions affecting the profit and loss statement automatically affect the balance sheet, and why the reverse situation does not hold. Ilustrate your answer using the following transactions:

Cash sales	$ 1 000
Credit sales	3 000
Purchases on credit	2 500
Wages paid	800
Purchase of land on credit	10 000
Payment of creditors	6 000
Cash collected from debtors	5 000
Withdrawals	1 000

6.23   *Capital maintenance and profit*

CASE A—LAWRANCE LTD

Using the following data for Lawrance Ltd, show how, under the historical cost accounting system, *profit is the increase in the net assets over a period*, using both the events approach and the stock approach to profit calculation:

Sales of inventory for cash	$140 000
Cost price of goods sold	100 000
Wages paid	18 000
Rates paid	1 000
Purchases of merchandise on credit	80 000
Cash paid to creditors	76 000

There were no other operating items during the period. The balance sheet *at the beginning of the period* was:

Cash	$ 31 000	Creditors	$ 25 000
Inventories	34 000	Capital	115 000
Buildings	75 000		
Total assets	**$140 000**	**Total funds**	**$140 000**

What is the profit for the period and the capital maintenance amount? Prepare a profit and loss statement and an end-of-period balance sheet as part of your answer.

CASE B—MACALISTER LTD

Lin Tan owns 5 per cent of the issued shares of MacAlister Ltd. When the company released its results for the year ending 31 December 20X1, Lin Tan was holidaying on Paradise Island. Lin Tan was very keen to learn the company's profit for 20X1, but was only able to obtain the following information from the rather limited communications facilities available on the island:

	30 Dec. 20X0	30 Dec. 20X1
Sales	$120 000	$130 000
Total assets	240 000	250 000
Total liabilities	190 000	160 000

Lin Tan received a cash dividend of $1000 during June 20X1 and during November 20X1 the company's shareholders contributed an additional $20 000 (in proportion to their previous holdings) in cash.

(a) What *profit* did MacAlister Ltd earn during the year ending 31 December 20X1?
(b) What was the amount of the *total expenses* incurred during the same period?

Case studies

6.24 *Profit measurement and performance*

As a financial adviser you have a client who owns 10 per cent of the shares in Universal Products Ltd. The client is quite happy with the company, as '*their assets keep growing, they always pay a good dividend and they don't ask the shareholders for much*'. On request, your client provides you with the following information about Universal Products Ltd:

	Dec. 20X1	Dec. 20X2	Dec. 20X3
Total assets	$260 000	$270 000	$290 000
Total liabilities	160 000	170 000	185 000

Your client received a cash dividend of $1000 in 20X2 and in 20X3. In 20X3 Universal Products Ltd's shareholders contributed an additional $8000 (in proportion to their previous share holdings) in cash.

Required

Advise your client about his assessment of the company.

6.25 *Profit measurement*

You have a 20 per cent interest in Lazar Lights Ltd and are re-evaluating your investment. Unfortunately, you have lost all but the following data:

	20X1	20X2
Sales	$130 000	$142 000
Total assets	260 000	276 000
Total liabilities	180 000	160 000

Sales are the only form of revenue for Lazar Lights Ltd.

Required

(a) Assuming that there were no dividends paid and no contributions made by shareholders to the company during 20X2, calculate the company's 20X2 profit figure.

(b) Assuming that there were no dividends paid, but that the company's shareholders contributed an additional $14 000 (in proportion to their previous shareholdings) in cash during 20X2, what would be the company's net profit for 20X2?

(c) Assume the same facts as in (b), except that you now recall that you received a cash dividend of $3000 during 20X2. What would be the 20X2 profit for the corporation now?

(d) Using the conventional accounting profit figure derived in (c), what would be Lazar Lights Ltd's total expenses for 20X2?

(e) You suspect that the sales figure given for 20X2 is wrong. You are also satisfied that the figure for profit that you derived in (c) is correct. If the total expenses incurred by Lazar Lights Ltd for 20X2 were $100 000, what should the sales figure have been?

6.26 *When is an expense an asset?*

Shedding light on tooling costs

A recent research note from UBS throws some interesting light on how Mayflower, the engineering group, accounts for tooling.

Normally, the up-front cost involved in the design and production of an automotive part is invoiced to the customer as incurred. This cost will include engineering design work and the purchase of equipment and tooling, such as press dies. Mayflower usually passes all such costs through its p&l account.

But it makes exceptions in the case of the MGF and Mercedes M-class contracts, where the recovery of tooling costs is undertaken via the balance sheet rather than the p&l account.

The MGF contract was awarded to Mayflower by Rover when it was owned by British Aerospace. At the time, Rover was under tight cash limits, so the agreement was that Mayflower would fund the upfront costs of £28.4m, but would recover these costs from Rover over a contracted volume. Mayflower accounted for these costs as long-term work in progress, making them visible as a separate item in the balance sheet.

SCSM had agreed to a similar contract with Mercedes for the M-class sport utility and had chosen the same accounting treatment. When Mayflower acquired SCSM, it simply merged the MGF and M-class long-term work in progress into one item.

UBS says that probably the best way to think of long-term work in progress is that Mayflower will receive £20m over the next 18 to 24 months from Rover and Mercedes in addition to reported revenues, as the work in progress reduces against the agreed production volumes.

Mayflower discloses movements in long-term work in progress in its annual report, while UBS includes it as a separate item in its cash flow forecasts.

Accountancy (International Edition), November 1997, p. 78

Required

(a) Which assumptions or principles of the historical cost accounting system are illustrated in this newspaper article?

(b) Do you agree with how Mayflower Ltd reported the normal tooling costs? Justify your answer.

(c) Do you agree with how Mayflower Ltd reported the MGF and Mercedes tooling costs? Justify your answer.

6.27 *Profit measurement—a challenging problem*

K. T. Lowe had the following assets and liabilities at 1 July 20X2:

Sundry debtors	$ 16 000
Stock on hand	34 000
Business premises and fittings	140 000
Home and furnishings	98 000
Bank overdraft	15 000
Sundry creditors	19 200
Mortgage on the house	40 000

During the next three years Lowe's profits from trading (their only source of income) were reported as follows:

20X2–X3	$19 380
20X3–X4	28 960
20X4–X5	27 300

By 30 June 20X5 Lowe's position had changed in the following manner:

- Sundry debtors were $14 400.
- Stock on hand was $35 800.
- Business premises had been extended at a cost of $32 200.
- Cash at bank was $10 480.
- Sundry creditors were owed $12 800.
- The mortgage on the house had been reduced to $24 000.

In answer to your questions, Lowe informs you that a legacy of $24 000 was received in 20X3 and that their personal expenditure had been somewhere between $1200 and $1400 per month.

Required

Do you think that Lowe's disclosed profit for the last three years is an accurate assessment? Explain your answer.

CHAPTER 7
End of period adjustments

Introduction

In earlier chapters, the recording process has been simplified by ignoring the problems of transactions that affect more than one accounting period. With the framework established in Chapter 6, it should now be clear that revenue and expense transactions often need to be apportioned over more than one period.

These types of transactions require adjustment at each period end to ensure that profit is measured in accordance with the principles established in Chapter 6, and that the balance sheet reflects faithfully the assets and equities of the entity at that date.

Adjusting entries

Adjusting entries are required to enable period reports to be prepared in accordance with the *accounting period concept*, which states that the life of an entity is broken up into periods for the purposes of measurement and reporting. Transactions may cross these finite periods and therefore must be adjusted so that only the relevant portion is recorded as revenue or an expense in the profit and loss statement.

The accrual accounting system

Expenses and revenues need not involve cash in the current period. An expense arises when resources acquired through an external transaction have been consumed. Expenses do not need to be paid for in the period in which they appear in the profit and loss statement. They may have been paid in a past period (wages in advance) or they may be payable in some future period (wages owing).

Wages incurred during the current period are expenses whether they are paid or not, because the benefit of the wages was gained during this period. Conversely, an amount paid this period for the next period's rent is not an expense, because the benefit from the rent payment will be gained in the next period.

Similarly, revenue is recognised when it is earned and can be measured reliably rather than simply when the cash has been received. Thus, a credit sale in March for which payment is received in June is regarded as revenue in March and not June.

As expenses differ from cash paid for resources and as revenues differ from cash received from customers, the resulting system of accounting is known as the *accrual accounting* system. 'Accrue' means to increase by growth or addition. Wages accrued, for example, are wages owing at the end of the period, indicating that the debt has been allowed to grow.

This system may be contrasted with a *cash accounting* system where profit (or the increase in cash) is measured as the difference between cash received and cash paid. This system was once used in government entities, but in recent times accrual accounting has gained favour as more accurately reflecting the operating activities of an entity.

Comparison of cash and accrual accounting systems

	PROFIT AND LOSS STATEMENT for October			
Transactions	Accrual accounting system		Cash accounting system	
	Revenue	Expense	(Receipts)	(Payments)
1. October cash sales	✓		✓	
2. October credit sales	✓		✗	
3. Cash from September credit sales	✗		✓	
4. Paid September wages		✗		✓
5. Paid October wages		✓		✓
6. October wages owing at month end		✓		✗
7. Paid September rent		✗		✓
8. Paid October rent		✓		✓
9. Pre-paid November rent		✗		✓

It can be seen that the differences between the *accrual accounting* and the *cash account-ing* systems lie in the timing of the recognition of revenue (instead of cash receipts) and expenses (instead of cash payments). However, the accrual accounting system is widely believed to provide a more relevant measure of profit and financial position for the purposes of making economic decisions and accountability assessments by users.

The principles of accrual accounting will now be applied to the various entries within the accounting system to adjust transactions.

Recording adjustments

In earlier chapters it was shown how the recording cycle commences with the following steps:

1. journal entries
2. ledger entries
3. trial balance

At each period end the accountant scrutinises the records and the situation as revealed by the trial balance and determines which accounts require adjustment. The recording process is then expanded to:

4. adjustments
5. adjusted trial balance
6. closing entries
7. financial statements

The following analysis outlines the seven major adjustments and the procedures to be followed.

Adjustment 1: Expenses that have been paid but not incurred

A prepayment arises whenever a payment is made in the current period for items that will benefit a future period. Prepayments include rent and wages paid in advance. In a sense, inventory on hand and productive assets are also prepayments of future expenses, although these items are large and are treated as separate categories. The term 'prepayments' normally refers to items the benefits of which are expected to expire within the next period.

Example: *Prepayments*

The following information concerns insurance paid by a company on its buildings. The company's year ends on 31 December.

20X1	January 1	Paid 18 months premium	$3600
20X2	June 30	Paid 12 months premium	$3200

If the benefits from insurance are expected to expire evenly over time, then the insurance expense for 20X1 should be two-thirds of $3600, or $2400. The $1200 carried forward to 20X2 becomes part of the expense for 20X2, together with half of the amount paid on 30 June 20X2, that is, $1600. The total expense for 20X2 will therefore be:

Insurance prepaid from 20X1	$1200
plus Insurance paid in 20X2	3200
	4400
less Insurance prepaid at the end of 20X2	1600
Insurance expense for 20X2	$2800

The ledger entries to make these adjustments appear on pages 199–200. The explanation will be assisted by showing the entries first in general journal form.

JOURNAL ENTRIES				
			Debit	Credit
20X1				
1.	Jan. 1	Insurance expense	3600	
		Cash		3600
		(Payment of insurance)		
2.	Dec. 31	Prepaid insurance (asset)	1200	
		Insurance expense		1200
		(Adjusting entry for 6 months insurance prepaid)		
3.	Dec. 31	Profit and loss summary	2400	
		Insurance expense		2400
		(Closing entry)		
20X2				
4.	Jan. 1	Insurance expense	1200	
		Prepaid insurance (asset)		1200
		(Reversal of adjustment)		

continues

JOURNAL ENTRIES

20X2			Debit	Credit
5.	June 30	Insurance expense	3200	
		Cash		3200
		(Payment of insurance)		
6.	Dec. 31	Prepaid insurance (asset)	1600	
		Insurance expense		1600
		(Adjusting entry)		
7.	Dec. 31	Profit and loss summary	2800	
		Insurance expense		2800
		(Closing entry)		
20X3				
8.	Jan. 1	Insurance expense	1600	
		Prepaid insurance (asset)		1600
		(Reversing entry)		

This example demonstrates how the adjusting entries (numbers 2 and 6) ensure that the unused portion of the insurance payment is transferred to the asset account for prepaid insurance, leaving the remainder in the insurance expense to reflect the expense for the year. This amount is then transferred to the profit and loss account along with the revenue accounts and all other expense accounts as part of the closing process, as discussed in Chapter 6.

The reversing entries (4 and 8) are made on the first day of each new year. They are a method of ensuring that the prepayment brought forward from the previous year becomes an expense in the current year.

Unused stocks of stationery, cleaning supplies and advertising brochures are also a form of prepayment and may be treated similarly. Payments are entered into an expense account and, at the end of the year, any unused supplies are transferred from the expense account to an asset such as stationery on hand.

LEDGER ACCOUNTS

		Debit	Credit	Balance
Assets	**Cash**			
20X1				
Jan. 1	Insurance expense		3600	
20X2				
June 30	Insurance expense		3200	
	Prepaid insurance			
20X1				
Dec. 31	Insurance expense	1200		1200 DR
20X2				
Jan. 1	Insurance expense		1200	–
Dec. 31	Insurance expense	1600		1600 DR
20X3				
Jan. 1	Insurance expense		1600	–

continues

LEDGER ACCOUNTS

		Debit	Credit	Balance
Owners' equity	**Insurance expense**			
20X1				
Jan. 1	Cash	3600		3600 DR
Dec. 31	Prepaid insurance		1200	2400 DR
Dec. 31	Profit and loss summary		2400	–
20X2				
Jan. 1	Prepaid insurance	1200		1200 DR
June 30	Cash	3200		4400 DR
Dec. 31	Prepaid insurance		1600	2800 DR
Dec. 31	Profit and loss summary		2800	–
20X3				
Jan. 1	Prepaid insurance	1600		1600 DR
	Profit and loss summary			
20X1				
Dec. 31	Insurance expense	2400		
20X2				
Dec. 31	Insurance expense	2800		

There are alternative ways of recording the events relating to prepayments. For example, in the method shown below, the insurance payment is debited directly to the asset account and is adjusted at year end to show the part that has been treated as an expense.

			Debit	Credit
20X1				
1.	Jan. 1	Prepaid insurance (asset)	3600	
		Cash		3600
2.	Dec. 31	Insurance expense	2400	
		Prepaid insurance		2400
		(Adjusting entry for 1 year's insurance expense)		
3.	Dec. 31	Profit and loss summary	2400	
		Insurance expense		2400
20X2				
4.	Jan. 1	No entry required		
5.	June 30	Prepaid insurance (asset)	3200	
		Cash		3200
6.	Dec. 31	Insurance expense	2800	
		Prepaid insurance (asset)		2800
		(Adjusting entry for 1 year's insurance expense)		
7.	Dec. 31	Profit and loss summary	2800	
		Insurance expense		2800
		(Closing entry)		
20X3				
8.	Jan. 1	No entry required		

It can be seen that both the expense method and the asset method result in the same amounts being reported in the profit and loss statement and in the balance sheet.

Adjustment 2: Expenses incurred but not paid

Accrued expenses are the opposite of prepayments. They represent expenses incurred during the current period which have not yet been paid. These include wages owing and rent unpaid. An adjusting entry is made to record the amounts owing in a liability account. This account is often called 'accrued expenses'.

Example: *Accrued expenses*

The following information concerns wages paid by a company. The company balances its accounts on 31 December.

20X1	Wages paid during the year	$24 000
	Wages owing at 31 December	3 000
20X2	Wages paid during the year	35 000
	Wages owing at 31 December	8 000

The wages expense consists of the total cost of wages related to the current year, whether paid or not. The expense for 20X1 is therefore $27 000. In calculating the expense for 20X2, it is necessary to adjust the wages paid in 20X2 to take account of the payment of $3000 that had been included as an expense in 20X1. The calculation is:

Wages paid in 20X2	$35 000
less Wages owing from 20X1	3 000
Wages paid for 20X2	32 000
plus Wages owing at 31 December 20X2	8 000
Wages expense for 20X2	$40 000

These adjustments are recorded in the journal and the ledger as shown on the following pages.

JOURNAL ENTRIES FOR ACCRUED WAGES			
20X1		*Debit*	*Credit*
1. During year	Wages expense	24 000	
	Cash		24 000
	(Wages paid)		
2. Dec. 31	Wages expense	3 000	
	Accrued expenses		3 000
	(Adjusting entry)		
3. Dec. 31	Profit and loss summary	27 000	
	Wages expense		27 000
	(Closing entry)		
20X2			
4. Jan. 1	Accrued expenses	3 000	
	Wages expense		3 000
	(Reversing entry)		

continues

JOURNAL ENTRIES FOR ACCRUED WAGES

20X2

5.	During year	Wages expense	35 000	
		Cash		35 000
		(Wages paid)		
6.	Dec. 31	Wages expense	8 000	
		Accrued expenses		8 000
		(Adjusting entry)		
7.	Dec. 31	Profit and loss summary	40 000	
		Wages expense		40 000
		(Closing entry)		

20X3

8.	Jan. 1	Accrued expenses	8 000	
		Wages expense		8 000
		(Reversing entry)		

LEDGER ACCOUNTS: ACCRUED WAGES

		Debit	Credit	Balance
Assets	**Cash**			
20X1				
During year	Wages expenses		24 000	
20X2				
During year	Wages expenses		35 000	
Liabilities	**Accrued expenses**			
20X1				
Dec. 31	Wages expenses		3 000	3 000 CR
20X2				
Jan. 1	Wages expenses	3 000		–
Dec. 31	Wages expenses		8 000	8 000 CR
20X3				
Jan. 1	Wages expenses	8 000		–
Owners' equity	**Wages expense**			
20X1				
During year	Cash	24 000		24 000 DR
Dec. 31	Accrued expenses	3 000		27 000 DR
	Profit and loss summary		27 000	–
20X2				
Jan. 1	Accrued expenses		3 000	3 000 CR
During year	Cash	35 000		32 000 DR
Dec. 31	Accrued expenses	8 000		40 000 DR
	Profit and loss summary		40 000	–
20X3				
Jan. 1	Accrued expenses		8 000	8 000 CR

continues

LEDGER ACCOUNTS: ACCRUED WAGES			
	Debit	Credit	Balance
Profit and loss summary			
20X1			
Dec. 31 Wages expense	27 000		
20X2			
Dec. 31 Wages expense	40 000		

An alternative to reversing the adjusting entry on 1 January 20X1 is to debit $3000 of the wages paid during 20X2 to the wages payable account to write off the liability. However, human memory being unreliable, it is safer to adopt the method illustrated here. It permits all wages paid to be debited to wages expense, since the reversal entry ensures the automatic deduction from that amount of wages owing at the beginning of the period.

Adjustment 3: Revenues that have been received but not earned

It is possible to receive an amount prior to providing a service or selling a product. When cash is received in advance by the business, the accountant has to decide whether to record the cash initially as revenue or as a liability. If the revenues received in advance are recorded initially as a liability, this will be adjusted when it is deemed that the amount has been earned.

Example

On 1 May the entity received $2000 in advance for services to be rendered. By 30 June 20 per cent of the services have been performed.

May 1	Cash	$2000	
	Unearned service revenue		$2000

(This is not an adjusting entry—it is simply the recording of the original transaction.)

June 30	Unearned service revenue	$400	
	Service revenue		$400
	(Adjusting entry)		

Note

The service revenue account has risen by 20 per cent and the liability has fallen by 20 per cent to reflect the recognition of revenue and the consequential reduction in the liability.

Case 7.1 Revenue received in advance

The Auburn Valley Recreation Club (AVRC) has experienced a year of declining membership following a population drift in the district to larger regional cities.

The 20X1/X2 Annual Report of the AVRC showed in the comparative balance sheet as at 30 September 20X1 the item 'subscriptions paid in advance' of $22 500 as a component of total members' equity. An accounting policy note stated the following change in accounting policy for the year ended 30 September 20X2 relating to the treatment of members' subscriptions:

> All subscriptions are included in revenue wholly in the period of receipt. Previously, subscriptions paid annually were allocated to the period to which they related.

There was no amount shown for 'subscriptions paid in advance' in the balance sheet as at 30 September 20X2.

The 'Accounting Policies' note in the Annual Report indicated that the 'accounts are prepared under the historical cost convention and are in accordance with the accounting standards issued by the professional accounting bodies'.

Using the information discussed in the text:

(a) Outline the commonly accepted criteria for the recognition of revenue.
(b) Critically evaluate the revenue recognition accounting policies of AVRC as outlined.
(c) Prepare a draft letter to the Secretary of the AVRC giving your views on the accounting policy change which occurred for the year ended 30 September 20X2.

The alternative method of recording revenue received in advance is to record it initially as revenue and make an adjustment at year end to record the amount that still remains unearned.

The journal entries relating to this method are shown below.

May 1	Cash	2000	
	Service revenue		2000
June 30	Service revenue	1600	
	Unearned service revenue		1600
	(Adjusting entry)		

Note

The service revenue has fallen by 80 per cent and the liability has risen by 80 per cent to reflect the recognition of the liability and the consequential reduction in the revenue.

Adjustment 4: Revenues that have been earned but not received

At the period end it is possible to have provided services or sold goods and be awaiting payment. In this circumstance revenue is recognised immediately because it has been earned.

Example

Provided services on credit for $3000 as yet unrecorded.

June 30 Revenue receivable	$3000	
Service revenue		$3000
(Adjusting entry)		

Note

- Revenue receivable and service revenue have both risen.
- Service revenue has risen because it was *earned*, even though cash has not yet been received (consistent with accrual accounting).

Adjustment 5: Accounting for supplies

During a typical year the balance of the supplies account at the end of a period will be different from the balance at the beginning of that period. At year end a stocktake is undertaken to determine the balance of supplies on hand. An adjusting entry is required to reconcile the difference between accounting records and physical supplies on hand.

Example

The supplies inventory had an opening balance of $800. During the year $500 worth of supplies was purchased and at year end $400 worth of supplies remained. Supplies information can be summarised as follows:

Beginning	$ 800
Purchased	500
	1300
Used	?
Remaining	$ 400

From the above analysis, it is obvious that $900 worth of supplies was used for the period.

June 30 Supplies inventory expense	$900	
Supplies inventory		$900
(Adjusting entry)		

Note

- Supplies expense has risen and supplies inventory (assets) has fallen. The asset and expense have an inverse relationship.
- Supplies inventory expense rises because it has been *incurred*; that is, the resource has been consumed (consistent with accrual accounting).

In Chapter 5 it was shown how inventories can be recorded using two different inventory systems: the perpetual and periodic systems. The point was made that the system should be appropriate to the needs of the business. This also applies to stocks of supplies and other consumables which a business might keep on hand. In the example above, the periodic rather than the perpetual method has been demonstrated to show the recording of the adjustment for supplies used.

Adjustment 6: Bad and doubtful debts

Just as expenses need not be paid in the current period, revenue need not be received in cash during the period in which it is recognised in the profit and loss statement. The inevitable consequence is that an overstatement of sales revenue in previous periods will have been recognised should debtors later fail to pay their accounts and be declared bad.

It is desirable to anticipate these bad debts for two reasons. First, in accordance with the matching concept, the bad debts are costs of the period in which the sale was first made. Second, it is desirable to avoid overstating profits and accounts receivable. In several recent cases in Australia, the poor financial state of some companies was concealed from shareholders by a decision not to write off accounts receivable that were bad. Once the extent of uncollectable accounts became known, it was apparent that these companies were faced with major cash flow problems.

To lessen the risk of bad debts credit should be offered to customers only after checking their credit rating with a reputable credit agency or by contacting supplied referees.

In a world of uncertainty it cannot be known what bad debts will result from current sales, but experience will enable a good estimate to be made of the likely percentage of credit sales that will not be paid for. The following example illustrates one means by which an estimate of likely credit losses can be incorporated into the financial statements.

Example: *Anticipation of bad debts*

The credit manager of Never-Never Sales has noticed that some customers are failing to pay their accounts and have even given fictitious names and addresses. Some 5 per cent of sales is lost in this way and it is desired to implement a system that accounts for anticipated bad debts.

Data supplied are as follows:

Relevant balances at 1 January 20X7, the start of a new year:	
Accounts receivable	$30 000
(None are doubtful or bad at this date)	
Transactions to 31 March 20X7	
Sales (all on credit)	
January	10 000
February	14 000
March	12 000
Receipts from accounts receivable	
January	15 000
February	18 000
March	11 600

On 31 March an ageing analysis of accounts receivable revealed that debts totalling $640 were bad and should be written off. Further debts totalling $1400 were considered doubtful and should be provided for. Show the relevant ledger accounts and portions of financial statements at 31 March.

In providing for uncollectable accounts, a percentage of sales is written off tentatively each month in anticipation of eventual losses. The Never-Never Sales company estimates that on average 5 per cent of credit sales become bad debts. Hence, on 31 January 5 per cent of the January credit sales of $10 000, or $500, will be deducted from sales and from accounts receivable by means of the following entry:

Bad and doubtful debts	500	
Allowance for doubtful debts		500
(Routine provision at 5 per cent credit sales)		

The charge for bad and doubtful debts will appear in the January profit and loss statement as a contra account deducted from sales revenue to reveal net sales. The allowance for doubtful debts is also a contra account, which is deducted from accounts receivable to show the amount expected to be realised from accounts owing. It is not appropriate to credit accounts receivable at this stage, because the reduction is only tentative and no specific accounts are being written off.

The percentage procedure facilitates the preparation of monthly interim reports. Each month 5 per cent of credit sales is tentatively written off, so by 31 March the major accounts affected are (entries marked * are explained below and on page 208):

BAD AND DOUBTFUL DEBTS: NEVER-NEVER SALES
PORTION OF GENERAL LEDGER

			Debit	Credit	Balance
Assets		**Accounts receivable**			
Jan.	1	Balance			30 000 DR
	31	Sales revenue	10 000		40 000 DR
		Cash		15 000	25 000 DR
Feb.	28	Sales revenue	14 000		39 000 DR
		Cash		18 000	21 000 DR
Mar.	31	Sales revenue	12 000		33 000 DR
		Cash		11 600	21 400 DR
		*Allow. for doubtful debts		640	20 760 DR
		Allowance for doubtful debts (contra to accounts receivable)			
Jan.	31	Bad and doubtful debts		500	500 CR
Feb.	28	Bad and doubtful debts		700	1 200 CR
Mar.	31	Bad and doubtful debts		600	1 800 CR
		*Accounts receivable	640		1 160 CR
		*Bad and doubtful debts		240	1 400 CR
Owners' equity		**Sales revenue**			
Jan.	31	Accounts receivable		10 000	10 000 CR
Feb.	28	Accounts receivable		14 000	24 000 CR
Mar.	31	Accounts receivable		12 000	36 000 CR
		Bad and doubtful debts			
Jan.	31	Allow. for doubtful debts	500		500 DR
Feb.	28	Allow. for doubtful debts	700		1 200 DR
Mar.	31	Allow. for doubtful debts	600		1 800 DR
		*Allow. for doubtful debts	240		2 040 DR

It is necessary to check periodically on the accuracy of the procedure of estimating uncollectable accounts as a percentage of sales. This is done by direct examination of the debtors accounts, perhaps by an *ageing* procedure, in which the age of an account is determined as the number of months it has been owing. Very old accounts may be regarded as bad, while various percentages will be applied to the schedule of aged accounts to reflect the likely losses within each category. In Never-Never Sales an ageing analysis was conducted on 31 March, and as a result $640 of debts were considered bad and $1400 were considered doubtful. Entries to record these adjustments to the amounts established by the percentage method are then made, beginning with the writing off of bad debts.

Allowance for doubtful debts	640	
Accounts receivable		640
(Writing off of bad debts)		

This entry reduces accounts receivable by transferring $640 from the contra account. It is not necessary to make a further charge against revenue, since this amount forms part of the previous amount provided by means of the monthly percentage charge. The uncollectable accounts were anticipated in this way and the occurrence of a bad debt merely causes a transfer between accounts receivable and its contra account. The net amount for accounts receivable, less the allowance for doubtful debts, will remain unchanged, the reduction in the receivable having been anticipated (see page 209).

The allowance for doubtful debts must now be adjusted to reflect the new estimate of doubtful debts provided by the ageing analysis. After writing off the bad debts, this account has a remaining balance of $1160 (page 209). This balance may be thought of as the amount charged against profits to provide for future bad debts, less amounts actually written off. The unused allowance will rarely agree with the independent estimate of doubtful debts provided by the ageing analysis. In this case the allowance is $1160, whereas the ageing analysis states that it should be $1400. The allowance is brought up to this amount by transferring an additional amount of $240, as follows:

Bad and doubtful debts	240	
Allowance for doubtful debts		240
(Adjustment of provision)		

In this example the allowance account had to be increased. Sometimes the percentage method may produce a balance that is too high and this is corrected by the reverse entry: the allowance for doubtful debts is debited and the bad and doubtful debts account is credited by the amount of the over-provision.

These entries assist in the preparation of interim reports for each month and a report for the quarter (see following). For illustrative purposes, the interim reports for March were prepared before the ageing analysis, but the quarterly report incorporates the adjustments.

PORTIONS OF FINANCIAL STATEMENTS OF NEVER-NEVER SALES PROFIT AND LOSS STATEMENT				
	Jan.	Feb.	Mar. (1)	Qtr. (2)
	$	$	$	$
Sales revenue	10 000	14 000	12 000	36 000
less Bad and doubtful debts	500	700	600	2 040
Net sales	9 500	13 300	11 400	33 960

continues

PORTIONS OF FINANCIAL STATEMENTS OF NEVER-NEVER SALES				
	Jan.	Feb.	Mar. (1)	Qtr. (2)
	$	$	$	$
Balance sheets				
Assets				
Accounts receivable	25 000	21 000	21 400	20 760
less Allowance doubtful debts	500	1 200	1 800	1 400
	24 500	19 800	19 600	19 360

(1) Before adjustments resulting from ageing analysis.

(2) After adjustments.

Adjustment 7: Depreciation

IAS 4, 'Depreciation' (para. 4), defines depreciation as a process of allocation of the cost of an asset over its estimated useful life. Thus depreciation is the term used to write off productive assets such as equipment over their active lives.

Assets have been defined as economic resources, consisting of a bundle of future benefits. As the benefits are used up, the assets expire and become expenses. The accounting period concept requires this expiry to be recognised each period by an allocation of the cost of the asset. The cost is allocated according to the benefits given by the asset in each period, in accordance with the matching concept.

A rational basis of allocation

A means must be found of allocating the cost of a wasting asset over its life. In the case of prepaid rent, the basis is time alone. If rent of $2400 is prepaid for the next 12 months, it is presumed that a fair allocation of the cost is $200 per month. The rent has 12 'bundles of service' to deliver, and one bundle is delivered each month.

Matching becomes more difficult with productive assets. Equipment may not distribute its benefits evenly over time. If equipment is more productive early in its life and gradually becomes less useful, it may be argued that the earlier periods should bear a greater proportion of the costs because they receive more of the benefits from the equipment.

It would distort the trend in profits if the whole cost were written off at once. Also, in accordance with the definition of an asset, while there is future value in use remaining in the equipment, an asset should be recognised for the unused services. Under the continuity assumption, the venture is assumed to continue and the unexpired portion of the asset's cost therefore may be carried forward to be charged against income in future periods. Within the historical cost accounting system, then, depreciation may be defined as: *the process of allocating the cost of an asset, less its estimated residual value, over its life in accordance with benefits derived.*

The cost of the asset will include any costs of installation required to place the asset in a condition required for use. The amount to be written off is reduced by any residual value expected to be recovered at the end of the asset's life.

Although residual value is often not material and in practice is frequently ignored the concept should nonetheless be understood.

Depreciation methods

The following example will be used throughout this discussion.

Example: *Depreciation*

On 1 January 20X1 equipment was purchased for $36 000. It was expected to have a three-year life and a residual value of $6000.

Since $6000 is expected to be recovered at the end of the equipment's life, $30 000 must be written off over the three years.

To achieve matching, some assumptions must be made about the future pattern of benefits.

1. *Straight-line method*

   If it is assumed that the asset will be equally beneficial each year, then the $30 000 will be written off as $10 000 depreciation each year. The formula to calculate depreciation under this straight-line method is:

   $$\text{Annual depreciation} = \frac{\text{cost} - \text{residual value}}{\text{years}}$$

   $$= \frac{36\,000 - 6\,000}{3}$$

   $$= \$10\,000$$

   This is a very popular method of depreciation as many assets are believed to be equally useful each year. Straight-line depreciation is also used when it is impossible to estimate the pattern of benefits and the equal benefits assumption is believed to be as sound as any other.

   In practice, residual value is often ignored and the depreciation rate set as a fixed percentage of the original cost to be written off each year.

2. *Reducing-balance method*

   Some assets are of greatest benefit in their early years after which they decline steadily in productivity. A method which allocates depreciation according to this benefit pattern is known as the declining-balance or reducing-balance method.

   The declining charge is achieved by writing off a set percentage of the written-down or 'book' value (cost less accumulated depreciation) each year. The appropriate percentage is arrived at by the following formula:

   $$\text{Depreciation (\%)} = 1 - \sqrt[n]{\frac{\text{residual value}}{\text{cost}}}$$

   $$= 1 - \sqrt[3]{\frac{6\,000}{36\,000}}$$

   $$= 45\% \text{ (approximately)}$$

Applying this to the problem, the depreciation is:

$36 000	Opening book value
16 200	Depreciation year 1 (45%)
19 800	Book value beginning year 2
8 910	Depreciation year 2
10 890	Book value beginning year 3
4 900	Depreciation year 3
5 990	Book value end year 3

This method produces a reducing charge each year until the estimated residual value (or nearly so) is reached at the end of the third year. The method is often favoured for taxation since it writes off a heavy charge in the early years, securing higher taxation savings in those years which may be reinvested to earn interest. For financial reporting purposes, its use must be justified in terms of the pattern of service benefits from an asset and many assets would fit the pattern of declining benefits.

3. *Production-units method*
Sometimes there may be a direct indicator of the use of an asset. An aeroplane may have a projected life measured in flying hours, a vehicle in kilometres and equipment in units produced. Annual depreciation may then be assessed in proportion to 'production units' consumed during the period, compared with the expected lifetime production.

Suppose the equipment in the example is expected to have a lifetime production of 200 000 units. First, a unit depreciation rate will be set:

$$\text{Unit depreciation} = \frac{\text{cost} - \text{residual value}}{\text{lifetime units}}$$

$$= \frac{36\,000 - 6\,000}{200\,000}$$

$$= \$0.15 \text{ per unit}$$

The annual depreciation charge depends on the number of units produced. For example:

Year	Units produced	×	Unit charge	=	Depreciation expense
			$		$
1	50 000	×	0.15	=	7 500
2	125 000	×	0.15	=	18 750
3	25 000	×	0.15	=	3 750
	200 000				30 000

This method is claimed to provide the closest link with the usage of the asset. It relies, however, on the assumption that the unit basis chosen is the best measure of the 'benefits' provided by the asset.

4. *Other methods*
Various other methods are used. The sum-of-the-digits approach allocates the cost as follows. For a three-year life, the sum of the digits is 6 (1 + 2 + 3). With $30 000 to be written off, annual depreciation is:

Year	Proportion	Depreciation amount
1	3/6 × $30 000	$15 000
2	2/6 × $30 000	10 000
3	1/6 × $30 000	5 000
		$30 000

This method may be applied in either direction, depending on whether benefits are assumed to be increasing or decreasing over time.

The availability of a wide variety of depreciation methods attests to the fact that the service lives of depreciable assets exhibit different patterns. A movie film, for example, might experience great popularity, a quick decline, and a later resurgence of interest when it becomes a 'classic'. It is difficult to anticipate such a pattern.

Depreciation methods disclosed by publicly listed companies in 1997 annual reports

The sample of companies shown below indicates that most select the straight-line method of depreciating property, plant and equipment.[1]

Company	Depreciation method
Burns, Philp and Company	Straight-line
Crown Ltd	Straight-line
CSR Ltd	Straight-line
Email Ltd	Straight-line
Fosters Brewing Group Ltd	Reducing-balance and straight-line
Harvey Norman Holdings Ltd	Straight-line
Mayne Nickless Ltd	Straight-line
National Australia Bank	Straight-line
Pacific Dunlop Ltd	Straight-line
Qantas Airways Ltd	Straight-line
Rio Tino Ltd	Units of production and straight-line
South Corp Holdings Ltd	Straight-line
Tabcorp Holdings Ltd	Straight-line
Village Roadshow Ltd	Reducing-balance and straight-line
Woolworths Ltd	Straight-line

Can you suggest a reason why so many public companies use the straight-line method?

Recording depreciation in the ledger

The twofold effect of depreciation is to reduce the asset and to reduce the owners' equity through an expense for depreciation. Rather than deduct depreciation from the asset itself, a contra account known as accumulated depreciation is created. In this way, the original cost of the asset is preserved in the accounts.

---

[1] This was also reported in G. Peirson and A. Ramsay 'Depreciation of Non-Current Assets', Discussion Paper No. 20, Australian Accounting Research Foundation, Melbourne, 1994.

The relevant entries are shown below, using the production-units method for illustration. The entry for 20X3 is:

20X3			
Dec. 31	Depreciation expense	3750	
	Accumulated depreciation—equipment		3750
	(Annual depreciation charge)		

The following are the ledger entries and the relevant portions of the balance sheet.

DEPRECIATION
EXTRACT FROM GENERAL LEDGER

			Debit	Credit	Balance
Assets		**Equipment**			
20X1	June 1	Cash	36 000		36 000 DR
		Accumulated depreciation: equipment			
20X1	Dec. 31	Depreciation expense		7 500	7 500 CR
20X2	Dec. 31	Depreciation expense		18 750	26 250 CR
20X3	Dec. 31	Depreciation expense		3 750	30 000 CR
Owners' equity		**Depreciation**			
20X1	Dec. 31	Accumulated depreciation	7 500		7 500 DR
		Profit and loss summary		7 500	–
20X2	Dec. 31	Accumulated depreciation	18 750		18 750 DR
		Profit and loss summary		18 750	–
20X3	Dec. 31	Accumulated depreciation	3 750		3 750 DR
		Profit and loss summary		3 750	–

EXTRACTS FROM FINANCIAL STATEMENTS
PROFIT AND LOSS

		20X1	20X2	20X3
Depreciation expense		$ 7 500	$18 750	$ 3 750
Assets	**Balance sheet**			
Equipment		36 000	36 000	36 000
less Accumulated depreciation		7 500	26 250	30 000
		$28 500	$ 9 750	$ 6 000

At the end of each year the depreciation expense account is transferred to the profit and loss summary account as part of the closing entry process. The accumulated depreciation account continues to grow until it reaches $30 000 at the end of 20X3, which is the total amount to be written off. In the balance sheet the accumulated depreciation is offset against the asset to reveal the written-down value, or the unexpired cost of the asset. This is often referred to as the 'book value'. Note that this term emphasises the value at which the asset is shown in the books, thereby drawing attention to the fact that this is not necessarily the market value.

Sale of an asset

Suppose the equipment in the previous example is sold on 1 January 20X4 for $4700 cash. To record the disposal it is useful to open a sale of equipment account.

Cash at bank	4 700	
Sale of equipment		4 700
(Proceeds from the sale)		

Then the following entries would be made:

Sale of equipment	36 000	
Equipment		36 000
(Transfer of the cost of the equipment)		

Accumulated depreciation: equipment	30 000	
Sale of equipment		30 000
(Transfer of the accumulated depreciation)		

Loss on sale of equipment	1 300	
Sale of equipment		1 300
(Recording the loss on sale)		

Alternatively the entries could be combined. The first entry shows the transfer of the original cost of the equipment from the equipment account and the accumulated depreciation on that equipment from the accumulated depreciation account, as follows:

Accumulated depreciation: equipment	30 000	
Sale of equipment	6 000	
Equipment		36 000
(Transfer of equipment and accumulated depreciation)		

This reveals the written-down cost of $6000. Once the proceeds of $4700 are entered, as shown below, a shortfall of $1300 is revealed, which becomes a loss on sale.

Cash at bank	4 700	
Loss on sale of equipment	1 300	
Sale of equipment		6 000
(Recording of proceeds and loss)		

Rarely will the estimated residual value equal the final proceeds of sale. A loss on sale is therefore equivalent to an additional depreciation charge not anticipated at the time of purchase. Conversely, a gain on sale would be a reversal of depreciation charges that were too high.

Gains and losses on sale appear in the profit and loss statement.

SALE OF DEPRECIATING ASSET			
EXTRACT FROM GENERAL LEDGER			
Assets	**Equipment**		
20X4 Jan. 1 Balance			36 000 DR
Sale of equipment		36 000	–
Accumulated depreciation: Equipment			
20X4 Jan. 1 Balance			30 000 CR
Sale of equipment		30 000	–

Owners' equity	**Sale of equipment**		
20X4 Jan. 1 Equipment	36 000		36 000 DR
Accumulated depreciation		30000	6 000 DR
Cash at bank		4700	1 300 DR
Loss on sale		1300	–
Loss on sale of equipment			
20X4 Jan. 1 Sale of equipment	1 300		1 300 DR
Dec. 31 Profit and loss summary		1300	–

Reporting of sales of assets

Note that under this approach the proceeds from the sale of non-current assets will not appear as an item in the profit and loss statement. This approach complies with the accounting standards AASB 1021 and AAS 4, 'Depreciation of Non-current Assets'. However, the disclosure requirements of AASB 1004 and AAS 15, 'Disclosure of Operating Revenue', suggests that the gross proceeds of the disposal should be displayed under 'other revenue'. In order to comply with both depreciation and disclosure of operating revenue standards, the gross proceeds would have to be shown as a note to the accounts.

Some misconceptions about depreciation

Misunderstandings about what is measured

Not all assets are depreciated. Accounts receivable and land, for example, are usually not wasting assets. Equipment, however, must eventually be replaced, due to wear and tear and obsolescence. These factors reduce the future benefits to be derived, so that the proceeds of sale will normally be below the original cost, creating an expense to be charged over the life of the asset.

In the present example, the difference between cost and estimated residual value is $30 000, and this must be charged against income over the three-year life of the equipment.

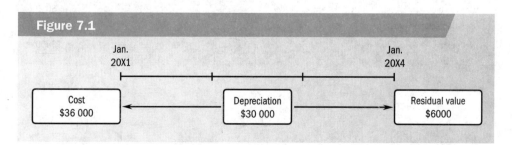

Figure 7.1

Although obsolescence, wear and tear and consequent loss of market value explain the total lifetime depreciation, the allocation of this cost over the three years of the asset's life is not based on annual changes due to these factors. Under the historical cost accounting system, the matching concept causes the allocation to be made each year according to an assumption about the benefits gained from the asset in each period. If the asset is expected to be equally beneficial to operations each year, the depreciation is spread evenly, without regard to annual changes in market value.

Market values fluctuate in response to various external pressures not necessarily related to the use made of the asset by the entity. If the asset were depreciated according to the decline in its market value, the following might result:

Date		Market value	Depreciation for year
1 Jan.	20X1	$36 000	–
1 Jan.	20X2	17 000	$19 000
1 Jan.	20X3	15 000	2 000
1 Jan.	20X4	4 700	10 300

The second year escapes heavy depreciation because the market value was relatively stable. Clearly, market-value depreciation may be incompatible with allocation of the cost according to benefits derived. Historical cost accounting favours the benefit approach and therefore depreciation is not based on the change in market value. It follows that the written-down value of an asset in the balance sheet bears no relationship to its market value except by coincidence.

Of the two sources of value, value in use and value in exchange, the historical cost system gives preference to the former.

Does depreciation provide funds to replace an asset?

The depreciation charge reduces profit and it may be thought that this provides funds for replacement. An example will test this belief.

Example: *Depreciation and replacement*

Regina Winter bought a taxi for $5000. It was expected to have a two-year life, no residual value and to be equally beneficial each year. Hence, depreciation charged was $2500 per year.

In each year, Regina had identical operating results:

Cash fares received	$9000
less Cash expenses	3000
Cash surplus	6000
less Depreciation expense	2500
Net profit	$3500

Each year she withdrew the profit for living costs at the beginning of the new year. Her balance sheets were as shown below.

The effect of depreciation is to recover the cost of the asset from revenue over its life. In this example, the depreciation charge prevents the full $6000 annual cash surplus being withdrawn and the taxi is gradually replaced as an asset by cash. In this way, capital is maintained by the recovery of the outlay.

Nevertheless, depreciation does not necessarily cause the retention of funds to replace the taxi. The price of a new taxi may have risen, so that the $5000 available is insufficient. Furthermore, this is an unusual business. In most businesses, profits retained through depreciation charges are reinvested in other assets or used to repay liabilities. Consequently, many businesses will have no cash available. Finally, the obvious point may be made that the depreciation charge generates nothing and that the funds are actually provided by the revenue.

Despite these facts, it is often claimed that depreciation provides funds to replace an asset. It is more correct to regard depreciation as a charge against profits that maintains capital by recovering the cost of an asset from revenues earned over its effective life.

BALANCE SHEETS: WINTER'S TAXI SERVICE					
	Beg. Year 1	End Year 1	Beg. Year 2	End Year 2	Beg. Year 3
	$	$	$	$	$
Assets					
Cash	–	6000	2500	8500	5000
Taxi	5000	5000	5000	5000	–
less Accum. depn	(–)	(2500)	(2500)	(5000)	(–)
	5000	8500	5000	8500	5000
Liabilities					
Owners' equity					
Capital	5000	5000	5000	5000	5000
plus Profit retained	–	3500	–	3500	–
	5000	8500	5000	8500	5000

Is depreciation an exact calculation?

Few would harbour this misconception. Depreciation charges must be based on three estimates of future events:

1. the life of the asset
2. its residual value
3. the pattern of its benefits

Annual depreciation charges are no better than an estimate. Over the life of the asset, however, the errors will balance out and any residual will be accounted for as a gain or loss on sale. Alternative depreciation methods may affect the trend in profits, but they will not affect profits over the life of the enterprise.

Case 7.2 Some misconceptions

A recently incorporated business, Really Wet Pty Ltd, purchased an organisation called 'Natural Spring Water' on 1 October 20X1 for a consideration of $260 000. Balance date is at 30 June 20X2. Among the assets acquired were the following:

Delivery vehicles	$70 000
Prepaid rent of premises	6 000
Aquawhiz Water Filters	30 000

The accountant of Really Wet, Kim Meng, believes that the delivery vehicle should be written off over three years using the sum-of-the-digits method. The application of the method will result in lower profits in the first years of operation of the business but the profits will thereafter improve. Kim believes this to be the appropriate method as shareholders will not be expecting good operating results in the first few years.

Kim also argues that the water filters, which are hired to customers on a one-year lease, are current assets and therefore should not be depreciated, as nearly 40 per cent of customers exercise the purchase option which is part of the lease agreement.

The prepaid rent relates to the period 1 October 20X1 to 31 July 20X2. Kim believes that the entire amount should be expensed during the current period even though the lease will not have expired. The reason for this opinion is based on the knowledge that Really Wet could not legally recover any of the rent if it decided to vacate the premises at balance date.

(a) What is the purpose of charging depreciation?
(b) Assess the appropriateness of selecting a depreciation method in order to achieve a particular profit.
(c) Distinguish between current and non-current assets and discuss this criterion for deciding whether the water filters should be depreciated.
(d) How much of the prepaid rent should be shown in the profit and loss statement for the period ending 30 June 20X2? Justify your answer.

Adjusting entries and the worksheet

The worksheet is a separate working paper used by the accountant to summarise accounting information. Although it is not a part of the ledger, it serves as a useful summary of post-trial-balance procedures, especially in the preparation of interim reports. Worksheets are also used when preparing final reports. Here, when the worksheet has been completed, adjusting and closing entries must be recorded in the general journal and general ledger prior to drafting the financial statements in proper form.

Example

Sam Danes operates a merchandising enterprise, Sam Danes Products, which adopts a perpetual inventory system. At 30 June 20X6 the following trial balance was presented:

TRIAL BALANCE: SAM DANES PRODUCTS		
as at 30 June 20X6		
Account	Debit	Credit
Cash at bank	$ 15 000	
Accounts receivable	8 400	
Supplies	500	
Prepaid insurance	1 000	
Inventory	12 500	
Motor vehicle	25 000	
Accum. depn—motor vehicle		$ 10 000
Equipment	40 000	
Accum. depn—equipment		20 000
Unearned revenue		400
Accounts payable		2 500
Loan payable		5 000
Capital		30 000
Drawings	3 700	
Sales revenue		110 000
Sales returns	3 100	
Cost of goods sold	48 000	
Insurance expense	4 700	
Wages expense	16 000	
	$177 900	$177 900

The following adjustments need to be taken into account:

(a) A count of inventory on 30 June 20X6 revealed a balance of $12 150 on hand.
(b) A stocktake on 30 June revealed that $100 worth of supplies remained.
(c) Fifty per cent of the prepaid insurance had expired by 30 June.
(d) Wages of $700 were owing at 30 June.
(e) Services provided on the last day of the month totalling $600 had not been received or recorded.
(f) Twenty per cent of unearned revenue had been earned by 30 June.
(g) Depreciation per annum on motor vehicle is $5000.
(h) Depreciation per annum on equipment is $10 000.
(i) Sam Danes estimated that 1 per cent of accounts receivable were doubtful by year end.

These events affect the current period's results, so that adjustments are required to the trial balance figures. At year end these would be made in the formal accounting records, including the ledger. For interim reports, however, no entries are made. A worksheet may be used instead to adjust the trial balance figures, using the adjustments columns. It is sometimes known as the 'twelve-column trial balance'. The worksheet may be completed in this sequence:

1. Enter the account names and trial balance figures.
2. Make adjusting entries in the adjustments column, adding new accounts as required. Note that the adjustments may be classified into numbers consistent with the analysis at the beginning of the chapter, such as:

   (a) and (b) —Adjustment 5
   (c)   —Adjustment 1
   (d)   —Adjustment 2
   (e)   —Adjustment 4
   (f)   —Adjustment 3
   (g) and (h) —Adjustment 7
   (i)   —Adjustment 6

3. Revenues and expenses are recorded in the profit and loss statement columns.
4. Capital, drawings and net profit (transferred from the profit and loss statement) are recorded in the capital statement columns.
5. Assets, liabilities and capital (transferred from the capital statement columns) are recorded in the balance sheet.
6. Financial statements may now be prepared from the worksheet, which is shown on page 221.

Account	Trial balance		Adjustments		Adjusted trial balance		Profit & loss statement		Capital statement		Balance sheet	
	Debit	Credit	Debit	Credit	Debit	Credit	Debit	Credit	Debit	Credit	Debit	Credit
Cash at bank	15 000				15 000						15 000	
Accounts receivable	8 400		600 (e)		9 000						9 000	
Supplies	500			400 (b)	100						100	
Prepaid insurance	1 000			500 (c)	500						500	
Inventory	12 500			350 (a)	12 150						12 150	
Motor vehicle	25 000				25 000						25 000	
Accum. depn–vehicle		10 000		5 000 (g)		15 000						15 000
Equipment	40 000				40 000						40 000	
Accum. depn–equipment		20 000		10 000 (h)		30 000						30 000
Unearned revenue		400	80 (f)			320						320
Accounts payable		2 500				2 500						2 500
Loan payable		5 000				5 000						5 000
Capital		30 000				30 000				30 000		
Drawings	3 700				3 700				3 700			
Sales revenue		11 000		600(e)/80 (f)		110 680		110 680				
Sales returns	3 100				3 100		3 100					
Cost of goods sold	48 000				48 000		48 000					
Insurance expense	4 700		500 (c)		5 200		5 200					
Wages expense	16 000		700 (d)		16 700		16 700					
	177 900	177 900										
Stock loss			350 (a)		350		350					
Supplies expense			400 (b)		400		400					
Wages payable				700 (d)		700						700
Depn expense–vehicle			5 000 (g)		5 000		5 000					
Depn expense–equipment			10 000 (h)		10 000		10 000					
Bad and doubtful debts			90 (i)		90		90					
Allowance for doubtful debts				90 (i)		90						90
			17 720	17 720	194 290	194 290						
Net profit							21 840			21 840		
							110 680	110 680	48 140			
									51 840	51 840		
Capital (end of period)												48 140
											101 750	101 750

PROFIT AND LOSS STATEMENT: SAM DANES PRODUCTS
for year ended 30 June 20X6

Sales revenue		$110 680
less Sales returns		3 100
Net sales		107 580
less Cost of goods sold		48 000
Gross profit		59 580
less Expenses		
Insurance expense	$ 5 200	
Wages expense	16 700	
Stock loss	350	
Supplies expense	400	
Depreciation expense—vehicle	5 000	
Depreciation expense—equipment	10 000	
Bad and doubtful debts	90	37 740
Net profit		$ 21 840

BALANCE SHEET: SAM DANES PRODUCTS
as at 30 June 20X6

Assets	$	$	Liabilities	$	$
Current			Current		
Cash		15 000	Unearned revenue	320	
Accounts receivable	9 000		Wages payable	700	
less Allowance for			Accounts payable	2500	
doubtful debts	90	8 910	Loan payable	5000	8 520
Supplies		100			
Prepaid insurance		500			
Inventory		12 150			
		36 660			
Non-current					
Motor vehicle	25 000		Owners' equity		
less Accum. depn	15 000	10 000	Capital	30 000	
Equipment	40 000		*plus* Net profit	21 840	
less Accum. depn	30 000	10 000		51 840	
		20 000	*less* Drawings	3 700	48 140
		56 660			56 660

In summary, the interim and final reporting processes are compared in the following diagram:

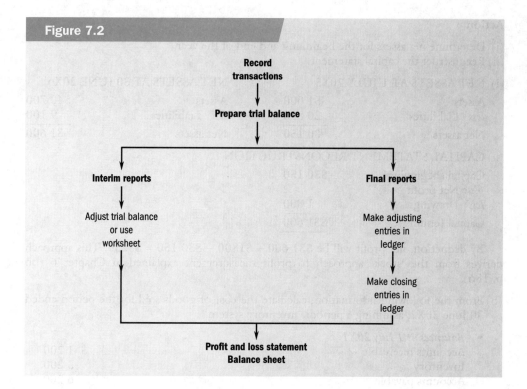

Figure 7.2

Incomplete records

The term 'incomplete records' refers to accounting systems that do not include or maintain an accurate record of events. Incomplete records tend to be evident when personnel are technically inefficient or when records have been lost or destroyed. Analysing incomplete records requires structured and logical thinking. The following examples show where the accountant must rely on logical accounting principles and procedures.

Missing information

Example 1

(a) The assets and liabilities of O. Limpic Trading at 1 July 20X5 were:

Cash	$14 000
Accounts receivable	1 200
Inventory	14 100
Prepaid rent	700
Equipment	21 000
Accounts payable	17 000
Loan payable	3 850

During the year O. Limpic withdrew $1800 for personal use. By 30 June 20X6 the assets and liabilities of O. Limpic Trading were cash $7100, inventory $11 300, prepaid rent $200, equipment $21 000, accounts receivable $1100, accounts payable $6000 and loan payable $3100.

Determine the profit or loss for O. Limpic Trading for the year ended 30 June 20X6. The principle to apply here is:

Net assets equals capital (equivalent here to owners' equity)

Action

(i) Determine net assets for the beginning and end of the year.
(ii) Reconstruct the capital statement.

(i) NET ASSETS AT 1 JULY 20X5   NET ASSETS AT 30 JUNE 20X6

Assets	$51 000	Assets	$40 700
less Liabilities	20 850	*less* Liabilities	9 100
Net assets	30 150	Net assets	31 600

(ii) CAPITAL STATEMENT RECONSTRUCTION

Capital (beginning)	$30 150
plus Net profit	?
less Drawings	1 800
Capital (ending)	$31 600

By deduction, net profit will be $31 600 + $1800 − $30 150 = $3250. This approach derives from the 'stock' approach to profit measurement explained in Chapter 6 (on p. 186).

(b) From the following information, calculate the cost of goods sold for the period ended 30 June 20X2, assuming a periodic inventory system.

- *Balances at 1 July 20X1*

Accounts receivable	$ 1 200
Inventory	5 200
Accounts payable	6 700

- *Transactions during the year*

Sales on credit	$17 000
Payments of accounts payable	11 400
Freight paid in cash	320
Purchase returns on credit	400
Cash purchases	920

- *Balances at 30 June 20X2*

Accounts payable	$ 4 900
Inventory	4 300

Action

(i) Calculate credit purchases for the period.
(ii) Calculate cost of goods sold for the period.

(i) Reconstruct the accounts payable ledger account.

ACCOUNTS PAYABLE			
	Debit	Credit	Balance
Balance (beginning)			6 700 CR
Cash	11 400		4 700 DR
Purchase returns	400		5 100 DR
Purchases		10 000 *	4 900 CR
*Balancing item			

(ii) Reconstruct cost of goods sold section of the profit and loss statement.

Opening inventory		$ 5 200
plus Purchases (cash and credit)	$10 920	
Freight in	320	
	11 240	
less Purchases returns	400	10 840
		16 040
less Closing inventory		4 300
Cost of goods sold		$11 740

Example 2

W. A. Worry commenced business on 1 July 20X1. Unfortunately some records were destroyed in a fire and the only information available is the following. Prepare a profit and loss statement and balance sheet from the incomplete records, assuming a periodic inventory system.

- *Balances at the beginning of the year*

Cash at bank	$11 000
Accounts receivable	700
Inventory	6 000
Accounts payable	450
Supplies	900
Plant and equipment	7 000

- *Transactions for the year*

Cash sales	$14 000
Payments of accounts payable	4 000
Payment of expenses	1 200
Cash purchases	4 300
Purchase returns on credit	520
Sales returns on credit	300
Receipts from accounts receivable	13 000

- *Other information to be noted*
  The depreciation of plant and equipment is at 10 per cent per annum on cost.

- *Balances at the end of the year*

Inventory	$ 2 000
Plant and equipment	7 000
Accounts receivable	14 000
Accounts payable	7 100
Supplies	300

Action

(i)   Calculate credit sales and purchases.
(ii) Summarise the cash and supplies information.
(iii) Prepare the profit and loss statement.
(iv) Prepare the balance sheet.

Answers

(i)   Reconstruct the accounts receivable and accounts payable ledger accounts.

ACCOUNTS RECEIVABLE

	Debit	Credit	Balance
Balance (beginning)			700 DR
Cash		13 000	12 300 CR
Sales returns		300	12 600 CR
Sales	26 600 *		14 000 DR

*Balancing items

ACCOUNTS PAYABLE

	Debit	Credit	Balance
Balance (beginning)			450 CR
Cash	4 000		3 550 DR
Purchase returns	520		4 070 DR
Purchases		11 170 *	7 100 CR

*Balancing items

(ii) Summarise cash and supplies information.

CASH

	Debit	Credit	Balance
Balance (beginning)			11 000 DR
Accounts payable		4 000	7 000 DR
Expenses		1 200	5 800 DR
Purchases		4 300	1 500 DR
Accounts receivable	13 000		14 500 DR
Sales	14 000		28 500 DR

SUPPLIES

	Debit	Credit	Balance
Balance (beginning)			900 DR
Supplies expense		600 *	300 DR

*Supplies expenses found by account reconstructions

(iii) Prepare the profit and loss statement.

PROFIT AND LOSS STATEMENT: W. A. WORRY
for year ended 30 June 20X2

Sales revenue (cash and credit)			$40 600
less Sales returns			300
Net sales			40 300
less Cost of goods sold			
Inventory (beginning of period)		$ 6 000	
plus Purchases (cash and credit)	$15 470		
less Purchase returns	520	14 950	
		20 950	
less Inventory (end of period)		2 000	18 950
Gross profit			21 350
less Expenses (including supplies and depreciation)			2 500
Net profit			18 850

(iv) Prepare the balance sheet.

CALCULATION OF OPENING CAPITAL	
	$
Assets at beginning	
Cash at bank	11 000
Accounts receivable	700
Inventory	6 000
Supplies	900
Plant and equipment	7 000
	25 600
less Liabilities	
Accounts payable	450
Capital at beginning	25 150

BALANCE SHEET: W. A. WORRY					
as at 30 June 20X2					
Assets	$	**Liabilities**	$		$
Cash	28 500	Accounts payable			7 100
Accounts receivable	14 000				
Supplies	300	**Owners' equity**			
Inventory	2 000	Capital		25 150	
Plant and equipment	6 300	plus Net profit		18 850	44 000
	51 100				51 100

Case 7.3 Cash and accrual–based accounting reports

Corporate Internet Services Co. (CIS) opened a consulting business on 1 July 20X1. The owner contributed $50 000 cash as capital. The business borrowed $40 000 from Western Banking Corporation (WBC) on 1 September 20X1. The loan is repayable on 1 July 20X3. The interest rate on the loan was 10 per cent per year.

On 1 July the business rented an office and paid three months rent in advance, totalling $2400. It was agreed that for the remainder of the one-year rental agreement the monthly rental fee of $800 would be paid at the beginning of each month. On 2 July office equipment with a three-year life was purchased on credit for $3600. Credit terms were 60 days. By 8 July the business had begun providing services to clients and by 31 December 20X1 had invoiced customers for $170 000 worth of services at year end, all but $22 000 of which had been received.

Costs incurred and paid by cheque by the end of the year were as follows:

- secretarial assistance, $10 000
- office supplies, $900
- electricity and other utilities, $700.

At the end of the year further information was available:

- accrued secretarial expenses, $800;
- accrued electricity and other utilities, $100;
- office supplies on hand were valued at $150;
- depreciation is charged on a straight-line basis with no residual values.

(a) Prepare a profit and loss statement for the half-year ended 31 December 20X1. Assume that the business uses the accrual basis of accounting, with revenue recognised at the time services are rendered.
(b) Prepare a statement of cash flows for the half-year ended 31 December 20X1.
(c) Prepare a balance sheet as at 31 December 20X1.
(d) One of the major shareholders has argued that the cash basis of accounting, with revenue being recognised at the time cash is received, should have been used in preparing the profit and loss statement. Write a reply justifying the use of the accrual method in preparing the profit and loss statement.

Ethical issues

A junior auditor of a large accounting firm uncovered what she believed to be a questionable valuation of an asset by a company whose accounts were presently under audit. The company had reported accounts receivable of $17 million. The auditor could find active debtors' cards totalling only $11 million. On inquiry, a trolley was wheeled out containing debtors' cards totalling $6 million in outstanding debts. These debts had all been outstanding for at least three years. The junior auditor suggested to her supervisor that the $6 million should be written off. She was told to keep quiet or the accounting firm would lose the audit assignment and the valuable fees received. The auditor is tempted to believe that, having reported the matter to her supervisor, she need take no further action. Do you agree? What are the possible consequences in either case?

Summary

The discussion in this chapter has applied the concepts discussed in previous chapters to derive the rules of accounting. The definition of an expense as a charge arising when the benefit is consumed, rather than when payment is made, requires certain adjustments at the end of the accounting period in order to determine profit and loss for the period. The recognition of revenue in periods prior to the receipt of cash requires the introduction of procedures to cope with anticipated bad debts and discounts. The chapter also considers the appropriate recording of receipt of revenues that have not been earned. Finally, the concept of an asset as the cost of future benefits carried forward and allocated over future accounting periods as the benefits are consumed, creates the need for depreciation.

All of these procedures have the effect of causing revenues recognised to differ from cash received during a period and for expenses of a period to differ from amounts paid. This system of accounting is known as accrual accounting.

Review exercises

Discussion questions

7.1 Explain the difference between expenses paid in advance and accrued expenses.

7.2 What are the reasons for making adjusting entries?

7.3 What is meant by the term 'accrual accounting'?

7.4 What type of account is unearned revenue? Explain why.

7.5 What purpose(s) does a worksheet serve?

7.6 Why are supplies that are used recorded as expenses?

7.7   Why do firms record bad and doubtful debts as an expense? How is the amount of this expense typically determined?

7.8   'I know this equipment will be useless in 10 years time but the fact is that in this its first year it has suffered no wear and tear and its market value is presently above its original cost. In other words, it has not depreciated and no such expense should be recorded.' Discuss.

7.9   A firm rents out breeding boars to farmers, taking one piglet per litter as rent. It accumulates all costs of raising such a hog in an asset account, then depreciates these costs over the boar's service life. Under what circumstances would conventional accounting thought find it appropriate for the firm to use (a) straight-line depreciation, (b) reducing-balance depreciation and (c) the production method? Assume that piglets bred from an elderly hog are just as valuable as those bred from a juvenile hog.

7.10   What method of depreciation seems to be the most appropriate for each of the following assets, and why is it the most appropriate?

(a) A motion picture film entitled *Son of Star Wars*.
(b) A standby electricity generator to be used in the case of power failure.
(c) An aeroplane designed to fly 40 000 hours in its lifetime.
(d) Office furniture for the managing director. As it becomes older it will be passed on to the secretary.
(e) A church bell.
(f) Equipment, the full benefits of which can be gained only after operators have been trained and have experience in operating the equipment.

7.11   What is depreciation? Why is it charged as an expense?

7.12   Explain the theoretical justification for adopting each of the four commonly used methods of depreciation.

7.13   'The amount of depreciation should always be related to the remaining useful life of the asset rather than to its age. Old equipment is worth just as much as new equipment if neither one has been used.' Do you agree? Explain fully.

Problems

7.14   On 1 April 20X4 Glenview Wholesalers paid its annual rent, $36 000, and recorded it as an expense. Show the journal entries to:

(a) record the transaction
(b) adjust the expense figure as at 30 June 20X4
(c) close the account as at 30 June 20X4
(d) reverse the entry as at 1 July 20X4

7.15   CAMS Company pays its insurance annually in advance on 1 May each year and records it as an expense. Its financial year ends on 30 June. On 1 May 20X4 the annual premium was $2400, but the following year the premium paid increased to $2700.

(a) Calculate the insurance expense for the year ending 30 June 20X5.
(b) Prepare the general journal entries required at 30 June 20X5 and 1 July 20X5.

7.16 On 1 November 20X2 MANCO Ltd paid $24 000 for a one-year lease. Show all the appropriate journal entries up to and including 1 July 20X3 using:

(a) the expense method

(b) the asset method

Note: the end of the financial year is 30 June 20X3.

7.17 *Preparation of adjusting entries*

1. Given the following information, prepare the relevant adjusting journal entries. (Assume that 30 June is the year end.)

(a) The electricity account for June of $400 is unpaid and unrecorded.

(b) On 1 May, six months rent was paid in advance totalling $2400.

(c) DB Ltd has four employees who each earn $400 a day. They have all worked the last three days of June for which they have not been paid.

(d) Rent of $1200 for the six-month period ending 30 September is due to be paid in November.

(e) On 1 July (beginning of year) the supplies account had a $200 debit balance. During the year $1300 worth of supplies were purchased and a 30 June stock-take revealed $400 worth of supplies on hand.

(f) On 1 March purchased a 36-month insurance policy for $7200.

2. Given the following information, prepare the relevant adjusting journal entries. (Assume that 30 June is the year end.)

(a) On 1 February received $1200 cash from a client as payment in advance for services to be performed. By 30 June, 40 per cent of the work was completed.

(b) Provided services on credit totalling $1100. This information was unrecorded at 30 June.

(c) On 1 April received six months rent in advance totalling $12 000. This was recorded by a credit to rental revenue.

(d) On 30 June it was estimated that $600 of accounts receivable were doubtful and that $200 of accounts receivable should be written off.

3. Fitts Shoes Ltd closes its accounts at 31 December. On 1 January 20X9 it owed $30 000 for wages but had prepaid its rent for the next two months, amounting to $42 000. During the year, wages paid were $480 000 and rent payments amounted to $231 000. At 31 December 20X9 wages unpaid were $14 000 and three months rent was prepaid, amounting to $63 000.

(a) Calculate the wages and rent expenses for 20X9.

(b) Show by means of journal entries or ledger accounts how these events would be recorded.

4. Oriel Industries closes its accounts at 30 June. On 1 July 20X0 it had prepaid its rent for the next month, amounting to $3000 and owed $2000 for rates relating to the previous year. During the year rates paid were $8000 and rent paid amounted to $49 000. At 30 June 20X1 four months rent was prepaid, amounting to $12 000, and rates unpaid were $3000.

    (a) Calculate the rent and rate expenses for the year ended 30 June 20X1.

    (b) Show by means of journal entries or ledger accounts how these events would be recorded.

  5. A company carries a number of insurance policies on its property as follows:

	at 1 Jan. 20X8	at 31 Dec. 20X8
Insurance prepaid	$ 5 000	$9000
Insurance owing	13 000	8500
Insurance paid in 20X8	142 000	

    Calculate the insurance expense for 20X8.

7.18 On 1 June 20X1 R.G. Computer Services signed a six-month contract to perform services for a customer at $400 per month, and received in advance the total contract price. The end of the financial year is 30 June. Show all the appropriate journal entries up to and including 1 July 20X1, using:

    (a) the liability method
    (b) the revenue method

7.19 T. Doery operates Ringwood Realty. At 30 June 20X3 the balance in the Commission Revenue account was $50 000. At this date Ringwood Realty was owed $4000 which has not been included in the records of the business. Show all the appropriate journal entries up to and including 1 July 20X3. Explain the reason why a reversal of the 30 June balance-day adjustment is necessary.

7.20 The accounting period of the Burwood Motor Co. ends on 30 June 20X6. The office supplies on hand account has a debit balance of $820 on 1 July 20X5. Supplies of $720 were purchased during the year and $220 of supplies are on hand on 30 June 20X6. Prepare the adjusting journal entry to record supplies expense. Assume the firm uses an asset approach to recording inventories of supplies.

7.21 *Accounting for bad and doubtful debts*

  1. John Farmer's retail store is about to permit credit sales for the first time and is anxious to provide for possible bad debts. Bad debts are expected to average 8 per cent of credit sales and are to be provided for monthly.

      Opening balances of relevant accounts at 1 April 20X1 are:

Cash sales	$150 000
Credit sales	Nil

    Monthly figures are as follows:

20X1		
April	Cash sales	$ 60 000
	Credit sales	130 000
	Cash received from debtors	53 000
May	Cash sales	81 000
	Credit sales	90 000
	Cash received from debtors	62 000
June	Cash sales	47 000
	Credit sales	170 000
	Cash received from debtors	79 000

A debtor has been declared bankrupt and the debt of $5700 must be written off. A review of debtors at 30 June reveals that $30 000 of debts are doubtful.

(a) Record the above transactions in the appropriate ledger accounts, including the relevant 'closing entries'.

(b) Show appropriate extracts from the profit and loss statement and balance sheet at 30 June 20X1.

2. R. U. Kareful runs a retail business. It has not been her policy to allow credit sales. However, since she is losing business she has now chosen to permit sales on credit. Bad and doubtful debts will be allowed for on the basis of 10 per cent of sales, and will be provided for on a monthly basis.

Opening balances of the relevant accounts are:

Cash sales	$400
Credit sales	Nil

Monthly figures are as follows:

April	Cash sales	$150
	Credit sales	330
	Cash received from debtors	130
May	Cash sales	200
	Credit sales	230
	Cash received from debtors	150
June	Cash sales	120
	Credit sales	420
	Cash received from debtors	190

H. Case, a debtor, has been declared bankrupt and the debt of $50 must be written off. A review of debtors at 30 June reveals that $100 of debts are doubtful.

(a) Record the above transactions in the appropriate ledger accounts.

(b) Show appropriate extracts from the profit and loss statement and balance sheet at 30 June.

3. Balances in the following accounts of the Thermal Appliances Co. Ltd on 31 May were:

Accounts receivable	DR	$ 246 000
Allowance for doubtful debts	CR	12 300
Sales	CR	1 420 000
Bad and doubtful debts	DR	14 200

Transactions for June were:

(i) Sales (all credit) $160 000

(ii) Cash collected from customers $134 000

(iii) $1500 was collected from a former customer who had been declared bankrupt in the previous year and whose debt had been written off as bad.

The directors expect doubtful debts to average about 1 per cent of sales and they provide for this regularly each month. The figures are reviewed at the end of the year after an analysis of debtors' accounts. The review on 30 June revealed the following situation:

Age of accounts	Accounts receivable	Uncollectable estimate (%)
0–1 month	$160 000	0.5
1–6 months	84 000	6
6–12 months	25 000	12
Over 1 year	3 000	100
	$272 000	

It was decided to write off all debts more than one year old as bad, and to revise the estimate of doubtful debts on remaining debtors' balances in accordance with the ageing schedule.

(a) Record the above information in ledger accounts.
(b) Show the relevant parts of the final accounting reports on 30 June.
(c) Briefly explain what the figures for net revenue and net debtors mean.

4. The following balances appeared in the ledger of Lo Gloss and Co. on 31 May:

Accounts receivable	DR	$ 354 360
Bad and doubtful debts	DR	16 840
Allowance for doubtful debts	CR	12 310
Sales	CR	2 648 420

Transactions for June were:

(i) Sales—cash $123 570
           credit $ 98 000
(ii) Cash collected from customers—$114 630.
(iii) A cheque for $300 (not included in (ii)) was received from a debtor whose debt of $800 had been previously written off. A letter attached to the cheque indicated that the balance would be paid in the near future.

Doubtful debts are normally provided for each month at the rate of 1 per cent of credit sales.

An analysis of accounts receivable balance on 30 June (after the transactions for June had been recorded) showed:

Age of accounts	Accounts receivable	Uncollectable estimate (%)
0–1 month	$ 95 000	0.8
1–6 months	188 500	4
6–12 months	48 400	10
Over 12 months	?	80

It was decided to write off all debts over 12 months as bad and to adjust the allowance for doubtful debts to agree with the uncollectable estimate given by the accounts receivable age analysis.

(a) Record the above information in the appropriate ledger accounts.
(b) Show the relevant parts of the final accounting reports for the year ended 30 June.
(c) Give a brief explanation for the use of contra accounts in making adjustments to sales and accounts receivable balances.

5. Guard & Co. Ltd had the following account balances on 1 July 20X3:

Accounts receivable	$94 200
Allowance for bad and doubtful debts	16 700
	$77 500

During the year the company's sales totalled $165 400. Cash sales for the period were $9300, and the company collected $123 000 from its customers. Sales returns for the year were $5900, which all related to credit sales during the year. The company's policy on bad and doubtful debts is to provide two per cent of net credit sales as an allowance. On 4 December 20X3 the company was informed that one of its debtors, Frances Williams, had been declared bankrupt and her debt of $1900 was to be written off. To the company's surprise, on 3 June 20X4 Ellen McKenna, whose $1400 account had been written off as bad in September, paid her account in full. An ageing analysis of accounts receivable performed on 30 June 20X4 by the company revealed bad and doubtful debts of $16 770.

(a) Record each of the above transactions in the appropriate ledger accounts.
(b) Show how accounts receivable and allowance for bad and doubtful debts would appear in the company's balance sheet as at 30 June 20X4.

7.22 *Correction of profit and loss report—all adjustments*

Hogan, trading as Hogan Stores, submits to you draft accounts for the year ended 31 December 20X7 and a balance sheet at that date. He explains that towards the end of the financial year his accountant resigned and he had 'finished off' the books himself. He thinks that errors have occurred and asks for your help. An examination of the books reveals the following:

(i) Rent due by B. Crow amounting to $480 is not included in the accounts.
(ii) A payment of $1800 for new computers has been debited to the sundry expenses account. Payment was made 31 December 20X7.
(iii) Commission due to staff for the month of December, $1000, has been overlooked.
(iv) Repairs to owner's private motor car, $640, have been debited to motor expenses account.
(v) A payment of $30 000 on 1 January 20X7 for additions to buildings has been debited to repairs and maintenance.
(vi) Allowances for doubtful debts is shown at $6000. Total debtors at 31 December were $72 500. The provision is to be increased to 10 per cent of debtors.
(vii) A fire insurance policy covering buildings was taken out on 31 October, the annual premium of $480 being paid in advance on this date, and is included in full in the accounts. The $480 was debited to insurance.
(viii) Interest of $100 on Wellington City Council Debentures was due, but has not been received.
(ix) No depreciation charges have been made for the year ending 31 December 20X7.

The draft balance sheet shows:

Buildings (at cost)	$830 000	
less Accumulated depreciation	80 000	$750 000
Office Furniture and Equipment (at cost)	105 000	
less Accumulated Depreciation	57 000	48 000

Depreciation expense is to be made as follows:
Buildings, 2 per cent per annum on cost
Office furniture and equipment, 20 per cent per annum on their carrying amount.

(a) Show the journal entries required to make the necessary adjustments in the books.

(b) Prepare a statement showing the effect of the adjustments on the net profit figure of $7520 as shown in the draft accounts.

7.23   *Calculating and accounting for depreciation*

1.   On 1 January 20X1 a company purchases an executive jet aeroplane for $500 000. The aeroplane was expected to have a life of 8000 flying hours spread over a five-year period. Its estimated residual value was $30 000. The flying hours were expected to be:

Year	Hours
20X1	2000
20X2	1000
20X3	3000
20X4	Nil
20X5	2000
	8000

(a) Calculate annual depreciation according to the following methods:

(i)   straight-line
(ii) production units
(iii) reducing-balance at a depreciation rate of 40 per cent
(iv) sum-of-the-digits.

(b) Assuming the reducing-balance method was adopted and the aeroplane was sold on 31 December 20X3 for $100 000, show the ledger accounts to record the purchase, depreciation and sale.

2.   A company bought equipment on 1 January 20X1 for $30 618. It is expected to last six years and to have a residual value of $2688.

     The production manager expects it to have a life of 10 000 running hours, distributed as follows:

Year	Hours
20X1	4000
20X2	2000
20X3	1000
20X4	1000
20X5	1000
20X6	1 000
	10 000

(a) Prepare a schedule of the annual depreciation charges (working to the nearest dollar) under the following methods:

(i)   straight-line
(ii) reducing-balance
(iii) production-units

(b) The company adopted the reducing-balance method. On 31 December 20X4 the equipment was sold for $8000. Show the relevant ledger accounts to record the depreciation and sale of the equipment.

7.24 *Accounting for the sale of an asset*

(a) Fiery Ltd began January 20X5 with the following balances, among others:

Equipment	$192 000
Accumulated depreciation: equipment	$ 79 000

On 30 June 20X5 equipment that had cost $80 000 on 1 January 20X2, and which had been depreciated at 30 per cent per annum on the reducing-balance basis, was sold for $5600.

Show the relevant ledger accounts to record the sale of the asset.

(b) The following balances appear in the ledger at 31 December 20X7:

Office equipment	$160 000
Accumulated depreciation: office equipment	$ 84 000
Depreciation expense: office equipment	$ 12 800

On that date equipment that cost $6000 and had been depreciated by $3500 was sold for $1850.

Show journal entries to record the sale.

(c) Once Again Ltd had the following balances at 1 January 20X7, the start of a new accounting period:

Equipment	$150 000
Accumulated depreciation: equipment	$ 42 000

On that date equipment that had cost $12 000 two years previously and had been depreciated at 20 per cent per year on the reducing-balance method was sold for $5500. It was half-way through its expected life of four years.

(i) Present journal entries to record the sale.
(ii) Give possible reasons for the discrepancy between the book value of the asset and the cash received on its disposal.

7.25 *Calculating depreciation and accounting for sale*

Timbertop Ltd had the following fixed assets as at 30 June 20X0:

Office equipment	$144 800
Accumulated depreciation	39 440
	105 360
Furniture and fittings	61 200
Accumulated depreciation	26 500
	34 700
Motor vehicles	28 000
Accumulated depreciation	10 080
	17 920
Total fixed assets	$157 980

The company depreciates its office equipment and furniture and fittings using the straight-line method. Office equipment has a useful life of 10 years and its estimated residual value is $1700. Furniture and fittings have a useful life of 15 years and no residual value. Motor vehicles are depreciated at 20 per cent per annum using the reducing-balance method.

On 1 November 20X0 the company purchased a new photocopier for $3856. The company anticipates using the copier for eight years, at which time it expects to dispose of it for $650.

On 31 December 20X0 the company sold a motor vehicle for $9800 that it had purchased for $15 000 on 1 July 20X8.

(a) Calculate the company's depreciation expense for each fixed asset for the year ending 30 June 20X1.

(b) Record the transactions relating to the sale of the motor vehicle in the appropriate ledger accounts.

7.26 *Analysis and meaning of depreciation*

On 1 January 20X1 William Tipp began business as Ace Rubbish Removals with a capital contribution of $100 in cash. He then borrowed $18 000 from a finance company to purchase a used truck. The truck was expected to have a three-year life and no residual value, and straight-line depreciation would be appropriate. The business was entirely 'cash and carry'. The operating results for each year were:

	20X1	*20X2*	*20X3*
Revenue	$28 000	$32 000	$49 000
Cash expenses	13 000	19 000	22 000
Cash surplus	$15 000	$13 000	$27 000

William Tipp argues that he should be able to withdraw the entire cash surplus and still maintain his capital.

(a) Is William Tipp correct?

(b) Compute the profit and loss statements and balance sheets for each year after making appropriate charges for depreciation. Tabular presentation is satisfactory, that is:

	20X1	20X2	20X3
Revenue	X	X	X
less Expenses, etc.			

Assume William Tipp withdraws his entire accumulated profit at the end of each year.

(c) Explain why there is cash on hand at the end of 20X3.

(d) After the loan is repaid, how much cash will be available to replace the asset? What does this imply for the meaning of depreciation?

7.27 *Analysis of the concept of depreciation*

Robin Nowall bought equipment on 1 January 20X1 for $22 000 that was expected to have a four-year life and a residual value of $2000. She used it evenly throughout its life and, at your insistence, employed straight-line depreciation. Now that it has been scrapped she complains about this practice as follows:

(a) Depreciation does not involve a current cash outlay. It is, therefore, a fictitious charge and I am unimpressed with your accountant's magic.

(b) If you had to charge depreciation, why was it not based on the change in selling price, which went as follows:

Date	Selling price of used asset
31 Dec. X1	$6000
31 Dec. X2	7000
31 Dec. X3	3000
31 Dec. X4	2000

(c) The equipment was as good as new until the last year. Why did you depreciate it in its early years?

Prepare a brief reply to each of these propositions.

7.28 *Using a worksheet to prepare financial statements for a merchandiser*

From the following information prepare a profit and loss statement and a balance sheet for the year ended 30 June 20X5. It is suggested that a worksheet be used in preparing these statements.

TRIAL BALANCE: ANGELIC CURIOS		
as at 30 June 20X5		
	Debit	Credit
Accounts payable		$ 9 690
Accounts receivable	$ 13 200	
Capital: R. Hill		54 000
Cash at bank	14 000	
Cost of goods sold	123 420	
Drawings	31 680	
Insurance expense	13 090	
Interest expense	2 300	
Inventory	43 450	
Property	140 000	
Mortgage loan		20 000
		continues

TRIAL BALANCE: ANGELIC CURIOS		
as at 30 June 20X5		
	Debit	Credit
Sales returns	6 350	
Sales revenue		375 800
Wages expense	72 000	
	$459 490	$459 490

Further information at 30 June 20X5:

(a) A count of the inventory on hand revealed a value, at cost, of $41 000.

(b) The insurance expense includes an annual policy costing $340 which was taken out on 1 January 20X5.

(c) Wages of $2000 were owing to employees.

(d) Interest due but unpaid on the loan was $500.

7.29 *Using a worksheet to prepare financial statements*

From the following information prepare a profit and loss statement and a balance sheet for the year ended 30 June 20X6. It is suggested that a worksheet be used in preparing these statements.

TRIAL BALANCE: EAST SHORE PAVING		
as at 30 June 20X6		
	Debit	Credit
Accounts payable		$ 17 300
Accounts receivable	$ 222 450	
Bank		30 100
Capital: C. Slab		487 780
Contract revenue		465 000
Drawings	51 440	
Insurance expense	16 090	
Land	300 000	
Materials used	20 000	
Office expenses	31 200	
Rental of equipment	113 000	
Subcontractors' fees	174 000	
Wages expense	72 000	
	$1 000 180	$1 000 180

Further information at 30 June 20X6:

(a) The insurance expense includes an annual policy for $3000 that was taken out on 1 January 20X6.

(b) Wages of $8500 were owing to employees.

(c) Revenue of $5000 due from a small job done in June has not yet been recorded.

(d) The office expenses include stationery unused at year end that is estimated to have cost $400.

7.30   *The accounting process for a merchandiser*

The following events concern the Bear Boutique, a sole trader run by Teddy Lockes. The Bear Boutique began 20X8 with the following assets and liabilities:

Cash	$47 000
Accounts receivable	2 000
Inventory	26 000
Accounts payable	8 000

- Purchased a delivery van on credit for $23 000. The vehicle is expected to have a five-year life and a residual value of $3000. Straight-line depreciation is deemed appropriate.
- Purchased goods on credit for $16 000.
- Sold goods on credit for $185 000. They originally cost $21 000.
- It was desirable to provide for doubtful debts at one per cent of sales.
- Returned goods that cost $800 to suppliers and received credit.
- Customers returned goods with a retail value of $1300 and a cost of $300 to the Bear Boutique and received credit.
- Receipts from customers totalled $159 500. Discounts allowed amounted to $1200. Other payments were:

Accounts payable	$11 900	
Wages	22 300	
Rent	18 200	
Personal drawings	32 000	$84 400

At the end of 20X8:

1. A count of the stock revealed $18 500 on hand at cost.
2. Wages owing amounted to $700.
3. Rent was prepaid by $1500.
4. An ageing of accounts receivable revealed that debts totalling $1400 were bad. Doubtful debts were estimated to be $2470.
5. Depreciation was to be recorded as above.

(a) Enter the above in general ledger accounts.

(b) Prepare a trial balance.

(c) Make adjusting entries.

(d) Prepare closing entries.

(e) Prepare financial statements for the year ended 31 December 20X8.

7.31   *Profit and loss statement for a merchandiser*

On 31 December 20X7 Ian, who owns Triumph Spare Parts, drew up a balance sheet for his business.

Assets		Liabilities	
Cash	$ 3 000	Accounts payable	$ 450
Merchandise	7 750	Delivery expenses payable	270
Prepaid telephone rental	30	Loan from bank	8 000
Fixtures and fittings	1 200		8 720
less Accumulated depn	(120)	**Owners' equity**	3 140
	$11 860		$11 860

Additional information:

1. All sales are paid for in cash. Cash refunds are available if customers are dissatisfied. Sales for January 20X8 were $4395, and sales returns were $115.
2. $630 was paid out for delivery expenses during January. Delivery charges of $140 remained outstanding at the end of the month.
3. Accumulated depreciation of fixtures and fittings totalled $180 at the end of January.
4. The prepaid telephone rental was for the period 1 January to 31 March 20X8.
5. An additional $1360 worth of spare parts was purchased and paid for during January; $6900 worth of merchandise was still on hand at the end of January.
6. The interest rate on the loan was 15 per cent per annum. Ian paid the bank $100 on 31 January.

(a) Produce a profit and loss statement for Ian's business for the month of January 20X8.

(b) Show the entries in the cash ledger account for the month.

7.32 *Balance day adjustments*

Potters are seeking your help. You have previously supplied them with end-of-year reports. They have since misplaced the balance sheet that you prepared for them. You are required to prepare another balance sheet as at 31 December 20X8.

TRIAL BALANCE: POTTER FINANCIAL ADVISORS as at 31 December 20X8		
	Debit	Credit
	$	$
Cash	70 000	
Accounts receivable	60 000	
Prepaid expenses (insurance)	10 000	
Supplies	30 000	
Equipment	380 000	
Accumulated depreciation—equipment		20 000
Accounts payable		60 000
Capital—Potter		220 000
Drawings—Potter	70 000	
Service revenue		742 000
Salaries expense	220 000	
Advertising expense	82 000	
Rent expense	70 000	
Miscellaneous expense	50 000	
	$1 042 000	$1 042 000

PROFIT AND LOSS STATEMENT: POTTER FINANCIAL ADVISORS		
for the year ended 31 December 20X8		
	$	$
Revenue		
Service revenue		742 000
Expenses		
Salaries expense	245 000	
Advertising expense	84 000	
Rent expense	70 000	
Insurance expense	6 000	
Interest expense	500	
Depreciation—equipment	90 000	
Supplies expense	15 000	
Miscellaneous expense	50 000	560 500
Profit		$181 500

7.33 *Adjustments, adjusted trial balance and preparation of financial statements for a merchandiser—periodic*

Angie Trader has owned a shoe store in Marton since July 20X1. The following is its trial balance as at 30 June 20X4, before any end-of-period adjustments.

	Debit	Credit
Cash at bank	$ 10 550	
Accounts receivable	4 200	
Allowance for doubtful debts		$ 850
Stock 1 Jan. X4	22 100	
Office equipment	37 100	
Accumulated depreciation—office equipment		4280
Motor vehicle	17 500	
Accumulated depreciation—motor vehicle		3 550
Accounts payable		5 400
Mortgage		15 000
Capital—A. Trader		50 000
Drawings—A. Trader	8 900	
Retained profits 1 Jan. X4		6 870
Sales revenue		100 300
Purchases	37 900	
Advertising	1 760	
Cleaning	980	
Interest	1 950	
Bad and doubtful debts	560	
Rent	5 400	
Repairs and maintenance	1 020	
Telephone	890	
Electricity	940	
Stationery	530	
Wages	31 910	
Insurance	2 060	
	$186 250	$186 250

Additional information:

1. Stock on hand 30 June 20X4 was $19 900.
2. Prepaid advertising totalled $490.
3. Stationery remaining on hand at the end of June had cost $140.
4. Office equipment is depreciated on a straight-line basis with no residual value and an estimated useful life of 10 years. Motor vehicles are depreciated at 20 per cent reducing-balance.
5. Rent expense for the year includes rent on premises for July 20X4 of $415.
6. Wages owing at 1 January 20X4 amounted to $890 and electricity accrued $210.
7. B. Burton, a debtor, was declared bankrupt on 30 June 20X4. He owed the shop $95.
8. An ageing analysis of debtors at 30 June 20X4 revealed bad and doubtful debts of $970.

(a) Make all adjusting entries.

(b) Prepare an adjusted trial balance.

(c) Prepare financial statements for the half-year ending 30 June 20X4.

7.34 *Analysis of poorly kept accounting records*
You have been asked to investigate Midas Ltd by a client who is interested in acquiring it. He considers the threefold increase in profit in 20X2 an indication of good prospects.

You discover that the president, Mr Midas Murdoch, has some strange ideas about accounting. He believes revenue is recorded only when cash is received and that expenses occur whenever cash is paid out (except in the case of equipment, which he regards as an asset).

INCOME STATEMENTS

	20X1		20X2	
	($000)	($000)	($000)	($000)
Revenue				
Cash received from customers		80		150
less Cash expenses				
Merchandise paid for	35		90	
Wages paid	20		24	
Rent paid	15		9	
Dividend paid	3	73	3	126
Net cash income		7		24

BALANCE SHEETS

	20X1		20X2	
	($000)		($000)	
Assets				
Cash	17		41	
Equipment	20	37	20	61
Liabilities		Nil		Nil
Shareholders' equity				
Capital	30		30	
Retained profit	7	37	31	61

Other information, not disclosed in the statements:

1. The company commenced business on 1 Jan. 20X1.

2.

	31 Dec. X1 ($000)	31 Dec. X2 ($000)
Customer accounts owing	30	10
Inventory on hand	12	28
Wages due to employees	3	7
Amounts payable to suppliers	2	12

3. The rental contract was for $1000 per month, commencing 1 Jan. 20X1.
4. The equipment, purchased on 1 Jan. 20X1 for $20 000, is expected to give four years of uniform service, after which it will be scrapped for about $4000. Murdoch says it is currently as good as new and talk of depreciation is so much nonsense.

(a) Present revised statements for 20X1 and 20X2 based on the principles of accrual accounting.

(b) Is Midas Ltd still showing a good profit trend?

CHAPTER 8
The principles applied: owners' equity

Learning objectives

In this chapter you will be introduced to:

1. the formation of a partnership

2. how to appropriate profits among partners

3. the report of appropriations for both a partnership and a company

4. the difference between the financial statements of a partnership and those of a sole proprietor

5. how to account for the admission of a new partner, and the dissolution and liquidation of a partnership

6. the meaning of 'goodwill'

7. how to apply the basics of partnership liquidation to various situations, such as the selling of the partnership as a going concern

8. the characteristics of a company

9. the advantages and disadvantages of companies when compared with partnerships

10. the incorporation of companies

11. the takeover of an existing business by a company

12. the issue of shares by instalments

13. how to report the shareholders' equity section for a company in its balance sheet

14. how to account for income tax expense, payment of dividends, and transfers to reserves.

Introduction

This chapter extends the broad rules of accounting for owners' equity beyond the simple situation of a sole trader to consider partnerships and companies. In general, the complications arise because of the need to account for several or many owners in terms of capital subscribed and the distribution of profits. The reader will acquire new knowledge about accounting for ownership interest and other transactions particular to:

- partnerships
  - their formation
  - the appropriation of profit between the partners
  - the admission of a new partner
  - the dissolution of a partnership
- companies
  - their formation
  - the appropriation of profit
  - the meaning of 'shareholders' equity'

Partnerships

Before commencing to consider differences in accounting for ownership interests and profit distribution for partnerships it is appropriate to consider the partnership form of business ownership. A partnership is defined by the *Partnership Act*[1] as the relationship that 'subsists between persons carrying on a business with a view to profit'. The relationship may be formed with as few as two people but may have many more. For example, many nationally known firms of accountants have a hundred or more partners.

Formation of a partnership

The basic motivation for individuals forming a partnership is mutual advantage. These advantages usually relate to the pooling of the capital and skills of its members. Partners with restricted capital resources can raise larger amounts if they pool their capital contributions. Note, however, that although involving additional people would normally provide more capital than a single owner could provide, the partnership form of business does not bestow any special method such as that provided by companies for bringing additional resources into the business.

Forming a partnership is relatively easy. It is desirable that the agreement be in writing but this is not a legal requirement. A partnership may be formed verbally or may even be inferred from the actions of the partners. For example, the opening of a joint bank account might be sufficient evidence of the existence of the partnership. Although the individual state Partnership Acts contain no special provisions for formation, they each contain provisions that regulate the relations of partners with each other and with others outside the partnership. The written agreement should be reached at the commencement of the partnership and should include all matters that may result in possible disagreement. Apart from the obvious inclusion of the names and addresses of the partners, the business name and the purpose of the business, it should address such matters as the distribution of profit, the investment and withdrawal of funds, the admission of new partners and provisions relating to the death, bankruptcy or retirement of partners. This is by no means a comprehensive list of matters that prospective partners should discuss on formation.

---

[1] All states of Australia have adopted a uniform Partnership Act (with minor modifications in some states).

Example: *Partnership formation*

G. Slamm had been operating as a wrecker of houses. On 1 January 20X5 he took his nephew, T. Crunch, into the business as his partner. At that date, Slamm's assets and liabilities, as revealed in a balance sheet, were as follows:

Cash at bank		$ 12 000
Accounts receivable		34 000
Equipment	$300 000	
less Accum. depn	69 000	231 000
		277 000
Accounts payable		47 000
Owner's equity		$230 000

In negotiation, it was agreed that the assets and liabilities of Slamm should all be taken over by the partnership, but that certain of the asset values should be adjusted as follows:

- Accounts receivable: $3000 should be regarded as doubtful.
- Equipment: the fair market value is $164 000, and the remaining life is estimated to be ten years.

T. Crunch was to contribute cash of $20 000 as capital.

In law, the partnership will not exist separately from the partners. However, in accordance with the entity assumption, a separate partnership entity is assumed to exist for accounting purposes. It is this entity for which the accounts will be prepared in this example.

A new set of accounts will be opened for the partnership and the first entries will record the capital contributions of each partner. They are shown below in general journal form, before posting to the general ledger.

20X5		$	$
Jan. 1	Cash at bank	12 000	
	Accounts receivable	34 000	
	Equipment	164 000	
	Allowance for doubtful debts		3 000
	Accounts payable		47 000
	Capital: Slamm		160 000
	(Capital contribution)		
Jan. 1	Cash at bank	20 000	
	Capital: Crunch		20 000
	(Capital contribution)		

It should be noted that the accounts receivable from Slamm's former sole proprietorship have been brought in at their original value, since it is possible that all debtors will pay their accounts, but an allowance for doubtful debts has also been created as agreed by the partners. The equipment is brought into the partnership at its fair market value. The allowance for depreciation shown in Slamm's balance sheet is not brought in, since, from the partnership's point of view, the equipment is a new asset acquired for $164 000. Finally, it should be noted that the 'owner's equity' shown in Slamm's balance sheet is not recorded in the partnership accounts. It is reflected in the credit to the partner's capital amount of $160 000, being the difference between the assets and liabilities taken over by the partnership.

Now that the partnership has been formed, trading can commence and transactions are recorded in the normal way in the partnership records.

Appropriation of profits

Partners may agree to distribute profits among themselves in any agreed way. They may award themselves salaries, to allow for the differing workloads undertaken by each partner. They also may award themselves interest on capital, to allow for differences in the capital contributions of each partner. The partnership agreement may also provide for interest to be allowed on advances (loans) made by the partners to the business. Finally, the partners may agree to share the residual profit in whatever proportions they desire.

In the absence of a formal partnership agreement, the applicable state's Partnership Act normally requires that profits and losses be shared equally between the partners and that no salaries or interest on capital may be provided to individual partners, although stipulated interest percentages are provided on advances.

Whatever the arrangement, all remuneration of partners, whether as salary, interest or shared profits, is usually classified as a withdrawal and not a business expense. As the partners and the partnership are the one legal entity, the partners are free to determine their own remuneration and could therefore manipulate their agreed salaries or interest to produce whatever profit they desire. It is therefore more informative to calculate profit before any remuneration to partners and to regard their remuneration as a distribution of the profit. The distribution to partners is known as the appropriation of the profit.

Separate capital accounts are maintained for each partner. Also, since it is often desired to preserve the amounts of the contributed capital separately in the records, current accounts may be established to record withdrawals of profit on the debit side and profit appropriations as credits.

Example: *Partnership profit appropriations*

Slamm and Crunch, the partners in the previous example, have agreed to share profits as follows:

	Slamm	Crunch
Salaries	$80 000	$20 000
Interest on capital	6% per year	6% per year
Share of profits	50%	50%

In computing the interest on capital, the partners need to decide whether to base the computation on contributed capital, or capital after deduction of the balance in the current accounts. They must also decide whether to use opening capital, closing capital or an average of the two. In this instance the partners have agreed to calculate interest on the opening balances in the capital accounts.

On 31 December 20X5 the books were closed for the year and relevant balances, after transferring revenue and expense accounts to the profit and loss summary account, were as follows:

Capital: Slamm	$160 000 CR
Crunch	20 000 CR
Current: Slamm	134 000 DR
Crunch	145 000 DR
Profit and loss summary	370 000 CR

The profit and loss summary account balance represents the net profit for the year. The next stage in the closing process is to apportion the profit between the partners. To appropriate the profit, a new statement, known as an appropriation statement, is drawn up to link the profit and loss statement with the balance sheet. This replaces the capital statement prepared for a sole proprietorship.

APPROPRIATION STATEMENT: SLAMM AND CRUNCH as at 31 December 20X5				
Net profit				$370 000
less Appropriations				
Salaries:	Slamm	$80 000		
	Crunch	20 000	$100 000	
Interest:	Slamm	9 600		
	Crunch	1 200	10 800	110 800
				259 200
Profit share:	Slamm		129 600	
	Crunch		129 600	259 200

The ledger entries in the relevant accounts reflect the items appearing in the appropriation statement. The net profit is transferred to an appropriation account and the appropriations are transferred to each partner's current account. As with a sole proprietorship, the entire profit must be appropriated to the owners.

PORTION OF GENERAL LEDGER: SLAMM AND CRUNCH			
Current account: Slamm			
	Debit	Credit	Balance
	$	$	$
Dec. 31 Balance			134 000 DR
Appropriation		80 000	54 000 DR
Appropriation		9 600	44 400 DR
Appropriation		129 600	85 200 CR
Current account: Crunch			
Dec. 31 Balance			145 000 DR
Appropriation		20 000	125 000 DR
Appropriation		1 200	123 800 DR
Appropriation		129 600	5 800 CR
Appropriation account			
Dec. 31 Profit and loss summary		370 000	370 000 CR
Current: Slamm	80 000		290 000 CR
Crunch	20 000		270 000 CR
Current: Slamm	9 600		260 400 CR
Crunch	1 200		259 200 CR
Current: Slamm	129 600		129 600 CR
Crunch	129 600		—

The owners' equity section of the balance sheet will appear as follows:

PORTION OF BALANCE SHEET: SLAMM AND CRUNCH
as at 31 December 20X5

Owners' equity		
Capital: Slamm	$160 000	
plus Current	85 200	$245 200
Capital: Crunch	20 000	
plus Current	5 800	25 800
		$271 000

Note in this example salary entitlements have not been withdrawn. If they had been drawn they would have been closed off as debits to the partner's current accounts and hence partner's equity would have been reduced.

The current accounts will then be carried forward to 20X6, along with the capital accounts.

Case 8.1

The partners of the Windy Hill accounting practice have recently retreated to conference at a resort in Northern Queensland to consider how partnership performance might be improved. Much to the reluctance of some partners, the thorny subject of profit sharing was raised. It appeared that the partners fell into three 'groups'—those who wished to maintain the status quo of equal profit sharing, those who believed that there should be differential profit sharing and those who had not quite made up their minds which was better as they could see merit in both.

The proponents of equal profit sharing argued that equal profit sharing avoided this most unpleasant task which usually worked itself out anyway as the good years usually balanced with the not so good. They also argued that it was difficult to assess the relative contributions of individual partners and it usually only led to antagonism and was detrimental to firm morale. They stressed that equal profit sharing led to the partnership working as a unified team and engendered in staff a sense of camaraderie and reduced the rivalry between the partners which would result from differential profit sharing.

The proponents of differential profit sharing argued strongly that profits in the firm should be divided among the partners on the basis of their individual performance and that not all partners are equal in their contribution. They argued that the profits accruing to partners should be influenced by who obtained the business, who did the work and how profitable it was. Although most partners agreed that these three factors did contribute to the success of the firm, they could not agree on the relative importance of them.

Some partners felt that even if some form of formula could be worked out it would probably not adequately account for meaningful management time, training, team spirit or attitude. Others argued that most formulas only measured those aspects of performance that were easy to measure and ignored the difficult to measure factors. One of the founding partners argued that loyalty and years of service should be reflected in any compensation arrangements.

The conference convenor agreed that the discussion had been very fruitful and that as there were many other matters to be considered a policy decision should be deferred until the next meeting.

(a) Adopt the view of those partners arguing for equal profit sharing and put forward a case which supports their views.

(b) Evaluate the suggestion that partnership profit distribution should be influenced by:

(i) who obtained the work
(ii) who did the work
(iii) how profitable it was

(c) Discuss this issue with an accountant in public practice and present your views on partnership profit sharing.

Admission of a new partner

Suppose that on 1 January 20X6 Slamm and Crunch decided to admit J. Tinkle to the partnership upon payment by him of a capital contribution of $25 000. The full partnership balance sheet based on the previous events is:

BALANCE SHEET: SLAMM AND CRUNCH as at 31 December 20X5		
Assets		
Cash at bank		$ 6 400
Accounts receivable	$ 53 000	
less Allowance for doubtful debts	4 000	49 000
Equipment	284 000	
less Accumulated depreciation	28 400	255 600
		311 000
Liabilities		
Accounts payable		40 000
Owners' equity		
Capital: Slamm	160 000	
plus Current	85 200	245 200
Capital: Crunch	20 000	
plus Current	5 800	25 800
		$311 000

These balances represent the book values of the assets at that date, based on the original cost prices to the partnership. Since, effectively, a new partnership venture is to begin, the existing and the new partners may agree to revalue the partnership assets to their fair market values so that the existing partners' capital accounts may reflect the current market values of the partnership assets. In following this policy, the following revaluations were agreed upon with the incoming partner:

• Accounts receivable: increase the allowance for doubtful debts to $5000.
• Equipment: the fair market value is estimated to be $250 000.

These changes to the recorded assets will usually not be sufficient to recognise the full market value of the partnership. Normally, a purchaser would pay for another asset also: the 'goodwill' of the partnership. Assuming they have been successful, the existing partners will have established a reputation for the business that will lead to further profits in the future. There may also be such benefits as the accumulation of special skills, and a team of competent and loyal employees that a purchaser would be willing to pay for. These intangible factors that make up the value of goodwill are difficult to identify and, since their value lies in the unknown future, it is difficult to set a value on goodwill. In practice, various 'rule of thumb' formulas are used within different industries, often based on some multiple of past profits earned by the business. For example, goodwill might be calculated as four times the average profits over the past six years. Whatever the method used, the partners in this example have agreed that:

- Goodwill of the existing partnership should be valued at $30 000.

All of the above revaluations to reflect the market values of the existing assets and to introduce goodwill are made before the admission of the new partner and are taken up entirely in the capital accounts of the existing partners, Slamm and Crunch. As the partners have agreed to share profits and losses equally, the net surplus or deficit on revaluation will be divided equally between the two capital accounts. After these entries, the records will be up to date, and ready for the admission of Tinkle to the partnership.

The changes are made by means of a capital adjustment account and are in general journal form:

20X6		$	$
Jan. 1	Capital adjustment	1 000	
	Allowance for doubtful debts		1 000
	(To increase allowance for doubtful debts)		
	Capital adjustment	5 600	
	Accumulated depreciation:		
	Equipment		5 600
	(Revaluation of the equipment)		
	Goodwill	30 000	
	Capital adjustment		30 000
	(Recognising goodwill of Slamm and Crunch)		
	Capital adjustment	23 400	
	Capital: Slamm		11 700
	Crunch		11 700
	(Allocating surplus on capital adjustment between partners)		

The capital adjustment account in the ledger will appear as:

	CAPITAL ADJUSTMENT			
		Debit	Credit	Balance
20X6		$	$	$
Jan. 1	Allowance for doubtful debts	1 000		1 000 DR
	Accumulated depreciation	5 600		6 600 DR
	Goodwill		30 000	23 400 CR
	Capital: Slamm	11 700		11 700 CR
	Capital: Crunch	11 700		–

The journal entry to account for Tinkle's entry to the partnership is:

20X6		$	$
Jan. 1	Cash at bank	25 000	
	Capital: Tinkle		25 000
	(Admission of new partner)		

As explained, Tinkle does not benefit from the revaluation of the assets of the existing partners. A balance sheet after the admission of Tinkle would appear as:

BALANCE SHEET: SLAMM, CRUNCH AND TINKLE as at 1 January 20X6			
Assets		$	$
Cash at bank			31 400
Accounts receivable		53 000	
less Allowance for doubtful accounts		5 000	48 000
Equipment		284 000	
less Accumulated depreciation		34 000	250 000
Goodwill			30 000
			359 400
Current liabilities			
Accounts payable			40 000
Owners' equity			
Capital: Slamm		171 700	
plus Current		85 200	256 900
Capital: Crunch		31 700	
plus Current		5 800	37 500
Capital: Tinkle			25 000
			359 400

These entries may appear to violate the principles of the historical cost system by permitting:

1. assets to be revalued
2. internally generated goodwill to be introduced
3. a 'surplus' not based on external transactions to be credited to capital

This criticism would be true were we accounting for an existing business. In this instance, however, one partnership entity is effectively being dissolved and replaced by a new partnership entity. In a sense, the assets of the 'old' partnership are being transferred to the 'new' partnership at their current market values, including an asset for goodwill. This is no different in principle to the situation we began with when the partnership of Slamm and Crunch acquired the assets of Slamm at their fair market values. (See page 247 for this example.) Nevertheless, practice varies, and there is some reluctance to introduce goodwill formally to the partnership records when admitting a new partner.

The final matter to consider is the sharing of profits and losses in the new partnership. Let us assume that the new partnership agreement contains the following provisions:

	Slamm	Crunch	Tinkle
Salaries	$80 000	$20 000	$20 000
Interest on capital	nil	nil	nil
Interest on advances	nil	nil	nil
Share of residual profits	one-third	one-third	one-third

Annual profit appropriations will thenceforth be made according to this agreement, using the procedures described above.

Dissolution of a partnership

In many cases the retirement, death or bankruptcy of a partner will require the partnership to be dissolved. Alternatively, the partners may agree to dissolve the partnership, or be forced to do so as a result of an inability to meet partnership debts. Another instance, to be considered below, is where it is desired to convert a partnership into a company.

These varied reasons why partnerships are dissolved give rise to a variety of methods for disposing of assets and paying off the liabilities. For example:

1. The assets might be sold in the normal way, and the partnership liabilities paid from the proceeds.
2. One of the partners might continue with the business alone, by buying the partnership assets and taking over the liabilities.
3. The partnership business might be sold as a going concern to another party or to a company incorporated for that purpose.

Regardless of the means of disposing of the assets and liabilities, the same principles apply from the viewpoint of the partnership entity, and hence in the partnership accounts. The partnership assets are sold, the debts repaid or transferred to some external party, and capital repaid or deficits made good by the partners.

Example: *Dissolution of partnership: assets sold individually*

After three years of trading, a downturn in the building industry brought difficulties to the partnership of Slamm, Crunch and Tinkle and it was decided to cease trading and to dissolve the partnership on 31 December 20X8. The trial balance as at that date was:

Cash at bank	$ 21 000	
Accounts receivable	36 300	
Allowance for doubtful debts		$ 5 000
Equipment	350 000	
Accumulated depreciation—equipment		113 000
Goodwill	30 000	
Accounts payable		52 000
Advance—Crunch		21 000
Revenue		550 000
Operating expenses	473 000	
Capital: Slamm		171 700
Crunch		31 700
Tinkle		25 000
Current: Slamm	22 000	
Crunch	4 600	
Tinkle	32 500	
	$969 400	$969 400

Further information:

1. Depreciation of 10 per cent is to be charged on the cost of the equipment.
2. Expenses of the dissolution amounted to $4500.
3. The equipment was sold for $190 000.
4. The accounts receivable realised $32 800, the remainder being bad debts.

The various steps will be illustrated by means of general journal entries. All entries are made as at 31 December 20X8. The partnership ledger is shown on pages 258–60.

1. Closing entries

Before any entries are made to close the partnership, its normal records are brought up to date as at the date of the dissolution. A trial balance is taken out, any necessary adjustments are entered, and closing and appropriation entries are made to allocate the trading profit or loss among the partners. In the example, the necessary entries are:

	$	$
Depreciation expense	35 000	
Accumulated depreciation		35 000
(Adjustment for depreciation)		
Revenue	550 000	
Operating expenses		473 000
Depreciation expense		35 000
Profit and loss summary		42 000
(Closing entries)		
Profit and loss summary	42 000	
Appropriation		42 000
(Transfer of net profit)		
Appropriation	120 000	
Current: Slamm		80 000
Crunch		20 000
Tinkle		20 000
(Salaries as per partnership agreement)		
Current: Slamm	26 000	
Crunch	26 000	
Tinkle	26 000	
Appropriation		78 000
(Appropriation of residual loss)		

To honour the terms of the partnership agreement, the partners' salaries are appropriated even though the profit is insufficient to cover them. Regarding the partners, Slamm is entitled to a credit for his salary, which no doubt reflects his greater work contribution, and Crunch and Tinkle will have to bear a larger share of the resulting residual loss.

2. Transfer of assets to realisation account

As the dissolution involves the disposal of assets, it is customary to open a realisation account to account for gains and losses on their sale.

The balances of all assets to be sold (including any associated contra accounts) are transferred to the realisation account, thus closing off the individual accounts. Normally the cash at bank account will remain open, unless, of course, the bank account is itself to be transferred to a new entity. In that case, a new cash at bank account will be opened to account for any cash received or dispersed as part of the realisation of the partnership. The entries in the present example are:

	$	$
Realisation	263 300	
Allowance for doubtful debts	5 000	
Accumulated depreciation	148 000	
Accounts receivable		36 300
Equipment		350 000
Goodwill		30 000
(Transfer of assets)		

3. Proceeds of realisation of assets

The proceeds of the disposal of the assets are debited to the cash at bank and credited to the realisation account.

	$	$
Cash	222 800	
Realisation		222 800
(Sale of equipment for $190 000 and		
receipts from receivables of $32 800)		

4. Expenses of realisation

Any expenses of the partnership dissolution, such as legal and accounting fees, or costs of disposal, are charged to the realisation account.

	$	$
Realisation	4 500	
Cash		4 500
(Expenses of realisation)		

5. Apportionment of loss on realisation between the partners

The balance of the realisation account after all of the above represents the profit or loss on realisation, and it is transferred to the partners' current accounts in proportion to the agreed sharing of profits and losses.

	$	$
Current: Slamm	15 000	
Crunch	15 000	
Tinkle	15 000	
Realisation		45 000
(Allocation of loss on realisation)		

6. Repayment of liabilities and partners' advances

It is not unusual for partners to lend money to the partnership, such loans being known as partners' advances. These are treated as liabilities of the partnership. However, on the dissolution of the partnership the outside liabilities must be repaid before the advances. Provided funds are available, advances are then repaid before capital.

	$	$
Accounts payable	52 000	
Cash		52 000
(Repayment of liabilities)		
Advance: Crunch	21 000	
Cash		21 000
(Repayment of liabilities)		

7. Transfer of current to capital accounts

In preparation for the final settlement of the partners' capital accounts, the current accounts are transferred to their respective capital accounts.

	$	$
Current: Slamm	17 000	
Capital: Slamm		17 000
(Transfer of current account to capital)		
Current: Crunch	25 600	
Capital: Crunch		25 600
(Transfer of current account to capital)		
Current: Tinkle	53 500	
Capital: Tinkle		53 500
(Transfer of current account to capital)		

8. Repayment of capital

Providing there is sufficient cash to settle all of the liabilities from 6 (previous), the only accounts now remaining open should be the cash at bank account and the partners' capital accounts. If a partner's capital account is in debit, perhaps because of losses or excessive drawings by the partner, then that partner is required to contribute cash to the partnership equal to the debit balance. Once this is done, the remaining cash should be sufficient to pay to the partners the amounts of the credit balances in their capital accounts. Then, since debits equal credits, all ledger accounts will have been closed.

	$	$
Cash	28 500	
Capital: Tinkle		28 500
(Contribution from Tinkle to meet deficit of capital)		
Capital: Slamm	188 700	
Crunch	6 100	
Cash		194 800
(Repayments of capital)		

These journal entries will be posted to the general ledger, which is shown on pages 258–60.

GENERAL LEDGER: SLAMM, CRUNCH AND TINKLE

Assets sold individually

Realisation

20X8		Debit $	Credit $	Balance $
Dec. 31	Accounts receivable	36 300		36 300 DR
	Allowance doubtful debts		5 000	31 300 DR
	Equipment	350 000		381 300 DR
	Goodwill	30 000		411 300 DR
	Accum. depn—equipment		148 000	263 300 DR
	Cash		190 000	73 300 DR
	Cash		32 800	40 500 DR
	Cash	4 500		45 000 DR
	Current: Slamm		15 000	30 000 DR
	Crunch		15 000	15 000 DR
	Tinkle		15 000	–

Cash at bank

20X8				
Dec. 31	Balance			21 000 DR
	Realisation	190 000		211 000 DR
	Realisation	32 800		243 800 DR
	Realisation		4 500	239 300 DR
	Accounts payable		52 000	187 300 DR
	Advance: Crunch		21 000	166 300 DR
	Capital: Tinkle	28 500		194 800 DR
	Slamm		188 700	6 100 DR
	Crunch		6 100	–

Accounts receivable

20X8				
Dec. 31	Balance			36 300 DR
	Realisation		36 300	–

Allowance for doubtful debts

20X8				
Dec. 31	Balance			5 000 CR
	Realisation	5 000		–

Equipment

20X8				
Dec. 31	Balance			350 000 DR
	Realisation		350 000	–

Accumulated depreciation: equipment

20X8				
Dec. 31	Balance			113 000 CR
	Depreciation expense		35 000	148 000 CR
	Realisation	148 000		–

continues

GENERAL LEDGER: SLAMM, CRUNCH AND TINKLE
Assets sold individually

Goodwill

20X8		Debit $	Credit $	Balance $
Dec. 31	Balance			30 000 DR
	Realisation		30 000	—

Accounts payable

20X8				
Dec. 31	Balance			52 000 CR
	Cash	52 000		—

Advance: Crunch

20X8				
Dec. 31	Balance			21 000 CR
	Cash	21 000		—

Revenue

20X8				
Dec. 31	Balance			550 000 CR
	Profit and loss summary	550 000		—

Operating expenses

20X8				
Dec. 31	Balance			473 000 DR
	Profit and loss summary		473 000	—

Depreciation expense

20X8				
Dec. 31	Accumulated depreciation	35 000		35 000 DR
	Profit and loss summary		35 000	—

Capital: Slamm

20X8				
Dec. 31	Balance			171 700 CR
	Current		17 000	188 700 CR
	Cash	188 700		—

Current: Slamm

20X8				
Dec. 31	Balance			22 000 DR
	Appropriation (salary)		80 000	58 000 CR
	Appropriation (loss)	26 000		32 000 CR
	Realisation	15 000		17 000 CR
	Capital	17 000		—

Capital: Crunch

20X8				
Dec. 31	Balance			31 700 CR
	Current	25 600		6 100 CR
	Cash	6 100		—

continues

GENERAL LEDGER: SLAMM, CRUNCH AND TINKLE

Assets sold individually

Current: Crunch

		Debit	Credit	Balance
		$	$	$
20X8				
Dec. 31	Balance			4 600 DR
	Appropriation (salary)		20 000	15 400 CR
	Appropriation (loss)	26 000		10 600 DR
	Realisation	15 000		25 600 DR
	Capital		25 600	—

Capital: Tinkle

		Debit	Credit	Balance
20X8				
Dec. 31	Balance			25 000 CR
	Current	53 500		28 500 DR
	Cash		28 500	—

Current: Tinkle

		Debit	Credit	Balance
20X8				
Dec. 31	Balance			32 500 DR
	Appropriation (salary)		20 000	12 500 DR
	Appropriation (loss)	26 000		38 500 DR
	Realisation	15 000		53 500 DR
	Capital		53 500	—

Profit and loss summary

		Debit	Credit	Balance
20X8				
Dec. 31	Revenue		550 000	550 000 CR
	Operating expenses	473 000		77 000 CR
	Depreciation expense	35 000		42 000 CR
	Appropriation	42 000		—

Appropriation

		Debit	Credit	Balance
20X8				
Dec. 31	Profit and loss summary		42 000	42 000 CR
	Current: Slamm	80 000		38 000 DR
	Crunch	20 000		58 000 DR
	Tinkle	20 000		78 000 DR
	Current: Slamm		26 000	52 000 DR
	Crunch		26 000	26 000 DR
	Tinkle		26 000	—

Partnership dissolution: other possibilities

Some of the other possible means of dissolving the partnership of Slamm, Crunch and Tinkle will now be considered. All introduce only minor variations to the above treatment.

1. Partnership sold as a going concern

Suppose a buyer were found for the business as a going concern. The buyer would normally take over all of the assets of the partnership, including the existing cash balance, and would pay off the outside liabilities as part of the consideration. Suppose, for example:

- Leviathan Ltd agrees to take over the partnership business, for the payment of $199 000 in cash.
- There were no expenses of realisation to be paid by the partnership.

The major changes to the first example are the transfer of the opening cash balance and the accounts payable to the realisation account, since these are now being taken over as part of the realisation. The ledger account for realisation will appear as follows:

PORTION OF GENERAL LEDGER: SLAMM, CRUNCH AND TINKLE			
Partnership sold as a going concern			
Realisation			
	Debit	Credit	Balance
20X8	$	$	$
Dec. 31 Cash at bank	21 000		21 000 DR
Accounts receivable	36 300		57 300 DR
Allowance for doubtful debts		5 000	52 300 DR
Equipment	350 000		402 300 DR
Accumulated depreciation		148 000	254 300 DR
Goodwill	30 000		284 300 DR
Accounts payable		52 000	232 300 DR
Cash (from Leviathon)		199 000	33 300 DR
Current: Slamm		11 100	22 200 DR
Crunch		11 100	11 100 DR
Tinkle		11 100	–

2. Partnership taken over by one of the partners

Suppose that Slamm had agreed to take over the partnership business as a going concern for consideration of $199 000. The only change to the above would be that instead of bringing cash of $199 000 in directly, that amount would be debited to Slamm's capital account. The amount of cash to be paid in would then be determined by the balance in Slamm's capital account after appropriations of profits and losses and after transfer of the balance in the current account to capital.

Companies

In Chapter 1 various forms of business ownership were discussed, including limited liability and unlimited liability companies, as well as the legal procedures for registering a company and some aspects of the respective roles of directors, auditors and shareholders.

The relevant sections in Chapter 1 might need to be reviewed prior to proceeding with your reading of this chapter. The following section compares companies with two other forms of ownership studied in previous sections of the text.

Comparison of companies with other forms of business ownership

1. Limited liability of shareholders

Most companies are limited by shares. In these companies, the liability of shareholders to the company and its creditors is the amount of the unpaid portion of the issue price of their shares. For example, a shareholder holding 1000 $1 shares paid to 60 cents on each share is liable to pay the unpaid amount (i.e. 40 cents × 1000 shares = $400). The shareholder may lose $1000 (1000 × $1) if the company fails but cannot be compelled to contribute further. A sole proprietor is liable for all the debts of the business. Partners are jointly and severally liable for all the debts of the partnership.

2. Perpetual succession and transferability of shares

A company may continue indefinitely and is not affected by the death of individual share-holders. With a sole proprietor business and a partnership (unless otherwise agreed) death or retirement brings the business to an end. The continuity of companies enables them to avoid the problems of divisions of property experienced by the other forms of ownership. Furthermore, the separation of the company from its shareholders enables easier transfer of ownership (shares). A shareholder may (subject to the instructions in the constitution) sell or otherwise dispose of shares at any time. In the case of public companies this transferability might be made easier by stock exchange listing.

In the case of a sole proprietor it is certainly possible to sell or transfer ownership but not always with the ease that a shareholder can sell or transfer shares in a listed company. In many cases partners are not permitted to sell or transfer their ownership in the business.

3. Raising additional finance

Publicly listed companies may be able to obtain additional funds by the issue of further shares and debentures to the public. Such an advantage is not available to proprietary companies. In these circumstances a small company has similar access to funds as a sole proprietor or a partnership business.

4. Ownership and management

The Board of Directors acts as the management of the company and hence is responsible for the affairs of the company. Ultimate control of the company rests with the shareholders as they have the collective right to elect the directors. However, a shareholder may decide not to vote or attend annual general meetings of the company yet still remain an owner and a recipient of company profits. This is unlikely to be the case in a sole proprietor business where the owner generally takes a major part in management. Similarly, in partnerships both management and control are shared by all partners (subject to the partnership agreement).

5. Tax savings advantages

Many family companies are formed in order to gain tax saving advantages. However, a detailed analysis of how a corporate structure may be used to lessen personal taxation is beyond the scope of this text.

In certain circumstances some of the points made above may provide little advantage to shareholders. They may argue that, as owners, they have insufficient say in management and that their companies are subject to too much regulation (e.g. Corporations Law, stock exchange regulations) and public scrutiny.

Contracts with resource providers—shareholders and lenders

Equity and debt

Debt
As discussed in previous chapters, debt involves a credit relationship whereby funds lent may be secured by a mortgage, a lien, a floating charge or the guarantee of another person or

entity. In the case of a public company part of their long-term funds may be raised by issuing debentures or unsecured notes to individual financial institutions or by issuing them to the public at large. This process allows a company to raise large sums of money by involving many lenders; some lenders may contribute only a relatively small amount—perhaps a few hundred dollars. These securities are often listed and traded on the stock exchange.

Debentures are a commonly used security issued to raise funds. The amount borrowed or deposited is secured by a mortgage or a floating charge over all of the assets. The contract requires that the borrowing company will repay the debt on an agreed date or under certain conditions. Until repaid, interest is paid at defined intervals. This method of finance provides relatively cheap finance as the interest expense on the debt is tax deductible. Often debenture holders require the borrowing company to maintain certain financial stability ratios. This type of condition is sometimes described as a debt covenant.

Unsecured notes are debts which do not possess a floating charge over the assets of the business but in other respects are similar to debentures.

Equity

As described in Chapters 1 and 2, equity finance consists of share capital, retained profits and reserves of the entity. Ordinary shares represent the majority of share capital for most companies. This class of shares possesses no preference rights over other classes of shares as to either dividends out of profits or capital on winding up.

Share capital may consist of several distinct classes, each with specific rights and obligations. For example, preference shares may receive priority over ordinary shares in matters of dividend payments and sometimes the distribution of assets should the company be wound up. Within these preference shares may be those classified as participating preference shares. Some preference shares are called 'cumulative', meaning that the annual dividend accumulates if it was unable to be paid in prior periods. Some are redeemable, meaning that they may be redeemed for cash at a certain future date. Such additional rights received by the investor might be at the expense of a right to take part in the management of the company (i.e. they might forgo voting rights at the annual general meeting).

Hybrid debt instruments

Some financial instruments possess some of the characteristics of debt and equity. For instance, redeemable preference shares have those characteristics in that they are shares but have a limited life. Similarly, some preference shares possess a fixed dividend rate and may deny any voting rights to their holders.

Preference shares might have debt-like characteristics, but there is a kind of debt that has some of the characteristics of equity. For example, convertible notes give creditors the right at the end of the note's fixed term to convert their security not to cash but to company shares. It could be said that such convertible notes have more of the characteristics of equity than debt.

In such circumstances, the distinction between debt and equity becomes less clear and understanding financial reports more difficult.

Debt and equity—the appropriate mix

The use of debt in an organisation's financial structure is often described as leverage. It enables the organisation to hold a greater level of assets than it could if it had to rely solely on owners' equity. Where the profit from the use of the additional assets is greater than the cost of the debt (interest) used to finance the assets, the additional profits flow to the shareholders. Of course the use of debt financing involves risk. The greater the level of debt the greater the risk that the company will not be able to meet its interest commitments or repayments of the debt. This dilemma for management is further discussed in Chapter 11. Table 8.1 shows shareholders' equity as a proportion of total assets for a sample of listed companies in Australia. Note that the nature of the industry or industries with which a business entity is concerned has an important impact on the financial structure of the entity. This issue will be discussed in more detail in Chapter 12.

Table 8.1 Shareholders' equity to total assets

Company	Shareholders' equity ($m)	Total assets ($m)	Shareholders' equity: total assets (%)
Coles Myer	2 516.3	6 696.6	37.6
Colonial	2 141	34 248.0	6.3
David Jones Ltd	469.1	941.3	49.8
Email Ltd	725.0	1 539.6	47.1
Foodland Associated Ltd	554.7	1 464.7	37.9
Foster's Brewing Group Ltd	2 800.4	4 145.9	67.5
GIO Australia Holdings Co.	1 569.7	6 631.4	23.7
Great Central Mines	284.7	460.0	61.9
Harvey Norman Holdings Ltd	257.5	514.4	50.1
Hills Motorway Group	141.3	478.3	29.5
Incitec Ltd	279.7	556.6	50.3
National Australia Bank Ltd	12 581	201 969.0	6.2
Pacific Dunlop Ltd	1 846.8	5 592.9	33.0
Qantas Airways Ltd	2 671.0	9 912.0	26.9
Southcorp Holdings Ltd	1 392.6	2 840.8	49.0
WD & HO Wills Ltd	261.6	497.2	52.7
Westpac Banking Corporation Ltd	7 380 (av)	124 778 (av)	5.9
Woolworths Ltd	1 225.7	3 563.5	34.4

Company share issues

In Australia, all shares have been required to have a par value. This is generally referred to as the legal value or 'face value' per share. Par value is the smallest unit of share capital that can be acquired. Traditionally, companies in Australia have often issued shares at par value in cases where shares were issued immediately on incorporation or soon afterwards. However, when successful companies or those expected to be successful in the future issued shares they usually issued them at a premium (i.e. the amount by which the price payable exceeded the par value). In practical terms par values have diminished in importance as Corporations Law has been modernised, and often par values have been somewhat trivial. For example, National Australia Bank Ltd shares are shown on the Issuer Sponsored Holding Statement as $1 (see p. 265), but their last issue price in the share top-up plan was $19.33.

In Australia, par values have been removed and we have followed the example of the United States and New Zealand where shares are now issued with no par value. This means that shares will no longer be issued at a premium. Likewise, as was sometimes the practice, dividends will no longer be expressed as a percentage of par value but simply as an amount (e.g. 47c per share).

Furthermore, the Australasian method of recording issues of shares, a method commonly described in accounting texts, will become less appropriate as the concept of authorised capital will no longer exist. Authorised or registered capital represented the number of shares times par value per share. While the requirement to state the authorised share capital in the company's constitution is abolished, the company's constitution will be able to set a numerical limit on the number of shares a company might issue.

Transferring ownership

The Issuer Sponsored Holding statement replaces the share certificate as proof of ownership. This holder statement is part of a new system called CHESS (Clearing House Electronic Sub-register System). Under this system paper transfers of ownership are eliminated for market transactions, as these transactions will take place electronically. The glossary that accompanies the National Australia Bank Issuer Sponsored Holding Statement (see p. 266) lists terms that describe the types of transactions and events that might affect share ownership. It is beyond the scope of this text to discuss each in detail.

The ledger entries to form a company will follow the 'direct method' rather than the traditional 'Australasian method', which is sometimes used in other textbooks on corporate accounting.

Figure 8.1 National Australia Bank Issuer Sponsored Holding Statement and glossary

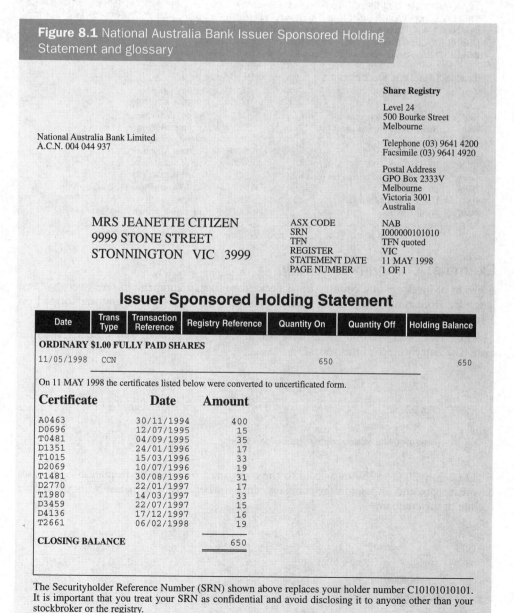

Share Registry

Level 24
500 Bourke Street
Melbourne

Telephone (03) 9641 4200
Facsimile (03) 9641 4920

Postal Address
GPO Box 2333V
Melbourne
Victoria 3001
Australia

National Australia Bank Limited
A.C.N. 004 044 937

MRS JEANETTE CITIZEN
9999 STONE STREET
STONNINGTON VIC 3999

ASX CODE	NAB
SRN	I000000101010
TFN	TFN quoted
REGISTER	VIC
STATEMENT DATE	11 MAY 1998
PAGE NUMBER	1 OF 1

Issuer Sponsored Holding Statement

Date	Trans Type	Transaction Reference	Registry Reference	Quantity On	Quantity Off	Holding Balance
ORDINARY $1.00 FULLY PAID SHARES						
11/05/1998	CCN			650		650

On 11 MAY 1998 the certificates listed below were converted to uncertificated form.

Certificate	Date	Amount
A0463	30/11/1994	400
D0696	12/07/1995	15
T0481	04/09/1995	35
D1351	24/01/1996	17
T1015	15/03/1996	33
D2069	10/07/1996	19
T1481	30/08/1996	31
D2770	22/01/1997	17
T1980	14/03/1997	33
D3459	22/07/1997	15
D4136	17/12/1997	16
T2661	06/02/1998	19
CLOSING BALANCE		650

The Securityholder Reference Number (SRN) shown above replaces your holder number C10101010101. It is important that you treat your SRN as confidential and avoid disclosing it to anyone other than your stockbroker or the registry.

continues

Figure 8.1 continued

Glossary of terms

ASX CODE – the Australian Stock Exchange code for security.

SRN – (Security Reference Number) a number which uniquely identifies a holding within a register. **It is important that your SRN be regarded as confidential. Avoid disclosing it to anyone other than the registry or your stockbroker.**

TFN – Whether a Tax File Number or Exemption has been recorded by the issuer.

REGISTER – the reigster on which the securities are recorded.

STATEMENT DATE – the date the statement is issued.

PAGE NUMBER – information may continue onto other pages and for your reference, pages are numbered.

DATE – the date the transaction was recorded on the register.

TRANS TYPE – please refer to the 'Transaction Type Descriptions' listed below.

TRANSACTION REFERENCE – supplementary reference.

REGISTRY REFERENCE – the transaction reference relevant to the registry.

QUANTITY ON – the number of securities registered into the holding

QUANTITY OFF – the number of securities registered out of the holding.

HOLDING BALANCE – the balance of the holding after each transaction has been recorded.

Transaction Type Descriptions

ADJ	– Adjustment		OCN	– Option Conversion
ALT	– Allotment		OMT	– Off Market Transfer
BON	– Bonus Issue Allotment		OPT	– Option Allotment
BSP	– Bonus Share Plan Allotment		REV	– Allotment Reversal
BYB	– Buyback		RLS	– Release of Employee Share Plan Shares
CAL	– Call Paid		SCD	– Dividend Allotment
CCN	– Conversion from Certificate(s)		SOS	– Sale of Staff Shares
DRP	– Dividend Reinvestment Plan Allotment		SPP	– Share Purchase Plan
DVM	– Divestment		STP	– Share Top Up Plan
HSC	– Holding Status Change		TRF	– Transfer
NMC	– Name Change		UCN	– Conversion to/from Issuer Sponsorship
SUR	– Survivorship			

Example: *Company formation*

A group of investors in a country town decided to form a company to take over the local hardware store run by Pop Hoff, who was about to retire. The company was formed on 1 July 20X1 as Pleasant Company Ltd.

On 2 July 20X1, 40 000 shares were issued at an issue price of $1 to the investors for cash. The entry to record this was:

20X1		$	$
July 2	Cash at bank	40 000	
	Paid-up capital		40 000
	(Issue of 40 000 ordinary shares at issue price of $1)		

On 2 July 20X1, $2500 was paid to the company's solicitors for formation costs. This payment represents an asset to the company, since the benefits of formation will extend over the life of the company.

20X1		$	$
July 2	Formation costs	2 500	
	Cash at bank		2 500
	(Costs of formation)		

On 3 July 20X1 the company purchased, as a going concern, the business of Mr Hoff, whose balance sheet at that date was as follows:

BALANCE SHEET: P. HOFF'S HARDWARE					
as at 3 July 20X1					
Assets	$	$	**Liabilities**	$	$
Cash at bank		2 000	Accounts payable		21 000
Inventory		32 000			
Equipment	42 000		**Owners' equity**		
less Accum. depn	24 000	18 000	Capital	25 000	
			plus Profit	6 000	31 000
		52 000			52 000

As consideration, Mr Hoff was to receive $40 000 cash, plus 10 000 ordinary shares in Pleasant Company Ltd valued at $1. The total consideration was therefore $50 000. Since the takeover reflects a new purchase, the assets were revalued at their 'fair market' values to the following:

Inventory	$27 000
Equipment	$ 9 000

The old 'historical costs' of Mr Hoff are no longer relevant and the fair market values will be adopted by the company. As the entire business is taken over, the entry to record the purchase takes in all assets and all liabilities. The owners' equity accounts are not entered in the purchaser's books, since they are Mr Hoff's own record of the difference between his assets and his liabilities. In the equation assets − liabilities = owners' equity, the left-hand side records the net assets of the business, whereas the right-hand side merely explains the residual claim of the owner.

The net tangible assets acquired were therefore valued at $17 000, as follows:

Assets		
Cash	$ 2 000	
Inventory	27 000	
Equipment	9 000	$38 000
less Liabilities		
Accounts payable		21 000
Net tangible assets acquired		$17 000

The agreed consideration, however, was $50 000. The difference of $33 000 represents payment for an asset that did not appear on Mr Hoff's books, known as his *goodwill*. As explained previously in regard to partnership goodwill, it is usual to pay an amount above the value of the net tangible assets acquired to cover such intangible factors as the good name of the business, customer contacts and secret processes. These factors are not identified specifically, but are included together as goodwill.

The entries for the purchase and payment of the vendor are:

20X1		$	$
July 3	Cash at bank	2 000	
	Inventory	27 000	
	Equipment	9 000	
	Goodwill	33 000	
	Accounts payable		21 000
	Liability to vendor		50 000
	(Purchase of business)		
July 3	Liability to vendor	50 000	
	Cash at bank		40 000
	Paid-up capital		10 000
	(Payment of vendor)		

Mr Hoff receives $40 000 additional cash and he is the holder of 10 000 $1 ordinary shares in the company.

Appropriation of profits

Unlike sole traders and partnerships, a company is a separate legal entity, apart from its shareholders. This has implications for the appropriation of profits. A sole trader may withdraw profits at will and this right is recognised by transferring all profits to the capital account. Similarly, partners may withdraw profits with ease and hence all profits are appropriated to the partners' current accounts. In a company, however, the shareholders do not gain specific entitlement to a distribution of the profits until the directors have recommended a dividend and it is agreed to at the annual meeting of shareholders. During the year the directors may pay an interim dividend in anticipation of the final profit, but this is entirely at the discretion of the directors. The unappropriated profits might never be distributed to shareholders and many companies have financed continuing operations to a considerable extent by retained profits.

The fact that shareholders do not have a present entitlement to the profit is recognised by creating a separate account for retained profits. Traditionally, this has been called an 'appropriation' account, although modern usage is tending towards more descriptive titles such as 'retained profits' or 'unappropriated profits'.

In a company, the owners' equity is commonly referred to as shareholders' equity. This section of the balance sheet will report both the contributed capital and the retained profits.

Example: *Profit appropriations*

The example of the Pleasant Company Ltd will be extended by considering the closing entries and the financial statements at the end of its first year of operations, on 30 June 20X2. The trial balance at that date was:

TRIAL BALANCE (AFTER ADJUSTMENTS): PLEASANT COMPANY LTD as at 30 June 20X2		
	Debit	Credit
Cash at bank	$ 13 500	
Inventory	32 000	
Equipment	9 000	
Accum. depn equipment		$ 4 500
Land	25 000	
Formation costs	2 500	
Goodwill	33 000	
Accounts payable		34 000
Paid-up capital		50 000
Revenue		48 000
Cost of goods sold	10 000	
General expenses	7 000	
Depreciation expense	4 500	
	$136 500	$136 500

Additional information:

1. Income taxation payable for the current year is estimated to be $7000.
2. A final dividend of $2000 is to be provided for.
3. $13 500 is to be transferred to a general reserve.

The journal entries to record the adjusting, closing and appropriation entries are:

Income taxation expense	7 000	
Taxation payable		7 000
(Adjustment for taxation payable)		
Revenue	48 000	
Profit and loss summary		48 000
(Closing entry)		
Profit and loss summary	28 500	
Cost of goods sold		10 000
General expenses		7 000
Depreciation expense		4 500
Taxation expense		7 000
(Closing entry)		
Profit and loss summary	19 500	
Retained profits		19 500
(Transfer of net profit)		
Retained profits	15 500	
Dividend payable		2 000
General reserve		13 500
(Appropriation of profit)		

The first entry is an adjustment to incorporate the accrual for taxation payable. This is an estimate at present, as the amount payable has not been assessed by the taxation authorities. As a separate legal entity, a company is required to pay income tax on its taxable income. Sole traders and partnerships are not taxed as operating entities because they do not have a separate legal identity.

The second and third entries are routine closing entries, and the fourth entry transfers the net profit to the retained profits account. As this is the first year of operations, this account will not have an opening balance of retained profits brought forward from previous years.

The final entry appropriates the profit. The capital maintenance requirement means that dividends may be paid only out of profits. These profits may have been earned in the current year or in the past. The balance in the retained profits account represents the total available for distribution as dividends, since payment of a higher dividend would amount to a distribution of the capital.

From the unappropriated profit after taxation of $19 500, the directors have decided to recommend a dividend of $2000. Although this amount is not final until ratified by shareholders at the annual meeting, variations are rare and it is customary practice to appropriate profits for the dividend in anticipation of approval. The credit appears as a dividend payable and thus is shown as a liability. The directors' recommendation is thought to be sufficient evidence to create a liability to shareholders. After this transfer, $17 500 of retained profits still remain, from which future dividends could be provided.

The directors of Pleasant Company Ltd have decided to inform shareholders that they intend to 'reserve' $13 500 of these profits and not pay them out as a dividend. This decision is communicated in the financial statements by the transfer of $13 500 to a general reserve. This is a confusing entry, since it accomplishes nothing in real terms. No funds are invested elsewhere (the cash account is unaffected by the entry), nor are specific funds 'earmarked' for future use. The entry's only effect is to give a message to shareholders of the restrictions on future dividends from available profits.

Both the general reserve account and the retained profits account report retained profits and they appear together in the shareholders' equity section of the balance sheet. The difference is that profits remaining in the retained profits account may subsequently be distributed to shareholders, whereas it is not intended to base dividends on the amount allocated to the general reserve. Even this difference is unimportant, since directors may transfer amounts back from reserves to the retained profits account at any time.

PROFIT AND LOSS STATEMENT: PLEASANT COMPANY LTD		
for year ended 30 June 20X2		
Revenue		$48 000
less Cost of goods sold		10 000
Gross profit		38 000
less General expenses	$7 000	
Depreciation expense	4 500	11 500
Net profit before taxation		26 500
less Taxation expense		7 000
Net profit		$19 500

RETAINED PROFITS STATEMENT: PLEASANT COMPANY LTD

as at 30 June 20X2

Retained profits at 1 July 20X1		$ Nil
plus Net profit		19 500
		19 500
less Appropriations		
Dividend payable	$ 2 000	
General reserve	13 500	15 500
Retained profits at 30 June 20X2		$ 4 000

BALANCE SHEET: PLEASANT COMPANY LTD

as at 30 June 20X2

Assets	$	$	Liabilities	$	$
Cash at bank		13 500	Accounts payable	34 000	
Inventory		32 000	Tax payable	7 000	
Equipment	9 000		Dividends payable	2 000	43 000
less Accum. depn	4 500	4 500			
Land		25 000	**Shareholders' equity**		
Formation costs		2 500	Paid-up capital	50 000	
Goodwill		33 000	Retained profits	4 000	
			General reserve	13 500	67 500
		110 500			110 500

Following the appropriation of profits, the financial statements (previous) are prepared to convey the information established in the ledger accounts.

Interpretation of shareholders' equity

In the example, shareholders' equity is composed of two parts: the contributed capital, known as the issued capital, and retained profits, consisting of the balance of unappropriated profits plus profits transferred to reserves.

The separation of retained profits from contributed capital is an important aspect of company accounting, reflecting the capital maintenance and profit assumption established in Chapter 6. In companies, dividends may be paid only when there are retained profits to support them, that is, they may not be paid out of capital. This ensures capital maintenance and provides a protection to creditors, in that the amount of the capital is always available somewhere in the net assets to cover the repayment of debts (except where there are accumulated losses). Contributed capital may not be returned to shareholders except by formal resolution of the shareholders and in agreement with creditors and perhaps the courts.

The general reserve and the retained profits accounts together indicate the maximum dividend that the company may declare. Whether the company can afford to pay a dividend depends on factors such as the liquidity of its assets, or priorities for expenditure of resources.

The categories within shareholders' equity explain the means by which the net assets have been funded. They are not in themselves hoards of cash or other assets. In the ownership equation, assets – liabilities = owners' equity, the 'reality' belongs on the left-hand side, with the owners' equity entries merely explaining how the present level of net assets was raised.

Example: *The meaning of shareholders' equity*

Bland Ltd began operations on 1 January 20X1 with a capital contribution in cash of $100 000. This amount was invested immediately in a block of land. During the year, rental revenue from the land provided cash of $40 000 and there were no expenses. This amount was used to purchase some further land for cash.

The entire profit for the year consisted of the $40 000 revenue and it was decided to transfer $26 000 of the profit to a reserve. The financial statements appear as follows:

RETAINED PROFITS STATEMENT: BLAND LTD	
as at 31 December 20X1	
	$
Retained profits at 1 January 20X1	Nil
plus Net profit	40 000
	40 000
less Appropriations	
General reserve	26 000
Retained profits at 31 December 20X1	14 000

BALANCE SHEET: BLAND LTD				
as at 31 December 20X1				
	$		$	$
Assets		**Liabilities**		Nil
Land	140 000	**Shareholders' equity**		
		Paid-up capital	100 000	
		Retained profits	14 000	
		General reserve	26 000	140 000
	140 000			140 000

This example shows that the retained profits and the general reserve merely explain that the entity was able to finance the additional block of land from trading profits. They are not in themselves assets. To find the substance to these accounts it is necessary to examine the net assets, which in this case are entirely land. Despite the presence of retained profits, there is no cash. Furthermore, the transfer to the general reserve has no immediate effect on the composition of assets, nor even the total of shareholders' equity. It is merely a book entry to rearrange the shareholders' equity.

To avoid confusion, the term 'shareholders' equity' will generally be used in preference to the more traditional term 'shareholders' funds', which implies falsely that the accounts therein represent funds of some kind.

Profit appropriations: later years

In general, the profit appropriations in each year follow the same pattern. However, in later years there will be a balance of unappropriated profits (or losses) brought forward from previous years. It will be necessary also to account for dividends and taxes paid during the year, for which appropriations had previously been made. A further example will illustrate these problems.

Example: *Profit appropriations in later years*

The Cathy Co. Ltd has been in operation for several years. At 1 January 20X5 its balance sheet was as follows:

Assets	$100 000	Liabilities		
		Tax payable	$16 000	
		Dividend payable	9 000	$ 25 000
		Shareholders' equity		
		Paid-up capital	40 000	
		General reserve	17 000	
		Retained profits	18 000	75 000
	$100 000			$100 000

During 20X5 the following occurred:

February 12	Dividend paid	$ 9 000
March 31	Taxation paid	15 600
August 12	Interim dividend paid	4 500
Net profit before tax for year		73 000
Adjustments and appropriations required:		
	Tax payable for 20X5	33 000
	Final dividend for 20X5	10 000
	Transfer to general reserve	2 500

The relevant ledger accounts are displayed below and the financial statements on page 274.

	GENERAL LEDGER ACCOUNTS			
Liabilities	**Tax payable**			
		Debit	Credit	Balance
		$	$	$
Jan. 1 Balance				16 000 CR
Mar. 31 Cash		15 600		400 CR
Dec. 31 Profit and loss summary		400		–
Income tax expense			33 000	33 000 CR
	Dividend payable			
Jan. 1 Balance				9 000 CR
Feb. 12 Cash		9 000		–
Dec. 31 Retained profits			10 000	10 000 CR
Shareholders' equity	**General reserve**			
Jan. 1 Balance				17 000 CR
Dec. 31 Retained profits			2 500	19 500 CR
	Retained profits			
Jan. 1 Balance				18 000 CR
Dec. 31 Profit and loss summary (net profit)			40 400	58 400 CR
Dividend payable		10 000		48 400 CR
Interim dividend paid		4 500		43 900 CR
General reserve		2 500		41 400 CR
				continues

GENERAL LEDGER ACCOUNTS

Shareholders' equity (continued)

Interim dividend paid

		Debit	Credit	Balance
		$	$	$
Aug. 12	Cash	4 500		4 500 DR
Dec. 31	Retained profits		4 500	–

Income tax expense

Dec. 31	Tax payable	33 000		33 000 DR
	Profit and loss summary		33 000	–

Profit and loss summary

Dec. 31	Balance			73 000 CR
	Tax payable		400	73 400 CR
	Income tax expense	33 000		40 400 CR
	Retained profits	40 400		–

ABBREVIATED PROFIT AND LOSS STATEMENT: CATHY CO. LTD
for the year ended 31 December 20X5

Net profit before taxation	$73 000
plus Excess taxation provided in 20X4	400
	73 400
less Taxation expense for 20X5	33 000
Net profit after taxation	$40 400

RETAINED PROFITS STATEMENT: CATHY CO. LTD
as at 31 December 20X5

Retained profits at 1 January 20X5		$18 000
plus Net profit		40 400
		58 400
less Appropriations:		
Final dividend payable	$10 000	
Interim dividend paid	4 500	
Transfer to general reserve	2 500	17 000
Retained profits at 31 December 20X5		$41 400

PORTION OF BALANCE SHEET: CATHY CO. LTD
as at 31 December 20X5

Liabilities	$
Tax payable	33 000
Dividend payable	10 000
Shareholders' equity	
Paid-up capital	40 000
General reserve	19 500
Retained profits	41 400

The tax payable account began with a balance of $16 000, which was the amount provided for estimated tax payable at the end of 20X4. The actual taxation paid in 20X5 was only $15 600, leaving $400 over-provided in the liability account. This amount is transferred back to the credit of the profit and loss summary account at the end of 20X5. The estimate of taxation payable for 20X5, $33 000, is then debited against income tax expense and credited to the tax payable account. In Australia, company law requires that the profit and loss statement clearly shows the amount of taxation expense for the current year ($33 000) as illustrated in the above profit and loss statement.

Three events affect dividends. First, the dividend paid on 12 February refers to the final dividend provided at the end of 20X4, so that it is only necessary to debit the payment to the liability account for dividend payable established at the end of 20X4. Second, the dividend paid on 12 August of $4500 was an interim dividend for 20X5. This dividend was paid in anticipation of profits for 20X5 and is entered initially in an interim dividend paid account. At the end of 20X5 it must be appropriated. Third, the directors recommended a final dividend for the year of $10 000. This is appropriated in the normal way, by debiting the retained profits account and crediting a liability for dividend payable.

Further aspects of share issues

Reserves created by the appropriation of profits are known as profit or revenue reserves. The latter are available for distribution as a cash dividend.

These revenue reserves may be converted into share capital by a bonus issue. Suppose that, at a later stage, a company decided to make a bonus issue of one $1 share for each ten shares held by the owners of its paid-up capital of $130 000, the bonus to be made out of the general reserve account. The value of the new shares is, in total, $13 000, and the entry to record the issue will be:

	$	$
General reserve	13 000	
Paid-up capital		13 000
(Bonus issue)		

Shareholders have gained little from the bonus issue, apart from the conversion of the general reserve account to share capital. They will gain only if the stock-market value of the new shares plus the existing shares is greater than the total value before the issue. Normally the stock market will adjust prices to prevent this from occurring, unless it is believed that the bonus issue will be supported by an increase in total dividends.

In these cases, the shareholder forgoes forever the right to receive a cash dividend based on the reserve and the profits become permanent capital of the company. It is difficult to see how shareholders should be elated at the receipt of such a 'bonus', especially since it is subject to taxation as income of the investor.

Issue of shares by instalments

Companies will sometimes issue shares for payment by instalments. The instalments may be due at three stages:

1. *Application*. An amount due with the application for shares.
2. *Allotment*. A payment due when the shares are formally allotted to applicants.
3. *Calls*. Amounts due when they are called for by the company.

As instalments due on allotment are relatively rare, they are not considered in this book.

Example: *Issue of shares by instalments*

Carrington Ltd, a company specialising in information technology, has been operating for several years since its formation in 20X3. On 15 January 20X3, $10 000 ordinary shares had been issued and paid in full.

Issue of shares

The initial issue of $10 000 of ordinary shares would have been recorded as:

20X5		$	$
Jan. 1	Cash at bank	10 000	
	Paid-up ordinary capital		10 000
	(Issue of 10 000 $1 ordinary shares)		

The paid-up capital would be revealed in each succeeding balance sheet, thus:

Shareholders' equity	
Issued and paid-up capital	
10 000 $1 ordinary shares	$10 000

On 1 January 20X8 the company announced in a prospectus its intentions of expanding into the field of computer-aided instruction, for which more capital was required. It proposed to offer, for subscription by the public, 20 000 ordinary shares at the issue price of $1.25 per share. The terms of the issue were:

- 40 cents per share on application
- 85 cents per share at call (second instalment).

Applications closed on 31 January 20X8.

The response to the prospectus was very satisfactory, with applications being received for 45 000 shares. On 15 February 20X8 the directors resolved to allot the 20 000 shares. Unsuccessful applicants received a refund of their application monies.

On 15 June 20X8 the company made a call for the second instalment of 85c, due on 30 June 20X8. By that date call monies had been received from all but the holder of 2500 shares.

Issue of prospectus

No entry is made when the prospectus is released, since at that date no transaction has taken place, merely an invitation to apply for shares. Moreover, it is always possible that the issue will be undersubscribed.

Receipt of applications

As applications are received, the application monies are held in trust in a special bank account. They are not available to the company until the shares have been formally allotted. Hence, in total, applications are accounted for as:

20X8		$	$
Jan. 31	Cash trust	18 000	
	Application		18 000
	(Applications received for 45 000		
	shares at 40 cents per share)		

Allotment of shares and transfer of application monies

Once the shares are allotted, the shares are issued to the successful applicants and hence the application account is reduced by $8000 (40c × 20 000 shares) and is recognised as capital.

20X8		$	$
Feb. 15	Application	8 000	
	Paid-up ordinary capital		8 000
	(Issue of 20 000 $1.25 shares payable		
	40 cents on application and the balance at call)		

Note that the Corporations Law requires the separate disclosure of share capital relating to different classes of shares. It is therefore necessary to establish separate accounts for each class of shares.

Once the shares have been allotted, the trust cash account is closed, with application monies being returned to unsuccessful applicants, and application monies from successful applicants being transferred to the company's operating cash account.

20X8		$	$
Feb. 15	Application	10 000	
	Cash at bank	8 000	
	Cash trust		18 000
	(Return of excess application		
	monies of 40 cents on 25 000		
	shares and transfer of monies on		
	20 000 shares now issued)		

The entries on 15 February to allot the shares would result in a transfer from the application account to recognise the increase in paid-up capital.

Call on shares and receipt of call

The entries to make the shares fully paid are:

20X8		$	$
June 15	Call No. 1	17 000	
	Paid-up capital		17 000
	(Call of 85 cents on 20 000 shares)		
June 30	Cash at bank	14 875	
	Call No. 1		14 875
	(Receipt of call monies on 17 500 shares)		

The balance in the call account, representing the amount unpaid on the call, will be described in the shareholders' equity section of the balance sheet as 'Call No. 1 in arrears'.

	PORTION OF GENERAL LEDGER: CARRINGTON LTD	Debit	Credit	Balance
20X8	**Cash trust**	$	$	$
Jan. 31	Application	18 000		18 000 DR
Feb. 15	Cash at bank		8 000	10 000 DR
	Application		10 000	—
20X8	**Cash**			
Feb. 15	Cast trust	8 000		8 000 DR
June 30	Call No. 1	14 875		22 875 DR
20X8	**Application**			
Jan. 31	Cash trust		18 000	18 000 CR
Feb. 15	Cash trust	10 000		8 000 CR
	Paid-up capital	8 000		—
20X8	**Paid-up capital**			
Feb. 15	Application		8 000	8 000 CR
June 15	Call No. 1		17 000	25 000 CR
20X8	**Call No. 1**			
June 15	Paid-up capital	17 000		17 000 DR
June 30	Cash at bank		14 875	2 125 DR

Disclosure of shareholders' capital

The Australian Accounting Standards Board AASB 1034, 'Information to be Disclosed in Financial Reports', requires companies to disclose the number of each class of shares and the amount of paid-up capital and calls in arrears. The following will meet this requirement. Note that exempt proprietary companies are not required to disclose this information.

PORTION OF SHAREHOLDERS' EQUITY SECTION OF BALANCE SHEET: CARRINGTON LTD		
as at 30 June 20X8		
Shareholders' equity		
Issued and paid-up capital		
10 000 ordinary shares fully paid	$10 000	
20 000 $1.25 ordinary shares	25 000	
	35 000	
less Call No. 1 in arrears	2 125	
Paid-up capital		$32 875

Pro-rata allotments

Instead of allocating the full number of shares applied for to some applicants and declaring the remainder unsuccessful, a company could have spread the shareholding by allocating to some or all applicants a proportion of the shares applied for. The excess application monies could then have been credited against any subsequent call.

Ethical issues

Oliver Lee is an accountant in public practice. One of his clients is a computer software company, Spieks Pty Ltd. The company is highly successful and is about to be listed on the stock exchange. Shares are being offered to the public at $3 per share. The managing director has confirmed that he wishes Mr Lee to remain as the accountant and, as a gesture of goodwill, has offered him 10 000 shares at $1 per share. What should Mr Lee consider in making his decision?

Summary

The introduction of more than one owner and of the concept of incorporation and limited liability creates the need for more sophisticated procedures for recording and reporting capital and profits. In partnerships, each partner has separate capital and current accounts, to which all profits are appropriated in accordance with the partnership agreement and against which partners' drawings are offset. Since the partners and the partnership are one in law, all profits must be appropriated.

In companies, the shareholders' capital contributions are shown in paid-up capital accounts. As a separate legal entity, a company may retain profits from shareholders and this is recognised by the creation of a retained profits or appropriation account. In addition, profits may be transferred to a reserve, such as a general reserve. Such transfers are book entries, involving no current movement of assets. Distributions to shareholders, known as dividends, are appropriated from profits and regarded as a liability pending ratification at the next annual meeting of shareholders.

Review exercises

Discussion questions

8.1 Discuss whether partners' salaries should be regarded as expenses of the partnership.

8.2 Why are company directors' fees an expense, whereas partners' salaries are not?

8.3 Compare and contrast the major characteristics of a registered company and a partnership agreement.

8.4 In Australia all registered companies are required to disclose information for each class of shares on issue. What is the meaning of class in this context?

8.5 'A company's shareholders' equity consists of retained profits and contributed capital. Because dividends are payments to shareholders, they can be paid from either account.' Do you agree with this statement? Explain your answer.

8.6 Distinguish between debentures, preference shares and convertible notes.

8.7 'The distinction between debt and equity is not clear.' Discuss.

8.8 A company has decided to issue shares for payment by instalments. Discuss the three stages at which the instalments may be due.

8.9 A public company's shares have two values: an issue price and a market value. Explain what is meant by each of these terms and why it is unusual for the share's issue price to equal its market value.

8.10   What purposes are achieved by the following?

(a) transferring profits to a general reserve

(b) making a bonus issue of shares from a general reserve

8.11   In what circumstances would a bonus issue arise?

8.12   What do the following items represent, and why are they regarded as assets?

(a) formation costs

(b) goodwill

Problems

8.13   *Formation of partnership*

T. Kaur is an electrical contractor who operates a small business in the Sydney suburb of Bondi. He finds that he has insufficient cash to continue operating at the present level of activity. He is considering various ways to overcome the cash shortage.

(a) Kaur is considering taking a partner into the business.

(i)   What would be the advantages of this proposal?

(ii) Would there be any disadvantages of this proposal?

(iii) If Kaur decides to admit a partner into the business what would have to be agreed on before the business could commence to operate as a partnership?

(b) What other possibilities are available to Kaur to overcome the cash shortage?

8.14   *Formation of partnership*

K. Lin conducts a photography studio. He has arranged to combine his business with a photography supplies and services firm which is operated by M. Moon. The partnership is to commence on 1 March 20X9. Lin supplies the following information about his business:

BALANCE SHEET: K. LIN PHOTOGRAPHER
as at 1 March 20X9

ASSETS	$	$	EQUITIES	$
Bank		3 400	Creditors	4 600
Debtors	4 900		Capital—K. Lin	46 800
Less Allowance for				
doubtful debts	100	4 800		
Equipment	39 000			
Less Accumulated				
depreciation	10 800	28 200		
Motor vehicle	17 000			
Less Accumulated				
depreciation	2 000	15 000		
		$51 400		$51 400

M. Moon supplies the following information about her business:

BALANCE SHEET: M. MOON PHOTO SUPPLIES
as at 1 March 20X9

ASSETS	$	$	EQUITIES	$
Debtors		2 700	Bank overdraft	1 300
Inventory		11 400	Creditors	1 700
Equipment	14 300		Capital—M. Moon	28 600
Less Accumulated				
depreciation	11 400	2 900		
Motor vehicle	16 000			
Less Accumulated				
depreciation	2 000	14 000		
Furniture	900			
Less Accumulated				
depreciation	300	600		
		$31 600		$31 600

The partners decide to do the following:

(i) Provide for doubtful debts of $300 on Lin's debtors.

(ii) Revalue Lin's motor vehicle at $14 500 for the partnership.

(iii) Provide for doubtful debts of $200 on Moon's debtors.

(iv) Value Moon's motor vehicle at $10 000.

(v) Value Moon's equipment at $3300.

(vi) All other assets and liabilities are to be taken over at book value.

The partners ask you to:

(a) Prepare the opening journal entries for the partnership.

(b) Present the balance sheet of the partnership at 1 March 20X9.

8.15 *Partnership appropriations*

1. Hume and Hovell are in partnership, trading as Outback Treks. In the partnership agreement the following provisions apply:

(i) Partners' salaries: Hume, $24 000; Hovell, $13 000.

(ii) Interest is credited on capital account balances at the rate of 11 per cent per year.

(iii) Residual profits are shared in the proportions: Hume, three-fifths; Hovell, two-fifths.

TRIAL BALANCE as at 30 June 20X7		
B. Hume: Capital		$ 80 000
L. Hovell: Capital		50 000
B. Hume: Current	$ 34 000	
L. Hovell: Current		2 000
Cash at bank	6 000	
Accounts receivable	9 000	
Motor vehicles	17 000	
Land	140 000	
Accounts payable		1 000
Profit and loss summary		73 000
(Profit before appropriation)		
	$206 000	$206 000

(a) Prepare the appropriation account and partners' capital and current accounts in the general ledger of the partnership.

(b) Present a balance sheet as at 30 June 20X7.

2. V. Blues and C. Hawkes are in partnership. The partnership agreement provides for:

(i) Partners' salaries: Blues, $18 000; Hawkes, $9000.

(ii) Interest on the opening balances of capital at 12 per cent per annum.

(iii) Residual profits to be distributed: Blues, three-fifths; Hawkes, two-fifths.

Capital at the beginning of the year was: Blues, $40 000; Hawkes, $80 000. Net profit for the year was $80 000. During the year the partners had withdrawn: Blues, $16 000; Hawkes, $11 000.

(a) Record this information in the relevant ledger accounts.

(b) Prepare an appropriation statement and an extract of the owners' equity section of the balance sheet.

8.16 *Partnership: profit appropriations*

H. Hogg and N. Nolan operate Hognol Fax Repairs. The following information has been extracted from the books of the partnership on 30 June 20X8.

	Debit	Credit
	$	$
Capital—Hogg		130 000
Capital—Nolan		110 000
Current—Hogg	2 900	
Current—Nolan	700	
Advance salary—Hogg		13 000
Salary—Hogg	32 000	
Salary—Nolan	28 000	
Drawings—Nolan	2 000	
Net profit (before partners' salaries, interest)		24 000

From the partnership agreement the following details are obtained:

(i)   Interest on capital is to be allowed at the rate of 10 per cent per annum.

(ii) Interest on advances is to be allowed at the rate of 10 per cent per annum.

(iii) Interest on drawings is to be charged at the rate of 10 per cent per annum. (Nolan's drawings were made on 1 January 20X8.)

(iv) The partners are entitled to these salaries:

Hogg—$32 000 per annum

Nolan—$28 000 per annum

(v)   Residual profits and losses are shared equally.

(a) Prepare an appropriation statement for the year ended 30 June 20X8.

(b) Show the current accounts of Hogg and Nolan at 30 June 20X8.

(c) Show the owners' equity section of the balance sheet at 30 June 20X8.

8.17   *Profit determination and appropriations*

Sass and Toll are operating in partnership the MidCity Carpet Store. From the following information you are required to prepare:

(a) a profit report for the year ended 30 June 20X8

(b) (i)   appropriation statement

(ii) partners' current accounts

(c) a balance sheet at 30 June 20X8

The following details are obtained from the partnership agreement:

- Interest will be allowed at 10 per cent per annum on partners' advances to the firm and 10 per cent per annum on capital, with current accounts free of interest.
- Salaries will be paid as follows:

Sass—$17 000 per annum

Toll—$15 000 per annum

- Profits and losses are to be shared equally.

BALANCE SHEET: MIDCITY CARPET STORE			
as at 30 June 20X7			
CURRENT ASSETS	$	$	$
Cash on hand		50	
Cash at bank		800	
Trade debtors		15 200	
Inventory		43 750	59 800
NON-CURRENT ASSETS			
Delivery vans	16 500		
Less Accumulated depreciation	1 500	15 000	
Furniture and fittings	18 000		
Less Accumulated depreciation	950	17 050	
Freehold property	68 000		
Less Accumulated depreciation	3 740	64 260	96 310
			156 110

continues

BALANCE SHEET: MIDCITY CARPET STORE
as at 30 June 20X7

	$	$	$
CURRENT LIABILITIES			
Trade creditors			37 750
NON-CURRENT LIABILITIES			
Advance—Sass (due 30 June 20X9)			4 000
OWNERS' EQUITY			
Capital—Toll	40 000		
Current—Toll	25 240	65 240	
Capital—Sass	25 000		
Current—Sass	24 120	49 120	114 360
			156 110

The following details relate to transactions for year ended 30 June 20X8:

- The firm purchased $250 000 of inventory. The following payments were made during the period:

	$	$	$
Creditors for inventory		190 000	
Rent		12 780	
Salaries to sales personnel		30 000	
Office expenses		3 201	
Salaries —Toll	15 000		
—Sass	15 000	30 000	265 981

- The firm's receipts for the period were:

	$	$
2-year bank loan (due 30 Sep 20X9, interest payable 12 per cent per annum)	20 000	
Cash sales	175 000	
Debtors	125 000	320 000

Additional information:

(i) Debts outstanding at the end of the year (not including interest)

	$	$
Creditors		97 750
Salaries—sales personnel	2 250	
Office expenses	4 250	6 500

(ii) Inventory at end totalled $63 200.

(iii) Debtors at 30 June 20X8 totalled $37 600.

(iv) Cash in the till at 30 June 20X8 totalled $50.

(v) Depreciation is to be charged as follows:

Delivery vans—10 per cent per annum on cost

Furniture and fittings—10 per cent per annum on reducing balance

Buildings—$3400

(vi) Salary entitlements and interest on the advance are to be treated as appropriations of profit.

8.18   *Partnership and admission of a new partner*

1.   Spic and Span are partners who operate a cleaning business. They decided to admit Sparkle as a partner on 1 January 20X8. The partnership balance sheet at that date was as follows:

Assets		
Cash at bank		$10 530
Cleaning materials		3 100
Accounts receivable		19 480
less Allowance for doubtful debts		(2 670)
Cleaning equipment		26 800
less Accumulated depreciation		(5 390)
Cleaning van		8 000
less Accumulated depreciation		(5 600)
		54 250
Liabilities		
Accounts payable		11 240
Bank loan		9 000
Owners' equity		
Capital–Spic	$15 000	
plus Current	5 630	20 630
Capital–Span	10 000	
plus Current	3 380	13 380
		$54 250

Sparkle has agreed to contribute $15 000 capital, which is comprised of a new cleaning van worth $10 000 and cash of $5000.

The partners reviewed the value of the partnership's assets on 1 January 20X8 and decided to increase the provision for doubtful debts to $3500, revalue the existing equipment to $18 000 net and to value goodwill at $7000. They also decided to sell the old cleaning van, as Sparkle was contributing a new one. The proceeds of the sale were $3000.

Spic and Span share the business's profits on a 2:1 ratio.

Prepare the general journal entries to record these events and a balance sheet for the new partnership after the admission of Sparkle.

2. Taylor and Jones decided to admit Hayes to their partnership. Their balance sheet at that date was:

TAYLOR AND JONES				
Assets		*Equities*		
Accounts receivable	$25 000	Accounts payable		$10 000
Inventory	36 000	Bank overdraft		5 000
Equipment	24 000	Capital		
		Taylor	$40 000	
		Jones	30 000	70 000
	$85 000			$85 000

Hayes agreed to contribute $25 000 as capital for a one-fourth share of the profits. Goodwill was to be valued at $10 000, and was to be raised in the partnership books. The other assets were to be revalued at book value, except for machinery, which was agreed to be worth $19 500.

Show the general journal entries required to record these transactions.

3. The assets and liabilities of W. Boarder as at 31 March 20X1 were as follows:

Accounts receivable	$11 700	
less Allowance for doubtful debts	600	$11 100
Inventory		19 550
Equipment	23 000	
less Accumulated depreciation	11 600	11 400
Total assets		42 050
Bank overdraft		6 025
Accounts payable		9 300
Loan payable		2 675
Total liabilities		$18 000

Boarder agreed to admit L. Lord into partnership as from 1 April 20X1 on the following conditions:

(i) Estimated doubtful debts on Boarder's debtors to be increased to $1000, inventory to be revalued at $15 000, and accumulated depreciation of equipment to be written up to $12 500. Goodwill of $6000 to be credited to Boarder.

(ii) Lord to bring into the partnership inventory at a value of $9250 and delivery vans, which had cost $8000, at a market value of $6000, together with sufficient cash to bring his capital up to $25 000.

(iii) Boarder's capital to be adjusted to the same amount as that of Lord, any excess or deficiency to be contributed or withdrawn in cash.

Show the general journal entries to give effect to the above transactions.

8.19 *Dissolution of partnerships*

1. The assets, liabilities and capital of Cutt and Forrest as at 30 September 20X6 were as follows:

Cash at bank		$ 7 000
Accounts receivable		340 000
Inventory		520 000
Plant and equipment	$620 000	
less Accumulated depreciation	360 000	260 000
Delivery vans	185 000	
less Accumulated depreciation	105 000	80 000
Total assets		1 207 000
Creditors		265 000
Advance: Cutt		83 000
Total liabilities		$ 348 000
Capital—Cutt	$600 000	
Capital—Forrest	200 000	$ 800 000
Current account—Cutt	12 500	
Current account—Forrest	46 500	59 000
Total partners' interests		$ 859 000

The partners, who shared profits in the proportion of Cutt two-thirds and Forrest one-third, dissolved the partnership as at 30 September 20X6, and Cutt agreed to take over the inventory at a valuation of $500 000. $325 000 was received from accounts receivable and the plant and delivery vans were sold for $295 000 and $102 500 respectively.

Show the ledger accounts to close the books of the partnership.

2. Bond and Parry were partners, sharing profits and losses equally. The trial balance of their books as at 30 June 20X5 was as follows:

Capital—Bond		$ 250 000
Capital—Parry		250 000
Current—Bond	$ 126 250	
Advance—Parry		50 000
Sales		1 069 800
Purchases	861 700	
Inventory, 1 July 20X4	123 600	
Wages	104 700	
Expenses	120 500	
Accounts payable		246 300
Accounts receivable	225 500	
Allowance for doubtful debts		12 500
Plant and equipment	157 500	
Delivery vans	52 500	
Accumulated depreciation—vans		17 500
Accumulated depreciation—plant		27 500
Goodwill	150 000	
Bank	1 350	
	$1 923 600	$1 923 600

(i)   The inventory on hand at 30 June 20X5 had cost $157 100.
(ii) Wages of $5000 were owing.
(iii) The partnership was dissolved as at 30 June 20X5. Parry took over the delivery vans at $28 000 and the remaining assets were sold.
(iv) Book debts realised $187 500, inventory $112 000, and machinery $105 000.
(v)   The cost of liquidating the business was $6500.

Show:

(a) General journal entries to close the books of the partnership.
(b) Ledger accounts for realisation, cash, and partners' capital and current accounts.

3. Gina Green and Beth Brown are partners operating a graphic design studio. On 30 June 20X8 they decided to close their business as they wanted an early retirement. Their balance sheet at that date was as follows:

	DR				CR
Cash	$ 4 900	Accounts payable			$ 5 880
Accounts receivable	1 200	Mortgage loan			25 000
less Allowance for		Loan–G. Green			5 000
doubtful debts	(340)	G. Green–capital	$16 000		
Inventory	7 560	–current	8 420	24 420	
Fixtures and fittings	21 400				
less Accum. depn	(6 210)	B. Brown–capital	12 000		
Studio premises	50 000	–current	6 210	18 210	
	$78 510				$78 510

Additional information:

(i)   Gina and Beth were each owed $800 wages.
(ii) All of the business's accounts receivable were realised in full. Fixtures and fittings were sold for $12 000. Gina agreed to take $3000 worth of inventory, the remaining inventory was sold for $3800, and the studio premises were disposed of for $70 000.
(iii) Expenses incurred from the realisation of the assets and the dissolution of the partnership amounted to $2700.

Prepare the general journal entries to record the above transactions and post them to the appropriate ledger accounts to terminate the partnership.

8.20 *Company formation*

BALANCE SHEET: TOMLINSON INDUSTRIES LTD as at 30 June 20X8					
CURRENT ASSETS	$	$	CURRENT LIABILITIES	$	$
Bank	50 000		Creditors		240 000
Debtors	420 000		NON-CURRENT LIABILITIES		
Inventory	980 000	1 450 000	12% Debentures		
			(repayable 20X8)		200 000
NON-CURRENT ASSETS			SHAREHOLDERS' EQUITY		
Land and buildings	600 000		Paid-up capital	2 000 000	
Equipment (book value)	550 000	1 150 000	(2 000 000 ordinary		
			shares of $1 each)		
			Retained profits	160 000	2 160 000
		$2 600 000			$2 600 000

(a) What form of business organisation is Tomlinson Industries? What evidence do you have for your answer? Do you think this is the most suitable form of business organisation for this firm? Why?

(b) What term would be used in other forms of business to describe the Shareholders' Equity section of the balance sheet?

(c) How would you describe the capital structure of this company?

(d) What are debentures? Why are they classified as liabilities? What rights would the holders of debentures in this business have?

(e) What is the significance, if any, of the use of the word 'ordinary' to describe the shares?

(f) What does the item 'retained profits' in the shareholders' equity section of the balance sheet represent?

8.21 *Company formation*

Hadrian Jones has been a sole trader selling computing equipment for several years. Convinced of the virtues of incorporation, he resolved to form a proprietary company with his wife, Esmeralda. The following events occurred in 20X6:

Jan. 2 Jones Computing Pty Ltd was incorporated.

3 The company purchased the business of Hadrian Jones. His balance sheet at that date was:

Assets			Liabilities		
Cash at bank		$12 000	Accounts payable		$ 5 000
Accounts					
receivable		4 000	*Owners' equity*		
Inventory		7 000	Capital	$10 000	
Equipment	$10 000		Retained profit	14 000	24 000
less Accum. depn	4 000	6 000			
		$29 000			$29 000

For the purchase, the vendor and the purchaser agreed that the assets should be revalued to fair market values as follows:

Inventory	$6500
Equipment	$9000

The vendor, Mr Jones, was to receive as consideration 28 000 shares in the company, fully paid and issued at $1, and $10 000 cash. The shares were issued immediately and the cash was to be paid on 7 January.

Jan. 4 Mrs Jones purchased one share in the company for the payment of $1.

5 An additional 5000 shares were issued to Mr A. Goodfriend at $2 per share, for the payment of $10 000 cash.

6 The company's solicitors were paid $3400 for their work in forming the company.

7 Paid the vendor his cash consideration.

(a) Show general journal entries to record the above events.

(b) Present a balance sheet for the company as at 7 January 20X6.

8.22 *Company takeover of partnership*

Jill and Megan operated a hairdressing salon in partnership. On 1 March 20X9 a company was formed that acquired the assets of their partnership and assumed its liabilities. In exchange, Jill and Megan each received 12 500 shares valued at $1. The trial balance for Jill and Megan's salon on the date of acquisition was as follows:

TRIAL BALANCE: JILL AND MEGAN'S SALON as at 1 March 20X9	Debit	Credit
Jill–Capital		$ 3 000
Megan–Capital		3 000
Cash at bank	$ 4 300	
Accounts receivable	600	
Allowance for doubtful debts		100
Supplies	4 200	
Equipment	8 900	
Accumulated depreciation		1 400
Accounts payable		800
Profit and loss summary		9 700
	$18 000	$18 000

It was decided that the market value of the equipment was $12 000, that $150 of outstanding accounts receivable could now be considered bad debts, and that $200 worth of supplies were no longer useable.

(a) What is the value of the salon's goodwill?

(b) Prepare journal entries to close the partnership and to open the books of the acquiring company.

8.23 *Company formation*

1. On 1 July 20X8 Smithers Bros Ltd took over the business of Hunk Ltd for $8000 cash plus 60 000 $1 shares in Smithers Ltd. At that date Hunk Ltd had the following balance sheet:

Assets		Liabilities	
Cash	$ 5 000	Accounts payable	$ 7 000
Equipment	40 000		
		Shareholders' funds	
		Paid-up capital	30 000
		Retained profits	8 000
	$45 000		$45 000

The equipment was valued by Smithers Bros Ltd at $18 000. Show the journal entry or entries to record the takeover in the records of Smithers Bros Ltd.

2. Show journal entries to record the following transactions in the books of Junket Pty Ltd.

20X7

July 1 A. Kurts formed a company, Junket Pty Ltd. It issued 150 000 $1 shares for cash.

2 Paid formation expenses of $8000.

4 Purchased the business of A. S. Way, whose balance sheet at that date was:

Assets	$	$	Liabilities	$	$
Inventory		15 000	Accounts payable		18 000
Equipment	45 000				
less Accum. depn	13 000	32 000	Owners' equity		
			Capital	20 000	
			plus Profit	9 000	29 000
		47 000			47 000

The equipment was revalued at $27 000. All other assets and liabilities were taken over at book values. Mr Way was paid $30 500 for the business.

8.24 *Company formation from partnership*

Harriet Small and George Long have been operating a successful dressmaking business for the past five years in partnership. Due to a rapid growth in their business over the last two years, Harriet and George decided to incorporate the business as a private company, Leave Pty Ltd. Harriet and George were equal partners in their business. The business's balance sheet as at this date appeared as follows:

Cash at bank	$10 500
Accounts receivable	17 310
less Allowance for doubtful debts	(4 140)
	continues

Sewing supplies		7 280
Equipment		25 700
less Accumulated depreciation		(9 440)
Delivery van		17 600
less Accumulated depreciation		(5 200)
Premises	$35 000	
less Accumulated depreciation	5 000	30 000
		89 610
Accounts payable		12 850
Mortgage loan		14 000
Capital–H. Small	23 000	
plus Current	8 380	31 380
Capital–G. Long	23 000	
plus Current	8 380	31 380
		$89 610

At the date of incorporation the business assets were revalued to fair market values as follows:

Premises	$40 000
Equipment	$14 000
Delivery van	$10 000

Harriet and George received 30 000 ordinary shares in the company at $1 fully paid and $20 000 cash each, as consideration on the sale of the business. Formation costs amounted to $4500.

(a) Prepare the general journal entries to record the above events.
(b) Prepare a balance sheet for the company as at its incorporation date.

8.25 *Meaning of shareholders' equity*
Target Ltd, a real estate developer, has the following balance sheet as at 30 June 20X3:

Assets		Liabilities		
Cash	$ 1 000	Accounts payable		$ 3 000
Land	86 000			
		Shareholders' equity		
		Paid-up capital	$ 5 000	
		Retained profit	40 000	
		General reserve	39 000	$84 000
	$87 000			$87 000

The company wishes to expand by purchasing a further block of land for $20 000. One director has suggested that the purchase be financed from the retained profits. Alternatively, the general reserve might be used, although it was not established for that purpose.

The managing director has sought your advice on the suggestion. Prepare a brief report in reply to the request.

8.26 *Company takeover*

Lloyd Ltd purchased the net assets and assumed the liabilities of Gomez Ltd on 3 March 20X6, when the book value and agreed market values of Gomez's net assets were as follows:

	Book value	Market value
Inventory	$ 32 000	$ 36 000
Land	18 000	24 000
Buildings	100 000	120 000
Equipment	40 000	50 000
Patents	5 000	15 000
Total	195 000	245 000
Accounts payable	30 000	30 000
Net assets	$165 000	$215 000

Lloyd Ltd paid $235 000 for the net assets of Gomez Ltd. Prepare the journal entry to record the purchase of Gomez Ltd in the books of Lloyd Ltd.

8.27 *Company adjustments and profit appropriation*

1. Calgary Ltd imports maple syrup from Canada. Its trial balance at 30 June 20X4 includes the following entries:

Paid-up capital		$300 000
Profit and loss summary		149 000
(Net profit before taxation)		
General reserve		65 000
Retained profits		823 000
Dividend paid	$12 000	
Tax paid	22 000	
Tax payable		24 000

The directors propose to:

(i)   Provide for tax payable for the current year, estimated at $72 000.
(ii) Transfer $5000 to a general reserve.
(iii) Provide for a final dividend of $28 000.

(a) Prepare journal entries for the above.
(b) Present a statement of retained profits as at 30 June 20X4.
(c) Show the liabilities and shareholders' equity sections of the balance sheet as at 30 June 20X4.

2. The following information relating to the year ended 30 June 20X6 has been obtained from the records of Macrash Ltd:

Net profit for the year (before taxation)	$120 000 CR
Appropriation balance, 1/7/X5	42 500 CR
General reserve	10 000 CR
Asset replacement reserve	55 000 CR
Interim dividend paid	25 000 DR
Goodwill	30 000 DR
Formation expenses	4 500 DR

On 30 June 20X6 the directors decided that the following should be done before the preparation of the final accounting reports:

(i)   Recommend a final dividend of $35 000.
(ii) Reduce formation expenses balance to $2000.
(iii) Write down goodwill by $8000.
(iv) Increase general reserves by $5000 and asset replacement reserve to $65 000.
(v)   Provide for estimated tax liability of $50 000.

Record the adjustments in the ledger accounts and prepare a revised profit and loss statement and a retained profits statement for the year ended 30 June 20X6.

3. The following information relates to the Cosy Co. Pty Ltd:

BALANCE SHEET			
as at 1 January 20X3			
Assets	$124 000	*Liabilities*	
		Dividend payable	$ 18 000
		Tax payable	11 000
			29 000
		Shareholders' equity	
		Paid-up capital	60 000
		General reserve	23 000
		Retained profits	12 000
			95 000
	$124 000		$124 000

During the year the following occurred:

- 12 February dividend paid $ 18 000
- 31 March tax paid   17 200
- 12 August dividend paid   9 000
- Net income for year before tax   156 000
- Adjustments and appropriations required:
  - Tax payable estimation   33 000
  - Final dividend to be provided for   10 000
  - Transfer to general reserve   2 500

(a) Show relevant ledger accounts to record the closing and appropriation entries.
(b) Prepare a retained profit statement and a balance sheet as at 31 December 20X3.

8.28 *Company taxation*
At 31 December 20X6 a company estimated its tax payable for 20X6 as $19 000. In 20X7 it paid tax of $19 300. It estimates that its taxation for 20X7 will be $35 000.

What items will appear in the profit and loss statement in relation to the above for the year ended 31 December 20X7?

8.29   *Company formation*

PART A

The following events relate to the formation of Milko Pty Ltd in 20X1:

July 1   Milko Pty Ltd was formed to take over the milk delivery partnership of Peters and Street.

BALANCE SHEET: PETERS AND STREET					
as at 1 July 20X1					
Assets			Liabilities		
Cash		$1000	Accounts payable		$2000
Van	$19 000				
less Accum. depn	14 000	5000	Owners' equity		
			Capital—Peters	$2500	
			Capital—Street	1500	4000
		$6000			$6000

(i)   The vendors were paid a total of $18 000
        comprising fully paid $1 ordinary shares: 200
                                                    cash: 17 800

(ii)   They agreed to lend $17 800 to the company.

(iii)   The van was valued for the takeover at $3000.

        July 2   Sold 10 shares to A. Stilton for $50 cash.
            3   Paid solicitor formation costs of $500.

PART B

After one year of trading, the trial balance was as follows:

TRIAL BALANCE: MILKO PTY LTD		
as at 30 June 20X2		
	Debit	Credit
Cash	$ 21 810	
Van	3 000	
Formation costs	500	
Goodwill	16 000	
Accounts payable		$ 4 260
Shareholders' loans		17 800
Paid-up capital		250
Sales revenue		84 000
General expenses	65 000	
	$106 310	$106 310

The following adjustments and appropriations were deemed necessary:

1.   Depreciation of $200 to be charged.
2.   Goodwill to be amortised over 10 years.
3.   Tax of $4700 to be provided for.

4. $2000 to be transferred to a general reserve.
5. Dividend of $3000 to be provided for.

(a) Prepare journal entries to record the events in Part A.
(b) Prepare a balance sheet as at 3 July 20X1.
(c) Prepare journal entries for adjusting, closing and profit appropriation entries as at 30 June 20X2.
(d) Present financial statements for the year ended 30 June 20X2.

8.30 *Company adjusting, closing and appropriation*

The following information relates to Henri Ltd, a company that has been trading for several years.

TRIAL BALANCE: HENRI LTD		
as at 30 June 20X8		
Cash at bank	$ 17 000	
Accounts receivable	8 000	
Inventory	4 000	
Rent prepaid	5 000	
Land and buildings	81 200	
Goodwill	7 000	
Formation costs	2 500	
Accounts payable		$ 8 700
Paid-up capital		50 000
Dividend paid	3 000	
Retained profits		36 000
General reserve		11 000
Sales revenue		145 000
Cost of goods sold	68 000	
Wages expense	31 000	
Rent expense	24 000	
	$250 700	$250 700

Adjustments required:

1. Inventory on hand at 30 June 20X8 is valued at $3600.
2. The rent prepaid related to the period ending 30 June 20X8.
3. Wages of $3100 are owing.
4. Goodwill is to be written down by $1000 and $500 is to be written off the formation costs.
5. Taxation for the year is estimated to be $8400.
6. A final dividend of $3000 is to be provided for.
7. $1500 is to be transferred to the general reserve.
8. The company desires to make a bonus share issue immediately from the general reserve totalling $6000.

(a) Present journal entries to incorporate the adjustments in the records of the company.
(b) Present financial statements for the year ended 30 June 20X8.

8.31   *Company appropriations, bonus issue*

The following balances were extracted from a trial balance prepared for Generous Ltd on 1 January 20X1, the first day of a new year.

Cash	$54 000
Other assets	70 000
Accounts payable	2 000
Dividends payable	4 000
Paid-up capital	60 000
General reserve	50 000
Retained profits	8 000

On that day the directors decided to:

(i)   Transfer $3000 to the general reserve.

(ii) Make a bonus issue of one new share for every six shares currently issued, the bonus to be made from the general reserve.

Show the balance sheet of Generous Ltd after these changes have been made.

8.32   *Company takeover, intangible items*

The Intermittent Electricity Commission (IEC) is a statutory corporation established by the government of the State of Chaos to take over the provision of electricity services to consumers. This function was previously undertaken by a privately owned company, Stokers Ltd, which was acquired by the Electricity Commission.

	In the records of Stokers Ltd $m	Revaluation on purchase $m
Assets acquired		
Cash	12	12
Equipment	39	25
Patented processes	–	12
Liabilities assumed	nil	nil

1.   Stokers Ltd was to be paid $80 million in cash.

2.   The commission was financed by a non-repayable loan from the state government of $100 million. An interest return of 12 per cent is required.

3.   The Commission's engineers have provided the following estimates of the lives and usage patterns of the assets:

Equipment	10 years life, used equally each year
Patents	5-year life

4.   Apart from the above, annual operating costs are likely to be:

	$m
Fuel	4
Wages and salaries	6
Other expenses	3

5. Annual production is expected to be 350 million kilowatt hours.

   (a) List the assets of the Intermittent Electricity Commission as they would appear after the takeover has been completed and funding obtained from the government, but before the commencement of operations.

   (b) Assuming that there is no inflation in the economy and that the Commission desires to achieve a return that meets annual costs exactly, without any profit or loss, prepare a statement showing the price it should set per kilowatt hour for the first year of operations.

   (c) Briefly state the reasons for your treatment of the intangible items.

   (d) What other factors should be considered in setting the appropriate price?

8.33 *Company share issue, calculation of book value*
On 1 March 20X1 Grantham Enterprises Pty Ltd sold an additional 2000 ordinary shares. The new shares were sold at the current market price of $4.50 per share. Before the sale the shareholders' equity of the company could be summarised as:

Shareholders' equity	*28 February 20X1*
Issued and paid-up capital (7000 shares at $1 value)	7 000
Retained profit	29 800
	36 800

   (a) Record the journal entry for the share issue and show how the sale of the shares will affect the shareholders' equity of the firm.

   (b) The 'book value' of shares is often calculated by dividing the total of shareholders' equity by the number of shares issued. How did the sale affect the book value of the ordinary share of Grantham Enterprises? Is the book value of shares important to shareholders?

8.34 *Company accounting*

1. July   1   Render Ltd was formed in 20X1 stating in its prospectus that share capital would consist of ordinary shares and preference shares.

   10   Issued 12 000 preference shares at an issue price of $2 to the directors for cash.

   14   Released a prospectus inviting applications for 40 000 ordinary shares to be issued at $1, payable:

   20 cents per share on application
   80 cents at call

   31   Applications were received for 63 000 shares.

   Aug. 15   Directors allotted the 40 000 shares. Applications for 3000 shares were unsuccessful and applicants received a refund. The remaining applicants were allotted 2 shares for every 3 applied for.

20X2
   Mar. 7   A first call of 40 cents was made on the shares.
   31   The call had been received on all but 1000 shares.

Show:

(a) Journal entries to record the above.

(b) The shareholders' equity section of the balance sheet as at 31 March 20X2.

2. Downhill Ltd has been operating for many years as a supplier of skiing equipment. On 1 January 20X1 the share capital was as follows:

	$1 Ordinary shares	*$1 Preference shares*
Issued and paid-up capital	280 000	75 000

The company decided to make an issue of shares.

Jan. 15   Released a prospectus offering 60 000 ordinary shares at $1.20 per share, payable as:

50 cents on application
70 cents at call

Jan. 31   Applications were received for 80 000 shares.

Feb. 7   The directors allotted 60 000 ordinary shares pro rata, awarding 3 shares for every 4 applied for. Excess application monies were returned to unsuccessful applicants.

Nov. 10   Made a call of 70 cents per share on the new issue of ordinary shares.

Dec. 15   Call received from all but the holder of 12 000 shares.

Show:

(a) Journal entries to record the above.

(b) The capital account in the shareholders' equity section of the balance sheet as at 15 December 20X1.

CHAPTER 9
The structure and content of financial reports

Introduction

To complete an introduction to the basic framework of accounting, four further issues are discussed:

- The preparation and presentation of accounting reports.
- The presentation of consolidated statements for groups of companies.
- The preparation of accounting reports for manufacturing organisations.
- Reporting by non-profit organisations and public sector organisations.

The first section deals with the preparation of financial statements and the classification and disclosure of information within those reports. The issues discussed in this section affect almost all reporting entities. The remaining three sections of this chapter deal with more specialised reports that are prepared by specific groups of entities to disclose information in ways that best permit informed judgements by the various users of that information.

Preparation and presentation of accounting reports

In this topic practice varies considerably between countries and this discussion emphasises the pronouncements of the International Accounting Standards Committee (IASC) on disclosure in the profit and loss statement and balance sheet. Reference will be made to Australian Accounting Standards where appropriate.

Profit appropriations distinguished from profit and loss statement items

Charges deducted from revenue before profit is determined must be distinguished from appropriations of the profit. Both will result in a reduction in the retained profit, but charges before profit (expenses and losses) will reduce the net profit, whereas appropriations of profit will not. The term 'above the line' is often used to describe items appearing before the determination of profit and 'below the line' to describe items that are appropriations of profits.

The IASC accounting standard on profit and loss disclosure, International Accounting Standard IAS 8, 'Net Profit or Loss for the Period, Fundamental Errors and Changes in Accounting Policies',[1] embraces the 'all-inclusive' concept of profit. The standard requires that the entity's profit or loss for the financial year reported in the profit and loss account includes all items of revenue and expense that relate to that financial year (para. 7).[2] The all-inclusive concept is based on the notion that the sum of the annual profits determined for a company should equal its total lifetime surplus. If items of revenue or expense were not included when determining the annual profit, this equality would not exist, since the items would affect the lifetime profit of the enterprise but not the individual annual profits. Another justification for the all-inclusive concept is that it prevents manipulation of profits by arbitrary decisions to include or exclude particular items from profit.

The most difficult decisions concern expense and profit appropriation items. Some items, such as dividends and reserve transfers, should not affect profit and some principles are required to identify them. The following are derived from the principles and assumptions established in earlier chapters.

---

[1] The profit and loss statement is known by many titles. International accounting standards refer to this statement as the income statement.

[2] The Australian accounting standard on this topic is Australian Accounting Standards Board, AASB 1018, 'Profit and Loss Accounts'. See also AASB 1034, 'Information to be Disclosed in Financial Reports'.

An item must appear as a charge before profits when either of the following conditions is met:

1. *the item represents a consumption of resources incurred in the process of deriving revenue*
2. *the item represents a charge that must be recovered from revenue so as to maintain capital*

Items that meet neither test are appropriations of profit.

The first test is based on the entity concept and has been discussed previously as the distinction between expenses and withdrawals.

The second test is derived from the concept of capital maintenance. In order to maintain capital intact, expenses are deducted to recover from revenue the cost of resources consumed in the period. The depreciation charge, for example, is designed to recover the cost of an asset over its effective life. By lowering profits an expense charge causes dividends to be lower. Resources retained in this way build up the net assets to maintain capital as assets are consumed.

These principles will now be applied to certain key items.

Losses

No clear distinction has been made between losses and expenses. Both involve the consumption of resources, but one possible distinction is to define a loss as a consumption of resources that does not assist in the revenue-generating process. Losses so defined may include stock losses, fire losses, losses on the disposal of obsolete equipment and the incurrence of legal damages in a law suit.

These losses do not meet the first test for a charge before profits, since they are not incurred to generate revenue. However, they do meet the second test in that they must be recovered from revenue to maintain capital.

Suppose a company had the following assets at 31 December 20X1:

Assets	
Shares in X Ltd (at original cost)	$10 000
Shares in Y Ltd (at original cost)	2 000
	12 000
Shareholders' equity	
Issued capital	12 000

During 20X2 a dividend of $5000 was received from X Ltd but Y Ltd collapsed and the entire investment had to be written off as a loss. This loss of capital must be recovered before capital is maintained and the profit for 20X2 must therefore be:

Revenue from dividends received	$5 000
less Loss on investment in Y	2 000
Net profit	3 000

The maximum dividend that may be paid while maintaining capital is $3000. The remaining $2000 of the dividend from X is required to replace the resources lost in Y. To regard the loss as an appropriation of profit would be to deny the capital maintenance assumption discussed in earlier chapters.

Nevertheless, there are examples in practice where losses on investments have been regarded as appropriations on the grounds that the event is unusual or that the loss is unrelated to the main operations of the business. These practices lack theoretical support and suggest strongly that the real intention is to shield profits from the consequences of an embarrassing loss. This practice is also contrary to the requirements of the accounting standard on profit and loss accounts.

Dividends

The charge to create a liability for dividends payable to shareholders in the case of a company, or to the government in the case of a public sector business enterprise, fails both tests for a charge before profits. The dividend is not related to the consumption of resources in the process of deriving profit. It may be levied only after the profit has been determined and represents a distribution of the profit to the owners, analogous to drawings by a sole trader.

The dividend also fails the second test in that it is payable only once capital has been maintained. It therefore cannot be a necessary charge for the maintenance of capital.

Salaries and other emoluments to shareholder employees

In partnerships and sole traders, all remunerations to owners, whether as salaries, interest or profit shares, are usually treated as distributions of the profit and not expenses. This practice recognises that the unincorporated business and its owners are inseparable in law.

In the case of a company, a separate legal entity exists apart from the shareholders, so that remuneration to a shareholder who is also an employee of the company is regarded as an expense. The directors of the company, who may be shareholders, receive directors' fees for services rendered and these also are business expenses. If shareholders also lend money to the company, they are entitled to interest, which again is an expense.

Large companies are usually independent of their shareholders. Many employees become shareholders in a small way and it would be ridiculous to regard their salaries as withdrawals, just because they held a small parcel of shares. In general, the possibility of manipulation of profits by declaring as salary expense a payment that would otherwise be a dividend is unlikely to exist in a large company.

Transfers to reserves

A transfer to a general reserve is no more than an allocation of the profit to another account to inform shareholders and other users of accounting reports that it is not intended to distribute all of the retained profits. In this 'book entry' no resources are consumed or transferred anywhere. Accordingly, a reserve transfer cannot be a charge against revenue, since it neither consumes resources nor is it an essential charge for the maintenance of capital. It is a discretionary entry, in contrast to an expense such as wages which represents the actual consumption of resources during the period which must be recovered from revenue.

Some reserves are given specific titles, such as a reserve for replacement, which may at first appear to have close links with capital maintenance. However, whereas depreciation is charged to recover the cost of a former purchase, a reserve for replacement is a retention of profits to provide for replacement. This is a future resource outflow, having no effect on the present stock of capital.

A dividend equalisation reserve is created to ensure that retained profits are always available to maintain a given dividend. In good years transfers are made to the reserve, and in bad years profits are transferred back to the retained profits account to increase the level of retained profits available for dividends. These entries again achieve no more than an allocation of the profit in the accounting records.

Many other names for reserves will be found in practice, including 'revenue', 'development', 'special', 'tooling reserve', and so forth. Despite the names, all such reserves are basically the same in their origin and effect. The entries to create these reserves are not expenses.

Income taxation

Is income taxation an expense or an appropriation of profit? Certain academic writers have regarded taxation as an appropriation; however, in practice, companies report taxation as an expense and this approach has been endorsed by the pronouncements of the accounting standard-setting bodies.

Taxation payments undoubtedly consume resources, but are the resources consumed in the process of deriving revenue? Those proposing that taxation is an expense argue that it is levied to provide government services such as roads, communications, law-enforcement facilities, health and education services and other services which enable an ordered society to exist and which permit companies to operate and derive revenue. In this view, taxation covers a general set of expenses necessary to carry on a profitable business. The contrary argument is that taxation charges are not related to services provided to individual companies. Companies that make losses pay no taxation, yet they remain heavy consumers of government services (and, if in liquidation, they may be very heavy consumers indeed).

Furthermore, it is argued that if taxation is based on profits it cannot be a charge before profits. These arguments lead to the conclusion that taxation is a distribution of the profit: the government expropriates its share of profits through taxation, and the shareholders appropriate their portion through dividends.

The second test, relating to the maintenance of capital, is less clear. As taxation is a charge that must be deducted before dividends are declared, it cannot be regarded as a discretionary transfer. This seems to indicate that taxation is a charge that must be recovered to enable capital to be maintained and hence that it is an expense. However, this test relates to charges against revenue, whereas taxation is a charge against profits. If taxation were allowed as an expense, then all compulsory charges would need to be similarly regarded. These would include dividends on preference shares, which are similar to taxation in that they must be paid if profits exist.

These arguments are not accepted in practice and, since the dispute is a longstanding one, a compromise is recommended. In Australia AASB 1018 requires companies to report their net profit (or loss) before and after tax (para. 12). This enables the user of the information to select either figure.

Write-downs of intangibles of indefinite life

Intangible assets of indefinite life include costs of incorporation and goodwill arising on a purchase. Formation costs are a long-term asset similar to equipment. The difference is that, whereas equipment normally has a finite life over which the benefits from its use are obtained, the costs of forming the company may be said to benefit the company for as long as it continues to exist. Since the company's life is indeterminate, it is impossible to establish a life over which the costs may be allocated and accurate amortisation is therefore impossible. Similarly, with goodwill the benefit of having purchased a business and its associated goodwill may extend indefinitely into the future.

Companies consider it desirable to remove these 'soft' assets from the balance sheet and a practice had grown in past decades whereby arbitrary amounts were written off as appropriations of profit whenever the directors so desired. Since the costs were not charged as expenses, the profit was unaffected and the need to 'match' was avoided.

These practices conflict with the criteria enumerated above. Payments for formation costs and goodwill represent outlays to acquire resources. If, like land, their benefits never expire, there is no case for writing them off either as expenses or appropriations. If, instead, they are assumed to expire, then the cost of resources consumed must be recovered from revenue over the life of the enterprise if capital is to be maintained. Under the all-inclusive profit concept these should be treated as charges before profit accounting. In practice, formation costs are usually written off as incurred or within a relatively short time. The accounting standards on goodwill typically regard goodwill as a wasting asset that must be amortised so that it is recognised as an expense in the profit and loss account on a straight-line basis, over a period from the date of acquisition to the end of the period of time during which the benefits are expected to arise. In Australia the period over which goodwill is to be amortised shall not exceed twenty years.[3]

Correction of prior period errors

When a company decides that previous profits were incorrect, due to some omission or error, or because an assumption later proved unrealistic, it is difficult to correct the error because the previous results are a matter of record. The alternative actions are to restate the previous results, to make the adjustment by means of a profit appropriation, or to allow the adjustment to affect the current profit determination.

Suppose a company has owned equipment for three years. The equipment originally cost $20 000 and was to be depreciated straight-line over 10 years, with a residual value assumed to be nil. The company now finds that the equipment will last only four years. This change will affect both the current depreciation charge and prior charges, as reflected in the accumulated depreciation account.

The original depreciation was $2000 per year ($20 000/10) whereas, in the light of the new estimated life of four years, it should have been $5000 ($20 000/4). The effect on previous charges is:

Actual balance in accumulated depreciation (3 × $2000)	$ 6 000
Required balance if life were four years (3 × $5000)	15 000
Under-charged depreciation in previous years	9 000

The first alternative, of revising the financial statements for the previous three years, is not favoured since this results in two conflicting financial statements, each purporting to cover the same period. An adjustment in the current year gives explicit recognition to the change and enables analysts to make their own adjustments to prior results if they wish.

The second alternative is to debit the retained profits account with the $9000 and to credit accumulated depreciation. In this way the prior adjustments would not distort the current profit, which would be affected only by the higher depreciation for the current year. Further, since the ultimate effect of the restatement is to reduce the unappropriated profits brought forward from previous periods, it appears reasonable to make the adjustment in the retained profits statement.

The disadvantage of this approach, however, is that the total of the annual declared net profits will no longer be equal to the lifetime profit of the enterprise. Consistent with the all-inclusive profit concept, prior period adjustments are to appear in the profit and loss statement.

As a general rule, under the all-inclusive concept, the only items that may appear 'below the line' in the retained profits statement are appropriations for dividends and transfers to or from reserves. All other items are normally charges before profit.

Classification within financial statements

The form of presentation of the information within an accounting report will affect the comprehension of that information by users. To improve the effectiveness of communication, accounting reports should disclose significant relationships, should concentrate

---

[3] Australian Accounting Standards Board, AASB 1013, 'Accounting for Goodwill', para. 35. IAS 22, Business Combinations, states that the amortisation period should not exceed five years unless a longer period, not exceeding twenty years from the date of acquisition, can be justified (para. 42).

on items of material significance and should strive for comparability. Finally, they should be understandable.

Disclosure of significant relationships: the profit and loss statement

Certain figures should be related to understand their significance. The cost of goods sold, for example, should be deducted from sales to determine the gross profit. Cost of goods sold will include all costs necessary to place the goods in condition for sale. Similarly, sales returns and discounts are related directly to sales.

Within the operating expenses, it is useful to group together items that come under the one responsibility, or are related to the same function. For a retailer, for example, expenses may be subdivided into categories such as selling expenses, administrative expenses and finance expenses according to the predominant purpose of the item. The headings must be chosen as the most suitable for the organisation concerned.

The grouping of expenses permits the organisation to allocate responsibility for individual items to particular department heads. The sales manager, for example, might be expected to assume responsibility for costs of running the retail store, including wages, lighting and losses through theft. For purposes of analysis it may be useful to compare the growth in selling expenses and administrative expenses in response to an increase in sales revenue.

Disclosure of significant relationships: the balance sheet

The balance sheet is intended to communicate information about the financial position of the entity. A critical issue is to determine whether the entity has the assets to cover its liabilities, and especially whether adequate liquidity is available to pay immediate debts. Accordingly, the assets in the balance sheet are subdivided on the basis of their liquidity and according to how soon they are expected to be sold or used up in the operating cycle of the enterprise.

Typically these assets and liabilities are classified as current and non-current. This classification and the reasons for doing so was discussed in Chapter 2, so it will not be discussed here. However, it is important that this process is understood before reading the rest of this chapter.

Materiality

If all possible items were reported, the financial statements would be extremely long and important information would be hidden beneath the detail. Items that are small, and which will not materially influence the interpretation of the financial statements, are commonly grouped together or aggregated under one heading. For example, it may not be important to report the cost of each piece of equipment owned by a large factory.

Materiality may also influence the treatment of minor items. The purchase of tools, for example, in theory ought to be regarded as an asset, but because the cost is small in comparison with total assets it may be expensed immediately.

The IASC *Framework* states: 'Information is material if its omission or misstatement could influence the economic decisions of users taken on the basis of the financial statements'.[4] The IASC *Framework* is shown in Appendix 2.

---

[4] See also Australian Accounting Standards Board and Public Sector Accounting Standards Board, Statement of Accounting Concepts, Qualitative Characteristics of Financial Information, SAC 3, Australian Accounting Research Foundation, 1990, para. 5.

Comparability

The headings used should be comparable from year to year and between companies, otherwise comparisons will be difficult. Moreover, similar items should be treated consistently.[5]

This requirement is paramount in the reporting of extraordinary items. An analyst who desires to determine the trend in profits of a company over time does not wish to be influenced by unusual and non-recurring events, such as a large gain on the sale of a major division of the company. In Australia AASB 1018 provides details as to how the profit and loss statement should be classified to improve comparability. The broad structure is shown in the following table:

OUTLINE OF PROFIT AND LOSS STATEMENT IN CONFORMITY WITH AASB 1018	
Operating profit (loss) before abnormal items and tax	X
Abnormal items before income tax	X
Operating profit (loss) before tax	X
less Tax on operating profit (loss)	X
Operating profit (loss) after tax	X
Profit (loss) on extraordinary items	X
less Tax on extraordinary items	X
Operating profit (loss) and extraordinary items after tax	X

It should be noted that a profit and loss statement prepared in accordance with AASB 1018 does not require disclosure of the entity's expense items. Hence, although management will prepare profit and loss statements with a detailed expense classification for its own planning and control purposes, for external reporting purposes such disclosure is not required by AASB 1018. However, with a view to promoting management accountability to shareholders and other external users, AASB 1034, 'Information to be Disclosed in Financial Reports', specifies a list of expense and revenue items that must be disclosed. These include, for example, directors', executives' and auditors' remuneration. This standard does not prescribe the format for the presentation of profit and loss items but states that it should be developed having regard to the particular circumstances of the entity. The appendixes of the standard provide for illustrative purposes an example of a profit and loss account (statement) and a balance sheet. These are shown on pages 320–322 of this text.

There are three main components of the AASB 1018 profit and loss statement. These are operating profit/loss, abnormal items and extraordinary items. These are discussed in turn.

Operating profit or loss includes all revenues and expenses (and gains and losses) arising from the entity's ordinary operations. Ordinary operations are defined in AASB 1018 as 'operations of a kind carried on regularly from financial year to financial year to achieve the objectives of the company or economic entity' (para. 9). 'Ordinary operations' is a very

---

[5] See paras 39–42 of the IASC *Framework*.

broad term. The vast majority of a company's revenue and expense items will relate to its ordinary operations. Operating profit or loss will include, for example, sales revenue and the expenses customarily incurred in running the business. Also included would be dividend and interest income, stock losses, bad debts, and gains and losses on the sale of machinery, since all occur within the normal operations of the entity.

Abnormal items form part of the operating profit or loss. They arise from ordinary operations but must be separately disclosed because they are unusually large in the current period and hence have a significant impact on the operating profit or loss for the period. Examples of abnormal items provided in AASB 1018 include unusually large bad debt losses or inventory write-downs, foreign currency exchange gains or losses and gains or losses from the sale of investments or properties.

AASB 1018 defines *extraordinary items* as revenue and expenses (and gains and losses) that are attributable to transactions or other events of a type that are outside the ordinary operations of the company or economic entity and are not of a recurring nature. An event or transaction that would be outside the ordinary operations of one company may well be part of the ordinary operations of another. However, it should be noted that for an item to be classified as extraordinary it must be both outside the ordinary operations of the company and the underlying transaction or event must be one that is not of a recurring nature. According to AASB 1018, the following are examples of items that may fall within the definition of extraordinary items:

(a) The sale or abandonment of a significant segment of a business or all the assets associated with such a business.
(b) The condemnation, expropriation or unintended destruction of a property.[6]

The AASB 1018 standard on profit and loss statement disclosure illustrates the complexities involved in attempting to separate ordinary items from extraordinary items for the benefit of analysts and other users. With reference to the items encountered in earlier chapters, stock losses, which are inevitable in any business, are regarded as normal operating losses unless they are unusually large, when they would be abnormal items. Gains or losses on the routine sale of non-current assets are ordinary operating items, but gains and losses on the sale of a major part of the business may be extraordinary items. The amortisation of goodwill would be a normal operating expense item, whereas uninsured losses in a fire or flood may qualify as extraordinary items.

When the distinction between ordinary and extraordinary was introduced in Australia there was widespread use of the extraordinary classification. Some managements preferred to treat significant losses and write-downs as extraordinary items because analysts tended to disregard extraordinary items when assessing ongoing performance prospects. If the losses had been treated as part of ordinary operations such disclosures risked damaging the share price. The reverse was true of gains. Because of changes in the definition of extraordinaries in the standard, the use of the term is now severely restricted and there is less scope for accountants to exercise professional judgement. The following table illustrates the significance of items classified as abnormal and extraordinary. Note for the year in question none of the companies listed in the table classified gains or losses as extraordinary.

---

6 AASB 1018 Commentary (xv).

CLASSIFICATION OF REVENUES AND EXPENSES (GAINS AND LOSSES) AS ABNORMAL OR EXTRAORDINARY IN ANNUAL REPORTS OF AUSTRALIAN PUBLIC COMPANIES IN 1997

Company	Net profit before tax $m	Abnormal items $m	Extraordinary items $m
ANZ Bank Ltd	1 576	(182)	–
BHP Ltd	2 539	(1 046)	–
Burns Philp & Co. Ltd	(900.5)	(923.4)	–
Crown Ltd	(117.6)	(187)	–
CSR Ltd	322	–	–
David Jones Ltd	11.4	(37)	–
North Ltd	279.7	–	–
Pacific Dunlop Ltd	96.2	(5.0)	–
Qantas Airways Ltd	517.2	(17.2)	–
Rio Tinto Ltd	2 675	–	–
The Seven Network Ltd	142.1	(1.6)	–
Tabcorp Holdings Ltd	156.7	–	–
Westpac Banking Corporation Ltd	1 786	–	–
WMC Ltd	384.5	40.5	–
Woolworths Ltd	407.8	–	–

( ) denotes losses

Source: 1997 annual reports.

Understandability

The statements must be understandable by readers.[7] This concept affects the choice of words and the arrangement of the items. In recent years attempts have been made to recast the balance sheet in a more readable style and as one that highlights significant relationships. The International Accounting Standards have not presently specified the format of a balance sheet. However, the appendix to IAS 1 (revised 1997) gives an example of a balance sheet, but also clarifies that it is an example. In general, there are two types of presentation: the narrative or report form and the account form.

In the account form the balance sheet appears with assets on the left and liabilities and equity on the right. This is the form that has been adopted in earlier chapters. It appears as follows:

	$	$		$	$
Assets			**Liabilities**		
Current	XXX		Current	XXX	
	XXX	XXX		XXX	XXX
Non-current	XXX		Non-current	XXX	
	XXX	XXX		XXX	XXX
			Shareholders' equity	XXX	XXX
Total assets		XXX		XXX	XXX

Traditionally in Australia the sides have been reversed, with assets appearing on the right. This is an historical custom stemming from an old practice of inserting a balance sheet account in the ledger at the start of every year. This account would provide the double entry for inserting the opening balances. The balance of cash at bank, for example, would appear as a debit to cash at bank and a credit to the balance sheet account. The balance of accounts payable would be entered as a credit to that account and a debit to the balance sheet account. Hence, the balance sheet account has its assets on the right and its liabilities on the left.

It is less confusing to place the assets on the left side, where they appear in the ledger. It also seems reasonable to list first the resources held by the entity and then to consider the claims on those resources. This practice is common in the United States.

Other forms of arrangement of the balance sheet have also been adopted by entities wishing to remove its mystique for users. A 'narrative form' is shown below.

NARRATIVE FORM OF BALANCE SHEET		
Shareholders' equity		XXXX
Represented by:		
Current assets	XXX	
less Current liabilities	XXX	XXX
Non-current assets	XXX	
less Non-current liabilities	XXX	XXX
Total of net assets		XXXX

The possible variations are limited only by the imagination of the accountant.

The following is the format of the balance sheet as illustrated by the appendix to IAS 1 (revised 1997):

CONSOLIDATED BALANCE SHEET: XYZ LIMITED *as at 31 December 20X2* *(in thousands of currency units)*				
	20X2	20X2	20X1	20X1
Assets				
Current assets				
Inventories	X		X	
Trade and other receivables	X		X	
Prepayments	X		X	
Cash and cash equivalents	X	XX	X	XX
Non-current assets				
Property, plant and equipment	X		X	
Goodwill	X		X	
Investments in associates	X		X	
Other financial assets	X	XX	X	XX
Total assets		XX		XX
Liabilities and equity				
Current liabilities				
Trade and other payables	X		X	
Short-term borrowings	X		X	
Current portion of interest-bearing borrowings	X		X	
Warranty provisions	X	XX	X	XX
				continues

CONSOLIDATED BALANCE SHEET: XYZ LIMITED				
as at 31 December 20X2				
(in thousands of currency units)				
	20X2	20X2	20X1	20X1
Liabilities and equity (continued)				
Non-current liabilities				
Interest-bearing borrowings	X		X	
Deferred taxes	X		X	
Retirement benefit obligations	X	XX	X	XX
Capital and reserves				
Issued capital	X		X	
Reserves	X		X	
Accumulated profit (losses)	X	XX	X	XX
Minority interest		XX		XX
Total equity and liabilities		XX		XX

Report preparation from trial balances

Trial balances can be used in the preparation of both interim and final financial reports. Interim reports are usually prepared from trial balances since it is not usual to close the ledger except at the end of the year. To ensure accuracy and to provide evidence of the process adopted, it is necessary to have a formal means of adjusting the trial balance and classifying the items into financial statements. One such means is the worksheet, or eight-column trial balance, which was explained in Chapter 7.

The worksheet is useful in practice, but may be cumbersome for the solution of student exercises, where the problems tend to be simplified. Nevertheless, a systematic approach is always desirable and the following is one possible method.

This method of preparing interim financial reports from trial balances can also be applied to the preparation of final reports from trial balances in student exercises, as is illustrated below. Report preparation from trial balances involves the following steps.

1. Determine the type of business. A partnership or company will require profit appropriation statements. Different businesses will require different expense classifications.
2. Determine the accounting period. The period may be less than a year, which will affect adjustments such as depreciation. Also, the period may be over a calendar year (January–December), a financial year (July–June) or some other time span.
3. Determine, where relevant, the inventory method that is being used. A perpetual inventory method should have a trial balance account for cost of goods sold. A periodic inventory method will have a purchases account and an inventory account showing the opening balance of inventory.
4. Decide on a system of classification for the financial statements, especially expenses in the profit and loss statement. This will require a glance through the list of accounts.
5. Enter the adjustments on the trial balance as new accounts or additions to or deductions from existing balances. In this way the adjustments will not be forgotten when preparing the statements.
6. Take note of the requested appropriations.
7. Classify the trial balance using symbols. This will make items easier to locate when preparing the statements. The symbols used in the following illustration are:

R = Revenue
C = Cost of goods sold
S = Selling and delivery expenses
G = General and administrative expenses
A = Appropriation
CA = Current asset
NCA = Non-current asset
CL = Current liability
NCL = Non-current liability
OE = Owners' equity

8. Prepare the financial statements.

Example: *Comprehensive preparation and presentation of accounting reports*

From the following information, prepare the final accounting reports for the Bedrock Store Ltd.

	TRIAL BALANCE: BEDROCK STORE LTD as at 30 June 20X4				
		Debit		Credit	
S	Advertising	$ 7 400			
A	Appropriation 1/7/X3			$ 16 700	
G	Audit fees	1 900			
NCA	Accum. depn–buildings			27 000	+3 780
NCA	Accum. depn–delivery vans			5 200	+2 300
NCA	Accum. depn–store fittings			3 400	+ 820
CA	Bank	14 300			
NCA	Building	90 000			
G	Directors' fees	3 000			
A	Interim dividend	5 000			
NCA	Deposit with United Building Society	18 000			
NCA	Delivery vans	23 000			
NCA	Goodwill	10 000	– 6 000		
R	Insurance recovery from theft			1 300	
S	Lighting	2 700			
S	Municipal rates	1 400	– 300		
NCL	Mortgage			30 000	
G	Office expenses	4 300			
G	Office salaries	6 600	+ 100		
OE	Paid-up capital			85 000	
C	Purchases	182 100			
OE	Reserve for contingencies			17 000	
R	Sales			286 700	
S	Salespersons' salaries	23 600	+ 300		
R	Sales returns	12 400			
NCA	Store fittings	8 200			
C	Stock of inventory 1/7/X3	44 700			

continues

TRIAL BALANCE: BEDROCK STORE LTD
as at 30 June 20X4

		Debit	Credit
CL	Trade creditors		19 700
CA	Trade debtors	33 400	
CL	Sundry creditors		400
		$492 000	$492 000
CA	Prepayments	300	
S	Depreciation—vans	2 300	
	—fittings	820	
	—buildings	3 780	
A	Goodwill write-down	6 000	

Additional information to be incorporated in the reports:

1. Stock of inventory on hand 30 June 20X4, $53 600.
2. Office salaries $100 and salespersons' salaries $300 are owing on 30 June.
3. Municipal rates are paid up to 30 September next, and $300 relates to 20X5.
4. Depreciation is to be charged at 10 per cent per annum on cost of delivery vans and store fittings, and at 6 per cent per annum on net book value of buildings.
5. Goodwill is to be written down by $6000.
6. Provide for company tax at 40 cents in the $ of net profits.
7. A final dividend of $7000 is recommended for payment by directors.
8. $10 000 is to be transferred to reserve for contingencies.

PROFIT AND LOSS STATEMENT: BEDROCK STORE LTD
for the year ended 30 June 20X4

Sales revenue			$286 700
less Sales returns			12 400
Net sales			274 300
less Cost of goods sold			
Inventory 1/7/X3		$ 44 700	
plus Purchases		182 100	
		226 800	
less Inventory 30/6/X4		53 600	173 200
Gross profit			101 100
less Selling and delivery expenses			
Advertising	$ 7 400		
Lighting	2 700		
Rates	1 100		
Sales salaries	23 900		
Depreciation—vans	2 300		
—fittings	820		
—buildings	3 780	42 000	

continues

PROFIT AND LOSS STATEMENT: BEDROCK STORE LTD
for the year ended 30 June 20X4

less General and administration expenses			
Audit fees	1 900		
Directors' fees	3 000		
Office expenses	4 300		
Office salaries	6 700		
Goodwill	6 000	21 900	63 900
Net operating profit			37 200
plus Insurance recovery			1 300
Net profit before taxation			38 500
less Taxation expense			15 400
Net profit			$ 23 100

RETAINED PROFITS STATEMENT: BEDROCK STORE LTD
as at 30 June 20X4

Balance of retained profits 1/7/X3		$16 700
plus Net profit		23 100
		39 800
less Appropriations		
Interim dividend	5 000	
Dividends payable	7 000	
Reserve for contingencies	10 000	22 000
Balance end		$17 800

BALANCE SHEET: BEDROCK STORE LTD
as at 30 June 20X4

Current assets			
Bank		$14 300	
Debtors		33 400	
Prepayments		300	
Inventory		53 600	$101 600
Non-current assets			
Buildings	$90 000		
less Accum. depreciation	30 780	59 220	
Delivery vans	23 000		
less Accum. depreciation	7 500	15 500	
Store fittings	8 200		
less Accum. depreciation	4 220	3 980	
Deposit with building society		18 000	
Goodwill		4 000	100 700
			202 300

continues

BALANCE SHEET: BEDROCK STORE LTD as at 30 June 20X4		
Current liabilities		
Trade creditors	19 700	
Sundry creditors	400	
Tax payable	15 400	
Dividend payable	7 000	42 500
Non-current liabilities		
Mortgage		30 000
Shareholders' equity		
Paid-up capital	85 000	
Reserve for contingencies	27 000	
Retained profits	17 800	129 800
		$202 300

This example has illustrated the preparation of final reports from a trial balance, and has presented these financial statements in a way that discloses significant pieces of financial information clearly and logically. Note that the final preparation and format of financial statements depend on the entity involved. For example, some entities may disclose certain items in the profit and loss statement; others may disclose them in the notes to the accounts.

Consolidated financial statements

Many companies own controlling interests in other entities. As the company's own financial statements may not provide an adequate overview of the economic activity controlled by the company, consolidation is performed in an attempt to give investors a more accurate picture of the entire operations of the group of entities.

Consolidation accounting is a method of combining the financial statements of two or more entities that are controlled by the same owners. The assets, liabilities, revenues and expenses of each subsidiary are aggregated with the parent company's accounts. Each account balance of the subsidiary thus loses its identity in the consolidated statements and the resultant consolidated statements represent the whole group of companies as a single economic entity. International Accounting Standard IAS 27, 'Consolidated Financial Statements and Accounting for Investments in Subsidiaries', is concerned with the preparation and presentation of consolidated financial statements for a group of entities under the control of the parent.[8] A parent entity as defined by AASB 1024, 'Consolidated Accounts' (paragraph 9), is *an entity which controls another entity*, and a subsidiary entity is defined as *an entity which is controlled by a parent entity*.[9] Therefore, it is control which is the criterion that determines whether a group of related entities should prepare consolidated financial reports. Control is defined in AASB 1024 (paragraph 9) as *the capacity of an entity to dominate decision making, directly or indirectly, in relation to financial and operating policies of another entity so as to enable that other entity to operate with it in pursuing the objective of the controlling entity.* Therefore, it is control over decision making rather than ownership that determines the need for consolidated reports.

---

[8] The Australian accounting standard on this topic is Australian Accounting Board, AASB 1024, 'Consolidated Accounts'.

[9] IAS 27 defines 'control' in the same vein as 'the power to govern the financial and operating policies of an enterprise so as to obtain benefits from its activities' (para. 6).

Thus, under the Australian Corporations Law, parent companies, in addition to presenting their profit and loss statement and balance sheet to shareholders, must also present consolidated financial statements for the group of entities.In principle, the balance sheets and profit and loss statements of the entities within the group are added together to produce group financial statements. However, the individual reports of members of the group will contain some items that relate entirely to entities within the group and which therefore do not exist outside the group. Entities will borrow within the group, sell goods within the group, and so forth. The consolidated process must therefore eliminate these inter-entity items, as the following example illustrates.

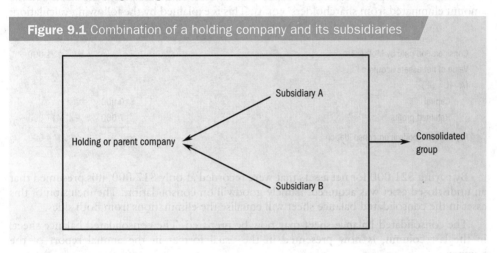

Figure 9.1 Combination of a holding company and its subsidiaries

Example: *A simple consolidation*

On 1 January 20X1 Mother Ltd acquired all of the issued shares in Son Ltd for the payment of $21 000. The respective balance sheets at that date were:

	Mother Ltd	Son Ltd
Assets		
Loan to Son Ltd	$ 2 000	
Investment in Son Ltd	21 000	
Other assets	29 000	$20 000
	52 000	20 000
Liabilities		
Loan from Mother Ltd	–	2 000
Other liabilities	4 000	1 000
	4 000	3 000
Shareholders' equity		
Issued capital ($1 par)	30 000	10 000
Retained profits	18 000	7 000
	48 000	17 000
	$52 000	$20 000

The inter-company loan from Mother Ltd to Son Ltd must be eliminated from the consolidated assets and the consolidated liabilities. No asset or liability exists outside of the group in relation to this loan.

The second elimination concerns the fact that Mother Ltd now holds the shares of Son Ltd and has a claim on the net assets, as represented by its shareholders' equity $(SE = A - L)$. No ownership claim exists outside the consolidated group. On the other hand, the asset 'Investment in Son Ltd' is also held entirely within the group. Accordingly, the investment account is eliminated from the consolidated assets, reducing them by $21 000. On the other side, the shareholders' equity accounts of Son Ltd are eliminated, amounting to $17 000. In effect, the shareholders' equity of Son Ltd is represented in the consolidated statements by the net assets.

There is a discrepancy of $4000 between the amount eliminated from the assets and the amount eliminated from shareholders' equity. This is explained by the following calculation:

Consideration paid by Mother Ltd		$21 000
Value of net assets acquired		
$(A - L = SE)$		
Capital	$10 000	
Retained profits	7 000	17 000
Payment for goodwill on consolidation		$ 4 000

By paying $21 000 for net assets that were recorded at only $17 000, it is presumed that an undisclosed asset was acquired, namely goodwill on consolidation. The inclusion of this asset in the consolidated balance sheet will equalise the eliminations from both sides.

The consolidated balance sheet may now be prepared. The consolidated balance sheet, in the last column, is now presented in the usual format in the annual report of the company.

Many large corporate undertakings are conducted through a holding (or parent) company and a series of subsidiaries. Sometimes the purpose may be to operate different divisions as separate legal entities in case of failure by one division. In other instances the subsidiary entities have arisen through the takeover of existing entities which have retained their separate legal existence. Whatever the reason, it is believed that investors in the holding company are best served by financial statements covering the operations of the entire group of entities. Financial analysis is mostly conducted on the consolidated statements rather than on those of the parent company alone.

	Mother Ltd $	Son Ltd $	Elimination $	Consolid. statement $
Assets				
Loan to Son Ltd	2 000	–	– 2 000	–
Investment in Son Ltd	21 000	–	– 21 000	–
Goodwill on consolidation	–	–	+ 4 000	4 000
Other assets	29 000	20 000		49 000
	52 000	20 000		53 000
Liabilities				
Loan from Mother Ltd	–	2 000	– 2 000	–
Other liabilities	4 000	1 000		5 000
	4 000	3 000		5 000
Shareholders' equity				
Issued capital ($1 par)	30 000	10 000	– 10 000	30 000
Retained profits	18 000	7 000	– 7 000	18 000
	48 000	17 000		48 000
	52 000	20 000		53 000

PREPARATION OF CONSOLIDATED BALANCE SHEET
at 1 January 20XX

The following appendix to AASB 1034, 'Information to be Disclosed in Financial Reports', is provided as an illustration. 'Outside equity interest' in the profit and loss statement and the balance sheet represent the equity in the entity other than that which can be attributed directly or indirectly to the parent entity.

Appendix to AASB 1034

The appendix is provided for illustrative purposes only and does not include every possible disclosure that might be appropriate. Other methods of presentation, which comply with the disclosure requirements in this Standard, may be appropriate in the particular circumstances of the entity.

Example of consolidated profit and loss account and a consolidated balance sheet

PROFIT AND LOSS ACCOUNT: XYZ CONSOLIDATED LIMITED					
for the financial year ended 30 June 19X7					
		Consolidated		Company	
		19X7	19X6	19X7	19X6
	Note	$'000	$'000	$'000	$'000
Sales revenue	2	X	X	X	X
Cost of sales		(X)	(X)	(X)	(X)
Gross profit		X	X	X	X
Selling, general and administrative expenses		(X)	(X)	(X)	(X)
		X	X	X	X
Other revenue	2	X	X	X	X
Operating profit before abnormal items		X	X	X	X
Abnormal items	3	X	X	X	X
Operating profit before income tax		X	X	X	X
Income tax expense	4	(X)	(X)	(X)	(X)
Operating profit after income tax		X	X	X	X
Profit on extraordinary items after income tax	5	X	X	X	X
Net profit		X	X	X	X
Outside equity interests in net profit		(X)	(X)	–	–
Net profit attributable to members of the parent entity		X	X	X	X

BALANCE SHEET: XYZ CONSOLIDATED LIMITED
as at 30 June 19X7

		Consolidated		Company	
		19X7	19X6	19X7	19X6
	Note	$'000	$'000	$'000	$'000
Current assets					
Cash		X	X	X	X
Inventories	6	X	X	X	X
Receivables	7	X	X	X	X
Property, plant and equipment	8	X	X	X	X
Other	9	X	X	X	X
Total current assets		X	X	X	X
Non-current assets					
Investments	10	X	X	X	X
Property, plant and equipment	8	X	X	X	X
Intangibles	11	X	X	X	X
Future income tax benefits	12	X	X	X	X
Research and development expenditure capitalised	13	X	X	X	X
Other	14	X	X	X	X
Total non-current assets		X	X	X	X
Total assets		X	X	X	X
Current liabilities					
Accounts payable	15	X	X	X	X
Borrowings	16	X	X	X	X
Provisions	17	X	X	X	X
Other	18	X	X	X	X
Total current liabilities		X	X	X	X

continues

	Note	Consolidated		Company	
		19X7 $'000	19X6 $'000	19X7 $'000	19X6 $'000

BALANCE SHEET: XYZ CONSOLIDATED LIMITED
as at 30 June 19X7

	Note	Consolidated 19X7 $'000	Consolidated 19X6 $'000	Company 19X7 $'000	Company 19X6 $'000
Non-current liabilities					
Borrowings	16	X	X	X	X
Provisions	17	X	X	X	X
Other	18	X	X	X	X
Total non-current liabilities		X	X	X	X
Total liabilities		X	X	X	X
Net assets		X	X	X	X
Equity					
Parent entity interest					
Issued capital	19	X	X	X	X
Reserves	20	X	X	X	X
Retained profits/ accumulated losses		X	X	X	X
Parent entity interest in equity		X	X	X	X
Outside equity interest					
Issued capital	19	X	X	–	–
Reserves	20	X	X	–	–
Retained profits/ accumulated losses		X	X	–	–
Outside equity interest		X	X	–	–
Total equity		X	X	X	X

Note: Entities may disclose categories of assets, liabilities and equity which are additional to those specified in section 5 of this Standard.

The following case illustrates many of the concepts discussed relating to companies and demonstrates the role of professional judgements in determining the 'bottom line'.

Case 9.1 Asset write-downs

BHP writes off $3b

by LEONIE WOOD

BHP yesterday acknowledged it made serious mistakes with major copper and iron ore projects as it slashed more than $3 billion from asset values, dragging its bottom line to a loss of $1.47 billion for the May year.

And the directors warned that world markets would remain under severe pressure for at least three years, putting strain on BHP's ability to grow revenue in the short term.

The ratings agency Standard & Poor's affirmed BHP's long-term credit rating at A, but indicated the next move would be down unless costs and debt eased and cash flows improved.

Although BHP has cut more than $400 million of costs from its businesses, its outlook is depressed, with commodity prices still sliding and economic turmoil in Asia dampening demand for products such as copper, steel and manganese.

The loss, which compared with a net profit of $410 million in 1996–97 marked BHP's second only loss since it was formed in 1885. It dropped £1006 in 1923.

The cathartic $3.05 billion of write-downs emerged after BHP's board completed a comprehensive review of assets and made substantial changes to their long-term economic and pricing assumptions. BHP also adopted a more conservative valuation method, bringing it into line with industrial companies.

Copper assets were written down by more than $1.6 billion, indicating Magma Copper is now worth just 33 per cent of the $3.2 billion that BHP forked out in early 1996.

BHP's hot-briquetted iron project in the Pilbara, where costs have blown out by more than $500 million, was written down by $590 million. The HBI plant still does not have a single buyer for its briquettes.

Despite the gloom, BHP's shares added 19 cents to $13.70 as investors welcomed the board's recognition of the severity of the problems.

BHP's chief operating officer, Mr Ron McNeilly, said the write-downs amounted to 'a very, very serious and significant decision' but was absolutely vital to help 'set the house in order'.

'We really do believe the Asian situation is very serious,' he said.

He said BHP would cut at least another $400 million from costs this year, restructure its assets portfolio, try to squeeze early revenue from developing projects, and lower debt.

Net operating profit of just over $1.3 billion was slightly above analysts' forecasts and 6 per cent below last year's $1.39 billion.

Revenue eased 10.5 per cent to $26.66 billion.

BHP sold about $3 billion of assets last year—including a $1.75 billion stake in Foster's Brewing

Group—and at least another $4 billion will go before 2001. Signfiicantly lower copper and oil prices cut about $521 million from operating profits, but BHP clawed back about $232 million through cost cuts, and a further $143 million from a lower Australian dollar.

BHP's ferrous minerals division posted profits of $327 million before abnormals ($265 million last year) and the coal group reported profits of $110 million ($166 million previously).

World minerals lost $111 million (a loss of $6 million last year) due to difficulties starting up the Hartley platinum project and engineering problems at Beenup mineral sands.

Integrated steel returned $168 million ($160 million a year ago) and the steel products division lifted profits 66 per cent to $287 million.

Copper earned $171 million ($542 million). Oil earned $672 million ($693 million), or more than half group earnings.

Australia's biggest corporate losses

Bond Corp	1990	$2.2 bn
State Bank SA	1991	$2.18 bn
Westpac	1992	$1.9 bn
Adsteam	1991	$1.58 bn
BHP	1998	$1.47 bn
State Bank Vic	1990	$1.35 bn
Elders-IXL	1990	$1.3 bn
Bell Resources	1990	$1.1 bn
Foster's	1992	$950m
Ariadne	1988	$640m

Age, 27 June 1998

(a) Briefly outline why BHP experienced a loss of $1.47 billion for the year ended May 1998.

(b) Define extraordinary and abnormal operating items.

(c) Explain whether the financial impact of the write-downs described in the newspaper report give rise to abnormal or extraordinary items.

(d) In the *Australian* just four days before the announcement by BHP of a $3 billion write-down, it was reported that BHP was preparing to cut its asset values by up to $2.0 billion. What was the impact on BHP's share price of the actual write-down of $3 billion?

(e) The financial press believed that BHP might have decided to write down its assets by a significantly lower amount than $3 billion. Suggest possible reasons for the financial press being so inaccurate in their estimation of the asset write-downs.

Manufacturing organisations

A specific type of organisation for which accounting reports are required is the manufacturing organisation. There are many similarities between accounting for manufacturing organisations and accounting for merchandisers (retailers or wholesalers). Both types of organisations have sales revenues and incidental gains to be accounted for, and the normal expenses involved in selling operations such as cost of goods sold, selling and distribution expenses, general and administrative expenses and finance expenses. Both require the measurement of profit and the measurement of assets, liabilities and owners' equity.

The major difference between the merchandiser and the manufacturer is that the former buys in goods and sells them in the same form whereas the manufacturer buys in goods and materials and transforms them through the manufacturing process into other goods to be sold. Labour and equipment of various kinds are used in the course of the transformation process, or manufacturing cycle. This gives rise to a difference in accounting for merchandising and manufacturing organisations in respect of the computation of the cost of goods sold.

For a merchandiser:

> *cost of goods sold* = *beginning inventory of merchandise*
> + *purchases of merchandise*
> − *ending inventory of merchandise*

For a manufacturer:

> *cost of goods sold* = *beginning inventory of finished goods*
> + *cost of goods manufactured*
> − *ending inventory of finished goods*

In the profit and loss statement, then, the cost of goods manufactured appears for a manufacturer where purchases appear for a retail company.

Determining cost of goods manufactured

The cost of goods manufactured must be computed before cost of goods sold can be calculated. There are three major elements of manufacturing cost: direct materials, direct labour and manufacturing overhead.

Direct materials cost

This is the cost of those raw materials which may be physically and economically traced to individual units of production. Examples would be the timber, leather or other covering material used in the construction of a custom-made chair.

Direct labour cost

This is the cost of labour that may be specifically identified with, or traced to, units of production, for example the cost of machine operators or assemblers involved in producing the chair. These costs can be identified with physical units of production through the use of time sheets to indicate the number of hours spent on a specific product, activity or job.

Manufacturing overhead cost

This category covers all manufacturing costs other than direct materials and direct labour—that is, all costs necessary for the production process, but not identifiable with or traceable to specific units of production. These costs can be termed 'indirect product costs'.

Included in this category are such costs as indirect materials (materials needed in the manufacture of all products but not able to be related to specific product units), indirect labour (for example supervisory salaries), repairs and maintenance of machines, factory heating and lighting, insurance on the manufacturing facilities and premises, and depreciation of manufacturing plant.

Also included are some costs that can be directly identified with specific units of production but not conveniently or economically (for example the cost of glue used in manufacturing the chairs).

Manufacturing costs are clearly distinguished from other costs of operating the company. The costs that normally appear after gross profit, such as selling and distribution costs, general administration and office expenses, and interest expense, are not 'manufacturing' costs, and therefore are not part of manufacturing overhead. They may be described as overhead costs of the business as a whole.

Depreciation expense, for example, is a part of manufacturing overhead if it relates to the factory building or to any item of plant or equipment used in the production process. However, depreciation of the administrative or sales office buildings or salespersons' cars are not manufacturing overhead expenses.

The cost of goods manufactured statement

It was noted earlier that the cost of goods sold for a manufacturing organisation for a particular period is found by adjusting the cost of goods manufactured during the period by the beginning and ending inventories of finished goods.

However, the cost of goods manufactured during the period cannot be determined simply by accumulating the costs of direct materials, direct labour and manufacturing overhead for the period. Some of the raw materials (the direct materials) purchased during the period may not have been used in production within that period, but instead may remain as part of a stock or inventory of raw materials for use in future production. The cost of raw materials used in production during the period will be calculated as:

> *raw materials inventory at beginning*
> *+ purchases of raw materials during the period*
> *− raw materials inventory at end*

Additionally, not all of the manufacturing activity during the period will have resulted in fully completed products. At balance date a manufacturer may have a stock of partly completed production, known as 'work-in-progress'. Some materials, labour and overhead services will have been used in producing this work-in-progress, but more will be required in a future period to complete the product and to have it in a form ready for sale.

The cost of goods manufactured (completed) during the period will therefore be calculated as:

> *work-in-progress at beginning*
> *+ manufacturing costs incurred during the period*
> *– work-in-progress at end*

The total cost of goods manufactured for the period may be reported in the form of a cost of goods manufactured statement or manufacturing statement. This statement is illustrated below. Note what this statement contains and its format.

The manufacturing statement begins with the opening balance of work-in-progress inventory, $70 000. Added to this is the total of manufacturing costs incurred during the period, $590 000. These costs comprise direct (raw) materials, direct labour and manufacturing overhead. The latter two costs are unproblematic—they are simply the accumulation of these costs for the period. However, the cost of raw materials used during the period has to be computed from the purchases and beginning and ending inventory figures.

STATEMENT OF COST OF GOODS MANUFACTURED		
for the current year		
Work-in-progress inventory,		
beginning of year		$ 70 000
Raw materials		
Beginning raw materials inventory	$ 50 000	
Purchases	97 000	
plus Transportation-in	5 000	
Cost of raw materials available for use	152 000	
less Ending raw materials inventory	42 000	
Cost of raw materials used		110 000
Direct labour		230 000
Manufacturing overhead		
Indirect labour	$ 60 000	
Supervisory salaries	100 000	
Heat, light and power	18 000	
Repairs and maintenance	12 000	
Rates and taxes	18 000	
Insurance on equipment	15 000	
Depn. on factory building	6 000	
Depn. on machinery and equipment	3 000	
Amortisation of patents	2 000	
Factory supplies used	8 000	
Miscellaneous factory costs	8 000	
Total manufacturing overhead		250 000
Total manufacturing costs		590 000
		660 000
less Work-in-progress inventory, end of year		60 000
Cost of goods manufactured		$600 000

The amount of $660 000 represents the total costs associated with work-in-progress. It is not the same as the costs of (fully) manufactured goods if, and because, some of the goods remain unfinished (in progress) at the end of the period. In the example we are discussing, the ending inventory of work-in-progress is costed at $60 000, meaning that the cost of goods manufactured for the period is computed at $600 000.

Recall that if we were now to go on to prepare a profit and loss statement for the manufacturing organisation in our example, the cost of goods manufactured (cost of finished goods) figure would appear where purchases normally appears for a merchandising organisation.

At this stage we can take as given the cost or value of inventories, particularly work-in-progress inventory. However, a major task in accounting for manufacturing organisations is the calculation of these inventory values. This issue will be returned to in Chapter 23, when we will deal with methods of cost accumulation, product costing and inventory valuation for manufacturing organisations in more detail.

Non-profit organisations and public sector organisations

The emphasis to date has been on the accounting system used by commercial organisations in the private sector and by most public sector entities, a system known as the 'accrual accounting system'. It is a system in which all transactions between the entity and external parties are recorded, whether they are for cash or for credit. The record is made at the time of the transaction. Various internal adjustments to the records are also made in order to measure periodic profit from operations and the organisation's assets and equities at the end of the period.

However, there are also a large number of organisations within the economy that are not motivated by profit. The special case of public sector enterprises, which report on similar bases to commercial enterprises although not entirely motivated by profit considerations, was briefly introduced in Chapter 1. Other non-profit organisations are clubs and societies, charities, universities, museums, trustees and executors of deceased estates, and bodies corporate. For these organisations the accrual approach to accounting, with its emphasis on the derivation of profit for the accounting period, has not traditionally been considered appropriate, and a cash accounting system has usually been adopted. Cash accounting involves the recording of only cash receipts and cash payments. Instead of a profit and loss statement and balance sheet, the reports produced are 'cash receipts and payments' and 'statement of cash balances'. An example of these reports is provided on page 328.

Cash accounting is not used by non-profit organisations alone. It is also used by some small profit-making businesses, such as professionals (i.e. doctors, solicitors, accountants), by small firms with few resources, and by entities that deal exclusively in cash transactions. For these businesses a modified cash accounting system is deemed sufficient. An estimate of profit is calculated as the cash surplus from operations, adjusted for accounts receivable and accounts payable.

All organisations need information about their cash inflows and outflows. The cash flow statement is examined in Chapter 10.

Example: *Cash accounting reports*

NORTHVILLE WOMEN'S AUXILIARY

STATEMENT OF CASH RECEIPTS AND PAYMENTS FOR 20X2

Receipts		Payments	
Sale of school calendars	$ 620	PCA donation	$7500
Sponsorship of school calendar	1500	Craft supplies	100
Mother's Day stall	1440	Hire of trestles	140
Father's Day stall	1200	Advertising	150
Raffles	650	Morning teas	20
Lamington drive	2200	Calendar production	150
Cake stall	410	Lamington drive	1700
Second-hand clothing sales	170		
Interest	50		
	$8240		$9760

STATEMENT OF CASH BALANCES AND RECONCILIATION TO BANK ACCOUNT

Balance brought forward from 12 December 20X1		$3000
plus Receipts	$8240	
less Payments	9760	(1520)
Balance as at 15 December 20X2		1480
represented by Balance at bank		1430
Cash on hand		50
		$1480

Detailed comparison of cash and accrual accounting

The aims, assumptions and concepts of the accounting system used by non-profit organisations can be compared with the aims, assumptions and concepts of commercial organisations, to highlight the features of both.

Aims

Whenever the structure of the organisation is commercial or performance-oriented accrual accounting techniques are used. This is to fulfil the purpose of accounting to communicate economic information (i.e. the results of financial transactions and events) in order to permit informed judgements and decisions by users of that information.

As has been explained, reports are prepared for the purposes of stewardship, control and planning. They report the results of management's actions to shareholders and other users of accounting reports, describing the uses of funds and disclosing whether a profit or a surplus has been earned.

Control is exercised over the operations of the organisation by both its owners and its managers. In the case of a company, its directors are ultimately controlled by its shareholders, who vote for the directors at the annual general meeting. The exercise of control by managers is like a pyramid structure, with each level of management being responsible for the employees and operations under its control, and responsible to those managers above them. Accounting information is used to prepare budgets (short-term plans) and to plan future investments (long-term plans).

Non-profit organisations exist to satisfy a variety of objectives. A wider range of factors needs to be considered, for example the social, political and welfare aspects of the organisation's activities. A charity's objectives might be to raise funds for a target beneficiary or cause by means of social activities and fund-raising ventures organised by members. Although it would be important to report on the financial success of the fundraising activities, other reported information would include the uses made of the funds after they had been handed to the beneficiary or cause, the level of success of social activities, and the growth in membership and contributors. Hence, accounting by non-profit organisations differs from accrual accounting in that information is required on other aspects of the organisation's activities than just economic events, and profit is not the only, or even a necessary, measure of performance.

In a non-profit organisation, reports are still prepared for the purposes of stewardship, control and planning. However, the contributors of the funds are different: for example, instead of shareholders they might be government, members or trustees. The question of interest is now not 'how much' but 'how were the funds spent?'

Planning by non-profit organisations is usually on a shorter time horizon, with the coming twelve months being the usual period of concern.

Assumptions

Cash accounting also differs substantially from accrual accounting in its assumptions. Under cash accounting the continuity assumption is not necessary, because for decision-making purposes the existence of the organisation cannot be assumed in the following accounting period. Although it can be reasonably assumed at the practical level that most organisations will still exist in the following period, such an assumption is not relevant to the measurement of current performance, nor is it an indication of the certainty of future funding. Continuity becomes an important consideration only when one seeks to value assets and obligations, since future expectations can affect their values.

One of the consequences of not assuming continuity is that no assets are recognised, because all cash payments are written off, or recorded as outflows to the organisation, when they occur. Any future benefits to be gained from different payments are not recorded. For example, wages for the period and the purchase of furniture, while both outflows of cash, are not differentiated for recording purposes, as they would be under the accrual system.

Public sector reporting

At all levels of government, most of its functions are carried out by different departments that have responsibility for a particular area of concern to that governmental level (e.g. defence, social welfare, housing, education and transport).

Traditionally, government department finances have operated on:

1. A yearly cash allocation from the funding authority (Treasury).
2. An approved budget that has detailed how the cash allocation is to be spent in the process of fulfilling the department's objectives.

Each department has been required to account for expenditure of its cash allocation and to report this in a statement of cash receipts and payments.

Within each department the process of reporting on and controlling expenditure is similar to the process that occurs in commercial organisations. There is a hierarchy of responsibility and delegated authority. Documentary evidence (such as receipts) has been required to verify expenditures, and reports of expenditures at each level have been prepared for those at the next highest level of responsibility. These reports have been subsequently used in the planning process (i.e. preparing the budget for the following year).

One interesting aspect of the financing of government departments has been that any unspent funds at the end of the year reverted back to the funding authority. This occurred because of the absence of the continuity assumption: projects and policies were not necessarily ongoing. Each year was considered to be a separate venture for a government department or program, and in theory a new case needed to be made each year for an allocation of funds.

In recent years the nature of public sector accounting in many countries including Australia has changed in quite a dramatic way. As private sector organisations have realised the importance of measuring cash flows and maintaining solvency, governments have begun to use accrual techniques of various types to improve efficiency and accountability in the public sector.

The traditional use of cash accounting had led to government departments operating as if their role was to spend the total funds allocated. Issues such as efficiency and effectiveness had not ranked highly. Such problems were recognised and in recent years have been addressed in Australia, for instance, at the state, federal and local government levels. Programs involving managerial reform, reorganising and restructuring have been implemented. Accounting systems have been changed to reflect varying degrees of compliance with accrual concepts, as befits the nature of the organisations.

The introduction of accrual accounting to the public sector enables the full cost of their operations to be identified. Costs not accounted for under a cash accounting system include those related to the use of assets, for example depreciation, rent on government offices, and employee-related costs such as health and superannuation. The introduction of accrual accounting techniques ensures that there is continued recognition within the accounting system of assets held, the utilisation of these assets, and a focus on the cost to the nation of services provided by the public sector.

The benefits of changing the techniques employed in public sector accounting towards accrual accounting techniques may include improved information for decision making (especially on underutilised and surplus assets), better maintenance and replacement planning, more effective risk management and insurance practices, and the provision of full-cost information on operations and programs, especially those that could be used for 'on-charging' under 'user pays' regimes. Costs of such a change include the direct system development costs, the need to develop human resource skills, and the ongoing costs of accounting and reporting valuations. In addition, the application of 'commercial accounting' in the public sector increases the contestability of the reported figures in view of the arbitrary allocations involved and may in fact narrow the accountability focus with such entities.[10]

Operating statements for government departments

The format for profit and loss statements and balance sheets discussed earlier in this chapter is also relevant for public sector business enterprises such as Telstra and Australia Post in the case of Australia. For government departments using accrual accounting, the balance sheet format would be relevant, but the profit and loss statement format is less appropriate. Government departments are typically not profit-making ventures. Departments such as the Department of Social Security and the Department of Water Resources are established to provide essential services to the community. Although departments may charge for some of the services they provide, they are generally dependent on government consolidated funds for at least 50 per cent of their revenues. For these government departments the focus is on the 'net cost of services' provided for the period. This represents the amount of funds the

10 Concerns about 'limited-scope' financial accounting in the public sector are discussed in G. D. Carnegie and P. W. Wolnizer, 'Enabling Accountability in Museums', *Accounting, Auditing and Accountability Journal*, Vol. 9, No. 5, 1996 and L. D. Parker, 'Broadscope Accountability: The Reporting Priority', *Australia Accounting Review*, Vol. 6, No. 1, March 1996.

government will need to allocate to the department to allow it to provide the desired level of services to the community. The general format of an operating statement for a government department is shown below.[11] Note that this is only one possible alternative.

OPERATING STATEMENT: DEPARTMENT XYZ
for the reporting period ended 30 June 20X1

	Note	20X1 $000	20X1 $000	20X0 $000	20X0 $000
Operating expenses					
Employee entitlements		(429 605)		(336 935)	
Depreciation	5	(27 289)		(25 689)	
Supplies		(27 000)		(25 000)	
Other	6	(43 187)		(30 512)	
Total cost of services			(527 081)		(418 136)
Operating revenues	7				
User charges, fees and fines		33 190		17 675	
Other revenue		80	33 270	70	17 745
Net cost of services			(493 811)		(400 391)
Revenues from government	3				
Recurrent appropriations		375 000		292 851	
Capital appropriations		47 000		13 000	
Other appropriations		19 000		7 000	
Assumption of liabilities		94 567	535 567	84 130	396 981
Net revenues from disposal of non-current assets	7(c)		2 890		–
Change in net assets before restructuring			44 646		(3 410)
Net revenues from restructuring	7(d)		1 923		–
Change in net assets after restructuring	12		46 569		(3 410)

For government departments the term 'operating statement' is usually used instead of profit and loss statement. The operating statement is a bit like an 'upside-down' profit and loss statement. Expenses are shown first, itemised by major category. From total cost of services, user charges and other non-government sources of revenue (revenue inflows) are deducted to determine the department's net cost of services. This is a key figure. It reveals how much it has cost the government, and ultimately the taxpayer, to provide the services of the department to the community. The net cost of services is funded by the recurrent allocation to the department from the government. The recurrent allocation is a source of revenue, and the departments are required to budget their recurrent needs very carefully. The capital allocation shown in the operating statement represents amounts paid by the government to the department to allow it to replace or expand its non-current asset base as necessary. Both recurrent and capital allocations are sources of revenue for the department; however, the capital allocation is provided for specified asset replacement and expansion purposes, whereas the operating grant is provided to cover the day-to-day operations of the entity.

---

[11] This example is shown in the appendix to Australian Accounting Standard AAS 29, 'Financial Reporting by Government Departments', reissued October 1996.

Statements of financial position for government departments

A sample 'balance sheet' for a government department is shown below.[12] It is usually referred to as a statement of financial position. The standard AAS 29 requires that departments disclose assets, liabilities and equity as at the reporting date. Note that infrastructure assets and works of art are disclosed as separate items, but in most respects this example is similar to the balance sheets of private sector entities.

		20X1		20X0	
	Note	$000	$000	$000	$000
STATEMENT OF FINANCIAL POSITION: DEPARTMENT XYZ *as at 30 June 20X1*					
Current assets					
Cash on hand and deposit accounts		9 196		1 103	
Receivables	9	5 500		1 000	
Other	10	13 139	27 835	14 239	16 342
Non-current assets	11				
Plant, equipment and vehicles		31 547		25 626	
Land and buildings		471 234		429 700	
Infrastructure		555 819		566 319	
Works of art		156	1 058 756	150	1 021 795
Total assets			1 086 591		1 038 137
Current liabilities					
Payables		116		929	
Employee entitlements		1 500		1 462	
Finance leases	18	500	2 116	500	2 891
Non-current liabilities					
Finance leases	18		4 500		4 000
Total liabilities			6 616		6 891
Equity	12				
Accumulated surplus		948 104		901 535	
Asset revaluation reserve		131 871	1 079 975	129 711	1 031 246
Total liabilities and equity			1 086 591		1 038 137

Ethical issues

Extraordinary items. Why shouldn't the gain on the sale of motor vehicles appear as an extraordinary revenue item in the financial statements of the Department of Road Construction? The Department has a regular program of updating their fleet of vehicles, purchasing at sales-tax-exempt prices and selling at a higher price three years later. After all, they are not in the business of selling motor vehicles, so gains on motor vehicles sales shouldn't be treated as operating revenue. Should they?

---

[12] This example is shown in the appendix to Australian Accounting Standard AAS 29, 'Financial Reporting by Government Departments' (reissued October 1996).

Summary

Three issues surrounding report preparation were the focus of this chapter. First, the preparation and presentation of profit and loss statements and balance sheets were discussed, including issues such as the distinction between profit appropriations and profit and loss statement items, and classification and disclosure in financial statements. A comprehensive example of report preparation from trial balances was provided. Next, the preparation of consolidated financial statements and the presentation of accounting reports for a manufacturing organisation were introduced and illustrated. Finally, the methods of financial reporting by non-profit organisations and public sector organisations were presented as specialised types of accounting reports. Hence the issues discussed in this chapter affect the structure and content of almost all accounting entities.

Review exercises

Discussion questions

9.1 Why is it considered important to deduct cost of goods sold to arrive at a gross profit?

9.2 Distinguish the category of cost of goods sold from other expenses and indicate to which category each of the following items belongs:

(a) Import duties paid on purchases of inventory.
(b) Freight on purchases of inventory.
(c) Freight on sales deliveries to customers.
(d) Costs of wrapping paper and string.
(e) Wages paid to the company's own employees to assemble for sale furniture purchased in individual pieces.
(f) Costs of storing goods in the warehouse prior to placing them on sale.

9.3 (a) For what purpose might it be useful to classify expenses into various classes?
(b) Suggest some possible expense classification headings appropriate to the following business enterprises:

(i) a large department store that offers home delivery and after-sales service
(ii) a bus company
(iii) a real estate agency
(iv) a funeral parlour.

9.4 Why is a distinction made between current and non-current items in the balance sheet? How would the following be classified?

(a) Land held for resale within the current year.
(b) Land held for development and resale in the distant future.
(c) Rent prepaid for the next three years.
(d) A mortgage liability on which annual repayments are made and which has five years to run.
(e) A bank overdraft that the company has had for many years but which may be recalled at short notice.
(f) Directors' fees unpaid.
(g) A loan to a shareholder of the company that is repayable at call.

9.5   'Expenses and profit appropriations are both debit entries and both result in a reduc-
       tion in the profits available for dividend. The distinction between the two is therefore of
       little importance.' Discuss.

9.6   'All credits arising from unusual items, such as gains on foreign currency translation,
       ought to be reported in the retained profits statement since they are not revenue from
       ordinary trading operations.' Discuss.

9.7   Patron Ltd has held an investment of $500 000 in ordinary shares of Struggling Ltd for
       10 years, and since that company has just entered liquidation with a large deficit the
       accountants of Patron Ltd believe that the investment should be written off in the cur-
       rent profit and loss statement. The directors of Patron Ltd argue, instead, that the loss
       should be regarded as an appropriation of profits, since:

       (a) Struggling Ltd has been deteriorating for some years and it would be unfair to
           recognise the entire loss in the current year's determination of profit.
       (b) The loss is unusual and its inclusion in the profit and loss statement would distort
           the results.
       (c) The loss is not yet certain.
       (d) The write-down does not affect capital maintenance since Patron Ltd will not be
           required to outlay any cash as a result of the collapse of Struggling Ltd.

       Prepare a reply to the directors' assertions.

9.8   The directors of Pinchpenny Wholesalers Pty Ltd have informed shareholders in the lat-
       est annual report that they must, with regret, reduce the dividend payment due to a fall
       in profits. The statement of profit and loss included several charges related to the
       company's major asset, a warehouse building, which has been in operation for some
       20 years:

Depreciation on building (1.5% per year)	$ 1 500
Repairs to building	27 000
Provision for extensions due next year	121 000
Provision for replacement (10% of estimated future cost)	49 000

       A shareholder has argued that the profit has been understated as a result of these
       charges. In reply, the directors stated that they are legitimately 'providing for the
       future'. Discuss.

9.9   Determine, giving reasons, how each of the following items should be classified in the
       financial statements:

       (a) An uninsured loss by fire of the company's premises.
       (b) Dividends paid on preference shares.
       (c) Interest paid on debentures.
       (d) Salaries paid to directors as full-time employees of the company.
       (e) Correction of an item incorrectly included as revenue in a previous period.
       (f) Income taxation payable on the current year's profits.
       (g) An amount written off goodwill.

9.10   Discuss, giving reasons, your view on how each of the following items should be clas-
       sified in the financial statements.

(a) Land held by a land developer to be sold in the coming year.

(b) A mortgage loan the company obtained ten years ago which is due to be paid off in the coming year.

(c) Accounts receivable on instalment sales, the amount to be received progressively over five years.

(d) Uninsured loss of inventory in a fire.

(e) Uninsured loss of inventory by theft.

(f) Duty paid on inventory imports.

(g) Warehousing charges on inventory held in store on behalf of the company because its own storage area is full.

(h) Interest received on surplus funds invested in Treasury Bonds by a manufacturing company.

(i) Interest received by a finance company on funds invested in listed company debentures.

(j) Inventory write-down of $8000. The average amount of inventory write-downs over the past five years has been $7800.

(k) Reduction of accumulated depreciation by $20 000 following a decision to correct excessive depreciation charges in the last two years. The depreciation expense should have been $15 000 in each of those years.

(l) A customer who was written off as a bad debt pays his account.

(m) A shareholder borrows money from the company for three years.

(n) A shareholder lends money to the company for six months.

(o) A company desires to retain $100 000 of profits to finance future growth.

(p) A company desires to retain $20 000 from profits to provide for holiday pay to which staff are presently entitled.

9.11 Happy Valley Motors Ltd in the notes to the financial statements stated in Note 3 that extraordinary items included the following expenses and revenue items:

(a) bad debt write-offs

(b) depreciation of revalued premises

(c) interest received on bonds

(d) loss on sale of plant and equipment

(e) foreign currency losses on overseas borrowings

(f) dividends declared on preference shares

Identify whether any of these items could be classified as extraordinary items and the circumstances under which this might be possible.

 Problems

9.12 *Report preparation from trial balance*

From the following information relating to Bubbles Bottles wine distributors and retailers, prepare appropriately classified accounting reports, and show journal entries where necessary.

TRIAL BALANCE: BUBBLES BOTTLES
as at 30 June 20X2

	Debit	Credit
Accounts payable		$ 27 400
Accounts receivable	$ 10 000	
Advertising	480	
Allowance for doubtful debts		3 600
Bank	2 000	
Cost of goods sold	126 000	
Doubtful debts expense	2 000	
Electricity	420	
Insurance	300	
Inventory	128 900	
Investments	4 000	
Paid-up capital		60 000
Salaries	105 600	
Sales		294 000
Shop fixtures	4 000	
Shop fixtures accumulated depreciation		1 500
Shop rental	2 200	
Telephone rental	600	
	$386 500	$386 500

Additional information:
1. Interest accrued on investments amounted to $250.
2. Advertising materials on hand as at 30 June 20X2 amounted to $80.
3. Unpaid shop rental for June was $200.
4. Insurance is charged to an expense account when paid. The amount prepaid at the end of June was $150.
5. Unpaid bills for electricity and telephone totalled $245.
6. Salaries of $800 were unpaid at the end of the year; the bottleshop manager's annual bonus of $2500 was to be paid in July 20X2.
7. Depreciation of shop fixtures is $500 for the year.
8. An ageing of accounts receivable revealed that $1200 should be written off as bad debts. Doubtful debts amounted to $2150.

9.13 *Report preparation from trial balance*
The following information has been obtained from the ledger accounts of the Wellington Woggle Co. Ltd. Prepare suitably classified final accounting reports.

TRIAL BALANCE
as at 31 December 20X6

	Debit	Credit
Accounts payable		$ 43 820
Accounts receivable	$ 62 240	
Accum. depreciation—buildings		16 450
Accum. depreciation—vehicles		5 130
Accum. depreciation—showroom fittings		1 230
Advertising	15 420	
Allowance for doubtful debts		3 590
Audit fees	1 800	
Bank		12 560
Buildings	85 600	
Cost of goods sold	338 570	
Debentures (Interest 9% p.a., due 20X8)		40 000
Doubtful debts expense	5 780	
Formation costs	3 500	
General reserve		14 000
Goodwill	20 000	
Interest	3 000	
Inventory	112 750	
Office expenses	9 610	
Office salaries	67 430	
Issued capital		100 000
Retained profits 1/1/X6		11 860
Sales		586 280
Sales returns	9 520	
Salespersons' salaries	76 570	
Showroom fittings	4 800	
Vehicles	18 330	
	$834 920	$834 920

Additional information:

1. Inventory on hand at 31 December 20X6 was $110 000.

2. Expenses unpaid on 31 December 20X6:

Office salaries	$550
Salespersons' salaries	280

   2 months interest on debentures

3. Expenses paid but relating to next year:

Advertising	$1000

4. Depreciation to be charged at 5 per cent per annum on cost of buildings, 10 per cent per annum on cost of showroom fittings and 20 per cent per annum on net book value of vehicles.

5. Goodwill and formation costs to be written down by $5000 and $1500 respectively.

6. $6000 to be transferred to general reserve.

7. Dividend of 12½ per cent on paid-up capital and company tax of $30 000 to be provided for.

9.14 *Report preparation from trial balance for a partnership*

Prepare half-yearly accounting reports for W. Pat and G. Slam who are in partnership as sporting goods retailers. They share profits and losses in the ratio of one-third and two-thirds respectively, after deducting salaries of $7500 each and after charging interest of 11 per cent per annum on advances from partners.

TRIAL BALANCE as at 31 December 20X5	Debit	Credit
Accum. depreciation —delivery van		$ 3 280
—office furniture		480
Advertising	$ 1 088	
Allowance for doubtful debts		1 300
Bad and doubtful debts expense	570	
Bank		920
Cartage on purchases	460	
Cost of goods sold	143 280	
Creditors		23 490
Debtors	11 552	
Delivery van	19 600	
Insurance	280	
Interest	70	
Inventory—1 July 20X5	52 460	
Office stationery	570	
Office furniture	1 640	
Office salaries	14 800	
Pat, W. —advance		17 000
—capital		20 000
—current	7 130	
Rent	7 800	
Sales returns	440	
Sales revenue		229 620
Sales staff's salary	12 100	
Slam, G. —capital		12 000
—current	6 250	
Wages—van drivers	28 000	
	$308 090	$308 090

Adjustments:

1. Inventory on hand at 31 December 20X5, according to a stock count, was $51 800.

2. Stationery on hand at 31 December 20X5 was $32.

3. Further bad debts of $150 to be written off. Doubtful debts at 31 December 20X5 are estimated to be $960.

4. Depreciation to be charged:

   Delivery van: 20 per cent per annum on straight-line method

   Office furniture: 10 per cent per annum on reducing-balance method

5. One month's rent, $600, has been paid in advance.

6. Office salaries of $120 were owing at 31 December 20X5.

9.15 *Report preparation from trial balance*

From the following information, prepare appropriately classified accounting reports for Cassidy Co. Ltd. The company is a wholesale distributor of cane furniture.

TRIAL BALANCE AS AT 30 JUNE 20X8		
	Debit	*Credit*
Accounts payable		$ 16 200
Accounts receivable	$ 61 400	
Accrued management consultant fees 1/7/X7		600
Accumulated depreciation:		
Office furniture		2 400
Warehouse equipment		11 200
Advertising	35 000	
Allowance for doubtful debts		4 800
Bank	74 400	
Damages awarded in law suit		24 200
Doubtful debts expense	7 200	
Freight on purchases	4 000	
General reserve		17 800
Insurance	12 000	
Interest	3 200	
Interim dividend	4 000	
Management consultant fees	35 600	
Mortgage		40 000
Office furniture	12 000	
Paid-up capital		100 000
Preliminary expenses	16 000	
Purchases	228 400	
Rent: Office	8 400	
Warehouse	14 800	
Retained profits 1/7/X7		17 000
Salaries: Office staff	29 000	
Warehouse staff	95 000	
Sales revenue		566 600
Sales returns	33 000	
Stock on hand 1/7/X7	72 800	
Tax payable		1 400
Warehouse equipment	56 000	
	$802 200	$802 200

Additional information:

1. The inventory on hand at 30 June 20X8 was estimated to be worth $86 000 at cost.

2. Depreciation is to be charged as follows:

    Warehouse equipment, 10 per cent on cost

    Office furniture, 20 per cent on reducing-balance

3. An ageing of accounts receivable at 30 June 20X8 revealed that $800 should be written off as bad debts. Doubtful debts amounted to $3400.

4. Rent on the office, at $600 per month, was prepaid to 31 August 20X8.

5. Salaries unpaid at 30 June 20X8 were:

    Office staff $1400

    Warehouse staff $1740

6. Included in the insurance payment is $1000 covering July 20X8.

7. $2000 is to be written off preliminary expenses.

8. The damages awarded in a law suit were the first in the company's history and legislative changes make it most unlikely that this action will ever have to be taken by the company again.

9. A final dividend of $10 000 is to be provided for.

10. $8000 is to be transferred to the general reserve.

11. Tax payable for the current year is estimated to be $15 600.

9.16 *Report preparation from trial balance*

From the following information relating to Guiselle's French Caterers Ltd, prepare appropriately classified accounting reports.

TRIAL BALANCE as at 30 June 20X7		
	Debit	Credit
Accounts payable		$ 9 000
Accounts receivable	$ 29 300	
Accumulated depreciation:		
Delivery vans		46 000
Kitchen equipment		36 300
Allowance for doubtful debts		6 300
Bank		3 400
Delivery vans	96 000	
Deposit with Flexible Building Society	60 000	
Doubtful debts expense	8 700	
General reserve		20 000
Goodwill	11 000	
Insurance expense	19 300	
Interest received		4 000
Interim dividend	5 000	
Kitchen equipment	81 000	
Paid-up capital		20 000
Prepaid insurance 1/7/X6	1 000	
Purchases	33 500	
		continues

Rent expense	30 000	
Retained profits 1/7/X6		32 300
Sales revenue		270 000
Stock cooking materials 1/7/X6	8 500	
Van running expenses	7 400	
Wages: Chefs	42 300	
Van drivers	14 300	
	$447 300	$447 300

Additional information:

1. The stock of cooking materials at 30 June 20X7 was estimated to be $11 200 at cost.

2. Wages unpaid at 30 June 20X7 were:

    Chefs $2900

    Van drivers $3300 $6200

3. Rent payable, $2000 per month, is paid to 30 September 20X7.

4. Included in the insurance payment is $1200 covering July 20X7.

5. Depreciation to be charged as follows:

    Delivery vans, 10 per cent on net book value

    Kitchen equipment, 20 per cent on cost

6. An ageing of accounts receivable at 30 June 20X7 revealed that $400 should be written off as a bad debt. $4800 of accounts receivable should be considered doubtful.

7. Tax payable for the current year is estimated to be $42 000.

8. A final dividend of $10 000 is to be provided for.

9. $15 000 is to be transferred to the general reserve.

10. $3000 is to be written off goodwill.

9.17 *Report preparation from trial balance*

From the following information, prepare appropriately classified accounting reports for Skinner Ltd. The company is a wholesaler of the 'Stickup' range of glues that bond permanently on contact.

TRIAL BALANCE
as at 30 June 20X8

	Debit	Credit
Accounting fees	$ 17 800	
Accounts payable		$ 8 100
Accounts receivable	30 700	
Accrued accounting fees 1/7/X7		300
Accumulated depreciation:		
Office equipment		1 200
Showroom equipment		5 600
		continues

TRIAL BALANCE as at 30 June 20X8	Debit	Credit
Advertising	23 500	
Allowance for doubtful debts		2 400
Bank	27 200	
Damages paid in law suit	14 200	
Debentures (due 31/12/X9)		20 000
Doubtful debts expense	3 600	
Formation expenses	8 000	
Freight on purchases	2 000	
General reserve		11 000
Interest	1 600	
Interim dividend	2 000	
Office equipment	6 000	
Paid-up capital		50 000
Purchases	110 000	
Rent: Office	4 200	
Showroom	7 400	
Retained profits		8 500
Salaries: Office staff	47 500	
Showroom staff	44 500	
Sales revenue		323 300
Sales returns	16 500	
Showroom equipment	28 000	
Stock on hand 1/7/X7	36 400	
Tax payable		700
	$431 100	$431 100

Additional information:

1. The inventory on hand at 30 June 20X8 was estimated to be worth $43 000 at cost.

2. Salaries unpaid at 30 June 20X8 were:

   Office staff $700
   Showroom staff $870 $1570

3. Rent on the office, at $300 per month, was prepaid to 31 August 20X8.

4. Advertising brochures costing $200 were to be issued in July 20X8.

5. Depreciation is to be charged as follows:
   Showroom equipment, 10 per cent on cost
   Office equipment, 20 per cent on reducing-balance

6. An ageing of accounts receivable at 30 June 20X8 revealed that $400 should be written off as bad debts. Doubtful debts amounted to $1700.

7. The damages in this law suit were the first for many years and steps have been taken by the chief executive officer of the company to ensure that this problem will not occur.

8. Tax payable for the current year is estimated to be $7800.

9. A final dividend of $5000 is to be provided for.
10. $4000 is to be transferred to the general reserve.
11. $1000 is to be written off formation expenses.

9.18 *Report preparation from trial balance*

New Town Co. Ltd has chosen to appoint you as their auditor. The company has agreed to pay $5000 audit fees and an additional $2000 for accountancy services rendered. New Town Co. Ltd expects you to complete their accounts and prepare the necessary financial statements in good narrative form for presentation to their board of directors.

TRIAL BALANCE: NEW TOWN CO. LTD
as at 30 June 20X4

	Debit	Credit
Paid-up capital		$140 000
Retained profits 1/7/X3		15 000
General reserve		14 200
Income tax paid	$ 18 000	
Income tax payable 1/7/X3		19 500
Capital reserve		10 000
Sales		250 000
Sales returns	1 500	
Purchases	100 000	
Purchases returns		620
Cartage inwards	600	
Cartage outwards	700	
Advertising	1 000	
Preliminary expenses	3 000	
Goodwill	13 400	
Buildings	160 000	
Selling expenses (sundry)	1 000	
Sales staff's salaries	40 000	
Sales staff's car expenses	2 500	
Sales staff's entertainment expenses	3 000	
General expenses (sundry)	3 250	
Insurance	2 000	
Rates	1 000	
Discount allowed	1 270	
Accounts receivable	29 000	
Allowance for doubtful debts		6 250
Accumulated depreciation—motor vehicles		6 000
—office furniture		2 800
Accounts payable		6 000
Bills payable		1 000
Petty cash	100	

continues

TRIAL BALANCE: NEW TOWN CO. LTD as at 30 June 20X4		
	Debit	Credit
Bank		9 700
Motor vehicles (used by managers)	30 000	
Office furniture	14 000	
Inventory 1/7/X3	20 800	
Bad and doubtful debts	7 500	
Office salaries	25 000	
Interest on overdraft	200	
Payroll tax—sales staff	1 250	
—office	1 100	
Bad debts recovered		100
	$481 170	$481 170

The following additional information was made available to you:

1. Inventory on hand at 30 June 20X4 was $10 000.

2. Adjustments in relation to depreciation are to be made. Depreciation is calculated on a straight-line basis:

Motor vehicles	5 years
Office furniture	10 years

    (Assume there is no scrap value.)

3. Write off preliminary expenses by $500.

4. Expenses incurred but not yet paid as at 30 June 20X4 include:

Office salaries	$2400
Sales staff's salaries	1600
Interest on overdraft	1164

5. Insurance paid in advance as at 30 June 20X4 was $400.

6. Provide for a final dividend of 10 cents per issued share. The company has 140 000 issued shares.

7. Provision should be made for audit and accounting fees owing.

8. The estimated taxation on company profits is $15 000.

9. Two companies owing a total of $4800 went into liquidation and New Town Co. Ltd has no chance of recovering any amount.

10. The company's allowance for doubtful debts is inadequate. You suggest that the provision be $6000.

9.19   *Report preparation from trial balance*

From the following information relating to Calliope Traders Pty Ltd, prepare the final accounting reports.

TRIAL BALANCE: CALLIOPE TRADERS PTY LTD as at 30 June 20X5		
	Debit	Credit
Accounts payable		$ 18 600
Accounts receivable	$ 22 250	
Accumulated depreciation on office equipment		1 390
Accumulated depreciation on vehicles		3 580
Advertising	4 530	
Allowance for doubtful debts		2 050
Bank	11 270	
Cost of goods sold	148 380	
Doubtful debts expense	1 320	
Government bonds	6 000	
Interest received		420
Inventory	52 720	
Office equipment	4 880	
Office salaries	68 140	
Paid-up capital		50 000
Rent	3 460	
Reserve		12 200
Retained profits		6 120
Sales		304 400
Sales staff's salaries	60 230	
Vehicles	15 580	
	$398 760	$398 760

Additional information:

1. Expenses unpaid on 30 June 20X5: office salaries $250, advertising $1400.
2. Rent payment of $1200 (already included in rent account) was for period 1 May 20X5 to 31 July 20X5.
3. Depreciation to be charged on office equipment at 12½ per cent on cost, and on vehicles at 15 per cent on net book value.
4. Dividend of $4500 and company tax of 40 per cent of net profit to be provided for.
5. $3000 to be transferred to reserve.
6. Directors' fees of $2200 have been incorrectly included in office salaries.

9.20   *Disclosure in the profit and loss statement*

Warrnambool Ltd disclosed the following items that were required to be shown in the profit and loss statement for the year ended 30 June 20X2. Show the correct order in which they would appear.

- Retained profits 1 July 20X1
- Abnormal items before income tax
- Operating revenue
- Operating profit before abnormal items and income tax

- Profit on extraordinary items before income tax
- Income tax attributable to operating profit
- Operating profit before income tax
- Retained profits 1 July
- Transfers to reserves
- Income tax expense attributable to profit on extraordinary items
- Amounts transferred from reserves
- Total available for appropriation
- Operating profit and extraordinary items after income tax
- Profit on extraordinary items after income tax
- Dividends declared
- Retained profits 30 June 20X2

9.21 *Report preparation from trial balance for a public sector entity*

TRIAL BALANCE: DEPARTMENT FOR CULTURAL CONSERVATION as at 30 June 20X2		
	Debit	Credit
	$000	$000
Accumulated surplus		4 000
Accum. depn—buildings		41 460
Accum. depn—fittings		3 420
Advertising and public notices	24 000	
Audit fees	3 600	
Buildings	171 200	
Capital works allocation		30 140
Cash	2 000	
Contributed capital		116 000
Depreciation expense	9 520	
Fittings	9 600	
Heat, light and power	20 000	
Interest expense	7 200	
Donations from industry		500
Recurrent allocation		130 000
Salaries expense	71 600	
Sundry creditors		2 800
Trade debtors (current)	13 600	
Travelling expenses	16 000	
User charges		20 000
	$348 320	$348 320

Prepare an operating statement for the department for the year ending 30 June 20X2 and a statement of financial position as at 30 June 20X2.

9.22   *Problems and questions on consolidated reports*

1.   Predator Ltd owns a controlling interest in two other companies. One of its sub-sidiary companies is Predator's supplier of plastic, the main material used by Predator in manufacturing a variety of toy animals. The other subsidiary is a trans-port company that Predator Ltd uses to transport its products to wholesalers.

As the major shareholder in Predator Ltd, why might you want to have the oper-ating results of all three companies combined in a set of consolidated accounts, rather than just have the separate accounts of each company to study?

2.   On 1 January 20X8 Ron Ltd purchased all of the issued shares of Eff Ltd for $4 600 000. The following balance sheet shows the position immediately after the acquisition.

	Ron Ltd	Eff Ltd
	$000	$000
Paid-up capital	9 000	1 125
Retained profits	3 350	2 500
Accounts payable	3 400	1 450
	15 750	5 075
Cash at bank	3 050	2 075
Investment in Eff Ltd	4 600	
Land and buildings	8 100	3 000
	15 750	5 075

Prepare the consolidated balance sheet as at 1 January 20X9.

9.23   *Problems and questions on manufacturing reports*

1.   Compare a manufacturing organisation with a merchandising organisation in terms of the nature of business activity and the types of inventories held.

2.   Define direct materials cost, direct labour cost, and manufacturing overhead cost.

3.   The following information is available from the accounting records of the Archway Company for the year ended 30 June 20X1.

Cost of raw materials purchased	$ 495 000
Manufacturing overhead costs	417 500
Total manufacturing costs	1 635 000
Finished goods inventory	
30 June 20X1	237 500
1 July 20X0	275 000
Work in progress inventory	
30 June 20X1	200 000
1 July 20X0	175 000
Raw materials inventory	
30 June 20X1	237 500
1 July 20X0	225 000

From the information provided, calculate:

(a) the cost of raw materials used during the year
(b) the direct labour costs incurred during the year
(c) the cost of goods manufactured during the year
(d) the cost of goods sold during the year

4. The Westminster Manufacturing Company commenced operations in July 20X0. The following information is available from the accounting records at the end of the first year of operations (i.e. 30 June 20X1).

Sales	$42 000
Advertising	6 000
Depreciation on office equipment	1 800
Depreciation on plant and equipment	4 800
Direct labour	12 000
Plant supervisory salary	4 000
Purchases of direct materials	7 500
Other manufacturing overhead	2 100
General and administrative expenses	3 600
Inventories at 30 June 20X1	
Direct materials	900
Work in progress	1 300
Finished goods	4 000

(a) Prepare a statement of cost of goods manufactured for the year ended 30 June 20X1.
(b) Prepare a profit and loss statement for the year ended 30 June 20X1.

5. The following data are available for the Mornington Company:

	Account balances	
	30 June 20X0	30 June 20X1
Work in progress inventory	$ 35 000	$ 7 000
Finished goods inventory	140 000	42 000
Accounts receivable	175 000	105 000
Accounts payable	140 000	70 000
Raw materials inventory	105 000	17 500
Raw materials purchased		280 000
Selling and administrative expenses		245 000
Direct labour		245 000
Indirect materials		21 000
Insurance on factory		3 500
Plant supervision salaries		17 500
Indirect labour		70 000
Depreciation on plant and equipment		31 500
Sales		1 825 000
Other manufacturing overhead		35 000

(a) Prepare a statement of cost of goods manufactured for the year ended 30 June 20X1.
(b) Prepare a profit and loss statement for the year ended 30 June 20X1.

9.24 *Problems and questions on non-profit and public sector reporting*

1. Why does the continuity assumption not apply to non-profit organisations?
2. What type of organisations prepare accounting reports on a cash basis? Give two examples not mentioned in the textbook.
3. Why did the use of cash accounting in the public sector encourage departments to spend the total amount of funds allocated to them? (Do you know of any examples of this type of behaviour in the public sector or elsewhere?)
4. Explain the rationale for the 'upside down' type of profit and loss statement prepared by many government departments.
5. Obtain a copy of the annual report of a major government trading enterprise, such as Australia Post. Compare it with the annual report of a major private sector corporation. Are there more similarities or more differences? Comment on the reasons for the differences you find.
6. For each of the following entities, identify:

   (a) the persons or other entities with an interest in obtaining financial information about the entity
   (b) the major purposes to be served by the presentation of financial reports
   (c) the nature of the resulting financial statements of:

      (i) a small tennis club
      (ii) a charitable institution
      (iii) a union of students within a tertiary institution

7. Why might it be useful for the following information on public sector assets and services to be known? Discuss any problems associated with finding this information and choose the best method of valuation for:

   (a) the value of the land over which an existing major road runs
   (b) the value of the land left vacant for the future construction of a major road
   (c) the 'full cost' of employing staff, including salary and current and future leave entitlements
   (d) the value of public transport vehicles
   (e) the full cost of a job creation scheme, including subsidies given and the full cost of employing staff to administer the scheme
   (f) the full cost of a garbage collection service provided by council, including the full cost of employees and the vehicles used
   (g) the full cost of defending Australia militarily

8. Using the example of cash accounting statements in the chapter (see page 328), present this information more meaningfully. For example, offset receipts and payments for the same ventures so that the financial results of each of the activities for the year can be clearly seen.

9.25 *Preparation of cash accounting reports*

The following cash payments and receipts for the Peninsula Bowling Club were recorded for the month of March.

Peninsula Bowling Club

March

1	Received annual membership fees	$1500
4	Bar receipts for past week	6600
5	Paid account from Liquor Wholesalers for liquor supplies	8600
7	Paid staff wages	2100
11	Bar receipts for past week	7200
12	Payment of accounts by Mr Beer and Ms Glass	220
14	Paid greenkeeping service fee for March and April	6000
	Paid staff wages	2100
18	Bar receipts for past week	6900
21	Paid staff wages	2100
25	Bar receipts for past week	7100
27	Purchased outdoor furniture, to replace identical furniture purchased five years earlier (by cheque)	5000
28	Paid staff wages	2100

(a) Prepare a statement of cash receipts and payments, presenting the information as meaningfully as you can.

(b) If you were required to present this to the Board of Directors, what other information and/or method of presentation would you wish to include in your report?

(c) Assuming there are no stocks, prepayments or accruals, or debts outstanding, prepare a statement of revenue and expense for the month for Peninsula Bowling Club.

9.26 *Accounting for clubs*

As treasurer of the Western Tennis Club it is your job to prepare the financial statements to present at the annual meeting, this year to be held on 29 November 20X1. The statements you are required to prepare include receipts and payments, revenue and expense, and assets and liabilities.

The following information is obtained from the club's records, which were closed on 31 October, the end of the financial year.

Receipts for year ended 31 October 20X1

Subscriptions	$3330
Interest	60
Donations	180
Sale of refreshments	1580
Sale of tickets for social and raffles	340
Court fees	1750

Payments for year ended 31 October 20X1

Refreshment purchases	$1120
Expenses for sale of refreshments	110
Purchase of seats for courts	400
Hire of hall for socials	210
Expenses in connection with social	35
Stamps and stationery	65
Sundry expenses	275
Repayment of loan	250

Balance of assets and liabilities at:

	1 November 20X0	31 October 20X1
Bank	$ 317	?
Stock of refreshments	680	$ 510
Furniture	350	?
Equipment	2700	2700
Loan from A. Bank	1500	?
Members' funds	2547	?

(a) Prepare a statement of receipts and payments for the year ended 31 October 20X1.

(b) Prepare a statement of revenue and expenses for the year ended 31 October 20X1.

(c) Prepare a statement of assets and liabilities at 31 October 20X1.

Case studies

9.27 *Abnormal and extraordinary items*

The Redland Pastoral Company Ltd (RPC) holds seven pastoral properties in the Far North region. In February 20X8 the company indicated in general terms the potential impact of drought. In May the chairperson reported that between 25 000 and 28 000 head of cattle had succumbed to disease and drought. The preliminary result reported for the year ending 31 December 20X7 was a loss of $3 million, a $10.2 million reversal from the previous year.

Required

(a) Outline the definition of 'abnormal' and 'extraordinary' items as used in financial reporting.

(b) Explain whether or not the financial impact of the conditions described in the case give rise to abnormal or extraordinary items in Redland Pastoral Company's accounts.

9.28 *Asset write-downs*

Brierley braced to cut assets

Richard Gluyas

SPECULATION is mounting that Brierley Investments in poised to hack into its asset base and announce writedowns of around $NZ1 billon ($870 million) next week.

The writedowns, which would reportedly be the biggest in New Zealand corporate history, will form part of the embattled investment group's 1998 annual result.

Sources in New Zealand said a $NZ1 billion writedown would place Brierley in breach of its banking covenants, which stipulate, among other things, that bottom line profit for the past two years should exceed $NZ300 million.

The more optimistic analysts are forecasting a pre-abnormals result for 1998 of about $NZ400 million, up from $NZ311 million in 1997, when the company reports on Thursday.

However, the emerging consensus is for a figure around $NZ300 million.

One New Zealand-based source said Brierley had already had preliminary discussions with its bankers about the looming breach of at least one of its covenants.

The banks, he said, would waive the breach as the writedowns related to accounting matters and in no way impaired Brierley's ability to service its debt.

Company representatives could not be reached for comment yesterday.

Brierley's main assets include 46 per cent of the Thistle Hotels chain in the UK, a 42 per cent stake in Air New Zealand, a 24 per cent holding in media group John Fairfax and a 28 per cent interest in building products company James Hardie.

Meanwhile, there were indications of unease emerging from Brierley's big shareholders yesterday about the prospect of Roger Douglas remaining chairman, even in an interim capacity, and indeed retaining a directorship. Sir Roger's demise as chairman was negotiated at a fiery boardroom meeting last Monday.

But as part of a compromise deal with hostile 10 per cent shareholder Camerlin Group, it was agreed he would vacate the position after a new chairman and chief executive were found. Camerlin, in return, withdrew its notice for an extraordinary general meeting seeking Sir Roger's removal as a director.

It was claimed after the board meeting that Sir Roger would retain the Brierley board position he has held since the early 1990s.

But if speculation about the size of the writedowns proves correct and negative market reaction to Monday's peace deal persists, Sir Roger could be placed under renewed pressure. A source close to one of the big, non-Camerlin investors in Brierley said: 'He (Sir Roger) has been a director for some time and he should take responsibility, as has happened with other directors of major corporations in the region.'

In line with a stronger overall market, Brierley gained 3c yesterday to 57c. The stock was trading at 88c in April after Sir Roger headed a boardroom coup that ousted chief executive Paul Collins and chairman Bob Matthew.

The loss in market capitalisation over that period has been more than $900 million, principally because of the collapse of the Thistle deal but also due to skittish world markets.

A research report by Salomon Smith Barney yesterday calculated there was now a $NZ1.7 billion gap between the book value of Brierley's assets and their market value.

Australian, 3 September 1998, p. 23

Required

(a) Why would Brierley Investments contemplate writing down its assets?

(b) Would such asset write-downs represent an extraordinary item? Explain.

(c) Define 'loan covenant'.

(d) How does the writing down of assets result in a breach of loan covenants?

(e) What are the possible financial implications of a company breaching loan covenants?

(f) Do substantial write-downs of assets impair ability to service debt?

(g) How is it possible for a shareholder with only 20 per cent shareholding to force a chairman of a public company to resign?

9.29 *Abnormal items*

Ups and downs for Ridley

ABNORMAL losses of $6.6 million incurred by Ridley in relation to writedowns of goodwill in its Pet Products division, the departure of its managing director and the restructure of the corporate office dragged down its annual net profit by 23.5 per cent to $15.3 million.

But the rapid expansion of Ridley's Canadian operations and a record performance from Cheetham Salt operations helped lift net pre-abnormal profit by 9 per cent to $21.9 million.

Sales for the 12 months to June 30 rose 45 per cent to $929.2 million.

Directors declared a final dividend of 3.75c a share fully franked, taking the annual dividend to 7.5c fully franked.

Australian, 8 September 1998

Required

(a) Does the abnormal loss of $6.6 million incurred by Ridley comply with pronouncements of the accounting profession? Discuss.

(b) Sales for the 12 months to June rose 45 per cent. Should part or all of this sales increase be considered abnormal revenue? Explain.

9.30 Consolidated financial statements

News faces rival offer for United

CLIVE MATHIESON

THE News Corporation Ltd faces a potential bidding war for English Premier League soccer club Manchester United, with diversified leisure group Enic emerging as a rival suitor.

News subsidiary British Sky Broadcasting and Manchester United yesterday confirmed discussions 'which may or may not lead to an offer being made' for the club.

Press speculation suggested BSkyB—40 per cent owned by News—had already negotiated a £575 million ($1.64 billion) takeover deal with United chairman and 14 per cent shareholder Martin Edwards.

However, a report in the *Financial Times* said Enic, a company with extensive interests in European football, was poised to make a rival bid for United, which is easily the most successful English football club of the 1990s.

The *Financial Times* said Enic was considering the bid after an angry reaction to the BSkyB bid for the richest club in the game.

Shares of United, which was listed on the London Stock Exchange in 1991, soared more than 35 per cent last night after confirmation of talks between News and the club.

In early London trading, the stock was 57p higher at 221p—just 4p short of the amount News is expected to pay for United shares, according to an article in *The Times* yesterday. Other listed UK soccer teams were also sharply higher. Tottenham Hotspur, also the subject of recent speculation about a takeover bid from News, was trading 3.25p higher at 63.75p. Chelsea was up 11p to 82.5p and Aston Villa 40p higher at 602.5p.

The Enic group already owns Vicenza of Italy, Slavia Prague of the Czech Republic, AEK Athens of Greece and a 25 per cent stake in Glasgow Rangers. According to the FT, Enic would look for financial backing from US entertainment group Time Warner.

Fans and others criticised the bid from BSkyB because of fears that the acquisition would give the satellite broadcaster too much influence in the lucrative television rights market.

Ownership of a Premier League club would also give News clout in the establishment of a proposed European Super League competition.

News has used a similar strategy in the US to secure content for its television interest there.

Earlier this year, News paid about $415 million for the Los Angeles Dodgers baseball team. It also owns stakes in the LA Lakers basketball and LA Kings ice hockey teams, and the New York Knicks basketball and New York Rangers ice hockey teams.

British Sports Minister Tony Banks said a deal between United and News could be subjected to an investigation by the Office of Fair Trading.

Australian, 8 September 1998

Required

(a) Why would News Corporation Ltd wish to acquire Manchester United?

(b) Why is British Sky Broadcasting considered a subsidiary of News Corporation Ltd if News Corporation Ltd owns only 40 per cent of BSkyB?

(c) How is it possible that News Corporation could have a controlling interest in Manchester United if BSkyB was negotiating the takeover deal with the soccer club?

CHAPTER 10
Statement of cash flows

Learning objectives

In this chapter you will be introduced to:

1. the purposes of a statement of cash flows

2. the relationship between the statement of cash flows and other general purpose reports

3. a definition of cash and cash equivalents and how they are treated in a statement of cash flows

4. the classification of cash flows as operating, investing and financing and the significance of these distinctions

5. the preparation of statements of cash flows using the transactions-based method and the financial-statement-based method

6. how to determine cash flow from operations using two methods described as the direct and indirect methods

7. the schedules required by the accounting standards to accompany the statement of cash flows

8. the use of a worksheet to prepare a statement of cash flows applying the financial-statement-based method.

Introduction

Another major accounting report, the statement of cash flows, is introduced in this chapter. Cash flow reporting is now a requirement of the International Accounting Standards Committee.[1] In Australia this statement is required for all reporting entities which are subject to approved accounting standards. The uses and functions of the cash flow statement will be explained. Two approaches to the preparation of such a statement are illustrated, and a comprehensive example of how to prepare and interpret a statement of cash flows is provided.

Two major financial reports are described in the previous chapters: the profit and loss statement, which purports to measure the increase in net assets arising from the entity's revenue-producing activities, and the balance sheet, which measures the stock of resources controlled by the entity and the claims against those resources. These reports assist users to make and evaluate decisions about the financial performance of the entity including the stewardship of management.

Another important function of accounting is to indicate the entity's liquidity and solvency, or its ability to pay debts when they fall due. This information is sought by both short-term and long-term lenders, trade creditors, employees and owners. In assessing the entity's future liquidity position, details of past cash movements are essential. This information is not provided in sufficient detail by the other major financial reports discussed so far.

The balance sheet is prepared as at a particular point in time; it does not explain how and why changes have taken place in reaching that financial position. It provides the balance of the entity's cash account, but does not explain how cash has varied over the accounting period or how the final balance of cash was generated. The profit and loss statement gives changes in net assets due to operating activities, but many items represent non-cash transactions or adjustments that do not affect the entity's cash position. On the other hand, many cash transactions do not affect the profit and loss statement. The profit and loss statement focuses on the entity's operating activities and does not include the effects of financial or investment transactions, such as the purchase of land or the repayment of a large debt. There is a need, then, for an additional statement that gives an account of the movements in cash that have brought changes from one balance sheet to the next.

More specifically, the statement of cash flows assists in assessing the ability of the entity to:

- generate positive net cash flows in the future
- meet its financial commitments as they fall due, including the servicing of borrowings and the payment of dividends
- fund changes in the scope and/or nature of its activities
- obtain external finance where necessary.

Put simply, it reports the effects of all transactions involving a flow of cash into or out of the entity, whether those transactions relate to operating, financing or investing activities. By highlighting the changes in the cash position over the accounting period, the statement of cash flows explains where cash was generated and how it was used.

Definitions

A statement of cash flows reports movements in cash under three headings:

1. operating activities
2. investing activities
3. financing activities

It also reports the total movement in the entity's cash balance over the accounting period.

---

[1] The IASC issued its revised IAS 7, 'Cash Flow Statements', in 1992.

The following definitions are from the Australian accounting standard on the statement of cash flows.[2] *Cash* includes both cash on hand and cash equivalents. *Cash on hand* means notes and coins held, and deposits held at call with a bank or financial institution. *Cash equivalents* mean highly liquid investments with short periods to maturity which are readily convertible to cash on hand at the investor's option and are subject to an insignificant risk of changes in value. Cash equivalents include borrowings which are integral to the cash management function and which are not subject to a term facility.

This definition of cash equivalents needs further consideration. Items that usually satisfy this definition include cash at bank and investments in money-market instruments with up to three months maturity. Borrowings integral to the cash management function would include bank overdrafts. It is considered that investments in short-term money-market instruments such as short-term bank and non-bank bills involve little risk in terms of price changes and thus do not warrant being shown as a cash outflow. Such movements of cash are considered only a transfer within the cash and cash equivalents category. Note, however, that the purchase of shares listed on the stock exchange, even though the intention might be to hold them for only a short period, would not be considered a cash equivalent because of likely changes in market value.

Investing activities relate to the acquisition and disposal of non-current assets, including property, plant and equipment, and other productive assets. Investments (other than those considered to be part of the entity's cash resources) and shares and ownership interests in other entities are also investing activities. Examples of investing activities are the purchase and disposal of vehicles, machinery, land and buildings, the purchase and sale of marketable securities issued by other entities, the acquisition of other entities, and the disposal of segments of an entity's own operations.

Financing activities relate to the size and composition of the financial structure of the entity. They include transactions in which the entity obtains resources from its owners and pays dividends to its owners, and also transactions involving borrowings and repayments other than those considered to be part of cash. Examples of financing activities are the issue of shares, the issue and redemption of debentures and unsecured notes, and the payment of dividends.

Operating activities involve receipts and payments for the production, sale and delivery of goods and services. Movements in certain working capital accounts due to cash transactions are considered to be operating activities. Working capital accounts include inventory, accounts receivable and accounts payable, and prepayments and accruals. Also included in operating activities are the payment of interest and taxes. Examples of operating activities are receipts of cash from customers (operating inflows) and payments for inventory, employee wages and insurance premiums (operating outflows).

Preparation of a simple statement of cash flows

There are two ways of preparing a statement of cash flows. The first way, the *transactions-based method*, analyses each transaction in terms of its effects on the entity's cash position. The second way, the *financial-statement-based method*, works from existing financial statements which have already summarised the effects of cash (and other) transactions on the entity.

---

[2] Australian Accounting Standards Board, Approved Accounting Standard, AASB 1026, 'Statement of Cash Flows', 1997.

The transactions-based method of preparation

In order to use the transactions-based method of preparing a statement of cash flows, the complete set of cash transactions must be obtained. Each transaction is then classified and grouped according to the activity that it affects: operations, finance or investment.

The transactions-based method of preparing a statement of cash flows is illustrated in the following example.

Example: *Rosetree Student Care Centre*

The Rosetree Student Care Centre provides before-school and after-school care for the students at Rosetree Primary School. Fees can be paid either on the day of attendance, or by the term, in which case an account is sent. The following information on cash payments and receipts was collected for the month of October.

ROSETREE STUDENT CARE CENTRE	
Cash payments and receipts for October	
October	$
2 Received casual fees since beginning of October	50 (O)
3 Paid wages to staff	450 (O)
Obtained a long-term loan from the local council	1 000 (F)
4 Receipt of fees on accounts	530 (O)
7 Purchased games and play equipment	630 (I)
9 Received casual fees for past week	62 (O)
10 Paid wages to staff	450 (O)
15 Receipt of fees on accounts	345 (O)
16 Received casual fees for past week	46 (O)
17 Paid wages to staff	450 (O)
23 Paid rent for October to Rosetree Primary School	60 (O)
Received casual fees for past week	72 (O)
25 Receipt of fees on accounts	480 (O)
28 Paid wages to staff	450 (O)
31 Paid cleaning fees for October and November	640 (O)
Received casual fees for past week	48 (O)

These cash transactions are grouped and classified into one of three categories to which they primarily relate: operations (O), finance (F) or investment (I). The classification chosen is indicated in the right-hand column in the table above. The two additional pieces of information needed to prepare a statement of cash flows are the opening and the closing balance of the cash account. The cash account balance was $1215 at the beginning of October and $718 at the end of October. The completed statement of cash flows is shown below.

STATEMENT OF CASH FLOWS: ROSETREE STUDENT CARE CENTRE		
for the month of October		
Cash flows from operating activities		
Receipts		
Casual fees received	$ 278	
Receipts on accounts	1355	
	1633	
Payments		
Wages	(1800)	
Rent	(60)	
Cleaning	(640)	
	(2500)	
Net cash used by operating activities		$ (867)
Cash flows from investing activities		
Payment for games and play equipment	(630)	
Net cash used by investing activities		(630)
Cash flows from financing activities		
Proceeds of loan from local council	1000	
Net cash provided by financing activities		1000
Net increase (decrease) in cash held		(497)
Cash at beginning of month		1215
Cash at end of month		$ 718

Rosetree Student Care Centre's statement of cash flows for October shows which activities were net providers (inflows) of cash and which activities were net users (outflows) of cash. Outflows are shown in parentheses to indicate that payments must be subtracted. Operating cash flows are listed first because they are usually the largest and most important source of cash for most entities.

This statement reveals that, during October, the operations of the centre used cash because receipts were insufficient to cover payments. The $1000 provided by the loan from the local council was used to purchase games and play equipment, and also helped to offset the use of cash in operating activities.

For larger entities, accounting computer software can be prepared to simplify the preparation of cash-flow statements from transactions data. This is done by identifying and coding each transaction involving a cash flow at the point of analysis and original entry to the accounting system. However, the development of such software is a specialist task.

The purpose and use of the statement of cash flows

A statement of cash flows provides a link between successive balance sheets and presents a dynamic picture of the entity's flows of cash over a period. It indicates how the entity's control over a major economic resource (cash) has changed, and it provides a basis for predicting how this may change in the future, as a result of the cash flows from the entity's operating, investing and financing activities.

Statements of cash flows permit a wider understanding of the entity's activities for both internal and external purposes. They provide users with information that may assist them in assessing the ability of the entity to generate positive cash flows into the future in order to meet its financial commitments, to fund changes in the scope of the entity and to obtain external finance, where necessary.

The cash flow from operations provides external users of the information with a measure of the entity's financial viability. An entity that has been able to provide positive cash flows from operations over a number of years would be of interest to a potential shareholder, a trading partner or an employee. An unstable pattern of positive and negative cash flows from operations over a number of years (even if it is accompanied by a stable pattern of profits) might indicate difficulties in some aspects of the entity's business.

By examining cash flow statements, external users may receive answers to both general and specific questions, such as:

- Were operations the major source of cash receipts?
- Were any debts repaid?
- Why is the entity short of cash despite making record profits?
- How was it possible to pay a dividend when the organisation made a loss?
- What use was made of the proceeds of borrowings?

Cash flow statements can be used internally to plan future financing needs, cash forecasts and cash control. In budgeted form, statements of cash flows are frequently used for planning the future activities of the organisation. In projecting the future expansions of an entity, statements of cash flows assist in determining the extent to which additional finance is needed. Budgeted statements of cash flows can vary in length from weekly cash flow projections to 20-year forecasts for strategic purposes.

A *bank overdraft* can be used to cover short periods when cash receipts are insufficient to cover cash outlays. The bank allows its client to overdraw the bank account to a set limit. The limit cannot be exceeded, and the client must repay the overdraft as required by the bank. This means that over the budget period cash receipts plus the opening cash balance need to be greater than cash payments, or the entity will get into financial difficulty. Prolonged financial difficulty or distress can result in insolvency, a situation in which an entity is unable to pay its debts as they become due. In this event, the entity may need to be liquidated.

Even profitable organisations can suffer from inadequate cash flow. Poor planning or unforeseen circumstances might mean that there is insufficient cash available to cover payments as they fall due. Profits do not guarantee cash availability. For example, profits may arise from credit sales, but collecting cash from debtors may be difficult. In recent times large organisations have been forced to sell major assets to generate cash. Although such self-administered treatment might seem drastic, the 'doctor's' treatment (whoever the doctor might turn out to be: the banks, the government or the stock market) could be far worse for the future of the organisation.

Statements of cash flows in Australia

In the early 1990s the failure of several large Australian companies highlighted the need for cash flow information to identify cash problems as early as possible. The statement of cash flows replaced the funds statement in 1991. International Accounting Standard IAS 7 provides guidance on the preparation and presentation of cash flow statements. In Australia, entities are required by Corporations Law to comply with AASB 1026 to present a statement of cash flows in their annual financial statements.

A case study[3] of the collapse of Hooker Corporation in 1989 revealed that funds from operations provided much the same information as did net profit in the years prior to the collapse. Neither measure gave any warning of financial distress. In contrast, the usefulness of cash flow information to shareholders was evident. Cash flows from operations were negative from 1985 to 1989. This reflected the same story as movements in the share price of Hooker.

---

[3] Jack Flanagan and Greg Whittred, 'Hooker Corporation: A Case for Cash Flow Reporting?', *Australian Accounting Review*, Vol. 1, No. 3, May 1992.

A statement of cash flows produced in accordance with AAS 28 and AASB 1026 will have the following features:

- Cash flows are classified into operating, financing and investing activities.
- Cash inflows and cash outflows are separately disclosed.
- Cash flows from operating activities are presented using the direct approach, which shows gross operating cash inflows less gross operating cash outflows. The indirect approach is required as a note to the statement of cash flows.
- Comparative data from the prior accounting period are presented.
- Notes to the statement provide information about external non-cash financing and investing transactions, details of credit standby facilities, and details about used and unused loan facilities.
- Certain cash flows must be separately identified. These are:
  - interest (and other items of a similar nature) received
  - dividends received
  - interest (and other costs of finance) paid
  - dividends paid
  - income taxes paid.

Although different entities may choose to classify certain items in different ways, the standard emphasises the importance of consistency over time within an entity.

The following case study illustrates the presentation of the cash flow statement and demonstrates how it assists business decision making.

Case 10.1 Cash and profit

The Empire Trading Company has submitted the following information relating to its first three months of operations.

Trading information

	January	February	March
	$	$	$
Sales	40 000	44 000	50 000
Purchases	32 000	38 000	41 000
Expenses:			
Depreciation	250	250	250
Wages	8 000	8 000	8 000
Rent	600	600	600
Other expenses	275	200	190

Purchase of equipment: $10 000 (payment in January). Bank Loan: $20 000.

Insurance (annual): $1500 paid in January

Collection period on sales is two months after purchase. Payments to suppliers is in the month after purchase.

| Inventory levels at end of month | 2 000 | 10 000 | 18 000 |

The accounting firm has provided monthly profit and loss statements and a statement of cash flows as requested.

Profit and loss statements prepared from information supplied

	January $	February $	March $
Sales	40 000	44 000	50 000
less Cost of sales	30 000	30 000	33 000
Gross profit	10 000	14 000	17 000
less Expenses:			
Depreciation	250	250	250
Wages	8 000	8 000	8 000
Insurance	125	125	125
Rent	600	600	600
Other	275	200	190
	9 250	9 175	9 165
Net profit	750	4 825	7 835

STATEMENT OF CASH FLOWS: EMPIRE TRADING COMPANY
for the months of January, February, March

	January $	February $	March $
Cash flows from operating activities			
Receipts:			
Customers	–	–	40 000
Payments:			
Suppliers	–	(32 000)	(38 000)
Wages	(8 000)	(8 000)	(8 000)
Rent	(600)	(600)	(600)
Insurance	(1 500)	–	–
Other	(275)	(200)	(190)
Net payments	(10 375)	(40 800)	(46 790)
Net cash used by operating activities	(10 375)	(40 800)	(6 790)
Cash flows from investing activities			
Purchase of equipment	(10 000)	–	–
Net cash used by investing activities	(10 000)	–	–
Cash flows from financing activities			
Bank loan	20 000		
Cash provided by owners	20 000		
Net cash provided by financing activities	40 000	–	–
Net increase (decrease) in cash held	19 625	(40 800)	(6 790)
Cash balance at beginning of year	–	19 625	(21 175)
Cash balance at end of year	19 625	(21 175)	(27 965)

Management was horrified to discover that although profit has increased tenfold they now have an overdraft of $27 965 in addition to still owing $20 000 on the bank loan. By comparing the profit and loss statement and the cash flow statement it is evident that profit and cash are not the same.

> The accountants have reminded management of the following facts:
>
> - Revenue is recognised in the month of sale but does not become a cash receipt until 60 days later.
> - Payments are made to suppliers in the month following purchase.
> - Payment of $10 000 for equipment was made in January, whereas it becomes an expense only by means of a depreciation charge over its useful life.
> - There is a recognition of expenses such as insurance in January even though payment is made in a later month.
>
> From the facts presented:
>
> (a) Is it likely that the company will have a positive cash flow in April?
> (b) Is it likely that the business's cash situation will get progressively worse?
> (c) State your assumptions in answering (a) and (b).

The financial-statement-based method of preparation

In the absence of the appropriate computer software, the transactions-based method of statement of cash flows preparation replicates much of the work already undertaken by the accountant, in that the effects of all transactions on the entity have already been classified in the ledger and summarised in the profit and loss statement and balance sheet. Another way to prepare a statement of cash flows is to use the information in these reports (the financial-statement-based method). But not all transactions reported involve cash. In using this method, therefore, the accountant must be careful to isolate only the cash effect of transactions.

This second way of preparing a statement of cash flows involves analysing the changes from one balance sheet to the next and eliminating known transactions not involving cash flows. This approach is illustrated using the financial statements of Rosetree Student Care Centre which have been prepared using the list of transactions given previously.

PROFIT AND LOSS STATEMENT: ROSETREE STUDENT CARE CENTRE *for the month of October*		
Revenue		$1478
less Expenses		
Wages	$2070	
Rent	60	
Cleaning	320	
Depreciation—games and play equipment	37	2487
Net loss		$1009

BALANCE SHEET: ROSETREE STUDENT CARE CENTRE						
as at						
	End September		End October		Difference	
	Debit	Credit	Debit	Credit	Debit	Credit
Assets	$	$	$	$	$	$
Cash	1215		718			497
Debtors	780		625			155
Prepayments			320		320	
Games and play equipment	4150		4780		630	
less Accumulated depreciation		1325		1362	37	37
Liabilities						
Accrued wages		90		360		270
Council loan				1000		1000
Equity						
Capital		2000		2000		
Retained profits		2730		1721	1009	37
Total	6145	6145	6443	6443	1959	1959

The following steps are necessary to prepare a simple statement of cash flows from financial statements. They will be explained in turn.

1. Calculate the differences columns

These show the debit and credit changes between the two consecutive balance sheets, as shown previously. The figures in the differences columns (other than those in the high-lighted boxes, which will be explained later) show all net movements in balance-sheet accounts during the year. These are the result of both cash and non-cash ledger entries.

2. Identify the non-cash items and remove their effects from both sides of the ledger

Non-cash items are an integral part of the accrual accounting system, and fall into two categories:

(a) *Book entries*. These are adjustments made to the accounts that are not prompted by external transactions.
(b) *Non-cash transactions with external parties*. These are transactions with external parties that do not involve cash (these entries are sometimes called accruals). They are integral to the accrual accounting system and involve operating working capital accounts.

* *Book entries*. In the example, the depreciation expense of $37 has affected two balance-sheet accounts: accumulated depreciation and retained profits. However, this change does not represent a cash transaction. Such an entry is a book entry because it is not prompted by an external transaction with another entity. Before completing the cash-flow statement, therefore, it is necessary to remove or eliminate the effects of this book entry from the differences columns. (Since every entry has offsetting debits and credits, the elimination will also require offsetting debits and credits in the differences columns.) The remaining differences will then represent the effects of transactions with external parties.

In more complex situations, the identification of non-cash items may necessitate the reconstruction of certain accounts. This is illustrated in a later section.

In order to eliminate the effect of charging depreciation, the original entry needs to be reversed. The original entry for the depreciation expense would have been:

DR   depreciation expense
CR   accumulated depreciation

However, the depreciation expense account has been closed to the profit and loss summary account, which in turn has been closed to the retained profits account. So the depreciation entry is eliminated by debiting accumulated depreciation and (to remove the effect of the deduction of the expense for depreciation) by crediting retained profits in the differences columns. This elimination is shown in the highlighted boxes on page 364.

After the elimination of book entries, the remaining figures in the differences columns should represent the effects of both cash and non-cash transactions with external parties.

- *Non-cash transactions.* The next step is to remove the non-cash (accrual) effects of transactions with external parties from revenue and costs of operations, which will indicate cash inflows and outflows for the period.

  Cash inflows and outflows are discovered by combining information revealed in the differences between successive balance sheets and the profit and loss statement. The following relations between account balances, the profit and loss statement movements and cash flows can be seen.

- *Cash from customers.* Revenue normally includes both cash and credit sales. Revenue is related to cash receipts from customers by the change in accounts receivable or debtors, thus:

$$\text{sales revenue} = \text{cash from customers} \left[\begin{array}{l} + \text{ increase in accounts receivable,} \\ \text{or} - \text{decrease in accounts receivable} \end{array} \right.$$

  This relation can also be expressed another way. Note that an increase in an asset account is recorded as a debit, and a decrease in an asset is recorded as a credit. Information in the differences columns on net debit or credit movements in accounts receivable, along with the revenue figure, can be used to discover cash from customers:

$$\text{cash from customers} = \text{sales revenue} \left[\begin{array}{l} - \text{ debit difference in accounts receivable,} \\ \text{or} + \text{credit difference in accounts receivable} \end{array} \right.$$

- *Payments for expenses.* The three items affected are discussed in the following list. For cash receipts from customers, a debit difference in accounts receivable is subtracted from the sales revenue to derive cash from customers; however, on the payments side, debit differences in balance-sheet items are added to the profit and loss statement items to derive the cash payments.

1. Payments to suppliers

   The charge matched against revenue for accrual accounting purposes is not payments to suppliers or even purchases, but cost of goods sold. Cost of goods sold is related to purchases by the change in inventory during the period.

$$\text{cost of goods sold} = \text{purchases} \left[\begin{array}{l} - \text{ increase in inventory,} \\ \text{or} + \text{decrease in inventory} \end{array} \right.$$

   In turn, purchases of inventory and other items are derived from cash paid to suppliers by adjusting for changes in accounts payable or creditors.

$$\text{purchases} = \text{cash paid to suppliers} \left[\begin{array}{l} + \text{ increase in accounts payable,} \\ \text{or} - \text{decrease in accounts payable} \end{array} \right.$$

   These relations can also be expressed differently. Recall that an increase (decrease) in an asset is a debit (credit) entry, and note that an increase (decrease) in a liability is a credit (debit) entry. The information in the differences column on debit or credit differences, along with cost of goods sold, can be used to discover cash payments to suppliers:

$$\text{cash payments to suppliers} = \text{cost of goods sold,} \left[\begin{array}{l} \text{+ debit difference in inventory,} \\ \text{or − credit difference in inventory} \end{array} \right.$$

$$\left[\begin{array}{l} \text{+ debit difference in accounts payable,} \\ \text{or − credit difference in accounts payable} \end{array} \right.$$

2. Accruals

As current liabilities, these are treated in the same way as accounts payable. For example, wages expense consists of:

$$\text{wages expense} = \text{wages paid} \left[\begin{array}{l} \text{+ increase in wages accrued,} \\ \text{or − decrease in wages accrued} \end{array} \right.$$

So, in terms of the differences columns,

$$\text{wages paid} = \text{wages expense} \left[\begin{array}{l} \text{+ debit difference in wages accrued,} \\ \text{or − credit difference in wages accrued} \end{array} \right.$$

3. Prepayments

As current assets, these are treated identically to inventory.

$$\text{prepaid expense} = \text{fee paid} \left[\begin{array}{l} \text{− increase in prepayments,} \\ \text{or + decrease in prepayments} \end{array} \right.$$

So, in terms of the differences columns,

$$\text{fee paid} = \text{prepaid expense} \left[\begin{array}{l} \text{+ debit difference in prepayments,} \\ \text{or − credit difference in prepayments} \end{array} \right.$$

3. Classify the remaining movements in cash as operating, financing, investing or cash, and prepare a statement of cash flows

After elimination of book entries and adjustment for non-cash transactions, the statement of cash flows may be prepared as shown in the following statement. Accounts with debit movements represent users of cash during the period, and accounts with credit movements represent providers of cash during the period.

This statement of cash flows shows the two ways of presenting cash flows from operations. In the statement the direct method has been applied, that is, subtracting cash outflows from cash inflows. In the reconciliation schedule cash flow from operations has been determined by adding back non-cash transactions and changes in operating working capital accounts, to reconcile the net profit from the profit and loss statement to the net cash flow from operations. This is known as the indirect method.

STATEMENT OF CASH FLOWS: ROSETREE STUDENT CARE CENTRE		
for the month of October		
	$	$
Cash flows from operating activities		
Cash receipts[1]	1633	
Payments		
Wages[2]	(1800)	
Rent	(60)	
Cleaning[3]	(640)	
	(2500)	
Net cash used by operating activities		(867)
Cash flows from investing activities		
Purchase of games and play equipment	(630)	
Net cash used by investing activities		(630)
Cash flows from financing activities		
Proceeds of loan from local council	1000	
Net cash provided by financing activities		1000
Net decrease in cash held		(497)
Cash at beginning of month		1215
Cash at end of month		$ 718

The calculation of the cash inflows and outflows in this statement of cash flows are explained below.

1. *Cash receipts* = revenue ($1478) + decrease (credit difference) in debtors ($155). Therefore, cash receipts equal $1633.
2. *Wages paid* = wages expense ($2070) – increase (credit difference) in accruals ($270). Therefore, wages paid equal $1800.
3. *Cleaning fee paid* = prepaid expense ($320) + increase (debit difference) in prepayment ($320). Therefore, fee paid equals $640.

RECONCILIATION OF CASH FLOW FROM OPERATIONS TO OPERATING PROFIT AFTER TAX		
	$	$
Net loss		(1009)
Depreciation		37
Adjustments for changes in operating working capital		
Increases in current assets		
Prepayments	(320)	
Decreases in current assets		
Debtors	155	
Increases in current liabilities		
Accrued wages	270	105
Cash flow from operations		$(867)

Cash flow from operations can be reconciled to net profit, as shown in the preceding illustration.

Two steps are involved. The first is to eliminate the effects of book entries from net profit. The resulting figure is the difference between revenue and all the costs associated with sales, in both cash and credit (or accrual) terms.

The second step is to remove the effects of non-cash transactions. These transactions are of two types. The first type consists of increases in current assets (other than cash itself) and decreases in current liabilities. These transactions have either used cash or represent a delay in the receipt of cash. These movements cause the cash flow figure to be lower than the net profit figure, and so they are deducted from the profit figure in calculating cash flow from operations. Note that the first type of deductions all involve debits in the differences columns.

The second type of non-cash transaction consists of decreases in current assets (other than cash) and increases in current liabilities. These transactions have either provided cash for the entity or represent a delay in the payment of cash. The effect of these transactions is opposite to that of the first type: they cause the cash flow figure to be higher than the net profit figure, and so they are added back to the profit figure in calculating cash flow from operations. Note that the second type of deductions all involve credits in the differences columns.

The final result is cash flow from operations, which confirms the calculations of operating cash inflows and outflows presented in the statement of cash flows.

Non-cash items

There is one disadvantage to preparing a statement of cash flows from financial statements. All movements identified by differences between consecutive balance sheets are in fact net movements and may disguise large offsetting transactions, which may or may not be cash transactions. It is not possible using the financial-statement-based method to identify such offsetting transactions, or to identify whether or not they involve cash. In the preceding example of the Rosetree Student Care Centre, it is not possible to determine whether the increase in games and play equipment of $630 involved a flow of $630 cash out of the centre, or whether it was explained by a larger purchase of games and play equipment, either for cash or on credit, and the disposal of older items. In order to eliminate significant non-cash flows such as this, additional information would be needed.

The classification of more complicated accounts or transactions as cash or non-cash items is discussed further.

Book entries

1. Depreciation and other write-downs

The entry for depreciation represents an allocation of the cost of an asset acquired in a previous external transaction. Depreciation is a book entry that does not involve any cash flows. Similar book entries occur in relation to the amortisation of intangible assets, such as goodwill, patents or formation costs.

Gains or losses on the disposal of depreciable assets should also be regarded as book entries, since they are merely adjustments for over- or under-depreciation in previous periods. In many cases it will be necessary to reconstruct the sale of asset account to identify the reported gain or loss on disposal. The appropriate amount to show on the statement of cash flows is the cash proceeds from the sale. The loss or gain on disposal, and the writing off of the accounts for the asset and its accumulated depreciation, are all book entries.

The entry for bad and doubtful debts expense is an allocation of an anticipated loss as an expense of the period in which the credit sale occurs, and therefore it is also a book entry.

2. Transfers to reserves

Reserve transfers are entries designed to allocate amounts from the retained profits account to a reserve account within owners' equity. Such entries do not arise from an external transaction, nor do they involve cash; they are therefore book entries.

Asset revaluation is also a book entry, since it does not reflect an external transaction that will be recorded in the books of another entity. Occasionally, assets are revalued by an entry such as:

Land	$50 000	
Asset revaluation reserve		$50 000
(Revaluation of asset)		

3. Provisions

Provisions for dividends and for taxation are both book entries until it is known that the other party to the transaction, the owners or the government, has made corresponding entries in their own accounts. In the case of owners, this would occur when the dividend is ratified, such as at the annual general meeting. In the case of the taxation department, this would occur when the tax assessment is made. Later in the next financial year, when the payments for dividends and for taxation are made, cash flows are recorded. So the cash flows for these accounts relate to events in the previous financial year. In the case of provision for taxation, it may be necessary to reconstruct the account to determine the actual cash flow, if an under-provision or over-provision for taxation has occurred.

Non-cash transactions

1. Bonus issues of shares

A bonus issue is an external transaction between the company and its shareholders. However, the transfer of shares is without cost to the shareholders, and so bonus issues are non-cash transactions that need to be eliminated in the preparation of a statement of cash flows.

2. Takeovers involving share or debenture issues

The acquisition of another entity is, of course, an external transaction. The purchase price may be paid to the owners in cash, but it is not uncommon for (at least part of) the payment to be in the form of shares or debentures issued by the acquiring company. This is a cashless transaction, and therefore its effects also need to be eliminated in the preparation of a statement of cash flows.

A comprehensive example

A statement of cash flows is to be prepared from the comparative trial balances of Clearview Ltd, shown on page 370. As transactions data are not available, it will be necessary to prepare the statement using the financial-statement-based method. While the techniques illustrated below will identify for elimination the major book entries and non-cash transactions, it is possible that other non-cash entries remain.

Additional information for transactions during the year:

1. Land that cost $1000 was sold.
2. Plant that cost $7500 was sold.
3. A final dividend of $10 000 is to be provided for.
4. $14 000 is to be transferred to the general reserve.

	1 January 20X2 Debit $	1 January 20X2 Credit $	31 December 20X2 Debit $	31 December 20X2 Credit $	Differences Debit $	Differences Credit $
TRIAL BALANCE: CLEARVIEW LTD						
Sales revenue				361 000		361 000
Cost of goods sold			200 000		200 000	
Selling expenses			68 000		68 000	
General expenses			48 000		48 000	
Interest expense			7 000		7 000	
Taxation expense			9 000		9 000	
Amortisation of goodwill			5 000		5 000	
Depreciation of buildings			6 000		6 000	
Depreciation of plant			4 000		4 000	
Loss on sale of plant			1 000		1 000	
Gain on sale of land				1 000		1 000
Cash	23 000		20 000			3 000
Prepayments	1 000		4 000		3 000	
Accounts receivable	60 000		56 000			4 000
Inventory	34 000		43 000		9 000	
Plant	72 000		82 000		10 000	
Accum. depn plant		30 000		31 000		1 000
Buildings	90 000		119 000		29 000	
Accum. depn buildings		37 000		43 000		6 000
Land	40 000		39 000			1 000
Goodwill	15 000		10 000			5 000
Trade creditors		40 000		54 000		14 000
Accrued expenses		–		2 000		2 000
Short-term loans		20 000		16 000	4 000	
Taxation payable		12 000		8 000	4 000	
Dividends payable		7 000		–	7 000	
Debentures		44 000		20 000	24 000	
Mortgage		20 000		35 000		15 000
Paid-up capital		67 000		92 000		25 000
Retained profits		33 000		33 000		
General reserve		20 000		20 000		
Asset revaluation reserve		5 000		5 000		
	335 000	335 000	721 000	721 000	438 000	438 000

CLEARVIEW LTD
Statement of cash flows worksheet

	Differences		Non-cash items		Cash flows	
	Debit	Credit	Debit	Credit	Debit	Credit
	$	$	$	$	$	$
Sales revenue		361 000				361 000
Cost of goods sold	200 000				200 000	
Selling expenses	68 000				68 000	
General expenses	48 000				48 000	
Interest expense	7 000				7 000	
Taxation expense	9 000			9 000 (8)		
Amortisation of goodwill	5 000			5 000 (3)		
Depreciation of buildings	6 000			6 000 (4)		
Depreciation of plant	4 000			4 000 (1b)		
Loss on sales of plant	1 000			1 000 (1a)		
Gain on sale of land		1 000	1 000 (2)			
Cash		3 000				3 000
Prepayments	3 000				3 000	
Accounts receivable		4 000				4 000
Inventory	9 000				9 000	
Plant	10 000		7 500 (1a)		7 500	
Accum. depn–plant		1 000	4 000 (1b)	3 000 (1a)		
Buildings	29 000				29 000	
Accum. depn–buildings		6 000	6 000 (4)			
Land		1 000	1 000 (2)			
Goodwill		5 000	5 000 (3)			
Trade creditors		14 000				14 000
Accrued expenses		2 000				2 000
Short-term loans	4 000				4 000	
Taxation payable	4 000			4 000 (8)		
Dividends payable	7 000				7 000	
Debentures	24 000				24 000	
Mortgage		15 000				15 000
Capital		25 000				25 000
Retained profits						
General reserve						
Sale of plant				3 500 (1a)		3 500
Sale of land				2 000 (2)		2 000
Taxation paid			13 000 (8)		13 000	
Totals	438 000	438 000	37 500	37 500	429 500	429 500

The table above again shows the differences in the comparative trial balances of Clearview, with a second set of columns for the adjustments for non-cash items, and a third set of columns showing the net effect of the first two sets of columns. These adjustments are explained below. The numbers in parentheses refer to the items in the statement of cash flows similarly identified.

The three major steps in the preparation of a statement of cash flows from consecutive trial balances or balance sheets and additional information are:

1. The incorporation of the additional information.
2. The elimination of book entries.
3. The adjustments for non-cash transactions.

Incorporation of additional information

1. Changes in plant accounts

In this instance, three necessary amounts are not disclosed:

(a) the proceeds of the sale of plant
(b) the accumulated depreciation on the plant sold
(c) additional purchases of plant during the year

These amounts may be discovered as the balancing items (*) by reconstructing the relevant ledger accounts.

RECONSTRUCTION OF LEDGER ACCOUNTS FOR PLANT			
	Debit	*Credit*	*Balance*
Plant account			
Balance (beginning)			72 000 DR
Sale of plant		7500	64 500 DR
Cash/accounts payable	17 500*		82 000 DR
Accumulated depreciation of plant			
Balance (beginning)			30 000 CR
Depreciation expense		4000	34 000 CR
Sale of plant	3 000*		31 000 CR
Sale of plant			
Plant	7 500		7 500 DR
Accumulated depreciation		3000	4 500 DR
Loss on sale		1000	3 500 DR
Cash (proceeds of sale)		3500*	

The following eliminations are made to the differences columns to remove the book entries associated with the changes in plant accounts. For accounts that have been closed prior to the preparation of the trial balance, the account name can be entered at the bottom of the worksheet. Alternatively, entries to accounts that were later closed to the profit and loss summary account and then to the retained profits account can be eliminated directly from retained profits.

(a) *Sale of plant*

  CR Loss on sale $1000
  DR Plant $7500
  CR Accumulated depreciation—plant $3000

The net effect of these transactions is a debit of $3500, and so the credit entry of $3500 for the proceeds from the sale of the plant maintains the balance.

(b) *Depreciation of plant*

The differences columns would now show the net movement in the accumulated depreciation of plant account to be $4000; this is confirmed in our account reconstruction. This revealed book entry is reversed by a debit of $4000 to the plant's accumulated depreciation account and a credit of $4000 to the depreciation of plant account.

(c) *Purchase of plant*

Again, the differences columns and our account reconstruction of the plant account both show that purchases of plant during the year amounted to $17 500.

No further entries are required, as this cash (or accrual) transaction has been revealed by the entries to reverse the sale of the plant.

2. Sale of land

The additional information discloses that land which cost $1000 was sold. The trial balance for 31 December 20X2 reveals a gain on sale of land of $1000. Reconstruction of the land account (not shown) would reveal the following information:

Cost of land sold	$1000
Gain on sale (profit and loss statement)	$1000
Proceeds of sale	$2000

The recording of the gain on sale needs to be eliminated in a similar way as the loss on sale of plant, presented above. A debit of $1000 goes to the land account, and a debit of $1000 also goes to the gain on sale account. The balancing entry of a $2000 credit is recorded as the proceeds on the sale of the land.

Elimination of remaining book entries

The trial balance is now searched for other book entries that must be eliminated. The following reversals of book entries are made:

3. DR Goodwill	$5000
CR Amortisation of goodwill	$5000
4. DR Accumulated depreciation on buildings	$6000
CR Depreciation expense	$6000

Adjustment of operating working capital accounts

5. *Cash receipts* = revenue ($361 000) + decrease in accounts receivable ($4000). Therefore, cash receipts equal $365 000.
6. *Purchases* = cost of goods sold ($200 000) + increase in inventory ($9000). Therefore, purchases equal $209 000.
    Cash payments = purchases ($209 000) – increase in trade creditors ($14 000). Therefore, cash payments equal $195 000.
7. *Expenses* = selling expenses ($68 000) + general expenses ($48 000) = $116 000. Cash payment = expenses ($116 000) + increase in prepayments ($3000) – increase in accruals ($2000). Therefore, cash payment equals $117 000.
8. *Taxation paid*
    The cash flow for taxation is discovered by a reconstruction of the account for taxation payable, thus:

TAXATION PAYABLE

	Debit	Credit	Balance
Balance (beginning)			12 000 CR
Taxation expense		9000	21 000 CR
Cash (payment for previous year)	13 000		8 000 CR

A payment of $13 000 reconciles the opening and closing balances after entering the known credit for the tax expense for the year. The equality of debits and credits in the differences column is preserved by the following:

Insert:	Tax paid	$13 000 DR
Delete:	Tax expense	9 000 DR
	Decrease in taxation payable	4 000 DR
		$13 000 DR

STATEMENT OF CASH FLOWS: CLEARVIEW LTD

for the financial year ended 31 December 20X2

Cash flows from operating activities		
Receipts from customers[5]	$365 000	
Payments to suppliers and employees[6][7]	(312 000)	
Interest paid	(7 000)	
Taxes paid[8]	(13 000)	
Net cash provided by operating activities		$33 000
Cash flows from investing activities		
Payment for buildings	(29 000)	
Payment for plant[1]	(17 500)	
Proceeds from sale of plant[1]	3 500	
Proceeds from sale of land[2]	2 000	
Net cash used by investing activities		(41 000)
Cash flows from financing activities		
Proceeds from mortgage issue	15 000	
Proceeds from share issue	25 000	
Repayment of short-term loans	(4 000)	
Repayment of debentures	(24 000)	
Dividends paid	(7 000)	
Net cash used by financing activities		5 000
Net decrease in cash held		(3 000)
Cash balance at the beginning of the year		23 000
Cash balance at the end of the year		$20 000

continues

STATEMENT OF CASH FLOWS: CLEARVIEW LTD

for the financial year ended 31 December 20X2

Notes to the statement of cash flows
Reconciliation of net cash provided by operating
activities to operating profit after income tax

Operating profit after income tax*		$14 000
Depreciation[4]		10 000
Amortisation[3]		5 000
Loss on sale of plant[1]		1 000
Gain on sale of land[2]		(1 000)
Decrease in tax payable[8]		(4 000)
Decrease in accounts receivable[5]		4 000
Increase in prepayments[7]		(3 000)
Increase in inventory[6]		(9 000)
Increase in trade creditors[6]		14 000
Increase in accrued expenses[7]		2 000
Net cash provided by operating activities		**$33 000**
*Operating profit after income tax: Revenue		$361 000
less COGS	$200 000	
Selling expenses	68 000	
General expenses	48 000	
Interest	7 000	
Amortisation	5 000	
Depreciation	10 000	338 000
Operating profit		23 000
less Taxation		9 000
Operating profit after income tax		$14 000

The completed statement of cash flows is shown above, with a note reconciling net cash provided by operating activities to operating profit after income tax.

Clearview's operating activities provided a cash surplus during the year. Its financing activities, involving the repayment of debt and the issue of further debt and capital, provided a net amount of $5000. The major area in which cash was used during the year was investment in buildings and plants. This investment used a net amount of $41 000 cash, which was provided partly by operating and financing activities, and partly by reducing the cash balance.

The reconciliation of net cash provided by operating activities to operating profit after income tax explains the relatively large difference of $19 000 between the two figures. Charges against profit not involving cash were depreciation and amortisation. Gains and losses on sales of assets exactly offset each other. Taxation payable fell by $4000, partly due to an over-provision in the previous year, and partly because of lower profits this year. Other reasons for the relatively large difference between net cash provided by operating activities and net profit after tax are the changes in operating working capital accounts: that is, the decrease in accounts receivable and increases in trade creditors and accrued expenses (providers of cash), which exceeded the increases in prepayments and inventory (users of cash).

Case 10.2 Cash flows and decision making

An acrimonious business dispute between Kristy Williams and her business partners has intensified in recent weeks. Both Kristy and her partners have rejected attempts to settle the matter. The business has been very successful in the past three years manufacturing costume jewellery and focusing marketing efforts on Australian youth.

Kristy has requested further injections of cash to support the steady growth. Her partners, Ivor and Aaron Frew, are not convinced that more cash is required and believe that Kristy has not enlisted their help in management of the business. They state that 'a bad chemistry' has developed between them and Kristy which 'can only be resolved by greater disclosure of the business's financials'.

Kristy retorts that she has in the past provided the Frews with audited profit and loss statements and balance sheets, and that in her review of the company has pointed out that the volume of sales has increased by 133 per cent in the past three years and that profit margins have been well maintained. Kristy also has stated that past reviews have reported the substantial requirements for more working capital and the increasing debt levels necessary to finance the purchase of plant and equipment.

However, Ivor and Aaron Frew are unconvinced, saying that in each year dividends as a percentage of trading profit have declined (50 per cent in 20X2, 42.1 per cent in 20X4) and that retained profits should have been sufficient to fund further asset purchases.

The financial statements of Kristy's Costume Jewellery Co Pty Ltd are shown below:

PROFIT AND LOSS STATEMENTS			
	20X2	20X3	20X4
	$000	$000	$000
Sales	2520	3900	5880
less Cost of sales	1500	2270	3460
Expenses (excluding depreciation)	720	1120	1700
Depreciation	60	120	150
Trading profit	240	390	570
less Dividends	120	180	240
Retained profits	120	210	330

continues

BALANCE SHEETS

	20X2		20X3		20X4	
		$000		$000		$000
Accounts receivable		300		480		750
Inventory at cost		240		750		1380
Plant at cost	720		1200		1440	
less accumulated depreciation	60	660	180	1020	330	1110
Property at cost		600		600		600
		1800		2850		3840
Bank overdraft		–		200		280
Bank loan (short term)		60		100		530
Accounts payable		120		270		420
		180		570		1230
Share capital		1500		1950		1950
Retained profits		120		330		660
		1800		2850		3840

The Frew brothers have made the following assessment of the business's cash flow. 'Although we can draw some information from the reports relating to the company's cash flow position, insufficient details are available to prepare a cash flow statement and this should be provided to the partners. However, we note that:

- There is no long-term debt, thus short-term loans from the bank appear to have financed long-lived assets, namely additional plant purchases. This is unwise as the company has given itself little time to generate sufficient funds from the use of the purchased assets to repay the debt. Long-term funds should have been used.
- Funds provided by retained profits have not been sufficient to fund the increasing gap between current assets and current liabilities. That is, in 20X2 this was $360 000 (current assets $540 000 less current liabilities $180 000) but in 20X4 this had extended to $900 000 ($2 130 000 – $1 230 000). During this period increases in retained profits equalled only $210 000 ($330 000 (X4) – $120 000 (X2). A statement of cash flows which showed the cash flow from operations would highlight this deficiency.
- Investment in plant has doubled in the three-year period and although owners have contributed additional capital in 20X3 presumably to assist the purchase of plant they have not done so to finance further purchases during 20X4.'

After several aborted meetings between the owners the Frew brothers and Kristy have finally agreed to employ you as a consultant to advise them on the additional disclosure which could be provided and to consider whether additional funds are required by the business. In your report comment on the accuracy of the Frews' assessment. Suggest what information other than cash flow should be provided to the brothers.

Published company reports and cash flow

The example of Clearview Ltd shows the significant differences that may exist between operating profit after tax and cash provided by operating activities. The following companies listed on the Australian Stock Exchange also show significant differences between net cash provided by operating activities and operating profit after income tax. Note that in the examples given only one company, National Australia Bank Ltd, shows an operating profit greater than net cash provided by operating activities. Suggest possible reasons for this.

Company	Net cash provided by operating activities	Operating profit after income tax
	$m	$m
Boral Ltd	458.7	406.0
Coles Myer Ltd	908.4	389.4
Fosters Brewing Group Ltd	255.5	248.0
National Australia Bank Ltd	2190.0	2221.0
Western Mining Company Ltd	825.4	297.7
Qantas Airways Ltd	1110.8	252.7

(Results drawn from 1997 annual reports)

 Summary

The statement of cash flows can be a most useful report. It may be used by management in both a budgeted and historical form for planning and controlling the financial activities of the entity and for explaining the changes that have occurred. For external analysis, the statement of cash flows helps in assessing the solvency and liquidity of the entity and significant changes in the entity's activities.

 **Review exercises**

Discussion questions

10.1 What is the purpose of preparing a statement of cash flows?

10.2 Explain the difference between net profit and cash provided by operations.

10.3 Explain in your own words what is meant by the definition of cash used in this chapter. How does the accountant decide what to classify as cash?

10.4 Give two examples of activities that may be classified as investing for one entity and operating for another.

10.5 Give two examples of activities that may be classified as financing for one entity and operating for another.

10.6 What is the difference between the direct and indirect methods of reporting cash flows from operations? Which is the preferred method? Why?

10.7 How do interim cash dividends affect the statement of cash flows?

10.8 Explain the effect upon cash flows of using reducing-balance rather than straight-line depreciation.

10.9 What is a non-cash transaction? Provide examples of such an item.

10.10 Explain why an increase in the paid-up capital account may not be a cash flow.

10.11 A bonus issue of shares increases capital, yet is not considered to be a cash flow. Comment on this statement.

10.12 For each of the following, indicate whether the event involves a cash flow.

(a) Appropriation of profits for future asset replacement.

(b) An increase in inventory.

(c) An entity exchanges a building for land.

(d) The purchase of a machine on credit.

(e) An increase in the expected residual value of a piece of equipment.

(f) Sale of goods on credit.

(g) Sale of goods for cash.

(h) An increase in prepaid expenses.

(i) An increase in net profit.

10.13 An investment newsletter contained the following statement: 'Despite a poor sales performance Edtech Ltd maintained a strong cash flow of $4 000 000 with net income of $1 000 000 and depreciation charges of $3 000 000. Even if sales remain stagnant next year, cash flow should increase because Edtech's continuing investment program will lead to substantially increased depreciation charges.' Comment on this statement. Assume that depreciation charges increase by 50 per cent next year, while other expenses and sales remain unchanged.

Problems

10.14 *Identifying cash flows*

Little Ltd, a company formed to speculate in the property market, was taken over by Big Ltd. Information relating to the takeover is given below:

	Little Ltd	Big Ltd
Net worth (prior to takeover)		
30 June 20X0	$1 million	$2 million

Between 30 June 20X0 and 25 July 20X0 the following events took place:

30 June 20X0 Big took over Little for $1.2 million. This gave rise to $200 000 goodwill in the books of Big. Little's shareholders received $200 000 in cash and $1 million in 10 per cent debentures issued by Big, redeemable in 20X5.

1 July 20X0 Big sold some of Little's assets, which had originally cost $800 000; these assets had been depreciated by $300 000. Big was paid in cash and made $150 000 profit on the sale. Big wrote off the $200 000 goodwill that had arisen as a result of acquiring Little.

> 2 July 20X0 Big revalued the remainder of Little's assets by $400 000.
>
> 20 July 20X0 Big sold Little to Superior Ltd for $700 000 cash.
>
> 21 July 20X0 Big offered to redeem the $1 million in debentures that it had issued to Little's shareholders.
>
> 25 July 20X0 All the $1 million in debentures had been redeemed by this date, but Big had to pay an additional $50 000 as a penalty for early repayment.

Identify the cash flows for Big.

10.15 *Completing a cash flow statement*

The accountant of Eglwys Ltd has suddenly disappeared. Fraud is suspected because details of the firm's cash account disappeared at the same time. The accountant was preparing a cash flow statement and left behind the following information, which is believed to be reliable and contains details of all cash movements for the period, except the change in the cash account.

Cash flow from operations	$60 000
Increase in paid-up capital	40 000
Increase in debentures	50 000
Increase in property, plant & equipment	80 000

It is known that the opening cash balance for the period was $20 000 and cash on hand and at bank now totals $15 000. To determine whether a fraud has been committed, complete the cash flow statement, highlighting the actual change in cash balance, and hence determine how much cash the firm should now have.

10.16 *Classification of cash flows*

Classify the following transactions as operating, investing or financing activities and indicate whether each represents an inflow or an outflow.

- Receipts from customers
- Payments for property, plant and equipment
- Proceeds from borrowings
- Dividends received
- Borrowing costs
- Proceeds from the sale of property, plant and equipment
- Proceeds from issue of shares
- Repayment of borrowings
- Payment for a subsidiary
- Dividends paid
- Payments to suppliers and employees
- Interest received
- Income tax paid
- Proceeds from court settlement

10.17 *Preparation of cash flow statement*

The following statement of receipts and payments shows the cash flows of Malaysian Toys Emporium.

STATEMENT OF RECEIPTS AND PAYMENTS
for June 20X7

	$	$
Bank balance 1 June 20X7		87 400
plus Receipts		
Cash sales	250 000	
Bank loans received	30 000	
Capital contributions	10 000	
Commissions received	7 000	
Interest received	10 000	
Proceeds from sale of investments	5 000	312 000
		399 400
less Payments		
Payments to suppliers	192 000	
Loan repayment	20 000	
Equipment purchases for cash	60 000	
Drawings	90 000	
Interest paid	32 000	394 000
Bank balance 30 June 20X7		5 400

(a) Prepare a classified statement of cash flows for June 20X7 to show the flows from operating, investing and financing activities.

(b) What conclusions can be drawn relating to the adequacy, source and disposition of the cash flows of the business?

10.18 *Preparation of statement of cash flows*

The accountant of the Hong Kong Music Emporium has used a computer software package to identify cash transactions and classify them into accounts, but further classification of the cash flows into the groups illustrated in the accounting standard (namely operating, investing and financing activities) has been neglected. Prepare a statement of cash flows for the year ended 30 June 20X2 in accordance with accounting standards.

Cash at bank balance 1 July 20X1	$ 15 000
Cash sales	198 600
Wages paid	17 200
Cash purchase of equipment	48 200
Interest paid on bank loan	1 700
Cash dividend paid	54 000
Payment to repay bank loan	18 100
Cash from accounts receivable	85 300
Cash purchases of inventory	11 000
Income tax paid	23 000
Payments to suppliers for inventory	99 400
Cash sales of equipment	4 900
Received loan from Victoria Bank Ltd	51 000
Cash paid for miscellaneous expenses	41 200
Received dividends on investments	14 900
Cash from share issue	70 000

10.19 *Indirect method—cash flows from operations*

You are provided with the following information for Jackson Ltd:

	30 June 20X6	30 June 20X7
Net profit	–	$1 800
Inventory	$2 000	3 000
Accounts receivable	500	1 500
Depreciation expense	–	200
Wages payable	600	3 000
Equipment purchased for cash	1 000	1 000
Proceeds from share issue	2 000	2 000
Dividends received	–	100
Prepaid rent and insurance	3 600	3 000

Determine the net cash provided by operating activities for Jackson Ltd for the year ended 30 June 20X7.

10.20 *Reconciling operating cash flows to operating profit*

Fricke Enterprises reported an operating profit after tax of $49 000, but net cash flows from operating activities were $39 000. Prepare a reconciliation of net cash from operating activities to operating profit after tax using the information selected from the accounting records shown below:

	$
Interest payments	11 000
Loss on sale of property, plant & equipment	6 000
Cash sales	20 000
Dividends received	8 000
Depreciation	24 000
Decrease in current liabilities	10 000
Increase in current assets other than cash	30 000
Payments of dividends	20 000
Payments to suppliers and employees	66 000
Receipts from customers	100 000
Payment of taxation payable	12 000
Purchase of property, plant & equipment	50 000

10.21 *Accompanying schedules*

The Hung Kai Telecommunications Co. has received from their accountants information relating to its trading activities for the year ended 30 June 20X3. Management are disturbed by the significant differences between the cash flows from operating activities shown in the cash flow statement and the new operating profit after tax. The following information has been extracted from the company's reports.

Net profit	$124 000
Issued shares to extinguish long-term debt	90 000
Depreciation for the year	20 000
Long-term investment sold	15 000
Proceeds from collection of loan	10 000
Dividends paid	41 000

Long-term debt paid	50 000
Share dividend	13 000
Long-term investments purchased for cash	45 000
Bill payable (long-term) issued to acquire property	105 000
Acquisition of fixtures and fittings for cash	55 000
Cash proceeds from the issue of shares	37 000
Gain on sale of investments	5 000
Amortisation expense for year	3 000
Proceeds from issue of long-term debt	20 000

Details of current assets and current liabilities as at June 20X1 and 20X2 are:

	20X1	20X2
Cash	$27 000	$ 38 000
Accounts receivable	71 000	74 000
Inventories	88 000	199 000
Prepaid expenses	3 800	1 800
Bills payable	38 000	38 800
Accounts payable	69 000	57 000
Income tax payable	6 000	7 300
Accrued expenses	27 000	23 100

Prepare schedules to accompany a statement of cash flows for:

(a) Reconciliation of net profit to cash flows from operating activities
(b) Schedule of non-cash investing and financing items

10.22 *Cash flow analysis*

STATEMENT OF CASH FLOWS: ORAM DISCOUNTS LTD
for the year ended 30 June 20X4

	20X4
	$000
Cash flows from operating activities	
Inflows	
Receipts from customers	7 900
Dividends received	100
Outflows	
Payments to suppliers (purchases/expenses)	(10 950)
Interest paid	(250)
Income taxes paid	(400)
Net cash provided by operating activities	(3 600)
Cash flows from investing activities	
Inflows	
Proceeds from sale of land	1 800
Outflows	
Payments for equipment	(2 000)
Payments for listed company shares	(2 000)
Net cash provided by investing activities	(2 200)
	continues

STATEMENT OF CASH FLOWS: ORAM DISCOUNTS LTD
for the year ended 30 June 20X4

	20X4
	$000
Cash flows from financing activities	
Inflows	
Proceeds from long-term loans	2500
Proceeds from issue of shares	2500
Outflows	
Dividends paid	(440)
Net cash provided by financing activities	4 560
Net increase (decrease) in cash held	(1 240)
Cash at beginning of the financial year	540
Cash at end of the financial year	(700)

Notes to the statement of cash flows

1. Reconciliation of cash

   Cash at the end of the financial year as shown in the statement of cash flows is reconciled to the related items in the balance sheet as follows:

	20X4	20X3
	$	$
Cash	200	1000
Bank overdraft	(900)	(460)
	(700)	540

2. Reconciliation of net cash provided by operating activities to operating profit after income tax

	20X4
	$
Operating profit after income tax	1050
Depreciation	600
Gain on sale of land	(300)
Increase in taxes payable	100
Increase in prepaid rent	(50)
Increase in accounts receivable	(2000)
Increase in inventory	(2000)
Decrease in creditors	(1000)
Net cash provided by operating activities	(3600)

(a) Why is it regarded as necessary to distinguish between cash flows from operating, investing and financing activities?

(b) Analyse the 20X4 cash performance of Oram Discounts based on the above statement of cash flows.

10.23 *Cash flow analysis*

STATEMENT OF CASH FLOWS: PENANG IMPORTS CO. LTD
for the year ended 30 June 20X5

	20X5	20X4
	$000	$000
Cash flows from operating activities		
Inflows		
Receipts from customers	7 000	10 980
Dividends received	310	410
Outflows		
Payments to suppliers	(6 460)	(7 140)
Interest paid	(1 615)	(170)
Income taxes paid	(1 105)	(1 020)
Net cash provided by operating activities	(1 870)	3 060
Cash flows from investing activities		
Inflows		
Proceeds from sale of investments	3 740	850
Outflows		
Payments for plant & equipment	(6 800)	(1 700)
Net cash provided by investing activities	(3 060)	(850)
Cash flows from financing activities		
Inflows		
Proceeds from new borrowings	2 550	–
Net cash provided by financing activities	2 550	–
Net increase (decrease) in cash held	(2 380)	2 210
Cash at beginning of the financial year	2 380	170
Cash at end of the financial year	–	2 380

Notes to the statement of cash flows	20X5	20X4
	$000	$000
1. Reconciliation of cash		
Cash	340	2 720
Bank overdraft	(340)	(340)
	–	2 380
2. Reconciliation of net cash provided by operating		
activities to operating profit after income tax		
Operating profit after income tax	3 587	2 057
Depreciation	2 040	1 700
Gain on sale of investments	(2 465)	(85)
Increase in prepayments	(17)	(34)
Increase in accounts receivable	(4 250)	(935)
Increase in inventory	(3 570)	(374)
Increase in creditors	2 805	731
Net cash provided by operating activities	(1 870)	3 060

(a) Evaluate the cash-flow performance and position of Penang Imports Co. Ltd from the above statement of cash flows.

(b) Cash-flow statements are a reporting requirement in addition to the traditional balance sheet and profit and loss statement. Why is there seen to be a need for this additional statement?

10.24 *Cash flow analysis*

STATEMENT OF CASH FLOWS: QUALITY DISCOUNTERS CO. LTD
for the year ended 30 June 20X4

	20X4	20X3
	$000	$000
Cash flows from operating activities		
Inflows		
Receipts from customers	4300	6700
Outflows		
Payments to suppliers	(3800)	(4200)
Interest paid	(950)	(100)
Income taxes paid	(650)	600
Net cash provided by operating activities	(1100)	1800
Cash flows from investing activities		
Inflows		
Proceeds from sale of investments	2200	500
Outflows		
Payments for plant and equipment	(4000)	(1000)
Net cash provided by investing activities	(1800)	(500)
Cash flows from financing activities		
Inflows		
Proceeds from new borrowings	1500	–
Net cash provided by financing activities	1500	–
Net increase (decrease) in cash held	(1400)	1300
Cash at beginning of the financial year	1400	100
Cash at end of the financial year	–	1400

Notes to the statement of cash flows	20X4	20X3
	$000	$000
1. Reconciliation of cash		
Cash	200	1600
Bank overdraft	(200)	(200)
	–	1400

continues

Notes to the statement of cash flows	20X4	20X3
	$000	$000
2. Reconciliation of net cash provided by operating activities to operating profit after income tax		
Operating profit after income tax	2110	1210
Depreciation	1200	1000
Gain on sale of investments	(1450)	(50)
Increase in prepayments	(10)	(20)
Increase in accounts receivable	(2500)	(550)
Increase in inventory	(2100)	(220)
Increase in creditors	1650	430
Net cash provided by operating activities	1100	1800

(a) Comment on the cash-flow performance and position of Quality Discounters Co. Ltd as depicted in the above statement of cash flows.

(b) Evaluate the following statement made by a supplier of goods to companies:
'I prefer to examine cash-flow reports rather than profit and loss statements and balance sheets because cash-flow information removes the impact of arbitrary allocations which occur under accrual accounting.'

10.25 *Identifying cash flows as components of a statement of cash flows*

1. Identify the cash flow in each of the following and prepare a profit and loss statement and a statement of cash flows from operations.

   (a) Revenue for the period was $5800; the balance of accounts receivable at the beginning of the period was $460 and at the end of the period was $840.

   (b) Cost of goods sold for the period was $2500; there was a decrease in inventory of $245, and an increase in accounts payable of $1290.

   (c) Taxation payable at the beginning of the period was $500 and at the end of the period was $540. The next tax expense charged against income for the period was $480.

   (d) Rent was prepaid $300 at the beginning of the period and was $50 in arrears at the end of the period. The rent expense for the period was $500.

2. Identify the cash flow in each of the following and prepare a profit and loss statement and a statement of cash flows from operations.

   (a) Revenue for the year was $278 000. The balance of accounts receivable at the beginning of the year was $13 200 and at the end of the year was $107 200.

   (b) Cost of goods sold for the year was $146 000; there was an increase in inventory of $9600 and an increase in accounts payable of $32 700.

   (c) Taxation payable at the beginning of the year was $43 000 and at the end of the year was $40 500. The tax expense charged against income for the year was $46 900.

   (d) Rent was prepaid $12 600 at the beginning of the year and $8700 at the end of the year. The rent expense for the year was $35 700.

   (e) Dividends payable were $20 000 at the beginning of the year and $20 000 at the end of the year. Interim dividends of $5000 were paid.

10.26 *Identifying cash flows*

1. Toptown Holdings Pty Ltd has the following balances relating to land and buildings:

	31 December 20X7	31 December 20X8
• Land and buildings	$350 000	$490 000
• Accum. depn buildings	$ 12 000	$ 15 000

   - Depreciation expense charged on buildings in 20X8 was $7000.
   - Land at Yarraville was revalued upwards by $8000.
   - Land and buildings at Mentone were sold for $94 000, at a gain of $30 000.

   Identify the cash flows.

2. Identify the cash flows in the following data. Provide clear details of any necessary reconstruction of accounts.

   Equipment account:

Balance 1 July 20X1	$37 500
Balance 30 June 20X2	$55 000

   During the year the following occurred:
   - Equipment were revalued upwards by $5000.
   - Equipment that had originally cost $22 500 and had been depreciated to $20 000 was sold for a loss of $5000. Assume that any purchases or sales of equipment were cash transactions.

10.27 *Determining profit and loss statement and balance sheet from cash flow information*

You have been asked to investigate Midas Ltd by a client who is interested in acquiring it. She considers the threefold increase in profit in 20X2 an indication of good prospects.

You discover that the president, Midas Murdoch, has some strange ideas about accounting. He believes revenue is recorded only when cash is received and that expenses occur whenever cash is paid out (except in the case of equipment, which he regards as an asset).

PROFIT AND LOSS STATEMENTS				
	\$000	20X1 \$000	\$000	20X2 \$000
Revenue: Cash received from customers		80		150
less Cash expenses:				
Inventory paid for	35		90	
Wages paid	20		24	
Rent paid	15		9	
Dividend paid	3	73	3	126
Net cash income		7		24

BALANCE SHEETS

	20X1		20X2	
	$000	$000	$000	$000
Assets: Cash	17		41	
Equipment	20	37	20	61
Liabilities		Nil		Nil
Owners' equity				
Capital	30		30	
Retained profit	7	37	31	61

Other information, not disclosed in the statements:

	31 Dec. 20X1	31 Dec. 20X2
	$000	$000
(i) Customer accounts owing	30	10
Inventory on hand	12	28
Wages due to employees	3	7
Amounts payable to suppliers	2	12

(ii) The rental contract was for $1000 per month, commencing 1 January 20X1.

(iii) The equipment, purchased on 1 January 20X1 for $20 000, is expected to give four years of uniform service, after which it will be scrapped for about $4000. Murdoch says it is currently as good as new and talk of depreciation is so much nonsense.

(iv) The company commenced business on 1 January 20X1.

(a) Present revised statements for 20X1 and 20X2 based on the principles of accrual accounting.

(b) Is Midas Ltd still showing a good profit trend?

10.28 *Determining a profit and loss statement and balance sheet for a public sector business enterprise from cash flow information*

The government has requested an investigation of the operations of State Publishings, a wholly-owned government printing business, which it is considering for privatisation because of its declining financial performance since its commencement on 1 January 20X1.

You are asked to examine their accounting reports for the past two years. You discover that State Publishings has been reporting on a strangely modified cash basis. Under its accounting policies, revenue is recorded only when cash is received, and expenses occur whenever cash is paid out (except in the case of equipment, which is treated as an asset).

From the following reports, prepare revised statements for 20X1 and 20X2 based on the principles of accrual accounting. Would you agree that State Publishing's financial performance is declining?

Other information, not disclosed in the statements is:

1.

	31 Dec. 20X1 $m	31 Dec. 20X2 $m
(a) Clients' accounts owing	2	10
(b) Supplies on hand	5.6	2.4
(c) Wages due to employees	1.4	0.6
(d) Amounts payable to suppliers	2.4	− 0.4

2. The maintenance contract was for $0.15 million per month, commencing 1 January 20X1.

3. The equipment, purchased on 1 January 20X1 for $4 million, is expected to give four years uniform service, after which it will be scrapped for about $0.8 million. State Publishings has not charged depreciation because the equipment is as good as new.

PROFIT AND LOSS STATEMENTS

	20X1 $m	20X1 $m	20X2 $m	20X2 $m
Revenue				
Cash from clients		30		16
less Cash expenses				
Supplies paid for	18		7	
Wages paid	4.8		4	
Maintenance fees paid	1.8		3	
Delivery paid	0.6	25.2	0.6	14.6
Net cash income		4.8		1.4

BALANCE SHEETS

	20X1 $m	20X2 $m
Assets		
Cash	6.8	8.2
Equipment	4	4
	10.8	12.2
Liabilities	Nil	Nil
Equity		
Capital	6	6
Retained profits	4.8	6.2
	10.8	12.2

10.29 *Preparing and interpreting a statement of cash flows from financial statements*

Spread Ltd has been growing rapidly for the last five years and each year profits have increased. However, the managing director is extremely concerned about the firm's liquidity position and finds it difficult to understand why the firm is short of cash after five years of profitable growth. From the information given here, prepare a cash flow statement and use it to explain to the managing director why there is a cash shortage.

BALANCE SHEET AS AT 30 JUNE 20X5

	20X5 $000	20X4 $000		20X5 $000	20X4 $000
Current assets			Current liabilities		
Cash	–	250	Trade creditors	2 000	750
Accounts receivable	1 550	750	Overdraft	625	
Inventory	2 500	1 250			
	4 050	2 250		2 625	750
Non-current assets			Long-term debt	3 750	
Plant (net of			Owners' equity		
deprec.)	2 500	1 250	Capital	2 500	2 500
Property	5 000	1 250	Retained profit	2 675	1 500
	7 500	2 500		5 175	4 000
Total assets	11 550	4 750	Total equities	11 550	4 750

For the year ended 30 June 20X5:

	$000
Revenue	12 000
Net profit	1 350
Depreciation	500
Dividends paid	175
Long-term assets purchases	5 500

10.30 *Preparing a statement of cash flows from financial statements*

From the following information relating to Richmond Ltd, prepare a cash flow statement. Include a reconciliation of net profit to cash flow from operations.

BALANCES AS AT 30 JUNE 20X1

	20X0 $000	20X1 $000
Cash	112	120
Investments	72	100
Accounts receivable	316	260
Inventory	500	580
Equipment	1600	2200
	2600	3260
Allowance for depreciation on equipment	800	940
Trade creditors	360	520
Debentures	500	780
Retained profits	440	480
Paid-up capital	500	540
	2600	3260

PROFIT AND LOSS STATEMENT
for year ended June 20X1

	$000	$000
Sales revenue		2940
less Cost of goods sold		1960
Gross profit		980
less Expenses		
Selling and administrative expenses	616	
Depreciation on equipment	240	856
		124
plus Gain on disposal of equipment		16
Net profit		140

Additional information:

1. Dividends paid were $100 000
2. Equipment acquisitions cost $700 000

10.31 *Preparing a statement of cash flows from financial statements*

1. Prepare a cash flow statement from the following information. Include a reconciliation of net profit to cash flow from operations.

PROFIT AND LOSS STATEMENT: CRANE LTD
for the year ended 30 June 20X4

Sales		$130 000
less Sales discounts	$ 4 320	
Sales returns	9 570	13 890
Net sales		116 110
less Cost of goods sold		
Opening inventory	36 400	
plus Purchases	76 200	
less Purchase returns	9 100	
Closing stock	45 700	57 800
Gross profit		58 310
Profit on sale of office furniture		800
		59 110
		continues

PROFIT AND LOSS STATEMENT: CRANE LTD
for the year ended 30 June 20X4

less Expenses:		
Advertising	$ 4 260	
Cleaning	3 380	
Interest	7 000	
Salaries and wages	11 430	
Depreciation —furniture and fittings	1 840	
—equipment	2 920	
—floor coverings	890	
Goodwill amortisation	4 000	
Stationery	2 620	
Insurance	2 810	
Rent	8 520	$ 49 670
Net profit		9 440
less Tax expense		3 400
		6 040
less Final dividend proposed		2 500
Interim dividend paid		1 000
Retained profit		$ 2 540

BALANCE SHEETS: CRANE LTD
as at 30 June 20X4

	20X3	20X4
Cash at bank	$ 22 600	$ 19 280
Trade debtors	26 300	34 600
Inventory	36 400	45 700
Furniture and fittings	42 000	36 300
Accumulated depreciation	(6 800)	(7 640)
Equipment	48 900	66 800
Accumulated depreciation	(9 820)	(12 740)
Floor coverings	13 300	13 300
Accumulated depreciation	(3 340)	(4 230)
Goodwill	42 000	38 000
	211 540	229 370
Trade creditors	30 120	24 410
Bills payable	25 000	15 000
Debentures (10%)	60 000	75 000
Taxation payable	2 600	3 100
Dividend payable	2 000	2 500
Paid-up capital	90 000	105 000
Retained profits	1 820	4 360
	$211 540	$229 370

The following transactions occurred during the year:

- Sold office furniture, which had cost $5700.
- A new issue of debentures was made. In addition, debentures of $10 000 matured and were paid.
- An interim dividend of $1000 was paid during the year.

2. From the following information prepare a cash-flow statement for 20X1. Include a reconciliation of net profit to cash flow from operations.

BALANCE SHEETS: VICTORIA LTD as at 31 December		
	20X6	20X7
Cash	$10 000	$16 000
Accounts receivable	4 000	3 000
Inventory	15 000	16 000
Prepayments	600	800
Land	20 000	20 000
Equipment	20 000	35 000
less Accum. depn	(14 000)	(14 700)
Goodwill	8 000	6 000
	63 600	82 100
Accounts payable	3 000	8 000
Tax payable	7 000	9 200
Dividend payable	5 000	6 000
Paid-up capital	30 000	30 000
General reserve	1 000	9 000
Appropriation	17 600	19 900
	$63 600	$82 100

Additional information:

- Tax paid in 20X7 was $6500.
- Dividends paid during 20X7 totalled $5000.
- Goodwill was written down by $2000. Revenue was $36 000.

3. From the following information prepare a cash flow statement for 20X7. Include a reconciliation of net profit to cash flow from operation.

BALANCE SHEETS: SPRING LTD
as at 31 December

	20X6	20X7
Cash	$14 000	$22 300
Accounts receivable	8 000	3 000
Inventory	15 000	26 000
Prepayments	600	800
Land	20 000	30 000
Equipment	30 000	35 000
less Accum. depn	(24 000)	(25 000)
Goodwill	8 000	6 000
	71 600	98 100
Accounts payable	13 000	8 000
Tax payable	7 000	9 200
Dividend payable	3 000	2 000
Paid-up capital	30 000	50 000
General reserve	1 000	9 000
Appropriation	17 600	19 900
	$71 600	$98 100

Additional information:

- The reduction in goodwill was treated as an expense.
- Equipment that cost $10 000 and had a book value of $7000 was sold for $5000.
- Tax paid in 20X7 was $6500.
- Dividends paid during 20X7 totalled $3000. Revenue was $41 800.

10.32 *Preparing a statement of cash flows from trial balances*

TRIAL BALANCES: LEMRAC PTY LIMITED
as at 30 June

	20X7		20X8	
	$	$	$	$
Assets				
Cash at bank	13 000		–	
Prepaid insurance	4 500		2 900	
Accounts receivable	33 200		29 900	
Provision for doubtful debts		4 100		3 880
Inventory	41 200		50 800	
Motor vehicles	24 800		27 600	
Accum. depn: motor vehicles		5 840		6 560
Plant and equipment	35 200		56 500	
Accum. depn: plant		12 300		16 200
Property	105 000		145 000	
Patents	33 000		29 000	

continues

TRIAL BALANCES: LEMRAC PTY LIMITED as at 30 June				
	20X7		20X8	
	$	$	$	$
Liabilities				
Bank overdraft		–		3 500
Sundry creditors		5 300		3 900
Accounts payable		29 400		39 900
Mortgage–18%		70 000		54 000
Provision for taxation		7 900		9 100
Provision for dividend		6 000		9 000
Shareholders' equity				
Paid-up capital		100 000		120 000
Retained profits		27 060		30 660
General reserve		12 000		15 000
Asset revaluation reserve		10 000		30 000
	289 900	289 900	341 700	341 700

Additional information:

- During the year the company purchased a new motor vehicle for $11 000, and sold an old motor vehicle that had a net book value of $6150 and made a $1300 profit on the sale.
- Property was revalued during the year and part of the revaluation increment was distributed as a bonus issue of shares.
- Revenue for the year was $274 900.
- During the year the company paid an interim dividend of $4000, company income tax of $8200 and declared a final dividend of $9000.

Prepare a cash-flow statement for Lemrac Pty Limited for the year ending 30 June 20X8. Include a reconciliation of net profit to cash flow from operation.

10.33 *Preparing a statement of cash flows from financial statements*

1. Prepare a cash flow statement for the Wattle Company Ltd, where only the following information is available. Include a reconciliation of net profit to cash flow from operations.

COMPARATIVE BALANCE SHEETS: WATTLE COMPANY LTD				
	30 June 20X8		30 June 20X9	
	$	$	$	$
Current assets				
Cash at bank	4 680			
Debtors	9 440		15 360	
Stock	23 600		33 200	
Prepayments	180	37 900	240	48 800
				continues

COMPARATIVE BALANCE SHEETS: WATTLE COMPANY LTD				
	30 June 20X8		30 June 20X9	
	$	$	$	$
Non-current assets				
Delivery vans	13 600		18 000	
less Accumulated depreciation	2 600	11 000	4 200	13 800
Fixtures and fittings	16 000		16 000	
less Accumulated depreciation	4 000	12 000	7 000	9 000
Land		40 000		40 000
Goodwill		8 600		8 000
		109 500		119 600
Current liabilities				
Sundry creditors	2 400		2 900	
Bank overdraft	–		3 600	
Provision for tax	3 600		4 000	
Provision for dividends	5 000	11 000	6 000	16 500
Debentures		20 000		
Shareholders' equity				
Paid-up capital		60 000		80 000
General reserve		8 000		10 000
Profit and loss appropriation		10 500		13 100
		109 500		119 600

Additional information:

- The dividend paid in 20X8–X9 was $5000 as provided.
- Tax paid in 20X8–X9 was $3000.
- During the year a delivery van that had cost $4800 and had been depreciated to $4000 was sold for $3600, and a new delivery van bought in its place.
- Revenue for the year was $63 000.

2.

BALANCE SHEETS: HALFCASE LTD		
as at 31 December		
	20X3	20X4
Cash at bank	$ 24 900	$ 32 800
Trade debtors	44 200	38 700
Provision for doubtful debts	(3 300)	(4 850)
Inventory	37 900	43 400
Investment in Review Ltd	29 000	25 000
Property	142 000	167 000
Store equipment	38 100	30 900
Accumulated depreciation	(11 400)	(11 560)
	301 400	321 390

continues

BALANCE SHEETS: HALFCASE LTD as at 31 December		
	20X3	20X4
Trade creditors	35 600	30 200
Short-term loan	–	8 000
Accrued expenses	1 200	1 050
Provision for taxation	5 500	6 300
Provision for dividend	3 000	3 000
Mortgage	90 000	80 000
Paid-up capital	120 000	140 000
Retained earnings	41 100	42 840
Capital asset reserve	5 000	10 000
	$301 400	$321 390

Additional information:

- On 31 December 20X4 store equipment that had cost $1200 was sold, resulting in a loss on sale of $1000. Store equipment (all purchased at the same date) is depreciated on a straight-line basis over 15 years. No new equipment was purchased during the year.
- The company revalued its investment in Review Ltd downward due to a share price decline of Review Ltd's shares.
- The company issued 10 000 shares at $2 each.
- The company's tax expense for the year was $6100 and a final dividend of $3000 was proposed.
- Revenue for the year was $89 500.

Prepare an appropriately classified cash-flow statement for Halfcase Ltd for the year ending 31 December 20X4, including a reconciliation of net profit to cash flow from operations.

3. Prepare a cash flow statement for Quicksmart Ltd, including a reconciliation of net profit to cash flows from operations.

COMPARATIVE BALANCE SHEETS: QUICKSMART LTD as at 31 December				
	20X7		20X8	
	$	$	$	$
Shareholders' equity				
Paid-up capital		318 000		334 000
Asset revaluation reserve		–		10 000
Profit and loss appropriation		36 000		40 200
		354 000		384 200
				continues

COMPARATIVE BALANCE SHEETS: QUICKSMART LTD
as at 31 December

	20X7		20X8	
	$	$	$	$
Current liabilities				
Bank overdraft		–		23 260
Sundry creditors		42 000		64 000
Accrued charges		2 520		1 660
Provision for tax		20 200		30 000
		64 720		118 920
Non-current liabilities				
Debentures		–		50 000
		418 720		553 120
Current assets				
Bank		10 240		
Accounts receivable	64 200		101 000	
less Provision for doubtful a/cs	7 000	57 200	10 000	91 800
Stock		71 200		83 200
Prepayments		1 680		1 840
		140 320		176 840
Fixed assets				
Plant and equipment	212 000		252 000	
less Accumulated depreciation	17 600	194 400	19 720	232 280
Land and buildings		42 000		64 000
		236 400		296 280
Investments		–		50 000
Intangibles				
Goodwill		42 000		30 000
		418 720		553 120

Additional information:

- During the year a dividend of $28 040 had been paid.
- Taxation paid during the year was $18 400.
- Buildings had been revalued by $10 000 and $12 000 had been written off goodwill.
- Revenue for the year was $126 400.

10.34 *Preparing and analysing a statement of cash flows from financial statements*

Prepare a cash flow statement for Expansive Ltd. Briefly comment on the firm's growth in 20X3 and explain how it was financed. Include a reconciliation of net profit to cash flow from operations.

BALANCE SHEET: EXPANSIVE LTD
as at 30 June

	20X2		20X3	
	$	$	$	$
Current assets				
Accounts receivable	595 000		755 000	
less Bad debt allowance	45 000	550 000	82 500	672 500
Marketable securities		57 500		145 000
Inventories		412 500		422 500
Long-term assets				
Plant and equipment	305 000		370 000	
less Accum. depn	127 500	177 500	160 000	210 000
Vehicles	215 000		347 500	
less Accum. depn	120 000	95 000	145 000	202 500
Land and buildings		467 500		467 500
Goodwill		100 000		75 000
Total assets		1 860 000		2 195 000
Current liabilities				
Overdraft		28 750		132 500
Accounts payable		236 250		408 750
Tax payable		45 000		36 250
Dividend payable		75 000		25 000
Long-term liabilities				
Debentures		125 000		75 000
Unsecured notes		75 000		75 000
Shareholders' equity				
Paid-up capital		1 110 000		1 250 000
Contingency reserve		125 000		162 500
Retained profits		40 000		30 000
Total equity		1 860 000		2 195 000

APPROPRIATION STATEMENT
for the period ended 30 June 20X3

Balance of retained profits 30 June 20X2		$ 40 000
plus Net profit after tax		102 500
plus Interim dividend paid	$50 000	
Final dividend proposed	25 000	
Transferred to contingency reserve	37 500	112 500
Retained profits 30 June 20X3		30 000

The following charges were deducted from revenue:

Depreciation of plant and equipment	$32 500
Depreciation of vehicles	65 000
Audit fees	12 500
Directors' fees	20 000
Loss on sale of vehicles	10 000
Goodwill written down	25 000
Taxation expense (net)	30 000

During the year vehicles, which originally cost $60 000 and had a book value of $20 000, were disposed of. Revenue for the year was $540 000.

PART 3
Financial management

CHAPTER 11
Accounting and financial management

Introduction

The focus of the chapters to this point has been on understanding what accounting is, how to record accounting information and how to prepare financial statements from the information recorded. However, the field of accounting goes beyond the keeping of records and the provision of accounting reports, and includes the very important function of the interpretation of that information. Chapters 11 and 12 discuss the uses of accounting information for financial management. In Chapter 12 the use of accounting reports to analyse the performance of the organisation is explained and illustrated. In Chapter 11 the use of accounting data for the management of the financial function within the organisation is considered; this encompasses an understanding of the appropriate goals for the organisation and the management of risk and return. The three aspects to the role of financial management are financing, dividends and investment. Some aspects of investment analysis are considered in Chapter 24. Our focus in this chapter will be on financing decisions and dividend policy.

Accountants fulfil a diverse range of roles, from acting as financial analysts for shareholders who wish to know the implications of the financial statements of a company, to being members of management teams as they attempt to plan and control an organisation's activities, but the common factor is that each role involves decision making based on accounting information.

How useful is accounting information for decision making? We have seen in earlier chapters that at least a few of the accounting numbers in financial statements are not the result of an external transaction but are arbitrarily allocated or assigned by the accountant, and as such may be seen as less than objective. Is accounting information therefore of limited relevance for decision making? On the contrary, research studies have shown that accounting provides a good summary of economic events and provides information that is used. William Beaver, in a well-known study in 1968 of share-market reactions to information about entities, showed that announcements of earnings convey information to the share-market that is relevant to the valuation of securities.[1] Provided the limitations of accounting information are recognised and allowances made for it, Beaver concludes that financial reports are useful for decision makers. They do provide information, although that information needs to be analysed and often adjusted to suit the particular purposes of the user.

Another way to view accounting reports is as a product, produced by the entity for two reasons:

1. to fulfil legal reporting requirements (external reporting)
2. to provide information about the entity to assist decision making (both externally for investment and internally for financial and other management decisions).

Naturally external reporting will be less detailed than internal reporting, to prevent competitors and other external parties gaining inside information.

An understanding of the principles of financial accounting will assist in conducting financial analyses, utilising the techniques to be discussed in Chapter 12. Conversely, an appreciation of financial management will aid in understanding the purpose of financial accounting and reporting. To make the process of producing accounting reports a more meaningful and informed one, accountants need to understand the process of decision making using accounting data, that is, the uses to which their product is put, giving greater meaning to the various accounting procedures outlined so far in this book and pursued in greater depth in subsequent chapters. By taking the role of a user of accounting information in this and the next chapter, we hope you will gain a better appreciation of the importance of reporting profit, financial position and cash flows and the significance of the concepts behind the reporting.

---

[1] W. Beaver, 'The Information Content of Annual Earnings Announcements', *Empirical Research in Accounting: Selected Studies, 1968*, supplement to Vol. 6 of *Journal of Accounting Research*, 1968.

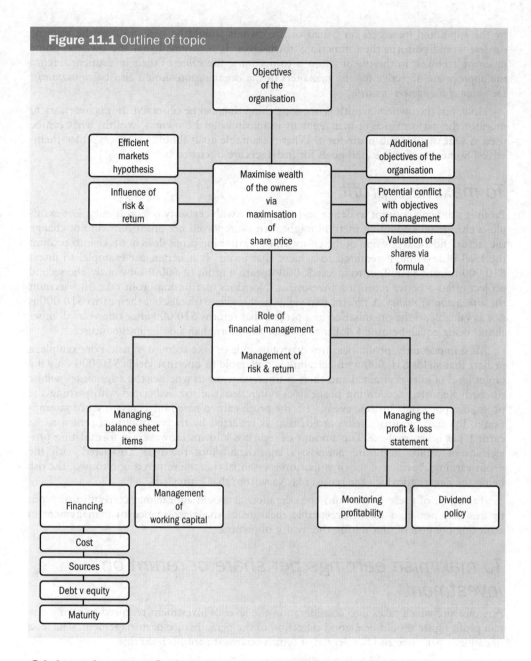

Figure 11.1 Outline of topic

Objectives of the organisation

The organisation has a number of objectives regarding products, employment, market position and numerous other functions. Financial management is the process of planning, controlling and evaluating financial decisions in order to achieve the financial objectives of the organisation.

An understanding of financial management begins with an appreciation of the organisation's objectives. Large organisations are usually managed by their employees, who are answerable to the owners of the organisation. For example, companies have managers appointed to run the company in the best interests of the owners, its shareholders, via a board of directors elected by the shareholders. The operations and management performed by the appointed managers on behalf of the owners should be very close to the way the owners would perform these functions themselves. It is assumed that the owners' prime incentive to invest in the organisation is to maximise the value of their investment. Hence the appropriate objective for the managers of the organisation should also be *to maximise the value of the owners' wealth.*

However, the owners' wealth is not something that can be observed. If it is necessary to monitor the performance of management in maximising the owners' wealth, what can be used as a measurable substitute for it? What measurable goals should managers set for themselves? Some commonly stated goals for managers are discussed below.

To maximise profit

Profit is a difficult concept to define and to measure with certainty or consistency. For example, a change of accounting method might increase reported net profit but will not change the 'actual' financial position of the entity. Also, maximising profit does not take into account the level of investment required to achieve that profit. Is it better, for example, to invest $10 000 to earn $1000, or to invest $5000 to earn a profit of $600? Obviously, the second project offers a better return on investment. Nor does maximising profit take into account the *time value of money*. A project that yields nothing for 10 years but then earns $10 000 is not as valuable to the organisation as a project that returns $10 000 after one year, all other things being equal, because a dollar today is worth more than a dollar in the future.

Most importantly, profit measures do not include or take account of risk. For example, a project that yields $10 000 with certainty is preferable to one that yields $10 000 only if a target level of sales is attained and there is uncertainty as to whether the sales target will be reached. Reported accounting profit does not reflect the risk associated with earning the profit; it reports only historic events (i.e. the profit earned based on a certain set of assumptions). By the time profit is reported, risk, as reflected by the variability of return to be earned, has been resolved. The amount of return is known. However, in formulating projections of profits in future periods, a consideration of the risks associated with the profit-earning activities of the organisation is essential (i.e. the return is not known, the risk being the degree to which the return may vary from that expressed).

Taking all of these factors into consideration, it would appear that conventional profit figures may not be a totally acceptable measure of the performance of management in achieving the goal of maximising the wealth of owners.

To maximise earnings per share or return on investment

Any measure which takes into consideration the level of investment required to earn a certain profit figure should be a good reflection of the performance of management. The level of earnings per share and the degree of return on investment both do this.

Earnings per share (EPS) is measured as:

$$\frac{\text{profit available to ordinary shareholders}}{\text{number of ordinary shares}}$$

Return on investment (ROI) is measured as:

$$\frac{\text{earnings before interest and taxes}}{\text{total assets}}$$

Although both measures scale the profit earned by the level of investment necessary to achieve it, EPS depends on the relative amounts of debt and equity finance that have been used in the organisation's capital structure. Increasing the use of debt finance increases the potential for improved EPS, by limiting the number of shares on issue, but it also increases the risk associated with future earnings, as is explained in a later section. ROI is a pure measure of operating performance, regardless of the source of the organisation's funds. Neither measure includes or takes account of risk. In addition, they both still depend on accounting profit. As such, they have all the problems associated with measuring accounting profit.

It would appear, therefore, that neither of these two measures, nor the measurement of profit alone, would be an acceptable basis for the maximisation of owners' wealth. Another measure needs to be identified in order to judge the performance of management in achieving the objective of the firm.

How is owners' wealth maximised?

In an actively trading share-market, the share price indicates the market's assessment of the value of the organisation. Hence by maximising the organisation's share price, managers can maximise the value of shareholders' wealth as perceived by the market.

Unless an entity is issuing shares, either when it is first incorporated or subsequently to expand in some way, its finances are not directly affected by the value of its shares. It receives cash only when the shares are initially issued, not when they are traded between investors on the share-market. Hence the organisation's concern with the price of its shares on the share-market is motivated by concerns such as the value of shareholders' wealth.

It seems logical that managers should aim to maximise the entity's share price, thereby maximising the wealth of its shareholders. It also seems sensible that shareholders would perceive their wealth, not only in terms of how profitable the organisation is now or is likely to be in the future, but in terms of the value of their shares if they sold them. As we shall see later when we derive a formula to value a share, the value of a share takes into account the time value of money and the risk of investing in that share, neither of which are considered by the other two measures discussed above.

What about organisations without shares traded on a share-market? Such organisations would include small privately owned companies, public sector business enterprises and government agencies and departments. Without a market-based assessment of performance to guide them, these organisations need to set goals that relate their efficiency and performance to that of their competitors, comparable organisations, 'world-best' practice, or some other high standard. Telstra, for example, might use a comparison with Bell Canada because both are telecommunications entities operating in markets with similar demographics such as long distances and a dispersed population. Local and municipal councils might 'benchmark' their activities and processes, such as rate notice issuance, against each other to determine the most efficient process and to use these comparisons to set efficiency and performance levels against which to judge their managers. Efficiency and performance measures are discussed in more detail in Chapter 12.

If an organisation with traded shares chooses to maximise its share price in order to maximise shareholders' wealth, it is relying on the share-market to be an efficient judge of the worth of the organisation. It is thus relying on what is known as the *efficient market hypothesis.*

The efficient market hypothesis

The efficient market hypothesis states simply that information is reflected in prices. In an efficient market the price of a security reflects its true value. If a new piece of information becomes available, that information might change the future earnings potential or risk (and hence the value) of the security. For example, if a toy manufacturer's product is announced 'Toy of the Year', its expected Christmas sales and future earnings potential could be much higher. Investors in shares will use the new information to calculate the new value of the share based on their assessment of the effect of this information.

Figures 11.2 and 11.3 provide examples of information, or the lack of it, appearing to affect share prices.

Figure 11.2

Coke dives on paucity of detail

Analysts have blamed poor communications skills and a lack of marketing expertise for Coca-Cola Amatil's disastrous share price performance since releasing its interim profit results last week. The share price fall has come despite what was generally perceived as a good profit result, coming in above market expectations...But the performance of CCA scrip has not matched that view and the share price has fallen more than 14 per cent since... 'They are not offering us any clarity or detail,' one analyst said. Another analyst said: 'They are one of the pre-eminent marketers in the world, but they have not sold that result at all well.'

Australian, 11 August 1998, p. 23

Figure 11.3

Buoyant Woolworths bucks trend

Investors yesterday welcomed a strong annual profit performance from the nation's biggest supermarket chain, Woolworths, pushing its shares sharply higher on an otherwise dismal day for the stock market. Boosted by a reduction in its cost base, Woolworths announced a net profit of $279.6 million for its 12 months to June 28, up from $258.3 million previously ... It was enough to lift Woolworths shares 15c higher to $5.23, defying a weaker broader market.

Australian, 1 September 1998, p. 21

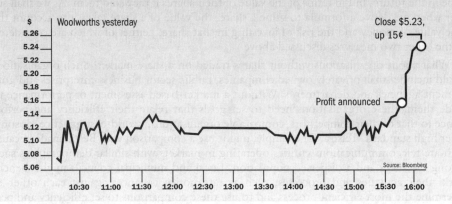

In the context of financial markets the term market efficiency usually refers to the efficiency with which markets process information. In a fully efficient market the prices of all securities at all times would fully reflect all the information relevant to determining the prices of those securities. In such a market there would be no securities that are underpriced and no securities that are overpriced. All securities would be fairly priced in the sense that they offer expected returns that are commensurate with their level of risk. Thus all securities with the same level of perceived risk would offer the same expected return. There is, of course, no guarantee that actual returns will match expected returns, except for securities with no risk. For example, a bank term deposit is risk free as the return expected on making the deposit will be the return actually received on maturity.

In an efficient market there should be no opportunities to make abnormal profits (i.e. returns consistently in excess of those commensurate with the level of perceived risk that the investor accepts). An opportunity to earn abnormal profits should be instantaneously traded away as soon as information becomes available that such an abnormal profit opportunity exists. If information that is favourable to the organisation becomes available, demand for its shares at the existing price will be high, and investors will quickly buy the shares. On the other hand, if the information is unfavourable to the organisation, demand will be low, and traders will quickly sell the shares at the existing price. The process of buying or selling will increase or decrease the price because of the effect on relative supply and demand. This process will stop when there is neither excess demand nor excess supply at the new share price. Even if only one investor obtains a piece of information and acts on it, other investors may mimic his or her actions, because they will assume that the informed investor has some secret information that he or she has effectively revealed to them by buying or selling certain shares. The overall result is that the prices of shares in the market quickly incorporate new information. Note also that the information does not need to be 'true' or confirmed— rumours also affect share prices.

In studies of information and financial markets, the level of efficiency has been found to be 'semi-strong form' where all *publicly available* information is incorporated into the current price. For example, newspaper reports on the organisation and its accounting report data would be quickly absorbed by the market and the price of the share would reflect them. Financial markets have been found to operate at better than 'weak-form efficiency' (where the current price includes only information from past trading) but not at 'strong-form efficiency' (where the price would include *all* private and public information about the organisation).

The concept of market efficiency has several implications for financial managers. The most important is that the manager, whether issuing or purchasing securities, can expect those securities to be fairly priced. The only way abnormal profits are likely to be obtained by buying securities is if the manager has private or 'inside' information. Similarly, it is unlikely that financial managers will be able to obtain cheap finance by selling securities for more than they are really worth. The financial manager's efforts are best devoted to keeping the transaction costs of security issues down and structuring financial packages to obtain the maximum tax advantage.

Additional organisation objectives

Increasingly important is the issue of secondary objectives that organisations may wish to pursue. In particular, are objectives related to social responsibility inconsistent with owners' wealth maximisation or efficiency and performance maximisation? Obviously such objectives and the resulting policies that the organisation may adopt have a cost, and that cost is borne by the owners. Nevertheless, the organisation has other interest groups to consider: customers, suppliers and employees are also important. The interests of these groups are best met by the organisation's ability to generate earnings, and the overall performance of the organisation will be enhanced by the coordinated efforts of the various interest groups. So the various secondary objectives of the organisation are not inconsistent with the maximisation of owners' wealth, or the maximisation of efficiency and performance.

Organisation versus management objectives

We have indicated that the most appropriate objective for the organisation is to maximise the owners' wealth by maximising its share price (or to pursue efficiency and performance maximisation if the organisation does not have issued shares). But does this happen in practice? Is this the objective that management does pursue?

Many large organisations have diverse shareholdings, with many small shareholders who do not concern themselves with the details of the activities of the organisation. Similarly, the owners of public sector business enterprises are the governments acting on behalf of their constituents. These owners have little contact with or direct influence over the operational decisions made in the business. Such organisations are run by their managers who are in an autonomous position regarding decision making. These managers receive no personal reward for taking risks on behalf of the owners. If a risky project undertaken by the organisation is successful, owners gain through the increased value of the organisation; if it is not successful, managers risk losing their jobs. The separation of the organisation's ownership and control gives the managers the opportunity to *pursue their own objectives*. There is obviously an incentive for such managers to act in their own interests and not in the owners' interests. Instead of vigorously seeking to maximise share price, profits or growth, they may seek only to improve the position of the organisation at a comfortably steady pace that will satisfy owners and creditors, with few risks taken.

There is obviously a conflict of interests between owners and managers in such circumstances. This makes it essential for owners to monitor financial performance, not only to determine whether the owners' goals are being met, but also to discover whether they are even being pursued.

This potential conflict of interest has been limited in practice by three means: the threat of takeovers, the cost of obtaining external finance, and management compensation plans.

Threat of takeovers

The threat of one organisation being purchased by another, known as a takeover, provides a powerful incentive for managers to aim to maximise the organisation's share price or performance. If, for example, a firm is mismanaged, and the full potential of its assets is not being realised, then its share price will be lower than it could be under more effective management. This might mean that all of its shares could be bought for less than the value of its assets (either value in use or value in exchange), which is obviously a 'bargain', and is one motive for takeovers. In the event of a takeover, the managers of the target organisation might lose their jobs, as management will in future be performed by the acquirer. Takeovers therefore are an incentive to efficient management.

Cost of obtaining external finance

When the organisation needs to approach the market for additional finance (either debt or equity) in order to expand, poor management will be reflected in either the high cost or the unavailability of such finance, and owners may be alerted to this. Loans may be available only at higher rates of interest than expected, because of the greater risk involved in making a loan to a poorly managed organisation. Shares may need to be sold at quite a low price compared with the current price to induce new shareholders to invest, which substantially 'waters down' or dilutes the proportion of the organisation that existing shareholders own.

In either case, management's actions would be brought to the attention of the owners and the market in general, providing an incentive for managers to act in the owners' interests. Although dismissal is unlikely to be a problem for the management of large public companies with diverse ownership, shareholders still possess a potent weapon. They may exercise their vote in the market place by selling shares and thus cause a fall in the company's share price. In the case of public sector business enterprises, adverse public focus on management may lead to political pressures that do result in the replacement of managerial staff.

Example: *Dilution of shareholders' relative ownership of the company*

If Spot Ltd has 100 000 shares currently trading at $2 per share, it is valued in the market at $200 000. If, in order to raise an additional $50 000, Spot needs to set the price of new shares at $1, it will issue an additional 50 000 shares.

However, it has sold at $1 what its shareholders previously valued at $2. The value of Spot has increased from $200 000 to $250 000 because of the receipt of the additional $50 000, but the number of shares issued has increased from 100 000 to 150 000, so now each share is worth only $250 000/150 000 shares or $1.67. The value of Spot's shares has been *diluted* from $2 to $1.67.

Management compensation plans

Specific policies of the organisation linking managerial incomes to the organisation's performance are frequently used. The objective is to link managers' interests to those of the owners. The linkage instrument must be carefully chosen, to ensure that it is consistent with the maximisation of owners' wealth and that it is not under the control of the management and therefore subject to possible manipulation. Examples of linkage instruments that are under management's control include reported profit, growth in sales, and other accounting numbers. Two of the most effective motivators are to issue shares to managers free of charge, or to sell shares to them at a reduced price. In this way a direct link is formed between managers' and owners' wealth.

Research shows that executive compensation plans help align managers' and owners' interests. Executive compensation is positively related to share-price performance, and the adoption of compensation plans is associated with increases in owners' wealth.

The influence of risk and return on share prices

Given that the financial objective of the organisation should be to maximise owners' wealth, and that this objective can be met by policies that maximise the organisation's share price where applicable, what factors influence the share price? The primary factor is the interaction of risk and return.

Risk is defined in terms of variability of outcome. A risky return is one that varies and is therefore difficult to predict. One of the advantages of the maximisation of the share price as the objective of the organisation, rather than maximising accounting numbers, is that this objective includes an assessment by the market of the riskiness of the organisation. Risk is not directly measured by accounting reports. The risk level of any organisation depends upon a combination of three different types of risk: business risk, financial risk and management risk.

Business risk

This arises from the investments the organisation makes. The organisation is faced with a wide range of possible investments, including physical assets such as land, buildings and inventory, intangible assets such as trademarks, or financial assets such as cash, securities and accounts receivable. Some assets offer less certain returns than others; for example, an organisation that invests in minerals exploration is riskier than one that holds only government bonds. Business risk is affected by factors such as the industry the organisation operates in, and the type of products or services it produces and sells.

Financial risk

This arises from the way the investments are financed. Differing forms of finance involve differing contractual obligations, which may influence the organisation's riskiness and profitability. For example, whereas failure to pay interest on debts may lead to a firm's liquidation, failure to pay dividends is likely to cause nothing worse than a decline in its share price. Hence, an organisation that has chosen a high level of debt finance may be more risky than if it had chosen to use equity finance. Financial risk is affected by factors such as the level of the organisation's borrowings, when they are due to be repaid, and the required level of current assets.

Quality of management

This refers to the effectiveness with which the assets and liabilities are managed. Management must constantly review the performance of the organisation's assets, the structure of its liabilities and the balance between them. Effective management is the major prerequisite to successful financial performance. Management risk is affected by factors such as the competency and ingenuity of management.

The importance of risk in decision making

To highlight the importance of risk in decision making, a 'Statement of Business Risk' has been suggested for inclusion in company financial reports.

> Investors need to know about risk and return, but to understand one, you have to know about the other. Currently, financial reporting pronouncements have much to say about measuring and analysing the returns a business makes, yet they say precious little about risk. To help put this right, the ICAEW (Institute of Chartered Accountants of England & Wales) has issued a discussion paper, *Financial Reporting of Risk—Proposals for a Statement of Business Risk*.
>
> Its vision is a new statement in the annual report in which companies would identify key risks, report actions they have taken to manage them and describe how they measure those risks. In highlighting risks, the statement of business risk would pick out the sources of uncertainty and volatility that have the greatest impact on return...
>
> Should companies adopt the statement, investment markets would see fewer surprises, better informed reaction to external news, stronger investor protection and more visible reporting on stewardship.[2]

A formula for share valuation

In order to value a share, a number of assumptions are made. One of those assumptions is market efficiency, as discussed earlier, and another is that all investors are 'risk averse'. Risk aversion means that people do not like risk and prefer a certain or less risky return to a more risky return that has the same expected payoff. For example, given the certainty of receiving $50, or the gamble on the flip of an unbiased coin of receiving $100 for heads and $0 for tails, risk-averse investors will choose the certain receipt of $50, even though the expected payoff of the gamble is also $50 (expected payoff = 0.5(100) + 0.5(0) = 50). In this example, it usually takes a reduction in the certain amount to $30 or so for most investors to prefer to take their chances with the gamble.

Estimating the appropriate price for an organisation's shares is a most difficult task, although the principles governing the valuation of shares are relatively simple. When we estimate the value of a share, we are really determining what the purchaser is willing to pay for it. This, in turn, depends on what cash flows the purchaser is going to get from the share. The cash flows would normally be dividend payments while the share is owned and then the price at which it can be sold in the future. To allow for the 'time value of money', both of these cash returns must be discounted to give their equivalent value today, commonly known as present value. An explanation of present value computations may be found in Appendix 3.

Before developing a share valuation formula, some symbolic notation must be introduced:

D_t = Cash dividends to be received in year t. Thus D_1 represents dividends to be received at the end of year 1.

P_t = Share price in year t. Thus P_1 represents the share price at the end of year 1.

r = The discount rate, or the return investors require from their investment.

---

[2] R. Hodgkinson, in *Accountancy* (International Edition), February 1998, p. 73.

Investors buying a share now for P_0 and holding it for one year expect to earn rate r on the original investment of P_0, so they will receive $P_0 + rP_0$ at the end of one year, or $P_0(1 + r)$. The expected returns are paid in the form of a dividend, D_1, and resale of the share at a price P_1. We can use this relationship to define the price of a share in terms of its future cash flows.

$$P_0(1 + r) = D_1 + P_1$$

$$P_0 = \frac{D_1}{(1 + r)} + \frac{P_1}{(1 + r)} \tag{1}$$

Equation (1) states that the price of a share today is determined by discounting expected future cash receipts at the investor's *required rate of return*. Thus, if a share is expected in one year's time to pay a dividend (D_1) of $0.70, to sell for a price (P_1) of $10.30, and investors require a return (r) of 10 per cent, the share value can be calculated as:

$$P_0 = \frac{0.70}{(1 + 0.1)} + \frac{10.30}{(1 + 0.1)}$$

$$P_0 = \$10$$

P_1, the price received at the end of one year, is the amount another investor will be willing to pay in one year's time; that is, the value of future dividends and the second investor's final selling price. This involves the same formula as for the first investor, with different subscripts for time. P_1 will therefore depend upon dividends to be received in year 2 and the price at the end of year 2, thus:

$$P_1 = \frac{D_2}{(1 + r)} + \frac{P_2}{(1 + r)} \tag{2}$$

Using equation (2) to replace P_1 in equation (1) gives:

$$P_0 = \frac{D_1}{(1 + r)} + \frac{1}{(1 + r)} \left[\frac{D_2}{(1 + r)} + \frac{P_2}{(1 + r)} \right]$$

$$P_0 = \frac{D_1}{(1 + r)} + \frac{D_2}{(1 + r)^2} + \frac{P_2}{(1 + r)^2} \tag{3}$$

Applying the same logic to replace P_2 and all future prices gives:

$$P_0 = \frac{D_1}{(1 + r)} + \frac{D_2}{(1 + r)^2} + \frac{D_3}{(1 + r)^3} + \quad \ldots \tag{4}$$

This general formula is:

$$P_{t-1} = \sum_{t=1}^{n} \frac{D_t}{(1 + r)^t} \tag{5}$$

If the same level of dividends is expected to be received forever (which is unlikely in most cases), equation (5) reduces to a perpetuity and can be written as:

$$P_t = \frac{D}{r}$$

Equation (5) states that the price of a share is determined by the *discounted value of all expected future dividends*. Thus, to estimate a share value, all that is required is a knowledge of future dividends and the appropriate required rate of return. This is where the difficulties begin!

Future dividends depend on two factors: future earnings of the organisation and the payout ratio (i.e. the proportion of earnings that are paid out in dividends). This is measured as d:

$$d = \frac{\text{dividends per share}}{\text{earnings per share}} = 1 - b$$

where b is the 'retention ratio' or rate of retention of profits in the firm

There is a trade-off between paying dividends now and paying them in the future. Higher levels of profit retention reduce the current dividends but increase the potential for larger dividends in the future as a result of better returns on the higher investment. Although dividends now are attractive to shareholders, if the organisation does not retain some profits for reinvestment, then future profits will suffer. As is discussed below, whereas future dividends are likely to stay the same over time, future earnings will not. The growth in future earnings (g) is a function of the retention ratio (b) and the organisation's profitability or its return on its investment (r). The relationship between these variables is $g = b \times r$.

The rate used to discount expected future dividends is composed of the time value of money, which is measured by the risk-free rate of return (R_f), and the riskiness of the organisation's dividend payments. This is much the same as the way the rate of return on an investment includes both a risk-free rate and a premium for the riskiness of the investment. This discount rate is known as the *required rate of return*, because it is the minimum rate that investors require to be compensated for investing in the organisation. If they do not anticipate earning this rate, they will not invest in that organisation.

The requirement of an additional return in order to compensate for risk introduces the relationship between risk and return. Because investors are assumed to be risk averse, as discussed earlier in this section, they must be compensated for taking a risk. The higher the risk of the investment, the higher the rate of return required.

Case 11.1 Required rate of return

Consider the current interest rate you can receive by depositing $10 000 in a major bank for six months. Now consider what you would want as a return for investing in the following alternatives:

(a) an unsecured loan
(b) a major company listed on the stock exchange
(c) an unknown diamond exploration company in Iceland

Why has your required rate of return changed (assuming it has)?

Both future dividends and the required rate of return are going to be influenced by factors affecting the organisation and by those affecting the whole economy. Some factors affecting the organisation will be captured by accounting numbers; others will not. Those not captured by accounting numbers include changes to the level of risk, the quality of management, and changes to the demand for the organisation's product. Factors affecting the whole economy include the state of the economy, the level of interest rates and inflation, wages policies, taxation policies and the current stage in the economic cycle.

Changes in either expected future dividends or the required rate of return will change the share price now. For example, the perceived riskiness of the organisation may change because of the bankruptcy of another organisation in the same industry, and this will increase the required rate of return for owners. This in turn will decrease the organisation's share price, other things being equal.

Rates of return

In order to understand the behaviour of share prices, a clear distinction must be drawn between *realised rates of return, expected rates of return* and *required rates of return*. The meaning of the term 'required rate of return' has already been discussed. This is the investor's minimum rate of return to compensate for the risk of the investment.

Two other rates of return often referred to relate to the organisation or investment. The expected rate of return is the rate that an organisation or investment is expected to earn, before the event. It relates to the future. The realised or actual rate of return is the rate that the organisation or investment actually realised or earned. It is measured after the event, and so relates to the past. It is a guide, though often unreliable, as to what investors will receive in the future. The expected rate of return will equal the actual rate only if expectations are correct. In equilibrium, the required rate equals the expected rate of return for an organisation's shares (and all other assets). The formula for expected rate of return is:

$$E(R) = \frac{E(P_1) - P_0 + E(D_1)}{P_0}, \text{where } R = \text{return and } E(\ ) \text{ refers to an expected value.}$$

This means that expected return is the difference in share price expected over the period plus the dividends expected, relative to (or scaled by) the initial investment in the share.

The relationship between expected return and share price is negative. If a share price goes up, the expected return goes down, because the dollar returns received are scaled by a larger initial investment. Conversely, if a share price goes down, the expected return goes up, because the dollar returns are a relatively greater proportion of the lower share price.

As new information is received about an organisation, it changes either the required rate of return (if the information changes the risk factor) or the expected rate of return (if the information changes the expected future dividends).

For example, if investors expect that the future returns from an organisation will exceed the return they require for an investment of that type, they will buy that organisation's shares, bidding up the share price and thus driving the expected rate of return downward. This process will continue until the expected rate of return is equal to the required rate of return, at which point the share price is in equilibrium. For example, suppose an organisation's shares are selling for $10 each and for companies of this type investors require a 10 per cent return. If investors expect to be able to sell each share in one year's time for $12, the expected return is 20 per cent:

$$
\begin{aligned}
E(R) \quad &= \quad \frac{E(P_1) - P_0 + E(D_1)}{P_0} \\[2mm]
&= \quad \frac{(\$12 - \$10)}{\$10} \\[2mm]
&= \quad \frac{\$2}{\$10} \\[2mm]
&= \quad 20\%
\end{aligned}
$$

Investors will therefore wish to buy the share at its current price of $10, and the buying pressure will rapidly push up the price to $10.91. At this new price the expected return is 10 per cent.

$$
\begin{aligned}
E(R) \quad &= \quad \frac{(\$12 - \$10.91)}{\$10.91} \\[2mm]
&= \quad \frac{\$1.09}{\$10.91} \\[2mm]
&= \quad 10\%
\end{aligned}
$$

Expected and required returns are now equal and the share price is in equilibrium. Alternatively, if actual future returns are less than expected and therefore do not match investors' required returns, investors will revise their expectations downwards. They will sell the organisation's shares, driving prices down. The lower share price will result in a higher expected return. This process will continue until share prices fall to a level at which expected and required returns are again in equilibrium.

In general, a disequilibrium is restored to equilibrium by an excess of buying (if expected rate of return is greater than required rate of return) or an excess of selling (if expected rate of return is less than required rate of return). The excess of buying or selling changes the price and realigns the expected rate of return with the required rate of return.

The management of risk and return

Financial managers can seek to maximise owners' wealth by choosing financial policies that increase expected future earnings and/or decrease risk, in order to maximise the organisation's share price.

However (except for monopolies), once the assets of the entity are being combined in the most efficient way, in an efficient market, future earnings from these assets can be increased only if risk is increased, and risk can be decreased only if expected future earnings are decreased. The higher the expected return (reflected in R), the higher will be the price of the share. The higher the expected risk (reflected in r), the lower the price of the share. An organisation that may achieve high expected returns, but at great risk of failure, may have a share price that is less than that of an organisation offering modest but more certain returns.

Changing both return and risk will change both expected and required rates of return, but shareholders may not be any better off.

So the implication for financial managers seeking to act in the owners' best interests is to organise all of the organisation's activities efficiently and to manage the risks taken in line with the expected profitability of the organisation's projects. An important function of financial management is therefore to appraise the risk–return trade-off, and determine whether changes in return are desirable after allowing for changes in risk. In some cases it may be acceptable for management to reduce returns, providing the reduction in risk offers sufficient compensation. The objective to be pursued, then, is the attainment of maximum return at an acceptable level of risk.

The role of financial management

The major areas of responsibility in financial management are:

1. Financing or capital structure decisions (i.e. how the organisation is financed).
2. Dividend decisions, or how much dividend should be paid.
3. Investment decisions, or which projects or activities the organisation should undertake.

These three areas will be discussed separately, but such a clear division of roles does not exist. The elements of financial performance form an integrated system, and financial decision making interacts with all the organisation's activities, as illustrated in Figure 11.4.

Financial managers are unlikely to have control over all the decisions to be discussed, but they will usually be able to make suggestions and apply pressure to managers in areas where performance could improve.

The first step is to formulate strategies to achieve the objective of owners' wealth maximisation. This includes the assessment of and choice between alternative avenues for investment of funds. This important function of management planning is discussed more fully in Chapter 24, on long-term planning. The financial manager can be expected to aid in the identification of alternatives, opportunities and constraints. This involves an appraisal of

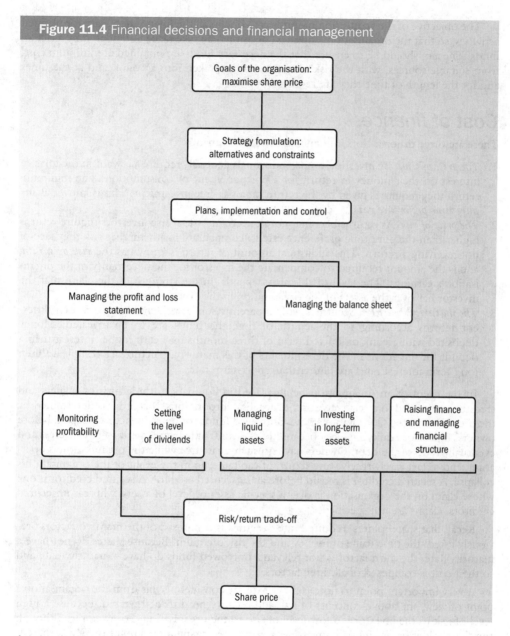

Figure 11.4 Financial decisions and financial management

the organisation's present and future economic environment, including factors such as the availability and cost of finance, the levels of demand for the organisation's products, and whether a boom or slump is anticipated.

Financial management and the balance sheet

The financing decision

The investment strategy chosen by management will require both an investment decision and a financing decision. The investment decision refers to the choice of the activity in which to engage and Chapter 24 discusses techniques to assist in this process. The financing decision concerns the means by which the project is financed and is the focus of this section.

The objective of the acquisition of funds is to obtain all the finance necessary for planned activities, so that the organisation's business decisions can take place unhindered by a lack of funds. The aim should be to ensure that the necessary funds are obtained at minimum cost, from suitable sources, with the risk of such financing taken into account, and at the times and for the length of time they are required.

Cost of finance

There are three major factors influencing the cost of finance.

1. *The price of time.* By investing funds, individuals generally require a reward in the form of interest on their money in return for a postponement of consumption. The minimum return they require is given by the return on a risk-free investment. This is known as the *pure time preference rate.*
2. *The price of risk.* As returns become more uncertain, risk-averse investors require returns higher than the pure time preference rate to compensate for the higher risk they face of not receiving a return. This additional amount of return is known as the *risk premium*, and is the amount required to compensate the investor for the uncertainty of the organ-isation's earnings. The level of this also depends on the strength of the claim that the investor has over the assets of the organisation in the event of its collapse.
3. *The maturity structure.* Securities with apparently similar risk characteristics offer differ-ent returns according to the length of time the funds are to be invested. Money deposited with a bank on a fixed term of three months may earn higher interest than a deposit for one month. The determinants of this maturity structure are complex. Often long-term interest rates are higher than short-term rates.

In the event of an organisation being placed in liquidation, the claims of owners and creditors are settled in a relatively strict order. For corporations, this order is determined by the provisions of the Corporations Law. Borrowed funds (or debt finance) are repaid before owners' funds (or equity finance) because of the contractual agreement to pay interest and eventually redeem the debt. Owners have no such guarantee while the organisation is oper-ating, and in fact rarely receive any return of capital, even in the event of the organisation's collapse. A secured creditor is repaid before an unsecured creditor. A secured creditor is one whose claim on the organisation is over a specific asset or level of assets, whereas unsecured creditors' claims are not specified.

Recall that shareholders' required rate of return is composed of the first two factors pre-viously listed: the time value of money and the risk premium. Because shares do not have a maturity date, the third factor is not relevant. Borrowed funds do have a maturity date and so their cost is composed of all three factors.

A very important point to note is that, if we are considering this from the organisation's point of view, the above concepts of risk and security need to be reversed, because a high level of risk to the investor is a low level of risk to the organisation. For example, although the shareholder has a high-risk investment, from the organisation's point of view a share is the safest source of finance because it cannot be forced to pay regular dividends to share-holders and shareholders cannot force it to repay their capital.

However, this does not mean that equity finance is a *free* source of funds just because there is no obligation to pay dividends. In fact, consistent with the relationship between risk and return, low risk to the organisation is accompanied by a high cost. The cost of equity finance is higher than the cost of debt finance, because of the higher risk premium required by the owners. This is consistent with what we have already noted regarding the risk–return relationship. Rates of return for various sources of finance vary according to the riskiness of the claim, with the secured debt holder accepting a comparatively low return, whereas the owner expects a high return to compensate for the lack of security. The cost of equity finance is implicit rather than explicit.

For example, shareholders expect to receive their required rate of return from their investment either in the form of dividends or in the increased value of their shares. The share price can be expected to increase if the organisation is profitably reinvesting its earnings, because the future economic value or market value of the organisation has increased and this will be reflected in a higher share price. If shareholders do not receive their required rate of return, by the process described earlier, demand for the organisation's shares will fall, causing the share price to fall. This fall in the share price is an illustration of the implicit cost of equity finance.

In addition to the high implicit cost of equity finance, borrowed funds have the advantage of interest payments usually being tax deductible, which lowers the effective (or after-tax) cost of this source of finance to the organisation if it is subject to taxation.

Level of debt

The use of debt in an organisation's financial structure is known as leverage. It gets its name from the effect it has of 'levering up' (or increasing) returns to owners on a given level of equity investment by increasing the asset base from which earnings are generated. Because debt requires only a fixed rate of return, if the organisation can earn more than this fixed return on its borrowed funds, the return to owners will increase without a change in their investment.

If, for example, an organisation borrows at 8 per cent and invests at 10 per cent, shareholders need to contribute no additional funds but will receive an increase in income of $2 for every $100 that the organisation borrows and invests. This effect can be further magnified by the tax deductibility of interest payments effectively increasing the net gain and hence the amount available to shareholders. But recall that in an efficient market the return to an efficient organisation cannot be increased without also increasing risk. The increase in risk that occurs in the case of leverage is part of the organisation's *financial risk* (as discussed earlier in the chapter). It is the risk that, if the organisation cannot employ its borrowed funds to earn more than it has to pay in interest payments, the returns to owners are reduced by the use of leverage. In the previous example, should the return on investments fall to 6 per cent, part of the earnings from other ventures that were previously accruing to shareholders would be diverted to pay debt holders. Also, the ultimate risk to owners from the use of leverage is the loss of control of the organisation. If sufficient funds are not available to meet interest charges and if creditors are not paid, they have rights to claim those payments from the organisation. In particular, secured creditors have the right to seize control of the organisation and to liquidate it if necessary.

Example: *The effects of leverage*

Ivan Ltd, a new firm, is going to invest in a project costing $1 million that is expected to earn $200 000 per annum. Two alternative methods of financing are:

(a) Issue 1 million shares at $1.
(b) Issue 500 000 shares at $1 and borrow $500 000 at 10 per cent.

The effects of these alternatives on the return to the firm and the return to shareholders can be forecast as follows:

	CAPITAL STRUCTURE	
	A	B
	(Unlevered structure)	*(Levered structure)*
Earnings before interest and tax	200 000	200 000
less Interest	–	50 000
Net profit before tax	200 000	150 000
less Tax (40%)	80 000	60 000
Net profit after tax	120 000	90 000
divided by	1 million shares	500 000 shares
Earnings per share	**12c**	**18c**

Net profit after tax is higher if the firm is all equity financed, because no interest charges are made against profit. However, when assessed on a per-share basis, in terms of earnings the effects of leverage in amplifying shareholders' returns can be clearly seen.

The effect on the share price of the two levels of EPS depends on the required rate of return at each level of financial risk. The result of the financial risk involved with option B can be seen by forecasting the situation in which the project does not return its expected $200 000, but returns only $80 000 instead.

	CAPITAL STRUCTURE	
	A	B
	(Unlevered structure)	*(Levered structure)*
Earnings before interest and tax	80 000	80 000
less Interest	–	50 000
Net profit before tax	80 000	30 000
less Tax (40%)	32 000	12 000
Net profit after tax	48 000	18 000
divided by	1 million shares	500 000 shares
Earnings per share	**4.8c**	**3.6c**

When earnings before interest and tax (EBIT) are lower, the interest charges have reduced the earnings per share of option B to below that of option A.

It is extremely difficult to determine the optimal amount of leverage for an organisation to adopt, as it is determined by four factors, each with its own variables:

1. The expected difference between the return on investment and the cost of debt. This gives a greater range for EBIT to vary before the levered option reduces returns to owners below that of the unlevered option.
2. The size and stability of the organisation's earnings stream. This is because a high and/or steady level of earnings can be relied on to meet the necessary interest payments, whereas a volatile and/or low level of earnings may more readily produce a negative earnings number after interest payments have been met. This is demonstrated in the example of 'Unstable Earnings' below. The two firms are identical except for the stability of their earnings streams. It is obvious that Stable Ltd can safely sustain a higher level of leverage than Unstable Ltd, which could encounter problems in year 4. If creditors take control of Unstable Ltd in year 4, the profits of year 5 may never eventuate.

3. The liquidity of the organisation's assets. The higher the cash flow of the organisation and/or the more liquid its assets, the more likely it is to be able to meet its interest payments when they are due. Interest payments can be met by converting liquid assets into cash when funds are not flowing in from trading operations.

4. The use of short-term debt. The use of short-term debt increases the need for the organisation to be reasonably liquid, because both interest and principal must be repaid over a shorter period.

Example: *Unstable earnings*

The following are details of two similar firms:

	Stable Ltd (A)	Unstable Ltd (B)
Earnings	$1 000 000	$1 000 000
Investment	$2 000 000	$2 000 000
Debt finance as % of investment	50%	50%
Debt finance in dollars	$1 000 000	$1 000 000
Interest rate on debt	10%	10%
Annual interest bill	$100 000	$100 000
Earnings stream	Even	Uneven

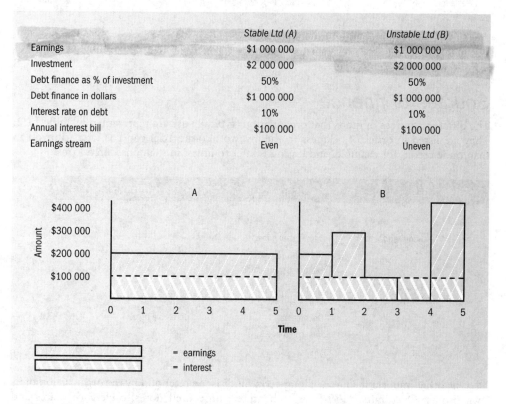

The effect on the organisation's share price of its use of leverage depends on how the market assesses the trade-off between the increased risk and the expected increase in return. The above discussion focuses on the EPS effect even though, as we have observed earlier in this chapter, an increase in EPS does not necessarily imply that shareholders' wealth is being maximised. The effect on its share price of a change in the organisation's policies cannot be determined in a simple example, because the risk–return trade-off determined by shareholders depends on a vast number of factors that are impossible to summarise or simplify. However, the likely maximum and minimum effects on shareholders' earnings from the increased risk can be determined. This is why it is useful to calculate the EPS effect.

As the percentage of leverage used by an organisation increases, owners' returns are initially 'levered up'. However, once a certain critical level of leverage is reached, any further borrowing will decrease returns to owners. At high levels of debt the amount of earnings committed to interest payments is high; further debt finance can only be obtained at a high price and the risk of bankruptcy is also quite high. The level of leverage that produces diminishing returns to owners cannot be deduced from a set of data. However, it seems likely that this level might differ between industries. Differences in the levels of leverage are observed to be quite high between different industries, whereas the differences within any industry are quite small, as illustrated in Table 11.1 which compares the percentage of debt finance used by banking companies with that used by media companies. Differences between industries' usage of leverage might be based on the riskiness of the industry and the type of assets each industry invests in.

Table 11.1 Debt as a percentage of total investment, 1997

Banking		Media	
Commonwealth Bank	94.2%	News Corporation	46.2%
Westpac	93.1%	Fairfax	49.6%

The decision rule regarding the effects of leverage on EPS and share price is quite simple: increasing amounts of leverage that increases EPS should be used as long as the effects on the share price are positive.

Sources of finance

The different sources of funds that organisations typically use are represented in Table 11.2. They are listed in order of riskiness to the investor: commercial paper is safer to invest in than trade credit, for example, and leasing is safer to invest in than unsecured loans.

Table 11.2 Sources of funds used by organisations, in order of riskiness

	Debt	Equity
Short term	Commercial paper	
	Overdraft	
	Factoring, trade credit	
Long term	Lease	
	Mortgages	
	Debentures	Convertible notes
	Unsecured notes	Preference shares
		Ordinary shares

One other important source of long-term funds is the retention by the organisation of its own profits. Overdrafts, mortgages, debentures, unsecured notes, preference shares and ordinary shares are defined in the Glossary. Commercial paper describes short-term securities issued by an organisation on which the issuer promises to pay the holder the face value of the security at maturity. Factoring is the purchase of accounts receivable. Trade credit is the use of credit terms granted by suppliers as a source of finance for the length of the credit period. A lease is an agreement to grant the use of property to a lessee in exchange for a series of payments over a period of time. Convertible notes are debt instruments that can be changed into ordinary shares.

Maturity structure

Maturity structure decisions involve questions about whether investing and financing should be short-term or long-term and whether the maturity of liabilities should be matched with the maturity of assets. In most cases the maturity of assets is substantially determined by the nature of the organisation's activities. For example, steel-making requires a heavy investment in long-term productive assets such as blast furnaces, whereas a retail store has substantial short-term assets such as inventory.

Finance raised as short-term debt is often cheaper than long-term debt and some short-term sources of finance are free. For example, the use of trade credit as a source of finance has no cost provided payments are made prior to the due dates. One reason for short-term debt being cheaper is that the organisation is not charged a liquidity premium by its creditors. It might therefore appear that the best financial policy would be to finance with as much short-term debt as possible. However, the financing of long-term investments, such as a new factory, entirely from short-term sources of finance, such as overdrafts and trade credit, would create a number of problems, including:

- There would be uncertainty about the future availability of finance.
- The future cost of finance would be unknown.
- There would be the constant problem of refinancing when debts mature.

There are, therefore, considerable risks in using short-term sources of finance for long-term investments. These risks are increased by long-term assets not usually being very liquid and hence unable to be readily sold to meet a shortfall in the organisation's finances.

Long-term finance for long-term investment assures continuity of funding and known finance costs. Conversely, it is generally undesirable to use long-term finance for temporary investments because this would entail a continuing burden of finance costs and the repayment of debt, long after the need for the borrowed funds had ceased. An idealised financing pattern is represented in Figure 11.5. Here, long-term finance is used for all long-term assets and *permanent current assets*. Permanent current assets are also known as working capital and represent that level of current assets permanently held by the organisation. Although current assets are constantly being converted into cash, a certain proportion represents a permanent investment. If inventory, receivables and other current assets are reduced below some minimum level, the organisation's operating activities will be disrupted. For example, organisations need a minimum level of inventory and cash at bank to operate successfully. Current asset requirements above this level, caused by seasonal factors or by a particular project or customer, are considered temporary and may be financed by short-term sources of funds. Organisations may experience seasonal demand patterns; breweries, for example, have peak activity and require higher current assets in the summer months. At the end of the peak season these current assets will have been converted into cash and need not be replaced. If these temporary assets have been financed short-term, the cash received can then be used to repay the finance.

The idealised pattern of Figure 11.5 is hardly ever encountered in practice because of the difficulty of determining accurately the temporary need for current assets. Furthermore, different industries and management objectives might require different policies regarding this. A conservative management, with a heavy investment in fixed assets, might wish to protect itself from the possibility of having to repay short-term borrowings when it has little or no cash reserves. This could be achieved by financing some temporary current assets from long-term sources of funds. The volume of short-term credit required during peak seasons would be reduced and the organisation would have surplus finance in periods of little activity. This surplus could be invested in marketable securities, to provide a store of liquidity that was available for conversion to cash as required. A more aggressive management, with substantial current assets, might finance some permanent current assets short-term, to minimise financing costs. The organisation would rely on liquidating current assets if difficulties arose in refinancing.

The appropriate policy to adopt is related to the method of managing current assets, which is discussed in the next section. The most important pitfall to avoid is the excessive use of short-term finance for permanent or long-term investments. At the same time, within the limits of prudence it is desirable to make as much use as possible of 'free' sources of finance such as trade credit.

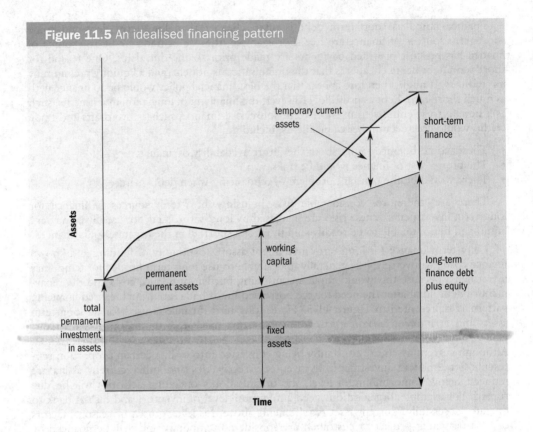

Figure 11.5 An idealised financing pattern

Other factors influencing the choice of finance

There are a number of other factors influencing the choice of finance, including:

1. The volume of funds required. Share issues, for example, are costly and time consuming to arrange and are used only to raise large amounts of money to be invested in long-term projects.
2. Transaction costs involved with raising the finance, for example the cost of negotiation, legal fees, stamp duties and bank fees.
3. Any restrictive conditions placed on the organisation by creditors such as in debenture trust deeds.
4. How permanent the source of funds is.
5. Prevailing conditions in the capital markets. For example, if an organisation wishes to issue shares, but management believes that the shares are currently undervalued, the firm may temporarily use debt finance in the hope that share prices will shortly rise.
6. Tax effects. Organisations seek to gain the tax advantage or to give the tax advantage to creditors/owners and thus lower the cost of funds. Tax effects are of major importance in financing decisions and considerable effort is devoted to structuring financing arrangements so as to maximise tax advantages.
7. The anticipated growth of the organisation, to ensure that funds are available to enable growth to occur.

Managing current assets

Current asset management, also known as working capital management, is linked with the management of liquidity. The organisation's working capital (the excess of current assets over current liabilities) shows the extent to which short-term assets are 'covered' by short-term liabilities and, as a result, the extent to which they are financed from long-term sources of funds. The term 'working capital' is used because it refers to that portion of long-term finance or capital that is constantly being converted from assets to cash and back to assets.

Current assets typically represent 40 per cent or more of an organisation's assets. They are constantly changing and therefore require careful attention. One of the most common causes of business failure is *under-capitalisation*. This means that insufficient long-term finance has been raised to support operations and there is therefore little or no working capital. The consequence is a relentless sequence of refinancing and liquidity problems. *Over-capitalisation* is less common but can also be a problem. If an organisation has excess working capital and an accumulation of liquidity, the liquid assets are likely to be earning less than it costs to finance them.

Another common cause of business failure is inefficient management of current assets. Excessive inventories and poor control over accounts receivable lead to an increased volume of current assets, to increased costs and perhaps to liquidity problems.

Current asset management is closely related to the organisation's operating cycle and the associated pattern of cash flows. A typical operating cycle for a manufacturing concern is shown in Figure 11.6. Ordinarily the organisation is required to expend cash on acquiring assets before it can produce and receive payment for its products. This is a particular problem if it is rapidly growing, since increasing sales require an immediate expansion of accounts receivable and inventories. As full operating capacity is approached, new fixed assets must also be acquired. As there will be a delay before cash inflows from sales occur, finance has to be obtained for this asset expansion. This in turn entails an obligation to service the finance obtained. Growth can therefore lead to serious cash-flow problems unless there is effective management of current assets and maintenance of adequate liquidity.

The primary activities involved in current asset management are the selection of the optimal quantities of each current asset to be held, and raising the finance required to fund those assets. The financing question having been previously considered, it remains to discuss the setting of optimal asset quantities.

Figure 11.6 The cash-flow cycle for a manufacturing organisation

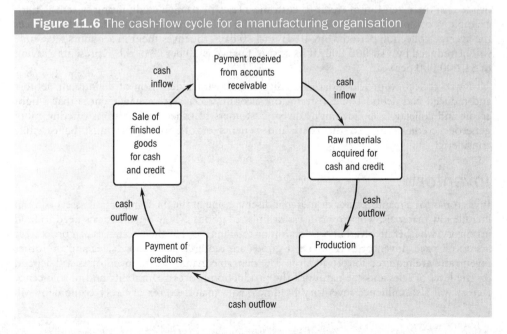

Cash and marketable securities

These represent the organisation's primary source of liquidity. Sufficient cash must be held to enable the organisation to conduct its normal cash transactions. The receipt of cash from debtors and sales cannot be relied upon entirely to meet cash payments as they become due, as asset purchases and unforeseen expenses might arise and a sudden shortage of cash might endanger relations with employees or suppliers if wages or accounts cannot be paid on time. Also, the loss of discounts can prove costly and damage to a credit rating may prove constricting in arranging future finance. In addition to normal needs, organisations sometimes hold cash and marketable securities for precautionary and speculative purposes. Precautionary holdings are particularly necessary when cash flows are unpredictable and sudden shortages arise. Speculative holdings by business enterprises are not common, but an increase in cash and marketable securities may precede new initiatives such as takeover activity.

The disadvantage of holding cash is that it generates little or no return, while it costs as much to finance as any other asset. Costs of holding cash include bank charges, transaction costs and opportunity costs such as interest forgone. For this reason organisations endeavour to minimise their cash balances and hold marketable securities as reserves of liquidity. The financial manager's task is greatly simplified when a line of credit such as a bank overdraft can be established, for use whenever unanticipated liquidity needs occur. This enables the organisation to borrow funds as and when they are needed, up to a certain limit, and to pay interest only on the funds that are actually borrowed. However, fees such as unused-limit fees apply to overdraft limits that are not being drawn on. The decision as to what level of cash should be held is a complex and important one, and a cash budget should be prepared to enable efficient planning. Preparation of the cash budget is dealt with in Chapter 25.

Accounts receivable

Credit facilities are offered to customers to increase profitability through increased sales as customers are attracted by the convenience of buying on credit. Against the increased revenue, however, must be offset the costs of financing the funds tied up in receivables, the costs of administering customers' accounts and the losses through bad debts. These costs are reduced by ensuring strict credit control (e.g. by collecting debts rapidly) and by being prudent in the extension of credit to customers (e.g. by using a credit rating system). If, for example, a company makes an average of $1 000 000 of credit sales per day and it reduces the average collection period from 40 days to 30 days, the investment in accounts receivable will be reduced by $10 000 000. If its cost of finance is 10 per cent, this represents a saving of $1 000 000 per year.

Rapid collection provides better credit control, earlier detection of delinquent debtors and reduced bad debts. The constraint on accounts receivable management is that a tight credit and collections policy might divert customers to other organisations offering more generous credit terms, so the costs and benefits of offering credit must be carefully considered.

Inventory

Inventories for a manufacturer or merchandiser are one of the most important assets and can include raw materials, work in progress or finished goods. Many organisations need to hold inventory, whether involved in production or retailing, so that their activities can proceed at a smooth pace. Inventories of finished goods are required to support sales and the other inventories are required for production. The desirable magnitude of inventories will depend on the level of sales and the nature of the production process. Durability and obsolescence factors will also influence inventory holdings, so a manufacturer of heavy equipment will have a very different inventory policy from a producer of dairy products. Inventory holdings involve significant carrying costs, such as the cost of the funds invested in inventory, storage, insurance and losses due to theft, deterioration and obsolescence. In order to minimise these costs, it is desirable to *turn inventory over* (sell and replace) rapidly. However, there are limits on the reduction of inventory that can be achieved. As inventory is reduced, re-orders must be made more frequently, and ordering and shipping costs increase. There is also a greater probability of inventory shortages, leading to lost sales and disruption of production. The appropriate level of inventory minimises all of these costs, balancing the benefits of carrying inventory against the costs.

In summary, the organisation needs to ensure that it has an adequate level of working capital and that sufficient liquidity is maintained, or that a line of credit has been established. For each class of current assets a balance must be struck between the cost of holding too much of the asset and the cost of holding too little.

Financial management and the profit and loss statement

The financial manager will generally have little direct control over revenues and operating costs, as these will be in the hands of sales and operating managers. There is, however, a strong indirect influence via the effect of balance-sheet decisions about current and long-term assets, because these decisions are an important determinant of the organisation's sales capacity and cost structure. The one cost over which the financial manager does have some direct influence is the cost of finance, which may substantially affect profitability.

The financial manager may also be required to monitor profitability in order to determine whether investments are performing as planned and to ensure that appropriate financing decisions are being made.

Dividend policy

After profits have been earned, one further important decision to be made by corporate entities is the proportion of profit to be distributed to the owners and the proportion to be reinvested within the organisation. The decision should depend on which alternative, either dividend payments or reinvestment, will ultimately produce the greater wealth for the owners. There are a number of different points of view about the value and effect of a corporation's dividend policy and these are discussed in the next sections.

Dividends increase share price

Dividends are often viewed as the return to the owners in much the same way that interest is earned on funds deposited in a bank account. From this viewpoint, organisations that pay higher dividends would be valued more by shareholders and would generally command a higher share price, other things being equal. A variation of this viewpoint is that earnings that are paid as dividends are less risky than earnings that are retained in the organisation.

However, the total return to shareholders is based on all of the earnings of the organisation, and is returned to them both as dividends and as the change in share price. The share valuation model that we discussed earlier in this chapter depends only on dividends, but it is not just the current dividend that determines the value of the share but also the sum of future dividends over the life of the organisation. The claim that dividend payments are less risky ignores the fact that both dividends and share price changes are generated by the organisation's earnings, and therefore all are equally risky.

The article featured in Figure 11.7 appears to suggest that the prospect of greater dividends will lead to a change in the share price.

Figure 11.7 Do dividends affect share prices?

Shares ride higher on hopes of bigger payout

For the third consecutive year speculators are fuelling a record run-up in Common-wealth Bank shares amid expectations of a surprising profit, due next week...

Recurrent speculation that CBA could increase its dividend payout ratio or pay a special dividend at its August 12 profit result has not impressed bank executives, who fear investors are clamouring for shares to take advantage of any special payout...

In the weeks leading to the 1995–96 full-year results, the shares gained more than $1.50, rising from about $10 in early June to nudge the $11.50 mark.

Last year, the price jumped from $14 in early June to a high of $16.80 by mid-August when the full-year profit was announced...

Despite warnings of tough trading conditions and flat earnings for the current financial year, investors traditionally rush the stock for the dividend payout.

Australian Financial Review, 3 August 1998

Dividends do not affect share price

Following the preceding argument, it could be asked why shareholders should care whether they are paid a dividend or whether the funds are retained in the organisation and used to earn higher amounts in the next year. (If the funds cannot be used to earn at least share-holders' required rate of return, they should be paid to shareholders.) If shareholders want to receive a cash flow from their investment they can sell some of their shares and create their own dividend. In this scenario it is assumed that there are no taxation effects that would induce shareholders to prefer dividend income or capital gains, and there are no transaction costs. For example, if a shareholder owns 100 shares valued at $1 each in a company that pays no dividends but earns 20 per cent return in 20X1, then at the end of 20X1 the shares should have increased in value to $1.20 each. If the shareholders would prefer to have received a 12 per cent dividend, they can (costlessly) sell ten shares, which would provide (in the absence of a taxation effect) an income of $12 and thus a cash return on investment of 12 per cent. The remaining shares are worth $108 ($1.20 \times 90$ shares), so the value of the shareholder's investment has also increased. This is an illustration of the famous Modigliani–Miller argument of 'dividend irrelevance', which claims that the dividend policy of the organisation doesn't matter.

Clientele effect

In practice dividend policy does matter because shareholders are subject to income tax and cannot sell their shares to gain income or reinvest dividends in shares without incurring transaction costs. The organisation also incurs transaction costs if it pays a dividend and then raises new finance to replace these funds (e.g. to finance its growth). A 'clientele effect' has been described, which suggests that an organisation will choose a dividend policy that is attractive to a particular group of shareholders, and will continue with that policy. There is a diversity of shareholder preferences with respect to dividends (ranging from no income/all capital gain to all income/no capital gain), preferences for current income, taxation effects, and so on. Given this diversity, no organisation could appeal to all shareholders, so each organisation chooses a clientele from this range and targets that group with its dividend policy.

Signalling

Another use of dividends, apart from satisfying the preferences of shareholders, is to signal information to the market. For example, a change in the amount of the dividend may signal that increased future earnings are anticipated. It has been observed that the actual amount of dividend per share paid by organisations is more stable over time than their earnings. Dividends do not vary from year to year in line with variations in earnings, but remain stable for a number of years. This implies that organisations aim at a steady pay-out amount. Adjustments to dividends, for example, if earnings have increased, occur only once it is evident that the increase in earnings is a sustainable one.

Reductions in dividends are viewed by the market as 'bad news' or an indication that the organisation is having considerable difficulties; hence they only occur in the most extreme circumstances. Increases in dividends, on the other hand, are viewed as 'good news', implying that the future prospects for the organisation are considered to be good. However, it has also been shown that dividend policy cannot 'fool' the market: an increase in dividends in the face of decreasing earnings would not normally result in a higher share price.

Dividend imputation

The introduction of dividend imputation in Australia in 1981 has removed the 'double taxation' of dividends, whereby dividends were paid out of after-tax profits and then taxed again as part of the shareholder's personal income. Now shareholders are entitled to receive a 'tax credit' for taxes paid at the company level. Dividends are now taxed only once, either at the level of the company or at the level of the shareholder. In effect, dividend imputation passes taxes paid at the company level on to shareholders.

The effects of dividend imputation on dividend policy in Australia are the subject of continuing investigation and research. Clearly, there is now a greater incentive for companies to pay as high a dividend to shareholders as possible, to maximise the benefit to shareholders. However, not all companies will have tax credits to pass on to their owners, and not all owners will benefit from receiving tax credits, because of the variety of tax situations possible for companies and for individuals. It is likely, therefore, that the clientele effect will remain an accurate description of the way diverse shareholder preferences and companies' payments of dividends are matched.

Ethical issues

1. Any time the directors of organisations initiate an increase in directors' fees, there is a conflict of interests between owners and management. Do you agree?
2. As a senior executive with Achieve Ltd, a company listed on the stock exchange, you have seen an internal document indicating that the soon to be reported profit figure for the current period is about 20 per cent higher than most analysts and commentators are expecting. You have the opportunity to buy a large number of shares in the company today, before the public announcement, and make a very large profit. Would you make the investment? Justify your actions.

Summary

This chapter has introduced you to many aspects of financial management. The financial manager's task is primarily concerned with investment, financing and dividend decisions in an endeavour to achieve the aim of the maximisation of wealth for the entity's shareholders. Decisions about the maturity of finance, the degree of leverage (or mix of debt and equity finance), the management of current assets and the maintenance of liquidity are crucial to financial performance and hence shareholder wealth. The unifying theme of the chapter was the interaction of risk and return. The balance struck between these two factors ultimately determines whether the organisation, and hence the financial manager, succeeds or fails in the goal of maximising owners' wealth.

 **Review exercises**

Discussion questions

11.1 What are some of the ways in which the financial manager can help to improve profitability?

11.2 Why is the management of *liquidity* and *leverage* important?

11.3 'Even if an organisation has excellent operating management, the quality of financial management will still be crucial to the organisation's success.' Discuss.

11.4 How might the managers' and shareholders' financial interests in an organisation differ? What steps may be taken to align their interests? Give some examples.

11.5 How might the cash-flow cycle of a retailer and manufacturer differ, and do the differences have any implications for financial management?

11.6 What is *business risk* and how does it differ from other types of risk an organisation may be subject to?

11.7 Which of the following items would be used *directly* in calculating the price of an organisation's shares in an efficient market?

(a) total sales
(b) last year's profit
(c) expected future profits
(d) last year's dividend
(e) expected future dividends
(f) the interest rate
(g) shareholders' required rate of return
(h) the organisation's rate of return on its investments

11.8 Why do share prices depend on expectations about risk and return? Use an example to assist with your explanation.

11.9 A major importing company, Wagner Trading Ltd, is planning a large expansion of its operating capacity and the board of directors is considering how the expansion should be financed. The head of the finance function has provided information that shows that the liquidity and leverage of the company compare favourably with the industry average figures. In the light of this information, one of the directors has suggested that they should finance the expansion using a short-term loan supported by a bank overdraft. Give reasons why you either agree or disagree with this suggestion.

11.10 'An adequate amount of working capital is essential to the continued well-being of an organisation.' Comment on this statement, using examples of different businesses, and discuss the factors that influence the level of working capital required.

11.11 'Retained earnings represent a free source of finance'. Explain why you agree or disagree with this statement.

11.12 From the viewpoint of the holder, rank claims against an organisation in order of riskiness. Very briefly explain why the risk differs between claims at the top and bottom of your ranking.

11.13 From the viewpoint of the organisation, rank the claims it issues in order of riskiness. Explain why you have ranked the claims in the order you have.

11.14 It is sometimes said that from the *owners'* point of view borrowing is a 'two-edged sword'. Explain what is meant by this statement.

11.15 The Glamorous Garment Co. Ltd experiences wide fluctuations in profits as fashions change. Nevertheless, the firm has embarked on a major expansion program and intends to build a new factory. Glamorous Garment's level of leverage is about average for the clothing industry, but in order to increase the benefits of leverage the firm's management intends to finance the new factory by making an issue of debentures. As consultant to the firm, do you consider debenture finance appropriate? Justify your answer.

 Problems

11.16 *Share price calculations*

Assuming other things remain equal, explain the effect on an organisation's share price of the following:

(a) Investors think the organisation has become less risky.
(b) Leverage is reduced.
(c) Asset turnover is increased.
(d) Investors become more risk averse.
(e) The return on government securities increases.
(f) The organisation's earnings exceed investors' expectations.
(g) Good news is received about future profits.
(h) Profit retention is increased.

11.17 *Financing decisions*

KL Ltd has issued capital valued at $500 000. It is seeking an additional $500 000 to finance a scheme which has been projected to have the following variations in earnings before interest and taxes (EBIT).

(a) How will shareholders' earnings per share (EPS) be affected if the firm finances the project by issuing $500 000 debentures at a rate of 15 per cent? Use the format illustrated to calculate your answer.

	A	B	C
EBIT	$100 000	$150 000	$200 000
Interest			
Net profit before tax			
Tax at 40 per cent			
Net profit after tax			
EPS			

(b) If EBIT is only $100 000, would EPS have been higher if the project had been financed by issuing an additional 500 000 $1 shares in KL Ltd, and not issuing the $500 000 debentures? (Ignore the dilution effect on the price of the shares in this question.)

11.18 *Share price calculations*

Calculate the expected share price of London Investments Ltd for each of the following, adopting the share valuation model described in the chapter.

(a) Dividends expected in perpetuity = 20 cents
Investors' required return = 10 per cent

(b) The dividend expected next year = 20 cents
The selling price expected next year = $2
Investors' required return = 10 per cent

(c) As a result of good news, investors expect dividends to rise to 30 cents in perpetuity. The required rate of return remains at 10 per cent.

(d) As a result of good news, investors expect dividends to rise to 30 cents next year and then fall back to 20 cents in future years. The required rate of return remains at 10 per cent.

(e) Although the expected dividend remains at 20 cents in perpetuity, investors think the firm has become more risky and raise their required rate of return to 20 per cent.

11.19 *Financing decisions*

The board of directors of Darwin Ltd is considering an expansion of the company. $2.5 million will be needed to finance this expansion. The existing capital structure comprises 2 million ordinary shares and no interest-bearing debt. Two methods of financing the expansion are under consideration:

(i) Issue 500 000 shares at $5 per share.

(ii) Issue 18 per cent 10-year debentures.

The company expects to pay company taxes at the rate of 40 cents in the dollar.

(a) Calculate the *earnings per share* under each alternative, assuming that the estimated earnings before interest and taxes after the expansion will be $1.8 million.

(b) If it is company policy to choose the alternative that maximises expected earnings per share, which method of financing would be selected?

11.20 *Dividend decision analysis*

At the annual general meeting of Retention Ltd a shareholder complained that no dividends had been paid for the last four years. The managing director replied that the policy of no dividends had been justified by increased profits and a steadily increasing return on paid-up capital. Using the following data, comment on the managing director's reply.

	Balances as at 30 June			
	20X1	20X2	20X3	20X4
	$000	$000	$000	$000
Net profit	100	100	120	130
Paid-up capital	1000	1000	1000	1000
Retained profits	100	210	330	460
Return on paid-up capital	10%	11%	12%	13%

11.21 *Share Price calculations*

Izarki Ltd has 50 000 issued shares, currently valued at $3.70 per share. It needs to raise an additional $40 000 to open a new showroom in a rural area. It has been advised to make a public issue of shares at the lower price of $3.20 in order to make the issue an attractive one to investors.

(a) What is the *market value* of Izarki Ltd prior to the new issue?

(b) How many shares must it issue at $3.20?

(c) What is the *new share price* likely to be, immediately after the new shares are issued?

(d) Why might the directors of Izarki Ltd be concerned about this new share price?

11.22 *Expected rate of return calculation*

The required return for shareholders in Lamplight Ltd is 12 per cent. The share price is currently $4 and the expected dividend is 20 cents per share. If the share price is forecast to increase by 10 per cent in the next twelve months, what is the expected rate of return implied by this forecast? (The riskiness of Lamplight is not expected to change.) Do you agree with the share price forecast? Why or why not?

Case studies

Case 11.23 *Towards happier returns*

We have been painfully slow, but a significant policy change is at last taking place in the boardrooms of many large Australian corporations. It is going to have a profound long-term beneficial effect on Australian share prices …

One by one, Australia's large companies are now following the United States pattern and dedicating their enterprises to increasing shareholder returns, rather than empire-building or concentrating excessively on governance theories.

Among the techniques being embraced are the traditional cost-cutting; outsourcing; selling businesses where the company has found it can't get good returns to those who believe they can; working on ways to reduce the amount of assets required to run the businesses; leveraging balance sheets and returning the money to shareholders; and changing the domicile of the business to countries like the US where they understand that growth and employment come with lower taxes.

But focusing on shareholder returns also coincides with an increased awareness of sustainable development by Australian corporations. Achieving sustainable development means first realising that governments have less power and so therefore enterprises must be seen to be in tune with the interests of local communities if they are to be viable in the long term.

Robert Gottliebsen, 'Comment: Towards happier returns', *Business Review Weekly*, 27 July 1998, p. 8

Required

(a) This commentator believes that Australian companies have not been dedicating their enterprises to increasing shareholder returns. Why would they not have this as their major aim?

(b) Why would shareholders not have introduced measures to change this attitude beforehand.

(c) What changes can directors and shareholders put in place to change this attitude?

Case 11.24 *Keeping stock of inventory*

In recent years, Australian businesses have learnt to carefully manage their working capital—and, in particular, holding of stocks. But stocks, or inventories, have increased sharply so far this year, with powerful implications for businesses and the national economy.

The chart shows the long-term decline in the ratio of business stocks to sales. (It excludes stocks of farm products, which have varied with seasonal conditions or with the floor-price scheme for wool.) In the early 1980s, stocks held by businesses—manufacturers, wholesalers, retailers and miners—were equal to 1.4 times their revenue for the quarter. In March, the figure was only 0.88.

The impressive decline in stocks as a proportion of sales in recent years reflects three things: the widespread use of computers; the adoption of just-in-time management of stocks, and the effect of painfully high interest rates in the late 1980s. For a time, Australian businesses lagged behind overseas moves towards frugality in holding stocks—then quickly caught up.

Many businesses have reported a sharp increase in stocks for the early months of this year.

Don Stammer, 'Economist: Keeping stock of inventory', *Business Review Weekly*, 6 July 1998, p. 20

SLOPPINESS CREEPS BACK IN

Ratio | Stocks-to-sales ratio

Sources: ABS, DEUTSCHE BANK

Required

(a) Why is the management of working capital so important to organisations?

(b) Inappropriate management of inventory will affect a number of aspects of the financial well-being of an organisation. Explain why this is so.

(c) Why is the commentator suggesting that the large decrease in inventory holding as a percentage of sales is a good sign?

(d) What are the implications for business and the economy to which the commentator refers, if inventory holdings increase again?

Case 11.25 *Tasty but forbidden morsels*

In the race to know what is happening in the sharemarket, the field is crowded. Journalists, analysts, stockbrokers, competitors, regulators and investors all want to get the news first. To make things a little fairer, the law tries to handicap the race: disclosure rules require companies to reveal price-sensitive information immediately a company is aware of it; and insider-trading rules prevent those who know the secrets from trading on them.

But it is never going to be an equal contest.

Those who have wire services on the screens on their desks, 40-page daily updates and invitations to private briefings are the unbackable favourites. As *Animal Farm* author George Orwell put it: 'All animals are equal, but some animals are more equal than others.'

Lucinda Schmidt, 'Tasty but forbidden morsels', *Business Review Weekly*, 17 August 1998, p. 54

Required

(a) What are the implications of some people knowing and acting on information about corporations before others?

(b) What is/can be done to prevent this from occurring?

(c) How does the efficient markets hypothesis relate to this situation?

CHAPTER 12
Financial statement analysis

Learning objectives

In this chapter you will be introduced to:

1. the users of financial statement analysis and how they use it

2. a plan for financial statement analysis

3. various techniques used for analysis

4. the limitations of analysis using financial ratios

5. a range of financial ratios

6. ratios for public sector organisations

7. the uses of ratio analysis.

Introduction

In the previous chapter we found that investment decisions are based on the mix of risk and return in relation to various alternatives. We also found that these were the determinants of the value of the firm, as assessed by financial markets and reflected in its share price, and that management was judged on its performance in managing the mix of risk and return.

The financial statements of a firm are seen as a major source of information by many users for judging the risk and return elements of the organisation. Although some very important information is explicitly stated in the statements, there is a wealth of additional information available only if the statements are analysed in certain ways. It is this analysis of the financial statements that this chapter concentrates on.

We begin with an overview of the users (management, owners, creditors, customers, employees etc.) and uses of the analysis of financial statements. Users have specific reasons for seeking information about the organisation and hence the type of analysis carried out should reflect the purpose for which it is being done. The procedure of analysing financial statements needs to be well planned, with a series of clearly defined steps being taken, so that the appropriate outcome from the analysis is achieved for the end user. We will identify such a plan to aid in the analysis process. As different outcomes are required from the process, the most appropriate techniques need to be chosen; techniques such as cross-sectional and time-series comparisons, common-size financial statements and ratio analysis are reviewed and illustrated.

Ratio analysis is the most common technique used and the chapter spends most of the discussion on the different categories of ratio to be used, what each ratio tells us about the financial state of the organisation and the limitations inherent in this type of analysis. You should keep in mind throughout this chapter that the techniques introduced here do not reduce the inherent limitations of financial statements produced under historical cost accounting. We have previously noted that such financial statements produce contested information and when used in any other form, for example when converted to ratios, the resulting information will still produce differing views regarding its accuracy and interpretation. The chapter concludes with a comprehensive example which provides the reader with an illustration of a carefully worked analysis of two organisations in the same industry.

The users and uses of financial analysis

Accounting information is produced to provide information for both management (internal users) and external users. In earlier chapters it was established that accounting reports are a product of the accounting system, produced by the organisation for two reasons: to fulfil legal reporting requirements and to provide information about the entity to assist decision making for investment (by external users) and financial management (internal users). It was concluded that accounting reports provide information, although that information needs to be analysed and often needs adjustment to suit the particular purpose of the user.

Management uses financial information in its planning and control of the entity. This includes monitoring current performance, diagnosing problems and revising plans accordingly. The great variety of reports presented to management will be discussed in detail in Chapters 21 to 26. Management is also interested, however, in the overall summary provided by the published reports.

External users fall into two broad groups:

1. Those making investment or lending decisions—essentially owners and creditors. For public sector entities and enterprises, the owners may be viewed as the entire Australian population represented by the appropriate level of government through the Minister or officer in charge of that area.
2. Those interested in the organisation's performance because of its effect on a specific interest group or the public interest in general. They include employees, customers, consumer groups, statutory authorities and trustees.

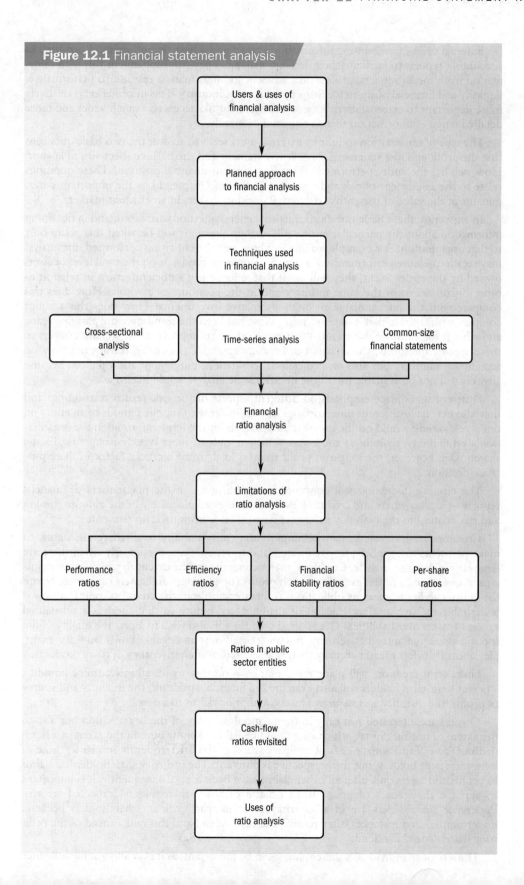

Figure 12.1 Financial statement analysis

External users of accounting information extract and adjust the information provided in accounting reports to facilitate their decision making. They will supplement this with information from media reports, professional advisers and information relating to performance, liquidity and financial position for firms in the specific industry. This information is relatively more important to external users because management has access to a much wider and more detailed range of information than is reported externally.

The type of information sought by external users seeks to answer the two basic questions that the profit and loss statement, cash flow statement and the balance sheet aim to answer: How well has the entity performed? What is its present financial position? These questions relate to the assessment of risk and return, discussed in Chapter 11 as the important determinants of the value of the entity to external decision makers in an efficient market.

In answering these basic questions, further general questions are asked, and in obtaining information about the particular entity, still further questions will be asked that relate only to that organisation. For example, to find out how well the entity has performed, the analyst may seek to measure performance as a return on owners' funds, or on the total level of assets owned by the entity. Next, they will ask if that amount is a sufficient return in relation to other organisations in the same industry and in the economy as a whole. How does this compare with the rate available through alternative investments? How does this amount compare with the rate that owners require? What has been the trend over the past five years, and what is the cause of this trend? What can be done to improve it? In seeking answers to these specific questions, the analyst can learn more about the entity, relying not only on accounting numbers but also on professional evaluation, judgement and opinion, because answers will not be available for all the questions the analyst would like to ask.

Different users place emphasis on different aspects of the risk–return relationship and they also may have different time horizons. A wholesaler who supplied goods to an entity on one week's credit would not be greatly concerned about the long-run trend in the organisation's profitability, so long as there was sufficient cash to meet weekly payments. To the shareholder, however, the long-run profit trend is likely to be a crucial factor in share purchase decisions.

The ensuing discussion will concentrate on the needs of the major users of financial reports—that is, owners and creditors. Both are interested ultimately in the amount, timing and risk relating to the cash flows they expect to receive from their investment.

Creditors are interested in such things as the entity's ability to discharge its debts, to make payments to suppliers, to pay interest and to repay loans, particularly when there are large claims about to mature. Creditors' major concerns are the extent to which other claims rank above theirs, and the extent to which profits (or earnings) and assets can shrink before the entity's ability to meet its obligations is threatened. From the creditors' point of view it is desirable to have a safety cushion of shareholders' equity so that there is a substantial excess of assets over liabilities. The secured creditor will also wish to assess the quality of the specific assets guaranteed as security. A loan secured over an organisation's land, for example, normally offers greater security than one secured over an inventory of dairy products.

Short-term creditors will place more emphasis on the organisation's current liquidity, whereas long-term lenders will also examine the financial structure, the quantity and source of profits, the quantity and nature of assets, and prior claims to assets.

Owners are interested not only in the financial solvency of the organisation but also in the extent of unpaid capital, which they could be liable to contribute in the event of a liquidation. The informational needs of ordinary shareholders are frequently similar to those of long-term debt holders, but the perspective is different. The ordinary shareholder has claims to profits and assets only after all other claims have been met. Consequently, it is important to appraise the impact of prior claims on the ordinary shareholders' expected returns. Preference shareholders are in a less risky position than ordinary shareholders because, under normal circumstances, they receive a fixed dividend and this ranks ahead of the ordinary shareholders' dividend.

The size of an individual's shareholding can be important, as it may allow some influence to be exerted on the policies of the organisation. If the shareholding is small then the shareholder is at the mercy of policies dictated by others. Important components of the shareholders' returns are capital gains obtained from increases in share prices. Thus, the shareholder has to be aware of the likely impact of the organisation's activities on its share price. In particular, it is necessary to determine whether retention of earnings has resulted in a growing earnings stream and a corresponding increase in the share price.

As owners of public sector entities on behalf of the people, governments are interested in the financial performance and solvency of these entities. On the positive side, dividends paid by government business enterprises assist in balancing state or federal budgets. On the negative side, the failure or financial distress of a government-backed organisation can have severe implications, not only for the public purse but also for the political credibility of the government.

A planned approach to financial analysis

A financial analysis should follow an orderly progression. A question should be posed, data should be obtained and analysed, and a conclusion reached. An example of a planned approach might be:

1. The first step involves identifying the users the analysis and report are being prepared for and their relationship to the organisation.
2. This step is most important to the type of analysis carried out and to the recommendations made in the report, as it is here that the decision to be ultimately made by the user is clearly identified. For example, is it a decision to buy shares or is the user a banker needing to decide whether to lend to the organisation?
3. Prior to the above decision being made, a number of questions will inevitably need to be answered. Some of the more frequently asked questions are:

   (a) How is the entity financed?
   (b) How profitable is the entity and how is the profit earned?
   (c) How efficient is the entity?
   (d) How solvent is the entity?
   (e) Is performance in the above areas satisfactory?
   (f) What may the entity's assets be sold for?
   (g) What appear to be the entity's future prospects?
   (h) What does the return on the entity's securities indicate about its rating in financial markets?
   (i) Are there any factors likely to distort the interpretation of the available financial data?

4. Although the financial statements will provide the majority of the information to answer the designated questions, they may need to be supplemented with data such as financial details relating to prior years, other organisations in the same industry, industry averages or economic indicators. All this information needs to be put into a suitable format before the analysis can be carried out efficiently.
5. The interpretation of the analysed information is of critical importance. Part of this interpretation will be to identify how significant the information is in relation to the questions we are trying to answer. Its significance should be measured against some 'benchmark' such as the averages for the industry as a whole, a key competitor, prior years results etc.
6. This step involves using the information from the analysis that is deemed significant to answer the question originally posed at point 2.
7. One of the most important stages for any analysist is the communication of their findings to the people relying on it to make a decision. The most complete and accurate analysis will be of little use if it is not communicated in a form and language that is easily understood by the user. The report should detail the process of the analysis, the outcomes relevant to the decision to be made and some recommendations regarding courses of action.

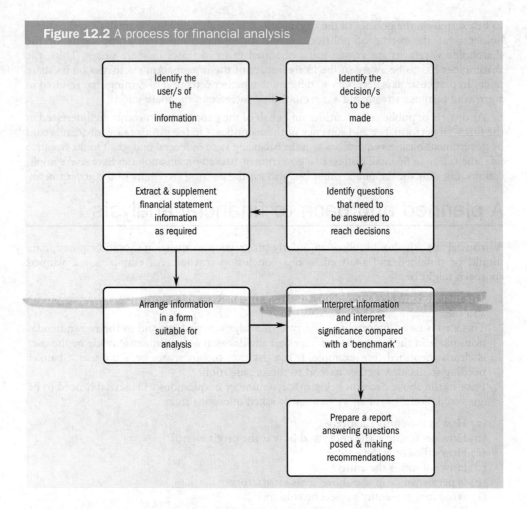

Figure 12.2 A process for financial analysis

Techniques used in financial analysis

The most common form of financial analysis is carried out using *ratios*. These are calculated using the data from financial statements and other sources to show the relationship between two figures. They aim to produce information in an understandable form to assess the firm's financial condition and performance. The result of the ratio calculation can be expressed in a number of forms, depending on what is seen as the most appropriate for the situation. For example, the relationship between the two figures may be expressed:

- as a pure ratio, such as 3:1
- as a certain number of units, such as 3 cents per share or 30 days
- as a percentage, such as 300 per cent
- as an index number.

Of these, the percentage is perhaps the most common and easiest to understand for comparisons of the same units, but it is not appropriate in all situations, as we will see later in the chapter. Analysis using ratios is carried out to control for the effects of size between organisations. Ratios also standardise data and this facilitates comparisons between organisations, comparison against established standards and comparisons over time.

Case 12.1 Comparing performance

Suppose that two companies in the same industry, Hi Ltd and Lo Ltd, each earned a net profit of $1 million in the current year. *Is their performance identical?*

Based on the limited information given, all we can say is that they both earned the same dollar amount of net profit. If it is also known that the total funds invested were $5 million in Hi Ltd and $10 million in Lo Ltd, would the answer to the question be the same?

A convenient means of comparison is to calculate ratios to reflect the relationship between profit and investment. It will be found that Hi Ltd obtained a higher return on invested funds (20 per cent) than Lo Ltd (10 per cent) and hence may be said to have the better performance.

However, if it is also known that the average rate of return for the industry during the year was 25 per cent, it might be claimed that neither company performed well. Ratio analysis also raises questions such as, 'Why was Hi Ltd's return on investment five percentage points below the industry average?'

Financial analysis should be carried out using some predetermined basis for comparison, for example national or world best practice, averages for the industry, other organisations in the same industry, the one organisation over a number of years, or alternative forms of investment. These comparisons will be either *cross-sectional* or *time-series*.

Cross-sectional comparisons will show the relationship between one organisation and another at a particular point in time. It may also show the relationship with some 'benchmark' such as world best practice or industry averages at a single point in time. The example of Hi Ltd and Lo Ltd above is an illustration of the use of cross-sectional analysis. Time-series comparisons generally relate to the performance of one organisation over a period of time, often several years. An illustration of time series can be seen in the Eight Year Financial Summary of Coca-Cola Amatil Ltd (Appendix 1, page 921). This technique lends itself to the use of index numbers, where one year (usually the first in the series) is chosen as the 'base' year with all figures for that year being expressed as 100. Figures in the other years are then expressed as index numbers, in relation to how they compare with the corresponding figure in the base year.

The following example illustrates the use of index numbers in a time-series analysis and shows that the profit has not kept pace with the sales growth because costs have been growing at a faster rate than sales.

	20X1		20X2		20X3	
	$	Index	$	Index	$	Index
Sales revenue	120 000	100	140 000	117	160 000	133
Cost of sales	20 000	100	30 000	150	32 000	160
Other expenses	30 000	100	46 000	153	45 000	150
	50 000		76 000		77 000	
Net profit	$ 70 000	100	$ 64 000	91	$ 83 000	119

Whether a cross-sectional comparison or a time-series comparison is carried out in a particular analysis will depend on the purpose of the analysis and the data provided.

The use of *common-size financial statements*, in conjunction with either cross-sectional or time-series comparisons, enables organisations of different sizes to be compared by standardising the various items in the financial statements in terms of their relationship to the size of the entity. In preparing common-size statements, each component figure of the profit and loss statement is expressed as a percentage of revenue and the figures representing the components of the balance sheet are each expressed as a percentage of total assets. The financial statements of Westcoast Ltd below illustrate how financial statements can be recast in the form of common-size statements. The percentages highlight the relative importance of individual expense items and individual assets and liabilities.

PROFIT AND LOSS STATEMENT: WESTCOAST LTD
for year ending 30 June 20X1

	$	%
Sales (all credit)	3 000 000	100.0
less Cost of goods sold	1 800 000	60.0
Gross profit	1 200 000	40.0
less Expenses		
Selling	600 000	20.0
Administration	300 000	10.0
	900 000	30.0
Profit before interest and tax	300 000	10.0
less Interest	90 000	3.0
Taxable profit	210 000	7.0
less Taxation	50 000	1.7
Net profit after taxation	$ 160 000	5.3

Notes:
1. A dividend of $80 000 was paid.
2. Selling expenses include a lease charge for sales premises of $100 000 per annum. The lease has 10 years to run.
3. The market price per share is presently $4.80.

BALANCE SHEET: WESTCOAST LTD
as at 30 June 20X1

Assets	$	$	%
Current assets			
Accounts receivable	400 000		20.0
Inventory	300 000		15.0
		700 000	35.0
Fixed assets			
Buildings	800 000		40.0
Equipment	500 000		25.0
		1 300 000	65.0
Total assets		$2 000 000	100.0
Liabilities			
Current liabilities			
Accounts payable	250 000		12.5
Bank overdraft	100 000		5.0
		350 000	17.5
Long-term liabilities			
Debentures (interest rate 10%)		850 000	42.5

continues

| BALANCE SHEET: WESTCOAST LTD | | | |
as at 30 June 20X1			
Shareholders' equity	$	$	%
Paid-up capital			
(200 000 $3 ordinary shares)	600 000		30.0
Retained profits	200 000		10.0
		800 000	40.0
Total equities		$2 000 000	100.0

| STATEMENT OF CASH FLOWS: WESTCOAST LTD | | | |
for year ending 30 June 20X1			
	$	$	%
Cash flows from operations			
Receipts from customers	2 880 000		
Payments to suppliers	(2 420 000)		
Interest paid	(90 000)		
Taxation paid	(50 000)		
Net cash flow from operations		320 000	200.0
Cash flows from investing		(980 000)	(612.5)
Cash flows from financing			
Dividends paid	(80 000)		
Other financing cash flows	580 000		
Net cash flow from financing		500 000	312.5
Net cash flow for period		(160 000)	(100)
Cash balance at beginning of period		60 000	
Cash balance at end of period		**($100 000)**	

The financial statements of Westcoast Ltd will be used in the remainder of the chapter to illustrate the calculation of various ratios.

The following very simple example illustrates how common-size statements provide a means of comparing entities of different size. Suppose Big Ltd had $20 million of debt and Little Ltd owes $5 million. It may seem that Big Ltd is more heavily in debt. However, if total equities (liabilities plus shareholders' equity) were $80 million for Big Ltd and only $10 million for Little Ltd, the component percentages would reveal that Little Ltd is the more highly levered, thus:

	Big Ltd		Little Ltd	
	$m	%	$m	%
Liabilities	20	25	5	50
Shareholders' equity	60	75	5	50
	80	100	10	100

Ratio analysis of financial statements

As indicated earlier, ratio analysis takes two figures, generally from the financial statements, and shows the relationship between them. This is then compared either with an industry standard, with other firms in the industry or with figures from prior years for the same firm. There is a wide range of ratios used to answer specific questions about the entity and the effectiveness of its management, especially in relation to its decision making in the three areas discussed in Chapters 11 and 24: financing, dividends and investment.

The range of ratios is usually divided into five groups:

- performance (or profitability)
- operating efficiency
- financial stability (or liquidity/solvency)
- cash flow ratios
- per-share ratios.

As will be seen, however, they are not independent divisions.

Prior to discussing each of these groups of ratios, it is appropriate to identify some of the limitations of this type of analysis. It is important that ratio analysis is not seen as being a totally accurate, scientific approach. It must be carried out with the full knowledge of what it can and cannot do for us. Knowing the limitations before embarking on a study of the ratios will enable you to make the appropriate use of the ratios and to interpret the information they reveal in a fully informed manner.

Limitations of ratio analysis

The limitations of ratio analysis can be broadly classified into problems of timing, the information base and end use.

Timing problems

Timing problems arise because the analysis is basically a static one. The report from which the balance sheet ratios are produced shows the entity's financial position at a point in time. This may not be typical of the entity's normal situation, perhaps because of seasonal factors. The profit and loss statement is a summary of all the transactions for a period and does not indicate any trend during the period (e.g. was gross margin increasing or decreasing in the later months of the year?).

These distortions can be heightened by deliberate attempts to 'window-dress' the financial reports. Window-dressing is temporarily changing the appearance of the financial statements by engaging in activities that have an effect for only a short period around the entity's balance date. For example, cash balances and the quick ratio can temporarily be increased by allowing inventory to run down or by delaying the payment of suppliers. Window-dressing is unethical because its purpose is to misinform users of financial statements. It is quite difficult to show that an entity has engaged in window-dressing using publicly available information.

Additional timing problems can be caused by the often significant delay between the production of the financial reports and their publication. On average this delay is about three months, during which period the circumstances of the entity may have changed considerably. Also the *timing* of future receipts and payments, which is crucial to the interpretation of current and quick ratios and cash-flow ratios, is not included in these calculations.

The information base

The problems of the information base stem from several causes, including:

- lack of disclosure generally and of specific detail in published financial statements
- variation in valuation methods
- variation in classification of information
- use of historical cost accounting information.

Legal disclosure requirements are restricted to a minimum of detail and are designed to display the discharge of fiduciary responsibilities rather than providing information for investment analysis. Although many entities report more than the minimum required by law, important information is frequently not disclosed, such as the cost of goods sold.

The data that is disclosed lacks detail. It consists of summaries of many transactions and totals of often diverse items within a class. The lack of detail relates both to trends within an accounting period (e.g. the pattern of sales or cash receipts over the period) and to the breakdown of sales by product, market segment or country. This also means that averages often have to be used because no further details are available.

The comparison of entities is often difficult because of the length of time the asset has been held or because of the different valuation policies adopted by the entities. For example, two organisations might hold identical blocks of land which are shown at entirely different book values because they were purchased at different times. In an effort to overcome the problems of historical cost valuations of long-lived assets, private sector organisations have adopted a system of ad hoc revaluations. This also causes problems for analysts; for example, the ratio analysis is carried out when an organisation revalues its assets upwards. This can cause difficulties when comparing an organisation's performance over time. Further, there is no recognition of general price-level changes and their effect on the purchasing power of the dollar. Other comparisons may also be invalid if different accounting policies (such as inventory valuation or depreciation method) have been used. These problems make both time-series and cross-sectional comparisons difficult.

Public sector and government business enterprises are increasingly using current values of assets in their reported ratios. Analysts comparing ratios calculated over a period of time and between entities will encounter difficulties if they are unaware of differences in the accounting policies used in the calculations, particularly in relation to valuations.

Deliberate manipulation of the data and of accounting methods may also be used to distort results, such as deferring the writing-off of bad debts until after the current balance sheet has been produced. Once again, practices that deliberately set out to misinform users of financial statements are clearly unethical.

A number of ratios require the use of the total of a particular classification of items, for example current assets or current liabilities. The items that are included in each classification will therefore affect the outcome of the calculation. When comparisons are then made between firms, using this ratio, any variation in the interpretation of items to be included in the classification by each firm will make the comparison less meaningful.

Chapters in Part 4 will analyse the quality of information contained in published accounting reports and will suggest, in further detail, the deficiencies in the information that make analysis difficult.

End use

There are several problems relating to the end use of financial ratios. First, the ratios use information from the past and so are not necessarily good indicators of the future. However, for many decisions, users are interested in the information for predicting future events. Any factor that causes the future to differ from the past can invalidate the use of ratio analysis for such prediction, unless that factor is specifically taken into account. For example, an entity may have opened a new outlet, it may have changed its management, it may have extended its product line, or it may have automated certain procedures. Any of these events could invalidate the use of past ratios as an indicator of the future.

Second, no evaluation can take place until some standard for evaluation has been established. However, determining guidelines to identify a 'good' ratio is extremely difficult. Rapid inventory turnover, for example, may indicate either an efficient management or an inadequate stock level. Frequently we turn to industry average ratios as a standard for comparison, but this has its drawbacks. It might reasonably be expected that half the entities will be above the industry average and half below. Deviation may be what makes an organisation the industry's performance leader rather than being seen as not meeting the 'standard' for the industry.

A final problem with the use of ratios arises when some ratios appear 'satisfactory' and some appear 'unsatisfactory'. In this situation it can be most difficult to reach an overall conclusion about the entity's financial performance.

The limitations of ratio analysis are many, but their impact can be reduced if the following points are borne in mind:

1. The behaviour of ratios is interrelated, thus ratios should never be analysed in isolation.
2. Ratios create no additional information; they merely help to reveal the relationships of interest already in the data. Any problems caused by the production of accounting data are not avoided by using ratio analysis.
3. The function of ratios is usually to raise questions; they act as clues that suggest further investigations are needed, rather than providing clear answers.
4. Ratios mean little on their own; they require comparison with past performance, another entity's performance or some standard.
5. The key to analysis is not the knowledge of a set of ratios but the development and exercise of judgement in interpreting what the ratios mean.

The next section uses the financial statements of Westcoast Ltd, detailed in an earlier section, to illustrate the calculation of various financial ratios and to identify what they reveal about the organisation.

Ratios used to assess performance

- What has been the entity's performance in the past in relation to the investment in the entity?
- What is the trend in profitability?
- What strengths or weaknesses exist that could affect future performance?

These are some of the questions to be answered by an analysis of past results. Performance is important, not only because it determines investment returns but also because the analysis of performance may provide a good indicator of the risk of bankruptcy.

Ratios that assist in assessing performance include:

- gross profit margin
- expense ratios
- net profit margin
- quality of income ratio
- asset turnover
- cash return on assets
- return on assets
- return on equity
- cash return to shareholders.

The analysis may begin by calculating percentages, using the profit and loss statement, which relate the expenses and the profit margins to sales revenue. The *gross profit margin* is 40 per cent, indicating that every dollar of sales returns 40 cents after deduction of the cost of the goods sold.

$$\text{Gross profit margin} \quad = \quad \frac{\text{Gross profit}}{\text{Sales}}$$

$$= \quad \frac{1\ 200\ 000}{3\ 000\ 000}$$

$$= \quad 0.40 \text{ or } 40\%$$

A decline in the gross profit margin over time could indicate that the sales price has been falling, perhaps due to discount operations to counter new competition. Alternatively, the buying costs of inventory could be rising, with the entity unable or unwilling to recover increased costs through higher prices.

An analysis of the individual expense components reveals their relative importance in the earning of profit. In Westcoast Ltd, selling expenses are more significant than administrative costs.

$$\begin{array}{rl} \text{Expense ratio} & = \quad \dfrac{\text{Selling expenses}}{\text{Sales}} \\ \text{(Selling expenses in this case)} & \end{array}$$

$$= \quad \frac{600\ 000}{3\ 000\ 000}$$

$$= \quad 0.20 \text{ or } 20\%$$

A change in the component percentages over time could indicate changes in future returns and prompt further investigation. If, for example, the selling expenses increased in proportion to sales, the analyst might decide to investigate several possible explanations, such as an increase in advertising that might improve future sales, or an increase in sales staff that may or may not be warranted by the results obtained. The financial statements merely indicate the need for further investigation. Perhaps no further investigation is possible, in which case the analyst can only list any suspicions and leave it to the user to decide which explanation is the most likely.

The interaction of all the profit and loss statement components produces the *return on sales* or *net profit margin*.

$$\text{Net profit margin} \quad = \quad \frac{\text{Earnings before interest and tax}}{\text{Sales}}$$

$$= \quad \frac{300\ 000}{3\ 000\ 000}$$

$$= \quad 0.10 \text{ or } 10\%$$

Using net profit (or 'earnings') before interest and tax (EBIT) reflects the return on sales from the operations of the organisation, without taking into consideration the effects of company taxation and the cost of gearing. This ratio can also be calculated using net profit after interest and tax which will reflect the final return available to owners earned on sales. Appropriate comments must be made relevant to whichever 'net profit' is used.

$$\text{Net profit margin} \quad = \quad \frac{\text{Earnings after interest and tax}}{\text{Sales}}$$

$$= \quad \frac{160\ 000}{3\ 000\ 000}$$

$$= \quad 0.533 \text{ or } 5.33\%$$

Whether the 5.33 per cent for Westcoast Ltd is satisfactory depends partly on previous results but also on the type of enterprise. An enterprise with a high turnover of inventory, such as a grocery store, normally expects to earn a lower profit per unit sold than a music store selling pianos. The music store sells fewer units but it expects to earn a higher profit margin on each unit sold.

The quality of the income generated can be gauged by the calculation of the following ratio:

$$\text{Quality of income/operations index} \quad = \quad \frac{\text{Cash flow from operations}}{\text{Earnings after interest \& tax}}$$

$$= \quad \frac{320\ 000}{160\ 000}$$

$$= \quad 200\%$$

This is a reflection of the relationship between cash flow generated from normal operations and the income generated from the same source. Operating income of course includes a number of items not included in the calculation of cash flow from operations. Organisations can be very profitable but can still have difficulty paying their debts if they cannot turn their profits into cash. This ratio is a measure of management's efficiency in achieving this aim.

How effective the organisation is in generating sales from its total investment in assets can be gauged by calculating its *asset turnover ratio*. This is measured by the relationship of sales to total assets:

$$\text{Asset turnover} \quad = \quad \frac{\text{Sales}}{\text{Total assets}}$$

$$= \quad \frac{3\ 000\ 000}{2\ 000\ 000}$$

$$= \quad 1.50 \text{ or } 150\%$$

The cash-generating ability of the assets should also be taken into account, as it is cash which is used to meet the firm's obligations. Substituting cash flow from operations (before interest and taxation) for sales can be used to indicate this:

$$\text{Cash return on assets} = \frac{\text{Cash flow from operations (before interest and tax)}}{\text{Total assets}}$$

$$= \frac{460\ 000}{2\ 000\ 000}$$

$$= 23\%$$

The interpretation of these ratios is dependent on the industry. It is not possible to say, for instance, that an asset turnover of 150 per cent is good or bad, unless it has been compared with the trend over time for the organisation, another similar organisation or an average for organisations in that industry. The grocery store would be expected to have a higher asset turnover ratio that the music store.

However, does its higher turnover compensate for its lower profit margin? This question is answered by computing the overall *return on assets (ROA)*, which results from the interaction of the profitability of sales with the rate at which sales occur. The normal ratio for return on investment is:

$$\frac{\text{Earnings before interest and tax}}{\text{Average (or year end) total assets}} = \frac{\text{Earnings before interest and tax}}{\text{Sales}} \times \frac{\text{Sales}}{\text{Average (or year end) total assets}}$$

('Average total assets' is calculated by adding opening and closing asset totals and dividing by 2.)

$$\frac{300\ 000}{2\ 000\ 000} = \frac{300\ 000}{3\ 000\ 000} \times \frac{3\ 000\ 000}{2\ 000\ 000}$$

$$0.15 \text{ or } 15\% = 0.10 \text{ or } 10\% \times 1.5 \text{ or } 150\%$$

This relationship is known as the *Dupont formula*, after the company which first introduced ratio analysis into performance measurement for management control. It used a system of ratios to reflect the effect of various outcomes on the final return to shareholders. The above formula shows that the earnings from using the total investment in assets is a product of the earnings the firm can generate from sales and the sales it can generate from its asset base. It can be used as a benchmark to compensate for different sized firms and firms in different industries, as illustrated with the grocery store and the firm selling pianos. One would be expected to have a low return on sales but a high asset turnover, whereas the other would normally have a high return on sales but a low asset turnover rate. By combining these two ratios, we can compare the firms on their performance in generating profit from their individual investments in assets. As will be seen below, the return on assets is used in combination with a measure of leverage to show the return on equity.

Westcoast Ltd has achieved a 15 per cent return on its total investment in assets, which results from the interaction of a 10 per cent return on sales and a 150 per cent turnover of sales in relation to assets. The measure of earnings used in this formula is earnings before the deduction of interest and taxation (EBIT). Interest is the return to lenders and taxation is the amount expropriated by the government. As the denominator of the ratio represents the funds provided both by creditors and owners, it is logical to measure the numerator as the return before any distributions are made, whether as interest or dividends. The profitability of sales may be an indicator of the performance of the sales department or the sales manager, and this performance should be assessed without considering how inventory and other assets were financed, and without considering the impact of tax on return. So the profit margin is a measure of the performance of sales or a measure of the investment decision to sell/produce those items. Since earnings is a flow measured over a period, it can be argued that the investment shown in the denominator should be measured as an average of assets held over the period. However, the year-end balance is frequently used.

Case 12.2 The Dupont formula

The following details are available for the 1997 financial year:

Coles Myer Ltd (major Australian retail company)

	$m
EBIT	615.3
Total assets (year end)	6 696.6
Sales	19 224.8

Broken Hill Proprietory Ltd (international resources company)

	$m
EBIT	2 099
Total assets (year end)	36 735
Sales	20 947

Use the Dupont formula to compare the performance of these two companies of different size and from different industries. What conclusions can be drawn from the different ratios?

EBIT to total assets measures the return achieved by the entity as an economic unit regardless of the source of its funds. In disregarding the influence of financial structure, it provides a measure of pure operating performance. The time series of these ratios indicates whether the organisation is maintaining its profit margin and sales turnover over time. A decline in the ratio indicates to owners and creditors alike that the organisation's operating performance is deteriorating.

Operating performance undoubtedly affects the return to the owners of an entity, but this return is also influenced by the *financial structure*. As discussed in Chapter 11, the astute use of leverage may improve the return on shareholders' equity in the absence of any improvement in operating performance. The ratio of the *return on equity* captures this factor, as follows:

$$\text{Return on equity} = \frac{\text{Earnings after interest and tax}}{\text{Ordinary shareholder equity}}$$

$$= \frac{160\ 000}{800\ 000}$$

$$= 0.20 \text{ or } 20\%$$

The analytical perspective usually taken is that of the ordinary shareholder, so the numerator is usually the return that is available to the ordinary shareholder, net profit after interest and tax. Also preference dividends are generally deducted from the numerator and preference share capital from the denominator. As shareholders' equity consists of contributed capital, reserves and retained earnings, this is the most appropriate figure to use in the denominator as an indication of the total ordinary shareholders' equity in the organisation.

Sometimes the return on shareholders' equity is computed with only contributed (paid-up) capital in the denominator. The exclusion of retained earnings from the equity figure means that the resulting ratio overstates the return on equity and should not be used.

A similar ratio is the *cash return on shareholders' equity* which shows the return in cash available to the shareholders from their investment. A healthy cash return is more likely to result in cash dividends continuing to be paid:

$$\text{Cash return to shareholders} = \frac{\text{Cash flow from operations}}{\text{Shareholders' equity}}$$

$$= \frac{320\ 000}{800\ 000}$$

$$= 40\%$$

The return on shareholders' equity combines the effects of operating performance and financial structure. As a result, when compared with the rate of return on total assets, the return on shareholders' equity shows the success or failure of management in using leverage to improve owners' returns. If, after allowing for the effect of taxes, the return on equity exceeds the return on investment, this is due to the successful use of leverage. *This can occur only if the interest cost of debt finance is less than the rate earned by the entity on these borrowed funds.* The entity should earn more on the invested borrowed funds than the owners could obtain by investing elsewhere, otherwise the funds should have been remitted as dividends.

The effect of leverage can most clearly be seen by breaking down the return on shareholders' equity into the profit margin after interest and tax, the total asset turnover and the ratio of total assets to equity. The latter ratio is sometimes called the equity multiplier. The relationship derived is:

$$\frac{\text{Net profit after interest and tax}}{\text{Owners' equity}} = \frac{\text{Net profit after interest and tax}}{\text{Sales}} \times \frac{\text{Sales}}{\text{Total assets}} \times \frac{\text{Total assets}}{\text{Owners' equity}}$$

$$= 5.33 \times 1.5 \times 2.5$$

$$= 0.20 \text{ or } 20\%$$

The equity multiplier is by definition always greater than 1.0. It indicates the proportion of assets financed by borrowing. The relation between return on investment and return on equity depends both on the successfulness of the use of leverage and the extent of the leverage (i.e. the size of the equity multiplier).

If leverage is used successfully, the higher the equity multiplier the higher the return on shareholders' equity. If leverage is not used successfully, however, the return on equity will be lower than the return on investment, because net profit after interest and taxes is either lower than EBIT or not sufficiently higher than EBIT to compensate owners for the higher level of assets financed by borrowing. For example, if Westcoast had achieved a net profit after taxation of only $60 000 instead of $160 000, the result would be:

$$\frac{\text{NPAT}}{\text{OE}} = \frac{\text{NPAT}}{\text{Sales}} \times \frac{\text{Sales}}{\text{TA}} \times \frac{\text{TA}}{\text{OE}}$$

$$\frac{60}{800} = \frac{60}{3000} \times \frac{3000}{2000} \times \frac{2000}{800}$$

$$= 0.075 \text{ or } 7.5\%$$

In this situation, leverage would have been used unsuccessfully, as the ROE is lower than the ROA. Perhaps the additional funds were not wisely employed, and additional earnings were insufficient to cover the interest cost of the loans.

Case 12.3 Two measures of return

Tennis Producers Ltd has total assets of $10 million and the ratio of net profit to total assets is 5 per cent. However, the return on shareholders' equity is 20 per cent. Explain how this situation can occur. (Assume the company pays no income tax.)

Ratios used to assess operating efficiency

Operating efficiency refers to the ability of the entity to manage its assets so that the maximum return is achieved for the lowest possible level of assets.

Ratios to assist in assessing operating efficiency include:

- inventory turnover (times and days)
- accounts receivable turnover (times and days)
- cash flow to sales
- accounts payable turnover.

The ratio of sales to total assets provides the first indication of the entity's success in controlling its assets, but more specific measures of control over assets exist, in particular the *turnover of inventory* and the *turnover of accounts receivable*. These assets were discussed in Chapter 11 as being an extremely important part of current asset management.

The desirable level of inventory depends largely on the volume of sales. In general, the larger the sales volume the more inventory that must be carried. These factors are related by means of the *inventory turnover ratio*.

— note

$$\text{Inventory turnover} = \frac{\text{Cost of goods sold}}{\text{Average (or year end) inventory}}$$

$$= \frac{1\ 800\ 000}{300\ 000}$$

$$= 6 \text{ times per year}$$

This can also be expressed in the number of days, on average, the inventory is on hand before sale:

$$\text{No. of days inventory is on hand} = \frac{365}{\text{Inventory turnover}}$$

$$= \frac{365}{6}$$

$$= \text{approximately 61 days}$$

Inventory turnover measures the efficiency of inventory management. It shows the relationship between inventory and the sales volume (at cost prices) by calculating the length of time it takes the entity to 'turn over' its inventory (or sell the same amount as its inventory value). For Westcoast Ltd the inventory has turned over, on average, once every 60 days. Some items will sell immediately and others may take months to sell, but the *average* turnover is a useful representation of the overall situation. The ideal turnover ratio, as with many others, depends on the type of business; 60 days would be excessive for a bread manufacturer, but might be satisfactory for a retailer of washing machines.

Where available, cost of goods sold rather than sales should be used as the numerator, because the inventory accounts are kept at cost. The average of opening and year-end inventory or, alternatively, year-end inventory alone, may be used in the denominator, whichever is thought to be more representative of 'normal' inventory levels. In interpreting the inventory turnover ratio it must be borne in mind that the value computed for the ratio may be distorted if the entity has a cyclical or seasonal sales pattern. Just prior to the peak selling season inventory is likely to be abnormally high and therefore the inventory turnover ratio will seem low. After peak sales, exactly the reverse situation will occur.

A low inventory turnover indicates that inventory levels are high in relation to sales and may signal poor inventory management. Inventory holding costs will be high and there may be obsolete stock that is difficult to sell. A high inventory turnover may indicate good management, but it may also indicate inadequate stock levels, causing lost sales and excessive restocking costs.

The *turnover of accounts receivable* or debtors is another commonly used efficiency ratio:

$$\text{Accounts receivable turnover} = \frac{\text{Gross credit sales}}{\text{Average (or year end) gross accounts receivable}}$$

$$= \frac{3\,000\,000}{400\,000}$$

$$= 7.5 \text{ times}$$

Gross figures are used when computing the accounts receivable turnover and it is important to ensure that allowances for bad debts are not deducted when computing the ratios. The control of these difficult customers is a significant determinant of the level of the accounts receivable turnover. Again, there is a problem for entities with seasonal activity, in that the accounts receivable figure when the ratio is calculated may not be typical of normal levels. This is a particular danger with accounts receivable, because attempts to 'window-dress' the balance sheet may well involve a temporary speeding up of debt collection at the end of the financial year, in order to reduce debtors and increase cash balances.

Generally, a rapid turnover of accounts receivable is desirable, but it should not be so rapid as to require credit terms that deter prospective customers. The turnover ratio may be converted to a measure of the average collection period:

$$\text{Average collection period} = \frac{360 \text{ or } 365}{\text{Accounts receivable turnover}}$$

$$= \frac{365}{7.5 \text{ times}}$$

$$= \text{approximately 49 days}$$

If the average collection period greatly exceeds the normal credit period allowed, it indicates poor control over accounts receivable. This may result in extensive write-offs of bad debts. An excessive collection period should therefore lead the analyst to query whether adequate allowances for bad debts have been made.

The efficiency of management in generating cash from its sales is reflected in the *cash flow to sales* ratio:

$$\text{Cash flow to sales} = \frac{\text{Cash flow from operations}}{\text{Sales}}$$

$$= \frac{320\,000}{3\,000\,000}$$

$$= 10.7\%$$

A calculation can also be made to determine the efficiency of management in paying its creditors. Inefficiency in this area may result in discounts for early payment being missed. It may also lead to the entity gaining a poor reputation for the payment of debts, which may lead to difficulties in gaining finance from suppliers and financiers in the future. Once such a reputation is earned, it is very difficult to change.

$$\text{Accounts payable turnover} = \frac{\text{Gross credit purchases*}}{\text{Average (or year end) gross accounts payable}}$$

$$= \frac{1\,800\,000}{250\,000}$$

$$= 7.2 \text{ times or approximately 50.7 days}$$

*Assuming opening inventory was the same as closing inventory and that all purchases were on credit, gross credit purchases would equal cost of goods sold.

This would have to be compared with the normal credit terms that have been negotiated with suppliers. In some industries this would be considered excessive, whereas in others it would be quite acceptable. The trend of this measure over time would also be vital for Westcoast Ltd, with an increasing number of days representing a potential problem area.

Ratios used to assess financial stability

Questions raised under this heading focus on the riskiness of the entity, for example whether it can pay its immediate debts and whether the degree of risk arising from its financial structure is acceptable. Financial stability ratios fall into two categories:

- measures of short-term liquidity:
  - current ratio (working capital ratio)
  - quick asset ratio
  - cash-flow ratio.
- measures of financial structure and long-term solvency:
  - debt to assets ratio
  - debt to equity ratio
  - times interest earned ratio
  - cash interest coverage
  - fixed charge coverage.

Measures of short-term liquidity

Liquidity ratios aid in the assessment of short-term solvency. They relate the level of short-term assets to the level of short-term claims. These ratios indicate whether the entity has managed its liquidity or cash flows properly, and measure its ability to repay its short-term debts. One commonly used ratio is the *working capital* or *current ratio*:

$$\text{Current ratio} = \frac{\text{Current assets}}{\text{Current liabilities}}$$

$$= \frac{700\ 000}{350\ 000}$$

$$= \text{2:1 or 200\%}$$

This ratio shows how well current liabilities are covered by current assets. It is interpreted as the percentage of debts arising within the next 12 months which can be met by assets expected to be liquidated within the same period. Although it is desirable to have current claims well covered (2:1 is a common 'rule-of-thumb'), a high ratio may indicate excessive current asset holdings, perhaps due to a poor turnover of inventory or accounts receivable. The 'ideal' current ratio may vary widely between organisations, depending on how readily inventory and debtors can be converted into cash and how rapidly sales can be converted to a cash flow into the organisation.

The current ratio includes assets expected to be turned into cash and liabilities due to be repaid within one year. A more immediate measure of liquidity is obtained by excluding the less liquid current assets and the less pressing current liabilities in a ratio of *quick assets to quick liabilities*, which is known as the *quick asset* or *acid-test ratio*:

$$\text{Quick asset ratio} = \frac{\text{Quick assets}}{\text{Quick liabilities}}$$

$$= \frac{400\ 000}{250\ 000}$$

$$= \quad 1.6:1 \text{ or } 1.6 \text{ times or } 160 \text{ per cent}$$

The difference between 'current' and 'quick' is the speed with which a conversion can be made to or from cash. Items normally excluded from the numerator include inventory and hire-purchase debtors. Bank overdrafts are often excluded from the denominator in the belief that banks rarely demand sudden repayment. A factor requiring consideration is the availability of unused credit facilities. An apparent liquidity shortage may be completely offset by a standby credit facility, such as an unused portion of a bank overdraft, or a guarantee from a parent company. As with the current ratio, the ideal ratio must take account of the individual circumstances of the entity.

In interpreting liquidity ratios, the quality of the current assets must always be borne in mind. High quick and current ratios are of little comfort if inventory cannot be sold and debtors will not pay. Thus, the liquidity ratios should be analysed in conjunction with the turnover ratios for current assets discussed earlier in the chapter.

Another ratio which can be used to show the degree of reliance on cash generated from activities other than operations of the firm and which overcomes the assumption that current assets can be liquidated at or close to their book value is the following:

$$\text{Cash flow ratio} = \frac{\text{Cash flow from operations}}{\text{Current liabilities}}$$

$$= \frac{320\ 000}{350\ 000}$$

$$= \quad 0.91 \text{ or } 91.4\%$$

A measure less than one would indicate some reliance on cash flow from sources other than operations to meet short-term debt and this is not reflected in the other two liquidity ratios.

Measures of financial structure and long-term solvency

One of the important tasks of financial management was said to be balancing the maturity structures of assets and liabilities so that, for example, long-term assets would not be financed from short-term sources of funds. In the balance sheet, the component percentages show the maturity structure of assets and liabilities and the way the entity is financed. Westcoast Ltd has nearly twice as many long-term assets (65 per cent) as it has short-term assets (35 per cent). Finance is predominantly long-term (82.5 per cent) and 60 per cent of total finance has been raised from a combination of short- and long-term debt.

The measurement of the extent of leverage deserves particular attention because of its critical influence on *long-term solvency*. Two types of measurement exist. One is a stock measure that is derived from the component percentages in the balance sheet, and the other is a flow measure that is drawn from the profit and loss statement as a measure of the extent to which the profits cover the interest commitment.

The *debt to assets* ratio measures the percentage of total funds provided by creditors:

$$\text{Debt to assets ratio} = \frac{\text{Total debts}}{\text{Total assets}}$$

$$= \frac{1\ 200\ 000}{2\ 000\ 000}$$

$$= 0.60 \text{ or } 60\%$$

Total debt is measured as the sum of all liabilities, both long-term and short-term. Total assets are measured as the sum of all assets, which is equivalent to the sum of all sources of finance (i.e. liabilities plus shareholders' equity).

An alternative way of measuring the extent of leverage is to use the *debt to equity* ratio. This ratio indicates the quantity of debt finance in proportion to owners' funds.

$$\text{Debt to equity ratio} = \frac{\text{Total debt}}{\text{Owners' equity}}$$

$$= \frac{1\ 200\ 000}{800\ 000}$$

$$= 1.51 \text{ or } 150\%$$

The higher these ratios, the higher the leverage of the entity. It should be recalled from Chapter 11 that initial increases in leverage are usually beneficial, but beyond a critical level, increases in leverage increase the cost of finance as well as the amount of income committed to interest payments and the risk of bankruptcy. The higher the ratio of debt, the more likely it is that, should the entity fail, the proceeds from liquidation will be insufficient to repay all debts. A high debt to total assets ratio or debt to equity ratio may therefore indicate that the entity could have difficulty borrowing further funds or, at the least, must accept higher interest charges or stringent conditions on loans. Moreover, if it defaults in payment of debenture interest, the creditors are more likely to take action to appoint an official receiver or liquidate the organisation.

From the owners' perspective, although leverage is undertaken to raise their return, the higher return must be viewed in relation to the higher risk of insolvency and liquidation should profits falter. The amount of profits committed to interest payments is an important factor in determining the impact of leverage and it is common to measure leverage, in terms of its effect on profits, in a ratio known as times interest earned:

$$\text{Times interest earned ratio} = \frac{\text{Earnings before interest and taxes}}{\text{Interest charges}}$$

$$= \frac{300\ 000}{90\ 000}$$

$$= 3.33 : 1 \text{ or } 3.33 \text{ times}$$

This ratio measures the safety margin of profit over interest payments, or the extent to which profit can decline before the entity will find it difficult to meet interest payments from current profits.

Alternatively, cash flow from operations before interest and tax can be used as the numerator of this ratio, to better reflect the fact that interest payments are provided for by cash flows not profits.

$$\text{Cash interest coverage} = \frac{\text{Cash flow from operations (BIT)}}{\text{Interest}}$$

$$= \frac{460\ 000}{90\ 000}$$

$$= 5 \text{ times}$$

It is useful to examine several years data to discover the ratio in the worst year and make comparisons with that for other years. A minimum of 3:1 is often considered desirable, but again there is no absolute standard.

A closely related ratio is the *fixed charge coverage ratio*. This ratio includes various fixed charges including lease payments:

$$\text{Fixed charge coverage} = \frac{\text{Earnings before interest and taxes and fixed charges*}}{\text{Interest and fixed charges}}$$

$$= \frac{300\,000 + 100\,000}{190\,000}$$

$$= \text{2.11:1 or 2.11 times}$$

*This is calculated by taking EBIT and adding back any fixed charges such as lease payments.

The inclusion of these fixed charges is important for an entity that leases a large proportion of its assets, since the lease commitments may exceed the interest bill. Again, cash flow from operations may be used as the numerator to provide a more meaningful measure of the entity's ability to meet its financing costs.

Case 12.4 CCA performance ratios

Refer to the Eight Year Financial Summary for Coca-Cola Amatil Ltd in Appendix 1. Study the 'Performance Ratios' section. What conclusions can be drawn about this organisation from these ratios?

Per-share ratios

The analysis so far will have created a general picture of past performance, the present financial position and some of the factors that account for the entity's performance.

This type of analysis is useful to all external users of accounting information for all types of entities. For shareholders in particular, another set of ratios can be calculated that link accounting measures of the earnings and dividends of the organisation with the market's assessment of the value of the organisation, its share price. Many of these ratios are quoted in newspaper reports of share-market trading.

Where a share is traded on a stock exchange, market analysts undertake their own analyses of the organisation and these will influence the actions of share traders. The collective judgement of all traders on the 'value' of the organisation will be reflected in the share price. The relationships between the share price and various items in the published reports may give us an insight into the market's judgement of the company's future return.

Earnings

The performance of the organisation on a per-share basis may be measured in a number of ways:

- earnings per share
- cash flow per share
- earnings yield
- price earnings ratio.

Earnings per share (EPS) measures profit on a per-share basis, giving an indication of the earnings available to the ordinary shareholders for each share owned. This may be compared with the share price, which is also on a per-share basis. Whereas earnings reflect the past performance of the organisation, its share price should reflect its expected future performance:

$$\text{Earnings per share} = \frac{\text{Net profit after interest and tax}}{\text{Number of ordinary shares}}$$

$$= \frac{160\ 000}{200\ 000}$$

$$= \$0.80 \text{ per share}$$

The numerator reflects profits earned for the ordinary shareholder, so any preference dividend must also be subtracted from net profit after interest and tax. EPS is a function of leverage, which increases risk as well as return. An increasing level of earnings per share may seem to be a sign of a healthy organisation, but this is not always true. As the performance analysis showed, the growth in earnings may not represent improved operations. The return on investment (EBIT to total assets) might be stable or declining, but an increase in EPS may be achieved by the use of leverage or by reinvesting profits in the organisation rather than paying dividends. If an organisation with one million shares earns $1 million profit and reinvests that amount to yield a 1 per cent return in the next year, then its earnings per share will increase by 1 cent, but this could hardly be considered a profitable course of action.

The effect of a change in EPS on the value of the organisation's shares must also include an assessment of the change in risk, and this assessment occurs in the share market. The unreliability of EPS as a measure of improved performance means that the share price would not be expected to react favourably every time EPS increases.

The behaviour of share prices over time is of some use for analysis. The degree of price fluctuation, relative to general trends in the market, provides a measure of the relative volatility of the share price and is a useful indicator of the organisation's riskiness. Shares with highly volatile price movements are the most risky. One measure of volatility that is widely used is known as the *beta factor*. Beta measures the volatility of total returns (dividends and price movements) from an organisation relative to the volatility of the total market. Thus an organisation with a beta of one, on average displays the same volatility in returns as the stock market. Organisations with betas less than one display less volatility; returns rise more slowly and fall less sharply than the market. Shares in such organisations are sometimes known as defensive securities, while shares in organisations with betas greater than one are called aggressive securities because they display more volatility than the market. The higher the beta, the higher the rate of return required by investors in order to compensate for the greater risk. The beta measure plays an important role in modern finance, but further discussion is beyond the scope of this text.

The level of cash generated on a per-share basis can provide additional information regarding the level of cash generated from operations which is available to be distributed for each share held. This is a more specific indication than the cash-flow return to shareholders' equity.

$$\text{Cash flow per share} = \frac{\text{Cash flow from operations}}{\text{No. of ordinary shares}}$$

$$= \frac{320\ 000}{200\ 000}$$

$$= \$1.60 \text{ per share}$$

As with earnings per share, however, share prices alone are a poor basis for comparing organisations. The share price depends on an organisation's total market capitalisation and the number of shares on issue. If Westcoast Ltd made a one-for-one bonus share issue its merits as an investment would remain unchanged but its price would fall to $2.40, other things being equal. This is illustrated in the following equation:

Total market capitalisation = Market price per share × no. of shares on issue

Pre-bonus:
$960 000 = $4.80 × 200 000

Post-bonus:
$960 000 = $2.40 × 400 000

Earnings per share—IAS 33

From 1 January 1998 this standard becomes operative. Its objective is stated as:

...to prescribe principles for the determination and presentation of earnings per share which will improve performance comparisons among different enterprises in the same period and among different accounting periods for the same enterprise...Even though earnings per share data has limitations because of different accounting policies used for determining 'earnings', a consistently determined denominator enhances financial reporting.

(International Accounting Standards Committee, International Accounting Standards 1997, IAS 33, p. 603)

The standard indicates that in calculating the 'basic EPS', the earnings part of the calculation should be the net profit for the period after preference dividends have been deducted and the denominator of the ratio should be the weighted average number of ordinary shares on issue for the period.

The standard also requires the calculation and presentation of 'diluted EPS', which takes into account the effect of the conversion into ordinary shares of such instruments as options, share warrants, certain debt or equity capable of conversion.

Note the inclusion of 'Basic EPS' and note regarding 'Diluted EPS' at the foot of the profit and loss statement in the Coca-Cola Amatil Ltd financial statements in Appendix 1.

Some of the difficulties of comparison between organisations are overcome by relating the earnings per share figure to the market price of the share. The resulting *earnings yield* is independent of the number of shares on issue.

$$\text{Earnings yield} = \frac{\text{Net profit after interest and tax/no. of shares}}{\text{Total market value of the firm's shares/no. of shares}}$$

$$= \frac{\text{Earnings per share}}{\text{Market price per share}}$$

$$= \frac{0.80}{4.80}$$

$$= 16.66\%$$

The 16.66 per cent yield for Westcoast Ltd can be interpreted to mean that, for every dollar invested in the share at the current price, the company has earned (although not necessarily distributed) 16.66 cents. Organisations that are regarded favourably by investors will have high share prices in relation to current earnings, resulting in a lower earnings yield. Investors in such organisations are willing to accept a low current return because they expect future returns to be higher. Growth stocks, for example, sell at low earnings yields because rapid growth demonstrates the potential for high future returns.

The earnings yield also has a risk dimension, in that securities thought to be risky will sell at a higher earnings yield. The market requires higher returns from organisations believed to be financially risky because there is doubt as to whether the current earnings will continue.

Thus, if an organisation offers a current earnings yield well above those of similar organisations, this should be regarded as a cue for careful analysis rather than an invitation to invest. The crucial task for the analyst is to calculate what the earnings yield will be, based on prospective earnings rather than historical earnings.

It is quite common to calculate the inverse of the earnings yield and this is called the *price earnings ratio (PER)*:

$$\text{Price earnings ratio} = \frac{\text{Share price}}{\text{Earnings per share}}$$

$$= \frac{4.80}{0.80}$$

$$= 6 \text{ times}$$

If it is assumed that earnings will continue at their current level, then the price earnings ratio indicates how many years earnings it will take before the total of earnings generated is equal to, or will pay back, the current share price. For Westcoast Ltd, it would be said that anyone buying the shares at the current price would be paying six years earnings. As the inverse of the earnings yield, a high price earnings ratio reflects willingness by investors to pay a high price in relation to current earnings because of confidence in the growth of future profits. Conversely, low price earnings ratios are reserved for unprofitable or very risky organisations.

The price earnings ratio can be thought of as a measure of the organisation's expected future profitability. In Chapter 11 it was shown that the share price is a discounted measure of expected future dividends; the ratio of expected future dividends to current earnings per share indicates the market's level of confidence in the organisation's future ability to generate earnings.

The price earnings ratio may be used to estimate an appropriate level for a share price by using the relationship:

$$\text{Estimated share price} = \text{Price earnings ratio} \times \text{earnings per share}$$

For example, if an entity's earnings per share is currently 10 cents and similar organisations in the industry sell at a price earnings ratio of 20, then an appropriate share price is estimated to be about $2.

Dividends

An organisation's dividend policy can be assessed using the following:

- dividends per share
- cash dividend coverage
- dividend yield
- dividend pay-out ratio.

The only cash that investors normally receive while they continue to hold their shares is in the form of dividends. Thus, investors are interested in the organisation's *dividend per share (DPS)* as a measure of the cash flow from their investment. For example:

$$\text{Dividends per share} = \frac{\text{Ordinary dividend}}{\text{No. of ordinary shares}}$$

$$= \frac{80\,000}{200\,000}$$

$$= \$0.40 \text{ per share}$$

Dividend per share is the most common way to assess an organisation's dividend policy. As discussed in Chapter 11, it is this figure that many entities endeavour to maintain from year to year. Most organisations prefer to maintain stable dividend policies and are most reluctant to cut dividends. Accordingly, dividends tend to change more gradually than profits, being increased only when management is convinced that recent profit increases will be maintained into the future. A change in dividend may be seen therefore as signalling a long-term effect, while a sudden and substantial change reflects some major upheaval.

The *cash dividend coverage ratio* gives a measure of the ability of the firm to meet current dividends from cash generated from its operating activities:

$$\text{Cash dividend coverage} = \frac{\text{Cash flow from operations}}{\text{Dividends paid}}$$

$$= \frac{320\ 000}{160\ 000}$$

$$= 4 \text{ times}$$

A *dividend yield* may be computed to measure the dividend component of shareholders' total returns. The other component of their returns is in the form of capital gains, for which cash is received only when shares are sold. The dividend yield therefore relates the dividends earned to the current price quoted for the shares of the entity:

$$\text{Dividend yield} = \frac{\text{Dividends per share}}{\text{Share price}}$$

$$= \frac{0.40}{4.80}$$

$$= 8.33\%$$

It is also useful to relate the level of dividends to the level of earnings in a *dividend pay-out ratio*:

$$\text{Dividend pay-out ratio} = \frac{\text{Total ordinary dividends}}{\text{Total profits earned for ordinary shareholders}}$$

$$= \frac{\text{Dividends per share}}{\text{Earnings per share}}$$

$$= \frac{0.40}{0.80}$$

$$= 50\%$$

This ratio shows the percentage of earnings paid out as dividends. Some analysts prefer to use the inverse of the ratio, which is called the *dividend cover ratio*. However, both ratios provide the same information, indicating the organisation's policy on profit retention and the extent to which earnings could decline before dividends might be threatened. The level of payout should be interpreted in association with the organisation's reinvestment opportunities, as previously discussed.

If an organisation is facing financial difficulties and is attempting to conserve cash, this might result in a low pay-out ratio. Organisations in this situation are often characterised by poor liquidity, declining profitability and high levels of leverage. Highly profitable organisations may also have a low pay-out ratio, with the object of retaining profits to finance expansion. Thus, dividend policy must always be related to the financial situation of the entity.

One other per-share statistic that is often used is the *net asset backing per share*.

$$\text{Net assets per share} = \frac{\text{Ordinary shareholders' equity}}{\text{Number of ordinary shares}}$$

$$= \frac{800\ 000}{200\ 000}$$

$$= \$4 \text{ per share}$$

Intangible assets such as goodwill are frequently excluded to produce a ratio called *net tangible assets per share*. This ratio is of limited application. It can be used by shareholders to compare the current share price with the per-share book value of the entity's net tangible assets. However, unless assets are measured at current selling prices, no guidance is given as to the amount a shareholder would receive in the event of a liquidation. An organisation in good economic health will normally have a share price in excess of the book value for net assets per share. This is due partly to the conservative valuation of assets inherent in historical cost balance sheets during periods of inflation, and partly to the omission of internally developed goodwill. Shares are valued in the market in terms of future prospects, not past events. If, however, shares are selling at a substantial discount on net asset backing, the organisation may become a takeover target, particularly if its assets are liquid.

Case 12.5 CCA information on shares

Refer to the Eight Year Financial Summary for Coca-Cola Amatil Ltd in Appendix 1. Study the 'Share Information' section. What conclusions can be drawn about this organisation from these ratios?

Cash flow ratios revisited[1]

The statement of cash flows is now an integral part of the financial statements of all companies and any analysis should reflect this. We have included a number of cash flow ratios within each group of ratios illustrated so that they assist to identify additional features of that type of analysis. However, it is also possible to carry out a separate analysis of cash flow ratios to highlight whether their level is sufficient and whether their management has been carried out efficiently. An example of the range and classification of ratios used for this purpose is shown below.

Cash flow sufficiency ratios

$$\text{Cash flow adequacy} = \frac{\text{Cash flow from operations}}{\text{Long-term debt paid} + \text{acquisitions of assets} + \text{dividends paid}}$$

$$\text{Debt coverage} = \frac{\text{Total debt}}{\text{Cash flow from operations}}$$

$$\text{Dividend payout} = \frac{\text{Dividends}}{\text{Cash flow from operations}}$$

---

[1] For our discussion here and earlier in the chapter, we have relied in part on the following articles, which should be referred to for a more in-depth discussion of this area: C. A. Carslaw and J. R. Mills, 'Developing Ratios for Effective Cash-Flow Statement Analysis', *Journal of Accountancy*, November 1991, pp. 63–70; R. Juchau and P. Ross, 'Putting Cash into Ratios', *The Australian Accountant*, November 1994, pp. 29–31; D. E. Giacomino and D. E. Mielke, 'Cash Flows: Another Approach to Ratio Analysis', *Journal of Accountancy*, March 1993, pp. 55–58.

$$\text{Long-term debt payment} \quad = \quad \frac{\text{Long-term debt payments}}{\text{Cash flow from operations}}$$

$$\text{Reinvestment ratio} \quad = \quad \frac{\text{Purchase of assets}}{\text{Cash flow from operations}}$$

Cash flow efficiency ratios

$$\text{Quality of income/operations index} \quad = \quad \frac{\text{Cash flow from operations}}{\text{Earnings after interest and tax}}$$

$$\text{Cash flow to sales} \quad = \quad \frac{\text{Cash flow from operations}}{\text{Sales}}$$

$$\text{Cash return on assets} \quad = \quad \frac{\text{Cash flow from operations (before interest and tax)}}{\text{Total assets}}$$

Other ratios

In the foregoing sections we have introduced some of the more popular ratios, but the number of possible ratios is almost without limit. Some ratios are industry-specific and combine both financial and physical operating characteristics in computing performance measurements. A commonly used ratio in the retailing industry, for example, is the ratio of sales to floor space, which is used to assess selling efficiency. We remind you that it is necessary to choose the appropriate ratios for any analysis based on the questions you are trying to answer, the type of information available and the type of organisation being analysed.

Ratios in public sector entities

The example of Westcoast Ltd is an illustration of ratio analysis applied to a private sector entity. The majority of ratios discussed for Westcoast Ltd apply equally to public sector entities, but there are differences in public sector and private sector entities. One, for example, is that whereas private sector entities typically have only commercial objectives, public sector ones have community service obligations (e.g. local councils and hospitals), or a combination of commercial and community service obligations.

Another difference is that public sector entities frequently have constraints such as ceilings on the prices they can charge for services. These differences, however, do not translate into differences in the importance of many of the ratios discussed in this chapter. Return on assets is an example. A private sector entity may have the flexibility to accept or to reject the provision of a new product or project, and will accept it if the prices it can charge and the revenue it can generate will produce an acceptable return on the assets required. This organisation will be seeking to maximise the numerator of the return on assets relative to the denominator.

A public sector organisation may be required, under its community service obligations, to provide a new product or project, and may then be constrained in the prices it can charge or the revenue it can generate from the product or project. Nonetheless, the return on assets ratio is still an important one. Here the emphasis will still be on maximising the numerator (through minimising expenses) and on minimising the denominator. That is, the public sector organisation will be seeking to minimise the assets invested and the resources consumed while providing the required product or service. Similarly, of course, the motivations for concern with efficiency, short-term liquidity and financial structure and long-term solvency ratios are exactly the same for public sector entities as for private sector ones.

There are some differences in the nature of public sector entities relative to private sector ones that affect the ratios calculated by and for those entities, including:

- Few public sector entities pay income tax at the present time, and therefore the EBIT calculation becomes EBI only for these entities.
- Public sector entities do not have shares traded on share-markets, so the per-share ratios discussed in the chapter are not applicable to these entities.
- There is a tendency for public sector entities to report and be evaluated on a variety of ratios other than the ones discussed in this chapter. The community service obligations of these entities give rise to the development of specific ratios, both financial and non-financial, to evaluate the efficiency and effectiveness with which the community services are being provided.

Uses of ratio analysis

Given an efficient stock market, as discussed in Chapter 11, it is unlikely that the analysis of published annual reports will lead to large gains in the stock market. Some additional information may be obtained from knowledge of the exact profit figure, or other items in the financial statements, but the opportunity to make gains from such information is usually short-lived because of the gap between the close of the accounting period and the publication of the financial statements.

However, financial analysis has many other uses. These include using ratios:

- as performance indicators
- as predictors of financial distress
- in making credit decisions.

Their use as performance indicators involves the trend in certain ratios over time being presented, and future performance being predicted. This is useful to both management and external users. For example, some parts of the financial press rank the top Australian companies for investment purposes, based on ratio analysis. Companies may be ranked by market capitalisation or by profitability (measured by return on equity); other ratios used in such analyses may include trend ratios to measure growth/decline, component ratios such as return on sales, and special relationship ratios such as price earnings ratio, dividend yield and interest cover.

> Note that the daily Sharemarket Report in the *Australian Financial Review* includes the following ratios for all listed companies: dividend per share, dividend coverage, net tangible assets per share, dividend yield, earnings per share and price earnings ratio.

Financial analysis can be used in the prediction of financial distress in two ways. First, ratios are used to compare different entities, usually in the same industry at one point in time, in order to determine which of those entities' ratios are out of line with the others. However, the problem with cross-sectional analysis is that a benchmark is needed for comparative purposes. Usually an industry average is used. Deviations from the industry average have a number of possible explanations. The deviation may be temporary and the entity's performance will revert towards the industry average at a later stage, or the entity may be in financial difficulty. Second, ratios are used as the explanatory variables in econometric models that attempt to predict financial distress. It has been shown that key ratios may diverge from industry averages up to four years before an entity actually fails. Multivariate analysis is one estimation technique that has used financial ratios in such a way.

Signs of financial distress include diminishing cash flows, the delayed release of audited accounts, avoiding recognising expenses, and the use of 'creative accounting'. An organisation can avoid recognising expenses by the creation of deferred assets such as advertising and research and development, for which the future benefits are possible but not probable. Creative accounting includes such practices as the expedient choice of depreciation rates and the capitalisation of expenses, which reduce reported losses.

Third, ratios can be used to predict the success or failure of a loan from the perspective of the bank or other financial institution. In general, in the analysis and negotiation of a large loan between a bank and a corporate client, the bank will invariably request a current set of financial statements to help assess their risk exposure, and also to determine any special conditions that may be attached to the loan.

Discriminant analysis is one specific technique that has been used to assist financial institutions in deciding whether or not to make a loan to an applicant. Financial ratios are used in the discriminant analysis as discriminating variables in order to initially assess the likelihood of the loan being repaid. Financial ratios can also assist in the subsequent decision of what interest rate to charge, and the security and/or restrictive covenants required over the applicant's assets.

Within the entity, management can use financial analysis when alternative courses of action are being contemplated. Analysis of projected financial statements under each alternative can be critical to the decision process. Financial analysis is often used by management to help diagnose problems such as poor performance because of inadequate inventory turnover.

Thus, even with efficient markets, there is no shortage of useful work for the financial analyst. Paradoxically, it is the competition between analysts who are trying to out-perform the market that maintains the level of market efficiency.

An example of a complete analysis of two companies

The following example is given to draw together the various types of analysis and range of ratios discussed in this chapter. It is representative of the type of comparative analysis between two companies which may be carried out for a prospective investor. It presents a discussion of the ratios under appropriate headings and indicates the limitations, areas for additional investigation and some conclusions.

Summary data: Cool Water Ltd & Sparkling Drinks Ltd

	Cool Water Ltd		Sparkling Drinks Ltd		Industry average
	$000	%	$000	%	%
Cash and liquid assets	113	0.1	–	0.0	1.0
Accounts receivable	14 225	12.5	42 003	21.7	11.3
Inventories	17 753	15.6	7 921	4.1	6.8
Other current assets	3 278	2.9	–	0.0	1.5
Investments	247	0.2	3 620	1.9	3.5
Land	45 062	39.5	122 407	63.3	55.2
Plant and equipment	25 659	22.5	17 042	8.8	14.4
Other tangible assets	–	0.0	–	0.0	1.4
Intangible assets	7 826	6.9	500	0.3	4.8
Total assets	**$114 163**	**100%**	**$193 493**	**100%**	**100%**

continues

	Cool Water Ltd		Sparkling Drinks Ltd		Industry average
	$000	%	$000	%	%
Accounts payable	9 781	8.6	13 982	7.2	6.6
Other current liabilities	19 358	17.0	34 019	17.6	14.2
Long-term liabilities	22 086	19.4	–	0.0	10.8
Shareholders' equity	62 938	55.1	145 492	75.2	68.4
	$114 163	100%	$193 493	100%	100%
Sales revenue	195 360	100.0	146 868	100.0	100.0
Depreciation	2 926	1.5	5 448	3.7	2.0
Interest expense	2 119	1.1	930	0.6	0.7
Other expenses	181 281	92.8	121 912	83.1	89.3
Taxation	3 919	2.0	8 375	5.7	3.6
Net profit (after tax)	5 115	2.6	10 203	6.9	4.4
Dividends	3 170		7 208		
Market price (at 31/7/X1)	$1.40		$1.74		
Number of shares (millions)	45.3		70.4		
Balance date	31/7/X1		31/3/X1		

Relevant ratios

	Cool Water Ltd	Sparkling Drinks Ltd	Industry average
Performance ratios			
Profit margin on sales (before tax)	5.70%	13.28%	8.74%
Total asset turnover (sales/total assets)	1.71 times	0.76 times	1.31 times
Return on investment (EBIT/total assets)	9.77%	10.10%	11.49%
Return on equity (pre-tax)	14.35%	12.77%	15.36%
(after tax)	8.12%	7.01%	8.45%
Efficiency ratios			
Inventory turnover	11.0 times	18.54 times	19.23 times
Accounts receivable turnover	13.73 times	3.50 times	11.61 times
Average collection period	26 days	102 days	31 days
Liquidity ratios			
Current ratio	1.21	1.04	0.99
Quick asset ratio	0.61	0.87	0.66
Stability ratios			
Debt to total assets	44.9%	24.8%	37%
Times interest earned	5.26 times	20.97 times	11.76 times
Per-share ratios			
Earnings per share (in cents)	11.3	14.5	
Earnings yield	8.07%	8.03%	n.a.
Dividend per share	7.00 cents	10.24 cents	n.a.
Dividend cover	1.62 times	1.42 times	n.a.
Net asset backing per share	$1.39	$2.07	n.a.

Leverage ratios →

Notes:

1. The quick asset ratio includes other current assets.
2. Times interest earned, profit margin on sales and return on investment were calculated using earnings before interest and taxes (EBIT).
3. As cost of goods sold was not available, inventory turnover was based on sales.

Report on Cool Water Ltd & Sparkling Drinks Ltd

The purpose of the report

It will be assumed that the analyst has been approached by an investor interested in purchasing shares in one or other of the two companies. For this purpose, a full analysis of performance and financial stability has been undertaken.

Limitations of the analysis

The different balance dates may affect the comparison of the two companies. Sparkling Drinks Ltd's balance date is 31 March, after the peak summer sales season, whereas Cool Water Ltd's is 31 July, after the winter season, which would be a quiet sales period. Cool Water Ltd would be expected to show a build-up of inventory and a run-down of debtors, whereas Sparkling Drinks Ltd would be expected to have a run-down of inventory and a build-up of debtors. This is exactly the picture revealed by the component percentage analysis of the current assets section of the balance sheet (see preceding financial statements).

Differing accounting methods may also distort comparisons between organisations or influence the industry averages.

The published information concerning the companies is incomplete. Further information will be required to complete the analysis. The search for such information would normally be concentrated in those areas where the ratios indicate some peculiarity and, in the following discussion, the need for further investigation is indicated by (?).

One factor that may influence the analysis is the extent to which leased assets are used instead of those purchased outright. Whereas 'finance leases' must be recorded in a similar way to a purchased asset, 'operating leased' assets are not disclosed on the balance sheet as assets, nor are any associated payment commitments shown as liabilities. The rental payments would simply be shown as expenses in the profit and loss statement. If operating leases are used, this affects comparisons of return on investment and leverage ratios. Cool Water has a low investment in land in comparison with Sparkling Drinks Ltd and the industry generally, which suggests that leasing of property may have been used. Without details of the 'Other expenses' category, it is not possible to draw any firm conclusions (?).

Another possibility is that Cool Water Ltd acquired its land much earlier than Sparkling Drinks Ltd, resulting in lower costs. Valuation at current market prices might show that Cool Water's holding of land is proportionately greater than the historical cost figures indicate (?).

Performance

Sparkling Drinks Ltd has achieved a much higher profit margin on sales than Cool Water Ltd and it compares favourably with the industry average. This may reflect good pricing policy or expense control. Cool Water Ltd's low margin merits further investigation. It could be due to heavy advertising expenditure, to leasing of outlets with heavy lease rental commitments, or to poor cost control (?).

A factor that is disclosed is the interest burden facing Cool Water Ltd because of its heavy reliance on debt. Interest represents 1.1 per cent of sales revenue, compared with an industry average of 0.7 per cent. This is the first indication that Cool Water Ltd is more highly levered than the industry average, an observation that will be confirmed in later analyses.

The total asset turnover for Cool Water Ltd is excellent, exceeding the industry average, whereas for Sparkling Drinks Ltd it is disappointing. A major cause of variation is the substantial difference in the ownership of freehold land. An examination of total assets and total sales reveals that Sparkling Drinks Ltd is the bigger company in terms of assets, but that Cool Water Ltd is larger in terms of sales. This is quite an impressive performance by Cool Water Ltd, as its sales are 133 per cent of Sparkling Drinks Ltd's sales, while its assets are only 59 per cent of Sparkling Drinks Ltd's assets. Part of the difference may reflect leasing activities by Cool Water Ltd.

The return on investment, which is the product of the profit margin and the turnover ratios, is similar for both companies, but somewhat below the industry average. The similarity in overall operating profitability arises because the better turnover ratio achieved by Cool Water Ltd is offset by the superior profit margin earned by Sparkling Drinks Ltd.

Cool Water Ltd, however, achieves a much better return on equity (pre-tax) because of its use of leverage and, although taxes substantially reduce the after-tax return to equity, Cool Water Ltd manages to achieve a return close to the industry average. Sparkling Drinks Ltd, on the other hand, with its less risky capital structure, earns an after-tax return on equity about 1.5 per cent below the industry average.

For earnings per share, the relative positions reverse, with Sparkling Drinks Ltd offering the high return, apparently because it has financed expansion more through retained profits than through share issues. The relative proportions of share capital to total shareholders' funds are 71.9 per cent (45.3/62.938) for Cool Water Ltd and 48.4 per cent (70.4/145.492) for Sparkling Drinks Ltd, indicating the high profit retentions by Sparkling Drinks Ltd.

Efficiency

Some variation from the industry averages is evident, but may simply reflect seasonal sales fluctuations. Cool Water Ltd's inventory turnover seems low by industry standards, but could reflect slack winter sales and a build-up of inventory for the summer (?). The low turnover of accounts receivable and the extended collection period for Sparkling Drinks Ltd could suggest slack credit management, but probably reflects a seasonal sales bulge resulting in a temporarily inflated level of accounts receivable (?).

Financial stability

1. Short-term liquidity
Although adequate by industry standards, the liquidity ratios for both companies would normally be considered low. However, the beverage industry has a very good cash flow and relies on this to meet its bills rather than using a store of liquid assets. Cool Water Ltd's quick asset ratio would fall to an unhealthy 0.49 if the 'other current assets' were not readily convertible into cash, so that it is relevant to investigate the nature and liquidity of those assets (?). Sparkling Drinks Ltd's quick ratio is bolstered by the high level of debtors and could fall dramatically if there was substantial bad-debt experience (?). The lack of cash in Sparkling Drinks Ltd is a little worrying, but presumably the company is operating on a temporary bank overdraft which will be paid off as the receipts from credit sales start to flow in (?).

2. Asset structure
In the long-term assets section of the balance sheet, Cool Water Ltd has a substantially lower than average investment in land (39.5 per cent), possibly a reflection of its greater involvement in leasing of premises than Sparkling Drinks Ltd (63.3 per cent) (?). Cool Water Ltd also has relatively more plant and equipment (22.5 per cent) than either Sparkling Drinks Ltd (8.8 per cent) or the industry average (14.4 per cent). Sparkling Drinks Ltd, on the other hand, has relatively less plant and equipment than the industry average (?). Cool Water Ltd's level of intangible assets (6.9 per cent) is quite substantial. What are they (?). Do they have any resale value (?).

3. Leverage ratios
There is a striking difference between the leverage ratios of Cool Water Ltd and Sparkling Drinks Ltd and both diverge from the industry average. Sparkling Drinks Ltd has a very conservative capital structure, with no long-term debt, and this is reflected in a low leverage

ratio. Cool Water Ltd, on the other hand, has a much more highly levered capital structure, with levels of debt above the industry average.

These differences in leverage are reflected by the times interest earned ratios. The Sparkling Drinks Ltd interest bill is well covered and the use of more debt in the company could be beneficial to shareholders. Although the interest coverage for Cool Water Ltd is well below the industry average, it appears that an adequate level of cover is currently being maintained; however, any decline in profitability or increase in leverage would be cause for caution. For Cool Water Ltd, an investigation of the size of any lease payments and the fixed charge cover ratios seems desirable (?).

Market price ratios

Sparkling Drinks Ltd pays a higher dividend per share and commands a higher price. Comparing the two firms' earning yields, it can be seen that they are very close, indicating that the market views the two firms as roughly equivalent. Cool Water possibly offers the higher return, through its use of leverage, but at greater risk. The dividend from Cool Water Ltd is slightly better covered than the dividend from Sparkling Drinks Ltd, but this is not a major factor.

Cool Water Ltd's shares are selling for slightly more than their net asset backing and the difference would increase if intangible assets were excluded. This means that the market values Cool Water Ltd at a figure higher than the book value of Cool Water Ltd's assets. Since book values would be expected to reflect historical costs and since prices generally have risen over time, it could be expected that the market value of the company will exceed book value. Moreover, shares are valued principally on the basis of the future dividend stream of the company, rather than on the book value of the company's assets. The market is generally more concerned with what the company's assets can earn than with their depreciated historical cost.

Sparkling Drinks Ltd's shares are selling below the net asset backing. Perhaps a takeover offer, followed by the liquidation of some of the company's assets, is a possibility (?).

Conclusions

With the exception of some of the ratios involving current assets, which may have been distorted by seasonal trends, both firms compare reasonably well overall with the industry averages, although there is room to improve performance and perhaps adjust leverage. The significant differences between the two firms are found in the debt ratio, the profit margin and the asset turnover. There are major differences in current assets, but these are probably seasonal.

Cool Water Ltd could possibly improve performance by examining its inventory turnover to determine whether funds are needlessly tied up in slow-moving stock. The low profit margin also merits investigation. If profit margins can be increased, performance could improve. There is no apparent scope, however, for further benefits to shareholders through increased leverage.

Sparkling Drinks Ltd may have excessive accounts receivable and, if so, a tightening of credit policy may release funds for more profitable use. Asset turnover might also be examined. The return to shareholders might also be improved by an increase in leverage.

Overall, balancing risk and returns, there seems little to choose between the two companies. This is reflected in the similarity of the earnings yields. Cool Water Ltd seems the more active, more aggressive company and, if margins are improved, profits will rise sharply, but the company is more risky than Sparkling Drinks Ltd. Sparkling Drinks Ltd resembles a slumbering giant, with more conservative policies than Cool Water Ltd, and is therefore less risky and less profitable. Should the management awaken to the possibilities of increased leverage and faster asset turnover, the potential for improved profitability may be substantial.

Ethical issues

The use of management compensation plans that are in some way linked to the financial performance of the organisation might encourage the practices of creative accounting and window-dressing. The question is, do we expect accounting reports to be prepared by management and presented by directors with high ethical considerations? Do we expect them to present a true and fair view of the organisation's activities and financial position? Or does the mere existence of management compensation plans, annual bonuses and similar schemes rely on and therefore encourage a different set of values?

Summary

This chapter has provided an introduction to some of the techniques that can be used to determine how effective the management of organisations have been in applying the sound financial management principles discussed in Chapter 11. These chapters complement one another by drawing together the use of accounting numbers in financial management and in analysing its effectiveness.

One of the major techniques discussed was the use of ratio analysis of financial statements. A number of limitations to the use of this technique were identified prior to the discussion of various ratios. These ratios show the relationships between items in the financial statements and other relevant information to reveal information relating to performance, efficiency, financial stability and data per share. This information, within the acknowledged limitations, when used for comparative purposes over a period of time or with similar organisations, can assist in decision making.

Although the form of the analysis must depend on the information required for a particular decision, an analysis of performance and financial stability will usually be relevant. Where possible, it will also be appropriate to relate the accounting results to the share price to gauge the market's impression of the organisation.

No analysis is other than a tentative investigation. Rarely is sufficient information available to answer every query, and the financial reports themselves are subject to limitations arising from the accounting methods used. Financial ratios are a valuable tool of financial analysis, but need to be used with care, intelligence and judgement, all of which improve with experience. They add to the pool of information that can be directed towards the making of better informed and hence more accurate financial decisions.

Review exercises

Discussion questions

12.1 It has been suggested that financial analysis would be more useful if 'liquidation values' were available. Do you agree with this position? Justify your response.

12.2 Why is it said that the key to successful financial analysis is the ability to ask the right questions, rather than the memorising of a list of ratios?

12.3 What alternatives are there to traditional ratio analysis in interpreting financial statements?

12.4 How can industry-average ratios be obtained, and what are the drawbacks to using industry averages as standards for comparison?

12.5 Explain, using an example, why a choice must be made between using an average of beginning- and end-of-year balances, or end-of-year balances only, in computing some ratios.

12.6 Slow Ltd has a return on investments of 10 per cent and a profit margin of 10 per cent. Quick Ltd also a return on investment of 10 per cent but only a 2 per cent profit margin. Explain how this is possible.

12.7 'The inclusion of cash flow data adds little to the outcome of financial analysis.' Discuss this statement, illustrating with examples as appropriate.

12.8 A financial analyst has predicted financial disaster for your company, based solely on a ratio analysis of data in published financial reports. How would you defend the company against such a judgement if you believed it not to be true?

12.9 Explain how the following are possible:

(a) An organisation has a high current ratio, but has difficulty paying its bills.
(b) An organisation has a high quick asset ratio, but has difficulty paying its bills.
(c) An organisation has a low quick asset ratio, but has no difficulty paying its bills.

12.10 Briefly explain the differences in profit margins, total asset turnover and level of accounts receivable that you would expect to find between retailers of consumer durables and retailers of alcoholic beverages.

12.11 What is the difference between dividend cover and dividend yield? Why is a change in the level of dividends an important indicator to financial analysts?

12.12 Explain the circumstances under which slowing down the payment of suppliers can help boost the quick ratio.

12.13 What factors, other than financial ratios, could be taken into consideration in predicting the future viability of an organisation?

 Problems

12.14 *Company evaluation based on ratios*
For the year ended 30 June 20X3 the following ratios have been calculated for River Ltd and Lake Ltd. Using this information, make an evaluation of the performance, efficiency and financial position of both companies.

	River Ltd	Lake Ltd	Industry averages
Return on total assets	17.04%	17.10%	17.00%
Total asset turnover	1.74 times	0.92 times	1.36 times
Return on shareholders' equity	17.50%	13.00%	15.65%
Current ratio	179.0%	236.0%	184.0%
Quick asset ratio	91.0%	177.0%	95.0%
Inventory turnover	6.88 times	8.36 times	6.99 times
Inventory turnover	53 days	44 days	52 days
Accounts receivable turnover	8.80 times	4.40 times	7.50 times
Accounts receivable turnover	42 days	83 days	49 days
Debt/equity ratio	53.0%	26.0%	45.3%
Times interest earned	5.0 times	18.0 times	12.8 times

12.15 *Dupont formulae analysis*

The following financial data are available for the financial year 20X2 for Africa Ltd and Britain Ltd which are fierce competitors in the same industry.

	Africa Ltd	Britain Ltd
	$000	$000
Sales	500	300
Cost of goods sold	200	220
EBIT	50	15
Total assets	250	75
Total debt	50	25
Shareholders' equity	200	50

(a) Use the Dupont formulae (based on EBIT) to compare the performance of each firm in 20X2. Do their performances differ and, if so, in what way?

(b) Assume that the interest rate on debt is 10 per cent and that the tax rate is 40 per cent of net profit. Calculate net profit after tax for each company and compare the performance of each from the point of view of an external shareholder.

12.16 *Calculation of per-share ratios*

With a current share price of $4, Kwan Trading Ltd has a price earnings ratio of 10. It has 1 million shares on issue which are fully paid at $2 each. It has maintained a dividend payout ratio of 50 per cent for a number of years.

(a) Calculate the

- earnings per share
- earnings yield
- dividend yield
- total net profit for the year.

(b) If the earnings yield that investors require from Kwan Trading's shares falls to 8 per cent, by how much will the firm's share price change and what will be the earnings per share?

12.17 *Ratio analysis and comparison with industry averages*
  The following financial statements are for Roulette Importers Ltd. Carefully analyse the
  statements and answer the questions below:

BALANCE SHEET: ROULETTE IMPORTERS LTD
as at 30 June 20X8

Current assets	$ 000	Current liabilities	$ 000
Cash	2 000	Bank overdraft	1 000
Shares in other companies	8 000	Short-term loans	10 000
Accounts receivable	15 000	Accounts payable	14 000
Inventories	20 000		
Total current assets	45 000	*Total current lliabilities*	25 000
Non-current assets		**Non-current liabilities**	
Property	30 000	Mortgage loan	25 000
Plant & equipment	40 000	Long-term loan	5 000
Computing equipment	10 000		
Total non-current assets	80 000	*Total non-current liabilities*	30 000
(net of accumulated depreciation)			
		Shareholders' equity	
		Paid-up ordinary capital	20 000
		Share premium reserve	18 000
		Retained earnings	32 000
		Total shareholders' equity	70 000
		Total liabilities and	
Total assets	**$125 000**	**shareholders' equity**	**$125 000**

PROFIT AND LOSS STATEMENT: ROULETTE IMPORTERS LTD
for year ended 30 June 20X8

	$ 000
Sales (80% on credit)	70 000
Less Cost of goods sold	50 000
Gross profit	20 000
Less Operating expenses	10 000
Earnings before interest and taxes	10 000
Less Interest	2 000
	8 000
Less Taxes (50%)	4 000
Earnings after interest and taxes	**$ 4 000**

Cash flow statement information

Cash flow from operations $2.5 million

(a) Calculate the following ratios for Roulette Importers Ltd (assume closing balances are representative of average balances):

	Industry averages
Long-term debt to equity	167%
Times interest ratio	1.33 times
Current ratio	180%
Quick asset ratio	125%
Inventory turnover	3.60 times
Inventory turnover	101 days
Accounts receivable turnover	2.15 times
Accounts receivable turnover	170 days
Operating expenses to sales	17.1%
Current liabilities to total assets	20.0%
EBIT to total assets	3.2%

(b) Evaluate Roulette's position in relation to the industry averages.

(c) What additional information would you like to have access to so that a more informed recommendation could be made?

12.18 *Interpretation of ratios*

The following financial ratios have been prepared from the financial statements of Vijay Ltd for the years 20X2, 20X3 and 20X4.

	20X2	*20X3*	*20X4*
Current ratio	4.1	1.6	1.3
Quick asset ratio	1.07	0.83	0.32
Debt to equity	10.1%	23.8%	35.1%
Inventory turnover (times)	2.4	2.9	1.4
Accounts receivable turnover (times)	10.9	7.8	6.2
Gross profit margin	33.3%	35.6%	39.4%
Profit margin on sales	21.5%	17.8%	14%
Return on equity (before tax)	16.7%	17.8%	27.3%
Times interest earned	4.8	3.9	2.8
Total asset turnover (times)	0.62	0.8	1.56
Return on investment	13.4%	14.2%	21.8%

(a) Using these ratios, comment on the company's profitability, liquidity and efficiency for the period and particularly 20X4.

(b) 'These financial ratios can be relied on because the financial statements from which they were calculated were prepared on the basis of generally accepted accounting principles and the relevant accounting standards.' Do you agree with this statement? Justify your comments.

12.19 *Assessment of a financing plan using ratio analysis*

The directors of Amazon Ltd have decided to finance the $12 million expansion of their production plant in Thailand by using long-term debt at an interest rate of 10 per cent. Comment on their decision, using the following information.

Balance sheet
(prior to the expansion)

Assets	$m	Equities	$m
Current assets	22	Current liabilities	15
Fixed assets	53	Long-term liabilities	15
		Shareholders' equity	45
	75		75

Present interest bill = $2 million

Present EBIT = $9 million

The new investment is expected to generate a similar rate of return to existing investments.

12.20 *Methods of improving current ratio*

One of the terms of the trust deed associated with the issue of debentures by Keat Ltd is that the company must maintain its current ratio at 3:1. Recent sales for the wholesaler have not been good, resulting in the current ratio falling to 2:1. At this time the current assets were $2 million and current liabilities amounted to $1 million.

Three suggestions have been made to rectify the situation:

• The accountant suggests that buying additional inventory on credit will rectify the situation.
• The treasurer suggests selling off inventory at cost and building up the firm's cash balance.
• The managing director favours the treasurer's plan but proposes that the cash generated should be used to reduce accounts payable.

Which plan if any should be adopted and by how much must inventory change to achieve the required ratio?

12.21 *From ratios back to financial statements*

This is something a little different, to make you think about the relationships involved with ratios from financial statements. Use the following ratio details to determine the missing figures in the financial statements for Hardy Trading Ltd.

Total assets turnover	3.0 times
Inventory turnover (based on cost of goods sold)	10 times
Quick ratio	1:1
Accounts receivable turnover	20 times
Gross profit margin	10%
Total debt to shareholders' equity ratio	3:4

BALANCE SHEET: HARDY TRADING LTD as at 30 June 20X1			
	$		$
Cash	???	Accounts payable	100 000
Accounts receivable	???	Long-term debt	50 000
Inventory	???	Paid-up capital	
Fixed assets	???	Retained profits	150 000
	$???		$???

PROFIT AND LOSS STATEMENT: HARDY TRADING LTD for year ended 30 June 20X1	
Sales	???
Cost of goods sold	???
Gross profit	???

Assume all sales are made on a credit basis.

12.22 *Cash flow and accrual ratios*

Using the following financial information from the financial statements of an organisation in the entertainment industry, calculate appropriate ratios and briefly comment on significant outcomes.

	$000
Net cash flow from operating activities	59 130
Net cash flow from investing activities	(154 707)
Net cash flow from financing activities	207 551
Total current assets	439 770
Total current liabilities	180 110
Total assets	1 126 440
Total shareholders' equity	755 000
Operating profit before interest and tax	83 330
Interest paid	12 020
Sales	298 000
Number of ordinary shares on issue:	177 650

12.23 *Investment evaluation using ratio analysis*

Your client has been approached by J. Wittoos with an offer to subscribe for 9 million $1 ordinary shares in Tasman Ltd, an importer/exporter in the Pacific Rim region.

J. Wittoos assumed control of this company in January 20X5 by purchasing all of the issued shares and it is claimed that since then the company has been modernised. After an initial development period results have improved dramatically. Your client's funds would provide additional working capital for the business.

The following information has been made available:

PROFIT AND LOSS STATEMENTS
for year ended 31 December

	20X4		20X5		20X6	
	$000	%	$000	%	$000	%
Sales	60 000	100.0	75 000	100.0	130 000	100.0
less Cost of sales	33 000	55.0	46 500	62.0	80 600	62.0
	27 000	45.0	28 500	38.0	49 400	38.0
less Expenses						
Selling	8 000	13.3	11 000	14.7	15 000	11.5
Administration	3 000	5.0	3 500	4.7	3 700	2.9
Financial (interest)	–	–	1 000	1.3	4 800	3.7
Total expenses	11 000	18.3	15 500	20.7	23 500	18.1
Net profit before tax	16 000	26.7	13 000	17.3	25 900	19.9
less Taxation	7 600	12.7	6 000	8.0	12 800	9.8
Net profit after tax	**$ 8 400**	**14.0**	**$ 7 000**	**9.3**	**$ 13 100**	10.1

BALANCE SHEETS
as at 31 December

	20X4		20X5		20X6	
	$000	%	$000	%	$000	%
Current assets						
Bank	5 500					
Accounts receivable	5 000		7 500		14 000	
Inventories	8 000		6 500		15 700	
	18 500	38.1	14 000	18.7	29 700	26.3
Long-term assets						
Land and buildings	17 000		34 000		44 000	
Motor vehicles and equipment (net)	13 000		26 900		24 300	
Shares in Oilsearch Pty Ltd	–		–		15 000	
	30 000	61.9	60 900	81.3	83 300	73.7
Total assets	**$48 500**	**100.0**	**$74 900**	**100.0**	**$113 000**	**100.0**
Current liabilities						
Bank overdraft	–		16 000		14 000	
Accounts payable	5 000		7 400		6 100	
Tax payable	8 000		6 500		12 950	
Dividend payable	3 000		6 000		10 000	
	16 000	33.0	35 900	47.9	43 050	38.1
Long-term liabilities						
Secured notes	–	0.0	6 000	8.0	24 000	21.2
Shareholders' equity						
Paid-up capital (10 million shares)	10 000		10 000		10 000	

continues

BALANCE SHEETS

as at 31 December

	20X4		20X5		20X6	
	$000	%	$000	%	$000	%
Retained profits	22 500		23 000		25 950	
Asset revaluation reserve	–		–		10 000	
	32 500	67.0	33 000	44.1	45 950	40.7
Total funds	**$48 500**	**100.0**	**$74 900**	**100.0**	**$113 000**	**100.0**

Additional information:

(i)   Inventory balance at 1/1/X4 was $4 000 000.

(ii) All sales were on 30 days credit.

(iii) The secured notes are held by J. Wittoos. Interest payable is 18 per cent per annum and the notes are due for repayment in 20X7 and 20X8.

(iv)

	20X5	20X6
	$000	$000
Cash flow from operating activities	$ 7 700	$ 5 000
Cash flow from investing activities	($32 200)	($15 000)
Cash flow from financing activities	$ 3 000	$12 000

Prepare a report to your client including:

(a) The calculation of any additional ratios you deem necessary. Display the formula and the results clearly as follows:

Ratio	Formula	20X4	20X5	20X6

(b) An analysis of the performance and financial stability of the company. Explain the significance of each ratio mentioned.

(c) A recommendation on whether the shares should be purchased, supported by reasons for the recommendation.

Case studies

12.24 *Which is which?*

The recent balance sheets of five entities have been standardised to derive the figures shown on page 483. Instead of being the reported balance-sheet figures, the figures shown are in percentage form based on the reported results.

- National Australia Bank is a large banking institution and one of the largest public companies by market capitalisation in Australia.
- Qantas is Australia's largest airline with an excellent international reputation.
- Coles Myer Ltd is one of the major retailing companies in Australia.
- Ashton Mining Ltd is a major diamond producer with worldwide exploration sites.
- Coca-Cola Amatil Ltd is based in Australia, operates in 18 countries and is an 'anchor bottler' within the Coca-Cola world system.

The five entities and their stated total assets on the dates indicated are:

	Total assets	
National Australia Bank	$201 969 million	(30.9.97)
Qantas	$9 912 million	(30.6.97)
Coles Myer	$6 697 million	(27.7.97)
Ashton Mining	$548 million	(31.12.97)
Coca-Cola Amatil Ltd	$9 466 million	(31.12.97)

Required

Which standardised balance sheet relates to each of the above companies? Justify your conclusions.

	A	B	C	D	E
	%	%	%	%	%
Assets					
Non-current assets:	79.1	2.7	76.3	64.4	53.0
Current assets:					
Inventories/stores	1.5	–	8.6	22.0	37.7
Debtors	16.6	64.5	8.0	4.2	5.0
Cash and near cash	2.4	27.4	4.6	8.8	2.7
Other assets	0.4	5.4	2.5	0.6	1.6
Total	100.0	100.0	100.0	100.0	100.0
Liabilities and shareholders' funds					
Shareholders' equity	27.0	6.2	57.3	48.1	37.6
Non-current liabilities	41.6	93.8	24.9	43.6	27.0
Current liabilities	31.4	–	17.8	8.3	35.4
Total	100.0	100.0	100.0	100.0	100.0

12.25 *Analysis of CCA annual report*

Refer to the financial statements of Coca-Cola Amatil Ltd in Appendix 1.

Required

(a) Using the CCA Group reports, compute the following ratios for the last two years at least:

   (i)   current ratio

   (ii) quick asset ratio

   (iii) debt/equity ratio

   (iv) net profit/sales

   (v) sales/total assets

   (vi) net profit/shareholders' equity

   (vii) ordinary earnings per share

   (viii)ordinary dividend per share

   (ix) interest cover

   (x) dividend cover

   (xi) net asset backing per share

(b) Find a recent share price from the daily paper and compute the current:

   (i)   earnings yield

   (ii) dividend yield

(c) Calculate appropriate ratios using available cash flow data and comment on the additional information they give.

(d) What are your overall impressions of the performance and financial stability of the company? Make reference to specific ratios computed above.

12.26 *Analysis of Coles Myer Ltd summary data*

Coles Myer Ltd is the leading retailing company in Australia. The following is the five-year review data from their annual report:

COLES MYER LTD: COMPARATIVE STATISTICS
5-YEAR REVIEW

	Notes		Year	1997	1996	1995	1994	1993
			Weeks	52	52	52	53	52
Profitability								
Sales		$m		19 224.8	13 175.0	16 801.6	15 921.4	15 168.1
EBITDA (EBIT before depreciation and amortisation)		$m		999.7	932.5	1 067.9	985.5	919.8
Retail EBIT and abnormals		$m		642.2	534.6	629.0	577.1	591.3
Increase/(decrease) on prior year				20.1%	(14.8)%	9.0%	(2.4)%	(10.3)%
Ratio to sales				3.3%	2.9%	3.7%	3.5%	3.9%
Operating profit before interest, income tax,								
abnormals and gain on sale of property		$m		615.3	542.0	686.5	658.5	638.4
Increase/(decrease) on prior year				13.5%	(21.0)%	4.3%	3.1%	(2.4)%
Operating profit before interest								
and income tax (EBIT)		$m		669.1	546.9	717.7	661.3	627.0
Increase/(decrease) on prior year				22.3%	(23.8)%	8.5%	5.5%	(4.9)%
Operating profit before income tax		$m		549.5	400.3	575.1	611.5	582.4
Operating profit after income tax		$m		389.4	280.4	423.4	424.2	411.6
Increase/(decrease) on prior year				38.9%	(33.8)%	(0.2)%	3.0%	11.1%
Basic earnings per ordinary share	(a)	Cents		34.0	24.1	36.5	31.3	30.4
Increase/(decrease) on prior year				41.1%	(34.0)%	16.6%	3.0%	3.4%
Investment								
Total assets		$m		6 705.3	7 069.7	6 568.4	6 910.1	6 234.6
Retail		$m		5 507.1	5 009.7	4 618.3	4 193.6	3 904.2
Property		$m		793.1	1 464.4	1 200.5	1 491.3	1 432.3
Unallocated		$m		405.1	595.6	749.6	1 225.3	898.1
Capital employed	(b)	$m		3 842.2	4 406.9	4 223.4	4 219.4	3 764.4
Net debt	(c)	$m		1 325.9	1 959.4	1 796.8	844.9	520.0
Shareholders' equity		$m		2 516.3	2 447.5	2 426.6	3 374.5	3 244.4
Market capitalisation	(d)	$m		7 564.1	5 140.1	4 875.9	5 803.1	6 649.1
Shareholder value								
Return on equity	(e)			15.9%	11.5%	15.4%	13.1%	13.4%
Return on capital employed	(f)			10.1%	6.4%	10.0%	10.0%	10.9%
Ordinary share price—closing		$		6.61	4.43	4.24	4.24	4.88
Ordinary dividend per share		Cents		22.5	22.0	22.0	20.0	19.5
Price/earnings ratio	(a) (g)	Times		19.4	18.4	11.6	13.5	16.1
Price/cash flow ratio	(a) (h)	Times		9.2	9.5	7.3	9.1	9.7
Dividend cover	(l)	Times		1.6	1.2	2.0	1.6	1.6
Cash flows								
Operating cash flow	(j)	$m		784.3	501.5	641.4	602.9	649.0
Investing cash flow	(k)	$m		120.4	(459.3)	(26.2)	(510.2)	(465.2)
Free cash flow	(l)	$m		904.7	42.2	615.2	92.7	183.8
Group capital expenditure	(m)	$m		706.7	676.7	605.4	563.2	457.0

continues

COLES MYER LTD: COMPARATIVE STATISTICS
5-YEAR REVIEW

		Year	**1997**	1996	1995	1994	1993
		Weeks	**52**	52	52	53	52
Financial strength	Notes						
Net debt/net debt and equity			**34.4%**	44.5%	42.5%	20.0%	13.8%
Net liabilities/net tangible assets	(n)		**61.1%**	63.6%	62.5%	45.6%	42.7%
Net finance cover	(o)	Times	**5.1**	3.9	5.1	11.1	14.4
Cash flow/debt service ratio	(p)	Times	**6.6**	3.4	4.5	10.0	14.6
Fixed charges cover	(o) (q)	Times	**2.1**	2.1	2.4	2.6	2.7
Net tangible assets per share	(r)	$	**2.13**	2.20	2.22	2.58	2.49
Statistics							
Total stores	(s)	No.	**1 891**	1 861	1 787	1 725	1 683
Selling area		sq.m. 000s	**3 526**	3 461	3 376	3 284	3 240
Increase on prior year			**1.9%**	2.5%	2.8%	1.4%	0.4%
Sales per square metre		$	**5 452**	5 251	4 976	4 647	4 681
Increase/(decrease) on prior year			**3.8%**	5.5%	2.7%	3.5%	(0.5)%
Ordinary shareholders		No.	**211 816**	171 877	128 715	66 579	59 748
Sales comparatives							
Increase/(decrease) on prior year—actual			**5.8%**	6.2%	5.5%	5.0%	(0.1)%
Increase/(decrease) on prior year—equivalent weeks			**5.8%**	8.2%	7.4%	3.2%	(0.1)%

Notes to comparative statistics

(a) Basic earnings per ordinary share is calculated in accordance with Accounting Standard AASB 1027.

(b) Capital employed represents net debt and shareholders' equity.

(c) Net debt is total debt adjusted for cash and short-term deposits.

(d) Market capitalisation is calculated as the number of fully paid ordinary shares and fully paid converting preference shares (subsequently converted) multiplied by the closing market prices.

(e) Earnings rate on shareholders' equity is calculated as operating profit after income tax divided by opening shareholders' equity (adjusted for the Kmart Buy-Back in 1995).

(f) Return on capital employed ratio is calculated as operating profit after income tax as a percentage of capital employed.

(g) Price/earnings ratio is the ratio of closing ordinary share price to earnings per ordinary share.

(h) Price/cash flow ratio is the ratio of closing ordinary share price to earnings per ordinary share calculated using cash flow from operating activities (see (j) below).

(i) Dividend cover is the ratio of operating profit after income tax to the ordinary dividend.

(j) Cash flow from operating activities is as defined in Accounting Standard AASB 1026.

(k) Investing cash flow represents net flows arising from the acquisition and sale of assets.

(l) Free cash flow represents the net of operating and investing cash flows.

(m) Group capital expenditure represents the total additions to property, plant and equipment during the year, at cost, other than those assets brought to account as a result of the acquisition of controlled entities.

(n) Net liabilities and net tangible assets are adjusted for cash and short-term deposits.

(o) Net finance cover is calculated as the operating profit before abnormal items, net finance expense and income tax divided by net finance expense. 1993 has not been recalculated for the finance charges and hedge costs which form part of net finance expense.

(p) Cash flow/debt service ratio is the cash flow from operating activities divided by net finance expense.

(q) Fixed charges cover is the ratio of operating profit before abnormal items, fixed charges, depreciation, amortisation and income tax to fixed charges (comprising lease rental costs and net finance expense—figure for 1993 has not been recalculated (see (o) above)).

(r) Net tangible assets per share is shareholders' equity less intangible assets divided by the fully paid ordinary shares at year end.

(s) Store numbers include free standing K Auto and Tyremaster stores.

Source: Coles Myer Annual Report 1997.

Required

(a) Using this data, prepare a summary time-series table containing relevant ratio figures for the five-year period.

(b) Comment on any significant trends or features which would be of particular interest to existing or potential shareholders.

(c) List any data not in the five-year summary that would add value to your analysis.

12.27 *S&P downgrade upsets Amcor*

by LEONIE WOOD

Amcor has angrily denounced Standard & Poor's decision to lower its ratings for the second time in a month, claiming the ratings agency has assumed an overly pessimistic view of its prospects.

S & P yesterday clipped Amcor's long-term credit rating by one notch to BBB+ from A–, describing its earnings and ratios, such as pre-tax interest cover and cash flow to debt, as 'very weak' but likely to improve in the next few years.

The new rating brings Amcor into line with other paper and packaging groups rated by S & P, such as Carter Holt Harvey (BBB–), Southcorp (BBB+) and Fletcher Challenge (BBB). But it is a rebuke for Amcor, which has been closing plants, cutting costs and restructuring work methods to improve margins in a highly competitive market.

Amcor finance director Mr David Meiklejohn strongly disagreed with S & P's assumptions and conclusions about its industries and financial profile. He also disputed S & P's method of including all cash and non-cash write-downs and abnormal charges when calculating pre-tax interest cover ratios.

'The competitive pressures have not increased, they have not got worse', he said. 'We believe [S & P] are much too pessimistic in their assumptions but in any event the financial impact will be minimal because we are not going to the market to raise new funds anyway.'

S & P said the downgrade reflected continuing pricing pressures and intense competition in Australia and NZ. S & P has taken Amcor off creditwatch and declared a stable outlook. It did not alter the company's short-term ratings.

The *Sydney Morning Herald*,
25 September 1998

Required

(a) What is meant by 'ratings' in the context of this article and why is it important to a company?

(b) What does the 'cash flow to debt' ratio and 'pre-tax interest cover' indicate about the financial situation of a company?

(c) Do you agree with the method of calculating the interest cover ratio indicated in the article? Justify your view.

(d) In this article, the analysis of accounting information has been used to make an important decision, yet it is 'contested' by the rated company itself. What does this indicate to you about the nature of accounting information generally and the interpretation of it?

12.28 *Financial analysis for a loan application*

Omega Fashions Pty Ltd manufactures women's fashion wear for sale in major retail outlets, with items appealing to the 25+ years age group and priced at the upper end of the range. The items are sold at wholesale prices to retailers, who can return unsold items at the end of the season and receive full credit. At the end of each manufacturing cycle, in May and November, the company has 'factory sales' to partly clear its stores of the season's excess production.

Omega's seasonal working capital needs have been financed primarily by loans from the Australian Commercial Bank, and the current line of credit permits the company to borrow up to $1 million. In accordance with standard banking practices, however, the loan agreement requires that the bank loan be repaid in full at some time during the year, in this case by 30 June 20X5.

Omega Fashions experienced steady growth in the five years prior to 20X2. An economic downturn from 20X2 until the end of 20X4 caused the company considerable difficulty in marketing its production, both to retailers and at its clearance sales. Having increased production during these years in expectation of a revitalisation of demand, out-of season stocks accumulated, in spite of the price discounts and more liberal credit terms offered to retailers in an effort to promote sales. As economic conditions improved again at the end of 20X4, Omega's demand began to increase.

The Australian Commercial Bank requires quarterly financial statements (balance sheets and profit and loss statements) from each of its major loan customers. It uses a computer analysis program to calculate key financial ratios, to chart trends in these ratios, and to compare the statistics of each company with the average ratios and trends of other companies in the same industry. If any ratio of any company is significantly worse than the industry average, the computer output highlights that fact. If the terms of a company's loan require that certain ratios be maintained at specified minimum levels and these minimums are not being met, this is also highlighted. Omega's financial statements and industry averages are shown on pages 488–90.

Omega's loan agreement specifies that its current ratio be at least 2.5. In 20X4 Omega's current ratio was below this level and the bank's local branch manager, Tony Milton, contacted Omega's managing director, Hecter Isaacs. Milton requested that Isaacs examine the company's situation and suggest immediate corrective action. He decided not to call for immediate repayment of all loans, because Omega was one of the bank's longstanding customers.

Although confident that Omega's financial position could be improved as a result of the recent recovery in the fashion industry, Hecter Isaacs realised the potential danger of losing the bank loan. However, the company's financial commitments were greater than Tony Milton realised. Isaacs had recently signed a firm contract for the modernisation of the factory equipment that would require another $200 000 of capital, which she had planned to obtain as a short-term bank loan, to be repaid from the profits generated by the increased efficiency of the new equipment. It now seemed doubtful to Isaacs that such a loan could be obtained.

Omega's projections for 20X5 are for growth of 8 per cent in net sales, cost of goods sold and other expenses. Isaacs plans to reduce accounts receivable and inventories by June 20X5 to levels that would yield ratios in line with industry averages.

Required

(a) Taking the viewpoint of a bank officer, prepare the necessary information for the bank manager to evaluate an application from Omega Fashions to extend the current line of credit and asking for an additional $200 000 with interest at 10 per cent effective from 1 January 20X5. This information should include the following:

(i) Omega's key financial ratios for 20X2, 20X3 and 20X4, with trends in these ratios graphed against industry averages.

(ii) What are Omega's strengths and weaknesses? What factors contributed to these? In answering this question use the ratios you calculated and include the Dupont ratios:

- to analyse the performance of the company over the three years (Dupont equation based on EBIT)
- to pinpoint the factors that caused Omega Fashions' ROE to fall below the industry average (extended Dupont equation based on net profit after tax).

(iii) If the bank were to maintain the current line of credit and grant an additional $200 000 with interest effective from 1 January 20X5, would the company be able to retire all short-term loans on 30 June 20X5? What do you recommend to your manager about the application?

To answer question (iii), consider the likely cash position under these assumptions:

- *Cash from operations.* The 20X4 inflow of $372 000 is projected to increase by 8 per cent in 20X5, less interest payments on the additional loan. Make allowance for payment in April of the tax already provided for.
- *Reduction in current assets.* The amount of inventory and accounts receivable that would be held if inventory turnover and the average collection period were at industry average levels—that is, if the company generated internal funds by reducing inventories and receivables to industry averages. Calculate inventory turnover using COGS as 70 per cent of sales. Use data from December 20X4, not forecast figures for this purpose. Assume that all of Isaacs' plans and predictions materialise.

(b) If the credit extension is not made, what alternatives are open to Omega Fashions?

(c) Under what circumstances might the validity of Omega's comparative ratio analysis be questionable?

BALANCE SHEETS: OMEGA FASHIONS PTY LTD

as at 31 December

	20X2	20X3	20X4
	$000	$000	$000
Current assets			
Cash	794	952	1001
Accounts receivable	205	336	501
Inventory	683	1051	1654
Prepayments	775	756	946
	2457	3095	4102

continues

BALANCE SHEETS: OMEGA FASHIONS PTY LTD

as at 31 December

	20X2 $000		20X3 $000		20X4 $000	
Non-current assets						
Land and buildings	500		500		500	
less Acc. depn	280	220	285	215	290	210
Equipment and other						
fixed assets	403		526		723	
less Acc. depn	354	49	393	133	436	287
		269		348		497
Total assets		**$2726**		**$3443**		**$4599**
Current liabilities						
Bank line of credit		340		580		940
Accounts payable		97		135		290
Taxation payable		279		273		246
Dividends payable		24		24		24
Accruals and other						
current liabilities		29		101		446
		769		1113		1946
Non-current liabilities						
Mortgage		183		179		175
Total liabilities		952		1292		2121
Shareholders' equity						
Paid-up capital		400		400		400
Retained earnings		1374		1751		2078
		1774		2151		2478
Total liabilities and						
shareholders' equity		**$2726**		**$3443**		**$4599**

PROFIT AND LOSS STATEMENTS: OMEGA FASHIONS PTY LTD
for year ended 31 December

	20X2 $000	20X3 $000	20X4 $000
Cash sales	360	244	274
Credit sales	3952	4026	4070
Total sales	4312	4270	4344
less Sales discounts	201	135	157
Net sales	4111	4135	4187
less Cost of goods sold	3018	3008	3072
Gross operating profit	1093	1127	1115
General and administrative expenses	303	317	349
Depreciation	42	44	48
Miscellaneous expenses (incl. $15 000 interest for each yr)	50	98	133
	395	459	530
Net profit before tax	698	668	585
Taxes (40%)	279	267	234
Net profit	**$ 419**	**$ 401**	**$ 351**

RETAINED PROFITS STATEMENTS: OMEGA FASHIONS PTY LTD
for year ended 31 December

Retained profits 1 January	979	1374	1751
plus Net profit	419	401	351
	1398	1775	2102
less Dividends payable	24	24	24
Retained profits 31 December	**$1374**	**$1751**	**$2078**

INDUSTRY AVERAGES FOR KEY FINANCIAL RATIOS[a]: LADIES FASHION WEAR

Current ratio	3
Quick ratio[b]	1.8
Inventory turnover[c]	4 x
Average collection period[c]	25 days
Fixed asset turnover[c]	10
Total asset turnover[c]	1.3
Return on total assets[d]	12.7%
Return on equity	25.5%
Debt ratio	50%
Profit margin on sales[d]	9.8%

[a] Industry average ratios were constant for the years 20X2–20X4.
[b] Quick ratio equals current assets less inventory divided by current liabilities.
[c] Based on year-end balance-sheet figures.
[d] Based on net income (after tax) figures.

PART 4

The conceptual framework applied

CHAPTER 13

Sources of authority in accounting

Learning objectives

In this chapter you will be introduced to:

1. the different sources of accounting regulation in Australia

2. the nature and purpose of accounting standards

3. the types of accounting standards that have so far been issued in Australia

4. the role of various institutions involved in setting accounting standards

5. the relationship between Australian and international accounting standards

6. why standard setting has become an increasing political activity both in Australia and overseas

7. the limitations of existing standard-setting processes

8. recent attempts by the Commonwealth government to reform accounting standard setting

9. the pros and cons of adopting international accounting standards as the basis of accounting practice in Australia.

Introduction

The work of the practising accountant is governed by a myriad of accounting regulations. These regulations set out the rules and principles which govern the preparation, disclosure and audit of financial statements. They also set out, among other things, the legal and ethical responsibilities of accountants in performing their professional duties. Accountants are obliged to follow accounting regulations or risk punitive measures, which can be imposed by the law and/or by the disciplinary processes of the accounting profession in Australia.

In Australia there are essentially three main sources of accounting regulation: (1) the requirements of companies legislation, (2) the Australian Stock Exchange listing requirements for public companies, and (3) accounting standards issued by the standard-setting body.

This chapter examines each of these sources of accounting regulation. Particular emphasis is given to the nature and role of accounting standards and the standard-setting process both in Australia and in other countries. Preparing financial statements that are consistent with accounting standards dominates the activity of the financial accountant. Generally speaking, the requirements of companies legislation and Stock Exchange regulation deal only with the broad principles of accounting measurement and disclosure. Accounting standards apply these broad principles to the many and varied accounting transactions and other events that arise in practice.

There are numerous accounting standards currently in existence in Australia and in other industrialised countries such as the United States and the United Kingdom. Practitioners need to know the requirements of accounting standards in order to adhere to the professional, ethical and legal requirements of their profession. The accounting standards of other jurisdictions and countries can also be important. Of much interest to Australian standard setters are the requirements of international accounting standards (IAS). International accounting standards are issued by the International Accounting Standards Committee (IASC). Australian standard setters have been anxious to ensure that Australian accounting standards are consistent with IASC standards. It has long been recognised by standard setters that major differences between Australian accounting standards and IASC standards can impact adversely on the Australian economy. For example, if the accounting practices of Australian companies are not seen to conform to what are regarded as best international practices, Australia could be less attractive to foreign investors.

This chapter also discusses the nature and limitations of existing standard-setting processes and arrangements in Australia, including recent initiatives proposed by the Australian government to formally adopt IASC standards as the norm for accounting practice in Australia.

Sources of authority in accounting

Corporations Law

A particularly important source of authority for accounting principles in Australia and overseas is the requirements of companies legislation. The requirements of companies legislation differ from country to country. In Australia the legislation governing companies is known as the *Corporations Law*. The constitutional power to legislate with respect to companies vests in the States, and for many years each Australian State formulated and administered its own corporate legislation. In the early 1990s, however, the Commonwealth government and the State governments agreed to a regime of applied law that has effectively created a national scheme of corporate legislation operated by the Commonwealth government. In summary, it involves each State adopting the Corporations Law formulated by the Commonwealth government and recognising the Australian Securities and Investments Commission (ASIC) as the sole administrator of the Corporations Law. The ASIC is an independent statutory commission accountable to the Commonwealth parliament.

As the major legislation affecting financial reporting by Australian companies, the Corporations Law is primarily concerned with the financial information that companies should disclose in their annual reports to shareholders, rather than with how specific financial transactions are taken into account.

Under the Corporations Law directors are required to present to shareholders an audited profit and loss statement and a balance sheet. These financial statements must comply with the detailed requirements for disclosure contained in Australian accounting standard AASB 1034 'Information to be Disclosed in Financial Reports'. This standard lists those items that must be shown either in the financial statements themselves or in notes accompanying the statements. There is a comprehensive list of what assets and liabilities must be disclosed and how they are to be broken up into groups and classes. In contrast to these requirements to disclose a detailed balance sheet, the items to be disclosed in the profit and loss statement are relatively few. Revenue must be shown, but not cost of sales or other operating expenses, except for specified items such as depreciation, auditors' fees and directors' fees.

The Corporations Law also requires that the profit and loss statement and balance sheet prepared by directors comply with the accounting standards issued by the Australian Accounting Standards Board (AASB) (to be discussed shortly) and that they give a 'true and fair view' of the company's affairs. The term 'true and fair view' is rather vague and is not defined in the legislation; greater reliance is generally placed on compliance with accounting standards. The requirement that financial statements comply with accounting standards issued by the AASB is particularly important as it gives legal backing to these standards and endorses their role in specifying what accounting methods can (and cannot) be used to account for particular types of financial transactions affecting corporate entities.

The disclosure practices of public sector entities such as statutory authorities and departments are also affected by legislation. For example, in New South Wales the *Annual Reports (Statutory Bodies) Act 1984* and similar legislation for government departments, together with the *Public Finance and Audit Act 1983,* specify a comprehensive list of financial and non-financial information that must be disclosed in the annual reports of statutory authorities and government departments. Other State governments and the Commonwealth government have similar requirements. Public sector entities are expressly directed to accounting standards for detailed guidance on the appropriate method of accounting for particular types of financial transactions.

Australian Stock Exchange listing regulations

The Australian Stock Exchange (ASX) is a non-profit, private sector body comprising over 100 stockbroker corporations and partnerships. The conduct of the exchanges and their members is governed by securities legislation that forms part of the Corporations Law. Within this legislative framework, the ASX operates effectively as a self-regulatory body with its own strict and comprehensive listing requirements. The ASX is oriented towards the protection of shareholders and investors as well as the promotion of share-market efficiency. This orientation is reflected in the ASX's concern with timely disclosure, as seen in its requirement for half-yearly and preliminary final reports in addition to the annual report. The ASX regulates corporate financial disclosure through its listing requirements. These requirements, like those of the Corporations Law, have traditionally been concerned with disclosure rather than with technical accounting issues such as measurement in the financial reports. In its concern with corporate disclosure, the ASX to a large extent has relied on compliance with accounting standards and corporate legislation. However, where it has considered that these regulatory mechanisms have lagged behind, it has been quick to insert additional disclosure items into the listing requirements. For example, turnover (total revenue) and funds statements (since replaced by cash flow statements) were included in the listing requirements many years before they were required disclosure in accordance with accounting standards.

Accounting standards

Although the Corporations Law provides authoritative direction on required disclosure in the annual financial statements prepared by entities, it has generally not dealt with detailed accounting principles and rules. This role has generally been filled by accounting standards. Accounting standards provide detailed rules on how particular types of financial transactions and other events should be dealt with in an entity's accounting records. Accounting standards, for example, explain how inventory should be valued, and how costs should be allocated between the cost of goods sold and the cost of inventory on hand. Accounting standards are very important in ensuring that an entity's profit and loss statement, balance sheet and statement of cash flows is an accurate and fair representation of its performance and financial position. In the absence of principles covering the major aspects of valuation in accounting reports, companies are free to take advantage of the 'gaps' and to choose valuation and accounting methods that achieve a desired reported profit.

Accounting standards were first issued in Australia in the late 1960s and early 1970s. In the 1970s, and through to 1983, 13 accounting standards were developed and issued by the two professional accounting bodies: the Institute of Chartered Accountants of Australia (ICAA) and the Australian Society of Certified Practising Accountants (ASCPA). The professional bodies jointly established the Australian Accounting Research Foundation (AARF) to carry out their standard-setting activities. The standards issued by the accounting profession are referred to as the 'AAS' series of standards and are binding only on members of the accounting profession. However, company directors who are legally responsible for the preparation of a company's profit and loss statement and balance sheet are frequently not members of either professional body.

Recognising the limitations of their powers of enforcement, the professional bodies requested the Commonwealth government to give legislative support to accounting standards by making them law and prescribing legal penalties if they were not followed. The government agreed with this on the condition that the standards were reviewed by a government-appointed board before they became law. The government was unwilling to make the accounting profession's standards law without ensuring that they were logically derived, consistent, and unlikely to have undesirable commercial or economic consequences.

Thus the Accounting Standards Review Board was created in 1984. The board initially consisted of seven members representing interested parties such as companies, the accounting profession and users of accounting information. This Board was appointed by the Ministerial Council and was charged with the responsibility of reviewing accounting standards submitted to it by the professional bodies through the AARF and other groups. Standards subsequently passed by the Board were submitted to the Ministerial Council, which could veto the standards within 60 days. If a standard was not vetoed, it became an Accounting Standard with the prefix ASRB. By December 1989 22 accounting standards had been approved.

In 1989 the structure of standard setting in Australia changed yet again. It was considered that the separation of the standard-setting functions of the AARF and the ASRB was inefficient, and that standards would be formulated more efficiently and effectively if the standard-setting activities of the AARF and the ASRB were merged. As a result of this merger, standard setting in Australia may currently be described as a joint venture between the government and the accounting profession. Accounting standards are developed jointly by the AARF and the ASRB, which in 1991 was reconstituted under the Corporations Law as the Australian Accounting Standards Board (AASB). The AASB currently has 11 members. Once a standard has been formulated it is referred to both the Commonwealth government (represented by the Federal Attorney-General and the ASC) and the two professional accounting bodies for a 30-day period of comment. Following this period the standard is issued as:

(a) an AASB accounting standard by the AASB. These standards apply to corporate entities and have the legal backing of the Corporations Law.
(b) an AAS accounting standard by the AARF on behalf of the ICAA and ASCPA. The AAS series of standards are professional accounting standards and do not have legal backing under the Corporations Law. They are applicable to all non-corporate entities including the large number of public sector entities that have recently adopted accrual accounting.

Figure 13.1 below provides a list of existing accounting standards which have been issued by the AASB and are currently in force. The list demonstrates both the broad range and the nature of accounting transactions and other events which have so far been subjected to standard-setting regulation in Australia.

Figure 13.1 AASB Accounting Standards

AASB 1001:	Accounting Policies
AASB 1002:	Events Occurring after Reporting Date
AASB 1003:	Foreign Currency Translation—Disclosure (Withdrawn)
AASB 1004:	Disclosure of Operating Revenue
AASB 1005:	Financial Reporting by Segments
AASB 1006:	Accounting for Interests in Joint Ventures
AASB 1007:	Financial Reporting of Sources and Applications of Funds (Withdrawn)
AASB 1008:	Accounting for Leases
AASB 1009:	Accounting for Construction Contracts
AASB 1010:	Accounting for the Revaluation of Non-Current Assets
AASB 1011:	Accounting for Research and Development Costs
AASB 1012:	Foreign Currency Translation
AASB 1013:	Accounting for Goodwill
AASB 1014:	Set-off and Extinguishment of Debt
AASB 1015:	Accounting for the Acquisition of Assets
AASB 1016:	Disclosure of Information about Investments in Associated Companies
AASB 1016:	Disclosure of Investments in Associates (Gazettal Deferred)
AASB 1017:	Related Party Disclosures
AASB 1018:	Profit and Loss Accounts
AASB 1019:	Measurement and Presentation of Inventories in the Context of the Historical Cost System
AASB 1020:	Accounting for Income Tax (Tax-Effect Accounting)
AASB 1021:	Depreciation
AASB 1022:	Accounting for the Extractive Industries
AASB 1023:	Financial Reporting of General Insurance Activities
AASB 1024:	Consolidated Accounts
AASB 1025:	Application of the Reporting Entity Concept and Other Amendments
AASB 1026:	Statement of Cash Flows
AASB 1027:	Earnings Per Share
AASB 1028:	Accounting for Employee Entitlements
AASB 1029:	Half-Year Accounts and Consolidated Accounts
AASB 1030:	Application of Accounting Standards to Financial Year Accounts and Consolidated Accounts of Disclosing Entities other than Companies
AASB 1031:	Materiality
AASB 1032:	Specific Disclosures by Financial Institutions
AASB 1033:	Presentation and Disclosure of Financial Instruments
AASB 1034:	Information to be Disclosed in Financial Reports
AASB 1035:	Amendments to Accounting Standard AASB 1034

Structure and format of an accounting standard

An accounting standard has a typical structure and format. The structure of an accounting standard normally includes (1) an explanation of the main features of the standard, that is, what the standard broadly requires; (2) which entities the standard applies to (in the case of AASB standards, they only apply to corporate entities or public companies); (3) when the standard takes force, or the operative date (most accounting standards become operative anywhere between six months and a year after its release); (4) the purpose or rationale for the standard; and (5) the detailed requirements of the standard including relevant commentary explaining, where appropriate, the purpose of the requirement. Figure 13.2 below demonstrates this structure with respect to a section taken from the International Accounting Standard IAS 7, 'Cash Flow Statements'.

Figure 13.2 Structure of Accounting Standard IAS7, 'Cash Flow Statements'

Cash Flow Statements

The standards, which have been set in bold italic type, should be read in the context of the background material and implementation guidance in this Standard, and in the context of the Preface to International Accounting Standards.

Objective

Information about the cash flows of an enterprise is useful in providing users of financial statements with a basis to assess the ability of the enterprise to generate cash and cash equivalents and the needs of the enterprise to utilise those cash flows. The economic decisions that are taken by users require an evaluation of the ability of an enterprise to generate cash and cash equivalents and the timing and certainty of their generation.

The objective of this Standard is to require the provision of information about the historical changes in cash and cash equivalents of an enterprise by means of a cash flow statement which classifies cash flows during the period from operating, investing and financing activities.

Scope

1. *An enterprise should prepare a cash flow statement in accordance with the requirements of this Standard and should present it as an integral part of its financial statements for each period for which financial statements are presented.*

2. The Standard supersedes International Accounting Standard IAS 7, Statement of Changes in Financial Position, approved in July 1997.

3. Users of an enterprise's financial statements are interested in how the enterprise generates and uses cash and cash equivalents. This is the case regardless of the nature of the enterprise's activities and irrespective of whether cash can be viewed as the product of the enterprise, as may be the case with a financial institution. Enterprises need cash for essentially the same reasons however different their principle revenue-producing activities might be. They need cash to conduct their operations, to pay their obligations, and to provide returns to their investors. Accordingly, this Standard requires all enterprises to present a cash flow statement.

Benefits of Cash Flow Information

4. A cash flow statement, when used in conjunction with the rest of the financial statements, provides information that enables users to evaluate the changes in net assets of an enterprise, its financial structure (including its liquidity and solvency) and its ability to affect the amounts and timing of cash flows in order to adapt to changing circumstances and opportunities. Cash flow information is useful in assessing the ability of the enterprise to generate cash and cash equivalents and enables users to develop models to assess and compare the present value of the future cash flows of different enterprises. It also enhances the comparability of the reporting of operating performance by different enterprises because it eliminates the effects of using different accounting treatments for the same transactions and events.

5. Historical cash flow information is often used as an indicator of the amount, timing and certainty of future cash flows. It is also useful in checking the accuracy of past assessments of future cash flows and in examining the relationship between profitabilty and net cash flow and the impact of changing prices.

Definitions

6. **The following terms are used in this Standard with the meanings specified:**

   Cash comprises cash on hand and demand deposits.

   Cash equivalents are short-term, highly liquid investments that are readily convertible to known amounts of cash and which are subject to an insignificant risk of changes in value.

   Cash flows are inflows and outflows of cash and cash equivalents.

   Operating activities are the principle revenue-producing activities of the enterprise and other activities that are not investing or financing activities.

   Investing activities are the acquisition and disposal of long-term assets and other investments not included in cash equivalents.

   Financing activities are activities that result in changes in the size and composition of the equity capital and borrowings of the enterprise.

Cash and Cash Equivalents

7. Cash equivalents are held for the purpose of meeting short-term cash commitments rather than for investment or other purposes. For an investment to qualify as a cash equivalent it must be readily convertible to a known amount of cash and be subject to an insignificant risk of changes in value. Therefore, an investment normally qualifies as a cash equivalent only when it has a short maturity of, say, three months or less from the date of acquisition. Equity investments are excluded from cash equivalents unless they are, in substance, cash equivalents, for example in the case of preferred shares acquired within a short period of their maturity and with a specified redemption date.

8. Bank borrowings are generally considered to be financing activities. However, in some countries, bank overdrafts which are repayable on demand form an integral part of an enterprise's cash management. In these circumstances, bank overdrafts are included as a component of cash and cash equivalents. A characteristic of such banking arrangements is that the bank balance often fluctuates from being positive to overdrawn.

9. Cash flows exclude movements between items that constitute cash or cash equivalents because these components are part of the cash management of an enterprise rather than part of its operating, investing and financing activities. Cash management includes the investment of excess cash in cash equivalents.

Presentation of a Cash Flow Statement

10. **The cash flow statement should report cash flows during the period classified by operating, investing and financing activities.**

11. An enterprise presents its cash flows from operating, investing and financing activities in a manner which is most appropriate to its business. Classification by activity provides information that allows users to assess the impact of those activities on the financial position of the enterprise and the amount of its cash and cash equivalents. This information may also be used to evaluate the relationships among those activities.

12. A single transaction may include cash flows that are classified differently. For example, when the cash repayment of a loan includes both interest and capital, the interest element may be classified as an operating activity and the capital element is classified as a financing activity.

Operating Activities

13. The amount of cash flows arising from operating activities is a key indicator of the extent to which the operations of the enterprise have generated sufficient cash flows to repay loans, maintain the operating capability of the enterprise, pay dividends and make new investments without recourse to external sources of financing. Information about specific components of historical operating cash flows is useful, in conjunction with other information, in forecasting future operating cash flows.

Whether or not Australian accounting standards are consistent with IASC standards is clearly an important issue to the AARF and the AASB. As previously stated, departure from IASC standards could create, under some circumstances, adverse perceptions about the quality of Australian company financial statements. For example, in the Australian standard on cash flow statements, AASB 1026, 'Statement of Cash Flows', we find the following statement:

Conformity with International Accounting Standards

As of the date of issue of this Standard, compliance with this Standard will ensure conformity with International Accounting Standard IAS 7, Cash Flow Statements.

The role and importance of international accounting standards will be examined in more detail in the following section.

The role of international accounting standards

International accounting standards are issued by the International Accounting Standards Committee (IASC) which was founded in 1973. The IASC was established largely as a response to the growing worldwide importance of various international accounting issues and events. In particular, there were many concerns voiced at this time, as they still are today, about divergences in the disclosure and financial accounting practices of companies operating in different countries. Furthermore, the accounting standards set by different standard-setting bodies around the world have tended to differ, sometimes quite markedly, due to a host of cultural, legal, political and economic factors. These divergences can adversely impact on user interpretations of company financial statements which have foreign-based or multinational operations.

An illustration of divergences in international accounting practices and standards is provided by the financial statement for year ended 31 December 1997 of Rio Tinto Ltd, shown below in Figure 13.3.

Figure 13.3 Case illustration of international differences in GAAP: financial statement of Rio Tinto for year ended 31 December 1997

Reconciliation with Australian GAAP

31 December

1997 A$m	1996 A$m	1997 £m	1997 £m		1997 US$m	1996 US$m
1 646	1 403	**744**	701	Net earnings reported under UK GAAP	**1 220**	1 096
				Increase/(decrease) net of tax in respect of:		
(224)	(215)	**(101)**	(108)	Goodwill amortisation	**(166)**	(168)
3	(1)	**1**	(1)	Taxation	**2**	(1)
3	4	**1**	2	Other	**2**	3
1 428	1 191	**645**	594	Net earnings under Australian GAAP	**058**	930
102.0c	85.1c	**46.1p**	42.5p	Earnings per ordinary share	**75.6c**	66.5c
11 262	9 506	**4 460**	4 413	Shareholder's funds under UK GAAP	**7 337**	7 551
				Increase/(decrease) net of tax in respect of:		
2 901	2 568	**1 149**	1 192	Goodwill	**1 890**	2 040
(78)	(69)	**(31)**	(32)	Taxation	**(51)**	(55)
(14)	(14)	**(5)**	(6)	Other	**(9)**	(11)
14 071	11 991	**5 573**	5 567	Shareholders' funds under Australian GAAP	**9 167**	9 525

The Group's financial statements have been prepared in accordance with generally accepted accounting principles in the United Kingdom (UK GAAP), which differ in certain respects from generally accepted accounting principles in Australia (Australian GAAP). These differences relate principally to the following items, and the approximate effect of each of the adjustments to net earnings and shareholders' funds which would be required under Australian GAAP is set out above.

Goodwill

For 1997 and prior years, UK GAAP permitted the write-off of purchased goodwill on acquisition directly against reserves. Under Australian GAAP goodwill is capitalised and amortised by charges against income over the period during which it is estimated to be of benefit, subject to a maximum of 20 years. Goodwill previously written off directly to reserves in the accounts has been reinstated and amortised for the purpose of the reconciliation statements.

Taxation

Under UK GAAP provision is made for deferred tax under the liability method where, in the opinion of the directors, it is probable that a tax liability will become payable within the foreseeable future. Under Australian GAAP deferred tax is provided in full on the liability method.

Equity Accounting

Following an announcement by the Australian Securities Commission in June 1997, accounts incorporating the results of associated companies on the equity accounting basis now satisfy Australian accounting regulations. Accordingly, the Australian GAAP information set out above includes associated companies on the equity accounting basis.

You will notice that Rio Tinto's statement provides a reconciliation for differences in results obtained by accounting standards adopted in Australia and those adopted in the United Kingdom. As the notes in Figure 13.3 demonstrate, the reconciliation is needed because application of the British accounting standard on goodwill resulted in a less conservative measure of profit (but a more conservative measure of assets) when compared with the requirements of the Australian goodwill standard.

Today, the importance of international accounting and international accounting standards is even more widely recognised and understood by standard-setting bodies around the world. This has partly been due to the significant economic and political influence exercised by multinational corporations around the world. It can also be attributed to the increasing globalisation of the world's financial, business and consumer markets. The rapid globalisation of financial markets has created numerous interdependencies between national and international economies and business practices. Hence, the need for harmonisation, compatibility and transparency in accounting principles around the world is now widely appreciated. In fact, the establishment of a uniform set of 'world accounting standards' to be observed by all countries has been the long-term goal of the IASC. The original charter of the IASC listed the following objectives:

1. To formulate and publish in the public interest accounting standards to be observed in the presentation of financial statements and to promote their worldwide acceptance and observance.
2. To work generally for the improvement and harmonisation of regulation, accounting standards and procedures relating to the presentation of financial statements.[1]

The harmonisation of accounting regulation and standards essentially requires all countries in the world to adopt the same or a similar set of accounting standards. In an attempt to achieve this objective, the IASC has issued a number of international accounting standards. In many instances, these standards have attempted to reflect generally accepted international accounting practices around the world. As of September 1998, the IASC had

---

[1] International Accounting Standards Committee, *Objectives and Procedures*, London, IASC January 1983, para. 8.

IAS 1   Presentation of Financial Statements
IAS 2   Inventories
IAS 4   Depreciation Accounting
IAS 5   Information to be Disclosed in Financial Statements
IAS 7   Cash Flow Statements
IAS 8   Net Profit or Loss for the Period, Fundamental Errors and Changes in
         Accounting Policies
IAS 9   Research and Development Costs
IAS10   Contingencies and Events Occurring after the Balance Sheet Date
IAS 11   Construction Contracts
IAS 12   Income Taxes
IAS 13   Presentation of Current Assets and Current Liabilities
IAS 14   Segment Reporting
IAS 15   Information Reflecting the Effects of Changing Prices
IAS 16   Property, Plant and Equipment
IAS 17   Accounting for Leases
IAS 18   Revenue
IAS 19   Retirement Benefits Costs
IAS 20   Accounting for Government Grants and Disclosure of Government
         Assistance
IAS 21   The Effects of Changes in Foreign Exchange Rates
IAS 22   Business Combinations
IAS 23   Capitalisation of Borrowing Costs
IAS 24   Related Party Disclosures
IAS 25   Accounting for Investments
IAS 26   Accounting and Reporting by Retirement Benefit Plans
IAS 27   Consolidated Financial Statements and Accounting for
         Investments in Subsidiaries
IAS 28   Accounting for Investments in Associates
IAS 29   Financial Reporting in Hyperinflationary Economies
IAS 30   Disclosure in the Financial Statements of Banks and Similar
         Financial Institutions
IAS 31   Financial Reporting of Interests in Joint Ventures
IAS 32   Financial Instruments: Disclosure and Presentation
         Statement of Intent: Comparability of Financial Statements
IAS 33   Earnings Per Share
IAS 34   Interim Financial Reporting
IAS 35   Discontinuing Operations
IAS 36   Impairment of Assets

It should be noted that IASC standards do not have the force of law. Nations around the world are not obliged to observe them. Hence, whether or not IASC standards will achieve worldwide acceptance and observance largely depends on the commitment by national standard-setting bodies to the virtues of international harmonisation. In recent years there has been much debate on the issue of international harmonisation and on whether countries like Australia should adopt IASC standards as the basis for accounting practice. There appear to be pros and cons to such a move.

Some of the benefits of Australia adopting IASC standards might include the following:

- It will save money, time and resources because Australia will not have to produce its own accounting standards.
- Foreign investment might improve if there are perceptions that Australian companies are conforming with best international accounting practices.

- The Australian accounting profession could gain more prestige if it is seen to be emulating internationally accepted professional standards of behaviour and conduct.
- It could legitimise Australia's status as an active and compliant member of the international community.

Some problems of adopting IASC standards might include the following:

- Certain industrialised nations, such as the United States, have not perceived IASC standards to be of sufficient quality to warrant worldwide observance. In short, IASC standards are considered to be too permissive and flexible. In order to achieve international harmonisation with various standard-setting bodies around world, IASC standards have tended to permit companies to adopt a number of accounting alternatives or choices for the same accounting transaction. For example, Australian accounting standards do not permit the use of LIFO valuation for inventories, whereas it is permitted by accounting standards in the United States. In order to achieve international harmonisation, the IASC standard on inventories permits the use of either FIFO or LIFO. This approach of 'trying to please every nation' has adversely impacted on perceptions about the quality of IASC standards.
- The wholesale adoption of IASC standards could stifle debate by national standard setters on how best to regulate accounting practices.
- Some countries have unique political and economic arrangements/objectives, which may render international harmonisation a difficult if not impossible task. For example, variations in income tax laws around the world have been an important factor in explaining the emergence of differences in accounting principles. Unless all nations are prepared to adopt the same principles and bases for income tax assessment, harmonisation of accounting principles appears unlikely.

Notwithstanding some inherent difficulties in achieving an internationally compatible set of accounting standards, the IASC has pushed ahead with its objectives. Currently, the IASC is working at full speed to develop a core set of internationally compatible accounting standards by 31 December 1998. The IASC hopes to convince powerful organisations such as the International Organisation of Securities Commissions (IOSCO) to endorse this body of accounting standards. If this endorsement is achieved, the IASC will have achieved a major milestone in reaching its harmonisation objectives.

Institutions involved in the setting of Australian accounting standards

Several institutions and organisations are involved in the setting of accounting standards in Australia. An appreciation of the role and function of these institutions will lead to a better understanding of the nature of accounting standards and the standard-setting process.

Key institutions and organisations currently involved in the standard-setting process include the AARF; the executive Boards of the AARF (including the AASB and the PSASB); the accounting profession, as represented by the Institute of Chartered Accountants in Australia (ICAAs) and the Society of Certified Practising Accountants (ASCPAs); and the government, as represented by the Federal Attorney-General's Department. Some of these institutions have already been discussed. Their respective roles are now examined in more detail.

Figure 13.4 describes the administrative and organisational relationships between these institutions. The ICAA and ASCPA bodies are listed at the top of the diagram because both these bodies currently provide joint funding to the AARF. The Federal Attorney-General's Department is also listed at the top of the diagram because it represents the government's authority in the accounting standard-setting process. The government provides legal backing to AASB accounting standards.

Figure 13.4 Institutions involved in accounting standard setting

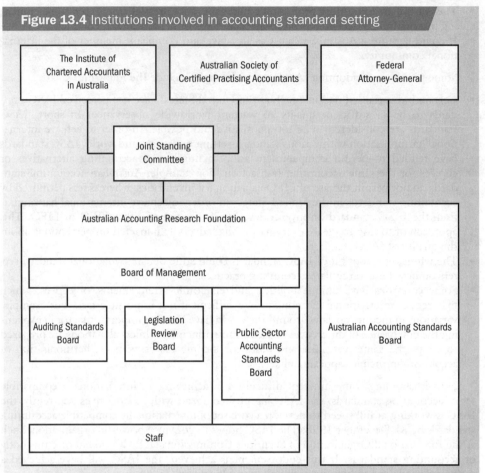

Source: Accounting Policy Statement APS 1, 'The Development of Statements of Accounting Concepts and Accounting Standards', AARF, 1993, p. 13. Reproduced with the permission of the ASCPA and the ICAA.

The Australian Accounting Research Foundation (AARF)

The ASCPA and the ICAA currently fund the majority share of the AARF's annual operating budget. The primary function of the AARF is to act as a secretariat to the AASB, the Public Sector Accounting Standards Board (PSASB) and other Boards of the AARF. The principle duties of the AARF include the provision of relevant technical advice on accounting and policy matters to the AASB and other Boards, including international accounting practice; to help establish the work programs of the AASB and other Boards; to organise meetings of the Boards and carry out their executive decisions; to develop discussion papers and accounting theory monographs; to develop exposure drafts; and to release accounting standards on behalf of the Boards. It is noteworthy that the AARF has no official powers to issue or amend accounting standards in its own right. Although the official or designated function of the AARF is one of technical assistance, it is widely understood that the AARF has been influential in providing policy recommendations and advice to the Boards on a range of accounting issues.

The Australian Accounting Standards Board

It was previously mentioned that the Australian Accounting Standards Board (AASB) was created under statute by virtue of the Australian Securities Commission Act in 1989. The creation of the AASB replaced the existing Accounting Standards Review Board (ASRB) which was subsequently disbanded. The standards issued by the AASB are referred to as 'Approved Australian Accounting Standards'. In Figure 13.4, it can be seen that, in contrast to other Boards of the AARF, the AASB is responsible directly to the government, not the accounting profession. The differences between the AASB and other Boards exist because the AASB has been created under legislation and has its functions defined by statute. Under statute, the accounting standards issued by the AASB are legally enforceable on publicly listed companies. In other words, if a listed company does not comply with AASB standards it can be prosecuted by the Australian Securities Commission. The Attorney-General and Federal Cabinet must approve all 11 members of the AASB and they also appoint the chairperson. The chairperson and members are expected to have relevant experience in accounting, law or business. The AASB is charged with the following specific functions under the Australian Securities Commission Act 1989 (section 226):

(a) to develop a conceptual framework, not having the force of an AASB Standard, for the purpose of evaluating proposed AASB Standards;

(b) to review proposed AASB Standards;

(c) to sponsor or undertake the development of possible AASB Standards;

(d) to engage in such public consultation as may be necessary to decide whether or not it should make a proposed AASB Standard; and

(e) to make such changes to the form and content of a proposed AASB Standard as it considers necessary.

It should be noted that under point (a) the AASB has also been afforded responsibility for the development of a conceptual framework which will guide the standard-setting process. Although the conceptual framework does not have the force of law, it has proven to be a very important development in standard setting in Australia and elsewhere. The nature and role of the conceptual framework is discussed in detail in Chapter 14.

The Public Sector Accounting Standards Board

The potential need for a separate standard-setting Board for the public sector was extensively discussed by the accounting profession and the AARF in the early 1980s. Also discussed was the need for a set of accounting standards that would be relevant to public sector entities (such as a government department or a local government authority) and not-for-profit entities in the private sector (such as clubs and associations). These deliberations resulted in the creation by the ICAA and the ASCPA of the Public Sector Accounting Standards Board (PSASB) as a Board of the AARF. Under the AARF's constitution, the PSASB has responsibilities for developing accounting standards for the public sector and not-for-profit entities. The accounting standards produced by the PSASB are known as AAS standards.

A major difference between AASB and AAS standards is that the former must legally be complied with by all publicly listed companies. It is obligatory but not compulsory on members of the accounting profession (whether in the capacity of account preparers or auditors) to comply with AAS standards in respect of public sector entities and not-for-profit entities. However, it is widely envisaged that if account preparers for public sector entities do not comply with AAS standards they may attract disciplinary action from the Australian accounting profession.

One final point with respect to the PSASB deserves special mention. Australia is one of the few countries in the world which has attempted to develop a common set of accounting standards for the private and public sectors. This is reflected in the fact that there are few if any significant differences in the accounting requirements of AASB and AAS standards.

Commentators on public sector accounting issues have noted both the benefits and the limitations of having a common set of accounting standards for the private and public sectors. Critics of the move argue, among other things, that commercial accounting principles (embodied in accrual accounting procedures) are not necessarily relevant to public sector entities. Public sector entities are argued to be service providers, not profit makers. Advocates of accrual accounting in the public sector argue, among other things, that accrual accounting will lead to fuller disclosure of the assets, revenues, expenses and particularly the unfunded liabilities of government entities (such as the superannuation entitlements of public service employees). Accrual information is seen to be essential for evaluating, in a financial sense, the efficiency and effectiveness of government entities in achieving their service delivery objectives. Because AASB and AAS standards are essentially the same in their requirements, there has been much discussion lately about merging the AASB and PSASB into a single nationwide standard-setting body. We will see later in the chapter that such a merger now appears imminent.

Other Boards of the AARF

The Auditing Standards Board (AuSB) and the Legislative Review Board (LRB) both have specific functions as Boards of the AARF. The primary responsibility of the AuSB is the promulgation of Statements of Auditing Practice (AUPs) and a conceptual framework for auditing practice in Australia. The primary function of the LRB is to review relevant companies legislation for its consistency and applicability to existing accounting standards (and vice versa), and to continually monitor the interface between the accounting standards developed and released by the AARF and the relevant companies legislation.

Urgent Issues Group

A major criticism of the work of the AASB and PSASB in recent years relates to the slow release of accounting standards. An accounting standard can take considerable time to develop and pass through the sometimes cumbersome due process procedures. These 'due process' procedures typically involve a number of steps which can take a considerable period of time, including (1) the commissioning of a discussion paper to be written on the subject of interest; (2) circulation of the discussion for public comment, and interpreting comments and other feedback on the discussion paper; (3) developing an exposure draft of an accounting standard based on the isssues raised in the discussion paper; (4) circulating the exposure draft for public comment, and making changes where appropriate; and (5) finalising an accounting standard based on an exposure draft.

Furthermore, the AASB and PSASB Boards are made up of part-time members only, which greatly reduces their capacity to work speedily in developing and issuing accounting standards. Criticisms of tardiness have been the catalyst for the formation in 1995 of an Urgent Issues Group (UIG) by the AARF and its Boards. The UIG does not appear in Figure 13.4 because its authority is delegated from the AASB and PSASB. The main function of the UIG is to provide timely guidance releases on urgent accounting issues to interest groups (such as users, account preparers and auditors) affected by accounting standards. UIG guidance releases do not have the force of an accounting standard. The UIG comprises 16 voting members and an official observer from the ASC. The UIG will release consensus views on the interpretation of accounting standards. To achieve a consensus, 11 members must vote in favour of a proposed guidance release *and* not more than two members can vote against it. As the AASB and PSASB have delegated their authority to provide guidance on accounting issues to the UIG, the Boards retain the right to veto any decision of the UIG.

Limitations of the present system for standard setting

The present institutional arrangements for standard setting in Australia suffer from certain fundamental deficiencies. The AARF and its Boards have been conscious of these limitations for a considerable period of time now. Formal recognition of these defects was given expression in the recommendations of the Peirson Report (1990). The Peirson Report was sponsored by the AARF, the AASB and the accounting profession as a review of the Australian standard-setting process. A major purpose of the Report was to compare the effectiveness of Australian standard setting arrangements with other countries, particularly the United States. The Peirson Report concluded that there were some major deficiencies with Australian standard setting when compared with similar arrangements in the United States. These deficiencies are highlighted in Figure 13.5.

Case illustration: comparison of standard-setting arrangements in Australia and the United States

Figure 13.5 highlights differences between Australian and various international standard-setting models. Compare and contrast the differences between Australian and US accounting standard-setting arrangements. Note that the US equivalent of the AASB is the Financial Accounting Standards Board or FASB. What potential limitations in Australian standard-setting arrangements can you see? How would you evaluate these limitations?

As can be seen from Figure 13.5, the major differences between Australian and US standard-setting arrangements are as follows:

1. The FASB is made up of full-time members, whereas the AASB is made up of members who work on a part-time basis for their Board. Because FASB members work full-time for their Board, they cannot also work for any other organisation, such as public companies or accounting firms. Members of the AASB all work full-time for other organisations. It has been suggested that this can undermine the independence of AASB members because their views on important accounting issues could potentially be influenced by the institutions they work for or the professions they represent. A full-time membership (as in the case of FASB members) may also sponsor greater commitment to the standard-setting process, and enable the Boards to have more frequent meetings, issue more standards and respond to constituent interests more quickly.
2. As full-time members, the FASB members are fully remunerated, whereas the AASB Board members receive a small sitting fee. Again, this could undermine the independence of AASB members.
3. The FASB's funding is broad-based (funded partly from business, the profession, government and other interest groups). The AASB currently receives its funding from a much narrower base: the accounting profession and, to a lesser extent, the government. This is perceived by many to be a limitation of Australia's standard-setting arrangements. Accounting standards affect a wide range of interest groups (particularly users of the accounts and account preparers). Hence, some believe it is not equitable or appropriate that standard setting should be in the hands of only one or two interest groups, such as the accounting profession.
4. Unlike the FASB, the AASB is not perceived to be (for the reasons listed above) an autonomous Board which is independent of business, the profession and government.

On the basis of these differences, the Peirson Report (1990) made a number of recommendations, which included:

1. That the AARF and the AASB should become independent of the accounting profession, business and government.
2. That the funding for the AARF and AASB should become broadly based.
3. That the AASB become a full-time Board with appropriate remuneration to its full-time members (see the Peirson Report, 1990, p. 5).

Figure 13.5 Accounting standard-setting boards and committees

	Australia	United States	Canada	United Kingdom	New Zealand
Number of members by Board/Committee	9 AASB 9 PSASB	7 FASB 5 GASB	21 AcSC 19 PSAAC	9 ASB	13 ASRB
Full-time/Part-time	Part-time	FASB: full-time GASB: Chairman full-time, others part-time	Part-time	Chairman and Technical Director full-time, others part-time	Part-time
Remunerated	AASB: Chairman receives a salary and members receive sitting fees PSASB: No	Yes	No	Yes	No
Consultative body	No	Yes	Yes	Yes	No
Funding	By the profession and government	Broadly based	By profession	By profession, business and government	By profession
Number of Boards/ Committees (by type)	2, AASB & PSASB	3, FASB, GASB & GAO	2, AcSC & PSAAC	1, ASB	1 Board, 3 Committees (Farm, Financial & Public Sector Accounting)
Voting	Simple majority	Simple majority	Complex rules	Two-thirds majority	Usually 8 out of 13
Legislative backing	Yes, AASB No, PSASB*	Yes	Yes, AcSC No, PSAAC	No	No
Standards issued by	AASB and AARF	Boards	Boards	Board	NZ Society of Accountants
Non-accountant members possible	Yes	Yes	Yes	Yes	Yes
Independent of the profession, business and government	No	Yes	No	Yes	No

* Although Australian accounting standards developed by the PSASB are not given legislative backing as such, in a growing number of jurisdictions they are being given legal endorsement in respect of particular categories of public sector reporting entities.

Source: Adapted from 'An Invitation to Comment on Proposals for Reform of the Institutional Arrangements for Accounting Standard Setting in Australia', Board of Management of the AARF, 1990.

The Report recommended that the AARF and its Board should be free from the exclusive control of the accounting profession and the government. Again, the rationale for this recommendation is that the standard-setting process is perceived to be largely in the hands of particular interest groups (notably the accounting profession) which are not perceived to represent the wider constituency affected by accounting standards. It was noted in the Report that funding for the FASB is broad-based, rendering the FASB largely independent of government, business and the profession.

One further recommendation of the Peirson Report actually represented a significant departure from the standard-setting arrangements in the United States. The Report had recommended the merger of the AASB and PSASB into a single national accounting standard-setting body. A major rationale for proposing the merger of the AASB and the PSASB (see Peirson Report, 1990, pp. 35–36) was the perception that it was unnecessary to develop separate accounting standards for the public and private sectors. After all, AASB and AAS standards are essentially the same. Given that this is the case, much of the work of the PSASB involves endorsing AASB standards for application in the public sector. Merging the AASB and the PSASB would therefore avoid any duplication of effort and save valuable resources.

For the recommendations of the Peirson Report to be implemented, the government's approval was essential. The Report was considered by the Federal Attorney-General's Department in 1991. Although the Report received wide support from the accounting profession and other interest groups in Australia, the Attorney-General's Department was less enthusiastic and largely rejected the substance of the recommendations in a written memorandum to the AARF in December 1991. The precise reasons why the government rejected the Report have never been published or publicly released. One problem the government may have had with the proposals was that they were too far-reaching and ambitious for the time. Furthermore, there may also have been a perception that the status quo was working satisfactorily and circumstances that would justify radical change had not been presented to the government. Another obstacle to federal support is that the pursuit of an independent standard-setting body would, by necessity, force the government to relinquish its control over the standard-setting process.

Although the Peirson Report was shelved by the federal government in the early 1990s, the pressure for change did not abate. Recently, new initiatives have been take to reform the standard-setting process in Australia. However, this time the reform process was initiated by the government itself, not the accounting profession. Some of the recent recommendations to reform accounting standard-setting in Australia are now examined.

Impending changes to institutional arrangements for standard setting in Australia

The desire for change reflected in the Peirson Report has recently reappeared under a new guise. In early 1997 the Federal Treasurer, Mr Peter Costello, announced a wide-ranging reform program to examine accounting standard setting in Australia. The program is known as the *Corporate Law Economic Reform Program*.[2] The program addressed, among other things, such issues as the current funding arrangements of the AARF and the AASB, the relevance of accounting standards to current commercial conditions in Australia, the effectiveness and quality of Australian accounting standards, and the need to extend user participation in the standard-setting process. The important issue of international harmonisation was also addressed in the program. That is, to what extent should Australia adopt IASC standards as the basis for accounting practice? The Treasurer released a position statement entitled 'Accounting Standards' (1997). The position statement considered a number of recommendations including:

---

[2] For a more detailed discussion, see G. Peirson, 'Proposed New Institutional Arrangements for Accounting Standard Setting', *Communiqué*, No. 82, March 1998.

1. The current AASB would be replaced by a new Board to be called the Australian Accounting Standards Committee (AASC). It is widely expected that the newly established AASC would incorporate a merger of the current AASB and PSASB Boards into a single nationwide standard-setting Board.
2. The AASC would be established under legislation and have powers of a body corporate or statutory authority. This body would be ultimately accountable to parliament.
3. The chairperson would be full time, but the proposed seven-member Board would be part-time.
4. The newly established AASC would be managed by a council, to be named the Financial Reporting Council (FRC). The proposed FRC would represent a number of interest groups involved in standard setting, including users of the financial statements, the accounting profession, regulators such as the ASX, and representatives of public companies and accounting firms.
5. The proposed FRC would have broad management responsibilities, such as appointing members of the AASC, setting the work program of the AASC and so on. However, the proposed FRC would not be given powers to veto or approve accounting standards. Current powers of veto belong to the accounting profession but would not continue under the new arrangements.
6. The funding base for the newly established AASC would be broadened. It is proposed that funding would be provided in equal proportions from the government, the accounting profession, and by a levy to be imposed on account preparers, securities advisors and security dealers.
7. The position paper also provides for a secretariat to the AASC. The AARF currently provides this role for the AASB, but it is unclear whether this role would continue.
8. The UIG would continue, but under a different guise. The chairperson of the newly established AASC would also be chairperson of the UIG.
9. There would be a major new commitment to the harmonisation of Australian accounting standards with IASC standards. The purpose for adopting IASC standards as the basis for accounting practice is to strengthen the international standing of Australian capital markets and to ensure that Australia does not fall out of alignment with international capital markets. It is presumed that a major task of the newly established AASC would be to influence the development of high-quality IASC standards, with the end objective that IASC standards be adopted for domestic purposes in Australia. The proposed deadline for harmonisation has been set for 1 January 1999.

It is clear that the above proposals will fundamentally restructure current standard-setting arrangements in Australia. Some of the changes will lead to certain improvements originally recommended by the the Peirson Report (1990). For example, the appointment of a full-time chairperson, a broadening of the funding base of the standard-setting body, and increasing user participation in the process may improve the independence of standard-setting arrangements in Australia.

Undoubtedly, point 9 above (the adoption of IASC standards by 1999) has proven the most controversial aspect of the Treasurer's reform proposals. Concern has been expressed recently that the wholesale adoption of IASC standards by Australia in 1999 could be a little premature. We have already examined some potential problems which national standard-setting bodies might encounter if they attempt to adopt all IASC standards. A major problem is that leading industrialised nations such as the United States, Japan and the United Kingdom are yet to endorse or approve IASC standards as the basis of accounting practice in their respective countries. The United States, for example, has expressed concern about the quality of IASC standards, rendering it unlikely that they will be adopted as a replacement for FASB standards. Most Australian businesses that seek overseas investment do so in the United States, where FASB standards, not IASC standards, are in force. Hence, the premature adoption of IASC standards could adversely affect Australia's foreign investments and international perceptions about the quality of company financial statements.

The 'politicisation' of accounting standard setting

Much has been written in recent years about the 'politicisation' of the accounting standard-setting process. Politicisation has occurred because the financial statements of entities impact on a number of competing economic interests in society. Company managers, for example, are concerned with the financial statements because these statements disclose vital information which reflects on managerial performance (such as a firm's profitability and financial position). Shareholders and creditors are concerned with financial statements in order to assess the value and riskiness of their investments or loans. Potential investors use financial statements to assess the potential spread of risk and return on their investments. Employees also have a pecuniary interest in financial statements. Many employees are concerned with such issues as job security, the state of their superannuation plans, the ability of their companies to pay bonuses and so on. Consumers are interested in whether firms will continue to provide goods and services, and financial statements can provide valuable clues about a firm's future prospects. Governments are interested in financial statements for regulatory purposes and for such activities as granting funding assistance to certain industries. Enviromental groups are interested in the financial statements of companies in assessments and evaluations of an entity's contribution to the physical environment that it operates in. Auditors are interested in financial statements to the extent that they comply with relevant accounting regulations and provide a 'true and fair' view of the company's affairs. These economic interests often conflict. For example, a manager's interest can conflict with that of the shareholder. Managers tend to be concerned about their tenure with the firm, which can create a higher or lower degree of risk aversion than the shareholder has. Hence, managers may avoid riskier investment projects which, although having the potential to provide higher returns to the shareholder, could jeopardise their job security and vice versa.

Because so many interests are affected by published financial statements, it is perhaps not surprising that accounting standards have become more politically sensitive for companies today. Accounting standards have consequences to a company, and some of these consequences are economic in nature. For example, accounting standards impose a financial cost on companies in terms of a compliance cost (e.g. information collection and processing to meet the requirements of a new regulation). Also, accounting standards can (and often do) affect the profitability and financial position of companies, which, in turn, influences the resource allocation decisions and assessments of various users. Consider an accounting standard which increases a company's debt levels or reduces profit. Such a standard is likely to be extremely distasteful to managers who may want to negotiate with bankers for a significant loan advancement. The company's debt level may prompt the banker in question to increase the interest rate on the loan or request greater security. Furthermore, managers may be concerned about the adverse affects of such a standard on perceptions of their own performance in the marketplace or on the share price of the company.

Indeed, it is common for powerful business groups to lobby against the standard-setting bodies to prevent an 'unpopular' accounting standard from being released. Because of these developments, standard setters have become obliged to consider the impact of their standards on a wide range of conflicting economic interests in society. Achieving general acceptance or a consensus on new accounting standards has now become an important part of the AARF's standard-setting activity. However, in many instances this has proved an extremely difficult task for standard setters. Because of their growing political importance, accounting standards are now being regularly challenged by powerful interests in the world of business and accounting. The function, purpose and ongoing relevance of accounting standards has become an issue of considerable controversy. A good case illustration of the conflicts and tensions in standard setting can be seen in Figures 13.6 and 13.7.

Figure 13.6 highlights concerns expressed by the Big Six accounting firms about the increasingly technical and rigid nature of accounting standards, and the fact that accounting standards are becoming incomprehensible, even to qualified accountants. Figure 13.7 represents the response to these criticisms by the AARF. The AARF claims that these criticisms are unfounded, and that Australian accounting standards are not as restrictive or as technical as those required by other leading industrialised nations such as the United States.

Figure 13.6

Accountants baffled by standards code

by NICK TABAKOFF

AUSTRALIA'S accountants are losing control of their profession because of the dominance of the current accounting standards regime, according to one of its most senior figures.

Mr John Harkness, the executive chairman of one of Australia's largest accounting firms, KPMG, said he believed guidelines rather than the imposition of black-letter law should be the means of ensuring accounting practitioners performed in the interests of their clients and the community.

'Self-regulation is one of the cornerstones of a profession. The accounting profession itself is the right body to determine if any practitioners have transgressed ethics,' he said after a conference at the St James Ethics Centre in Sydney yesterday.

The accounting profession regulated itself until 1977, when accounting standards were first introduced to ensure correct behaviour by practitioners.

'Before then, the professionals had general concepts of behaviour, instilled by the profession over many years,' he said.

But Mr Harkness said that matters had now moved to the stage that accountants themselves could not understand the codes of behaviour they were meant to subscribe to, because of the increasingly technical and incomprehensible nature of accounting standards.

Legally binding standards were an unnecessary imposition on accountants, who were 'mature enough' not to be governed by black-letter law. 'We've swung too far trying to codify everything,' he said.

Mr Harkness said regulation of accountants should err on the side of simplicity, moving towards 'concepts' rather than specifics.

There was also a disturbing tendency towards having a number of matters settled in the courts. While in the past the profession dealt with cases of misconduct by professionals, it was now 'the courts who seem to have taken over that role', he said.

But he warned that the future of the profession was dependent on accountants keeping a balance between profit and public-interest considerations.

'Efficiency is but one value and it must not be at the top of the list [of considerations by practitioners],' he said.

Australian Financial Review, 3 March 1998

Figure 13.7

Watchdog bites back at big six rigid claims

by NICK TABAKOFF

AUSTRALIA'S accounting regulators have hit back at claims by the corporate sector and Big Six firms that accounting standards have become too rigid, arguing instead that regulations in the area may be too weak and in need of tightening. Mr Warren McGregor, the executive director of the Australian Accounting Research Foundation—the body whose work forms the basis of Australian accounting standards—told the *Australian Financial Review* that the quality of reporting in countries like the United States was 'far higher' than in Australia, and that an 'odour' remained around many Australian corporates.

His comments came in response to criticisms of the scope and direction of the local accounting standards regime in recent days by director representatives and senior accountants, including Mr Graham Stubington, the chief executive of the Australian Institute of Company Directors, and Mr John Harkness, the executive chairman of the Big Six firm KPMG.

Mr Harkness claimed that accounting standards were becoming so complicated that not even accountants could understand them, and called for a return to a set of non-binding concepts rather than standards.

Mr Stubington contended the Corporations Law should be the only overriding law on what disclosures are required by companies, with accounting standards only 'setting the standard' of disclosures necessary under the Corporations Law.

But Mr McGregor has come out fighting following the recent claims, saying arguments over the application of standards were damaging the reputation of Australia's corporate sector internationally.

'Our companies are being penalised because of the bad odour surrounding Australian reporting,' he said.

He cited recent instances where bodies such as the Australian Securities Commission had become embroiled in stand-offs with companies over their standards of corporate reporting as—'rightly or wrongly'—creating concern internationally about the general quality of the accounts of Australian companies.

'The requirements in the US are far more extensive, and the demands are far more onerous,' he said. 'Consequently, their capital markets are much better informed.'

US accounting standards called for a strict 'cookbook' approach to corporate reporting—involving companies following them almost to the letter of the law—something that Australian standards had so far avoided.

Australian Financial Review, 10 March 1998

Summary

This chapter has attempted to trace the sources of accounting regulation in Australia. The main sources of regulation include the Corporations Law, the Stock Exchange listing requirements for public companies and the accounting standards issued by the AASB and PSASB. Emphasis was given to accounting standards and the standard-setting process because the requirements of the Corporations Law and Stock Exchange regulations only deal with the broader principles of accounting measurement and disclosure. Accounting standards apply these broad principles to the many and varied accounting transactions, events and circumstances which continually arise in practice. Accounting standards are a steadily growing body of accounting regulation. Not only are new accounting standards continually appearing on a variety of topics, but public companies are legally obliged to follow the standards issued by the AASB.

There are numerous bodies and institutions involved in accounting standard setting, each performing its own role and function, and the limitations of current institutional arrangements for standard setting were discussed. One major limitation is that the AARF and the AASB are not perceived to be sufficiently independent to adequately represent all the interest groups affected by accounting standards. This lack of independence can be highlighted in at least two ways. First, the AARF and AASB are currently funded mainly from the accounting profession (with a small amount of funding from government). This has led to the perception that standard setting is largely in the hands of one major interest group: the accounting profession. However, many other interest groups are affected by accounting standards, such as the users of financial statements and account preparers. It is widely believed that these parties are generally not well represented by current standard-setting arrangements. Second, the AASB and PSASB are made up of part-time members who are fully employed in the commercial, business or government sectors. This may compromise their independence because, among other things, Board members may potentially be influenced by the institutions they work for. Attempts to reform standard-setting arrangements started with the Peirson Report (1990). More recently, the *Corporate Law Economic Reform Program* was introduced and is likely to lead to wide-ranging changes to standard-setting arrangements in Australia. These reforms are likely to improve the independence of the standard-setting process to some degree, namely by (1) broadening the funding base for the standard-setting body, (2) the appointment of a full time chairperson, and (3) the establishment of a Financial Reporting Council that will increase user participation in the standard-setting process.

As well as the many accounting standards that have so far been issued by the AARF and the AASB, the international accounting standards issued by the the International Accounting Standards Committee (IASC) have also been of paramount concern to Australian standard setters. The AARF and the AASB have been anxious to ensure that Australian accounting standards are generally consistent with IASC standards. The important issue of international harmonisation has been linked to improving foreign investment in Australia and lifting perceptions about the quality of Australian company financial statements overseas. More recently, the Corporate Law Economic Reform Program has initiated significant debate in Australia as to whether Australia should be adopting IASC standards as the basis for accounting practice.

Finally, this chapter briefly addressed the politicisation of accounting standard setting. Accounting standards have economic consequences to a firm. For instance, accounting standards impose a financial cost on firms in terms of compliance costs. Moreover, numerous parties are affected by accounting standards because these standards impact on the measurement of an entity's profitability and financial position, which in turn influences the resource allocation decisions of various user groups. Hence, when releasing new accounting standards, standard setters have become more conscious of the need to achieve general acceptance or a consensus view from those interest groups most affected by the accounting standards.

 **Review exercises**

Discussion questions

13.1 Identify and discuss the three main sources of accounting regulation. How do they differ?

13.2 What is the role and purpose of accounting standards?

13.3 Explain the role of the AARF, the AASB and the PSASB in accounting standard setting.

13.4 Why was the Urgent Issues Group (UIG) established?

13.5 What is the difference between AASB and AAS standards? Should there be a difference?

13.6 Why do all Australian accounting standards provide a statement of conformity with international accounting standards? Do you believe this is necessary?

13.7 What is the role and purpose of international accounting standards?

13.8 Why was the IASC established? What are the objectives of the IASC?

13.9 What were the recommendations of the Peirson Report (1990)? What was the purpose for these recommendations?

13.10 What are the limitations of current standard-setting arrangements in Australia?

13.11 Explain why the issue of 'independence' is important for a standard-setting body. Can current arrangements for standard setting in Australia be described as independent?

13.12 How does the *Corporate Law Economic Reform Program* propose to alter existing arrangements for standard setting in Australia? Are these reforms wise? Explain your answer.

13.13 Discuss the pros and cons of Australia adopting ISAC standards as the basis for accounting practice.

13.14 Explain the concept of international harmonisation of accounting standards. What are the goals of international harmonisation? Are these objectives realistic?

13.15 'Accounting standards have resulted in very technical financial statements which few accountants and users can now comprehend.' Discuss.

13.16 'Legally binding standards are an unnecessary imposition on accountants who are now mature enough not to be governed by black-letter law.' Discuss.

13.17 What is meant by the politicisation of accounting standards? Illustrate your answer with examples.

13.18 Why do you think standard setting has become a political activity? Do you think standard setting should be a political activity?

CHAPTER 14

A conceptual framework for financial accounting and reporting

Learning objectives

In this chapter you will be introduced to:

1. the nature and structure of the IASC conceptual framework

2. the purpose of a conceptual framework

3. various motives for the development of a conceptual framework

4. the definition of financial reporting and the reporting entity

5. the objectives of financial statements

6. definitions of recognition criteria for assets, liabilities, equity, revenues and expenses

7. the qualitative characteristics that information should possess before its inclusion in the financial statement

8. the limitations of a conceptual framework

9. the impact of the conceptual framework on accounting and business practice.

Introduction

It was mentioned in Chapter 13 that an important part of accounting standard setting, both in Australia and in other countries, has been the development of a *conceptual framework* for financial accounting and reporting. Conceptual framework projects have been developed in numerous countries, and are in varying stages of completion. Notwithstanding some individual differences, most of these projects share similar underlying rationales, purposes and objectives. The conceptual framework proposed by the International Accounting Standards Committee (IASC) tends to reflect many of the basic commonalities shared by frameworks in various jurisdictions. Consequently, the IASC *Framework* (see Appendix 2), with its international focus, will be emphasised in this chapter.

A conceptual framework is often described as or likened to a coherent body of accounting theory or a set of *interrelated concepts*. The primary purpose of this theory or set of interrelated concepts is to *define* the nature, scope and purpose of financial accounting and reporting. For example, a conceptual framework seeks to answer questions such as: What types of entities should be required to prepare financial statements and follow accounting standards? What are the objectives of financial statements? Whose interests should the financial statements serve? What are the qualitative characteristics of useful information? What types of information should be included in financial statements?

In answering these questions, conceptual frameworks can adopt different approaches. Some frameworks are essentially *descriptive*, while others are more *prescriptive*. There are also frameworks that attempt to blend both approaches.

A *descriptive* framework is one which essentially describes or codifies existing accounting practices. Rather than seeking to change accounting practice, descriptive frameworks attempt to explain existing practices in a logical and rational manner. A *prescriptive* conceptual framework is one which attempts to impose changes on accounting practice by explaining what accounting practices *should* or ought to be.

It will be seen that the development of a conceptual framework by standard setters has been an attempt to infuse a higher degree of formalisation and rigour into accounting regulatory processes and company accounting practices. A conceptual framework for financial accounting and reporting is widely expected to result in more consistent and logical accounting standards and accounting practices, with the end objective of improving the overall quality of information provided to users of company financial reports.

Although standard setters have expended considerable time and resources in developing a conceptual framework, the implementation of such a framework in practice has tended to generate considerable debate and controversy within the business community. A case study illustration of the Australian conceptual framework project highlights the nature of such controversy and evaluates the future of the conceptual framework.

Purposes and motivations for a conceptual framework

The primary purpose of a conceptual framework is to define the nature, scope and purpose of financial accounting and reporting. Implicit in efforts of accounting standard setters to develop a conceptual framework is the recognition that a number of fundamental issues in accounting remain either unresolved, are poorly understood or have failed to achieve general consensus by the community of accounting and business practitioners, academics and regulators.

Some of the fundamental questions that a conceptual framework attempts to answer include:

1. What types of entities should be required to prepare financial statements and follow accounting standards? For example, should a local tennis club, church or family business be required to prepare financial statements and follow accounting standards?
2. What is the primary purpose or objective of financial statements? Should the primary objective be to serve the economic decision making of users, or are there other purposes that need to be contemplated?
3. What qualities should financial information possess before it is included or *recognised* in the financial statements? For example, should the information be *relevant* for economic decision making? Is the reliability of information a consideration? Is the understandability of information important?
4. How should the basic elements of financial statements (i.e. assets, liabilities, equity, revenue and expenses) be defined and recognised? For example, is an asset a future economic benefit, or is some other definition appropriate? What should be the basis for revenue recognition?
5. How should the elements of financial statements be measured? Should the historical cost basis of measurement continued to be used or should some other measurement basis, such as current market valuation, be adopted?

Standard-setting bodies have long asserted that lack of resolution on these and other fundamental conceptual issues will cause confusion and uncertainty and ultimately impede the development of logical, consistent and comparable accounting standards and accounting practices. The major beneficiaries of improving the quality and consistency of accounting standards are expected to be the users of financial statements.

The Australian Accounting Research Foundation (AARF) expects the conceptual framework project to have a number of other distinct advantages. For example, a conceptual framework can also lead to better understanding among accountants, auditors and users because all parties would be using a common set of definitions and criteria when interpreting company financial statements. The AARF's *Guide to Proposed Statements of Accounting Concepts* states the potential benefits of the conceptual framework as follows:

(a) reporting requirements should be more consistent and logical, because they will stem from an orderly set of concepts;
(b) avoidance of reporting requirements will be much more difficult because of the existence of all-embracing provisions;
(c) the Boards which set down the requirements will be more accountable for their actions in that the thinking behind specific requirements will be more explicit, as will any compromises that may be included in particular accounting standards;
(d) the need for specific accounting standards will be reduced to those circumstances in which the appropriate application of concepts is not clear-cut, thus mitigating the risks of over-regulation;
(e) preparers and auditors should be able to better understand the financial reporting requirements they face; and,
(f) the setting of requirements should be more economical because issues should not need to be re-debated from differing viewpoints.

The IASC stressed additional goals for their conceptual framework to reflect the Committee's international focus. These international goals included:

1. to assist the Board of IASC in promoting harmonisation of regulations, accounting standards and procedures relating to the presentation of financial statements by providing a basis for reducing the number of alternative accounting treatments permitted by International Accounting Standards; and
2. to assist national standard-setting bodies in developing national standards [paragraph 1 (b) (c)].

Improvement in the overall quality of financial reporting has been argued to be the primary motivation for a conceptual framework. However, other potential motivations need to considered. The development of a conceptual framework by institutions such as the IASC and the AARF is not without its 'political' connotations and purposes. Hence, the conceptual framework has *strategic* as well as technical purposes and functions. Some commentators have argued that the conceptual framework is an attempt by standard setters to assert greater authority in the setting of accounting standards, to ward off public criticism of the accounting profession and to maintain the authority and legitimacy of accounting standards.[1] As was mentioned in Chapter 13, accounting standards are now being set in an increasingly political environment, and numerous conflicting economic interests and competing regulatory bodies or agencies are now involved in the standard-setting process. Politicisation of the process inevitably occurs because standard setters must actively strive to gain general acceptance from these diverse interests in order for their outputs, such as the conceptual framework, to have any hope of success in practice.

The conceptual framework of the International Accounting Standards Committee

The following section outlines the structure of the conceptual framework proposed by the IASC. Emphasis is given to the IASC *Framework* because it encapsulates developments in various international conceptual framework projects. It should be noted that, although the IASC and Australian conceptual frameworks are essentially the same, the Australian framework is relatively more advanced in its development. Contrasts between the IASC *Framework* and Australian framework will be made where relevant. The structure of a conceptual framework is illustrated in Figure 14.1.

Figure 14.1 emphasises all the stages necessary to complete a conceptual framework project. It does not necessarily indicate that the IASC, the AARF or other standard-setting bodies have already addressed every part of the figure. In fact, most conceptual framework projects, including the IASC's *Framework*, are still in a process of development.

Scope of financial reporting

As shown by Figure 14.1, the highest level of the conceptual framework defines the *scope* of financial reporting. The scope of financial reporting deals with the type of information that should be included in *general purpose* financial statements. As discussed in Chapter 2, a distinction needs to be drawn between *general purpose* financial statements and *special purpose* financial statements. General purpose financial statements are designed to serve users who lack the necessary resources or authority to demand accounting information from companies. Traditional balance sheets, profit and loss accounts and cash flow statements are generally referred to as general purpose financial statements. Special purpose financial reports, on the other hand, are designed for those users who do possess the necessary power and authority to demand any accounting information they need from companies. For example, tax authorities, state parliament and the federal parliament and, in some cases, powerful institutional investors would qualify as special report users. Standard setters have confined the scope of financial reporting to general-purpose financial reporting. Special purpose financial reporting is excluded from the standard-setting process.

The scope of financial reporting is of keen interest to standard setters because it determines what kinds of accounting information, transactions and events should be subjected to standard setting. The history of accounting reveals that the scope of company financial reporting has changed greatly over the years. In the early decades of the twentieth century it was common for companies to disclose profit and loss accounts as well as balance sheets. By the 1950s many companies started disclosing additional information in the form of a funds flow statement. Today the scope of financial reporting has widened to embrace cash flow

1 See R. Hines, 'The FASB's Conceptual Framework, Financial Accounting and the Maintenance of the Social World', *Accounting Organisations and Society*, Vol. 16, 1991, pp. 313–31.

Figure 14.1 Tentative building blocks of a conceptual framework for general-purpose financial reports

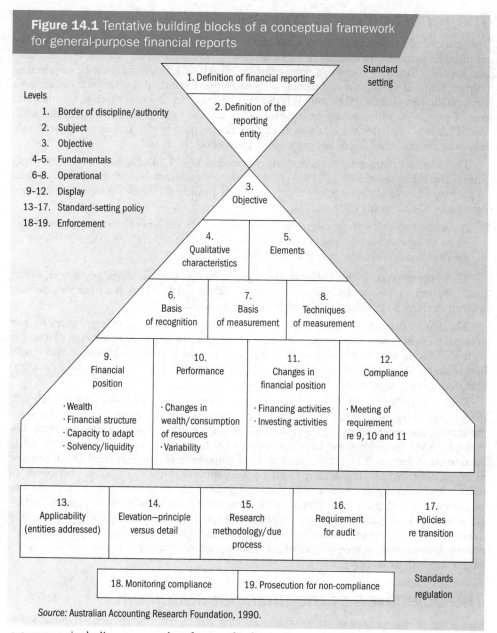

Source: Australian Accounting Research Foundation, 1990.

statements, including many other forms of information such as financial summaries, environmental disclosures and market-based information (e.g. earnings per share and the price/earnings ratio).

Herein lies the fundamental difficulty in defining the scope of financial reporting. In fact, neither the IASC nor the AARF have so far attempted to provide a rigid definition. The major definitional problem is that the scope of financial reporting is dynamic and constantly changes over time. New forms of company disclosure are continually appearing. These disclosures include environmental disclosures, value-added statements, trend data, future-oriented information and non-financial performance indicators. Any definition of scope will have to be sufficiently elastic to capture dynamic new developments in company disclosure as well as anticipate future developments.

The next two levels shown in Figure 14.1 define the concept of the *reporting entity* and the *objectives* of financial statements.

The reporting entity concept

This part of the conceptual framework deals with the types of entities that should be required to prepare financial statements and comply with accounting standards. For example, should a local city council, a tennis club, a church or a family business be required to prepare financial statements and comply with accounting standards in the same manner as a large public corporation? This issue is important because, among other things, the financial cost of complying with accounting regulations tends to be more prohibitive for smaller entities. The IASC has not yet dealt with this particular part of the conceptual framework. Australia, on the other hand, has made some ground on this issue.

The Australian Statement of Accounting Concepts SAC 1, 'Definition of the Reporting Entity' (issued by the AARF in 1990), states that only *reporting entities* should be required to prepare financial statements and comply with accounting standards. A reporting entity is defined by SAC 1 as any entity:

> in respect of which it is reasonable to expect the existence of users dependent on financial statements for information which will be useful to them for making and evaluating decisions about the allocation of scarce resources (paragraph 40).

These users would include shareholders, potential investors, analysts, regulators, creditors, suppliers, employees and other users who need financial reports as a basis for assessing an entity's financial position, profitability and performance.

The SAC 1 definition implies that, for those entities where major external users are *not expected* to exist, these entities should not have to prepare financial statements or comply with accounting standards. For example, private companies, trusts, sole traders and family businesses would not qualify as reporting entities under SAC 1, because it would be reasonable to assume that there will be no major external users.

Some writers have argued that a major limitation of SAC 1 is that it does not provide sufficient guidelines as to what constitutes a reporting entity. In particular, guidelines for identifying dependent users are expressed in *qualitative* rather than quantitative terms. For example, SAC 1 does not indicate how large a company must be before it can be safely assumed that there will be major external users. Furthermore, the reporting entity concept as enunciated in SAC 1 is underpinned by assumptions about the information needs of users. Some commentators have been concerned about the degree of 'use' which needs to be exercised before it can be concluded that users make economic decisions based on financial statements. For example, would an entity still qualify as a reporting entity if users only made very modest use of the financial reports? Because SAC 1 guidelines are coined in such generic phraseology, determination of whether a reporting entity exists or not becomes a largely subjective exercise.

The objectives of the financial statements

This stage of the conceptual framework deals with the overall objectives of financial statements, the users of these reports and their information needs.

The IASC *Framework* defines the objectives of financial statements in terms of two qualities: economic decision making and managerial accountability (paragraphs 12–14):

1. The objective of financial statements is to provide information about the financial position, performance and changes in financial position of an enterprise that is useful to a wide range of users in making economic decisions.
2. Financial statements also show the results of the stewardship of management, or the accountability of management for the resources entrusted to it. Those users who wish to assess the stewardship or accountability of management do so in order that they may make economic decisions; these decisions may include, for example, whether to hold or sell their investment in the enterprise or whether to reappoint or replace the management.

The vision behind the IASC objectives for financial statements (as is the case of SAC 2) is that the provision of relevant financial information by companies to users will ultimately enhance the efficient allocation of scarce resources throughout national and international economies, thus contributing to economic growth. For example, relevant financial information will assist investors to make informed portfolio decisions concerning the spread of risk and return, and assist creditors to make informed lending decisions.

Because efficient resource allocation is the ideal, the IASC states that the primary objective of financial statements is to provide relevant information to various external users so that they can make and evaluate decisions about the allocation of scarce resources.

As discussed in Chapter 1, the IASC *Framework* defines the following external users as being dependent on company financial statements (paragraph 9):

(a) *Investors:* The providers of risk capital and their advisers are concerned with the risk inherent in, and return provided by, their investments. They need information to help them determine whether they should buy, hold or sell. Shareholders are also interested in information which enables them to assess the ability of the enterprise to pay dividends.

(b) *Employees:* Employees and their representative groups are interested in information about the stability and profitability of their employers. They are also interested in information which enables them to assess the ability of the enterprise to provide remuneration, retirement benefits and employment opportunities.

(c) *Lenders:* Lenders are interested in information that enables them to determine whether their loans, and the interest attaching to them, will be paid when due.

(d) *Suppliers and other trade creditors:* Suppliers and other creditors are interested in information that enables them to determine whether amounts owing to them will be paid when due. Trade creditors are likely to be interested in an enterprise over a shorter period than lenders unless they are dependent upon the continuation of the enterprise as a major customer.

(e) *Customers:* Customers have an interest in information about the continuance of an enterprise, especially when they have a long-term involvement with, or are dependent on, the enterprise.

(f) *Governments and other agencies:* Governments and their agencies are interested in the allocation of resources and, therefore, the activities of enterprises. They also require information in order to regulate the activities of enterprises, to determine taxation policies and as the basis for national income and similar statistics.

(g) *Public:* Enterprises affect members of the public in a variety of ways. For example, enterprises may make a substantial contribution to the local economy in many ways including the number of people they employ and their patronage of local suppliers. Financial statements may assist the public by providing information about the trends and recent developments in the prosperity of the enterprise and the range of its activities.

The IASC envisages that a wide-ranging community of interest is affected by the disclosure of company financial statements. This also suggests that general-purpose financial statements are potentially useful for a wide variety of economic and social decisions. This view is consistent with the *entity concept* in accounting. Under the entity concept, economic interests or stakeholders in the business corporation extend beyond the owners and managers, and include other participants or affected parties such as employees and consumers. This can be contrasted with the *proprietorship* view of accounting, which posits that the major stakeholder in a company is the shareholder or owner. Under the entity view, all the users have the same priority or importance. Under the proprietorship view, shareholders are considered to be the primary users. Nearly all standard-setting bodies around the world have endorsed the entity concept of accounting.

Level 4 of Figure 14.1 deals with the qualitative characteristics that financial information should possess before inclusion in financial statements. Level 4 also covers the definition of basic elements of financial reports—the assets, liabilities, equity, revenues and expenses of an entity. We will now deal with each of these issues in turn.

Qualitative characteristics of financial statements

The IASC *Framework* notes (paragraph 24) that qualitative characteristics 'are the attributes that make the information provided in financial statements useful to users'.

The *Framework* (paragraphs 26–42) specifies four basic qualitative characteristics, all of which are needed to present a 'true and fair' view of a company's financial affairs. These are (1) understandability, (2) relevance, (3) reliability and (4) comparability. The IASC *Framework* adopts very similar guidelines to SAC 3, 'Qualitative Characteristics of Financial Information', in Australia.

1. *Understandability*

An essential quality of the information provided in financial statements is that it is readily understandable by users. For this purpose, users are assumed to have a reasonable knowledge of business and economic activities and accounting and a willingness to study the information with reasonable diligence. However, information about complex matters that should be included in the financial statements because of its relevance to the economic decision-making needs of users should not be excluded merely on the grounds that it may be too difficult for certain users to understand.

2. *Relevance*

To be useful, information must be relevant to the decision-making needs of users. Information has the quality of relevance when it influences, or has the capacity to influence, the economic decisions of users by helping them evaluate past, present or future events or confirming or correcting their past evaluations.

3. *Reliability*

To be useful, information must also be reliable. Information has the quality of reliability when it is free from material error and bias and can be depended on by users to represent faithfully that which it either purports to represent or could reasonably be expected to represent.

Information may be relevant but so unreliable in nature or representation that its recognition may be potentially misleading. For example, if the validity and amount of a claim for damages under a legal action are disputed, it may be inappropriate for the enterprise to recognise the full amount of the claim in the balance sheet, although it may be appropriate to disclose the amount and circumstances of the claim.

4. *Comparability*

Users must be able to compare the financial statements of an enterprise over time in order to identify trends in its financial position and performance. Users must also be able to compare the financial statements of different enterprises in order to evaluate their relative financial position, performance and changes in financial position. Hence, the measurement and display of the financial effect of like transactions and other events must be carried out in a consistent way throughout an enterprise and over time for that enterprise and in a consistent way for different enterprises.

In addition, the IASC *Framework* stresses that accounting information should reflect, among other things, substance over form, neutrality and completeness.

Substance over form implies that transactions should be 'accounted for and presented in accordance with their substance and economic reality and not merely their legal form'. The substance of transactions can be inconsistent with legal form. For example, as was seen in Chapter 6, the historical cost basis of reporting non-current assets may be consistent with the legal form of the transaction, but this measurement basis often does not reflect the economic substance of the transaction.

Neutrality implies that the information contained in financial statements must be free from bias. The IASC framework notes (paragraph 36): 'Financial statements are not neutral if, by the selection or presentation of information, they influence the making of a decision or judgement in order to achieve a predetermined result or outcome.'

Completeness implies that information in financial statements 'must be complete within the bounds of materiality and cost'. Any significant omissions can result in accounting information being misleading and thus unreliable.

The IASC *Framework* does not rank the qualitative characteristics in any order of importance. Although the four basic characteristics are considered primary, there is acknowledgement that possible 'trade offs' between the qualitative characteristics may be essential in many practical situations. The *Framework* states (paragraph 45): 'In practice a balancing, or trade-off, between qualitative characteristics is often necessary. Generally the aim is to achieve an appropriate balance among the characteristics in order to meet the objective of financial statements. The relative importance of the characteristics in different cases is a matter of professional judgement.'

The only substantive difference between the IASC *Framework* and SAC 3, 'Qualitative Characteristics of Financial Information', is that SAC 3 gives more emphasis to relevance and reliability as primary information characteristics.

Definition and recognition of elements of financial statements

As found in Chapter 2, the elements of the financial statements embrace assets, liabilities, equity, revenues and expenses. Definitions and rules for the recognition of accounting elements are essential for determining the content of financial statements, or those transactions which should be included in or excluded from the financial statements. Not surprisingly, the definition and recognition criteria for accounting elements have so far proven the most controversial aspect of the conceptual framework project. This stands to reason given that the underlying profitability and financial position of companies can be materially affected depending on which definition and recognition criteria are used. The IASC *Framework* sets out definitions and rules for the recognition of accounting elements that are broadly consistent with Australia's SAC 4, 'Definition and Recognition of the Elements of Financial Statements'.

The IASC guidelines are as follows (paragraphs 70–81):

(a) An *asset* is defined as a resource controlled by the enterprise as a result of past events and from which future economic benefits are expected to flow to the enterprise.

Control relates to the capacity of the entity to benefit from the asset in the pursuit of its objectives, and to deny or regulate the access of others to that benefit. The concept of control is not constrained to legal ownership or possession. Hence, the IASC *Framework* completely avoids a legally rigid definition. 'Future economic benefits' is considered to be the essence of assets. It constitutes the scarce capacity of assets to provide benefits to an entity. The future economic benefits are used to provide goods and services for exchange with the objective of generating positive net cash inflows.

The application of the IASC definition of assets will result in certain changes to conventional accounting practice. For example, some forms of deferred charges do not represent economic resources available to the firm, and would therefore be excluded from the balance sheet. These 'dangling debit balances' are traditionally included on the balance sheet to assist in a proper matching of revenues and expenses.

(b) A *liability* is defined as a present obligation of the enterprise arising from past events, the settlement of which is expected to result in an outflow from the enterprise of resources embodying economic benefits.

This definition stresses the obligation to pay to parties external to the entity. Most obligations are legally enforceable because they result from legally binding contracts or are government imposed—such as income taxes or employer superannuation contributions. However, the definition of liabilities extends beyond the concept of legal enforceability and could include equitable obligations (arising from moral or social sanctions) and constructed obligations. Constructed obligations are inferred or construed from the facts of a particular situation rather than contracted by agreement with an external party. For example, a constructive obligation exists where an entity adopts a practice of paying year-end bonuses to employees even though the company is not contractually bound to do so.

(c) *Equity* is defined as the residual interest in the assets of the enterprise after deducting all its liabilities.

Equity is therefore determined by subtracting the total liabilities from the total assets of an entity. This net amount constitutes a claim or right to the net assets (the total assets minus total liabilities) of an entity. One rationale for defining equity as a residual is that equity ranks after liabilities as a claim to the assets of the entity. An entity's equity is increased by profitable operations (revenues exceed expenses) and contributions by owners. Conversely, equity is diminished by distributions to owners and unprofitable operations (expenses exceed revenues).

(d) *Revenue* is the increases in economic benefits during the accounting period in the form of inflows or enhancements of assets or decreases of liabilities that result in increases in equity, other than those relating to contributions from equity participants.

The definition of revenues is therefore driven by or derived from the definition of assets. The logical application of this definition in practice could result in important items not previously treated as revenues (under conventional accounting) being treated as such. For example, incremental increases in the value of non-current assets above book value could justifiably be treated as revenues under the IASC definition.

(e) *Expenses* are decreases in economic benefits during the accounting period in the form of outflows or depletions of assets or incurrence of liabilities that result in decreases in equity, other than those relating to distributions to equity participants. Similar to the definition of revenues, the definition of expenses follows the definition of liabilities.

Recognition of the elements of financial statements

According to the IASC *Framework*, an item that meets the definition of an element should be recognised if:

(a) it is probable that any future economic benefit associated with the item will flow to or from the enterprise; and
(b) the item has a cost or value that can be measured with reliability (paragraph 83).

Recognition criteria apply only to assets, liabilities, revenues and expenses. Because equity is defined as a residual, the recognition criteria will be consequential to procedures used to recognise assets and liabilities.

The IASC recognition criteria have proven very controversial in practice, as we will see in the case illustration of SAC 4 in the next section. The main controversy surrounds the word 'probable'. The word simply means 'more likely than less likely' (more or less than 50 per cent). This conceptualisation represents a fundamental departure from conventional accounting practice. Consider the example of revenue recognition. Conventional practice has long adopted the principle of revenue realisation, which requires revenue to be recognised only when there is a reasonably high degree of certainty of cash being received. The notion of 'probable' could result in some less scrupulous companies bringing to account doubtful revenues and assets.

Level 5 of Figure 14.1 deals explicitly with how assets, liabilities, revenues and expenses are to be measured. Lower levels of the framework deal with the display (disclosure) of information, standard-setting policy and policy enforcement procedures.

Measurement of the elements of financial statements

With respect to the bases and techniques of measurement, the fundamental question is how to value assets and liabilities given the objective of financial reporting and the qualitative characteristics of financial information? Should assets and liabilities be measured at some market-determined value or at historical cost? This area of the *Framework* is undoubtedly the most contentious. At the time of writing, the measurement of assets, liabilities, equity, revenues and expenses had not been explicitly dealt with by the IASC *Framework* or the Australian conceptual framework. However, the IASC *Framework* does at least describe some of the basic measurement models that are available in practice. These models include the following (see paragraph 100):

(a) *Historical cost:* Assets are recorded at the amount of cash or cash equivalents paid or the fair value of the consideration given to acquire them at the time of their acquisition. Liabilities are recorded at the amount of proceeds received in exchange for the obligation, or in some circumstances (for example income taxes) at the amounts of cash or cash equivalents expected to be paid to satisfy the liability in the normal course of business.

(b) *Current cost:* Assets are carried at the amount of cash or cash equivalents that would have to be paid if the same or an equivalent asset was acquired currently. Liabilities are carried at the undiscounted amount of cash or cash equivalents that would be required to settle the obligation currently.

(c) *Realisable (settlement) value:* Assets are carried at the amount of cash or cash equivalents that could currently be obtained by selling the asset in an orderly disposal. Liabilities are carried at their settlement values: that is, the undiscounted amounts of cash or cash equivalents expected to be paid to satisfy the liabilities in the normal course of business.

(d) *Present value:* Assets are carried at the present discounted value of the future net cash inflows that the item is expected to generate in the normal course of business. Liabilities are carried at the present discounted value of the future net cash outflows.

Historical cost is the most prevalent measurement base used in accounting practice. However, the historical cost principle is not followed too rigidly by accountants. For example, it is conventional for inventories to be carried at the lower of cost and net realisable value; marketable securities are often carried at market value and pension liabilities are carried at their present value. In Australia, Approved Accounting Standard AASB 1010, 'Accounting for the Revaluation of Non-current Assets', encourages companies to revalue their non-current assets on a regular basis. Hence, the system of measurement used in Australia is sometimes referred to as 'modified historical cost'.

Display of financial information

The final level of the main body of the framework shown in Figure 14.1 is the display level. This level considers in detail the nature of the information to be displayed in financial reports. As Figure 14.1 demonstrates, this involves identifying the appropriate information groupings (financial position, performance, investing and financing and compliance) and analysing the components of those selected groupings. This is envisaged to provide a rational basis for disclosures required by Australian accounting standards. The display level of the conceptual framework is naturally closely related to the objective of general-purpose financial reporting, concerning as it does the information to be displayed and the format of the disclosure.

Standard-setting policy and enforcement

The lowest levels of the conceptual framework consider policy issues, that is, issues such as the audit status, applicability and timing of financial reporting, and, lastly, enforcement of policy. Clearly, different levels of the framework will be, to a large extent, interdependent and interrelated. For example, the objectives of financial reports will have a bearing on the definition of the scope of financial reporting. Another example is that the qualitative characteristics of financial information will influence various measurement alternatives, and measurement alternatives will impinge on auditor verification and policy enforcement issues. Hence, it will be essential that decisions made at one level of the framework are reviewed for consistency and applicability with other levels.

The IASC *Framework* is still in the process of development. Figure 14.1 illustrates all the parts or aspects that standard setters need to address in order to complete a conceptual framework. However, we have seen that many areas of the conceptual framework structure outlined in Figure 14.1 are not yet covered by existing IASC conceptual statements or by the Australian SACs.

Implementation of the conceptual framework: the Australian case

So far we have discussed the nature, purposes and possible motivations for a conceptual framework. We have also discussed the contents of the IASC *Framework*, including the IASC's position on the objectives of financial statements, and definition and recognition criteria for the elements of financial statements.

The goal of standard setters is not only to develop a conceptual framework but to see that the framework is successfully implemented in practice. The following case illustration outlines attempts by the AARF to implement the Australian conceptual framework. The Australian case is instructive and interesting for at least three reasons. First, Australia was the only country in the world to attempt to implement a conceptual framework having *mandatory* status. That is, professional accountants were required to follow the requirements of the conceptual framework in a similar fashion to the mandates of accounting standards. Second, the Australian conceptual framework was more prescriptive in its requirements than many other conceptual frameworks around the world, particularly when compared with frameworks developed in the United States and the United Kingdom. Finally, Australia is one of the few countries in the world that has committed itself to an accelerated conceptual framework program. The AARF is seeking to address each part of Figure 14.1 as speedily as possible.

Background of Australia's conceptual framework

In Australia the development of a conceptual framework followed a similar pattern to events occurring in the United States around the 1970s and beyond. In a similar vein to the American Accounting Association, the Australian accounting profession also recognised the need to develop a system of coordinated concepts and objectives which would guide the development of consistent accounting standards and practices. The absence of what Paton and Littleton had referred to as 'a coherent, coordinated, consistent body of doctrine' within which to develop accounting standards was seen as the root cause of many inadequacies in Australian accounting practices.

In the United States, the Financial Accounting Standards Board (FASB) accelerated work on the development of a conceptual framework during the 1970s, and the Australian profession followed suit. Although American developments were important, other factors also influenced the early development of Australia's conceptual framework. Academic writers such as Mathews and Grant and Chambers were highly critical of the perceived limitations of conventional accounting practices during the 1960s and 1970s. They drew attention to the deficiencies of historical cost accounting, particularly in times of changing price levels, and the lack of a sound conceptual basis underpinning many accounting practices. Their work proved to be very influential. Largely as a response to this academic push, the Australian accounting profession commissioned John Kenley, the director of the

Accountancy Research Foundation (later reconstituted as the AARF), to formally examine the FASB's conceptual framework developments. This led to Kenley's adaptation of the American studies of Paul Grady, which had formed the basis of the FASB conceptual framework project. This adaptation by Kenley was followed by a further influential study by Kenley and Staubus. Although the study was intended to be an Australian adaptation of FASB proposals, the book ended up adopting a more *prescriptive* approach to accounting concepts and objectives.

The adoption of this more prescriptive approach represented a fundamental departure from the FASB model which had attempted to blend descriptive and prescriptive elements to enhance the operationality and general acceptance of the conceptual framework. In hindsight, the works of Kenley and Kenley and Staubus have proven very influential, as the AARF to this day has persisted with the development of a largely prescriptive framework.

Significant progress on the Australian conceptual framework was made during the 1980s. The Australian strategy to develop a conceptual framework has been stated by a previous director of the AARF. Two elements of this strategy included: (1) to maximise the use of FASB thinking; and (2) the notion that the importance of a conceptual framework would not be over sold, but gradually unveiled.

The AARF kept to its game plan. In the late 1980s six exposure drafts were released for public comment. Exposure drafts ED 42A (objectives of financial reporting), ED 42B (qualitative characteristics of financial information), 42C (definition and recognition of assets) and ED 42D (definition and recognition of liabilities) were all released simultaneously in December 1987. Exposure drafts ED 46A (definition of the reporting entity) and ED 46B (definition and recognition of expenses) were released together in May 1988. Exposure drafts ED 51A (definition of equity) and ED 51B (definition and recognition of revenues) were released in August 1990. All of these exposure drafts were preceded by discussion papers and accounting theory monographs commissioned by the AARF from academics within Australia and in other countries. Furthermore, in August 1990 three Statement of Accounting Concepts (or SACs) were released having mandatory status:

SAC 1 'Definition of the Reporting Entity'
SAC 2 'Objectives of General Purpose Financial Reporting'
SAC 3 'Qualitative Characteristics of Financial Information'

In the early 1990s greater momentum was instilled into the development of a conceptual framework arising from certain amendments to Australian corporations law. In addition to developing accounting standards, Section 226(1) of the *Corporations Law* (1991) specifically charged the AASB with the responsibility of developing a conceptual framework for financial reporting. This gave added authority to the AARF to develop further SACs. Furthermore, the share-market collapse of 1987, followed by the collapse of numerous companies in Australia in the late 1980s and early 1990s, also precipitated greater efforts by the AARF to accelerate development of the conceptual framework.

The controversial SAC 4, 'Definition and Recognition of Elements of Financial Statements' (which combined exposure drafts ED 42B–D, ED 46B and exposure drafts 51A–B), was released in March 1992. It had mandatory status on its release. The SACs had initially been made mandatory under APS 1, 'Conformity with Statements of Accounting Concepts and Standards', and AASB Release 100, 'Nature of Approved Accounting Standards and Statements of Accounting Concepts and Criteria for the Evaluation of Proposed Approved Accounting Standards'.

The first release of SAC 4 symbolised the AARF's ideological commitment to a largely prescriptive or normative conceptual framework. Implicit in the requirements of SAC 4 were significant departures from conventional accounting practices.

Requirements of SAC 4

SAC 4 deals with the definition and recognition of assets, liabilities, equity, revenues and expenses. It was mentioned above that the IASC *Framework* is essentially the same as SAC 4's requirements. For example, in the case of assets, SAC 4 defines them in a similar way to the IASC as future economic benefits controlled by the entity as a result of past transactions or other past events. With respect to recognition criteria, SAC 4 stipulates that an asset should only be recognised in the balance sheet when:

(a) it is probable that the future economic benefits embodied in the asset will eventuate; and
(b) the asset possesses a cost or other value that can be measured reliably.

Reactions from the business community to SAC 4

The only aspect of the Australian conceptual framework to attract significant corporate concern was SAC 4. SACs 1–3 were issued by the AARF with little objection or protest from the business community, but SAC 4 created a storm of protest. The corporate backlash to SAC 4 took the AARF and its Boards by surprise, as earlier exposure drafts of SAC 4 (which were widely circulated for public comment) did not attract significant commercial opposition. The commercial reaction to the requirements of SAC 4 became evident only when the Statement was officially released by the AARF in August 1992.

There were 108 public submissions relating to SAC 4 during 1993. The submissions contained a variety of criticisms from leading accounting firms, companies, local and federal government agencies and departments, and interest groups and representative bodies such as the Australian Institute of Directors, the Government Accountants Group Committee and the Australian Merchant Bankers Association. Furthermore, the AARF received considerable feedback from a number of workshops and seminars it conducted on SAC 4 in all major States and Territories throughout Australia in 1993. Many of the concerns with SAC 4 were captured in a statement from a submission by a major public company: '[SAC 4] is a laudable aim but I contend it does not address commercial reality, or focus on that very important issue of the credibility of the accounting profession in Australia'.

The Group of 100 (a group representing the 100 largest public companies in Australia) also reflected the prevailing climate of corporate opinion at this time, as Figure 14.2 shows:

The following outlines some of the specific corporate concerns with SAC 4 as they appeared in the corporate submissions of 1993. Some of these concerns are also reflected in Figure 14.2.

1. *Expected changes to accounting practice*. There were concerns that SAC 4's definition criteria for assets, liabilities, revenues and expenses departed too much from accepted commercial practice. Consider the following two examples:
    (a) *Revaluation practices*. There were concerns from companies that SAC 4 provided insufficient guidance on selective asset revaluation practices widely adopted by Australian companies. The existing Accounting Standard AASB 1010, 'Accounting for the Revaluation of Non-current Assets', permits companies to revalue their non-current assets, but does specify the valuation base to be employed. Some respondents believed SAC 4 was too vague and generic to provide guidelines on what valuation model should be used as the basis for asset revaluation. A more serious concern with SAC 4 was that AASB 1010 does not permit revaluation increments above book value (historical cost less accumulated depreciation) to be treated as revenue. However, under SAC 4 revenues are defined in terms of enhancements of assets, which would clearly include revaluation increments. The practical application of SAC 4 would therefore contradict the requirements of AASB 1010.
    (b) *Treatment of debt/equity items*. Of concern to standard setters in recent years has been the growing practice of companies disclosing certain types of 'hybrid' securities as equity items when they possess all the essential characteristics of liabilities (for

Figure 14.2

G100 pulls the rug on SAC 4

by DOREEN SOH

Corporate Australia, represented by The Group of 100, has declared that it will not support Statement of Accounting Concepts number Four, 'Definition and Recognition of the Elements of Financial Statements', in its present form.

In a letter to the Australian Accounting Standards Board, G100 president, Graeme Standish, says the group wants to achieve in-principle agreement in four areas before it examines the details in SAC 4. G100 wants assurances that:
- international compatibility will be maintained;
- SACs will not be mandatory;
- SAC 4's undue bias towards the balance sheet at the expense of the profit and loss statement would be corrected; and
- a measurement standard would be fast tracked.

Standish, who who is the finance controller for the Shell Company in Victoria, says AASB chairman Peter Day has replied and the group is seeking further discussion.

Privately, some G100 members say Day's reply—a five-page letter in response to a two-page letter—was 'unsatisfactory'.

Day, who was himself president of G100 before accepting the chairmanship of the AASB, is saddened by the group's approach.

'The group has got its message across pretty clearly—"reject" is a big message', says Day.

'It's one thing to reject SAC 4, it's another thing to identify areas of similarity which should be supported and areas of differences where things can be treated in a more gradual way'.

New Accountant, 15 April 1993
Published with permission from Australian Financial Press

example redeemable preference shares, convertible debt). A potential motivation for such practices is improvement in the debt/equity ratio and the rate of return on assets (which will improve because interest expenses are excluded from the profit and loss account). To some extent SAC 4 had tried to tackle this problem. For instance, equity is defined in SAC 4 as the residual of assets minus liabilities. Hence, the test for classification of equity items is based on whether or not they meet the definition of liabilities. SAC 4 also suggests that a security could be classified as either debt or equity during the lifetime of those securities. However, many commentators were concerned with SAC 4's handling of the debt/equity classification controversy. Some companies remarked that reclassification could easily occur depending on the volatile nature of stock-market conditions, or with the circumstances of the entity or management intent. Many of these events are outside an entity's control and are difficult to anticipate. As such, commentators noted that reclassification can be extremely subjective.

2. *Recognition criteria for elements of financial statements.* Many submissions were concerned that SAC 4's recognition criteria for assets, liabilities, revenues and expenses were too permissive. Take the example of revenue. Recall from the above-mentioned discussion that SAC 4 stipulates the 'probability' test for recognition of revenue. Probable means 'more likely than less likely' or more than less of 50 per cent. The SAC 4 probability test therefore relaxes conventional accounting practice, which follows the revenue realisation principle. As one submission noted, the SAC 4 probability test 'will undoubtedly be subjected to abuse and exploitation by the less scrupulous operators'. The SAC 4 probability test was also seen to undermine the principle of prudence or conservatism, which indicates that more stringent criteria should be applied in respect of the recognition of revenues and assets than for expenses and liabilities.

3. *SAC 4 inconsistent with existing accounting standards.* Following the release of SAC 4 many of the public submissions stated that inevitable clashes would arise between certain accounting standards and the concept statements. Most of Australia's accounting standards are based on the historical cost model and associated principles of matching, realisation and conservatism (none of these concepts were mentioned in the 1992 version of SAC 4). The inconsistencies between SAC 4 and accounting standards were seen

by many companies to result in conflict, confusion and uncertainty in practice. Hence, the relevance and commercial realism of SAC 4 was questioned.

4. *Departure from international accounting standards and practices.* There were also concerns from respondents (as was seen in the Group of 100 extract above) that SAC 4 would result in significant departures from accepted international accounting practices. For example, the FASB conceptual framework adopts more restrictive recognition criteria than SAC 4. Furthermore, while the IASC *Framework* adopted the same recognition criteria as SAC 4, this framework was not issued with mandatory status. The problem of international comparability raised fears that foreign investors, rating agencies and analysts may not readily comprehend Australian financial statements. The competitive advantage of Australian companies could be adversely affected, for example, by foreign investors raising the cost of capital requirements for Australian firms.

The withdrawal of SAC 4

Faced with what appeared to be overwhelming criticism, the Australian accounting profession acted swiftly. In late 1993 a Joint Standing Committee of the Australian Society of Certified Practising Accountants (ASCPA) and the Institute of Chartered Accountants in Australia (ICAA) considered the 1993 submissions and decided that, as from 31 December 1993, the SACs should no longer have mandatory status for members of the accounting profession.

Furthermore, to quell industry discontent with the conceptual framework efforts, the AARF decided to significantly revise SAC 4. Work on these revisions progressed through most of 1994 and involved an extensive consultative process between the AARF, its Boards, representatives of the Big Six accounting firms, the Group of 100 and the Australian Securities Commission. An amended SAC 4 was released by the AARF in March 1995. These amendments were accompanied by an AARF release entitled 'SAC 4: Definition and Recognition of the Elements of Financial Statements—Background and Basis for Conclusions' (March 1995). This document set out the specific changes to SAC 4 and provided discussion on why the Boards arrived at particular conclusions.

Changes to SAC 4 were reported by the financial press, as seen in Figure 14.3.

The revision of SAC 4

As can be seen from Figure 14.3, some of the changes made to SAC 4 were substantive and others were more superficial. However, the overall change to SAC 4 was the AARF's endorsement of a more descriptive and internationally compatible conceptual framework. The substantive changes to SAC 4 can be summarised from Figure 14.3 as follows:

1. Removal of mandatory status
2. Removal of an operative date (which would no longer be appropriate to a document which does not have mandatory status)
3. Removal of the detailed Appendix attached to the 1992 version of SAC 4. This Appendix provided guidance on the interpretation and application of SAC 4 concepts to a number of specific accounting transactions. These detailed interpretations were no longer considered appropriate to a statement designed to set out broad concepts. It was concluded that interpretations of SAC 4 to specific accounting issues are better reserved for accounting standards and other AARF releases.
4. Greater attention given to conventional accounting principles, such as matching and periodicity. This gives SAC 4 a more descriptive flavour.

It is noteworthy that, with respect to the more controversial issue of recognition criteria and the probability test, the AARF and its Boards made no alterations to SAC 4, other than to provide additional explanation for their particular policy stances. Although the AARF acknowledged that their probability test was more permissive than all other international conceptual frameworks, it justified its position as follows:

(the AARF) ... decided against the adoption of a conservative approach in the recognition of revenues, for the following reasons (paragraph A31):

(a) it would conflict with the qualitative characteristic of reliability, which requires *inter alia* that financial information is neutral. Accordingly, it would conflict with the qualitative characteristics set out in SAC 3;

(b) it would conflict with the Boards' goal of a balance between the quality of information reported in the statement of financial position and in the operating statement; and

(c) it would specify two-tier criteria for the recognition of assets and liabilities instead of the general criterion of probability. That is, the criteria for the recognition and derecognition of assets and liabilities would differ according to whether a revenue or expense is involved.

Figure 14.3

Back from the dead: the new SAC 4

A revised version of Statement of Accounting Concepts 4 should appease the corporate sector, which loudly condemned the original version. As PATRICIA HOWARD reports, now there are plans for SAC 5.

The storm that surrounded Statement of Accounting Concepts 4, or SAC 4, for at least three years should at last be settled by the recent release of a revised version. The more controversial sections of the original have been dropped, and instead of being mandatory on accountants it has now been described as 'a general guide'.

The new version, redrawn in response to widespread criticism, relaxes the tough stance that had been taken by the Australian Accounting Research Foundation on liabilities, particularly the inclusion of lease agreements and forward contracts on corporate balance sheets.

The one area that AARF has toughened relates to the general definition of liabilities: this will now include obligations under legislation, such as a mine licence condition to rehabilitate a mining site. As a result, the revised document, released last month, is very much in line with the demands put forward by both accountants and the business community generally.

For Ken Spencer, who only recently took over from Peter Day as Chairman of the Australian Accounting Standards Board, these decisions reflect the board's pragmatic nature. 'SAC 4 is important as a general guide on such issues as assets, liabilities and expenses', Spencer says.

'The revisions that have been put in place are due to comments by people within the profession and business community and the now accepted need to make SAC 4 non-mandatory. The areas that have been amended are basically areas where the board received lots of comments and it felt it was productive to change them.

'It's important though, that people don't overlook that the really important aspect of SAC 4 is in providing a framework for standard setters so their standards can be as consistent as possible, and for the business community to have appropriate guidance on specific issues.'

SAC 4 is now very similar to conceptual frameworks adopted by the International Accounting Standards Committee and the US Financial Accounting Standards Board.

'In an environment where people are saying we should be harmonising our accounting standards with those overseas, then this is a very good result', says Warren McGregor, the AARF's executive director.

'The great potential of SAC 4 that many people have overlooked is that it means that the US, New Zealand, South Africa, England, Australia and the International Standards Committee have the same framework in place.'

Financial Forum, Vol. 4, June 1995

Questions arising from the case illustration

Why did the Australian business community's concerns about the conceptual framework not become apparent until SAC 4 was issued in 1992?

It is true that when the earlier exposure drafts on SAC 4 were released companies and other interest groups did not raise many objections to the proposed requirements of SAC 4. The AARF was taken by surprise when the 1993 submissions revealed great opposition to SAC 4 by commercial interests in Australia. It was only after SAC 4 was officially released in 1992 that companies realised there was going to be considerable difficulty in applying this part of the conceptual framework in accounting practice. There is a difference between a proposal for regulation and the actual release of a mandatory regulation in practice! People tend to pay more attention when they actually have to do something. The release of SACs 1–3 in 1990 raised no real concerns from the business community. However, SAC 4 was by nature more controversial than the previous SACs. Unlike previous SACs that were issued, SAC 4 deals with the pragmatic questions of the definition and recognition of elements of financial statements, which directly impact on the measurement of a company's financial results and performance.

What were the major concerns with SAC 4 arising from the public submissions in 1993?

As the case illustration indicates, at least three interrelated concerns arose from the 1993 submissions. First, the definition and recognition criteria adopted for elements of financial statements were considered too permissive or broad. This is particularly true of the recognition criteria, which adopt the 'probability' test (or the 50 per cent rule). Furthermore, some companies believed that the definitions were too vague or generic to provide realistic guidelines on when or when not to include accounting elements in the financial statements. A second concern related to the fact that SAC 4, if literally applied, would contradict a number of conventional accounting practices and principles. A third concern, which relates to the second, is that most existing accounting standards are based on traditional accounting principles such as historical cost, revenue realisation and conservatism. SAC 4 did not adopt or endorse these principles in 1992, thus rendering the statement inconsistent with the body corpus of accounting standards.

Why did the AARF and the accounting profession withdraw the mandatory status of the conceptual framework?

By the end of 1993 the AARF and the accounting profession knew they had little support from the business community for SAC 4. There were really only two major choices available to the AARF. The first choice was to ignore the criticism and keep SAC 4 unchanged with mandatory status. The second choice was to appease the groundswell of criticism and withdraw the mandatory status of the document.

The first course of action would probably have resulted in protracted lobbying by business interests to remove the conceptual framework, as well as increasing the incidence of non-compliance with SAC 4 by professional accountants and the business sector. Furthermore, if the AARF ignored the criticism of SAC 4, it would most likely have diminished the standing and authority of the AARF in the eyes of the business community. This could have led to future challenges to the AARF's role as the primary standard-setting body in Australia. The second choice, while less distasteful than the first, was nevertheless a major embarrassment for the AARF which had invested considerable time and resources in developing SAC 4.

How would you assess the usefulness and influence of a conceptual framework without mandatory status?

With the withdrawal of its mandatory status, the conceptual framework statements have been reissued by the AARF as a 'guide' to account preparers and users. A guidance statement clearly will not have the same influence and impact as a mandatory statement, so the conceptual framework's relevance in practice will be much diminished. However, although the conceptual framework (without mandatory status) will probably be taken less seriously by practitioners and the business community, it is widely expected that standard setters will continue to make considerable use of the conceptual framework in the setting of accounting standards.

How would you assess the future of Australia's conceptual framework project?

The setback on SAC 4 has left the AARF undeterred in its pursuit of the conceptual framework. In fact, the much anticipated release of SAC 5 dealing with accounting measurement is close to final completion. Notwithstanding the AARF's commitment to developing the conceptual framework, the previous experimentation with a radically prescriptive framework is not likely to gain general acceptance in accounting and business practice. In order to achieve general acceptance by the accounting and business communities in Australia, it may be necessary for the AARF to develop a more descriptive conceptual framework.

Summary

A major purpose of a conceptual framework is to facilitate the resolution of conceptual disputes in accounting and hopefully create more consistent and logical accounting standards and accounting practices. Ultimately, the major beneficiary of the conceptual framework will be the external user, who will benefit from the overall improvement in the quality of company financial reporting.

As we have seen in the case of SAC 4, to be effective the conceptual framework must gain general acceptance in the business community. The capacity for the conceptual framework to achieve general acceptance is probably the most critical factor facing its future. Can this realistically be achieved? Many problems confronting general acceptance of a conceptual framework relate to the realities of political processes. In a similar fashion to accounting standards, the conceptual framework is set in a political environment of conflicting economic interests. Reconciling these diverse interests will pose considerable challenges to standard setters, but is essential if a conceptual framework is to have any hope of influencing accounting practice in a significant way.

The general acceptance or workability of a conceptual framework may also be hampered by the inability of standard setters to provide clear-cut technical and conceptual guidance for resolving a number of financial reporting controversies. As we have seen with SAC 4, the definition and recognition criteria for elements of financial statements appeared to be too prescriptive and vague to resolve controversial accounting problems.

Australia's experimentation with a mandatory and prescriptive framework provides insights into the many difficulties facing standard setters in achieving the implementation of a generally accepted conceptual framework. The amended SAC 4 will undoubtedly quell widespread concerns and disgruntlement with the Australian conceptual framework project. Although the Boards have met the industry only halfway on these amendments, the real substantive change to SAC 4 is the removal of its mandatory status and its relegation to a mere 'general guide'.

With the removal of the mandatory status of the SACs, the accounting bodies have effectively dismantled the conceptual framework. The future of the framework is now less certain. Although it is clear that the conceptual framework will play less of a role in guiding company financial reporting and disclosure practices, it is widely understood that the AARF will continue to develop SACs and continue to use the conceptual framework in the standard-setting process.

 **Review exercises**

Discussion questions

14.1 Define in your own words a conceptual framework.

14.2 What are the goals of a conceptual framework?

14.3 What motives have stimulated the development of the Australian conceptual framework?

14.4 What is meant by the 'politicisation' of accounting? Provide some examples.

14.5 Is it important to define the scope of financial reporting? How would you define it?

14.6 Do you think financial statements should include non-financial as well as financial information?

14.7 What is the difference between general purpose and special purpose financial statements? Do standard setters distinguish between the two? If so, in what way?

14.8   What is meant by a reporting entity?

14.9   Define, in your own words, a prescriptive and a descriptive conceptual framework. On what premises is a prescriptive framework founded?

14.10   Why do you think international standard setters have devoted so much time and resources to the development of a conceptual framework project? Do you consider it time and money well spent?

14.11   What are the objectives of financial statements as proposed by the IASC conceptual framework? Are these objectives consistent with your own view?

14.12   Explain clearly why each of the qualitative characteristics discussed in the IASC *Framework* is important. Which characteristic do you think is the most important? Why?

14.13   Why is there frequently a conflict between the qualitative characteristics of relevance and reliability? Use examples to illustrate your answer.

14.14   Refer to the user groups identified in the IASC conceptual framework. Think of some examples of specific decisions that each group of users might want to make. In what ways might general-purpose financial statements help them in making the decisions?

14.15   A large paper manufacturer is releasing toxic wastes into the river next to which it is located. Is it the function of external financial reporting to report on this polluting activity?

14.16   A large public chemical company, several kilometres from an orchard district, is releasing into the air toxic fumes which are believed to be contaminating the fruit at the orchards. Would information regarding this situation be relevant to investors in evaluating the company for investment purposes?

14.17   'Overly pessimistic reports may be detrimental to the interest of those presently holding shares in the company concerned, but overly optimistic reports may be detrimental to the interest of prospective investors. How then can accountants maintain a neutral stance?' Discuss.

14.18   Assume that your entire savings are invested in the shares of a public company which states in its annual report that it has not disclosed estimates of its future trading activities because such information is not verifiable. Discuss whether you would prefer to have been informed of such estimates. Why?

14.19   What definition and recognition criteria for elements of financial statements is proposed by the IASC *Framework*? Will these criteria result in any departures from conventional accounting practices? Explain your answer.

14.20   Why was the Australian business community avidly opposed to SAC 4?

14.21   Is SAC 4 consistent with Australian accounting standards? If not, why not?

14.22   How would you assess the future of the Australian conceptual framework project?

CHAPTER 15
Assets and expenses

Learning objectives

In this chapter you will be introduced to:

1. the nature of assets

2. the nature of expenses

3. the difference between assets and expenses

4. the criteria for the recognition of assets and expenses

5. the influence of conservatism in accounting for assets and expenses

6. the allocation problems in asset and expense determination, especially in the cases of inventories, marketable securities, depreciable assets and intangible assets

7. the lack of precision generally in accounting for assets and expenses.

Introduction

The next three chapters explore in greater detail the principles and rules applicable to the historical cost system of accounting for assets, expenses, revenues and liabilities. These *elements* of financial statements will be discussed in terms of their definition and recognition. A *definition* permits the identification of the attributes the financial statement element should possess to be identified as such. An asset, for example, must represent a future economic benefit to the entity. *Recognition* is the process of recording an asset (or other element) in the body of the financial statements.

The separation of the definition and recognition components allows a transaction or other event to be analysed in terms of whether it gives rise to an asset, liability, expense or revenue. Having identified the nature of the item, it can be asked whether and how it is to be reported in the financial statements.

After highlighting the assumption of conservatism implicit in historical cost accounting, this chapter explores in depth the definition and recognition criteria for assets and expenses. A number of examples are discussed, with explicit attention given to inventory costing, marketable securities, depreciation and intangible assets.

Conservatism

Uncertainty about recognition of an item is inevitable whenever reliance is placed on expected future events such as the continued usefulness of production equipment over its expected life, the ability to sell inventory at market value, and the ability of the firm to continue to operate. Variations in estimates cannot be avoided whenever an asset is deemed to represent future economic benefits or the amount of a liability depends on future occurrences. This uncertainty has given rise to a further assumption in conventional accounting, that of conservatism. Most people exercise caution when faced with uncertainty and accountants are no exception.

Conservatism means caution or prudence. Prudence is perhaps a more commonly used term today to describe such caution. Whenever conservatism or prudence is mentioned, it implies that accountants should always anticipate losses and never anticipate gains, and that when a choice of values exists for an asset, the lower value should be chosen. Conversely, liabilities are stated at values in order to prevent their understatement.

The assumption of conservatism is believed to result in more useful data because it enhances the reliability of the reported results. Moreover, it is believed that users are harmed more by results that are over-optimistic than by those that are pessimistic. The resulting financial statements represent 'safe estimates' in that the underlying financial position and the profit performance might be better than reported but they should not typically be worse.

Conservatism modifies the sense of the historical cost system from that of valuation at original cost to valuation at *recoverable amount*, in instances where recoverable amount is less than the original cost. Recoverable amount is the net amount likely to be recovered through an asset's continued use and disposal. If any doubt exists about whether an asset's cost will be recovered, either through sale or continued use, then a conservative approach is to write it down. This policy was encountered earlier in the discussion on doubtful debts and is enforced rigorously in respect of current assets. Case 15.1 provides a context in which to consider the writing-down of assets.

Case 15.1 Foster's Brewing Group Ltd

Foster's Brewing Group Ltd reported a net profit of $446.6 million including abnormal items for the financial year ended 30 June 1998. This represented a rise in profits from $250.5 million recorded in the previous financial year. Foster's Asia, including the group's operations in China, lost $42.2 million. Much of this operating loss occurred in China. In response to loss-making in China, the group wrote off more than $150 million of its China assets as an abnormal item and announced plans to sell two of its three breweries there.

As stated in a report in the *Age* of 25 August 1998: 'Foster's entered China in 1993 declaring it would report profits in China in 1999. However, it was forced to defer profit forecasts indefinitely after a series of losses, which have amounted to more than $80 million.' The report also quoted Foster's managing director, Mr Ted Kunkel, as stating that the group ' "put a stake in the ground" and wanted to halve the [China] losses within the next year'.

Explain why Foster's took this action of writing down the value of its China assets when its overall profitability increased in 1997/98.

Source: Helen Shield, 'Foster's profits surge', *Age*, 25 August 1998, p. 2B; 'Brewer moves to stem China losses', 25 August 1998, p. 2B.

In the difficult choice between assets and expenses, the impact of conservatism is to make the transition to expenses more rapid. The test is: 'How likely are the anticipated future economic benefits?' In the case of research and development expenditure it might seem reasonable to capitalise the cost of an experimental program that seems likely to lead to a profitable new product, but under the influence of conservatism the research costs may be charged to expense unless, for example, future benefits are assured 'beyond any reasonable doubt'. A beyond any reasonable doubt test is, of course, more stringent than a test concerned with the prediction of 'probable' future economic benefits.

Similarly, when it is believed that the goods will be sold at below cost, the conservative action is to write them down to their net realisable value.

The definition and recognition of assets and expenses

In this and following chapters, material will be drawn from the IASC *Framework* (see Appendix 2) and International Accounting Standards (IAS) of the International Accounting Standards Committee (IASC). Where relevant, reference will be made to the Australian statements of accounting concepts (SACs).

Assets

From the assumptions and principles presented in Chapters 6 and 14 it was suggested that an asset must have the following characteristics:

- It must be a resource offering future economic benefit through its use or exchange.
- It must be under the control of the entity.
- It must have been acquired in a past, external transaction.

The measurement rules provide that the relevant property of an asset to measure is its unexpired original cost, and the appropriate unit of measurement (in Australia) is the dollar.

With the introduction of conservatism, when the net realisable value of an asset falls below its original cost, the property to be measured becomes the recoverable amount.

Expenses

Definition and measurement rules for expenses were also drawn from the assumptions and principles addressed earlier. For an item to be identified as an expense it must satisfy the following criteria:

- It must represent economic benefit that has been consumed or lost during the period.
- The benefit must have been acquired in a past, external transaction.
- Withdrawals by owners are not expenses but reductions in capital.

The measurement rule provides that the appropriate measure of an expense is the original cost of the economic resources consumed. Following conservatism, a resource will be considered as an expense when there is reasonable doubt about the existence of future benefits.

Stability of asset definitions

A review of accounting textbooks published this century reveals a number of definitions of assets that differ in various ways from those provided above. This should not be taken, necessarily, as evidence that accountants are unable to make up their minds about assets, nor does it mean that one of the many definitions is right and that the others are incorrect. What it may indicate is that accounting is not insulated from the changes that occur in the world, and that the definitions may change as accountants refine their activities and expand their influence, and as the commercial framework within which the system operates changes and develops.

A definition issued by the American Institute of Certified Public Accountants states that assets are:

> economic resources of an enterprise that are recognised and measured in conformity with generally accepted accounting principles. Assets also include certain deferred charges that are not resources but that are recognised and measured in conformity with generally accepted accounting principles.[1]

Although this definition provides little information about the properties of an asset, it does recognise that assets cannot be defined in isolation from other generally accepted accounting principles. Presumably, then, as these principles change, it may be necessary at times to modify asset identification and measurement rules.

One of the earliest definitions of assets this century, and perhaps one of the most enduring, was offered by W. A. Paton in 1922. Paton defined assets as:

> any consideration, material or otherwise, owned by a specific business enterprise and of value to that enterprise.[2]

This definition was provided in an era when an entity's ownership of its resources was the normal situation and it may not be entirely appropriate for a modern economy where entities frequently lease economic resources rather than purchase them outright. Otherwise, Paton's definition may be viewed as compatible with the notion of assets as future economic benefits. It refers to assets as being of value to the enterprise. In terms of the assumptions and principles of the historical cost system, 'value to the enterprise' must be yielded in the

---

1 American Institute of Certified Public Accountants, *Accounting Principles Board Statement No. 4*, 'Basic Concepts and Accounting Principles Underlying Financial Statements of Business Enterprises', American Institute of Certified Public Accountants, New York, 1970, para. 132.

2 W. A. Paton, *Accounting Theory*, The Ronald Press Company, New York, 1922, p. 30.

form of economic benefits derived from the asset's use or its exchange in the marketplace. Hence, value to the enterprise and economic benefits may be viewed as different approaches to describing the same property of an asset.

Some later definitions of an asset focused on the process whereby an asset appears in the accounting records and financial statements rather than on the inherent properties that an item should possess to be called an asset. Paton and Littleton, for example, state that:

> assets are those factors acquired for production which have not reached the point in the business process where they may be treated as 'costs of sales' or 'expenses'. Under this usage, assets or costs incurred would clearly mean charges awaiting future revenue, whereas expenses and costs applied would mean charges against present revenue.[3]

The American Institute of Certified Public Accountants issued a similar definition, although it also offered some ideas about the properties of an asset. The definition states that an asset is:

> something represented by a debit balance that is or would be properly carried forward upon a closing of books of account according to the rules or principles of accounting (provided such debit balance is not in effect a negative balance applicable to a liability) on the basis that it represents either a property right or value acquired, or an expenditure made which has created a property right or is properly applicable to the future.[4]

The emphasis by some authors in the 1940s and 1950s on defining assets in terms of their role in the recording process is perhaps partly attributable to the view that the profit and loss statement was more relevant to investment decisions than the balance sheet. This perspective is captured, a little dramatically perhaps, in a comment by Baxter:

> Conventional accounting 'tends to dismiss the balance sheet as a mere appendage of the revenue account—a mausoleum for unwanted costs that the double-entry system throws up as unregrettable by-products'.[5]

In more recent years there has been a marked trend towards defining assets not merely as part of the recording process but in terms of their inherent properties. The balance sheet seems to have been restored to a position of importance, and is considered by most accountants to be, in intent if not in fact, a statement of financial position rather than a list of balances. Contemporary definitions support the notion of assets as 'future economic benefits'.

Conceptual framework projects undertaken in certain countries have articulated definitions of the elements of financial statements. The definitions are closely similar for each financial statement element. Such high-profile definitions have also been criticised for being abstract and vague. For instance, P. W. Schuetze, the then chief accountant of the Securities and Exchange Commission (SEC) in the United States, expressed dissatisfaction with the conventional notion of assets as probable 'future economic benefits' in stating:

> Defining an asset as probable future economic benefit is to use a high-order abstraction ... I suggest that we try the following definition [of assets]: cash, contractual claims to cash or services, and items than can be sold separately for cash. The suggested definition would comprehend only real things, not abstractions ... Abstract probable future economic benefits cannot be sold, pledged, or given away.[6]

---

[3] W. A. Paton and A. C. Littleton, *An Introduction to Corporate Accounting Standards*, American Accounting Association, Florida, 1940, pp. 25 and 26.

[4] The Committee on Terminology, 'Review and Reserve', *Accounting Terminology Bulletin No. 1*, American Institute of Certified Public Accountants, New York, 1953, p. 73.

[5] W. T. Baxter and S. Davidson, *Studies in Accounting Theory*, Sweet and Maxwell Ltd, 1962, p. viii.

[6] W. P. Schuetze, 'What Is an Asset?', *Accounting Horizons*, September 1993, p. 69.

In fact, Scheutze argued that the conventional definition of assets:

… is so complex, so abstract, so open-ended, so all inclusive, and so vague, that we cannot use it to solve problems … The definition does not discriminate and help us to decide whether something or anything is an asset.[7]

Being similarly critical, R. A. Samuelson explained that the definition 'is therefore used to justify the recognition of assets which have little if any relevance to an assessment of the financial position of an enterprise'.[8]

Properties of assets and expenses and their recognition

The IASC *Framework* defines an asset as:

a resource controlled by the enterprise as a result of past events and from which future economic benefits are expected to flow to the enterprise.[9]

Similarly, SAC 4 in Australia defines assets as:

future economic benefits controlled by an entity as a result of past transactions or other past events.[10]

Assets may have other characteristics that can help identify them. For example, they may have been acquired at a cost, or they may be tangible, exchangeable or legally enforceable. These features, however, are not deemed essential characteristics of assets and therefore do not constitute sufficient grounds for the identification of assets. For example, an asset need not be acquired at a cost, but may be obtained as a gift. The essential characteristics of an asset as contained in the IASC *Framework* definition are:

- future economic benefit
- control by the entity
- arises from past events (including transactions).

We now consider each of these essential characteristics in more detail.

Future economic benefit

Conceptual framework statements on assets denote 'future economic benefit' as the essence of assets. This feature typically applies to both private and public sector entities. The IASC *Framework* attempts to clarify the notion of 'future economic benefit' as follows:

The future economic benefit embodied in an asset is the potential to contribute, directly or indirectly, to the flow of cash and cash equivalents to the enterprise. The potential may be a productive one that is part of the operating activities of the enterprise. It may also take the form of convertibility into cash or cash equivalents or a capability to reduce cash outflows, such as when an alternative manufacturing process lowers the costs of production (para. 53).

[7] Ibid., p. 66.

[8] R. A. Samuelson, 'The Concept of Assets in Accounting Theory', *Accounting Horizons*, September 1996, p. 148.

[9] International Accounting Standards Committee, 'Framework for the Preparation and Presentation of Financial Statements', *International Accounting Standards 1997*, IASC, London, 1997, para. 49(a).

[10] Australian Accounting Standards Board and Public Sector Accounting Standards Board, Statement of Accounting Concepts SAC 4, 'Definition and Recognition of the Elements of Financial Statements', Australian Accounting Research Foundation, 1995, para. 14.

For profit-making or commercial entities their assets are used to provide goods and services for exchange that will generate net cash inflows. For non-business entities such as the Department of Social Security, the State Emergency Service, public libraries, art galleries and charities, the provision of goods and services may not result in direct cash inflows from the recipients. These entities typically rely on appropriations of cash from the government or donations from the public to supplement exchange prices or to negate the need for price charging at all.

In dealing specifically with not-for-profit entities, SAC 4 states that resources held by such entities 'benefit the entities by enabling them to meet their objectives of providing needed service to beneficiaries' (para. 21). Items such as cathedrals, monuments, museum collections and archaeological remains certainly provide needed or desired services to the general public. Although the services provided by these items are more social than economic in nature, it is asserted that they still meet the asset definition in that they provide benefits to their controlling entities in enabling them to fulfil their objectives. Such objectives are non-commercial in nature and typically exclude reference to financial wealth creation or wealth maximisation, profitability, surplus distribution and revenue maximisation. The use of SAC 4 and also accounting standards based on its definition of assets and allied interpretations to require monetary values to be placed on cultural, heritage and scientific collections of not-for-profit public museums for financial reporting purposes has been hotly debated in Australia.[11]

Control

By control is meant the capacity of the reporting entity to benefit from the asset and to deny or regulate the access of others to that benefit. The entity's capacity to control the future economic benefit will frequently stem from legal rights. However, legal enforceability of a right is not always necessary for the establishment of control, since control may be secured through other means. For example, research and development costs may qualify as an asset where an entity exercises control over the future economic benefit by keeping particular know-how a secret.

An interesting example is that of leased property. In this case the future economic benefits in the property are 'unbundled' through the lease agreement. The lessor as legal owner of the property records an asset, lease receivable, which represents the right to receive periodic lease payments from the lessee. The lessee, through the lease agreement, has the right to hold and use the property and, in most situations, records a lease asset in acknowledgment of this future economic benefit. Accounting for leases and the circumstances in which leased assets should be recorded are discussed further in Chapter 17.

Control is crucial in establishing the existence of an asset for an entity. For example, in Australia public highways and the land and recreational facilities in national parks, for instance, may qualify as assets of the government units that control them, in this case the Roads Authority in each state and the National Parks and Wildlife Service. However, they should not be recorded as assets of other reporting entities that derive benefits from them, since these other entities cannot deny or regulate access to these benefits.

---

11 G. D. Carnegie and P. W. Wolnizer, 'The Financial Value of Cultural, Heritage and Scientific Collections: An Accounting Fiction', *Australian Accounting Review*, June 1995; F. Micallef and G. Peirson, 'Financial Reporting of Cultural, Heritage, Scientific and Community Collections', *Australian Accounting Review*, May 1997; P. Hone, 'The Financial Value of Cultural, Heritage and Scientific Collections: A Public Management Necessity', *Australian Accounting Review*, May 1997; G. D. Carnegie and P. W. Wolnizer, 'The Financial Reporting of Publicly Owned Collections: Whither Financial (Market) Values and Contingent Valuation Estimates?', *Australian Accounting Review*, May 1997; G. D. Carnegie and P. W. Wolnizer, 'Unravelling the Rhetoric about the Financial Reporting of Public Collections as Assets: A Response to Micallef and Peirson', *Australian Accounting Review*, March 1999.

Occurrence of past transaction or other event

The third essential characteristic of an asset is that the transaction or event giving the entity control over the future economic benefit must have occurred. Most assets are obtained by a reporting entity from cash, credit or barter transactions. Alternatively, the transactions may be non-reciprocal transfers of assets to the entity, for example donations, grants and contributions by owners or members. Assets may also result from discovery, for example the discovery of mineral resources or a new formula or process.

A future economic benefit not controlled at the present time by the entity would not meet the conventional definition of an asset. Thus, transactions or other events expected to take place in the future do not, in themselves, give rise to assets for the entity. For instance, a management decision to acquire equipment in the future does not of itself create an asset for the entity. The entity needs to actually acquire the equipment (through purchase or lease) and have present control over its use.

Recognition of assets

The IASC *Framework* specifies the following criteria for the recognition of financial statement elements:

> An item that meets the definition of an element should be recognised if:
>
> (a) it is probable that any future economic benefit associated with the item will flow to or from the enterprise; and
> (b) the item has a cost or value that can be measured with reliability (para. 83).

Thus, an asset shall be recognised in the financial statements if, and only if, '… it is probable that the future economic benefits will flow to the enterprise and the asset has a cost or value that can be measured reliably' (para. 89).[12] 'Probable' is used to refer to that which can be reasonably expected on the basis of available evidence or logic. In terms of probability levels it means that the chance of the benefit arising is more likely than less likely (that is, a greater than 50 per cent chance).

Where expenditure has been incurred, but at the time the entity is preparing its financial statements it is not considered 'probable' that future economic benefit will flow to the entity, an asset is not recognised. This does not necessarily mean that the item fails to satisfy the asset definition. It may well represent future economic benefit under the control of the entity. The only implication is that, on the basis of available evidence, the necessary degree of certainty for the item to be recognised as an asset does not exist. In this case the expenditure involved would be recorded as an expense of the period.

Some research and development expenditure may fall into this category, for example. The importance of the distinction between the issues of asset definition and asset recognition should be noted here.

Expenses

The IASC *Framework* offers guidance on the nature of expenses and when they should be recognised. In particular it defines expenses as follows:

> Expenses are decreases in economic benefits during the accounting period in the form of outflows or depletions of assets or incurrences of liabilities that result in decreases in equity, other than those relating to distributions to equity participants (para. 70(b)).

---

12 The term 'probable' does form part of the definition of an asset under the IASC *Framework* and also the Australian conceptual framework, as is the case in the United States.

Similarly, SAC 4 in Australia provides the following definition:

'Expenses' are consumptions or losses of future economic benefits in the form of reductions in assets or increases in liabilities of the entity, other than those relating to distributions to owners, that result in a decrease in equity during the reporting period (para. 117).

The definition of expenses encompasses items that have typically been reported in financial statements as 'losses'. These include, for example, losses on foreign currency transactions, losses resulting from the write-down of assets to a recoverable amount, and losses from natural disasters such as fires and floods. As with all types of expenses, losses represent expired economic benefits and are not, therefore, regarded as constituting a separate element of the financial statements. Any separate identification of losses is a matter of presentation or display.

Recognition of expenses

The IASC *Framework* states that an expense should be recognised in the financial statements if, and only if, '… a decrease in future economic benefits related to a decrease in an asset or an increase in a liability has arisen that can be measured reliably' (para. 94).

Assessments of the probability that economic benefits have been consumed or lost will vary. In some cases there will be agreement that assets have yielded economic benefits during a period, but a substantial amount of uncertainty will surround the issue of 'how much' benefit has been consumed or lost. For example, it may be difficult to determine the extent to which the economic benefits relating to a non-current asset have expired during the period. The importance of this issue is discussed at a general level in the next section in relation to the allocation problem, and more specifically in later sections in relation to inventory, depreciable assets, intangible assets, and research and development. For now, form a view on Case 15.2 which addresses the asset versus expense decision in the airline industry.

Case 15.2 KK Air Ltd

KK Air Ltd is a national air carrier that has recently experienced some adverse publicity following certain breaches of safety. The adverse publicity has impacted on sales of air tickets which has affected the company's profitability. KK's directors decided to change the company's name in an attempt to create a new image for the struggling carrier. A consultant was appointed to provide advice on a new trading name.

KK's financial accountant, J. Boon, was required to treat the consultant's fee for services relating to changing the company's trading name—amounting to $2.3 million—as an asset rather than an expense. Although the consultant had undertaken market research on a new name—'KK Airlines'—and designed new signs and stationery featuring the new name, the directors decided to change the name from 'KK Air' to 'KK Air' with a large full stop added ('KK Air.'). Having queried this accounting treatment with the company's finance director, the following written response was received:

The $2.3 million cost should be capitalised as an asset in the year-end accounts and written off over an arbitrary period of three years. Although you correctly point out that the actual name recommended by the consultant was not adopted by the directors, the entire review process was valuable and resulted in the adoption of a different name which is likely to improve the company's public profile and enhance its overall profitability.

Boon remains unconvinced and seeks your view on the appropriateness of treating this $2.3 million cost as an asset rather than an expense of the year.

Resource consumption and the allocation problem

To apply the principles of asset and expense identification, it is necessary to separate costs into those that relate to benefits that have been consumed (an expense) and those that relate to benefits available for consumption in the future (an asset). In some cases it is very difficult to apportion benefits in this manner because of the presence of what is commonly referred to in accounting as the allocation problem.

The allocation problem is associated with revenue recognition as well as asset and expense determination, and its impact on revenue recognition will be discussed in Chapter 16. The allocation problem stems from the nature of the assumptions of the historical cost system and in particular from the assumptions of continuity, the accounting period and capital maintenance. The assumption of continuity provides for the life of the firm to stretch into the future so that the firm is assumed to have continuing and incomplete ventures at balance date. The accounting period assumption allows for the life of the entity to be broken into discrete periods and this necessitates reporting on the progress to date of incomplete ventures.

Under the capital maintenance assumption, the capital of the entity must be maintained intact before any profit is declared. Capital maintenance is achieved through the process of matching expenses with revenue for the period. It requires that the cost of the economic benefits consumed in the process of generating the revenue earned for the accounting period be deducted as expenses from that revenue before any profit is determined.

The cost of used benefits must be recovered from revenue to maintain capital and the costs of unused benefits are to be carried forward to the future as balance-sheet assets. The allocation problem is one of deciding which benefits have been consumed in the period and which remain unconsumed. The problem arises with all resources, but particularly with inventories, marketable securities, depreciable assets and intangible assets.

Inventory

Inventory accounting is concerned with keeping a record of the goods on hand available for sale (inventory) and the goods that have been sold (cost of goods sold expense). The inventory recording process has a direct impact on an entity's measure of (net) income and its financial position, in that:

$$income = sales - cost\ of\ goods\ sold - other\ expenses$$

and

$$inventory + other\ assets = liabilities + owners'\ equity.$$

The identification and measurement of inventory on hand and cost of goods sold have a cost and a quantity dimension. First, it is necessary to identify the quantity of goods on hand and the quantity sold. The second step is to measure the cost of goods sold and the cost of goods on hand. The two most popular methods of recording the movement of goods for sale into and out of the entity, the perpetual and the periodic inventory recording systems, were discussed and illustrated in Chapter 5, so it remains to discuss the valuation of inventory and cost of goods sold.

In accordance with the principles of the historical cost system, the appropriate cost figures for the quantities of goods sold and the quantities of goods in inventory are the original purchase costs. Careful selection of the cost figures is essential to the capital maintenance objective, since it requires the matching of the original purchase cost of each item sold with the period in which the revenue earned from the item is recognised. To achieve a matching of revenue and expenses in this manner, it is necessary for one of the following conditions to hold:

1. All units of the same type of inventory purchased over the life of the firm are purchased at the same price.

2. The purchase price of each individual item of inventory can be identified with certainty.

In an economy characterised by inflation and shifts in supply and demand patterns, the first condition is unlikely to hold. The second condition may hold for firms dealing in goods that typically have a relatively high market value, for example motor vehicles, jewellery and aircraft. This method identifies the purchase cost of each item as it comes into inventory. When an item is sold its identified cost is transferred to cost of goods sold.

In many other types of firms inventory turnover is much higher and the individual items of a particular type of inventory are frequently identical, interchangeable and stored together. Some examples are cans of paint, brushes, bricks, tiles, blue metal nails, petroleum and chemicals. Different lots of each type of inventory may be purchased at different prices during the period. For example, a building supplier might purchase a number of different batches of tiles, of the same type and colour, at varying prices during the period. It is impractical to tag each tile with its actual cost, especially since the costs involved would outweigh any benefits from the exercise.

An alternative to specific identification to is make an assumption about the order in which the goods are sold and to expense the purchase costs in that order.

Inventory cost allocation methods

There are three commonly used methods, each of which is based on a different assumption about the physical flow of goods. FIFO (first in, first out) assumes that the goods first received into inventory are the first to be sold. LIFO (last in, first out) assumes that the goods most recently received into inventory are the first to be issued for sale. WAC (weighted average cost) assumes that all items purchased go into a common pool and lose their separate identities.

The methods are applied in the following example.

Example: *Inventory valuation*

During its first three months of operations Doodle Ltd made the following purchases and sales of pencil cases.

Date		Cost	Total
	Number units purchased	$	$
June 1	500	0.20	100
July 15	300	0.25	75
August 17	800	0.30	240
Total purchased	1600		415
	Number units sold		
July 17	400		
August 20	500		
Total sold	900		

FIFO

FIFO is based on the assumption that the oldest stock is sold first, thus leaving the most recent costs to be allocated to the inventory on hand, thus:

DOODLE LTD			
FIFO inventory valuation method			
	Units sold	Unit cost	Total cost
Cost of goods sold	500	$0.20	$100
	300	0.25	75
	100	0.30	30
Total units sold	900		205
Cost of inventory on hand	700	0.30	210
Total units available	1600		415

LIFO

Under LIFO the cost of sales is charged at the most recent purchase prices, leaving the cost of items that have been in inventory the longest to be applied to inventory on hand.

DOODLE LTD			
LIFO inventory valuation method			
	Units sold	Unit cost	Total cost
Cost of goods sold			
July 17	300	$0.25	$ 75
	100	0.20	20
August 20	500	0.30	150
Total units sold	900		245
Cost of inventory on hand	400	0.20	80
	300	0.30	90
Inventory on hand	700		170
Total units available	1600		415

Comparison of FIFO and LIFO

The comparative figures are:

	FIFO	LIFO
Cost of goods sold	$205	$245
Ending inventory	210	170
Total available for sale	$415	$415

This example is typical of inflationary periods when prices are rising. In these circumstances, LIFO generally yields a higher cost of goods sold than FIFO because the costs are the more recent, higher costs. This reduces reported profit.

The major support for LIFO as an inventory valuation method is based on the claim that, by using recent prices, LIFO enables the current cost of goods sold to be deducted from revenue, making it easier to maintain 'real' capital in times of rising prices. In the United States this argument was used to obtain permission to use LIFO for taxation purposes and the higher deduction for taxation explains its widespread use in that country.

However, LIFO does not always achieve a higher cost of goods sold. When prices fall, LIFO will produce lower cost of goods sold than FIFO, higher profits, and thus higher taxation! At such times there is a demand to return to FIFO valuation.

LIFO is inconsistent with the principles of historical cost accounting, which endeavour to measure historical costs rather than current costs. If current cost measures are widely desired, the historical cost system should be abandoned in favour of one of the alternative systems to be discussed in later chapters.

LIFO is artificial in that it is rare to find situations in which the most recently acquired goods are sold first. The artificiality is particularly apparent in the balance sheet, which reports inventory at the oldest values available. When prices are rising, valuation under LIFO will result in the reporting of inventory values below the FIFO values and sometimes at ridiculously low values. In a company with continually expanding inventory levels, the oldest purchase prices will remain on the books for many years. In practice, some American companies have price 'layers' that were added over thirty years previously. An anomalous situation can arise when a 'stock-out' causes very old cost prices to be used for the calculation of cost of goods sold in the current period. Suppose a company had a beginning inventory valued on the LIFO basis as follows:

100 units at 1968 prices of $1	$ 100
200 units at 1978 prices of $2	400
300 units at 1998 prices of $30	9000

Now suppose that on the first day of 1999 it sold 550 units for $100 each. On the first 300 units, it would declare a normal profit of $70 per unit ($100 – $30) and a profit of $98 per unit ($100 – $2) on the second 200 units, while the profit on the last 50 units in the batch sold would be $99 per unit ($100 – $1). Thus, when there is a 'stock-out', LIFO will produce higher profits than FIFO. This anomaly again points to the artificiality of the LIFO method.

To guard against reaching back into opening inventory prices, LIFO is usually applied as a 'periodic' approach at the end of the year, so the timing of purchases and sales during the year is ignored. In the case of Doodle Ltd, discussed earlier, the LIFO figures would be computed at year end as follows:

DOODLE LTD
LIFO applied on a periodic basis

	Units sold	Unit cost	Total cost
Cost of goods sold	800	$0.30	$240
	100	0.25	25
Total units sold	900		265
Cost of inventory on hand	200	0.25	50
	500	0.20	100
Inventory on hand	700		150
Total units available	1600		415

Under the periodic approach, the LIFO cost of sales rises by $20 in comparison with the previous LIFO calculation because it is not necessary to reach back to the first purchase price of $0.20.

International Accounting Standard IAS 2, 'Inventories', permits the use of LIFO as an 'alternative' treatment (para. 23) to FIFO and WAC which are preferred as 'benchmark' treatments (para. 21). In Australia LIFO is not accepted by the taxation authorities as a valid method of inventory costing. The Australian accounting standard on the valuation and presentation of inventories in the context of the historical cost system does not allow LIFO to be used for inventory costing.[13]

Weighted average cost (WAC)

Under this approach, inventory on hand and cost of goods sold are determined by applying the weighted average cost of all items in inventory, at the time a sale is made, to the respective quantities sold and on hand. Where the weighted average cost method is applied as sales are made, that is, in a perpetual inventory system, the weighted average cost of inventory and goods sold must be recalculated each time a purchase is made at a different price.

DOODLE LTD
WAC (perpetual approach)

	Units sold	Unit WAC		Total cost
		$		$
Cost of goods sold				
July 17	400	$\frac{500 \times 0.20 + 300 \times 0.25}{800}$	= 0.219	88
August 20	500	$\frac{400 \times 0.219 + 800 \times 0.30}{1200}$	= 0.273	136
	900			224
Inventory on hand	700	$\frac{700 \times 0.273}{700}$	= 0.273	191
Total units available	1600			415

Where the weighted average cost method is applied at the end of the period, the calculation of cost of goods sold and cost of inventory is much simpler:

$$\text{Weighted average cost (periodic approach)} = \frac{\text{total purchase cost}}{\text{total inventory available}}$$

$$= \frac{\$415}{1600}$$

$$= 0.259 \text{ dollars per unit}$$

$$\text{Cost of goods sold} = \text{units sold} \times \text{WAC}$$

$$= 900 \times 0.259$$

$$= \$233$$

$$\text{Inventory on hand} = \text{units on hand} \times \text{WAC}$$

$$= 700 \times 0.259$$

$$= \$182$$

[13] Australian Accounting Standards Board, AASB 1019, 'Valuation and Presentation of Inventory in the Context of the Historical Cost System', para. 30.

Lower of cost or net realisable value

Under IAS 2, 'inventories should be measured at the lower of cost and net realisable value (para. 6)'.[14] Conservatism implies that assets should not appear at amounts in excess of recoverable amount. If the market value has fallen, the cost may not be recovered when the goods are sold.

This rule is also consistent with the general rules for measuring assets, since the definition of assets emphasises the attribute of future economic benefits arising from use or exchange. The benefits associated with inventory are normally derived through exchange in the market in the short term. If there is strong evidence to support a belief that the value of the inventory in exchange is less than its cost, the cost will actually be a joint measure of future economic benefits and lost economic benefits. In this situation the accountant is justified in recording the inventory at net realisable value (which is also its recoverable amount) and treating the difference between cost and net realisable value as a loss in the profit and loss statement for the current period.

This treatment is also consistent with the principle of capital maintenance, in that it ensures that not only the cost of benefits consumed in the process of generating revenue but also the cost of benefits lost during the period are recouped from revenue over the asset's useful life. In this sense, the write-down of inventory is similar to the treatment of stock losses due to theft or wastage, although in those cases the net realisable value is zero and the loss is equivalent to the entire original cost.

Marketable securities

Marketable securities include all investments in securities that can be sold readily through a stock exchange or other organised market. Frequently traded shares, listed debentures and government bonds are examples.

Short-term holdings of marketable securities encounter the same valuation dilemmas as inventory. The identification problem arises where several lots of a security are purchased at different prices over time. For example:

1 January	Bought 1000 shares in F Ltd for $1.39 each.
31 March	Bought 2500 shares in F Ltd for $1.76 each.

If 500 shares in F Ltd are sold on 14 June, it becomes necessary to identify a cost of sale. Since the securities bought at different dates are otherwise identical, a 'flow' assumption is required. In these circumstances, the FIFO method of cost allocation is usually adopted, there being no systematic advantages to the use of LIFO (share prices do not necessarily move upwards in inflationary periods).

In practice, marketable securities are also affected by the lower of cost and net realisable value rule, reflecting the underlying principle that assets should not be recorded in the balance sheet above their recoverable amount. If management views marketable securities as current assets, they may be regarded as inventory in that they are bought and sold and their economic benefits are yielded through exchange in the short term. If a security was purchased for $1.20 and is quoted on a stock exchange at $1.05 at balance date (and thus can be sold at that price), it should be written down and a loss recognised of $0.15 per share.

This raises the question of the unit being dealt with in the accounts. A prudent company recognises that some marketable securities will fall in price and it guards against this risk by holding a portfolio of securities rather than 'placing all its eggs in the one basket'. Over time, it is hoped that the losses on one security will be compensated for by gains on others. Suppose a company held two securities with the following price histories:

---

[14] ASRB 1019 also requires inventories to be measured on this basis.

	Cost	Present market value	Change
	$	$	$
S Ltd	10 000	8 000	− 2 000
M Ltd	45 000	61 000	+ 16 000
Total portfolio value	55 000	69 000	

Proponents of the portfolio approach to value would argue that it is inconsistent to recognise the decline in S Ltd without taking into account the gain on M Ltd, especially when the company regards the marketable securities as a portfolio. This view has now been adopted in the United States, but the Australian accounting regulators have yet to rule on the matter. In practice, Australian accountants would usually treat each security independently and write down the above portfolio by $2000.

Depreciating assets

The issues to be considered in this section are the methods by which asset costs are allocated over their lives and the determination of the costs that give rise to depreciable assets.

Allocating the cost of a depreciating asset over its life

In Chapter 7 depreciation was defined as the process of allocating the cost of a non-current asset over its life in accordance with the benefits derived. Hence, the depreciation expense for each period should reflect the following relationship:

$$\frac{\text{economic benefits consumed during the period}}{\text{total economic benefits expected over the asset's life}}$$

The more of an asset's economic benefits that are consumed in generating revenue, the greater the portion of total costs that should be matched as depreciation expense in that period. If, for example, an asset has an expected lifetime benefit of 100 units and 20 units are gained in the first year, then the depreciation in that year should equal 20 per cent of the asset's cost (or cost less scrap value).

This seems straightforward until it is asked what these benefits are and how their consumption is to be identified. The consumption of an asset's economic benefits over its useful life results from both use and obsolescence. Obsolescence, the process of becoming out of date, is often a more important determinant of the decline in an asset's economic benefits than physical deterioration. Obsolescence relates to the purpose for which an asset was purchased. The future economic benefits of an asset might decline because it is not as useful to the entity as a new, technically superior alternative. Obsolescence is readily observable in the computer and electronics industries. Obsolescence cannot be measured accurately in its own right, since it exists only in relation to other assets.

Consumption of benefits through usage might be approached by adopting a production units method and finding some physical record of output such as units produced. This task is complicated by the fact that the one item of equipment might produce a variety of different products. Paper producing equipment, for example, can be set to produce various thicknesses or compositions of paper. Each product will fetch different prices, suggesting that the ultimate benefit is not the production of a good but its sale. This leads to the identification of 'gross sales revenue of goods produced' as the measure of an asset's benefits; from there it is but a small step to argue that, since production and selling costs differ between products and over time, the benefit contribution of the goods produced should be the net profit contribution from the equipment's productive output.

At this point it becomes obvious that the profit contribution from a particular item of equipment cannot be isolated from that contributed by other items of equipment and by the people who operate them. For example, a firm might have a number of non-current assets (equipment, delivery vehicles, factory, warehouse, buildings, etc.) and current assets (labour, fuel, raw materials, etc.) which interact to generate revenue. A productive process is interactive and the individual contribution of each factor cannot be separately identified. The front wheels of a motor vehicle, for example, contribute nothing unless the rear wheels are also in operation.

The presence of interaction in the profit-generating processes means that the benefits produced by a particular asset cannot be identified, and neither can the pattern in which the benefits decline be determined. The choice between the various methods of depreciation is supposed to be guided by the pattern of usage; an asset offering equal annual benefits is depreciated on a straight-line basis, an asset offering higher benefits in earlier years is depreciated on the reducing-balance basis, and so on. Since the pattern of benefits cannot be discovered, it follows that any method of depreciation can be justified for any depreciating asset.

The annual depreciation charge, therefore, represents an arbitrary allocation of the cost. It cannot meet the standard of verifiability such that independent experts would agree that the allocations are reasonable approximations of the expected pattern of benefit consumption.

In practice, a number of other factors, such as taxation requirements and expediency, have an important impact on the selection of a depreciation method. To avoid dual depreciation calculations, the taxation rates are sometimes used for accounting purposes as well. For reasons of expediency, some firms will use the same depreciation method for all non-current, depreciable assets, although the write-off term is varied according to the estimated period over which benefits are expected to arise.

Case 15.3 illustrates the adoption of different write-off periods for deferred expenditure (i.e. expenditure which is expected to provide benefits in periods beyond the current accounting period).

Case 15.3 The Australian Gas Light Company

The Australian Gas Light Company (AGL) is an owner and operator of energy infrastructure. The 1997 Annual Report of the AGL stated the following accounting policy on 'deferred expenditure' in note 1(g):

> Borrowing expenses relating to long-term facilities are capitalised and amortised over periods not exceeding the term of the borrowing.
>
> Other expenditures which provide benefits beyond the current accounting period are deferred and amortised over the periods during which the benefits are expected to arise, ranging from three to twenty years. These expenditures principally relate to computer software development, research and development and gas utility operations (the connection of new customers to the gas system, the conversion of existing customers' appliances to the use of natural gas and other gas industry expenditures).

What future benefits might be expected to arise from incurring up-front borrowing fees relating to long-term loan facilities?

Explain the implications for financial statement analysis of deferring expenditure of the kind mentioned in this note to future financial years.

The meaning of profit or loss on the sale of a depreciable asset

Depreciable assets are purchased to interact with other current and non-current assets to generate the entity's revenue. The cost of the resources (including an allocated portion of the cost of depreciable assets) consumed in generating the revenue is matched against the revenue to determine the entity's profit (or loss) from its major operating activities. The profit or loss recorded on the sale of a non-current, depreciable asset is of a different nature to the profit (or loss) the entity earns from its major operating activities. It is effectively a prior-period adjustment made necessary by the understandable inability of the entity to predict accurately the actual scrap value of the asset or its actual useful life.

Variations between estimated and actual residual value may be attributed partly to differences between estimated and actual useful life. An asset's useful life may have been estimated as four years, for example. If the actual life is six years, then by the end of the fourth year the asset's cost less accumulated depreciation will be equal to its estimated residual value and no depreciation expense will be recorded in the fifth and sixth years. Hence, profit in years 1 to 4 will be underestimated, and profit in years 5 and 6 will be overestimated. The situation would be reversed if the asset's life was overestimated.

An interesting situation arises when one asset is traded in for another. Suppose a motor vehicle, which originally cost $18 000 and on which there was accumulated depreciation of $8400, giving a book value of $9600, was traded in for an agreed value of $10 000 on a new vehicle with a list price of $22 000. The balance owing, $12 000, was paid in cash. Is the gain on disposal $400 ($10 000 – $9 600)?

It is known that trade-in values may be inflated so as to give a discount on the new purchase, but the amount of the discount can be determined only by comparing either:

1. The trade-in value ($10 000) with the real market price of the vehicle traded in ($X); or
2. The listed price of the new vehicle ($22 000) with the price that would be paid without a trade-in ($Y).

If there is no trade-in, car dealers will often give a discount on the list price.

As values X and Y are not part of the exchange agreement, a verifiable price in an exchange transaction is not readily determinable. Hence, any gain on sale resulting from the difference between book value and trade-in value is not easy to verify. Accordingly, following conservatism, accountants often do not recognise a gain on sale in the above example and regard the 'value' of the vehicle traded in as identical to the book value. The journal entry to record the sale is, then:

	$	$
New vehicle	21 600	
Accum. depreciation	8 400	
Old vehicle		18 000
Cash at bank		12 000
(Disposal of old vehicle by trade-in)		

The supposed 'gain' on the sale of the old asset has been absorbed by reducing the cost of the new vehicle from $22 000 to $21 600, which is the actual purchase price only if the fair market value of the old vehicle is its book value.

When the trade-in value falls below book value, a loss on disposal will result. Under conservatism, this loss will be allowed to stand, and the agreed trade-in value will be accepted as the proceeds of the sale.

Which costs give rise to an asset?

As a general principle, assets are recorded on acquisition at their original cost. Sometimes a number of different costs are incurred when assets are acquired and it is necessary to determine which costs form part of the original cost of the asset and which costs should be treated as an expense (or loss) of the period. In subsequent years of an asset's life further costs might be incurred and it will be necessary to make the asset or expense decision in relation to these costs. The decisions have a direct impact on the measures of profit and financial position, with an expense giving an immediate deduction from revenue and an asset spreading the deduction over several periods as depreciation. A third choice also exists between regarding the payment as giving rise to a depreciating asset (such as buildings) or a non-depreciating asset (such as land).

The asset and expense definitions discussed earlier in this chapter provide us with general guidelines for the identification and recognition of assets. In some situations the decision as to whether an item should be recorded as an asset or an expense is by no means clear-cut. This section outlines and illustrates a set of working rules to guide the consistent and logical application of the general principles of asset and expense identification and recognition.

Example: *Installation costs*

A firm purchased a photocopier for $5000 and incurred the following additional costs:

1. Freight on photocopier	$100
2. Insurance in transit	20
3. Cost of installation and testing materials	100
4. Cost of labour to install	150
5. Cost of carpet shampoo in photocopier room prior to installation	50

Rule no. 1—Installation costs: The cost of an asset includes all costs necessary to render an asset suitable for its intended use.

Without costs 1 to 4 the photocopier would not have been in a suitable condition to provide its future economic benefits. Hence, these costs should be added to the original purchase price of the asset and the total progressively allocated to depreciation expense over the life of the asset. The cost of shampooing the carpet should be treated as part of the ordinary maintenance expense of the period, since it was not 'necessarily incurred' under rule number 1. The photocopier could have been installed just as effectively on a carpet that had not been shampooed.

The following example presents more difficult choices.

Example: *Assets versus expenses*

Chris's City Crepe and Pancake Restaurant has become very popular in recent years. After discussing the matter with a friend and a bank manager, Chris decided to establish another crepe restaurant in the suburbs. Chris purchased a block of land with a former butcher's shop on it and then hired contractors to demolish the old shop and construct a new restaurant.

At the time of acquisition, an independent valuation placed a value of $80 000 on the land and $40 000 on the shop.

Chris incurred the following costs in relation to the new and old restaurants:

New restaurant

1. Land and old butcher's shop	$130 000
2. Demolition of old butcher's shop	5 000
3. Construction of new restaurant	10 000

4. Compensation to passer-by hit by a falling tile during construction	2 000
5. Decoration and furnishing interior	10 000
6. Painting exterior red, white and blue	1 000

In addition, Chris received $500 for the sale of scrap materials from the old butcher's shop.

Old restaurant

7. Painting ceiling in old restaurant	1 500
8. Painting exterior red, white and blue	1 000
9. New cooking utensils for kitchen	2 000

Expenditure on the new restaurant

In accordance with rule number 1, the purchase price of the land and building should be recorded as an asset, since it was necessary to acquire the land and old butcher's shop before Chris could put the plan into action. Now, since land is not depreciated but buildings are, it becomes important to decide whether the old butcher's shop is part of the asset, land, or a separate asset, buildings. Rule number 2 may provide some useful guidance in these types of situations.

> Rule no. 2—Group asset costs: Where a group of assets is acquired for the purpose of acquiring only one of the assets, the entire purchase price relates to the desired asset.

Chris acquired one asset, land, at a cost of $130 000. This decision is consistent with the basic asset definition that describes assets as future economic benefits for the entity. The land will provide future economic benefits for Chris and is therefore an asset; however, the butcher's shop is of no use to Chris on its own and is a necessary cost in acquiring the land.

If Chris had intended to use the butcher's shop, either in its purchased condition or after renovations, both the land and the shop would be classified separately and it would be necessary to apportion their joint cost in some systematic and reasonable manner. One such method is the relative market value method which assumes that the total joint cost of the asset is based on the relative cost relationship that would exist between the assets if they were purchased individually. In this example, the relative cost relationship between the land and the buildings is 2:1, based on the relationship between the independent market values of each at the time of acquisition ($80 000 and $40 000 respectively). Hence, one-third of the purchase cost of the land and building ($43 333) would be classified as an asset, buildings; and two-thirds ($86 667) as an asset, land.

The cost of constructing the new restaurant is an asset cost in accordance with rule number 1. The $5000 cost of demolishing the butcher's shop is also classified as an asset under rule number 1 in that it was necessary to remove the old building before construction of the new building could begin. The question arises, however, as to which asset the cost of demolition relates to. Is it part of the cost of the land or part of the cost of the new restaurant? Since the intended use of the land was to accommodate a new restaurant, which necessitated the removal of the butcher's shop, the cost of demolition should be included in the cost of the land. The cost of the land, then, is $130 000 plus the net cost of demolition after sale of scrap materials ($5000 – $500), totalling $134 500. After all, the owner would have been prepared to purchase a vacant block in an equivalent location if one were available and should have been prepared to pay up to $134 500 for the convenience of not having to demolish an old building.

Under rule number 1 the cost of decorating and furnishing the interior and the cost of painting the exterior would be included as part of the asset cost of the new restaurant, as they represent expenditure necessary to render the restaurant suitable for its intended purpose.

The compensation paid to a passer-by hit by a falling tile during construction does not meet the test of rule number 1. It is not a cost necessary to render the asset suitable for its intended purpose. The restaurant could have been constructed just as effectively without this misadventure. The cost should be treated as a loss in the profit and loss statement for the current period.

Expenditure on the old restaurant

Rule number 3 might provide some guidance as to how the cost of painting the ceiling in the old restaurant should be recorded.

> **Rule no. 3—Maintenance versus improvements:** Any cost incurred to obtain the benefits initially expected from an asset is a maintenance expense of the current period. Any cost incurred to increase lifetime benefits beyond the original expectation gives rise to an additional asset for improvements.

Lifetime benefits may be increased by enlarging productive capacity, by extending the economic life or by reducing operating costs.

In the case of Chris's crepe restaurant, if the ceiling was repainted in the expectation that it would increase the number of restaurant customers, by either attracting new customers or enticing old customers to dine more frequently, it should be regarded as an improvement and hence recorded as an asset. On the other hand, the ceiling might be old and crumbling and the paintwork might be an expected cost of maintaining the restaurant through its original expected life. It is helpful to ask of all such payments whether it should have been anticipated at the time of purchase that such payments would have to be made from time to time during the original expected life of the building. A taxi requires batteries and tyres over its life and these are normal maintenance expenses, but if the owner installs luxury seating this might be regarded as an improvement that increases the lifetime income-earning potential of the taxi.

In the case of the old restaurant, the repainting of the ceiling would most likely be a maintenance cost. The new exterior painting, however, might qualify as an improvement if it was intended to give the restaurant a new image and a new class of customer. The dividing line is indeed fine in such cases, since it is reasonable to assume that Chris would not expect the original coat of paint to be suitable for the entire life of the restaurant, which would make it a maintenance expense.

The different circumstances relating to the exterior painting of the old and new restaurants indicate that the improvement–maintenance decision has a time dimension. Expenditure on a new asset, such as the new restaurant, gives rise to an asset since it is either a further cost of installation or an improvement aimed at extending the condition and potential of the asset at the date of purchase. As time passes, outlays such as painting and other repairs take on the character of maintenance costs attributable to wear and tear since the date of purchase.

The time perspective also affects the purchase of new cooking utensils (item 9). Cooking utensils for a new restaurant are assets, but it is reasonable to assume that established restaurants will from time to time replace different pieces of their kitchen equipment. With reference to rule number 3, this cost could be treated as a maintenance expense necessary to obtain the service initially expected from the restaurant, providing the cooking utensils were originally identified as being part of a larger asset such as kitchen equipment.

However, on the initial purchase of cooking utensils for the restaurant, Chris could have chosen to record the equipment as a separate asset because the various items in the kitchen, such as stoves, refrigerators and cooking utensils, had separate identities, performed different functions and, above all, because they had different life expectancies and hence their economic benefits would be used at different rates. Rule number 4 is concerned with the number of separate assets a firm may choose to record when asset costs are initially incurred.

Rule no. 4—The unit being accounted for: Where the objects associated with the costs arising out of a related set of transactions have either different life expectancies or different identities, the firm may choose to recognise more than one asset.

The application of rule number 4 may result in a very large number of assets being recorded in a given cost situation. For example, Chris may choose to recognise each item of cooking utensils (pots, pans, dishes, etc.) as a separate asset. The decision is arbitrary, since one cannot say that the recognition of any given number of assets is superior to any other number. The constraint is that the greater the detail, the more complex the accounting task becomes with associated cost implications. The implications of the decision are important, however, since the decision affects not only the number of assets recorded but also the treatment of subsequent expenditure in the manner outlined in rule number 5.

Rule no. 5—Replacement versus maintenance: Where the expenditure results in the replacement of an entire asset, the old asset is removed from the accounts and the cost of the new asset is capitalised.

Where the expenditure results in the replacement of only part of an asset, it is treated as a maintenance expense of the period, unless the expenditure is expected to increase materially the asset's condition and potential.

The treatment of the cost of the new cooking utensils would therefore depend on whether the old utensils had been recognised as a separate asset. If it was regarded as part of the cost of a comprehensive asset such as kitchen equipment, then, under rule number 5, the replacement cost would be treated as a maintenance expense and hence current profit would be reduced by $2000. If, instead, the cooking utensils were regarded as a separate asset, then the replacement cost would be treated as an asset and written off over its life as depreciation expense.

There is a tale of a tramways company that charged its customers twice for the cost of the trams. The fare structure took into account the recovery of the original outlay on the trams, through depreciation, and it also charged as a repairs expense the costs of replacing parts of the tram such as seats, wheels and motors. At no time were any trams replaced in their entirety and customers travelling on trams 80 years old and older could only speculate on why they were paying for depreciation. To add further insult, the company included an additional charge to a sinking fund to cover the eventual replacement of the trams!

Major overhauls

The distinction between the improvement of assets and maintenance expenses has been discussed earlier and it is now necessary to consider the effects of these principles on the procedures for calculating depreciation and asset values.

During the useful life of an asset, management may decide to overhaul the asset extensively and thereby extend its useful life, as an alternative to disposing of the asset as originally intended and replacing it with a new, but similar, asset. If, for example, the existing equipment is carrying out its assigned task quite adequately and there has been a large price increase in replacement equipment, it may be more economical to overhaul the dated equipment than to buy new equipment. A major overhaul differs from maintenance expense in that the latter is undertaken to obtain the economic benefits initially expected from the asset, whereas the former either extends the useful life of the asset, increases its productive capacity or reduces the operating costs. Hence, a major overhaul possesses the properties of an asset and therefore the cost of the overhaul should be allocated over the remaining life of the asset. The effect of a major overhaul on the calculation of depreciation expense is illustrated in the following example.

Example: *Major overhauls*

A firm purchased an item of equipment for $100 000. It had an estimated scrap value of $20 000 and a useful life of eight years. Using the straight-line method of depreciation the annual expense would be $10 000. At the beginning of the sixth year, $70 000 was expended on overhauling the equipment, extending its estimated useful life by six years.

The cost of the overhaul would be added to the cost of the equipment and would be allocated over the revised remaining life of the asset, together with an unallocated portion of the original cost.

The annual depreciation expense for years 6 to 14 would be calculated as:

$$\frac{\text{cost} - \text{scrap} - \text{accumulated depreciation} + \text{cost of overhaul}}{\text{remaining useful life}}$$

$$= \frac{100\ 000 - 20\ 000 - 50\ 000 + 70\ 000}{9}$$

$$= \$11\ 111$$

Intangible and other non-current assets

Intangible assets may be classified into two broad types, identifiable and unidentifiable. Identifiable intangible assets include brand names, intellectual property, licences, mastheads, patents and trademarks. The main unidentifiable intangible asset is goodwill. Both identifiable intangible assets and goodwill are either purchased (i.e. acquired from another party) or internally generated through the ordinary operations of entities.

Goodwill

Goodwill is generated by the interaction of human and other resources directed towards the earning of revenue in a going concern. It can be acquired either by purchasing a going concern with which the goodwill is associated (called purchased goodwill) or it can be generated internally by the ongoing, positive interaction of the entity's resources (called self-developed goodwill). Usually it is not possible to sever goodwill from the other assets of the entity and thus it is a difficult asset to measure. The generally accepted approach to measuring goodwill is to regard it as a residual value. It is the amount by which the purchase consideration of a group of assets exceeds the aggregated fair market value of the individual net assets acquired. Hence, only acquired or purchased goodwill is recorded on the face of the balance sheet.

Goodwill may be described as comprising future benefits from unidentifiable assets which because of their nature are not normally recorded individually in the accounts. These unidentifiable assets include effective advertising, good labour relations and a superior management team.

Historically, the treatment of purchased goodwill has varied considerably. Some firms have carried it on their books at cost indefinitely; some have treated the total cost as an expense in the period of acquisition; some have amortised goodwill systematically over an arbitrary period; others have amortised goodwill in an ad hoc manner. Underlying the recording of goodwill at original cost for an indefinite number of periods is an assumption that goodwill, like land, is not a wasting asset. Recording the total cost of goodwill as an expense of the period of acquisition is consistent with the belief that the benefits associated with purchased goodwill have a very short life. If, however, goodwill is viewed as an asset whose benefits are consumed in the process of generating revenue, then it is necessary to amortise goodwill in some manner that will reflect the pattern of benefit consumption. Given that the measure of purchased goodwill is a derived figure, that it is only a partial measure of goodwill since self-developed goodwill is excluded, and that the nature of good-will is very difficult to describe, it is hard to envisage how one method of amortisation could be defended as providing a superior approximation of benefit consumption over any other method. Faced with this problem, one approach is to select an arbitrary number of years over which to allocate the cost of goodwill using the straight-line method of amortisation. This capitalise and amortise approach is consistent with accounting standards on goodwill, which typically require purchased goodwill to be amortised, by systematic charges against income, over the period of time during which the benefits are expected to arise.[15]

In Australia the maximum period over which goodwill is to be amortised is twenty years.

Identifiable intangible assets

These are intangible assets that are capable of being both individually identified and specifi-cally brought to account. Although the difference between goodwill and the so-called identifiable intangible assets is not always clear-cut, the main distinction would seem to be that concrete evidence is available to support the separate existence of 'identifiable' intangi-bles such as patents, brand names, licences and newspaper mastheads. The separate existence of the identifiable intangible asset of intellectual property would appear to be more difficult to justify.

Identifiable intangible assets may be purchased or internally developed. Purchased intan-gibles, such as licences, may simply be recorded at their original cost. However, the reliable measurement of internally developed identifiable intangibles will be more difficult to deter-mine because often these assets cannot be directly associated with transactions entered into by the entity. For example, the value of the mastheads of a newspaper corporation will have been developed over time as the individual newspapers controlled by the corporation have built up their circulation and reputations. This process will have involved a multitude of transactions and events which, in interaction, have established the market positions of the newspapers and which in turn give value to their mastheads.

The appropriate treatment of internally developed, identifiable intangible assets has been a controversial issue in Australia and internationally. In Australia an exposure draft on the topic was released in 1989 but withdrawn in 1992 for further consideration by the account-ing standard setters. The view taken in the exposure draft that 'internally developed identifiable intangible assets which are brought to account as assets shall initially be recorded at the lowest cost at which the assets could currently be obtained in the normal course of business as determined by independent valuation'.[16] It was envisaged that identifi-able intangible assets brought to account 'should be amortised over the period of time during which the benefits embodied in the asset are expected to arise'[17] and that in the vast majority of cases this period should not exceed twenty years. In the past many Australian companies that have put identifiable intangible assets such as brand names and mastheads on their balance sheet have tended not to amortise these assets. For example, the 1997 Annual Report of Adelaide Brighton Ltd stated the accounting policy for brand names thus: 'Brand names valued at $9 060 000 with an indefinite life are not amortised.'

---

15 International Accounting Standard IAS 22, 'Business Combinations', para. 42; Australian Accounting Standards Board, AASB 1013, 'Accounting for Goodwill', para 5.2. Under IAS 22 the preferred amortisa-tion period is five years and a maximum amortisation of 20 years is permitted where it 'can be justified' (para. 42).

16 Australian Accounting Research Foundation, 'Proposed Approved Accounting Standard, Accounting for Identifiable Intangible Assets', ED 49, 1989, para. 21.

17 Ibid., para. 40.

Research and development costs

Many firms carry on a more or less continuous research and development program. Research may be regarded as the search for new knowledge that might lead to the development of a new product or process or that will significantly improve existing products or processes. Development is concerned with putting the positive results of research into practice, which includes designing and testing product alternatives, and constructing and operating pilot plants.

In practice, research and development activities tend to be carried on interactively and hence the distinction between the two tends to be blurred. International Accounting Standard IAS 9, 'Research and Development Costs', provides the following definition of 'research' and 'development':

> *Research* is original and planned investigation undertaken with the prospect of gaining new scientific or technical knowledge and understanding.
> *Development* is the application of research findings or other knowledge to a plan or design for the production of new or substantially improved materials, devices, products, processes, systems or services prior to the commencement of commercial production or use (para. 6).

In determining whether research and development costs should be treated as assets or expenses, reference may again be made to the asset recognition tests. However, estimating the likelihood of future economic benefits at the time research and development costs are incurred is especially difficult in view of the experimental and speculative nature of much of this activity. There is frequently much uncertainty as to whether the research and development carried out by an entity will provide future economic benefits and, if benefits are forthcoming, what magnitude of benefits will be provided and in what periods the benefits will be derived.

Because of this uncertainty, IAS 9 requires *all* research costs to be charged to expense in the period they are incurred (para. 15). However, as development costs are incurred following the research phase of the activities, entities can often more readily ascertain the probability of receiving future economic benefits. Thus, development costs may be recognised as assets (para. 17) if, and only if, *all* the following criteria are met:

(a) the product or process is clearly defined and the costs attributable to the product or process can be separately identified and measured reliably;
(b) the technical feasibility of the product or process can be demonstrated;
(c) the enterprise intends to produce and market, or use, the product or process;
(d) the existence of a market for the product or process or, if it is to be used internally rather than sold, its usefulness to the enterprise, can be demonstrated; and
(e) adequate resources exist, or their availability can be demonstrated, to complete the project and market or use the product or process.

Australian Accounting Standards Board AASB 1011, 'Accounting for Research and Development Costs', requires research and development costs to be carried forward as assets to the extent that 'such costs, together with unamortised deferred costs in relation to that project, are expected beyond any reasonable doubt to be recoverable (para. 31)'.[18] This test is more restrictive than the asset recognition criteria in SAC 4 and also the IASC *Framework*, which only require the likelihood of future benefits to be probable.[19] AASB 1011 also does not prohibit research costs to be carried forward as assets, while IAS 9 specifically requires these costs to be written off as expenses in the period they are incurred.

---

[18] Evidence of Australian practice in accounting for research and development costs is found in G. D. Carnegie and S. Turner, 'Accounting for Research and Development Costs: Company Response to AAS 13, Part II—Impact of AAS 13: Study's Results', *Australian Accountant*, May 1987.

[19] A discussion of inconsistent asset recognition criteria in the context of Australian accounting standards is found in G. D. Carnegie and G. L. Wines, 'Inconsistent Standard Setting: The Case of Asset Recognition Criteria in Australia (1970 to 1992)' *Accounting History*, Vol. 4, No. 2, 1992.

Ethical issues

This year has not been one of the best. In completing the working papers for the end-of-year stocktake, the accountant draws the conclusion that the net realisable value of a substantial portion of the inventory on hand would appear to be well below its cost. The directors, however, are reluctant to write down the inventory to the lower of cost and net realisable value as this would further depress the profit figure for the year. They favour the option of leaving the inventory stated at cost and letting the impact on profit occur when the inventory is actually sold. In addition they argue that 'the demand for the inventory items concerned may pick up next year. You accountants worry too much'. The directors' optimism is not shared by the accountant. The accountant, having an overriding concern with presenting a *true and fair* view of the company's performance and financial position, asks you what action should be taken. Advise the accountant.

Summary

To apply the principles of asset and expense identification it is necessary to separate costs into those that relate to benefits consumed and those that relate to benefits available for consumption in the future. In many situations the accountant will not be able to allocate the costs of benefits other than by arbitrary means. Such decisions usually involve judgements that are inherently subjective about what is likely to happen in the future. This problem arises with all resources but particularly with inventories, marketable securities, depreciable assets and intangible assets.

As a general principle, assets are recorded on acquisition at their original costs. Sometimes a number of different costs are incurred when assets are acquired and it is necessary to determine which costs form part of the original cost of the asset and which costs should be treated as an expense (or loss) of the period. In subsequent years of an asset's life further costs may be incurred and it will be necessary to make the asset or expense decision in relation to these costs. This chapter outlined a set of working rules to guide the application of the general rules of asset and expense identification and measurement in these situations. It also examined accounting for specific types of non-current assets.

 ## Review exercises

Discussion questions

15.1 Refer to the ethical issue above and discuss the issues involved.

15.2 'The concept of assets has changed over time.' Discuss.

15.3 Contemporary definitions of assets emphasise control over future economic benefits. How relevant is this definition to our contemporary environment, and what problems might be encountered in the application of such definitions of assets under the historical cost system of accounting?

15.4 'The vehicles and equipment of the metropolitan fire brigade and the police are really assets of all entities. After all, we all receive services and associated social benefits from the fire brigade and the police.' Is this a correct interpretation of the asset definition? Explain your answer.

15.5 'Acquisition at cost', 'exchangeability', 'tangibility' and 'legal enforceability' have been described as non-essential characteristics of an asset. Clearly explain why these characteristics are non-essential.

15.6 'FIFO, LIFO and WAC are cost allocation methods not valuation methods.' Explain this statement in terms of the historical cost system, relating it directly to the assumption of capital maintenance and the unit of measurement principle.

15.7 'The LIFO method of inventory cost allocation is more relevant to our contemporary commercial environment than other methods. It should be used in all inventory costing situations.' Do you agree with this statement? Explain your view.

15.8 'Inventory on hand is written down to the lower of market and cost only when the assumption of liquidation is more relevant than the assumption of continuity.' Is this a correct interpretation of the historical cost system as it is usually practised? Explain your view.

15.9 'The uncertainty and disagreement surrounding the selection of appropriate depreciation and inventory costing policies arise primarily from the allocation problem.' Explain the nature of the allocation problem and discuss its impact on the choice of either depreciation or inventory costing policy.

15.10 'The only important requirement for a capitalisation policy is consistency; that is, the details of the policy are unimportant so long as it is applied consistently from year to year.' Discuss.

15.11 Why is the inherent level of uncertainty over future benefits to be derived from research and development expenditure reflected in the more restrictive asset recognition criteria specified for such expenditure compared with the criteria normally applied.

 Problems

15.12 *Inventory costing and valuation*

1. During its first three months of operation, Calver Pty Ltd made the following purchases of walking sticks:

	Number of units		
	Purchased	Cost	Total
Jan. 2	300	$8.00	$2400
Feb. 4	100	7.00	700
Mar. 8	250	6.00	1500
	650		4600

	Number of units sold
Feb. 6	150
Mar. 3	200
Mar. 9	100
	450

There was no opening inventory.

(a) Calculate the cost of goods sold, using FIFO, LIFO and WAC methods of inventory allocation. The periodic approach may be used in each case.

(b) A count of inventory on hand revealed a shortage of 20 walking sticks. Prepare journal entries to show how this information should be taken into account under each of the three inventory allocation methods.

2. Kimberley Pty Ltd distributes green tea to restaurants in the national capital. The records for November show the following purchases and sales of bales of green tea:

Purchases of green tea:		Sales of green tea:	
Nov. 3	40 bales @ $50	Nov. 5	25 bales
11	45 bales @ $52	12	50 bales
14	30 bales @ $54	16	10 bales
23	40 bales @ $56	25	50 bales

There was no opening inventory.

(a) Calculate the cost of goods sold under the FIFO, LIFO and WAC methods of inventory allocation.

(b) A count of inventory on hand revealed a shortage of two bales of tea. Show by way of journal entries how this shortage should be accounted for under each method of inventory allocation.

3. The Martini Company Ltd sells Kangbats and Womaroos. Purchases and sales of the items for the last quarter of 20X7 were as follows:

Purchases	Kangbats	Womaroos
October	3000 @ $28	2500 @ $54
November	4000 @ $33	3000 @ $50
December	2000 @ $35	1000 @ $48

Sales		
October	2750 @ $50	1250 @ $60
November	2000 @ $50	1750 @ $60
December	4000 @ $50	2000 @ $50

There was no opening inventory.

(a) Calculate the cost of goods sold under the FIFO, LIFO and WAC methods of inventory allocation. The periodic approach may be used in each case.

(b) A count of inventory on hand at 31 December 20X7 recorded 245 Kangbats and 1490 Womaroos. The current market selling price of Womaroos is $50. Prepare journal entries to show how this information should be taken into account under each of the three inventory allocation methods.

(c) Calculate the profit figure for the quarter under each inventory allocation method.

4. P. Scipione trades in the shares of two companies, Abet Ltd and Cann Ltd. Scipione's dealings in the shares of each company for the year ending 31 December 20X4 are as follows:

Abet Ltd

	Purchases		Sales	
	Number	Price per share ($)	Number	Price per share ($)
Jan.	100	30	50	35
April	200	32		
July			250	34
Sept.	100	31		
Dec.	100	36	150	40

Cann Ltd

	Purchases		Sales	
	Number	Price per share ($)	Number	Price per share ($)
Feb.	200	15		
Mar.	150	18	100	20
May	300	16	200	22
Oct.			200	25
Dec.	100	19		

There is no opening inventory of shares. On 31 December 20X4 the market selling price was $40 for Abet Ltd shares and $17 for Cann Ltd shares.

(a) Calculate the cost of shares sold in each company using the FIFO method of inventory costing and determine the profit earned on share trading for the year ending 31 December 20X4.

(b) At what amount should the shares be recorded in the balance sheet as at 31 December 20X4?

15.13 Depreciation policy

1. The Kanga Company purchased a small aircraft 15 years ago for $300 000. At that time it was estimated that the useful life of the aircraft would be 20 years and that its residual value would be $30 000. The company uses straight-line depreciation.

State, with reasons for your answers, whether each of the following events necessitates a revision of the original depreciation rate. Treat each event separately.

(a) The present replacement cost of the aircraft is $700 000.

(b) The directors estimate that, due to recent technical advancements in the industry, the aircraft will have a total useful life of only 15 years and a residual value of $10 000.

(c) The company could sell the aircraft now for $100 000.

(d) At the end of the fourteenth year the aircraft was thoroughly overhauled at a cost of $50 000. As a result, the directors expect to use it for 11 more years, retiring it when it is 25 years old.

2. On 1 January 20X5 a company bought equipment for $25 000 that was expected to last for five years. The following data are available concerning what actually occurred.

	Year 1	2	3	4	5
No. of hours run	2000	3000	4000	5000	6000
No. of units produced	1000	1000	2000	2000	3000
Selling price per unit	$1	$1	$3	$4	$6
Gross profit/unit	$0.20	$0.30	$1.50	$2.00	$1.00
Year-end selling price	$10 000	$10 000	$11 000	$2000	–
Cost to replace (used)	$12 000	$12 000	$14 000	$4000	$1000
Total profit (with equipment)	$1m	$1m	$2m	$2m	$4m
Total profit (without equipment)*	$0.5m	$0.6m	$1m	$1.2m	$3m

* An estimate made in retrospect by management

Assuming that historical cost accounting is in use, which basis of depreciation do you believe will yield the correct measure of annual depreciation? Calculate the amounts and give reasons for your answer.

3. Since firms buy depreciable assets in order to obtain their economic benefits, most accounting theorists agree that the depreciation patterns chosen for these assets should parallel the pattern of their expected benefits as closely as possible. Since the goal of a profit-seeking firm is profits, it must ultimately be possible to interpret these economic benefits as contributions to profits.

   Musgrove Structural Arts Ltd operates in a highly unstable industry; during some years even well-managed companies suffer net losses. The firm's managing director subscribes so strongly to the interpretation of depreciation outlined in the first paragraph that she refuses to recognise any depreciation at all during loss years:

   > We aren't in business for the fun. We bought buildings and equipment in order to make profits, not to make losses. So when we don't make profits it's obviously completely wrong to charge any depreciation.

   Exactly how does the managing director's position conflict with the traditional rationale for depreciation?

15.14 *Asset acquisition cost on a trade-in*

Wallabi Ltd owns a yacht rental business near a major coastal city. On 27 February 20X2 it purchased a new yacht for $250 000, less a trade-in allowance of $30 000 on an old yacht. The balance owing, $220 000, was paid in cash. The old yacht had cost $120 000 and had been depreciated by $110 000. A prospective buyer had offered $20 000 for the old yacht last week. The name *Wallabi* was painted on the side of the new yacht at a cost of $500 and new jackets and caps to match the colour of the *Wallabi* were purchased for the crew at a cost of $600. A 12-month insurance premium of $3000 was paid for the yacht and it was registered to operate as a commercial vehicle at a cost of $1000. The registration fee is paid only once.

(a) Prepare journal entries to record the purchase of the new yacht and the trade-in of the old yacht.

(b) What assets did Wallabi Ltd acquire and at what cost?

15.15 *Asset acquisition cost*

The Waterloo Wagon Company bought three truck chassis on 1 January 20X4 for a total cost of $60 000. Identical bodies were installed on them on the day of purchase for a total cost of $15 000, of which $4000 was paid to the company's own employees. The vehicles had an expected life of five years and were to be depreciated on a straight-line basis. Their salvage value was estimated to be $5000 each.

On 30 June 20X5 two vehicles were sold for $35 000 cash and the third truck was overhauled and modified at a cost of $7000. It was then expected to have a service life of four years and a salvage value of $6000.

(a) Record the above information in the appropriate ledger accounts.

(b) Show the relevant parts of the final accounting reports for each of the three years ended 30 June 20X4, 20X5 and 20X6 respectively.

15.16 *Asset versus expense decisions*

1. The Nepean Company purchased five robots to perform routine assembly tasks within its production plant. The robots cost $50 000 each and installation costs amounted to $10 000. The employees effectively replaced by the robots were transferred to another division. The transferred employees were retrained at a cost to the factory of $12 000 and each employee was paid a $500 relocation bonus. What cost figure should be attached to the five robots?

2. How would you classify (i.e. asset or expense) each of the following costs at the time of its incurrence? Explain your answer.

   (a) A major overhaul of heavy earthmoving equipment is estimated to have increased the productive capacity of the equipment by twenty per cent and to have increased its useful life to the firm by three years.

   (b) Rivers Ltd recently purchased a computer for $300 000 and spent $30 000 to train three employees to operate it. One month later two of the trained employees left the firm and a further $20 000 was spent to train two new employees.

   (c) Davey Ltd recently purchased two new cars for its managers at a cost of $100 000. The two cars were air-conditioned at a cost of $5000 and a telephone was installed in one car for $300.

   (d) Ronin Ltd purchased all the shares in Julien Ltd for $3 million. The book value of the net tangible assets at the time of purchase was $2.75 million. A director suggested that the self-developed goodwill in Ronin Ltd was probably worth twice as much as the goodwill they had just purchased.

3. Hotsprings Ltd spent $229 500 in 20X9 on its guesthouse that it had built near a lake 12 years ago. Expenditure consisted of:

   (i) Painting of old bedroom units $ 20 000

   (ii) Replacing the wooden window frames on
   the old units with aluminium frames   30 000

      (iii) Purchase of new carpet for the bedroom
           floors of the old units   15 000

      (iv) Purchase of new bedding for one unit whose occupant
           had accidentally set the bedclothes on fire   500

      (v) Demolition of two old sheds to make space for new units   4 000

      (vi) Construction of new units   100 000

      (vii) Painting of new units   20 000

      (viii) Deemed wages of own employees assisting in
           building operations   30 000

      (ix) Damages paid to a guest in the old units who suffered
           injuries from a flying tile   10 000

    (a) For each item state whether, at the end of 20X9, it is an asset or an expense. Explain the rules governing your decision and how the rules apply in the particular case. (You may group items to which identical rules apply.)

    (b) Would any of your answers to (a) have been different if the guesthouse had been purchased by Hotsprings Ltd just prior to the expenditure?

4. The Dagnell Association recently constructed a new stadium. They purchased a block of land with an old factory on it. They hired contractors to demolish the factory and erect the stadium. The following costs were incurred:

    (i)   Land and factory $ 480 000

    (ii) Legal fees and stamp duty   30 000

    (iii) Rates and taxes   12 000

    (iv) Demolition of factory   7 000

    (v) Construction of stadium   1 000 000

    (vi) Landscaping   40 000

    (vii) Electricity and telephone connection   1 000

    (viii) Interest on loan raised to finance construction of
        stadium   50 000

        In addition, the following revenue was earned:

    (ix) Sale of salvage materials from factory   2 000

    At the time of the acquisition, an appraisal of the property placed the value of the land at $400 000 and the value of the old factory at $10 000.

    (a) What assets did the company acquire?

    (b) Calculate the cost of each asset identified.

Case studies

15.17 *Changing accounting policies at KK Air Ltd*

Turn again to Case 15.2, KK Air Ltd, on page 545 of this chapter and read the first paragraph only and what follows here:

Another concern raised by Boon related to a change in accounting policy for the depreciation of aircraft. The previous policy was to charge depreciation on a usage basis where the annual expense was determined according to the proportion of actual flying hours per year per aircraft to the total expected flying capacity of each aircraft. Boon's research indicated that this policy is common in the aviation industry. For the current year, depreciation was calculated on a straight-line basis over an arbitrary period of 20 years for each aircraft in service. This accounting policy change contributed a total of $5.8 million to the unaudited profit before tax of $5.9 million. (The operating profit before tax was $21.9 million in the previous year.) In response to Boon's concerns about this policy change, the finance director wrote:

> The depreciation expense on aircraft may be calculated using a variety of methods all of which are arbitrary. In addition, KK aircraft are all of a similar age and are rotated on flight routes to ensure that standardised usage patterns emerge in the long term.

Once again, Boon was not satisfied with this explanation.

Required

Provide written advice to Boon which sets out your opinion on whether this change of policy is appropriate in the circumstances.

15.18 *Queensland Fire and Rescue Authority*

The 1996/97 Annual Report of the Queensland Fire and Rescue Authority (QFRA) stated the following accounting policies for 'acquisitions of assets' and 'property, plant and equipment':

- *Acquisitions of assets.* The cost method of accounting is used for the initial recording of all acquisitions of assets controlled by the authority. Cost is determined as the fair value of the assets given as consideration plus costs incidental to the acquisition, including architects' fees and engineering design fees and all other costs incurred in getting the assets ready for use.
- *Property, plant and equipment.* All items of property, plant and equipment with a cost, or other value, in excess of $2000 are recognised in the year of acquisition. All other such items with a cost, or other value, less than $2000 are expensed.

Items or components that form an integral part of an asset are recognised as a single asset (functional asset). The recognition threshold is applied to the aggregate cost of each functional asset.

A full set of tyres for a typical fire appliance is obtainable at a current cost to QFRA in excess of $2000. Fitting costs are typically included in the overall cost of the new set of tyres.

Required

Discuss and agree upon the accounting treatment of the costs of new sets of tyres.

15.19 *Burns Philp & Company Ltd*

Burns Philp & Company Ltd is a global food ingredients company headquartered in Australia which has operations in 30 countries and customers in over 60 countries. The company's accounting policies on 'goodwill' and 'trademarks, trade names, brand names and technological assets' were stated in its 1997 Annual Report (note 1) as follows:

Goodwill

Purchased goodwill, being the excess of purchase consideration over the fair value attributed to net assets acquired, is amortised on a straight-line basis over the period of expected benefit, not exceeding 20 years. In addition, the carrying value of goodwill is reviewed annually by the directors and adjusted where necessary. In determining the value of purchased goodwill on acquisition, appropriate consideration is given to assigning a fair value to trademarks, trade names, brand names, fermentation technology and other technologies acquired.

Trademarks, trade names, brand names and technological assets

Burns Philp develops and acquires products and businesses with registered trademarks, trade names and brand names. Acquired trademarks, trade names and brand names are included in the financial statements at the lower of cost of acquisition and recoverable amount.

At the present time, no value has been placed on trademarks, trade names and brand names developed by Burns Philp from its own resources.

Burns Philp also develops and acquires fermentation technology and other technologies. These assets are included in the financial statements at either independent valuation or cost, neither of which exceeds their recoverable amount.

No amortisation is provided against the carrying value of trademarks, trade names, brand names and technological assets. The directors believe that the life of these assets is of such duration and the residual value would be such that the amortisation charge, if any, would not be material.

The directors have, however, adopted a policy of regular independent review of the value of trademarks, trade names, brand names and technological assets and disclose the independent valuations of these assets in the financial statements (refer note 13).

Where the independent valuation, of any individual trademark, trade name, brand name or technological asset is less than its carrying amount, that asset is written down to its independent valuation, notwithstanding that the overall class of asset to which it belongs shows a valuation surplus.

Expenditure incurred in developing, maintaining or enhancing trademarks, trade names, brand names and technological assets is written off against the consolidated result.

Required

1. Which of the following are recognised as assets by Burns Philp:
   - purchased goodwill?
   - internally generated goodwill?
   - purchased identifiable intangible assets?
   - internally generated identifiable intangible assets?

2. Is the apparent inconsistency in accounting for purchased goodwill and purchased trademarks, trade names, brand names and technological assets justified? Explain.

15.20 *Amortising the costs of tooling*

A story titled 'Tooling costs amortised' appeared in the April 1987 issue of *Accountancy* and stated, in part, the following:

> Reliant Motor launched the Scimitar SS1 sports car in April 1985 and is hoping it will be enthusiastically received by the North American and European markets.
>
> The net book value of the group's tooling—Pnds 1.080m at 30 September 1986—wholly relates to Scimitar SS1 and is being amortised at the rate of Pnds 200 (1985 Pnds 100) for each car sold.
>
> The company's accounting policy for tooling is to amortise it so as to recover the costs rateably on anticipated sales of the model concerned.
>
> The note adds that future sales of the Scimitar are uncertain. 'However, sales of Scimitar SS1, since its launch in April 1985 to 30 September 1986, amount to 913 units. In the event of sales continuing at a similar level in the future, the cost of tooling would be wholly written off over the next 10 years' (p. 44).

Required

1. What are 'tooling costs'?
2. On what basis may tooling costs be recorded as assets?
3. Evaluate the basis of amortising tooling costs as explained in the story.
4. What reliance should be placed on sales forecasts in ascertaining the period over which systematic charges will be made against income? Justify your view.
5. What consideration should be given to plans to introduce new models of vehicles in determining accounting policies to write off the tooling costs related to current models? Support your view.

15.21 *Coca-Cola Amatil Ltd and Burns Philp & Company Ltd*

The accounting policies on research and development expenditure adopted by these two companies are stated in their respective 1997 annual reports as follows:

CCA Ltd: Research and development

All expenditure on research and development is written off in the period in which the expenditure is incurred except where future benefits can be assured beyond reasonable doubt.

Burns Philp & Company Ltd (1997 Annual Report): Research and development

Research and development expenditure, including expenditure on developing, maintaining, enhancing and protecting fermentation technology and other technologies, is charged against the consolidated result.

Required

1. Why is the 'beyond any reasonable doubt' test applied in Australia in the case of expenditure on research and development when the 'probable' test applies generally in recognising financial statement elements?
2. Compare and contrast the research and development accounting policies of these two companies.

15.22 *Placing financial values on publicly held museum collections*

The following article titled 'What the market can't bear' by Geoffrey Maslen appeared in the *Bulletin* of 8 April 1997, p. 20.

Priceless: A multi-million-dollar project to put a ticket on Victoria's cultural assets is posing problems for valuers and institutions alike

Andrew Broadway was stumped. What possible value, the Melbourne antiques expert wondered, could he place on Steve Hart's armour? Here were 41 kilograms of forged iron the Kelly gang outlaw had donned during the shootout at Glenrowan in 1880. It was in good condition and, apart from a couple of dents where police bullets had struck, it looked almost brand new. But nothing like the massive metal outfit had ever appeared in an Australian saleroom, so there was no market price.

Nor were there sales figures for the revolver that William John Wills gave to his friend Robert O'Hara Burke, which was found in the dead explorer's hands at Cooper Creek in 1861. It was not even in original condition, as the gun had been stolen from the State Library of Victoria in 1944. The thieves had cut the barrel down, converted the gun to a rimfire weapon and used it in a foiled hold-up, which was how it came to be returned. It had cost the crooks 10 years in prison, but what was it worth today?

EPIC: Broadway also pondered over Douglas Mawson's oak skis, which the Antarctic explorer used during his epic journey across the ice-bound continent early this century. And what about the fragment of Mawson's sled that some-one had cut into four and given to various bodies, including the library?

Such puzzles constantly confront Broadway and a dozen experts putting prices on the hundreds of thousands of books, manuscripts, paintings, prints, photographs, bones, rocks, machinery and innumerable other objects held by Victoria's major institutions.

In 1995 the Kennett government told the library, the Museum of Victoria, the Australian National Gallery, the Performing Arts Museum and the Public Records Office that they would have to value their collections and to be the first institutions in Australia to include them as assets in annual reports. While Victoria has taken the lead in assigning sums to all its assets—including roads, bridges, buildings and cultural items—the other states are now following suit. Under a new standard issued by the Australian Accounting Research Foundation three years ago, all government departments are supposed to list heritage items in their financial statements after 31 December 1996.

The institutions were shocked and horrified. They estimated the total cost of the process at $30 million and declared they could not afford it. The library calculated that using independent valuers to assess its 3 million or so items would cost $12.5 million—more than its annual government grant. Curators at the gallery claimed that to obtain a market value for its 55 000 works of art would take years and cost $11 million.

Following the protests, the state arts department commissioned a study by two senior Deakin University academics, Garry Carnegie and Peter Wolnizer. Their report, however, condemned the proposal. It said no other country apart from New Zealand had attempted such a task and the cost would be considerably more than the 'dubious benefits likely to be gained'.

UNIQUE: After three months searching the academic literature and surveying arts institutions in the United States, Britain, New Zealand, Spain and across Australia, the academics concluded that cultural and heritage items could not be regarded as assets in any financial or commercial sense. As many of the objects held by the organisations were unique, and therefore irreplaceable, how could a value be placed on them?

But the government insisted and promised to pay external assessors to do the job. As well, the estimated time and expense was cut to a fraction using random sampling. At the library, only the most rare and expensive items are being individually valued. A figure for the worth of the rest is achieved by sampling at different rates across the various collections and extrapolating the results.

So far, the library's holdings have been valued at $100 million. For Broadway, the solution to his conundrums involved inspired guesswork. He knew four suits of armour worn by the Kelly gang still existed; the one in private hands had once been insured for $500 000, so he figured Steve Hart's suit must be worth $800 000. Wills' revolver he valued at $25 000, the Mawson skis at $20 000 and the quarter-sled at $10 000. 'I would have liked to have seen Ned Kelly's Colt revolver which the library used to have,' Broadway muses. 'But it was loaned to the Americans during their bicentenary in 1976 and was stolen in Chicago.'

Following publication of this article, the letter to the editor reproduced below appeared in the *Bulletin* of 22 April 1997 (Forum, p. 8):

Unwanted expertise

Your article on the accounting valuation of public heritage assets ('What the market can't bear', *B*, April 8) provides a compelling illustration of the uncritical acceptance of professional 'expertise'. Nothing else can explain how the Australian accounting profession, apparently unperturbed and unsullied by the private sector accounting debacles it perpetrated during the 1980s, now enjoys government-sanctioned authority to inflict its ideology on the public sector.

Valuing Douglas Mawson's oak skis at $20 000 might give some satisfaction and comfort to accountants, but does it really mean anything to anybody else? Perhaps as a 'thank you' to the accounting profession for the distraction and other costs it has imposed within the public sector, representatives of Australian museums could curate a special exhibition. It could feature unique and irreplaceable heritage items, but without the usual descriptive information that accompanies such exhibits. Instead, each item would have a price tag. It would be an 'accountants only' exhibition and a celebration of their success in expanding the market for their professional services. Would anybody else want to attend?

Brian West
University of Ballarat, Vic.

Required

Does the monetary valuation of collections of not-for-profit public museums for financial reporting purposes 'mean anything to anybody else' as queried in this letter? Justify your view.

CHAPTER 16
Revenue

Introduction

The nature of revenue, or income, is explored in greater depth in this chapter, and the criteria for the recognition of revenue are discussed. While an item that meets the definition of revenue is to be recognised when the commonly accepted criteria for revenue recognition are met, we emphasise in this chapter the elimination of uncertainty as to the amount of revenue ultimately to be received by an entity. A set of tests is developed to assist in applying the criteria for the recognition of revenue.

Having developed and discussed rules for the recognition of revenue, the remainder of the chapter explains and illustrates the accounting entries for recognising revenue in particular circumstances. These include, for example, the recognition of revenue on instalment sales and hire purchase and the recognition of revenue on long-term construction contracts.

The definition of revenue

The IASC *Framework* provides the following definition of revenue:

> *Income* [i.e. revenue] is increases in economic benefits during the accounting period in the form of inflows or enhancements of assets or decreases of liabilities that result in increases in equity, other than those relating to contributions from equity participants.[1]

Similarly, SAC 4 in Australia provides the following definition:

> 'Revenues' are inflows or other enhancements, or savings in outflows, of future economic benefits in the form of increases in assets or reductions in liabilities of the entity, other than those relating to contributions by owners, that result in an increase in equity during the reporting period.[2]

These two definitions are complementary and are helpful in gaining an understanding of the nature of revenue. Revenue can be earned in many different ways such as the provision of goods and services, the sale of a long-term asset or investment and the receipt of a grant or allocation from a government funding authority. Revenues arise from a range of different transactions and events and are commonly referred to by a number of different names. The IASC *Framework* provides the examples of sales, fees, interest, dividends, royalties and rents (para. 74). Applying the assumptions and principles of historical cost accounting and drawing on the definitions of revenue, the following key points are made:

1. Revenue increases owners' equity, so it follows that a revenue-producing transaction or other event must be one that increases net assets. This eliminates from consideration, for example, the receipt of cash by way of a loan because this transaction does not result in any change to an entity's net assets position.
2. Contributions of capital are not revenue. Net assets increase either by capital contributions or profit, and revenue is concerned with the latter change.
3. The form of consideration ultimately received is immaterial; it might be cash, the reduction of a liability or an exchange of services. Any of these can lead to an increase in net assets.

Having identified the inflow of net assets that are not capital inflows, a further step of discriminating between *revenues* and *gains* might be undertaken. Gains also arise from an entity's activities, for example gains arising from the disposal of non-current assets and gains earned on the disposal of investments not acquired for resale.

---

[1] International Accounting Standards Committee, 'Framework for the Preparation and Presentation of Financial Statements', *International Accounting Standards 1997*, IASC, London, 1997, para. 70(a).

[2] Australian Accounting Standards Board and Public Sector Accounting Standards Board, Statement of Accounting Concepts (SAC) 4, 'Definition and Recognition of the Elements of Financial Statements', Australian Accounting Research Foundation, 1995, para. 111.

The IASC *Framework* states that 'gains represent other items that meet the definition of income [i.e. revenue] and may, or may not, arise in the course of the ordinary activities of an enterprise' (para. 75). In conceptual terms, gains are therefore not regarded as different in nature from revenue. Given this view, there is no reason why revenues and gains should not follow the same rules for their recognition and measurement. Fundamentally, both represent increases in net assets and should therefore be treated identically. They may, of course, be disclosed separately.

Alternative points for revenue recognition

A popular belief is that revenue should be recognised in the period in which it is 'earned' so that the profit and loss statement reflects the 'accomplishment' of an entity during the period. However, the earning process is very often a continuous one, in which no point can be identified as the moment when the revenue is earned. The typical earnings cycle for a manufacturer is depicted in Figure 16.1.

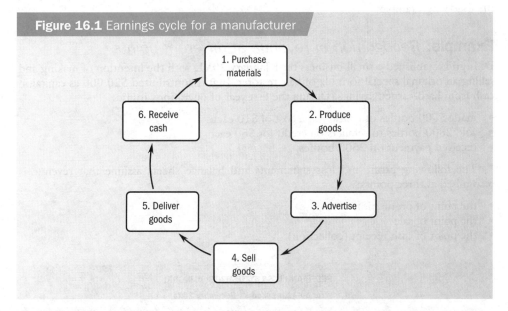

Figure 16.1 Earnings cycle for a manufacturer

As all of these activities may have contributed to the earning of revenue, all are part of the 'accomplishment', and the problem of allocating the eventual revenue over the earnings cycle in some rational way is therefore overwhelming. In practice, the allocation is not usually made, due to the lack of verifiable evidence of the amount of revenue earned at each point.

Emphasis has been placed throughout this book on the need for verifiable evidence to support a primary entry. The verifiable evidence of revenue often consists of an external sales transaction, so revenue cannot usually be recognised before the point of sale, no matter how much has been 'accomplished' in earlier stages.

In general, as a firm moves through the revenue-earning cycle, the certainty that revenue has been earned increases. The receipt of cash usually represents the point where uncertainty is fully resolved. However, absolute uncertainty is not achieved in cases where a full refund is available when customers are not completely satisfied. Unfortunately, though, in terms of the magnitude of effort expended in earning the revenue, the cash receipt, although vital to a firm's survival, may be regarded as the least important step in the earning process. The effort of producing goods may have contributed most to the successful venture. There is, therefore, a conflict between the goals of recognising revenue when the major effort is expended and recognising revenue when it is certain.

Inevitably, judgements must be made in deciding the timing of revenue recognition, that is at what point revenue should be recorded in the financial statements. Such decisions clearly have direct impacts on the amount of reported profit for any accounting period and the net assets position of an entity at the end of that period. The temptation to recognise revenue prematurely may prove to be too great in certain cases. Sometimes unfortunate consequences may arise for those who base decisions on results that were more favourable than was warranted in the circumstances.

Different activities present a different mix of problems. A mining company operating under a standing contract to supply at a fixed price would achieve certainty as soon as the ore is extracted. A dentist, however, faced with clients who are uninsured, may not be certain of the amount that will ultimately be derived until the cash is received. A set of tests is required that will cope with all of these possibilities in a systematic way.

Recognising revenue at different points

The importance of determining the point at which to recognise revenue is brought out in the following example.

Example: *Recognition of revenue at different points*

D. Ingrid established a small business on 1 January 20X1, with the intention of making and selling an original special formula of hair restorer. Ingrid contributed $20 000 as capital in cash from hard-earned savings. During the first year of operations Ingrid:

- made 5000 bottles of restorer at a cost of $10 each
- sold 2800 bottles to retailers on credit for $50 each
- received payment on 2500 bottles.

The following profit and loss statements and balance sheets assume that revenue is recognised at three points:

- the point of production
- the point of sale
- the point of cash receipt (collection).

	Production	Sale	Collection
PROFIT AND LOSS STATEMENTS: D. INGRID			
for the year ended 31 December 20X1			
Units recognised	(5 000)	(2 800)	(2 500)
Revenue ($50/unit)	$250 000	$140 000	$125 000
less Cost of goods ($10)	50 000	28 000	25 000
Net profit	$200 000	$112 000	$100 000

BALANCE SHEETS: D. INGRID as at 31 December 20X1				
	Production	Sale		Collection
Assets				
Cash at bank	$ 95 000	$ 95 000		$ 95 000
Inventory	110 000	22 000		22 000
Accounts receivable	15 000	15 000	$ 15 000	
less Deferred income			12 000	3 000
	220 000	132 000		120 000
Shareholders' equity				
Capital	20 000	20 000		20 000
plus Profit	200 000	112 000		100 000
	$220 000	$132 000		$120 000

Production basis compared with the sales basis

The production basis recognises revenue on the goods produced but not yet sold, whereas the sales basis recognises revenue only on goods sold. Revenue on 2200 unsold units, at $50 per unit, amounts to $110 000. However, this is not the addition to profit, since the production costs of these units, totalling $22 000 (2200 × $10), must be matched against the revenue, so the increase in profit compared with the sales basis is therefore only $88 000. The consequent increase in shareholders' equity is matched in the balance sheet by an increase in the valuation of stock on hand. Since the production basis regards the profit as having been 'earned' on the unsold stock, the value placed on the stock must be its market value.

When future costs are to be incurred that will affect the profit from the goods, such as costs of delivery, these should be anticipated in the current period and the inventory valued at its selling price after deduction of future costs. This is often termed the *net realisable value*.

Collections basis compared with the sales basis

Under the collections basis, the recognition of profit is deferred beyond the point of sale until the cash has been received. At balance date, 300 units have been sold but not yet been paid for and the profit on these units of $12 000 (300 × $40) is deferred. The reduction in shareholders' equity by comparison with the sales approach is matched by a reduction in accounts receivable to remove from it the deferred profit element. In effect, accounts receivable is valued at the original cost of those sales. If the profit from the sales is not yet 'earned', then accounts receivable cannot be increased by the amount of that profit.

As a general rule, the production basis recognises revenue before the point of sale and is accompanied by the valuation of inventory at net selling price. This is a departure from the cost basis of valuation adopted in the historical cost system. The collections basis defers profit beyond the point of sale and reduces the balance sheet valuation of accounts receivable.

The point at which revenue is recognised will not affect the lifetime profit of the enterprise, but it will affect the trend in revenue from year to year. Since the trend in profits is useful information for analysis purposes, it is important to derive some tests to determine the point at which revenue should be recognised in an historical cost accounting system.

The recognition of revenue

The literature contains a variety of suggested tests that attempt to reconcile the desire to recognise revenue at the moment of its accomplishment with the need for reliability. They include tests for a sale transaction, realisation and the critical event. As this is a study of an existing accounting system, involving inductive reasoning, the procedure will be to study various events on which revenue is recognised immediately in practice and events on which recognition is denied (Table 16.1). Each of the proposed tests will be examined to determine its effectiveness in discriminating between events that give rise to revenue and those that do not.

Table 16.1 Selection of events on which revenue is recognised or denied

	Test	
	External *sale transaction?*	*Realisation?* *(cash or a claim to cash)*
Revenue recognised immediately		
1. Retail credit sales	Yes	Yes
2. Sales under warranty	Yes	Yes
3. Primary production for marketing board, selling price is known	?	?
4. Perform service and invoice customer	Yes	Yes
Revenue denied at present		
5. Increase in market value of asset	No	No
6. Advance sales of magazine subscription	Yes	Yes
7. Sales order received, with deposit	Yes	Partially
8. Sales on approval	Yes	No
9. Sales where collection dubious	Yes	Yes

External transaction test

In the framework adopted in Chapter 5 a transaction must occur before a primary entry is made. A revenue event is a primary entry because it increases the net assets and a transaction is necessary before revenue may be recognised. However, it will be found that a transaction alone is not sufficient to justify the recognition of revenue.

In an increasingly complex world the transaction test is not easily applied, because of difficulties in identifying a revenue-producing transaction. An agreement to sell a product in three months time is a type of transaction, but few accountants would accept that a sale has occurred until the product has been delivered. The transaction must be of a certain type before revenue can be recognised.

In all of the cases listed in Table 16.1 in which revenue is recognised in practice, it may be argued that an external transaction has taken place. Only item 3 is dubious, although there may be a standing arrangement with the marketing board to supply all production and this might be regarded as a transaction. With regard to the events that are not recognised immediately as revenue, the sales transaction test explains why the increase in the market value of an asset that is held (item 5) is not recognised as revenue. However, in each of the items numbered 6 to 9, a transaction seems to have occurred. Magazine subscriptions have been sold, goods have been sold on approval, and a deposit has been received with an order.

Nevertheless, the immediate recognition of revenue is denied in these cases, apparently because the 'right' type of transaction has not yet taken place.

Clearly, some transactions create binding obligations while others do not. To delve deeper, it must be asked what characteristics an external transaction must possess for it to justify the immediate recognition of revenue. Some higher principle must guide the selection of an 'appropriate' transaction. Some have called this principle the 'realisation' test.

Realisation

The terms 'realisation' and 'recognition' often have been used interchangeably in the accounting literature with the result that it has become increasingly difficult to distinguish between them. In our view, *realisation* should refer to the conversion of an asset into cash or a claim to cash, while revenue *recognition* will be at the point in the operating cycle at which it is deemed appropriate to recognise revenue. The two are not always identical. Revenue realisation normally arises in the final stages of the operating cycle and is only one possible point for revenue recognition. For example, a miner might choose to recognise revenue from the mining of gold in the accounts as soon as the gold is discovered, but it will be realised only when the ore is sold.

The realisation test implies that revenue should be recognised only when there is an external transaction that results in the receipt of cash or a claim to cash. Item 1 in Table 16.1 produces a claim on the customer, an account receivable, and this satisfies the realisation test. Similarly, sales under warranty (item 2) and the performance of a service (item 4) produce valid claims on outsiders. Item 3 is more dubious, since the claim on the marketing authority will not exist until the product is delivered.

The adoption of a strict realisation test is effective in identifying cases where revenue *may* be recognised, but it is less successful in indicating when revenue *may not* be recognised. In each of items 6, 7 and 9, realisation seems to have occurred. The advance magazine sales have resulted in the receipt of cash, the receipt of a cash deposit with a sales order amounts to a partial realisation of the sale, and sales to customers where collection is dubious do result in a claim to cash on the customer.

It is apparent that a simple realisation test, requiring the receipt of cash or a claim to cash, will not be a sufficient test for the recognition of revenue. Yet the literature in accounting makes constant reference to realisation being required. Over time, the meaning of realisation has changed as the inadequacies of the simple test have become apparent. Hence its meaning is now unclear. It is useful to make reference to realisation of revenue in some circumstances, but the word should be carefully defined to mean 'the receipt of cash or a claim to cash'. Furthermore, this term should not be used as a synonym for the recognition of revenue.

Accomplishment: the critical event criterion

Myers[3] has suggested a test for the *critical event* as a measure of the point at which revenue is 'earned'. Under this approach, 'profit is earned at the moment of making the most critical decision or of performing the most difficult task in the cycle of a complete transaction'.

In most cases, the sale is the most critical event (items 1, 2 and 4 in Table 16.1). Excellent ideas, huge time and energy contributions, and a sound production process are worthless unless the goods can be sold. Accordingly, many firms place great emphasis on the marketing of their products and for them the sale is the critical event in the earning process.

However, as has been noted, the sale is not always the point at which revenue is recognised in practice and the critical event approach attempts to provide a more comprehensive test. Where the collections basis is used (as in item 9), the critical event notion suggests that collection is the critical event since, in those situations, collection is the hardest step in the earning process. Similarly, when the production basis is used (as in item 3), it is asserted that the remaining stages are not of great importance. In the cases of advance magazine sales and deposits, the critical task may be to complete the production process so as to be permitted to retain the cash.

The critical event approach seems to provide a sensible criterion for recognising revenue when it is earned, until the question is asked: What is there about an event that makes it critical to the earning of revenue? This question can be answered only by delving deeper still.

Resolution of uncertainty

The concept of recognising revenue when it is accomplished has intuitive appeal as an attempt to provide an indication of comparative performance between firms and over time. However, the search for the 'earning point' might be pursued to its logical conclusion, regardless of the difficulties of valuation that would result. Profit might even be regarded as earned from the moment the product is first conceived. Within the historical cost accounting system, however, there are limitations imposed that limit recognition to a point where it may be recorded with sufficient reliability. Sufficient *uncertainty* must have been eliminated before revenue is recognised.

Before uncertainty is resolved, a change in net assets must be *measurable* and it must be *permanent*. To be measurable, a change must be verifiable; that is, it must appear substantially the same to all accountants examining it. To be permanent, the change must be unlikely to be reversed.

To illustrate, a contract to supply 5000 units in three months time at $12 per unit has a measurable revenue of $60 000 that may be verified by trained observers. However, a contract to supply 5000 units in three months time at the then ruling price is not measurable at present. Here, uncertainty exists as to the amount of revenue that will be derived and no revenue may be recognised until verifiable figures are available.

The test for permanence takes account of uncertainty as to the occurrence of future events necessary to secure any revenue. Continuing the previous example, a contract to supply 5000 units in three months time at $60 per unit, subject to cancellation at the buyer's request, is not yet permanent. A sale may be for a set price, but there may be great uncertainty as to whether the product can be built to the customer's requirements, or whether the customer will pay the account, and trained observers may be forced to the conclusion that the increase in net assets cannot yet be considered permanent.

The measurement of a price and the obtaining of certainty that the amount of revenue thus recorded will not need to be cancelled at some future time are thus different and complementary aspects of the resolution of uncertainty.

3 J. M. Myers, 'The Critical Event and the Recognition of Net Profit', in S. Zeff and T. Keller, *Financial Accounting Theory*, McGraw-Hill, New York, 1964.

In our view, the resolution of uncertainty is the most basic requirement for the recognition of revenue. The transaction and realisation tests exist because they help to resolve uncertainty. Similarly, it is believed that the critical event approach is ultimately a test for the resolution of uncertainty.

The following simple example might clarify the issue. A firm enters a raffle by signing a contract that requires it to contribute $10 000, which it duly does. It stands to earn $20 000, $100 000 or nothing. At what point should revenue be recognised, and why?

Recognition would normally be deferred until the prize has been determined. Two alternative reasons may be given. The uncertainty view is that the revenue is not measurable at a specific price until the raffle is drawn and that no revenue is permanent until then. The 'earning point' interpretation must be that performance is not complete until the prize has been determined. Yet no further actions are required of the firm other than to receive the prize. This suggests that the performance of the contract is deemed incomplete essentially because of the uncertainty surrounding the outcome. Uncertainty is the critical factor.

This example demonstrates also that the meaning of an exchange transaction is unclear, since three transactions have occurred:

1. The signing of the contract.
2. The contribution of $10 000 by the entity.
3. The receipt of the proceeds (if any) of the raffle.

The selection of the third transaction as the relevant transaction for revenue recognition is justified only because it is the moment when the uncertainty is resolved.

If the events cited in Table 16.1 are now viewed from the perspective of the resolution of uncertainty, it may be argued that the first four events produce immediate revenue because there is no uncertainty as to the amount of revenue they will produce, or the permanence of that revenue. The remaining five events are denied immediate recognition either because the claim is not yet permanent (6, 7, 8) or because the amounts receivable ultimately are not yet measurable (5 and 9).

If the resolution of uncertainty is the underlying criterion for the recognition of revenue, the task becomes one of establishing specific tests consistent with this overriding principle.

Cases 16.1 and 16.2 provide contexts within the transportation industry to evaluate the revenue recognition policies adopted.

Case 16.1 SAS Ltd

The 1997 Annual Report of air carrier SAS Ltd (Scandinavian Airlines System) reported the 'traffic revenue' policy as follows:

> Ticket sales are reported as traffic revenue only upon completion of the air travel in question. The value of tickets sold but not yet used is reported as unearned transportation revenue. This item is reduced either when SAS or another airline completes the transportation or after the ticket holder has requested a refund.

Outline a likely explanation for the recognition of traffic revenue on completion of air travel.

Case 16.2 TNT Ltd

The 1987 Annual Report of the transporter TNT Ltd contained the following policy statement relating to the 'recognition of income':

> Revenue is recognised, other than from vessel operations, when freight commences its longhaul movement. Estimated costs of performing the transportation services are then accrued. Revenue from vessel operations by way of charter hire is recognised on an accrual basis and from cargo on a terminated voyage basis. General and administrative expenses are charged to profit as incurred.

Give likely reasons for the adoption of different points for the recognition of revenue from vessel operations compared with longhaul (trucking) operations.

Tests for the resolution of uncertainty

No accounting system that relies on the continuity assumption can produce firm rules to cover every revenue-earning venture that will be resolved only by the occurrence of future events. The only point at which all uncertainty will be removed is when the cash (or other consideration) has been received, the customer no longer has any ground for recovery of any amount by way of returns, legal action or allowances, and no further warranty work is necessary. This is an ultra-conservative and impracticable requirement and is softened by permitting revenue to be recognised earlier in the operating cycle when a certain level of uncertainty has been removed.

This philosophy is embraced in the recognition criteria adopted in the IASC *Framework* which states that:

> An item that meets the definition of an element should be recognised if:
> (a) it is probable that any future economic benefit associated with the item will flow to or from the enterprise; and
> (b) the item has a cost or value that can be measured with reliability (para. 83).

Specifically in connection with revenue, the *Framework* states:

> Income [i.e. revenue] is recognised in the income [i.e. profit and loss] statement when an increase in future economic benefits related to an increase in an asset or a decrease of a liability has arisen that can be measured reliably (para. 92).

The revenue recognition criteria provided by the IASC are quite general. However, the criteria focus on the measurability and permanence of the change in net assets associated with revenue.

In 1982 Martin and Coombes[4] developed a set of tests for determining whether the uncertainty associated with the measurability and permanence of a change in net assets had been reduced to a tolerable level, thus allowing the recognition of the revenue. This set of tests has been adopted in SAC 4 in Australia to provide *guidance* as to whether the revenue recognition criteria have been met (see para. 130). Revenue should be recognised at the earliest point at which all of the following tests have been satisfied:

1. An agreement has been entered into by the entity with one or more independent parties.
2. Cash has been received, or the entity has a claim on another party or parties that:
   (a) is for a specific consideration, either in cash, other assets, or a reduction in debt owing by the entity; and
   (b) may not be cancelled at will by either party.

---

4 C. A. Martin and R. J. Coombes, *The Definition and Recognition of Revenue*, Accounting Theory Monograph No. 3, Australian Accounting Research Foundation, Melbourne, 1982.

3. All acts of performance necessary to establish a valid claim on the other party have been completed.
4. It is possible to estimate to a satisfactory extent the uncollectability of debts or the return of goods sold.[5]

The first test remains faithful to the transaction test, which is a mandatory requirement in an historical cost system. An agreement also provides verifiable evidence of a measurable price, as well as evidence that may help determine whether the transaction will lead to a permanent increase in net assets.

The second test is related to the realisation test. Until cash is received, or an irrevocable claim exists, there is insufficient evidence of a permanent change, and unless the consideration is specified it will not be measurable.

The third test incorporates the accomplishment test, but only because the permanency of the revenue is in doubt until performance is complete.

The fourth test softens the uncertainty criterion by permitting some uncertainty to remain whenever a satisfactory provision for subsequent reductions in the revenue can be made. Practices such as the provision for doubtful debts, discounts and returns are well established, although judgement will be required in individual cases.

Some applications

Increases in values of assets

As a general rule, increases in the market values of assets will fail the tests for revenue recognition. No sale agreement exists with an independent party to verify the gain, no non-cancellable claim exists and not all acts of performance have been completed to secure the revenue or gain. These tests will not be met until a sale has been made.

A block of land may have appreciated in value by $60 000, but until the land is sold there is uncertainty as to the amount of the ultimate gain to be made and as to whether it will be permanent.

Marketable securities, such as publicly listed shares which are traded frequently, represent a challenge to this position. If a company holds a small parcel of shares, it is known at balance date that they can be sold for about the market price. Where, then, is the uncertainty? The uncertainty must relate to whether the gain will evaporate before the shares are actually sold.

Instalment sales or real estate

In Australia and the United States a variety of land sale practices create doubt as to the appropriateness of recognising revenue at the point of sale.

In some contracts the purchaser pays a low deposit and, should any future repayment be missed, the land is forfeited and no further action may be taken against the purchaser. In these circumstances, a purchaser who subsequently discovers that the land is unsuitable, perhaps because it is swamp land, may abandon the contract with little loss. There is no certainty, then, that the seller will receive the whole of the revenue.

At one time real estate developers of unattractive land commonly recognised the entire purchase price as immediate revenue as soon as the deposit was received. This gave an apparently attractive earnings per share outcome, the developer sold the company for a good price and it was left to the new owner to discover that the land purchasers would not be proceeding with their contracts. Applying the tests for revenue recognition, where there is no binding contract, revenue should not be recognised immediately (rule 2(b)).

---

[5] Ibid, p. 3.

Another condition of a land sale contract may be that the seller has to fulfil some further obligations before the sales contract becomes binding. The land may have to be cleared, and until then the necessary acts of performance have not been met (rule 3).

Because of the uncertainty surrounding instalment sales, three different methods of revenue recognition are in use. For illustration, assume land that cost $10 000 is sold for $50 000, to be received in 10 annual instalments of $5000. No interest is charged on the loan.

The sale method

Under this approach, the profit of $40 000 is recognised immediately and a receivable raised for the $50 000 to be received by instalments. The entries follow the principles of the sales basis illustrated on page 579.

Instalment receivable	50 000	
Sale revenue		50 000
(Recording the sale)		
Cost of sales	10 000	
Land inventory		10 000
(Cost of sale transfer)		

The instalment method

The entries follow the principles of the collections basis (page 579), including the creation of accounts for deferred income. The first two entries are as above, followed by:

Deferred income (profit and loss statement)	40 000	
Deferred income (balance sheet)		40 000
(Deferral of unearned income)		

The profit and loss statement reports the sale and cost of sale normally, but the deferred income is deducted before the net profit is determined. In the balance sheet the deferred income account appears as a contra to the instalments receivable account.

As payments are received, the profit is gradually recognised, so that it is spread evenly over the repayment period by means of the following entries each year:

Cash at bank	5 000	
Instalment receivable		5 000
(Receipt of instalment)		
Deferred income (balance sheet)	4 000	
Instalment income		4 000
(Recognition of proportion of income earned on instalment sale)		

The justification for this method may be that each instalment represents a new transaction to which some of the profit attaches. Alternatively, it may be thought that the income is progressively 'realised' with each instalment. Whatever the reason, it is a more conservative method than the sale approach.

From the perspective of uncertainty resolution, there is no clear reason why the instalment method is appropriate. The receipt of an instalment gives no guarantee that future instalments will be paid. If they are not, and if the total instalments received are insufficient to cover the cost of the sale, the profits declared on receipt of earlier instalments will have to be reversed.

Where a conservative approach seems prudent, the cost recovery method is favoured.

The cost recovery method

The entries under this approach are similar to the instalment method, except that no profit is recognised until all of the costs have been recovered. In the example, the first two instalments of $5000 each are recovering the cost. The profit of $40 000 is then recognised evenly over the remaining eight repayment periods.

The relative effects of each approach on profit each year are:

		PROFITS DECLARED AT END OF		
		Year 1	Year 2	Years 3–10
		$	$	$
1.	Sales method	40 000	–	–
2.	Instalment method	4 000	4000	4000 per year
3.	Cost recovery method	–	–	5000 per year

The cost recovery method is appropriate where there is extreme doubt as to whether the debtor will pay. It has been practised recently in Australia, when several finance companies considered that borrowers were unlikely to meet either their capital repayments or the interest due on their loans. Accordingly, the interest was not recognised until the capital was repaid.

The cost recovery method is extremely conservative and may be justified only when there is great doubt as to the likelihood of repayment. This applies to land sales on cancellable contracts and to payment contracts that depend on the borrower remaining in business. An agreement to pay $10 000 per year for 20 years for the use of a business name is a good example. It is obviously premature to recognise $200 000 revenue immediately, when the business may not survive for more than a few years. The conservative approach is first to recover the costs and then to recognise annual profits as the fees are received.

Hire-purchase transactions and similar financing arrangements

A hire-purchase transaction is an arrangement whereby the purchaser of goods pays by instalments. Legally, the goods are hired over the repayment period and ownership is not obtained until payments have been completed. Where hire-purchase arrangements are not permitted by law, there may be an alternative means of financing a sale which raises problems in accounting similar to those to be discussed.

Two elements of profit exist. First, there is the *trading profit* on the sale of goods and, second, there is an interest charge, known as the *hiring charge*, over the period of the hire-purchase contract.

Suppose that goods with a cash price of $8000 and that originally cost $5000 are sold through a hire-purchase contract that requires monthly repayments over six months of $2000 per month. The total repayment will therefore be $12 000. The trading profit and the hiring charge are determined thus:

	$	$
Cost of goods sold	5 000	
		3000 trading profit
Cash selling price	8 000	
		4000 hiring charge
Instalments due	12 000	

Consider first the question of when the trading profit should be recognised. If a 'sale' is required, then that event will not occur until all payments are made and the hiring period is over. If a realisation test is applied, it would be concluded that no gain is 'realised' until the contract is complete.

From the perspective of the resolution of uncertainty, the date of sale or realisation is of less concern than the degree of uncertainty at various points. In most cases, sufficient certainty exists at the date the contract is entered into. A right exists of repossession and recovery of losses from the purchaser. Moreover, in any business in which hire purchase is a frequent transaction, it ought to be possible to estimate satisfactorily the likely extent of bad debts (rule 4). It therefore seems appropriate to recognise the trading profit at the date the contract is signed, in accordance with the sale method.

Turning now to the hiring charge of $4000, it should be noted that the client has the option of early repayment, which would reduce the interest burden. Interest becomes due and payable period by period and it therefore is logical to spread the interest commitment over the loan as the certainty of achieving each period's interest becomes known. This also accords with the intuitive idea that interest is 'earned' progressively over the period of the loan. By contrast, the trading profit is earned at the moment of sale.

The interest amount may be spread evenly over the six-month period at approximately $667 per month ($4000/6). A conceptually superior method, however, is to determine the compound interest rate and to allocate the interest according to a table of present values. This approach will be demonstrated in the next chapter, on liabilities.

Long-term construction projects

The discussion has indicated that revenue nominally is recognised at a fixed point and should not be allocated over the earning period. Contracts that extend over a number of years, such as a long-term construction contract, are important exceptions. To prevent the situation in which no revenue is recognised until the final year, it is common to allocate revenue over the project life.

Since the activities are continuous, it is impossible to allocate the revenue on any natural basis and two methods of revenue recognition may be found in practice. The *completed contracts* method recognises no revenue until the contract has been completed. The alternative is the *percentage of completion* method, which attempts to take account of the progress during each period of the contract by allocating the revenue in accordance with some measure of the proportion of the contract completed in each period.

Example: *Bridge building contract*

Capable Builders Ltd began business on 1 January 20X1 with contributed capital, in cash, of $3 000 000. They agreed to build a bridge over the Weary River for the sum of $8 000 000, payable in instalments as follows:

20X1	$ 600 000
20X2	7 400 000
	8 000 000

Costs over the two-year construction period were:

20X1	$ 750 000
20X2	250 000
	1 000 000

Under the completed contracts method, the entire revenue is recognised in the year of completion. In accordance with the matching concept, the production costs incurred in the first year are carried forward as an asset and matched against the revenue in the second year. The asset, contracts in progress, is reduced by the amount billed to the client in the first year.

The percentage of completion method frequently uses the costs incurred as an indicator of the proportion of the contract completed in each period. The total revenue from the project is then allocated to each period in accordance with the costs incurred. Since 75 per cent of total costs were incurred in the first year, 75 per cent of the revenue is recognised. The amount of revenue recognised in excess of the amount billed is included as a contract receivable in the balance sheet. Costs are expensed as incurred and no inventory appears in the balance sheet.

Ideally, some basis other than cost would be adopted as an indicator of progress to date. An engineer's or an architect's estimates of the stages completed, in proportion to the stages yet to complete, might be adopted.

The consensus is that the percentage of completion approach is generally superior because it relates revenue more directly to the effort and hence the accomplishment in any period. However, in times of inflation or industrial disputes the total costs of a project may be difficult to reliably estimate and thus the proportion of revenue to be recognised in each period is similarly difficult to estimate. The resulting uncertainty surrounding the ultimate outcome of the project suggests that the completed contracts method may be more suitable in such cases.

The accounting period concept is difficult to comply with in long-term ventures and some have suggested that companies engaged in prolonged projects should abandon annual reporting in favour of reporting periods that coincide with the completion of projects.

CAPABLE BUILDERS LTD
Completed contracts method

Profit and loss statements

	20X1	20X2	Total
Revenue	$nil	$8 000 000	$8 000 000
less Production costs	nil	1 000 000	1 000 000
Net profit	$nil	$7 000 000	$7 000 000

Balance sheets

		20X1	20X2
Assets			
Cash at bank		$2 850 000	$10 000 000
Contracts in progress	$750 000		
less Billings to date	600 000	150 000	–
		3 000 000	10 000 000
Shareholders' equity			
Capital		3 000 000	3 000 000
Retained profit			7 000 000
		$3 000 000	$10 000 000

CAPABLE BUILDERS LTD

Percentage of completion method

Profit and loss statements

	20X1	20X2	Total
Revenue	$6 000 000	$2 000 000	$ 8 000 000
less Production costs	750 000	250 000	1 000 000
Net profit	$5 250 000	$1 750 000	$ 7 000 000

Balance sheets

	20X1	20X2	Total
Assets			
Cash at bank		$2 850 000	$10 000 000
Contract receivable	$6 000 000		
less Billings to date	600 000	5 400 000	–
		8 250 000	10 000 000
Shareholders' equity			
Capital		3 000 000	3 000 000
Retained profits		5 250 000	7 000 000
		$8 250 000	$10 000 000

Ethical issues

The Hemisphere Building Society often charged borrowers substantial loan establishment fees of between 6 and 12 per cent of the loan amount. Its competitors
normally charged a maximum loan establishment fee of 3 per cent. However, borrowers from Hemisphere were charged interest rates on loans which were always
lower than those charged by Hemisphere's competitors. Hemisphere's accounting
policy for loan establishment fees was thus: 'Establishment fees on loans are recognised as revenue on approval of the loan after making appropriate allowance for
any loans not expected to proceed'. Evaluate Hemisphere's approach to revenue
recognition.

Summary

This chapter examined the nature of revenue and the criteria for its recognition in financial statements within the historical cost accounting system. The recognition of revenue results in an increase in owners' equity and, therefore, an increase in an entity's net assets. Unfortunately, discussions of revenue have been cluttered with vague criteria, such as the need for realisation or an external sales transaction. These terms are inadequate as tests for the recognition of revenue. We advocate the resolution of uncertainty as the fundamental principle which underlies revenue recognition in the historical cost system.

The general principle of uncertainty resolution involves considerable judgement in making assessments of the measurability and permanence of revenue and involves the adoption of four specific tests designed to pinpoint the earliest moment at which revenue may be recognised in the operating cycle of any business. The great variety of profit-making activities and the need to make assumptions about future events mean that the tests can only be applied with judgement and experience and that differences of opinion will be inevitable. Any assumptions about the future must inevitably be conjectures.

Review exercises

Discussion questions

16.1 What are the main differences between the production, sales and collection bases of revenue recognition?

16.2 What is meant by 'the resolution of uncertainty' and why is this criterion important to the recognition of revenue?

16.3 An economist would argue that revenue is created or earned by a wide variety of the firm's activities (such as production, sales, delivery, etc.), yet the accountant typically selects one of these activities to signal the time at which all revenues are to be recognised. What are the obstacles to a practical implementation of the economist's concept of revenue recognition? How should the accountant select the appropriate point of revenue recognition?

16.4 The National Postal Authority recognises revenue when it sells stamps. Is this a violation of the revenue recognition criteria outlined in the text? Explain your answer.

16.5 Refer to the ethical issue in this chapter and complete the requirement presented.

Problems

16.6 *Revenue realisation*

What conditions must have been satisfied before revenue may be said to have been 'realised'? Discuss whether realisation has occurred in the following cases.

(a) ABC Ltd has received payment in advance for specialised machinery it has agreed to manufacture and deliver to a customer.

(b) DEF Ltd has sold goods on credit to J. Joyce on the understanding that she may return them within three days if they are unsuitable.

(c) GHI Ltd has sold land to Z. Chow for a 1 per cent deposit and the contract of sale stipulated that a further 1 per cent must be paid each month, in default of which the contract is void and the ownership of the land will revert to GHI Ltd.

16.7 *Applying the tests for revenue recognition*

1. Identify the point at which revenue should be recognised in each of the following cases and justify your decision:

   (a) *Tame Magazine* sells subscriptions through newspaper advertisements.

   (b) Zottos Mail Order sells goods by mail in response to orders accompanied by full monies. The promise is given that an unsatisfied customer may receive a refund.

   (c) The Exclusive Club charges new members a joining fee of $400 and demands a subscription for the first year in advance of $250.

   (d) Al Betts is a bookmaker at a racecourse. Betts accepts bets for up to a week before a race is conducted, but does not grant credit.

   (e) The Superb Engineering Shop receives orders from customers, accompanied by deposits, for its custom-made machinery.

   (f) A grape farmer works under a contract with a winemaker wherein each crop is delivered immediately after harvest and the farmer is paid the then ruling price.

   (g) An insurance salesperson receives commission on each new policy written provided the insured continues with the policy for at least two years.

   (h) A company services small computers for customers, who undertake a service contract that is renewed annually.

   (i) A coal-mining company mines and ships coal in accordance with a long-term contract to supply a large manufacturing company at a set price.

2. The following events occurred in the business of V. Targe and Sons, Winemakers, with regard to a special bottling of fine cabernet wine.

   20X1 Grapes are harvested and wine bottled.

   20X3 Wine is exhibited at National Wine Show and a bronze medal awarded.

   20X5 Wine is sampled and appraised by experts who claim it is comparable with another wine presently on sale for $8 per bottle.

   20X6 Wine is released to the public for the first time, available at the cellar only for $7.50 per bottle.

   20X7 A trial shipment is sent to a large city wine merchant who agrees to return unsold bottles within two months. The price is now $8.20.

(a) At what point or points should revenue be recognised, and why?

(b) Does the answer you have given provide the best indication of the comparative performance of the winery over time? If not, why was another method not chosen?

3. In each following case, discuss whether there has been a violation of the principles of revenue recognition under historical cost accounting. If so, how should the transaction have been recorded?

(a) MS Ltd held shares in X Ltd which had cost them $8 each. They were sold to A. Friend, a broker, for $20 each. The next day, a subsidiary of MS Ltd purchased the shares from the broker for $20 each. MS Ltd reported a profit of $12 per share.

(b) Iniquity Ltd purchased shares in Opportunity Ltd for $8 million. Shortly thereafter the shares were revalued at $13 million and the $5 million difference included as profit.

(c) Quickclaim Insurance Ltd suffered a loss of $20 million when it wrote off its investment in H. O. Ribble Traders Ltd, which was liquidated. The loss was offset by a revaluation of other investments by $30 million. The net credit of $10 million went to an asset revaluation reserve.

(d) Grandscale Developers Ltd sold land on the Tourist Coast for $100 000 under the following conditions:

(i) Five per cent deposit and the balance over 20 years. Failure to meet two consecutive payments resulted in forfeiture of the land.

(ii) At the time of sale the land was under water and Grandscale undertook to reclaim the land.

(iii) At the time of sale, Grandscale had not itself acquired title to the land, though the funds received from the sale now enabled it to do so.

The entire $100 000 was treated as revenue at the date of sale and a receivable was created for the balance owing by the customer.

4. K. Walnut planted 100 macadamia nut trees in 20X0, at a total cost of $10 000. The macadamia is a highly prized nut with a ready market at all times and it sells at a high price. The tree is hardy and once planted is subject to practically no pests or diseases. Unfortunately, it does not bear nuts for several years. In 20X4 an advance order was received for 5000 kg of nuts at $6 per kg. In 20X6 the first crop was harvested, yielding 15 000 kg of nuts. The cost of harvesting was $2 per bag. The nuts were delivered a month later. The purchaser paid for the nuts in 20X7.

(a) Identify three possible points at which revenue might be recognised. For each point, state an advantage and a disadvantage of recognising revenue at that point.

(b) When should revenue be recognised if the conventional criteria for revenue recognition are applied?

(c) Which method would yield the greater total profit over the life of the plantation?

16.8   *Revenue recognition at different points in the cycle*

1.   Cuddly Toys Ltd commenced business on 1 January 20X1 as a manufacturer of toy wombats. The transactions for 20X1 were:

   - Issued shares for $100 000 cash.
   - Manufactured 8000 wombats at a cost of $3 each.
   - All costs were paid in cash.
   - Sold 6000 wombats for $5 each.
   - Collected cash on 3500 of the wombats sold.

   Prepare profit and loss statements and balance sheets for 20X1 assuming that revenue is recognised at the point of:

   (a) production
   (b) sale
   (c) cash collection

2.   Galactic Ltd commenced business on 1 January 20X1 as a manufacturer of toy spaceships. The transactions for 20X1 were:

   - Issued shares for $400 000 cash.
   - Manufactured 32 000 spaceships at a cost of $10 each.
   - All costs were paid in cash.
   - Sold 18 000 spaceships for $20 each. Costs of delivery were $2 per unit.
   - Collected cash on 10 000 of the spaceships sold.

   Prepare profit and loss statements and balance sheets for 20X1 assuming that revenue is recognised at the point of:

   (a) production
   (b) sale (delivery)
   (c) cash collection

3.   Alton Ltd commenced business on 1 January 20X3 as a manufacturer of umbrellas. Transactions for 20X3 were:

   - Issued shares for $1 000 000 cash.
   - Manufactured 40 000 umbrellas at a cost of $4.00 each. All costs were paid in cash.
   - Sold 25 000 umbrellas for $7.00 each. Delivery costs were $180 per 1000 units and were paid by Alton.
   - Collected cash on 7000 units sold.

   Prepare profit and loss statements and balance sheets for 20X3 assuming that revenue is recognised at the point of:

   (a) production
   (b) sale
   (c) cash collection

16.9   *Revenue recognition for construction contracts*

1.   Edensor Ltd began with a capital contribution in cash of $80 million. It contracted to build a bridge over the river Wyenot for $120 million. Costs incurred over the three years of the contract were:

	$ million
Year 1	20
Year 2	50
Year 3	10

All costs were paid in cash.

The contract revenue was received as follows:

	$ million
Year 1	12
Year 2	33
Year 3	75

Prepare a profit and loss statement and a balance sheet at the end of each year under:

(a) the percentage of completion method

(b) the completed contracts method

2. On 1 January 20X1 Tracklayers Ltd signed a contract worth $1 000 000 to build a rail line from Eastwood to the University. The company had been formed on 1 January 20X1 with a capital contribution of $6 000 000. The line was to be built over two years with payments of $500 000 to be made at the end of each year. Costs incurred and paid by Tracklayers Ltd were, as estimated:

20X1	$600 000
20X2	$200 000
	$800 000

(a) Show profit and loss statements and balance sheets for each year under the following bases of revenue recognition:

(i)   completed contracts method

(ii) percentage of completion method

(b) For what reasons would it be inappropriate to recognise the entire profit at 1 January 20X1, the contract date?

3. Young Ltd began with a capital contribution in cash of $20 000 000. It contracted to build a recreation centre for $6 000 000. Costs incurred over the three years it took to build the centre were:

Year 1	$ 800 000
Year 2	1 000 000
Year 3	200 000
	$2 000 000

The progress payments were received as follows:

Year 1	$ 500 000
Year 2	1 200 000
Year 3	4 300 000
	$6 000 000

All costs were paid in cash.

(a) Prepare a profit and loss statement and a balance sheet at the end of each year under:

    (i) the completed contracts method

    (ii) the percentage of completion method

(b) Which method would you recommend?

16.10 *Revenue recognition for instalment sales*

1. Uplift Importers Ltd sold excavating equipment that had cost $160 000 to Dig Deep Ltd for $340 000. The terms of sale called for a deposit of $40 000 and monthly instalments of $50 000 at the end of each of the following six months. No interest was charged on the extended payments.

    (a) Prepare schedules of the monthly revenues and expenses for the six-month period under:

        (i) the sale method of profit recognition

        (ii) the instalment method of profit recognition

        (iii) the cost recovery method of profit recognition

    (b) Which method appears to be the most appropriate in this case? Give reasons.

2. On 30 June 20X4 Holmes Ltd sold a parcel of land adjacent to its factory to Marshall Developments Pty Ltd for $4 million. The contract provided for a deposit of 10 per cent and a three-year loan was raised for the balance remaining with interest charged on the loan at the rate of 15 per cent per annum. Each six months Marshall was to pay $600 000 principal plus interest on the unpaid balance. Should Marshall default on any payment, the title would revert immediately to Holmes Ltd. The land had originally cost Holmes Ltd $1.6 million.

    (a) Prepare schedules showing how the profit and interest would be recognised on this transaction under:

        (i) the sale method of profit recognition

        (ii) the instalment method of profit recognition

        (iii) the cost recovery method of profit recognition

    (b) Which method would be the most appropriate in the present circumstances? Why?

Case studies

16.11 *The Australian Gas Light Company*

The 1997 Annual Report of the Australian Gas Light Company (AGL) stated the following policy on 'accounting for gas sales':

> Gas revenue is not brought to account until customers' meters are read and bills rendered. Meters are read on monthly or quarterly cycles and no revenue is accrued in respect of gas consumed after each customer's last reading date for the respective financial year.
>
> The cost of gas (including) overheads supplied to customers but not billed at year end is estimated and treated as a prepayment in accordance with the principle of matching costs and revenue in each accounting period.

Required

Why do the profit and loss statements of AGL not include revenue accrued in respect of gas consumed after each customer's last reading date for each respective financial year and the costs associated with the delivery of gas supplied but not billed at each year end?

16.12 *Jo Polimeni seeks your advice*

Southern Growers (SG) Pty Ltd owns and operates a chicken growing farm under a contractual agreement with Prime Chickens (PC) Ltd, a national producer and distributor of frozen chickens. PC contracts with over 100 chicken farm operators across the country. In the case of SG, PC delivers approximately 120 000 few-day-old chicks to SG on regular eight-week cycles and also supplies all the chicken feed required to fatten the chickens in accordance with strict feed specifications. After approximately seven weeks, the chickens fattened by SG are collected by PC and slaughtered at PC's processing plant for immediate delivery to retail outlets. SG cleans the growing sheds and conducts the required maintenance during the following week in preparation for the arrival of the next batch of chicks. Throughout the fattening process, the chickens remain under the ownership of PC.

For its services, SG is paid at nominated contract rates based on the average weight of chickens collected for slaughter. PC makes such payments almost immediately on clearing the sheds and, in the past, SG has recognised revenue on receipt of cash.

A director of SG, Jo Polimeni, seeks your advice as the company's potential new accountant. Jo wishes to ensure SG adheres to recognised accounting. A second-year undergraduate student majoring in accounting at a local university has informed Jo of the need to account for chickens on hand as an asset. The student had stated that 'this asset should be recognised in the accounts at each balance date and stated at nominated contract rates based on the average weight of a representative sample of chickens'.

This notion appealed to Jo who believed chicken fattening was the key process undertaken by SG and that the company's accounts, prepared on a monthly basis for management purposes, should reflect actual growing performance. Jo now seeks your views on this idea.

Required

(a) Advise Jo on appropriate accounting policy selection for SG given the alternatives presented. Justify your recommendations.

(b) Irrespective of your response to (a), outline the implications for financial statement analysis of implementing the policies advocated by Jo.

16.13 *Revenue recognition at Gillette Co*

Gillette Co announced in September 1998 that it expected to record 'dismal' quarterly earnings. The *Herald International Tribune* of 30 September 1998 carried a story titled 'Gillette Issues Warning, Analysts Say "Too Late"' by Dana Canedy. In the story, Alfred Zeien, the chairman and chief executive officer of Gillette, was quoted as calling it a 'very poor quarter we'd like to forget' and indicated several factors for the results.

The article reported these factors as follows:

First, the company's strategy to accelerate the introduction of its Mach 3 shaving system resulted in huge one-time costs. At the same time, Mr Zeien said, as consumers have been stocking up on the new razor, which was sold with at least a month's worth of blades, many have not yet had to purchase replacements. In addition, economic instability in some countries has hurt wholesale demand overseas.

Required

Suggest a revenue recognition policy for Gillette based on the extract from the above-detailed press report and outline the implications of this policy on quarterly profits when new shaving systems are launched.

16.14 *Frequent Flyer programs*

The following article titled 'Impact of Frequent Flyers Compels Program Revision' by James Ott appeared in *Aviation Week & Space Technology*, 11 April 1988 (pp. 130–31).

Frequent flyer programs are due for significant change as a result of proposed standards that airlines will adopt to account for accumulated and future mileage benefits in an airline's financial statements.

The perceived effects of ballooning frequent flyer programs on airline earnings also are pressuring airline officials to restrict program benefits and lessen their financial impact.

Airline accountants have been advised by their peers on the Accounting Standards Executive Committee of the American Institute of Certified Public Accountants to adopt new accounting methods including:

- A deferred revenue method to reflect actual use of mileage benefits at a future time.
- A requirement that airlines in some way account for the large backlog of accumulated mileage benefits that have been awarded from the various programs.

In each case, the accounting methods will have an effect on earnings, taking 'the bloom off the frequent flyer rose', according to a top official at the Air Transport Association.

Seat availability

Since the start of the frequent flyer programs seven years ago, airlines have considered mileage benefits on an incremental cost basis that has shown little or no effect on financial statements. The method has allowed airlines to regard the use of a free ticket earned through mileage benefits as filling an empty seat on an airplane.

At a time of medium load factors in the 50–60 per cent range, the accounting method was regarded as valid. Sufficient seats were available for a program of mileage awards to be implemented without displacing a large number of fare-paying passengers. Thus, a passenger redeeming a travel award was basically considered a non-revenue passenger.

The new triple mileage programs begun this year that offer three times actual miles for qualified frequent flyer club members are causing a re-evaluation of the accounting process among professional accountants.

One accountant close to task force activities said that the triple mileage provision has changed the nature of frequent flyer programs. Multiplication of mileage credits by the triple mileage provision is greatly increasing the backlog of unredeemed travel awards and increasing the chances that the holder of a free ticket will displace a fare-paying passenger, affecting airline costs.

'Frequent flyer programs, which began as a way of building brand loyalty, have become a form of price cutting, and price cutting among a group of similar companies is easily and always matched,' Candace Browning, airline analyst for Wertheim Schroder & Co., New York, said.

Redemption of frequent flyer benefits can significantly displace fare-paying passengers when an airline achieves a 65 per cent load factor, according to Browning. She estimates that US airlines will operate at an average load factor of approximately 61 per cent in 1988, which will still lead to displacing about 10 per cent of the fare-paying passengers.

She refers to frequent flyer programs as 'self-propagating monsters' with an off-balance sheet liability of more than $1 billion, and expects airlines to keep the programs but reduce award benefits.

The first change in accounting standards—use of the deferred revenue method—was recommended by the Institute's Task Force on Airlines, whose members are accountants working for airline auditing companies. Under this change, the airline would allocate a portion of the revenue from ticket sales to a future time when a frequent flyer is able to use the mileage benefits.

Revenue spreading

The change would spread out the revenue to the flights that are now considered non-revenue.

The Accounting Standards Executive Committee concurred with the task force on adoption of the deferred revenue method, but the committee asked the task force to take into account the accumulated mileage benefits as well. The task force is expected to respond to the committee with a set of recommended practices by early summer.

The effects of the triple mileage award will continue throughout 1988, and redemption of mileage awards can occur years from now in most programs. Airlines have required passengers to qualify for triple mileage by flying in the first quarter, which ended March 31. Continental and Eastern airlines have extended the qualification privilege to some of their OnePass members if they manage to fly at least twice on one or the other airline before May 15.

Triple mileage benefits will be accorded to all qualified members for every flight taken this year.

Delta Air Lines introduced the triple mileage provision that requires the passenger to purchase the airline ticket with an American Express card. Delta officials defend the triple mileage program as a competitive stroke against the 'affinity' credit cards introduced last year by United and American airlines that award one mile for every $1 spent using the credit cards.

The major carriers have matched the Delta provision but allowed for other ways of payment and have required that qualifying flying take place in the first quarter.

Delta has added 700 000 members to its frequent flyer club, 150 000 of whom came from other frequent flyer clubs, according to W. W. Hawkins, Delta senior vice-president of marketing. Hawkins contends the triple mileage has aided Delta's average yield per passenger mile since most of the qualifying flying was done by business flyers wanting to qualify for triple mileage benefits while paying full fare.

Robert Oppenlander, Delta's chief financial officer, said the triple mileage program would not harm Delta financially and that as a promotion it would end within the year.

Not everyone agrees

Other airlines are taking a different view. In general, the carriers have been concerned about the growing backlog of mileage awards for some time (*AW & ST*, January 4, p. 74). In a recent publication of United Airlines, new chairman Stephen Wolf said, 'The triple mileage offer is not a mistake, it is a disaster.'

A United official said the airline plans shortly to 'return to the original objective' of frequent flyer programs and will reward passengers who are frequent travellers on the carrier. A restructuring of United's Mileage Plus program is under study. American Airlines has set aside two special periods, in spring and in fall, for its frequent flyer members to use travel awards at reduced mileage requirements.

ESTIMATED COST OF TRIPLE MILES

Airlines	1987 Market share	Cost of triple mileage ($million)	Dilution per share	1988 Estimated EPS*	Dilution as a per cent of 1988 EPS*
American	17.1%	$ 17.1	$0.28	$2.20	13%
Delta	13.8	13.8	0.28	3.50	8
Northwest	7.8	7.8	0.26	3.00	9
Pan Am	7.8	7.8	0.06	−1.00	−
TWA	9.8	9.8	0.32	1.50	21
Texas Air	19.7	19.7	0.47	−2.70	−
United	16.7	16.7	0.78	5.36	15
USAir	7.3	7.3	0.17	4.00	4
Total	100.0	100.0			

Estimate of costs is $100 million a year if each benefit mile were to be redeemed.

* Earnings per share
Source: Wertheim Schroder

Required

(a) Evaluate the appropriateness of the 'deferred revenue method' described in the article in accounting for the benefits to members of frequent flyer programs.

(b) How is the proportion of revenue to be deferred ascertained in such cases?

(c) What alternative methods of accounting may be adopted in accounting for the benefits arising under such programs?

(d) What might be the impact on organisational functioning of introducing a method to account for the benefits arising under frequent flyer programs?

CHAPTER 17
Liabilities

Introduction

The first part of this chapter deals with the definition and recognition of liabilities. The issues of definition and recognition are separated in this discussion because each raises problems of importance for the reporting of liabilities. Following this discussion, consideration is given to techniques of measurement that are relevant to liabilities. In particular, measurement issues associated with debentures and leases are discussed.

There are a number of unsettled issues in relation to liabilities. Often the decision to record a liability is made because an asset is to be recognised on the other side of the accounting equation, or because an expense should be recorded or because some item of revenue should be deferred. The release of accounting concepts statements addressing liabilities has provided guidance in accounting for liabilities. However, the definition, recognition and measurement of liabilities are issues which continue to arouse controversy.

The definition of liabilities

Nature of liabilities

It may seem logical to regard liabilities simply as legal debts or legal obligations. These descriptions would cover, for example, bank overdrafts, mortgages, wages payable and accounts payable. Some items that are recorded as liabilities, however, are not legal debts if a debt is given its usual legal definition of 'a sum of money due from one person to another'.

The provision for taxation payable is recorded as a liability before the legal debt is assessed, and dividends payable are reported as liabilities before they are ratified at meetings of shareholders. Liabilities also include other provisions for future payments assumed to be related to the activities of the current and past periods but for which there is some uncertainty about the amount to be paid. Provisions are made for future warranty service, even though no legal debt will be established unless the product requires warranty service. These liabilities are not legal debts at the present time.

Since liabilities are not necessarily legal debts, a broader definition of liabilities is required. The IASC *Framework* provides the following definition of a liability:

A *liability* is a present obligation of the enterprise arising from past events, the settlement of which is expected to result in an outflow from the enterprise of resources embodying economic benefits.[1]

Liabilities are similarly defined in SAC 4 in Australia:

'Liabilities' are the future sacrifices of economic benefits that the entity is presently obliged to make to other entities as a result of past transactions or other past events.[2]

The essential characteristics of a liability are the existence of a present obligation and the requirement that the obligation is settled in the future through the disposition of economic resources. We now discuss each of these characteristics in more detail. In doing so, we draw on the liability definition and recognition criteria in the IASC *Framework*, and on the assumptions and principles of the theoretical framework developed in Chapter 6.

---

1 International Accounting Standards Committee, 'Framework for the Preparation and Presentation of Financial Statements', *International Accounting Standards 1997*, IASC, London, 1997, para. 49(b).

2 Australian Accounting Standards Board and Public Sector Accounting Standards Board, Statement of Accounting Concepts (SAC) 4, 'Definition and Recognition of the Elements of Financial Statements', Australian Accounting Research Foundation, 1995, para. 48.

Existence of a present obligation

A liability must result from a past transaction or other event. It must be a present obligation and not be dependent on the occurrence of a future event. Most obligations recorded as liabilities are legally enforceable. These obligations either stem directly from a legal contract or are imposed by an authorised body or statute.

Although most obligations that fall within the definition of liability are legally enforceable, obligations may also be equitable or constructive. An equitable obligation is governed by social or moral sanctions or custom rather than by legal sanction. It is an obligation to do what an entity considers ought to be done in the situation rather than what the entity is required to do on legal grounds.[3] Hence ethical considerations arise in the recognition of liabilities.

For example, an entity may have a policy based on moral and social considerations to make good any defects in its goods or services even when these defects are discovered after the legally imposed warranty period has expired. Hence, in relation to goods and services supplied by the entity, an estimate will be made of the costs involved in honouring this policy. This estimated amount would represent an equitable obligation and would be recorded as a liability, 'provision for non-warranty service and repairs', or similar title. In accordance with the matching concept, the corresponding debit entry would be to an account titled 'estimated non-warranty service and repairs expense'. This would allow recognition that these expected future outlays comprise part of the total costs incurred in generating revenue from the supply of goods and services in the current period. When the entity fulfils a claim for repairs outside the warranty period, the cost of the repairs is debited to the provision account, since the entity is extinguishing, in part, a previously recorded liability.

In practice, we may find that an entity does not distinguish in its accounts between its legal obligations and the equitable obligations associated with service or product defects discovered after sale. Hence, a liability account provision for warranty commitments may include amounts that represent both equitable and legal obligations.

Another liability that may be partly an equitable obligation and partly a legal one is a provision for environmental restoration. For example, legislation might impose certain minimum requirements for environmental restoration on mining companies and on public sector entities concerned with the construction of roads, dams and other major infrastructure. The more environmentally conscious of these entities might, however, adopt a policy of restoring the environment to a level above the legally required minimum. The entry to record the legal and equitable obligation in relation to restoration would be a debit to estimated restoration costs and a credit to provision for restoration costs. In the example given, this entry would be made each period during which the entity was involved in mineral extraction or infrastructure construction. In accordance with the matching principle, this ensures that each period takes a fair share of the final cost of the restoration. When the restoration is finally undertaken it would be recorded as a credit to cash or payables, reflecting the cost of the restoration, and a debit to provision for restoration, reflecting the extinguishment of the liability as the restoration work is carried out.

In addition to legal and equitable obligations, constructive obligations may also qualify as liabilities. A constructive obligation is created, inferred or construed from the facts in a particular situation, rather than contracted by agreement with another entity or imposed by government.[4] A common example of a constructive obligation is the practice whereby Australian companies record in their end-of-year financial statements a proposed final dividend as a current liability. Legally the company is not bound to pay the dividend until it is ratified by its shareholders at the annual general meeting and, hence, at the time the liability is initially recorded in the financial statements, a legal obligation does not exist. However, the established practice of directors proposing a final dividend, which is later ratified by

---

[3] ibid., para. 55.

[4] ibid., para. 56.

shareholders and then paid by directors in the following period, allows the existence of an obligation to be inferred or construed at the time the financial statements are being prepared.

Some companies record provisions in the liability section of their balance sheet that do not appear to satisfy the formal definition of a liability. Examples include provisions for overhauls and provisions for repairs and renewals of major equipment in relation to work to be undertaken in the future.[5] In neither case does the entity have a present obligation to an external party. Such an obligation would only arise in the future when the overhaul or repair work was undertaken. Only then would the entity have a present obligation to sacrifice economic resources to an external party.

Case 17.1 provides two contexts in which provisions were recognised as liabilities. It presents the opportunity to evaluate whether these provisions, based on the information disclosed, satisfy the typical definition of liabilities found in accounting concepts statements.

Case 17.1 SAS Ltd and Adelaide Brighton Ltd

SAS Ltd (Scandinavian Airlines System) reported the following accounting policy note on 'maintenance costs' in its 1997 Annual Report:

> Routine aircraft maintenance and repairs are charged to income [i.e. revenue] as incurred. Accrual accounting is carried out for future external costs for heavy maintenance including engine maintenance of aircraft of the MD-80 and MD-90 type. This maintenance is carried out on average every tenth year and the annual provision per aircraft is MSEK 1.5 [i.e. Swedish Kroner]. Provisions for future engine maintenance are made for Boeing 767s and provisions for future maintenance costs are made for Fokker F-50s.

Provisions for aircraft maintenance were not shown as a separate item in the SAS financial statements for the years ended 31 December 1996 and 1997.

Adelaide Brighton Ltd, whose core business is cement, lime and related products and technologies, included the following accounting policy note on 'provision for workers compensation' in its 1997 Annual Report:

> Provision is made for estimated amounts outstanding on existing claims and an assessment of unreported accidents for which the economic entity may become liable.

The provision for workers compensation was shown as a current liability at $487 000 in the consolidated balance sheet as at 30 June 1997. This represents a reduction from $3.1 million as at 30 June 1996.

Discuss whether the provisions recognised in these two instances satisfy the commonly-advocated definition of liabilities.

Obligations must be settled in the future through the disposition of economic resources

An essential characteristic of a liability is that satisfaction of the obligation requires sacrifice of economic resources by the entity. This characteristic follows from the assumption that accounting is concerned with economic resources and the claims of 'owners' and 'creditors' on those resources. Here we are concerned with 'creditors' claims'.

---

[5] ibid., para. 60.

The settlement of a present obligation can occur in many different ways. The IASC *Framework* provides the following examples of different ways to satisfy the claims of other parties:

(a) payment of cash;
(b) transfer of other assets;
(c) provision of services;
(d) replacement of that obligation with another obligation; or
(e) conversion of the obligation to equity.

An obligation may also be extinguished by other means, such as a creditor waiving or forfeiting its rights (para. 62).

A claim for warranty service, for example, will require the entity to sacrifice resources such as employee time and spare parts to meet that claim. Similarly, an obligation to a creditor who is also a debtor of the entity may be settled by offsetting the two amounts.

The rules for the identification and recognition of revenue also provide instances in which liabilities are not discharged by the payment of cash. When a deposit is received for work to be performed in the future, the amount received is recorded initially as a credit to a liability account, unearned revenue, and as a debit to cash. The liability is discharged and the revenue earned by the performance of the service. At this time a debit entry is made to the unearned revenue account and a corresponding credit is made to a revenue account.

As noted earlier, the obligation to dispose of economic resources in the future may be a legal, equitable or constructive obligation. In Australia, SAC 4 notes that an obligation comprises a liability when the obligation is such that the legal, social, political or economic consequences of failing to honour the obligation leave the entity with little, if any, discretion to avoid the disposition of economic benefits to another entity.[6]

The recognition of liabilities

Having identified the essential characteristics of a liability, attention is now turned to the tests for the recognition of liabilities in the financial statements. Recognition refers to the decision to include or exclude the liability from the face of the balance sheet.

The IASC *Framework* provides the following tests:

An item that meets the definition of an element should be recognised if:
(a) it is probable that any future economic benefit associated with the item will flow to or from the enterprise; and
(b) the item has a cost or value that can be measured with reliability (para. 83).

Especially in connection with liabilities the IASC *Framework* states:

A liability is recognised in the balance sheet when it is probable that an outflow of resources embodying economic benefits will result from the settlement of a present obligation and the amount at which the settlement will take place can be measured reliably (para. 91).

The term 'probable' means that the chance of the disposition of economic benefits occurring is *more* likely rather than *less* likely. That is, there exists a greater than 50 per cent chance of the disposition taking place.

---

6 ibid., para. 61.

The second liability recognition test can be broken into two parts. The first part is that the amount of consideration should be known or capable of close estimation. The second is that the identity of the other party, or the group concerned, should be known. Satisfaction of both parts is necessary to ensure verifiability. Unless the amount of the obligation can be estimated, and unless the claimant, or the potential group of claimants, is known, it is not possible to provide sufficient evidence to support a verifiable measurement of the obligation. Moreover, an inability to estimate the amount or to nominate the creditor suggests that further events have yet to occur before an obligation exists.

It is not required that the amount payable be known exactly, or that the name of the specific claimant be known; merely that the class to which the claimant belongs is known. This flexibility is required to ensure compatibility with the rules for expense recognition. In accordance with the matching concept, all expenses incurred in the earning of revenue should be recognised in the period in which the revenue is reported. Since it is not necessary that expenses be paid in the period of recognition, accruals are recorded for an obligation to pay wages, rent and so forth in future periods if the services are received in the current period.

However, as noted earlier, the concept of matching also reaches into vaguer areas such as warranty (and non-warranty) commitments arising from sales of the current period. Another example is long-service leave. During the current period employees may accumulate entitlements towards long-service leave. Many organisations in Australia, for example, grant three months of leave after every 10 years of service. This future commitment is related to every year of service by the employee and it is usual to recognise some of the future payments as an expense in each year of service, or after an arbitrary period of say five years service, rather than recognise a large expense in the year the leave is actually taken. Again, the logical credit entry for this provision is a liability account for future long-service leave payments. Accrued holiday pay and superannuation provisions are similarly regarded. When an employee takes long-service leave a credit entry is made in the cash account and a debit entry in the provision for long-service leave account to reflect a reduction in the liability.

A strict set of criteria for liabilities that insisted on exact knowledge of the amounts payable on these items and the names of those to whom payment should be made would cause all of the above estimates to be omitted. For example, it is not known at present who will claim warranty service and for what amount. The exact amount to be paid for long-service leave is also unknown as employees may leave before they have served the requisite 10 years and general wage levels usually change over time. Similarly, it would not be possible to record an exact liability for taxation since the amount will not have been assessed at balance date.

Executory contracts

Although in general legal debts constitute liabilities, the case of *executory contracts* requires special consideration. An executory contract is one in which the performance depends on some future action by both parties to the contract. With a contract for goods to be purchased in the future, for example, the purchaser must pay and the seller must deliver the goods and ownership documents to the buyer. Until then, the contract is executory. Future work remains to be carried out by the seller and non-performance of that work would breach the contract. An agreement to sell land, subject to the clearance of the land by the seller, is another example of an executory contract. Employment agreements are also executory contracts. The employee agrees to provide specified services over time and the employer agrees to pay wages and salary in return for those services.

Accepted practice in relation to executory contracts is that no obligation exists on the part of the purchaser of goods and services to pay the seller (as creditor) until the creditor has performed services for the purchaser. Hence, no liability is recorded until this time. As services are performed a liability is recognised. For example, as an employee provides services to the entity, a liability to pay for those services accrues. Similarly, under a contract for the construction of equipment or a building, the purchaser would usually recognise a liability to pay the contractor as stages of the work are completed and progress payments fall due under the terms of the contract.

The IASC *Framework* considers the application of the liability (and asset or expense) recognition criteria to executory contracts. That is, obligations (liabilities) and related rights (assets) or expenses under contractual agreements should be recognised at the earliest stage at which the recognition criteria for a liability and also an asset or an expense are satisfied (para. 91).

Application of the liability (and asset or expense) recognition criteria to executory contracts focuses on the degree of certainty associated with the obligations (and rights or expenses) under the contract at its inception. For many executory contracts assessments of whether the items meet the liability (and asset or expense) recognition criteria will be difficult to make. We are dealing with the likelihood of future benefits eventuating or not and future obligations becoming enforceable: is it probable or is it not? Such decisions are not always straightforward and will involve the use of judgement within the specific organisational context.

Contingent liabilities

The first test for the recognition of a liability requires that it be a *probable* future commitment. At balance date, other *possible* commitments to outlay resources might also exist that are not sufficiently definite at present to be reported as liabilities in the balance sheet. Where it is possible that an entity will be obliged to outlay resources in the future, but is not currently obligated to do so, and the amounts are potentially material, the disclosure of the existence of these *contingent liabilities* in a note to the balance sheet is generally accepted practice. They are not entered into the accounts and, therefore, are not incorporated in the calculation of an entity's net assets based on balance sheet figures.

A contingent liability is an obligation that will occur in the future *only* if some particular event occurs. A company may have guaranteed the repayment of a loan to one of its subsidiaries and, should the subsidiary default, the loan will become repayable by the company. Similarly, a company that is the defendant in a lawsuit should disclose the likely obligation in the event that the judgement is unfavourable. These cases should be distinguished from situations in which an obligation already exists, such as a judgement involving damages and costs having been determined in a lawsuit. Such an obligation should be recognised in the balance sheet as a liability.

A second test is required to limit the scope of a contingent liability and to remain faithful to the principles of the historical cost system. The contingent liability must relate to a past event. An obligation expected to arise when a purchase contract is signed in the future is not a contingent liability.

Case 17.2 Coca-Cola Amatil Ltd

The *Australian* of 9 September 1998 carried a story titled 'Cole flattens Coke with $50m damages suit' by Michael McGuire. The article is reproduced below.

> Coca-Cola Amatil will defend vigorously a massive damages claim lodged by sacked chief executive Norb Cole, who alleges chairman Dean Wills and the US-based parent company interfered in his running of the local soft drink bottler.
>
> Mr Cole, who was dismissed in March, has filed six claims totalling more than $50 million, according to documents filed yesterday in the NSW Supreme Court. The claims are:

- Three of $16.9 million each alleging breach of contract.
- One of $2 million alleging injury to reputation.
- One of $1.89 million for lost salary.
- One of $2.13 million for his 'total cost of employment' multiplied by 24 months.

CCA and Atlanta-based The Coca-Cola Co. (CCC) are fighting all claims related to Mr Cole's dismissal.

In a separate document, CCA revealed Mr Cole had received a termination payout of more than $1 million and would continue to receive a monthly pension of $US13 397.47 ($22 000) to be paid by CCA and CCC.

Texas-based Mr Cole, who was not in court, is pursuing his claim through law firm Atanaskovic Hartnell.

He is endeavouring to have clauses retrospectively inserted in his employment contract, which he alleges was 'unfair, harsh and unconscionable'. Among the clauses sought is one specifying Mr Cole be re-employed by CCC for three years in the event of being sacked by CCA for any reason apart from embezzlement.

When Mr Cole's sacking was announced by Mr Wills, it coincided with CCA breaking itself in separate Asian and European companies.

Mr Cole was allegedly approached by CCC in February 1994 about becoming joint chief executive at CCA and signed a five-year contract in May that year. But Mr Cole said he was not allowed to carry out his duties fully.

'The first respondent (CCA) did not give the applicant (Mr Cole) the full opportunity to carry out his duties by reason of interference by Mr Wills and by representatives of the second respondent (CCC)', the affidavit says.

The affidavit also alleges Mr Cole was given no indication by CCA at any time that his performance was unsatisfactory. Mr Cole alleged an employee of CCC threatened to have him sacked by CCA and that the parent company also helped CCA find his eventual replacement in David Kennedy.

'The above facts lead to the overall strong inference that the second respondent (CCC) played a role in the termination of the applicant's employment with the first respondent', the affidavit says.

Mr Wills has always defended the independence of CCA, which is 40 per cent owned by CCC (p. 41).

Consider how CCA will treat this legal action from an accounting perspective.

The measurement of liabilities

The measurement, or valuation, of a liability is made difficult because the payments will be made in the future. As the future is uncertain, these payments may not be met at their due dates, liquidation may ensue or the company might decide to pay off the obligation ahead of time. These events could affect the amount to be repaid.

Another aspect to be considered is the timing of the payment. A payment of $1000 due next week places a greater burden on present resources than an identical payment to be made in one year's time since, in the latter case, the company may earn interest on the cash during that year. The valuation of a liability must therefore take into account the interest element inherent in future payments.

Future interest commitments

The discussion in this section requires a knowledge of techniques of discounting future cash flows and the calculation of present values. A brief discussion of this topic is contained in Appendix C.

Suppose a company issues debentures with a par value of $10 000, at an interest rate of 15 per cent per annum, repayable at the end of three years. The total repayment commitment is $14 500 ($10 000 + (3 × $1500)) but, for accounting purposes, the liability is valued at the capital sum repayable of $10 000 and the future interest commitments are omitted. Interest commitments are not regarded as liabilities until the accounting period in which the interest falls due for payment.

Given the conventional asset and liability definition and recognition criteria, a case could be made for recording a liability for the $4500 future interest commitments when the debentures are issued. The $4500 would represent a present obligation to pay a total of $4500 over a three-year period according to the terms of the debenture agreement. A corresponding asset could also be recorded representing future benefits arising from the right to use the debenture-holders' monies for three years. The right would expire over time as the entity had the use of the borrowed money and at the end of each year $1500 would be transferred from the asset account to an interest expense account to be matched against the period's revenue.

Accountants typically do not observe this treatment of interest under a loan or debenture agreement. In practice the liability is recorded at the amount of the loan or debenture raised and an interest liability and interest expense are recorded as the interest falls due and payable. Hence, in this example a debenture liability for $10 000 would be recorded at the beginning of the agreement. Interest expense of $1500 would be recognised at the end of each year and a corresponding liability for interest payable recorded as a current liability until the interest is paid. The measurement of liabilities is an important consideration here.

The task of liability measurement in practice is one of separating the capital from the interest elements inherent in future payment commitments. Segregating these components may be achieved by valuing the liability as the present value of the future payments stream, using as a discount rate the effective rate of interest ruling at the time the debentures were issued.

In the above example, $10 000 was borrowed from debenture-holders for three years at 15 per cent annual interest. Hence, the company has to meet a stream of cash flows of $1500 each year for three years, and to repay $10 000 at the end of the three-year period. The present value of the debenture liability consists of the present value of a stream of three cash outflows of $1500 paid at the end of years 1, 2 and 3, plus the present value of a cash outflow of $10 000 at the end of year 3. Using the present-value tables in Appendix C, the calculations may be summarised as:

Table	Present value of liability	Yr 1	Cash payments Yr 2	Yr 3
A.4	$ 3 425	$1500	$1500	$ 1 500
A.2	6 575			10 000
	10 000			

The debenture liability is recorded at the amount of the present value of the future cash outflows associated with the liability. Since the actual interest payments are in line with the discount rate of 15 per cent, the present value is the capital sum raised. This is straightforward, but it demonstrates that the present value is equivalent to the debt before future interest payments are considered.

Debentures may be issued at a premium or a discount but the discussion of these topics is beyond the scope of this book.

The irrelevance of possible future actions

The second valuation issue is whether to make allowance for uncertain future events such as early repayment. The discussion on debentures has assumed that the debt will be held until maturity but, in reality, any of the following might occur:

1. The company might seek to repay the debentures early and perhaps incur a penalty for payment before maturity.
2. The company might repurchase the debentures on the open market at an amount other than face value. If the market price falls, due to rising interest rates or other factors, the company might seek to gain by repurchasing the debentures for less than their issue price.
3. The company may enter liquidation.

In determining whether these possible actions should influence the valuation of a liability under historical cost accounting, reference is made again to the assumptions of the historical cost system. Continuity is the most relevant assumption since it states that in the absence of evidence to the contrary, the entity is viewed as remaining in operation indefinitely. In normal circumstances, then, liquidation of the company (possibility 3) is not contemplated and in conventional accounting this implies that asset and liability values in a forced liquidation may be ignored.

The list of possibilities can be reduced further if the continuity assumption also implies that each individual liability will be repaid only at maturity and again current practice with respect to assets seems consistent with this assumption. A depreciating asset, for example, may have no immediate resale value, yet it is carried in the books at unexpired cost on the assumption that it will be held for the duration of its planned life. For liabilities, then, it may be assumed that each debt issue will be held to maturity and that values arising from early repayment or repurchase may be ignored.

It seems, then, that liabilities should be valued on the assumption that they will be held until maturity. Accordingly, it is appropriate to value the stipulated future cash payment flows at discounted present value. Thus, liabilities are valued at the present value of those commitments.

The discount rate

The last issue to resolve is the rate at which to discount the future payments. Following the tenets of the historical cost system, the interest rate should be the effective rate at the date the debt was issued and this rate should remain unchanged throughout the period of the loan. In the above example, the rate of interest implicit in the loan was the effective interest rate payable on the debt at the date of issue.

The rate that equates the current quoted price of debt with the future payment commitments may fluctuate over time, due mainly to market forces. In a historical cost system these changes are usually ignored, just as changes in asset prices are ignored. Continuity implies that year-to-year fluctuations in interest rates are irrelevant when the debt is assumed to be held to maturity.

Where no interest rate is stated, it is necessary to infer one. If, for example, a used motor car was purchased for the payment of $200 per month for 30 months, the total repayment will be $6000, but what is the interest component? If no interest rate is stated, the best approximation is to find the cash price of the car. If it could be purchased outright for $4200, then the $1800 difference can be regarded as the future interest commitment.

A specific application of the recognition and measurement principles: leases

Most liabilities will present few problems, since the face values and present values at the date of issue will be identical. However, the present value approach does provide a means of valuing liabilities that have no obvious face value, or in which the interest and capital repayments are intertwined. These include accounts payable, where discounts for early settlement are offered. Here the net price method might be applied to show the liability as net of discount receivable, which is in reality future interest payable if the payment is delayed and the discount is lost.

Leases take many forms, but all consist of rental agreements whereby periodic payments are made by a lessee for the use of an asset that remains, in law, the property of the owner or lessor. In some cases the lessee has a right of purchase at the end of the lease, perhaps for a small additional payment. In such cases the lease is, in substance, a purchase financed by a loan to be repaid in instalments. Leases of this type are known as *finance leases*.

Where the purpose of the lease is not to gain ownership or long-term use but merely to obtain the use of an asset for a short period of time, an *operating lease* exists. Operating leases are essentially rental agreements, such as the rent of a building for two years or the hire of heavy equipment for a particular project. In a world of rapid technological change, it is common to lease computers rather than to purchase them and be left within a short period of time with outmoded equipment. Accounting standards on leases typically prescribe practice for both finance and operating leases.[7]

Operating leases are accounted for as with any rental agreement. Rental payments are charged to expense in the periods in which they are due. If the current period's lease rental is unpaid, it will appear as a liability. Future rental payments are not recorded as a liability, and an asset itself does not appear in the lessee's balance sheet.

A finance lease agreement is based on the understanding that the lessee will make periodic lease payments with the aim of eventually acquiring the asset or at least acquiring the right to the use of the leased property's future economic benefits. This changes the substance of the lease from a short-term rental agreement to a 'purchase'. If the asset were purchased outright, the entire cost would appear as an asset and the capital amount repayable as a liability. It is argued that if the lease is in effect a purchase, the future payments should be capitalised to produce the same balance sheet as would appear if a purchase had been recorded.

The following example contrasts the effect of treating a finance lease as a rental agreement with the effect of treating it as a purchase.

Example: *A finance lease*

A Ltd agreed to lease a piece of equipment to B Ltd for three years in return for an annual lease payment of $3880 payable at the end of each year. At the end of the third year ownership of the equipment would pass to B Ltd for the payment of one cent. The equipment could be purchased today for $10 000 cash and has an expected life of five years.

The rental approach

Under this approach the lease is treated in B Ltd's books as a rental contract, as if it were an operating lease, as follows:

---

7 See International Accounting Standard (IAS) 17, 'Accounting for Leases', and Australian Accounting Standards Board, AASB 1008, 'Accounting for Leases'.

		ANNUAL RENTAL REPAYMENTS		
		December		
		20X0	20X1	20X2
DR	Lease expense	$3 880	$3 880	$3 880
CR	Cash	3 880	3 880	3 880

No record is made in the accounts of B Ltd's right to the use of the equipment for three years or of its legal obligation under the agreement to make an annual payment of $3880 for three years.

The purchase approach

If the lease is regarded as essentially a 'purchase' under a finance lease arrangement, future lease obligations are capitalised as if the asset had been purchased. The asset and the liability relating to the lease are valued at the present value of the future payments, discounted at the rate of interest implicit in the lease contract.[8] Since no discount rate is identified in the example, the cash price is used as a measure of the present value.

The finance lease in this example is equivalent to a three-year $10 000 loan obtained by B Ltd to purchase the equipment, where the loan is repayable in three annual instalments of $3880.

The rate of interest implicit in the loan and lease agreement is 8 per cent, since $10 000 is the present value of an annuity of $3880 for three years discounted at 8 per cent.

The principal sum repayable ($10 000) is recorded as a liability, while the interest component ($1640) of the total amount payable ($11 640) is recognised progressively as an interest expense over the three years. The calculations are:

	SCHEDULE OF LEASE REPAYMENTS UNDER THE PURCHASE APPROACH			
Year	Lease liability at beginning	Lease payment	Interest (8% of beg. bal.)	Principal repaid
1	$10 000	$ 3 880	$ 800	$ 3 080
2	6 920	3 880	554	3 326
3	3 594	3 880	286	3 594
		11 640	1640	10 000

The appropriate entries for B Ltd would be:

January 20X0	DR	Leased equipment	$10 000		
	CR	Lease liability	10 000		
			December		
			20X0	20X1	20X2
	DR	Lease liability	$3080	$3 326	$3 594
	DR	Interest expense	800	554	286
	CR	Cash	3880	3 880	3 880

---

[8] IAS 17 defines 'the rate implicit in the lease' as: 'the discount rate that, at the inception of the lease, causes the aggregate present value of (a) the minimum lease payments, from the standpoint of the lessor; and (b) the unguaranteed residual value to be equal to the fair value of the leased asset, net of any grants and tax credits receivable by the lessor'.

The remaining item to be considered is the amortisation of the lease asset. Assuming straight-line amortisation, the annual charge will be based on the allocation of $10 000 over a five-year life resulting in an amortisation charge of $2000 per year.

EFFECT ON FINANCIAL STATEMENTS	Rental approach	Purchase approach
Profit and loss statement extract for year 1		
Lease rental expense	$3880	–
Interest expense	–	$ 800
Amortisation expense	–	2 000
Balance sheet extract at end of year 1		
Assets		
Leased asset	–	$10 000
less Accumulated amortisation	–	2 000
	–	8 000
Liabilities		
Lease liability	–	6 920

Comparison of approaches

The profit and loss statements and balance sheets under each approach appear above. If the rental method is used, the company is not forced to reveal its payment commitments and the full extent of the assets under its control. This keeping of liabilities off the face of the balance sheet, or 'off-balance-sheet' financing, improves the debt/equity ratio and increases the EBIT/total assets formula. Accounting standards on leases require that the purchase approach be used for recording finance leases. The variety of lease arrangements makes it very difficult in practice to distinguish finance from operating leases. Some firms have restructured their lease agreements as operating leases in order to avoid bringing a lease asset and liability on to the balance sheet.

Ethical issues

'We have done well this year,' one of the company directors concludes on examining a draft copy of the company's financial statements. 'Perhaps even too well! Maybe we should have a look at some of the provision accounts and check whether we can increase them. If we increase the provision for doubtful debts beyond what is really necessary on the basis of current expectations we can build up some slack for future years.' One of the other directors looks puzzled and asks, 'But shouldn't the charges to the provision account reflect the activities and circumstances of the period? I think we should ask the accountant for some advice.'

What advice would you give the directors?

Summary

In the modern commercial world it is not adequate to define liabilities simply as legal debts. Liabilities may be more broadly described as obligations to make payments or render services in the future as a result of a past transaction or other event. While a clearly specified definition of a liability and agreed recognition criteria for liabilities are intended to facilitate full and consistent reporting of liabilities across entities, in practice a certain amount of judgement is involved in their implementation. As elucidated in this chapter, the definition, recognition and measurement of liabilities remain contentious topics in accounting.

Review exercises

Discussion questions

17.1 'Liabilities are legal debts.' Is this an adequate definition of liabilities for our contemporary commercial environment?

17.2 Discuss briefly the essential characteristics of a liability. Use examples to illustrate your answer.

17.3 What is an executory contract? Why is its accounting treatment controversial?

17.4 The application of the matching principle may sometimes result in the recording of a liability. Why is this? Use examples to illustrate your answer.

17.5 Explain the main differences between each of the following and provide examples to illustrate your answer:

    (a) a contingent liability and a current liability

    (b) a liability and a legal debt

    (c) a finance lease and an operating lease

17.6 Outline the main arguments for and against presenting the lessee's obligation under a finance lease on the balance sheet.

17.7 Refer to the ethical issue on page 613. How would you advise the directors?

Problems

17.8 *Identifying liabilities: annual report exercise*

Obtain a recent annual report for two large publicly listed companies. Look through the reports for examples of current liabilities, non-current liabilities, contractual commitments and contingent liabilities. Study the items listed, analysing their relative significance to the overall financial position of the firm. Explain clearly the differences between the four items.

17.9 *Identifying liabilities*

    1. Kim Jessie is the accountant for Taliana Co. Ltd. How would you advise Jessie to account for the following items in the financial statements as at 31 December 20X2?

        (a) Gooch and Sons is suing Taliana Co. Ltd for breach of contract. Jessie thinks Gooch and Sons will probably lose the case.

        (b) A new financial controller was appointed on 1 October 20X2 under a three-year contract that specifies an annual salary of $70 000 for each of the three years. The contract can be terminated by three months notice from either party.

        (c) Taliana Co. Ltd signed a contract with a building firm to construct a new warehouse at a cost of $100 000. Construction will commence in January 20X3.

        (d) A subsidiary of Taliana Co. Ltd has just been placed in receivership. In September 20X1 Taliana Co. Ltd signed as guarantor for a $50 000 two-year loan to the subsidiary from a finance company.

(e) Based on personal experience in previous years, the service department manager expects warranty claims against sales made during 20X2 to amount to $30 000.

(f) On 15 October 20X2 Taliana Co. Ltd issued (at par value of $100) 20 000 five-year debentures carrying an interest rate of 15 per cent per annum.

2. Which of the following items meet the tests for a liability?

(a) Debentures maturing in three years time
(b) Provision for warranty claims
(c) Accounts payable
(d) Holiday pay accrued
(e) Reserve for replacement of equipment
(f) Provision for deferred maintenance and repairs
(g) Provision for long-service leave
(h) Accumulated depreciation
(i) Reserve for environmental protection
(j) Provision for taxation

17.10 *Leasing*

1. On 1 January 20X1 Poppy Ltd agreed to lease a piece of equipment to Violet Ltd for three years in return for an annual lease payment of $5000 at the end of each year. At the end of the third year ownership of the equipment will pass to Violet Ltd for the payment of one cent. The equipment could be purchased today for $12 435 cash and has an expected life of three years. Violet Ltd uses straight-line depreciation. The interest rate implicit in the lease agreement is 10 per cent per annum. Prepare journal entries for 20X1, assuming Violet Ltd desires to recognise a lease asset and liability in its balance sheet.

2. On 1 January 20X0 Stony Ltd leased a piece of equipment from Point Ltd. The lease contract provided for five annual payments (at the end of each year) of $2000 each. The interest rate implicit in the lease was 20 per cent per annum and the cash purchase price of the equipment on 1 January 20X0 was $6000. Stony Ltd estimated that the economic life of the equipment was five years and the end-of-life salvage value was nil.

    Prepare journal entries for the years 20X0 and 20X1 assuming Stony Ltd desires to recognise the leased asset and liability in its balance sheet. Assume also that for accounting purposes the leased equipment is amortised over its economic life of five years.

3. On 1 January 20X0 Murray Ltd leased a tour bus from Darling Ltd for six years. The terms of the lease required six annual payments (at the end of each year) of $8000. The cash purchase price of the bus on 1 January 20X0 was $30 000. Murray Ltd estimated that the economic life of the bus was six years and that it would have a zero residual value. The interest rate implicit in the lease agreement was 15.25 per cent per annum.

    (a) Assuming that Murray Ltd wishes to recognise the leased asset and liability in its balance sheet, calculate the annual interest expense and the reduction in lease obligation at the end of each year.

(b) Prepare journal entries for the years ending 31 December 20X0 and 20X4. The company uses straight-line amortisation for its leases.

4. On 1 January 20X6 R. J. Earthmoving signed a lease contract to lease a bobcat, with annual lease payments of $8000 per annum for three years, after which ownership of the machine would pass to R. J. Earthmoving. The company's accountant has advised that the correct treatment of the lease is to recognise both the company's rights to use the bobcat and its legal obligation to make the annual repayments. The cash purchase price of the bobcat on 1 January 20X6 was $18 265 and its expected life was three years with $4000 estimated salvage value. The accountant has recommended the use of reducing-balance amortisation to match the expected pattern of service benefits.

Prepare journal entries for 20X6.

Case studies

17.11 *Is there a 'correct' policy?*

In researching the topic of provisions for a first-year accounting assignment, a student came across two company annual reports whose stated accounting policies with respect to provisions for service warranties were different. The policy of the first company was stated as:

> Provision is made, out of revenue, for the estimated costs of future warranty service on all products sold but still under warranty at balance date. The amount of the provision is based on the company's experience with service warranty claims over the past three years.

The other company's annual report stated the following policy:

> Costs of servicing products under warranty are charged against revenue as they are paid or provided for on the basis of known claims. In addition, a general provision is made to cover costs of an exceptional nature including costs which relate to any claims on products which are outside their warranty periods.

Concerned at this apparent diversity of practice, the student has asked you to advise the 'correct' policy.

Required

Advise the student using any relevant accounting pronouncements to justify your views.

17.12 *RGC Ltd*

RGC Ltd is a diversified Australia-based mining company. Its 1997 Annual Report included the following accounting policy note on 'rehabilitation and restoration costs':

> Expenditures relating to ongoing rehabilitation and restoration programs are provided for or charged to costs of production as incurred. Other restoration costs are accrued over the life of the mine. The estimated costs are reassessed on a regular basis and changes are dealt with progressively.
>
> The expenditures and accruals include costs of labour, materials and equipment required to rehabilitate disturbed areas, to remove the plant and equipment and for subsequent environmental monitoring. The estimates are not discounted and are based on current costs, legislative and community requirements and technology.

As at 30 June 1997 the provision for rehabilitation and site restoration recorded in the consolidated financial statements (note 15) totalled $48.5 million (current $13.9 million; non-current $34.6 million).

Required

Evaluate whether the provision for rehabilitation and site restoration satisfies the typical definition of liabilities found in accounting concepts statements. Justify your view.

17.13 *Accounting for the millennium bug*

The *Australian* of 2 July 1998 carried a feature story titled 'Curing the Bug Bite'. The article is reproduced in part below:

The millennium bug is already biting into balance sheets

JOHN MACLEAY reckons up the bill so far

After a last-minute flurry, most of Australia's 1205 listed companies have made the June 30 deadline to report on their year 2000 programs.

Surprisingly, what they had to report was mostly good news—and that is precisely what worries the experts, who warn that corporate Australia may still not be taking the threat seriously enough.

Some say the final cost of eradicating the bug, that pesky computer glitch that threatens to send every date-sensitive computer program haywire on New Year's Eve 1999, could be up to double what we expect now.

In the three months to June 30 every listed company in Australia was required to lodge a report with the stock exchange disclosing its potential bug problems, what it was doing about them and how much it thought it would cost.

As of yesterday, 1130 listed companies had complied with the stock exchange requirements and only 75 had failed to comply, all of them relatively small companies.

The disclosures have yielded some useful data. For example, we now know that the top 100 companies are facing a bill in excess of $2 billion, with the banks, Telstra and Qantas accounting for almost a third of that, or $647 million.

However, given the nature of the problem, with many companies finding remediation and testing are taking longer than first anticipated, experts believe the total cost is likely to rise over the next 18 months.

Last November, Coopers & Lybrand estimated the total cost to fix the problem would be at least $5 billion. New estimates put the figure closer to $10 billion.

Telstra tops the list of big bug spenders, with a budget of $500 million, reflecting its size and crucial position within the national electronic network.

National Australia Bank, with a budget of $255 million, comes in at second place, followed by ANZ at $183 million and AMP, which, although it is spending $135 million, cannot guarantee that it will be ready before the December 31 1999 deadline.

Other big spenders include Qantas ($147 million), Commonwealth Bank ($115 million) and Coles Myer ($90 million).

Judging by their disclosures, other top 50 companies have a very minor exposure; those that are budgeting to spend $5 million or less include Tabcorp, AGL, John Fairfax and Southcorp ...

Counting the cost

Company	Approx. Cost ($m)	Company	Approx. Cost ($m)
1. News Corp	not given	26 Colonial	40
2. NAB	255	27. GPT	3
3. BHP	85	28. Pioneer	9.2
4. AMP	135	29. PBL	2
5. Westpac	57	30. Boral	40
6. Telstra	500	31. AGL	1
7. ANZ	183	32. Dairy Farm	not given
8. Commonwealth	115	33. Comalco	<10
9. BTR	not given	34. Wesfarmers	5–7.5
10. Rio Tinto	not given	35. Santos	18
11. CC Amatil	30	36. Southcorp	2.2
12. Lend Lease	55	37. Mayne	18
13. Coles Myer	90	38. GoodmanFielder	10
14. Brambles	not given	39. Qantas	147
15. Foster's	25.8	40. PacDun	15.43
16. Woolworths	30	41. Tabcorp	2
17. Nat Mutual	36	42. Carter Holt	not given
18. WMC	30	43. Orica	120
19. Woodside	20	44. GIO	6
20. St George	50	45. North	15
21. CSR	20+	46. Macquarie Bank	10
22. Amcor	17.5	47. Fairfax	3.8
23. Placer Dome	not given	48. Normandy	not given
24. Westfield Holdings	not given	49. Brierley	not given
25. Westfield Trust	not given	50. QBE	not given

Required

Discuss whether the estimated costs shown in the table meet the formal definition of a liability and the criteria for recognition in the financial statements. Should the liability definition be changed if you believe the estimated costs do not meet the definition? Justify your view.

17.14 *Jo Polimeni seeks your advice again*

Turn to case study 16.12 and read the case again. Jo Polimeni requests your advice on another matter. He has believed for some time that stores of chicken feed held at balance date should be valued and stated as a liability because they constitute a loan in kind rather than cash from PC. SG's former accountant evidently believed the recognition of a liability 'was simply not worth the bother' and had encouraged Jo to drop the idea. Jo was not convinced by what he perceived as a lack of attention to detail.

Required

Advise Jo on the appropriateness of changing the accounting policy on stores of chicken feed. Justify your recommendation.

17.15 *Pioneer International Ltd*

Pioneer International Ltd is a global building materials company. Note 24 to the financial statements published in the company's 1997 Annual Report pertained to 'contingent liabilities'. The note included particulars on 'other contingent liabilities' as follows:

> There are contingent liabilities arising in the normal course of business in respect of legal actions or other claims being undertaken by or against the parent entity and its controlled entities. The total maximum amount for which these entities could become liable is not considered material.

Required

Discuss the role of materiality in applying recognition criteria.

17.16 *Burns Philp & Company Ltd*

The 1996 Annual Report of Burns Philp & Company Ltd stated that 'Burns Philp is a significant global food ingredients company with operations in 30 countries and customers in over 60 countries'. An item 'commitments and contingent liabilities' appeared below the 'total shareholders' equity and convertible notes' totals in the balance sheets published in this annual report. Of four notes (19, 20, 27, 30) pertaining to this item, note 27 stated:

Burns Philp Trustee Company Limited and Estate Mortgage Trusts
In 1938, Burns, Philp & Company Limited established a separate trustee company, Burns Philp Trustee Company Limited (now called BPTC Limited (In Liquidation) (BPTC)). Because of the special nature of BPTC's activities and the particular responsibilities imposed on trustee companies by Acts of Parliament, Burns, Philp & Company Limited established a separate and independent board of directors to oversee BPTC. Burns, Philp & Company Limited oversaw the broad direction and general policies of its subsidiary, but had no involvement in the discharge of the day to day trustee responsibilities.

In 1983 BPTC became trustee for the first of the six Estate Mortgage Trusts (now called Meridian Investment Trusts) (the Trusts). Early in 1990 the Trusts ran into severe liquidity problems and the manager of these trusts, Estate Mortgage Managers Limited, began to get into serious difficulties in maintaining the stability of the operations, due to abnormally high calls for repayment of investors' funds. As a result of these problems BPTC removed the manager of the Trusts and carried out certain functions of the Trusts' management pending the appointment of a new trust manager.

By the end of September 1990, BPTC was involved in defending a large number of legal actions brought by borrowers and lenders relating to the Trusts. In addition, the Corporate Affairs Commission of NSW had announced a private inquiry into BPTC's actions in relation to the Trusts.

In October 1990 a newly appointed board of directors of BPTC determined, after a due diligence investigation, that the appropriate course of action was to seek the appointment of a provisional liquidator to BPTC. The Trusts continue operations under the management of Global Funds Management (NSW) Limited with J. W. Murphy and P. B. Allen (Murphy & Allen) of Arthur Andersen, Chartered Accountants, acting as court-appointed trustees.

In October 1991 the new trustees commenced legal action seeking compensation for breaches of trust and other alleged breaches from BPTC and a number of other parties including Burns, Philp & Company Limited. They have amended their statement of claim several times since then, removing or limiting a number of the claims made.

In 1993 the new trustees sought to have their rights to pursue certain claims (their 'standing') confirmed as a preliminary issue.

After several hearings, appeals and reformulations of the issues the Victorian Court of Appeal decided in 1995 that the questions of standing can only finally be determined once the facts have been established at trial. The effect of this outcome is that Murphy and Allen's standing to pursue several of the claims remains uncertain. It is thus possible that at the end of a long trial the Court will hold that the new trustees are not entitled to pursue those claims, and that for lack of standing to sue those claims will fail.

In 1994 the Court ordered that mediation take place under Sir Laurence Street. Mediation is a structured negotiation process to assist the parties to identify the matters really in dispute and to reach a settlement if possible. After extensive preparations formal mediation meetings were held in May 1996 but ended after several days of discussions, as the parties were unable to conclude a settlement.

The proceedings are being defended vigorously by the company. The hearing of the case together with related proceedings has been scheduled to start on 3 February 1997, and is estimated to continue for 9 to 12 months. At present the parties are engaged in pre-trial preparation, including the discovery and inspection of documents and assembly of witnesses' statements and experts' reports.

Since the claims against the company were first made, the company has obtained legal advice and has updated that advice regularly. During the last three years the legal advice has been provided by Clayton Utz and by Senior Counsel who maintain their advice that on the facts as known and the present state of the law, the claims against the company will fail.

The auditors of Burns, Philp & Company Limited, KPMG, have independently sought and obtained an opinion from another Senior Counsel in regard to the proceedings. The opinion concurs that the company has sound prospects of succeeding in resisting the claims which have been made against it.

The *Australian* of 22 July 1997 carried a story titled 'Burns to pay out $116m in Estate Mortgage battle' by Michael McGuire. The article began thus:

The influence of new major shareholder Graeme Hart is believed to be behind the sudden decision by Burns Philp to strike a $116 million settlement with the former Estate Mortgage group after a seven-year legal battle.

Burns Philp announced yesterday it would pay the trustees of Meridian Investment Trust, formerly Estate Mortgage, $90 million in cash and would issue the trust 12 million five-year convertible notes at $2.20 a note.

The settlement comes despite the company's repeated denials of any responsibility for the Estate Mortgage collapse in April 1990, when the Burns Philp Trustee Co. (BPTC) was its trustee.

The 1997 Annual Report of Burns Philp & Company Ltd explained the details of the settlement made. Note 27, in part, stated:

The settlement, as it meets all the claims against the company in respect of the Estate Mortgage case, eliminates the risk of a more substantial award being made against the company. The directors considered the settlement was in the best interests of the company and its shareholders and received legal advice recommending it.

© The Australian

Required

Discuss the judgements made by the management of Burns Philp and the associated implications for financial statement analysis in applying the conventional criteria for the recognition of liabilities and expenses in connection with the 'Estate Mortgage' battle.

CHAPTER 18
Appraisal of the historical cost system

Introduction

This chapter reviews the historical cost system of accounting and evaluates how well the system fulfils its role. The historical cost system is reviewed against the objectives of accounting discussed in earlier chapters. The provision of relevant and reliable information for stewardship (accountability) purposes and for the evaluation of an entity's financial performance and financial stability are identified as key objectives of accounting. The historical cost system is evaluated in terms of its successes and failures in fulfilling these objectives.

The historical cost system is analysed first in its pure form and then in the modified form found in practice. In discussing the modified historical cost system, or conventional accounting, particular attention is given to the seemingly conflicting philosophies of conservatism, which tends to state asset values below their historical cost, and revaluations, which restate asset values above historical cost.

The evaluation of the historical cost system in this chapter provides the basis for an examination of alternative accounting systems in Chapter 19.

A detailed set of objectives for investors and creditors

The Australian *Corporations Law* requires all public companies and certain proprietary companies to have their annual financial statements audited. The auditor is required to determine whether the accounts comply with accounting standards, and whether they present a 'true and fair' view of the state of a company's affairs at balance date and the results of its operations for the financial year. However, the expression 'true and fair' is an undefined and ambiguous term that is subject to interpretation in practice.

There is no such thing as a single 'true' profit or value in accounting. Profit is calculated based on various underlying assumptions, and the profit figure therefore depends on the assumptions made. The usefulness of a particular theory of profit depends on the extent to which it satisfies the needs of accounting information user groups. These needs depend on the decisions that individual users must make and the information required for those decisions. Thus:

useful accounting information ➡ decision models ➡ decision

The conceptual framework regards relevance and reliability as two of the primary qualities that make accounting information useful for making decisions. The assumptions in traditional accounting designed to promote relevance and reliability have been discussed in detail in Chapters 6 and 14, but now that the sections on financial analysis and valuation have explored more fully the decision processes of investors and creditors, a more comprehensive statement may be made of the sub-objectives of accounting.

To promote relevance, investors and creditors require information on stewardship, financial performance and financial stability. To promote reliability, investors require information that is verifiable, free from bias and a faithful representation of transactions and other events.

Relevance

Stewardship

A shareholder has rights as a part-owner of the enterprise to vote on the appointment and replacement of the directors. The directors, and the managers they appoint, are entrusted with resources and must, as a minimum, account for their 'stewardship' over those resources. This has been the traditional function of accounting. Stewardship includes not only the custody of an organisation's resources, but also their efficient and profitable use and protection from the unfavourable impact of factors in the economy such as inflation and technological and social change. This is all part of 'accountability', or making managers responsible for resources under their control and for providing information to enable users to make informed decisions.

Owners and creditors alike desire to know whether, as a result of these activities, capital has been maintained. Dividends may be paid only out of profits, so the dividend, or profit distribution, decision requires knowledge of the surplus after capital is maintained. Since creditors' claims on the assets of a company rank ahead of shareholders' claims in the event of liquidation, maintenance of capital provides protection for creditors. Shareholders and creditors need information relating to the assets in which their funds have been invested. To meet these requirements, accounting reports must disclose:

1. what management has done with the cash entrusted to it
2. the resources held and the claims thereon
3. the surplus (if any) after capital has been maintained

These traditional objectives of accounting are met, in general, by the preparation of a cash flow statement (for 1), a balance sheet (for 2) and a profit and loss statement (for 1 and 3).

Performance evaluation

The modern investor is interested in stewardship reports but often for a different purpose. Rather than exercising the rights of a shareholder to appoint directors, ratify dividends and so forth, the investor may prefer to leave these functions to the major shareholders. If the company's management is disappointing, the investor's reaction may be to sell the shares.

This leads to a different decision model based on a comparison of the price to be obtained by selling a share with an investor's estimate of its 'value'. The estimated value of a share depends on assessments of the future cash flows that will flow from ownership, in the form of dividends and the proceeds from eventual sale of the share.

The investor must predict the future dividends to be received from the company. The factors influencing dividends include the availability of cash and the priority of investment projects financed through retained earnings, but the ultimate source of cash returns to investors must be profitable trading. Hence, the investor must predict the future profits of the enterprise. Without profits, there can be no dividends, and losses will eventually erode the capital base to the extent that commitments cannot be met.

The earning of future profits is dependent on effective management and often the best guide to management is the trend in past profits. In financial analysis, an organisation's reported profit is considered in relation to some standard, such as the amount invested in the entity, so that a further objective of accounting must be to provide reliable measures of the funds invested in the enterprise by owners and creditors.

Analysts seek to rank organisations according to their performances and to compare current with previous profit results to determine the trend in performance. It should, therefore, be an objective of accounting to provide measures of profit and investment that facilitate valid comparisons between organisations (inter-entity comparisons) and over time (inter-temporal comparisons).

These accounting measures will supply only part of the required information. Investors will also refer to other information sources, such as trade reports, economic statistics and advice from financial analysts. Nevertheless, the financial statements provide the record of past achievement upon which to base future expectations. In addition, financial analysts also rely on accounting information in forming their opinion.

What of the needs of creditors? Again, the discussion of financial analysis revealed that they share with investors the need to predict the amounts and timing of cash flows to the enterprise so as to ascertain the likelihood of repayment of their debt. Performance evaluation assists in this task. Creditors differ from investors, however, in that their concern is with the adequacy of the return to meet fixed commitments (interest and debt repayment) rather than with achieving the maximum return.

Financial stability

In general, high-income prospects are associated with high risk, because parties dealing with a risky entity require higher returns to compensate them for accepting high risks. Speculative mining ventures, for example, are regarded as high-risk investments. Risk analysis relies upon measures designed to assess financial stability, such as the working capital ratio and the debt/equity ratio. A company that is financially unstable is fundamentally riskier no matter what investment prospects it might offer.

In the analysis of long-term stability, users are concerned with information relating to the way in which an entity is financed, whether it be by short-term or long-term debt or owners' equity, and with the principal repayment commitments relating to borrowings. For the immediate future, users are concerned to discover whether short-term assets comfortably exceed short-term commitments.

As well as relying on balance sheet analysis, risk assessment is largely dependent on profit analysis. An organisation's capacity to meet interest commitments depends on its profitability, and, although current debt may be repaid out of the proceeds of further borrowings, current profit is an important factor affecting the organisation's ability to repay debt.

Reliability

The qualitative characteristic of reliability requires information to be free from material error and bias. Reliability implies that accounting information can be relied on for decision-making purposes as it faithfully represents transactions and other events. The principle of 'substance over form' is also a component of reliability. This notion means that the genuine economic nature and effect of transactions and other events should be reported, irrespective of their legal form.

Reliability implies the appropriate measurement of revenues and expenses and the appropriate valuation of assets and liabilities in accordance with the above principles. In this respect, a major component of reliability is verifiability, which is the extent to which independent experts arrive at the same measurement or conclusion from an examination of any given data. Accordingly, the measurement and valuation assumptions and rules adopted in preparing the financial statements should be verifiable, free from material error and bias and faithfully represent the substance of transactions and other events.

The pure historical cost system

The historical cost system in its pure form values assets at their original buying prices established by actual transactions with other entities. The original purchase transactions provide objective evidence on which to base the valuations. The valuations of individual assets in an organisation's financial statements are not changed from original purchase cost under a pure historical cost system, irrespective of changes in the general price level or the specific prices of the relevant assets.

Relevance to stewardship

Stewardship, or accountability, refers to management's responsibility for the safekeeping, protection and the efficient utilisation of the organisation's assets. The historical cost concept of profit gives management the responsibility for maintaining intact the original monetary amount contributed by shareholders and invested in the net assets—that is, the historical monetary capital.

Assume a retailer commences the accounting period by buying 10 units of inventory for $200 each (total cost $2000), and then sells them all for $3500. According to the historical cost system, $2000 must be recovered from revenue to maintain 'money' capital before any profit may be recognised. The profit, calculated as the excess of sales revenue over the historical cost of the inventory sold, amounts to $1500. A dividend of $1500 could be paid in the knowledge that the original money capital of the organisation has been maintained.

Suppose, however, that when the inventory is replaced the retailer finds that it now costs $240 per unit rather than $200 per unit. It then becomes clear that the $2000 capital recovered is insufficient to provide capital to maintain the ongoing operations of the business. The owner will be forced to contribute $400 additional capital to maintain the stock of inventory. One may well argue that there is more to capital maintenance than simply maintaining the original monetary amount invested, and that the increasing costs of maintaining the 'physical' capital should be considered.

This example contrasts two views of profit and capital that depend on how the commercial (that is, profit-making) venture is defined. Under the traditional view, the venture begins and ends with cash and the profit of $1500 arises naturally from that assumption.

cash		inventory		cash
$2000	➡	10 units	➡	$3500
				Profit = $1500

The opposing view is that, in a continuing venture, the capital consists not of cash but of the various assets the enterprise must hold to conduct its continuing operations. Under this view, profit appears as only $1100.

Inventory		cash		inventory + cash
10 units	➡	$3500	➡	10 units + $1100*
				Profit = $1100

(*10 units cost $2400 to replace, leaving $1100)

The $400 by which the two profit figures differ represents the amount that must be retained in the business to replace the inventory. A business that maintains only the original money capital in times of rising factor prices, especially in periods of high general inflation, may find itself unable to maintain its stock of assets without additional contributions of capital.

The alleged inadequacies of the historical cost capital maintenance concept may also be argued from the shareholder's viewpoint. A shareholder who contributes $2000 to a company when the price of goods that constitute the investor's personal consumption are rising at 10 per cent annually may not recognise a growth in the investment unless the annual growth in the equity in the company exceeds 10 per cent. Suppose the company reported that the initial $2000 had grown to $2050 by the end of the year and that the historical cost profit was therefore $50. An investor arguing in purchasing power terms could assert that, rather than earning a profit, a loss of $150 had occurred. To maintain the purchasing power of the investment, the owners' equity should have grown by 10 per cent to $2200. Instead, it has grown to only $2050.

This may be illustrated as:

	Initial wealth	Ending wealth	Profit (Loss)
In dollars	$2000	$2050	$50
In equivalent purchasing power (at year end)	2200	2050	(150)

If management is to account for its stewardship in terms of maintaining and increasing the net economic resources of the enterprise, the above arguments suggest that the historical cost system of accounting is an inadequate basis for stewardship reporting. Measurement of capital in original cost terms will maintain neither the physical assets of the entity nor the purchasing power of the shareholder's investment.

If the assets of a business are eroded by paying as dividends the full amount of the declared historical cost profits, creditors' security will also be eroded. The constant diminution of an organisation's operating capability in this way has important implications for its prospects of survival in the longer term. In turn, this could have deleterious effects for organisations in an economic and social context. Financial institutions and other creditors could become less willing to lend to organisations, and organisations themselves could find it more difficult to operate within the economy.

Further, outside bodies whose decisions affect organisations, such as trade unions and a prices surveillance authority, consider the profitability of organisations in making decisions. Overstatement of profits under inflationary conditions may result in decisions being made that are unduly onerous for an organisation. For example, trade unions may argue for wage rises based on overstated profits in financial statements, or governments may reduce certain benefits or advantages for those companies.

Relevance to performance evaluation

The criticism that under inflationary conditions historical cost profit may result in an overstatement of the profit from a capital maintenance viewpoint is relevant also to performance evaluation. Critics argue that expenses should be increased from the historical cost to the current cost of replacing the resources consumed, so as to provide a measure of profit in terms of contemporary prices.

The failure to account in current terms makes comparison between entities difficult. Consider the case of New Ltd and Old Ltd. They are in identical businesses and enjoy identical operating results except that Old Ltd was established in 20X1 and New Ltd was established in 20X5. At the end of 20X5 details of assets held were as follows:

		Old Ltd	New Ltd
Equipment:	Purchased in	20X1	20X5
	Cost	$2000	$10 000
	Life	10 years	10 years
	Depreciation	straight-line	straight-line
Inventory:	Units at beginning of 20X5	700	700
	Cost price/unit	$1.00	$1.25

In both companies all inventory was sold during 19X5 for $2 per unit and no replacements were made.

PROFIT AND LOSS STATEMENTS: OLD LTD AND NEW LTD for year ended 20X5		
	Old Ltd	New Ltd
Sales revenue	$1400	$1400
less Cost of sales	700	875
Depreciation expense	200	1000
	900	1875
Net profit (loss)	$ 500	$ (475)

Under the above scenario, Old Ltd recorded a profit and New Ltd incurred a loss. From the analyst's perspective, however, the question may be which company performed better in the 20X5 financial year. Old Ltd earned the higher profit simply because it had been trading longer and purchased its resources in periods when prices were lower. In contemporary terms, there is no difference between the performance of either company in 20X5.

The difference in recorded performance becomes greater if the return on investment calculation is used, since Old Ltd will have a lower investment cost, the denominator of the return on investment ratio, than New Ltd, for identical assets. If analysts seek to compare entities on the basis of current performance alone, then in inflationary times historical cost results will usually be biased in favour of older or mature organisations.

Another way in which it is claimed that historical cost accounting distorts profit measurement is in the failure of the system to account for gains when prices of assets rise. According to the historical cost criteria for revenue recognition, no gain may be recognised until an exchange transaction occurs to substantiate the gain. Price changes above or below historical cost result in 'holding' gains and losses, so called because they occur as assets are held over time rather than through productive activities. They are also sometimes called 'capital' gains and losses, but this term will be avoided to prevent confusion with other uses of the word 'capital'.

To illustrate, suppose two companies with no debt, Quicksale Ltd and Slowsale Ltd, invest their total capital, of $80 000 each, on 1 July 20X1 in identical blocks of land located next to each other in the same street. On 30 June 20X2 either block may be sold for $110 000. On that day Quicksale Ltd sells its block and reinvests the proceeds in another identical block in the same street. Slowsale Ltd retains its original block on the basis of different expectations of future land prices.

Quicksale Ltd's balance sheet at 30 June 20X2 shows land of $110 000 and owners' equity of $110 000, consisting of $80 000 originally invested capital plus retained profits for the year of $30 000. Slowsale Ltd's balance sheet at 30 June 20X2 comprises land of $80 000 and capital of $80 000. Slowsale shows no retained profit for the year.

Using the traditional terminology, historical cost accounting is said to recognise profit from a holding gain only when it is 'realised' rather than when the change in the price of the asset occurs. When unrealised holding gains occur, it is difficult to assess the performance of an entity and its management. Quicksale and Slowsale began and ended the year in identical positions, but their financial reports disclose different results solely due to a transaction by Quicksale, which placed it, in substance, in no better position at the end of the year.

The failure to report holding gains when they occur is claimed to impede the comparison of a single entity's performance over time (inter-temporal comparability) and the comparison between organisations at one point in time (inter-entity comparability).

Changing price levels create a further difficulty in comparing the performance of organisations over time. In inflationary periods an entity would need to increase annual profits in money terms by an amount sufficient to cover the rate of inflation, otherwise the purchasing power of its profits will be falling in real terms. For example, assume an entity's profit for the previous financial year amounted to $10 000 and the annual rate of inflation is 10 per cent. That entity's current year profit would need to amount to $11 000 to have the same general purchasing power as the prior year's profit of $10 000. The distorting effects of inflation on the trend in profits will be removed only if the dollar is indexed for inflation, so that it becomes a measure of constant purchasing power. On the contrary side, it may be argued that analysts are well aware of the effects of inflation and can and do make their own adjustments to historical cost reports.

Relevance to financial stability

The problems of capital maintenance and performance measurement discussed above also influence the assessment of financial stability. A long-established firm that seems to be maintaining capital intact, and which is disclosing large profits following conventional accounting techniques, may be enjoying the benefits of past cost levels (for example as Old Ltd was in the earlier example), but may be unable to meet the current replacement costs necessary to remain in business. Measures of interest and dividend cover may therefore be overly optimistic.

The analyst also uses the balance sheet in the assessment of the long-term and short-term liquidity of the enterprise. Long-run solvency may be measured by the debt/equity ratio and many debenture trust deeds specify limits on the size of this ratio as a condition for continuance of a debenture loan. This is referred to as a debt covenant. In such ratios, assets are valued predominantly at cost, when the relevant figure to assess the availability of cash to meet commitments would be the proceeds to be obtained from selling the entity's assets. The net realisable values, or market values, of assets would provide a better indication of the debt-paying ability of the enterprise at balance date, as the following example shows.

On 30 June 20X1, Misstatement Ltd had the following historical cost balance sheet:

BALANCE SHEET: MISSTATEMENT LTD			
Cash	$ 2 000	Mortgage	$16 000
Land (6 blocks @ $3000)	18 000	Paid-up capital	3 000
		Retained earnings	1 000
	$20 000		$20 000

It appears from this balance sheet that Misstatement Ltd is highly leveraged and hence risky, having a debt/total assets ratio of $16 000/$20 000 or 80 per cent (otherwise expressed as a debt/equity ratio of 400 per cent, calculated as $16 000/$4000).

Using current market (selling) prices and assuming each block of land to now be worth $8000, and recognising revenue as prices rise, the balance sheet at 30 June 20X1 would appear as follows:

BALANCE SHEET: MISSTATEMENT LTD			
Cash	$ 2 000	Mortgage	$16 000
Land (6 blocks @ $8000)	48 000	Paid-up capital	3 000
		Retained earnings	31 000
	$50 000		$50 000

The change affects both the land and the shareholders' funds, increasing the profit by $30 000 ($5000 × 6). The firm now appears less risky, having a debt/total assets ratio of 32 per cent (or a debt/equity ratio of 47 per cent). Furthermore, the higher profit would indicate a greater capacity for interest payments and debt repayment as profit is recognised each year.

Consider also the position where a company owns land that has a present resale value below cost. In these circumstances, which have occurred all too frequently in the past in respect of land held by development companies and long-term equity investment companies, the historical debt/total assets ratio is less than the market value debt/total assets ratio. Accounting regulators are now more vigilant in these matters. The relevant accounting standards now clearly require that a non-current asset shall be revalued downwards when its carrying amount is greater than its recoverable amount. In this situation the asset is to be revalued to its recoverable amount.[1] This requirement is, however, a modification to the pure historical cost system.

Another class of asset that confounds solvency analysis is the intangible asset, goodwill. In an historical cost balance sheet, the goodwill amount represents the cost of purchasing the goodwill. An organisation's own 'internally generated' goodwill is not recognised, even though it may be substantial. Since the objective of solvency analysis is to explore the worst eventuality, goodwill is regarded as likely to evaporate on liquidation of the organisation and is therefore disregarded. The same may be said of other intangible assets, such as research and development costs, trademarks and exploration expenditure. In practice, analysts tend to base their ratios on the tangible assets so as to avoid the 'softness' that intangible assets typically introduce in the figures. In fairness, it should be added that the proponents of alternatives to the historical cost system also have difficulty in valuing intangibles.[2]

Short-term liquidity assessment using the current, or working capital, ratio (current assets/current liabilities) is also affected by the method of valuation. Short-term monetary assets such as cash and accounts receivable are disclosed at estimated realisable values, but inventory is at cost. The current ratio attempts to match the expected inflows from assets that are to be liquidated during the year with the outflows to settle liabilities to be repaid over that period. The liabilities all appear at the amounts of the prospective outflows, but inventory will not unless it is reported at net realisable value. Allowing that selling prices will normally exceed cost, the current ratio consistently understates the expected inflows in comparison with expected outflows.

Reliability

The aforementioned weaknesses notwithstanding, the case for historical cost accounting rests on its reliability. It is characteristic of the system that all primary entries, those that increase net assets, must be supported by transactions. Current market value systems, which restate the values of assets to reflect their current market prices, depart from this test by introducing price changes not experienced directly by the entity through an external transaction.

Generally, some type of documentation will exist against which transactions can be verified. Such documents include invoices, receipts, contracts of sale, delivery dockets, cheque butts and transactions appearing in bank statements. Under current market value systems, however, accounting entries are required for unrealised gains and losses, which are not supported by external transactions.

Historical cost accounting also requires secondary reallocation entries to arrive at periodic profit, and reflection on these entries must place doubt on the verifiability of the outputs of the historical cost accounting system. Consider the need for future estimates in establishing depreciation rates, anticipating bad debts, providing for such items as long-service leave and warranty commitments, and in providing for items such as future mine-site rehabilitation. Consider also the assumptions underlying the treatment of exploration and drilling costs, research and development costs and computer software development costs as assets rather than expenses.

The impact of these secondary reallocations on historical cost values is considerable. The resulting balance sheet is not verifiable directly by external evidence. A computer, for example, appears on the balance sheet at unexpired cost (written-down value less accumulated depreciation), a value that has no reference to any external market price. Capitalised intangibles, such as purchased goodwill, are similarly valued at past purchase prices, which may have been partly written off using an arbitrary amortisation policy.

---

[1] Australian accounting standard AASB 1010, 'Accounting for the Revaluation of Non-Current Assets', 1996 and international accounting standard IAS 16, 'Property, Plant and Equipment', 1993.

[2] G. D. Carnegie and R. W. Gibson, 'The Evolution of Accounting Standards for Goodwill in the English-Language Countries Following APB Opinion No. 17 (1970)', *Advances in International Accounting*, Vol. 4, 1991, pp. 3–17.

Thus, although inputs to the historical cost system may be verifiable, the subjection of these costs to allocation on the basis of expectations of the future, and the creation of provisions for events not to be known until the future, means that the outputs of the system, such as residual asset values and expense allocations, are not verifiable by reference to evidence outside the entity regarding contemporary prices and conditions.

Benefits of the historical cost system

Despite the apparent weaknesses of the historical cost system, it is still the system most used throughout the world. Its persistence indicates that it has some positive features.

It is based on a simple capital maintenance concept, which is a necessary, if not a sufficient, basis for assessing management's stewardship performance. Suppose, for example, a person invests $10 000 in a firm. Although concerned with the likely return on that investment, the investor's first concern is that the $10 000 will not be misappropriated or otherwise eroded by losses. Anyone dealing with a firm expects that, before all else, the historical cost of the firm's capital will be maintained intact.

Similarly, maintenance of the historical cost of an entity's net assets means that creditors are protected to this extent. Legally, dividends may not be paid out of capital and, in determining what constitutes the capital of a company, courts have generally relied on the historical cost concept of capital.

Whichever system is used for external reporting, an entity must maintain historical financial records for internal administrative purposes. Trade debtors and trade creditors are collected and paid in terms of the transaction amount. Historical costs are necessary also for the efficient running of the organisation. Detailed historical cost records of labour, materials and overhead costs are necessary for identifying and acting upon variances between actual and budgeted costs.

The historical cost system has been widely used for many years and therefore cannot be lightly dismissed. The system's deficiencies discussed in the chapter have been recognised in practice and various modifications have been made to make the system more relevant.

The modified historical cost system

The historical cost system has been modified in practice in two major ways. The first involves the introduction of conservatism, or prudence, in certain circumstances, and the second is the practice of revaluing assets upwards without the existence of an external transaction. The two modifications are in obvious conflict, making it difficult to achieve a coherent framework of accounting in what is generally described as the modified historical cost system.

Influences on accounting practice

A number of parties are both influenced by and in turn influence accounting. External reporting, for example, is influenced by accounting standards, companies legislation, stock exchange listing requirements, and a variety of what might be called 'political' influences, such as public opinion, which might, for example, influence a company to report in detail on its expenditure for the public good. Further, external reporting is often influenced by taxation law.

At the same time, however, management indirectly influences accounting. The way in which management accounts to external parties determines the stock of presently used accounting principles and techniques, and so influences any formalising or modifying of these principles through the publication of accounting standards, as well as legislation related to accounting. Furthermore, all the factors influencing accounting interact with one another. For example, a spate of company crashes may cause public opinion to be critical of accounting reports which, in turn, may precipitate amendments or additions to stock exchange listing requirements, company law, accounting standards and even possibly taxation law.

One unfortunate, but perhaps inevitable, result of this pragmatic evolutionary process is that accounting has developed as a piecemeal set of practices that lack consistency with one another. The pure historical cost system, which does possess a certain degree of logical consistency, is generally not the system of accounting used in practice. Rather, it has been modified in an ad hoc way by the above-mentioned influences, largely to overcome its most serious limitations. Consequently, the 'modified' historical cost system, as used in practice, is not a logically consistent set of practices.

Conservatism

Most people exercise caution when faced with uncertainty. Accountants and managers are no exception. The future of any organisation is uncertain, and for this reason accountants have a propensity to adopt a conservative, even sometimes pessimistic, approach to preparing accounting reports on the present financial situation of an organisation and its results for the year.

When making the many subjective estimates required by the historical cost system, a conservative manager or accountant will generally choose the lowest feasible value for assets and revenue, and the highest for liabilities and expenses, thus tending to understate net assets and profit. The most common modifications to the pure historical cost system inspired by conservatism are the following:

- Holding losses. Although the pure historical cost system rules that holding gains may not be recognised until a sale is made, conservatism adds the condition that holding losses on short-term assets should be recognised as soon as the market price falls. The most common instance of this type of downward bias is the valuation of inventory according to the 'lower of cost or net realisable value' method. Stocks are written down when the expected resale value is below cost, but are not written up when resale value exceeds cost.
- Expenditures that will benefit future periods and which should therefore be capitalised are often expensed as they are incurred. Research and development costs and software development costs are often written off immediately, even when the likelihood exists that this expenditure will prove fruitful.
- Long-term intangible assets, such as goodwill, may be written off as soon as profits will absorb them, or over a shorter period of time than their expected beneficial life.
- Expenses and their associated provisions may be overestimated deliberately. Bad debts and allowances for doubtful debts, for example, may be inflated, thus understating net assets and profit. Depreciation charges may be accelerated by underestimating the expected lives of assets or by choosing low, even nominal, residual values.
- Liabilities may be overstated. Provisions for 'repairs' or 'contingencies' do not normally meet the tests for a liability because they are seldom associated with specific amounts expected to be paid to known parties. They are, rather, cautious estimates built into the system in case difficulties arise. Moreover, if there is a greater than 50 per cent chance of a contingent liability being incurred, such as lawsuit damages, the liability is provided for in the financial statements together with a charge for the associated expense. On the other hand, contingent assets (assets that may potentially arise, such as the possible recovery of damages in a lawsuit instigated by the organisation) are not usually reported.

Case 18.1 Inventory valuation

In addition to other assets, Yannagawa Ltd holds inventory of two products, products A and B. Inventory is valued at the lower of cost or net realisable value in Yannagawa's balance sheet as at 30 June 20X2.

The inventory of product A, a highly successful product which is sold at a 60 per cent mark-up on cost, is listed in the balance sheet at cost of $180 000. The inventory of product B, which had a total cost of $190 000 but which is beginning to become obsolete, has been written down to the directors' estimate of net realisable value of $80 000.

An extract from Yannagawa's balance sheet reveals the following balances at 30 June 20X2:

	$
Inventory —Product A	180 000
—Product B	80 000
	260 000

Discuss the appropriateness of the account balances for inventory for the purpose of presenting the financial position of Yannagawa Ltd as at 30 June 20X2.

Case 18.2 Software development and exploration costs

Agostini Software Ltd is a computer software development company. It has been involved in the development of general computer software and specialised computer programs for individual clients over the past 10 years. The company, with shareholders' equity of $2 500 000 at 30 June 20X4, incurs software development costs of approximately $400 000 per annum. Even though these development costs will provide future economic benefits, the company has an accounting policy of immediately expensing these costs to the profit and loss account.

Shiyan Mining Ltd is involved in the exploration and mining of gold, silver, nickel and zinc in Australia and South-east Asia. The company, with shareholders' equity of $3 500 000 at 30 June 20X4, has incurred exploration costs averaging approximately $500 000 per annum over the past seven years. Exploration costs are capitalised by Shiyan Mining as assets where exploration activities have not reached a stage that allows a reasonable assessment of whether economically recoverable reserves exist or where such exploration costs are expected to be recouped through successful development of the area. This accounting policy has resulted in the balance of the capitalised exploration costs (asset) account amounting to $1 750 000 in Shiyan Mining's balance sheet as at 30 June 20X4.

Comment on the accounting policies for software development and exploration costs adopted by Agostini Software and Shiyan Mining respectively from the viewpoint of an investor considering investing in these companies.

Claimed advantages of conservatism

Today, organisations operate in a volatile global environment which makes the future even less certain than it was previously. By stating net assets and profits conservatively, accountants believe they are partially protecting themselves and the organisation against this uncertainty. They are also mindful of the legal liability for negligence in reporting, which punishes an overstatement but never, it seems, a cautious statement.

A traditional view of the balance sheet is that the actual unstated financial position of an entity will normally be better than stated, but it should not be worse. The amounts by which the balance sheet understates the position that would be revealed by the pure historical cost system are known as 'secret' reserves. These should be contrasted with what may be called 'hidden reserves', which arise as the difference between historical cost values and market values, thus:

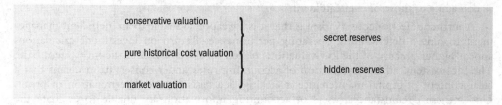

Secret reserves consist of such items as productive assets depreciated excessively, overstated allowances for doubtful debts, inventory written down unnecessarily below its historical cost, and liabilities that may never need to be paid, such as contingent liabilities. It might be suggested that this is to provide an 'inner strength' to be called upon in times of adversity and to provide a buffer against the uncertainty of the future.

The practice of conservatism also contributes to the large variety of alternative accounting rules that provide management with the means to manipulate profits. Secret reserves may be 'released' as the situation demands. An entity that has been accelerating its depreciation in good trading years, for example, is able to reduce the depreciation in poor years to maintain a desired trend in profit. Allowances for doubtful debts can also be adjusted downwards if they were previously excessive and if profits fall. The possibilities are many and derive from the fact that, since the total amount to be written off an asset is a finite amount, higher charges in earlier years will result in lower charges in later years.

Management may use a variety of alternative accounting rules to 'smooth' profits. By this means, the entity may appear to be more stable and less financially risky than it would otherwise appear. This could produce a higher value for its shares, which is particularly advantageous when the company requires further share capital. Moreover, it may lead to an improved credit rating and a lower interest cost on borrowed funds.

Conservatism is also thought to aid in overcoming the deficiencies in capital maintenance of the historical cost system. The overstatement of expenses under the modified historical cost system reduces profits and dividend payments, conserving funds in the organisation that may help to meet higher replacement costs. It should be noted, though, that eventually these overstated charges will be reversed and become understated charges, so the relief is only temporary.

Finally, the understatement of profit provides, to varying degrees, a measure of protection for the organisation against the demands of pressure groups such as trade unions.

Arguments against conservatism

A moment's reflection on the supposed advantages of conservatism will reveal an underlying theme of deliberate understatement that must deceive certain parties. In so far as conservatism leads to the smoothing of a trend, investors and creditors acting on reported information may be misled into investing in an apparently stable entity. On the other hand, the understatement of profits below pure historical cost levels may cause current and potential shareholders to underestimate the company's potential, or government committees concerned with levels of industry assistance to gain the impression that the organisation is in need of support when this may be far from the case.

A consequence of conservatism is that balance sheets can depart materially from market valuations and, historically, conservatively valued companies have been the subject of takeover bids. Astute 'predators' have discerned that the undisclosed market values of the assets of their 'victims' exceed the market values of shares in such companies. When an attractive takeover offer is made to the shareholders of the offeree company, the directors of the company may find it extremely difficult to explain to the shareholders that the conservative figures they have presented for years were in fact an understatement. As a consequence, shareholders may accept a takeover price below the current market value of the net assets. It seems that conservatism cuts both ways and that the consequences of understatement can be as damaging as those of overstatement.

A further defect of conservatism is that it is a weapon available to an inefficient management to hide a deteriorating operating performance. Return on investment calculations appear higher because of the low valuations placed on assets, which is the investment base. The inconsistent, ad hoc application of accounting rules under conservatism means that a clear concept of capital maintenance is lacking as a basis for the determination of profit. Under these circumstances, users of accounting information are unable to evaluate the extent to which management has satisfactorily performed the stewardship function of protecting the assets of an organisation. Performance measurement is similarly distorted, with expenses attributed to one period that might on more objective analysis be applied in another. Inter-entity and inter-temporal comparisons are made more difficult by the varying degrees of conservatism applied between entities and over time.

More objectionable still is the presumption that it is appropriate to deceive certain parties for the benefit of others. This contradicts the assumption of freedom from bias, which was cited as a quality that gives reliability to accounting.

The distortion cannot easily be corrected by the user. It cannot be assumed that profit is understated, since conservatism is merely one of the influences affecting profit and certain of the estimates may prove adequate. Moreover, when a choice of valuations must be made, it may be justifiable to choose the least favourable outcome when conditions are highly uncertain. This is different from an act of deliberate misstatement at an amount below any likely outcome. It therefore cannot be said that every conservative statement is made with the intention of deceiving the user.

Asset revaluation

The second major modification of the pure historical cost system is the practice of upward asset revaluation of long-term assets such as land and investments. Revaluation is now widely practised in Australia, the United Kingdom and New Zealand but is not permitted in the United States. Revaluations are undertaken ostensibly to overcome the deficiency of historical cost accounting that, in a period of rising prices, historical costs lose much of their relevance. In effect, holding gains are recognised before realisation, although the tests for revenue are not violated as the gain is credited to a reserve, thus:

DR Asset		
CR Asset revaluation reserve		

Hence, if, for example, a company's land was to be revalued in the accounts from $100 000 to $150 000, the entry would be:

DR Land	50 000	
CR Asset revaluation reserve		50 000

In this way, the land asset account is increased by $50 000 to $150 000 and an asset revaluation reserve, an equity account, is created. The asset revaluation reserve may be used for the issue of bonus shares in a firm, thus transforming the reserve into paid-up capital.

Is revaluation beneficial?

In principle, market value disclosures are desirable since persistence with long-outdated cost figures, including written-down cost figures, for assets that have appreciated considerably hides the asset backing of the company in contemporary prices. Current market prices are useful information for anyone making investment, credit and other decisions relating to a firm.

These advantages will exist, however, only when revaluations are consistently and universally applied. This is rarely the case. Some firms never revalue their assets, whereas others revalue every few years. More objectionable still is the practice of selective revaluation to offset the reduction in reported assets resulting from the writing down of other investments. Companies also use revaluation as a takeover defence, disclosing at the last minute the company's 'inner strength' to show that the takeover offer is unattractive.

Although the relevant accounting standards (AASB 1010 and IAS 16) have brought a greater sense of fairness to the way in which upward revaluations are to be undertaken, the standards still allow management considerable flexibility. For example, revaluations could be determined by independent valuers or by company directors, and there is a degree of flexibility in the timing of revaluations.

When viewed in conjunction with the flexibility of accounting rules afforded by conservatism, revaluation gives management the capacity to manipulate figures at will under the guise of presenting more relevant data. To be completely consistent, either a strict historical cost approach should be adopted or a complete current valuation system should be enforced.

Ad hoc asset revaluation practices reduce the usefulness of the balance sheet. The pure historical cost system has a clearly defined and interpretable concept of asset valuation at unexpired cost. However, when some assets are revalued and others are not, the balance sheet becomes a mixture of different valuation bases, as the following demonstrates.

Example: *Mixed valuation bases*

The modified historical cost balance sheet of Chaos Ltd at 30 June 20X8 was:

BALANCE SHEET as at 30 June 20X8			
Assets		**Liabilities**	$ 9 500
Inventory	$ 4 000	**Shareholders' funds**	
Plant	7 000	Paid-up capital	5 000
Land	11 000	Retained earnings	6 000
		Asset revaluation reserve	1 500
	$22 000		$22 000

Notes to the balance sheet indicate that:

1. Inventory was valued at the 'lower of cost and net realisable value'.
2. Plant was purchased in 20X2 and is at written-down cost.
3. Land —at directors' revaluation 20X6 $ 2 000
          —at original cost, purchased 20X8   9 000
                               $11 000

What meaning may be drawn from this balance sheet? Assets are valued at $22 000, but this consists of a mixture of costs and market values. Fundamentally, the balance sheet is not additive because it contains amounts representing different properties of the assets. It is meaningless to add together a person's height, weight and age. Why then would it be more meaningful to add a current market value to a written-down historical cost, a market value prevailing two years ago and a current market value, and call the total the 'value' of the assets held?

Consider also the problems of comparing companies. If company A has revalued its assets but company B has not, A will show a lower return on investment, all other things being equal, solely because it has revalued. An analyst must therefore discount the effect of company A's revaluation or attempt a revaluation of company B's assets for comparability purposes. Further, within a company, the practice of revaluing every, say, three to five years, rather than annually, makes it difficult to assess the trend in return on investment, the debt/equity ratio and other key measures of financial stability.

 ## Summary

In attempting to overcome the deficiencies of the historical cost system, accountants have adopted conservatism, which tends to state net asset values below their historical cost levels, and revaluation, which increases values above historical cost. The two practices reflect conflicting philosophies, the one of caution, the other of recognition of unrealised capital appreciation. The consequence they share is that both sever historical cost accounting from its logical structure, replace it with inconsistent practices, and provide greater flexibility to management in smoothing or otherwise manipulating reported profits.

In the wake of these changes, the opportunities for manipulation to suit the ends of some users and not others have increased and the ability to interpret the resulting statements has been impaired. The cure is arguably worse than the disease. Conservative understatement may actually harm the interests of users, while revaluations make it impossible to add up the total assets in any meaningful way.

The proper choice must inevitably be between the historical cost system strictly applied and a complete change to a current valuation system of accounting, such as those addressed in the next chapter.

 ## Review exercises

Discussion questions

18.1 Explain the following concepts in relation to the pure historical cost system of accounting:

(a) assets
(b) capital maintenance
(c) profit

18.2 'In times of inflation the pure historical cost accounting system loses its relevance for investment decisions.' Discuss, giving examples to support your analysis.

18.3 'During inflationary periods, the overstatement of profit under the pure historical cost system may cause users of the reports to form inaccurate impressions of the company's performance, resulting in poor investment decisions.' Discuss, giving examples.

18.4 Discuss the extent to which reports prepared under the pure historical cost system are useful for making comparisons between different companies at the same point in time, and the same company over time. Give examples to illustrate your answer.

18.5 'Whether a firm uses assets purchased recently or some time ago may radically affect its pure historical cost balance sheet and profit and loss statement.' Explain this statement.

18.6   If you were a shareholder in a large public company, would you be satisfied to receive accounting reports prepared on the basis of historical costs? Explain your answer.

18.7   Assume you are a bank manager and are approached for a loan by a large manufacturing company in a capital-intensive industry, where the company's plant and equipment are offered as security for the loan. Copies of the company's most recent balance sheet and profit and loss statement are provided and they have been prepared according to generally accepted accounting principles by a reputable firm of accountants. Would you make the lending decision solely on the basis of these statements? If not, what other information would you require?

18.8   Explain the concept of depreciation used in pure historical cost accounting. Are there other concepts of depreciation that might be more relevant for the information needs of financial statement users?

18.9   On 1 January 20X1 a small hardware store purchased 100 packets of nails for $5 each. During the year all of the nails were sold for $8 per packet and the supply was replaced for $6 per packet.

(a) What cost of sales would be recorded under historical cost accounting and what 'capital' is to be maintained under that system?

(b) What, in your opinion, was the 'real cost' of selling the nails? Justify your answer.

18.10   'Financial statements result from subtractions and additions. Under inflationary conditions, preparing balance sheets and profit and loss statements on the basis of measurements in dollars makes about as much sense as adding yards and metres together.' Discuss.

18.11   'The adoption of a "modified" historical cost system has led to the adding up of items in a way that is no more sensible than adding a person's age, height and weight together in order to describe their appearance.' Critically evaluate this assertion.

18.12   Assume that your savings are invested in a company that was formed during the year, and which invested its entire share capital of $1 million in highly specialised equipment that probably has no resale value. It has not yet begun production, and the financial statements that you receive at the end of the year disclose share capital and assets of $1 million.

(a) Are these valuations justified under historical cost accounting?

(b) To what extent will these statements provide the information you require to make an appropriate assessment of the company?

(c) If you consider the information is inadequate, what other information should the accountants provide?

18.13   Is it a wise policy for a company to distribute to shareholders its entire after-tax pure historical cost income? Explain your answer.

18.14   'The pure historical cost system is often defended on the grounds that it is at least verifiable.'

(a) Why might accountants and auditors be disinclined to report current market values?

(b) To what extent is the information provided within the pure historical cost system verifiable?

18.15 Why might managers favour a conservative approach to financial reporting? Is conservatism in the best interests of decision makers who use accounting information in making their decisions? Explain your answer.

18.16 To what extent is a system of accounting which adheres basically to historical cost principles but which permits assets to be revalued on occasions an improvement on a pure historical cost system?

18.17 'Two major influences have led to modifications in the historical cost system of accounting: conservatism and the revaluation of assets. In general they have been opposing influences, although this they have in common: both result in arbitrary and inconsistent practices that destroy the integrity of the accounting reports.' Discuss, with examples, whether you agree with this statement.

Problems

18.18 Two companies, A Ltd and B Ltd, were formed on 1 January 20X1, each with contributed capital of $100 000. On the next day, each company invested its capital as follows:

- A Ltd purchased 100 000 shares in Y Ltd for $1 per share
- B Ltd purchsed 100 000 shares in Z Ltd for $1 per share.

On the last day of 20X1, A Ltd sold its shares in Y Ltd for $125 000 and invested the entire proceeds in Z Ltd at $1.25 per share. B Ltd had held its original investment intact.

(a) Determine the profit and prepare the balance sheet for each company under the historical cost system of accounting.

(b) How useful are these reports in enabling investors to compare the performance and financial position of the two companies?

18.19 Gasp Ltd has been operating a quarry for many years. On 1 January 20X8 it had the following assets:

Land, purchased in 20X1 for $1500; two per cent written off annually as a depletion allowance.

Unsold rock on hand at cost at date of mining:

Mined in 20X6	$6000
Mined in 20X7	$9000

Grabbit Ltd commenced operations on 1 January 20X8 with the purchase of a quarry for $50 000. This was expected to be depleted over a period of 50 years.

During 20X8 both companies mined identical amounts of ore at an identical cost of mining (excluding depletion charges) of $14 000. Both companies sold identical quantities of rock for identical revenue of $38 000. Gasp Ltd, however, took the opportunity to dispose of its oldest stock, so that its sales consisted of all the rock mined in 20X6. Grabbit Ltd sold all of the rock mined in 20X8.

The FIFO method of inventory valuation is normal in this industry.

Neither company had assets or liabilities other than those mentioned. All transactions were for cash.

(a) Prepare profit and loss statements for 20X8 for each company according to the principles of historical cost accounting.

(b) Do the comparative statements provide an accurate guide to the performance of each company in 20X8? If not, in what ways could the statements have been improved?

(c) Is sufficient information supplied to assess the financial position of each company? If not, what other information should have been provided?

Case studies

18.20 *Comparison of accounting policies*

Two companies, Sherwood Ltd and Kepler Ltd, have been operating successfully since they were incorporated within weeks of each other approximately 10 years ago. Sherwood operates in the electronics industry while Kepler is in the pharmaceuticals industry. Both companies have successfully transformed initial discoveries in their respective fields into commercially successful products, and hold various copyrights and tradenames to protect their commercial interests. Sherwood produces specialised computer hardware components that are used by many computer manufacturers. Kepler produces a number of anaesthetics for use in medical operations and various medicinal products, the latter principally for the treatment of asthma and migraines. The companies are also involved in ongoing research and development activities, and have been since their inception. Their balance sheets as at 30 June 20X4 appear below:

BALANCE SHEETS

as at 30 June 20X4

	Sherwood Ltd		Kepler Ltd	
	$	$	$	$
Assets				
Current assets				
Cash		10 000		15 000
Accounts receivable	33 000		20 000	
Less Provision for doubtful debts	(4 000)	29 000	–	20 000
Inventory	41 000		50 000	
Less Provision for obsolete/damaged stock	(3 000)	38 000	–	50 000
Total current assets		77 000		85 000
Non-current assets				
Plant and equipment (cost)	120 000		120 000	
Less Accumulated depreciation	(60 000)	60 000	(40 000)	80 000
Buildings	100 000 [a]		200 000 [b]	
Less Accumulated depreciation	(10 000)	90 000	(2 000)	198 000
Land		60 000 [a]		110 000 [b]
Research and development costs		–		100 000
Patents and trademarks	9 000 [a]		75 000 [b]	
Less Accumulated amortisation	(2 000)	7 000	–	75 000
Total non-current assets		217 000		563 000
Total assets		294 000		648 000

continues

BALANCE SHEETS
as at 30 June 20X4

	Sherwood Ltd		Kepler Ltd	
	$	$	$	$
Liabilities				
Current liabilities				
Creditors and borrowings		15 000		30 000
Provisions for employee entitlements		2 000		–
Total current liabilities		17 000		30 000
Non-current liabilities				
Borrowings		20 000		45 000
Provisions for employee entitlements		5 000		–
Total non-current liabilities		25 000		45 000
Total liabilities		42 000		75 000
Net assets		252 000		573 000
Represented by:				
Shareholders' equity				
Share capital		120 000		150 000
Retained earnings		132 000		223 000
Asset revaluation reserve		–		200 000
Total shareholders' equity		252 000		573 000

ª Cost   ᵇ Directors valuation

Required

Evaluate and comment on the financial position of Sherwood Ltd and Kepler Ltd as portrayed in the balance sheets. In the course of completing the case, refer to the accounting policies adopted by the two companies and the effects of such policies on the analysis of the financial position of each company.

18.21 *Goodwill and identifiable intangible assets*

Madura Ltd and Serang Ltd are companies of similar size operating in the same industry. Both companies have had very similar reported profitability over the past three years. Their gearing ratios, as calculated from their latest balance sheets, are also very similar.

Madura depreciates its plant and equipment over a five-year period assuming nil residual values, and amortises its goodwill and other intangible assets (patents and trademarks) over a period of 10 years. Serang depreciates its plant and equipment over an eight-year period assuming residual values of 20 per cent of cost, amortises its goodwill over a period of 20 years, and does not provide for any amortisation on its other intangible assets (copyrights and trademarks).

Required

Comment on the depreciation and amortisation policies adopted by Madura and Serang, and the issues to be considered, from the viewpoint of (a) an investor considering investing in these companies, and (b) a financial institution considering additional lending to these two companies.

18.22 *Provisions*

Elko Ltd and Klamath Ltd are large retailing companies operating in the same State. While Klamath is approximately twice the size of Elko, its profitability, measured by return on sales and return on equity, has been only approximately one-half of Elko's over the past three years. In addition, the following ratios have been calculated for the two companies for the year ended 30 June 20X3:

	Elko	Klamath
Provision for doubtful debts/Accounts receivable	5.1%	2.5%
Provision for stock obsolescence and damage/Inventory	10.0%	5.2%
Provision for warranty claims/Sales	4.3%	1.7%
Provision for employee entitlements/Payroll expense	7.5%	3.3%

Required

Discuss the accounting treatments adopted in these four areas by Elko and Klamath. Comment on the effects of these treatments on the reported profitability and financial position of the two companies.

CHAPTER 19
Alternative accounting systems

Introduction

In the previous chapter, the historical cost system of accounting was reviewed and evaluated. In its pure form, the historical cost system has its strengths in its simplicity and its reliability, while its principal weaknesses are the result of its lack of relevance during periods of changing price levels. Attempts have been made to overcome these weaknesses by certain ad hoc modifications to the historical cost system; conservatism on the one hand and asset revaluations on the other.

In this chapter, various alternative systems of accounting are presented. It was noted in the previous chapter that the capital maintenance concept underlying the historical cost system is one of maintaining money capital. Three alternative accounting systems that have received the most attention, and that have an alternative capital maintenance concept to that underlying the historical costs system, are analysed in this chapter.

Measuring profit and wealth

The search for a measure of profit and value should begin with a very basic model. Hicks, a prominent economist, defined a person's income as the maximum value they could consume during a period and be as well off at the end of the period as they were at the beginning.[1] Hicks noted that the purpose of income calculations in practical affairs was to give people an indication of the amount they could consume without impoverishing themselves.[2] Using similar reasoning, the profit of a business entity for a period is the amount that could be distributed to owners during the period while still leaving the entity with the same wealth as existed at the commencement of the period. It represents the amount that could be distributed to owners without depleting the entity's capital base. In this respect, business income has been defined as the increment in net wealth over a period after maintaining intact the firm's capital.[3] Hence:

> After removing the effects of any additional capital contributions or withdrawals by owners from the initial capital investment ... the increase in net wealth is the income of the period.[4]

Accordingly, there is general agreement that profit represents a growth in wealth over time, as depicted in Figure 19.1.

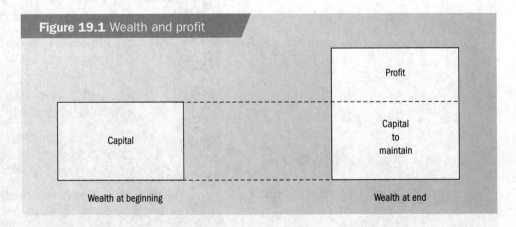

Figure 19.1 Wealth and profit

Profit

Capital

Capital to maintain

Wealth at beginning

Wealth at end

[1] J. Hicks, *Value and Capital: An Inquiry into Some Fundamental Principles of Economic Theory*, 2nd edn, Clarendon Press, Oxford, 1946, p. 172.

[2] Ibid.

[3] A. Barton, *The Anatomy of Accounting*, 3rd edn, University of Queensland Press, St Lucia, 1984, p. 90.

[4] Ibid., pp. 89–90.

It was noted in the previous chapter that the capital maintenance concept underlying the historical cost system is that of 'money' capital. That is, historical cost profit is the amount by which the closing balance of money capital exceeds the opening balance of money capital. Assume, for example, that Varapik Ltd commenced business on 1 January 20X3 with contributed capital of $50 000. At 31 December 20X3 the company has money capital (equal to assets less liabilities) of $55 000. Assume also that there were no further capital contributions from, or profit distributions to, the owners during the year. Varapik's historical cost profit amounts to $5000, representing the amount by which the closing money capital of $55 000 exceeds the opening money capital of $50 000.

Of course, Varapik's revenues less expenses for the period, calculated according to the historical cost system, would also have amounted to $5000. This is because the measurement of revenues and expenses, representing increments and decrements of wealth, must be consistent with the capital maintenance concept adopted.

Assume now the same facts as above with the exception that Varapik's owners had contributed additional capital of $2000 and received a profit distribution of $1000 during the year. In this case, the periodic profit under the historical cost system amounts to $4000, calculated as follows:

	$
Money capital at 31 December 20X3	55 000
Money capital at 1 January 20X3	50 000
Total increase in capital	5 000
Less increase due to additional capital contribution	(2 000)
Add decrease due to profit distribution	1 000
Net increase in money capital (historical cost profit)	4 000

The discussion in the previous chapter hinted that there might be alternative capital maintenance concepts to that of money capital. For example, should profit measurement consider changes in the replacement cost of goods consumed in the income-generation process, or should changes in the general price level or in the market prices of the entity's assets be considered? It was noted in the previous chapter that the measurement of profit depends on the various assumptions adopted. At a fundamental level, these assumptions depend on the capital maintenance concept selected. In this respect, three questions must be answered in measuring profit:

1. What property of the asset represents its wealth?
2. In what unit of measurement shall that wealth be measured?
3. Is capital to be maintained in terms of its financial value or the physical operating capacity it provides?

The property of an asset

An asset such as land has many physical properties, including area, circumference and crop-holding capacity. Accountants are concerned, however, with a range of 'value' properties, including the land's initial cost, its current replacement cost, its net realisable value and the present value of the cash flows it is expected to produce in the future.

More than one value property may be claimed to be the measure of wealth at any time. If asked what an entity's motor vehicle was worth, a person might make any of the following claims:

- It is worth what I can sell it for (net realisable or market value) since I value it for the cash I can obtain from it.
- It is worth what it would cost to replace (current replacement cost) since if deprived of the vehicle I would need to purchase another of the same type.

- Its worth consists of future cash flows it will generate from my business activities (present value of future cash flows) since I intend to use it for that purpose.
- It is worth what I paid for it (historical cost) since that was the sacrifice I made to obtain it.

Importantly, all of these valuations represent information for different purposes, and the valuation that is appropriate in any situation will depend on the purpose for which the information is required. The term 'value' refers to any value property chosen for measurement. Thus, the cost of a motor vehicle is a value just as much as the present market price or the current replacement cost is a value.

Although individual decisions require different valuations, the present task is to discover the value to be selected from this range to represent the wealth of an asset for the purpose of measuring income and financial position. However, the view taken throughout this book is that there is no single correct or true value of an asset. It all depends on the nature of the decision to be made, although the asset valuation method ought to be consistent with the capital maintenance concept selected.

The unit of measurement

The unit of measurement refers to the unit that will be adopted to measure the chosen attribute. Alternative measures exist. If, for example, the attribute of land to be measured is its area, the possible units of measurement that might be adopted include the hectare and the acre. Similarly, the circumference of the land might be measured in kilometres or miles.

When the attribute is a value, it seems natural to choose the currency unit of the country concerned (dollar, pound, yen, ringgit, etc.) as the unit of measurement, since it will be used universally in commercial dealings in that country. To simplify the discussion, the 'dollar' will be assumed to be the unit of currency.

An alternative to adopting the unit of currency is to adjust the currency unit for changes in its purchasing power over time. This unit of measurement will be called the 'constant' or 'price-level adjusted' dollar. It is well known that the purchasing power of the dollar diminishes with increases in the general level of prices and, by indexing the dollar for price-level changes, the constant dollar measurement represents a constant unit of purchasing power.

As with the choice of a property to be measured, the choice of the appropriate unit of measurement must depend on the use to which the information will be put. The dollar may be appropriate for some uses and the constant dollar for others.

The property to be measured and the unit of measurement should not be confused, for, as will be shown, some systems of accounting allow for price changes by the choice of a current price property to be measured, while others adjust the measurement unit.

Maintenance of financial value versus physical operating capacity

The capital to maintain is the benchmark by which to determine the increase in wealth; that is, the profit. Broadly, the choice lies between maintaining the financial value of capital or maintaining the ability to replace the physical assets held by the entity.

The maintenance of the financial value of capital is the approach adopted in most accounting systems. For example, profit is measured as the increase in the money (financial) capital of the entity under the historical cost system.

An alternative financial capital concept, touched on in the previous chapter, is to measure income as the increase in opening capital adjusted for changes in its purchasing power (note the interaction with the unit of measurement described above). For example, returning to the earlier Varapik Ltd example where opening money capital was $50 000 and closing money capital was $55 000 (with no profit distributions or additional capital contributions), assume now that the general rate of inflation for the year ended 31 December 20X3 was 4 per cent. This implies that, if the general price-level index was 100 at the commencement of the year, it would be 104 at the end of the year. If profit for the period was to be measured as the increase in the opening capital adjusted for changes in the purchasing power of the dollar, the 'real' (i.e. inflation adjusted) profit would amount to $3000 (and not $5000 as under the historical cost system), calculated as follows:

	$
Capital at 31 December 20X3	55 000
Purchasing power adjusted opening capital ($50 000 × 104/100)	52 000
Current purchasing power (price-level adjusted) profit	3 000

The above profit figure of $3000 can be explained as follows. The adjustment of opening capital from $50 000 to $52 000 has adjusted for the effects of inflation and has restated the opening capital into the same 'constant dollar' units as closing capital. The $3000 profit represents the amount of profit that could be distributed while maintaining intact the general purchasing power, or the 'real' value, of the company's capital. Accordingly, if a $3000 dividend was distributed to Varapik's shareholders on 31 December 20X3, the company's closing capital would amount to $52 000 (i.e. $55 000 less the $3000 dividend). This amount of closing capital would be assumed to have the same purchasing power at 31 December 20X3 as had the opening capital at 1 January 20X3.

Consider now the maintenance of the physical operating capital rather than the financial value of capital. Under this alternative, capital is measured by reference to the so-called physical operating capacity of the entity's net assets rather than by reference to financial value (whether or not adjusted for the effects of inflation). Profit is measured as the amount that could be distributed while maintaining intact the physical ability of the entity to continue operations into the future (i.e. maintaining the operating capability of the entity).

Operating capability has been defined as 'the aggregate utility, to the entity, of the service potential of the resources under the command of the entity'.[5] The service potential of assets means their 'economic utility to the entity, based on the total benefit expected to be derived by the entity from use (and/or through sale) of the asset'.[6] Hence, the physical operating capability of the entity's capital (i.e. its net assets) could be, for example, the capacity to manufacture 500 computers per week, produce 1000 motor vehicles per month, build 50 houses per year, or provide services to 2000 clients per year. The profit would be the amount that could be distributed to owners while still maintaining the operating capability of the entity's net assets in terms of these service or production volumes.

Case 19.1 Accounting for the effects of inflation

Lee Chen Ltd manufactures electronic circuit boards for use by several computer manufacturers. The company, using highly automated and computer-controlled manufacturing procedures, produces approximately 80 000 circuit boards per year.

The specialised plant and equipment used in the manufacturing process was purchased only 12 months ago but, given the rapid advances in technology, is expected to require replacement within approximately two to three years. The company operates from its own premises which were purchased eight years ago. The general rate of

[5] The Institute of Chartered Accountants in Australia and the Australian Society of Certified Practising Accountants, *Guidance Notes on Statement of Accounting Practice SAP 1, 'Current Cost Accounting'*, Melbourne, 1989, para. 4.

[6] The Institute of Chartered Accountants in Australia and the Australian Society of Certified Practising Accountants, *SAP 1, Current Cost Accounting*, Melbourne, 1989, para. 49.

> inflation over the past financial year has been officially determined at 7 per cent.
>
> Discuss, in general, the factors to be considered by Lee Chen Ltd if the company is to account for the effects of inflation when calculating its annual profit result.

An analysis of the major alternative systems

Various alternatives to the capital maintenance concept of money capital, as employed by the historical cost accounting system, have been briefly introduced to this point. It has been noted that accounting systems can differ either with respect to the property of the asset measured (original cost, replacement cost, net realisable value, etc.), the unit of measure adopted (the dollar or the price-level adjusted 'constant' dollar), or in the concept of capital (financial value or physical capital).

From the various combinations that result from these choices, measures of profit may be drawn that have different characteristics. The choice must be governed by the information needs of users of accounting information. With this background in mind, it is now possible to focus attention on the three alternatives to historical cost accounting that have achieved most support. These are current purchasing power (CPP) accounting, continuously contemporary accounting (CoCoA) and current cost accounting (CCA). If historical cost accounting is to be supplemented or replaced, it will probably be by one of these three systems. It should be emphasised here that, although many variations on these systems are possible, the balance of this chapter will examine these alternatives in only their basic form.

Each system is explained more fully by an example and evaluated against the general objectives established in the previous chapter. Each deserves a fuller analysis than can be given at an introductory level and it must be emphasised that the issues are complex. To simplify the discussion, the treatment of each system will be restricted to the capital maintenance concept, its suitability for financial analysis and its reliability.

CPP: current purchasing power accounting

1. PROPERTY MEASURED: Original cost
2. UNIT OF MEASUREMENT: The constant dollar
3. CAPITAL MAINTENANCE CONCEPT: Financial value

CPP measures the original cost of an asset, but indexes the cost so that it always represents a unit of constant purchasing power. Figures established in the past are restated in end-of-period purchasing power. The CPP system is illustrated in the following example.

Example: *Concert Promotions Ltd*

Concert Promotions Ltd commenced business on 1 January 20X1 with paid-up capital of $20 000 and the following assets:

Cash at bank	$6000
Motor vehicle	5000
Land	9000

The motor vehicle will be depreciated on the straight-line basis of depreciation over a period of 10 years (nil residual value).

The transactions all occurred on 30 June 20X1 and consisted of:

Cash received from rock concert	$2000
Cash expenses incurred on concert	300

An index of the general price level was:

1 January 20X1	100
30 June 20X1	105
31 December 20X1	120

To restate the dated dollar amounts recorded during the year in equivalent year-end purchasing power, each entry must be converted using the purchasing power index applicable at the date the entry was made. The financial statements before and after restatement appear below. Amounts have been rounded upwards to the nearest dollar.

Notes

1. *The opening balance sheet*. The first entry calculates a 'capital maintenance reserve' by restating the opening balances in equivalent year-end purchasing power. This is done by adding 20 per cent to the opening net assets of the entity as follows:

	DR	CR
Cash at bank ($6000 × 20%)	$1200	
Motor vehicle ($5000 × 20%)	1000	
Land ($9000 × 20%)	1800	
Capital maintenance reserve		$4000

A capital maintenance reserve is established to record the increase in the capital to be maintained.

2. *Revenues and expenses*. These are restated from middle-of-year purchasing power dollars to end-of-year dollars by multiplying them by the ratio of the index values at the two dates. They then purport to measure the equivalent end-of-year purchasing power gained through the revenue and sacrificed through the expenses when the transactions took place. It should be noted that, if revenue and expense transactions had occurred evenly throughout the year, they would be adjusted by the average rate for the year. This is exactly the same adjustment as for transactions occurring in the middle of the relevant year, as in the Concert Promotions example.

3. *Depreciation*. As depreciation is based on the motor vehicle (asset) figure recorded at the beginning of the year, it is restated to end-of-year dollars by the full change in the price index over the year.

4. *Cash and the purchasing power loss*. So far every entry has been indexed, but monetary assets and liabilities are an exception. *Monetary* items are defined as claims of fixed amounts and include cash at bank, accounts receivable and accounts payable. *Non-monetary* items, such as inventory, land and buildings, will change in value due to inflation and other causes, but monetary items will not. Therefore, monetary items do not require indexation. If a debtor is contractually bound to pay $10 000, that is the amount to be paid, regardless of changes in the purchasing power of the debt over time.

PROFIT AND LOSS STATEMENTS: CONCERT PROMOTIONS LTD
for the year ended 31 December 20X1

	Dollars	Restatement formula	Constant dollars	
Revenue	2000	120/105	2286	(2)
Less Cash expenses	300	120/105	343	(2)
Depreciation	500	120/100	600	(3)
	800		943	
Gross profit	1200		1343	
Purchasing power loss			(1443)	(4)
Net profit (loss)	1200		(100)	

BALANCE SHEETS: CONCERT PROMOTIONS LTD
as at 31 December 19X1

	Dollars		Restatement formula	Constant dollars	
Assets					
Cash at bank		7 700	–	7 700	(4)
Vehicle	5000		120/100	6000	(1)
less Acc. depn	500	4 500	120/100	600	5 400	(3)
Land		9 000	120/100	10 800	(1)
		21 200		23 900	
Owners' equity					
Capital		20 000		20 000	
Capital maintenance					
reserve			120/100	4 000	(1)
Retained profit (loss)		1 200		(100)	
		21 200		23 900	

In the example, cash at bank is the only monetary item. To account for this monetary item, the accounts are first indexed completely (refer note (1)) and then an adjusting entry is made to restore the balance of cash to the legally fixed amount. The bank account would be adjusted on a worksheet as follows:

CASH AT BANK ACCOUNT

				$	Restatement	Constant $
(1)	Jan. 1	Balance	DR	6000	120/100	7200
(2)	June 30	Revenue	DR	2000	120/105	2286
(3)	June 30	Expenses	CR	(300)	120/105	(343)
	Dec. 31	Balance	DR	7700		9143
(4)	Dec. 31	Purchasing power				
		loss	CR			1443
	Dec. 31	Balance	DR			7700

The adjusting entry (number 4) represents the difference between the actual amount of the claim and what it would have been if all claims were indexed. Because the bank will not recognise a claim for $9143, the entity has suffered a loss of $1443 ($9143 less $7700) by holding cash in high inflationary times. This is known as a purchasing power loss and it will arise whenever monetary assets exceed monetary liabilities. Conversely, a purchasing power gain arises when monetary liabilities exceed monetary assets, since the debtor repays fewer units of purchasing power than were originally borrowed. The moral is that it may be better to owe money in times of inflation rather than to hold cash, subject, of course, to consideration of such factors as the level of interest rates, one's own short-term commitments and the ability to repay borrowed funds.

The purchasing power gain or loss is charged against profit and becomes a factor in the evaluation of management performance.

Case 19.2 Current purchasing power accounting

Summarise the nature of the various adjustments to the historical cost financial statements made under the CPP system and state the reasons for the specific adjustments. For our purposes, summarise adjustments using the following headings:

- adjustments to profit and loss for revenues, depreciation and other expenses
- purchasing power gain or loss included in the calculation of profit or loss
- monetary assets and liabilities in the balance sheet
- adjustments to non-monetary assets in the balance sheet
- adjustment to owners' equity through the capital maintenance reserve.

An evaluation of the CPP system

Capital maintenance

As the property measured is cost and as capital is maintained in real value terms (i.e. adjusting for changes in the general level of prices), the major difference between CPP and historical cost accounting is that CPP measures in constant dollars. The effect is that the capital to be maintained is the purchasing power of the contributed capital. In the example, $24 000 is the amount of capital to be maintained before any profit is declared. This partially overcomes the criticism that historical cost accounting does not make any allowances for cost increases due to inflation. Further, from the owners' perspective it ensures that profit represents an increase in the purchasing power of the owners' equity.

Financial analysis

CPP seeks to correct a major defect of the historical cost system. Critics claim that a 20X1 dollar amount and a 20X6 dollar amount should not be added because these two amounts represent different purchasing power. To say that a block of land purchased in 20X1 for $50 000 cost more than a similar block purchased 10 years previously for $20 000 is at least mathematically correct, but it is misleading in purchasing power terms because the earlier purchase required a greater sacrifice of purchasing power. The dollar is not a constant measurement standard because it represents different purchasing power at different times. It is as if a rubber band were used to measure a distance: it will take on different lengths as it is stretched and, depending on the stretch applied, a table length might be measured as 10 'rubber-band lengths' or two. The conversion of dollars to constant dollars creates a measurement unit of constant purchasing power, in which the total cost of assets purchased at different times may be added.

Under this view, profit measures should therefore represent real growth in purchasing power rather than simply an increase in dollar income. This ought to assist the evaluation of the trend in profits. Inter-organisational comparisons should also improve, since the effect on reported values of lower price levels prevailing in previous years will have been eliminated.

Performance measurement under CPP also includes the gain or loss on purchasing power arising from monetary items. This results in large purchasing power gains for organisations that are heavily in debt and large purchasing power losses for organisations that hold large stores of cash and/or have high debtors or other monetary assets. The impact of this on the financial analysis of any entity should be considered. For example, should management be 'rewarded' with higher reported CPP profits by engaging in high-risk borrowing practices in times of inflation, or does this actually reflect sound policy when operating in an inflationary environment? Similarly, should management be 'penalised' with lower reported profits for holding high cash reserves, or does this reflect the fact that management has not utilised its resources in the most effective manner?

Many organisations have large amounts of long-term debt that far exceed their holdings of monetary assets. Surveys of the likely impact of CPP have found that large purchasing power gains will arise in such cases and that the CPP profit will exceed that recorded under historical cost accounting. Since the original perception of CPP was that it would overcome capital maintenance problems by reducing profit and maintaining higher capital, the surveys raised doubts about the 'reality' of purchasing power gains. The gain is never 'realised' in dollars, but rather stands always as a notional difference between the stated debt and what would have to be repaid if the debt were indexed. Expressed in this way, there seems to be no economic substance to the gain.

As to the denominator of the return on investment calculation, it is claimed by proponents of CPP that, by converting historical costs into current purchasing power units, the balance sheet becomes more useful for comparative purposes, and that the individual assets can at least be legitimately added because they are expressed in constant dollars.

Against this, it may be argued that the indexation of cost figures by a general index may not represent the sum total of the effects of specific price changes on an entity's individual assets and thus adds an overlay of artificiality to the exercise. What is the meaning of an asset amount restated for the effects of inflation? The restatement of land in the example from $9000 to $10 800 signifies that this higher amount must be recouped from the proceeds of the sale of the land before any profit is recognised, but as a measure of the investment in the land it is neither the original cost and most probably not its current market value.

Constant dollar amounts reported are not identifiable with any known prices or transaction figures. Sales are reported in the example at $2286, which is not the actual amount of the sale. There is sufficient mystery in the historical cost system without injecting constant dollar values that do not relate to actual transactions.

The artificiality of the figures produced by price-level adjustments does little to assist in assessing current financial stability, a process that requires knowledge of current prices and estimates of future prices.

The ultimate source of these problems is that, apart from introducing purchasing power gains and losses and standardising the measurement unit, CPP is still an historical cost measurement system. The property measured is unexpired original cost, and the revenue recognition principles are unchanged, thus prohibiting recognition of specific price gains on assets such as shares and land until they are sold. To the extent that these are defects of the historical cost system, CPP represents no improvement.

Reliability

CPP retains the arbitrary allocations inherent in historical cost accounting and the multiplicity of generally accepted accounting principles available under that system.

Although the index used may be verified as an independent measure, the choice of index, general or consumer price, adds a further element of subjectivity to the reporting process. In Australia, for instance, the inflation rate on goods and services in general may be represented by the Gross Domestic Product Implicit Deflator, which is calculated each quarter by the Commonwealth Statistician. This is a measure of the weighted average change in the prices of most of the goods and services produced in the economy. An alternative index is the Consumer Price Index, which measures the change in the ability of the dollar to buy consumer goods. The choice depends on whether the intention is to maintain the capital from the entity's point of view, for which the general price index would be the more appropriate, or from the owners' perspective, which may require use of the Consumer Price Index.

Developments in CPP

A number of countries, and particularly Australia, the United Kingdom and the United States, considered the adoption of CPP accounting because of the high rates of inflation in the early 1970s. For example, the Australian accounting profession in 1974 produced an exposure draft on CPP.[7] An exposure draft is preliminary in nature and is designed to test reaction to a proposed standard. This exposure draft was not adopted, and was followed shortly afterwards by the first of several exposure drafts and provisional standards on current cost accounting (CCA).

An international accounting standard, IAS 15, 'Information Reflecting the Effects of Changing Prices', has been issued concerning accounting for price-level changes. IAS 15 applies generally to 'enterprises whose levels of revenues, profit, assets or employment are significant in the economic environment in which they operate',[8] but the standard also encourages other entities to comply. The standard recommends that supplementary information prepared under either a CPP or a CCA approach be provided in the entity's financial statements, although few entities seem to follow its guidance.

CoCoA: continuously contemporary accounting

1. PROPERTY MEASURED: Current cash equivalent
2. MEASUREMENT UNIT: Constant dollar
3. CAPITAL MAINTENANCE CONCEPT: Financial value

There are a number of systems based on current selling prices, but the most popular of these is the system known as continuously contemporary accounting (CoCoA), which was proposed by R. J. Chambers.[9] CoCoA values each asset at its 'current cash equivalent' (CCE), which usually refers to the net realisable value of the asset if sold in the ordinary course of business. This is not the same as a liquidation value in a forced sale, nor does it represent the cash to be obtained by selling the assets as a group rather than individually.

An evaluation of CoCoA

Capital maintenance

The capital to be maintained consists of the total of the current cash equivalent values (sometimes called 'exit prices') of the individual assets held at the beginning of the year, less the liabilities at that date. In this context, therefore, 'capital' means net assets or total owners' equity, not just directly contributed or paid-up capital. This capital is indexed for the price-level changes during the year.

The CoCoA capital maintenance concept is often referred to as that of 'adaptive' capital. As the net assets of the entity are valued at their current cash equivalents (and as revenues and expenses are measured in a manner that is consistent with such a method of valuation), CoCoA portrays an entity's financial position as a measure of that entity's ability or capacity to adapt to a changing environment. The capacity to adapt to changing circumstances depends on the saleability of the entity's assets.

Suppose an entity's assets consist entirely of land that had a net realisable value of $10 000 at the start of the current year and could now be sold for net proceeds (sale price less selling costs) of $18 000. Suppose also that prices rose generally by 20 per cent over the year. The gain may be represented as shown on the following page:

---

[7] The Institute of Chartered Accountants in Australia and the Australian Society of Accountants, *Preliminary Exposure Draft: A Method of Accounting for Changes in the Purchasing Power of Money*, Melbourne, December 1974.

[8] IAS 15, 'Information Reflecting the Effects of Changing Prices', para. 3.

[9] R. J. Chambers, *Price Variation and Inflation Accounting*, McGraw-Hill Book Company, Sydney, 1980.

	Capital to maintain	Wealth at end	Profit
In dollars	10 000	18 000	8 000
In constant dollars	12 000	18 000	6 000

The entity began the year with the ability to obtain cash of $10 000. At that date, this cash had purchasing power equivalent to the purchasing power of cash of $12 000 held at the end of the year. The growth in command over goods generally was, therefore, $6000.

By ensuring that no profits are declared for distribution unless net assets with current cash equivalents of at least $12 000 are present at the end of the year, the CoCoA system goes further than historical cost accounting in ensuring that adequate funds are retained to continue the operations of the entity. That is, CoCoA ensures that the return on owners' funds is calculated after adjustment for inflation. The entity is regarded as an adaptive system, responding to changing opportunities and pressures by means of sale of its assets to obtain new investments. Its activities are seen as involving actions in markets, hence the need for regular information about what it may obtain by selling its assets.

The entity's ability to adapt through the resale of assets is revealed by the balance sheet and thus the general purchasing power of capital is maintained. Proponents of CoCoA argue that the method provides a continuous source of financial information, and that this information is necessary to guide the entity in the action it may take in markets in the future. The neutrality of information is stressed and it is pointed out that the CCE values are necessary for any decisions concerning assets. For example, even in a replacement decision it is necessary to know the resale or disposal value of an existing asset.

From the owners' perspective, the presence of retained CoCoA profits gives assurance that, if the assets of the entity were sold individually at balance date and the cash distributed to owners and creditors, the owners would receive cash representing greater purchasing power than they originally contributed. Historical cost retained profits do not carry this assurance, since neither price-level changes nor realisable values are taken into account.

Financial analysis

The measure of profit under CoCoA is unlike that under historical cost systems, principally because it bases the recognition of revenues and expenses on changes in market prices, as the following example will illustrate.

Example: *Creeley's Chewing Gum*

The initial capital of Creeley consisted of cash of $42 000. The company commenced its second year of business in 20X1 with assets of:

Equipment $28 000 at cost
          23 000 CCE
Cash at bank 14 000

The equipment was acquired on the first day of 20X1 and is expected to have a five-year economic life. It would be depreciated on the straight-line basis under historical cost accounting.

During the year, cash payments, all of which related to production, were $95 000 and sales of gum generated cash receipts of $113 000.

At 31 December 20X1 the assets were as follows:

	At cost	*CCE*
Cash at bank	$32 000	$32 000
Raw materials	3 000	nil
Finished goods	6 000	17 000
Equipment	28 000	19 000
		$68 000

A general price level index disclosed a rise of 10 per cent over the year. The CoCoA profit may be derived as follows:

Wealth at end		
Sum of closing CCE values		$68 000
Capital to maintain		
Opening CCE values	$42 000	
plus Price level adjustment (10%)	4 200	46 200
CoCoA net profit		$21 800

A number of important differences between CoCoA and historical cost are revealed in the following comparison.

COMPARISON OF CoCoA AND HISTORICAL COST RESULTS
Profit and loss statement for 20X1: Creeley's Gum Pty Ltd

	Historical cost		CoCoA	
	$		$	
Sales		113 000		113 000
Cost of goods sold				
Opening stock		0		0
plus Purchases				
(production costs)		95 000		95 000
		95 000		95 000
less Closing stock				
Raw materials	(3 000)		(3 000)	
Finished goods	(6 000)	(9 000)	(6 000)	(9 000)
Cost of goods sold		(86 000)		(86 000) (1)
Gross profit		27 000		27 000
less Expenses				
Depreciation expense		(5 600)		(9 000) (2)
Price-level adjustment				
(10% opening capital)				(4 200) (3)
Price-variation adjustment				
(+ 11 000 − 3 000)				8 000 (5)
Net profit before taxation		21 400		21 800

	Historical cost	CoCoA
BALANCE SHEET *as at 31 December 20X1*		
Assets	$	$
Cash at bank	32 000	32 000
Raw materials	3 000	–
Finished goods	6 000	17 000
Machine (net of depreciation)	22 400	19 000 (7)
	63 400	68 000
Owners' equity		
Capital	42 000	42 000 (6)
Capital maintenance reserve	–	4 200
Retained profit	21 400	21 800
	63 400	68 000 (4)

Notes

1. *Cost of goods sold.* One of the criticisms of CoCoA is that it is inconsistent not to value cost of goods sold (COGS) at its CCE. However, it becomes obvious that since the CCE is the net selling price of an asset, if COGS was shown at its selling price then, under CoCoA, any gross profit would always be zero. CoCoA, therefore, continues to record COGS at book (historical cost) value and allows for changes in the general level of prices in the 'price variation adjustment' and asset accounts (to be explained in point 5 below).

2. *Depreciation expense.* Historical cost accounting regards depreciation as an allocation of costs according to benefits derived, and accordingly the $28 000 cost is apportioned over five years at the rate of $5600 per year. No attempt is made to allow for the annual decline in market value. CoCoA depreciation, however, is based solely on the decline (price variation) in the current cash equivalent of the asset. The decline of $9000 is said to be the cost of using the asset over the year. The company forfeited an opportunity to obtain cash of $23 000 for the asset at the start of the year, and it can obtain only $19 000 for it at the end of the year. The company has suffered a $4000 reduction in its ability to adapt through the resale of its assets. This loss in command over goods is recovered from revenue (i.e. expensed to profit and loss) before any profit is declared.

   This notion of depreciation may be closer to the layman's concept of depreciation as a loss in market value. It also avoids the difficulties encountered in the historical cost system of allocating costs where the benefit pattern and the life of the asset can only be approximated. In this sense, CoCoA depreciation is a more reliable measure of what it purports to measure than historical cost depreciation.

3. *Price level adjustment.* Unlike CPP, CoCoA does not require the conversion of every financial statement measurement to constant dollars. The balance sheet is already in end-of-20X1 dollars, as assets are valued by reference to their current cash equivalents as at balance date.

   The profit and loss statement could have been restated where items were incurred at earlier price levels, such as sales revenue, but it is preferred to leave the revenues and expenses at their transaction amounts rather than introduce artificiality into the accounts.

In the case of Creeley's Chewing Gum above, it may be assumed that the first entry for the company would have been:

	DR	CR
DR Cash	42 000	
CR Capital		42 000

and then:

	DR	CR
DR Equipment	28 000	
CR Cash/Creditors		28 000

Therefore, opening capital is $42 000 and the price-level adjustment is $4200 (calculated as the opening capital multiplied by the 10 per cent increase in the price index). The entry for this is:

	DR	CR
DR Price-level adjustment (10% of opening capital)	4 200	
CR Capital maintenance reserve		4 200

4. It is important to note that the indexation applies to total owners' equity, not just to contributed capital. The opening balance of owners' equity in 20X2, for instance, will be $68 000 and, therefore, the price-level adjustment debited to the CoCoA profit and loss statement at 31 December 20X2, assuming that inflation remains at 10 per cent, will be $68 000 × 10% = $6800.

5. *Price variation adjustment and inventory.* The CoCoA system values assets, and therefore inventory in the balance sheet, at market selling price (current cash equivalent). In the present example, CoCoA calculates that raw materials have decreased in value by $3000 and finished goods have increased in value by $11 000. Therefore the net increase of $8000 is recognised in the calculation of profit, even though it is an *unrealised gain.* This procedure is equivalent to the recognition of revenue at the point of production under an historical cost system. In that system, it was argued that the moment of production is normally too early in the operating cycle for uncertainty to have been reduced sufficiently to enable a measurable and permanent gain to be recorded. Advocates of CoCoA contend, however, that an independent, measurable market price normally exists which provides the basis for a CoCoA measurement.

Another relevant question is whether revenue is 'accomplished' before the point of sale and whether management ought to be rewarded for the profit before a sale occurs. As previously discussed, it is most difficult to determine the moment of accomplishment but critics of CoCoA argue that, for inventory at least, the sale is more likely to be the appropriate point.

In the above example there could just as easily have been a decrease in the CCE value of finished goods, which would have resulted in a debit to the profit account. Critics of CoCoA should have no argument with this procedure since writing down to 'lower of cost or market' is an accepted historical cost practice. In this case, raw materials have no market value and the CoCoA system does not place a financial value on them. The traditional historical cost view that such assets have 'future benefits' in contributing to future production and sales is not part of CoCoA, given the capital maintenance concept of adaptive capital. Although it is recognised that an outlay may produce such future benefits in various forms, including production, the only benefit of relevance under CoCoA is the cash that can be obtained by its resale. The fact that the company probably does not intend to scrap its raw materials but will use them in production is considered irrelevant.

6. *Contributed capital.* The balance sheet always shows the owners' paid-up or contributed capital at face value. Adjustments for the effects of inflation are taken to the capital maintenance reserve.

7. *Asset values.* In the balance sheet, the CCE value is reported for the machine from the actual date of purchase, creating an instantaneous loss, since the write-down must be from historical cost. If the usual format of 'asset less accumulated depreciation' is preserved, the total write-down to balance date will be shown in the accumulated depreciation account, giving a net book value which is the asset's CCE. Instantaneous losses on purchases of productive assets are common under CoCoA and do much to change the character of the profit figure that is reported. Some people advocate that such losses should be charged directly against capital; however, there is no apparent reason why gains and losses at the moment of purchase should be treated differently from those that occur over time.

Case 19.3 Continuously contemporary accounting

Summarise the nature of the various adjustments to the historical cost financial statements made by the CoCoA system and state the reasons for the specific adjustments. For our purposes, summarise the adjustments using the following headings:

- adjustments to profit and loss for changes in the CCE of non-monetary assets
- price-level adjustment on opening capital included in the calculation of profit or loss
- monetary assets and liabilities in the balance sheet
- valuation of non-monetary assets in the balance sheet
- adjustment to owners' equity through the capital maintenance reserve.

Other features of CoCoA for financial analysis

CoCoA has a number of important advantages over the historical cost system. It produces a balance sheet measuring the same property of each asset, its CCE, whereas the conventional balance sheet represents a mixture of properties. The CCE amounts, being current prices, are already measured in units of comparable purchasing power, whereas historical cost balance sheets contain dollar amounts of varying purchasing power. Asset values may therefore be added meaningfully to show the total assets of a business in terms of their CCE values.

The CoCoA balance sheet estimates what the entity would receive if it sold its assets individually. This informs creditors and owners of the cash available to the entity, through sale of its assets, to meet its debts or reinvest elsewhere. An entity with large growth prospects, but possessing assets such as specialised equipment or mining prospects that cannot be sold in markets, will be revealed as having low liquidity. Investors cannot expect a large cash return if the entity is liquidated in the near future. This information is useful in assessing the risk of investing in the entity, with investors still being able to make their own assessments of future growth prospects.

The financial statements of several large companies that have collapsed in recent years have been criticised for providing cost-based information that failed to indicate the extent of the likely deficit on liquidation. As the review of the historical cost system revealed, it is possible to retain costs on the balance sheet in the face of declining market prices whenever the decrease is considered temporary. Moreover, the continuity assumption prevails until evidence to the contrary arises. Even then, it would be suicidal for any management hoping to rescue a failing enterprise to adopt a liquidation assumption. The signal to the market would be so overwhelming as to ensure liquidation. The auditors also are placed in an impossible position since, if they insist on a change, they may subsequently be sued for the losses that occur from this decision. CoCoA requires the reporting of realistic values in all circumstances.

Net realisable values are also relevant to financially stable entities. Entities sometimes adapt to changing conditions by selling assets and investing the cash elsewhere and CCE prices indicate their ability to adapt in these ways. On the other hand, the sale of fixed assets is not a common occurrence and entities often finance new ventures by the sale of shares or by borrowing. Hence, the capacity to adapt includes the ability to raise new finance and this depends on the evaluation of the entity's performance and prospects.

Many investments fit the CoCoA model of adaptation by resale. Investments in listed shares may be sold through an organised exchange and changes in portfolios are often undertaken without disturbing the long-term production plans of an entity. Moreover, if the entity is entirely engaged in the purchase and sale of investments, it is essentially committed to a constant review of its activities, arising from which any investment may be sold.

In the review of the historical cost system it was indicated that the rules for revenue recognition produced apparent distortions when holding gains and losses on equity investments were ignored for an entity that held its shares, but included for an entity that traded securities. The CoCoA system recognises unrealised holding gains in the period when the price change occurs. Investment portfolio performance may, therefore, be compared between entities and over time on the assumption that an entity always has the opportunity of liquidating investments at the market price.

Suppose a company began 20X1 with shares with a market value of $20 000, that the value rose to $30 000 by the end of that year, but that it fell to $4000 in the next year. As a measure of performance, it is possible to report a profit of $10 000 in 20X1 followed by a loss of $26 000 in 20X2 caused by the failure, in 20X2, to sell the shares before the price fell dramatically.

On the other hand, entities engaged in manufacturing make long-term commitments to investments and rarely contemplate selling off productive assets for the low salvage values they may offer. A number of items conventionally thought of as assets are omitted from CoCoA balance sheets because they do not possess reliable prices or prices set in markets. Highly specialised assets, such as a computer program written for an individual purpose, may have no resale market. Research and development costs, life-extending overhauls, exploration costs and the like are similarly omitted. Critics of CoCoA argue that the public disclosure of these instantaneous write-downs may deter management from engaging in long-term ventures, notwithstanding the likely benefits of these projects.

The disclosure of net selling prices in the balance sheet reduces the possibility of an entity being taken over by a corporate raider for the purpose of 'asset-stripping'. If owners know that, as a minimum, the entity's assets may be sold individually to produce a return to owners greater than the takeover offer, they are unlikely to accept a takeover. There have been many instances in Australia of entities taking over other entities and liquidating the assets for a profit.

Reliability

Historical cost has the advantage that primary entries are based on verifiable transactions. Under CoCoA, the price adopted for an asset will not be directly experienced by the entity unless the asset is sold at that price. For frequently traded securities, a market price exists that will suffice unless the shareholding represents a substantial portion of the issued capital, in which case the sale could influence the market price. Productive assets, however, are less frequently traded and obtaining a realistic resale price can be difficult. Even with inventory, the advertised price may reflect what the entity hopes to sell the goods for, not what the likely sale price will be. Sometimes, also, different prices prevail, depending on the market and in what lot sizes the inventory is sold.

With respect to primary entries, then, historical cost is based on verifiable past transactions whereas CoCoA is reliant on current market price data. However, in another respect, CoCoA is the more reliable system. Unlike historical cost accounting, CoCoA is not dependent on unverifiable cost and revenue allocations. Profits are calculated based on the changes in market price between two dates. Depreciation, for example, is simply the decline in market value of the asset. No choice between straight-line or reducing-balance methods, or estimation of residual value, is required. Periodic profit is therefore likely to be more volatile under CoCoA compared with historical cost systems.

CCA: current cost accounting

1. PROPERTY MEASURED: Current replacement cost
2. MEASUREMENT UNIT: The dollar
3. CAPITAL MAINTENANCE CONCEPT: Physical maintenance

Whereas the two systems examined previously employ a financial value concept of capital, the current cost system (CCA) adopts a physical concept of capital maintenance. It attempts to maintain the initial operating capability of an entity by recovering from revenue the current costs of replacing resources at the time they are consumed. This provides the capability to replace assets, if desired, although actual replacement is not assumed.

Replacement-cost-based systems gained favour both in the United Kingdom and in the United States. In the United Kingdom, SSAP 16,[10] released in March 1980, required all listed and large unlisted entities to publish a current cost balance sheet and profit and loss statement. In the United States, ASR 190,[11] released in March 1976 by the Securities and Exchange Commission, required the footnote disclosure of replacement cost accounting data by large entities. This was followed in 1979 by FASB Statement Number 33[12] which required supplementary disclosure not only of replacement cost data but also of CPP data. All of these statements have now been withdrawn.

The accounting profession in Australia has also acted. In 1976 the Australian profession released two statements,[13] which were amended and reissued in 1978, 1983 and 1989, on a system of accounting similar to other current cost systems. However, while SAP 1 remains as a 'Statement of Accounting Practice' which strongly recommends that entities present CCA supplementary statements in addition to their conventional financial statements, virtually no companies follow its guidance.

While a comprehensive current cost accounting system has not received acceptance, one aspect has been adopted in Australian public sector accounting. The recommended method of valuing public sector assets is that of 'deprival value'. Deprival value refers to the loss to the entity if deprived of the particular asset. In most cases, particularly for assets such as infrastructure and other non-monetary assets, public sector entities would replace their assets if, for some reason, they were deprived of them. Hence, the appropriate asset valuation method in these circumstances is replacement cost, the method adopted under current cost accounting.

As noted in the discussion of current purchasing power accounting, the international accounting standard IAS 15, 'Information Reflecting the Effects of Changing Prices', recommends that certain companies should disclose supplementary information prepared under a CCA or CPP approach. Once again, few companies follow its guidance. Accordingly, it may be concluded that there is no agreement on the form of CCA nor even whether it should be introduced, although it is the method that has received the most support from the professional accounting bodies internationally.

The discussion below will concentrate on the general principles found in most of the proposed CCA systems. Although further adjustments may also be made in current cost

---

[10] The Institute of Chartered Accountants in England and Wales, *Statement of Standard Acounting Practice No. 16, 'Current Cost Accounting'*, March, 1980.

[11] Securities and Exchange Commission, *Accounting Series Release No. 190*, New York, March 1976.

[12] Financial Accounting Standards Board, *Statement of Financial Accounting Standards No. 33, 'Financial Reporting and Changing Prices'*, Stamford, Connecticut, 1979.

[13] The Australian Society of Accountants and the Institute of Chartered Accountants in Australia, *Statement of Accounting Practice, SAP 1, 'Current Cost Accounting'*, Melbourne, 1989, and *Explanatory Statement PAS 1.2, 'The Basis of Current Cost Accounting'*, Melbourne, 1978.

systems for monetary items and the adoption of values for non-monetary assets other than replacement cost, a discussion of these items is beyond the scope of this text. The following represents a very simple example of CCA.

Example: *Tan Lee Ltd*

On 1 January 20X8 Tan Lee Ltd was established with the following assets at original cost:

Cash at bank	$ 2 000
Inventory (300 units × $10)	3 000
Office equipment	9 000
	$14 000

On 30 June 20X8, the inventory was sold for $25 per unit and replaced immediately at a cost of $15 per unit. At 31 December 20X8 the inventory would cost $22 per unit to replace and new office equipment of similar capacity to that already held would cost $11 000. The office equipment is to be depreciated on the straight-line basis over a period of 10 years. The comparative statements follow.

PROFIT AND LOSS STATEMENT: TAN LEE LTD
for the year ended 31 December 20X8

	Historical cost	CCA
Sales	$7500	$7500
less Cost of goods sold	3000	4500 (1)
Gross profit	4500	3000
less Depreciation	900	1000 (2)
Net profit	$3600	$2000

BALANCE SHEETS
as at 31 December 20X8

	Historical cost		CCA	
Assets	$	$	$	$
Cash		5 000		5 000
Inventory		4 500		6 600 (4)
Equipment	9000		11 000	(3)
less Acc. depn	900	8 100	1 100	9 900 (3)
		17 600		21 500
Shareholders' equity				
Paid-up capital		14 000		14 000
Current cost adjustment		–		5 500 (5)
Retained profits		3 600		2 000
		17 600		21 500

Notes

1. *Cost of goods sold.* The replacement cost of inventory applicable at the time of its sale is charged against revenue as cost of goods sold. This is to maintain the ability to replace the goods. Thus, cost of goods sold is $4500 (300 × $15) under CCA, compared with $3000 (300 × $10) under historical cost. If historical costs are recorded in the entity's

books of account through the year (which is the usual situation), the CCA adjustment may be made at balance date by adding $1500 to the cost of goods sold and crediting an account for capital maintenance, known as the 'current cost adjustment' account (see note 5 below), as follows:

DR	Cost of goods sold	$1500
CR	Current cost adjustment	$1500

2. *Depreciation.* Replacement costs for expenses are calculated as at the date the resource is consumed. The asset in the example was used throughout the year, presumably evenly, so that depreciation is based on the average replacement cost of the asset during the year, approximated by averaging the beginning and ending prices. This gives a CCA depreciation charge of $1000 for the year (10% of 1/2 ($9000 + $11 000)). Again, this may be accomplished as a balance-day adjustment to the historical cost records, as follows:

DR	Depreciation expense	$100
CR	Current cost adjustment	$100

3. *Balance sheet value of office equipment.* Since the balance sheet shows end-of-year asset values, it is necessary to use the end-of-year replacement cost of the office equipment of $11 000. This requires the following adjustment:

DR	Equipment	$2000
CR	Current cost adjustment	$2000

It is also necessary to disclose accumulated depreciation of 10 per cent of the replacement cost valuation; that is, $1100 ($11 000 × 10% × 1 year). Under historical cost accounting, depreciation of $900 would have been debited to depreciation expense and credited to accumulated depreciation. To base accumulated depreciation on the year-end replacement cost of $11 000, the following entry is necessary to increase the balance in the accumulated depreciation account from $900 to $1100:

DR	Current cost adjustment	$200
CR	Accumulated depreciation	$200

4. *Balance sheet value of inventory.* Cost of goods sold is calculated using the replacement cost of inventory at the time of the sale. As the balance sheet is drawn up at the end of the year, the end-of-year replacement cost of inventory, amounting to $6600 (300 × $22), must be used. The historical cost inventory value must therefore be written up by $2100 and the credit transferred to the current cost adjustment account, as follows:

DR	Inventory	$2100
CR	Current cost adjustment	$2100

5. *Current cost adjustment account.* After all the preceding entries, the account will appear as follows:

CURRENT COST ADJUSTMENT ACCOUNT				
		DR	CR	BAL.
Dec. 31	Cost of goods sold		1500	1500 CR
	Depreciation expense		100	1600 CR
	Inventory		2100	3700 CR
	Equipment		2000	5700 CR
	Accumulated depn	200		5500 CR

Case 19.4 Current cost accounting

Summarise the nature of the various adjustments to the historical cost financial statements made by the CCA system and state the reasons for the specific adjustments. For our purposes, summarise the adjustments using the following headings:

- adjustments to profit and loss for cost of goods sold
- adjustments to profit and loss for depreciation
- monetary assets and liabilities in the balance sheet
- valuation of non-monetary assets in the balance sheet
- adjustment to owners' equity through the capital cost adjustment account.

An evaluation of CCA

Capital maintenance

CCA represents a capital maintenance concept concerned with maintaining the operating capacity of the entity. Entities are normally established with the expectation that they will be profitable and will continue to exist indefinitely. Indeed, one of the major factors underlying the rapid growth of the corporate sector has been the separate legal identity of a company, which permits the transfer of ownership and therefore gives the company a legal life that is not necessarily terminated by the death or bankruptcy of an owner.

A continuing entity must maintain at least its operating capacity to ensure a viable future. Under the historical cost system, managers generally prevent the gradual contraction of the entity during inflationary periods by retaining additional profits for asset replacement, or by issuing further shares or increasing debt. If maintenance of operating capacity is intended by these actions, there is an advantage in adopting an accounting system that indicates whether the profits are sufficient to cover the replacement of productive factors consumed during the period.

Whether operating capacity is the type of capital maintenance an investor believes is relevant has yet to be determined. Owners may prefer, for example, that the entity maintain the general purchasing power of their investment rather than the entity's own operating capability. The conflict between the entity's viewpoint and that of the owner is therefore relevant to the choice of the method of capital maintenance.

CCA will not provide literally for replacement of productive assets as they fall due for replacement. Suppose that on 1 January 20X1 a company bought a machine possessing a two-year life, for $10 000, and that its replacement cost at the end of each succeeding year was:

End of 20X1	$11 000
End of 20X2	$16 000

Depreciation (50% per year) at the average replacement cost would be:

20X1 (10 000 + 11 000)/2 × 50%	=	$ 5 250
20X2 (11 000 + 16 000)/2 × 50%	=	6 750
Total depreciation		$12 000

Since the actual replacement cost at the end of the asset's life is $16 000, there is a shortfall of $4000, known as the 'depreciation gap' or 'depreciation backlog'. It arises because depreciation is levied on the average, current replacement cost in each year, not on the higher, future replacement cost. Strictly speaking, then, the CCA system covers replacement only if it takes place immediately the resource is consumed.

CCA falls short of providing for actual replacement. It must also be acknowledged that assets are rarely replaced with exact counterparts. For example, technological change produces different and superior machines which often have a greater capability than those held, and it is very often impossible to replace an asset held for several years with an identical new one. CCA merely ensures that sufficient funds are retained, on average, to maintain the purported operating capacity of the entity.

In times of inflation, business people become aware of the increasing cash requirements to maintain their assets and of the fact that the government, which levies taxes largely on historical cost profits, is thus depleting cash resources that are otherwise required to replace assets. This has given impetus to the promotion of CCA for taxation as well as for external reporting.

Taxation relief from higher replacement costs has been granted in the United States through the adoption of LIFO for inventory valuation, and accelerated depreciation. In the United Kingdom, taxation deductions are allowed in respect of part of the increase in cost of holding inventory and for accelerated depreciation. The Australian government permitted, in 1976, a 50 per cent deduction of the difference between historical and current costs of inventory, but this scheme was soon abandoned. Advocates of CCA argue that the system should be adopted for both taxation and external reporting. The business community seems unwilling to adopt CCA for financial reporting, in the absence of a legal requirement, until and unless a similar system may be used for taxation purposes.

Financial analysis

By valuing all expenses, whenever incurred, at current cost, CCA ensures that the profit and loss statement contains representations in contemporary terms. The influence of costs established in previous periods is eliminated, making it possible to compare entities of different ages on their contemporary performance.

Assets are measured in contemporary prices in end-of-year dollars. The denominator for the calculation of return on investment represents the outlay currently required to secure the assets of the entity. The return on investment therefore represents the return achieved after covering costs of replacement, as a percentage of the current cost of the assets employed.

CCA removes the discretion given under historical cost as to whether and when to revalue assets. Revaluations are required each period, and holding gains and losses are recognised as they occur rather than when they are realised or when the entity chooses to revalue assets. Under CCA, these holding gains and losses generally form part of the current cost adjustment and do not affect periodic profit. Holding gains must be retained as capital to support the higher cost of maintaining the assets.

CCA may also provide a better measure of an entity's financial stability than does historical cost. A measure of profit using current market costs is claimed to give a better indication of the entity's ability to cover higher operating costs in the future, together with interest and dividend payments.

Reliability

A deficiency of the CCA system is that it relies on many of the allocations found in historical cost accounting. Depreciation, for example, is still usually calculated as an allocation of cost over the beneficial life of the asset, the only difference being that the cost figure is now measured as current replacement cost. The rules for revenue recognition are also unaffected by the introduction of CCA. Some allocations, however, are eliminated. For example, the choice between FIFO and LIFO for inventory is unnecessary, since inventory costs are now at current prices and not at allocated historical costs.

There are difficulties in estimating the current replacement costs of some assets, especially highly specialised assets or those that have been superseded by new models with different operating characteristics and capabilities. These are not insurmountable problems, however, because the replacement cost of a new model may be adjusted, albeit on an arbitrary basis, for such differences. If, for example, a new model is capable of producing twice as many components per hour as the model owned by an entity, then the applicable replacement cost of the entity's equipment may be regarded as half the replacement cost of the new equipment.

As with CoCoA, astute management should be aware of the current replacement costs of the entity's assets. Apart from decisions related to the possible sale or replacement of assets, managers need to be aware of replacement costs when making inventory pricing decisions.

 ## Summary

Changes to accounting practice will be slow, and apparent solutions may fail the test of practical experience. In describing each of the main alternatives to the historical cost accounting system, an endeavour has been made to present the advantages and disadvantages of each system in terms of the objectives of accounting.

The aim has been to impart some understanding of each alternative system. It is not possible, at present, to state which system, if any, is likely to replace the historical cost system in its entirety. Of the alternatives, CCA has received the most support in a number of countries. Its strongest attraction seems to be the maintenance of operating capacity in periods in which price changes, spurred by inflation, have been dramatic. The acceptance of CCA may nevertheless depend on its acceptance for taxation purposes, since many entities seem unwilling voluntarily to reduce their declared net profits without a tax benefit in return.

It is foreseeable that entities will increasingly be required to disclose net realisable values of at least certain assets.

In many instances when entities have collapsed, the financial press has criticised the accounting profession for failing to force the disclosure of liquidation values. CoCoA does not propose the disclosure of values obtainable in a forced liquidation, as it is more concerned with adaptability through the sale of assets in the ordinary course of business. Before a system based on realisable values is adopted, it will therefore be necessary to decide between forced liquidation values and realisable values in the ordinary course of business as the measure that will provide the more useful information for the investor. Nevertheless, a number of accounting standards on issue require the disclosure of market value information for certain items.

International consensus on alternatives to the historical cost system does not currently exist, but one of the opportunities to resolve the various issues, internationally, lies in the development of rigorous and robust statements of accounting concepts in addressing the measurement issue in accounting. A mature international accounting profession would do just that.

 ## Review exercises

Discussion questions

19.1 Explain the relationship between capital and profit.

19.2 'There is no one "true" value for an asset, and hence there is no one "true" profit figure.' Critically evaluate this statement. If it is true, how can the most 'appropriate' accounting system be identified?

19.3 What is meant by the term 'constant dollar'?

19.4 Distinguish between the maintenance of historical cost capital, constant dollar or real capital, and physical capital.

19.5 'Different values of an asset may be required for different decisions.' Explain and illustrate this statement by reference to equipment that a company has used for several years that is nearing replacement.

19.6 'Changes in the general price level may not always be reflected in changes in the buying prices of specific assets and, in fact, they may move in opposite directions.' Explain and illustrate this statement.

19.7 A company owns equipment that it uses to manufacture margarine.

(a) List at least six attributes of the equipment which it might be useful to measure. Do not restrict yourself to financial attributes.

(b) For each attribute, indicate at least two units of measurement that might be adopted.

(c) For each combination of attribute and measurement unit, indicate a possible use that might be made of the measure.

19.8 To measure profit, it is necessary to identify:

(a) whether the financial capital or the physical capital is to be maintained

(b) the property of assets which represents capital

(c) the unit of measurement

Explain why each of these choices is necessary before profit may be determined.

19.9 What are the reasons for the existence of alternative measures of profit?

19.10 'Current purchasing power accounting represents an improvement on historical cost accounting in that the figures in the balance sheet and in the profit and loss statement are in the same unit of measurement and can be added and subtracted legitimately.' Discuss.

19.11 Explain the concepts of capital maintenance and profit employed in the current purchasing power system of accounting.

19.12 Using current purchasing power accounting, a purchasing power gain is recorded on monetary liabilities such as mortgages and debentures. Explain this treatment.

19.13 Explain the concept of capital maintenance adopted in the CoCoA system. Is it a relevant and useful concept of capital for purposes of stewardship reporting and performance measurement?

19.14 How does the concept of capital maintenance adopted in the current cost accounting system differ from (a) the historical cost concept of capital, and (b) the CoCoA concept of capital? What implications does this difference have for the CCA profit and loss statement and the CCA balance sheet?

19.15 Explain the major differences between CoCoA and CCA accounting.

19.16 What are the advantages and disadvantages of current cost accounting compared with historical cost accounting?

 Problems

19.17 *Determining profit during time of inflation*

Assume that five years ago you purchased a house for $90 000, which you rented to a tenant for $8000 net per year. Each year the market price of the house has risen by $10 000 per year.

(a) What would you regard as the profit on the house in each year? Explain your answer.

(b) Would your answer be altered if either of the following occurred?

    (i) Today, after owning the house for five years, you have sold the house for $135 000 in order to purchase, also for $135 000, a similar home in a sub-urb closer to your place of work.

    (ii) Today, having owned the house for five years, it has been destroyed by fire.

19.18 *Determining profit on an investment in shares*

Shrewd Investments commenced business on 1 January 20X1 with capital of $60 000 invested in:

Shares in ABC Retailers Ltd	— cost $15 000
Shares in XYZ Manufacturers Ltd	— cost $32 000
Shares in IOU Financiers Ltd	— cost $13 000

The first two investments were considered to be long-term investments and the third, the shares in IOU Financiers Ltd, was a speculative purchase.

On 31 December 20X1 the following dividends were received:

ABC Retailers Ltd	$1500
XYZ Manufacturers Ltd	1600
IOU Financiers Ltd	–
	3100

The market values of the shares at that date were:

ABC Retailers Ltd	$25 000
XYZ Manufacturers Ltd	30 000
IOU Financiers Ltd	11 000

(a) What profit would be declared for the year using the historical cost system of accounting?

(b) What profit do you consider was made during the year? Give reasons for your answer.

(c) Assuming the shares were all sold on 31 December 20X1, what profit do you con-sider was made for the year ended 31 December 20X1?

(d) Does it make any difference to your answer to know that the average inflation rate over the year was 50 per cent? Explain your answer.

19.19 *Asset valuation under CPP*

1. On 1 July 20X5 Rent-It Ltd purchased a block of home units for $500 000. The general price-level index was 150 at that time and on 30 June 20X6 was 180. The estimated selling price of the block of units at 30 June 20X6 was $750 000.

    (a) Under the current purchasing power system, at what figure would the home units be shown in the balance sheet at 30 June 20X6? What does this figure represent?

    (b) Show the journal entry for the price-level adjustment. Explain the meaning of the journal entry.

2. A firm owns 100 000 shares in Investment Ltd, of which 40 000 shares were pur-chased for $10 000 on 1 July 20X1 when the general price-level index was 100, 20 000 shares were purchased for $10 000 on 1 July 20X5 when the general

price-level index was 120, and 40 000 were purchased on 30 June 20X7 for $40 000 when the general price-level index was 150.

(a) Using current purchasing power accounting, at what value would each parcel of shares be shown in the 30 June 20X7 balance sheet? What do these figures represent?

(b) To what extent would these values be useful for investment analysis?

(c) Show journal entries to record the price-level adjustments.

19.20 *Comparative financial statements: CoCoA and historical cost*

1. Uneedit Pty Ltd commenced business on 1 January 20X2 with the following assets:

Plant and equipment:	$50 000 at cost
	48 000 at CCE
Cash at bank:	15 000

The plant and equipment are expected to be used in the business for 10 years after which time they will have a zero scrap value. They are to be depreciated straight-line under the historical cost system.

During the year, cash payments for production costs totalled $100 000, and sales amounted to $145 000. Wages were $20 000. Uneedit Pty Ltd undertakes all its business on a strictly cash basis.

Assets at 31 December 20X2 were as follows:

	At cost	CCE
Cash at bank	$40 000	$40 000
Raw materials	10 000	2 000
Finished goods	15 000	25 000
Plant and equipment	50 000	30 000

The general price index rose from 100 to 110 over the year.

(a) Prepare a profit and loss statement and balance sheet for the year ended 31 December 20X2 under:

(i) the historical cost system

(ii) continuously contemporary accounting (CoCoA)

(b) What useful information is revealed by the statements prepared under CoCoA that was not available under historical cost accounting?

2. On 1 January 20X5 Ripoff Rents Pty Ltd began its second year of business with the following assets:

	At cost	CCE
Home units	$120 000	$245 000
Motor vehicle	15 000	14 000
Cash at bank	10 000	10 000
Mortgage	30 000	30 000

The motor vehicle, which was purchased on the last day of 20X4, was expected to be used in the business for three years, after which time its residual value would be $6000.

During the year, rents of $50 000 were received, interest of $10 000 was paid on the mortgage, and expenses totalling $15 000 were paid. A further $2000 interest was due at 31 December 20X5.

At 31 December 20X5 the non-monetary assets had the following current cash equivalent values:

Home units $340 000
Motor vehicle   8 000

The general price index rose 20 per cent during the year.

(a) Prepare a profit and loss statement and balance sheet for the year ended 31 December 20X5 under:

(i)   the historical cost system
(ii) continuously contemporary accounting (CoCoA)

(b) What useful information is revealed by the statements prepared under CoCoA that was not available under historical cost accounting?

3. Shady Gulch Ltd, an exploration company, commenced business on 1 January 20X7 with a capital contribution in cash of $1 000 000. Of this amount $750 000 was invested immediately in specially imported equipment for extracting and refining ore.

During the year the company spent cash of $120 000 in drilling for ore and at the end of the year the following was on hand:

		At estimate of
	Cost	Resale value
Unprocessed ore	$70 000	$ 3 000
Refined ore	50 000	260 000

The costs were obtained by allocating the outlays in accordance with hours spent on mining activities. The resale values were obtained by examining the current prices of similar ore sold by established companies at or about 31 December 20X7. They reflect the fact that the ore has practically no value until it has been refined. The company has not yet made any sales.

The equipment was estimated to have a resale value of approximately $40 000 at the end of the year. It should last approximately 20 years and it is thought proper to depreciate the equipment on the straight-line basis.

The price index rose by 10 per cent during the year.

(a) Prepare profit and loss statements and balance sheets under:

(i)   the historical cost method of profit determination
(ii) the CoCoA method of profit determination

(b) In your opinion, which, if either, system best measures the company's performance in its first year? Give reasons.

(c) Which method produces the more reliable results? Justify your view.

19.21 *Comparative financial statements: CPP and historical cost*

Rentals Pty Ltd began business on 1 July 20X1 with paid-up capital of $50 000 and the following assets:

Home units	$35 000
Vehicle	5 000
Bank	10 000

The vehicle will be depreciated on the straight–line basis over a period of four years after which time its residual value is expected to be no more than $1000.

Transactions for the year were:

Rents received 31 December 20X1	$5 000
Rents received 30 June 20X2	6 000
Cash expenses paid 31 December 20X1	4 000

An index of the general price level was:

1 July 20X1	100
31 December 20X1	120
30 June 20X2	150

(a) Prepare an historical cost profit and loss statement and balance sheet for the year ended 30 June 20X2.

(b) Prepare a current purchasing power profit and loss statement and balance sheet for the year ended 30 June 20X2.

19.22 *Comparative financial statements: CCA and historical cost*

1. The Makeit Manufacturing Company commenced business on 1 January 20X5 with the following:

Cash at bank	$ 8 000
Inventory (600 units @ $15)	9 000
Equipment (new—at cost)	20 000
Capital	$37 000

The equipment is to be depreciated on the straight-line basis over a 10-year period, and after that time is estimated to have no residual value.

Transactions for 20X5 were:

Sales (600 units at $35)	$21 000
Purchases (600 units @ $18)	
made immediately after sale	10 800

At 31 December 20X5, the replacement cost of inventory was $20 per unit. New equipment would cost $26 000. Sundry expenses totalling $1000 were paid during the year. All transactions were for cash.

(a) Prepare profit and loss statements and balance sheets for 20X5 under:

(i) the historical cost system
(ii) the current cost system

(b) Contrast the respective measures of financial performance given by each of the statements presented in (a). Would the availability of a current cost statement improve the quality of decision making and, if so, in what respects?

2. Speedy Sellers Pty Ltd commenced business on 1 January 20X5 with capital in cash of $100 000. On that day it purchased shop premises for $40 000, display shelves for $10 000 and 10 000 units of inventory at $4 per unit.

The total inventory was sold on 30 June 20X5 for $12 per unit, and was immediately replaced for $8 per unit (10 000 units). Wages for the year were $15 000 and other sundry expenses totalled $2000. All transactions were for cash.

At 31 December the replacement cost of the 10 000 units of inventory totalled $120 000; the replacement cost of the new shop premises was $65 000, and new display shelves $30 000. The display shelves are to be depreciated straight-line over four years, after which they will have zero residual value.

Prepare a profit and loss statement and balance sheet for the year ended 31 December 20X5 using:

(a) the historical cost method of accounting

(b) current cost accounting

Case studies

19.23 *Current purchasing power accounting*

Sugo Ltd commenced business on 1 January 20X5 with the following opening balance sheet.

BALANCE SHEET
as at 1 January 20X5

Assets	
Cash at bank	$15 000
Plant and equipment	50 000
Total assets	65 000
Shareholders' equity	
Paid-up capital	$65 000

The company's historical cost profit and loss statement for the year ended 31 December 20X5 and balance sheet as at that date appear as follows:

PROFIT AND LOSS STATEMENT
for year ended 31 December 20X5

Sales		$65 000
less Cash expenses	50 000	
Depreciation ($50 000 × 10%)	5 000	55 000
Net profit		10 000

(All sales were earned, and cash expenses incurred, evenly throughout the year.)

BALANCE SHEET
as at 31 December 20X5

Assets		
Cash at bank		$15 000
Investments		15 000
Plant and equipment	50 000	
Accumulated depn	(5 000)	45 000
Total assets		75 000
Shareholder's equity		
Paid-up capital		$65 000
Retained profits		10 000
		$75 000

Additional information

(i) The investments disclosed in the balance sheet were purchased by Sugo on 1 July 20X5.

(ii) An index of the general price level was:

1 January 20X5	100
1 July 20X5	107
31 December 20X5	114

Required

(a) Prepare Sugo Ltd's profit and loss statement for the year ended 31 December 20X5, and the balance sheet as at that date, under the current purchasing power (CPP) method of accounting.

(b) Summarise the rationale for the adjustments made to the financial statements under the CPP approach, and discuss the advantages and disadvantages of Sugo's financial statements as prepared under this alternative.

(c) How useful do you consider Sugo's financial statements, as prepared under CPP, to be in presenting the results of the company's operations for the year and its financial position at 31 December 20X5? Comment from the point of view of (i) a Sugo shareholder and (ii) a bank considering lending to Sugo.

19.24 *Continuously contemporary accounting and current cost accounting*

Saarinen Ltd commenced business on 1 July 20X5 as a toy retailer with the following opening balance sheet.

BALANCE SHEET
as at 1 July 20X5

Assets	
Cash at bank	$10 000
Plant and equipment	60 000
Total assets	70 000
Shareholders' equity	
Paid-up capital	$70 000

The company's historical cost profit and loss statement for the year ended 30 June 20X6 and balance sheet as at that date appear as follows:

PROFIT AND LOSS STATEMENT
for year ended 30 June 20X6

Sales		$80 000
Less Cost of goods sold		40 000
Gross profit		40 000
Less Cash expenses	28 000	
Depreciation ($60 000 × 10%)	6 000	34 000
Net profit		6 000

BALANCE SHEET
as at 30 June 20X5

Assets		
Cash at bank		$12 000
Inventory		10 000
Plant and equipment	60 000	
Accumulated depn	(6 000)	54 000
Total assets		76 000
Shareholders' equity		
Paid-up capital		$70 000
Retained profits		6 000
		76 000

Additional information

(i) The replacement cost of the goods sold on the date the sales were made was $44 000.

(ii) The replacement cost of physical assets at 30 June 20X6 was:

Inventory	$12 000
Plant and equipment	65 000

(iii) The net realisable value (current cash equivalents) of non-monetary assets at 30 June 20X6 was:

Inventory	$14 000
Plant and equipment	40 000

(iv) The general price-level index rose by 8 per cent during the year.

Required

(a) Prepare Saarinen Ltd's profit and loss statement for the year ended 30 June 20X6, and the balance sheet as at that date, under the continuously contemporary accounting (CoCoA) method of accounting.

(b) Prepare Saarinen Ltd's profit and loss statement for the year ended 30 June 20X6, and the balance sheet as at that date, under the current cost accounting (CCA) method of accounting.

(c) Summarise the rationale for the adjustments made to the financial statements under the CoCoA approach and the CCA approach.

(d) Discuss the advantages and disadvantages of Saarinen's financial statements as prepared under each of these alternatives.

(e) How useful do you consider Saarinen's financial statements, as prepared under CoCoA and CCA, to be in presenting the results of the company's operations for the financial year and its financial position at 30 June 20X6? Comment from the point of view of (i) a Saarinen shareholder, (ii) a bank considering lending to Saarinen, and (iii) an employee of Saarinen.

19.25 *Presentation of financial position and valuation: historical cost, CoCoA and CCA*

Chee Pty Ltd is a successful private company operated by its two shareholders, each of whom owns 50 per cent of the issued capital of the company. The company is well established and operates in a stable, steadily growing industry. Over the past five years the company's historical cost financial statements reveal that net profit after tax has averaged 26 per cent of shareholders' equity. This represents an excellent return given the stable industry in which Chee Pty Ltd operates and is reflective of the established client base the company has built up over the years.

Chee's shareholders have received a takeover offer of $170 000 each from Raider Ltd for their shares in the company (i.e. valuing the total company as a whole at $340 000). The managing director of Raider has told Chee's shareholders that the offer is a 'particularly good one because it represents a premium of $40 000 over the value of the company's net assets as disclosed in Chee's balance sheet for the latest financial year ended on 30 June 20X4'.

Chee's shareholders are seriously considering this offer, as they are both over 60 years of age and have been thinking about retirement in recent years. They also realise that the company's plant and equipment, although in sound working order, requires substantial upgrading and should be replaced within two to three years.

To assist them in deciding whether to accept the takeover offer, the shareholders have instructed their accountant to provide further relevant accounting information. In response, the accountant provided them with the following comparative balance sheets based on historical cost accounting, continuously contemporary accounting and current cost accounting.

BALANCE SHEET: CHEE PTY LTD
as at 30 June 20X4

	Historical cost	CoCoA $	CCA $
Assets			
Cash at bank	14 000	14 000	14 000
Accounts receivable	42 000	42 000	42 000
Inventory	40 000	55 000	43 000
Investments	34 000	66 000	66 500
Motor vehicles (net)	90 000	70 000	115 000
Plant and equipment (net)	130 000	35 000	190 000
Land and buildings	150 000	295 000	305 000
	500 000	577 000	775 500
Liabilities			
Creditors and borrowings	200 000	200 000	200 000
Net assets	300 000	377 000	575 500
Shareholders' equity			
Paid-up capital	210 000	210 000	210 000
Retained profits	90 000	70 000	65 000
Capital maintenance reserve		97 000	
Current cost adjustment			300 500
	300 000	377 000	575 500

Required

Discuss the financial factors to be considered by the shareholders of Chee Pty Ltd, given the above information, in assessing the attractiveness of the takeover offer from Raider Ltd.

PART 5

Accounting information systems

CHAPTER 20

Accounting information systems and internal control

Learning objectives

In this chapter you will be introduced to:

1. the relationship between the accounting information system and the management information system

2. the importance of internal control in accounting information systems

3. various internal control procedures

4. the importance of documents to an accounting information system

5. the importance of journals in a manual accounting information system

6. a range of special journals in a manual accounting information system

7. the advantages of special journals

8. the advantages, particularly for control purposes, of using subsidiary ledgers

9. the use of subsidiary ledgers in a manual accounting information system.

Introduction

The accounting system involves a process of input, processing and output, as illustrated below:

INPUT → PROCESSING → OUTPUT
(accounting events)   (accounting records)   (financial statements)

In previous sections of the book, emphasis has been placed on the output of the system, the design of financial statements to communicate relevant and reliable information to aid in the decisions of owners, managers and others.

In this chapter we turn to the input and processing stages of the system and begin by identifying the accounting information system as a subset of the management information system. Within the accounting information system, a series of controls, referred to as internal controls, are designed to protect the assets of the organisation and to ensure the accuracy of the recording and processing of data. The importance of documents to the accounting information system is discussed, as they are the initial source of data for the system and are an important element in the internal control procedures.

Although many accounting information systems are now computerised, we will explain some of the features of control built into a manual accounting system. These include the process of recording data into special journals which enables a large volume of data to be summarised prior to being posted to the ledger. Another feature that increases efficiency and control is the process of dividing the general ledger into subsidiary ledgers. Common subsidiary ledgers include those for accounts receivable, accounts payable and inventory.

The control of cash is of particular importance because this asset is a prime target for fraud and theft. Also, because of the large number of transactions involving cash, there is more likelihood of errors occurring in its recording and processing. For this reason we describe how a system of external verification can occur when we reconcile an organisation's cash records with those kept by the bank, again a very important part of control within the accounting information system.

The chapter concludes with a comprehensive example to illustrate the use of special journals, subsidiary ledgers and bank reconciliation statements in a manual accounting information system.

Management information systems (MIS) and accounting information systems (AIS)

Management has the task of planning, controlling and evaluating the activities of the organisation. In fulfilling these functions, management requires information which it may obtain through formal information systems or informal information systems. Informal information may arise from systems of communication such as discussions with staff at morning tea time. Informal systems might provide some important information that is capable of assisting with decision making, but they can be unreliable and because of their nature lack control features. The formal systems which provide management with more reliable information are structured to ensure accuracy. They encompass the process of data collection and processing and information generation and communication for the entire organisation. They would include systems to produce reports to management relating to the marketing of their service or product, details of personnel employed by the organisation and details of the production of their product. Included in these management information systems are the accounting systems. Although the boundaries between the systems are not necessarily fixed, the accounting systems generally concentrate on the generation and communication of relevant and reliable information on the financial aspects of the organisation. Accounting systems consist of a series of interrelated procedures for the collection and processing of financial

Figure 20.1

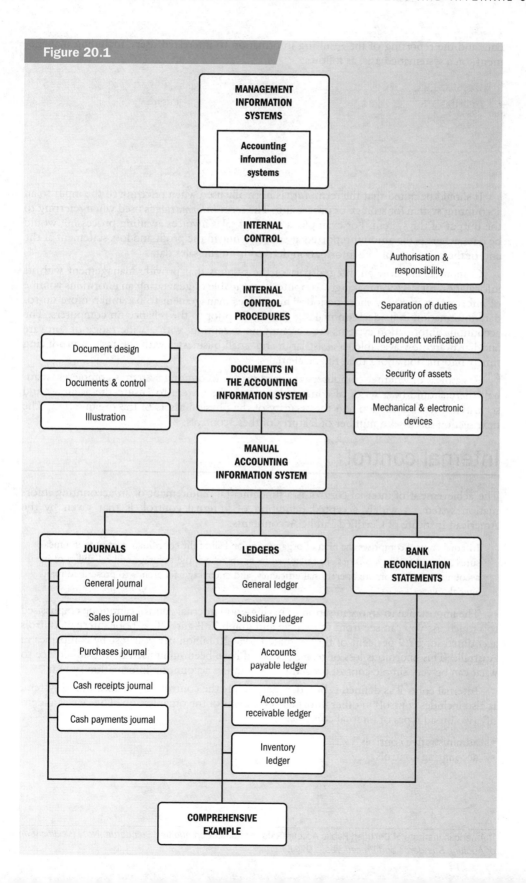

data and the reporting of the resulting information to interested users, including management, on a systematic basis, as follows:

It should be noted that the term *data* is normally used when referring to the input to an accounting system for storage or processing. The term *information* is used when referring to the output of the system. For example, a batch of sales invoices awaiting processing would be data, whereas the amount reported as sales revenue in the profit and loss statement at the end of the period would be information derived from the sales data.

Computers are now an integral part of the systems that provide management with its information for decision making. Computers are capable of generating an enormous volume of information in a very short period. This enables management to use much more up-to-date information in its decision making than it did prior to the reliance on computers. The accounting information systems are certainly no exception, with a wide range of software and hardware now available to assist large and small businesses with the task of producing timely information about their financial affairs.

Regardless of whether computers are used or the accounting system is completely manual, there should be a series of controls built into the system to ensure the accuracy and security of the information and the security of the physical assets of the organisation. The next section discusses a number of features of these controls.

Internal control

The achievement of internal control is a fundamental requirement of an accounting information system. A widely accepted definition of 'internal control' is that given by the American Institute of Certified Public Accountants:

> Internal control comprises the plan of organisation and all of the coordinate methods and measures adopted within a business to safeguard its assets, check the accuracy and reliability of its accounting data, promote operational efficiency, and encourage adherence to prescribed managerial policies.[1]

The importance to an organisation of having good internal control cannot be emphasised too much. As you can see from the article and graph in Figure 20.2, poor internal controls accounted for 57.9 per cent of the estimated $15–20 billion per year lost by companies in Australia. This enormous loss of resources could have been minimised by the adherence to what can be very simple control procedures within the accounting information system.

Internal control as defined is broader than simply the controls in the accounting system. It also includes controls in other information systems of the organisation. Thus we can identify two broad types of internal controls:

- administrative controls
- accounting controls.

---

[1] American Institute of Certified Public Accountants, *Statement on Auditing Standards, No. I (Codification of Auditing Standards and Procedures, 1973).*

Figure 20.2

Company fraud 'costs up to $20 billion'

Corporate crime

John MacLeay

CORPORATE fraud is costing the economy between $15 billion and $20 billion a year with as many as one in two companies experiencing significant losses, according to a survey by accounting firm KPMG.

The 480 big companies that took part in the survey, which is conducted every two years, reported losses due to fraud of at least $104 million during the past two years.

Patria Mann, co-ordinator to KPMG's forensic accounting unit, said the amount of fraud reported was only the tip of the iceberg, as many organisations were unaware of fraud or were reluctant to discuss their losses.

'The survey suggests the perpetrators of fraud were becoming more sophisticated', she said.

Poor internal controls and management override of these controls are the most common reasons for fraud, followed by collusion between employees and a third party, the survey finds.

About 70 per cent of companies experienced more than one fraud, with the majority experiencing between two and 10 frauds.

The average cost of fraud was $450 000, with the majority costing between $10 000 and $500 000, although 9 per cent of respondents put each fraud loss at between $500 000 and $10 million. One per cent of companies experienced individual frauds of more than $10 million.

Ms Mann said she suspected computer fraud was grossly under-reported, as only 7 per cent of respondents had experienced it.

She said companies were now more willing to instigate civil action to recover lost funds. However, there were some comments in the survey which suggested the police were under-resourced to investigate fraud.

KPMG director and forensic accountant John Banks said that while the level of fraud had remained at around the same level over the past few years, companies were now more willing to report the crime.

Mr Banks said fraud from the retail sector alone was estimated at $4 billion a year.

Of the 7771 frauds reported in the survey, 68.7

per cent were passed on to the police and criminal charges were laid in 57 per cent of those cases.

KPMG's principal consultant for information security, Peter McNally, said that by its very nature fraud was difficult to detect.

While most fraud—almost 50 per cent—was detected by a company's own internal controls, less than 1 per cent of fraud was discovered by external auditors.

Mr McNally said that downsizing and, in some cases, the abolition of internal company auditors had made it easier for fraud to flourish.

By industry group, all respondents in the tourism and hospitality and communications industries had reported fraud, while the highest average fraud occurred in the mining, manufacturing, automotive and communications industries.

Theft of inventory or plant was the most common type of fraud, which was consistent with KPMG's two previous fraud surveys. This was followed by misappropriation of funds and petty-cash fraud.

The Australian, 23 July 1997

continues

Figure 20.2 continued

FRAUD BY MANAGEMENT

Purchase for personal use	**13.5%**
Conflict of interest	**12.0%**
Expense account	**11.5%**
False invoices	**9.6%**
Misappropriation of funds	**9.1%**
Theft of inventory/plant	**8.2%**
Petty cash fraud	**7.7%**
Kickbacks	**7.2%**
Unnecessary purchase	**4.8%**
Cheque forgery	**3.8%**

**Other
12.6%**

FRAUD BY EMPLOYEES

Theft of inventory/plant	**17.8%**
Misappropriation of funds	**15.6%**
Petty cash fraud	**12.6**
Purchase for personal use	**8.0%**
Expense account	**7.6%**
False invoices	**6.2%**
Conflict of interest	**5.0%**
Kickbacks	**4.1%**
Unnecessary purchase **4.1%**	
Credit card fraud **3.7%**	

**Other
15.3%**

WHY FRAUD OCCURRED

Poor internal controls	**57.9%**
Collusion between employees & third party **29.6%**	
Management override of internal controls **23.2%**	
Poor inventory controls	**19.3%**
Type of industry	**18.5%**
Collusion between employees & management **16.7%**	
Poor hiring practices **15.0%**	
Other	**14.6%**
Lack of accountability **13.7%**	
Poor or non-existent corporate ethics **8.6%**	

*Note that in many
cases, respondents
indicated that more
than one factor
was responsible for
fraud occurring*

Source: KPMG

Administrative controls consist of all those controls in the organisation designed to promote efficient operations and to encourage the following of the policies of the organisation. A company will have a plan for the achievement of its goals and controls are necessary to ensure that the plan is carried out as intended and in the most efficient way. Administrative controls include quality control over the goods produced on the production line, policies governing the hiring of staff, and the comparison of operating results with budgets or standards.

Accounting controls are those controls intended to ensure that the accounting records and hence reports are accurate and reliable and to prevent the organisation's assets from being lost or stolen. The double-entry system provides one means of accounting control by requiring that transactions have two entries. Consequently, if the trial balance does not balance, this control feature tells us that the recording system needs to be checked for possible errors. Other accounting controls are instituted to ensure the safekeeping of assets, by requiring, for example, that lists of assets be kept and that the assets be inspected periodically.

Accounting and administrative controls are highly interrelated. Accounting information is used extensively for administrative control, such as in the preparation of budgets and in the evaluation of performance by analysis of the financial statements. To be useful for the evaluation of performance, however, the financial statements must be produced within an accounting information system that ensures reliability by means of accounting controls. Also, operational efficiency (an objective of administrative control) is impaired if adequate accounting controls do not exist to prevent misappropriation of the entity's assets. Good administrative control, therefore, requires sound accounting control.

Case 20.1 The diligent employee

Can you identify how the following fraud could have been prevented? Read through the case, then read the next section and see if some of your suggestions agree with any of the procedures in that section.

The record for the longest continuous career of theft by one employee must surely belong to a man who stole cash receipts totalling US$100 000 over a period of 29 years before being detected. The thefts took place over the employee's entire time with the company and were discovered only when the man retired.

The scheme involved using cheque receipts to cover the theft of cash, a process known as 'lapping'. The theft was possible because this employee was responsible for both cash receipts and the records establishing accountability for the receipts. He withheld cheques from accounts receivable collections, took cash from later collections, and then credited the previously withheld cheques to the accounts of customers who had paid cash. Later receipts were credited to the accounts of the customers who had sent in the first batch of cheques, and so on.

For this theft to have escaped detection for 29 years is remarkable. The employee had to be extremely careful. If customers who had paid by cheque received a second account, they would complain and the scheme would be discovered. The employee had to keep track of normal unpaid bills as well as deal with unexpected business disruptions such as strikes.

This employee was noted for his hard work and never required assistance. He also never took a long holiday, which was hardly surprising. The company trusted him, but because there were no controls in place, the company lost a lot of money.

Adapted from The Chubb Corporation 1989, 'White Collar Crime: Loss Prevention Through Internal Control', prepared by Ernst & Young for the Chubb Group of Insurance Companies (*http://www.chubb.com/library/crp15.html*)

Important internal control procedures

Certain procedures should be present in any good information system, but the complexity of the internal control procedures will depend on the size, complexity, type and operating functions of the organisation. For instance, the size of the organisation will affect the extent of the separation of duties, as in a small office there may be only one staff member. This does not mean that the employee's work cannot be verified; it simply means that the verification must be done by management.

Clear authorisation and responsibility

Management should ensure that any member of staff who has the authority to carry out certain tasks recognises the associated responsibility that goes with it. The lines of authority for tasks must be very clearly defined to ensure that staff are not confused about what they have the authority, and hence responsibility, for within the organisation. For example, two staff members might have the authority to issue petty cash, but it should be very clear which one is required to balance the petty-cash fund.

Separation of duties within the accounting system

This is a fundamental feature of a good system of internal control. If one person has the ability to make out cheques and also to sign them, the potential for fraud or error is very great. The potential is also there when one person in responsible for both the ordering and the receiving of goods for the organisation. By separating key tasks and making them the responsibility of different employees, errors are more easily detected and a potential fraud needs collusion between at least two people. The more people that are involved in the process from start to finish, the less likely fraud will occur without early detection. Duties should be separated on the basis of those who record details of an asset (cash, inventory, accounts receivable) and those who have access to the asset.

Independent verification

Independent verification should occur at various points throughout the system. This process is closely related to the separation of duties feature in that the performance of one employee can be evaluated or verified by the work of another employee who is independent of the subject and function. Examples of this include requiring each cheque issued to be signed by two responsible officers, the physical stocktake to be conducted by someone not involved in the record-keeping of stock, and the reconciliation of the cash record-keeping of the organisation with the bank statement by an employee not involved in recording the receipt or payment of cash. Internal verification might also include appointing staff within the organisation to act as *internal auditors* of the accounting records. The independence of this staff from the regular accounting staff is achieved by making them responsible directly to the upper levels of management of the organisation.

Adequate security for assets

Cash is one of the prime targets for fraud and theft, so it is important to have appropriate safeguards in place to minimise this possibility. For instance, cash registers should be used, cash should be banked daily, with the aid of security staff if necessary, and any cash left on the premises should be locked in a safe. Stock, vehicles, equipment and other physical assets should all be protected by appropriate safeguards such as locked buildings with security systems, security surveillance, regular physical checks, etc.

Use of mechanical and electronic equipment

The security of records and assets is greatly enhanced when appropriate and reliable mechanical and electronic devices are used. The use of cash registers, particularly those linked directly to the organisation's computers, will reduce the possibility of errors and theft by employees or people external to the organisation. The simple function of having the cash register display the amount of the sale not only protects the customer from an incorrect charge, but ensures that the correct amount is added to the internal record kept by the cash register, and hence the correctness of its daily total of receipts. The employee must account for the amount of cash as indicated by the daily total and embezzlement of funds therefore becomes more difficult. Security systems, surveillance cameras, time clocks, counters and measuring devices can all be used in various situations to minimise the loss of assets, both intentionally and unintentionally.

Internal control in the electronic environment

With much of the processing of accounting data now being carried out by computer systems, the internal control procedures relating to this type of processing need to be addressed. Many of the basic procedures still apply, but they may need to be varied slightly as much of the processing is done within the memory of the computer and there may not be as much evidence of the processing as when it is done manually.

The basic principles of separation of duties and internal verification are still vitally important. The person in charge of entering data, for instance, should not be responsible for banking receipts, and proper authorisation of purchases still needs to occur. However, new situations need to be taken into account. Once data is entered into a computer system there is less chance of errors in processing occurring, but there is also less chance of entry errors being detected. This places more importance on control over the accuracy of data entry, so a system of data-entry verification may be justified. Security over the entry of data also becomes important. Passwords may be used to limit access to various parts of the computer system or the system as a whole.

Two special problems of control relating to computer-based systems are the use by organisations and individuals of the Internet for transacting business and 'publishing' information about themselves, and the use of EDI (electronic data interchange). EDI involves organisations having their systems linked so that each has access to certain information on the others data files. This is happening between suppliers of goods and their customers. A retailer, for instance, can see what stocks and prices are available from the wholesaler and the wholesaler can monitor the stock levels of the retailer to ensure that levels are maintained. This might involve automatic reordering, invoicing and dispatch of goods, obviously creating a special set of control issues.

The area of control within computer-based systems is a very extensive and detailed one and a comprehensive discussion is beyond the scope of this text. However, as indicated earlier, humans are still involved and the basic procedures can still be applied to varying degrees to increase error detection and to safeguard assets.

Documents in the accounting information system

In designing an accounting information system that incorporates adequate internal control features, particular attention must be given to the documents to be produced. This will ensure that the data entering the accounting system are relevant to the information to be produced and are accurate. Different types of organisation will be involved in different types of transactions and transaction cycles. Thus their requirements in terms of the design and type of documents and the information contained in them will be very different.

Organisations are involved in a number of transaction cycles or chains of events that occur as a transaction proceeds to completion. Contrary to the impression that may have been given in the examples elsewhere in this book, transactions are not always single, instantaneous events. With the sale of goods, for example, the filling of a customer's order might be delayed while the goods are purchased from the wholesaler; the goods would then need to be delivered, and only then could the customer be sent an invoice. These events may take time to complete and may require the coordination of activities in the sales section, the production department, the dispatch department and the accounts department.

Some other examples of transaction cycles include:

- the production of goods, which requires materials to be obtained, production processes to occur and finished goods to be sent to the store (This cycle might take days or even months to complete. The production of wine, for example, often takes several years.)
- the payment of employees, commencing perhaps with the lodgment of a time sheet by the employee, indicating the hours of regular work and overtime completed, continuing with a calculation in the payroll office of the amount due to the employee, and ending with the insertion of the appropriate cash in a pay envelope by staff in the cashier's office and the receipt of that pay envelope by the employee
- the purchase of inventory and other supplies
- the incurring and payment of operating expenses
- the purchase of plant and equipment.

These cycles interact: in the payroll cycle, for example, employees are paid for their work in the production cycle. The data on hours worked are therefore required both for production statistics and for the payment of wages. It can be seen that the design of an accounting information system in a large organisation is a very complicated and specialised area, one that is beyond the scope of this text. In the next sections we discuss some general principles of document design and illustrate the interaction of documents and internal control within an accounting information system.

Document design

The coordination of activities to complete the various transaction cycles is achieved by the preparation of documents that flow within the organisation. There is no limit to the documents an organisation may produce to meet its particular needs. They include not only the familiar forms such as invoices to customers and receipts for payment but also purchase orders, employee time-sheets, materials requisitions, goods received reports and very specialised documents that would be appropriate for one particular organisation only.

Apart from their value in achieving coordination, documents provide the source of the data for entries in the accounting records. There may be a time lag between the occurrence of a transaction and the entry of that transaction in the accounts, which requires a written record to be kept pending the accounting entry. A sale, for example, might be made at the beginning of the week and written immediately on a sale docket, but the sale might not be entered into the accounting records until the end of the week when the accountant finds time to record all the sales for the week. So long as a sales docket exists, the sale can be recorded at a convenient later date.

Documents also supply the auditor with evidence in support of the accounting entry. In the above case, sales would be supported by invoices, which might in turn be supported by a bank deposit slip for the amount received from the customer.

The documents should be designed carefully in order to capture all of the required information. If the necessary pieces of data are not written on the originating document, they may be lost forever. If, for example, it is desired to know the weight of each item purchased so that it can be entered in the production records, the document must provide a space for the weight to be included.

The one document might provide information for several purposes, perhaps covering more than one transaction cycle. In designing the form, therefore, it is necessary to consider the data required to satisfy each purpose. A document to serve as a purchase order, for example, would require the entry of all data necessary to inform the supplier of exactly what goods are to be supplied. The purchase order might also need to include sufficient data to enable the purchase to be entered in the accounting records when the goods are received. In the case of sales, one copy of the sales invoice might be sent to the credit department to record the amount due from the customer, while another copy might be sent to the inventory control manager to enable the recording on the appropriate stock card of the goods issued to the customer.

Documents should also be designed to facilitate the orderly arrangement of data, making the data easier to enter, read and check. Recording time is reduced by the use of printed forms in an established format that can be followed routinely. The design should also take into consideration whether the document is to be computer-generated, as there may be special requirements to be allowed for.

Usually documents carry serial numbers. These numbers enable the documents to be cross-referenced in the journals and the subsidiary ledgers, and to be easily identified in any verbal or written communication in relation to them. They also have an inbuilt control feature in that each number must be accounted for. A missing numbered purchase order may provoke an inquiry as to whether the form has been taken by an employee to purchase goods for personal use. Cancelled forms should therefore be retained as proof that the form was not misused.

Documents and internal control

As the types of transaction cycles depend on the organisation, this book cannot describe them all. However, a cycle that occurs in most organisations is the purchase of goods and subsequent payment for those goods, so this will be used to illustrate the interaction of documents and internal control within an accounting information system.

Example: *Purchase of goods in a university*

The University of Leaning Tower has instituted an internal control system over its purchases and payment of accounts in accordance with Figure 20.3.

In the purchase of goods, a control objective must be to ensure that all activities are properly authorised. The purchase must be authorised by a responsible officer, and the payment may be authorised only when the goods have been received in good condition and in accordance with the purchase order. Six control points have been identified in Figure 20.3 (1 to 6 in parentheses). Each will be explained as the cycle is followed through for a typical transaction.

Several departments in the university participate in the purchase cycle. The duties of each department in relation to the purchase are arranged to achieve accounting control through internal verification, since the work of one department verifies the work of another. The departments to be encountered in the purchase transaction cycle and the functions to be performed are as follows:

UNIVERSITY DEPARTMENTS

Department	Function	Documents produced
Purchasing	Place orders for goods	Purchase order
Stores	Receive, store and issue goods	–
Accounts	Check and approve payments	Payment voucher
Cashier	Receive and disburse cash	Cheques
Various teaching depts	Teaching and research	Purchase requisition

Figure 20.3 Transaction cycle for the purchase of goods

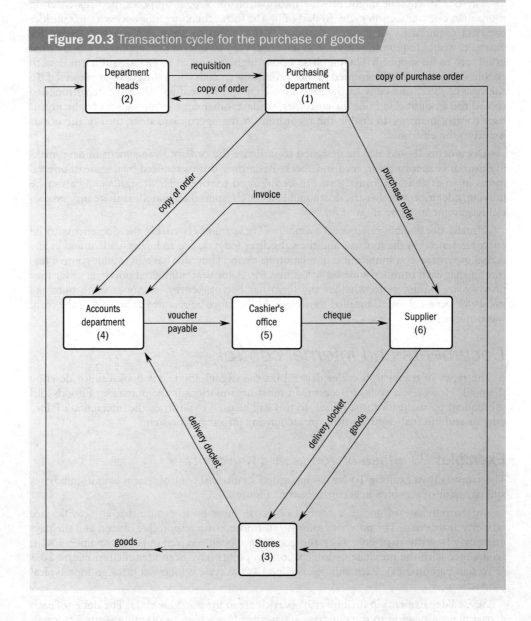

On 10 August 20Xl the Classics Department, within the Faculty of Arts, wished to order 49 binders for course notes to be given to students. The Professor of Classical Studies completed a *purchase requisition* (see Figure 20.4) that was duly countersigned by the Dean of the Faculty of Arts, who was authorised to approve expenditures. A copy was retained in the faculty and the original was sent to the purchasing department, which conducted the first control check.

Control 1

The purchasing department should check that the requisition has been signed by an authorised officer.

Next, the purchasing department determined the best source for the binders and the price and wrote these details on a *purchase order* (see Figure 20.5). Five copies of the purchase order were made and distributed as follows:

1. Sent to supplier.
2. Sent to stores department to be compared eventually with the actual goods delivered.
3. Sent to the Faculty of Arts for checking.
4. Sent to accounts department for later comparison with invoice.
5. Retained in purchasing department.

Control 2

Staff in the Faculty of Arts should check the purchase order against the original requisition to ensure that the correct goods have been ordered.

When the goods arrived from the supplier they were delivered to the stores department. With the goods, the supplier enclosed a *delivery docket* (see Figure 20.6) describing the goods and referring to the order number quoted on the university's purchase order.

Control 3

The stores department should check the physical quantity and quality of the goods against the supplier's delivery docket.

Once the stores department had made its checks, the goods were delivered to the Classics Department. The delivery docket was signed as being correct by a responsible officer in the stores department and sent on to the accounts department.

Later in the month an *invoice* (see Figure 20.7) was received by the accounts department from the supplier. The invoice referred to the goods, the order number, the delivery docket number and the price to be paid.

Control 4

Before approving payment, the accounts department must match the following documents:

(a) the supplier's invoice
(b) the original purchase order
(c) the delivery docket

Once a match was obtained, the accounts department made out a *voucher payable* (see Figure 20.8) and sent the completed file on the purchase to the cashier's office.

Control 5

The paying clerk should check that all documents have been verified, that is, that all of the required internal checks have been followed.

Once the paying clerk was satisfied, a cheque was prepared and signed by an independent officer. The details were checked by another officer, who countersigned the cheque. The cheque was posted to the supplier. All documents were then returned to the accounts department for cancellation and filing.

Control 6

The supplier will make an independent check for discrepancies in payments received.

This simplified example demonstrates how accounting control may be achieved by the division of duties in such a way that the work of one department must be checked by the work of another. The purchasing department, for example, orders goods, but it does not receive them, thus making it difficult for individuals to orders goods for their personal use. The cashier makes payments, but only when the accounts department has authorised payment, thus making it difficult to make unauthorised payments for the cashier's personal benefit.

Figure 20.4 Example of a purchase requisition form

LEANING TOWER UNIVERSITY

PURCHASE REQUISITION

SCHOOL: Arts
SCHOOL REQ NO: 330
ACCOUNT: Classics
DELIVER TO: W3A-318   DATE: 10/8/X1

QTY	PARTICULARS
49	Binders—A4–2ring standard Yellow with gold printing, 'Classics Course Notes'

AUTHORISED: Con Template
(Dean, Faculty of Arts)
REQUISITIONED BY: C. Dickens, Ext. 9123

Figure 20.5 Example of a purchase order

LEANING TOWER UNIVERSITY
NORTH BUSH

Avarice Industries Ltd
4 Dunk Street
RIVERVIEW

PURCHASE ORDER

ORDER NO: 14537
DATE: 12/8/X1

DELIVER TO: Store, University Drive.

QTY	PARTICULARS	UNIT PRICE	EXTENSION
49	Binders–A4–2ring standard Cat No 46	$1.58	$77.42
	Yellow with gold printing, 'Classics Course Notes'	$0.55	26.95
	Plus University logo		
	As previously supplied on 0/No 13908 dated 17/4/X0		
	NET FIS DEL: 2–3 weeks		104.37

SCHOOL: Arts   ACCOUNT: Classics
REQ NO: 330   A/C CODE: 805.006.401

Figure 20.6 Example of a delivery docket

Avarice Industries Ltd
4 Dunk Street
RIVERVIEW

DELIVERY DOCKET: 32832

DATE: 21/8/X1
CUSTOMER ORDER NO: 14537
SALES TAX: Exempt

| DESCRIPTION | PRODUCT | | | QUANTITY | UNIT PRICE |
	GROUP	NUMBER	COLOUR		
Binder Printing	01	46	Yellow	49 49	1.58 .55

DELIVER TO: Leaning Tower University, Store, University Drive

OFFICIAL INVOICE WILL FOLLOW

Figure 20.7 Example of an invoice

Avarice Industries Ltd
4 Dunk Street
RIVERVIEW

INVOICE NO: 94918

DATE: 12/8/X1
DELIVER TO: Store,
University Drive

INVOICE TO: Leaning Tower University
North Bush

CUSTOMER NO	DATE OF ORDER	CUSTOMER ORDER NO.	SALES TAX NUMBER	AREA	INTERNAL ORDER NO.	WAREHOUSE
LEANTOWOO	12/8/X1	14537	Exempt	122	32382	SYDSTA

STOCK CODE	DESCRIPTION	QTY ORD	QTY DEL	UNIT DESC	UNIT PRICE	GROSS AMOUNT	DISCOUNT SALES TAX	NET
0146 Yel	2 ring A4 Binder	49	49	Each	1.58	77.42		77.42
	Printing	49	49	Each	0.55	26.95		26.95

NO CLAIM ACCEPTED OVER 30 DAYS. TERMS: 30 DAYS NET.	TOTAL	$104.37

Figure 20.8 Example of a voucher payable

SUPPLIER NO: 1045

VOUCHER PAYABLE

CARD CODE	DOCUMENT NUMBER	ORDER NUMBER	ACCOUNT CODE	AMOUNT		ACCOUNT NAME
1	94918	014537	805006401	104	37	Classics

PREPARED BY:

CHECKED BY:

I CERTIFY THAT THE SERVICE
HAS BEEN PERFORMED

Control through the division of duties is a vital part of an effective internal control system, but the separation of functions requires the production of documents to enable communication between divisions to take place. The example shows how coordination is achieved by means of a well-designed set of documents and an orderly system for the transfer of those documents between various departments. No invoice ought to be paid until it is successfully matched with a purchase order, which confirms that the goods being charged for were actually ordered by the purchasing department, and a countersigned delivery docket, which confirms that the goods were received by the store in good order. The completion of a payment voucher by the accounts department provides the cashier with the authorisation to pay the account. Without these documents the various departments dealing with the purchase would not have been able to bring together the evidence to confirm that the payment should be made.

Manual accounting information systems

The previous section discussed the source documents used to identify and collect information about the transactions taking place in an organisation. This section describes how the accounting system processes the information from the source documents systematically and in a manner that:

- allows the preparation of the financial statements as the outputs of the process
- ensures accuracy and integrity in the collection and provision of accounting information.

Even though most accounting systems at this time involve, to at least some degree, the use of a computer, the system described here is a manual system. Computer-based systems allow greater efficiencies and economies in information processing than do manual systems, but many of the principles underlying manual systems are present in, and form the basis of, the logic of computer-based systems. For this reason, the illustration of a manual system is seen as being important in making visible the mechanisms needed to ensure the accuracy and integrity of information collection and provision.

The recording process

Although the manual recording process has been dealt with in various earlier chapters, it is appropriate to return to this process now to identify any added features as a result of the discussion of control in the previous section.

There are three sequential steps in the manual recording process:

1. Collect the documents or records providing evidence of transactions. These include invoices, delivery dockets, cheque butts and bank deposit slips. Otherwise, obtain authorisations from the responsible officers for the entries to be made.
2. Record the transactions in chronological sequence in a book of original entry, known as a journal.
3. Transfer the transaction detail from the journal to the ledger, making entries in appropriate accounts as established in the chart of accounts. This process is called 'posting'.

Accounting control over the recording process is strengthened by two important controls aimed at preventing error and fraud. To ensure that ledger entries are based on proper evidence and are consistent with the evidence provided by the documents and authorisations, the following must be adhered to:

- All ledger entries must be supported by journal entries.
- All journal entries must be based on documents or authorisations.

Journals

The general journal

The format of a general journal entry was described in Chapter 4, although more detail must now be added, as follows:

GENERAL JOURNAL				GJ12
Date	Description	Folio	Debit	Credit
20X8				
May 12	Equipment	128	$4000	
	Accounts payable	211		$4000
	(Purchase of Mark III Lathe			
	from Machinery Ltd—delivery			
	note 7732 dated 11 May)			

This entry describes a purchase of equipment on credit. It includes a narration containing the reason for the entry and making reference to the supporting documentary evidence. A link between the journal and the ledger is also provided by means of the folio column, which contains the numbers of the ledger accounts to which the journal entries have been posted. The number in the folio column next to 'Equipment', for example, indicates that a debit of $4000 has been made in the ledger account number 128, presumably the account for equipment.

There is now a chain of reference from the original evidence records to the ledger, which will aid in any examination of the records at a later stage. Moreover, the ledger entry will provide a cross-reference to the journal of origin by including the page number of the journal (GJ12) within the ledger entry.

The ability to trace a particular transaction from its source to the respective entries in the ledger and vice versa is referred to as the *audit trail* and is an important accounting control feature of an accounting information system.

Special journals

It would be possible to enter all transactions in a general journal before posting to the ledger as we have been doing to this point. However, the general journal is a most inefficient means of coping with the volume of transactions experienced in a modern organisation. Many types of business transactions occur frequently, and for ease of access to information and efficiency of recording it is useful to record various transactions in a series of *special journals*, each designed to record the details of a particular type of transaction, rather than recording them in the general journal. The major aim of the creation of these special journals is to take advantage of the summarising effect they have on the recording process. If designed correctly, these journals will not only group common types of transactions together, but will greatly reduce the amount of detail to be posted to the ledger.

The number and types of special journals to be used will depend on the needs of the organisation. For example, a company engaged in retail sales might typically have the following:

- *Cash receipts journal* —Records all receipts of cash, from whatever source.
- *Cash payments journal* —Records all payments of cash.
- (Credit) *Sales journal* —Records all credit sales of merchandise.
- (Credit) *Purchases journal* —Records all credit purchases of merchandise.

Other special journals might include those for sales returns and purchases returns, provided these occur frequently. A 'special' journal can be created for any type of transaction that occurs with sufficiency frequency to justify its use.

No transaction may appear in more than one journal, otherwise it will be posted more than once to the ledger. For this reason the sales journal is restricted to *credit sales*, with cash sales appearing in the cash receipts journal. Similarly, cash purchases appear in the cash payments journal and not in the purchases journal. It is normally considered preferable to keep all cash transactions together in the two cash journals so that the balance of cash may be computed with ease using the totals from these two journals only. The sales and purchases journals are also normally restricted to the recording of inventory transactions, leaving the purchase and sale of assets to be recorded in either the cash journals, if the transaction is for cash, or the general journal, if the transaction is on credit.

The format of each journal must be designed with the organisation's needs in mind and thus the designs will vary enormously. The following sales journal is, however, typical of one used by a retail business that does not have departments and adopts the periodic inventory method of recording inventory.

SALES JOURNAL			SJ23
Date	Accounts receivable	Folio	Amount
May 1	R. U. Reddy		$ 45.26
3	X. Pense		125.00
5	B. Hunter		24.18
7	I. Klass		236.21
			$430.65
			(112/331)

The design reduces the amount of detail that must be recorded, in comparison with the same entries in the general journal. Since all of the entries are credits to sales, it is only necessary to list the names of the customers in the journal.

Significant economies are also gained in the posting of this data to the ledger. If each sale had been entered as a separate general journal entry, eight individual entries would have been posted to the ledger (four debits to accounts receivable and four credits to sales revenue). However, with special journals all of the detailed information is available conveniently in the sales journal, and it is only necessary to post the total of $430.65 to the ledger, as a debit to accounts receivable and a credit to sales revenue. This procedure saves six entries in the above example but thousands of entries in a larger business entity. It therefore permits the size of the general ledger to be kept to manageable proportions.

The ledger postings are cross-referenced in the journal by placing the appropriate ledger account numbers below the totals posted to the ledger, that is (112/331).

The sales journal is easily posted, because all entries have common debits and credits. Similarly, in the cash payments journal illustrated in Figure 20.9, all of the entries involve cash payments. With the total cash payment being shown as one figure, it will result in just one credit entry to cash at bank of $3653.88. The debits, however, affect a number of ledger accounts. It is nevertheless possible to economise on ledger entries by providing columns for items that appear frequently. Since payments to suppliers occur frequently in the example, a special column is provided for accounts payable. In this way, the design of the journal will again reflect the type and frequency of transactions each organisation is involved in and will result in numerous designs for this journal.

Payments to suppliers are subject to the deduction of discounts, which are provided for by an additional column. Taking the payment to S. Smith & Co. as an example, $576.83 is entered in the accounts payable column to reduce that account, but only $566.63 is actually paid. This amount must be shown in the cash column, to be credited to cash at bank, with the remainder being entered in the purchase discount column, to be posted to an account of that title.

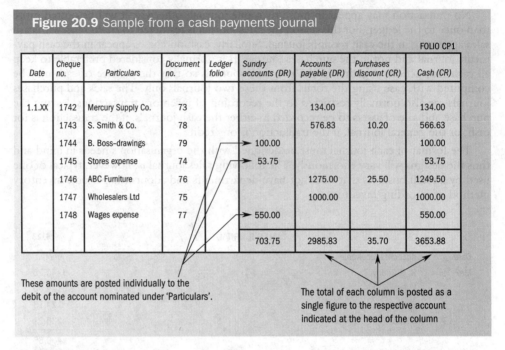

Figure 20.9 Sample from a cash payments journal

FOLIO CP1

Date	Cheque no.	Particulars	Document no.	Ledger folio	Sundry accounts (DR)	Accounts payable (DR)	Purchases discount (CR)	Cash (CR)
1.1.XX	1742	Mercury Supply Co.	73			134.00		134.00
	1743	S. Smith & Co.	78			576.83	10.20	566.63
	1744	B. Boss–drawings	79		100.00			100.00
	1745	Stores expense	74		53.75			53.75
	1746	ABC Furniture	76			1275.00	25.50	1249.50
	1747	Wholesalers Ltd	75			1000.00		1000.00
	1748	Wages expense	77		550.00			550.00
					703.75	2985.83	35.70	3653.88

These amounts are posted individually to the debit of the account nominated under 'Particulars'.

The total of each column is posted as a single figure to the respective account indicated at the head of the column

A large organisation will have columns in the cash payments journal for recurring items such as wages, salaries, rent and interest payments. In addition, it will be necessary to have a 'sundries' column in which to enter all payments that do not occur frequently enough to have a special column provided for them. These sundry items are posted individually to the particular ledger accounts concerned.

If the cash payments journal were to be posted after the transactions in the example, then the following amounts would be posted to the accounts indicated:

Ledger account	Amount
Debits	
B. Boss: Drawings	$ 100.00
Stores expense	53.75
Wages expense	550.00
Accounts payable	2985.83
Total debits	$3689.58
Credits	
Purchase discounts	35.70
Cash at bank	3653.88
Total credits	$3689.58

In the cash at bank account it is necessary to enter only the total amount with a description such as 'sundry payments' in the details column.

If these same transactions had been recorded individually as general journal entries, 16 ledger entries would have been required instead of the six actually made. This again demonstrates the efficiency of the summarisation effect of special journals in comparison with the general journal.

One cost of obtaining this efficiency is an increased possibility of error. Errors in entering columnar data in special journals, or in totalling columns, are easily made and difficult to detect because the debits and credits are no longer posted transaction-by-transaction in the ledger. Before posting, therefore, the individual columns in the special journal are reconciled with the cash column by a procedure known as *crossfooting* the journal. That is, the totals of the individual columns must equal the total of the cash column.

The audit trail is provided in the cash payments journal by columns referring back to the cheque numbers, and to the document authorising payment, which is often called the *payment voucher*. The link with the ledger is made, as before, by the insertion of the corresponding ledger account numbers next to the amounts when posted.

Irrespective of the extent to which special journals are used, it will always be necessary to retain the general journal for entries that occur infrequently and for which a special journal is not warranted. These entries include:

- non-recurring transactions, such as credit purchases of equipment and sales of items other than merchandise
- adjusting entries, such as depreciation expense, bad debts and recording of accruals and prepayments
- entries made to correct errors
- closing entries at the end of the period.

As all entries in the ledger must be supported by journal entries, and these entries do not have a special journal of their own, the general journal is provided for that purpose.

Advantages of special journals

Efficiency through summarisation
The economy of entries achieved by special journals is considerable and becomes greater as the volume of transactions increases. The ledger does not become cluttered with detail and is more easily maintained as a result. Moreover, as the name of the journal and its design make apparent what types of transactions are contained therein, the amount of detail necessary to describe each transaction is greatly reduced in comparison with general journal entries which must be supported by the naming of accounts and by extensive narrations.

Improved accessibility to information
Special journals also improve accessibility by providing convenient and readable summaries of like transactions. If all cash payments in the current month need to be scrutinised (see later section on bank reconciliation for example), the cash payments journal contains all of the relevant entries. Within the cash payments journal, for example, payments to suppliers are easily identified, as they have their own column. Accessibility to information is a feature of a well-designed special journal, making it unnecessary to refer to the ledger to discover the detail of any particular transactions during the current period.

Division of duties—efficiency
The usual advantages of division of labour apply to special journals. In any large organisation, the division of duties and the delegation of responsibility are essential for efficient operations and special journals enable the accounting functions to be shared by employees given independent responsibility for each journal. Employees might specialise in the work of recording one journal only, thus becoming expert in the area. Work is done more rapidly and with less likelihood of error.

Division of duties—better control
The subdivision of the journals also aids accounting control by facilitating internal verification. The possibility of embezzling the firm's cash is reduced if the cash receipts and payments journals are under the control of different employees, since it would require collusion to conceal fraudulent entries in the cash payments journal by the insertion of compensating entries in the cash receipts journal. Similarly, if the purchases and cash payments journals are in separate hands, it requires collusion to make a fictitious purchase for the benefit of an employee and to pay for it from the company's bank account.

General and subsidiary ledgers

So far the discussion has assumed the existence of a single ledger that contains all the accounts and which forms the basis of the main accounting reports. This main ledger is known as the *general ledger*. However, other ledgers are possible, since each of the general ledger accounts is capable of subdivision to provide greater detail.

It is obviously important for the company to have detailed knowledge of the amounts owing by each of its customers, and since the general ledger either does not maintain accounts for individual customers, or if it does, can do so for only a small number, some kind of subsidiary record must be kept. The establishment of a *subsidiary ledger* for accounts receivable enables that to be done in a way that enhances the control and convenience of the accounting system.

In principle, any account in the general ledger may be supported by a subsidiary record that provides greater detail about the composition of the account. Among the possibilities are:

- The *accounts receivable* account may be supported by individual records of customer accounts owing.
- The *accounts payable* account may be supported by records of individual accounts payable.
- The *merchandise inventory* account may be accompanied by a separate set of stock cards, recording the balances of individual items of stock.
- The *equipment* account may be supplemented by an equipment register, which provides more information on the types of equipment in use.
- The *paid-up capital* account may be supported by entries in the company's share register, which lists the owners of the shares and the size of each holding.

There are significant advantages to this arrangement of maintaining the general ledger in summary form and recording the detail for a number of elements elsewhere. If the general ledger contained individual accounts for every customer and every stock line, it would be very large and would be difficult to maintain. The task of manually posting to and balancing a ledger containing several thousand individual accounts would be enormous. Also, the possibility of error and the time to locate an error increase with the size of the ledger.

Subsidiary ledgers also allow for a greater division of labour and, as we have seen, this increases the control within the system. Different employees may be assigned responsibility for each of the detailed records. One officer might maintain the general ledger, while another might undertake responsibility for the recording in the accounts receivable subsidiary ledger.

To preserve control in the accounting system, the detailed subsidiary records may be designed in such a way that the individual balances must reconcile with the balance in the 'summary' account in the general ledger, which then becomes a *control account* over the subsidiary records, as Figure 20.10 illustrates by reference to accounts receivable.

Accounting entries for subsidiary ledger accounts

A subsidiary ledger may take any convenient form. In some cases, such as accounts receivable and payable, it might follow the normal ledger style, but in others, especially the recording of equipment or the share register, more appropriate forms might be devised.

Following is an example of the type of entries necessary to maintain a subsidiary ledger for accounts receivable. Very similar procedures would be used to record entries from the cash payments journal and the purchases journal into the accounts payable subsidiary ledger and the general ledger. The principles are the same no matter what type of subsidiary ledger is being used. Whenever an entry is made in the 'control' account in the general ledger, the individual amounts that formed this 'summary' entry must be entered into the appropriate individual accounts in the subsidiary ledger. Double entry is still maintained in the general ledger, but only one side of the entry is made in the subsidiary ledger accounts.

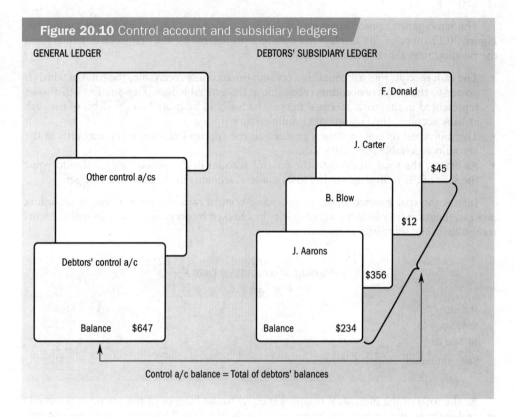

Figure 20.10 Control account and subsidiary ledgers

GENERAL LEDGER

DEBTORS' SUBSIDIARY LEDGER

F. Donald

J. Carter

$45

Other control a/cs

B. Blow

$12

J. Aarons

$356

Debtors' control a/c

Balance $647

Balance $234

Control a/c balance = Total of debtors' balances

Example: *Accounts receivable subsidiary ledger for Classic Communications Ltd*

Classic Communications Ltd has just commenced business. The accountant has established a general ledger. Within the general ledger there is a control account, entitled 'accounts receivable control'. A separate ledger is then established as a subsidiary ledger, known as the 'accounts receivable ledger' (or the 'debtors ledger').

There are a number of specialised journals, including those for credit sales and cash receipts. This example will consider the transactions in the first week of trading, commencing 1 July 20X1.

The sales journal entries are considered first. Figure 20.11 on page 703 illustrates the procedure for posting to the control account in the general ledger and to the individual accounts for customers in the accounts receivable ledger.

- The total of the amount column, representing the total for each invoice, is posted to the debit of accounts receivable control and to the credit of sales revenue in the general ledger.
- The relevant folio numbers are then placed below the total in the sales journal.
- The individual sales amounts are then debited to the relevant accounts in the accounts receivable ledger.
- The numbers of those accounts are placed in the folio column in the sales journal.
- The total of the individual debits in the subsidiary ledger must agree with the debit to accounts receivable in the general ledger. Hence, the accounts receivable control account 'controls' the entries in the subsidiary ledgers.

The same general procedures are followed in recording cash received from customers. Figure 20.12 on page 704 displays the cash receipts journal for the first week in January and the postings relevant to accounts receivable.

- The cash receipts journal contains a column for accounts receivable, the total of which is posted to the credit of accounts receivable in the general ledger. This amount will also be represented in the 'total receipts' figure which would be posted to the debit of the cash at bank account, thus maintaining double entry.
- The individual receipts are then credited to the appropriate customers' accounts in the accounts receivable subsidiary ledger.
- As before, the total credited to the control account in the general ledger should equal the sum of the individual credits to customers' accounts in the subsidiary ledger.

Just as the trial balance assists in providing control over the general ledger recording process, the subsidiary ledger recording may be checked by preparing a schedule of accounts receivable in the subsidiary ledger, thus:

SCHEDULE OF ACCOUNTS RECEIVABLE as at 7 July 20X1	
M. Smith	$154.32
Torrid Supply Co.	43.00
VIP Steel Ltd	nil
Balance in accounts receivable control account	$197.32

As the total of the individual balances is equal to the balance in the accounts receivable control account, the entries may be presumed to be accurate. However, just as the trial balance does not identify all errors within the general ledger, the schedule of accounts receivable may not identify all errors relating to the recording of accounts receivable. It is nonetheless a good guide to the accuracy of the records.

The subsidiary ledger for accounts payable may be kept in an identical way to that for accounts receivable, the source journals being the credit purchases journal and the cash payments journal. Similarly, provided a perpetual inventory approach is adopted, the balance in the merchandise inventory account in the general ledger may control the balances in a subsidiary ledger composed of individual stock cards for the items carried (which would record movements into and out of the business of each type of stock).

In summary, the use of subsidiary ledgers reduces the volume of entries in the general ledger, thus simplifying the recording process, increasing the control features and simplifying the preparation of accounting reports. By providing for a division of labour they can also lead to improved accounting and administrative control.

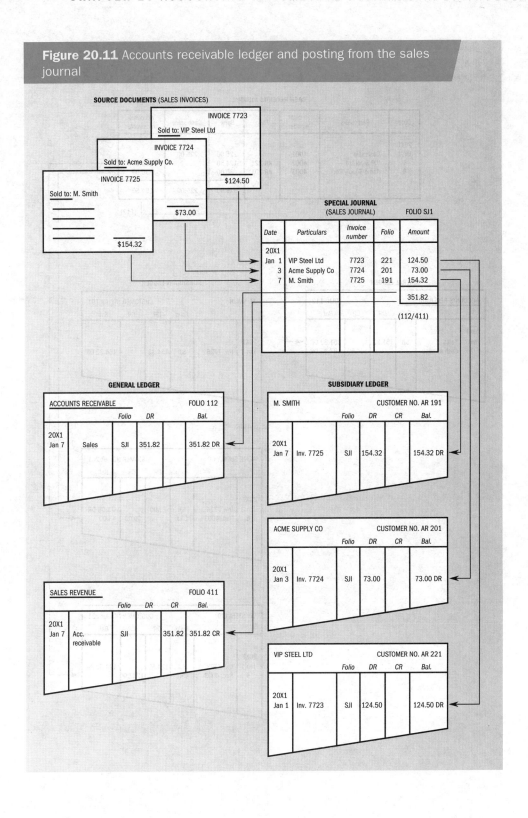

Figure 20.11 Accounts receivable ledger and posting from the sales journal

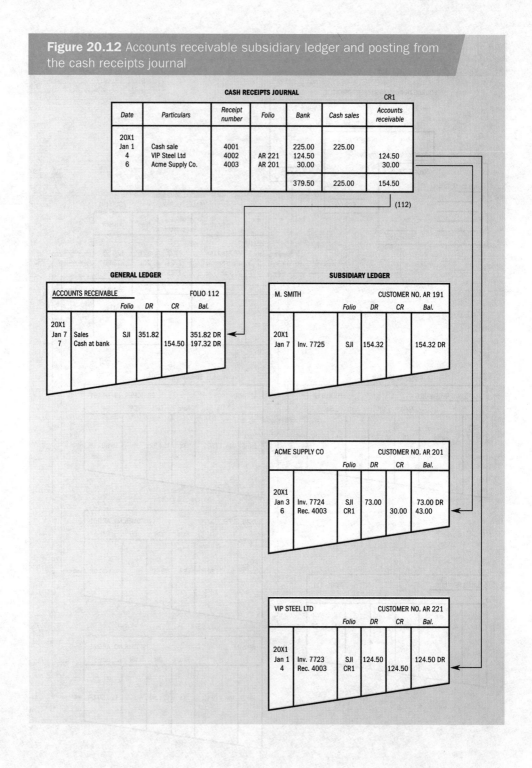

Figure 20.12 Accounts receivable subsidiary ledger and posting from the cash receipts journal

Control and verification of cash

Cash is the most negotiable of all assets and for this reason it should be the subject of rigorous internal control procedures. With cash all the basic features already discussed relating to internal control procedures should be implemented and strictly adhered to. Perhaps the most important is the separation of duties, to ensure that those responsible for handling cash do not have access to the recording systems for it. It is also important that roles are arranged in such a way that there is strict verification of tasks.

Important internal control features that specifically relate to cash are that all cash should be banked daily, and all payments should be made by cheque and the cheques signed by two members of staff.

Case 20.2 Cheque it out!

A few weeks ago British newspapers devoted excited columns to an investment fraud that had led to arrests in the London area. What seized the press's attention was not so much the fraud itself, as the sums involved were not vast. No, it was the fact that astute financial services companies could have been taken in by an elementary, almost childish, ruse.

It worked like this: a gang submitted multiple applications for certain investments, enclosing with each a cheque written on a closed or non-existent account. Then, taking advantage of the statutory cooling-off period, they asked for their money back. By the time the insurance companies discovered that the cheques were fakes, the refunds had been posted and the proceeds banked.

What simple controls could have prevented this fraud?

S. Burns 'Cheque it out', *Accountancy—International Edition*, December 1997, p. 38.

External verification of cash—the bank reconciliation statement

One of the unique features of cash systems is that there is a system of external verification of the organisation's or the individual's records. All our receipts and payments are not only recorded by us, but also by the bank we deal with. When the bank sends us a bank statement, we are receiving a copy of our ledger account as recorded by the bank. By cross-checking this record with our own records of the same transactions, we are able to verify that the two sets of records are in agreement, or, if they are not, we should be able to explain why. This process of verification of cash occurs when we prepare a bank reconciliation statement.

From the following example of a bank statement, it can be seen that it represents a copy of the account of the customer in the 'customer subsidiary ledger' of the bank.

	STATEMENT OF ACCOUNT			
	St Nab Bank			
Customer:	B. P. & H. Pty Ltd	Account no.:		Statement date:
	1024 Princes Highway	8134-567		31 March 20X2
	Westvic, 3999			
Date	Particulars	Debit	Credit	Balance
28-2	Balance forward			$1467.41 CR
1-3	Direct dep.–NK Ltd		$653.16	2120.57 CR
11-3	1741	$ 528.00		1592.57 CR
12-3	C/C		754.02	2346.59 CR
12-3	Bank fee	2.50		2344.09 CR
24-3	1742	21.60		2322.49 CR
25-3	1743	235.00		2087.47 CR
28-3	Govt tax	8.40		2079.09 CR
29-3	1745	321.60		1757.49 CR
30-3	1744	1800.00		42.51 DR
31-3	C/C		120.00	77.49 CR

You will notice that the account began with a credit balance and that the first transaction was a credit. This was as a result of a deposit by the customer of cash and cheques (C/C). This means that when a customer deposits money it increases the credit balance in the account. Remember that this account represents a liability to the bank, as they are obliged to pay back to the customer whatever they deposit. It is thus the direct opposite of the cash at bank account kept by the customer in their general ledger.

It follows that when an organisation has cash in the bank there will be a debit balance in the organisation's own records, corresponding to a credit balance shown on the bank statement, which is presented from the bank's point of view. If both sets of records are up to date and in agreement, a debit balance in the organisation's ledger account for cash should equal a credit balance for the same amount appearing on the bank statement.

In reality, timing discrepancies occur between the two sets of records. The customer may enter cheque payments in the cash payments journal immediately they are drawn, but they will appear in the bank's records only after they have been presented and cleared by the bank for payment. This may involve a delay of several days, or even weeks. At any one date, therefore, the two sets of records may disagree because of what are known as *unpresented cheques*.

Similarly, the customer may make an entry in the cash receipts journal immediately deposits are lodged with the bank. This amount may not appear on a bank statement prepared at the end of that day, appearing instead on the next day. Such discrepancies are termed *deposits not credited*.

Further differences between the two sets of cash records arise because of entries made by the bank without the customer's knowledge. These include *bank charges* for maintaining the account and deductions for *interest charges* due on bank loans and *government taxes*. They also include *direct deposits* made to the bank by an external party (see the first entry credited to the above account), such as interest received by the customer from an investment, where the borrower has agreed to transfer the interest directly to the customer's account.

Finally, differences may arise due to *errors in either set of records*. Errors by banks are rare, due to the high standards of internal control exercised within banks, although this should never be assumed. It is more likely, however, that the customer's records will be inaccurate.

The reconciliation of the accounting records with the bank statement requires three steps:

1. *The comparison step:* This identifies timing discrepancies (unpresented cheques and deposits not credited), unexplained items appearing on the bank statement and possible errors.
2. *The adjustment step:* This adjusts the organisation's records by including legitimate items appearing directly on the bank statement and correcting any errors identified in the organisation's records.
3. *The reconciliation step:* This explains why the two set of records still disagree, which should be due to unpresented cheques, deposits not credited and bank errors.

The comparison step may begin with a comparison of the bank deposits recorded in the cash receipts journal with the credit entries in the bank statement. Any differences are noted. Next, the cheques shown in the cash payments journal may be compared with the debits on the bank statement. This will enable the unpresented cheques to be identified, along with any direct debits made by the bank.

In the adjustment step, items on the bank statement but not appearing in the organisation's own records are scrutinised carefully to ensure that they are valid. A mysterious debit charge by the bank, for example using a cheque number that is not in a series of numbers on cheque forms issued to the company, should be referred to the bank as a possible error in their records. Once items are found to be valid transactions, they are entered in the cash journals of the organisation and the journals are totalled.

Similarly, errors in the cash journals are corrected. Suppose a cheque that appears in the bank statement at $221.50 was entered in the cash payments journal at $22.15. Once the difference has been investigated and the bank's entry found to be correct, a correcting entry is placed in the cash payments journal.

After all of these adjustments and corrections of errors, the only remaining differences between the two sets of records should consist of confirmed errors by the bank, which of course the organisation cannot adjust, unpresented cheques and deposits not credited. A statement may now be prepared to reconcile these differences. Assuming the organisation has a favourable balance with the bank, the form of the statement could be:

BANK RECONCILIATION STATEMENT	
as at...	
Balance as per bank statement (CR)	$XXXX
add Deposits not yet credited	XXXX
	XXXX
subtract Unpresented cheques	XXXX
Balance as per cash account (DR)	$XXXX

The statement begins with the bank statement balance, as that is assumed more likely to be correct than the organisation's own cash account balance. When the deposits lodged but not credited are finally acknowledged by the bank, the balance in the bank's records will increase. Conversely, when the unpresented cheques are lodged and debited by the bank, the balance in the bank's records will decrease. After allowing for these differences, and any errors by the bank, the balance according to the accounting records should have been reconciled with the balance shown in the bank statement, otherwise further investigation will be necessary.

When the bank statement reveals a *debit* balance in the bank's records, the organisation is 'in overdraft' and the above procedure of adding deposits not credited and deducting unpresented cheques will need to be reversed. Unpresented cheques will increase the overdraft and should be added to the bank statement balance and the deposits not credited will reduce the overdraft in the bank's records and should be subtracted from the balance in the reconciliation statement, to arrive at the organisation's own cash balance.

The bank reconciliation statement is one of the most important verification controls in any organisation. Reliance may be placed on a bank's records as an independent check on the accounting records of a business, and given the importance of the cash asset, this is a very valuable system of independent verification.

The manual accounting information system—a comprehensive example

The features of a manual accounting system will be demonstrated in a comprehensive example. Hope N. Shutt has been operating Hope N. Shutt Building Supplies for some years. His balance sheet at 30 June 20X2 was as follows:

Assets		Liabilities	
Cash at bank	$6500	Accounts payable	$3000
Accounts receivable	2000		
Inventory	1100	**Owners' equity**	
		Capital	6600
	$9600		$9600

The accounting records include special journals for credit sales, credit purchases, cash receipts and cash payments. A general journal is maintained for all other entries.

The organisation maintains a general ledger, supported by subsidiary ledgers for accounts receivable, accounts payable and inventory (in the form of stock cards). The balances in the subsidiary ledger accounts at 30 June 20X2 were:

Accounts receivable			
Hi Rise Ltd			$2000
Accounts payable			
All Needs Ltd			3000
Inventory			
Doors	10 @ $50	$500	
Windows	30 @ $20	600	1100

Journalising the transactions

The special journals appear below. The company uses a perpetual inventory system of recording, so the sales journal must provide information not only for the recording of the sales revenue but also for the transfer of the cost of sales from the asset account for inventory to cost of goods sold expense. In addition, the data recorded must be sufficient to enable the subsidiary ledgers for accounts receivable and inventory to be maintained.

SPECIAL JOURNALS

CREDIT SALES JOURNAL   SJ2

Date 20X2		Customer	Item no.	Inv. no.	Customer no. (folio)	Sale amount $	Qty	Cost $
July	1	Hi Rise Ltd	10	9041	12-501	1200	4	200
	4	Low Flats Ltd	20	9042	12-551	400	5	100
	6	Hi Rise Ltd	20	9043	12-501	160	2	40
	15	Bargain Cellars	20	9044	12-601	800	10	200
	22	Hi Rise Ltd	10	9045	12-501	300	1	50
	30	Low Flats Ltd	10	9046	12-551	600	2	100
						$3460		$690
						(12/41)		(15/51)

CREDIT PURCHASES JOURNAL   PJ2

Date 20X2		Supplier	Item no.	Order no.	Supplier no. (folio)	Qty	Amount $
July	1	All Needs Ltd	10	61	21-110	5	250
	3	All Needs Ltd	20	62	21-110	6	120
	22	All Needs Ltd	10	63	21-110	3	150
							$520
							(15/21)

CASH RECEIPTS JOURNAL   CR2

Date 20X2		Particulars	Receipt no.	Folio	Sales discount $	Accounts receivable $	Sundry	Bank $
July	4	Hi Rise Ltd	378	12-501	140	2000		1860
	12	Low Flats Ltd	379	12-551	28	400		372
	31	Hi Rise Ltd	380	12-501	84	1200		1116
					$252	$3600		$3348
					(42)	(12)		(10)

CASH PAYMENTS JOURNAL   CP2

Date 20X2		Particulars	Cheque no.	Folio	Wages $	Payable $	Rent $	Sundry $	Bank $
July	1	All Needs Ltd	432	21-110		2000			2000
	3	Rent	433				180		180
	7	Wages	434		200				200
	9	All Needs Ltd	435	21-110		1250			1250
	17	Rent	436				180		180
	19	Drawing	437					1500	1500
	21	Wages	438		400				400
	28	Insurance	439					90	90
	29	Bank charges						8	8
					$600	$3250	$360	$1598	$5808
					(52)	(21)	(53)		(10)

continues

Analysis of sundries column		
Drawings	(32)	$1500
Insurance	(54)	90
Bank charges	(55)	8
		$1598

Similarly, the credit purchases journal contains data to be entered in the general ledger as well as the subsidiary ledgers for accounts payable and inventory. Finally, the cash journals contain columns for recurring items.

Each journal contains columns for recording the reference numbers of original evidence records and for cross-referencing the ledger accounts to which the entries are posted.

Reconciling the bank balance

At the end of July the business received a statement from its bank (see below). This is compared with the cash journals and, for July, the following differences were detected:

- In bank statement but not in business records: July 29 Fee $8
- In business records but not in bank statement: July 28 Cheque 439 $90
  31 Bank deposit $1116

An entry is made in the cash payments journal to include the bank fee. The 'bank' columns in each cash journal are then totalled and an informal calculation of the cash balance according to the accounting records is made thus:

Cash at bank account balance 1 July 20X2	6500 DR
add Receipts (cash receipts journal)	3348
	9848
less Payments (cash payments journal)	5808
Balance as per accounting records	4040 DR

The correctness of this balance is then tested by the preparation of a bank reconciliation statement.

As the balances agree, it is concluded that the cash journals have been maintained correctly.

Within each journal, the journal columns are then *footed* by adding the totals of the individual analysis columns to ensure that the total equals the total of the main column.

BANK STATEMENT

Steep Bank

Seven Hills Branch

Customer: Hope N. Shutt Building Supplies

Number: 745.986.384.77771

20X2			Debit	Credit	Balance
July	1	Balance			$6500 CR
	3	432	$2000		4500 CR
	5	Deposit		$1860	6360 CR
	7	433	180		6180 CR
	10	435	1250		4930 CR
	11	434	200		4730 CR
	13	Deposit		372	5102 CR
	20	437	1500		3602 CR
	23	438	400		3202 CR
	25	436	180		3022 CR
	29	Fee	8		3014 CR

BANK RECONCILIATION STATEMENT

as at 31 July 20X2

Balance as per bank statement (CR)	$3014
add Deposits not yet credited	1116
	4130
less Unpresented cheques: No. 439	90
Balance as per accounting records (DR)	$4040

Posting the journals to the ledgers

The subsidiary ledgers after the posting of the journals appear on pages 712–13 and the general ledger is shown on pages 713–14.

The subsidiary ledgers are posted at frequent intervals during the month because current information is required. The exact amounts owing by customers should be determinable at short notice, so that customers' queries may be answered. Similarly, amounts owing to particular suppliers may need to be determined promptly. Current information on the balances of stock on hand is also useful as a check against stock shortages or excess stock holdings.

SUBSIDIARY LEDGERS: HOPE N. SHUTT BUILDING SUPPLIES

ACCOUNTS RECEIVABLE

Date		Reference	Debit	Credit	Balance
		HI Rise Ltd **Customer no. 501**			
20X2					
July	1	Balance			$2000 DR
	1	Invoice 9041	$1200		3200 DR
	4	Receipt 378		$2000	1200 DR
	6	Invoice 9043	160		1360 DR
	22	Invoice 9045	300		1660 DR
	31	Receipt 380		1200	460 DR
		Low Flats Ltd **Customer no. 551**			
20X2					
July	4	Invoice 9042	400		400 DR
	12	Receipt 379		400	–
	30	Invoice 9046	600		600 DR
		Bargain Cellars Pty Ltd **Customer no. 601**			
20X2					
July	15	Invoice 9044	800		800 DR

INVENTORY

Date		Reference	IN No.	IN $	OUT No.	OUT $	BALANCE No.	BALANCE $
		Doors **Item no. 10**						
20X2								
July	1	Balance					10	500
	1	O/N 61	5	250			15	750
	1	Invoice 9041			4	200	11	550
	22	Invoice 9045			1	50	10	500
	22	O/N 63	3	150			13	650
	30	Invoice 9046			2	100	11	550
		Windows **Item no. 20**						
20X2								
July	1	Balance					30	600
	3	O/N 62	6	120			36	720
	4	Invoice 9042			5	100	31	620
	6	Invoice 9043			2	40	29	580
	15	Invoice 9044			10	200	19	380

continues

ACCOUNTS PAYABLE

Date		Reference	Debit	Credit	Balance
		All Needs Ltd	**Account No. 21 110**		
20X2					
July	1	Balance			3000 CR
	1	O/N 61		250	3250 CR
	1	Cheque 432	2000		1250 CR
	3	O/N 62		120	1370 CR
	9	Cheque 435	1250		120 CR
	22	O/N 63		150	270 CR

GENERAL LEDGER: HOPE N. SHUTT BUILDING SUPPLIES

Date		Particulars	Folio	DR	CR	Balance
		Cash at bank	Account No. 10			
20X2						
July	1	Balance				6500 DR
	31	Sundry accounts	CR2	3348		9848 DR
	31	Sundry accounts	CP2		5808	4040 DR
		Accounts receivable	Account No. 12			
20X2						
July	1	Balance				2000 DR
	31	Sales revenue	SJ2	3460		5460 DR
	31	Cash & discount	CR2		3600	1860 DR
		Inventory	Account No. 15			
20X2						
July	1	Balance				1100 DR
	31	Accounts payable	PJ2	520		1620 DR
	31	Cost of goods sold	SJ2		690	930 DR
		Accounts payable	Account No. 21			
20X2						
July	1	Balance				3000 CR
	31	Inventory	PJ2		520	3520 CR
	31	Cash	CP2	3250		270 CR
		Capital	Account No. 31			
20X2						
July	1	Balance				6600 CR
		Drawings	Account No. 32			
20X2						
July	31	Cash	CP2	1500		1500 DR
		Sales revenue	Account No. 41			
20X2						
July	31	Accounts receivable	SJ2		3460	3460 CR

continues

GENERAL LEDGER: Hope N. Shutt Building Supplies					
Date	Particulars	Folio	DR	CR	Balance
	Sales discount		Account No. 42		
20X2					
July 31	Accounts receivable	CR2	252		252 DR
	Cost of goods sold		Account No. 51		
20X2					
July 31	Inventory	SJ2	690		690 DR
	Wages expense		Account No. 52		
20X2					
July 31	Cash	CP2	600		600 DR
	Rent expense		Account No. 53		
20X2					
July 31	Cash	CP2	360		360 DR
	Insurance expense		Account No. 54		
20X2					
July 31	Cash	CP2	90		90 DR
	Bank charges		Account No. 55		
20X2					
July 31	Cash	CP2	8		8 DR

The general ledger is posted less frequently, depending on the volume of transactions and on how often interim reports are required. In the present case, the company requires monthly profit and loss statements and balance sheets, so monthly posting is carried out.

In the example, an audit trail is provided by the insertion of folio numbers and references to original evidence documents. In the journals, posting references to the ledger account numbers appear against the amounts actually entered. Taking the cash payments journal as an example, the totals are posted to the general ledger accounts for wages, accounts payable and rent, and the bank account and the relevant general ledger account numbers are inserted underneath each column total in the journal. The items in the sundries column are analysed separately at the bottom of the journal and posted individually to the general ledger, with numbers appearing in brackets. The numbers appearing in the folio column of the journal refer to the entries in the subsidiary ledger for accounts payable.

Within the general ledger, the source journal for each entry is noted in the folio column. In the subsidiary ledgers, reference is made to the special journal from which the entry was posted and, where appropriate, reference is made also to the original evidence records.

Trial balance and schedules of subsidiary ledgers

Once the ledgers have been posted, accounting control is further strengthened by the preparation of a trial balance of the general ledger accounts (page 715). As the trial balance is in balance, it is concluded that the journals have been posted correctly and that no arithmetic error has occurred.

The subsidiary ledger accounts are then reconciled with the general ledger control accounts (page 715). As these agree, it is assumed that the individual balances in the subsidiary ledgers are correct.

TRIAL BALANCE: HOPE N. SHUTT BUILDING SUPPLIES

as at 31 July 20X2

	Debit	Credit
Cash at bank	$ 4 040	
Accounts receivable	1 860	
Inventory	930	
Accounts payable		$ 270
Capital		6 600
Drawings	1 500	
Sales revenue		3 460
Sales discount	252	
Cost of goods sold	690	
Wages expense	600	
Rent expense	360	
Insurance expense	90	
Bank charges	8	
	$10 330	$10 330

RECONCILIATION OF SUBSIDIARY LEDGERS

Schedule of accounts receivable

as at 31 July 20X2

Hi Rise Ltd	$ 460
Low Flats Ltd	600
Bargain Cellars Pty Ltd	800
Balance as per control account	$1860

Schedule of inventory on hand

as at 31 July 20X2

Doors	550
Windows	380
Balance as per control account	$ 930

Schedule of accounts payable

as at 31 July 20X2

All Needs Ltd	$ 270

Preparation of interim accounting reports: the worksheet

Before the profit can be computed, it is necessary to make adjustments for items such as depreciation, accruals and prepayments. In this example, two adjustments only will be introduced:

Wages owing at the end of July	$100
Insurance prepaid at the end of July	$85

As this accounting period covers only one month, adjusting and closing entries are not made in the ledger. Instead, interim reports are prepared directly from the trial balance. A convenient procedure for making the necessary adjustments to the trial balance is to prepare a *worksheet*, as discussed in Chapter 7. The worksheet, which is not part of the formal records but an adjunct to the trial balance, appears below. It is sometimes called the 'eight-column trial balance'. The first two columns record the trial balance, followed by two columns for entering the adjusting entries, for which the debits must equal the credits. The adjusted balances are carried across to either the profit and loss statement columns or the balance sheet columns. The link between the profit and loss statement columns and the balance sheet columns is provided by the figure for net profit.

The interim reports may now be prepared by presenting the data in the statement columns of the worksheet in properly classified statements as shown. The worksheet provides a convenient means of preparing the interim reports and, moreover, it discloses to an auditor the calculations that explain the items appearing in the financial statements.

WORKSHEET: HOPE N. SHUTT BUILDING SUPPLIES
as at 31 July 20X2

Account	Trial balance DR $	Trial balance CR $	Adjustments DR $	Adjustments CR $	P & L statement DR $	P & L statement CR $	Balance sheet DR $	Balance sheet CR $
Cash at bank	4 040						4 040	
Accounts receivable	1 860						1 860	
Inventory	930						930	
Accounts payable		270						270
Capital		6 600						6 600
Drawings	1 500						1 500	
Sales revenue		3 460				3460		
Sales discounts	252				252			
Cost of goods sold	690				690			
Wages expense	600		100		700			
Rent expense	360				360			
Insurance expense	90			85	5			
Bank charges	8				8			
	$10 330	$10 330						
Prepayments			85				85	
Wages payable				100				100
Net profit					1 445			1 445
			$185	$185	$3 460	$3 460	$8 415	$8 415

PROFIT AND LOSS STATEMENT: HOPE N. SHUTT BUILDING SUPPLIES

for the month ended 31 July 20X2

	$	$
Sales revenue		3460
less Sales discounts		252
Net sales		3208
less Cost of goods sold		690
Gross profit		2518
less Expenses		
Wages	700	
Rent	360	
Insurance	5	
Bank charges	8	1073
Net profit		$1445

BALANCE SHEET

as at 31 July 20X2

Current assets			**Current liabilities**		
Cash at bank	$4040		Accounts payable		$ 270
Accounts receivable	1860		Wages payable		100
					370
Inventory	930				
Prepayments	85				
			Owners' equity		
			Capital	$6600	
			plus Profit	1445	
				8045	
			less Drawings	1500	6545
	$6915				$6915

Final reports

On 30 June 20X3 Hope N. Shutt Building Supplies will prepare its final reports for the year. It will then be necessary to make formal entries in the general ledger for adjusting and closing entries (see Chapters 4 and 7). Since all ledger entries must be supported by journal entries, general journal entries are required for the adjusting and closing entries.

Ethical issues

1. Refer to the example of the Professor of Classical Studies and the purchase of 49 binders discussed earlier to illustrate the documents and control steps involved in purchasing equipment in the Faculty of Arts. A year after that purchase, the same Professor wants to buy another 35 binders. He calls in the departmental administrative assistant, and says:

We need 35 binders like the ones we bought last year for the course starting next week. If we go through the normal processes, as we did last time, we won't get them in time for next year's course, much less next week's. Plus I remember that last time we needed the 49 binders just to file the documents we had to fill out to buy the binders. Administration might have nothing better to do with their time than create paperwork and roles, but I have. Go over to Office Stationers in Emble and buy them in three lots. Get three receipts and put them through petty cash, a bit apart from each other. Gee, I wonder if I can buy the two new computers we need that way as well?

If you were the administration assistant, what would you do about the binders? What would you say to the Professor?

2. A customer in a retail store is buying a microwave oven. The tagged price on the oven is $180. When the sale is rung up on the cash register, the customer notices that the sales assistant, who seems a little preoccupied and not totally awake, has misread the price as $130. What should the customer do?

3. A customer is buying a dinner set at 9 am on Monday morning. The price is $150. The sales assistant says, 'You should have come in yesterday, we had a 10 per cent off everything sale'. The customer is charged $150, but notices that the cash register is rung up at $135. What, if anything, should the customer do?

4. You paid your membership subscription to the Australian Institute of CPAs six months ago and, although you have received a receipt from them, the cheque has never been debited against your account. Either the Institute's or the bank's system appears to have failed. What should you do?

5. Refer to question 4. Assume that you have checked with the bank and they say the Institute has not presented the cheque. You contact the Institute and tell them about it. Three months later, the cheque still hasn't been presented. What should you do now?

Summary

The province of accounting is not confined to decisions such as how to measure profit. The measurement of profit requires a system for the collection of relevant data and its processing into information.

The total set of information used by management is provided by the management information system (MIS). Within this system the accounting information system (AIS) is usually a major component. The accounting information system is normally restricted to information of a financial nature or based on transactions with external parties.

An important task of management is to achieve internal control within its information systems. Internal control embraces both accounting control and administrative control. Accounting control refers to control over the accuracy of the accounting records and the safeguarding of the assets. Administrative control is more concerned with ensuring that the objectives and plans of the organisation are carried out faithfully and as efficiently as possible. There are a number of basic internal control procedures that should exist in any good system.

Within an organisation, control procedures must accommodate the various transaction cycles experienced by that organisation, the chains of events that occur as transactions are completed. There is a need to coordinate activities between departments, a task that is accomplished by the provision of documents that flow between departments and to and from the organisation and the external parties with which it deals. Documents also provide the basis for the entry of data in the accounting records and provide, in turn, confirmation of those entries.

Accounting and administrative control are achieved in a manual accounting system through a carefully designed recording process. Individual systems may vary to suit particular needs, but common features include the requirement that ledger entries be supported by journal entries which are, in turn, supported by authorisations or original evidence records. An audit trail is provided by making references to the source and the destination of each entry in the journals and the ledgers.

Journals may be subdivided into various special journals, to achieve economies in the entry process, and to enable tasks to be allocated to different personnel, thus making the accounting task more efficient and permitting internal checks of the work of one person by that of another. Special journals also permit improved accessibility to desired data.

Similar advantages and controls are obtained by the creation of subsidiary ledgers to record detailed data on items such as customer accounts owing, while the general ledger functions as a summary that controls the detailed records.

Bank reconciliation statements are an important means of obtaining external verification, by reference to the records maintained independently by an organisation's bank.

Although many accounting information systems are now computerised, the principles demonstrated in the manual accounting information system are important, as they help us understand the processes occurring within the computer system. Internal control is an important issue which must be present whether the accounting system is manual or computer-based.

 **Review exercises**

Discussion questions

20.1 Distinguish between the terms 'data' and 'information' in relation to the following items:

(a) a set of duplicate bank deposit slips

(b) a summary of bank deposits for the week prepared by the computer

(c) a summary of sales for the day prepared by hand

20.2 The accounting information system is regarded as a subset of the management information system. Which of the following functions are part of the management information system but *not* part of the accounting information system?

(a) preparing a sales budget for the month

(b) preparing a budget of quantities of expected raw materials usage for the month

(c) monitoring the quality of output

(d) reporting on wastage of raw materials

(e) reporting on absences by employees

(f) preparing quotations for work to be done for customers

20.3 Explain why each of the following controls exists:

(a) Two officers share responsibility for the accounting function, a chief accountant and a finance manager.

(b) The cash register operators are required to give every customer a cash register sales slip.

(c) There is a requirement that all receipts be banked intact and that all payments be made by cheque.

(d) A separate list of mail collections of cash is prepared even though the bank deposit slip will contain the same data.

(e) Cheques and sales invoices must be pre-numbered.

20.4 (a) Explain why is it important to identify transaction cycles within a company.

(b) Identify several key transaction cycles likely to be encountered in a large retail store dealing in women's fashions.

20.5 (a) Explain the role of documents in achieving internal control.

(b) List the documents you might expect to find within the payroll cycle of a large manufacturing company.

20.6 Email Ltd deals exclusively in sales via the Internet, where payment is received in advance with the customer's order.

(a) Draw up a chart (similar to Figure 20.3) showing the allocation of functions for staff involved in the sale and delivery of goods by that company.

(b) Identify the major documents that would be required and the data they contain.

(c) Identify the key points of internal control which should be in place in such a system.

20.7 Explain why ledger entries should not be permitted until there are supporting journal entries.

20.8 (a) Justify the use of special journals instead of relying completely on the general journal.

(b) Why is a complete range of special journals not always necessary?

20.9 You are the accountant of a small retail store which sells on credit to its customers and uses a perpetual system for recording inventory. Justify to your general manager why you need to alter your accounting system to include subsidiary ledgers.

20.10 What contribution does a bank reconciliation statement make to the achievement of accounting control?

20.11 Assuming that a company has special journals, in which, if any, of the journals would the following entries be made?

(a) cash sales of merchandise

(b) credit sales of merchandise

(c) credit sales of old delivery vehicles

(d) cash sales of old delivery vehicles

(e) contribution of a block of land as capital of the business

(f) the write-off of a bad debt

(g) annual charge for depreciation

(h) a customer returns merchandise

(i) closing entries

(j) profit appropriation entries

Problems

20.12 *Special journals, posting to ledger accounts*

The Body Company Pty Ltd uses special journals and an accounts receivable subsidiary ledger in its accounting information system.

(a) Record the transactions for August in suitably designed special journals.

(b) Post the journals to the accounts receivable subsidiary ledger and the general ledger control account for accounts receivable.

Balances for accounts receivable at 31 July 20X1: R. Bones $220

Aug.	1	Sold goods on credit to:
		R. Bones for $260 (cost $120)—invoice no. 234
		L. Legge for $590 (cost $280)—invoice no. 235
		B. Neck for $340 (cost $130)—invoice no. 236
	2	Received cash from R. Bones after allowing 5 per cent discount.
	3	Sold goods for cash $267 (cost $35).
	4	Sold goods on credit to L. Legge for $750 (cost $420)—invoice no. 237.
	5	Cash sales $246 (cost $111).
	6	Received interest on bank loan $500.
	7	Received cash from B. Neck, less 5 per cent discount.

20.13 *Special journals and accounts payable ledger*

Sanctity and Sons uses special journals and an accounts payable subsidiary ledger in its accounting information system.

(a) Record the transactions for September 20X2 in suitably designed special journals.

(b) Post the journals to the accounts payable subsidiary ledger and the general ledger control account for accounts payable.

Balances for accounts payable at 31 August 20X2: R. Toombes $140

Sept.	1	Purchased goods on credit from:
		• H. Gravestones $350—purchase order no. 891
		• R. Toombes $460—purchase order no. 892
	2	Made the following payments:
		• week's wages $2000 (cheque no. 443)
		• week's rent $360 (cheque no. 444)
		• drawings $500 (cheque no. 445)
		• entertainment $140 (cheque no. 446)
	8	Purchased goods on credit from:
		• F. Hurst $400—purchase order no. 893
		• T. Ribute $870—purchase order no. 894
	9	Made payments:
		• week's wages $2000 (cheque no. 447)
		• week's rent $360 (cheque no. 448)
		• drawings $450 (cheque no. 449)
		• H. Gravestones, amount due (above) less 4 per cent discount (cheque no. 450)

15   Made payments:
* week's wages $2000 (cheque no. 451)
* week's rent $360 (cheque no. 452)
* R. Toombes, amount due (above) less 4 per cent discount (cheque no. 453)

17   A new machine was purchased on credit from Machines Galore Ltd for $10 000 (purchase order no. 895).

22   Made payments:
* week's wages $2000 (cheque no. 454)
* week's rent $360 (cheque no. 455)
* interest due on bank loan $100 (cheque no. 456)

20.14 *Special journals, posting to ledgers, internal control*

The following information relates to transactions of Hearty Traders Pty Ltd, a new company, in its first two weeks of operations, commencing 1 July 20X1. The company buys and sells goods on its own account and also receives commission for sales on behalf of other companies. The company intends to adopt the perpetual inventory method of recording.

* Summary of purchase orders that have been matched with invoices and delivery dockets:

Order no.	Date		Supplier	Item no.	Qty	Unit price $	Total $
81	July	1	Allgoods	42	10	1 700	17 000
82		2	Allgoods	43	6	5 200	31 200
84		6	Allgoods	44	8	3 000	24 000

* Summary of sales invoices:

Invoice no.	Date		Customer	Item no.	Qty	Sale amount $
124	July	1	D. Mence	42	2	5 600
125		5	G. Butler	42	6	16 300
126		7	M. Wether	44	1	8 000
127		11	D. Mence	44	1	7 700

* Summary of receipts issued for cheques received

Receipt no.	Date		Particulars	Discount $	Cash received $
74	July	1	Capital contribution		80 000
75		1	Commission received		1 500
76		3	D. Mence	120	5 480
77		9	Commission received		850
78		9	G. Butler	240	16 060
79		12	M. Wether		4 000
80		14	Commission received		2 600

- Summary of cheque payments:

Cheque				Amount
no.	Date		Particulars	$
251	July	2	Equipment	5 000
252		2	Rent	1 200
253		3	Allgoods	17 000
254		5	Wages	620
255			Cheque cancelled	
256		6	Withdrawals	3 000
257		8	Rent	1 200
258		10	Allgoods	31 200
259		11	Wages	620
260		13	Withdrawals	3 000

- Miscellaneous events:

July 5 Returned one unit of item number 43 to Allgoods and received a credit note for the cost of the unit.

13 D. Mence returned one of item number 44 and it was returned to stock. D. Mence was given an appropriate credit note.

(a) Record the transactions in appropriately designed special journals.

(b) For each journal, prepare a list of the postings that should be made to the general ledger.

(c) Identify the internal accounting controls present in this recording process.

20.15 *Bank reconciliation statements*

On 30 June 20X4 the cash at bank account in the ledger of Humble Pie Pty Ltd revealed an overdraft of $964.70, but a bank statement as at the same date showed a balance in favour of the company of $658.58. An examination of the records reveals the following differences:

(i) Entries in the bank statement but not in the journals:

June	6	Cheque book	$ 6.00
	12	Interest recorded by the bank on a fixed interest deposit with the bank	120.00
	18	Cheque 884765 debited	97.00
	19	Interest charged on bank overdraft	64.48
	21	Regular loan repayment to Shark Finance Co. paid directly by the bank	300.00
	29	Dishonoured cheque, no. 123654, E. Fled	20.50

(ii) Entries in the cash journals not recorded on the bank statement:

Cheque	667	drawn	28 May	60.00
	698		14 June	729.06
	734		30 June	960.00

Deposits entered in the cash receipts journal on 30 June but banked next day totalled $333.80.

The cheque debited on 18 June was not drawn by the company and, on inquiry, the bank manager admitted that it was the bank's error and would be corrected.

An error was detected in the cash payments journal in relation to a cheque, no. 702 issued to J. Luckless, which was entered as $640.00 instead of $64.00.

Calculate the revised balance in the cash at bank account and prepare a bank reconciliation statement as at 30 June 20X4.

20.16 *Bank reconciliations, subsidiary ledgers*
Refer to the journals prepared for Hearty Traders (question 20.14 above). The proprietor has now received a bank statement for the fortnight ended 14 July 20X1.

		THE PEOPLE'S BANK			
		Statement for Hearty Traders 14 July 20X1			
July	1	Deposit		$81 500	$81 500 CR
	2	Cheque book	$ 5		81 495 CR
	3	251	5 000		76 495 CR
	3	252	1 200		75 295 CR
	3	Deposit		5 480	80 775 CR
	5	254	620		80 155 CR
	5	253	17 000		63 155 CR
	10	Deposit		16 910	80 065 CR
	11	256	3 000		77 065 CR
	11	255	600		76 465 CR
	12	Deposit		4 000	80 465 CR
	13	258	31 200		49 265 CR
	14	260	3 000		46 265 CR

The proprietor mentioned in passing that he withdrew an additional $600 for personal use during the month, but cannot seem to find any record of the amount.

(a) Prepare a bank reconciliation statement as at 14 July 20X1, making any necessary amendments to the journals.
(b) Present general ledger accounts for accounts receivable and inventory and the subsidiary ledgers for each. Post the journals to their respective accounts. The full general ledger is not required.
(c) Prepare schedules of subsidiary ledger balances.
(d) What additional accounting controls apply to the above procedures?

20.17 *Cash journals, bank reconciliation statements*
The following information is available to you:

		LEDGER OF G. FIELDS	
		Cash at bank	
20X4			
July	1	Balance	$802 DR

JOURNAL OF G. FIELDS
Cash receipts Journal

Date	Particulars		Details	Bank
20X4				
July 3	H. Lauder		$ 33	
	Cash sales		45	$ 78
8	J. Ray		52	52
19	Q. Fox		201	201
31	K. Kong		85	85
			$416	$416

Cash payments Journal

Date	Particulars	Cheque no.	Details	Bank
20X4				
July 3	L. Pickles	101	$ 63	$ 63
5	Entertainment	102	15	15
9	M. Mouse	103	77	77
17	Advertising	104	25	25
27	Cash purchases	105	100	100
30	N. Mercury	106	33	33
			$313	$313

BANK OF HOPE BANK STATEMENT
Account of G. Fields

20X4		Debit	Credit	Balance
July 1	Balance b/f		$802	$ 802 CR
3	Deposit		78	880 CR
7	Cheque 102	$ 15		865 CR
8	Deposit		52	917 CR
9	Cheque 101	63		854 CR
12	Cheque 103	77		777 CR
19	Deposit		201	978 CR
24	Interest collected		50	1028 CR
27	Cheque 105	100		928 CR
30	Deposit (O. Pitt)		33	961 CR
31	Bank charges	4		957 CR
	Cheque book	2		955 CR

(a) Complete the cash journals and cash at bank account for July.

(b) Prepare a bank reconciliation statement as at 31 July 20X4.

20.18 *Division of responsibilities, review of an accounting system*

The Stingy Co. Ltd has three clerical employees who must perform the following functions:

(i)   maintain general ledger

(ii)   maintain accounts payable ledger

(iii) maintain accounts receivable ledger

(iv)   prepare cheques for signature

(v)   maintain cash payments journal

(vi)   issue credit notes for sales returns and allowances

(vii) reconcile the bank account

(viii) handle the deposit cash receipts

(a) Suggest an allocation of duties that should lead to adequate internal control and explain why you suggested the allocations were made in that way.

(b) Identify at least three sets of functions that should be combined and justify your choices.

Case studies

20.19 *The phony distributor*

A purchasing department employee set up a phony distributorship to provide his company with a much needed component that had previously been bought directly from the manufacturer. The employee was the only person in the company who dealt with the manufacturer, so it was a simple matter to persuade both his employer and the manufacturer that the other was in favour of the new setup. The employee made a handsome profit but eventually became overconfident and said that the manufacturer had put his prices up. When another employee complained about the price rise to the manufacturer the phony scheme was uncovered. In all, the company had lost over $1 million.

Required

(a) Identify the missing internal control feature/s that enabled this situation to occur.

(b) What procedures would you put in place to prevent this from occurring in the future? Justify your choice of procedures.

Adapted from The Chubb Corporation 1989, 'White Collar Crime: Loss Prevention Through Internal Control', prepared by Ernst & Young for the Chubb Group of Insurance Companies (*http://www.chubb.com/library/crp15.html*)

20.20 *Internal control features*

Kim Asher, the manager of Sublime Sausages Pty Ltd, has sought your advice on the company's purchases and creditors' system principally because of the following events:

(i) The company ran out of preservatives recently and the manager's investigation revealed that a payment had been made for sufficient quantities to cover their current needs.

(ii) Minced beef was received from a supplier but was of a lower quality than that ordered, a difference which is difficult to detect. The supplier's invoice was for the higher quality meat.

(iii) The manager suspects that dates are being changed on some old invoices and they are being presented for payment a second time.

The purchasing transaction cycle is monitored as follows:

- The purchasing officer, Robin Shaw, prepares two copies of the purchase order, one for the supplier and one for the files.
- Goods are delivered to the purchasing office where Shaw's assistant, Tran Fong, checks the quantities received and initials the supplier's delivery docket.
- When the invoice is received, the office clerk, Lesley Dry, checks the extensions and additions and forwards it to Robin Shaw for comparison with the purchase order and the delivery docket.
- If all is in order, Shaw initials the invoice and returns it to Lesley Dry, who prepares a cheque that Kim Asher signs. Robin Shaw then posts the cheque to the suppliers.

Required

(a) Explain how the circumstances (i) to (iii) outlined above might have occurred.

(b) Suggest what changes would be necessary to improve the system. Justify your suggestions.

20.21 *Above suspicion?*

Organisations must be able to trust their senior management, but there still needs to be some control over their activities. One chief financial officer (CFO) managed to defraud his employer of over $2 million because of a lack of internal controls.

The CFO had complete responsibility for the investment activities of his company and had been successful in this area in the past. So when he bought 1000 preference shares of an unknown company, assuring other senior managers that the company was sound, no one had reason to question his decision. And the 14% dividend promised by the company was very attractive.

In fact, the company had been set up some years previously by the CFO and had no assets or operations, the money from the sale of the shares being used by the CFO for personal investments.

The CFO was able to pay the 14% dividend at first simply from the money received for the shares. But when his personal investments proved unsuccessful he was unable to pay them and his deception was revealed.

Required

Identify the control procedures that would have prevented the above situation resulting in such a large loss to the company. Justify your choice of control procedures.

Adapted from The Chubb Corporation 1989, 'White Collar Crime: Loss Prevention Through Internal Control', prepared by Ernst & Young for the Chubb Group of Insurance Companies (*http://www.chubb.com/library/crp15.html*)

728 PART 5 ACCOUNTING INFORMATION SYSTEMS

20.22 *Review of an accounting system*

Crumbly Candies Pty Ltd, a wholesale confectionery company, has expanded its operations over recent months. The accounting records are diligently kept by the managing director's wife and consist of:

(i)   A ledger.
(ii) A cash book in which are entered all receipts deposited with the bank and all payments by cheque. Totals are posted to the ledger each month.
(iii) A notebook for recording the details whenever cash received from customers is used to pay a creditor's account. A summary of these transactions is posted to the ledger each month.
(iv) A file containing unpaid invoices. At the end of each year the unpaid invoices at that date are totalled and an adjusting entry is made in the ledger accounts for purchases and sundry creditors.
(v)   A file containing duplicates of all invoices sent to customers. When an account is settled, the word 'Paid' is written across the duplicate invoice.

Accounts outstanding at the end of the year are totalled and an adjusting entry is made in the ledger accounts for sundry debtors and sales. The company deals with 23 suppliers and, following the recent expansion, regular customers have grown from 20 to over 400. The managing director's wife is now grossly overworked and cannot cope with the sales transactions, which exceed 1500 per month. Arguments with debtors over outstanding accounts are becoming frequent. You have been asked to review the company's accounting system.

Required

(a) What changes in accounting procedures would you recommend to the company?

(b) Explain the advantages that would result from adoption of the improvements you have recommended.

PART 6

Accounting for management decisions

CHAPTER 21

Managerial decision making and the accountant

Learning objectives

In this chapter you will be introduced to:

1. the reasons why reports prepared for external reporting purposes are inadequate to serve the information needs of internal decision makers

2. the nature of decision making and the different stages in the decision-making process

3. the difference between planning and control

4. the advantages to be obtained from effective planning and the difference between strategic plans and operating plans

5. the effective use of a performance evaluation system within the management control system

6. the role of organisational control as a key source of persuasion influencing the decision maker in organisations

7. the importance of criteria of relevance to the user in the preparation of information for managerial decision making

8. the criteria governing the categorisation of responsibility centres as profit centres, expense centres and revenue centres

9. the need for decentralised decision making in some organisations and the impact decentralisation has on the appropriate organisational structure.

Introduction

The material you have covered so far in this book has focused on financial accounting for external reporting purposes. You have been given an understanding of the elements of financial statements, the preparation of financial statements, accounting regulations, financial management and alternative financial accounting systems. However, the focus has been on maintaining records and preparing accounts so that information can be reported to external users such as owners of the entity, potential investors, lenders and government agencies. The reports you have prepared have mainly been statements that portray what has happened during the past accounting period (e.g. the profit and loss statement and the cash flow statement) and the consequent financial position of the entity (the balance sheet).

You are now asked to consider how the statements you have been preparing would help managers to make daily decisions with regard to managing the organisation. The statements you have focused on have been designed to report on the *results* of management's decisions (remember that actions are the results of decisions). How could the information you have been recording assist the managers to make those decisions? First let us consider what decisions need to be made during the accounting period.

In a firm that manufactures goods, these decisions include:

- what products to make (product mix)
- what materials to use as inputs to production
- what price to charge for the product
- how many to make
- when to make them
- what lay-out the factory should have (i.e. the positioning of equipment and other work-stations)
- whether to work shifts or overtime.

In a service environment there is a need to decide:

- what products to offer (these are services rather than goods)
- what to charge
- how to deliver the service
- how to maintain the required quality
- how to manage demand (consider the special offers made by airlines and hotels to utilise what would be unused capacity at times of slack business demand)
- what resources are required at different times (e.g. how many nurses are required in different hospital wards).

In a retail outlet, managers need to decide:

- how much stock to order
- how much should be stored
- what price to charge
- whether to expand operations
- whether it is a good idea to offer a delivery service
- how to compete with the opposition.

None of these decisions are necessarily exclusive to any category. For instance, an accounting firm and an ice-cream manufacturer need to make decisions about whether to expand, just as the jeans shop proprietor does.

Case 21.1 Information for control decisions

Alex Mitchell is the new chief accountant for a firm that makes paper sacks. While reviewing the most recent profit and loss statement Alex notices that some expenses, such as power, seem high compared with other expenses. How would Alex get the information required to be able to contain the cost of electricity used?

Before turning to the discussion at the end of this chapter, make a note of the sort of information Alex would need, and then consider the information needs for some of the decisions listed above. Make a few notes and then read the discussion of this case before proceeding with the rest of this chapter.

This part of the text concentrates on accounting for internal decision making and other associated issues (e.g. the nature of decision making, the behavioural implications of manager involvement in planning processes, and the level of autonomy enjoyed by the decision maker). Consequently, building on the brief coverage in Chapter 2, this chapter distinguishes between the role of the management accountant (which will be defined to include the financial management function) and that of the financial accountant. It then provides the theoretical and organisational context for the material discussed in the other chapters in this part. Specifically, this chapter focuses primarily on the information-provider role of the management accountant, the information needs of the users of this information and the organisational impact of the requirements of the management control system, for which the chief management accountant is responsible.

The other chapters in this part illustrate and discuss a number of accounting methods used by management accountants in the fulfilment of their role, and the behavioural impact that the management control system and the work of the management accountant might have.

Informing internal decision makers

Looking back to your study of the external financial reports in earlier parts of this text, you will recall that the profit and loss statement is concerned with the depiction of revenue and resources used (expenses). However, how would a manager be able to ensure that the required resources are on hand when production is to occur? Financial accounting mainly focuses on past activity, but managers need information on what is happening currently in their organisations. They also need to be able to plan ahead. For such purposes managers rely on management accounting information. In this part of the book you will learn about recording data and reporting information that is designed to assist management decision making.

Note that information is what you have after raw data have been processed into a useable, useful communication. You also need to be clear about the nature of decision making and its consequences. A useful definition of decision making is the making of a choice between alternatives. To make 'informed decisions', managers need to be apprised of all alternative choices, as well as the outcome of adopting, or not adopting, each one of them. Such information should also be used after the decision has been made to compare the actual outcome with the anticipated outcome.

Figure 21.1 provides an illustration of the several stages of decision making. It can be seen that first the need to make a decision must be recognised before all alternative courses of action are determined and evaluated so that an *informed choice* can be made between them. The management accountant has a responsibility to identify alternatives and to provide as much timely and helpful guidance as possible in the selection of a course of action. This does not restrict the management accountant to the provision of financial information. As will become apparent in subsequent chapters, relevant information may include physical measures that have not been converted to financial data, and qualitative data as well.

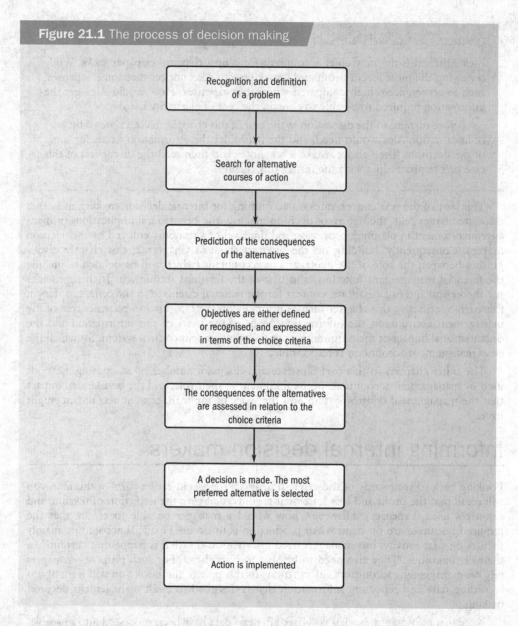

Figure 21.1 The process of decision making

Recognition and definition
of a problem

↓

Search for alternative
courses of action

↓

Prediction of the consequences
of the alternatives

↓

Objectives are either defined
or recognised, and expressed
in terms of the choice criteria

↓

The consequences of the alternatives
are assessed in relation to the
choice criteria

↓

A decision is made. The most
preferred alternative is selected

↓

Action is implemented

Figure 21.1 considers the stages that take a manager from identifying the need to take action, through deciding what action to take, to taking the action itself. Unfortunately, some managers then dismiss that issue from their minds until they are forced to reconsider it because of the occurrence of some other problem. As illustrated in Figure 21.2, it is preferable to monitor the outcome of any decision, to evaluate whether the action taken needs modification, and to identify the ways in which future decisions can be improved.

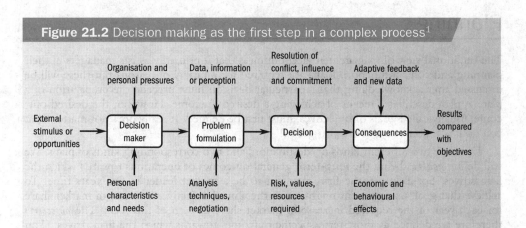

Figure 21.2 Decision making as the first step in a complex process[1]

The pressures on the decision maker outlined in Figure 21.2 are considered again later in this chapter. The other chapters in this last section of the text focus on:

- the data collection and analysis techniques referred to in the second stage of the figure (in particular Chapters 23, 24 and 25)
- the risk (i.e. feasibility) and resource usage plans relating to the alternative options as well as discussions on the influences and conflicts affecting the decision, as referred to in the third stage of the figure (primarily Chapters 24 and 25)
- the economic and behavioural consequences of the decision (Chapters 24, 25 and 26) and the need for monitoring the outcome and possibly adapting the adopted alternative course of action (i.e. the decision) (especially Chapters 24 and 25).

Because of its importance to management control, the behavioural consequences of what is done by management and the way it is done will be illustrated. For example, there is little point in measuring a manager's performance as a means of motivating a better performance level if the way it is done alienates the manager.

You will also find that the management function of 'control' is very much about the fourth stage depicted in Figure 21.2.

Before discussing and illustrating the different techniques used by management accountants we will consider the role of these accountants more closely. It will help you to comprehend the techniques if first you understand their function.

The management accountant must satisfy much of the information requirements of other managers. The information that is explained in Chapter 22 is designed to satisfy the needs of the financial accountant in the preparation of the financial statements. This manager needs to know the cost of goods sold in order to determine profit and also the inventory valuation for inclusion in the balance sheet. The way to derive these figures and make the necessary entries in the accounts will be explained in Chapter 22.

The provision of other information by the management accountant is directed at meeting the decision-making needs of managers. There are a multitude of decisions to be made by each manager and the management accountant can help in many of them. In fact, the main functions of management accounting relate to planning, control and decision making.

Although planning and control are identified separately from decision making, these two functions are merely formal, regular, and often regulated, decision-making processes, rather than individual-issue-resolving decisions. Planning and control will be considered holistically, giving a broad view of these particular processes that require a range of decisions to be made.

---

[1] A. J. Rowe, 'Making Effective Decisions', in A. L. Patz and A. J Rowe, *Management Control and Decision Systems*, Wiley, New York, 1971, p. 10.

Planning

The traditional view of management accounting is that it primarily assists managers in their planning and control function. Plans are required for a variety of reasons but these will be discussed after acknowledging that a particular decision must precede the preparation of a plan. A plan describes a means of achieving a desired outcome. However, the desired outcome, usually called goals or objectives, must first be defined. It really does not matter what you do if you don't care where you get to!

There are two different kinds of 'destination' and two corresponding kinds of plans. We will define *goals* as being the long-term general outcomes of operations towards which the firm strives. For example, the firm may aim to be a market leader in five years time. To achieve that goal, management might assess the annual objectives in terms of market share for each year or the required increase in market share in each of the years. The *objectives* therefore are defined as short-term specific outcomes towards which the firm strives. (You should be aware that some writers use the terms 'goals' and 'objectives' interchangeably and some reverse the meanings adopted here.)

The plans that are made to achieve goals are called *strategic plans*. They might relate to where to trade and what to make. They might reveal a need to build an extra factory or open more outlets. They are long-term in nature and have a broad impact. The *operating plans* (sometimes referred to as tactical plans) relate to short-term activity. They identify what resources will be needed to satisfy demand in the short term. The most common form of plan is the budget. The budget should not be regarded as a spending allowance. Rather, it is a resource usage plan. For example, suppose that the strategic plan is to sell two different kinds of bicycle, the Sprint and the Tourer. The marketing manager estimates the sales of each bicycle for each month of the year. From this information there needs to be an estimation of how far ahead the bicycles need to be made in order to have them in the correct places at the times they are needed. This reveals the latest time at which they must be made. Knowing this, the resource requirements of production can be determined.

The schedule of when to make each product is called a *production budget*. It is used to calculate:

- the monthly requirements of each component or direct material that goes into production
- what the demand for labour will be
- what the demands on equipment will be (and questions about whether there are enough of these resources or whether more equipment needs to be purchased months ahead)
- the requirements of all other 'ingredients' that are used in production.

Budgeted cash flow statements can be prepared to check whether there will be enough cash from sales to meet payments for resources when they have to be made. If not, advance arrangements may be made to borrow funds.

These budgets will be looked at more closely in later chapters, but they are being introduced here to illustrate why you need to learn the skills that are covered in later chapters.

A key advantage that can be derived from planning is lost if isolated plans are developed for different parts of the organisation, or if strategic plans are not used to guide the development of operational plans. Consistency and coordination are vital if goals are to be attained, and goals are vital for a positive direction of purpose. Furthermore, the way in which the planning function of management is carried out has an impact on whether the potential benefits of planning are realised.

Consistency

An organisation must identify its long-term goals and short-term objectives if there is to be a concerted effort not only on survival but advancement. When an organisation has defined its long-term goals it is able to determine short-term objectives that will advance the firm towards the ultimate goals. The objectives are therefore consistent with the goals. Once the aims are known by all managers they are able to make decisions that are consistent with the achievement of objectives in the short term. Defining managers' objectives and motivating managers to work towards the same goals promotes what is called *goal congruency*. This describes the situation in which managers make decisions that are in the best interests of the organisation.

Coordination, cooperation and communication

Coordination, cooperation and communication between managers is important in ensuring the achievement of objectives, and hence the achievement of goals. Musicians in an orchestra would make a terrible noise if they each 'did their own thing'. So that a beautiful sound reaches the audience, consistent with the desires of the composer, music is written down in a plan that coordinates the contribution of each player with that of others to achieve the objective of the composer. Similarly, the performances of ballet dancers, opera singers and actors are planned and written down in order to avoid confusion during the performance. This is achieved by communicating the plan to the performers so that they know what is required of them, thus promoting their cooperation with one another to achieve the desired effect. Planning is also required in a firm. A complete set of plans is written into a document called the *master budget*.

Formalised planning

An ad hoc approach to planning is not as effective as having a formal, documented planning process. A formalised approach to planning brings benefits such as the identification of needs and problems in advance, consequently minimising the need to operate in a reactionary mode. Decisions produce actions that are positive and preventative rather than curative. When designing a formal planning process it is necessary to determine the extent of lower-level management involvement in drafting budgets, and the level at which budget approval is given.

Manager participation

The level at which budget decisions are made differs between organisations. At one extreme all budget decisions are made by senior management and the resultant budget targets are imposed on lower-level managers. At the other extreme lower-level managers prepare draft budgets for their area of responsibility and submit them for minor adjustment and approval. Typically the situation will lie towards the first of these extremes (the disadvantages of adopting this approach are discussed in Chapter 25). An obvious advantage to be obtained from the greater involvement of lower-level managers in the budget-setting process is the utilisation of their better knowledge of their own department, its activities and its output. In deciding about the level at which budget drafting should take place consideration should be given to potential results.

It should be recognised that managers responsible for drafting budgets:

- are forced to think ahead
- have to ensure that they understand the goals and objectives of the organisation
- have to clearly define their own objectives (consistent with organisational goals and objectives)
- are required to come up with a plan of their own operations for the future period.

Planning techniques

Planning is a systematic decision-making process designed to establish strategies and objectives for all levels in the organisation. By planning, managers seek to identify and anticipate the organisation's future problems and opportunities and to develop courses of action that will enable the organisation to achieve its objectives. For this purpose it is useful to undertake a SWOT analysis, in which the firm's *internal* strengths and weaknesses are assessed and its *external* opportunities and threats identified.

Strategic decisions, such as a decision to diversify the company into new product areas, usually affect the organisation over a reasonably long time period, such as five years or more. Consequently, information needed for these decisions should include assessments of project costs and benefits resulting from the decision over an extended period of time. Some examples of decisions of this nature, and ways to develop cost and revenue information as inputs to the long-term planning process, will be considered in Chapter 24. Short-term planning is the main focus of Chapter 25.

Control

It is clear from the discussion of planning that certain elements of control are present in the planning process, since the plans are used to communicate to managers what is required of them and their departments, and to coordinate the efforts of managers towards common organisational goals.

Having used plans in this way, it is unwise to assume that 'things' are progressing according to plan without continually checking that this is the case. Mechanical control devices have the means of presetting the desired conditions (e.g. a central heating system requires the desired temperature to be preset), a way of measuring current conditions (e.g. the current temperature), a way of bringing about a correction if there is a mismatch between the first two elements (e.g. a heater), and a means of communicating between these other three elements (e.g. turn on the heater if the desired temperature is greater than the current temperature).

To some extent this is what happens in an organisation. Progress must be monitored and compared with the plan in order to identify any deviation from the plan. When a deviation occurs, a correction can be made to the activity, to return to the plan. Alternatively, an evaluation may reveal that the plan needs to be adjusted to allow for conditions that are different from those anticipated (e.g. the heater needs to be replaced by a cooler because of an unseasonal heat-wave).

The major difference between the mechanical control system and the management control system is that the management control system must allow for the uncertainties inherent in dealing with the human element. Correction will not be automatic; it will be due to a response made by a manager. One function of the management control system is to encourage managers to make the same decision that the chief executive officer would make in the same circumstances. If this occurs, goal congruency can be achieved.

It can be seen that there are two kinds of control being promoted by the management control system. The first is the control managers exercise over matters for which they have responsibility. This responsibility must be accompanied by appropriate influence over these matters. (Unfortunately some managers are inappropriately held accountable for matters over which they do not have control or at least significant influence.)

The second form of control is the influence (control) being exerted over the manager to make appropriate decisions. A way in which the management control system encourages managers to make goal-congruent decisions is by evaluating their performance. A key to doing this effectively is to first define clearly what constitutes desirable and reasonable 'performance'. Reasonableness relates to what is measured as part of the performance evaluation. Desirable performance relates to the acceptable level of performance.

What to measure

It is not reasonable, and is likely to be demotivating, to expect managers to control matters that are beyond their influence. For example, a manager running a department that manufactures standard goods will not have influence over selling prices and sales volumes, so does not have control over the revenue earned by the products made in the department. Hence it is sensible to evaluate the control this manager exercises over the costs incurred in the production of the goods, and not try to identify the profit earned by the department. (The revenue should be part of the performance evaluation of the marketing and sales department.)

Performance measures need not be financial measures. Non-financial measures such as physical volumes are useful (e.g. throughput times for production, ratios of inputs to outputs, staff turnover ratios and number of defects produced) and qualitative factors may be included (such as customer satisfaction levels identified by surveys).

Decisions about which factors appropriately measure performance have a direct impact on which structure is suitable for the organisation, a topic that is dealt with separately later in this chapter.

Evaluating the measured performance

A measure of performance does not indicate whether that performance is good or bad until it is compared with a standard. When watching swimming at the Olympic Games, for instance, the viewer can compare the performances of the swimmers in the same race, or compare the lead swimmers with the Olympic Games record, the national record, the world record, the swimmers' own previous best times and the times set in previous heats of the same event. A measure of performance does not, in itself, evaluate that performance.

With regard to evaluating the performance of managers, their performance measures can be subjected to three kinds of comparisons:

- with the manager's own past performance to identify a trend
- with the performance of other managers
- with predetermined objectives.

The first two methods can cause dysfunctional behaviour (i.e. the opposite of goal congruency). A manager's measured performance may change over time due to external influences (e.g. an exchange-rate change affecting imported material costs, or new staff who are not yet proficient at their jobs). Or different managers might be working with pieces of equipment that have different capabilities.

Ideally, a manager's performance will be compared with agreed targets. The way in which these targets should be set is covered in more detail in Chapter 25, where the advantages of participative decision making are discussed. Briefly, managers are likely to make a greater effort to achieve targets for which they feel some responsibility (i.e. they had an influence in the setting of them).

Departmental performance

An organisation might wish to prepare reports on the economic performance of departments, but these should not be confused with reports on the manager responsible for the department. Departmental reports are likely to include many items over which the manager does not have direct control (e.g. allocations of costs incurred in head office). The departmental economic report, therefore, does not equate with the performance report on the manager of the department.

Organisational control in context

Most of the material on the topic of control in this text will relate to organisational control. Organisational control is the kind of influence exerted by the management control system and the way it is utilised. It relates to the way performance is assessed, the structure of the organisation, and other formal means of control (e.g. the way the planning process is managed). In Chapter 26 it will be shown that organisational control is one of three major types of control that influence the decisions of managers. Consider Figure 21.3, in which the influences that impact on decisions are illustrated.

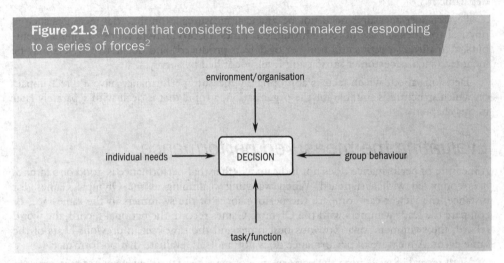

Figure 21.3 A model that considers the decision maker as responding to a series of forces[2]

The influences from the organisation, social/work group and the individual create what are called organisational control, social or group control and self control respectively. Organisational control is therefore only one form of persuasion to which managers are subjected when deciding how to act. An in-depth consideration of the forms of control that stem from individual and group influences is beyond the scope of this text, but they are discussed briefly in Chapter 26.

Decision making

There are particular decisions that are made as part of the planning and control processes. What is often referred to in management accounting as 'decision making' is the task of making one-off decisions (e.g. whether to discontinue selling a product or whether to dispose of a manufacturing plant or retail outlet) rather than decisions that are part of a formal, regular, decision-making sequence or process, such as the budgeting process (part of planning) and performance evaluation procedure (part of control).

The preparation of reports for internal decision making is not subject to prescribed methods or formats. The format used, and the information to be included, is at the discretion of the preparer, unless the organisation concerned has a preferred format. The information that should be included is determined by what is relevant. The inclusion of irrelevant information requires users to exercise discretion that may be beyond their capabilities. Such a report would certainly take longer to understand, and it may mislead.

The format used to present information should be easy to follow and should highlight key items. For example, in a report on the cash flow of a tennis club, it is useful to identify

---

[2] A. J. Rowe, 'Making Effective Decisions', in A. L. Patz and A. J. Rowe, *Management Control and Decision Systems*, Wiley, New York, 1971, p. 9. It will be noticed that most of the research on control that underpins current thinking and research on control systems was published during the first half of the 1970s.

the cash surplus/deficit from the year before adjusting it by the opening balance to derive the final cash balance. Other items may also be highlighted by the arrangement of items (e.g. whether competition fees cover competition expenses or whether 'pennant players' are subsidised by social members).

Two techniques for deriving useful information for specific decisions are explained in Chapter 25. A number of other techniques for various types of decisions may be found in management accounting texts.

Organisational structure

The success with which the management control system meets its purpose is heavily dependent on the organisational structure adopted by the organisation. Decisions to be made with regard to the organisational structure include the extent of centralised decision making and the use of decentralisation.

Decisions about centralisation/decentralisation are closely related to decisions about the nature of responsibility centres in the organisation. A responsibility centre is any part of the organisation that is the responsibility of one manager. The organisation therefore consists of responsibility centres within responsibility centres, all gathered together within the biggest responsibility centre, the whole organisation itself.

Figure 21.4 shows, in part, an organisation chart for a large bank. Only some units are named, for illustration purposes, but it can be seen that there are tiers of units. (Organisations now are typically 'flatter' than they were a decade or two ago—they have fewer layers in the hierarchy.) From Figure 21.4 it can be seen, for instance, that the manager of Group Services is responsible for 13 sub-units including the Training College, HR Services, Performance Measurement and Costing Services, each of which has its own manager. The manager of Group Services is responsible *to* the Group Chief Executive.

Responsibility centres

The growth and increasing diversity of activities within firms has made it progressively more difficult for one single manager to keep abreast of all decisions and developments. The need for delegation of responsibility has been met by the creation of departments, each with its own responsible manager. As small firms progressed over time to become large corporations, the nature and size of departments also changed. The management accounting literature now refers to functional units and business units. Within organisations, functional units often have the word 'department' in their title, whereas a business unit is often called a division.

- A functional unit is a segment of the organisation that is responsible for performing one function. It has specialist managers and may have specialist employees (e.g. the marketing department and research and development department) and often provides services to other parts of the organisation (e.g. the legal department and the personnel department).
- A business unit is a segment of the organisation that can be compared to an external business, as it undertakes its own research and development, production, marketing and sales. It is more self-contained than a functional unit.

Because of the nature of business units the business unit manager (often called the divisional manager) often has significant influence over profit generation within the unit. If the manager does have significant influence over (a) revenue and (b) costs that can be matched against revenue to give an indication of profit-generation success, the unit is called a *profit centre*. The success with which the business unit manager generates profit for the organisation should not be measured by the unit's profit as reported in external financial statements, because these statements include some items over which the manager has no control (see Chapter 23). The relevance of different methods of measuring profit generation (such as contribution margin, direct business-unit profit, controllable business-unit profit, return on investment and economic value-added) are more appropriately studied in a management

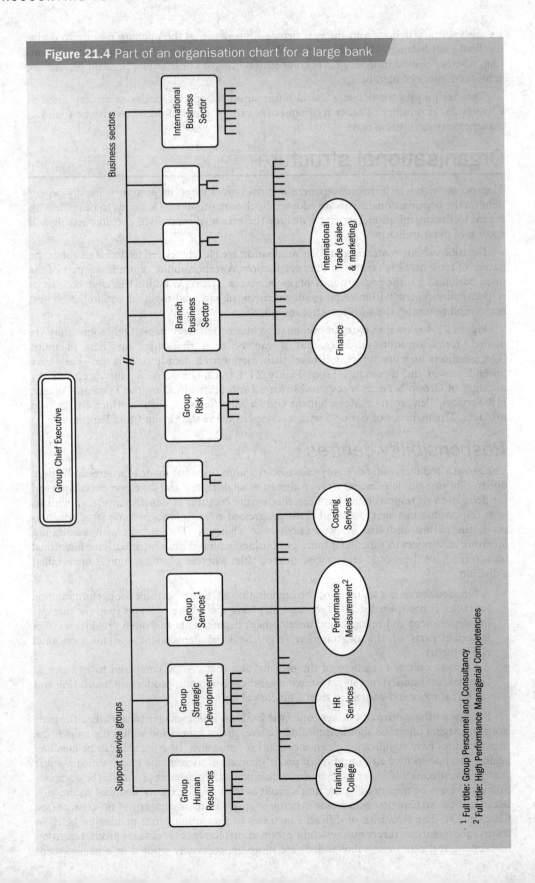

Figure 21.4 Part of an organisation chart for a large bank

1 Full title: Group Personnel and Consultancy
2 Full title: High Performance Managerial Competencies

accounting course, but we will briefly consider two essential elements of their calculation here:

- Influence over revenue generation is dependent on being able to make decisions that affect sales price, sales volume and the mix of products sold.
- The costs that are controllable by the manager (i.e. those the manager has significant influence over) must include product costs. A marketing department will have its own internal costs, but these could not be matched against revenue to measure profit generation.

Not all organisations have business units, but all organisations have some functional units (e.g. the head office functions). Regardless of whether the organisation has business units, functional unit managers normally have significant influence only over costs or revenue generation (i.e. in the marketing department). Functional units are therefore called expense centres, or revenue centres, respectively.

- In an *expense centre* the unit manager has significant influence over costs incurred in that unit but not over the generation of revenue (e.g. a research and development unit, or a manufacturing department that is not responsible for external sales and cannot take action that will significantly affect revenues).
- In a *revenue centre* the unit manager is primarily responsible for revenue generation. This manager will also have departmental costs that must be controlled, but these costs cannot be matched against revenue to indicate how profitable transactions have been.

The relationship between different units can be depicted in an organisation chart, as illustrated in Figure 21.4. The chart may show that there is, for example, a business unit that has a research and development department, two marketing departments serving different geographical areas, and three producing departments. This would depict one profit centre with two revenue centres and four expense centres within it (see Figure 21.5).

Alternatively, instead of having functional units within various business units, the chart might show that there is only one business unit, the organisation itself. In this case there will be a number of functional units all reporting to the chief executive officer.

An important aspect of the organisation chart is that it represents the line of responsibility and reporting. Thus, for example, J. Turner, the manager of the Marketing Department (Eastern Districts) would report to, and is held responsible to, the General Manager of the Plastic Film Division, T. Jones.

Although we have only briefly considered the nature of responsibility centres, it is important to be aware that the classification of them may have a major impact on the behaviour of managers. Such classification is directly related to the earlier discussion on the importance of assessing the performance of managers on the basis of items over which the managers have sufficient influence for the assessment to be fair. For example, an evaluation of the performance of a manufacturing manager on the basis of success in generating profit (i.e. as a profit-centre manager) when the sales effort and pricing are controlled by other managers can cause dysfunctional behaviour.

Centralisation and decentralisation

Since functional unit managers do not have the information or responsibility to make cost–revenue trade-off decisions, such decisions must be made centrally. However, profit-centre managers have a wide range of responsibilities and knowledge. They also require sufficient autonomy to maintain significant influence over profit generation. The delegation of a large amount of responsibility and authority to such managers is called decentralisation.

An important consideration with regard to decentralisation and the autonomy required by business-unit managers is the effect on the manager if a decision made by the manager on a matter normally within this manager's responsibility is overturned by head-office managers. Such action should not be taken lightly as it is likely to cause feelings of insecurity and frustration. It can also cause future dysfunctional behaviour.

Figure 21.5 Part of an organisation chart for a decentralised manufacturing firm

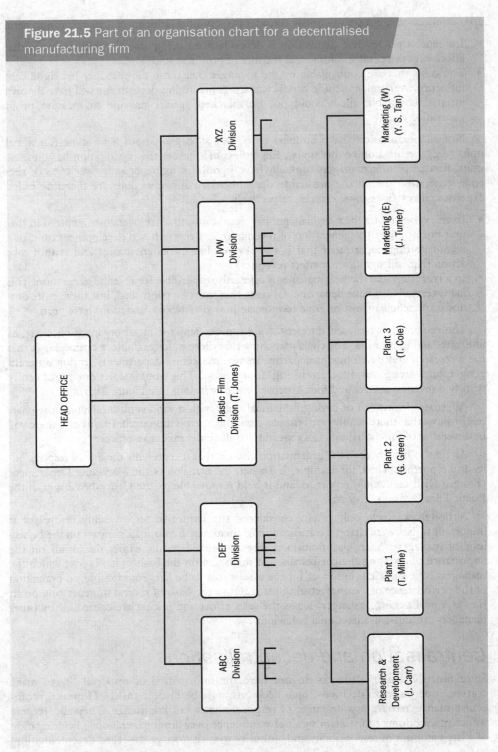

Other issues with regard to centralisation and decentralisation are dealt with in a number of management accounting texts[3] and will not be covered further here.

3 One of note is R. N. Anthony and V. Govindarajan, *Management Control Systems*, 9th edn, Irwin, Boston, 1998.

Ethical issues

The importance of accounting for the preparation and communication of financial information is critical within an organisation. All organisations have accounting systems and, as an organisation grows, the systems become more important. The complexity of decision making increases as members of the organisation are spread through various levels and when activities are conducted by individuals physically more remote from one another. There is a need to ensure that decisions are co-ordinated and that the organisation acts as one in achieving its goals. An information system is vital in planning the organisation's activities, in controlling operations so that plans are adhered to, and in evaluating performance so that plans can be improved and corrective action taken. The management accountant is a critical part of an organisation's information system.

Management accountants are called on to provide information to help make some important decisions. In most organisations they will be regularly preparing and providing financial information as an input into day-to-day operational decisions, and also into long-term strategic decisions. Decisions and outcomes are affected by accounting information and hence it is critical that the information provided by the accountant is prepared carefully and objectively. The accountant must check the source of information carefully and be aware that different groups and individuals in the organisation may wish to have a particular type of influence on a decision for which the accountant is providing information. For example, the marketing manager might be very keen for the company to manufacture a new product because he or she may want to have on offer all the products that a customer might ask for. However, from the company's point of view it is only worthwhile making a new product if it is going to be profitable. In calculating figures to determine the profitability of the proposed new product, the accountant needs to bear in mind that the marketing estimates of sales of the new product may be overly optimistic. In this situation it would be useful for the accountant to do some sensitivity analysis to show how the profitability of the product is affected by varying levels of projected sales. The possibility of introducing bias into forecasts is also a reason why it is important to monitor the outcome of decisions, and to identify the source of any inaccurate information on which the decision was based. Such feedback on the consequences of decisions allows steps to be taken to improve future decisions and discourages biased forecasts, as managers know that their errors will be identified with them.

Similar instances might arise when the accountant is involved in setting budgets. Groups and individuals who are evaluated on their ability to achieve budgeted output, costs or profit targets may have a vested interest in having budgeted targets set that are easy to meet. Budgets easily met, however, are not necessarily in the best interests of the organisation as a whole. Hence, the accountant must check carefully the information gathered in the budget-setting process to ensure that budget targets are fairly set. As a pivotal part of the organisation's information system, management accountants must use their skills to provide information that is accurate, fair and reliable.

Summary

This chapter has demonstrated the need for the adoption of particular accounting techniques that can meet the needs of internal decision making. The wide range of such decisions was demonstrated and the information needs of managers making those decisions was discussed. The chapter also explained the different stages of decision making and the different influences on those decisions. Organisational control, through the management control system, is but one source of these influences.

The management functions of planning, control and decision making were discussed and the behavioural implications of management action were considered. Further, issues with regard to the organisational structure, in the context of the management control system, were canvassed.

Accountants and accounting play an important role within the organisation. Beyond this, there is a need to consider the behavioural implications of decisions and the outcomes of decisions, including the monitoring of outcomes and possible adjustments to decision-related action.

Having identified various information requirements of managers, the remaining chapters of the text will clarify the ways that many of those information needs can be met. Chapter 22 looks at ways in which products (i.e. both goods and services) and projects can be costed, for the purpose of satisfying the information needs of external financial reporting. Chapter 23 introduces the ways in which costs can be categorised and analysed. Such analysis provides useful information about the behaviour of costs and the causes of costs. The use of this information for control purposes is then explored.

Control is further facilitated by the existence of plans. A comparison of what is happening with plans of what is expected to happen can highlight a need for corrective action. This action may be directed at returning the organisation to plan or taking the necessary moves to adjust the plans and strategies to allow for a changing environment. Chapters 24 and 25 present techniques used for developing and presenting long-term plans and short-term plans respectively.

Finally, Chapter 26 studies the role of management accounting information in management decisions relating to control and performance evaluation.

Discussion of in-text case

Case 21.1

As an expense, power would be one item in the profit and loss statement, although it is incurred in many different places for many different reasons. Alex would need to know the power *use* of each different department (i.e. the cost is controlled through monitoring and controlling power usage). Within departments the power may be identified with different causes (e.g. lighting, heating, computer power, other equipment usage). If this information is not being collected, it is difficult to know where excesses are occurring or how to control usage of the resource.

As a cost, power consumed in production would be part of the overhead costs and would be obscured in the profit and loss statement because it becomes part of cost of goods sold. Excess usage of power in production is therefore not identifiable from the profit and loss statement. However, production managers often do receive detail about the power usage of different equipment or processes. Provision of this information is part of the role of the management accounting system.

Power consumed in other parts of the firm would similarly become part of an aggregate figure in the profit and loss statement and would not be identifiable with any specific part of the firm. It may even be aggregated with other expenses.

With regard to the other decisions listed at the beginning of the chapter, the information required may be a combination of:

- the contribution to profit of each product
- the cost to produce the product and whether its production utilises excess capacity
- the current market price for the product
- the cost of preventing defects, the cost of identifying defects, the cost of correcting for defects, and the cost of lost sales when defects reach the customer

- forecasts of demand and knowledge of the resources needed to satisfy the demand (e.g. forecasts of claims levels in an insurance office and staffing requirements to cope with the claims need to be accurate two/three months in advance)
- long-term staffing requirements compared with fluctuating requirements
- the unnecessary costs caused by transferring materials, partly finished goods and finished goods between inventories and processes.

This is not a complete list of information for which the management accountant may be responsible, but you can see the wide range of decision-relevant information that is not available from the financial statements prepared for external purposes or the financial accounting system.

Review exercises

Discussion questions

21.1 What is the difference between strategic planning and operational planning?

21.2 Discuss the role of the accountant and of accounting information in planning the activities of an organisation.

21.3 What main type of budgets do you think would be prepared in a medium-sized retail store chain? What purpose would each budget serve and who would be most involved in its preparation?

21.4 (a) Explain the nature of control as it relates to the management control system.
(b) How is performance evaluation related to the control function of management?

21.5 What feedback reports do you think would be most useful within a small company that manufactures anti-glare screens for computers?

21.6 Pullit Ltd, a Sydney firm that manufactures tow-bars for cars, has decided to expand operations by opening a factory and sales office in Melbourne. Identify the major aspects in which planning will be required for both the long term and short term and, in each case, suggest some possible undesirable consequences of inadequate planning.

21.7 The managing director of A. B. Barker Ltd, manufacturers of superior dog kennels, decided to set a sales target of 14 000 kennels for 20X1. This plan was announced to shareholders at the annual meeting held at the end of 20X0 and was placed on the company's noticeboard for employees. During the year the following events occurred:

- It was discovered in January that a severe shortage of appropriate timber would continue until March.
- In February A. B. Barker Ltd had to arrange emergency finance from a merchant bank at a high interest rate when it was discovered that the company had insufficient cash to pay its wages.
- When timber was eventually obtained it was ordered in one consignment and most lay around until November.
- Only 10 000 kennels were completed during the year even though the factory was operating at maximum capacity throughout.
- Only 4000 kennels were sold, partly because the colour was unpopular and partly because they had a habit of collapsing on the occupant.

Discuss how these events could have been avoided.

21.8   What is meant by 'organisational structure'?

21.9   Distinguish between an expense centre, a revenue centre and a profit centre.

21.10   Why is it necessary for authority to be delegated as organisations grow? Why does delegation of authority give rise to the need for a formal management control system?

 Problems

21.11 *Product costing*

On a recent camping trip in the outback Rodney Saulwick marvelled at the camp bread baked by his wife, Jenny. 'We could go into business selling this bread to other campers and cover our costs throughout the camping season', he said. The occupant of the next tent, Simon Spoilsport, doubted this claim, whereupon Rodney collected the following data:

Average number of camping groups: 35
Cost of baking one loaf of bread:

White flour	250 g @ 40c per kg
Wholemeal flour	250 g @ 48c per kg
Honey	100 g @ $2 per kg
Yeast	One sachet @ 7c
Firewood	No cost
Salt	1c per loaf

Each loaf could be sold for 60c.
Each loaf takes 15 minutes to make.

Rodney estimates that it costs his family $45 each week to camp. Advise Rodney as to whether his idea is feasible. Give reasons.

21.12 *Organisational chart for a company*

In the mid-1970s Henry Ford II was the chair of the board of directors of the Ford Motor Company. Reporting directly to Henry Ford and the board was Lee Iacocca. His title was President, a term frequently used in North American companies and which equates with General Manager. Also reporting directly to Henry Ford was a finance department, comprising accounting and finance staff.

Mr Iacocca was responsible for overseeing the activities of the three major divisions in Ford Motor Company's organisational structure. These were:

(a) Ford International Automotive Operations

(b) Ford Diversified Operations

(c) Ford North America Automotive Operations

Alan Hampson was in charge of the third of these divisions. Reporting directly to Alan Hampson were three departments, or groups. These were the Product Development Group, responsible for the planning, design and engineering of new cars; the Manufacturing Group, responsible for vehicle production; and the Sales Group, responsible for vehicle promotion and selling.

Draw an organisational chart for the Ford Motor Company to reflect the above relationships and responsibilities.

21.13 *Accounting information and business decisions*

Bill ('Lucky') Bargwanna has just won Lotto and has bought a yacht marina at Paradise Bay. Existing facilities at the marina include moorings for privately owned yachts, a fully equipped workshop used to carry out repair and maintenance work on customers' boats, a shop selling things sailors seem to need (ranging from fuel to milk to blue caps with 'Captain' and 'Mate' in gold lettering on the peak), and a great lump of unused land.

Lucky had bought the marina on faith, as all the financial records had been destroyed by fire the day after the previous owner had received a letter advising of an impending tax audit. Fortunately the fire had done little other damage, being contained to the filing cabinets containing the financial records.

Lucky doesn't know anything about management but does want to run the marina himself. He has asked you to advise him on the sorts of things he should pay attention to in managing the marina, and what accounting records he should keep. He has also asked what he should do with the unused land. He has two bright ideas for it. One is to go into the business of buying and selling boats and use the land to store and display a range of new and used boats. The other is to diversify and build an amusement arcade with video games and pinball machines.

(a) Advise Lucky on the main functions of managing a business.
(b) What accounting information or financial records do you think would be helpful in managing the marina?
(c) What information and considerations would be relevant in deciding how to use the vacant land?

Case studies

21.14 *Accounting records and an expanding business*

Lee Strauss has owned and managed a jeans shop in Canberra for many years. Lee has recently sold out to True Blue Aussie Genes, a company based in Melbourne with a nation-wide chain of jeans shops. True Blue Aussie Genes is, in turn, owned by a New Zealand multinational.

Strauss is to be retained as the manager of the Canberra shop, but her accounting system is to be completely overhauled by True Blue. Strauss kept only minimal records—a cash book showing daily receipts and expenditures and a file of debtors. By contrast, True Blue wants a much more formal and detailed recording system and has sent one of its accountants to the shop to install the system. The accountant, with a gleam in her eye, is explaining to Strauss that once the system is up and running, not only will it provide full profit and loss statements and balance sheets on a regular and frequent basis to monitor the profitability and financial position of the shop, but it will also provide breakdowns of profit by product lines, by days of the week and month, and in relation to floor and shelf space. The accountant estimates it will take her about four weeks to get the accounting system operational and to teach Strauss how to use it.

Strauss goes to bed that night contemplating the merits of financial reporting. Before she sold out to True Blue, she didn't need this formality or detail. The shop must have been profitable or her bank manager would not have remained as good a friend over the years, nor would she have had enough money to buy a new Mercedes every three or four years. (She forgets for the moment that she won a small fortune in the lottery 10 years ago, which she invested successfully in rental property and shares—this might also account for her bank manager's attitude and the new cars.)

Strauss thought to herself that she certainly didn't need formal product profitability reports to know when she bought well or badly. The fact that she had had to walk past 10 dozen pairs of stretch jeans in the back room of her shop every day for six months was visible evidence of a wrong market judgement. She had bought them in anticipation of a fashion revival, but in the end had to throw them out.

All in all, Strauss couldn't see the need for all this information and record-keeping the accountant was implementing. Frankly, she couldn't see what the fuss was about.

Required

Explain to Lee Strauss what the fuss is about. That is, explain why a more systematic, formal and detailed accounting information system will be needed for her shop now that it is part of a national chain and owned by an overseas company.

21.15 *Responsibility centres, motivation*

The Jumbuk Paper Company has two manufacturing plants that each produce writing paper. The products from these plants are allocated different brand names and are targeted at different markets. One plant produces large-volume products in long production runs which are sold under the name 'Kangaroo' Paper Products. The 'Kangaroo' range of products includes lecture notepaper, standard-quality letter-writing pads, standard-quality airmail writing pads, and pads of graph paper used mainly by students. These products are sold through outlets such as supermarkets, newspaper agencies, university bookshops and school stationery and book suppliers.

The other plant produces high-quality writing paper in the 'Koala' range of products. There is only a small demand for each Koala product but the profit margin on sales is greater than for the Kangaroo products. Koala is designed for niche markets. For example, some of the products are designed to have the appearance of hand-made paper. These products are sold through specialist card and stationery shops and 'up-market' department stores.

The performance of the managers of these plants is evaluated on the basis of the profitability of their operations. Each year the performance of the managers is compared in order to identify which of them should receive a bonus holiday.

On one occasion the manager of the Kangaroo products plant, knowing that certain supplies were likely to become scarce due to an importation problem, purchased as much of that supply as was possible. The manager realised that such action was likely to halt production at the Koala plant, since the supply was vital to the production of most of the Koala products. This material could have been replaced by another for the purpose of making most of the Kangaroo products, but the manager of the Koala plant could not afford to substitute lower-quality materials. This was the only year in which the Kangaroo manager earned the bonus holiday.

Required

Identify any inadequacies of the performance evaluation system adopted for these two plant managers at the Jumbuk Paper Company.

CHAPTER 22
Costing systems

Introduction

This chapter examines particular product costing systems. The purpose of costing products and projects is to be able to accumulate and determine these costs as inputs to management decisions, and for financial reporting purposes.

Manufacturing organisations require such systems to determine the costs of the products they make and sell. Non-manufacturing organisations also require such systems. Organisations providing professional services to clients, such as accounting, law and architectural firms, need costing systems in order to determine the cost of specific client contracts. Engineering and construction organisations need them in order to determine the cost of engineering or construction projects. The systems discussed in the chapter are applicable to organisations in both the private sector and the public sector and for both profit-oriented and non-profit organisations.

We begin by examining costing systems for manufacturing organisations. Accounting for manufacturing organisations is discussed briefly in Chapter 9, and should be revised before proceeding with this chapter.

In Chapter 9 we noted the similarities and differences in accounting for a manufacturer and a merchandiser. The major difference, of course, was that, whereas a merchandiser buys and sells goods in essentially the same form, a manufacturer buys raw materials and then incurs labour and manufacturing overhead costs in converting the raw materials to a manufactured product for sale. This difference gives rise to some implications for accounting for manufacturing organisations.

First, the calculation of cost of goods sold is more involved for a manufacturer than for a merchandiser. Instead of depending on inventories and purchases for its calculation (as in the case of a merchandiser), cost of goods sold for a manufacturer depends on inventories and cost of goods manufactured. This latter cost must be computed by determining the raw materials, the labour and the overhead services (such as factory lighting and heating) consumed in manufacturing the product. The calculation of the cost of goods manufactured is often presented in a specific manufacturing statement, an example of which was given on page 326.

A second implication of the difference between a manufacturer and a merchandiser is that in accounting for a merchandiser we are concerned with only one type of inventory. In accounting for a manufacturing organisation we are concerned with three types of inventories:

- *Raw materials inventory*. These are materials that have been purchased but have not yet been used in the production process.
- *Work-in-progress inventory* (often called work-in-process inventory). These are goods for which the production process has begun but has not yet been completed.
- *Finished goods inventory*. These are goods for which the production process has been completed but which have not yet been sold.

The first two types of inventories are important in determining the cost of goods manufactured for any period, while the third is important in determining the cost of goods sold. In Chapter 9 we took as given the valuation or cost of these inventories. In the current chapter we will examine how the costs or values of these inventories, particularly work-in-progress and finished goods inventories, are determined.

This chapter, therefore, considers the methods of cost accumulation and product costing for the purposes of inventory valuation and profit determination. However, product costing information is also required for internal management purposes, such as cost control, performance evaluation and decision making. These will be discussed in later chapters in this section. The emphasis in this chapter, however, is on cost accumulation procedures and product costing methods for inventory valuation and profit determination. You have already been introduced to this use of the information for the purpose of external reporting.

The primary example used in the chapter is based on a manufacturing organisation. However, similar costing principles apply to conducting architectural consultancy projects as apply to manufacturing prefabricated houses. The cost categories, cost flows and allocation issues are essentially the same. You should note that products can be either goods or services, and that manufacturing firms often supply services as well as goods. Where differences in costing for services and activities exist relative to manufactured goods, these differences will be noted at the appropriate point.

Case 22.1 Basic costing decisions

Consider the situation in which you employ someone to make children's hats. Each hat takes, on average, 30 minutes to make and necessitates the use of 0.5 metres of felt and 0.6 metres of braid. The felt costs $10 per metre and braid costs $2 per metre. The labour cost is $16 per hour. You believe 3200 hats can be made and sold in the next year. During that period your other costs (rent of premises, equipment, power, thread) are expected to come to $5120.

How could you calculate the cost per hat? How could you use this information?

Consider these issues carefully before turning to the discussion at the end of this chapter.

Flow of costs in conventional product costing

The specific procedures for cost accumulation in product costing in manufacturing environments depend on the production process in use. Two different approaches to production will be described later in this chapter. The present discussion will develop a general approach to product costing based on the flow of manufacturing costs through the accounting system, as it reflects the production of goods through the manufacturing process. Figure 22.1 illustrates this flow, which involves four stages:

- *Stage 1.* The manufacturing costs are accumulated in terms of the nature of the resource to which the cost relates. The classifications of resources are materials, labour and manufacturing overhead. Hence, there are accounts for materials, labour and manufacturing overhead.

  The purchase of materials will be recorded as an increase in the materials control account, and the purchase of factory labour (represented by the payment of the factory payroll) will be recorded as an increase in the factory labour control account.

  The purchase of all manufacturing overhead services (represented by payments for factory rent, insurance on factory buildings and equipment, factory heating and lighting, and the like) will, similarly, increase the manufacturing overhead control account.

- *Stage 2.* As the resources are used in production, the accounts reflect this by recording decreases in the resource accounts and an increase in the work-in-progress inventory account. This asset account is a focal account into which all product costs are channelled.

  It should be noted that materials will include direct and indirect materials, and factory labour costs will include both direct and indirect labour. Direct materials and direct labour can be physically identified with units of product. Consequently the flow of these costs to products can easily be identified with the physical flow of materials and labour into production.

  The indirect materials and indirect labour costs cannot be so identified. For example, a supervisor may supervise the production of several different products but does not have a direct, identifiable relationship with any individual product. As a result, the indirect costs form part of manufacturing overhead, along with other costs incurred in production that do not have a measurable link with the product (for example the costs incurred in the provision of power, buildings and other facilities, and the lubricating oil applied to equipment). The manufacturing overhead costs need to be assigned (or applied) to units of product. This is usually done by a method of averaging these costs over total production. A method of assigning manufacturing overhead costs to products will be discussed in the job order costing section which follows.

- *Stage 3.* After the products have been completed and transferred physically to the warehouse for finished goods inventory, the cost of that production is transferred to an asset account for finished goods. The accounting records will then show a decrease in the work-in-progress account and an increase in the finished goods account.
- *Stage 4.* When the products are sold their cost is transferred to the cost of goods sold account.

Figure 22.1 The flow of manufacturing costs

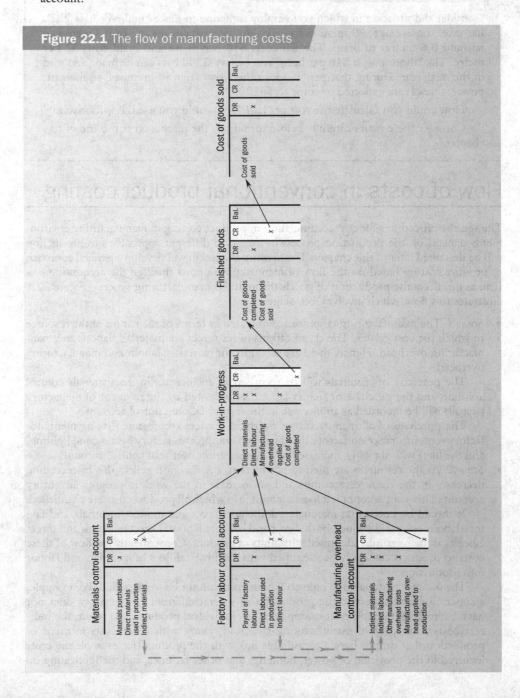

Product costing methods

Given this framework for the flow of manufacturing costs, specific systems of product costing for inventory valuation and profit determination may now be considered.

In practice, systems of product costing will be designed around the specific production processes of individual firms. However, they will be based on two general approaches to product costing: job order costing and process costing.

Job order costing should be used when products are readily identifiable as individual units or batches, each of which receives varying amounts of raw materials and labour inputs. Users of this method include organisations in the construction, printing, machinery manufacture or aircraft industries. Job order costing may also be used by service organisations. Examples are organisations providing professional services and consulting jobs for clients. Job order costing systems are appropriate only when individual jobs can be separately identified in the production or service provision departments. Organisations that produce customised products, such as Boral Elevators, Cummins Engines and NCR Automatic Teller Machines, need to use job order costing methods.

Process costing may be used when there is mass-production of like units. These units usually pass in continuous fashion through a series of uniform production steps, called operations or processes. Examples of such processes are found in the chemical, oil, textile, plastics, paint or food processing industries. Individual units or batches of products cannot be separately identified in production departments. Consequently firms such as Alcoa and Shell use a process costing approach.

A firm may use both job order costing and process costing methods. A plastic film manufacturer may use process costing for costing its mass-produced plastic food wrap, and job order costing to cost customised jobs such as printed plastic sacks in which potting mix is to be sealed. Alternatively, the supermarket plastic bag may be a standardised product that is printed with the supermarket chain's trademark. In this case, if the printing costs vary between orders due to the number of colours and size of design, the bags will be subject to process costing in all processes until the final printing process.

Job order costing

Job order costing attempts to trace or apply costs to specific jobs, which may consist of a single physical unit or a batch of like units. Each individual job or batch will have a job order or job cost sheet on which to accumulate all costs attributable to that job.

Direct materials are entered on a job cost sheet as they are issued to each job. For direct labour, time sheets, work cards or a computer spreadsheet may be made out for each factory worker. These will indicate the individual job on which a particular person worked, and for how long. Increasingly, computers are being used to automatically record this information in response to the use of a key card or a password.

An example will show that the system not only provides for the accumulation of costs on a job basis; it also enables the costs of all jobs to be summarised for the purpose of inventory valuation and profit determination.

The summary is maintained in the general ledger through the work-in-progress account. This account is supported by a subsidiary ledger (probably called a cost ledger) which consists of the individual job cost sheets. Thus, at any time the total cost of all jobs in production should equal the summarised total in the work-in-progress account in the general ledger.

Example: *A job order costing system*

You may benefit from recording entries in the subsidiary ledger while reading through this example. The job cost sheets will be shown after several entries are made.

- 1 July Purchased direct materials and factory supplies, $60 000.

The direct materials will be used directly in the production process, while the supplies will be indirect materials not related to specific jobs; they are therefore part of the manufacturing overhead.

Job cost sheets	Ledger	
(in the subsidiary ledger)		
No entry, as no materials	DR Materials control	$60 000
have been issued to any job	CR Cash (or accounts payable)	$60 000

- 4 July Issued materials $52 000, of which $48 000 was direct materials for specific jobs, and $4000 was for general factory supplies.

The direct materials were issued as follows:

$30 000 for job no. 101
$10 000 for job no. 102
$ 8 000 for job no. 103.

Job cost sheets	Ledger	
101-$30 000	DR Work-in-progress control	$48 000
102-$10 000	DR Manufacturing overhead control	$ 4 000
103-$ 8 000	CR Materials control	$52 000

- 7 July Paid wages $44 000. The time sheets disclosed the following:
$22 000 to job no. 101
$10 000 to job no. 102
$ 7 000 to job no. 103
$ 5 000 wages of factory supervisors, maintenance workers and storekeepers.

Job cost sheets	Ledger	
101-$22 000	DR Factory labour control	$44 000
102-$10 000	CR Cash	$44 000
103-$ 7 000		
	DR Work-in-progress control	$39 000
	DR Manufacturing overhead control	$ 5 000
	CR Factory labour control	$44 000

At this stage, the job cost sheets show, for each job, the costs of material and labour. The summary account, work-in-progress, shows the total of materials and labour charged to all jobs. The manufacturing overhead, however, has not been allocated to jobs.

- 9 July Incurred the following costs:
Factory lighting and power $11 000
Insurance on factory equipment $1000
Equipment repairs $6000

These non-traceable manufacturing overhead costs are accumulated in the manufacturing overhead control account.

Job cost sheets	Ledger	
No entry	DR Manufacturing overhead control	$18 000
	CR Light and power expense	$11 000
	CR Insurance expense	$ 1 000
	CR Repairs and maintenance expense	$ 6 000

Applying manufacturing overhead to production

The total manufacturing overhead cost for the period is the total of all costs accumulated in the manufacturing overhead control account.

These costs are not, however, physically traceable to individual product units. Consequently, a method of assigning or applying them to individual units or batches of product is required.

As an initial approach, the total manufacturing overhead cost could be divided by the number of units produced. However, the units are not necessarily identical in their demand for time, equipment usage, labour effort, and so forth, and the allocation of the overhead cost to units of product should attempt to allow for these differences.

A preferable approach is to relate manufacturing overhead costs to some other activity factor which can be directly identified with individual products or jobs. They could, for example, be related to machine hours if it is believed that the usage of overhead services depends on, or tends to vary with, the number of machine hours. In those circumstances, if job X required twice as many machine hours as job Y, it would be charged with twice as much overhead cost.

Alternatively, overhead costs could be related to direct labour hours if analysis indicated that overhead costs tended to vary with the number (or cost) of direct labour hours.

The means by which an activity is selected as the basis for overhead cost allocation may include detailed statistical analyses of the association between manufacturing overhead costs and relevant activity variables.

Predetermined overhead application rates

Suppose, in the example, that it was decided to apply overhead costs to products on the basis of direct labour hours. A rate for application would then be developed on the following basis:

$$\frac{\text{total manufacturing overhead for the period}}{\text{total direct labour hours worked during the period}}$$

The resulting rate would be used to apply overhead to product or jobs, based on the number of direct labour hours worked on each product.

To illustrate, if the total manufacturing overhead for the period was $200 000, and the number of direct labour hours worked was 100 000, then overhead would be charged to each product or job at the rate of $2 for each direct labour hour worked on the job. Job A may be charged with $6000 (3000 direct labour hours × by $2 per hour), and job B, $2000 (1000 hours × $2 per hour).

A complication of this procedure is that the actual overhead application rate cannot be determined until the end of the period, when the total overhead costs and the total hours of labour are known. As this period is usually a year (to smooth out any seasonal or cyclical variations in the monthly totals of overhead costs incurred), the problem exists of how to compute, *during* the year, the costs of individual jobs completed.

To avoid the delay of computing product costings, the normal method of charging overhead to jobs uses a predetermined application rate, based on the *expected* total annual manufacturing overhead costs, and the *expected* annual total of direct labour hours (or machine hours).

If, for example, the budgeted (i.e. expected) annual overhead is $2 400 000, and budgeted annual direct labour hours is 800 000, the predetermined rate for applying manufacturing overhead to jobs is $3 per direct labour hour. Thus, a job requiring 4000 direct labour hours would be charged with $12 000 for manufacturing overhead, irrespective of the actual level of overhead costs incurred during the period.

This method introduces an element of what is known as 'standard costing' into the cost accumulation system. The amount of overhead charged to jobs is, in effect, a standard charge based on a certain number of actual hours.

This method of overhead application will now be used in an example.

Assume that the budgeted manufacturing overhead for the year was $324 000, and the budgeted level of activity was 120 000 direct labour hours. The predetermined overhead application rate was calculated as $2.70 per direct labour hour ($324 000/120 000 hours).

The direct labour hours worked in July were 9800; 4000 on job no. 101, 3500 on job no. 102 and 2300 on job no. 103.

Job cost sheets	Ledger	
101 4 000 × $2.70 = $10 800	DR Work-in-progress control	26 460
102 3 500 × $2.70 = $ 9 450	CR Manufacturing overhead applied	26 460
103 2 300 × $2.70 = $ 6 210		

It is necessary to keep separate records of the overhead being charged to the jobs and the overhead costs actually being incurred. Hence, there are two manufacturing overhead accounts: the manufacturing overhead control account that is being used to accumulate the actual manufacturing overhead costs incurred during the period (hence, it normally has a debit balance), and a manufacturing overhead applied account, which is being used to charge or apply overhead to production using the predetermined overhead application rate (hence, it normally has a credit balance-see relevant journal entry above). These accounts will need to be reconciled at a later stage.

Following these entries the records will appear as follows:

Work-in-progress account		
Direct materials	48 000	48 000 DR
Direct labour	39 000	87 000 DR
Manufacturing overhead applied	26 460	113 460 DR

Job cost sheets	Job no. 101	Job no. 102	Job no. 103	Total
	$	$	$	$
Direct materials	30 000	10 000	8 000	
Direct labour	22 000	10 000	7 000	
Manufacturing overhead	10 800	9 450	6 210	
	62 800	29 450	21 210	113 460

Completion and sale of jobs

Assume that at 31 July jobs no. 101 and 102 have been completed, and that job no.101 has been sold. Job no. 103 is incomplete at that date. On completion, jobs 101 and 102 would have been physically transferred to the finished goods inventory. On sale, job 101 would have been dispatched from the finished goods inventory.

The accounting records must show the completion of jobs 101 and 102, and record their transfer from the work-in-progress account to the finished goods account.

Finished goods inventory	92 250	
Work-in-progress		92 250
(Transfer of jobs 101 and 102 to finished goods inventory)		

This leaves a balance of $21 210 in the work-in-progress account at the end of July, which is, of course, the current cost of job no. 103.

The accounting records must also record the sale of job no. 101. If it were sold for $85 000, two entries would be required:

1. To transfer the cost of the job sold to the cost of goods sold account.

Cost of goods sold	62 800	
Finished goods inventory		62 800

2. To record the sale.

Cash (or accounts receivable)	85 000	
Sales		85 000

This leaves a balance of $29 450 ($92 250 − $62 800) in the finished goods inventory account, which is the cost of job no. 102, completed but as yet unsold.

Preparation of the profit and loss statement

A partial profit and loss statement for July, showing the cost of goods manufactured, the cost of goods sold and the gross profit for the period is presented below. The statement recognises that:

- the cost of goods manufactured in the period (this expression refers to the goods that have been finished during the period) is the cost of opening work-in-progress, plus the cost of resources used in production during the period, less the closing work-in-progress;
- the closing work-in-progress is job no. 103 in the job cost sheet;
- the cost of finished goods inventory is the cost of job no. 102.

(PARTIAL) PROFIT AND LOSS STATEMENT FOR JULY				
	$	$	$	$
Sales				85 000
less Cost of goods sold				
Finished goods inventory (1 July)			–	
plus Cost of goods manufactured				
Work-in-progress inventory (1 July)			–	
Manufacturing costs				
Direct materials		48 000		
Direct labour		39 000		
Manufacturing overhead:				
Indirect materials	4 000			
Indirect labour	5 000			
Other	18 000	27 000		
		114 000		
less Work-in-progress (31 July)		21 210		
Cost of goods manufactured			92 790	
less Finished goods inventory (31 July)			29 450	
Cost of goods sold				63 340
Gross profit				21 660

Reconciliation of manufacturing overhead

If the gross profit is now computed from the sales and cost of goods sold accounts in the ledger, a difference of $540 will arise in comparison with the calculation of profit in the profit and loss statement on this page. In this case the cost of goods sold is, of course, the cost of job no. 101.

Sales	$85 000
less Cost of goods sold	62 800
Gross profit	$22 200

The difference represents the discrepancy between the total *actual* manufacturing overhead incurred for the month, which is accumulated in the manufacturing overhead control account ($27 000), and the overhead *applied* to work-in-progress on the basis of the predetermined overhead application rate, recorded in the manufacturing overhead applied account ($26 460). This discrepancy can be caused by inaccurate estimations of the overhead cost or of the direct labour hours. In Chapter 26 we will consider ways to analyse and use information about this difference between actual and applied overhead (called a variance).

In effect, the company has undercharged, or under-applied, manufacturing overhead to jobs for the period. In order to prepare a profit and loss statement on actual cost terms, therefore, this difference of $540 must be charged to the cost of goods sold account. Technically, the difference should be apportioned over cost of goods sold, finished goods inventory and the work-in-progress inventory, because the under-application relates to all three jobs, not just the one that has been sold. However, if the amount is not 'material' in terms of the prescribed financial accounting standards, it is normally adjusted as if it applied only to the goods that were sold.

Returning to the example, the manufacturing overhead control account and the manufacturing overhead applied account would appear as follows:

Manufacturing overhead control		
Indirect materials	4 000	4 000 DR
Indirect labour	5 000	9 000 DR
Light and power	11 000	20 000 DR
Insurance	1 000	21 000 DR
Repairs and maintenance	6 000	27 000 DR

Manufacturing overhead applied		
Work-in-progress	26 460	26 460 CR

Adjusting the difference to the cost of goods sold account would be achieved by the following journal entries:

Manufacturing overhead applied	27 000	
Manufacturing overhead control		27 000
Cost of goods sold	540	
Manufacturing overhead applied		540

This would result in the following accounts:

Manufacturing overhead control		
Indirect materials	4 000	4 000 DR
Indirect labour	5 000	9 000 DR
Light and power	11 000	20 000 DR
Insurance	1 000	21 000 DR
Repairs and maintenance	6 000	27 000 DR
Manufacturing overhead applied	27 000	–

Manufacturing overhead applied		
Work-in-progress		26 460	26 460 CR
Manufacturing overhead control	27 000		540 DR
Cost of goods sold		540	–

Cost of goods sold		
Finished goods inventory	62 800	62 800 DR
Manufacturing overhead applied	540	63 340 DR

If overhead had been over-applied, a credit would appear in cost of goods sold.

Case 22.2 Overhead allocation dilemmas

To test your understanding of the way manufacturing overhead can be under- or over-applied, calculate the under- or over-applied overhead in the following situation: At the start of the operating year it is estimated that the manufacturing overhead cost will be $325 000 for the coming year, and that 13 000 machine hours will be needed. It is believed that most overhead varies in proportion to machine hours so this is used as the application rate base. At the end of the year it is found that manufacturing overhead was actually $342 000 and there were 13 250 actual machine hours.

After calculating the extent to which manufacturing overhead is under- or over-applied, study the discussion of this problem at the end of the chapter. If you still do not understand this issue, re-read the last section of the discussion of Case 22.1 and the relevant material in the chapter so far.

Process costing

As discussed earlier, process costing is appropriate for organisations that use mass-production style methods to produce similar units. These units usually pass in continuous fashion through a series of uniform steps, called operations or processes. Examples include the processing of chemicals, oil, textiles and food.

The focal point in job order costing was the job itself, or the job order. Given the inability to identify individual products or batches of products in process manufacturing, the focal point shifts to the individual process or operation. These are usually self-contained within departments and, consequently, process costing concentrates on the accumulation of costs by departments. A brewery, for example, might have three departments—blending, brewing and bottling. The process of beer manufacture is continuous and the end products are homogeneous but the operations of blending, brewing and bottling are separable and identifiable.

Flow of costs in processing operations

The manufacturing cost elements (direct materials, direct labour and manufacturing overhead) are the same for process costing as for job order costing. So, too, is the basic flow of costs from the originating accounts for direct materials, labour and manufacturing overhead through to work-in-progress, finished goods and, finally, cost of goods sold.

Work-in-progress accounts are maintained for each separate operation or department. As these departments are linked in the chain of producing the final product, the completed output of the first process or department (the output of the blending department in the beer manufacturing example) becomes the input to the second process or department (the brewing department). Similarly, the output of the brewing department (the beer itself) becomes an input material for the final process (the bottling department). Only when the bottling operation is completed will the product move through to finished goods.

The accounting records need to reflect this movement of product between the three departments, from the final producing department to finished goods and, on sale, to cost of goods sold. The journal entries, given below, demonstrate the flow of costs. To simplify the analysis, it is assumed that there are no beginning or ending inventories in any of the three departments for the period, and that the entire output is sold during the period.

The process is shown diagrammatically in Figure 22.2.

Flow of process costs

Work-in-progress (Blending)	30 000	
Materials		15 000
Labour		10 000
Manufacturing overhead		5 000
(Manufacturing costs of the blending department)		
Work-in-progress (Brewing)	30 000	
Work-in-progress (Blending)		30 000
(Transfer of blended product from blending to brewing department)		
Work-in-progress (Brewing)	29 000	
Materials		5 000
Labour		16 000
Manufacturing overhead		8 000
(Additional manufacturing costs of the brewing department)		
Work-in-progress (Bottling)	59 000	
Work-in-progress (Brewing)		59 000
(Transfer of brewed product from brewing to bottling department)		
Work-in-progress (Bottling)	30 000	
Materials		11 000
Labour		9 000
Manufacturing overhead		10 000
(Additional manufacturing costs of the bottling department)		
Finished goods inventory	89 000	
Work-in-progress (Bottling)		89 000
(Transfer of finished product to finished goods inventory)		
Cost of goods sold	89 000	
Finished goods inventory		89 000
(Cost of goods sold)		

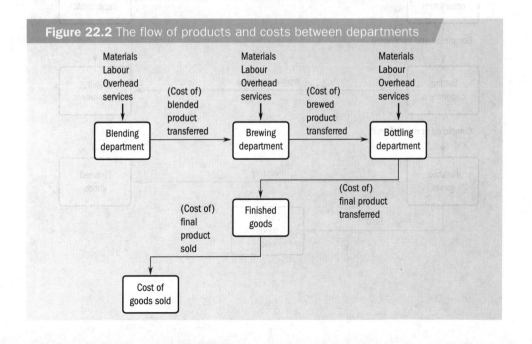

Figure 22.2 The flow of products and costs between departments

Inventory valuation in process operations

We assumed on page 762 that there were no inventories on hand. Process manufacture, however, is a continuous activity and at any selected balance date there will not only be finished goods inventory, but also work begun and not completed in all of the processing departments (work-in-progress inventories). This work will be completed in the subsequent period in that department and then transferred to the next processing department in the chain.

For example, during June the blending department will have been continuously involved in using its labour force as well as its physical equipment to blend or convert its basic ingredients (raw materials) into quantities of blended output. This output will have been transferred to the brewing department for further processing. However, at the end of June the blending operation for some quantities will have been begun but not finished. This will constitute the work-in-progress inventory for the blending department at the end of June, and will be completed and transferred to brewing during July.

A similar situation will exist for all departments in the chain, as depicted in Figure 22.3. This figure may be compared with Figure 22.2 to gain a perspective on the complicated flows of products and costs between departments and over time.

Figure 22.3 The flow of products and costs between departments over time

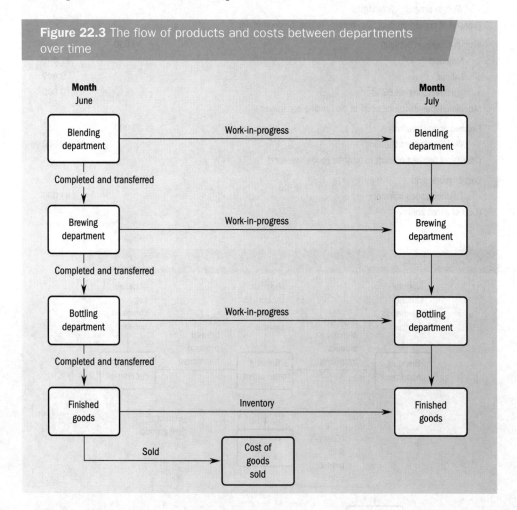

The problem facing the management accountant is how the manufacturing costs of a processing department for a period are to be split between:

1. the quantity of production completed and transferred to the next department during the period, and
2. the quantity of work-in-progress in this department at the end of the period.

This problem is approached by dividing the total manufacturing costs incurred in a department during the period by an estimate of the physical measure of the quantity of production achieved during the period. The result is a cost per quantity unit, which may then be applied to the relative physical quantities of completed (i.e. transferred) output, and work-in-progress.

For example, if in the previous example the total costs of the blending department for June were $30 000, and a physical measure of the amount of blended output, both completed and still in the process of completion, was 30 000 litres, the cost per unit would be $1 per litre. If 10 000 litres were still in the blending process at the end of June, the cost of work-in-progress could be calculated as $10 000, and the cost of blended output transferred to brewing as $20 000.

The cost per litre (unit) of $1 was derived from:

$$\frac{\text{total manufacturing costs}}{\text{total output}} = \frac{\$30\ 000}{30\ 000\ \text{litres}}$$

This simplistic example allows for reporting the finished units and the incomplete units (work-in-progress) separately, but does not take account of the difference in degree of completion. A further refinement to the calculation is therefore required and will now be explained.

Concept of equivalent units

Although the demonstrated 'averaging' approach forms the basis for valuing the output and inventories of processing departments, it rests on the assumption that the litres of product completed and transferred are equivalent to the litres still in process, with respect to the amount of productive effort devoted to them. Specifically, they are assumed to consume per litre the same amount of materials, the same amount of labour effort, and to have benefited from the same amount of overhead services.

In the calculation of $1 per litre in the example, the denominator consists of 20 000 litres of fully completed output and 10 000 litres of partly completed product. It has been assumed, then, that each 'unit' in the 20 000 is equivalent to each 'unit' in the 10 000.

An examination of the production process in this department shows that the units are not equivalent in their costs. During the period the department has used raw materials, labour and manufacturing overhead services to produce what will eventually be 30 000 fully completed (or equivalent) units of product. At the end of the period, 20 000 units have been completed and transferred to the next processing department. Each of these 20 000 units can be thought of as having received a 'full' benefit from the manufacturing resources (materials, labour and overhead), and consequently can be costed with a 'full' charge per unit for materials, labour and overhead.

The 10 000 units in work-in-progress are not complete and are therefore not equivalent to the finished units. If they were exactly half-finished in respect of all elements in the manufacturing process, they could be thought of as being equivalent to 5000 fully completed units at this stage. This way of thinking about partly completed production leads to a concept of 'equivalent full units' which may be used in determining the denominator for the calculation of manufacturing cost per unit.

There is an added complication. Work-in-progress at the end of a period may not be at the same stage of production in respect of each of the individual cost elements of materials, labour and overhead.

Assume that it is possible to divide the manufacturing process within the department into stages, as depicted in Figure 22.4.

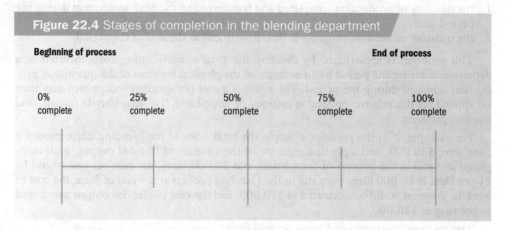

Figure 22.4 Stages of completion in the blending department

- *Direct materials.* All ingredients (raw materials) required in the blending process are used at the beginning of the process. No more materials will be added during the remainder of the process. Thus, although the work-in-progress may be only half-way through the production process, it may be thought of as being 100 per cent complete in respect of the total input of direct materials.
- *Direct labour.* Analysis of the production process may show that, to a greater or lesser degree, labour input is required continuously throughout the process. As far as the labour cost element is concerned, work-in-progress may be thought of as 50 per cent complete.
- *Manufacturing overhead.* Manufacturing overhead cannot be traced directly to the production process. Consequently, the assumption is usually made that the use of overhead services is distributed evenly throughout the process. Hence, in respect of the manufacturing overhead cost element, the work-in-progress may also be considered to be 50 per cent complete.

Because direct labour and manufacturing overhead are commonly regarded as occurring evenly throughout the period, they are often grouped together in the costing process and termed 'conversion costs'. They represent the cost of converting direct materials into the finished output.

We will look at an example that illustrates these concepts. The purpose will be to prepare departmental production reports, computing the costs of work-in-progress and of goods completed for departments.

Departmental production cost reports

The focal point of product costing for process manufacturing environments is the processing department. The most common report prepared for each department is the production cost report.

Example: *Departmental production cost reports*

The Plastic Paint Co. has two departments in its manufacturing process and uses a process costing system. Department 1 begins manufacture of the product, with materials applied at the beginning of the process and conversion resources (labour and manufacturing overhead combined) consumed uniformly throughout the process.

Production is then transferred to Department 2 for completion. In Department 2 further materials are added at the end of the process, while again conversion costs are assumed to be incurred uniformly.

The following data relate to the operations of both departments for the month of July:

Units (litres)	Dept 1	Dept 2
Work-in-progress 1 July	3 000 litres	4 000 litres
	(50% complete)	(50% complete)
Units started in production in July	14 000 litres	15 000 litres
Units completed and transferred	15 000 litres	16 000 litres
Work-in-progress 31 July	2 000 litres	3 000 litres
	(50% complete)	(66⅔ % complete)

Costs	Dept 1	Dept 2
Work-in-progress 1 July		
Direct materials	$ 3 000	–
Conversion costs	3 500	$ 3 800
Costs transferred from Dept 1	–	14 300
Current (July)		
Direct materials	15 700	14 400
Conversion costs	28 500	32 200

Prepare a production cost report for each department, showing the cost of goods completed and transferred and the cost of work-in-progress at 31 July.

Department 1

Preparing a production cost report for Department 1 may be approached in several stages.

- *Stage 1.* Trace the physical flow of production through the department and identify the absolute quantity of output completed and transferred to Department 2 and the absolute quantity of work-in-progress. In the example, this is given as:

Units completed and transferred	15 000 litres
Units in work-in-progress 31 July	2 000 litres
Total units worked on during July	17 000 litres

- *Stage 2.* Adjust the absolute number of units in work-in-progress to 'equivalent full units' in respect of materials, labour and manufacturing overhead inputs. The adjustment is made by determining the number of units that could have been produced had all productive inputs been devoted to making only fully completed units. Consequently, the units completed and transferred are already expressed in equivalent full-unit terms. With regard to partially complete units, 10 units that have received 50 per cent of their conversion resources are considered to be the equivalent of 5 units completely converted.

	Absolute units	Equivalent full units	
		Materials	Labour and overhead
Completed and transferred	15 000	15 000	15 000
Work-in-progress 31 July	2 000	2 000	1 000
	17 000	17 000	16 000

Although work-in-progress is only 50 per cent complete at the end of the period, all materials required for the production of these units have been used by this stage, and consequently the work-in-progress is considered to be 100 per cent complete in respect of direct material charges. The total equivalent full units of products for which direct materials cost has been incurred during the period is therefore 17 000.

As conversion costs (labour and overhead) are incurred evenly over the production process, on average they are 50 per cent complete and the work-in-progress is considered to be equivalent to 1000 fully completed units in respect of these costs. The total equivalent full units of production for which conversion costs have been incurred during the period is therefore 16 000.

- *Stage 3.* Determine an equivalent production cost per unit separately for materials and conversion costs. This is done by dividing the manufacturing costs (materials and conversion costs) by the previously determined equivalent full units of production in respect of materials and conversion costs respectively.

	Direct materials	Conversion costs
Manufacturing costs:		
From work-in-progress 1 July	$ 3 000	$ 3 500
Incurred in July	15 700	28 500
Total	18 700	32 000
Divided by:		
Equivalent full units	17 000	16 000
Cost per equivalent full unit	$1.10	$2.00

- *Stage 4.* Calculate the cost of production completed in Department 1 and transferred to Department 2 during the period, and the cost of work-in-progress in Department 1 at the end of the period. This is achieved by multiplying the costs per equivalent unit (determined in Stage 3) by the number of equivalent units in completed production and work-in-progress (determined in Stage 2).

			$
Cost of goods completed and transferred:			
Equivalent units (materials)	15 000		
× Cost per equivalent unit (materials)	$1.10	=	16 500
Equivalent units (conversion)	15 000		
× Cost per equivalent unit (conversion)	$2.00	=	30 000
			46 500

Note that as goods completed and transferred are always equivalent full units in respect of both materials and conversion costs (i.e. they are 100 per cent complete), the cost of goods completed and transferred may be calculated by the absolute number of units (15 000) multiplied by the total cost per equivalent unit ($3.10).

Cost of work-in-progress:			$
Equivalent units (materials)	2000		
× Cost per equivalent unit (materials)	$1.10	=	2200
Equivalent units (conversion)	1000		
× Cost per equivalent unit (conversion)	$2.00	=	2000
			4200

The total manufacturing costs for the department have now been apportioned over completed production and work-in-progress. This could be reconciled by comparing the total manufacturing costs incurred from Stage 3 ($18 700 + $32 000 = $50 700) with the total apportioned to goods completed and transferred, and work-in-progress ($46 500 + $4200 = $50 700).

The stages discussed provide the components for preparation of the departmental production report. The form of this report varies and is not prescribed in any accounting pronouncements; however, a common form is shown below.

Weighted-average and FIFO methods

In practice, the cost per equivalent unit may vary from one period to the next. For instance, it is possible that the conversion cost per equivalent unit of ending work-in-progress in November is $3.00, whereas the conversion cost per unit in December, during which they are completed, is $3.10 per unit. If they ended November (and hence entered December) 50 per cent converted, their final conversion cost per unit will be $3.05. This approach is called the FIFO (first in, first out) method.

A simplified method of dealing with this variation in unit cost is the approach adopted in the production cost report below. In this example the stage of completion of beginning work-in-progress has been ignored, as has the cost per unit of these units carried forward in production. For the purpose of costing completed units and work-in-progress at the end of July, the simplifying assumption has been made that all productive work on the beginning work-in-progress has been carried out in July. To be consistent, the costs of beginning work-in-progress have simply been added to the current costs for July, and the averaging process (the determination of equivalent costs per unit) has been based on the assumption that all work on beginning inventory and all costs associated with that work have been incurred in July.

Department 1
PRODUCTION COST REPORT—JULY

	Absolute units	Equivalent full units	
		Materials	Conversion
Units to account for:			
Work-in-progress 1 July	3 000		
Started July	14 000		
	17 000		
Units accounted for:			
Completed and transferred	15 000	15 000	15 000
Work-in-progress 31 July	2 000	2 000	1 000
	17 000	17 000	16 000

		Total costs	Material costs	Conversion costs
Costs to account for:				
Work-in-progress 1 July		6 500	3 000	3 500
Current costs July		44 200	15 700	28 500
		50 700	18 700	32 000
Cost per equivalent unit			$1.10	$2.00
Costs accounted for:				
Goods completed and				
transferred		46 500	15 000	+ 15 000
			× $1.10	× $2.00
Work-in-progress 31 July				
Materials	2 200		2 000	
			× $1.10	
Conversion cost	2 000	4 200		1 000
				× $2.00
Costs accounted for		50 700		

This is a common assumption made in process costing (called the 'weighted-average' assumption or method), and in practice is unlikely to distort significantly the resulting cost apportionments. If the accountant feels that this assumption may cause a significant distortion to the process costing apportionments, the alternative method using a 'first in, first out' assumption should be used. As explained, the FIFO method retains separate identification of the costs of beginning work-in-progress with the productive effort already carried out on that inventory. The FIFO method will not be discussed fully here, but it is covered in most management accounting textbooks. These specialised texts also cover extensions and complications of process costing systems, such as accounting for defective units, spoilage or scrap resulting from the production process.

Department 2

The production cost report for Department 2 in the Plastic Paint Co. is given on the following page.

Again, this production cost report is based on the weighted-average assumption. The major point to consider when examining this report is that the cost of goods completed and transferred from Department 1 forms an additional cost input for Department 2. This cost may be thought of as a material cost for Department 2, incurred at the beginning of the production process in that department.

Department 2
PRODUCTION COST REPORT—JULY

	Absolute units	Equivalent full units		
		Transferred-in	Materials	Conversion
Units to account for:				
Work-in-progress 1 July	4 000			
Transferred-in from Dept 1	15 000			
	19 000			
Units accounted for:				
Completed (finished goods)	16 000	16 000	16 000	16 000
Work-in-progress 31 July	3 000	3 000	0 *	2 000
	19 000	19 000	16 000	18 000

	Total costs	Transfer costs	Material costs	Conversion costs
Costs to account for:				
Work-in-progress 1 July	18 100	14 300	0	3 800
Current costs July	93 100	46 500 †	14 400	32 200
	111 200	60 800	14 400	36 000
Costs per equivalent unit		$3.20	$0.90	$2.00
Costs accounted for:				
Finished goods	16 000	16 000	16 000	16 000
	× $6.10 → 97 600	× $3.20 +	× $0.90 +	× $2.00
Work-in-progress 31 July				
Transferred-in cost	9 600	3 000		
		× $3.20		
Materials	0		0	
			× $0.90	
Conversion cost	4 000 → 13 600			2 000
				× $2.00
Costs accounted for	111 200			

* Although the production process in Department 2 is 66.66% per cent complete, the additional materials in this department are not added until the end of the process. Consequently, there is no materials cost element in either beginning or ending work-in-progress.

† Costs of goods completed and transferred from Department 1.

Some extensions of product costing

The foregoing discussion concentrated on the basic issues associated with job order costing and process costing in manufacturing environments. Some extensions to and complications of this basic process are now addressed.

First, a comparison between manufacturing and service environments reveals a difference in respect of the relative mix of resources and costs incurred in the manufacturing and service provision activities. Manufacturing environments, particularly as they become increasingly automated, will typically have much greater direct materials cost than labour costs in the product cost mix. By contrast, the key resource of many service organisations is labour (professional accountants, lawyers, architects, etc.), and in these organisations direct labour will typically be much greater than materials in the mix of service provision costs.

There are four points to be remembered with regard to the output of manufacturing and service environments:

1. The outputs of both environments are products, and they are distinguished by the terms 'goods' and 'services' respectively.
2. A service organisation may not be able to carry an inventory of its product, which is often delivered as it is produced.
3. The examples used in this chapter have illustrated that both job order and process systems may operate in a manufacturing organisation. Similarly, service organisations may both undertake job orders (for example legal representation and accounting advice) and operate processes (for example handling claims in an insurance firm and processing cheques in a bank).
4. Any organisation may have a combination of manufacturing and service provision units. In fact, all manufacturing organisations will have some service units that provide internal services such as human resource management. Many of them will also provide customer service departments that deal with external customers.

Second, we assumed that the application of all manufacturing overhead was done using a single application base. This single application base was used despite the qualification earlier in the chapter that, although some manufacturing overhead costs such as indirect labour may be appropriately applied to products or jobs on the basis of direct labour hours, other costs may not. Other costs, such as repairs and maintenance and perhaps power, may be more appropriately applied on a different base, for example direct machine hours. An extension of the approach taken in the example is that an organisation may use two (or more) application bases in its production and product cost determinations.

For process costing and job order costing, direct labour hours might be used to apply some manufacturing overheads, and direct machine hours to apply others. In process costing, it is likely that manufacturing overhead rates will be calculated independently for each department, based on the department's own overhead incurrence and appropriate base. The basis for application in each department (for example direct labour hours, direct labour cost, material usage or machine hours) may differ between departments. Furthermore, within departments there may be more than one application rate in use. A 'cost pool' for the aggregation of the relevant overhead costs is used for each rate.

Although the conventional approach to overhead application allows the separate application of overhead according to whether it varies with machine hours, direct labour hours or a variety of other bases, these bases are measures that change with the number of units of product manufactured or delivered (in the case of services). Some overheads do not change with the number of units produced. For example, production lines in a manufacturing environment are usually capable of adaptation so that different products can be manufactured at different times. The adaptation of the production equipment to accommodate a change in production is called 'set-up'. It is performed each time there is a change in product being produced and the cost of set-ups does not vary directly with anything that varies with the volume of production.

A contemporary approach to product costing will now be examined. It need not be an alternative to job order costing and process costing. Rather, it is a way of more accurately affixing costs to products and may be utilised within a job order costing or process costing system.

Activity-based costing

As a method of overhead application, activity-based costing (ABC) goes beyond using dual or multiple application bases, and examines the essential activity underlying each overhead item. The purpose is to be more discriminatory and accurate in the application of costs to products based on their relative need for, or use of, the underlying activity.

Thus, rather than classifying overhead costs as light and power, insurance and repairs and maintenance, as we did in the earlier example in the chapter, costs would be classified by an activity such as inspection and testing or material handling. The costs of inspection and testing for product quality would be separated from the other overhead costs and comprise their own cost pool for the purpose of application. This cost pool would then be applied to products based on their relative consumption of, or need for, the particular activity. The result could be to apply this pool on the basis of so many dollars per hour of inspection or testing required. Hence the term 'activity-based costing'.

Activity-based costing may be described as a system of cost accounting whereby the costs of a product are developed from the costs of the activities required to produce the product, whether it is a good *or* a service.

Example: *Activity-based costing*

The Coper Company manufactures a range of automotive products. Traditionally, materials and labour were traced to products and overhead applied on the basis of direct machine hours. A change to activity-based costing has resulted in the identification of the following operational activities and the factors driving the costs of those activities (the cost drivers).

Activity	Factor driving activity costs
Materials handling	Number of components or parts
Production set-up	Number of set-ups
Production (automated)	Number of machine hours
Dispatching	Number of orders dispatched

The following data relate to Coper's two products, A and B, for the forthcoming period in respect of each of the four activities and their identified cost drivers.

	A	B
Number of components or parts	50	85
Number of set-ups	175	90
Number of machine hours	12	14
Number of orders dispatched	2000	4000

The expected production during the period is 20 000 units of product A and 10 000 of product B. The total cost pools for each activity for the products are as follows.

Materials handling	$ 450 000
Production set-up	280 000
Production	6 000 000
Dispatching	370 000

We therefore have the following situation:

Activities	Cost	Driver	A	B
Materials handling	$ 450 000	Number of components or parts	50	85
Production set-up	280 000	Number of set-ups	175	90
Production	6 000 000	Number of machine hours	12	14
Dispatching	370 000	Number of orders dispatched	2000	4000

Using activity-based costing, a separate application rate would be developed for each activity. For example, the application rate for materials handling would be $0.24 per component part, calculated as $450 000 (total cost of the materials handling activity) divided by 1 850 000 parts to be handled (i.e. 20 000 units of product A multiplied by 50 component parts per unit, plus 10 000 units of B multiplied by 85 component parts per unit). The materials handling cost for product A would be $12 per unit (50 component parts by $0.24 per part) and for product B the cost would be $20.40 (85 × $0.24) per unit. The higher cost of materials handling per unit of product B is a consequence of the greater number of component parts in each unit of B.

The application of production set-up costs to the products will result in a lower cost for total production of product B in comparison with A—again a consequence of the greater number of set-ups required for product A. The total cost of this activity is estimated at $280 000 and the total number of set-ups is estimated at 265 (175 for product A plus 90 for B). The application rate for this activity is, therefore, $1056 (rounded) per set-up. The cost allocated or applied to product A for this activity will be $184 800 (175 set-ups by $1056 per set-up), and to product B, $95 040 (90 set-ups by $1056). (If the *average* set-up cost per unit is then calculated, the average set-up cost per unit of product B [$95 040/ 10 000 units] will be found to be greater than the average set-up cost per unit of product A [$184 800/20 000 units].)

This averaging of overhead costs over the units of production is sometimes misunderstood by non-accounting managers. It does not represent the cost incurrence per unit—if 100 fewer units of product B were produced, there may not be any change in the number of set-ups, and any change in the number of set-ups cannot be in direct proportion to the volume of production (you cannot have part of a set-up!). For many management decisions the need to find an *average* cost per unit does not exist, as the total cost of production for each product is the more relevant and reliable information. The use of ABC in decision making will be discussed further in later chapters of this book.

The data in this illustrative example form part of Review exercise 22.22, question 1. Application rates for the other activities will be calculated in that question, as will the average per-unit manufacturing costs for products A and B.

The benefit of activity-based costing is that it seeks to identify those factors that influence the overhead costs of a company and to use those factors in determining product costs. Reliance on a single activity base, such as direct labour hours for example, ignores the influence of those other factors and may misrepresent the cost of products that consume or need those other factors in differential amounts. Knowledge of the factors that influence overhead cost incurrence has an enormous impact that goes beyond improving product costing; knowledge of cost drivers focuses attention on ways to control costs and provides activity analysis that facilitates the improvement of 'the way things are done'.

The use of the activity analysis data for management purposes is called 'activity-based management'. An example of this use from the illustrative example could be the attempt to redesign product B to reduce the number of components used, since this has such an impact on materials handling costs.

It should be noted that, in the context of reporting inventory and using cost of goods sold to determine reported profit, the method of allocating overhead between products will not make a significant difference. This is because changing the method of allocation merely moves costs between products; it does not change the total cost that must pass through these accounts. The reported inventory balance and profit in published financial statements is normally an aggregate of many products and the shift[1] of cost between total inventory and total cost of goods sold because of the method of overhead allocation is normally very small. However, *internal* reports that focus on the profitability of individual products can change significantly as a result of changing the overhead allocation method. The decisions that are based on product profitability, and the information that assists in those decisions, are discussed in later chapters.

---

[1] This shift is simply a time difference in when the inventory cost is transferred to cost of goods sold, due to some of the cost being attached to different products.

Ethical issues

The accountant of the Mardi Medical Products company is seeking to introduce activity-based costing (ABC) into the cost determination of the company's products and product lines. She believes that the way in which many costs are simply lumped into overhead categories in the current system and the way in which those overheads are allocated to products have been significantly distorting the relative costs of the company's products. She has had her staff prepare a proposal arguing for the change to ABC. The proposal contrasts how a number of the company's product lines would be costed under ABC in comparison with the present system. There are some substantial differences. On seeing the proposal, the managing director's response was as follows:

> I might have been enthusiastic about ABC before. I'm not now. What it does here is decrease the costs of almost every product in the G1 and G2 codes. These are almost entirely government contract purchases and the contract prices are based, in part anyway, on our costs. We justify them on full cost recovery plus a negotiated margin. If we decrease the booked cost, we can't justify the price as easily and there will be pressure for us to reduce the price on these lines. We should be looking for ways to load the costs of the government product lines, not decrease them. Go back and tell your staff that we are not going ahead with ABC—tell them it isn't appropriate. Plus have a look at the overhead allocations again. We haven't had a price rise out of the government for a while. If we used a different basis of allocation, could we 'up' the cost of the G1 and G2 coded lines? Allocations are arbitrary anyway!

As the accountant, what would you do?

Summary

The purpose of this chapter has been to consider some accounting systems that cost products and projects. The emphasis has been on developing product and project costs for the purposes of determining the profit of the organisation and valuing its inventories.

Manufacturing organisations maintain three types of inventories (raw materials inventory, work-in-progress inventory and finished goods inventory). This contrasts with merchandising organisations, which typically maintain only one type. Additionally, developing the costs of those inventories requires analysis of the internal manufacturing cost elements (materials, labour and overhead).

The approaches taken to product costing (for both job order and process style manufacturing organisations) were based on an 'absorption costing' method, so called because total manufacturing overhead costs have been applied or absorbed into the cost of the product. This is the most commonly used method of product costing for profit determination and inventory costing for external reporting purposes.

This method contrasts with an approach to product costing known as 'variable costing', which will be discussed in later chapters of the book and in which the emphasis will move from product costing for external reporting purposes to costing for internal management decisions.

Case 22.1

Cost per unit

It is easy to identify the cost of direct material and direct labour per hat. The direct material will be the felt and the braid, and the direct labour will be the cost of employing the person who makes the hats.

The other costs are called 'indirect costs'. That is, either

(a) a direct link between the cost of the resource and the product cannot be identified, or
(b) it is not worth the effort of direct association.

However, you probably realised that you need to include these costs in the product costing if you are to know what sales price would be acceptable to you. You probably calculated the cost per hat as follows:

			$	$
Direct material:	felt	(0.5 m @ $10/m)	5.00	
	braid	(0.6 m @ $2/m)	1.20	6.20
Direct labour		(0.5 hrs @ $16/hr)		8.00
Overheads		($5120/3200 hats)		1.60
				$15.80

If the business employed many people and produced many products, there would be a need for a supervisor and the cost of employing that person would be considered an indirect cost for the hats.

The cost of thread can also be treated as indirect. Although it would be possible to calculate how much is used in the manufacture of each hat, on a cost/benefit basis the effort would not be adequately rewarded.

Note that the $15.80 represents an *average* cost per unit. It is not the cost of making each individual hat. In effect, we have averaged the cost of rent, for example, over the expected production for the period. Rent would not increase or decrease if a few more or a few less hats were made. Decisions that depend on more accurate product cost information will be discussed in later chapters.

Uses for the unit cost

If you are in a position to set the price, this cost per hat could be used to determine the selling price. In a market in which the market has determined the acceptable price for this product (i.e. it is a competitive market in which customer behaviour defines the price), you need knowledge of the cost to determine whether you can afford to be in the market. (Such decisions will be considered in later chapters.)

The cost can also be used for the financial recording of inventory and cost of goods sold (the focus of this chapter).

Complicating issues

If your hat-making concern was successful, you might decide to expand the business. This chapter considers more complicated circumstances than the one product, the one employee and the one process situation you have dealt with here. For example, suppose you start taking orders for customised hats. The customers are retailers who each change your basic design to one that will be identified with their outlets. They order many hats at a time, all identical within the one order. In this situation it would be necessary to identify costs with the order to which they relate.

Alternatively, you might employ many workers and produce a range of basic hats. The continuous processing requires a different approach to recording costs and calculating product costs. In particular, the above calculation of overhead per hat may not be considered appropriate if, for example, it takes twice as long to make one kind of hat as to make another—the power used for one hat would be greater than the power used for the other. Then you may think that overhead should be calculated per hat on the basis of how long it takes to make the hat.

A further complication may arise, even in the simplified situation in this task where one person is making one style of hat. Suppose the expected overhead cost is wrong, and the estimated number of hats made is wrong. These were both predictions made at the start of the year so that useful information on product cost could be derived long before the actual happenings during the year could be known. The recovery of overhead costs through the sale of hats was calculated at the rate of $1.60 per hat. If the inventory and cost of goods sold accounts during the year had recorded $1.60 per hat for overhead, and only 3000 hats had been made, then only $4800 would have been recorded in the inventory (and flowed through to cost of goods sold) for overhead. Furthermore, if the actual overhead costs for the year turned out to be $5400, the actual overhead incurred would be $600 more than was recorded as part of cost of goods sold. This would require an end of year adjustment to cost of goods sold to increase it by $600. This adjustment is usually required because it is unusual for the two estimates of overhead cost and volume of production to be correct. The adjustment may require either increasing cost of goods sold or decreasing it, depending on the nature of the prediction errors.

You should not be unduly concerned at failing to fully comprehend this material at present. This discussion merely alerts you to some of the complications that we need to address. These issues will be covered in this chapter.

Case 22.2

The predetermined application rate for manufacturing overhead

$$= \frac{\$325\,000}{13\,000 \text{ manufacturing hours (MH)}} = \$25 \text{ per manufacturing hour (MH)}$$

During the year the amount of manufacturing overhead applied

$$= 13\,250 \text{ MH @ \$25 per MH} = \$331\,250$$
The actual manufacturing overhead incurred $= \$342\,000$

As the manufacturing overhead incurred is more than the manufacturing overhead applied, it is *under*-applied, since the aim is to apply the amount actually incurred. In this case the manufacturing overhead is $10 750 under-applied.

As mentioned, the aim is to accurately apply overhead. However, as the application rate depends on two estimates, and each is likely to be at least slightly incorrect, it is usual to have what is called a 'variance'. This is the amount by which actual manufacturing overhead differs from the applied manufacturing overhead.

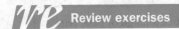

Review exercises

Discussion questions

22.1 Define direct materials cost, direct labour cost and manufacturing overhead cost.

22.2 Define raw materials inventory, work-in-progress inventory and finished goods inventory.

22.3 What types of manufacturing organisations are likely to use job order costing? Process costing?

22.4 Would an organisation designing and building yachts to customer specifications use job order costing or process costing? Explain your answer.

22.5 Explain the purpose and conventional method of applying manufacturing overhead costs to products.

22.6 Explain the concept of under- or over-applied manufacturing overhead, using the following data in your explanation:

Budgeted overhead	$1 500 000
Budgeted direct labour hours	250 000
Actual overhead	$1 700 000
Actual direct labour hours	250 000

22.7 If manufacturing overhead is over-applied for the year, the cost of sales account must be debited with the amount of over-application. Do you agree? Why or why not?

22.8 Product costing in process operations uses an 'averaging' approach. Explain and compare this approach with product costing in job order situations.

22.9 Explain the concept of 'equivalent units' in process costing. Use the following data in your explanation:

	Units of product
Work-in-progress 1 July	4 000
Started in production July	10 000
Work-in-progress 31 July	6 000
(Materials 100% complete	
Conversion 40% complete)	

22.10 Work-in-progress in a department at the end of a period might not be at the same stage of production in respect of each of the individual cost elements of materials, labour and overhead. Explain why this might be so.

22.11 As the accountant involved in the ethical issue on page 775, what would you do? Why?

Problems

22.12 *Process costing, equivalent units*
The Chalk Farm Company makes liquid fertiliser. It uses a process costing system. The following data relate to May 1998:

Work-in-progress 1 May	
(40% complete)	4 600 litres
Started during May	32 340 litres
Completed during May	27 600 litres
Work-in-progress 31 May	
(50% complete)	9 200 litres

Calculate the equivalent full units for materials and conversion costs under the weighted-average method and assuming materials are added at the beginning of the production process and conversion costs are incurred uniformly throughout the process.

22.13 *Cost of goods manufactured statement*

The following information is available from the accounting records of the Gunnersbury Company for the year ended 30 June 1998.

Cost of raw materials used in production	$ 551 250
Manufacturing overhead costs	267 750
Direct labour	416 500
Work-in-progress inventory:	
1 July 1997	56 000
30 June 1998	12 600
Finished goods inventory:	
1 July 1997	224 000
30 June 1998	63 000
Raw materials inventory:	
1 July 1997	157 500
30 June 1998	40 250
Sales	2 737 500
General and administrative expenses	382 200
Selling expenses	535 000

(a) Prepare a statement of cost of goods manufactured for the year ended 30 June 1998. (You may need to revise the format for this statement shown in Chapter 9 on page 326.)

(b) Prepare a profit and loss statement for the year ended 30 June 1998.

22.14 *Manufacturing overhead application*

The following information is available for the Wandsworth Company for the year 1998:

Budgeted manufacturing overhead cost	$243 000
Actual manufacturing overhead cost	276 750
Budgeted direct machine hours	110 000
Actual direct machine hours	130 000
Budgeted direct labour hours	270 000
Actual direct labour hours	303 750

(a) Assuming manufacturing overhead is applied to production on the basis of direct machine hours, calculate:

(i) the predetermined manufacturing overhead application rate

(ii) the manufacturing overhead costs applied to production during the year

        (iii) the amount of over-applied or under-applied manufacturing overhead cost

  (b) Calculate (i), (ii) and (iii) again, assuming manufacturing overhead is applied on the basis of direct labour hours.

22.15 *Job order costing*

  1. The Olympia Manufacturing Company uses a job order costing system for costing its products. The following information is available from the accounting records for the month of August 1998:

    (i) Direct materials purchased for cash $159 000.

    (ii) Factory supplies purchased on credit $15 000.

    (iii) Direct materials issued to production $136 800.

    (iv) Factory supplies issued to production $12 000.

    (v) Wages for factory workers for August paid in cash $103 350.

    (vi) Salaries of factory supervisors for August paid in cash $13 250.

    (vii) Other manufacturing overhead costs incurred and paid in cash during August $48 000.

    (viii) Manufacturing overhead is applied to production on the basis of $12 per direct labour hour. The number of direct labour hours worked during August was 6500.

    (ix) Jobs costed at $244 500 were completed during August.

    (x) Jobs costed at $166 400 were delivered and invoiced to customers during August. The invoice amounts for these jobs totalled $225 250. The customers are required to pay in September.

  (a) Prepare journal entries to record each of the above items. Assume under-applied or over-applied overhead is adjusted against cost of goods sold each month.

  (b) Assuming that the raw materials inventory at 31 July 1998 was $32 000, calculate the raw materials inventory at 31 August 1998.

  (c) Assuming that the work-in-progress inventory at 31 July 1998 was $25 000, calculate the work-in-progress inventory at 31 August 1998.

  2. The Kentish Company uses a job order cost system. Direct materials costs and direct labour costs are traced to individual jobs using job cost sheets and time sheets. Manufacturing overhead is applied to jobs using a predetermined annual application rate based on direct labour hours. At the beginning of the current year, 20X1, the company estimated that 160 000 direct labour hours would be worked and that manufacturing overhead costs would amount to $800 000.

The following information relates to the month of September 20X1.

Raw materials inventory 1 September	$ 14 200
Work-in-progress inventory 1 September	
(Job no. KC48 only)	72 900
Finished goods inventory 1 September	151 000
Raw materials purchased	182 250
Materials issued to jobs:	
Job no. KC48	61 600
Job no. KC49	50 600
Job no. KC50	34 400

Supplies purchased	20 000
Supplies issued to production	16 000
Direct labour costs	
(11 400 hours @ $6 per hour)	68 400
Supervisory salaries	28 350
Factory heating and lighting	12 000
Depreciation on factory equipment	2 400
Factory repairs and maintenance	2 000
Other factory overhead	3 750
Direct labour hours worked in September were:	
Job no. KC48	4 725
Job no. KC49	4 000
Job no. KC50	2 675

(a) Calculate the predetermined rate used to apply manufacturing overhead to jobs during 20X1.

(b) Calculate the amount of manufacturing overhead applied to production during September.

(c) Calculate the amount of under-applied or over-applied manufacturing overhead for September.

(d) Assuming job no. KC48 was completed during September, what was the total cost of this job?

(e) Assuming job no. KC48 was the only job completed during September, calculate the cost of work-in-progress inventory at the end of September.

22.16 *Job order costing, separate department application rates*
The Aldgate Company is a job order manufacturing organisation made up of two production departments.

Separate manufacturing overhead application rates are predetermined for each department and the rates are used to charge overhead to jobs as they move through each department. Overhead is applied on the basis of direct labour hours in Department 1, and direct machine hours in Department 2.

The rates are determined from the following budgets for each department for the current year, 20X1.

	Department 1	Department 2
Manufacturing overhead	$720 000	$630 000
Direct labour hours	180 000	105 000
Direct machine hours	36 000	126 000

The job order cost sheet for job no. 108, finished during March 20X1, showed the following:

	Department 1	Department 2
Direct materials	$64.00	$28.00
Direct labour	$36.00	$24.00
Direct labour hours	6	4
Direct machine hours	4	10

(a) Calculate the predetermined manufacturing overhead application rates for each department.

(b) Calculate the overhead charged to job no. 108.

(c) The following information is available at the end of 20X1:

	Department 1	Department 2
Actual total manufacturing overhead incurred	$680 000	$650 000
Actual total direct labour hours	160 000	100 000
Actual total direct machine hours	36 000	133 000

Calculate the under- or over-applied overhead for each department.

22.17 *Job order costing; process costing; hybrid systems*

Jan Jefferies needs to know how to cost a particular product. Jan is the management accountant for a firm that makes soap. One of the products is a small 'guest soap'. The firm has been requested by a well-known hotel chain to supply them with a large order of these soaps, but the hotel chain's name must replace the soap manufacturer's name on the packaging. Jan has a process costing system. It appears that branching out into the supply of customised orders will require a job order costing system for those orders. Jan is concerned about the time and cost involved in setting up and running a parallel system for costing.

Discuss whether it would be necessary to identify direct materials, direct labour and overheads separately for the mass-produced items and the customised orders. Explain and justify your answer fully.

22.18 *Production cost report*

The following data are taken from the records of Myall Park Ltd, a process manufacturing company.

Production data		Units
Work-in-progress 1 January		5 000
Work started during January		15 000
Work-in-progress 31 January		4 000

Cost data		Cost
Work-in-progress 1 January		
Direct materials	$10 000	
Direct labour	5 000	
Manufacturing overhead	7 500	$22 500
Direct materials issued to production during January		40 000
Direct labour costs incurred during January		30 700
Manufacturing overhead charged to production during January		43 500

All direct materials are used at the beginning of the production process. Direct labour and manufacturing overhead costs are assumed to be incurred uniformly through the process.

Work-in-progress at 31 January is estimated to be 25 per cent complete.

Prepare a production cost report for Myall Park Ltd for the month of January, showing the cost of goods completed during the month and the cost of work-in-progress at the end of the month.

22.19 *Job order costing, journal entries and ledger accounts*

Ashford Ltd, an engineering repair and reconditioning factory, uses job order costing.

Work-in-progress at the beginning of November consisted of two jobs, nos. 474 and 477, with the following costs:

	Job no. 474	Job no. 477
Direct materials	$3150	$ 600
Direct labour	3375	1122
Manufacturing overhead applied	1689	564
	8214	2286

During November both jobs were completed, job no. 474 requiring a further $2100 of direct materials and 200 labour hours, and job no. 477 requiring $900 of direct materials and 100 labour hours. Job no. 474 was invoiced at $18 000, and job no. 477 at $7200. Jobs no. 478 and 479 were commenced in November. The job cost sheets show the following direct materials and labour costs for these jobs:

	Job no. 478	Job no. 479
Direct materials	$1860	$2340
Direct labour	2250	1125

The labour rate is $15 per hour, manufacturing overhead is applied to jobs at the rate of $7.50 per direct labour hour, and actual manufacturing overhead incurred during November is $6600.

(a) Calculate the total cost of jobs no. 474 and 477, showing the breakdown into materials, labour and overhead.

(b) Calculate the cost of work-in-progress at 30 November.

(c) Prepare journal entries for November.

(d) Show the work-in-progress account in the general ledger for November.

22.20 *Process costing, weighted-average method*

The Fitzroy Company produces a specialised lubricating oil through two processing departments, a refining department and a blending department.

Raw fluid forms the direct material of the refining department and is required at the beginning of the refining process. Direct labour and overhead costs are assumed to be incurred evenly throughout the process.

Once the first process is completed, the refined product is transferred immediately to the blending department. Additional material is required midway through the blending process. Conversion costs are again assumed to be incurred evenly.

The following data relate to processing operations during the month of July 20X1.

	Refining Department	Blending Department
Litres		
Work-in-progress 1 July	50 000	60 000
	(¼ complete)	(⅔ complete)
Started during July	200 000	?
Completed in July	240 000	220 000
Work-in-progress 31 July	10 000	80 000
	(½ complete)	(⅜ complete)
Costs		
Work-in-progress 1 July		
Transferred-in costs	-	$ 49 000
Direct materials	$ 30 000	-
Conversion costs	7 500	56 000
Direct materials	110 500	70 000
Conversion costs	90 000	335 000

(a) Using the weighted-average method of product costing, prepare production cost reports for each department, showing the cost of goods completed in each department during the month, and the cost of work-in-progress for each department at the end of the month.

(b) The data given show the estimated stage of completion of work-in-progress on 1 July. Explain the significance of this data for the weighted-average method of product costing.

22.21 *Process costing*

The Camden Company has three departments in its manufacturing process, the third of which is the finishing department. The following data relate to February 20X1.

Production data	Units
Work-in-progress 1 February (75% complete)	16 000
Transferred-in from previous department	64 000
Completed and transferred-out	56 000
Work-in-progress 28 February (40% complete)	24 000

Cost data		Costs
Work-in-progress 1 February		
Transferred-in cost	$60 800	
Direct materials	34 400	
Direct labour	62 400	
Manufacturing overhead	67 200	$224 800
Cost of production transferred-in from		
previous department		215 000
Direct materials issued to production		112 000
Direct labour costs incurred		260 000
Manufacturing overhead charged to production		208 100

Direct materials are added at the 10 per cent stage of processing in the finishing department. Conversion costs are assumed to be incurred uniformly throughout the process.

Prepare a production cost report for the finishing department for the month of February, showing the cost of goods completed during the month and the cost of work-in-progress at the end of the month.

22.22 *Activity-based costing*

1. The Coper Company manufactures a range of automotive products. Traditionally, materials and labour were traced to products and overhead applied on the basis of direct machine hours. A change to activity-based costing has resulted in the identification of the following operational activities and the factors driving the costs of those activities (the cost drivers).

Activity	Factor driving activity costs
Materials handling	Number of components or parts
Production set-up	Number of set-ups
Production (automated)	Number of machine hours
DIspatching	Number of orders dIspatched

The following data relate to two of Coper's products, A and B, for the forthcoming period in respect of each of the four activities and their identified cost drivers.

	A	B
Number of component parts per unit	50	85
Number of set-ups	175	90
Number of machine hours per unit	12	14
Number of orders dIspatched	2000	4000

The expected production during the period is 20 000 units of product A and 10 000 of product B, and the total cost pools for each activity for the products are as follows:

Materials handling	$ 450 000
Production set-up	280 000
Production	6 000 000
DIspatching	370 000

(a) Calculate the application rate for each of the four activities based on the identified cost driver.
(b) Calculate the budgeted costs for each product for each activity for the forthcoming period, both in total and per unit. (Note that solutions to selected parts of this question were provided in the illustrative example in the chapter.)
(c) Recalculate the per-unit cost using an application rate based on machine hours.
(d) Comment on the difference between the per-unit costs derived under each method.

2. Medway Products manufactures two products, Doh and Soh. Overhead costs have traditionally been applied to each product on the basis of direct labour hours. A change to activity-based costing has resulted in the identification of the following operational activities and the factors driving the costs of these activities (the cost drivers):

Activity	Factor driving activity cost
Materials (inward handling)	Number of inward deliveries of materials
Production set-up	Number of production set-ups
Production (automated)	Number of machine hours
Inspection and testing	Number of inspections

The estimated costs of each activity for the forthcoming period and the relative consumption of, or need for, each activity by the two products are given thus:

Activity	Total cost	Relative consumption Doh	Soh
Materials handling	$125 000		
Number of inward deliveries		220	850
Production set-up	320 000		
Number of product set-ups		4 350	2 900
Production (automated)	440 000		
Number of machine hours		17 500	41 000
Inspection and testing	223 000		
Number of inspections		7 300	4 300

(a) Calculate the application rate for each of the four activities based on the identified cost driver.

(b) Calculate the budgeted costs of the activities for each product for the forthcoming period, both in total and per unit.

(c) Before introducing activity-based costing, Medway applied overhead on the basis of direct labour hours. Assuming that both products required two direct labour hours, determine the manufacturing overhead cost per unit of each product. Comment on the different costs per unit in this section in comparison to (b) above.

(d) Discuss any difficulties Medway might have experienced with regard to the selling price and sales of their products before adopting activity-based costing.

22.23 *Decision usefulness and the cost of errors*

Elcom Testers provides a testing service for firms that use electronic components in their products. Although the electronic components are inexpensive, when a faulty one is installed in a product the costs of correction or scrap can be very high. Consequently they are all tested prior to use in production. It is not economical for each firm that either makes or utilises these components to conduct the testing itself. Elcom Testers provides a testing service for a wide range of electronic components.

When Elcom Testers first provided this service tests were either manually performed or conducted on simple equipment. Overhead costs such as the cost of equipment and other facilities constituted a small proportion of overall costs. The testing services were costed as direct labour cost plus overhead costs. The application of overhead was on the basis of direct labour cost and was recalculated each year. This method continues to be used.

As total direct labour cost last year totalled $2 900 000 and all other costs (the overheads) totalled $4 495 000, overhead was allocated as 155% of direct labour cost. Hence, a job order (job X) with direct labour costs of $2900 would be allocated overhead costs of $4495.

Recently Lou Harris, the new management accountant at Elcom Testers, has been questioned about the product costing method used. Other managers have noticed that competitors quote lower prices than Elcom for simple tests and higher prices than Elcom for complex tests that use expensive equipment.

Lou has explained that the costing system was first designed to meet financial reporting requirements and is still accepted by the auditors as being adequate for this purpose. Inventory only consists of work in progress and tested components that have not been dispatched. Tested components may be stored for up to two days but are usually dispatched within a few hours of completion of testing.

Lou suggests that costing for the purposes of internal decision making, such as pricing, should adopt a more sophisticated approach. Such an approach could also be used for financial reporting, instead of having two different costing methods in use.

Lou has identified two different kinds of overhead cost: the costs incurred by the testing units themselves (referred to as test costs), and the administrative, technical support and other costs (generically termed support costs) incurred by the firm. Lou suggests that the costs directly linked to the testing process be allocated on the basis of machine hours, and that the other costs be allocated on the basis of direct labour dollars, as before. A total of 34 000 machine hours were used for the year.

Of the $4 495 000 overhead costs, $674 250 are support costs and $3 820 750 are test costs. Assuming that job X, with direct labour costs of $2900, uses 34 machine hours, it would be costed as follows:

Direct costs			
Direct labour			$2900.00
Indirect costs			
Test	$(34* (3 820 750/34 000))	$3820.75	
Support	$(2900* (674 250/2 900 000))	674.25	4495.00
			$7395.00

One of the engineers, Alex Walker, has been studying management accounting in an MBA program and draws up comparative costings for three different jobs completed last year—job no. 163, job no. 167 and job no. 171. As a result Alex claims that the inequities of the previous system would not be overcome by Lou's new method of costing. Alex suggests breaking the testing overhead costs into two separate cost pools, one for mechanical testing and one for electrical testing. Mechanical testing and electrical testing are already performed in separate test rooms so there are few joint costs (e.g. cleaning costs are easily identified with each test room).

Because there is not a direct link between the support costs and any job, test or product the application of these costs will be arbitrary. Alex suggests that continuing the use of direct labour dollars as the basis of this application is as good as any other method. However, Alex proposes that indirect testing costs should be allocated on the basis of machine hours. Electronic testing has a greater investment in equipment than mechanical testing and is using increasingly automated equipment, reducing the traditional direct labour allocation base and also increasing throughput time.

The relevant data for the three jobs costed by Alex are as follows:

		Testing machine hours	
	Direct labour $	Mechanical	Electrical
Job no. 163	875	13	6
Job no. 167	1805	12	28
Job no. 171	1254	4	5
Total for the year		20 000	14 000
Cost		$1 468 750	$2 352 000

Required

(a) Cost job nos. 163, 167 and 171 under each of the three methods.

(b) Explain why Elcom has been receiving an increasing number of complex electronic testing jobs but has seen a decline in the number of mechanical testing jobs received from customers.

(c) How would this impact on the profitability of the firm?

(d) How many machine hours would job X need of mechanical testing and electronic testing for it to cost $7395?

(e) Which of the three costing methods do you prefer? Why?

(f) Can you suggest a more accurate method? Would you recommend that Elcom adopt your costing method?

CHAPTER 23
Cost concepts for management decisions

Learning objectives

In this chapter you will be introduced to:

1. the need for different cost classifications according to their decision-making context

2. outlay costs and opportunity costs

3. costs as direct or indirect with regard to various identified cost objects

4. the behaviour of variable costs and fixed costs

5. controllable and non-controllable costs

6. the concept of costs being engineered, discretionary or committed

7. the benefits obtainable from deriving the cost of value adding and non-value adding activities

8. opportunity, incremental, differential and sunk costs.

Introduction

The previous chapter dealt with costs and costing systems to determine the cost of goods and services, specifically for externally reporting inventory and profit. This chapter examines a number of other purposes for which costs and cost information is required by the management of organisations, specifically for internal decision making. The chapter examines different ways of thinking about, classifying and analysing costs for different management purposes and decisions. Particular attention is given to the cost classifications of: variable and fixed; controllable and non-controllable; engineered, discretionary and committed; value adding and non-value adding; and incremental, differential and sunk costs.

Accounting systems within merchandising, manufacturing and service organisations identify, classify, accumulate and analyse cost (and revenue) data in organised, systematic ways for a variety of purposes.

The previous chapter considered two types of cost accounting systems (job order and process costing systems). These systems allowed the development of product costs on a per-unit basis, for the purposes of inventory valuation and profit determination. However, the methods of cost accumulation and analysis and the product costs developed for these external reporting purposes may not be appropriate for the many other purposes for which cost data are required, specifically internal management decision-making purposes.

One such purpose is product pricing. Do the product costing methods developed for inventory valuation and profit determination purposes provide a basis for setting prices for products? To examine this question, attempt the following short case.

Case 23.1 How cost behaviour affects decisions

Consider the example of C. Ashley, a tailor who makes and sells business suits from leased premises on an industrial estate. Ashley also leases all production equipment and employs skilled labour on an hourly basis. The estimated cost of making each suit during the coming year is:

Materials	$120
Labour	250
Overheads	80
	450

The labour cost is estimated as 10 hours per suit at a rate of $25 per hour. The overhead cost is determined by dividing Ashley's total lease costs for the year by the number of suits expected to be made and sold over the year. Ashley adds a 50 per cent mark-up and prices the suits at $675.

What should Ashley do if a price of $400 was offered for a single suit? On what circumstances does your answer depend?

Attempt these questions before turning to the discussion on the case at the end of this chapter.

The C. Ashley case is a relatively simplistic example which overlooks various factors. It demonstrates, however, that although product costing methods incorporating allocation of fixed overhead costs may be relevant for external reporting purposes, they may not be relevant for many internal management purposes. The preparation of information that is relevant to internal decision making requires an understanding of the behaviour of costs and a careful selection of the data that assist the decision maker with regard to a particular decision.

The objectives of this chapter are to reconsider the purposes for which cost information is required by management (already explained in detail in Chapter 21), and to examine different ways of classifying and analysing costs for those purposes. First we will consider the purposes for which the information may be used.

Management purposes: planning, decision making and control

Management's basic responsibility may be viewed as the acquisition and integration of all resources (technical and human) to accomplish specific objectives. Although these activities are highly complex and interactive, a way of making them operational is to consider management in terms of the functions a manager performs. In Chapter 21 these functions were seen to include planning, decision making and control. An integral part of control is performance evaluation, since control requires the evaluation of what is happening and the correction of undesirable activities and outcomes. Closely linked to performance evaluation is the development of the organisation structure: grouping the activities of the organisation into segments, such as departments and divisions; specifying the relationship between segments; and determining such issues as the degree of centralisation or decentralisation of decision-making authority. These issues are also discussed in Chapters 21 and 26.

Planning

Planning is a systematic decision-making process designed to establish objectives, strategies and tactics for all levels in the organisation, consistent with identified constraints and opportunities. The development of courses of action that will enable the organisation to achieve its objectives is also part of the planning process.

In Chapter 21 you discovered that planning can be broadly divided into two phases, strategic planning and operational or tactical planning. Operational or tactical planning is typically concerned with a shorter time period than strategic planning. It involves decisions about the allocation of the organisation's current resources with a view to achieving short-run targets. Theoretically, these short-run targets are viewed as steps to the achievement of long-term or strategic organisational objectives.

The cost accounting system is closely linked to the planning process at this operational level. For example, if management sets a profit target for the year, it must also determine how that target can be achieved. It must determine its product mix for the year (i.e. what products will be produced and sold), examine the resources that will be required in the producing and selling processes and their cost, and formulate ranges of selling prices. Management accountants are involved in preparing these plans and presenting them in operating budgets and capital expenditure budgets. The anticipated outcome of following these plans can then be presented in the budgeted profit and loss statement, balance sheet and cash flow statement. The budgeted financial statements forecast the outcome of operations for the coming year and, hence, the anticipated picture that will be presented to outside entities of what will occur during the year. However, it is the operating budgets and capital budgets that guide management activity during the year. All of the budgets, including the budgeted financial statements, are collected together in a document called the master budget. These aspects of operational planning will be discussed further in Chapter 25.

Decision making

The term 'decision making' has been used synonymously with planning in the preceding discussion. All planning does involve decision making, but some decisions are made in practice without detailed planning. An example of this kind of decision is the 'one-off' situation described in Case 23.1. In general, managers will want to avoid being forced to make decisions without adequate information. Indeed, expectations of management accountability creates the need for decisions to be rationalised and supported by appropriate information of sufficient comprehensiveness.

Decision making may be considered a separate management function to the extent that a manager can draw on a body of literature that examines the organisational process of decision making rather than simply the accounting data inputs to the decision-making model. This process involves the behavioural, political and organisational dimensions of decision making, such as the relative influence, at different stages in the process, of different managers and departments. Although the accountant needs to be aware of the organisational decision-making process, this section concentrates on the use of accounting data as inputs to the formalised decisional processes of planning and control.

Control

The purpose of the management function of control is to ensure that the events and activities occurring within the organisation are conforming to plans.

The control function is closely associated with the management accounting system because management receives the greatest quantity of data and reports pertaining to this function from the accounting system. This system is used to monitor events and activities. When there is a perceived deviation from plan, it is necessary to either take action to revert back to plan or revise the plan in the light of the changed circumstances that caused such deviation.

Control of many things is required, such as equipment at the operations (task) level, costs and activities (including people) at the managerial level, and managers at the organisational level. A management control system should be designed and used in such a way that managers are motivated to make the same decision that their chief executive officer would make.

Control of costs requires a comprehensive and detailed cost accounting system to determine when and where the costs were incurred and to compare actual cost levels with planned levels. Reports known as budgetary control and standard cost variance analysis reports are usually prepared for this purpose. These reports are examined in Chapter 26. Variance analysis reports may also be used in the evaluation of the performance of managers, typically to determine how well the managers controlled the matters over which they had responsibility and authority to act.

Evaluation

As noted in Chapter 21, evaluation covers the obtaining of feedback on the results of operations in order that decisions can be made about any changes to those operations that may be seen as desirable in the future. It is also used to determine the particular strengths and weaknesses of individual managers in the organisational context.

Cost classifications for different management purposes

Many complexities in the process of cost classification and analysis arise because of the differential nature of the costs themselves and the many ways in which they may be used. Costs may be collected and analysed effectively only if the analyst, the accountant, is fully aware of the management purpose underlying the exercise.

Some common classification categories relate to the nature of the cost (outlay and opportunity costs), the traceability of the cost to the activity under examination (direct and indirect costs), the behaviour of the cost in relation to the activity (variable and fixed costs), the controllability of the cost at a specific management level (controllable and non-controllable costs), the timing and nature of controllability (engineered, discretionary and committed costs), product enhancement (value adding and non-value adding costs), and the relevance of the cost to a specific decision (incremental, differential and sunk costs).

These categories are not exclusive; any one cost may fall into a number of categories depending on the purpose of the analysis.

Outlay and opportunity costs

Outlay costs involve actual financial expenditure to obtain goods and services. Opportunity costs do not represent financial expenditures, but are measures of the loss of benefits from a forgone alternative.

The cost of reading this chapter, for example, may be viewed as the loss of one hour's leisure time. In choosing between reading the chapter or having an hour's pleasure, you need to know the benefits lost from the second alternative by choosing the first. Opportunity costs, and varying perceptions of those costs, will therefore be an important concept in decision making.

As another example, assume a company is evaluating a proposal to produce a new product which requires two raw materials, A and B. Material A is bought from a supplier at $1.00 per unit. Material B is currently being produced and sold by the company. Material B costs $1.50 per unit to produce, and the company is able to sell all the units of B it can make at $3.00.

In evaluating the decision to produce the new product, the relevant cost for material A is $1.00 per unit, because this is the future, additional cost the company will incur if it chooses to produce the new product. However, the relevant cost for material B is $3.00 per unit, because each unit of B diverted to the production of the new product will decrease outside sales, and cause the company to forgo $3.00 sales revenue. Since it represents a lost opportunity to sell these units to an external customer, the $3 per unit of B is the opportunity cost of using it in the production of the new product.

Direct and indirect costs

Direct costs are those costs that are capable of being identified with or traced to an activity (repairing equipment), a project (building a bridge), a good (a 64 cm colour television set), a service (insuring a car), a sales territory (the Sydney metropolitan area), a department (the production quality control department or the advertising department), or any other segment or activity of the organisation that is the focus of management's attention.

These segments or activities may be known as 'cost objects', where the cost object is the basic unit for cost accumulation. In Chapter 22 the cost object was the product, and the purpose was product costing for profit determination and inventory valuation. Costs that were considered direct to the product were the materials and labour that could be readily identified with units of product.

However, as the cost object is broadened from the product, either to the department in which the product is produced, or to the division of the company (which may consist of this and other departments), then more costs become direct. This is illustrated in Figure 23.1 in which you can see that a cost may be direct to some cost objects while being indirect to others.

The department manager's salary is an indirect cost with respect to particular products, but a direct cost when the entire department is the cost object. The division manager's salary also becomes direct when the focus becomes the division.

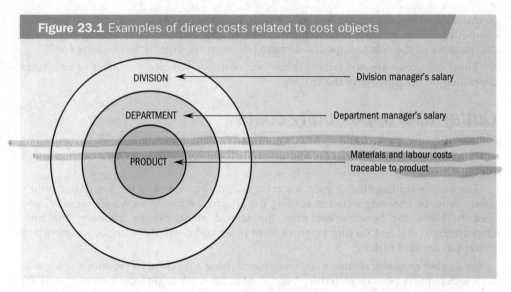

Figure 23.1 Examples of direct costs related to cost objects

If the cost object is a sales territory, the wages of sales staff who service that particular territory are direct costs. However, if those sales staff sell the entire range of the company's products in the territory, then their wages would not be a direct cost of marketing any one product, because it is unlikely that their wages could be identified specifically with any particular product line. The wages of sales staff would be considered direct to the territory, but indirect to any particular product. This distinction is illustrated in Figure 23.2.

The cost object must therefore be defined before a cost can be classified as direct or indirect.

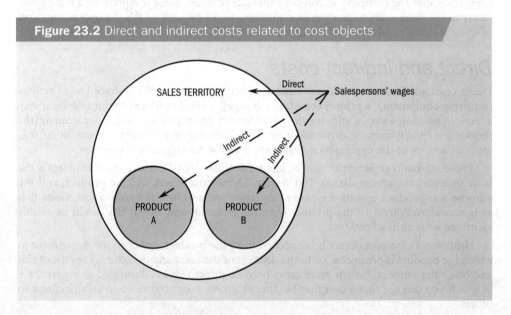

Figure 23.2 Direct and indirect costs related to cost objects

Variable and fixed costs

A critical distinction between costs for management purposes is based on how costs are expected to behave or change in response to changes in other relevant variables.

The behaviour of costs is usually referred to as their reaction to changes in an activity base, which may be the level of production, the volume of sales or the amount of material despatched. The activity base is also often referred to as the cost 'driver', because it is the factor that 'drives' movements in the cost item. Each of the cost drivers noted earlier in this paragraph are volume based. However, factors other than volume may often serve to drive costs. If two products differ in their level of complexity (e.g. a plain-legged table and one with ornately turned and decorative legs), their costs will differ, driven by the different levels of complexity.

Fixed costs

Fixed costs are costs that will not change in total amount with changes in the level of activity. For example, if the activity level is the volume of production, and the cost concerned is the lease of factory premises, the expected behaviour of this cost in relation to the activity level may be graphed as in Figure 23.3. Table 23.1 provides some examples of fixed costs in relation to selected activity bases. The vertical (or y axis) in Figure 23.3 represents dollars ($) and the horizontal (or x axis) represents units of activity (here, units of volume of production). The horizontal line in the graphically defined space depicts the behaviour of a fixed cost in response to changes in the level of activity. The line may also be thought of as a series of points, with x, y co-ordinates. A fixed cost is one where the y co-ordinate remains unchanged at different values of the x co-ordinate.

This strict description of fixed costs needs to be qualified. No cost is 'fixed' in the literal meaning of the word. For instance, a fixed cost may be changed by managerial decision. As an example, the production or sales manager's salary, or the wages of advertising production staff, may be altered by more senior management. In addition, insurance or lease costs may change as a result of marketplace changes. These changes are brought about not by changes in the activity level but by management's discretionary powers or by factors external to the firm.

A fixed cost may also change if the activity level falls below, or reaches beyond, a reasonable or 'relevant' range of activity. For example, if production output increases to a point where additional factory space is needed, the cost of leasing factory premises will rise by a discrete amount. If the level of advertising increases to the extent where the present advertising production staff can no longer cope, additional advertising staff may be hired.

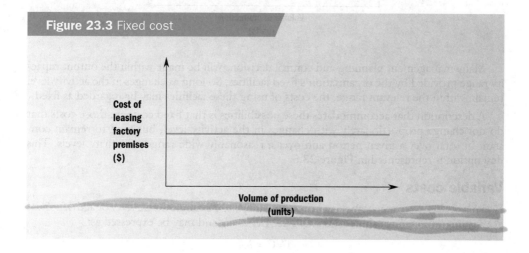

Figure 23.3 Fixed cost

Cost of leasing factory premises ($)

Volume of production (units)

Table 23.1 Examples of fixed costs in relation to selected activity bases

Activity base	Fixed costs
Volume of production output	Production manager's salary
	Depreciation on plant and equipment
	Insurance on plant and equipment
	Lease of factory premises
Level of sales activity	Sales manager's salary
Number of ads placed by advertising department	Wages of advertising production staff

Once these costs are adjusted to accommodate a higher level of activity they will again be 'fixed'.

The graph previously used to illustrate the behaviour of fixed costs should realistically be drawn to show a 'stepped' function, whereby increases in fixed costs will occur in discrete amounts, each addition providing sufficient capacity for a further range of output. This is shown in Figure 23.4. These costs are still regarded as fixed in that they do not change proportionately with each unit change in the activity level.

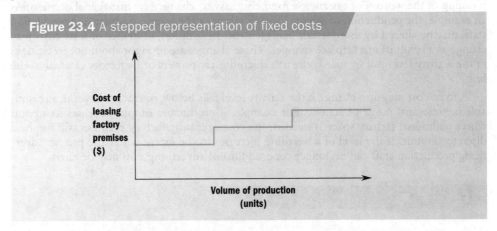

Figure 23.4 A stepped representation of fixed costs

Many management planning and control decisions will be made within the output capacity range provided by the organisation's fixed facilities. So long as changes in the activity level remain within the relevant range, the costs of using these facilities may be regarded as fixed.

A description that accommodates these possibilities is that fixed costs are those costs that do not change proportionately with changes in the activity level, but tend to remain constant in total over a given period and over a reasonably wide range of activity levels. This description is represented in Figure 23.5.

Variable costs

Variable costs are costs which vary proportionately with changes in the level of activity. They are assumed to be linear functions of the activity level, and may be expressed as:

$$TVC = b.x$$

where TVC is total variable cost, b is the cost per unit of activity base, and x is the level of activity. Examples of variable costs are direct materials and direct labour. Variable costs may be shown as Figure 23.6.

The assumption of linearity will not hold over the entire range of production volume because of economies and diseconomies of scale. Again, however, examination of the relevant range of volume will indicate that the true behaviour of variable costs can often be approximated as linear over this range. This assumption is shown in Figure 23.7.

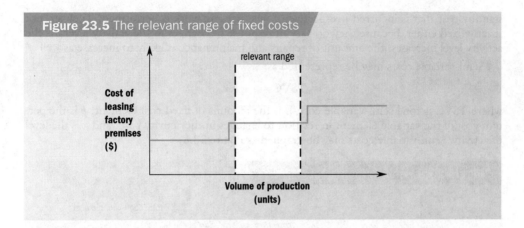

Figure 23.5 The relevant range of fixed costs

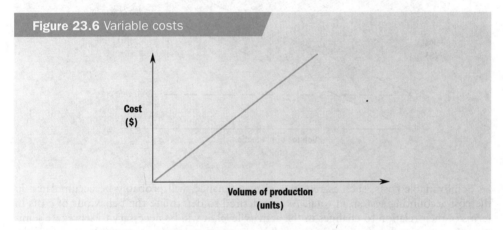

Figure 23.6 Variable costs

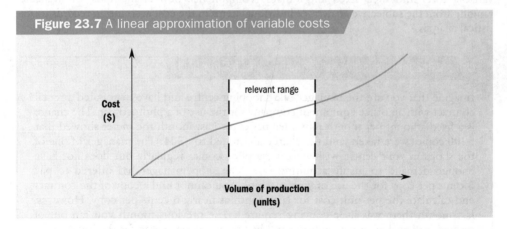

Figure 23.7 A linear approximation of variable costs

Semi-variable costs

Many costs are neither fully fixed nor fully variable, but contain both fixed and variable elements. For example, the cost of equipment repairs and maintenance may have a fixed element representing the cost of the maintenance staff employed full-time to service and repair equipment, and a variable element representing the increased cost of repairs and maintenance caused by increased usage of the equipment.

These costs possess attributes of both fixed and variable costs. They are not strictly variable, because they are not zero when the activity level is zero. Part of the cost represents a standby cost that is incurred irrespective of whether any work is performed. They are not strictly fixed either, because they do vary in response to changes in the activity level. As the activity level increases, the amount of repairs and maintenance is likely to increase as well.

Semi-variable costs may be represented as:

$$TSVC = a + b.x$$

where TSVC is total semi-variable cost, a is the amount of fixed cost element, b is the per-unit cost of the variable element in relation to changes in the activity base, and x is the level of activity. Semi-variable costs may be graphed as Figure 23.8.

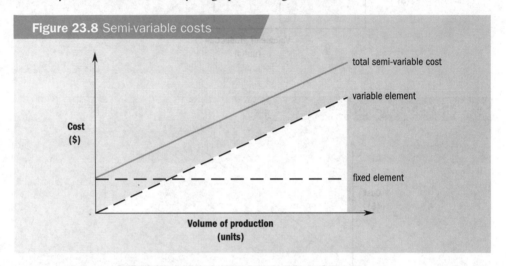

Figure 23.8 Semi-variable costs

Semi-variable costs, such as repairs and maintenance, will probably be accumulated in the cost accounting system in total. As it is desired to determine the behaviour of costs in terms of their relation to changes in the activity level, it will be necessary to segregate semi-variable costs into their fixed and variable components. Several methods are available, ranging from the subjective analysis of individual items in the cost accounting records to statistical analysis.

Case 23.2 Identifying cost behaviour and its impact

Imagine that you are the manager of a shopping centre and have negotiated a rental contract with an office equipment company for the use of a photocopier. The charge is a fixed amount per month plus a fee per copy. Last month the meter showed that 5200 copies were taken, and the charge amounted to $304. The manager of one of the shops in your centre wishes to use a photocopier regularly but does not have enough demand to justify acquiring one. The shop manager has offered to pay 5 cents per copy for the use of your machine. You cannot find a copy of the contract and calculate the per-unit cost for last month as nearly 6 cents per copy. However, last month there was little copying required. The previous month you ran out of printed leaflets during a promotion and had to photocopy some for the last day. On checking the figures for that month you find that 13 400 copies were made and the total charge was $468.

What is the fixed monthly charge and how much is paid per copy? Assuming that the shop manager's use of the machine would not hinder the efficient running of your office, should the offer of 5 cents be accepted?

A discussion on the case can be found at the end of this chapter. You should read the discussion after attempting these questions and before proceeding.

The utility of analysing costs into their fixed and variable elements for management decision-making purposes is illustrated in the following example.

Example: *Fixed and variable costs*

The Romiley Manufacturing Company makes executive toys. The company's projected profit and loss statement for the year, based on expected sales of 10 000 units, is as follows:

PROJECTED PROFIT AND LOSS STATEMENT	
Sales	$500 000
less Cost of goods manufactured and sold	375 000
Gross profit	125 000
less Selling and administrative expenses	100 000
Net profit	$ 25 000

A major retail store offers to buy 1000 toys from Romiley at a price of $35.00 per unit. This is below Romiley's normal selling price of $50.00 per unit, and below the company's manufacturing cost per unit of $37.50.

However, the manufacturing cost per unit includes both fixed and variable costs; it has been calculated as follows:

$$\frac{\text{total manufacturing costs}}{\text{total units produced}} = \frac{\$375\ 000}{10\ 000}\ \text{units}$$

An analysis of Romiley's costs show that they are made up of the following elements:

Variable costs:
Manufacturing	$30.00 per unit
Selling and administrative	$ 2.75 per unit

Fixed costs:
Manufacturing	$75 000 per year
Selling and administrative	$72 500 per year

Provided Romiley has sufficient production capacity to manufacture the additional 1000 units required by the retail store, the analysis of fixed and variable costs indicates that Romiley should accept the offer.

Only the variable costs of production and sale will increase if the order is accepted. The fixed costs will remain unchanged in total. Consequently, the price of $35.00 will cover the variable costs of production and sale ($32.75) and provide a contribution of $2.25 per unit to profit.

The concept of contribution per unit, or the 'contribution margin', is important in decisions of this nature. It is calculated as the sales price less the variable costs of production and sale. In this example the contribution margin per unit is $2.25 ($35.00 – $32.75), and the total contribution to be generated from the order is $2250.

The contribution margin concept may be formalised, for internal management decison-making purposes, by redrafting the projected profit and loss statement for the year, and by classifying costs on the basis of their fixed or variable behaviour. This is shown in the following projected profit and loss statements, with and without the retail store order. These statements confirm the increase in expected contribution and profit of $2250.

PROJECTED PROFIT AND LOSS STATEMENTS: ROMILEY MANUFACTURING COMPANY CONTRIBUTION FORMAT			
	Without retail order (10 000 units)	*With retail order (11 000 units)*	*Difference (1000 units)*
Sales	$500 000	$535 000	$35 000
less Variable costs			
Manufacturing	300 000	330 000	30 000
Selling and administrative	27 500	30 250	2 750
Total variable costs	327 500	360 250	32 750
Contribution margin	172 500	174 750	2 250
less Fixed costs			
Manufacturing	75 000	75 000	–
Selling and administrative	72 500	72 500	–
Total fixed costs	147 500	147 500	–
Net profit	25 000	27 250	2 250

Controllable and non-controllable costs

A major use of cost accounting data is to allow the performance of managers of each segment of the organisation to be evaluated. To achieve this, costs (and, where possible, revenues) should be identified with the manager responsible for their incurrence. This is known as 'responsibility accounting'. Managers should only be held responsible for costs over which they have control. Other costs are regarded as uncontrollable at that level of management.

A distinction needs to be made between direct and indirect costs, and controllable and non-controllable costs.

Direct costs were described as those costs capable of being identified with an activity or a segment (for example a department or division) of the organisation. Under this classification the salary of a segment manager would be a direct cost of the segment. If the purpose of analysis is to examine the viability of the segment, the salary of its manager would be relevant as a cost of continuing to operate the segment.

However, that same cost is not controllable by the segment manager, but by a manager at a higher level in the organisation. If the objective is to evaluate the performance of the segment manager in controlling costs, this manager's own salary would not be relevant because it is uncontrollable at that level. Performance evaluation requires the comparison of measured performance against some standard. The preferred basis for comparison is the desired performance that has been represented in the budget. Comparisons with that person's past performance or with the performance of others might be affected by external factors (for example a different economic environment or working with different equipment). Performance evaluation is part of the control function of management. The topic was introduced in Chapter 21 and is discussed more fully in Chapter 26.

This discussion further illustrates that the purpose of the analysis is critical in determining the relevant approach to cost classification and accumulation.

Engineered, discretionary and committed costs

Closely related to the variable and fixed, controllable and non-controllable cost classifications is the notion of engineered, discretionary and committed costs. They can be regarded as a more detailed analysis of variable and fixed costs, with an emphasis on controllability.

Engineered costs

Engineered costs are costs that have a direct relationship with a level of activity, and are directly determined by that level of activity. For example, the petrol consumption of a car is determined by the distance driven. Three kinds of decision determine petrol costs. The first of these decisions is made when the car is bought, since consumption rates vary with the type and model of vehicle. The second kind of decision, the one that determines how far the car is driven, is made regularly throughout the life of the vehicle. The third decision is the choice of petrol used. However, the fluctuating price of petrol is an external factor, rather than being the result of an internal decision.

The same range of decisions usually influence engineered costs in an organisation. The design of the product and the choice of processes to be used determine most product engineered costs before the launch of a product, for example, with regard to raw material, the decisions that determine the quantity and quality of material to be used per unit. The total amount that *should* be used is dependent on the volume of production (the number of units) required. A manager's control of the quantity *actually* used in production should therefore be monitored. Further, there is the danger that a manager might reduce costs by buying substandard material, so attention is also paid to savings on material prices. Differences between (a) planned activities and costs and (b) actual activities and costs are called variances. Variance analysis wil be discussed further in Chapter 26.

Table 23.2 Different decisions made at different times affecting one engineered cost

Decisions affecting personal petrol consumption costs	Decisions affecting material usage costs in production
Choice of vehicle	Design of product and production processes
Journeys to travel and route taken (distance travelled)	Efficient usage of material and control of waste (material volume usage)
Choice of petrol purchased (e.g. unleaded v. premium unleaded)	Choice of material purchased (standard, substandard or superior quality material)

It is the nature of engineered costs that the second decision in Table 23.2 provides a volume which is multiplied by a rate (price per unit) that is determined from the third decision. The multiple is the cost (of materials in this case). The major impact of the first decision has led to the use of 'life cycle costing' during the research and development phase of a product's life.[1]

Committed costs

Committed costs are predetermined and inflexible. Examples are: a three-year contract with an advertising firm, annual depreciation using the straight-line method and a five-year contract with a senior manager. Each of these items would stipulate the annual cost, frequently for more than the normal budget period (i.e. the short-term planning period). The amount cannot be changed during the period and, typically, is not even controllable at the time of setting the budget. Committed costs frequently relate to the provision of facilities that enable operations to take place (e.g. rent, rates, depreciation, and other plant, equipment and office costs). They have often been the subject of capital expenditure budgets in prior periods, since capital expenditure projects normally extend over several years.

---

[1] Life cycle costing and its associated technique—target costing—are outside the scope of this textbook. If you seek further information on them, you should refer to a contemporary management accounting textbook, such as Langfield-Smith, Thorne and Hilton, *Management Accounting: An Australian Perspective*, 2nd edn, Irwin McGraw-Hill, Sydney, 1998.

Since the committed cost itself is not manageable during the period, the manager may be held responsible for the efficient utilisation of the resource provided by the incurrence of the cost. The use of the resource is more readily controllable by the manager.

Discretionary costs

In the discussion of 'fixed costs' you found that some costs may be changed at the discretion of managers. Discretionary costs relate to the provision of resources that are not consumed in direct proportion to operations. The amount of the cost to be incurred is determined by what can be acquired, rather than by what must be incurred to maintain production in the short term (whether of goods or services). For example, advertising costs might be determined by the preferred placement and number of advertisements. If it is desired to reduce costs during the operating year, the manager may have the discretion to do so. Other costs that are determined in this way, and have the potential to be changed in a discretionary way, are training costs, entertainment costs and maintenance costs.

By their nature, short-term cuts in discretionary costs often cause long-term problems (e.g. inadequately trained personnel, falling sales and equipment break-downs). To managers who do not have the discretion to change these costs, they become 'committed' costs. It is important that managers' responsibility with regard to discretionary costs is clearly stated, and any change to these costs is justifiable.

Value-adding and non-value-adding costs

Activity-based costing was briefly introduced in Chapter 22. A full activity-based costing system would attempt to establish cost drivers for all costs, not just production costs. Such an analysis presents an opportunity to develop an activity chain. This chain links every activity with the activities that come before and after it.

For product costing, the relationships between activities and products are established, leading to the more accurate allocation of the costs to the products on the basis of the activity demand of each product. However, the activity analysis also provides an opportunity for cost control and the streamlining of activities. An activity is said to add value to the product if the activity causes the product to become more valuable to the consumer. For example, passing through a particular process converts the input of the process, advancing it towards completion. However, moving input material to the start of the process, or moving finished goods away from a process, does not add value to the product.

The costs of activities that add value can be termed 'value-adding costs' since they relate to 'value-adding activities'. The costs of activities that do not add value may similarly be called 'non-value-adding costs'. The value-adding costs classification is sometimes further extended to cover customer value adding (as defined above) and business value adding (necessary for the business but not adding value for the customer).

The control of customer value-adding activities and their associated costs means performing the activities as efficiently as possible. Business value-adding costs can be minimised without affecting the end product, while non-value-adding costs should, where possible, be eliminated (they do not add value to the product and are not essential to the organisation). Typical non-value-adding costs are the cost of maintaining work in progress inventories between processes. Where possible these should be eliminated by streamlining production.

If activity times are analysed to determine value-adding time and non-value-adding time, a useful analysis comes from a study of the length of time taken between raw material entering the first production process and the finished good exiting the last process. Typically the value-adding time for production of the item will be a small percentage of total throughput time. Value-adding and non-value-adding activities can be costed to focus attention on the areas with the most scope for improvement (i.e. assist decision making by prioritising action).

Incremental, differential and sunk costs

This classification of costs is related specifically to the decision-making purpose of cost analysis.

As you would have seen in attempting the task in Case 23.1, the costs that are relevant in making decisions are not necessarily the costs that are used in conventional accounting or for external reporting. Many of the costs relevant for decision making will never be recorded in the accounting records. Opportunity costs, for example, are important in decision making but are not recorded under the normal accounting procedures.

Again, some costs appearing in profit and loss statements are not relevant for decisions in other contexts. Depreciation is a prime example. The decision to buy the asset (e.g. a major item of equipment) has already been made, and that decision has committed the organisation to depreciate the asset until such time as the organisation chooses to dispose of it or it is fully depreciated.

For decisions made during the life of the asset, such as whether to increase or decrease production by the equipment or to alter the product mix, the annual recorded cost of depreciation on the equipment is irrelevant. It represents the allocation of a 'sunk' cost incurred in the past which will not change as a result of decisions on changes in production volume or mix in the short term.

In decision making, the emphasis is on the future. In the choice between alternatives (e.g. increase or decrease production volume, alter the product mix, make or buy a component part), the relevant costs are those that are expected to change as a result of the decision. These costs may be viewed as 'differential costs' (costs that will differ between decision alternatives) or 'incremental costs' (additional costs that will be incurred as a result of the decision). Costs that will be unaffected by the decision, either because they have been incurred in the past or because they will not change between decision alternatives, are irrelevant costs.

The following example illustrates the concept of relevant costs in a decision involving the production or purchase of a component part.

Example: *Relevant costs in 'make or buy' decisions*

The Sycamore Company manufactures bicycles. The company is organised into several departments, one of which produces saddles. The expected cost of producing saddles in the forthcoming period has been determined as:

	Total cost for 5000 saddles	Cost per unit
Direct materials	$ 10 000	$ 2
Direct labour	80 000	16
Departmental variable overhead	40 000	8
Departmental fixed overhead	20 000	4
Company fixed overhead charged to department	30 000	6
Total cost	$180 000	$36

The departmental fixed overhead consists of the cost of production supervision and the cost of leasing production equipment used exclusively for the manufacture of saddles. The company overhead charged to the department represents an allocation of company administration costs.

Birch Vale Products has offered to supply the Sycamore Company with the saddles at a price of $32 per unit. Should Sycamore continue to make the saddles or purchase them from Birch Vale?

The costs relevant to this decision are those costs that will differ between the decision alternatives.

The variable costs of materials, labour and variable overheads are relevant, because they will be incurred if Sycamore continues to produce the saddles but not if Sycamore decides to buy from Birch Vale.

The company fixed overhead charged to the department is not a relevant cost; it will be incurred irrespective of the decision. If Sycamore chooses to buy the saddles from Birch Vale and close down its saddle department, these costs will simply be reallocated to other departments within the company.

Determining whether the saddle department's fixed overhead cost is relevant to the decision is a greater problem. Although the behaviour of a cost provides an initial indication of its relevance (i.e. variable costs are frequently relevant, fixed costs irrelevant), this is not a sufficient criterion. The departmental fixed overhead cost items must be analysed to determine whether they will differ with each decision alternative.

If the Sycamore Company is able to avoid the lease costs and supervision salaries if it buys the saddles from Birch Vale, these costs are relevant. Assuming this is the case, a comparison of the relevant costs shows that the Sycamore Company should continue to produce the saddles. This comparison is shown below.

The decision to produce the saddles assumes that there are no alternative uses of the saddle department's fixed facilities. However, if the decision to manufacture necessitates the rejection of an opportunity to sub-lease the facilities for $12 000 per year, there is another relevant cost to consider. Incorporation of this cost in the analysis shows that Sycamore is better off, financially, if it purchases the saddles from Birch Vale. This analysis is also shown below.

MAKE OR BUY SADDLES

RELEVANT COST COMPARISON

(No alternative use of fixed facilities)

	Per unit	Total
Make		
Direct materials	$ 2	$ 10 000
Direct labour	16	80 000
Departmental variable overhead	8	40 000
Departmental fixed overhead (avoidable)	4	20 000
Relevant cost of making saddles	30	150 000
Relevant cost of buying saddles	32	160 000
Difference in favour of making	$ 2	$ 10 000

MAKE OR BUY SADDLES

RELEVANT COST COMPARISON

(Fixed facilities may be sub-let)

	Total
Make	
Direct materials	$ 10 000
Direct labour	80 000
Departmental variable overhead	40 000
Departmental fixed overhead (avoidable)	20 000
Opportunity cost of sub-leasing facilities	12 000
Relevant cost of making saddles	162 000
Relevant cost of buying saddles	160 000
Difference in favour of buying	$ 2 000

Qualitative and behavioural factors in management decisions

In this and subsequent chapters involving management decisions, it should be kept in mind that the analytical techniques and models discussed are adjuncts and aids to decision making. They are not substitutes for decision making. The techniques and models allow us to quantify the likely financial implications of particular decision alternatives. As such, they do not incorporate factors that are difficult or impossible to quantify in financial terms but which the decision maker regards as important.

In the example of the Sycamore Company, the relevant cost analysis showed a $2000 financial benefit of purchasing the saddles from Birch Vale Products if Sycamore's fixed facilities could be sub-let. Despite this financial advantage of buying, Sycamore's management might decide to continue to make the saddles because they consider that there are benefits of making that are not captured in the financial analysis. These benefits might include greater control over product quality and delivery if they make the saddles themselves, protection against price rises, and the desire to continue providing employment for their workers. Sycamore management may consider $2000 a small price to pay to obtain these less quantifiable but important benefits. Of course, if the relevant cost analysis showed a difference of $20 000, or $200 000, in favour of buying from outside, Sycamore's management might consider this too high a price to pay and decide to close the saddle department.

The output of the financial analysis is critical in providing management with a quantification of the expected financial implications of decision alternatives. This quantification serves as a reference point, a 'benchmark', which managers can use to weigh the importance to them of qualitative and/or non-financial factors.

Sometimes the qualitative or non-financial factors of importance to a particular manager may not seem rational or logical to others. Decisions are made by human beings and human beings have biases, prejudices, likes and dislikes. They often have political motivations and 'hidden agendas'. Perhaps the manager of the Sycamore Company dislikes the manager at Birch Vale Products intensely because they play squash regularly and the latter manager always wins and, worse still, boasts about it. As a result there is an impediment to Birch Vale Products gaining Sycamore's subcontracting business. For the Sycamore manager a $2000 financial advantage of subcontracting is easily outweighed by personal feelings. But perhaps the Sycamore manager has to defend the decision to reject the Birch Vale offer to the board of directors. An argument based on the relative squash abilities of the managers and a desire for personal revenge will not be very convincing to the board. There may be a political incentive for the Sycamore manager to 'review' the financial data used to compare the alternatives. Mysteriously, the review might find that the previous estimate of the benefits of sub-letting the released facilities was considerably overstated. The board may very well be presented with the following analysis.

MAKE OR BUY SADDLES RELEVANT COST COMPARISON (Fixed facilities may be sub-let)	
	Total
Make	
Direct materials	$ 10 000
Direct labour	80 000
Departmental variable overhead	40 000
Departmental fixed overhead (avoidable)	20 000
Opportunity cost of sub-leasing facilities	8 000
Relevant cost of making saddles	158 000
Relevant cost of buying saddles	160 000
Difference in favour of making	$ 2 000

The financial information and data that go into decision/analytical models are not always a determinant of the decision; sometimes they are the product of a decision that has already been taken. In these circumstances the role of accounting information and analytical models is not to assist in making the decision, but rather to support, justify or rationalise the decision to others in the organisation or to the decision maker him or herself. This often leads to ethical issues that the accountant must confront. Consider the following possible situation arising in the example of the Sycamore Company.

Ethical issues

The task of preparing the relevant cost comparisons as the basis of evaluating Birch Vale's bid to supply the saddles for the Sycamore Company was given to Sycamore's assistant accountant, Elmer Beechworth. The data Elmer gathered were based on his assumption that the fixed facilities could be sub-let for $12 000 and, therefore, showed a difference in favour of buying the saddles from Birch Vale of $2000. Elmer sent a draft copy of his calculations independently to both his boss, Frances Gipani, and the manager of the saddle department, Kit Willow, for their comments prior to preparing a formal proposal for the Board.

At 5.00 pm that afternoon his boss walked into the office. Her words were:

This is a good report on the Birch Vale bid. It can pretty much go to the Board as it is. Just one change I'd suggest. The opportunity cost of the space—it's way too conservative. I rang a couple of friends in property rentals today and both agreed with me that $30 000 would not be out of the question.

The problem we've got is that, if we use the $12 000, the difference in favour of buying from Birch is very small—it's line ball and the Board probably won't go for it. They'll say if that's all the difference is we should keep it in-house. But we really should be subcontracting a lot more than we are. I've been pushing this for a long time and the saddle department is a prime candidate to go. It gives us labour trouble and, quite frankly, I can't stand Willow—he's getting too powerful around here.

By the way, I'm writing your annual performance report at the moment. Let me see the revised figures before we finalise them for the Board please.

At home that evening, Elmer received a telephone call from Willow.

That's a good report you did on the Birch Vale bid. Just one change I'd suggest. The opportunity cost of the space—it's a bit optimistic, isn't it? I rang a couple of mates today and they said that, in the present climate, we'd be very lucky to get anywhere near $12 000. More likely, it would sit vacant for quite some time.

Given that, I don't think we should be giving the Board any false impressions here. If they do go with Birch and close my department down, they won't get it back in a hurry if we subsequently see Birch jack up the price when they've got us. And you won't look too flash if insult is added to injury through the facilities sitting idle. We'd be caught both ways, and you might have some answering to do.

I wouldn't like to see that happen because I think you've got a real future here. I hear that Gipani is thinking of leaving. You'd certainly have my vote for chief accountant. Let me see the revised figures before we finalise them for the Board. And don't forget to push what might happen to price and quality if Birch were to get the nod.

What should Elmer do?

Summary

The concepts discussed in this chapter provide the basis for the next three chapters, which are concerned with information for management decisions.

The management purposes for which accounting information may be required are planning, decision making and control. Costs may be classified and accumulated in different ways to make them relevant for different purposes. Cost classification schemes were approached from the concepts of the nature of the costs themselves, their traceability to cost objects, their behaviour patterns in relation to specific activity variables, their controllability at different management levels, and their relevance to specific decisions.

Discussion of in-text cases

Case 23.1

The cost per suit of $450 provides Ashley with useful information for setting the normal selling price for the year as it encompasses all the costs that need to be covered in order to remain in business. But it does not provide sufficient information about the nature of the costs to allow adjustments to the selling price during the year.

The direct materials and labour costs are different in nature from the lease costs. For each suit made, Ashley will incur costs of $120 for materials and $250 for labour. For each suit not made, Ashley will not have to incur these costs. By contrast, the lease costs are a fixed amount that must be met for the year irrespective of how many suits are made and sold.

We are to assume a price of $400 was offered for a suit. The price offered is well below the normal selling price and is also below the product cost. However, if at the time orders were below the level expected and there was considerable spare machine capacity, Ashley may decide to accept the offer. The price covers the costs of materials and labour required to make the suit and contributes a surplus of $30 to the fixed lease costs.

If already able to sell all that can be produced, it would be unwise to accept this offer as Ashley would need to forgo $675 to receive $400. However, if there is excess production capacity, Ashley will be $30 'better off' as a result of this sale. Apart from the financial analysis, Ashley needs to consider whether any of the regular customers are likely to be upset by the sale if they hear of it.

Case 23.2

When the number of copies decreased by 8200 (i.e. 13 400 – 5200), the cost dropped by $164. Hence, the charge per copy is 2 cents. This is the amount that is relevant to your decision since the fixed charge will have to be paid whether you allow others to

> use the machine or not. Assuming you will not be contravening the terms of your contract, you can make a 'profit' of 3 cents on every copy that the shop manager makes.
>
> If the variable cost is $0.02 per copy, the fixed monthly charge is $(304 − 0.02 × 5200)$. This is $200 per month. The same answer is obtained by calculating $(468 − 0.02 × 13\ 400)$.

Review exercises

Discussion questions

23.1 List and describe four functions of management.

23.2 Describe what is meant by and give an example of:

(a) an opportunity cost
(b) a direct cost
(c) a variable cost
(d) a semi-variable cost

23.3 Define and give some examples of a 'cost object'.

23.4 Sales staff's salaries may be considered as a direct or indirect cost depending on the object of analysis. Explain.

23.5 'A fixed cost is one which never changes.' Explain why you agree or disagree with this statement.

23.6 'The assumption of linearity of variable costs does not hold. Cost analysis based on this assumption is therefore simplistic and not very useful.' Explain why you agree or disagree with this statement.

23.7 Explain the following:

(a) contribution margin
(b) incremental costs
(c) relevant costs

23.8 'The training of staff does not change with the volume of production so it must be a fixed cost, but last year our manager cut staff training during the year because it looked as if other costs were going to exceed budgeted costs. Training doesn't seem to be fixed or variable! And now we are having equipment break-downs because of misuse.' Discuss the nature of the training costs and how the manager can be encouraged to maintain adequate training levels.

23.9 Lostralia Post offers a mail and package courier delivery service. It has been approached by Heaven's Devils, an entrepreneurial motorcycle club that has bought 50 metropolitan street directories and is planning on going into the courier business. Heaven's Devils has quoted Lostralia Post a weekly fee for carrying out all its courier delivery work. An analysis of existing costs, including the wages of its own couriers, the running costs of its courier vehicle fleet and the cost of funds tied up in the vehicles, shows that Lostralia Post would be well ahead financially if it accepted the Heaven's Devils offer. Identify and discuss any other factors Lostralia Post should take into account before making a decision.

23.10 Discuss the importance of opportunity costs in a 'make or buy' decision, and give some examples of such costs.

23.11 Describe what is meant by and give an example of value-adding and non-value-adding costs.

23.12 You wish to rent a car for three days, and have obtained prices from two rental companies. Company A quotes a rate of $90 per day all-inclusive for unlimited mileage. Company B offers a rate of $65 per day plus 25 cents per kilometre. Which company should you rent from?

 Problems

23.13 *Cost behaviour*

1. A. Romeo is complaining about the high cost of running a Ferrari. Romeo drives 30 000 kilometres a year and, based on the following costs, estimates the car is costing 30 cents per kilometre.

Petrol—5 000 litres @ 55c	$ 2 750
Services and tuning—3 @ $750	2 250
Tyre replacements—every 30 000 km	720
Insurance	1 200
Registration	450
Depreciation	4 000
	$11 370

Romeo's accountant suggests that the cost per kilometre would be halved if the car were driven twice as many kilometres.

Explain what is wrong with the accountant's reasoning. How would each item of cost change if Romeo drove the car twice as many kilometres?

2. Draw a graph, with total dollar cost on the vertical axis and units of production on the horizontal axis, to represent each of the following costs:

   (a) cost of direct materials used
   (b) cost of direct labour used
   (c) cost of electricity (a fixed base charge per period plus a variable charge after a certain level of kilowatt hours is reached)
   (d) rent on factory building
   (e) salary costs for supervisors (one supervisor is required for up to 1000 units of product, two if production is between 1000 and 2000 units, etc.)

3. Congleton Foods Ltd manufactures canned meat foodstuffs. Below is a selection of the costs accumulated by the accounting department for the company. Assuming the cost object is the product, classify each of these costs into direct or indirect. Also classify each cost as variable or fixed in respect of its expected reaction to changes in volume of production.

   (a) raw meat purchased for cooking and canning
   (b) salary of factory supervisor
   (c) electricity power costs of cooking equipment and can-filling equipment

      (d) depreciation on cooking equipment

      (e   cost of tin cans

      (f) salary of food taster and quality control supervisor

      (g) cost of labels for cans

      (h) lubricants for can-filling equipment

      (i)   cost of general manager's Rolls Royce

      (j)   cost of road freight for product distribution

4. H. Coppini owns a number of photocopying service shops. Coppini is trying to determine how specific items of cost in the business react to changes in the volume of photocopying carried out. Having seen the following graphs in a cost accounting textbook, Coppini is trying to match up specific cost items with the graphs.

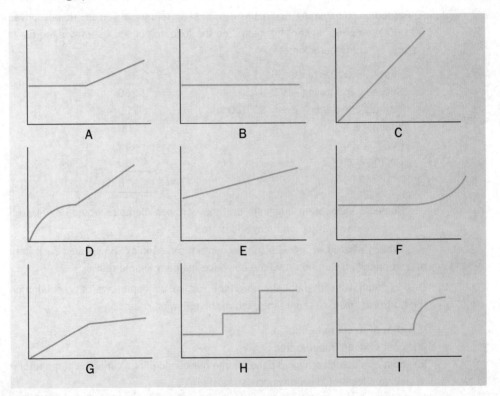

    The vertical axis on each graph represents total dollar cost and the horizontal axis represents volume of relevant activity.

    For each of the following nine cost items, determine which graph best represents the behaviour of the cost item in respect to changes in volume.

(a) The cost of paper used in photocopying, assuming Coppini has to pay the same price per ream irrespective of the quantity.

(b) The cost of paper used in photocopying, assuming Coppini pays one price per ream for the first thousand reams and a lower price per ream thereafter.

(c) The salary of Coppini's daughter who is an accountant employed by Coppini to do all the accounting reports and tax returns.

(d) Telephone expense that is based on a fixed rental and equipment charge each period plus a uniform charge per call.

(e) Electricity expense that is levied as a flat charge up to a specified number of kilowatt-hours, plus a variable cost per kilowatt-hour thereafter.

(f) The cost of service and repairs to the photocopy machines. A service contract with the suppliers requires Coppini to pay a fixed fee per period plus a charge for each service call.

(g) The wages cost of staff in the shops who carry out the photocopying work for customers. One person can handle about 20 hours of photocopying work each week. If volume goes above that in any shop Coppini has to put on a second person. If volume exceeds 40 hours, a third person is needed, and so on.

(h) Cost of toner for the photocopy machines. The supplier charges a lower cost per container as the number of containers bought increases. That is, one container costs $10, two cost $19.80, three cost $29.40, etc. There is a minimum cost per container of $9.

(i) Water rates that are levied as a flat rate up to a prespecified consumption and then charged as excess rates as follows:

> first 10 000 excess litres charged at x cents per litre
> second 10 000 excess litres charged at $2x$ cents per litre
> third 10 000 excess litres charged at $3x$ cents per litre.

5. In the context of engineered, committed and discretionary costs, explain what kind of costs are likely to be incurred in the following:

(a) a research and development department
(b) a marketing department
(c) an aircraft manufacturer
(d) an airline company
(e) a hotel.

23.14 *Contribution margin analysis*

Hill Farm Products produces two types of concentrate fertilisers, HFC1 and HFC2. They are made in the same factory and with the same production equipment. Only the raw materials and the direct labour times differ between the two products. Hill Farm's sales staff deal with produce stores, garden shops and nurseries and represent and sell both products. The accountant calculates the profit of each fertiliser as follows:

	HFC1	HFC2
	$ per kg	*$ per kg*
Sales price	89.00	62.00
less Costs:		
Raw materials	25.00	8.00
Direct labour	10.00	18.00
Variable factory overhead	23.00	11.50
Fixed factory overhead	8.90	4.45
Sales staff's salaries	14.00	10.00
Total costs	80.90	51.95
Profit	8.10	10.05

Variable and fixed overheads are apportioned to each product on the basis of the equipment time required to produce a kilogram of each product. Sales staff's salaries are apportioned to each product on the basis of the relative sales prices. Thus, the amount of $14 apportioned to HFC1 is the result of ($89/$151) × $24.

(a) Calculate the contribution margin for each product.

(b) Assume production capacity is limited, but market demand for either product is unlimited. How (i.e. in what proportion) should production capacity be allocated between the two products?

(c) Assume production capacity is limited and there is also a limit on the market demand for each product. How (i.e. in what proportion) should production capacity be allocated between the two products?

23.15 *Relevant costs, pricing decision*

At 30 June 1999 Oswell Products has 25 000 1999 diaries still in stock. Originally Oswell priced the diaries at $10 each, based on the following costs:

Variable production costs per unit	$5.00
Variable selling costs per unit	0.50
Fixed production costs per unit	1.00
Fixed selling costs per unit	1.50
	$8.00

Oswell realises that it cannot hope to sell the diaries at normal prices, and has to decide on one of the following alternative courses of action:

(i) Scrap the diaries immediately.

(ii) Sell the diaries to the Toland Department Store, which has offered $65 000 for the lot. Toland would collect the diaries from Oswell's warehouse.

(iii) Discount the diaries to $3.00 and attempt to sell them through normal channels.

(a) Identify the relevant costs and revenues of each alternative and suggest which alternative Oswell should take.

(b) If Toland Department Store withdrew its offer, what is the minimum discount price Oswell could use to be no worse off than if it scrapped the diaries?

23.16 *Relevant costs, special order*

Matsuya Products Ltd manufactures decorative rice-paper lanterns, which are sold to retail stores at $14 per unit. The manufacturing cost per unit has been determined at $8.75, made up as follows:

	Cost per unit
Direct materials	$2.50
Direct labour	3.00
Variable manufacturing overhead	2.00
Fixed manufacturing overhead	1.25
	$8.75

In addition, the company estimates the costs of selling and distributing the product as variable $1.75 per unit and fixed 50 cents per unit.

Dutton Department Store has offered to buy 2000 lanterns from Matsuya Products at $10.50 per unit. The lanterns will be stamped with Dutton's name and logo, and will be used for promotional displays within the store.

Determine whether Matsuya Products should accept the order from Dutton. Provide calculations and reasoning to support your answer.

23.17 *Relevant costing, make or buy decision*

Kehane Electronics develops and manufactures stereo sound equipment. One of the company's products, a portable long-range radio receiver, has the following costs per unit:

Direct materials	$12.50
Direct labour	15.00
Variable manufacturing overhead	10.00
Fixed manufacturing overhead	9.50
	$47.00

The radio is sold to retailers for $75.00 per unit. Variable selling and distribution costs are $4.50 per unit, and fixed costs $2.50 per unit.

Kehane has been approached by Waseda Ltd with an offer to produce the radios on a contracting basis for $45.00 per unit. Waseda would manufacture the radios and Kehane would continue to market and distribute them under the Kehane brand name.

Kehane's production manager favours rejecting the offer because it would result in idle production capacity. The marketing manager, however, claims that the idle capacity could be used to produce a new product, a personal stereo cassette unit which attaches to the wearer's belt and plays through a set of headphones. The marketing department is currently evaluating the feasibility of this new product, and estimates that it will yield a contribution margin per unit of $16.00.

(a) Assume Kehane decides not to produce the new product and will therefore have idle production equipment if Waseda's offer is accepted. Should Kehane accept Waseda's offer? Support your answer with calculations and reasoning.

(b) Assume the capacity released from the production of radios will be used to produce the new product. Should Kehane accept Waseda's offer? Show calculations and reasoning.

(c) What other factors should be taken into account before deciding to accept or reject Waseda's offer?

23.18 *Value-adding and non-value-adding costs*

Chris Tan was curious about the length of time taken in his department to convert raw materials into finished goods. In particular he was concerned with the high investment in work in progress inventories. Chris asked his management accountant to measure the throughput time for various batches of raw material during the week and to report on the average time taken. The management accountant recognised this as an opportunity to demonstrate the benefits of activity analysis. She therefore analysed the total throughput time and presented Chris with the following information:

Production line 1	25 minutes
Production line 2	55 minutes
Quality control inspection	35 minutes

Movements	45 minutes
Storing	55 minutes

(a) Calculate value-adding time as a percentage of throughput time.

(b) Identify the costs that will be incurred during non-value-adding time and discuss how they may be contained.

Case studies

23.19 *Marginal and full costing*

This case is based on an episode of the British television series *Yes, Prime Minister*, in which a dog gets through a security fence at a military installation on Salisbury Plain and becomes stranded inside a minefield. The dog is a child's pet and the local and national media become involved. Viewers of nationwide television watch live as the trapped animal races around inside the enclosure, its distraught young owner crying outside the fence and expecting her pet to be blown to pieces any second. Sniffing an opportunity for publicity and popularity, a government minister authorises a major military exercise to rescue the dog. The exercise involves three army helicopters and their crews, 100 personnel based at the installation deployed to traffic and crowd control, and a top veterinarian in private practice in London flown by the minister's personal jet to the scene of the incident.

The helicopters hover over the minefield while crew members are winched down to entice the dog with its favourite food. The dog is caught, strapped into a cradle, and swung over the enclosure fence, where it is checked out by the vet, and then returned to the child by the government minister to tumultuous acclaim. The exercise from conception through planning to execution took 15 hours.

The following day the media ask embarrasing questions about the cost of the rescue exercise. The government minister asks a staff member to work out the cost (and convert it to Australian dollars) and is horrified when the staff member presents the following:

1. *Personnel*

    (a) Army personnel deployed to crowd control

Average annual salary per man	$40 000
plus Provisions for employee benefits	$20 000
Effective annual salary costs	$60 000
Annual effective work hours per person—1350	
Cost per hour	$ 44.44
times 15 hours for operation	$666.60
times 100 personnel	$66 660

    (b) Helicopter crew

    - calculated on similar basis to army personnel $16 875

    (c) Rescue co-ordinator—commander of installation

    - calculated on similar basis to above $ 1 111

    (d) Veterinarian

    - cash paid to vet for services $ 250

2. *Non-personnel*

Fuel for helicopters	$ 600
Fuel for ministerial jet	$ 350
Lunch for veterinarian at local pub	$ 40
Cost of dog food	$ 2
Total cost of operation	$ 85 888

Required

(a) If you were a member of the opposition with access to the above information, what would you claim to be the cost of the rescue operation? What concept or classification of costs would you be using?

(b) If you were the minister, seeking to downplay the claim of the opposition member in part (a), what would you contend was the real cost of the rescue operation? What concept or classification of costs would you be using?

23.20 *Product profitability, retention or abandonment decision*

Hazel Grove Hardware Products manufactures two products, lawnmowers and garden mulchers. The two products are made in separate departments housed within the same factory. The profit of $772 000 recorded by the company for the last year has been broken down by product as follows:

	Lawnmowers $000s	Mulchers $000s	Total $000s
Sales	5850	1170	7020
less Costs:			
Direct material	2340	350	2690
Direct labour	580	55	635
Departmental variable overhead	468	82	550
Departmental fixed overhead	878	585	1463
Selling costs	175	35	210
Administrative costs	583	117	700
Total costs	5024	1224	6248
Net profit	826	(54)	772

The selling costs relate primarily to the salaries of the sales staff who handle both products. These costs are therefore apportioned to each product on the basis of sales revenue. Thus, the selling cost for lawnmowers was calculated as (5850/7020) × 210.

The same allocation basis is used to apportion the administrative costs of the company to each of the two products.

One of the company's directors, Chris Green, has made the comment that garden mulchers are unprofitable and that without them the company would have recorded a profit of $826 000 for the year. Another director, Les Fingers, says that Hazel Grove should stop making garden mulchers.

Required

(a) Do you agree with Chris's comment? If not, explain what is wrong with Chris's reasoning and determine what the profit of the company would have been last year without the mulchers. Attempt to devise a better format for the product profitability report that may help Chris understand the situation better.

(b) Do you agree with Les's comment? What other information or factors would you want to take into account before making a decision on the retention or abandonment of the mulchers?

23.21 *Product profitability and cost allocation*

To supplement a salary of $45 000 as a chartered accountant, G. Leslie runs a small business constructing concrete swimming pools. Leslie has enough labourers to keep construction on two pools going at any one time and each pool takes roughly a month to complete. The labourers are paid on an hourly basis.

Leslie has only one permanent employee, G. Foreman, to whom Leslie pays an annual salary. Foreman supervises the on-site constructions. All earthmoving equipment is hired as required.

Leslie has only two plans for the pools, a standard rectangular pool and a multi-level, oval-shaped pool.

In a conversation with Leslie one evening, Foreman says: 'In my opinion you should drop the oval pools completely and concentrate on the standard ones. They take about the same time to complete, but when we're working on one of each, I reckon I spend 80 per cent of my time making sure they get the oval pool right. If they don't get it right, an oval will crack when the water flows in. The standard ones are a dream by comparison. Ten minutes a day are all I need to know things are okay. There's plenty of demand for either pool; it's just a matter of talking the customer into one or the other. Plus you don't make nearly as much money on the ovals. Here's the figures to prove it.'

	Standard pool	Oval pool
Selling price	$10 000	$13 000
less Materials and labour	6 000	8 000
Supervision*	800	3 200
Profit	$ 3 200	$ 1 800

*Foreman has based the supervision cost on his own salary of $48 000 per year spread over 12 standard pools and 12 oval pools produced during a year.

Instead of dropping the oval pools, Leslie:

(i)   fires Foreman

(ii) gives up his job as a chartered accountant

(iii) drops the standard pools

Required

Explain why Leslie took each of these actions.

23.22 *Relevant costing*

The Ginza Company produces and distributes a range of automotive parts for Japanese motor vehicles. The unit costs of producing and selling one of Ginza's products, Product G–14, are as follows:

	Cost per unit
Production	
Direct materials	$2.50
Direct labour	3.00
Variable overhead	2.00
Fixed overhead	1.25
Selling	
Variable	3.75
Fixed	2.25

The fixed costs per unit are based on a monthly production and sales volume of 20 000 units. The normal selling price of the product is $15.

Each of the following questions is independent of the others.

(a) At what unit cost would G–14 appear in Ginza's balance sheet as inventory?

(b) What is the unit cost on which Ginza bases its normal price for G–14?

(c) Ginza's fixed costs per unit are based on a monthly production and sales volume of 20 000 units. What is the total cost of production and sale of:

(i) 20 000 units?

(ii) 19 000 units?

(iii) 21 000 units?

(d) Ginza currently sells to vehicle manufacturers and spare-part dealers in its home country. It is bidding for an export order for 5000 units of G–14 with a view to obtaining a foothold in the export market. Consequently Ginza is prepared to quote a break-even price for the order—that is, a price where it will make no profit but incur no loss on the order. The 5000 units can be produced from existing idle capacity in Ginza's plant. Costs of shipping the product to Ginza's agent in the foreign country are $2.00 per unit. Additionally, Ginza will pay the agent a flat fee of $5000 plus a commission of $1.00 per unit. What is the total price Ginza will quote for the order?

(e) Ginza has received a proposal from Hibiya Products Ltd, a company currently facing substantial excess production capacity. Hibiya has offered to act as a sub-contractor for Ginza, producing G–14 and distributing it directly to Ginza's customers. Ginza estimates that if it accepts Hibiya's offer:

(i) Ginza's fixed selling costs would remain unchanged, but variable selling costs for G–14 would be eliminated completely.

(ii) Ginza's plant would lie idle but a warehouse currently used by the section producing G–14 for the storage of materials would no longer be required. Ginza is currently leasing the warehouse for $2000 per month.

(iii) Of the three production supervisors currently required in the G–14 production section, two would be retrenched and one would be transferred to another section. Each supervisor is currently being paid $1250 per month.

Required

Hibiya has offered to produce and distribute G–14 at a price to Ginza of $12 per unit. Should Ginza accept Hibiya's offer?

23.23 *Controllable costs, manager performance evaluation*

T. Cole submitted the following estimate of costs for his department for the following year:

Materials	$ 467 000
Salaries	256 000
Cleaning costs (subcontracted)	24 000
Equipment depreciation	97 000
Building depreciation	112 000
Other occupancy costs (insurance, rates, etc.)	52 000
Training	25 000
Power	40 000
	$1 073 000

Cole's manager responded with a directive that the costs must not exceed $997 890 during the next year as management would only approve the cost budget if it were reduced by 7 per cent. In this firm, managers' performance evaluation is based on their ability to keep costs within their approved total cost budget.

Required

Discuss what Cole can do. Also evaluate the firm's policy with regard to budget approvals and manager performance evaluations.

23.24 *Activity-based management*

The management of Sevenoaks Shaving Products has predicted that the following activities and costs will apply to their three products in the year 200X:

	Smooth Shaver	Groovy Razor	Whisker Shaper
Direct materials per unit	$36	$28	$25
Direct labour per unit	$12	$10	$14
No. of units	100 000	75 000	30 000
No. of set-ups	100	120	150
Total machine hours	100 000	100 000	60 000
No. of parts per unit	6	5	10

After costing the products by using the activity-based costing method, and comparing the costs with the anticipated market prices for Smooth Shaver, Groovy Razor and Whisker Shaper, it appears that the Smooth Shaver will show a larger than average profit margin (i.e. profit as a percentage of sales price), that Groovy Razor will return a profit margin close to that desired, but that Whisker Shaper, designed for a specialist market among the bearded and moustached population, will not be a profitable line.

Required

Can you make any suggestions with regard to making the Whisker Shaper more profitable?

CHAPTER 24

Accounting for long-term management planning

Learning objectives

In this chapter you will be introduced to:

1. the role of long-term planning in an organisation

2. the benefits obtainable from long-term planning

3. the analysis of feasibility and benefit factors with regard to capital investment proposals

4. the relative advantages and disadvantages of using non-discounted cash flow and discounted cash flow methods of capital investment financial analysis

5. how to derive the after-tax net cash flows over the life of capital investment projects

6. how to calculate the accounting rate of return, payback period, net present value and internal rate of return for capital investment projects

7. discounted cash flow financial analysis methods

8. implementation audits and post-implementation audits.

Introduction

Planning is the process by which a manager considers the future, determines alternative courses of action, evaluates those alternatives and chooses among them. As a rational systematic approach to achieving objectives, planning is a basic management function that applies to managers at all levels in an organisation. Decisions to be made during the planning process include selection of objectives as well as determining the means of attaining them. The pre-determination of these objectives and preferred courses of action facilitates decision making during the period the plan is operational.

The need for planning arises from changes in the economic, technological, social, political and market environments confronting an organisation. Change provides both opportunities and risk for an organisation. Planning seeks to identify, anticipate and take advantage of the opportunities and to minimise the risk associated with them.

Management planning has two phases: strategic planning, involving long-term decisions, and operational planning, involving short-term decisions. This chapter examines the economic techniques designed to assist strategic planning through quantifying and evaluating the financial consequences of long-term decisions. The qualitative aspects associated with long-term management planning are also considered.

Elements in the planning process

The planning process includes the following steps:

1. Setting the primary goals and objectives. Primary goals are long term in nature and may relate to the growth of the company, its market position, rates of return on the funds invested in the company, or the market price of the company's shares. Objectives may be concerned with sales volume, production levels and financial performance in the immediate future period.
2. Determining specific paths to meet those goals and objectives. This involves a search for opportunities, which will be based on assumptions about the future and expectations arising from those assumptions. It also involves prediction of events both within the organisation and external to it, such as changes in demand, competition and technology.
3. Identifying specific alternative courses of action. Assumptions, expectations and predictions need to be translated into alternative possible courses of action for the organisation.
4. Evaluating the alternatives and selecting the best alternative in line with the goals of the organisation.

You will see from these elements of the planning process that both internal and external factors are concerned. It helps to perform a formal analysis of the relevant factors. A methodical approach to analysing the internal and external operating environment is called a SWOT analysis, in which the internal strengths and weaknesses of the organisation, and the external opportunities and threats, are identified. The analysis encourages planners to take advantage of internal strengths and external opportunities in their plans. It also draws attention to any plans that depend on areas of internal weakness being strengthened, or on external threats being overcome.

Advantages of planning

A formal planning process has several advantages.

1. Planning facilitates the systematic determination and regular review of long-term and short-term goals and objectives. Planning is directed towards achieving organisational goals and consequently focuses attention on those goals.

2. Planning stimulates the identification of contingencies that need to be covered, such as the possible need for additional finance.
3. Planning may relieve management of routine decisions. Plans, once formalised and communicated to people responsible for carrying them out, allow routine decisions to be delegated to lower levels of management.
4. Planning facilitates economic operations within the organisation. Effective planning results in the substitution of deliberate decisions for snap judgements, and directed effort and work flow for uncoordinated activity. This should allow effective use of organisational resources because of the emphasis on efficient and consistent operations.
5. Planning provides the ability to simulate activities in advance. Computers may be used to simulate wear and tear rates on equipment and estimate the timing of repairs and possible replacement. Simulation models may be used to incorporate a vast number of possible variations in sales and cost levels and facilitate production and marketing decisions.
6. Planning allows for 'lead time'; that is, the unavoidable time between taking a decision (to replace an item of equipment for example) and seeing that decision materialise (having the new equipment installed and ready for use).
7. Planning stimulates adherence to the achievement of goals and objectives and facilitates control. Control can only be exercised over future events and may be encouraged through the need for explanation when a divergence from formally presented plans occurs.
8. Planning provides a measure against which the performance of managers and economic units can be evaluated.

Long-term management planning

The planning function of management has two phases: strategic planning, involving long-term decisions, and operational planning, involving short-term decisions. Short-term decisions may be characterised by a relatively short time span (e.g. a year) and consequently need to be made within the constraints of the organisation's existing productive and technological capability as well as its existing product or service lines and markets.

Long-term decisions usually involve changes in the firm's productive or technological capability (e.g. to replace or purchase additional production equipment or to adopt new technologies) or in its product or service lines and markets (e.g. produce new products, provide new services or expand into new markets). These decisions typically require large investments of resources, which are committed for relatively long time periods.

Similarly, the benefits from these investments are expected to accrue over an extended time span. The resources invested in developing a new product or service and its market are expected to yield a return to the organisation in the form of worthwhile sales over the life of the product or service. The resources invested in replacing or acquiring additional production equipment allow the firm to operate at a higher level of capacity for the life of the equipment.

Decisions of this type, or similar decisions such as engaging in mineral exploration or undertaking major research and development projects, are termed 'capital investment decisions'. The process of analysing major long-term projects with the purpose of deciding on their acceptance or rejection is termed 'capital budgeting', or 'capital investment analysis'.

This evaluation of capital investments is important for organisations in both the private and the public sectors. A distinction between these organisations is that those in the private sector have predominantly commercial objectives, whereas those in the public sector have both commercial and social (or community service) objectives. Commercial ventures will require the selection of high-return investments, but even investments under community service obligations carry a responsibility to plan for the efficient use of resources and to select between alternative investments. Whether the undertaking of a project is discretionary or required, the economic analysis is equally important:

- In examining a project that is discretionary, management will seek to maximise the financial benefits from the investment needed for the project.
- In examining a project that is required, management will seek to minimise the investment for the level of benefit that is to be provided. There will typically be alternative ways of providing that level of benefit, with different investment or cost levels.

In either case, therefore, economic quantification of the benefits and costs of alternatives is required.

The question of whether a private sector steel manufacturing company should build another blast furnace, for example, is no different from whether a public sector power generation authority should build another power station. Both decisions require quantification of the economic costs and benefits of the increase in productive capacity resulting from the investment of capital required to provide the capacity. Although the ultimate decision may be made on different cost–benefit weightings, resulting from different expectations of the groups with vested interests in each organisation and the different governmental and political influences on each organisation, the economic analysis required to quantify those benefits and costs is equally important in each context.

Capital investment analysis

The purposes of capital investment analysis are to provide management with relevant information and criteria to enable:

- a decision to be reached on whether a specific capital investment proposal should be accepted or rejected
- a selection to be made among two or more mutually exclusive proposals. (Mutually exclusive proposals occur when the acceptance of one precludes the acceptance of the others, for example the choice between a 20 cm or a 25 cm gas pipeline.)
- a ranking of non-mutually-exclusive proposals where the resources of the organisation are not sufficient to undertake all projects.

Before subjecting a capital investment proposal to what may be a costly and time-consuming financial analysis, it should undergo other feasibility and benefit analyses. Only if the projects prove to be feasible and of benefit should they have full financial analyses performed on them.

Feasibility factors

A financial analysis of a project becomes irrelevant if the project will not meet requirements, or cannot be operated, financed or completed in time to meet its need. Failure for any of these reasons means that the project is not feasible, despite any projected financial advantage. A TOES[1] analysis considers these feasibility factors:

- Technical feasibility—does the necessary technology exist and will the project meet the identified needs of the organisation?
- Operational feasibility—do the necessary procedures exist for the successful implementation and operation of the project, do employees have the necessary skills or can they readily acquire them, and is there employee support for the project?
- Economic feasibility—does the organisation have the necessary funds for the project and will top management be prepared to direct such funds to the project?
- Schedule feasibility—can the project be implemented by the time it is needed to be operational?

---

[1] J. G. Burch, *Cost and Management Accounting: A Modern Approach*, West Publishing Company, St Paul, MN, 1994.

Benefit factors

Both tangible and intangible benefits should be itemised when assessing the viability of a project. Tangible benefits are directly attributable to the project and are measured, whereas intangible benefits are less readily linked to the project or measured.

Quantifying feasibility and benefit factors

Many managers are uncomfortable with making decisions based on data that is only qualifiable. Unfortunately the conversion of such data to numbers tends to be quite arbitrary yet gives an appearance of decisiveness. However, in the circumstance in which managers require quantified data, the feasibility and benefit factors can be presented by assigning the level of feasibility for each feasibility factor on a scale from 1 to 10, and similarly assigning the level of benefit for each identified benefit to be gained from the project. The whole may be reduced to one figure for comparison with alternative projects by weighting the importance of each factor (e.g. scheduling may sometimes be more important than others) and multiplying the weighting by the rate of that factor on the 10-point scale. These multiples are then added, as in Figure 24.1 in which the overall feasibility rating is 6.1. A similar overall rating can be derived for benefits.

Figure 24.1 Feasibility rating[2]

Feasibility factors	Rating	Weighting	Weighted value
Technical	9	10%	0.9
Operational	7	20	1.4
Economic	5	40	2.0
Schedule	6	30	1.8
		100%	6.1

Feasible projects that have sufficient projected benefits can proceed to a full financial analysis. Alternatively, the feasibility and benefit analyses may have been used to select the most feasible and beneficial projects from a wide range of alternatives, and this selection would proceed to a financial analysis for further prioritisation or selection.

Simple capital investment financial analysis

Two simplified approaches to capital investment financial analysis are the 'accounting rate of return method' and the 'payback' method.

Accounting rate of return method

The accounting rate of return method estimates and compares the long-term profitability of alternative capital investment proposals on a conventional accrual accounting basis. It is calculated as the ratio (or percentage) of the average annual profit generated by the investment to the amount of the initial investment. In some applications of the accounting rate of return the average investment in the project, rather than the initial investment, is used as the denominator in the ratio calculation.

---

[2] ibid., p. 1059.

Assume, for example, that the chief architect in a state government public works department is considering the purchase of some new computer-assisted design and drafting (CADD) equipment. This equipment will increase the productivity of the department and produce savings in both the staff architects' salaries and architectural consultants' fees. Two pieces of equipment are available, labelled CADD system A and CADD system B. Each system will cost $5000 initially, and will be depreciated using the straight-line method. However, it is estimated that the reduction in costs will occur differently over the five years of each system's expected life. The expected cost savings are as follows:

| System | Year | | | | |
	1	2	3	4	5
	$	$	$	$	$
A	5000	4000	3000	2000	1000
B	1000	2000	3000	4000	5000

Due to the investment, total operating costs decrease and total depreciation charges increase. The average change to the profit as a result of the investment may be calculated thus:

| | System | |
Average annual profit from investment	A	B
	$	$
Average annual cost savings ($15 000 ÷ 5)	3000	3000
less Annual depreciation	1000	1000
Average annual incremental profit	2000	2000

The accounting rate of return may therefore be calculated as follows

| | System | |
Accounting rate of return	A	B
	$	$
Average annual profit	2000	2000
Initial investment	5000	5000
Accounting rate of return	40%	40%

Based on accounting rate of return, the two systems are calculated to be equally profitable. However, there is a critical difference between system A and system B that is not reflected in the accounting rate of return. The accounting rate of return is based on an accounting profit measure, whereas it is the cash invested in and recoverable from the project that is important in management's planning decision.

Management invests cash in a capital investment project with the objective of generating an acceptably greater amount of cash from the project over its expected life. Cash is the critical variable in the decision because it has an opportunity cost to the organisation.

The use of cash in a capital investment project forgoes the opportunity to use that cash for another investment purpose.

Similarly, the cash released or recovered from a project may be reinvested by management. It is cash rather than accounting profit that may be reinvested. Consequently, accounting profit, which is derived from cash and non-cash items (for example depreciation), does not provide a valid basis for management's capital investment decisions.

Because the accounting rate of return does not recognise the importance of cash in investment decisions, it cannot accommodate differences in the timing of cash flows generated by capital investment projects. Management would prefer system A in the example because it generates greater cash cost savings in the earlier years. This means that management has more cash available for reinvestment earlier if it chooses system A over system B.

Consequently, it is not only the magnitude of cash flows that is important in capital investment decisions; the timing of cash flows is also important. One method of capital investment analysis that attempts to incorporate these criteria is the payback method.

Payback method

The payback method concentrates on the cash flows associated with a project and takes as its criterion for analysis the time it will require to recover the initial cash invested in the project.

The payback period for the systems in the previous example may be calculated by comparing the initial cash investment in each system with the accumulated cash recovered from cost savings.

	Cash investment	Accumulated cash recovered				
		Years				
		1	2	3	4	5
	$	$	$	$	$	$
System A	5000	5000	9000	12 000	14 000	15 000
System B	5000	1000	3000	6 000	10 000	15 000

The payback period for system A is one year, as the initial cash investment is recovered in the first year of operation. For system B, payback occurs in 2⅔ years (with $3000 recovered in the first two years, there is $2000 to recover in the third year, in which cash savings are $3000). The payback method prefers system A to system B, because the initial cash outlay is recovered more quickly.

The payback method, however, is an inadequate model for capital investment analysis because it fails to recognise the long-term worth of different projects. Assume, for example, that management is evaluating the purchase of one of two CADD systems. Both require an initial outlay of $6000. System X will generate cash savings of $2000 per year for six years; system Y, $2000 per year for ten years.

The payback period for each system is three years ($6000 ÷ 2000 per year), but this analysis does not recognise that system Y is preferable because it has the potential to generate cash savings for a longer period than system X. The payback period analysis ignores what happens after the payback period and is useful only when liquidity is critical or if the project entails a high degree of risk.

Case 24.1 Investment decisions are affected by the time value of money

Consider the situation in which you have $6200 in a bank account earning 5 per cent interest. You are given the opportunity to invest $6000 in one of two projects, each lasting four years. The first one has expected returns over four years of $3000, $2000, $1000 and $500. The second project has expected returns over four years of $1000, $2000, $3000 and $800. After working out the payback period and accounting rate of return you are unsure what to do.

What issues would influence you in your decision whether to invest in one of these projects, and which would you select if you decided to invest in one of them? Before turning to the discussion on the case at the end of this chapter, make notes of the matters you would consider in your deliberations.

Financial criteria for capital investment decisions

As you have seen, the accounting rate of return and payback methods fail to recognise explicitly that money has a time value—that a cash sum of $1 to be received in one or more years' time is not as valuable as $1 received now. Cash available at the present time may be invested and will accumulate to a greater sum at the end of one or more years. The concept of the time value of money is discussed in Appendix 3 and should be revised before proceeding.

Capital investment analysis needs to recognise formally the timing of cash flows as well as their magnitude. Additionally, the analysis needs to incorporate a method that will allow cash flows at any specific time to be compared with cash flows at any other time. This is achieved through the determination of present and future values of cash flows. Moreover, a valid method of capital investment analysis should take account of all the cash flows generated by a project over its expected life.

Methods of capital investment analysis which incorporate these criteria are known as discounted cash flow methods.

Financial information for capital investment decisions

In the capital investment decisions considered, we have included the initial investment and the annual cash benefits. The relevant annual cash flows are all cash flows that change as a result of the investment and are therefore called incremental cash flows. The estimates of the incremental cash flows associated with a capital investment project include the amount of the initial cash outlay (usually incurred at the present time), the amount and timing of cash inflows generated by the project, and the amount and timing of cash outflows required by the project in the future. We need to consider these individually.

Initial cash outlay

The initial cash outlay for a capital investment project will frequently be known or will be relatively simple to estimate. For example, the cost of buying and installing a new piece of equipment may be quoted at $25 000. However, there may be additional factors to consider. Purchase of the new equipment may allow the sale of an existing one at an estimated price of $2000 so that the initial net cash outlay is $23 000.

For other types of capital investment decisions, the initial outlay may be more difficult to determine. For example, in evaluating the feasibility of producing a new product, the initial outlay will consist not only of the cash outlays for new manufacturing equipment, but also the relevant outlays for product and market development. These may be more difficult to estimate than the cash outlay for machinery purchase.

Future cash inflows

The cash inflows to be generated by a project will occur over an extended number of years. In cases such as a decision to introduce a new product, the cash inflows will be represented by the cash sales revenue from the product. In other cases, such as a decision to replace an existing machine with a more efficient one, the cash inflows will be represented by the saving or reduction in cash outflows that the more efficient machine will make over the existing machine.

In each case, however, it is the incremental or differential cash flows generated by the project that are relevant to the analysis. In the case of a new product decision, marketing management may anticipate that sales of the new product will result in lower sales of one or more of the company's other products. If this is so, the incremental cash inflows from the new product would be calculated as the new cash sales revenue less the cash sales revenue that may be lost from other existing products.

The use of incremental cash inflows means that the analysis will examine only those cash flows that are estimated to occur in the future as a consequence of the proposed investment. By implication, the analysis will compare the difference between the total cash flows of the organisation with and without the investment project.

Future cash outflows

The relevant cash outflows needed for the analysis consist of the estimated future incremental cash outlays that will be incurred if the investment project is accepted. In the case of a new product decision, the relevant cash outflows would represent the future payments for production, distribution, advertising and selling costs that would occur over and above the estimated future level of these payments without the new product. Thus, if the product will be handled by the existing sales force, no incremental cash outlays for sales salaries will result from the decision to produce and market the new product. But if it is planned that the company will spend an additional $5000 on advertising the product in each of the first three years of market life, these would be incremental cash outflows.

Beyond the initial cash outlays required for the project, all subsequent cash outflows must be identified and estimated, both in terms of their expected amount and their timing. For example, in the case of a decision to purchase or construct a new warehouse, future estimates of maintenance, repairs, insurance and rate payments would need to be made.

Discount rate

The other informational requirement for discounted cash flow methods of capital investment analysis is the discount rate—that is, the rate at which future cash inflows and outflows will be discounted to make them comparable at a common point in time and to serve as a criterion for a project's desirability.

This rate will be predetermined by management, and will reflect a criterion for acceptance or rejection of an investment project based on the return management requires from the project. The required rate will typically take into account the returns expected by suppliers of debt and equity finance and the risk inherent in any particular project. These factors were discussed in Chapters 11 and 12.

Methods of discounted cash flow analysis

Two alternative approaches to discounted cash flow analysis are the 'net present value' method and the 'internal rate of return' method. These are demonstrated through the following example.

Example: *Discounted cash flow analysis*

Assume that management is considering the automation of one operation in its production process. One of two pieces of equipment may be purchased for this purpose. Each requires an initial cash outlay of $25 000. However, equipment A is estimated to produce equal cash savings in variable production costs over the four years of its expected life, whereas equipment B will produce no cash savings in the first year and increasing savings in the remaining years. The estimated cash flows associated with each piece of equipment are as follows:

| | Cash flows | |
Year	Equipment A	Equipment B
	$	$
0	− 25 000	− 25 000
1	10 000	–
2	10 000	5 000
3	10 000	9 000
4	10 000	35 000

The rate of return required by management is 12 per cent per annum.

The initial cash outlay for each piece of equipment is made at the beginning of the first year (time 0), and all subsequent cash flows occur at the end of the year to which they refer (time 1, 2, 3 etc.).

Net present value method

The net present value method discounts all future cash flows to their present value using the required rate of return as the discount factor. Any cash inflows or outflows occurring at the beginning of the first year (time 0), including the initial cash outlay for the equipment, are already expressed in present-value terms.

The present value of any future cash inflow or outflow is given by:

$$PV = \frac{FV}{(1+r)^n}$$

where PV = present value of the cash sum

FV = cash sum at point of time, n

r = required rate of return

In the example, the present value of the $10 000 at the end of year 4 for equipment A is given by:

$$PV = \frac{\$10\ 000}{(1+0.12)^4} = \$6353$$

The net present value of all cash flows associated with equipment A is given by:

$$NPV = \sum_{t=0}^{n} \frac{FV}{(1+r)^n}$$

Therefore:

$$NPV = -\$25\,000 + \frac{\$10\,000}{(1+r)^1} + \frac{\$10\,000}{(1+r)^2} + \frac{\$10\,000}{(1+r)^3} + \frac{\$10\,000}{(1+r)^4}$$

$$= -\$25\,000 + \$8\,929 + \$7\,974 + \$7\,117 + \$6\,353$$

$$= +\$5373$$

Further explanation

Note that if you invest $8929 at 12 per cent interest for one year, at the end of the year you will have $(8929 + 8929 × .12). This equals $(8929 × 1.12), or $10 000. Similarly, $7117 invested now at 12 per cent will be $10 000 in three years time. To obtain the present values of $10 000 in each of the years, this process was reversed, dividing by (1 + interest rate) for each year of discounting. Of course, this is the same as multiplying by $\dfrac{1}{(1 + \text{interest rate})}$ for each year of discounting:

$$\$10\,000 \times 1/1.12 = \$10\,000 \times 0.8929 = \$8929$$

Tables are available in Appendix 3 to enable the direct calculation of the present values of future cash flows. Using Table A.2 (present value of $1), the following discount factors for four years at a 12 per cent discount rate may be applied to the cash flows for equipment A and B.

Year	Discount factor 12%	Equipment A FV	Equipment A PV	Equipment B FV	Equipment B PV
		$	$	$	$
0	1.000	− 25 000	− 25 000	− 25 000	− 25 000
1	0.893	10 000	8 930	−	−
2	0.797	10 000	7 970	5 000	3 985
3	0.712	10 000	7 120	9 000	6 408
4	0.636	10 000	6 360	35 000	22 260
			5 380		7 653

The net present value (NPV) of the cash flows associated with equipment A is $5380, equipment B, $7653.

Because the cash inflows for equipment A are equal for each year, their present value may be calculated directly using Table A.4 (present value of annuity of $1 in arrears).

$$NPV = -\$25\,000 + \$10\,000\,(3.037)$$
$$= \$5370^3$$

---

[3] The difference in the net present values of equipment A, calculated by discounting single future cash flows and by using an annuity discount rate, results from the rounding of the discount factors.

Further explanation

For equipment A, since each discount factor is multiplied by the same number, you could add those discount factors and then multiply by $10 000. In Table A.4 you will see that this addition is done for you: (0.893 + 0.797) = 1.690, which is found in the 12 per cent column in the row for two periods (2 years in our example). You will find 3.037 in the same column, along the row for four years.

The net present values of both pieces of equipment are positive, indicating that both are acceptable projects when evaluated against management's criteria expressed in the required rate of return, the discount rate. Another way of viewing this is that the present value of estimated cash inflows from the project exceeds the present value of cash outflows.

The projects are mutually exclusive, however, and one piece of equipment must be chosen. Equipment B will be selected because it is estimated to result in a higher NPV than equipment A.

Internal rate of return method

This method also takes account of the amount and timing of cash flows, through the discounting process, in evaluating capital investment projects. The net present value method preselects a discount rate reflecting the acceptability criterion and discounts cash flows at this rate. The resulting NPV may be equal to or greater or less than zero.

By contrast, the internal rate of return method analyses the cash flows to determine the rate at which the NPV will be zero. By this means, it calculates the discount rate that equates the present value of cash inflows generated by the project with the present value of cash outflows. The calculated rate is then compared with management's required rate to determine whether the project is accepted or rejected.

The internal rate of return method sets the NPV formula equal to zero and solves for r, the discount rate:

$$\sum_{t=0}^{n} \frac{FV}{(1 + r)^n} = 0$$

Equipment A:

$$- \$25\ 000 + \frac{\$10\ 000}{(1 + r)^1} + \frac{\$10\ 000}{(1 + r)^2} + \frac{\$10\ 000}{(1 + r)^3} + \frac{\$10\ 000}{(1 + r)^4} = 0$$

$$\frac{\$10\ 000}{(1 + r)^1} + \frac{\$10\ 000}{(1 + r)^2} + \frac{\$10\ 000}{(1 + r)^3} + \frac{\$10\ 000}{(1 + r)^4} = \$25\ 000$$

Solving for r is essentially a trial-and-error process, for which computer programs are available. However, where the cash inflows are uniform, as in the case of equipment A, the internal rate of return (IRR) can be calculated by recognising that the inflows constitute an annuity.

Consequently, the internal rate of return for equipment A can be found from the equation:

$$\$25\ 000 = \$10\ 000(F)$$

where F represents the discount rate for an annuity of $10 000 for four years having a present value of $25 000.

$$F = \frac{\$25\ 000}{\$10\ 000}$$

$$= 2.5$$

By examining Table A.4 on the Year 4 line, it can be seen that a discount factor of 2.5 lies between 20 per cent (2.589) and 22 per cent (2.494).

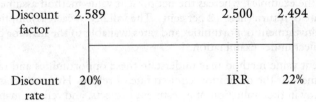

The IRR can be calculated by interpolation.

Discount rate	Discount factor	
20%	2.589	2.589
exact rate		2.500
22%	2.494	
Difference	0.095	0.089

$$\text{Exact rate} = \left(20 + \left(\frac{0.089}{0.095}\right) 2\right) \%$$

$$= 21.87\%$$

Further explanation

You should note that $0.089/0.095 = 0.937$. The temptation is to give an answer of 20.937, but 2.5 lies 93.7 per cent of the way from 20 to 22, not 93.7 per cent of the way from 20 to 21! For this reason, 0.937 must be multiplied by the gap between the discount rates for which annuity factors are known—in this case that gap is 2 per cent. The answer is therefore $(20 + 2 \times 0.937)$ per cent.

Where the cash inflows are not uniform, as in the case of equipment B, the trial-and-error process cannot take advantage of the annuity discount factor, and may be solved using a computer program. The internal rate of return for equipment B is 20.76 per cent.

Comparing the internal rate of return for equipment A (21.87%) and equipment B (20.76%) with the required rate of return (12%) indicates that automation of the process is desirable on this criterion. However, this method prefers equipment A to equipment B, a result which conflicts with the ranking of the equipment using the net present value method.

Comparison of net present value and internal rate of return methods

The net present value and the internal rate of return methods will provide consistent results when the decision is the acceptance or rejection of a single capital investment project. Where the decision involves selection among mutually exclusive projects, the two methods will also provide consistent rankings for selection in most cases.

However, as the example illustrates, there are some cases where the two methods will give inconsistent results. The difference arises from the assumptions about the rate of re-investment of cash inflows generated by projects, which are implicit in each method. The internal rate of return method assumes that cash inflows may be reinvested at the rate generated by the project (i.e. 21.87 per cent and 20.76 per cent respectively for the two pieces of equipment in the example), whereas the net present value method assumes reinvestment at the required rate of return (here 12 per cent). The validity of each assumption will depend on the specific reinvestment opportunities and rates available to the firm for cash flows generated by the project under examination.

The net present value method may understate these opportunities and rates, because it assumes reinvestment at the minimum required rate of return. However, this assumption is applied consistently in the evaluation of investment projects, and reflects management's criteria. By contrast, the opportunities and rates implicit in the internal rate of return method will differ, depending on the rate yielded by the specific project being considered. High-return projects will assume high reinvestment opportunities and rates; low-return projects will assume low reinvestment rates. This may be unrealistic if the project under examination is estimated to produce a very high rate of return, for example 50 per cent. Other opportunities available to the firm are unlikely to produce a similarly high rate on reinvestment.

The net present value method is generally preferred, although internal rates of return are commonly used in practice, because management is often more comfortable dealing with percentage rates of return on projects under examination.

Total and incremental cash flow analysis

Discounted cash flow analysis using the net present value method may be based either on the analysis of total cash flows or incremental cash flows. The total cash flows will be those that relate directly to an alternative course of action. However, when choosing between two alternatives the comparison can be made by evaluating the difference in annual cash flows if one alternative is selected. This option is not available when selecting between more than two alternatives, or when ranking a range of proposals.

Example: *Total versus incremental analysis*

Edale Steel Company currently owns and uses a wire-tying machine in its dispatch department to secure bundles of steel pipes. The machine cost $60 000 when it was purchased three years earlier and has an estimated remaining useful life of five years, at which time its estimated salvage value (realisable price on sale) will be $10 000. The cash operating costs of the machine are anticipated to be $40 000 per year. Also, a major overhaul will be required in two years' time at an expected cost of $11 000.

The company has the opportunity to buy a more efficient machine for $53 000, or for $33 000 if the existing machine is traded in at the time of purchase. The new machine is expected to reduce cash operating costs by $10 000 per year, should not require any major overhaul, and will have a salvage value of $4000 at the end of its expected five-year life.

The company's required rate of return is 16 per cent per annum.

Total cash flow analysis

This decision may be approached by examining the total cash flows of each alternative (keep the existing machine or replace it with the new one), and comparing these total cash flows in net present value terms. The cash flows and the net present value calculations are shown below.

	Cash flows (years)					
	0	1	2	3	4	5
	$	$	$	$	$	$
Keep existing machine:						
Cash operating costs		(40 000)a	(40 000)	(40 000)	(40 000)	(40 000)
Major overhaul			(11 000)			
Salvage value						10 000
Replace:						
Initial outlay	(33 000)b					
Cash operating costs		(30 000)	(30 000)	(30 000)	(30 000)	(30 000)
Salvage value						4 000

a Cash outflows are represented by figures in brackets.

b The trade-in value of the old machine may differ according to the replacement option selected, if more than one alternative were considered. If the old machine were to be sold for $20 000 rather than traded in, this would represent an opportunity cost (the amount forgone by not replacing the machine) that would be part of the cash flows for the old machine, and the initial outlay for the new machine would be $53 000. This would not change the difference between net present values in the next calculation.

NET PRESENT VALUE CALCULATION				
	Cash flow	Nature and timing of cash flow	Discount factor	Present value
Keep existing machine:	$			$
Cash operating costs	(40 000)	Annuity for 5 yrs at 16%	3.214	(130 960)
Major overhaul	(11 000)	Single sum, yr 2 at 16%	0.743	(8 173)
Salvage value	10 000	Single sum, yr 5 at 16%	0.476	4 760
PV of net cash outflows				(154 373)
Replace:				
Initial outlay	(33 000)	Single sum at time 0	1.000	(33 000)
Cash operating costs	(30 000)	Annuity for 5 yrs at 16%	3.274	(98 220)
Salvage value	4 000	Single sum, yr 5 at 16%	0.476	1 904
PV of net cash outflows				(149 316)
Difference in favour of replacement				5 057

Incremental cash flow analysis

Alternatively, the decision could be approached by examining only the incremental or differential cash flows between the alternatives of replacing and keeping the existing machine. The cash flows and the net present value calculations are shown below.

			Cash flows (years)			
	0	1	2	3	4	5
	$	$	$	$	$	$
Replacement cash flows						
less Keep cash flows:						
Initial outlay	(33 000)					
Cash operating costs		10 000	10 000	10 000	10 000	10 000
Overhaul saved			11 000			
Salvage value						(6 000)

	NET PRESENT VALUE CALCULATION			
	Cash flow	Nature and timing of cash flow	Discount factor	Present value
Replacement cash flows	$			$
less Keep cash flows:				
Initial outlay	(33 000)	Single sum at time 0	1.000	(33 000)
Cash operating costs	10 000	Annuity for 5 yrs at 16%	3.274	32 740
Overhaul saved	11 000	Single sum, yr 2 at 16%	0.743	8 173
Salvage value	(6 000)	Single sum, yr 5 at 16%	0.476	(2 856)
Net present value of replacement				5 057

Both approaches to analysing the alternatives reflect the relevance of incremental or differential cash flows, and produce the same net present value in favour of replacement. The incremental approach emphasises the relevance of the differential flows explicitly, and calculates only the net present value of the differences. The total approach calculates the net present value of each alternative. Both of these calculations have been based on pre-tax cash flows and the appropriate discount rate should allow for this. However, it is better to base decisions on analyses of after-tax cash flows, using an appropriate discount rate.

The effect of taxation

Analysis of cash flows for capital investment decisions should take account of the effect of taxation, since taxation payments represent cash flows and different projects will result in different tax payments.

Taxation normally has the effect of reducing the difference between the net present values of cash flows resulting from competing projects. Cash savings from automating a production process, for example, will result in an increase in taxable income, an increase in cash tax payments, and hence a decrease in the after-tax cash savings.

Taxation will affect capital investment analysis in two major ways. First, tax must be paid on any income generated by a capital investment project. Cash *inflows* from a project will *increase* the liability of the company for tax; cash *outflows* (provided they are tax deductible) will *reduce* that liability.

Second, although depreciation is a non-cash item, it is usually deductible from income for taxation purposes. The purchase of a piece of equipment to automate a production process enables the company to reduce its future tax payments through the depreciation allowance. Consequently, although the depreciation charge is not itself relevant in discounted cash flow analysis, its effect on cash flows, through reduced taxation payments, is relevant.

Discounted cash flow analysis should be based on after-tax cash flows. This will require the estimation of taxable income and taxation payments before the cash flows from the project can be analysed. The effect of taxation payments is shown in the next example.

Example: *Effect of taxation on cash-flow analysis*

Kinder Products is carrying out a feasibility study on the introduction of a new product. The product is expected to have a market life of 10 years and generate cash sales revenues of $75 000 in the first year, $90 000 in the second, and $130 000 in each remaining year.

The incremental cash costs of producing and selling the product are estimated to be $50 000 in year 1, $65 000 in year 2, and $90 000 per year from then on.

An initial investment of $100 000 is required for new machinery and equipment to produce the product. This equipment may be sold at the end of 10 years for $15 000. Additionally, a promotion campaign costing $30 000 will be carried out at the beginning of year 1 to launch the product.

The company currently pays tax of 50 per cent on its taxable income. For tax purposes, the promotion campaign costs may be deducted in full in the first year and the new equipment may be depreciated over the 10-year period using the straight-line method. Losses may be carried forward and offset against taxable profits of subsequent years.

ESTIMATION OF TAXABLE PROFITS AND TAX PAYMENTS

	Years		
	1	2	3–10
	$	$	$
Sales revenue	75 000	90 000	130 000
less Operating costs			
Production and selling	50 000	65 000	90 000
Depreciation	8 500	8 500	8 500
Promotion	30 000		
Total costs	88 500	73 500	98 500
Taxable profit (loss)	(13 500)	16 500	31 500
Loss carried forward		(13 500)	
Taxable profit	–	3 000	31 500
Tax payment (50%)	–	1 500	15 750

AFTER-TAX CASH FLOWS

	Time				
	0	1	2	3–10	10
	$	$	$	$	$
Initial outlay (equipment)	(100 000)				
Promotion outlay	(30 000)				
Salvage value (equipment)					15 000
Cash surplus from operations after tax		25 000	23 500	24 250	

The objective of the financial feasibility study is to determine whether the new product is economically worthwhile, given management's required rate of return of 10 per cent. The cash surplus from operations after tax is computed as sales revenue less cash operating costs and less the estimated tax payment for each year. For year 2, this is calculated as:

Sales revenue		$90 000
less Cash operating costs	$65 000	
Tax payment	1 500	66 500
		$23 500

To simplify the example, it has been assumed that the tax is paid in the same year in which the liability to tax arises. Note that the $30 000 promotion campaign costs are a cash outflow at time 0, although it is claimed against tax in the first year of operation.

The net present value calculation for the new product is shown below.

NET PRESENT VALUE CALCULATION

	Cash flow	Discount factor	Present value
	$		$
Initial outlay (equipment)	(100 000)	1.000	(100 000)
Promotion outlay	(30 000)	1.000	(30 000)
Salvage value (equipment)	15 000	0.386	5 790
Cash surplus from			
operations after tax:			
Year 1	25 000	0.909	22 725
Year 2	23 500	0.826	19 411
Years 3–10	24 250	(5.335)(0.826)	106 862
Net present value			24 788

The cash surpluses after tax for years 3–10 have been discounted as an annuity for eight years at 10 per cent per year (discount factor 5.335). The result represents a present value at the beginning of year 3, and this has been further discounted as a single sum at the end of year 2 at 10 per cent (discount factor 0.826).[4]

The net present value of the estimated cash flows for the new product is positive, indicating that the investment in the product is acceptable.

Case 24.2 Allowing for the time value of money

As in Case 24.1, consider the situation in which you have $6200 in a bank account earning 5 per cent interest. You are given the opportunity to invest $6000 in one of two projects, each lasting four years. The first one has expected returns over four years of $3000, $2000, $1000 and $500. The second project has expected returns over four years of $1000, $2000, $3000 and $800.

How would you use discounted cash flow analysis to make your decision? How do you explain the results that you get? Read the discussion of these issues at the end of this chapter before you proceed.

---

[4] An alternative means of calculating this is to take the discount factor for a 2-year annuity from the discount factor for a 10-year annuity, and multiply the difference by the annuity to get the present value: 24 250 (6.145 – 1.736) = 106 918 (difference between this and 106 862 is caused by rounding errors). This method recognises that 24 250 needs to be multiplied by the aggregate of the discount factors for years 3 to 10 inclusive.

Extensions of capital investment analysis

There are many extensions and complications in the analysis of capital investments. Some of the more significant of these are examined below.

Projects having unequal lives

The examples used in this chapter to compare alternative projects using discounted cash flow analysis have assumed that the alternative projects have equal lives or time horizons. A problem may arise when two projects that have different expected life spans need to be compared. Several methods are available to allow such projects to be compared. These include assuming replacement with identical projects up to a common terminal date, assuming infinite replacement with identical projects, and converting the NPV to an equivalent annual cash flow (i.e the annuity that would give the NPV as its present value).

Investment in working capital

Some projects, such as the introduction of a new product, will require the investment of working capital at the beginning of the project to finance inventories and sales. Unlike the investment in fixed assets, investment in working capital is usually viewed as being fully recoverable at the end of the project's life. Consequently the investment is considered as a cash outflow at time 0, and a cash inflow at the end of the project's life.

Estimation uncertainty

Although the estimates of cash flows in the examples so far have been treated as deterministic, usually there will be uncertainty associated with all projected cash flows. The further into the future for which projection must be made, the greater will be the degree of uncertainty. Estimation uncertainty may be accommodated subjectively by requiring a higher than normal rate of return on a project, by according greater weight to the project's payback period, or by making adjustments to the cash flows on a conservative criterion. Alternatively, more involved methods may be based on probabilistic estimates of cash flows or by simulation models.

Capital rationing

A desirable project in discounted cash flow terms may have to be rejected because of an overall limitation on resources available for investment. Although we have implied that all non-mutually-exclusive projects that promise positive net present values or internal rates of return greater than the target rate should be accepted, in reality the resources available for projects in any period will be constrained by the ability of the company to obtain resources and by budget 'ceilings' imposed by management.

In such cases, non-mutually-exclusive projects may be ranked in terms of their desirability on net present value or internal rate of return measures. The resources available will then be allocated to projects based on this ranking with the objective of obtaining the greatest aggregate net present value from the resources available.

Discounted cash flow analysis and the decision process

Discounted cash flow methods of capital investment analysis should be examined within the perspective of the decision-making process generally. Figure 21.1 in Chapter 21 provided an illustration of the several stages involved in this process.

Figure 21.1 indicated that formal quantitative methods of analysis, such as discounted cash flow methods, are typically part of the fifth stage in the decision process. Several stages precede this. For example, the analysis of benefit factors will be part of the third stage in that model. It should be recognised that decisions made in these earlier stages, such as which projects are proposed for analysis and which information is collected about the projects, may often predetermine the ultimate decision.

In the reality of the organisational decision-making process, perceptions of the desirability of a project are often formed during the earlier stages of the process. Those perceptions may often influence the collection of information needed to evaluate the project, perhaps by restricting the amount of information that is collected or by biasing the estimates in favour of the perception. Consequently, projects which reach the stage of formal evaluation, and the information provided for their evaluation, are often screened to the point that formal analysis will confirm their desirability.

None the less, the formal evaluation process is very important. First, that process may bring to light relevant factors that were not seen earlier. Second, decisions on the commitment of large sums of corporate capital to a project are not typically made by the person who thought the project up. Most organisations have formal requirements about which people or groups of people are able to authorise capital funding of different amounts. A request to spend $10 000 on a new fork-lift truck in a warehouse may be able to be approved by the warehouse manager or the plant manager. A proposal to spend $1 million on establishing a new outlet interstate may require authorisation by the board of directors.

In each case, the person or group authorising capital commitment to the project will want to see detailed documentation that provides evidence of the care and thoroughness which went into the process of information acquisition and decision analysis. The formal evaluation process provides evidence of such thoroughness and is important, therefore, not only in convincing the decision analyst of the worth of the project, but also in 'selling' the project to higher levels of management or the board of directors.

The need to convince others of the merit of a project explains why, in practice, we often see the proponents of a project gather and document far more supportive information and evidence than may be adjudged as necessary from an objective viewpoint. Another reason for paying for more information than may be seen as necessary at the decision stage is that it can be invoked in defence of the decision should the project turn out to be a failure. In this event the people responsible for the decision can point to 'the overwhelming evidence in favour of the project at the time' as a justification for their decision. These phenomena, often observed in practice, may be termed part of the 'sociology' of the decision-making process, and contrasted with the 'technology' of the process embodied in the analytical technique of discounted cash flow. See the 'ethical issues' section at the end of the chapter for further discussion.

Discounted cash flow analysis provides a quantification of the economic desirability of a decision; it rarely constitutes a sufficient criterion for the decision. If management rejects a decision despite the economic analysis, it does so on the assumption that the qualitative factors relevant to the decision outweigh the quantitative ones. In this case the formal financial analysis provides management with a measure of the economic opportunity costs of rejecting the decision.

In recent years there has been a changing approach to long-term planning by organisations, creating a changing role for staff in the finance department (the department in which various accountants and financial analysts are typically grouped) in those organisations. For example, Sportsgirl Sportscraft Group P/L promote the notion that 'finance' is a service group rather than a control group and that financial analyses should involve the business units. By broadening the responsibility for such analysis and, hence, the decisions, there is a broadening of responsibility for the outcome of the decisions.

The financial role of the accountant is also changing in the public sector. Apart from the current trend towards out-sourcing many activities (a decision that typically requires long-term financial analyses of the kinds described in this chapter), Yarra Valley Water Ltd identified changes such as the need to assess alternatives to the traditional sources of funding, the reassessment and redefinition of assets in the public sector (leading to the reassessment of what could be sold) and accountability requirements that create a need to rethink ways to assess performance when the chief goal is not profit. The latter change is partly responsible for the separation of service obligations from the business obligations of competitive operations at Yarra Valley Water. All of these changes have an impact on either the financial analysis itself or on the way it is used in the decision-making process.

Implementation audits and post-implementation audits

When a capital investment project is approved it becomes part of the capital budget. All budgets are resource-usage plans for the coming period. As with other plans, progress needs to be monitored and compared with the plan to determine whether the plan is being followed. If it is not, corrective action must be taken to return to plan, or it is recognised that conditions differ from those projected and the plans need to be changed.

During the period of implementing a capital project, the monitoring is done through implementation audits. These audits check that the project is going to be completed on time, within the projected cost, and will meet the needs of users.

Another audit should be conducted six to twelve months after the completion of implementation. This is a post-implementation audit during which all data used in pre-implementation analyses are checked for accuracy (i.e. the feasibility and benefit analyses and discounted cash flow analysis) and the project is evaluated to identify whether what was implemented meets requirements or whether improvement is possible. The post-implementation audit should identify any problems in the forecasting, budgeting and decision-making stages, with a view to improving the results of these processes in the future.

Qualitative factors in capital investment analysis

As in all decision making, qualitative factors may outweigh the financial criteria embodied in discounted cash flow analysis. The decision to automate an operation in the production process may be rejected if management does not want to retrench employees, or if it fears the consequences of potential industrial action. Product A may be chosen over product B, even though analysis showed product B to be economically more profitable, because A may be considered to give prestige to the company (these are intangible benefits).

One of the most important qualitative factors in this respect is the compatibility of the proposed project with organisational goals and strategic plans. A prestige car manufacturer may reject a proposal to build an inexpensive, lesser-quality vehicle that would appeal to the lower end of the motor vehicle market. Although the financial analysis might show that this car would be a volume seller and very profitable because of the reputation and name of the manufacturer, the company might reject the proposal on the grounds that it would prejudice and violate the corporate goal of excellence in motor vehicle design and engineering. If this corporate goal restricts the manufacturer to the upper end of the vehicle market, then this is a restriction the company may very explicitly accept.

This illustrates the need for projects in the capital budget to be consistent with the strategic plan adopted by the organisation. As explained in Chapter 21, the master budget is the collection of all budgets for the whole organisation, including the capital budget. The first part of the master budget is the statement of the corporate objectives, the strategic plan, and assumptions about the coming operating period on which the content of the budgets is based (e.g. economic environment and sales demand). The subsequent parts of the master budget, such as the capital budget, must be consistent with the objectives, strategic plan and assumptions as stated there.

Ethical issues

1. You are the accountant in the Australian subsidiary of a Europe-based multi-national. The general manager of the Australian subsidiary has the authority to spend up to $100 000 without approval from Europe. Any amount over that requires formal requests for approval, and those requests have to be supported by substantial documentation, arguments and financial calculations justifying why the amount should be spent. The Australian subsidiary needs to install some pollution-control equipment in its factory. Until it does, the company is in breach of Australian laws on pollution and is vulnerable to severe fines. The equipment costs $250 000. The European headquarters has been very reluctant to approve spending for these types of purposes in the past. If it does finally approve them, the experience is that it takes an inordinate amount of time. The general manager has suggested that the purchase of the equipment will be treated as if it were three separate pieces of equipment, each of which has a purchase and installation cost of less than $100 000. You are asked to organise it in the books so that it looks like three separate pieces of equipment were purchased at three separate invoice prices and for three separate purposes that were unrelated to each other. The general manager's argument is that the equipment has to be put in and if the capital investment approval system has to be 'got around' to do it, then that is the problem of the system.

   Do you do as the general manager asks?

2. You are an accountant attached to a government department. The responsible minister is an ex-sporting hero who wants to spend $100 million on a sports complex, which will be named after him. The government has said that it will consider the project so long as it is largely self-funding. You have been put in charge of examining whether it is likely to be financially self-sufficient. As you conduct your investigation, two things begin to happen. First, the minister's lobbying of other politicians starts to bear fruit in that the government collectively begins to get very enthusiastic about the idea. Their enthusiasm is such that announcements, which you think are premature, are made about the establishment of the complex, pointing out how much value it will provide to the community and, at the same time, how it will not cost the taxpayers anything. The other thing is that the more data you gather, the clearer it becomes in your mind and in the numbers you are generating that the complex is going to be a 'white elephant'.

   What do you do?

 Summary

This chapter has discussed the analyses that assist decision makers with regard to capital investment decisions. A four-stage capital investment model is illustrated in Figure 24.2. In stage one of this model the feasibility and benefit factors relating to capital investment proposals should be considered. Analyses of the financial results of these proposals are undertaken in stage two. Although methods such as the accounting rate of return and pay-back are found in the analysis of capital investment projects, the most appropriate methods are those based on the discounting of cash flows associated with the projects. These methods are the net present value and internal rate of return methods. The implementation of the project occurs during stage three, at which time implementation audits monitor the progress of the implementation. After implementation, in stage four, a post-implementation audit identifies ways in which future projects can be better selected, planned and implemented.

The chapter pointed out the importance of organisational and qualitative factors in the capital investment decision. In particular, there is a need for such decisions to be consistent with the organisation's strategic plan.

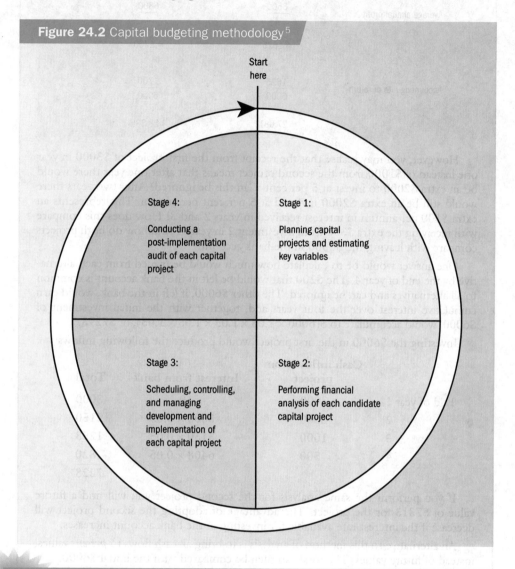

Figure 24.2 Capital budgeting methodology[5]

Start here

Stage 4:

Conducting a post-implementation audit of each capital project

Stage 1:

Planning capital projects and estimating key variables

Stage 3:

Scheduling, controlling, and managing development and implementation of each capital project

Stage 2:

Performing financial analysis of each candidate capital project

Discussion of in-text cases

Case 24.1

The payback period for each is exactly three years, but after payback the second project appears preferable, with a higher return in the fourth year. The accounting rate of return confirms this decision:

5 John G. Burch, *Cost and Management Accounting: A Modern Approach*, West Publishing Company, St Paul, MN, 1994, p. 1046.

	First project	Second project
Average annual profit	$\dfrac{6500}{4}$	$\dfrac{6800}{4}$
	$= 1625$	$= 1700$
Accounting rate of return	$\dfrac{1625}{6000}$	$\dfrac{1700}{6000}$
	$= 27.08\%$	$= 28.33\%$

However, you may realise that the receipt from the first project of $3000 in year one instead of $1000 from the second project means that after one year there would be an extra $2000 to invest at 5 per cent. Can this be ignored? After two years there would still be an extra $2000 invested at 5 per cent per annum. This represents an extra $100 per annum in interest received in years 2 and 3! How does this compare with receiving the extra $300 from investment 2 in year 4? And how do both projects compare with leaving the $6000 in the bank account?

One answer would be to calculate how much would be owned from each alternative by the end of year 4. The $200 that would be left in the bank account is common to all alternatives and can be ignored. The other $6000, if left in the bank, would earn cumulative interest over the four years and, together with the initial investment of $6000, would accumulate to $(6000 \times 1.05 \times 1.05 \times 1.05 \times 1.05)$, or $7293.

Investing the $6000 in the first project would produce the following inflows:

	Cash inflow from project	Interest from bank	Total
End of year 1	3000	0	3000
2	2000	3000×0.05	2150
3	1000	5150×0.05	1258
4	500	6408×0.05	820
			7228

If you perform the same analysis for the second project you will find a future value of $7313 for the project. The advantage of adopting the second project will decrease if the interest rate available for investing in the bank account increases.

An alternative to this method of analysis is to bring all cash flows to *present* values, instead of future values. The total can then be compared with the initial $6000.

Let us see how this works. We know that $6000 invested at 5 per cent per annum will become $7293 by the end of year 4. Reversing this we say that $7293 in year 4, discounted at 5 per cent per annum, has a present value of $6000, because discounting reverses the cumulative interest calculation. (Instead of multiplying $6000 by 1.05 four times, we divide $7293 by 1.05 four times, which is the same as multiplying $7293 by 0.8227.) As another example, how much must you invest today at 5 per cent per annum to receive $500 in four years time? (We will find later that $411 invested now at 5 per cent will increase to $500 in four years.)

All of the cash flows from the two projects under consideration can be discounted at 5 per cent to derive a total present value for each project. These totals are then compared with the $6000 to see if the projects are more profitable than leaving the money in the bank, revealing also that at a discount rate of 5 per cent the second project is slightly more profitable as an investment than the first alternative.

Case 24.2

		PROJECT 1		PROJECT 2	
Year	Discount factor	Cash flow	Present value	Cash flow	Present value
1	0.9524	3000	2857	1000	952
2	0.9070	2000	1814	2000	1814
3	0.8638	1000	864	3000	2591
4	0.8227	500	411	800	658
			5946		6016

This analysis reveals that:

- To have the same amount in the bank at the end of year 4 as you would receive from investing in the first project, you would need to deposit $5946 at 5 per cent per annum.
- The second project gives the same yield in year 4 as $6016 deposited now at 5 per cent per annum.

Since this is the result, in both cases, from investing $6000 in the projects, $6000 in the bank account will give a higher balance after four years than the first project, whereas from an investment of $6000, the second project gives the same results as if you had deposited $6016 in the bank account!

The second project is therefore preferable as far as the financial analysis is concerned.

 **Review exercises**

Discussion questions

24.1 'The accounting rate of return is the best method of evaluating capital investment proposals because it is consistent with conventional accounting concepts and information needed for evaluation is available from the accounting records.' Do you agree? Why or why not?

24.2 What are the advantages and disadvantages of the payback method of capital investment analysis?

24.3 Discounted cash flow methods of capital investment analysis often require the estimation of cash flows for many years in the future. One can rarely estimate these cash flows with confidence, and as a result there is little point in their use. Do you agree? Explain.

24.4 Refer to question 24.3. How may a decision maker incorporate an allowance for estimation uncertainty in the decision analysis?

24.5 Explain the criterion of 'relevance' in determining which cash flows should be incorporated in discounted cash flow analysis.

24.6 The internal rate of return method is preferred to the net present value method of capital investment analysis because it shows the percentage return expected from the project. Do you agree? Why or why not?

24.7 Discuss the significance of taxation for capital investment analysis.

24.8 Management often takes a decision on a capital investment proposal on criteria which are not incorporated in discounted cash flow analysis. Discuss the importance of qualitative factors in capital investment analysis.

24.9 Why is it cash and not accounting income that is important in capital investment analyses?

 Problems

24.10 *Present value calculations*

1. Using a discount rate of 10 per cent, calculate the present value of each of the following:

   (a) $1000 to be received one year from the present.
   (b) $1000 to be received four years from the present.
   (c) $1000 to be received twenty-five years from the present.
   (d) $1000 to be received immediately.

2. Using a discount rate of 14 per cent, calculate the present value of each of the following:

   (a) An annuity of $1000 for five years, the first payment being made immediately.
   (b) An annuity of $1000 for five years, the first payment being made at the end of the first year from the present.
   (c) An annuity of $1000 for five years, the first payment being made at the end of the second year from the present.

3. Assume you wish to take a round-the-world trip in five years time. Your travel agent estimates that the trip you want will cost about $50 000 in five years time. How much money would you have to invest now at 14 per cent per annum compound interest to be able to pay for your trip?

24.11 *Net present value and internal rate of return*

Two projects require the following initial cash outlays and are expected to generate the following net cash inflows:

			Year			
Project	0	1	2	3	4	5
	$	$	$	$	$	$
A	(2500)	250	250	250	250	2750
B	(2500)	600	600	600	600	600

(a) Using a discount rate of 10 per cent, calculate the net present value of each project.

(b) Calculate the internal rate of return for each project.

(c) Using a discount rate of 24 per cent, calculate the net present value of each project.

(d) Assuming A and B are mutually exclusive projects, compare and discuss your answers to parts (a) and (c) above.

24.12 *Project evaluation for a government business enterprise*

Telecommunications of Australia Ltd (TCA) is considering a request to establish tele-phone and telecommunications facilities at a rapidly growing but isolated tourist resort near a world-famous natural attraction.

TCA has estimated the following costs and revenues for the project over the next five years:

Initial cost of exchange and plant facilities	$1 050 000
Annual operating costs	150 000

Sales and service revenues:

Year 1	420 000
Year 2	435 000
Year 3	450 000
Year 4	480 000
Year 5	500 000

At the end of five years the residual value of recoverable equipment is estimated at $350 000.

An increase in working capital would be required to support the additional custom. This increase is estimated at $15 000 and would be recoverable at the end of five years.

(a) Using a required rate of return of 16 per cent and a five years time horizon, calcu-late the net present value of the project. Is the project worthwhile in financial terms?

(b) Assume TCA is worried about the riskiness of the project. How could it take account of this in its decision analysis?

(c) Other than financial feasibility, what other considerations should influence the decision?

(d) If the project is adopted, what role would implementation and post-implementation audits have to play?

24.13 *Comparison of project evaluation methods*

The following information relates to three mutually exclusive projects:

	Project A	Project B	Project C
Initial cash outlay	$30 000	$36 000	$40 000
Net cash inflows:			
Year 1	12 000	16 000	18 000
2	12 000	12 000	14 000
3	8 000	10 000	12 000
4	6 000	8 000	6 000
5	–	4 000	4 000
6	–	–	2 000
Salvage value year 6	2 000	2 000	2 000

(a) Calculate the payback period for each project.

(b) Using a required rate of return of 10 per cent, calculate the net present value of each project.

(c) Calculate the approximate internal rate of return for each project.

24.14 *Lease versus buy in a public sector entity*

The Lisworth Town Council is considering whether it should acquire a street sweeping and cleaning vehicle. It is also examining whether it would be cheaper to lease the vehicle or to buy it outright. If it bought the vehicle, the purchase price would be $90 000 with an estimated residual value after five years of $10 000. Service and maintenance costs are expected to be about $2500 per year. If it leased the vehicle, lease payments would be made on the first day of each year for the following amounts.

Year 1 $27 500
Year 2   25 000
Year 3   22 500
Year 4   22 500
Year 5   22 500

The lease payments include an annual service contract that would cover all service and maintenance on the vehicle. The council would employ a driver for the vehicle at an annual wage of $22 000.

(a) Calculate the net present values of the purchase and lease alternatives, assuming the council considers its cost of money to be 12 per cent.

(b) If the council acquires the vehicle, should it buy or lease it?

24.15 *Net present value analysis*

Berlina Plastics is evaluating two types of quality control systems for installation in its manufacturing plant. Each system is expected to have a useful life of eight years and to result in the incurrence of the following costs:

	System A	System B
Initial cost	$62 500	$100 000
Salvage value	Nil	25 000
Annual variable costs of operation	13 750	10 000
Annual cost of repairs and maintenance	6 250	3 000

(a) What feasibility issues should be considered by Berlina Plastics with regard to this proposed investment?

(b) What benefits may be derived from this investment?

(c) Calculate the cost of each system in net present value terms, using a required rate of return of 12 per cent.

(d) Which system of quality control would you recommend? Is there any other information you would wish to have before making a recommendation?

(e) Assuming one of the projects is adopted, what would be evaluated in an implemetation audit?

(f) When would a post-implementation audit be undertaken and what would it evaluate?

24.16 *Net present value and internal rate of return*

Giulia Nuvolari runs a business converting standard motor vehicles to high-perfor-mance specifications through engine and suspension modifications. The business is quite successful. Giulia is presently considering two proposals, each of which will require a capital outlay of about $1 million.

The first is to buy some new equipment that will bring the benefits of CAD/CAM (computer assisted design and manufacturing) to the business. Giulia quantifies the benefits from this equipment at $250 000 per year. These benefits include faster and more efficient work, labour cost savings and other operating cost savings. The equip-ment has an expected life of eight years and an estimated residual value of zero.

The second proposal is to expand into motor vehicle body conversions. She could do this by buying out an existing business, Unique Car Kits, which is in some financial difficulties. The present owner is prepared to accept $1 million to sell. Giulia thinks the business can be built up and estimates the following net cash inflows from the busi-ness over the next eight years.

Year 1	$ 0
Year 2	50 000
Year 3	200 000
Year 4	350 000
Years 5–8	500 000

Giulia is quite conservative and has placed a limit of $1 million on capital spend-ing at this time. Even if both proposals were financially attractive, only one can be chosen because of this self-imposed capital limit.

(a) Calculate the net present value of each of the two proposals assuming Giulia requires 14 per cent rate of return. Ignore taxation for the purposes of calculation.

(b) Which alternative should Giulia choose? What considerations other than the calcu-lations in part (a) would Giulia need to take into account?

(c) What would be the value of conducting a post-implementation audit in this case?

24.17 *Net present value and new product introduction*

Milan Manufacturing is evaluating the financial feasibility of introducing a new product to its product line. The sales department estimates that the product will be marketable for ten years and will probably be discontinued at that time.

An initial outlay of $850 000 will be required for equipment and facilities to manu-facture and distribute the product. The equipment and facilities are assumed to have a life of ten years and a salvage value of $100 000. An additional investment of $300 000 in working capital is also required to support higher levels of inventories and accounts receivable associated with the new product. This will be fully recovered when the product is abandoned in ten years time.

Sales revenue forecasts for the product are as follows:

Year 1	$ 600 000
Year 2	950 000
Years 3–10	1 250 000

Estimates of the total operating costs of manufacturing, distributing and selling the product are as follows:

Year 1	$ 400 000
Year 2	650 000
Years 3–10	800 000

An additional $200 000 will be spent in year 1 on an advertising campaign to launch the product.

The company's tax rate is 40 per cent. The equipment and facilities are depreciable for tax purposes over ten years using the straight-line method. Assume the cash payment for taxation occurs at the end of the same year in which the liability for tax arises. Tax losses in any year (arising where allowable deductions for expenses exceed assessable income in that year) may be carried forward and offset against profits of future years.

(a) Calculate the expected taxable profits and tax payments associated with the product for each year.

(b) Calculate the cash surplus generated by the product after tax payments for each year.

(c) Assuming that the required rate of return is 12 per cent, is the new product viable in financial terms? Use the net present value method of discounted cash flow analysis to determine your answer.

24.18 *Project selection, net present value and taxation*

Five projects being considered for inclusion in a capital expenditure budget have the following initial outlays and are calculated to yield the following net present values:

Project	Initial outlay	Net present value
A	$ 70 000	$19 250
B	187 500	54 375
C	45 000	12 000
D	50 000	12 750
E	105 000	23 750

A sixth project, expected to have a four-year life, has the following estimated data:

Project F

Initial outlay on capital equipment	$64 000
Gross cash inflow for each year of useful life	55 000

Gross cash outflow for each year of useful life:

Year 1	25 000
2	25 000
3	25 000
4	30 000
Proceeds from sale of equipment at end of year 4	15 000

Additional information

(i) Depreciation for taxation purposes will be calculated on a straight-line basis over the useful life of the project.

(ii) The rate of taxation is 50 per cent, and it may be assumed that taxation is paid at the end of the year in which the liability to tax arises.

(iii) The company's required rate of return after tax is 10 per cent.

(a) Calculate the net present value of project F.

(b) Management has restricted spending on new capital investment projects to $225 000. Which of the six projects should be undertaken? Explain.

24.19 *Project evaluation, net present value and taxation*

Alfetta Minerals Ltd is a mineral exploration and refining company, operating several open-cut mines. The company is considering the acquisition of another existing mine site. The cost of acquiring the mine and the plant and equipment already in use on the site is $2 400 000. The mine is expected to yield 50 000 tonnes of ore in the first year of operation, followed by tonnages of 50 000, 40 000, 30 000 and 20 000 in the remaining years of the mine's productive life.

The following estimates are available:

(i) Selling price per tonne of ore over the five years: $42
(ii) Fixed costs per year: $180 000
(iii) Variable costs per tonne: $10.80
(iv) Depreciation and depletion of the mine site and equipment is determined at $6 per tonne. However, for taxation purposes an additional allowance for depletion of $1.20 per tonne will be deductible.
(v) The company will have to pay royalties of $4.80 per tonne.
(vi) The company's current rate of taxation is 40 per cent. For purposes of analysis, assume tax payments are made in the same year in which the liability to tax arises.

Calculate the net present value of acquiring and operating the new mine using a required rate of return of 12 per cent.

24.20 *New product decision, net present value and taxation*

Giulietta Products Ltd is evaluating a proposal to add a new product to its existing range. The new product is expected to have a market life of five years and to generate the following net cash inflows before tax (sales revenues less cash operating costs):

Year	Net cash inflows
1	$ 62 500
2	100 000
3	125 000
4	125 000
5	50 000

The product will require new manufacturing equipment estimated to cost $225 000. The equipment should be able to be sold for $60 000 at the end of five years. For taxation purposes, the equipment must be depreciated over ten years using the straight-line method. Any loss on sale will be tax deductible at the end of the fifth year.

Additionally, the company would need to increase its level of working capital by $25 000 immediately if the new product is to be introduced, and by a further $30 000 at the end of the first year of operations. The investment in working capital is fully recoverable at the end of five years.

Production would take place in a building owned by Giulietta Products but currently leased to Sud Ltd for $2500 per year. The lease contract has a further five years to run; however, Giulietta could cancel the contract and obtain immediate possession of the building on payment of $5000 to Sud Ltd. The payment for cancellation would be an allowable deduction for taxation purposes.

A promotional campaign to launch the new product will be carried out at the beginning of the first year. This is expected to cost $37 500.

The company's current rate of taxation is 40 per cent and its required rate of return is 10 per cent after tax.

Using discounted cash flow analysis, determine whether the new product is an acceptable addition to the company's existing product lines. For the purpose of analysis, assume tax is paid in the same year in which the liability to tax arises.

Case studies

24.21 *Cost reduction in a government business enterprise*

The State Power and Electricity Commission has branch offices in two country towns, Rundown and Brokendown. As well as providing customer account payment services, the offices also serve as bases for technicians who do repair and maintenance work on power lines and equipment in the area.

The commission is considering closing down both these branch offices and building a new office at another town, Newtown. Newtown is halfway between Rundown and Brokendown and would be the base for customer and equipment maintenance services for all three towns. Part of the reason for considering the move at this time is that both the existing branch offices are in very poor shape. If the commission decides to retain the existing locations, the offices at Rundown and Brokendown will both need some structural repair and extensive renovations.

The commission, therefore, has two alternatives. The first is to retain the existing locations and carry out the renovations. The second is to sell the existing offices and build a new office at Newtown. One of the two alternatives must be chosen.

The following information is available to assist the decision.

	Rundown	Brokendown	Newtown
Renovations cost	$240 000	$370 000	
Building cost			$750 000
Site preparation cost			40 000
Sale price of properties if sold now	60 000	50 000	
Estimated residual value of properties in 10 years time	250 000	250 000	650 000
Annual repairs and maintenance costs	5 000 p.a.	4 000 p.a.	6 000 p.a.

If the new office at Newtown is built, one staff position can be saved. This saving should amount to $40 000 per year. However, the commission will have to pay additional travelling costs and expenses of $20 000 per year if the staff are relocated at Newtown.3

Required

(a) Calculate the net present value of the cash flows associated with each alternative. Assume a discount rate of 16 per cent. Which alternative is the least cost option for the commission?

(b) Assume it is not certain that the staff position can be saved under the relocation alternative. How would your answer to part (a) change if the staff saving could not be made?

24.22 *New product decision, net present value and taxation*

The GTV Manufacturing Company is considering a proposal to manufacture and market a new product.

The accountant has accumulated the following estimated data from the sales, production and cost departments. Sales levels and prices of the new product have been estimated for a ten-year period.

Year	Sales (units)	Selling price per unit ($) (net of selling costs)
1	200 000	7.00
2	200 000	7.00
3	200 000	7.00
4	300 000	6.80
5	300 000	6.80
6	300 000	6.80
7	350 000	6.60
8	350 000	6.60
9	350 000	6.60
10	350 000	6.60

The investment required to produce the new product consists of an initial outlay on manufacturing equipment of $660 000. This will provide an annual production capacity of 250 000 units. Major overhauls are planned at the end of the third and sixth years to increase annual capacity by 50 000 units each time. Each overhaul is estimated to cost $60 000.

Investments in working capital will also be required to support the new product. Initially, investment in raw material and product inventories will amount to $120 000. The level of accounts receivable and accounts payable will also rise by $240 000 and $20 000 respectively, and will remain at the increased levels during the expected ten-year life of the new product.

Additional investments in raw materials and product inventories will be required at the end of the third and sixth years. Additional investment of $40 000 will be required on each occasion. Alterations to existing buildings will need to be made at the end of the third year at an estimated cost of $100 000.

- The raw materials usage and cost have been estimated as follows:
The new product will require two raw materials, A and B, in the following standard quantities:
A—2 units per unit of finished product.
B—1 unit per unit of finished product.
There will be a spoilage factor of 10 per cent of the units of raw material A.
Material A will be purchased from outside suppliers at a price of $1.00 per unit.
Material B is currently being manufactured and sold by GTV Manufacturing

Company on an outside market. The company presently sells all material B it is capable of producing at the market price of $1.40 per unit, and any units diverted to the manufacture of the new product would reduce outside sales.

Material B has a variable cost of production of 90 cents per unit and variable selling costs of 10 cents per unit.

- Direct labour usage and cost have been estimated as follows:
  Direct standard labour time will be six minutes per unit of finished product. Applicable labour rates are currently $4.00 per hour, and lump-sum increases averaging 80 cents per hour are expected every three years.

- Other costs are expected as follows:
  Variable manufacturing overhead   —$0.30 per unit of finished product
  Repairs and maintenance   —$120 000 per year
  Insurance   —$ 80 000 per year
  Indirect labour   —$120 000 per year

Other information

(i) Estimated life of the production equipment is ten years, with no scrap value at the end of that time.
(ii) For taxation purposes, depreciation on equipment, including major overhauls, is based on a ten-year useful life, and is calculated by the straight-line method.
(iii) The company's current rate of taxation is 50 per cent. For purposes of analysis, assume that tax is paid in the same year in which the liability to tax arises.
(iv) The company's required rate of return is 14 per cent per annum.

Required

Using net present value analysis, determine whether the GTV Manufacturing Company should produce the new product.

CHAPTER 25
Accounting for short-term management planning

Learning objectives

In this chapter you will be introduced to:

1. the need for budgets
2. the structure of the master budget
3. the major operating budgets for a manufacturing environment
4. the budgeted financial statements and support budgets
5. cost-volume-profit analysis
6. the advantages of activity-based costing for budgeting and short- to intermediate-term decision making
7. the advantages to be derived from sensible budgeting processes and practices.

Introduction

Long-term planning was described in the previous chapter as involving decisions that affected the organisation for a reasonably long period of time, for example five years.

Short-term planning involves decisions that are designed to affect the organisation for periods typically of a year or less, depending on the operating cycle of the firm. These decisions must be made within the constraints of long-term plans. Plans for production levels, service levels and sales and cost levels for the year will be limited by the physical manufacturing capacity and the service provision capability available for that year. Profit and cash results for the year will, therefore, also be limited by manufacturing and service provision capacity. In the longer term, that capacity may be increased by additional equipment if the need is indicated by the short-term plans. The techniques discussed in Chapter 24 will then be employed.

This chapter concentrates on accounting information for short-term (operational) planning. The major accounting procedures involve budgeting.

Budgets for short-term planning

Budgets are management plans, expressed in financial terms, for the operations and resources of an organisation, for some specified period in the future.

Budgets should be prepared for different segments of the organisation (departments or divisions), as well as for the organisation as a whole. They are prepared for different activities (sales, cash, capital expenditure, production), for different purposes (responsibility budgets for control and performance evaluation, or program budgets for specific activities), and for different periods (monthly, annually). All budgets should be consistent with one another and with forecast conditions. At Phillips Lighting, for example, the financial controller places a focus on linking plans (budgets) and forecasts to the business plan at the corporate and functional levels. Part of the adopted strategy is to consider the 'bigger picture', using statistical analyses to forecast the likely future economic and business environment (this is consistent with the SWOT analysis discussed in Chapter 24). A 'rolling business plan' is frequently updated to account for changing business requirements and economic conditions.

Additionally, budgets serve a variety of functions within organisations, including authorisation, planning, coordination, communication, measurement, control and motivation.

Authorisation is the traditional function of government budgets under case-based accounting systems, which authorise a certain amount of funds to be allocated for an activity for a specified period. In business organisations some budgets have an authorising function, for example capital investment budgets and research and development budgets. Depending on how much a manager is allowed to diverge from the budget during the budget period, discretionary costs in an operating budget may take the form of a spending allowance. Discretion to change the incurrence of these costs is more likely in an environment where flexibility is required to meet changing conditions rather than in a stable industry.

The planning function requires the attempt, during the budgetary process, to forecast future events beyond the control of the organisation, and to determine other future events by coordinating resources to bring about desired objectives. The budget is therefore a resource usage plan.

Coordination is the formally planned linkage of all the factors of production and of all departments and programs of the organisation so that the organisational objectives may be attained. A comprehensive system of budgetary planning facilitates coordination by enabling the integration and communication of plans and activities between departments, such as sales and production for example; not producing according to sales demand can result in either overproduction and excess inventories or stock-outs. The budget also provides an overview of the resource allocation among departments and activities, facilitating the efficient utilisation of the organisation's limited resources.

Budgets fulfil a communication function by providing a formal mechanism whereby senior levels of management may convey general policies and specific instructions to subordinate levels of management, and managers on the same level can understand the relationship of their role with that of others.

The measurement function of budgets implies the use of a budget as a yardstick of performance; the budget may be compared against actual performance during the period to allow an evaluation. This monitoring of performance against plans is part of the control function of management. If performance is not consistent with preset plans it may be necessary to take corrective action to return to plan. However, the reasons for divergence from the plan should be assessed in case the plans were based on erroneous assumptions about the operating period (e.g. external economic environment, sales demand), in which case it may be necessary for management to alter the plans or recommend a change to them.

As discussed in Chapter 21, the control function of the budget also includes its use to evaluate the effectiveness with which individual managers meet their own control responsibilities, thus influencing the behaviour of the managers by encouraging them to make goal-congruent decisions (i.e. decisions that are in the best interests of the organisation).

Consequently, the types of budgets used, the level of performance represented by the budget, and the way in which the budget system is implemented and administered may have a significant effect on manager and employee motivation and performance. (For example, if the budget targets are perceived as impossible to achieve they may have an adverse effect, or if senior management does not pay serious attention to the budget, it will not have much influence over the behaviour of subordinate employees.) Issues concerning the behavioural impact of the budget will be further discussed later in the chapter.

Preparation of the master budget

The entire collection of financial plans for the organisation is called the *master budget*, or annual budget. It gives the complete picture of current long-term and short-term plans and the probable short-term outcome of following those plans. The master budget is normally prepared for the 12-month financial reporting period, with breakdowns into shorter time periods such as months or quarters. The practice of dividing the annual budget by 12 or 4 to obtain monthly or quarterly budgets respectively can produce misleading plans. Activity may be influenced by seasonal fluctuations and some cash flows (in the cash budget) will be paid at frequencies other than monthly (e.g. quarterly) or quarterly (e.g. annually). The monthly or quarterly budget breakdowns should be realistically prepared specifically for each individual time period.

The major part of the master budget will consist of short-term operating plans and the short-term financial outcome of operations. This chapter focuses on these short-term plans and outcomes, but to see them in context it is necessary to first consider the construction of the master budget and the relationship of the various components, one with another.

As Figure 25.1 illustrates, the master budget is likely to have four main sections: the budget bases, the operating budgets, the project budgets and the budgeted financial statements.

Budget bases

The first set of statements in the master budget should clarify the basis on which these budgets are prepared. Hence, the organisational goals should be clearly expressed and the strategic plan explained. This should be accompanied by the balance sheet for the start of the year. These statements give the reader an indication of the current position of the firm and what management hopes to achieve over the next year of operations.

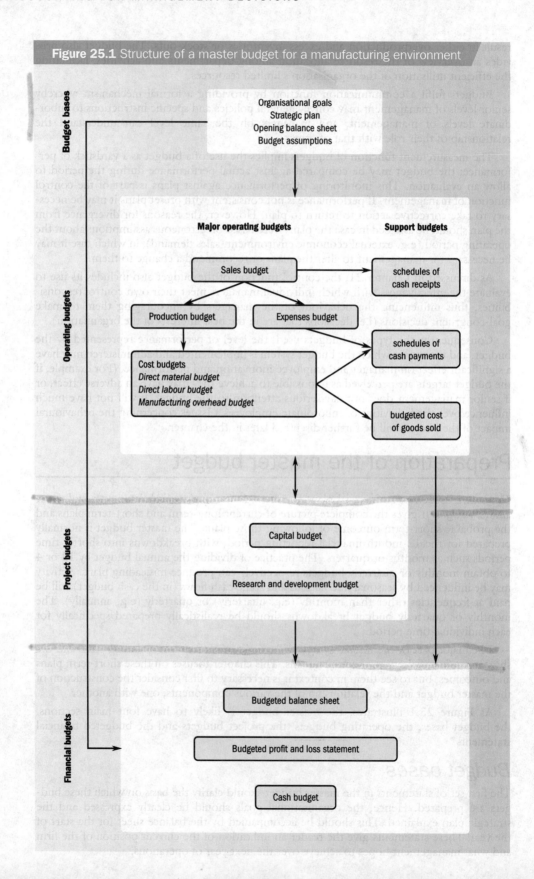

Figure 25.1 Structure of a master budget for a manufacturing environment

To understand the plans that constitute the rest of the master budget the reader also needs a statement of the assumptions that underpin the preparation of the plans. A critical part of this statement will be the sales forecast. This is likely to include projections and assumptions with regard to market trends, the general economic environment, the industry economic environment, the firm's market share, pricing policy, competition, advertising and product promotion, employment economic indicators, among other factors.

Operating budgets

The operating budgets guide the decisions of the managers of the organisation during the budget period. They are interdependent and serve to coordinate the efforts of the different operating segments of the organisation.

The first operating plan is the sales budget, which is directly based on realistic sales forecasts prepared by marketing managers for the first section of the master budget. Given the sales budget, the production budget must then plan for the timely production of products (i.e. it must ensure that sales demand is satisfied without causing the added expense of overstocking on any items). From this plan of what is to be made and when it is to be made, a plan for the use and provision of direct materials, direct labour and manufacturing overhead can be drawn up.

Decisions with regard to the level of costs in the budgets will depend on the nature of the cost (as discussed in Chapter 22). Many manufacturing costs change with the volume of production or other necessary activity. These are the engineered costs that are directly determined by the production plans. The costs that relate to the provision of capacity (costs such as those incurred in the acquisition of production equipment have normally been approved in capital budgets of prior periods) are usually committed and cannot be changed while setting the budget (unless the method of calculating depreciation is changed). Many other costs are discretionary and need to be carefully determined when drawing up the budget. Examples of discretionary costs are staff training and machine maintenance. Once approved in the budget, they may become committed costs and production managers not given the discretion to change them during the operating period. However, managers may be given autonomy with regard to these costs, or they may be permitted to vary them up to a set percentage (for example permission may be required to change them by more than seven per cent). The authority and responsibilities of managers must therefore be clearly understood.

The acquisition of resources used in production has an impact on the budgeted cash-flow statement (cash budget), but the timing of payments for resources varies. A schedule of payments assists in the preparation of the forecasts in the cash budget. Similarly, a schedule of receipts from sales is prepared, based on the sales budget.

Another budget that is based on the sales budgets and assists in the preparation of forecast cash flows is the expense budget, predominantly detailing sales, marketing and administration expenses for the budget period. Many of these expenses will be committed or discretionary in nature. Some sales expenses (especially commissions and freight out) will be engineered costs, as they change with the volume of sales.

Before budgeted financial statements can be prepared it is necessary to forecast unit costs from the cost budgets, similar to the product cost calculations described in Chapter 22. These calculations form part of the budgeted cost of goods sold calculation.

Project budgets

Projects are tasks that are defined in their objective, approach and duration. The project may relate to capital expenditure, in which case the item purchased will have its purpose, life span and the cash flows it generates detailed in its budget. The project may relate to research and development activities or to any other special task that needs resources allocated to it and may generate funds.

The budget for a project will not necessarily be for a 12-month period. Rather, it is more likely to be for a number of years. The preparation of the financial detail in these budgets was discussed in Chapter 24. As resources need to be made available during the coming master budget period (normally 12 months) and funds, it is to be hoped, will flow from the project, it will impact on other parts of the master budget, in particular the cash budget and other budgeted financial reporting statements.

The need for a project may be identified in the strategic plan. If the project relates to the provision of operating capacity, it will impact on decisions relating to the operating plans for this or later periods. It is also possible that in the preparation of operating budgets based on sales forecasts a lack of sufficient operating capacity is identified, in which case a capital expenditure project might arise.

Budgeted financial statements

To complete the picture of the year's activities there should be forecasts of the financial reporting statements. These will be the statements of where the operating and project plans are intended to take the organisation—the results of the year's activities and its intended position at the end of the year. The statements required are the budgeted balance sheet, the budgeted profit and loss statement and the budgeted cash-flow statement (usually called a cash budget).

Budgeted profit and loss statements and balance sheets predict the financial outcomes of management plans and allow management to evaluate and to revise those plans if the predicted outcomes are not satisfactory. However, those revisions must not lose sight of the realistic assumptions on which the budget is to be based.

Cash budgets enable management to predict the organisation's liquidity over the budget period. The forecast of the timing and amount of cash shortages and surpluses assists management to determine the best way of financing operations in the short-term, based on anticipated cash requirements.

Case 25.1 Planning needs of production

Chris Rousseau is the production manager at a plant that manufactures a range of balls for sports games including football and tennis. Chris has been asked to prepare a plan for production for the next 12 months, giving separate estimates of production for each month and for each product.

Before turning to the discussion at the end of this chapter, make a note of the kinds of information Chris will need when formulating the production schedule.

Preparing the major operating budgets

Example: Budget preparation

The Marple Manufacturing Company produces and markets a range of executive toys. It uses a formal budgeting system to assist profit planning and cash management. The company expects sales to grow rapidly over the first three months of the forthcoming year, commencing in July 20X1. It will need to replace an item of factory equipment in July, and this purchase will be financed through the company's normal bank overdraft facilities. The overdraft interest rate is 12 per cent per annum.

The balance sheet for the company as at 30 June 20X1 is given below. Other information relating to production costs and sales levels is provided as required.

BALANCE SHEET: MARPLE MANUFACTURING COMPANY
as at 30 June 20X1

Assets	$	$	$
Current assets:			
Cash		5 000	
Accounts receivable		5 000	
Raw materials inventory (1000 units)		3 000	
Finished goods inventory (100 units)		1 540	14 540
Non-current assets:			
Land		90 000	
Plant and equipment	180 000		
Accumulated depreciation	50 000	130 000	220 000
Total assets			234 540
Liabilities			
Current liabilities:			
Accounts payable		5 700	
Interest accrued		95	5 795
Non-current liabilities:			
Term loan			5 000
Total liabilities			10 795
Shareholders' funds:			
Paid-up capital		200 000	
Retained profits		23 745	223 745
Total liabilities and shareholders' funds			234 540

Sales budget

Using Figure 25.1 as a framework, the starting point in developing budgets for the period is the sales budget. The sales budget will be formulated by considering sales forecasts for the period. Sales forecasting is inherently difficult because sales depend partly on behaviour outside the control of the organisation, including consumer and competitor behaviour and the level of general economic activity, and partly on strategies and tactics used by the organisation to influence sales levels, such as pricing and promotional tactics.

The choice of sales forecasting methods is not usually the responsibility of the accounting function. These methods may be qualitative (i.e. developing the forecast from estimates by marketing management or field sales people) or statistical (i.e. analysing past sales data for trends and random elements and extrapolating these trends into the future period), or a combination of both.

The sales forecast may differ from the final sales budget for the period because of organisational constraints and management objectives. These will include production capacity limitations, inventory requirements, the ability to service different sales levels, and a consideration of production and selling expenses at different sales levels.

These expenses will determine the profitability of different possible sales levels after taking account of different prices, sales mixes, volumes and promotional tactics. It is not until these expenses have been considered that the sales budget can be assessed against organisational objectives. Consequently, the sales budget will be prepared more than once during the budget process.

The sales budget adopted for the Marple Manufacturing Company for the next five months is as follows:

SALES BUDGET					
	July	August	September	October	November
Sales units	1 000	2 000	4 000	5 000	5 000
Sales revenue	$25 000	$50 000	$100 000	$125 000	$125 000

The sales revenues are based on an unchanging selling price of $25 per unit. Sales in the immediately preceding month of June were 2000 units ($50 000).

Production budget

Once the sales budget has been prepared the production budget may be determined, setting the level of production in each month of the period. Units of product will be needed to meet the anticipated sales level for the month, and to provide the required level of finished goods inventory at the end of the month. However, not all these units will need to be produced in the current month: some will already be on hand in the form of finished goods inventory at the beginning of the month.

The number of units to be produced in any month can be computed as:

$$\text{anticipated sales level during month} + \text{required ending inventory} - \text{beginning inventory}$$

At the end of any month Marple Manufacturing Company wishes to maintain a basic inventory of finished goods equal to 10 per cent of the next month's anticipated sales. Accordingly, the production budget in units for July may be computed as:

$$\underset{\substack{\text{(anticipated sales} \\ \text{level, July)}}}{1000 \text{ units}} + \underset{\substack{\text{(10\% of anticipated} \\ \text{sales, August)}}}{200 \text{ units}} - \underset{\substack{\text{(finished goods} \\ \text{inventory, 1 July)}}}{100 \text{ units}} = 1100 \text{ units}$$

The finished goods inventory level at 1 July was given in the balance sheet at 30 June. The production budget for each month is as follows:

PRODUCTION BUDGET (UNITS)					
Month	Sales (current month)	+ Ending inventory	− Beginning inventory	=	Production (current month)
July	1 000	200	100		1 100
August	2 000	400	200		2 200
September	4 000	500	400		4 100
October	5 000	500	500		5 000

Direct materials usage and purchases budget

This budget determines the monthly costs of direct materials to be used in production and the cost of direct materials to be purchased. The two may be different because management may wish to purchase more direct materials than it needs in production, in order to have an inventory of direct materials at the end of the month and thus ensure continuous production at the beginning of the next month. The direct materials needed in any month's production will be drawn from the beginning inventory of direct materials and the current month's purchases of direct materials.

The direct materials usage in any month can be determined by multiplying the units to be produced by the quantity of direct materials required per unit. In the example, assume that each unit of finished product requires 2 kg of direct materials, with an expected purchase cost of $3 per kg. The direct materials usage in July is therefore 2200 kg (1100 units × 2 kg per unit), with a cost of $6600 (2200 kg × $3 per kg).

If Marple Manufacturing wishes to maintain an inventory of direct materials equal to 25 per cent of next month's expected usage, with a 1000 kg minimum, then the materials purchases (in units and cost) for July would be calculated as follows:

direct materials usage (July)	+	required ending inventory (25% of August usage of 4400)	−	beginning inventory	=	direct materials purchases (July)
2200 kg	+	1100 kg	−	1000 kg	=	2300 kg
$6600		$3300		$3000		$6900

The raw material usage and purchases budget for July, August and September is shown below:

	DIRECT MATERIALS USAGE AND PURCHASES BUDGET							
	Usage (current month)		+	Ending inventory	−	Beginning inventory	=	Purchases (current month)	
Month	kg	× $3		kg		kg		kg	× $3
July	2 200	6 600		1 100		1 000		2 300	6 900
August	4 400	13 200		2 050		1 100		5 350	16 050
September	8 200	24 600		2 500		2 050		8 650	25 950
		44 400							48 900

Direct labour budget

Assume that two hours of direct labour are required to manufacture one unit of product, and that the cost of direct labour is $2.50 per hour. Below is the budgeted direct labour cost for each month, based on the production levels previously determined.

	DIRECT LABOUR BUDGET		
	Production units	Direct labour hours	Direct labour cost
Month	(current month)	(2 hrs per unit)	($2.50 per hour)
July	1 100	2 200	$ 5 500
August	2 200	4 400	11 000
September	4 100	8 200	20 500
			$37 000

Manufacturing overhead budget

Assume that an analysis of the manufacturing overhead costs of the Marple Manufacturing Company has identified three items of semi-variable costs and three items of fixed costs.

The semi-variable costs are power, indirect materials and indirect labour. Each of these costs has a fixed component and a variable component that varies with changes in the volume of production. For each month in the budget period these costs are estimated as:

Power	$2000 + $0.25 per unit of production
Indirect material	$500 + $0.10 per unit of production
Indirect labour	$1000 + $0.20 per unit of production

The power costs for any month will be budgeted as $2000, representing the basic cost of power consumed in the factory irrespective of the production level, plus 25 cents for each unit of production. For July the production level is 1100 units and the budgeted power cost is:

$$\$2000 + \$0.25\ (1100) = \$2275$$

The fixed costs are identified as the cost of leasing factory premises, insurance, and depreciation on plant and equipment. Being committed costs, these costs will not change irrespective of the production levels, and are budgeted for each month of the period as:

Lease costs	$1000
Insurance	$1000
Depreciation	$4000

The budgeted level of manufacturing overhead costs for each month is shown below:

MANUFACTURING OVERHEAD BUDGET			
	July	August	September
Semi-variable costs			
Power	$ 2 275	$ 2 550	$ 3 025
Indirect material	610	720	910
Indirect labour	1 220	1 440	1 820
	4 105	4 710	5 755
Fixed costs			
Lease costs	1 000	1 000	1 000
Insurance	1 000	1 000	1 000
Depreciation	4 000	4 000	4 000
	6 000	6 000	6 000
Total	$10 105	$10 710	$11 755

Selling and administrative expenses budget

Although budgets for selling expenses and administrative expenses are normally prepared separately, for the purpose of this example they have been combined into one budget.

Analysis of the selling and administrative expenses of the company has again identified three items of semi-variable costs (sales staff's salaries, delivery expenses, and other expenses) and two items of fixed costs (advertising and rent). This analysis has shown that the variable components of semi-variable costs change in relation to sales volume in the period rather than production volume.

The following cost behaviours and levels are budgeted for each month in the period:

Semi-variable costs	
Salespeople's salaries	$1000 + $1.00 per unit of sales
Delivery expenses	$500 + $0.50 per unit of sales
Other expenses	$200 + $0.10 per unit of sales
Fixed costs	
Advertising	$2000
Rent	$600

The budgeted cost of sales staff's salaries in July is therefore $1000 plus $1.00 multiplied by the expected sales level in July of 1000 units.

Note a difference between the two fixed-cost items, advertising and rent. The former is a discretionary fixed cost; management exercises its discretion in deciding how much money will be spent on advertising in the coming period and can vary that amount, again by discretion, during the period. Rent is a committed fixed cost. It arises as a result of a previous and particular commitment to the rental or lease costs of property.

A consideration of these two items can illustrate the difference in decision making with regard to categories of costs. Budgeting the level of a committed fixed cost such as rent is not difficult as it will come directly from the terms and conditions of the rental contract. However, planning the level of advertising and many other discretionary fixed costs is a highly uncertain task. Two approaches to budgeting discretionary fixed costs are *incremental budgeting* and *zero-based budgeting* (ZBB). (Note that these budgets are likely to include engineered and committed costs. The level of engineered costs should be determined by the forecast level of activity, and committed costs are usually rigid, regardless of what misguided budget-setters insert in the budget—the habit of cutting or increasing each budget item by a set percentage produces an unrealistic budget.)

Under the incremental approach, the previous period's budget forms the starting point, and adjustments up or down are made at the margin to take account of known or anticipated changes in factor costs or circumstances. For example, the advertising budget for this period is initially based on the amount budgeted and/or spent last period and subsequent changes are made around this amount. Under ZBB, the starting point is set at zero and the entire budget allocation for the forthcoming period must be developed, proposed and defended from scratch. Under ZBB managers must justify the inclusion of each item in the budget as well as the amount budgeted for the item. The amount spent during the last period to sustain a particular level of activity, say advertising, is ignored in the determination.

A benefit of ZBB is that it forces the planners and managers to evaluate carefully all the projects and activities underlying the discretionary cost. An incremental approach requires them to evaluate and justify only the increments over the past period (this is sometimes called the 'use it or lose it' approach). However, ZBB is also the more costly and time-consuming of the two approaches.

SELLING AND ADMINISTRATIVE EXPENSES BUDGET			
	July	August	September
Semi-variable costs			
Salespeople's salaries	$2 000	$3 000	$ 5 000
Delivery expenses	1 000	1 500	2 500
Other expenses	300	400	600
	3 300	4 900	8 100
Fixed costs			
Advertising	2 000	2 000	2 000
Rent	600	600	600
	2 600	2 600	2 600
Total	$5 900	$7 500	$10 700

Preparing the budgeted financial statements and support budgets

Reference to Figure 25.1 will suggest that all the major operating budgets have been prepared. An expenses budget has also been prepared, and for the purposes of this example other expense budgets will be ignored.

In many organisations such as retailers the expenses budgets would be considered major operating budgets. In retailing, the manufacturing budgets would be replaced by a merchandise purchasing budget and marketing and selling activities would be a significant part of the operations of the organisation. In some organisations the expenses budgets may not be considered a major operating budget as they budget for a small percentage of the overall resource usage. The distinction made in this chapter between operating budgets and support budgets is that the major operating budgets are the budgets for operations that detail resource utilisation during the budget period. The support budgets predominantly provide the bridge between the major operating budgets and the budgeted financial statements.

Budgeted cost of goods sold

At this stage of our example the cost of goods *sold* for the period has not been determined. The expected cost of goods *produced* in the budget period may be determined by the addition of the budgeted cost for direct material usage, direct labour and manufacturing overhead (when appropriate the aggregate cost must be adjusted for opening and closing work in progress as described in Chapter 22, but this does not apply in our example). To find the cost of goods sold, the cost of goods produced must be adjusted for the change in the level of finished goods inventories from the beginning to the end of the budget period.

The valuation of inventory and hence cost of goods sold will require calculation of a unit cost of production. With respect to the manufacturing cost elements of direct materials and direct labour, and the variable component of semi-variable manufacturing overhead, the budgeted cost per unit of production can be calculated directly from the data provided.

Direct materials and direct labour can be traced physically to individual units of production, and cost analysis has provided information on the relationship between the variable components of manufacturing overhead and units of production. Consequently, a budgeted variable cost per unit of production can be calculated as follows:

BUDGETED PRODUCT COST		
Direct materials (2 kg per unit × $3 per kg)		$6.00
Direct labour (2 hours per unit × $2.50 per hour)		5.00
Variable manufacturing overhead:		
Power	$0.25	
Insurance	0.10	
Depreciation	0.20	0.55

The fixed component of semi-variable manufacturing costs and those items of manufacturing overhead that are fully fixed cannot be directly identified with individual units of product since they do not vary with changes in the number of units produced. If it is desired to include fixed costs in inventory valuation, an absorption costing basis, as described in Chapter 22, will be used, and a fixed overhead application rate must be developed to apply these costs to units of product.

A fixed overhead application rate can be determined for the Marple Manufacturing Company by relating the total budgeted fixed manufacturing overhead for the period to the total number of units budgeted for production. This simplified approach assumes away the difficulties of heterogeneous products, the choice of application bases and cost drivers, and the under-applied or over-applied manufacturing overhead discussed in Chapter 22, but to introduce these difficulties would complicate the present example.

Using this method, a budgeted rate for applying fixed manufacturing overhead to units of product could be developed as follows:

	Per month	Budgeted period
Budgeted fixed manufacturing overhead:		
Power	$ 2 000	$ 6 000
Indirect materials	500	1 500
Indirect labour	1 000	3 000
Lease costs	1 000	3 000
Insurance	1 000	3 000
Depreciation	4 000	12 000
		28 500
Budgeted units of production:		
July	1 100	
August	2 200	
September	4 100	7 400

$$\text{Budgeted fixed overhead application rate} = \frac{\text{Budgeted fixed manufacturing overhead}}{\text{Budgeted units of production}}$$

$$= \frac{\$28\ 500^*}{7\ 400}$$

$$= \$3.85 \text{ per unit}$$

* Note that in respect of the power, indirect materials and indirect labour costs, only the fixed component has been included in this computation.

The budgeted cost per unit of production may now be calculated:

BUDGETED PRODUCT COST	
Direct materials	$ 6.00
Direct labour	5.00
Variable manufacturing overhead	0.55
Fixed manufacturing overhead	3.85
	$15.40

The budgeted cost of goods sold for the period can now be determined:

BUDGETED COST OF GOODS SOLD *for the three months ending 30 September 20X1*		
Finished goods inventory 1 July*		$ 1 540
plus Cost of goods produced		
Direct materials used (p. 861)	$44 400	
Direct labour (p. 861)	37 000	
Manufacturing overhead (p. 862)	32 570	113 970
Cost of goods available for sale		115 510
less Finished goods inventory 30 September		
(500 units × $15.40 per unit)		7 700
Cost of goods sold		107 810
* From balance sheet as at 30 June		

Budgeted profit and loss statement

The budgeted profit and loss statement for the three-month period may now be commenced.

The projected interest expense has yet to be determined. It depends on the company's use of bank overdraft facilities during the period to finance the purchase of the new equipment in July ($16 000), and any cash deficits or shortages that may arise because of the timing of receipts of sales revenues and payments for the company's expenses.

In order to predict the usage and cost of bank overdraft facilities during the period, a projection of the cash flows for each month in the budget period still needs to be prepared.

BUDGETED PROFIT AND LOSS STATEMENT *for the three months ending 30 September 20X1*	
Sales (p. 860)	$175 000
less Cost of goods sold	107 810
Gross profit	67 190
less Operating expenses	
Selling and administrative (p. 863)	24 100
	43 090
less Interest expense	?
Net profit	?

Cash budget

The preparation of a budgeted cash flow statement assists the organisation in planning and managing its short-term financing methods. During the ordinary course of trading activities an organisation will encounter periods of cash surpluses and cash deficits, caused by the differential timing of its sales receipts compared with its expense payments, and by the need to make large lump-sum payments for specific purposes, such as the replacement of an item of equipment.

Predicting the frequency and significance of cash shortfalls will enable the company to plan the cheapest acceptable method of financing those shortfalls, for example through the use of bank overdraft facilities or through a fixed-term loan. Predicting the frequency and significance of cash surpluses will allow management to plan where, and for how long, it may be able to invest the surplus cash to best advantage, such as in the short-term money market.

With these objectives in mind, the monthly cash flow statements for the Marple Manufacturing Company will now be prepared. These statements will project the cash inflows for each month (e.g. from cash sales and the collection of accounts receivable), and compare them with the projected cash outflows for each month (e.g. payments to creditors for direct materials purchases, the company payroll and payment for the new machine to be purchased).

The budgets developed so far have been prepared on the basis of accrual accounting. These budgets have been concerned with the timing of revenues and expenses, with the objective of developing a projected profit and loss statement and balance sheet for the period. In developing cash flow projections, the focus changes from the timing of revenues and expenses to the timing of the cash flows associated with those revenues and expenses.

Schedule of cash receipts

The major item of cash inflow for most trading organisations, and the only one in the example of Marple Manufacturing, is cash collections from sales. In the example, assume that sales for any one month consist of 50 per cent cash sales and 50 per cent credit sales. Of the credit sales, 80 per cent are collected in cash in the month of sale, and 20 per cent in the following month.

Consequently, the cash collections from customers in July are made up as follows:

CASH COLLECTION—JULY	
Cash sales—July	
(0.5 × total sales July of $25 000)	$12 500
Credit sales—July	
(0.8 × 0.5 × total sales July of $25 000)	10 000
Credit sales—June	
(0.2 × 0.5 × total sales June of $50 000)	5 000
	27 500

The remaining 20 per cent of July credit sales will be collected in cash in August. The projection of cash collections from customers for each month in the budget period is shown below.

CASH COLLECTIONS FROM CUSTOMERS				
	June	July	August	September
	$	$	$	$
Total sales	50 000	25 000	50 000	100 000
Cash sales (0.5)		12 500	25 000	50 000
Credit sales (0.5):				
from current month (0.8)		10 000	20 000	40 000
from previous month (0.2)		5 000	2 500	5 000
Total cash collections		27 500	47 500	95 000

Schedule of accounts payable

The credit terms on purchases of raw materials by Marple Manufacturing are 'net thirty days'.[1] Marple pays 50 per cent of a given month's purchases in that month, and 50 per cent in the following month.

CASH PAYMENTS FOR PURCHASES				
	June	July	August	September
	$	$	$	$
Purchases	11 400	6 900	16 050	25 950
Cash payments:				
current month's purchases (0.5)		3 450	8 025	12 975
previous month's purchases (0.5)		5 700	3 450	8 025
Total cash payments		9 150	11 475	21 000

Schedule of payments for direct labour

In this example we will assume that the cash payments for direct labour are made in the same month in which the direct labour costs are incurred. The cash payments for labour in each month are, therefore, the same as the costs shown on page 861.

Schedule of payments for manufacturing overheads

Assume again that Marple Manufacturing pays for its manufacturing overhead services in the month in which they are incurred. This means that the cash payments for these services in each month are the same as the costs shown on page 862, with the exception that depreciation must be deducted as a non-cash expense.

CASH PAYMENTS FOR MANUFACTURING OVERHEADS			
	July	August	September
Total costs (p. 862)	$10 105	$10 710	$11 755
less Depreciation	4 000	4 000	4 000
Cash payments	6 105	6 710	7 755

Schedule of payments for selling and administrative expenses

Given the assumption that these costs are also paid in cash in the month in which they are incurred, the cash payments are as shown in the relevant budget (see page 863).

---

[1] This is the expression used to indicate to customers the time at which their account will be considered to be 'in arrears' or 'in default (of the trading agreement)'. 'Net 30 days' therefore means that the customer has 30 days to settle (pay) the account. To retain a good credit rating with this supplier (which often means trading at a preferential price) it is good practice to make payments within the period for which they are willing to grant credit.

Other cash payments

The Marple Manufacturing Company will pay accrued interest of $95, outstanding at 30 June, in July. The term loan of $5000 will be repaid in August, and payment for the new equipment ($16 000) will be made in July.

Additionally, the company wishes to maintain at least $5000 in cash at the end of each period. It uses bank overdraft facilities to finance short-term cash deficits. Overdraft facilities are drawn at the beginning of each month in anticipation of the cash deficit predicted for the month in the cash flow budget. Borrowings, together with interest, are repaid in multiples of $1000 at the end of the month in which surplus cash is generated. The interest rate is 12 per cent per annum.

Based on this information, the budgeted cash flow statement for each month may now be prepared:

BUDGETED CASH FLOW STATEMENT			
for the three months ending 30 September 20X1			
	July	August	September
	$	$	$
Opening balance	5 000	5 000	5 508
Cash receipts:			
Collections from customers (p. 867)	27 500	47 500	95 000
Total cash available	32 500	52 500	100 508
Cash payments:			
Purchases (p. 868)	9 150	11 475	21 000
Direct labour (p. 861)	5 500	11 000	20 500
Manufacturing overheads (p. 868)	6 105	6 710	7 755
Selling and administrative (p. 863)	5 900	7 500	10 700
Purchase of new equipment	16 000		
Payment of accrued interest	95		
Repayment of term loan		5 000	
Total payments	42 750	41 685	59 955
Minimum cash balance required	5 000	5 000	5 000
Total cash needed	47 750	46 685	64 955
Excess (deficiency) (1)	(15 250)	5 815	35 553
Borrowing (short-term)	15 250	–	–
Repayments (2)	–	5 307	10 353
—Interest		307 (3)	103 (4)
—Capital		5 000	10 250
Ending balance	5 000	5 508	30 200

Notes on budgeted cash flow statement:

(1) Total cash available minus total cash needed.
(2) Repayments of capital are made in multiples of $1000.
(3) Interest calculation for August:

$$\frac{\$15\ 250 \times 0.12}{12} \quad + \quad \frac{(\$15\ 250 + \$153) \times 0.12}{12}$$

$$= \quad \$153 + \$154$$

$$= \quad \$307$$

(4) Interest calculation for September:

$$\frac{\$10\,250 \times 0.12}{12}$$

$$= \$103$$

Note also that the cash flow statement must be prepared sequentially, as the predicted ending balance of cash in one month becomes the opening balance in the next month.

Completing the financial budgets

All the information required for the completion of the budgeted profit and loss statement, started on p. 866, and the budgeted balance sheet is now known.

BUDGETED PROFIT AND LOSS STATEMENT: MARPLE MANUFACTURING COMPANY	
for the three months ending 30 September 20X1	
Sales	$175 000
less Cost of goods sold	107 810
Gross profit	67 190
less Operating expenses:	
Selling and administrative	24 100
	43 090
less Interest expense	410
Net profit	$ 42 680

BUDGETED BALANCE SHEET: MARPLE MANUFACTURING COMPANY			
as at 30 September 20X1			
Assets	$	$	$
Current assets:			
Cash (1)		30 200	
Accounts receivable (2)		10 000	
Raw materials inventory (3)		7 500	
Finished goods inventory (4)		7 700	55 400
Non-current assets:			
Land (5)		90 000	
Plant and equipment (6)	196 000		
Accumulated depreciation (7)	62 000	134 000	224 000
Total assets			279 400
Liabilities			
Current liabilities:			
Accounts payable (8)			12 975
Non-current liabilities:			–
Total liabilities			12 975
Shareholders' funds			
Paid-up capital		200 000	
Retained profits (9)		66 425	266 425
Total liabilities and shareholders' funds			279 400

Notes on budgeted balance sheet:

(1) From cash budget.
(2) 20 per cent of September credit sales.
(3) 2500 units × $3 per unit.
(4) 500 units × $15.40 cost per unit.
(5) Unchanged from balance sheet as at 30 June.
(6) Plant and equipment at 30 June ($180 000) plus new equipment purchased ($16 000).
(7) Accumulated depreciation at 30 June ($50 000) plus depreciation expense for period ($12 000).
(8) 50 per cent of September purchases.
(9) Retained profits at 30 June ($23 745) plus budgeted income for three months ($42 680).

Budget decisions

The financial budgets developed in the Marple Manufacturing Company example project the probable outcome of management plans for the budget period. However, they reflect the outcome of only one set of plans from a wide range of alternatives available to management. When developing the budget, management must select between a wide variety of options relating to considerations such as product mix, sales price, direct material quality and marketing strategies. Consequently, if the predicted financial result does not meet management's target financial performance for the budget period, management may wish to consider alternative plans, such as a decrease in sales prices with the objective of raising sales volume, increased advertising expenditures, or the use of lower-cost raw materials.

Information will need to be provided to enable management to evaluate the projected financial outcome of any or all of these alternatives. Repeating the entire budget formulation process for alternative sets of plans is clearly possible, since budgets can be prepared using powerful spreadsheet packages that readily rework the entire master budget, given a change in data input. However, there are so many alternative courses of action to take into consideration that this can be a major task, even when using spreadsheets. It is preferable, both during the initial formulation of the budget and during any possible reworking of the budget, to focus on the information relating to individual choices.

A simplified model that concentrates on identifying a limited number of critical variables in the profit determination process, and examining the relationships among those variables, is known as 'cost-volume-profit analysis'.

Cost-volume-profit (CVP) analysis

This is a simple technique which enables management to predict the probable short-term effect on profit of changes in critical cost and revenue variables. The technique relies on what is known as the 'contribution margin' concept and has two main objectives: to determine the break-even level of operations in the short term, and to predict the effect on profit of changes in the level of activity, prices or the cost structure.

The break-even level of operations (or break-even point) is the point at which total revenue for the period is just equal to total costs and hence profit is zero. CVP analysis can be used to determine how many units of output must be produced and sold if the firm is to operate without a loss in the period. CVP analysis can also focus on particular segments of the organisation, or particular products, to identify how certain changes with respect to those segments or products will affect the total profit.

Example: *Cost-volume-profit analysis*

The Verry Firm manufactures and sells a single product at a price of $10 per unit. The variable costs of production and sale total $6 per unit, and the total fixed costs for the period are estimated at $100 000.

This information allows for a determination of the contribution margin. The contribution margin is the excess of the sales price per unit over the variable costs per unit of production and sale, and represents the amount each unit produced and sold contributes to the coverage of fixed costs and to profits.

In this example, the contribution margin is $4 per unit ($10 − $6), and the break-even point in units may be determined as:

$$\text{Break-even point (units)} = \frac{\text{Total fixed costs}}{\text{Contribution margin per unit}}$$

$$= \frac{\$100\ 000}{\$4}$$

$$= 25\ 000 \text{ units}$$

The firm must sell 25 000 units to cover its fixed costs and therefore to break even. Beyond that point, every additional unit sold contributes $4 to profit.

The break-even point in sales revenue terms is $250 000 (25 000 units × $10 per unit). This may be estimated directly using the contribution margin ratio, which is the proportion of the contribution margin per unit in relation to the sales price per unit ($4/$10 = 0.4).

$$\text{Break-even point (\$)} = \frac{\text{Total fixed costs}}{\text{Contribution margin ratio}}$$

$$= \frac{\$100\ 000}{0.4}$$

$$= \$250\ 000$$

The break-even point assists management planning. For example, a break-even point near the top end of the estimated sales level for the period indicates that profit is vulnerable to demand fluctuation, because fixed costs are a major component of total costs.

The main benefit of CVP analysis, however, is to provide management with an estimate of how profit will respond to changes in prices, costs and volume of production and sales in the short term.

Assume that the management of the Verry Firm estimates the sales level during the period to be 30 000 units. This could be increased to 32 000 units, either by spending an additional $10 000 on sales promotion or by decreasing the price by 10 cents per unit. CVP analysis may be used to evaluate these alternatives.

The estimated profit at 30 000 units sales volume is:

$$\begin{aligned}
\text{Profit} &= \text{total contribution} - \text{total fixed costs} \\
&= (\text{units sold} \times \text{contribution margin}) - \text{total fixed costs} \\
&= (30\ 000 \times \$4) - \$100\ 000 \\
&= \$20\ 000
\end{aligned}$$

Alternatively, profit could have been derived by:

$$\begin{aligned}
\text{Profit} &= \text{units sold beyond break-even point} \times \text{contribution margin per unit} \\
&= (30\ 000 - 25\ 000) \times \$4 \\
&= \$20\ 000
\end{aligned}$$

The estimated profit at 32 000 units sales volume with incremental sales promoti
costs of $10 000 is:

$$\begin{aligned} \text{Profit} &= \text{total contribution} - \text{total fixed costs} \\ &= (\text{units sold} \times \text{contribution margin}) - \text{total fixed costs} \\ &= (32\ 000 \times \$4) - \$110\ 000 \\ &= \$18\ 000 \end{aligned}$$

The increased sales promotion ($10 000) does not generate sufficient extra contribution
from sales (2000 units × $4 contribution margin per unit) to cover its cost. Consequently,
the estimated profit for the period is less than the profit estimated without the sales
promotion.

The estimated profit at 32 000 units sales volume, with a reduction in price of 10 cents
per unit is:

$$\begin{aligned} \text{Profit} &= \text{total contribution} - \text{total fixed costs} \\ &= (\text{units sold} \times \text{contribution margin}) - \text{total fixed costs} \\ &= (32\ 000 \times \$3.90) - \$100\ 000 \\ &= \$24\ 800 \end{aligned}$$

Although the contribution margin per unit has been reduced, the increase in volume of
sales is estimated to offset the lost per-unit margin, giving an increased total contribution
and, therefore, generating increased profit for the period.

CVP analysis may also be used to determine the level of sales volume required to earn a
target profit under specified revenue and cost conditions. Assume that the management of
the Verry Firm was considering a change in the basis of salespeople's remuneration, by discontinuing commission on sales (currently estimated at 50 cents per unit sold) and
increasing salaries to compensate. This would require a $20 000 increase in salaries and
would increase contribution margin per unit by 50 cents. Management wishes to earn a target profit of $20 000. The volume needed to earn this profit under the changed conditions
is calculated below:

$$\begin{aligned} \text{Total contribution} &= \text{total fixed costs} + \text{target profit} \\ (\text{Sales volume}) \times (\text{contribution margin per unit}) &= \$120\ 000 + \$20\ 000 \\ \text{Sales volume} &= \frac{\$140\ 000}{\$4.50} \\ &= 31\ 111\ \text{units} \end{aligned}$$

The interrelationships between costs, volume and profit may be shown graphically.
Figure 25.2 is based on the following data:

Sales price per unit	$10
Variable cost per unit	$6
Fixed costs per period	$50 000

The graph indicates that the break-even point is 12 500 units or $125 000. Beyond this
point each unit produced and sold contributes $4 per unit to profit.

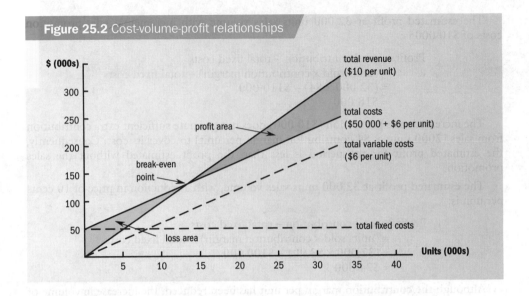

Figure 25.2 Cost-volume-profit relationships

Assumptions and limitations of CVP analysis

The assumptions and limitations of CVP analysis may be examined using Figure 25.2 as an illustration.

Linearity of cost and revenue functions

CVP analysis assumes linearity of the cost and revenue functions. If these functions are curvi-linear, under the assumptions of differential per-unit revenues and costs at different output levels, there may be two or more break-even points. This is shown in Figure 25.3.

The assumption of linearity may, however, be valid for the anticipated relevant range of activity during the period. If so, CVP analysis constitutes a useful basis for management information and decision making in the short term. The relevant range is shown in Figure 25.3 to indicate the tendency towards linearity over these levels of output.

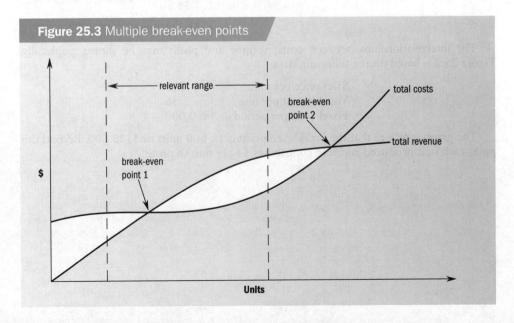

Figure 25.3 Multiple break-even points

Selling prices and cost elements remain unchanged

The relationships shown in Figure 25.2 apply to a unique combination of selling prices and costs. If any of these change, the determined relationships shown on the graph would no longer be relevant for predicting profit. This indicates the static nature of CVP analysis.

Single-product analysis

CVP analysis is valid only for single products or for multiple products that are sold in unchanging combinations (i.e. constant sales mix). Assuming a constant sales mix allows the calculation of an average contribution margin per unit, which may be used in the analysis in similar fashion to the contribution margin for a single product. However, if the sales mix changes, the basic CVP technique cannot accommodate the changing relativities among high-margin and low-margin products.

Equal sales and production volumes

The analysis assumes that sales and production levels are the same for the period, so sales revenues and costs may be related to the same level of activity. This assumption implies that changes in beginning and ending inventories during the period are insignificant.

Volume is the critical factor influencing costs

In earlier discussions it was indicated that the determination of cost patterns may depend on factors other than volume of production and sales. Variable overhead costs, for example, may be influenced by activity levels based on the number of set-ups and the number of components.

The utility of CVP analysis, like all simplified decision models, must be based on an evaluation of the assumptions in any specific situation. If any of the above simplifying assumptions are thought likely to be sufficiently unrealistic as to cause a significantly distorted result, the assumption should be modified. Extensions of CVP analysis relaxing the assumptions of linearity, unchanging prices and cost structures and single products are available. So, too, are extensions designed to allow formal recognition of uncertainty in the estimation of critical variables.

CVP analysis is a useful short-term planning technique for management, drawing its utility from the simplicity of its concept. Because of its potential assistance in making planning decisions, it can be a useful adjunct to the budget planning process.

Activity-based costing

Budgets based on activity-based costing principles (Chapter 22) are appropriately called 'activity-based budgets'. Such budgets are more detailed than those resulting from the traditional budgeting approach described earlier in the chapter. They forecast the volumes of all cost drivers such as machine set-ups, number of purchase orders and engineering changes. *Such detail facilitates the management of costs rather than just accounting for costs.* This was illustrated in Chapter 23, in the discussion on value-adding and non-value-adding costs.

As demonstrated in Chapter 23, activity-based costing (ABC) and activity-based management (ABM) are particularly helpful when making decisions affecting the intermediate term. For example, data on the length of time it takes to transport raw materials and partly completed goods around a factory highlight the need to streamline production. Other activity data may affect decisions made during research and development. For example, if the number of components is a cost driver, cost containment may be achieved by designing a product with fewer components (e.g. cars now have large moulded body components that save the costs of both transporting parts and welding parts together).

A further use of ABM is in attaining target costs. Target costing entails the design of products within three predetermined parameters: the function of the product, the quality of the product and the total cost to produce the product (including research, design, marketing, etc.). The cost parameter is determined by reference to the competitive price for which the product with these stated functions and quality can be sold in the marketplace. From the competitive price that the product could attain, it is possible to deduct the required profit margin to derive the average required cost of the product. ABM is one technique that assists designers to design a product within this target cost parameter.[2]

In many environments ABC achieves a better understanding of cost causation. First, in an environment in which all products cause costs in very similar ways (e.g. two different dining chairs made in similar ways will have similar relationships with overhead costs, whereas a manually produced dining chair will have a very different pattern of cost causation to a predominantly machine-worked chair) there is less opportunity for inaccurate costing than in an environment in which there is diversity of product. Second, any inaccuracy has less impact when overhead costs are a very small proportion of total costs. Finally, the effect on the firm of making erroneous decisions due to inaccurate costing depends on the competitiveness in the market in which the firm operates. Hence, ABC brings the greater decision-making benefits as product diversity, overhead costs and market competition increase.

A use of ABC for short-term decision making is in assessing how appropriate the selling price of the product is, given the best estimate of product cost. When competition is weak, this information may be used to guide the determination of the selling price. When competition is strong, the market sets the 'going price' and the best estimation of cost indicates how profitable the product is (i.e. whether the producer can afford to operate in that market, given the current product cost). It has been found that prices accepted on the basis of traditional costing (using the averaging of overhead costs as presented in Chapter 22) can lead to large-volume products subsidising small-volume products that are made in many small batches.

Although ABC was described in Chapter 22 as a product costing method, it can be used to trace costs to objects (called cost objects) other than products. For example, decisions often need to be made about which supplier to deal with, or the profitability of customers. The costs of dealing with suppliers are greater than the price paid to them for materials. Added costs come from receiving poor-quality items, the wrong amount of items, early or late deliveries, or inaccurate paperwork. Similarly, customers (in particular wholesale customers) can cause 'hidden costs' that are revealed by ABC—costs such as ordering irregularly, ordering small amounts frequently instead of fewer large orders, and the costs associated with engineering changes to the components they buy. An ABC system can associate such costs with the customers causing them, because it is able to identify the cause of the activities that cause the cost incurrence.

These decisions will impact on the construction of budgets and may be undertaken specifically as part of the budget planning process.

A full discussion of the wide range of uses of activity-based information in budgeting and other decision making are beyond the scope of this text.[3]

---

[2] In-depth coverage of target costing is beyond the scope of this book. Further detail on the way ABC and functional analysis can be used to achieve target costs can be found in J. G. Burch, *Cost and Management Accounting: A Modern Approach*, West Publishing Company, Saint Paul, MN, 1994.

[3] Two monographs that provide many case study examples of the use of activity-based techniques and the information derived from them are: A. L. Friedman and S. R. Lyne, *Activity Based Techniques: The Real Life Consequences*, 1995, and J. Innes and G. Norris, *The Use of Activity-based Information: A Managerial Perspective*, 1997, both published by The Chartered Institute of Management Accountants, London.

> **Case 25.2** Behaviour implications of budgeting
>
> Coming out of a meeting with senior managers 'Charlie' Charleston looked totally dejected. Charlie was responsible for the production of a line of women's garments and had just been to a budget meeting with other line managers and senior managers. The participation of the line managers at these meetings had started two years earlier, in an attempt to make the line managers feel a greater commitment to the budget targets.
>
> CJ, another line manager, suggested that Charlie's demeanour represented the way all the line managers felt. Charlie merely commented that they all had another year of impossible targets to reach and silently recalled the job advertisement in last weekend's newspaper for a production manager in a rival firm. Perhaps senior managers in that firm actually listened to production managers when they explained the difficulty of achieving top production rates when the staff were still learning how to use new equipment?
>
> Meanwhile CJ went off to call the rival firm, having also seen the advertisement last weekend. CJ was hoping that in the rival firm senior managers did not have their performance evaluated on the basis of comparisons between departments when those departments made different products, targeted different markets, and had equipment with varying production capacity.
>
> Before reading a discussion of this case at the end of the chapter, think about the issues raised here and make a note of the way you think the meeting was run, and the way you think the meeting should have been run. Also pay some consideration to the way the managers' performance seems to be assessed.

The behavioural aspects of budgeting

The discussion on budgets so far has concentrated on the construction of budgets and the data required. This may be called the 'accounting process' for budget preparation and may be contrasted with the 'organisational process' of budgeting. We have also looked at the operational use of budgets, which may be contrasted with the administrative and managerial use of budgets.

The organisational process of budgeting involves consideration of the complex interactions among managers that occur over the time between setting the initial budget guidelines and distributing the approved budgets. The final budgets provide not only formal estimates of profit and cash flows for the period but also targets of performance against which managers and employees will be evaluated. Use of the budget for control and evaluation purposes is designed to motivate lower-level managers and employees to perform to budget expectations. The budget preparation process and the way management uses the budget therefore have an enormous influence over the behaviour of those managers and employees who are expected to be guided in their decisions by the budget.

In practice, however, management's approach to budgets and the budgeting process may decrease rather than increase motivation to achieve the budget expectations. For example:

- The budget 'subjects', the people responsible for attaining budget performance, may reject budget targets if the budget is seen to be arbitrarily or unfairly created by senior managers and then imposed on lower-level managers and employees.
- If budget subjects regard the target levels of performance as unrealistically high, they may reject the levels set in the budget and substitute much lower levels.

- If senior managers do not appear to treat the budget as important, the budget subjects will not pay much attention to it or its contents either, so will not be motivated or guided by it.
- Lower levels of performance may result if undesirable pressures are exerted on people to abide by the budget, perhaps by linking financial rewards or penalties to performance against the budget.

Although pressure often provides a challenge and encourages innovation, different degrees of pressure cause individuals to react in different ways. Some people have a positive response to pressure and try to meet expectation levels, whereas others react unfavourably and perform below standard. Employees or lower-level managers may seek to relieve this pressure by forming coalitions or informal groups, whose aim is collective security through cooperative non-compliance. For example, employees could informally agree on group production standards different from those expressed in the budget.

The organisational process of budgeting is intended to ensure that the final budgets are acceptable not only to top-level management in terms of organisational objectives but also to the lower levels of management responsible for meeting those objectives. Some of the conditions that can influence the successful use of budgets will now be outlined.

Suitability of goals and objectives

The goals and objectives set by the company must be clearly defined and must be appropriate. They are inappropriate if they do not guide the managers in setting their own objectives or in designing their own operating plans for the coming period.

Budget emphasis in the organisation

In some organisations the preparation of annual budgets has become a routine matter and the budgets lack meaning. They may not even be referred to again for the whole year. In these circumstances there is a total lack of budget emphasis. The other extreme is that the budget may be expected to govern every movement of the managers.

For budgets to be influential there needs to be a *commitment* to them and *sensible use* of them by senior management. Senior managers demonstrate the importance of the budget to them if they are active in reviewing and approving budgets and in following up variances (i.e. differences between the budget and actual outcomes). The budget will become even more important to managers if it is used in performance evaluation.

The sensible use of budgets relates to perceptions of equity and control. For example, statements that report on the performance of the division, department or other segment of the organisation are economic statements of performance. They differ from statements on the performance of individual managers, since a manager should not be held responsible for any item over which he or she does not have control, or at least significant influence.

The performance report on a department may be adjusted to become suitable as a performance report on its manager by identifying the 'controllable items' (discussed in Chapter 23). The preparation and use of a performance report that includes only items over which the manager is held responsible is called *responsibility accounting*.

Even items that are within the control of managers may differ from the budget for good reasons. Indeed, if sales demand is 10 per cent greater than forecast, and operating capacity exists to meet this demand, management would want production engineered costs to be higher than in the budget as they would want that demand to be met. Similarly, if sales demand is 10 per cent less than forecast, it is reasonable for production to be down by 10 per cent, otherwise there will be an inventory build-up. Such fluctuations are taken into account by assessing performance against the *flexible budget* (a reworked budget that calculates the cost projections that would have appeared in the budget if demand had been accurately forecast). The flexible budget will be discussed fully in Chapter 26.

Involvement of managers in budget setting

There are practical advantages to be obtained from the involvement of lower-level managers in budget setting. As these managers are closer to the action being planned they can give useful feedback as to how reasonable the budget expectations are. Furthermore, there may be behavioural advantages to participative decision making with regards to the budget.

The extent to which lower levels of management participate in setting budget targets has been a subject of considerable research in management and management accounting. As a general statement, it has been agreed that if people subject to the budget are also involved in setting the budget they will 'internalise' the budget; they will come to regard the budget as their own and to feel more responsibility for meeting the budget targets, and will therefore strive harder to attain the levels of performance contained within the budget. This argument is often based on theories of individual motivation, which propose that people will be more motivated if they are given more responsibility, more autonomy, and more opportunity for achievement in their work. Participation is one way of doing this, because it increases the subject's responsibilities in the work situation and also increases his or her perceived control over the budgets and the level of performance built into the budgets.

As discussed in Chapter 21, the presence of influence in participatory decision making is very important if advantage is to be taken of the approach of involving managers in setting the budget. If, for example, managers are merely invited to attend meetings at which decisions are made, they will still feel that budget objectives are being imposed on them, and the budget objectives may still be unrealistic. In this context the notion of 'involvement' and 'participation' must include a reasonable level of influence over the decisions made.

Even so, the research findings are more complex than the above statement implies. Some research suggests that not all people are motivated by increased responsibility, autonomy and the need for achievement. Some people are quite happy to be told what to do in their job situation and to go about doing it within the hours for which they are paid. For these people, the opportunity for participation in the budget-setting process may have no positive effect on their motivation or commitment to the job. In fact, participation may be used here to negotiate less demanding levels of performance (called budget slack) in order to make life a little easier. Managers are even more likely to attempt to introduce budgetary slack when their performance is evaluated against the budget and they are subject to tight control (i.e. they are expected to conform exactly with the budget and are not given the discretion to deviate from it) or they operate in an environment that is subject to fluctuations.

It is important, therefore, that the accountant involved in the budgeting process in organisations understands the types of people, or the personalities of people, who are subject to the budget, and the stresses to which budget achievement is subject. This understanding will be critical to the organisational process of budgeting, particularly in respect of the motivational benefits expected to be gained from participation.

The accountant must understand the type of task or job for which budgets are to be established. Again, research in management accounting suggests that participation may be more effective in some tasks or jobs than in others. Some tasks are very complex and uncertain—it is difficult to know what actions to take in carrying out the task in order to bring about the desired result. An example might be research and development directed towards designing a new and technologically advanced computer system. Here, participation by all people involved, at all levels, would be valuable in clarifying the nature and problems of the task, how to go about the task, and how to set budgets and targets for resource needs and uses. Obviously the benefit of participation here would be one of bringing as much knowledge to bear on the task as possible in order to determine how best to approach it and how best to plan and budget for it, as much as for a motivational benefit.

By contrast, some tasks are quite predictable and certain—the brewing of beer would be an example. The technology underlying the task of brewing is well known; the physical relationships between the inputs of raw materials (such as hops and water) and the output can be specified with considerable certainty. Here it may be said that the 'path-goal' relationship is quite clear—we know exactly what path to take in terms of materials, processes and actions to attain the goal. Participation may not offer the same path-clarification benefit that participation offered in the previous example of designing a computer system.

Clear lines of authority and responsibility

To hold a manager responsible for a particular item in a performance report there must be a clear delineation of responsibility between different managers. Furthermore, being held responsible for an item also requires the possession of authority with regard to the control of, or influence over, that item.

Budgeting in perspective

Further details of the motivational and behavioural aspects of budgeting are beyond the scope of this text.[4] However, the examples above point to the importance for accountants involved in budgeting in organisations to understand the organisational process as well as the accounting process of budgeting.

In a highly complex organisation with many departments, activities and managers the organisational process may take several months and will entail a formal system of budget preparation, administration and review. This system may use budget committees, or may involve the creation of separate budget departments with their own managers and personnel.

These considerations indicate that, while the techniques of budget formulation are straightforward, the success of the budgetary process relies on careful analysis of the organisational process, including the ways in which budgeted levels of performance are set and the ways in which the budget system is administered and implemented.

Ethical issues

As the accountant within the sales division of a media advertising company, you have the responsibility of monitoring the performance of individual sales people against monthly financial targets for selling media advertising space. One of the sales staff has been of concern to you this year—a person who has been with the firm a little while and is very well liked. The person has been through difficult times in the last year or so with a divorce and property settlement that caused him both emotional and financial distress. For several months his sales performance has suffered, and he lost goodwill with his regular clients through unreliability brought on by his emotional state. He came very close to losing his job. However, for the last three months his sales figures have improved and he has reached budget on each occasion. It comes to your attention that, while part of this improvement is genuine and the salesman is clearly recapturing the client base he had previously, he has also been falsifying some of his accounts to ensure he reaches his target.

What do you do?

---

[4] A good reference for a reader interested in pursuing these aspects is L. D. Parker, K. R. Ferris and D. T. Otley, *Accounting for the Human Factor*, Prentice-Hall, Sydney, 1989, Chs 4 and 5.

Summary

This chapter has discussed accounting for short-term management planning. The major accounting procedures discussed were the preparation of operating budgets and financial budgets. The sub-budgets (support budgets) required in the process of preparing budgeted financial statements were also examined. The important short-term planning technique of cost-volume-profit analysis was discussed and the uses of ABC for short-term and intermediate-term decision making were considered. Finally, the chapter examined the organisational process of budgeting to complement the technical process of budget formulation. In particular it examined the way in which behaviour may be influenced by inappropriate budgeting techniques and emphasis.

Discussion of in-text cases

Case 25.1

To determine how many units of each product to make each month Chris needs to know how much of each product is expected to be in the finished goods inventory at the beginning of the budget year, how many units of each product are expected to be sold each month and what the minimum finished goods inventory balance ought to be each month (usually expressed as a percentage of total demand in the following month). The sales forecast is crucial to these calculations, as Chris needs to determine what production is required in order to maintain inventory levels while meeting this sales demand. Monthly forecasts will need to be separately calculated, as it is likely that there will be seasonal demands. Taking an annual production level and dividing it by 12 to derive the monthly production schedule does not allow, for example, for the demand for footballs increasing during the winter while the demand for tennis balls declines.

Chris may then draw attention to any problems that the budget reveals. It is possible that Chris does not have adequate equipment to meet the production needs, or overtime costs may need to be met to increase the production capacity of the plant.

Case 25.2

The problems that these line managers are experiencing seem to include:

- Participation does not mean having any influence over decision making. It appears to be merely a case of being present at the meeting where decisions are made or explained.
- Valid objections to budget targets are ignored and explanations dismissed, or senior management lacks the ability to understand production problems.
- Managers' performance is assessed by how well they 'do' compared with one another, even when these performances are not comparable due to working with different products and in different markets. (One may be experiencing a surge while another goes through a slump due to external factors not related to anything over which the managers have control.) Some managers are working with new, modern equipment, whereas others have equipment that is due for replacement, has low production capabilities and requires more frequent maintenance.

Senior managers will not achieve the commitment of subordinate managers to budget targets unless the subordinate managers have had some input into the budget figures. Imposing a budget on managers when they have been called to a meeting and ignored is likely to produce a worse effect than imposing budget figures on the managers without pretending to adopt participatory decision-making methods.

The senior managers have taken action that is sure to lose any respect their subordinate managers previously had for them.

> Comparing the performance of managers is dangerous because they operate under different conditions. It is far better to compare the performance of each manager against a fair evaluation of what their perfomance should be. This evaluation of what they should achieve can be derived from the budget.

 **Review exercises**

Discussion questions

25.1 State and briefly explain four functions of budgeting.

25.2 Describe the structure of the master budget, explaining the purpose of each section.

25.3 Examination of the budget projections for the Wood Green Company for the next three months shows differences between:

   (a) sales levels and production levels

   (b) raw material usage and raw material purchases

   (c) sales revenues and collections from customers.

     Provide reasons for each of these differences.

25.4 What are the purposes of preparing budgeted cash flow statements? What are the difficulties in preparing these statements?

25.5 Why is cost-volume-profit analysis a useful aid to budgetary planning?

25.6 Explain what is meant by each of the following:

   (a) Contribution margin

   (b) Contribution margin ratio

   (c) Break-even point

25.7 In respect of the ethical issue on page 880, what are you going to do? Why?

25.8 Compare and contrast the 'accounting process' of budgeting with the 'organisational process'.

25.9 'People who have to perform against budget targets should be allowed to participate in setting their budget targets.' Do you agree with this statement? Why or why not?

25.10 Explain four uses of activity-based information (such as ABC and ABM) in short- and intermediate-term decision making.

 Problems

25.11 *Missing data: CVP analysis*

Determine the missing data in each of the following cases:

	Case A	Case B	Case C
Sales price per unit	$12	?	?
Variable costs per unit	$8	$24	?
Contribution margin per unit	?	?	7
Contribution margin ratio	?	0.20	?
Total fixed costs	$60 000	?	$90 000
Break-even points (units)	?	?	30 000
Break-even point ($)	?	$240 000	$300 000

25.12 *CVP analysis*

Given the following data, determine the expected net profit for the period:

Variable costs per unit	$7
Contribution margin ratio	0.30
Break-even point ($)	$200 000
Anticipated sales	25 000 units

25.13 *Raw materials purchases budget*

Bramhall Manufacturing Company wishes to determine its requirements for raw materials over the three months January to March 20X1. The sales forecast for the first six months of 20X1 is as follows:

Month	Units
January	20 000
February	22 000
March	26 000
April	27 000
May	24 000
June	20 000

Each unit of product requires 0.5 kg of raw materials, expected to cost $12 per kg during the budget period.

Bramhall wishes to maintain raw materials inventory at the end of any month equal to 40 per cent of the next month's production requirements. At 31 December 20X0 inventory of raw materials stood at 4040 units.

The company also tries to maintain a finished goods inventory at the end of any month of 6000 units plus 10 per cent of the next month's forecast sales. Finished goods inventory at 31 December 20X0 was 8000 units.

Prepare a raw materials purchases budget, showing the quantity to be purchased in January, February and March.

25.14 *Budget preparation*

Manchester Products Ltd manufactures two products, MP1 and MP2. The following estimates have been made for the coming year.

	MP1	MP2
Sales volume in units	83 400	55 600
Sales price per unit	$170	$140
Finished goods inventories:		
Opening (units)	27 800	11 000
Closing (units)	35 000	12 500
Raw material requirements:		
Material A (kg)	$5\frac{1}{2}$	7
Material B (kg)	3	4
Direct labour requirements (hours)	$\frac{3}{4}$	$1\frac{1}{2}$

The cost of raw materials over the year is expected to average $11 per kg for Material A and $7 per kg for Material B. Inventories of Material A are estimated at 45 000 kg at the beginning of the year and 50 000 kg at the end of the year. Equivalent estimates for Material B are 40 000 kg (opening) and 44 000 kg (closing).

Direct labour rates over the year are expected to average $12 per hour. Variable manufacturing overhead is projected at $4 per direct labour hour and fixed manufacturing overhead is budgeted at $150 000 per month. Prepare the following budgets for the forthcoming year:

(a) sales budget
(b) production budget
(c) raw material usage and purchases budget
(d) direct labour budget
(e) manufacturing overhead budget

25.15 *Production and profit and loss statement budget*

Alderney Edge Company makes and sells a single product. The sales forecast for the three months October to December 20X1 is as follows:

	Units	
October	2500	$150 000
November	3000	180 000
December	3500	210 000

Sales during 20X2 are expected to average 4000 units per month. Standard costs and budget projections for production costs are:

Direct materials (5 kg at $3.00 per kg)	= $15 per unit
Direct labour (2 hours at $6.00 per hour)	= $12 per unit
Variable manufacturing overhead	= $4.50 per direct labour hour
Fixed manufacturing overhead	= $9000 per month

Selling and administrative costs are estimated at $30 000 per month plus 8 per cent of sales.

The company maintains finished goods inventories at 40 per cent of the next month's sales, and raw materials inventories at 30 per cent of the next month's requirements of materials. At the beginning of October the company had on hand 1600 units of finished goods, costed at $62 400, and 8000 kg of materials.

(a) For each of the three months prepare:

(i) production budget
(ii) raw material usage and purchases budget
(iii) direct labour budget
(iv) manufacturing overhead budget

(b) Prepare a budgeted profit and loss statement for the quarter.

25.16 *Cash inflow budget*

An analysis of accounts receivable for the Fallowfield Company at 31 December 20X2 shows the following:

Outstanding from sales of:	
December 20X2	$77 000
November 20X2	18 900
October 20X2	8 600
Prior to October 20X2	7 900

The sales forecast for the first three months of 20X3 are:

January	$210 000
February	135 000
March	160 000

All sales are on credit. Cash is normally collected from customers in the following pattern. Of the sales in any month, 65 per cent will be collected in the same month, 25 per cent in the month following sale, and 5 per cent in the second month following sale. The remaining 5 per cent generally proves to be uncollectable.

Prepare a statement showing the expected cash collections from customers for each of the first three months of 20X3.

25.17 *Cash flow budgets*

1. Given below is a balance sheet for Knutsford Products at 30 June 20X0 and a projected profit and loss statement for the company for July 20X0.

BALANCE SHEET
as at 30 June 20X0

	$	$		$	$
Non-current assets:			Non-current liabilities:		
Motor vehicles	20 500		Loan		7 000
less Accum. depn	9 000	11 500	Current liabilities:		
			Accounts payable	2 920	
			Interest payable	500	
Office furniture	7 500		Wages payable	1 200	4 620
less Accum. depn	7 500	–			
Current assets:					
Accounts receivable	2 340		Owners' equity:		
Cash	7 630		Capital and		
Inventory	4 200	14 170	retained profits		14 050
		25 670			25 670

PROJECTED PROFIT AND LOSS STATEMENT
for month of July 20X0

Sales		$8 600
less Expenses		
Cost of goods sold	$3 500	
Wages	1 800	
Advertising	450	
Depreciation	200	
Rent	850	6 800
Net profit before tax		$1 800

The following information is also available.

(i) Sales average 50 per cent cash, 50 per cent on credit with terms of net cash 30 days.
(ii) Bad debts are negligible.
(iii) The inventory balance expected at 31 July is $3400.

    (iv) The company intends paying cash for all expenses projected for July.

    (v) All purchases are on credit terms, payable within ten days of purchase.

    (vi) The current liabilities of interest and wages are due for payment in July. Prepare a cash flow budget for July 20X0.

2. The Ardwick Company wishes to forecast its cash receipts and payments for the first two months of the coming financial year, July and August 20X2.

An extract from the trial balance as at 30 June 20X2 shows the following balances:

Cash	$ 2 500
Accounts receivable	70 000
Allowance for doubtful debts	3 950
Inventory	21 815
Accounts payable	23 000

The company sells a single product at a price of $25 per unit. Actual sales for the last two months of the preceding financial year were $45 000 for May 20X2 and $62 500 for June 20X2. Forecast sales for July 20X2 are $75 000, for August $37 500, and for September $30 000. Total sales projected for July 20X2 to the following June are $375 000.

All sales are made on credit and a 2 per cent discount is allowed if cash is received within the first fifteen days of the month following the sale. The company's experience with the collection of cash from sales indicates that 70 per cent of the sales made in any one month will be collected within the discount period, 20 per cent by the end of the month following the sale, and 8 per cent in the second month after the sale. Two per cent of sales remain uncollectable.

Ardwick Company purchases its inventory at a unit cost of $11.50, and pays for all purchases within fifteen days. Consequently, approximately 50 per cent of any month's purchases are paid in the month, and the remainder in the following month. No discount is available to the company. At the end of any month Ardwick maintains an inventory of 500 units plus 25 per cent of forecast sales for the following month.

Total budgeted selling and administrative expenses for the year beginning July 20X2 are $100 000. This amount consists of $37 500 fixed costs, including depreciation expenses of $7500, and $62 500 variable costs. The variable component varies with the level of sales volume. All selling and administrative expenses are paid in the month in which they are incurred.

Ardwick has to repay a long-term loan of $25 000 on 27 August 20X2.

Prepare a budgeted cash flow statement for each month, July and August 20X2.

25.18 *CVP analysis*

1. The Stockport Novelty Company is considering a proposal to lease floor space in a large department store. It plans to sell T-shirts and print them on-the-spot with any slogan the customer requires. Stockport estimates that it can sell the printed shirts at $40 each. They cost $25 each from the wholesaler.

The department store has quoted a lease cost of $106 000 per year for the space Stockport needs. Stockport estimates other costs as follows:

Sales commissions	$1.90 per T-shirt
Sales promotion	$60 000 per year
Wages	$35 000 per year
Other	$38 000 per year

(a) What is the contribution margin per unit?

(b) What is the break-even point, in dollars and in units?

(c) If 17 500 T-shirts were sold, what would be Stockport's profit (or loss)?

(d) If the sales commission were to be discontinued and replaced by an increase in the wages cost of $10 000 and an increase in sales promotion cost by $40 000, what would be the break-even point, in units and in dollars?

2. Hulme Company produces and sells a single product. The following cost and revenue data are estimated for the forthcoming year 20X2.

Sales price	$15 per unit
Variable costs of production and sale	$10.50 per unit
Fixed costs	$900 000 per year
Annual volume	250 000 units

(a) Calculate:

  (i) contribution margin per unit

  (ii) contribution margin ratio

  (iii) break-even point in units

  (iv) estimated net profit for 20X2

(b) Calculate the break-even point and expected net profit for the year under each of the following alternatives:

  (i) decrease in sales price of $1.50 per unit

  (ii) increase in variable costs of $1.00 per unit

  (iii) twenty per cent increase in fixed costs

  (iv) ten per cent decrease in both sales price and variable costs

(c) Management believes that sales volume could be increased to 300 000 units for the year if the selling price were reduced by 50 cents per unit, or if an additional $10 000 per month was spent on advertising. Which, if either, alternative would you recommend?

3. New Mills Central Ltd produces petroleum products. The company is considering adding a high-octane racing fuel to its product line. The racing fuel will constitute only a small part of the company's total business, but will allow New Mills Central to offer a wider range of products to its customers.

Company management does not want a major feasibility study to be carried out for the new product as the additional investment in fixed facilities will not be substantial. However, management does require some basic sales and cost data to assess the likely profitability of the racing fuel.

Racing fuel of this type currently sells for $1.25 per litre, and is expected to require variable costs of $1.00 per litre for production and distribution. The company's current fixed costs are estimated to increase by $17 500 per month if the racing fuel is produced.

(a) Calculate the monthly break-even volume of sales for the racing fuel.

(b) Graph the relationship between costs, sales and volume.

(c) Although company management does not require the racing fuel to be as profitable as other products in its line, it has determined that production will go ahead only if the fuel will yield a minimum increase of $2500 per month in the net income of the company. What monthly volume of sales is required to meet this criterion?

(d) Sales management estimates the monthly demand for the fuel to be between 90 000 and 100 000 litres. What increase in monthly net income can the company expect?

(e) Sales management wants to launch the product using one of the following promotional schemes:

    (i) Spend $10 000 per month on advertising in the first three months.

    (ii) Price the fuel at $1.15 per litre in the first three months.

    (iii) Spend $5000 per month on advertising and price the fuel at $1.20 per litre in the first three months.

    It is estimated that each of these schemes will ensure sales of 90 000 litres per month over the promotional period. Which scheme should be adopted?

25.19 *Comprehensive budgets*

Wilmslow Ltd is preparing budgets for the first quarter of the coming year, 20X0, on the basis of the following estimations:

- *Sales*
  The company manufactures and sells a single product. Forecast sales during the period are 20 000 units at a price of $25 per unit.

- *Production costs*
  Direct materials: Each unit of product requires 1.5 units of raw materials at a cost of $5 per unit.
  Direct labour: Each unit of product requires 1 hour of labour at $7.50 per hour.
  Manufacturing overhead: Variable manufacturing overhead is estimated at $1.25 per unit of product. Fixed overhead is estimated at $37 500 for the quarter.

- *Inventories*
  Finished goods inventory at the beginning of the quarter is 9000 units costed at $159 750. It is desired to have an inventory of finished goods at the end of the quarter of 14 000 units.
  Raw materials inventory at the beginning of the quarter is 10 000 units. Desired inventory at the end of the quarter is 8000 units.

- *Selling and administrative expenses*
  Selling expenses for the period are expected to average $2.50 per unit and administrative expenses are estimated at $63 000.

Prepare the following budgets:

(a) sales budget

(b) production budget

(c) raw material usage and purchases budget

(d) direct labour budget

(e) manufacturing overhead budget

(f) selling and administrative expenses budget

(g) cost of goods sold budget

(h) budgeted profit and loss statement

Case studies

25.20 *CVP analysis*

Security Systems of Australia (SSA) Pty Ltd sells and installs security alarms for both residential and commercial properties. The company is adding to its product range a revolutionary component that will greatly boost the sensitivity and range of sensory detection devices in alarm systems. Called the 'Bionic Eye', this component can be added on to existing systems or installed as part of new systems.

SSA plans to sell the 'Bionic Eye' for $1198 installed, whether as part of a new or an existing system. At that price, demand is forecast at 5000 units per period. The component costs $580 to buy from the manufacturer and is expected to cost $120 to install (based on an average time to install of 2 hours at $60 per hour). SSA sales-people are to be paid a commission of $58 per unit.

It is proposed to spend $240 000 on advertising the 'Bionic Eye' each period, and that SSA will incur additional overhead costs of $200 000 each period as a result of carrying the product. Thus, based on an estimated sales volume of 5000 units per period, each unit bears a cost of $88 ($440 000/5000 units) for advertising and overheads.

Required

Unless otherwise stated, the following questions are independent of each other.

(a) At a price of $1198 per unit, how many 'Bionic Eyes' must SSA sell each period to reach the break-even point?

(b) SSA's marketing department wants the 'Bionic Eye' to be sold at a lower price than $1198 in order to capture more volume. The marketing people argue that the demand for alarm systems is expanding rapidly and that this will attract more com-panies into the industry. They also believe that a lot of new business comes from 'word of mouth' from existing customers. They contend that SSA should go for mar-ket share and should price the 'Bionic Eye' at $1050. At that price, they estimate sales volume will increase by 20 per cent to 6000 units per period.

Calculate the effect on sales revenue, total costs and profit per period if the units are priced at $1050 compared with a price of $1198. What price should be charged for the 'Bionic Eye'?

(c) A government authority with a very large number of premises around the country wants to place a bulk order with SSA for 250 'Bionic Eyes'. These are to be installed into existing alarm systems in the authority's multiple offices and build-ings in Sydney and Melbourne. The authority wants the units installed within a month and has offered a lump-sum payment of $250 000.

SSA cannot obtain any additional units from the manufacturer to meet the authority's needs. If it accepts the government contract it will have to divert 250 units from its normal sales and will lose those sales to competitors.

Should SSA accept the government authority's offer?

(d) A proposal has been received from Blackadder Alarms Ltd. Blackadder has offered to supply and install the 'Bionic Eye' to SSA customers for a fixed fee of $640 000 per 1000 units. SSA will still make the sale to the customers and collect the revenue.

If SSA does sub-contract supply and installation, its advertising costs of $240 000 per period could be reduced by 25 per cent and the overhead costs of $200 000 per period could be reduced by 30 per cent.

Should SSA become involved in the proposed arrangement?

25.21 *Comprehensive cash flow budgets*

The Moss Retail Company wishes to project its cash flows for the first three months of the coming financial year, July, August and September 20X1. The company's balance sheet as at 30 June 20X1 is as follows:

BALANCE SHEET: MOSS RETAIL COMPANY

as at 30 June 20X1

Assets			
Current assets:			
Cash		$ 35 000	
Accounts receivable		540 000	
Inventory		393 750	$ 968 750
Non-current assets:			
Land and buildings		250 000	
Other non-current assets	$200 000		
Accumulated depreciation	18 250	181 750	431 750
Total assets			$1 400 500
Liabilities			
Current liabilities:			
Accounts payable		214 375	
Dividends payable		30 000	244 375
Non-current liabilities:			
Term loan			100 000
Total liabilities			344 375
Shareholders' funds			
Paid-up capital		750 000	
Retained profits		306 125	1 056 125
Total liabilities and shareholders' funds			$1 400 500

The following projections and data are available:

- *Sales*

The sales price of Moss' product has been held at $20 per unit for the last six months and no change is expected in the price for the next six months. Sales revenue for the final three months of the last financial year have been:

April	$400 000
May	480 000
June	560 000

Sales forecasts for the next six months are:

	Units
July	35 000
August	45 000
September	60 000
October	40 000
November	40 000
December	40 000

Approximately 25 per cent of sales are made for cash. The remainder are made on credit terms of net thirty days. The company's experience is that two-thirds of the credit sales in any month are collected in the following month and one-third in the second month following sales. Bad debts have proved to be negligible.

- *Inventory*
  The company wishes to maintain an inventory at the end of any month equal to 90 per cent of the next month's sales.

- *Purchases*
  The purchase price of Moss' product is expected to remain unchanged at $12.50 per unit for the immediate future. Fifty per cent of any month's purchases are paid for in the same month, the remainder being paid in the month following purchase.

- *Operating expenses*
  The company's operating expenses per month are as follows:

Variable expenses:	
Commission on sales	$1.50 per unit
Fixed expenses:	
Salaries	$40 000
Depreciation	3 750
Other	10 500

  All cash operating costs are paid during the month in which they are incurred.

- *Overdraft facilities*
  The company finances its short-term operations through overdraft facilities. Overdraft facilities are drawn at the beginning of each month in anticipation of the cash deficit predicted for the month in the cash flow budget. Borrowings are repaid in multiples of $1000 at the end of the month in which surplus cash is generated. Interest at 16 per cent per annum is calculated and paid only when the principal is repaid.

- *Other information*
  (i) The company's minimum required cash balance at the end of each month is $25 000.
  (ii) Some fixed assets will need to be replaced during August at an estimated cost of $62 500.
  (iii) The dividend payable at 30 June 20X1 will be paid during July 20X1.

Required

For each of the months July, August and September prepare:

(a) a schedule of cash collections from customers

(b) a schedule of cash payments for purchases

(c) a budgeted cash flow statement

25.22 *Comprehensive budgets*

Maxine Kent is about to set up business manufacturing plastic cutlery that has the look and feel of sterling silver. She has asked you to prepare a cash budget and a budgeted set of financial statements for the next six months of operations. She provides you with the following estimates and data.

She has put $58 000 of her own money into the business and has borrowed a further $80 000 from her parents. They are well enough off to require no interest on the loan and to leave repayment until the business is successful.

Maxine has leased factory and office accommodation on an industrial estate at a cost of $38 700 per year, payable quarterly in advance, with the first payment to be made when she moves in next Monday, 1 July 20X0. The plant and equipment she needs have been ordered and will be delivered and installed early in July. The cost is $70 000 and she will pay the full amount in July. She estimates the life of the plant and equipment to be five years and to have negligible residual value. She has also arranged for office furniture costing $11 500 to be delivered and will again pay cash in July. She estimates a two-year life for the furniture with zero residual value. She has taken out a combined service contract and insurance policy on the plant, equipment and furniture at an annual premium of $9000. She will pay half this amount in July, the other half in January 20X1.

Maxine intends buying a small delivery van in July for $31 000 cash. She expects to replace it in two years time when its trade-in value is expected to be $15 500. The annual registration and insurance costs on the vehicle will be $2700, and will be payable in July.

Raw materials costing $46 000 will be purchased in July. Maxine estimates that about $19 000 worth of materials will be used in production each month. Orders will be placed for further deliveries of materials costing $39 000 in both September and November. The raw material supplier offers credit terms of 'net 30 days' and Maxine intends to take advantage of this.

Maxine will work full time in the business and her husband, who is a primary school teacher, will devote evenings and weekends. Maxine has also hired one employee at a wage of $2400 per month, which will be increased to $2800 a month if, after a three months trial, he should prove satisfactory. The employee will be paid on the last day of each month. Maxine estimates that all other expenses will be about $2000 per month and she will pay these monthly.

The following estimates of sales revenues for the first six months have been made:

Month	Sales revenues
July	$Nil
August	23 000
September	35 000
October	46 500
November	58 000
December	70 000

In order to encourage sales in the early months, Maxine will offer credit terms of sixty days. That is, payment for July sales will not be received until September.

Maxine has arranged an overdraft facility with her bank with a limit of $100 000. Interest will be charged at 1.5 per cent per month and may be assumed to be calculated for the month on the balance of the overdraft at the end of the month. The total interest for the six months will be paid in cash at the end of December 20X0.

Required

(a) Prepare a budgeted cash flow statement for each of the six months.

(b) Calculate Maxine's expected profit (or loss) for the six months ending 31 December 20X0.

(c) Prepare a budgeted balance sheet as at 31 December 20X0.

25.23 *Comprehensive budgets*

Maitland Manufacturing wishes to prepare comprehensive projections of income and cash flows for the first two months of the coming financial year, July and August 20X1. The projections are to be based on the following data:

- *Sales*
  Sales forecasts for the next four months are:

	Units	
July	11 000	$330 000
August	9 500	285 000
September	11 500	345 000
October	10 000	300 000

  Sales during June 20X1 were 10 000 units ($300 000).

  Approximately 50 per cent of Maitland's sales are for cash. Credit sales are invoiced at the end of the month in which the sale is made. A 2 per cent discount is offered on credit sales if payment is received within ten days of invoicing. The company's experience is that 30 per cent of credit sales are collected within the discount period, the remainder being collected before the end of the month following sale. Bad debts are negligible.

- *Production costs*
  Standard costs per unit of product are:

Direct material (0.5 kg × $15 per kg)	$ 7.50
Direct labour	6.00
Variable manufacturing overhead	3.00
Fixed manufacturing overhead	
(based on 10 000 units per month)	1.50
	18.00

  All raw materials are purchased for cash. Direct labour and manufacturing overhead costs are paid in the month in which they are incurred, with the exception of the depreciation cost within fixed manufacturing overhead of $2000 per month.

- *Inventories*
  The inventory of finished goods is maintained at 25 per cent of the next month's anticipated sales, and the inventory of raw materials at 35 per cent of the materials requirement for the next month's production. Inventories at 30 June 20X1 were 2750 units of finished goods costed at $49 500 and 1860 kg of materials.

- *Selling and administrative expenses*
  Selling expenses average 9 per cent of sales and are paid within the month of incurrence. Administrative expenses are expected to average $50 000 per month, of which $1500 represents depreciation. Administrative expenses are also paid as incurred.

- *Overdraft facilities*
  The company finances its cash deficits by a bank overdraft. The overdraft is assumed to be utilised from the beginning of the month in which a cash shortfall is anticipated, and repaid at the end of the month in which surplus cash becomes available. Interest at 14 per cent per annum is calculated and paid only when the principal is repaid.
  The balance of cash on hand at 30 June 20X1 is $15 000.

- *Additional information*
  During July 20X1 the following cash payments have to be met:

Repayment of term loan	$65 000
Purchase of replacement manufacturing equipment	$55 000

Required

(a) For each month, prepare a:

    (i)   production budget

    (ii) raw material usage and purchases budget

    (iii) direct labour budget

    (iv) manufacturing overhead budget

    (v) selling and administrative expenses budget

(b) For the two months period, prepare a budgeted profit and loss statement.

(c) For each month, prepare a:

    (i)   schedule of cash collection from customers

    (ii) cash flow budget

25.24 *Motivational impact of budget process*

Yarra College has seven departments, each of which attempts to attract international students into its courses. Of the international student fees received, a percentage is deducted by the college to cover extra costs incurred by them in promoting the courses and in providing administration services to these students. Also, part of these funds is put into a special fund that subsidises the activities of the departments that are unable to attract many international students. The balance is passed to the department in which the student enrols, to cover the costs of instructing and otherwise servicing these students and the costs of promoting the program locally. One department is much more successful at attracting these students than other departments, regularly exceeding the total budgeted revenue from this source. Over a few years, due to the department's success in attracting these funds, the college progressively reduces the percentage of the fees that are passed on to the department until the amount received by the department does not cover the costs incurred by their international students' program. Each year the Heads of Department are individually interviewed by the three most senior executive officers of the college and invited to voice their opinions about the budget decisions, but these opinions are disregarded and the budget remains unchanged.

Required

Discuss the behavioural aspects of the college's policy with regard to this department and its business acumen. What is the college budget-setting policy encouraging the Heads of Department to do?

CHAPTER 26
Accounting for management control

904 PART 8 ACCOUNTING FOR MANAGEMENT DECISIONS

Learning objectives

In this chapter you will be introduced to:

1. the function of a financial control system in an organisation

2. the guidelines that facilitate the design and operation of an effective financial control system

3. variance analysis and evaluation in the context of operational control

4. the need for non-financial controls

5. the differences between organisational control, social control and self control

6. the relationship between organisational control and social and self control.

Introduction

The management function of control ensures that the events and activities occurring within the organisation are conforming to plans. A variety of controls are designed to evaluate the performance of different segments of the organisation (e.g. different divisions of the firm), different activities (e.g. production or marketing) and over different periods of time (e.g. long term and short term).

In the long term, management may wish to evaluate the viability of different divisions in terms of their growth rates, market position, rate of new product introduction, and the extent to which divisions are adapting to new technologies. Management may decide subsequently to diversify into new areas, or to discontinue existing divisions or activities.

In the short term, management will want to ensure that the ongoing operations of the organisation are being carried out efficiently and in accordance with short-term planned performance. Specifically, management will require information on the efficiency with which resources are being used in the many operations of the organisation, particularly the manufacturing, marketing and administration activities.

The control function at this operational level is closely associated with the management accounting system. Control of the efficiency of resource utilisation will be based largely on cost and revenue control and much of the data and reports relevant to this function will be generated by the accounting system in the form of standard cost variance analysis reports and budgetary control reports.

This chapter examines methods of cost analysis for the purpose of facilitating management's short-term operational control function. These methods are generally set within a framework for organisational control systems. The chapter focuses primarily on financial controls associated with operational management of resource acquisition and use; however, attention is also given to non-financial controls, particularly as they relate to organisations pursuing strategies based on total quality management (TQM) and just-in-time (JIT) programs.

Essentials of a control system

If budgetary and standard cost control are to be considered as part of a total operating cost and performance control system, it is necessary to develop a framework within which these methods may be designed and administered. This framework will include the essential elements of any control system and will provide guidelines for the design and administration of control systems.

Any system of control, whether it be the control of temperature in an air-conditioning unit or the control of direct material costs in a production process, requires:

1. a planned level of performance
2. a means of measuring actual performance
3. a means of comparing actual with planned performance
4. a means of correcting performance or, alternatively, a means of correcting the plan.

In a financial control system for operating performance, the control system will rely on the effective accumulation and analysis of cost and revenue data.

Guidelines for organisational control

The following guidelines should also be considered in formulating a system of financial control over the operations of an organisation.

Strategic point control

Control should be directed to critical points of the operation. Establishing formal control mechanisms is expensive and it is not cost-effective to attempt to control continuously every activity in the organisation. Management will not seek to control the activities of a word processing operator in the administrative office on an hourly basis, but it will use sophisticated on-line monitoring equipment to control weld quality in a continuous steel-pipe-forming operation.

The selection of strategic points should take account of the costs of the control process, the expected frequency of variations from plans and the costs of such variations. Although this selection process will need to be approached differently for different organisations, or different activities within them, it will usually be based on the identification of separable and critical units of activity and on the timing of control.

Timing of control

For some activities the control system is designed to detect deviations before the activity occurs. A system of cash planning and control, using cash budgeting, may determine potential cash shortages in advance. In other cases the system detects deviations immediately they occur. In the earlier example, poor welding in a steel-pipe-forming operation will be discovered instantly by electronic sensing devices and the weld quality will be corrected with negligible time lag.

For some activities the system may entail a considerable time lag. An accounting cost system may accumulate and compare overhead expenses incurred with the budgeted expenses on a monthly basis. It may allow the possibility of unplanned expenditure to continue for some time before a deviation, or variance, is discovered and investigated.

The timing of the control process depends, again, on the amount of control for which management wishes to pay. This requires a balancing of the offsetting factors—that is, the cost of reducing the time lag and the expected benefits from that reduction.

The importance of the timing of control raises the question of the relative utility of financial and non-financial control data.

Financial control data require considerable preparation time, covering the accumulating, recording, analysing and presentation of cost and revenue data. Consequently, financial data will frequently be a secondary control rather than a primary one. For example, control of direct material usage in production will be primarily and critically controlled at the point of production. This will be achieved through production supervision using physical rather than financial measures of the relationship between inputs of direct materials and outputs of product.

Financial control of direct material usage will be a secondary control stage, adding a financial (cost) dimension to the measurement, and providing control of the aggregate usage of materials in production over a period, rather than direct control at the time of usage. To some extent, the financial control stage permits evaluation of the performance of the production manager in controlling the efficient use of resources at the primary control stage, rather than controlling the resource usage itself.

Identification of control units

Design of the system of controls in an organisation requires the identification of separable segments or activities for which management may wish control data to be accumulated. For a financial control system this requires the selection of activity units for which cost and possibly revenue data will be collected.

The selection of these units will be made in accordance with the organisational structure of the firm, in particular the way in which the organisation is segmented into departments or divisions (as discussed in Chapter 21). The control system should be consistent with that structure, and reflect the responsibility and authority assigned to segment managers. These units are often called 'responsibility units' or 'responsibility centres', and a financial reporting system designed to evaluate and control the operating performance of managers responsible for the activities of these centres is often called a 'responsibility accounting' system.

Identification of criteria for success

An effective control system should reflect the responsibilities of managers by incorporating criteria to reflect successful or unsuccessful performance.

For example, successful performance of a production unit manager may be gauged by the extent to which resources are used efficiently in the production process, product quality is maintained, production schedules are met, and the satisfaction and cooperation of employees are maintained. Not all of these responsibilities can be quantified in financial terms. Accordingly, the financial control system to be discussed in this chapter provides only part of the total control data that will be needed.

Successful performance of the research and development department may be reflected in the extent to which it keeps up to date with technological advances and applies them to improve the technical and engineering operations of the organisation. Again, these criteria cannot be effectively measured in financial terms. The added complication here is that there may be no direct relationship between units of input effort and units of productive output. Ideally, such a relationship is needed for an effective, formalised control system. In controlling the usage of direct materials in the production process, an identifiable relationship between inputs of materials and the output of product can be established. However, some research activities may yield no direct or immediate benefits to the organisation and some improvements to the firm's technical processes may result from a combination of research efforts or projects over many years.

The conclusion is that different methods of control will be needed to reflect the different activities of the organisation and the different responsibilities of their managers. For various reasons not all of these methods are amenable to quantitative or financial representation.

Direct control

The control system should be designed to maintain direct control between the controller and the activity being controlled. Therefore, at different levels in the organisational hierarchy the extent and nature of control data will be different.

A production supervisor may have direct control over an operation in the production process, an operations manager over the entire production process, and a plant manager over all operations, processes and sections in the plant. The production supervisor or operations manager may use physical quantity control data in controlling the usage of materials in the production operation, whereas the plant manager will probably require control data less detailed but covering a wider range of activities for a longer period, expressed in physical quantities *and* financial terms.

An implication of this for the control system is that control data will lose specific detail, encompass a wider range of activities and become more financially oriented as they proceed upwards in the organisational hierarchy, because of the different nature of responsibilities at each level.

A second implication is that control data for an activity must be provided directly to the level of management responsible for controlling that activity and in a form suitable for control.

Flexibility of control

The control process must be sufficiently flexible to allow for changes in the conditions underlying the plan. A production budget, for example, is prepared on the basis of budgeted sales for a future period. Once the production budget is set, material and labour quantity schedules and costs are budgeted as a function of planned production. In most cases these quantities and costs will be in direct relationship with planned production levels.

If the level of production is not met, or is exceeded, the base on which material and labour budgets were originally prepared will have changed, and a deviation from the original budgets will be expected. The control process should be flexible enough to enable those changes in the base to be absorbed and accounted for before comparisons and analyses are made and reported. Later in this chapter this concept will be examined in its application to cost control, particularly overhead cost control.

Exception reporting

The control system should report or highlight significant deviations or variances from plans so that the controller's attention can be directed towards those activities most in need of correction. Some variances from plan will arise randomly. They will be the result of chance and will have no determinable cause. Statistical analysis will often be used to determine the probability that a variance results from a random cause and this analysis may be built into the control system. Assessing the significance of variances will be considered later in this chapter.

Accounting for operational control

The role of accounting data in management control may be developed from the following guidelines.

Accounting control data are essentially concerned with evaluating the efficiency with which resources are being acquired and used in the operations of the organisation. The data are financial, resulting from the accumulation and analysis of costs and revenues. This entails a time lag between the occurrence of the activity and the analysis of the costs associated with that activity. Consequently, accounting control data represent a secondary stage in operational control and may be viewed as facilitating evaluation of how effectively the activity is being controlled, rather than providing a primary control over the activity itself.

Each of these control stages is important and the particular value of the accounting stage is that it adds the dimension of financial measurement to the control process. The overall control process, of which accounting is but a part, will include primary and secondary stages of control at different levels of the organisation and will use a variety of control mechanisms, including personal supervision, qualitative as well as quantitative data, and non-financial as well as financial data.

Cost classification and analysis for operational control

The emphasis in this chapter will be on cost classification and analysis, with the objective of facilitating the control of costs and operating performance. Most attention will be given to control of the costs of production operations, but financial control is equally relevant to marketing, distribution and administrative activities, and these will be discussed at various points in the chapter.

In analysing costs with a control objective, the emphasis will be on the cost classification categories that were discussed in Chapter 23. The direct and indirect cost classification allows the identification of costs within the organisational units or activities selected for control. This classification forms the initial basis for cost accumulation. Similarly, the ability to classify costs into controllable or non-controllable, at a particular management level, permits evaluation of the performance of managers of those units or activities.

An important method of cost classification for control purposes, however, is based on the expected behaviour of those costs in relation to changes in the level of activity, using the distinction between variable and fixed costs. The basis of cost control will be the predicted behaviour of costs and their budgeted levels during the control period and the subsequent comparison of actual cost behaviour and levels against those predicted.

Case 26.1 Behaviour and control

Kerry Cauberg is the production manager at a plant that manufactures rolls of plastic material. Each year Kerry is rewarded for careful control of production costs. When the chief engineer, who is responsible for performance evaluation, compares Kerry's costs with the original budget there is normally very little deviation. However, the plant management accountant, Pat Ho, is distressed that there is an inventory build-up of 20-tonne rolls of material and a stock-out of the 2-tonne rolls of material that customers are waiting for. Pat believes that Kerry should not receive bonuses for achieving the budget if customer demand is not being met by production.

Think briefly about the factors that may influence Kerry to produce the wrong product before turning to the discussion of the case at the end of this chapter.

Control of direct material and direct labour costs: standard costing

The costs of acquisition of direct materials and direct labour, and their usage in the production process, are usually controlled through a standard cost-accounting system.

These costs are directly traceable to the production operation and physically identifiable with individual units of product. Additionally, the levels of these costs vary proportionately with the number of units of output produced. Physical relationships between the inputs of direct materials and direct labour and the outputs of product may be established and used as the basis for control of the usage of these inputs.

The physical relationship between inputs and outputs that should be maintained under normal production conditions are termed physical standards. For example, if 12 kg of direct material are required to produce 10 units of finished product, the physical standard (or the standard input/output ratio) for material will be 1.2 kg per unit of product.

Physical standards for direct materials and direct labour will normally be set by engineering or production personnel on the basis of experimentation, using sample runs, theoretical calculation and work study. They take account of unavoidable spoilage (in the case of material standards), and assume an attainable level of performance (in setting direct labour standards).

Cost standards, or standard costs, are the dollar equivalents of the standard physical relationships between inputs and outputs. For example, if direct materials are predicted to cost $0.85 per kg on average over the period, the standard cost for direct materials per unit of production output is $1.02 (1.2 kg × $0.85 per kg).

The responsibility for setting cost standards will usually lie with the purchasing manager in respect of direct materials, and the personnel manager in respect of labour. In setting standard costs for materials, the purchasing manager will need to consider the average market price predicted for the period, the effect on unit prices of quantity discounts, and criteria other than simply minimum cost, including the assurance of continued supplies and maintenance of an acceptable quality of material. In setting direct labour cost standards, the personnel manager will need to take account of the local labour market, union contracts and awards, and appropriate labour skills.

The standard costs of direct materials and direct labour represent the cost levels that should be incurred per unit of production output under 'efficient' operating conditions and performance, hence the material and labour cost budgets discussed in Chapter 25 are based on them. They represent the costs that should be incurred if direct materials and labour are efficiently purchased and efficiently used in production during the control period. Consequently, they form the basis of evaluation and control through comparison with the actual cost levels incurred for the period.

Example: *Standard costs*

Joytime Ltd, manufacturers of camping equipment, produce a line of folding canvas chairs. Canvas is purchased in rolls, cut to the required size and fitted to the aluminium frames. Each chair requires 1.5 square metres of canvas at a cost of $12 per square metre. The predetermined standard cost of canvas for each chair is therefore $18.

During the last month 2000 square metres of canvas were purchased at a total cost of $22 800. Also during that period 1000 chairs were made and 1640 square metres of canvas were used.

This information is used to determine the level of efficiency in both the acquisition of canvas during the period and its usage in production. The responsibility for each of these activities lies with different departments and managers within the organisation. The purchasing department (or manager) will be responsible for buying materials at the 'right' price and the production manager for using them efficiently in production. Consequently, the functions of purchasing and usage must be evaluated separately by establishing a standard for each activity and comparing it with actual performance to determine deviations or variances from standard performance.

Direct materials price variance (MPV)

The efficiency of the purchasing manager in acquiring canvas may be evaluated by comparing the actual price paid for canvas with the standard price. This comparison will be a function of the standard price per square metre (SP), the actual average price per square metre (AP), and the actual quantity of material purchased (AQ).

$$MPV = (SP - AP)AQ$$

If SP is greater than AP, the resulting variance will be favourable (F) and will indicate a better than planned performance (less was paid for the material than expected); if SP is less than AP, the variance will be unfavourable (U).

For this example:

$$MPV = \left(\$12.00 - \frac{\$22\,800}{2000}\right) 2000$$

$$= (\$12.00 - \$11.40)\,2000$$

$$= \$1200\ (F)[1]$$

The initial conclusion may be that the purchasing manager's performance in acquiring canvas has been better than expected. The purchasing manager may have negotiated better credit terms or quantity discounts, or may have actively sought out and obtained better prices from different suppliers. The favourable variance, however, may not reflect increased

---

[1] The expected cost of 2000 kg of material at $12 per kg is $24 000, $1200 more than actually paid.

efficiency by the purchasing manager. The general level of market prices for canvas may have fallen during the period. Alternatively, the manager may have purchased poorer-quality canvas at a lower price, with the potential consequences of greater spoilage in the production process or reduced market acceptability of a lower-quality final product.

Examination of these factors will be necessary before the underlying reason for the variance can be determined. This may result in positive or negative appraisal of the manager's performance if the decreased price was attributable to his or her actions. Alternatively, it may lead to a revision of the standard cost if the decreased price was caused by a permanent decline in canvas prices generally.

Direct materials usage (quantity) variance (MQV)

The efficiency of the production manager in using canvas in the production process may be evaluated by comparing the actual quantity of canvas used (AQ) with the standard quantity specified for the final output achieved (SQ). Both quantities will be priced at the standard cost per square metre of canvas, in order that the usage variance will not be distorted by efficiencies or inefficiencies in purchasing.

$$MQV = (SQ - AQ)SP$$

For this example:

$$MQV = ((1000 \times 1.5) - 1640)\ \$12$$
$$= (1500 - 1640)\ \$12$$
$$= \$1680\ (U)$$

Again, this unfavourable variance may have been due to the inefficient performance of the production manager in controlling the levels of waste or spoilage in material usage, or in using inappropriate or inexperienced labour in the production process. However, it is also possible that the variation was due to causes not controllable by the production manager, such as the purchase of inferior-quality material with a correspondingly higher wastage rate.

Finding the reason for a variance is therefore a critical aspect of variance analysis. The analysis should recognise the potential interrelationships between departments and activities. For this reason the variances should be regarded as indicating what questions need to be answered; they are an attention-focusing device and should not be used as the sole arbiter of performance bonus payments.

Direct labour variances

The analysis of direct labour again involves a price and a quantity dimension. The price (or rate) variance compares the standard labour rate with the actual rate and measures the significance of the deviation by relating it to the total number of direct labour hours used in the activity. The quantity (or efficiency) variance holds the labour rate constant at the standard and compares the actual hours used with the standard hours allowed for production output.

In the example of Joytime Ltd, assume that 0.25 direct labour hours are required at standard operating performance to assemble each chair and that the standard rate (price) of direct labour is $5 per hour. During the production run of 1000 chairs, 325 hours of direct labour were charged to the chairs at a total cost of $1750.

Direct labour rate variance (LRV)

The $LRV = (SR - AR)AH$
where SR = standard rate per hour
AR = actual rate per hour
AH = actual hours worked.

For this example:

$$LRV = \left(\$5.00 - \frac{\$3750}{325}\right) 325$$

$$= (\$5.00 - \$5.38)\,325$$

$$= \$123.50\ (U)$$

Possible reasons for this unfavourable variance may include an award pay rise for workers in the industry, or the need to use higher skilled or casual labour, or to pay overtime rates, perhaps because of poor production scheduling or abnormal absenteeism.

Direct labour efficiency variance (LEV)

The $LEV = (SH - AH)SR$

where SH =   standard hours allowed for production

         AH =   actual hours used in production

         SR =   standard rate per hour.

For this example:

$$LEV = ((1000 \times 0.25) - 325)\,\$5$$

$$= (250 - 325)\,\$5$$

$$= \$375\ (U)$$

Possible reasons for an unfavourable efficiency (quantity) variance of direct labour may include ineffective supervision of workers during the process, poor-quality raw materials requiring longer assembly time per unit, or the use of workers inexperienced in the assembly process.

Standard costs may be used to control any activity for which physical relationships may be established between inputs of efforts and outputs of activity. For example, control of the dispatching operation may be achieved by establishing physical and cost standards for the amount of dispatching labour hours (inputs) required to dispatch a quantity of product (outputs).

Not all costs of the manufacturing operation, and very few of an organisation's non-manufacturing costs, are suited to the establishment of input to output relationships, and other methods of control need to be considered.

Control of manufacturing overhead costs: flexible budgeting

Manufacturing overhead costs are usually controlled in totals over the relevant period using a flexible budgeting system, rather than as costs per unit of activity using a standard cost control system, for two reasons. First, although control of individual items of manufacturing overhead is important, it is generally less critical in terms of the timing and form of control mechanisms than direct materials and direct labour. Second, no readily identifiable, precise input to output relationship can be prescribed between items of manufacturing overhead costs and activity levels.

The basis of the control process for manufacturing overhead costs is nevertheless similar to that for direct materials and direct labour. A planned cost level is established on the basis of the predicted behaviour of costs and this is compared with actual costs incurred. A flexible budget is established for overhead, based on the expected behaviour of costs in relation to changes in activity. As previously discussed, some overhead costs such as indirect labour and indirect materials or supplies may vary with the level of activity. Others, such as supervision salaries, rent and depreciation on equipment, may be fixed for the period, in the sense that they will not vary with changes in the level of activity during the period, at least over the relevant range. Other items of manufacturing overhead, including repairs and maintenance, may be semi-variable in behaviour. As the emphasis in the control process is on the predicted behaviour of costs, semi-variable costs will need to be segregated into their fixed and variable components.

A flexible budget is a series of individual budgets that indicate what the manufacturing overhead cost levels should be at various activity levels. They provide budget costs for a range of activity levels rather than one single activity level. This flexibility enables actual performance to be compared with expected performance at that level of activity. If actual production was 9000 units, but the budget had been calculated on 8000 units, variations would appear in variable overhead cost items such as lighting and power simply because production was higher than budgeted. The variances of significance for control purposes are those between the expected costs at the actual level of activity and the actual cost incurred.

An example of a flexible budget for a production department (Assembly Department) for a selected budgetary control period (April) is shown below.

The principle of flexible budgeting for control of overhead costs is that once the actual activity level for the period is known the target cost for overhead items for the period may be determined and compared with the actual cost. The only items of overhead costs that will be expected to change because of changes in the activity level for the period are the variable items. Fixed items of manufacturing overhead should not be affected by changes in the activity level.

Different items of variable overhead may vary with different measures of activity level. Indirect labour costs, for example, are likely to vary with the number of direct labour hours worked and repairs and maintenance costs are likely to vary with the usage of equipment.

The activity measure, with which individual items of variable overhead will tend to vary, and the rate of variability may be determined by a combination of logical reasoning and statistical analysis, for example, by regressing past levels of overhead costs against corresponding levels of activity. The objective of this analysis is to determine which activity level has the most influence over individual items of overhead cost.

		ASSEMBLY DEPARTMENT			
		Flexible budget—Manufacturing overhead for the month of April			
Activity level	Predicted rate of cost	Total predicted cost at activity level			
(units produced)	variability	5000	5500	6000	6500
Variable manufacturing overhead		$	$	$	$
Indirect labour	$1.20 per unit	6 000	6 600	7 200	7 800
Indirect material	$0.95 per unit	4 750	5 225	5 700	6 175
Repairs and maintenance	$0.50 per unit	2 500	2 750	3 000	3 250
Total variable overhead	$2.65 per unit	13 250	14 575	15 900	17 225
Fixed manufacturing overhead					
Rent	–	6 500	6 500	6 500	6 500
Depreciation on machinery	–	11 000	11 000	11 000	11 000
Supervision salaries	–	17 500	17 500	17 500	11 500
		35 000	35 000	35 000	35 000
Total manufacturing overhead		48 250	49 575	50 900	52 225

The relationships established by the analysis will never show perfect correlation because an individual overhead cost will be influenced by a combination of factors. For example, while repairs and maintenance costs may tend to vary with changes in the level of equipment usage, they will also be affected by other factors including the quality and age of the different equipment in use and decisions to accelerate or delay repairs and maintenance because of production constraints (i.e. they are discretionary costs).

Because of the uncertainties in determining patterns of variability for overhead costs, organisations often simplify the process. Instead of determining different activity measures for individual overhead cost items, a single activity measure is chosen. The statistically established variability of all variable overhead cost items with that single activity measure may then be used to predict overhead cost levels during the period.

This approach is based on the assumption that the benefits of simplifying and reducing the cost of the control mechanism for overhead costs outweigh the improvements in control that would result from more complex analysis. Suppose that direct labour hours are selected as the single activity measure. Some overhead cost items will correlate well with this activity measure (indirect labour for instance), others less well (repairs and maintenance). This approach is often satisfactory in predicting overhead cost levels for operations within the period and it is used in the following example. However, it places added importance on the variance analysis stage of control because there is now another potential explanation for an overhead cost variance. The variance may be the result of an invalid predictor relationship.

The person responsible for formulating or evaluating the control system should also recognise that if any item of variable overhead is of critical importance, it may have to be controlled separately.

Example: *Overhead variance analysis*

Assume that Joytime Ltd has scheduled the production of 1000 folding canvas chairs to require 250 direct labour hours (0.25 standard direct labour hours per chair). A statistical analysis of past levels of variable overhead costs has shown that these costs vary with the number of direct labour hours as follows:

Variable overhead cost	Cost per direct labour hour
Indirect labour	$3.50
Indirect material	1.70
Repairs and maintenance	0.80
Inspection and rework	0.60
	6.60

The fixed overhead costs for the production period were predicted to be:

Rent	$1500
Depreciation on equipment	1000
Supervision salaries	1200
	3700

The original budget projection for overhead costs (based on 250 direct labour hours) for the production period was, therefore, as follows:

Variable manufacturing overhead		
Indirect labour	$ 875	
Indirect material	425	
Repairs and maintenance	200	
Inspection and rework	150	
Total variable overhead		$1650
Fixed manufacturing overhead		
Rent	1500	
Depreciation on equipment	1000	
Supervision salaries	1200	
Total fixed overhead		3700
Total manufacturing overhead		$5350

The actual number of direct labour hours required to produce the chairs was 325, and the actual manufacturing overhead costs for the production period were:

Indirect labour	$1050
Indirect material	620
Repairs and maintenance	430
Inspection and rework	170
Rent	1650
Depreciation on equipment	1000
Supervision salaries	1300
	$6220

If the actual costs incurred during the period were compared with those predicted in the original budget they would be expected to be greater because of the fact that 325 hours were required to produce the output, rather than 250 as budgeted. Because variable overhead costs tend to vary with the number of direct labour hours, it is necessary to construct a budget based on the actual activity level during the period so as to compare the actual overhead costs incurred with expected (or predicted) costs at the same activity level. Flexible budgeting is used to construct a budget after the level of actual labour hours is known. This will provide a valid base with which to compare actual costs for variance analysis purposes. The budget prepared on this basis (i.e. 325 direct labour hours) is shown below.

Variable manufacturing overhead		
Indirect labour	$1138	
Indirect material	552	
Repairs and maintenance	260	
Inspection and rework	195	
Total variable overhead		$2145
Fixed manufacturing overhead		
Rent	1500	
Depreciation on equipment	1000	
Supervision salaries	1200	
Total fixed overhead		3700
Total manufacturing overhead		$5845

Note that expected fixed overhead costs do not change.

The use of flexible budgets permits the isolation of two types of overhead cost variances: a spending variance, which may be likened to the price and rate variances determined for direct materials and direct labour costs, and an efficiency variance, which is similar to the usage and efficiency variances. These variances are computed in the performance control report.

PERFORMANCE CONTROL REPORT

Manufacturing overhead

	(1) Budget based on 250 standard direct labour hours	(2) Budget based on 325 actual direct labour hours	(3) Actual costs	(4) Efficiency variance (1)-(2)	(5) Spending variance (2)-(3)
Variable overhead	$	$	$	$	$
Indirect labour	875	1138	1050	263 U	88 F
Indirect material	425	552	620	127 U	68 U
Repairs and maintenance	200	260	430	60 U	170 U
Inspection and rework	150	195	170	45 U	25 F
Total variable overhead	1650	2145	2270	495 U	125 U
Fixed overhead					
Rent	1500	1500	1650	–	150 U
Depreciation	1000	1000	1000	–	–
Supervision salaries	1200	1200	1300	–	100 U
Total fixed overhead	3700	3700	3950	–	250 U

Manufacturing overhead efficiency variance

The manufacturing overhead efficiency variance results from the comparison of the overhead costs predicted under efficient operating conditions (250 direct labour hours) with the costs that would have been expected at the actual activity level (325 direct labour hours). It relates only to variable items of manufacturing overhead, again because there is no change in expected fixed overhead costs resulting from a change in the level of activity. The overhead efficiency variance is a direct consequence of the excessive use of labour hours in producing 1000 units of product. It may therefore be computed in total as:

$$\left[\begin{array}{c} \text{standard direct labour} \\ \text{hours (for 1000 units)} \end{array} - \begin{array}{c} \text{actual direct labour} \\ \text{hours (for 1000 units)} \end{array} \right] \begin{array}{c} \text{variable} \\ \text{overhead} \\ \text{rate per hour} \end{array}$$

or, $(250 - 325)\ \$6.60 = \$495\ (U)$.

The excessive use of direct labour hours in producing 1000 units of product has resulted in two unfavourable variances: additional direct labour costs, measured by the direct labour efficiency variance (discussed earlier in the chapter), and additional variable overhead costs, measured by the variable overhead efficiency variance. The two unfavourable variances may be added to provide management with a measure of the total additional costs resulting from the failure to control the level of direct labour in production.

Manufacturing overhead spending variance

The spending variance results from the comparison of the actual overhead costs incurred with the predicted costs at the same activity level. It may indicate favourable or unfavourable performance in the acquisition of overhead services during the control period. It indicates whether excessive costs were incurred for their services, after allowing for the increased need for the quantity of services because of increased activity.

Unlike the overhead efficiency variance, no single explanation underlies the spending variance and analysis of individual variances is required to determine their cause. In the Joytime example, the variances for rent and supervision salaries may have resulted from unforeseen and unavoidable increases in market prices and wage rates. The unfavourable variance for repairs and maintenance may have resulted from the breakdown of a specific piece of equipment during the period, or may have been a carry-over effect from the previous period, when maintenance was deferred because of heavy production requirements. In the case of repairs and maintenance, direct labour hours may not be an entirely satisfactory predictor of cost levels and part of the variance may be attributable to an unsatisfactory prediction method rather than actual performance.

Significance of variance

The major purposes of the control system are to enable evaluation of the performance of responsibility centres and their managers and to indicate areas where corrective action may be needed. Variances from standard or planned performance are isolated for relevant responsibility areas, with a view to determining the underlying causes for those variances and improving future performance. It is important to regard variances as attention-focusing data that indicate what needs investigation (where and what questions to ask) rather than independent evaluators (they do not, themselves, provide answers).

Variance analysis involves examining the variance in respect of several attributes, its origin and cause, the person responsible and its significance. The variance may result from several causes, including better or poorer performance by people responsible for the activity, incorrect standards or plans, and uncontrollable events occurring outside the responsibility area (including decisions made by other managers who are not held directly responsible for this variance).

Analysis of a variance, however, may reveal no determinable underlying cause. Some variances will result from chance events. No corrective action will be necessary in response to these variances and ideally management would not want them to be analysed or investigated. In determining whether a variance is sufficiently large to warrant investigation, managers often use rule-of-thumb criteria based on the absolute amount of the variance, or on the percentage of the variance in relation to the standard or predicted cost. More formalised methods, based on statistical analysis, may be used to estimate how large a particular variance must be before it is likely to have a determinable, non-random cause that warrants investigation.

Also, management will not want a variance to be investigated if the costs of investigation and correction exceed the likely benefits from correcting the activity. The decision to investigate a variance should therefore be made on a cost-benefit basis. This topic is addressed further in a number of management accounting texts.

Strategic and non-financial controls

So far the chapter has focused primarily on financial controls associated with operational management of resource acquisition and use. Today, many organisations are broadening and refocusing their control systems to direct them at specific areas of strategic importance to the organisation and to incorporate non-financial controls.[2]

---

[2] For example, at a two-day conference on performance measurement in Sydney in 1997, presented by executive managers for executives and other senior managers, the need to monitor strategically linked performance indicators was addressed by speakers from Manatec, Telstra, Sportsgirl Sportscraft, Eli Lilly, BHP Australia Coal and Dyno Nobel Asia Pacific Ltd. Many of these speakers stressed the need for a balanced approach and for the use of non-financial as well as financial measures.

Quality and flexible responses to markets and customers are being increasingly identified as key strategies of many organisations contemporarily. Total quality management (TQM), just-in-time (JIT) and continuous improvement programs have brought with them an expanding set of performance indicators designed to promote and facilitate the implementation and maintenance of these programs and to measure their success. Some of these performance indicators retain a financial quantification. For example, cost of quality programs seek to quantify in financial terms the costs associated with the processes of preventing the production or provision of defective goods or services, and of detecting defective products or services, as well as the costs that are incurred when a defective product or service is found only after its production or provision. In respect of the latter situation, these programs would seek to include in the quantification of the cost of quality not only warranty and repair costs, but also the costs of potential liability claims brought by customers. They are further improved by the inclusion of estimates of future lost sales due to current poor quality.[3]

More frequently, however, the indicators designed for evaluation of performance against strategic variables are non-financial. TQM as a strategy requires the recording of the number of defects, and strives to progressively decrease these under its 'zero-defect' ideology. Flexible response as an identified strategy for example, might be appraised by time-related performance indicators, such as time-to-market. This is the time lag between the identification of a customer need or opportunity for a new product or service and its market introduction. For example, when the Ford Motor Company realised that its strategy had to be to increase its responsiveness to the market, Ford concentrated on reducing the lead time between the idea of a new car and its appearance in showrooms. Concentration on this key factor resulted in Ford taking some models from conception to market in two years, against a norm time-to-market for new models in excess of three years.

Time-based performance indicators are also often used to measure customer satisfaction as an input to quality management and measurement. A distributor of electrical energy and energy services, for example, has used the 'average duration of outage (loss of power) per customer per annum', measured in number of minutes, as an index of reliability of delivery of its product to its customers. Similarly, Telstra has used the percentage of faults cleared within two working days of notification as an indicator of its repair component of customer service quality.

JIT systems also rely on non-financial indicators of their successful operation. These systems seek to minimise inventories of direct materials or component parts by producing a sub-component on a production assembly line, for example, just at the time the part is needed to enter the next stage. If the sub-component is not available at the time it is needed, the production process is halted. Therefore, an indicator of throughput time, for example, or the time it takes from start to completion of a product, is often used as a measure of the effectiveness of a JIT system.

Controls and the process of organisational control

We said at the outset of this chapter that accounting control information constitutes a secondary rather than primary form of organisational control—that is, it provides an

---

[3] TQM is based on the philosophy that the costs of prevention are less than the costs incurred due to producing poor-quality output. In the past firms have been committed (usually legally) to correcting or compensating for defects that reach the customer. The costs of correcting defects discovered before dispatch are less than those discovered after dispatch (typically by the customer). However, it is usually even cheaper to make sufficient investment in processes, product design, training etc. to prevent defects occurring. This investment in prevention is a discretionary cost that has tended to be minimised in the past. For further coverage of TQM philosophy and techniques, refer to a modern management accounting textbook.

assessment of how well a specific activity is being controlled, rather than providing direct control over the activity itself. Accounting control data can also be termed *administrative controls* and contrasted and complemented with *social controls* and *self controls* in constituting the overall process of organisational control.[4]

Organisations are using administrative controls when they formulate rules, regulations and standard operating procedures to direct the actions of people in the organisation and to evaluate those actions. If the service section of a motor vehicle dealership sets a standard time allowance of 55 minutes to carry out a 20 000 kilometre service on a particular car, this is an administrative control. The time allowance both directs the behaviour of the mechanic in effecting the service and serves as a reference point to measure the efficiency of the mechanic's performance. This last section of the text has been concerned almost exclusively with administrative controls, such as formal budgets, plans, standards and variance analyses.

However, organisations also use other types of controls, such as social and self controls, in seeking to ensure that organisational members work towards the goals of the organisation. Social controls, or peer group controls, exist when the behaviour of a member of a social or work group is regulated by other members of the group. For example, a university student may work hard to try and gain good grades because other people in that student's circle of friends also work hard and value the attainment of good grades. If the student wishes to remain part of that circle, he or she must adopt the values of the group and act according to those values.

Self controls exist when, in the absence of interaction with or pressure from others, a person directs his or her energies to the task at hand in an efficient and effective manner. The image of the medical research scientist buried in the laboratory in the early hours of the morning and working laboriously on a problem or experiment is representative of self controls. The motivation to direct one's energies to the task at hand comes from within the person, not from without. The implications of the differences between the three types of control are illustrated in Table 26.1, based on work by Dalton and Lawrence in which they write about control emanating from the organisation (organisational control), informal groups (often called social, group or clan control) and the individual (self control).

Table 26.1 Three types of control in organisations[5]

Controls administered by	Organisation	Informal group	Individual
Direction for controls derive from:	Organisation plans, strategies; competitive demands	Mutual commitments, group ideals	Individual goals, aspirations
Behavioural and performance measures:	Budgets, standard costs, sales targets	Group norms	Self-expectations, intermediate targets
Signal for corrective action:	Variance	Deviance	Perceive impending failure, missed targets
Reinforcements or rewards for compliance:	Management commendation; monetary incentives; promotions	Peer-approval, membership, leadership	Satisfaction of 'being in control'
Sanctions or punishments for non-compliance:	Request for explanation; dismissal	Kidding; ostracism, hostility	Elation

---

4 A good review of these types of controls in organisations is provided by A. O. Hopwood, *Accounting and Human Behaviour,* Haymarket Publishing, London, 1974, and T. Lowe and J. L. J. Machin, *New Perspectives in Management Control*, MacMillan Press, London, 1983.

5 Based on G. W. Dalton and P. R. Lawrence, *Motivation and Control in Organisations*, Irwin, Homewood, Illinois, 1971.

These three types of control should be considered in the context of the influences on the individual when making decisions, as discussed in Chapter 21. Figure 21.3 illustrates four influence sources as being the environment/organisation, group behaviour, individual needs and the task or function. The first three of these relate to the need for the administrative, social and self controls discussed here.

Different types of controls may be appropriate for different types of people and for different work tasks. It is hard to imagine how one could design administrative controls for the task of the medical research scientist—we could hardly set a standard of one major medical breakthrough every 55 minutes. The scientific research task is non-routine, and unpredictable in terms of the time that will be required and the problems that will be encountered along the way. It requires creativity and flexibility—attributes that are not encouraged under administrative controls. Fortunately, people who become and remain scientific researchers are highly likely to be self-starters, to be motivated by the challenge of the task at hand and to impose their own (self) controls on their behaviour and efforts.

Consider the task of hospital nursing. Once again, it would probably be inappropriate to seek to develop administrative controls for many hospital nursing tasks. As different patients require different amounts of attention and time depending on their medical and emotional conditions, nurses must frequently make spontaneous and discretionary decisions in response to unexpected and emergency situations. Perhaps fortunately again, people who become and remain nurses are, in the main, motivated by genuinely held values of compassion and concern for the welfare of others. Also, as nurses tend to work in and with groups of people with similar values, social and peer group controls act as much stronger regulators of behaviour than administrative controls in hospital situations. One can imagine social controls working in many other organisations or situations where the organisational members share similar values and commitments. Charitable and church-based organisations would be likely examples.

Administrative control, therefore, has been the major topic of this chapter, but it is just one type of control mechanism operating in organisations. Administrative controls are well suited to tasks that are routine, are relatively predictable in their conduct and are unlikely to produce many exceptions or new problems for the people carrying them out. These controls are also suited to tasks that can be relatively clearly specified in advance in respect of the inputs of materials and efforts and the outputs of goods or services. Many production tasks have these characteristics. Administrative controls may also be more appropriate for people who have a calculative rather than a moral involvement with their organisation. That is, they are there for what they can get out of the organisation rather than for what they can put in. However, such controls can, if used in inappropriate circumstances, have adverse consequences. Imagine the reaction of the medical researcher if he or she was required to 'clock' on and off, and to account for time breaks out of the laboratory.[6]

In designing management control systems it is vital that the management accountant understand the types of people involved in the organisation or in particular parts of the organisation, and the types of tasks and work to be performed. Only with this understanding will the accountant be able to determine the appropriateness of administrative controls and their correct mix with social and self-controls in organisations.

---

[6] In fact many employees working in 'secure environments' do have their presence and absence recorded. Security is being maintained in many organisations by equipping employees with plastic cards that must be swiped through an electronic scanner to open doors. Even certain internal doors may require this kind of identification to allow movement between departments. Apart from maintaining security, the system electronically monitors the movements of employees. Care must be used in deciding how this information is acted upon.

Irrespective of the types of people or the work task involved, many organisations seek to create conditions within which self and social or peer group controls become important in motivating and directing organisationally valued behaviours. Organisations that emphasise TQM and JIT believe that by involving employees in the work situation both individually and collectively in work groups, people take responsibility for their actions, which is an integral and necessary component of the successful operation of TQM and JIT. These organisations believe that the power of self and social controls can be realised regardless of the type of task or the personal characteristics of the individuals concerned.

Summary

This chapter has considered methods of cost analysis for the purpose of facilitating management's short-term (operational) control function. Although the analysis has concentrated on the control of manufacturing costs (direct materials, direct labour and overhead), the approaches to cost control may be applicable to other non-manufacturing costs of the organisation.

The expected behaviour of costs is the important factor in the control process, not whether the costs are manufacturing or non-manufacturing. Consequently, control of non-manufacturing costs may be approached by examining the nature and expected behaviour of the costs of the operation under consideration, formulating expected levels of costs under predetermined levels of operating efficiency and comparing actual costs for these operations with the planned levels. For non-manufacturing operations, such as marketing, research and development, it should be appreciated that relationships between cost inputs and activity outputs may be very difficult to determine and that methods of control in these areas may have to rely more heavily on non-financial, non-quantitative criteria.

The discussion has also concentrated on cost control rather than revenue control. As a result, variances commonly known as sales mix, production yield, opportunity loss and forecast variances have not been discussed. These are beyond the scope of this text, but constitute important components of a comprehensive system of financial control of operations.

It should be appreciated that the identification of variances and the measurement of their significance are mechanical aspects of the control process. The critical tasks lie in the determination of acceptable levels of operating efficiency and in the investigation and analysis of the variances to determine their underlying causes.

Finally, these aspects of control relate to administrative or organisational control which needs to be seen in the context of all influences on the individual. Other forms of control which were touched on but not covered in detail were social control (also called group or clan control) and self control.

Discussion of in-text case

Case 26.1

This disfunctional behaviour was caused by the chief engineer sticking rigidly to the original budget as the standard against which Kerry's performance was to be evaluated. Budget forecasts are derived a few months before the start of the budget period, so they are set 15 months or more before the end of the budget period. It is unlikely that the forecast sales demand will be fully accurate. To achieve production costs close to those in the 'static budget' (i.e. those in the master budget) Kerry must produce the products on which that budget was based. While 100 2-tonne rolls of material may use the same material inputs as 10 20-tonne rolls of material, other costs are likely to be greater for the smaller rolls. For example, more rolls must be moved away from production into finished goods inventory, increasing overhead costs. Further, extra labour costs are incurred for changing the roll on the equipment 10 times more often.

In Chapter 24 it was stated that the use of the budget for control and evaluation purposes is designed to motivate lower-level managers and employees to perform to budget expectations. Care must be used in deciding what those 'budget expectations' were. Management would not 'expect' (i.e. desire) the budget to prevent managers from making decisions that are in the best interests of the firm (when managers make decisions in the best interest of the firm there is said to be goal congruence).

The static budget was based on estimates such as how much material is used per unit of output. The budget expectations are expressed in these standards and it is these expectations that should guide performance evaluation. Budget expectations are the budget cost and volume standards (e.g. the cost of material and the amount of material per unit) that, in total, should be adjusted for changing demand etc. The budget should be used to guide people to make goal-congruent decisions rather than used to demand budget-conforming decisions that are not goal congruent. The way this is achieved in the calculation of variances is the main focus of this chapter.

 **Review exercises**

Discussion questions

26.1   Standard cost variance analysis may be regarded as a secondary stage in controlling the acquisition and use of direct materials and direct labour. Explain.

26.2   Control is facilitated if a clear relationship can be specified between the input of production effort and the output of product. Explain in respect of control over:

(a) direct material usage in production
(b) manufacturing overhead costs
(c) research and development costs
(d) advertising costs

26.3   Control data lose specific detail, encompass a wider range of activities and become more financially oriented as they proceed upwards in the organisational hierarchy. Explain why.

26.4   Define the term 'standard cost'.

26.5   A favourable direct material price variance indicates that the purchasing department has performed better than expected during the period under review. Do you agree? Why or why not?

26.6   An unfavourable labour efficiency variance indicates inefficiency in the control of direct labour. Do you agree? Why or why not?

26.7   Explain why flexible budgets rather than standard costs are used to control manufacturing overhead costs.

26.8   Direct labour hours is the best measure of activity for the planning and control of manufacturing overhead. Do you agree? Why or why not?

26.9   The manufacturing overhead efficiency variance consists entirely of fixed overhead costs. Is this statement correct? Explain.

26.10 Explain, and suggest several possible reasons for, an unfavourable manufacturing overhead spending variance.

26.11 To ensure effective control, all variances from standard should be examined to determine their underlying cause. Do you agree? Why or why not?

26.12 What is meant by administrative controls, social controls and self controls? Give examples of each type of control.

26.13 Why must the accountant involved in designing a management control system for an organisation understand the types of people in the organisation and the nature of the tasks and work to be performed?

26.14 Out of the three types of controls—administrative, social and self—which do you think would be most appropriate in the following situations?

(a) claim processing in an insurance office
(b) secondary school teaching
(c) piloting a passenger jet
(d) working for 'meals on wheels'
(e) driving for a courier service

 Problems

26.15 *Standard costing, material and labour variances*

Upton Park Products makes football shirts. The standard requirement per shirt for polyester cotton cloth is 2 metres at $3.75 per metre, and for direct labour 1½ hours at $4.50 per hour.

During August 20X0 the company produced 800 shirts, purchased and used 1750 metres of cloth at a total cost of $5950, and incurred direct labour costs of $6682, representing 1350 hours.

(a) Calculate the following variances from standard for the month:

(i) direct material price variance
(ii) direct material usage variance
(iii) direct labour rate variance
(iv) direct labour efficiency variance

(b) Suggest two possible explanations for each variance.

26.16 *Standard costing, manufacturing overhead variances*

The Hawthornes Company segregates the manufacturing overhead costs of one of its production departments into their fixed and variable components. Fixed overhead costs are budgeted in total on an annual basis, and variable overheads are budgeted on a rate per direct labour hour.

Each unit of finished product requires two direct labour hours under standard operating conditions.

The departmental manufacturing overhead budget for 20X0 is based on the formula: $96 000 + $ 1.50x, where x represents the number of direct labour hours.

The following data are available for the first month of 20X0:

Units produced	1000
Direct labour hours worked	1900
Fixed overhead costs incurred	$7700
Variable overhead costs incurred	$3200

Calculate manufacturing overhead spending and efficiency variances for the month.

26.17 *Standard costing, variance analysis*

1. The Carrow Road Company produces metal model soldiers. The company uses standard costs to control direct materials and direct labour, and flexible budgets to control manufacturing overheads. Variable overhead costs have been found to vary with direct labour hours and are budgeted and controlled on this basis.

   The following data relate to the month of July:

Standard direct labour hours per unit of product	0.50
Standard direct labour cost per unit of product	$42.00
Variable overhead cost per direct labour hour	$5.80
Units produced	950
Direct labour costs incurred	$39 000
Actual direct labour rate per hour	$78.00
Actual variable overhead costs	$3100

   Calculate variances for direct labour rate and efficiency, and for variable overhead efficiency and spending.

2. Plough Lane Products Ltd uses a standard cost system to control the costs associated with manufacturing its single product. The following data relate to this product for the last period of operations.

Direct material cost at standard	$2.30 per kg
Direct materials required per unit of product at standard	3.2 kg
Direct labour cost per hour at standard	$9.25
Direct labour hours required per unit of product at standard	5
Direct materials purchased, 23 000 kg	$57 500
Units produced	3000
Direct materials used	10 200 kg
Direct labour hours worked	14 700
Direct labour costs incurred	$130 600
Variable overhead costs incurred	$18 750
Fixed overhead costs incurred	$33 150
Budgeted fixed overhead costs	$32 000

   Variable overhead is applied to product at the rate of $1.35 per direct labour hour.

   Calculate the following variances from standard for the period:

   (a) direct material price and usage variances
   (b) direct labour rate and efficiency variances
   (c) variable and fixed overhead spending and efficiency variances

3. The White Lane Company produces and sells a single product. The company uses standard costs as the basis of control over direct material and direct labour costs, and flexible budgeting to control manufacturing overhead costs.

The standard inputs per unit of product are:

Direct materials	1 kg at $5 per kg
Direct labour	1.6 hours at $10 per hour

The manufacturing overhead costs expected at the company's planned production level of 6000 units per year are:

Variable overhead	
Indirect labour: 30 000 hours at $10 per hour	$300 000
Indirect materials: 60 000 litres at $1.25 per litre	75 000
Other	75 000
Fixed overhead	
Supervisory salaries	67 500
Depreciation on factory	112 500
Other	37 500
	667 500

The following data are available from the company's records for the month of September 20X0:

	Quantity	
Production	5000 units	
Direct materials purchased	5200 kg	$27 300
Direct materials issued to production	5400 kg	
Direct labour	8200 hours	84 050
Indirect labour	2400 hours	24 600
Indirect materials	6000 litres	8 280
Other variable overhead		8 000
Supervisory salaries		6 200
Depreciation on factory		9 400
Other fixed overhead		3 125

(a) Calculate the following variances for the month:

    (i)   direct material price variance (*MPV*)

    (ii) direct material usage (quantity) variance (*MQV*)

    (iii) direct labour rate variance (*LRV*)

    (iv) direct labour efficiency variance (*LEV*)

    (v) manufacturing overhead efficiency variance

    (vi) manufacturing overhead spending variance

(b) Suggest reasons for each of the variances determined for the month.

4. Old Bar Ltd produces a single product in one of its manufacturing divisions. The company has a comprehensive cost control system using standard costing and flexible budgeting. Budgets are based on standard cost data and monthly performance reports are prepared highlighting variances from standard. The standard input of direct materials per unit of output is 5 kg at $1.60 per kg, and for direct labour, 0.30 hours at $8.00 per hour.

Manufacturing overhead costs are segregated into their fixed and variable elements. Variable overhead costs are expected to vary with machine hours. The expected behaviour of overhead costs is as follows:

Indirect material	$2400 per month	+ $1 per machine hour
Indirect labour	$6800 per month	+ $1.40 per machine hour
Supplies	$2800 per month	+ $0.80 per machine hour
Supervisory salaries	$14 000 per month	
Depreciation	$4000 per month	
Other overhead	$2000 per month	

Each unit of product requires 0.25 machine hours at standard operating efficiency. The following data are available for the month of July 20X0:

	Quantity	
Budgeted production	6600 units	
Actual production	6200 units	
Budgeted machine hours	1650 hours	
Actual machine hours	1500 hours	
Direct materials purchased	36 000 kg	$53 280
Direct materials used	32 500 kg	
Direct labour	2100 hours	17 325
Manufacturing overhead incurred:		
Indirect materials		4 000
Indirect labour		8 400
Supplies		4 000
Supervisory salaries		16 200
Depreciation		4 000
Other overhead		1 800

(a) Calculate variances for direct materials, direct labour and manufacturing overhead.
(b) Explain the purpose of, and suggest two possible reasons for, each variance.
(c) Write a brief report commenting on the efficiency and effectiveness of production operations during the month.

26.18 *Flexible budgeting, standard costing*
The Highfields Company produces footballs in one of its manufacturing departments. The company uses a system of flexible budgeting to control departmental manufacturing overhead costs. The activity measure used as the basis for developing the flexible budgets for the football department is direct labour hours.

The manufacturing overhead budget for September 20X0, based on expected production of 4000 footballs each requiring 0.20 direct labour hours, was as follows:

	Cost per direct labour hour	Budget for 800 hours
Variable overhead:		
Indirect labour	$3.00	$2400
Indirect material	0.20	160
Light and power	0.25	200
Repairs and maintenance	0.20	160
		2920
Fixed overhead:		
Supervisory salaries		2850
Property taxes		150
Depreciation on factory equipment		375
Insurance		300
		3675
Total budgeted manufacturing overhead		$6595

During September 3500 footballs were produced and 600 direct labour hours were worked in the department. Actual manufacturing overhead costs incurred were:

Indirect labour	$2100
Indirect material	160
Light and power	180
Repairs and maintenance	140
Supervisory salaries	2850
Property taxes	150
Depreciation	375
Insurance	300
	$6255

Prepare a performance control report for the overhead costs incurred by the department during September. The report should incorporate budget projections at relevant activity levels and highlight manufacturing overhead efficiency and spending variances.

26.19 *Standard costing and variance analysis*

Maine Road Manufacturing produces a single product which has the following standard cost per unit:

Direct materials:	5 kg at $2.00 per kg	$10.00
Direct labour:	2 hr at $15.00 per hour	30.00
Variable overhead:	$2.50 per direct labour hour	5.00
Fixed overhead:	$5.00 per direct labour hour	10.00
		$55.00

The following data relate to the month of August 20X0:

- Budgeted manufacturing overhead for August was $42 500 fixed, plus $2.50 per direct labour hour variable.
- Actual costs for August:

Material:	Purchased 25 000 kg at $2.12 per kg
	Used 23 100 kg
Labour:	8350 hours at $14.90 per hour
Variable overhead:	$20 250
Fixed overhead:	$45 000

- Actual production for August:

Work in-progress 1 August:	Nil
Units completed during August:	3800 units
Work-in-progress 31 August:	600 units

Work-in-progress at 31 August is assumed to be fully completed for materials and 50 per cent complete for labour and manufacturing overhead.

Calculate the following variances for August:

(a) direct material price variance
(b) direct material usage variance
(c) direct labour rate variance
(d) direct labour efficiency variance
(e) manufacturing overhead efficiency variance
(f) manufacturing overhead spending variance

Case study

26.20 *Flexible budgeting and standard costing*

Goodison Grains Ltd was formed six months ago by Mary Park to make granular fertiliser. Mary Park has had the dubious benefit of a husband who calls himself a self-taught accountant and who has insisted on preparing all the financial systems and reports. At the end of the first six months, Ron Park has produced the following financial performance report.

PROFIT AND COST ANALYSIS

July to December 20X0

(1)	(2)	(3)	(4)	(5)	(6)
		Total at standard cost and budgeted sales volume	Total at standard cost and actual sales volume	Total at actual	Variance from standard
Item	Standard per kg	(38 000 kg)	(35 000kg)		
	$	$000	$000	$000	$000
Sales revenue	25.00	950	875	875	Nil
Raw materials	3.80	144	133	147	(14)
Direct labour	3.35	127	117	153	(36)
Other variable costs	2.58	98	90	88	2
Total variable costs	9.73	369	340	388	(48)
Depreciation	5.08	193	178	192	(14)
Insurances	0.40	15	14	15	(1)
Interest	0.65	25	23	25	(2)
Research & development	2.97	113	104	114	(10)
Total fixed costs	9.10	346	319	346	(27)
Profit before tax	6.17	235	216	141	(75)

Mary Park does not understand this report and asks her husband to explain it to her. Unfortunately, on his way to her office he slips on a liquid asset, loses his balance, and falls down a flight of stairs. He suffers concussion and amnesia and can remember nothing about accounting.

Mary Park has therefore asked you to explain the report and answer the following questions for her. If you cannot answer any of the questions from the information Ron Park has provided, state how you would improve the report to help with these answers, by changing either the format or the content of the report.

Required

(a) Explain the meaning or significance of each of the columns in the report.

(b) What are the reasons for the negative variances of $14 000 and $36 000 for raw materials and direct labour respectively?

(c) What is the reason for the total variance of $27 000 in respect of fixed costs, and what can be done about it?

(d) The company failed to attain target volume of 38 000 kg because of equipment breakdowns. How much did this cost the company?

(e) Should Ron Park be allowed to prepare the reports again next year, assuming he regains his memory?

APPENDIX 1
Extracts from Coca-Cola Amatil Limited Financial and Statutory Reports

Eight Year Financial Summary

	1990	1991	1992	1993	1994	1995	1996	1997	Increase (Decrease) on Prior Year	Average Compound Growth Since 1990
Sales and profits:										
Sales volume (million litres)	1 363.0	1 622.0	1 929.0	2 181.0	2 515.0	3 334.0	4 315.0	**6 299.0**	46.0%	24.4%
Sales revenue ($ millions)	1 154.9	1 392.0	1 672.7	1 951.0	2 239.1	2 968.1	3 704.8	**4 828.4**	30.3%	22.7%
Cash operating profit ($ millions)	162.0	188.0	226.4	275.1	330.4	454.1	501.3	**784.7**	56.5%	25.3%
Trading profit ($ millions)	126.3	147.0	166.6	198.4	227.9	324.5	316.8	**528.0**	66.7%	22.7%
Net operating profit ($ millions) – CCA shareholders	59.8	65.9	63.7	93.8	109.0	136.3	139.9	**242.2**	73.1%	22.1%
Balance sheet:										
Total assets ($ millions)	1 746.3	2 013.9	2 289.8	2 903.3	3 222.8	4 651.1	6 091.7	**9 466.3**	55.4%	27.3%
Total liabilities ($ millions)	1 152.2	1 366.0	1 540.9	1 777.0	2 051.0	2 689.7	3 453.8	**4 043.5**		
Net assets ($ millions)	594.1	647.9	748.9	1 126.3	1 171.8	1 961.4	2 637.9	**5 422.8**	105.6%	37.1%
Borrowings ($ millions): —net of cash and cash equivalents	595.0	802.4	943.5	583.2	759.6	1 342.5	1 500.3	**1 942.0**		
CCA shareholders' equity ($ millions)	594.1	647.9	730.8	1 101.5	1 141.6	1 930.4	2 569.8	**5 344.8**		
Outside equity interests ($ millions)			18.1	24.8	30.2	31.0	68.1	**78.0**		
Total shareholders equity ($ millions)	594.1	647.9	748.9	1 126.3	1 171.8	1 961.4	2 637.9	**5 422.8**	105.6%	37.1%
Share information:										
Earnings per share	19.5¢	18.7¢	17.8¢	25.5¢	28.5¢	31.3¢	27.4¢	**31.5¢**	15.0%	7.1%
Dividends per share	9.3¢	9.9¢	11.2¢	14.4¢	18.0¢	19.0¢	19.0¢	**19.0¢**		10.8%
Net tangible asset backing per ordinary share	$1.66	$1.79	$1.99	$2.87	$2.93	$3.90	$4.69	**$6.30**	34.3%	21.0%
Share price—closing price	$3.31	$5.57	$4.80	$9.20	$8.20	$10.73	$13.45	**$11.47**	-14.7%	19.4%
Share price—high for year								**$17.20**		
Share price—low for year								**$10.25**		
Market capitalisation ($ millions)	1 155.1	1 974.0	1 734.8	3 488.0	3 160.3	5 273.8	7 345.0	**9 719.7**		
Performance ratios:										
Cash operating profit/sales	14.0%	13.5%	13.5%	14.1%	14.8%	15.3%	13.5%	**16.3%**		
Trading profit/sales	10.9%	10.6%	10.0%	10.2%	10.2%	10.9%	8.6%	**10.9%**		
Trading profit/average operating assets	11.9%	9.7%	9.5%	9.6%	9.5%	9.8%	6.9%	**7.6%**		
Debt/equity ratio	100.2%	123.8%	126.0%	51.8%	64.8%	68.4%	56.9%	**35.8%**		
Return on average shareholders' equity	14.8%	10.6%	9.2%	10.2%	9.7%	8.9%	6.2%	**6.1%**		
Interest cover (times)	1.9	2.1	2.4	3.5	3.9	3.1	2.8	**3.5**		

Profits and balance sheet have been adjusted retrospectively to comply with AASB1033 (preference dividends and capital reclassified to interest and borrowings as appropriate).

Share information has been notionally adjusted for 1991 share split and 1993 and 1994 bonus issues of shares where applicable.

Financial and Statutory Reports

For the Financial Year ended 31 December 1997

Profit and Loss Accounts

Coca-Cola Amatil Limited and its controlled entities

For the Financial Year ended 31 December 1997		CCA Group		CCA Entity	
	Refer Note	1997 $M	1996 $M	1997 $M	1996 $M
Sales revenue		4 828.4	3 704.8	–	–
Other operating revenue		137.1	75.7	1 420.4	323.4
Total operating revenue	2	4 965.5	3 780.5	1 420.4	323.4
Trading profit		528.0	316.8		
Finance expenses (other than interest)		1.0	(13.6)		
Operating profit before interest and tax		529.0	303.2		
Net interest expense	2&3	(151.4)	(106.6)		
Operating profit	3	377.6	196.6	332.5	83.9
Income tax expense applicable	4	(132.5)	(48.6)	(24.6)	(22.8)
Operating profit after income tax		245.1	148.0	307.9	61.1
Outside equity interests in operating profit after income tax		(2.9)	(8.1)		
Operating profit after income tax attributable to ordinary shareholders of Coca-Cola Amatil Limited		242.2	139.9	307.9	61.1
Retained profits at the beginning of the year		622.9	580.1	165.9	203.9
Aggregate of amounts transferred from reserves	19	14.6	2.0	–	–
Total available for appropriation		879.7	722.0	473.8	265.0
Dividends provided for or paid—					
Ordinary shares		(114.6)	(99.1)	(114.6)	(99.1)
Payable by controlled entity in lieu of dividend on suspended dividend shares	18	(18.3)	–	–	–
Retained profits at the end of the year		746.8	622.9	359.2	165.9
Earnings per share					
Basic earnings per share*		31.5¢	27.4¢		
Weighted average number of ordinary shares on issue used in the calculation of basic earnings per share (millions)†		769.6	510.5		

* Diluted earnings per share figures are unchanged from basic earnings per share.

† The weighted average number of shares used to calculate earnings per share has been notionally adjusted to include shares issued in respect of the Philippines transaction as from the effective date of acquisition, 3 April 1997.

Comparative figures have been adjusted to reflect reclassification of preference dividends to interest expense—refer Note 1, paragraph n.

Balance Sheets

Coca-Cola Amatil Limited and its controlled entities

As at 31 December 1997	Refer Note	CCA Group		CCA Entity	
		1997 **$M**	1996 $M	**1997** **$M**	1996 $M
Current assets					
Cash and cash equivalents	6	**435.6**	877.1	**116.0**	52.1
Receivables	7	**734.8**	645.9	**1 579.1**	889.3
Cross currency swap receivables relating to borrowings		**24.0**	0.6	**11.0**	0.6
Inventories	8	**817.3**	628.8	**0.1**	0.3
Prepayments		**235.3**	170.6	**14.5**	18.6
Total current assets		**2 247.0**	2 323.0	**1 720.7**	960.9
Non-current assets					
Receivables	7	**66.7**	13.3	**910.9**	870.2
Cross currency swap receivables relating to borrowings		**159.6**	1.1	**159.6**	–
Investments in securities	9	**15.7**	12.3	**6 503.7**	3 239.3
Investments in bottlers' agreements	10	**3 598.7**	1 376.0	**–**	–
Property, plant and equipment	11	**3 206.6**	2 247.7	**58.7**	62.6
Intangibles	12	**10.2**	10.8	**–**	–
Prepayments		**69.5**	30.0	**–**	–
Future income tax benefits	13	**92.3**	77.5	**12.4**	10.4
Total non-current assets		**7 219.3**	3 768.7	**7 645.3**	4 182.5
Total assets		**9 466.3**	6 091.7	**9 366.0**	5 143.4
Current liabilities					
Accounts payable	14	**591.2**	441.9	**922.8**	850.7
Borrowings	15	**478.1**	706.5	**329.7**	430.0
Provisions	16	**234.6**	166.1	**121.7**	88.1
Accrued charges		**386.3**	307.1	**88.1**	34.3
Total current liabilities		**1 690.2**	1 621.6	**1 462.3**	1 403.1
Non-current liabilities					
Accounts payable	14	**23.1**	25.3	**342.9**	385.6
Borrowings	15	**2 083.1**	1 672.6	**1 610.4**	1 072.9
Provision for deferred income tax	17	**226.8**	113.1	**8.6**	4.5
Provision for employee entitlements		**20.3**	21.2	**5.7**	5.4
Total non-current liabilities		**2 353.3**	1 832.2	**1 967.6**	1 468.4
Total liabilities		**4 043.5**	3 453.8	**3 429.9**	2 871.5
Net assets		**5 422.8**	2 637.9	**5 936.1**	2 271.9
Shareholders' equity					
Share capital	18	**467.4**	316.7	**467.4**	316.7
Reserves	19	**4 130.6**	1 630.2	**5 109.5**	1 789.3
Retained profits		**746.8**	622.9	**359.2**	165.9
Shareholders' equity attributable to ordinary **shareholders of Coca-Cola Amatil Limited**		**5 344.8**	2 569.8	**5 936.1**	2 271.9
Outside equity interests in controlled entities					
Share capital		**22.5**	17.6		
Reserves		**23.9**	34.3		
Retained profits		**31.6**	16.2		
Total outside equity interests		**78.0**	68.1		
Total shareholders' equity		**5 422.8**	2 637.9	**5 936.1**	2 271.9

Comparative figures have been adjusted to reflect reclassification of preference share capital to non-current loans—refer Note 1, paragraph n.

Statements of Cash Flows

Coca-Cola Amatil Limited and its controlled entities

For the Financial Year ended 31 December 1997	Refer Note	CCA Group 1997 $M	1996 $M	CCA Entity 1997 $M	1996 $M
Inflows (outflows)					
Cash flows from operating activities					
Receipts from customers		**4 745.7**	3 642.5	–	–
Receipts from related parties for management and guarantee fees				**215.3**	173.6
Payments to suppliers and employees		**(4 116.7)**	(3 416.7)	**(234.5)**	(117.0)
Dividends received		–	–	**530.0**	65.0
Interest and bill discounts received		**79.3**	35.1	**80.1**	83.2
Interest and other costs of finance paid		**(187.3)**	(154.4)	**(128.6)**	(138.8)
Income tax paid		**(87.3)**	(68.1)	**(0.3)**	(13.5)
		433.7	38.4	**462.0**	52.5
Cash flows from investing activities					
Proceeds from—					
sale of property, plant and equipment		**75.1**	23.6	**13.0**	1.5
settlement of legal claim (purchase price adjustment) .		–	11.6	–	–
sale of investments		–	–	**581.9**	–
Payment for—					
property, plant and equipment		**(777.9)**	(679.5)	**(12.5)**	(29.9)
investments		–	(2.4)	**(695.0)**	(1 022.6)
acquisitions of entities, net of cash acquired	29	**95.0**	(126.5)	–	–
goodwill		**(0.6)**	–	–	–
		(608.4)	(773.2)	**(112.6)**	(1 051.0)
Cash flows from financing activities					
Proceeds from issue of shares		**95.5**	750.0	**95.5**	750.0
Proceeds from borrowings		**656.7**	763.1	**839.6**	261.6
Borrowings repaid		**(583.6)**	(570.9)	**(275.8)**	(309.2)
Net increase in intragroup loans				**(544.0)**	(163.3)
Dividends paid		**(104.2)**	(97.3)	**(104.2)**	(94.0)
		64.4	844.9	**11.1**	445.1
Net increase (decrease) in cash held		**(110.3)**	110.1	**360.5**	(553.4)
Cash held at the beginning of the year		**406.4**	319.1	**(377.9)**	175.5
Exchange rate adjustments to cash held at the beginning of the year		**(24.2)**	(22.8)	–	–
Cash at the end of the year		**271.9**	406.4	**(17.4)**	(377.9)

Comparative figures have been adjusted to reflect reclassification of preference dividends to interest expense—refer Note 1, paragraph n.

Coca-Cola Amatil Limited and its controlled entities

	Refer Note	CCA Group 1997 $M	1996 $M	CCA Entity 1997 $M	1996 $M
Reconciliation of cash flows from operating activities to operating profit after income tax					
Operating profit after income tax		245.1	148.0	307.9	61.1
Depreciation and amounts set aside to provisions		297.6	202.4	707.7	(2.9)
Losses (profits) from disposal of non-current assets		(11.1)	4.8	(480.5)	(0.2)
(Increase) decrease in—					
interest receivable		17.3	(17.0)	(0.1)	(0.1)
other receivables		(114.6)	(140.9)	(229.1)	(824.1)
inventories		(154.9)	(145.9)	0.2	–
prepayments		15.0	(90.4)	4.1	(0.8)
Increase (decrease) in—					
interest payable		26.1	4.3	29.4	(0.4)
tax payable		45.2	(19.5)	24.3	9.3
other payables		95.6	37.8	72.4	821.2
accrued charges		(27.6)	54.8	25.7	(10.6)
Cash flows from operating activities		**433.7**	38.4	**462.0**	52.5

Changes in assets and liabilities are net of effects from
purchases of entities.

Reconciliation of cash

For the purposes of the statements of cash flows, cash
includes cash on hand and in banks and investments
in money market instruments, net of bank overdrafts
and short-term borrowings.

	Refer Note	CCA Group 1997 $M	1996 $M	CCA Entity 1997 $M	1996 $M
Cash and cash equivalents	6	435.6	877.1	116.0	52.1
Call deposits (included in loans)		(119.8)	(420.5)	(119.8)	(420.5)
Bank overdrafts		(43.9)	(50.2)	(13.6)	(9.5)
Cash at the end of the year		**271.9**	406.4	**(17.4)**	(377.9)

Non-cash financing and investing activities

During the year, the Group issued 275 million ordinary shares for the acquisition of 100% of the common shares of Coca-Cola
Bottlers Philippines, Inc and 18 million ordinary shares as consideration for a non-compete agreement from the San Miguel
Corporation in certain countries in Asia. These shares were issued at $11.52 each, amounting to a total of $3375.4M.

Notes to the Financial Statements

Coca-Cola Amatil Limited and its controlled entities

For the Financial Year ended 31 December 1997

1. **Statement of Accounting Policies**

   The financial statements are general purpose financial reports and have been prepared in accordance with applicable Accounting Standards, Urgent Issues Group Consensus Views and the Corporations Law. A summary of the significant accounting policies adopted by the Coca-Cola Amatil Limited Group is set out below. These policies have been consistently applied.

   a) **Historical cost**

   The financial statements have been prepared on the basis of historical cost and, except where otherwise stated, do not account for changing money values or valuations of non-current assets.

   b) **Principles of consolidation**

   The consolidated accounts of the economic entity referred to as the CCA Group include the chief entity, Coca-Cola Amatil Limited (CCA Entity), and its controlled entities. A list of controlled entities is contained in Note 28.

   The financial statements include the information and results of each controlled entity from the date on which the Company obtains control and until such time as the Company ceases to control the entity.

   In preparing the consolidated accounts, the effects of all transactions between entities in the Group have been eliminated.

   c) **Leased assets**

   Finance leases are those which effectively transfer from the lessor to the lessee substantially all the risks and benefits incidental to ownership of the leased property. There are no material finance leases within the Group.

   Operating leases are those where the lessor effectively retains substantially all the risks and benefits incidental to ownership of the leased property.

   Operating lease payments are charged against profits as incurred. Disclosure of the relevant details of operating leases is contained in Note 21.

   d) **Depreciation and amortisation of non-current assets**

   Non-current assets are depreciated or amortised over the useful life of each asset where the amount charged would be material. Where assets have been revalued, depreciation or amortisation is charged on the adjusted amount.

   e) **Valuation of non-current assets**

   Freehold land and buildings are revalued at three-yearly intervals. The value of the land and buildings is assessed on their worth to the Group on an existing use basis and does not exceed the net amount expected to be recovered from their continued use and subsequent disposal. Other non-current assets are carried at the lower of cost and recoverable amount. The expected net cash flows included in determining the recoverable amounts of non-current assets have been discounted to their present value.

   f) **Inventories**

   As a general principle, inventories are valued at the lower of cost (including fixed and variable factory overheads where applicable) and net realisable value. Cost is determined on the basis of first-in-first-out, average or standard, whichever is the most appropriate in each case.

   g) **Investments**

   Investments in securities are stated at cost. A provision for diminution in value is only made where the diminution is regarded as being other than temporary.

   Investments in bottlers' agreements are stated at cost. As more fully described in Note 10, bottlers' agreements document the relationship between The Coca-Cola Company (TCCC) and the CCA Group in relation to individual geographic markets. Cost comprises the purchase price for agreements acquired in previously developed markets as well as the cost of developing the market in regions in which TCCC has granted the CCA Group the right to develop an initial market, until such time as the basic infrastructure is in place. For the reasons described in Note 10, no amortisation is provided against the carrying value of these assets.

   h) **Foreign currency translations**

   Transactions in overseas currencies are converted to Australian currency at the rate of exchange ruling at the date of each transaction. Foreign currency items in the balance sheet are converted at rates of exchange ruling at balance date. Exchange rate gains or losses are brought to account in the profit and loss account, in the period in which they arise, as are exchange gains or losses relating to cross currency swap transactions on monetary items.

1. **Statement of Accounting Policies continued**

Exchange differences relating to hedges of specific transactions in respect of the purchase of inventories or other assets, to the extent that they occur before the date of purchase, are deferred and included in the measurement of the purchase transaction. Exchange differences relating to other hedge transactions are brought to account in the profit and loss account in the period in which they arise.

Foreign controlled entities are considered self-sustaining. Assets and liabilities are translated by applying the rate ruling at balance date and revenue and expense items are translated at the average rate calculated for the period. Exchange rate differences are taken to the foreign currency translation reserve.

Foreign controlled entities operating in hyperinflationary environments prepare separate accounts using a functional (hard) currency for inclusion in the Group consolidation. Adjustments resulting from translating net monetary items from the local currency to the functional currency are brought to account in the profit and loss account.

i)   Income tax

Tax effect accounting principles are observed by the Group whereby income tax expense for the period is matched with the pre-tax result adjusted for permanent differences. The account 'Provision for deferred income tax' records the income tax effect of items which will cause taxable income to be higher than book profits in the future and the account 'Future income tax benefits' records the income tax effect of items which will cause taxable income to be lower than book profits in the future.

Withholding tax and Australian tax payable upon the distribution of overseas earnings have been provided to the extent the earnings are planned to be remitted. No provision has been made on earnings that are expected to be retained by certain controlled overseas entities to finance their ongoing businesses.

j)   Self-insurance

The Group self-insures and funds certain insurable risks. All known self-insured losses have been brought to account and adequate provisions have been raised for self-insured losses not yet reported.

k)   Research and development

All expenditure on research and development is written off in the period in which the expenditure is incurred except where future benefits can be assured beyond reasonable doubt.

l)   Capitalisation of interest

Interest relating to the financing of major projects is capitalised in non-current assets up to the date of commissioning and subsequently amortised over the useful life of the asset.

m)   Employee entitlements

Provision is made for employee entitlement benefits accumulated as a result of employees rendering services up to balance date and an accrual is raised for related on-costs. The benefits include wages and salaries, incentives, annual leave, sick leave and long service leave, which are charged against profits in their respective expense category. Employer contributions to the employee share plan described in Note 18 are charged as an employee entitlement expense as incurred. No expenses are recorded in respect of the executive option plan. Employer contributions made to superannuation funds are charged against profits as incurred.

n)   Preference share capital—change in accounting policy

In accordance with Australian Accounting Standard AASB 1033 'Presentation and Disclosure of Financial Instruments', preference capital has been reclassified to non-current loans with a corresponding reduction in shareholders' equity and preference dividends have been reclassified to interest expense, non-allowable. As the reclassifications do not have a material effect on the current year or prior year accounts the comparative figures have been adjusted accordingly for the purpose of consistency and in order to achieve greater comparability. Details are as follows:

	1997 $M	1996 $M
Amounts reclassified to non-current loans	**39.6**	39.6
Amounts reclassified to interest expense	**1.8**	2.2

APPENDIX 2
IASC
Framework

Framework for the Preparation and Presentation of Financial Statements

Contents

Preface

Financial statements are prepared and presented for external users by many enterprises around the world. Although such financial statements may appear similar from country to country, there are differences which have probably been caused by a variety of social, economic and legal circumstances and by different countries having in mind the needs of different users of financial statements when setting national requirements.

These different circumstances have led to the use of a variety of definitions of the elements of financial statements; that is, for example, assets, liabilities, equity, income and expenses. They have also resulted in the use of different criteria for the recognition of items in the financial statements and in a preference for different bases of measurement. The scope of the financial statements and the disclosures made in them have also been affected.

The International Accounting Standards Committee (IASC) is committed to narrowing these differences by seeking to harmonise regulations, accounting standards and procedures relating to the preparation and presentation of financial statements. It believes that further harmonisation can best be pursued by focusing on financial statements that are prepared for the purpose of providing information that is useful in making economic decisions.

The Board of IASC believes that financial statements prepared for this purpose meet the common needs of most users. This is because nearly all users are making economic decisions, for example, to:

(a) decide when to buy, hold or sell an equity investment;
(b) assess the stewardship or accountability of management;
(c) assess the ability of the enterprise to pay and provide other benefits to its employees;
(d) assess the security for amounts lent to the enterprise;
(e) determine taxation policies;
(f) determine distributable profits and dividends;
(g) prepare and use national income statistics; or
(h) regulate the activities of enterprises.

The Board recognises, however, that governments, in particular, may specify different or additional requirements for their own purposes. These requirements should not, however, affect financial statements published for the benefit of other users unless they also meet the needs of those other users.

Financial statements are most commonly prepared in accordance with an accounting model based on recoverable historical cost and the nominal financial capital maintenance concept. Other models and concepts may be more appropriate in order to meet the objective of providing information that is useful for making economic decisions although there is presently no consensus for change. This framework has been developed so that it is applicable to a range of accounting models and concepts of capital and capital maintenance.

Introduction

Purpose and Status

1. This framework sets out the concepts that underlie the preparation and presentation of financial statements for external users. The purpose of the framework is to:

   (a) assist the Board of IASC in the development of future International Accounting Standards and in its review of existing International Accounting Standards;

   (b) assist the Board of IASC in promoting harmonisation of regulations, accounting standards and procedures relating to the presentation of financial statements by providing a basis for reducing the number of alternative accounting treatments permitted by International Accounting Standards;

   (c) assist national standard-setting bodies in developing national standards;

   (d) assist preparers of financial statements in applying International Accounting Standards and in dealing with topics that have yet to form the subject of an International Accounting Standard;

   (e) assist auditors in forming an opinion as to whether financial statements conform with International Accounting Standards;

   (f) assist users of financial statements in interpreting the information contained in financial statements prepared in conformity with International Accounting Standards; and

   (g) provide those who are interested in the work of IASC with information about its approach to the formulation of International Accounting Standards.

2. This framework is not an International Accounting Standard and hence does not define standards for any particular measurement or disclosure issue. Nothing in this framework overrides any specific International Accounting Standard.

3. The Board of IASC recognises that in a limited number of cases there may be a conflict between the framework and an International Accounting Standard. In those cases where there is a conflict, the requirements of the International Accounting Standard prevail over those of the framework. As, however, the Board of IASC will be guided by the framework in the development of future Standards and in its review of existing Standards, the number of cases of conflict between the framework and International Accounting Standards will diminish through time.

4. The framework will be revised from time to time on the basis of the Board's experience of working with it.

Scope

5. The framework deals with:

   (a) the objective of financial statements;

   (b) the qualitative characteristics that determine the usefulness of information in financial statements;

   (c) the definition, recognition and measurement of the elements from which financial statements are constructed; and

   (d) concepts of capital and capital maintenance.

6. The framework is concerned with general purpose financial statements (hereafter referred to as "financial statements") including consolidated financial statements. Such financial statements are prepared and presented at least annually and are directed toward the common information needs of a wide range of users. Some of these users may require, and have the power to obtain, information in addition to that contained in the financial statements. Many users, however, have to rely on the financial statements as their major source of financial information and such financial statements should, therefore, be prepared and presented with their needs in view. Special purpose

financial reports, for example, prospectuses and computations prepared for taxation purposes, are outside the scope of this framework. Nevertheless, the framework may be applied in the preparation of such special purpose reports where their requirements permit.

7. Financial statements form part of the process of financial reporting. A complete set of financial statements normally includes a balance sheet, an income statement, a statement of changes in financial position (which may be presented in a variety of ways, for example, as a statement of cash flows or a statement of funds flow), and those notes and other statements and explanatory material that are an integral part of the financial statements. They may also include supplementary schedules and information based on or derived from, and expected to be read with, such statements. Such schedules and supplementary information may deal, for example, with financial information about industrial and geographical segments and disclosures about the effects of changing prices. Financial statements do not, however, include such items as reports by directors, statements by the chairman, discussion and analysis by management and similar items that may be included in a financial or annual report.

8. The framework applies to the financial statements of all commercial, industrial and business reporting enterprises, whether in the public or the private sectors. A reporting enterprise is an enterprise for which there are users who rely on the financial statements as their major source of financial information about the enterprise.

Users and Their Information Needs

9. The users of financial statements include present and potential investors, employees, lenders, suppliers and other trade creditors, customers, governments and their agencies and the public. They use financial statements in order to satisfy some of their different needs for information. These needs include the following:

(a) *Investors.* The providers of risk capital and their advisers are concerned with the risk inherent in, and return provided by, their investments. They need information to help them determine whether they should buy, hold or sell. Shareholders are also interested in information which enables them to assess the ability of the enterprise to pay dividends.

(b) *Employees.* Employees and their representative groups are interested in information about the stability and profitability of their employers. They are also interested in information which enables them to assess the ability of the enterprise to provide remuneration, retirement benefits and employment opportunities.

(c) *Lenders.* Lenders are interested in information that enables them to determine whether their loans, and the interest attaching to them, will be paid when due.

(d) *Suppliers and other trade creditors.* Suppliers and other creditors are interested in information that enables them to determine whether amounts owing to them will be paid when due. Trade creditors are likely to be interested in an enterprise over a shorter period than lenders unless they are dependent upon the continuation of the enterprise as a major customer.

(e) *Customers.* Customers have an interest in information about the continuance of an enterprise, especially when they have a long-term involvement with, or are dependent on, the enterprise.

(f) *Governments and their agencies.* Governments and their agencies are interested in the allocation of resources and, therefore, the activities of enterprises. They also require information in order to regulate the activities of enterprises, determine taxation policies and as the basis for national income and similar statistics.

(g) *Public.* Enterprises affect members of the public in a variety of ways. For example, enterprises may make a substantial contribution to the local economy in many ways including the number of people they employ and their patronage of local suppliers. Financial statements may assist the public by providing information about the trends and recent developments in the prosperity of the enterprise and the range of its activities.

10. While all of the information needs of these users cannot be met by financial statements, there are needs which are common to all users. As investors are providers of risk capital to the enterprise, the provision of financial statements that meet their needs will also meet most of the needs of other users that financial statements can satisfy.

11. The management of an enterprise has the primary responsibility for the preparation and presentation of the financial statements of the enterprise. Management is also interested in the information contained in the financial statements even though it has access to additional management and financial information that helps it carry out its planning, decision-making and control responsibilities. Management has the ability to determine the form and content of such additional information in order to meet its own needs. The reporting of such information, however, is beyond the scope of this framework. Nevertheless, published financial statements are based on the information used by management about the financial position, performance and changes in financial position of the enterprise.

The Objective of Financial Statements

12. The objective of financial statements is to provide information about the financial position, performance and changes in financial position of an enterprise that is useful to a wide range of users in making economic decisions.

13. Financial statements prepared for this purpose meet the common needs of most users. However, financial statements do not provide all the information that users may need to make economic decisions since they largely portray the financial effects of past events and do not necessarily provide non-financial information.

14. Financial statements also show the results of the stewardship of management, or the accountability of management for the resources entrusted to it. Those users who wish to assess the stewardship or accountability of management do so in order that they may make economic decisions; these decisions may include, for example, whether to hold or sell their investment in the enterprise or whether to reappoint or replace the management.

Financial Position, Performance and Changes in Financial Position

15. The economic decisions that are taken by users of financial statements require an evaluation of the ability of an enterprise to generate cash and cash equivalents and of the timing and certainty of their generation. This ability ultimately determines, for example, the capacity of an enterprise to pay its employees and suppliers, meet interest payments, repay loans and make distributions to its owners. Users are better able to evaluate this ability to generate cash and cash equivalents if they are provided with information that focuses on the financial position, performance and changes in financial position of an enterprise.

16. The financial position of an enterprise is affected by the economic resources it controls, its financial structure, its liquidity and solvency, and its capacity to adapt to changes in the environment in which it operates. Information about the economic resources controlled by the enterprise and its capacity in the past to modify these resources is useful in predicting the ability of the enterprise to generate cash and cash equivalents in the future. Information about financial structure is useful in predicting future borrowing needs and how future profits and cash flows will be distributed among those with an interest in the enterprise; it is also useful in predicting how successful the enterprise is likely to be in raising further finance. Information about

liquidity and solvency is useful in predicting the ability of the enterprise to meet its financial commitments as they fall due. Liquidity refers to the availability of cash in the near future after taking account of financial commitments over this period. Solvency refers to the availability of cash over the longer term to meet financial commitments as they fall due.

17. Information about the performance of an enterprise, in particular its profitability, is required in order to assess potential changes in the economic resources that it is likely to control in the future. Information about variability of performance is important in this respect. Information about performance is useful in predicting the capacity of the enterprise to generate cash flows from its existing resource base. It is also useful in forming judgements about the effectiveness with which the enterprise might employ additional resources.

18. Information concerning changes in the financial position of an enterprise is useful in order to assess its investing, financing and operating activities during the reporting period. This information is useful in providing the user with a basis to assess the ability of the enterprise to generate cash and cash equivalents and the needs of the enterprise to utilise those cash flows. In constructing a statement of changes in financial position, funds can be defined in various ways, such as all financial resources, working capital, liquid assets or cash. No attempt is made in this framework to specify a definition of funds.

19. Information about financial position is primarily provided in a balance sheet. Information about performance is primarily provided in an income statement. Information about changes in financial position is provided in the financial statements by means of a separate statement.

20. The component parts of the financial statements interrelate because they reflect different aspects of the same transactions or other events. Although each statement provides information that is different from the others, none is likely to serve only a single purpose or provide all the information necessary for particular needs of users. For example, an income statement provides an incomplete picture of performance unless it is used in conjunction with the balance sheet and the statement of changes in financial position.

Notes and Supplementary Schedules

21. The financial statements also contain notes and supplementary schedules and other information. For example, they may contain additional information that is relevant to the needs of users about the items in the balance sheet and income statement. They may include disclosures about the risks and uncertainties affecting the enterprise and any resources and obligations not recognised in the balance sheet (such as mineral reserves). Information about geographical and industry segments and the effect on the enterprise of changing prices may also be provided in the form of supplementary information.

Underlying Assumptions

Accrual Basis

22. In order to meet their objectives, financial statements are prepared on the accrual basis of accounting. Under this basis, the effects of transactions and other events are recognised when they occur (and not as cash or its equivalent is received or paid) and they are recorded in the accounting records and reported in the financial statements of the periods to which they relate. Financial statements prepared on the accrual basis inform users not only of past transactions involving the payment and receipt of cash but also of obligations to pay cash in the future and of resources that represent cash to be received in the future. Hence, they provide the type of information about past transactions and other events that is most useful to users in making economic decisions.

Going Concern

23. The financial statements are normally prepared on the assumption that an enterprise is a going concern and will continue in operation for the foreseeable future. Hence, it is assumed that the enterprise has neither the intention nor the need to liquidate or curtail materially the scale of its operations; if such an intention or need exists, the financial statements may have to be prepared on a different basis and, if so, the basis used is disclosed.

Qualitative Characteristics of Financial Statements

24. Qualitative characteristics are the attributes that make the information provided in financial statements useful to users. The four principal qualitative characteristics are understandability, relevance, reliability and comparability.

Understandability

25. An essential quality of the information provided in financial statements is that it is readily understandable by users. For this purpose, users are assumed to have a reasonable knowledge of business and economic activities and accounting and a willingness to study the information with reasonable diligence. However, information about complex matters that should be included in the financial statements because of its relevance to the economic decision-making needs of users should not be excluded merely on the grounds that it may be too difficult for certain users to understand.

Relevance

26. To be useful, information must be relevant to the decision-making needs of users. Information has the quality of relevance when it influences the economic decisions of users by helping them evaluate past, present or future events or confirming, or correcting, their past evaluations.

27. The predictive and confirmatory roles of information are interrelated. For example, information about the current level and structure of asset holdings has value to users when they endeavour to predict the ability of the enterprise to take advantage of opportunities and its ability to react to adverse situations. The same information plays a confirmatory role in respect of past predictions about, for example, the way in which the enterprise would be structured or the outcome of planned operations.

28. Information about financial position and past performance is frequently used as the basis for predicting future financial position and performance and other matters in which users are directly interested, such as dividend and wage payments, security price movements and the ability of the enterprise to meet its commitments as they fall due. To have predictive value, information need not be in the form of an explicit forecast. The ability to make predictions from financial statements is enhanced, however, by the manner in which information on past transactions and events is displayed. For example, the predictive value of the income statement is enhanced if unusual, abnormal and infrequent items of income or expense are separately disclosed.

Materiality

29. The relevance of information is affected by its nature and materiality. In some cases, the nature of information alone is sufficient to determine its relevance. For example, the reporting of a new segment may affect the assessment of the risks and opportunities facing the enterprise irrespective of the materiality of the results achieved by the new segment in the reporting period. In other cases, both the nature and materiality are important, for example, the amounts of inventories held in each of the main categories that are appropriate to the business.

30. Information is material if its omission or misstatement could influence the economic decisions of users taken on the basis of the financial statements. Materiality depends on the size of the item or error judged in the particular circumstances of its omission or misstatement. Thus, materiality provides a threshold or cut-off point rather than being a primary qualitative characteristic which information must have if it is to be useful.

Reliability

31. To be useful, information must also be reliable. Information has the quality of reliability when it is free from material error and bias and can be depended upon by users to represent faithfully that which it either purports to represent or could reasonably be expected to represent.

32. Information may be relevant but so unreliable in nature or representation that its recognition may be potentially misleading. For example, if the validity and amount of a claim for damages under a legal action are disputed, it may be inappropriate for the enterprise to recognise the full amount of the claim in the balance sheet, although it may be appropriate to disclose the amount and circumstances of the claim.

Faithful Representation

33. To be reliable, information must represent faithfully the transactions and other events it either purports to represent or could reasonably be expected to represent. Thus, for example, a balance sheet should represent faithfully the transactions and other events that result in assets, liabilities and equity of the enterprise at the reporting date which meet the recognition criteria.

34. Most financial information is subject to some risk of being less than a faithful representation of that which it purports to portray. This is not due to bias, but rather to inherent difficulties either in identifying the transactions and other events to be measured or in devising and applying measurement and presentation techniques that can convey messages that correspond with those transactions and events. In certain cases, the measurement of the financial effects of items could be so uncertain that enterprises generally would not recognise them in the financial statements; for example, although most enterprises generate goodwill internally over time, it is usually difficult to identify or measure that goodwill reliably. In other cases, however, it may be relevant to recognise items and to disclose the risk of error surrounding their recognition and measurement.

Substance Over Form

35. If information is to represent faithfully the transactions and other events that it purports to represent, it is necessary that they are accounted for and presented in accordance with their substance and economic reality and not merely their legal form. The substance of transactions or other events is not always consistent with that which is apparent from their legal or contrived form. For example, an enterprise may dispose of an asset to another party in such a way that the documentation purports to pass legal ownership to that party; nevertheless, agreements may exist that ensure that the enterprise continues to enjoy the future economic benefits embodied in the asset. In such circumstances, the reporting of a sale would not represent faithfully the transaction entered into (if indeed there was a transaction).

Neutrality

36. To be reliable, the information contained in financial statements must be neutral, that is, free from bias. Financial statements are not neutral if, by the selection or presentation of information, they influence the making of a decision or judgement in order to achieve a predetermined result or outcome.

Prudence

37. The preparers of financial statements do, however, have to contend with the uncertainties that inevitably surround many events and circumstances, such as the collectability of doubtful receivables, the probable useful life of plant and equipment and the number of warranty claims that may occur. Such uncertainties are recognised by the disclosure of their nature and extent and by the exercise of prudence in the preparation of the financial statements. Prudence is the inclusion of a degree of caution in the exercise of the judgements needed in making the estimates required under conditions of uncertainty, such that assets or income are not overstated and liabilities or expenses are not understated. However, the exercise of prudence does not allow, for example, the creation of hidden reserves or excessive provisions, the deliberate understatement of assets or income, or the deliberate overstatement of liabilities or expenses, because the financial statements would not be neutral and, therefore, not have the quality of reliability.

Completeness

38. To be reliable, the information in financial statements must be complete within the bounds of materiality and cost. An omission can cause information to be false or misleading and thus unreliable and deficient in terms of its relevance.

Comparability

39. Users must be able to compare the financial statements of an enterprise through time in order to identify trends in its financial position and performance. Users must also be able to compare the financial statements of different enterprises in order to evaluate their relative financial position, performance and changes in financial position. Hence, the measurement and display of the financial effect of like transactions and other events must be carried out in a consistent way throughout an enterprise and over time for that enterprise and in a consistent way for different enterprises.

40. An important implication of the qualitative characteristic of comparability is that users be informed of the accounting policies employed in the preparation of the financial statements, any changes in those policies and the effects of such changes. Users need to be able to identify differences between the accounting policies for like transactions and other events used by the same enterprise from period to period and by different enterprises. Compliance with International Accounting Standards, including the disclosure of the accounting policies used by the enterprise, helps to achieve comparability.

41. The need for comparability should not be confused with mere uniformity and should not be allowed to become an impediment to the introduction of improved accounting standards. It is not appropriate for an enterprise to continue accounting in the same manner for a transaction or other event if the policy adopted is not in keeping with the qualitative characteristics of relevance and reliability. It is also inappropriate for an enterprise to leave its accounting policies unchanged when more relevant and reliable alternatives exist.

42. Because users wish to compare the financial position, performance and changes in financial position of an enterprise over time, it is important that the financial statements show corresponding information for the preceding periods.

Constraints on Relevant and Reliable Information

Timeliness

43. If there is undue delay in the reporting of information it may lose its relevance. Management may need to balance the relative merits of timely reporting and the provision of reliable information. To provide information on a timely basis it may often be

necessary to report before all aspects of a transaction or other event are known, thus impairing reliability. Conversely, if reporting is delayed until all aspects are known, the information may be highly reliable but of little use to users who have had to make decisions in the interim. In achieving a balance between relevance and reliability, the overriding consideration is how best to satisfy the economic decision-making needs of users.

Balance between Benefit and Cost

44. The balance between benefit and cost is a pervasive constraint rather than a qualitative characteristic. The benefits derived from information should exceed the cost of providing it. The evaluation of benefits and costs is, however, substantially a judgmental process. Furthermore, the costs do not necessarily fall on those users who enjoy the benefits. Benefits may also be enjoyed by users other than those for whom the information is prepared; for example, the provision of further information to lenders may reduce the borrowing costs of an enterprise. For these reasons, it is difficult to apply a cost-benefit test in any particular case. Nevertheless, standard-setters in particular, as well as the preparers and users of financial statements, should be aware of this constraint.

Balance between Qualitative Characteristics

45. In practice a balancing, or trade-off, between qualitative characteristics is often necessary. Generally the aim is to achieve an appropriate balance among the characteristics in order to meet the objective of financial statements. The relative importance of the characteristics in different cases is a matter of professional judgement.

True and Fair View/Fair Presentation

46. Financial statements are frequently described as showing a true and fair view of, or as presenting fairly, the financial position, performance and changes in financial position of an enterprise. Although this framework does not deal directly with such concepts, the application of the principal qualitative characteristics and of appropriate accounting standards normally results in financial statements that convey what is generally understood as a true and fair view of, or as presenting fairly such information.

The Elements of Financial Statements

47. Financial statements portray the financial effects of transactions and other events by grouping them into broad classes according to their economic characteristics. These broad classes are termed the elements of financial statements. The elements directly related to the measurement of financial position in the balance sheet are assets, liabilities and equity. The elements directly related to the measurement of performance in the income statement are income and expenses. The statement of changes in financial position usually reflects income statement elements and changes in balance sheet elements; accordingly, this framework identifies no elements that are unique to this statement.

48. The presentation of these elements in the balance sheet and the income statement involves a process of sub-classification. For example, assets and liabilities may be classified by their nature or function in the business of the enterprise in order to display information in the manner most useful to users for purposes of making economic decisions.

Financial Position

49. The elements directly related to the measurement of financial position are assets, liabilities and equity. These are defined as follows:

    (a) An *asset* is a resource controlled by the enterprise as a result of past events and from which future economic benefits are expected to flow to the enterprise.
    (b) A *liability* is a present obligation of the enterprise arising from past events, the settlement of which is expected to result in an outflow from the enterprise of resources embodying economic benefits.
    (c) *Equity* is the residual interest in the assets of the enterprise after deducting all its liabilities.

50. The definitions of an asset and a liability identify their essential features but do not attempt to specify the criteria that need to be met before they are recognised in the balance sheet. Thus, the definitions embrace items that are not recognised as assets or liabilities in the balance sheet because they do not satisfy the criteria for recognition discussed in paragraphs 82 to 98. In particular, the expectation that future economic benefits will flow to or from an enterprise must be sufficiently certain to meet the probability criterion in paragraph 83 before an asset or liability is recognised.

51. In assessing whether an item meets the definition of an asset, liability or equity, attention needs to be given to its underlying substance and economic reality and not merely its legal form. Thus, for example, in the case of finance leases, the substance and economic reality are that the lessee acquires the economic benefits of the use of the leased asset for the major part of its useful life in return for entering into an obligation to pay for that right an amount approximating to the fair value of the asset and the related finance charge. Hence, the finance lease gives rise to items that satisfy the definition of an asset and a liability and are recognised as such in the lessee's balance sheet.

52. Balance sheets drawn up in accordance with current International Accounting Standards may include items that do not satisfy the definitions of an asset or liability and are not shown as part of equity. The definitions set out in paragraph 49 will, however, underlie future reviews of existing International Accounting Standards and the formulation of further Standards.

Assets

53. The future economic benefit embodied in an asset is the potential to contribute, directly or indirectly, to the flow of cash and cash equivalents to the enterprise. The potential may be a productive one that is part of the operating activities of the enterprise. It may also take the form of convertibility into cash or cash equivalents or a capability to reduce cash outflows, such as when an alternative manufacturing process lowers the costs of production.

54. An enterprise usually employs its assets to produce goods or services capable of satisfying the wants or needs of customers; because these goods or services can satisfy these wants or needs, customers are prepared to pay for them and hence contribute to the cash flow of the enterprise. Cash itself renders a service to the enterprise because of its command over other resources.

55. The future economic benefits embodied in an asset may flow to the enterprise in a number of ways. For example, an asset may be:

    (a) used singly or in combination with other assets in the production of goods or services to be sold by the enterprise;
    (b) exchanged for other assets;
    (c) used to settle a liability; or
    (d) distributed to the owners of the enterprise.

56. Many assets, for example, property, plant and equipment, have a physical form. However, physical form is not essential to the existence of an asset; hence patents and copyrights, for example, are assets if future economic benefits are expected to flow from them to the enterprise and if they are controlled by the enterprise.

57. Many assets, for example, receivables and property, are associated with legal rights, including the right of ownership. In determining the existence of an asset, the right of ownership is not essential; thus, for example, property held on a lease is an asset if the enterprise controls the benefits which are expected to flow from the property. Although the capacity of an enterprise to control benefits is usually the result of legal rights, an item may nonetheless satisfy the definition of an asset even when there is no legal control. For example, know-how obtained from a development activity may meet the definition of an asset when, by keeping that know-how secret, an enterprise controls the benefits that are expected to flow from it.

58. The assets of an enterprise result from past transactions or other past events. Enterprises normally obtain assets by purchasing or producing them, but other transactions or events may generate assets; examples include property received by an enterprise from government as part of a programme to encourage economic growth in an area and the discovery of mineral deposits. Transactions or events expected to occur in the future do not in themselves give rise to assets; hence, for example, an intention to purchase inventory does not, of itself, meet the definition of an asset.

59. There is a close association between incurring expenditure and generating assets but the two do not necessarily coincide. Hence, when an enterprise incurs expenditure, this may provide evidence that future economic benefits were sought but is not conclusive proof that an item satisfying the definition of an asset has been obtained. Similarly the absence of a related expenditure does not preclude an item from satisfying the definition of an asset and thus becoming a candidate for recognition in the balance sheet; for example, items that have been donated to the enterprise may satisfy the definition of an asset.

Liabilities

60. An essential characteristic of a liability is that the enterprise has a present obligation. An obligation is a duty or responsibility to act or perform in a certain way. Obligations may be legally enforceable as a consequence of a binding contract or statutory requirement. This is normally the case, for example, with amounts payable for goods and services received. Obligations also arise, however, from normal business practice, custom and a desire to maintain good business relations or act in an equitable manner. If, for example, an enterprise decides as a matter of policy to rectify faults in its products even when these become apparent after the warranty period has expired, the amounts that are expected to be expended in respect of goods already sold are liabilities.

61. A distinction needs to be drawn between a present obligation and a future commitment. A decision by the management of an enterprise to acquire assets in the future does not, of itself, give rise to a present obligation. An obligation normally arises only when the asset is delivered or the enterprise enters into an irrevocable agreement to acquire the asset. In the latter case, the irrevocable nature of the agreement means that the economic consequences of failing to honour the obligation, for example, because of the existence of a substantial penalty, leave the enterprise with little, if any, discretion to avoid the outflow of resources to another party.

62. The settlement of a present obligation usually involves the enterprise giving up resources embodying economic benefits in order to satisfy the claim of the other party. Settlement of a present obligation may occur in a number of ways, for example, by:

    (a) payment of cash;
    (b) transfer of other assets;

(c) provision of services;
(d) replacement of that obligation with another obligation; or
(e) conversion of the obligation to equity.

An obligation may also be extinguished by other means, such as a creditor waiving or forfeiting its rights.

63. Liabilities result from past transactions or other past events. Thus, for example, the acquisition of goods and the use of services give rise to trade payables (unless paid for in advance or on delivery) and the receipt of a bank loan results in an obligation to repay the loan. An enterprise may also recognise future rebates based on annual purchases by customers as liabilities; in this case, the sale of the goods in the past is the transaction that gives rise to the liability.

64. Some liabilities can be measured only by using a substantial degree of estimation. Some enterprises describe these liabilities as provisions. In some countries, such provisions are not regarded as liabilities because the concept of a liability is defined narrowly so as to include only amounts that can be established without the need to make estimates. The definition of a liability in paragraph 49 follows a broader approach. Thus, when a provision involves a present obligation and satisfies the rest of the definition, it is a liability even if the amount has to be estimated. Examples include provisions for payments to be made under existing warranties and provisions to cover pension obligations.

Equity

65. Although equity is defined in paragraph 49 as a residual, it may be sub-classified in the balance sheet. For example, in a corporate enterprise, funds contributed by shareholders, retained earnings, reserves representing appropriations of retained earnings and reserves representing capital maintenance adjustments may be shown separately. Such classifications can be relevant to the decision-making needs of the users of financial statements when they indicate legal or other restrictions on the ability of the enterprise to distribute or otherwise apply its equity. They may also reflect the fact that parties with ownership interests in an enterprise have differing rights in relation to the receipt of dividends or the repayment of capital.

66. The creation of reserves is sometimes required by statute or other law in order to give the enterprise and its creditors an added measure of protection from the effects of losses. Other reserves may be established if national tax law grants exemptions from, or reductions in, taxation liabilities when transfers to such reserves are made. The existence and size of these legal, statutory and tax reserves is information that can be relevant to the decision-making needs of users. Transfers to such reserves are appropriations of retained earnings rather than expenses.

67. The amount at which equity is shown in the balance sheet is dependent on the measurement of assets and liabilities. Normally, the aggregate amount of equity only by coincidence corresponds with the aggregate market value of the shares of the enterprise or the sum that could be raised by disposing of either the net assets on a piecemeal basis or the enterprise as a whole on a going concern basis.

68. Commercial, industrial and business activities are often undertaken by means of enterprises such as sole proprietorships, partnerships and trusts and various types of government business undertakings. The legal and regulatory framework for such enterprises is often different from that applying to corporate enterprises. For example, there may be few, if any, restrictions on the distribution to owners or other beneficiaries of amounts included in equity. Nevertheless, the definition of equity and the other aspects of this framework that deal with equity are appropriate for such enterprises.

Performance

69. Profit is frequently used as a measure of performance or as the basis for other measures, such as return on investment or earnings per share. The elements directly related to the measurement of profit are income and expenses. The recognition and measurement of income and expenses, and hence profit, depends in part on the concepts of capital and capital maintenance used by the enterprise in preparing its financial statements. These concepts are discussed in paragraphs 102 to 110.

70. The elements of income and expenses are defined as follows:

    (a) *Income* is increases in economic benefits during the accounting period in the form of inflows or enhancements of assets or decreases of liabilities that result in increases in equity, other than those relating to contributions from equity participants.

    (b) *Expenses* are decreases in economic benefits during the accounting period in the form of outflows or depletions of assets or incurrences of liabilities that result in decreases in equity, other than those relating to distributions to equity participants.

71. The definitions of income and expenses identify their essential features but do not attempt to specify the criteria that would need to be met before they are recognised in the income statement. Criteria for the recognition of income and expenses are discussed in paragraphs 82 to 98.

72. Income and expenses may be presented in the income statement in different ways so as to provide information that is relevant for economic decision-making. For example, it is common practice to distinguish between those items of income and expenses that arise in the course of the ordinary activities of the enterprise and those that do not. This distinction is made on the basis that the source of an item is relevant in evaluating the ability of the enterprise to generate cash and cash equivalents in the future; for example, incidental activities such as the disposal of a long-term investment are unlikely to recur on a regular basis. When distinguishing between items in this way consideration needs to be given to the nature of the enterprise and its operations. Items that arise from the ordinary activities of one enterprise may be unusual in respect of another.

73. Distinguishing between items of income and expense and combining them in different ways also permits several measures of enterprise performance to be displayed. These have differing degrees of inclusiveness. For example, the income statement could display gross margin, profit from ordinary activities before taxation, profit from ordinary activities after taxation, and net profit.

Income

74. The definition of income encompasses both revenue and gains. Revenue arises in the course of the ordinary activities of an enterprise and is referred to by a variety of different names including sales, fees, interest, dividends, royalties and rent.

75. Gains represent other items that meet the definition of income and may, or may not, arise in the course of the ordinary activities of an enterprise. Gains represent increases in economic benefits and as such are no different in nature from revenue. Hence, they are not regarded as constituting a separate element in this framework.

76. Gains include, for example, those arising on the disposal of non-current assets. The definition of income also includes unrealised gains; for example, those arising on the revaluation of marketable securities and those resulting from increases in the carrying amount of long term assets. When gains are recognised in the income statement, they are usually displayed separately because knowledge of them is useful for the purpose of making economic decisions. Gains are often reported net of related expenses.

77. Various kinds of assets may be received or enhanced by income; examples include cash, receivables and goods and services received in exchange for goods and services supplied. Income may also result from the settlement of liabilities. For example, an enterprise may provide goods and services to a lender in settlement of an obligation to repay an outstanding loan.

Expenses

78. The definition of expenses encompasses losses as well as those expenses that arise in the course of the ordinary activities of the enterprise. Expenses that arise in the course of the ordinary activities of the enterprise include, for example, cost of sales, wages and depreciation. They usually take the form of an outflow or depletion of assets such as cash and cash equivalents, inventory, property, plant and equipment.

79. Losses represent other items that meet the definition of expenses and may, or may not, arise in the course of the ordinary activities of the enterprise. Losses represent decreases in economic benefits and as such they are no different in nature from other expenses. Hence, they are not regarded as a separate element in this framework.

80. Losses include, for example, those resulting from disasters such as fire and flood, as well as those arising on the disposal of non-current assets. The definition of expenses also includes unrealised losses, for example, those arising from the effects of increases in the rate of exchange for a foreign currency in respect of the borrowings of an enterprise in that currency. When losses are recognised in the income statement, they are usually displayed separately because knowledge of them is useful for the purpose of making economic decisions. Losses are often reported net of related income.

Capital Maintenance Adjustments

81. The revaluation or restatement of assets and liabilities gives rise to increases or decreases in equity. While these increases or decreases meet the definition of income and expenses, they are not included in the income statement under certain concepts of capital maintenance. Instead these items are included in equity as capital maintenance adjustments or revaluation reserves. These concepts of capital maintenance are discussed in paragraphs 102 to 110 of this framework.

Recognition of the Elements of Financial Statements

82. Recognition is the process of incorporating in the balance sheet or income statement an item that meets the definition of an element and satisfies the criteria for recognition set out in paragraph 83. It involves the depiction of the item in words and by a monetary amount and the inclusion of that amount in the balance sheet or income statement totals. Items that satisfy the recognition criteria should be recognised in the balance sheet or income statement. The failure to recognise such items is not rectified by disclosure of the accounting policies used nor by notes or explanatory material.

83. An item that meets the definition of an element should be recognised if:

   (a) it is probable that any future economic benefit associated with the item will flow to or from the enterprise; and
   (b) the item has a cost or value that can be measured with reliability.

84. In assessing whether an item meets these criteria and therefore qualifies for recognition in the financial statements, regard needs to be given to the materiality considerations discussed in paragraphs 29 and 30. The interrelationship between the elements means that an item that meets the definition and recognition criteria for a particular element, for example, an asset, automatically requires the recognition of another element, for example, income or a liability.

The Probability of Future Economic Benefit

85.   The concept of probability is used in the recognition criteria to refer to the degree of uncertainty that the future economic benefits associated with the item will flow to or from the enterprise. The concept is in keeping with the uncertainty that characterises the environment in which an enterprise operates. Assessments of the degree of uncertainty attaching to the flow of future economic benefits are made on the basis of the evidence available when the financial statements are prepared. For example, when it is probable that a receivable owed by an enterprise will be paid, it is then justifiable, in the absence of any evidence to the contrary, to recognise the receivable as an asset. For a large population of receivables, however, some degree of non-payment is normally considered probable; hence an expense representing the expected reduction in economic benefits is recognised.

Reliability of Measurement

86.   The second criterion for the recognition of an item is that it possesses a cost or value that can be measured with reliability as discussed in paragraphs 31 to 38 of this framework. In many cases, cost or value must be estimated; the use of reasonable estimates is an essential part of the preparation of financial statements and does not undermine their reliability. When, however, a reasonable estimate cannot be made the item is not recognised in the balance sheet or income statement. For example, the expected proceeds from a lawsuit may meet the definitions of both an asset and income as well as the probability criterion for recognition; however, if it is not possible for the claim to be measured reliably, it should not be recognised as an asset or as income; the existence of the claim, however, would be disclosed in the notes, explanatory material or supplementary schedules.

87.   An item that, at a particular point in time, fails to meet the recognition criteria in paragraph 83 may qualify for recognition at a later date as a result of subsequent circumstances or events.

88.   An item that possesses the essential characteristics of an element but fails to meet the criteria for recognition may nonetheless warrant disclosure in the notes, explanatory material or in supplementary schedules. This is appropriate when knowledge of the item is considered to be relevant to the evaluation of the financial position, performance and changes in financial position of an enterprise by the users of financial statements.

Recognition of Assets

89.   An asset is recognised in the balance sheet when it is probable that the future economic benefits will flow to the enterprise and the asset has a cost or value that can be measured reliably.

90.   An asset is not recognised in the balance sheet when expenditure has been incurred for which it is considered improbable that economic benefits will flow to the enterprise beyond the current accounting period. Instead such a transaction results in the recognition of an expense in the income statement. This treatment does not imply either that the intention of management in incurring expenditure was other than to generate future economic benefits for the enterprise or that management was misguided. The only implication is that the degree of certainty that economic benefits will flow to the enterprise beyond the current accounting period is insufficient to warrant the recognition of an asset.

Recognition of Liabilities

91.   A liability is recognised in the balance sheet when it is probable that an outflow of resources embodying economic benefits will result from the settlement of a present

obligation and the amount at which the settlement will take place can be measured reliably. In practice, obligations under contracts that are equally proportionately unperformed (for example, liabilities for inventory ordered but not yet received) are generally not recognised as liabilities in the financial statements. However, such obligations may meet the definition of liabilities and, provided the recognition criteria are met in the particular circumstances, may qualify for recognition. In such circumstances, recognition of liabilities entails recognition of related assets or expenses.

Recognition of Income

92. Income is recognised in the income statement when an increase in future economic benefits related to an increase in an asset or a decrease of a liability has arisen that can be measured reliably. This means, in effect, that recognition of income occurs simultaneously with the recognition of increases in assets or decreases in liabilities (for example, the net increase in assets arising on a sale of goods or services or the decrease in liabilities arising from the waiver of a debt payable).

93. The procedures normally adopted in practice for recognising income, for example, the requirement that revenue should be earned, are applications of the recognition criteria in this framework. Such procedures are generally directed at restricting the recognition as income to those items that can be measured reliably and have a sufficient degree of certainty.

Recognition of Expenses

94. Expenses are recognised in the income statement when a decrease in future economic benefits related to a decrease in an asset or an increase of a liability has arisen that can be measured reliably. This means, in effect, that recognition of expenses occurs simultaneously with the recognition of an increase in liabilities or a decrease in assets (for example, the accrual of employee entitlements or the depreciation of equipment).

95. Expenses are recognised in the income statement on the basis of a direct association between the costs incurred and the earning of specific items of income. This process, commonly referred to as the matching of costs with revenues, involves the simultaneous or combined recognition of revenues and expenses that result directly and jointly from the same transactions or other events; for example, the various components of expense making up the cost of goods sold are recognised at the same time as the income derived from the sale of the goods. However, the application of the matching concept under this framework does not allow the recognition of items in the balance sheet which do not meet the definition of assets or liabilities.

96. When economic benefits are expected to arise over several accounting periods and the association with income can only be broadly or indirectly determined, expenses are recognised in the income statement on the basis of systematic and rational allocation procedures. This is often necessary in recognising the expenses associated with the using up of assets such as property, plant, equipment, goodwill, patents and trademarks; in such cases the expense is referred to as depreciation or amortisation. These allocation procedures are intended to recognise expenses in the accounting periods in which the economic benefits associated with these items are consumed or expire.

97. An expense is recognised immediately in the income statement when an expenditure produces no future economic benefits or when, and to the extent that, future economic benefits do not qualify, or cease to qualify, for recognition in the balance sheet as an asset.

98. An expense is also recognised in the income statement in those cases when a liability is incurred without the recognition of an asset, as when a liability under a product warranty arises.

Measurement of the Elements of Financial Statements

99. Measurement is the process of determining the monetary amounts at which the elements of the financial statements are to be recognised and carried in the balance sheet and income statement. This involves the selection of the particular basis of measurement.

100. A number of different measurement bases are employed to different degrees and in varying combinations in financial statements. They include the following:

   (a) *Historical cost.* Assets are recorded at the amount of cash or cash equivalents paid or the fair value of the consideration given to acquire them at the time of their acquisition. Liabilities are recorded at the amount of proceeds received in exchange for the obligation, or in some circumstances (for example, income taxes), at the amounts of cash or cash equivalents expected to be paid to satisfy the liability in the normal course of business.

   (b) *Current cost.* Assets are carried at the amount of cash or cash equivalents that would have to be paid if the same or an equivalent asset was acquired currently. Liabilities are carried at the undiscounted amount of cash or cash equivalents that would be required to settle the obligation currently.

   (c) *Realisable (settlement) value.* Assets are carried at the amount of cash or cash equivalents that could currently be obtained by selling the asset in an orderly disposal. Liabilities are carried at their settlement values; that is, the undiscounted amounts of cash or cash equivalents expected to be paid to satisfy the liabilities in the normal course of business.

   (d) *Present value.* Assets are carried at the present discounted value of the future net cash inflows that the item is expected to generate in the normal course of business. Liabilities are carried at the present discounted value of the future net cash outflows that are expected to be required to settle the liabilities in the normal course of business.

101. The measurement basis most commonly adopted by enterprises in preparing their financial statements is historical cost. This is usually combined with other measurement bases. For example, inventories are usually carried at the lower of cost and net realisable value, marketable securities may be carried at market value and pension liabilities are carried at their present value. Furthermore, some enterprises use the current cost basis as a response to the inability of the historical cost accounting model to deal with the effects of changing prices of non-monetary assets.

Concepts of Capital and Capital Maintenance

Concepts of Capital

102. A financial concept of capital is adopted by most enterprises in preparing their financial statements. Under a financial concept of capital, such as invested money or invested purchasing power, capital is synonymous with the net assets or equity of the enterprise. Under a physical concept of capital, such as operating capability, capital is regarded as the productive capacity of the enterprise based on, for example, units of output per day.

103. The selection of the appropriate concept of capital by an enterprise should be based on the needs of the users of its financial statements. Thus, a financial concept of capital should be adopted if the users of financial statements are primarily concerned with the maintenance of nominal invested capital or the purchasing power of invested capital. If, however, the main concern of users is with the operating capability of the enterprise, a physical concept of capital should be used. The concept chosen indicates the goal to be attained in determining profit, even though there may be some measurement difficulties in making the concept operational.

Concepts of Capital Maintenance and the Determination of Profit

104. The concepts of capital in paragraph 102 give rise to the following concepts of capital maintenance:

    (a) *Financial capital maintenance.* Under this concept a profit is earned only if the financial (or money) amount of the net assets at the end of the period exceeds the financial (or money) amount of net assets at the beginning of the period, after excluding any distributions to, and contributions from, owners during the period. Financial capital maintenance can be measured in either nominal monetary units or units of constant purchasing power.

    (b) *Physical capital maintenance.* Under this concept a profit is earned only if the physical productive capacity (or operating capability) of the enterprise (or the resources or funds needed to achieve that capacity) at the end of the period exceeds the physical productive capacity at the beginning of the period, after excluding any distributions to, and contributions from, owners during the period.

105. The concept of capital maintenance is concerned with how an enterprise defines the capital that it seeks to maintain. It provides the linkage between the concepts of capital and the concepts of profit because it provides the point of reference by which profit is measured; it is a prerequisite for distinguishing between an enterprise's return on capital and its return of capital; only inflows of assets in excess of amounts needed to maintain capital may be regarded as profit and therefore as a return on capital. Hence, profit is the residual amount that remains after expenses (including capital maintenance adjustments, where appropriate) have been deducted from income. If expenses exceed income the residual amount is a net loss.

106. The physical capital maintenance concept requires the adoption of the current cost basis of measurement. The financial capital maintenance concept, however, does not require the use of a particular basis of measurement. Selection of the basis under this concept is dependent on the type of financial capital that the enterprise is seeking to maintain.

107. The principal difference between the two concepts of capital maintenance is the treatment of the effects of changes in the prices of assets and liabilities of the enterprise. In general terms, an enterprise has maintained its capital if it has as much capital at the end of the period as it had at the beginning of the period. Any amount over and above that required to maintain the capital at the beginning of the period is profit.

108. Under the concept of financial capital maintenance where capital is defined in terms of nominal monetary units, profit represents the increase in nominal money capital over the period. Thus, increases in the prices of assets held over the period, conventionally referred to as holding gains, are, conceptually, profits. They may not be recognised as such, however, until the assets are disposed of in an exchange transaction. When the concept of financial capital maintenance is defined in terms of constant purchasing power units, profit represents the increase in invested purchasing power over the period. Thus, only that part of the increase in the prices of assets that exceeds the increase in the general level of prices is regarded as profit. The rest of the increase is treated as a capital maintenance adjustment and, hence, as part of equity.

109. Under the concept of physical capital maintenance when capital is defined in terms of the physical productive capacity, profit represents the increase in that capital over the period. All price changes affecting the assets and liabilities of the enterprise are viewed as changes in the measurement of the physical productive capacity of the enterprise; hence, they are treated as capital maintenance adjustments that are part of equity and not as profit.

110. The selection of the measurement bases and concept of capital maintenance will determine the accounting model used in the preparation of the financial statements. Different accounting models exhibit different degrees of relevance and reliability and, as in other areas, management must seek a balance between relevance and reliability. This framework is applicable to a range of accounting models and provides guidance on preparing and presenting the financial statements constructed under the chosen model. At the present time, it is not the intention of the Board of IASC to prescribe a particular model other than in exceptional circumstances, such as for those enterprises reporting in the currency of a hyperinflationary economy. This intention will, however, be reviewed in the light of world developments.

APPENDIX 3
Interest tables

A brief explanation of interest computations

Reference is made frequently to the discounting of a series of cash payments or receipts expected to occur in the future to compute the 'present value'. In this context, the term 'present value' is used in its technical, mathematical sense to refer to the discounted present worth of a series of future cash flows. It does not mean 'present market value'.

Example: *Future and present values*

Bev Brown has cash on hand of $100 and has decided that, rather than spend it now, she will invest it to earn 12 per cent interest per annum with a building society. Interest is calculated annually.

After one year her investment will be worth $112 ($100 principal + $12 interest). In formal terms:

$$
\begin{aligned}
\text{Let} \quad P &= \text{the principal invested} \\
r &= \text{the rate of interest (as a decimal, i.e. 0.12)} \\
S &= \text{the future value of the investment.}
\end{aligned}
$$

Then,

$$
\begin{aligned}
S &= P + Pr \\
\text{Therefore} \quad S &= P(1 + r) \quad\quad (1) \\
&= 100(1 + 0.12) \\
&= \$112
\end{aligned}
$$

The relationship between the present amount (P) and the future amount (S) can also be considered from the opposite end by taking the future value as given. Suppose Bev Brown has to pay a debt of $112 at the end of the year. She knows that this future value must be available in one year's time and asks what she must invest at the beginning of the year, at 12 per cent interest, to ensure that the $112 will be available at the end. The answer, from the previous relationship, is obviously $100. This is the initial principal that must be invested and it is known as the *present value* of $112 at the end of one year, *discounted* at 12 per cent. The formula is derived from the future value formula as follows:

$$
S = P(1 + r) \quad\quad (1)
$$

$$
\text{Therefore} \quad P = \frac{S}{(1 + r)} \quad\quad (2)
$$

$$
= \frac{112}{(1 + 0.12)}
$$

$$
= \$100
$$

The future sum is divided by one plus the interest rate, to bring it back to its equivalent present value.

Future versus present values

There are many uses for present value analysis, especially when a choice must be made between cash amounts to be received over different time intervals. Suppose a choice was offered between receiving $200 today and $232 at the end of one year. In making the choice, both propositions must be considered at the one point in time to allow for the fact that money received today may be reinvested at the going rate of interest. Assume that the relevant interest/discount rate is still 12 per cent. Both propositions could be viewed at their future values at the end of the year, thus:

- *Alternative 1: Receive $200 today.*

$$\begin{aligned} S &= P(1 + r) \\ &= 200(1 + 0.12) \\ &= \$224 \end{aligned}$$

- *Alternative 2: Receive $232 at the end of the year.*

$$S = \$232 \text{ (as given)}$$

The second alternative is selected because it offers a greater future value (S) at the end of one year.

An alternative means of solving the problem is to express both propositions in terms of present values.

- *Alternative 1: Receive $200 today.*

$$P = \$200 \text{ (as given)}$$

- *Alternative 2: Receive $232 at the end of the year.*

$$\begin{aligned} P &= \frac{S}{(1 + r)} \\ \\ &= \frac{232}{(1 + 0.12)} \\ \\ &= \$207.14 \end{aligned}$$

Proposition 2 has the higher present value because, at 12 per cent interest, the future value of $232 could be achieved only by investing $207.14 today. Bev Brown ought to consider $232 to be received in one year's time as equivalent to $207.14 today. She should therefore prefer proposition 2 to proposition 1, which has a present value of only $200.

Later periods

Bev Brown might leave an investment to accumulate over several periods and, in so doing, earn interest on the interest, or *compound interest*. The future value formula may be extended as follows:

For one period:
$$S = P(1 + r) \tag{1}$$

For two periods:
$$\begin{aligned} S &= P(1 + r)(1 + r) \\ &= P(1 + r)^2 \end{aligned} \tag{2}$$

For n periods,
the future value must be:
$$S = P(1 + r)^n \tag{3}$$

This is a standard formula for compound interest computations. The present value formula may be derived from it by rearrangement:

$$P(1 + r)^n = S$$

Therefore,
$$P = \frac{S}{(1 + r)^n} \tag{4}$$

Mathematical tables

Calculation of future and present value is made easier by the availability of tables that show values of the formula for various combinations of periods and interest rates. Four such tables appear at the end of this appendix.

Table A. 1 calculates compound interest to derive the future value of a present sum. The formula values given are for the investment of $1 (i.e. $P = \$1$). To find the future value of a different present value, it is necessary to multiply the formula by that amount.

$$\text{Let } F = \text{formula value}$$

Then, in Table A. 1
$$S = P \times F$$

To calculate the future value of $400 invested for five years at 20 per cent, the first step is to find the formula value in Table 1 for five periods at 20 per cent, which is 2.488. The future value therefore is:

$$S = \$400 \times 2.488$$
$$= \$995.20$$

A similar process is followed to calculate present values from the figures given in Table A.2.

Annuities

An annuity is a fixed sum payable at specified intervals. Examples include annual repayments due on a loan, where each instalment is of the same amount.

Suppose Bev Brown is offered employment for three years, for which she will be paid $10 000 at the end of each year. She intends to reinvest the salary immediately each year at the interest rate of 12 per cent per annum. If Bev Brown desired to know the amount of cash she would hold after three years (S = the future value) she could make three separate future value computations, using Table A.1, thus:

	End of year		
0	1	2	3
	$	$	$
	10 000		12 540
		10 000	11 200
			10 000
Future value (S)			33 740

Bev Brown will have an investment of $33 740 at the end of three years. As the last amount is to be received at the end of the third year no interest will have accumulated.

Annuities involve identical calculations for each period, except for the value of n, and it is therefore possible to derive a formula to perform all of the calculations at once. The formula is complicated and it is not necessary to understand its derivation. The table of values for the future value of an annuity appears as Table A.3.

$$\text{Let } S_n = \text{the future value of an annuity}$$
$$A = \text{the annuity}$$
$$F = \text{the formula value}$$

Then, to find the future value of an annuity of $10 000 for three years at 12 per cent:

$$S_n = A \times F$$
$$= \$10\ 000 \times 3.374$$
$$= \$33\ 740$$

Problems with annuities also call for present value analysis. Bev Brown might have asked what the present value would be of an annuity of $10 000 per year at the end of each of the next three years. The present value could then be compared with the present values of other alternatives. Suppose, for example, that her employer offered her, as an alternative to the $30 000 salary in annual instalments, the entire salary in advance, provided she accepted $21 000. Her expected interest rate on investments is, as before, 12 per cent per annum.

To solve the problem it is necessary to discover the present value of the future salary payments. Since this is an annuity, a formula has been devised to discount the entire annuity stream in the one step. The appropriate table is Table A.4.

The present value of $10 000 per year at the end of each of the next three years is, at a discount rate of 12 per cent:

$$P = A_n \times F$$
$$= \$10\ 000 \times 2.402$$
$$= \$24\ 020$$

The annuity stream has a present value of $24 020. This is higher than the value of the immediate cash offer of $21 000 and Bev Brown would be advised to accept the annual payment, since its present equivalent is higher than the other alternative.

Understanding present values

Whenever the interest rate is positive, the present value will be less than the future value. Money has a time value and people must be compensated for postponing their consumption. An amount of $1 available today is worth more than $1 in one year's time because it may be invested and earn interest over the year.

When comparing two prospects, each of which promises cash returns, but over different time horizons, the influence of time must be removed by comparing values at a particular date. Present value analysis expresses all future cash flows in their equivalent present day values.

The further into the future a cash flow is expected to occur, the lower will be its present value. The longer the receipt of cash is delayed, the more interest is forgone. The formula takes account of this by dividing by one plus the interest rate.

It is also apparent from the formula that the higher the interest, or discount rate, the lower will be the present value. A person who is able to earn 20 per cent on investments is less willing to delay the receipt of cash than is a person who earns only 5 per cent. In practice, different returns are expected from each project according to the riskiness of the project. Higher returns are required to compensate for higher risk. Thus, the selection of a discount rate is influenced by the perceived riskiness of the project.

Table A.1 Future value of $1.00 $S = P(1 + r)^n$

Periods	1%	2%	3%	4%	5%	6%	7%	8%	9%	10%
1	1.010	1.020	1.030	1.040	1.050	1.060	1.070	1.080	1.090	1.100
2	1.020	1.040	1.061	1.082	1.102	1.124	1.145	1.166	1.188	1.210
3	1.030	1.061	1.093	1.125	1.158	1.191	1.225	1.260	1.295	1.331
4	1.041	1.082	1.126	1.170	1.216	1.262	1.311	1.360	1.412	1.464
5	1.051	1.104	1.159	1.217	1.276	1.338	1.403	1.469	1.539	1.611
6	1.062	1.126	1.194	1.265	1.340	1.419	1.501	1.587	1.677	1.772
7	1.072	1.149	1.230	1.316	1.407	1.504	1.606	1.714	1.828	1.949
8	1.083	1.172	1.267	1.369	1.477	1.594	1.718	1.851	1.993	2.144
9	1.094	1.195	1.305	1.423	1.551	1.689	1.838	1.999	2.172	2.358
10	1.105	1.219	1.344	1.480	1.629	1.791	1.967	2.159	2.367	2.594
11	1.116	1.243	1.384	1.539	1.710	1.898	2.105	2.332	2.580	2.853
12	1.127	1.268	1.426	1.601	1.796	2.012	2.252	2.518	2.813	3.138
13	1.138	1.294	1.469	1.665	1.886	2.133	2.410	2.720	3.066	3.452
14	1.149	1.319	1.513	1.732	1.980	2.261	2.579	2.937	3.342	3.798
15	1.161	1.346	1.558	1.801	2.079	2.397	2.759	3.172	3.642	4.177
16	1.173	1.373	1.605	1.873	2.183	2.540	2.952	3.426	3.970	4.595
17	1.184	1.400	1.653	1.948	2.292	2.693	3.159	3.700	4.328	5.054
18	1.196	1.428	1.702	2.026	2.407	2.854	3.380	3.996	4.717	5.560
19	1.208	1.457	1.754	2.107	2.527	3.026	3.617	4.316	5.142	6.116
20	1.220	1.486	1.806	2.191	2.653	3.207	3.870	4.661	5.604	6.728
25	1.282	1.641	2.094	2.666	3.386	4.292	5.427	6.849	8.623	10.835
30	1.348	1.811	2.427	3.243	4.322	5.744	7.612	10.063	13.268	17.449
40	1.489	2.208	3.262	4.801	7.040	10.286	14.975	21.725	31.409	45.259

continues

Table A.1 continued

Periods	11%	12%	13%	14%	15%	16%	17%	18%	19%	20%
1	1.110	1.120	1.130	1.140	1.150	1.160	1.170	1.180	1.190	1.200
2	1.232	1.254	1.277	1.300	1.323	1.346	1.369	1.392	1.416	1.440
3	1.368	1.405	1.443	1.482	1.521	1.561	1.602	1.643	1.685	1.728
4	1.518	1.574	1.630	1.689	1.749	1.811	1.874	1.939	2.005	2.074
5	1.685	1.762	1.842	1.925	2.011	2.100	2.192	2.288	2.386	2.488
6	1.870	1.974	2.082	2.195	2.313	2.436	2.565	2.700	2.840	2.986
7	2.076	2.211	2.353	2.502	2.660	2.826	3.001	3.185	3.379	3.583
8	2.305	2.476	2.658	2.853	3.059	3.278	3.511	3.759	4.021	4.300
9	2.558	2.773	3.004	3.252	3.518	3.803	4.108	4.435	4.785	5.160
10	2.839	3.106	3.395	3.707	4.046	4.411	4.807	5.234	5.695	6.192
11	3.152	3.479	3.836	4.226	4.652	5.117	5.624	6.176	6.777	7.430
12	3.498	3.896	4.335	4.818	5.350	5.936	6.580	7.288	8.064	8.916
13	3.883	4.364	4.898	5.492	6.153	6.886	7.699	8.599	9.596	10.699
14	4.310	4.887	5.535	6.261	7.076	7.988	9.008	10.147	11.420	12.839
15	4.785	5.474	6.254	7.138	8.137	9.266	10.539	11.974	13.590	15.407
16	5.311	6.130	7.067	8.137	9.358	10.748	12.330	14.129	16.172	18.489
17	5.895	6.866	7.986	9.277	10.761	12.468	14.427	16.672	19.244	22.186
18	6.544	7.690	9.024	10.575	12.376	14.463	16.897	19.673	22.901	26.624
19	7.263	8.613	10.197	12.056	14.232	16.777	19.749	23.215	27.252	31.948
20	8.062	9.646	11.523	13.744	16.367	19.461	23.106	27.393	32.429	38.338
25	13.586	17.000	21.230	26.462	32.920	40.875	50.659	62.669	77.388	95.397
30	22.893	29.960	39.116	50.951	66.213	85.851	111.067	143.373	184.675	237.380
40	65.002	93.052	132.780	188.886	267.871	378.730	533.884	750.395	1 051.667	1 469.798

continues

Table A.1 continued

Periods	21%	22%	23%	24%	25%	26%	27%	28%	29%	30%
1	1.210	1.220	1.230	1.240	1.250	1.260	1.270	1.280	1.290	1.300
2	1.464	1.488	1.513	1.538	1.563	1.588	1.613	1.638	1.664	1.690
3	1.772	1.816	1.861	1.907	1.953	2.000	2.048	2.097	2.147	2.197
4	2.144	2.215	2.289	2.364	2.441	2.520	2.601	2.684	2.769	2.856
5	2.594	2.703	2.815	2.932	3.052	3.176	3.304	3.436	3.572	3.713
6	3.138	3.297	3.463	3.635	3.815	4.002	4.196	4.398	4.608	4.827
7	3.798	4.023	4.259	4.508	4.768	5.042	5.329	5.630	5.945	6.275
8	4.595	4.908	5.239	5.590	5.960	6.353	6.768	7.206	7.669	8.157
9	5.560	5.987	6.444	6.931	7.451	8.005	8.595	9.223	9.893	10.605
10	6.728	7.305	7.926	8.594	9.313	10.086	10.915	11.806	12.761	13.786
11	8.140	8.912	9.749	10.657	11.642	12.708	13.863	15.112	16.462	17.922
12	9.850	10.872	11.991	13.215	14.552	16.012	17.606	19.343	21.236	23.298
13	11.918	13.264	14.749	16.386	18.190	20.175	22.359	24.759	27.395	30.288
14	14.421	16.182	18.141	20.319	22.737	25.421	28.396	31.691	35.339	39.374
15	17.450	19.742	22.314	25.196	28.422	32.030	36.063	40.565	45.588	51.187
16	21.114	24.086	27.446	31.243	35.527	40.358	45.800	51.923	58.808	66.543
17	25.548	29.385	33.759	38.741	44.409	50.852	58.166	66.462	75.862	86.506
18	30.913	35.849	41.523	48.039	55.511	64.073	73.871	85.071	97.862	112.457
19	37.405	43.736	51.074	59.569	69.389	80.732	93.816	108.891	126.243	146.195
20	45.260	53.358	62.821	73.865	86.736	101.723	119.146	139.380	162.853	190.054
25	117.392	144.212	176.860	216.546	264.699	323.051	393.642	478.908	581.761	705.659
30	304.486	389.762	497.916	634.833	807.797	1 025.950	1 300.533	1 645.518	2 078.231	2 620.077
40	2 048.439	2 847.080	3 946.463	5 456.064	7 523.199	10 347.483	14 195.857	19 426.895	26 521.098	36 120.340

Table A.2 Present value of $1.00 $P = \dfrac{S}{(1 + r)^n}$

Periods	1%	2%	3%	4%	5%	6%	7%	8%	9%	10%
1	.9901	.9804	.9709	.9615	.9524	.9434	.9346	.9259	.9174	.9091
2	.9803	.9612	.9426	.9246	.9070	.8900	.8734	.8573	.8417	.8264
3	.9706	.9423	.9151	.8890	.8638	.8396	.8163	.7938	.7722	.7513
4	.9610	.9238	.8885	.8548	.8227	.7921	.7629	.7350	.7084	.6830
5	.9515	.9057	.8626	.8219	.7835	.7473	.7130	.6806	.6499	.6209
6	.9420	.8880	.8375	.7903	.7462	.7050	.6663	.6302	.5963	.5645
7	.9327	.8706	.8131	.7599	.7107	.6651	.6227	.5835	.5470	.5132
8	.9235	.8535	.7894	.7307	.6768	.6274	.5820	.5403	.5019	.4665
9	.9143	.8368	.7664	.7026	.6446	.5919	.5439	.5002	.4604	.4241
10	.9053	.8203	.7441	.6756	.6139	.5584	.5083	.4632	.4224	.3855
11	.8963	.8043	.7224	.6496	.5847	.5268	.4751	.4289	.3875	.3505
12	.8874	.7885	.7014	.6246	.5568	.4970	.4440	.3971	.3555	.3186
13	.8787	.7730	.6810	.6006	.5303	.4688	.4150	.3677	.3262	.2897
14	.8700	.7579	.6611	.5775	.5051	.4423	.3878	.3405	.2992	.2633
15	.8613	.7430	.6419	.5553	.4810	.4173	.3624	.3152	.2745	.2394
16	.8528	.7284	.6232	.5339	.4581	.3936	.3387	.2919	.2519	.2176
17	.8444	.7142	.6050	.5134	.4363	.3714	.3166	.2703	.2311	.1978
18	.8360	.7002	.5874	.4936	.4155	.3503	.2959	.2502	.2120	.1799
19	.8277	.6864	.5703	.4746	.3957	.3305	.2765	.2317	.1945	.1635
20	.8195	.6730	.5537	.4564	.3769	.3118	.2584	.2145	.1784	.1486
25	.7798	.6095	.4776	.3751	.2953	.2330	.1842	.1460	.1160	.0923
30	.7419	.5521	.4120	.3083	.2314	.1741	.1314	.0994	.0754	.0573
40	.6716	.4529	.3066	.2083	.1420	.0972	.0668	.0460	.0318	.0221

continues

Table A.2 continued

Periods	11%	12%	13%	14%	15%	16%	17%	18%	19%	20%
1	.9009	.8929	.8850	.8772	.8696	.8621	.8547	.8475	.8403	.8333
2	.8116	.7972	.7831	.7695	.7561	.7432	.7305	.7182	.7062	.6944
3	.7312	.7118	.6931	.6750	.6575	.6407	.6244	.6086	.5934	.5787
4	.6587	.6355	.6133	.5921	.5718	.5523	.5336	.5158	.4987	.4823
5	.5934	.5674	.5428	.5194	.4972	.4761	.4561	.4371	.4190	.4019
6	.5346	.5066	.4803	.4556	.4323	.4104	.3898	.3704	.3521	.3349
7	.4817	.4523	.4251	.3996	.3759	.3538	.3332	.3139	.2959	.2791
8	.4339	.4039	.3762	.3506	.3269	.3050	.2848	.2660	.2487	.2326
9	.3909	.3606	.3329	.3075	.2843	.2630	.2434	.2255	.2090	.1938
10	.3522	.3220	.2946	.2697	.2472	.2267	.2080	.1911	.1756	.1615
11	.3173	.2875	.2607	.2366	.2149	.1954	.1778	.1619	.1476	.1346
12	.2858	.2567	.2307	.2076	.1869	.1685	.1520	.1372	.1240	.1122
13	.2575	.2292	.2042	.1821	.1625	.1452	.1299	.1163	.1042	.0935
14	.2320	.2046	.1807	.1597	.1413	.1252	.1110	.0985	.0876	.0779
15	.2090	.1827	.1599	.1401	.1229	.1079	.0949	.0835	.0736	.0649
16	.1883	.1631	.1415	.1229	.1069	.0930	.0811	.0708	.0618	.0541
17	.1696	.1456	.1252	.1078	.0929	.0802	.0693	.0600	.0520	.0451
18	.1528	.1300	.1108	.0946	.0808	.0691	.0592	.0508	.0437	.0376
19	.1377	.1161	.0981	.0829	.0703	.0596	.0506	.0431	.0367	.0313
20	.1240	.1037	.0868	.0728	.0611	.0514	.0433	.0365	.0308	.0261
25	.0736	.0588	.0471	.0378	.0304	.0245	.0197	.0160	.0129	.0105
30	.0437	.0334	.0256	.0196	.0151	.0116	.0090	.0070	.0054	.0042
40	.0154	.0107	.0075	.0053	.0037	.0026	.0019	.0013	.0010	.0007

continues

Table A.2 continued

Periods	21%	22%	23%	24%	25%	26%	27%	28%	29%	30%
1	.8264	.8197	.8130	.8065	.8000	.7937	.7874	.7812	.7752	.7692
2	.6830	.6719	.6610	.6504	.6400	.6299	.6200	.6104	.6009	.5917
3	.5645	.5507	.5374	.5245	.5120	.4999	.4882	.4768	.4658	.4552
4	.4665	.4514	.4369	.4230	.4096	.3967	.3844	.3725	.3611	.3501
5	.3855	.3700	.3552	.3411	.3277	.3149	.3027	.2910	.2799	.2693
6	.3186	.3033	.2888	.2751	.2621	.2499	.2383	.2274	.2170	.2072
7	.2633	.2486	.2348	.2218	.2097	.1983	.1877	.1776	.1682	.1594
8	.2176	.2038	.1909	.1789	.1678	.1574	.1478	.1388	.1304	.1226
9	.1799	.1670	.1552	.1443	.1342	.1249	.1163	.1084	.1011	.0943
10	.1486	.1369	.1262	.1164	.1074	.0991	.0916	.0847	.0784	.0725
11	.1228	.1122	.1026	.0938	.0859	.0787	.0721	.0662	.0607	.0558
12	.1015	.0920	.0834	.0757	.0687	.0625	.0568	.0517	.0471	.0429
13	.0839	.0754	.0678	.0610	.0550	.0496	.0447	.0404	.0365	.0330
14	.0693	.0618	.0551	.0492	.0440	.0393	.0352	.0316	.0283	.0254
15	.0573	.0507	.0448	.0397	.0352	.0312	.0277	.0247	.0219	.0195
16	.0474	.0415	.0364	.0320	.0281	.0248	.0218	.0193	.0170	.0150
17	.0391	.0340	.0296	.0258	.0225	.0197	.0172	.0150	.0132	.0116
18	.0323	.0279	.0241	.0208	.0180	.0156	.0135	.0118	.0102	.0089
19	.0267	.0229	.0196	.0168	.0144	.0124	.0107	.0092	.0079	.0068
20	.0221	.0187	.0159	.0135	.0115	.0098	.0084	.0072	.0061	.0053
25	.0085	.0069	.0057	.0046	.0038	.0031	.0025	.0021	.0017	.0014
30	.0033	.0026	.0020	.0016	.0012	.0010	.0008	.0006	.0005	.0004
40	.0005	.0004	.0003	.0002	.0001	.0001	.0001	.0001	.0000	.0000

Table A.3 Future value of annuity of $1.00 in arrears $S_n = \dfrac{(1+r)^n - 1}{r}$

Periods	1%	2%	3%	4%	5%	6%	7%	8%	9%	10%
1	1.000	1.000	1.000	1.000	1.000	1.000	1.000	1.000	1.000	1.000
2	2.010	2.020	2.030	2.040	2.050	2.060	2.070	2.080	2.090	2.100
3	3.030	3.060	3.091	3.122	3.152	3.184	3.215	3.246	3.278	3.310
4	4.061	4.122	4.184	4.246	4.310	4.375	4.440	4.506	4.573	4.641
5	5.101	5.204	5.309	5.416	5.526	5.637	5.751	5.867	5.985	6.105
6	6.152	6.308	6.468	6.633	6.802	6.975	7.153	7.336	7.523	7.716
7	7.214	7.434	7.662	7.898	8.142	8.394	8.654	8.923	9.200	9.487
8	8.286	8.583	8.892	9.214	9.549	9.898	10.260	10.637	11.028	11.436
9	9.369	9.755	10.159	10.583	11.027	11.491	11.978	12.488	13.021	13.579
10	10.462	10.950	11.464	12.006	12.578	13.181	13.816	14.487	15.193	15.937
11	11.567	12.169	12.808	13.486	14.207	14.972	15.784	16.646	17.560	18.531
12	12.683	13.412	14.192	15.026	15.917	16.870	17.888	18.977	20.141	21.384
13	13.810	14.680	15.618	16.627	17.713	18.882	20.141	21.495	22.953	24.523
14	14.948	15.974	17.086	18.292	19.599	21.015	22.551	24.215	26.019	27.975
15	16.097	17.293	18.599	20.024	21.578	23.276	25.129	27.152	29.361	31.773
16	17.258	18.639	20.157	21.825	23.657	25.673	27.888	30.324	33.003	35.950
17	18.431	20.012	21.762	23.698	25.840	28.213	30.840	33.750	36.974	40.545
18	19.615	21.412	23.414	25.646	28.132	30.906	33.999	37.450	41.301	45.599
19	20.811	22.841	25.117	27.671	30.539	33.760	37.379	41.446	46.018	51.159
20	22.020	24.297	26.870	29.778	33.066	36.786	40.996	45.762	51.160	57.275
25	28.244	32.030	36.459	41.646	47.727	54.865	63.249	73.106	84.701	98.347
30	34.786	40.568	47.575	56.086	66.438	79.059	94.461	113.284	136.308	164.494
40	48.888	60.402	75.401	95.027	120.799	154.763	199.636	259.058	337.882	442.594

continues

Table A.3 continued

Periods	11%	12%	13%	14%	15%	16%	17%	18%	19%	20%
1	1.000	1.000	1.000	1.000	1.000	1.000	1.000	1.000	1.000	1.000
2	2.110	2.120	2.130	2.140	2.150	2.160	2.170	2.180	2.190	2.200
3	3.342	3.374	3.407	3.440	3.473	3.506	3.539	3.572	3.606	3.640
4	4.710	4.779	4.850	4.921	4.993	5.067	5.141	5.215	5.291	5.368
5	6.228	6.353	6.480	6.610	6.742	6.877	7.014	7.154	7.297	7.442
6	7.913	8.115	8.323	8.536	8.754	8.978	9.207	9.442	9.683	9.930
7	9.783	10.089	10.405	10.731	11.067	11.414	11.772	12.142	12.523	12.916
8	11.860	12.300	12.757	13.233	13.727	14.240	14.773	15.327	15.902	16.499
9	14.164	14.776	15.416	16.085	16.786	17.519	18.285	19.086	19.923	20.799
10	16.722	17.549	18.420	19.337	20.304	21.322	22.393	23.521	24.709	25.959
11	19.562	20.655	21.814	23.045	24.350	25.733	27.200	28.755	30.404	32.151
12	22.713	24.133	25.650	27.271	29.002	30.850	32.824	34.931	37.180	39.581
13	26.212	28.029	29.985	32.089	34.352	36.787	39.404	42.219	45.244	48.497
14	30.095	32.393	34.883	37.581	40.505	43.672	47.103	50.818	54.841	59.196
15	34.406	37.280	40.417	43.843	47.581	51.660	56.111	60.966	66.261	72.036
16	39.190	42.753	46.672	50.981	55.718	60.926	66.650	72.940	79.850	87.443
17	44.501	48.884	53.739	59.118	65.076	71.674	78.980	87.069	96.022	105.931
18	50.396	55.750	61.725	68.394	75.837	84.142	93.407	103.741	115.266	128.118
19	56.940	63.440	70.749	78.970	88.213	98.604	110.286	123.415	138.166	154.741
20	64.204	72.053	80.946	91.025	102.445	115.381	130.035	146.630	165.418	186.690
25	114.415	133.335	155.619	181.872	212.797	249.218	292.110	342.608	402.042	471.987
30	199.024	241.335	293.197	356.790	434.755	530.321	647.453	790.961	966.712	1 181.898
40	581.838	767.100	1 013.695	1 342.040	1 779.141	2 360.812	3 134.613	4 163.305	5 529.824	7 343.991

continues

Table A.3 continued

Periods	21%	22%	23%	24%	25%	26%	27%	28%	29%	30%
1	1.000	1.000	1.000	1.000	1.000	1.000	1.000	1.000	1.000	1.000
2	2.210	2.220	2.230	2.240	2.250	2.260	2.270	2.280	2.290	2.300
3	3.674	3.708	3.743	3.778	3.813	3.848	3.883	3.918	3.954	3.990
4	5.446	5.524	5.604	5.684	5.766	5.848	5.931	6.016	6.101	6.187
5	7.589	7.740	7.893	8.048	8.207	8.368	8.533	8.700	8.870	9.043
6	10.183	10.442	10.708	10.980	11.259	11.544	11.837	12.136	12.442	12.756
7	13.321	13.740	14.171	14.615	15.074	15.546	16.033	16.534	17.051	17.583
8	17.119	17.762	18.430	19.123	19.842	20.588	21.361	22.163	22.995	23.858
9	21.714	22.670	23.669	24.713	25.802	26.941	28.129	29.369	30.664	32.015
10	27.274	28.658	30.113	31.644	33.253	34.945	36.724	38.593	40.557	42.620
11	34.002	35.962	38.039	40.238	42.566	45.031	47.639	50.399	53.318	56.406
12	42.142	44.874	47.788	50.895	54.208	57.739	61.502	65.510	69.780	74.328
13	51.992	55.746	59.779	64.110	68.760	73.751	79.107	84.853	91.016	97.626
14	63.910	69.010	74.528	80.497	86.950	93.927	101.467	109.612	118.411	127.914
15	78.331	85.193	92.670	100.816	109.687	119.348	129.863	141.304	153.750	167.289
16	95.781	104.935	114.984	126.012	138.109	151.378	165.926	181.869	199.338	218.476
17	116.895	129.021	142.430	157.255	173.636	191.737	211.726	233.792	258.146	285.019
18	142.443	158.406	176.189	195.997	218.045	242.589	269.892	300.254	334.009	371.525
19	173.356	194.255	217.713	244.036	273.556	306.662	343.763	385.325	431.871	483.983
20	210.760	237.991	268.786	303.605	342.945	387.395	437.579	494.216	558.114	630.178
25	544.249	650.961	764.609	898.107	1 054.794	1 238.659	1 454.228	1 706.814	2 002.625	2 348.864
30	1 445.171	1 767.102	2 160.505	2 640.972	3 227.187	3 942.115	4 813.083	5 873.279	7 162.865	8 730.256
40	9 749.709	12 936.729	17 154.186	22 729.434	30 088.797	39 794.168	52 573.543	69 378.195	91 448.617	12 0397.797

Table A.4 Present value of an annuity of $1.00 in arrears $P_n = \dfrac{1}{r}\left[1 - \dfrac{1}{(1+r)^n}\right]$

Periods	1%	2%	3%	4%	5%	6%	7%	8%	9%	10%
1	.990	.980	.971	.962	.952	.943	.935	.926	.917	.909
2	1.970	1.942	1.913	1.886	1.859	1.833	1.808	1.783	1.759	1.736
3	2.941	2.884	2.829	2.775	2.723	2.673	2.624	2.577	2.531	2.487
4	3.902	3.808	3.717	3.630	3.546	3.465	3.387	3.312	3.240	3.170
5	4.854	4.713	4.580	4.452	4.329	4.212	4.100	3.993	3.890	3.791
6	5.796	5.601	5.417	5.242	5.076	4.917	4.767	4.623	4.486	4.355
7	6.728	6.472	6.230	6.002	5.786	5.582	5.389	5.206	5.033	4.868
8	7.652	7.325	7.020	6.733	6.463	6.210	5.971	5.747	5.535	5.335
9	8.566	8.162	7.786	7.435	7.108	6.802	6.515	6.247	5.995	5.759
10	9.472	8.983	8.530	8.111	7.722	7.360	7.024	6.710	6.418	6.145
11	10.368	9.787	9.253	8.761	8.306	7.887	7.499	7.139	6.805	6.495
12	11.255	10.575	9.954	9.385	8.863	8.384	7.943	7.536	7.161	6.814
13	12.134	11.348	10.635	9.986	9.394	8.853	8.358	7.904	7.487	7.103
14	13.004	12.106	11.296	10.563	9.899	9.295	8.745	8.244	7.786	7.367
15	13.865	12.849	11.938	11.118	10.380	9.712	9.108	8.559	8.061	7.606
16	14.718	13.578	12.561	11.652	10.838	10.106	9.447	8.851	8.313	7.824
17	15.563	14.292	13.166	12.166	11.274	10.477	9.763	9.122	8.544	8.022
18	16.399	14.992	13.753	12.659	11.690	10.828	10.059	9.372	8.756	8.201
19	17.226	15.678	14.324	13.134	12.085	11.158	10.336	9.604	8.950	8.365
20	18.046	16.351	14.877	13.590	12.462	11.470	10.594	9.818	9.129	8.514
25	22.024	19.523	17.413	15.622	14.094	12.783	11.654	10.675	9.823	9.077
30	25.808	22.396	19.600	17.292	15.372	13.765	12.409	11.258	10.274	9.427
40	32.835	27.356	23.115	19.793	17.159	15.046	13.332	11.925	10.757	9.779

continues

Table A.4 continued

Periods	11%	12%	13%	14%	15%	16%	17%	18%	19%	20%
1	.901	.893	.885	.877	.870	.862	.855	.847	.840	.833
2	1.713	1.690	1.668	1.647	1.626	1.605	1.585	1.566	1.547	1.528
3	2.444	2.402	2.361	2.322	2.283	2.246	2.210	2.174	2.140	2.106
4	3.102	3.037	2.974	2.914	2.855	2.798	2.743	2.690	2.639	2.589
5	3.696	3.605	3.517	3.433	3.352	3.274	3.199	3.127	3.058	2.991
6	4.231	4.111	3.998	3.889	3.784	3.685	3.589	3.498	3.410	3.326
7	4.712	4.564	4.423	4.288	4.160	4.039	3.922	3.812	3.706	3.605
8	5.146	4.968	4.799	4.639	4.487	4.344	4.207	4.078	3.954	3.837
9	5.537	5.328	5.132	4.946	4.772	4.607	4.451	4.303	4.163	4.031
10	5.889	5.650	5.426	5.216	5.019	4.833	4.659	4.494	4.339	4.192
11	6.207	5.938	5.687	5.453	5.234	5.029	4.836	4.656	4.486	4.327
12	6.492	6.194	5.918	5.660	5.421	5.197	4.988	4.793	4.611	4.439
13	6.750	6.424	6.122	5.842	5.583	5.342	5.118	4.910	4.715	4.533
14	6.982	6.628	6.302	6.002	5.724	5.468	5.229	5.008	4.802	4.611
15	7.191	6.811	6.462	6.142	5.847	5.575	5.324	5.092	4.876	4.675
16	7.379	6.974	6.604	6.265	5.954	5.669	5.405	5.162	4.938	4.730
17	7.549	7.120	6.729	6.373	6.047	5.749	5.475	5.222	4.990	4.775
18	7.702	7.250	6.840	6.467	6.128	5.818	5.534	5.273	5.033	4.812
19	7.839	7.366	6.938	6.550	6.198	5.877	5.584	5.316	5.070	4.843
20	7.963	7.469	7.025	6.623	6.259	5.929	5.628	5.353	5.101	4.870
25	8.422	7.843	7.330	6.873	6.464	6.097	5.766	5.467	5.195	4.948
30	8.694	8.055	7.496	7.003	6.566	6.177	5.829	5.517	5.235	4.979
40	8.951	8.244	7.634	7.105	6.642	6.233	5.871	5.548	5.258	4.997

continues

Table A.4 continued

Periods	21%	22%	23%	24%	25%	26%	27%	28%	29%	30%
1	.826	.820	.813	.806	.800	.794	.787	.781	.755	.769
2	1.509	1.492	1.474	1.457	1.440	1.424	1.407	1.392	1.376	1.361
3	2.074	2.042	2.011	1.981	1.952	1.923	1.896	1.868	1.842	1.816
4	2.540	2.494	2.448	2.404	2.362	2.320	2.280	2.241	2.203	2.166
5	2.926	2.864	2.803	2.745	2.689	2.635	2.583	2.532	2.483	2.436
6	3.245	3.167	3.092	3.020	2.951	2.885	2.821	2.759	2.700	2.643
7	3.508	3.416	3.327	3.242	3.161	3.083	3.009	2.937	2.868	2.802
8	3.726	3.619	3.518	3.421	3.329	3.241	3.156	3.076	2.999	2.925
9	3.905	3.786	3.673	3.566	3.463	3.366	3.273	3.184	3.100	3.019
10	4.054	3.923	3.799	3.682	3.571	3.465	3.364	3.269	3.178	3.092
11	4.177	4.035	3.902	3.776	3.656	3.543	3.437	3.335	3.239	3.147
12	4.278	4.127	3.985	3.851	3.725	3.606	3.493	3.387	3.286	3.190
13	4.362	4.203	4.053	3.912	3.780	3.656	3.538	3.427	3.322	3.223
14	4.432	4.265	4.108	3.962	3.824	3.695	3.573	3.459	3.351	3.249
15	4.489	4.315	4.153	4.001	3.859	3.726	3.601	3.483	3.373	3.268
16	4.536	4.357	4.189	4.033	3.887	3.751	3.623	3.503	3.390	3.283
17	4.576	4.391	4.219	4.059	3.910	3.771	3.640	3.518	3.403	3.295
18	4.608	4.419	4.243	4.080	3.928	3.786	3.654	3.529	3.413	3.304
19	4.635	4.442	4.263	4.097	3.942	3.799	3.664	3.539	3.421	3.311
20	4.657	4.460	4.279	4.110	3.954	3.808	3.673	3.546	3.427	3.316
25	4.721	4.514	4.323	4.147	3.985	3.834	3.694	3.564	3.442	3.329
30	4.746	4.534	4.339	4.160	3.995	3.842	3.701	3.569	3.447	3.332
40	4.760	4.544	4.347	4.166	3.999	3.846	3.703	3.571	3.448	3.333

GLOSSARY

abnormal item an expense or revenue which, although relating to the ordinary operations of a business, is considered abnormal by reason of its size and effect on the results of the period

account a record of movements in the level of an individual element. *See also* elements of financial statements

accounting 'the language of business', having monetary measurement as its most distinguishing feature

accounting controls those controls intended to ensure that the accounting records and hence reports are reliable and to prevent the organisation's assets from being lost or misappropriated

accounting entity an area of activity in which users of accounting information are interested. Includes individuals, companies, company branch offices, professional practices, clubs, government departments and small business enterprises, not necessarily legal entities. *See also* entity

accounting equation the equating of a firm's assets with the claims on the assets:
assets = liabilities + proprietorship
assets = equities

accounting period assumption the assumption that the life of an entity can be broken into periods for the purpose of providing timely information on the entity's performance and financial position

accounting rate of return the accounting measure of income divided by an accounting measure of investment

accounting reports the outputs of accounting and the prime communication tools of accountants

accounting standard a technical document issued by an accounting standard setting body regulating some aspect of financial measurement and/or disclosure in financial reports. *See also* international accounting standards

accounts payable amounts owing to other entities, usually for inventory or other supplies. *See also* creditors

accounts receivable amounts owing from other entities, usually as a result of sales made on credit terms. *See also* debtors

accrual revenue earned or expense incurred before the associated cash flow occurs

accrual accounting the basis of accrual accounting is the recognition of transactions and other events as goods and services provided or consumed during an accounting period rather than when a flow of cash occurs. Revenues and expenses are recognised in the period in which they relate rather than when cash is transferred to or from the entity

accrual reporting incorporates the results of both external cash and credit transactions and other internal adjustments necessary to measure profit for the accounting period

accrued expense an expense incurred but unpaid at balance date

accrued revenue revenue recognised on work completed but not yet billed. *See also* unbilled revenue

accumulated depreciation the total of depreciation expense charged against revenues since the asset was acquired. It is shown in the balance sheet as a deduction from the asset to which it relates

accumulated surplus or deficit *see* retained profits (or loss)

activity-based budget a budget prepared by the application of activity-based costing principles

activity-based costing (ABC) a system of cost accounting whereby the costs of a product (i.e. goods or services) are developed from the costs of the activities required to produce the good or provide the service. It may also be used to trace costs to cost objects other than products

activity-based management management decision making influenced by activity analyses

administrative control consists of all those controls in the organisation designed to promote efficient operations and to encourage the following of the policies of the organisation

ageing analysis an analysis of the age of outstanding accounts receivable, usually by months since the credit was provided, prepared for credit control and also to calculate a more appropriate balance for the provision or allowance for bad and doubtful debts: different probabilities of default are applied to debts that have been outstanding for different lengths of time

allotment of shares the decision to allocate shares in a company to an applicant. Sometimes a sum of money becomes payable by the applicant at this time ('allotment money')

allowance for doubtful debts a contra or negative asset account arising from debts on which it is considered that a loss will be incurred through payment not being received in full. The contra account is shown as a deduction from the debtors (accounts receivable) in the balance sheet

amortisation a term used to describe the depreciation of intangible assets

annual budget master budget prepared for a 12-month period

applied overhead overhead costs applied (assigned or allocated) to products, jobs or projects on the basis of a predetermined formula rate

assets economic resources controlled by the entity for the purpose of providing future benefits to that entity

assumption statements accepted for a particular situation, as self-evident facts but may be changed for another situation

Australian Accounting Research Foundation the primary function of the AARF is to act as a secretariat to the Australian Accounting Standards Board (AASB), the Public Sector Accounting Standards Board (PSASB) and other boards. The AARF is currently funded primarily by the Australian Society of Certified Practising Accountants and the Institute of Chartered Accountants in Australia

Australian Accounting Standards Board consists of 11 members drawn from a wide spectrum of the community, including business, industry, accounting practice and academia. The Board has authority under the Australian Securities Commission Act (1989) to issue legally binding accounting standards on Australian listed companies. *See also* accounting standards

auditing the process of checking and verifying accounting entries and procedures

bad debt an amount owing by a specific debtor that the entity has determined will not be paid

balance day adjustments adjusting a business's records where revenues and expenses have been either overstated or understated for a period

balance sheet or statement of financial position, reports the resources of value controlled by the enterprise and the claims of owners and non-owners to those resources as at a given date

balancing an account the difference between the debit and credit sides of a ledger account is recorded in the account which is totalled and this balance is carried forward to future periods

bonus shares an issue of shares to an existing shareholder without cash being paid. Usually based on reserves held by the company

book entry an internal transaction, one that does not affect an external party, e.g. depreciation

book value the net amount reported for an asset; the cost of a non-current (fixed) asset less accumulated depreciation. *See also* net book value

break-even point the level of sales at which total revenue equals total cost and profit is zero

budget resource usage plan for the attainment of preset objectives

business risk the variability of returns from a business as a result of the type of industry it is involved in, its products or services and the type of investments it makes

business unit a segment of the organisation that can be compared to an external business as it undertakes its own research and development, production, marketing and sales. It has a high level of autonomy and often has 'division' in its name

capital budgeting the process of planning, evaluating and deciding on investments in long-term projects and their financing

capital maintenance ensuring that the level of owners' equity at the beginning of a period (however measured) is maintained at the end of the period, before recognising and profit

capital structure the mix of owners' equity and liabilities adopted in financing the entity's total assets

capital works grant a grant from the government to a public sector entity for works of a permanent nature

cash flow statement reports the effects of all transactions involving a flow of cash into or out of the entity, whether those transactions are operational, financial or investment in nature

cash reporting incorporates the results of only external cash transactions to measure cash surplus or deficit for the accounting period

chart of accounts a classification system for the individual accounts in the general ledger

closing entries the transfer of revenue and expense accounts to a summary account at the end of an accounting period or transferring profit or loss and drawings to the capital account

committed costs costs that an organisation is 'locked into' in the short run as a consequence of (a) past decisions such as the acquisition of non-current assets or entering into a long-term contract for services or (b) statutory charges such as rates

company a legal entity authorised by the Corporations Law to operate under the entity's charter and rules that are provided by its company constitution. *See also* proprietary companies, public companies

comparability accounting information should be comparable from business to business and a single business's statements must be comparable from one period to the next

conceptual framework a coherent body of theory or interrelated set of concepts which defines the nature, scope and purpose of financial accounting and reporting

contingent liability an obligation that will occur in the future only if some particular even occurs

continuity assumption the assumption that the entity's life continues beyond the current accounting period into the future

contra accounts an account linked to an original account, which is logically subtracted from that original account and has a balance of the opposite sign. For example:

- accumulated depreciation (CR) and (depreciable) assets (DR)
- provision or allowance for bad and doubtful debts (CR) and accounts receivable (DR)
- sales returns (DR) and sales revenue (CR)
- purchase returns (CR) and purchases (DR)

contribution margin sales revenue minus variable costs (may be expressed as total or per unit of activity)

contribution margin ratio the contribution margin divided by sales price

controllable cost the costs of a responsibility centre that can be changed, influenced or affected by the manager of the centre within that manager's sphere of responsibility

Corporations Law the Corporations Law is a statute passed by federal parliament, and is the highest level of regulatory authority over companies in Australia. The Corporations Law details numerous regulations relevant to the formation, conduct, administration and winding up of companies

costs economic resources consumed in selling goods or providing services

cost allocation the process of identifying, tracing or assigning costs to cost objects such as products, services, activities or organisational units

cost centre an organisational unit (e.g. department) for which the unit manager is held responsible for the costs of the unit only

cost driver a factor that causes a change in the total cost of a cost object

cost object any organisational activity, unit or item for which a separate measure of cost is determined (e.g. product, service, department, sales territory, operational activity)

cost of capital *see* required rate of return

cost of goods sold an expense account including all costs related to getting the goods into a condition and location for sale

cost of goods manufactured the cost incurred in producing the goods that were finished in the accounting period

cost-volume-profit analysis a technique used to predict the effect on profit of changes in critical cost and revenue variables

credit an entry in a ledger which shows an increase in a liability revenue or proprietorship, or a decrease in an asset or expense account; the allowance made to a purchaser to take possession of goods or services and make payment at a later date

creditors *see* accounts payable

current asset assets that are intended to be converted to cash or consumed within the next financial year (i.e. within 12 months)

current liability liabilities that must be discharged within 12 months

debentures financial instruments offered to the public or to financial institutions in exchange for loans of large amounts of money for a number of years and secured by a fixed or floating charge over the company's assets. The issue of debentures must be accompanied by a prospectus

debit an entry in a ledger account which shows an increase in an asset or expense account or a decrease in a liability, proprietorship or revenue

debtors *see* accounts receivable

decentralisation the process of devolving decision-making authority and autonomy to managers at lower levels in the organisational hierarchy

decision a choice between alternatives

deductive an approach which begins with a general statement and moves, by means of logical argument, to more specific statements

deferred shares similar to ordinary shares except that the entitlement to dividends is delayed for a specified period

deficit *see* loss

depreciation the process of allocating the estimated cost of a wasting non-current asset as an expense over the asset's useful life

deprival valuation stating assets at their current replacement cost

development involves putting the positive result of research into practice, which includes designing and testing product alternatives and constructing and operating pilot plans

differential costs costs that differ between decision alternatives

direct cost a cost item that can be identified with or traced to a cost object in an economically feasible manner

discounted cash flow (DCF) a technique that allows cash inflows and outflows to be received or paid in future years to be restated in comparable present value terms by discounting them to take account of the time value of money

discount rate *see* required rate of return

discretionary cost a cost that does not have a simple cause-and-effect relationship with the level of activity but is determined by a management decision to incur a particular cost for a particular purpose

dividend a distribution of profits to the shareholders of a company, or a share of profits payable to the Consolidated Fund by government commercial services, businesses and enterprises

double-entry recording the system of recording where a debit entry is matched by a corresponding credit entry. Total debit entries must equal total credit entries

doubtful debts an amount of total accounts receivable that is estimated to be unlikely to be collected

drawings *see* withdrawals

dysfunctional behaviour decisions made that are contrary to the best interests of the organisation

effectiveness the success with which an output or objective is achieved, irrespective of the inputs or effort required to achieve the output or objective

efficiency the ability to achieve a given output or objective with minimum inputs or effort

elements of financial statements the components of financial statements—assets, liabilities, equity, revenue and expense

engineered cost has a clear, measurable relationship with its cost driver

entity *see* accounting entity, legal entity

executory contract one in which the performance depends on some future action by both parties to the contract

expense an economic resource consumed in the process of generating revenue or in the process of providing services for which revenue has been granted

expense centre *see* cost centre

external transaction a transaction between the entity and another entity

extraordinary items those items of revenue and expenses not relating to the ordinary operations of the entity and which are of a non-recurring nature

financial lease a lease that is accounted for in the financial records by recognising both the asset associated with the right to use the leased property and the liability to make lease payments, which is the most appropriate accounting treatment for non-cancellable, medium- to long-term leases

financial management the process of planning, controlling and evaluating financial decisions in order to achieve the financial objectives of the organisation

financial ratio analysis involves taking two significant figures from the financial statements and expressing their relationship in terms of a ratio or percentage

financial risk the variability of returns from a business as a result of the mix of finance used to fund investments

financing activities those that relate to changes in the debt (excluding those arising from purchases stated under operating activities) and owners additions or withdrawals of equity. Examples of cash flows relating to financing activities would include inflows such as additional long-term borrowings or cash contributions by the owner. Cash outflows could include repayment of long-term debt and cash withdrawals by the owners. Note interest paid on loans is classified as a cash outflow from operating activities

fixed cost a cost that does not change in total amount with changes in the level of activity within the relevant range

freight inwards cartage costs on the acquisition of stock

full cost the cost of a cost object comprising both direct costs and allocation of indirect costs

functional classification grouping of expenses according to the purpose/role of the expenditure by the business, e.g. selling, administrative and finance expenses. Expenses are classified according to the purpose for which they were incurred

functional unit a segment of the organisation that is responsible for performing one function. It often has 'department' in its title and may provide services to other parts of the organisation

gearing *see* leverage

general journal a book of originating entry which records transactions not recorded in special journals. Also records adjusting, closing and reversing entries. *See* journal

general purpose financial reports reports designed to meet the information needs of a wide range of users who are unable to command (demand) the preparation of reports to satisfy their individual specific information needs

general reserve tax-paid profits separately set aside in the entity's accounts and designated for general purposes

goal congruency achieved when all decision making is consistent with the attainment of the stated goals of the organisation

goals long-term general outcomes of operations towards which the organisation strives

goodwill comprises future benefits from unidentifiable assets which because of their nature are not normally recorded individually in the accounts.

gross profit the difference between net sales and cost of good sold

group control the regulation of the behaviour of a member of a social or work group by peer group pressure

harmonisation of accounting standards harmonisation entails developing an internationally compatible set of accounting standards that every country can adopt

heritage assets include museums, art collections, historical documents and artefacts, monuments, landmarks and other priceless treasures, which are held in public ownership for the community as a whole

high-low approach a method of estimating the variable/fixed cost function of a cost item based on the highest and lowest values of the cost item and the activity levels at which the highest and lowest values were recorded

historical cost the figures stated in financial statements are obtained from the historical set of transactions engaged in by the business, i.e. valuation is at original cost

income statement *see* profit and loss statement

incremental budgeting the formulation of a budget based on the previous period's budget, making adjustments up or down at the margin to take account of known or anticipated changes in factor costs or circumstances

incremental cost the difference between the total cost of two decision alternatives. *See also* marginal cost, differential cost

indirect cost a cost item that cannot be identified with or traced to a cost object in an economically feasible manner. *See also* overhead cost

inductive an approach which begins with very specific and detailed statements and moves, by means of logical argument, to a general statement

intangible assets assets without physical existence, e.g. goodwill, patents and licenses

interim reports regular, short-term reports on cash, inventory profit, and the like prepared during an accounting period

internal control comprises the coordinated methods and measures adopted within a business to safeguard its assets, check the accuracy and reliability of its accounting data, promote operational efficiency and encourage adherence to prescribed managerial policies

internal rate of return (IRR) a method of evaluating capital investment projects based on determining the discount rate that equates the present value of cash inflows generated by a capital investment project with the present value of the cash outflows, and comparing the determined rate with the required rate of return

internal transaction a transaction that does not involve another entity

international accounting standards accounting standards issued by the International Accounting Standards Committee (IASC) based in London. International accounting standards (IAS) have been developed in an effort to reduce international financial reporting diversity

inventory supplies of items for sale or use in production. *See also* merchandise, stock

inventory accounting keeping records of the goods on hand available for sale (i.e. inventory) and of the goods that have been sold (i.e. cost of goods sold expense)

inventory shortage (gain) an adjustment to the stock control account where a physical stocktake differs from the calculated balance on the account

investment activities those which relate to the acquisition and disposal of non-current assets of a productive nature and to investments such as shares and debentures in other entities which are not defined as cash equivalents. Cash flows from (and to) investment activities relate to those activities stated above

job cost sheet the source document to record costs associated with a particular job or project

journal a record of all transactions affecting the entity in chronological order. These transactions are subsequently 'posted' to ledger accounts

ledger a collection of accounts. *See also* general ledger

legal entity a body recognised in law as having a separate identity, which entitles it to act in its own right, including contracting itself into debt, being able to be sued and ordered to pay damages, and taking legal action against another legal entity. *See also* accounting entity

leverage the use of debt in financing investments of the firm (also referred to as gearing)

liability an obligation to sacrifice economic resources

limited liability the shareholder, or club member, is not liable to contribute any more than agreed to when joining a club or purchasing a share

loss the result of operations for a period when expenses exceed revenue. *See also* deficit

management risk the variability of returns from a business as a result of the quality and effectiveness of its management

marginal cost *see* incremental cost

master budget full collection of budgets for the coming financial year

matching principle requires that resources consumed in earning revenue for the period be 'matched' against the revenue in determining profit or surplus for a period

materiality that test which is used to assess the extent to which relevant and reliable information may be omitted, misstated or not disclosed separately without having the potential to adversely affect the decisions about resource allocations by users

merchandise *see* inventory

mortgage loan a loan from another legal entity, whereby money is borrowed and property (such as land, buildings and equipment) is pledged in return as security for the loan

net book value the original (historical cost) value of an asset less any accumulated depreciation

net income *see* net profit

net present value method (NPV) a method of evaluating capital investment projects based on calculating the difference between the present value of the cash inflows and cash outflows associated with a project

net profit the net increases in earned resources of the entity. Combining revenue and expenses in the profit and loss statement results in the display of net profit

non-current asset an asset that is intended to be held for continuing use rather than exchange

non-current liability a liability that will mature at times beyond the next 12 months, including long-term borrowings, debentures and mortgages

non-wasting asset an asset whose benefits do not expire as it is used (e.g. land, artworks)

neutrality implies that financial information should be free from bias

objectives short-term specific outcomes towards which the organisation, organisational unit or manager strives

opening balance the balance in a ledger account at the beginning of a period

operating activities are those activities which relate to the ongoing provision of goods and services. The operating activities are typically shown in the profit and loss statement. The cash flows which are generated from operating activities include receipts from customers (sale of goods); cash payments to suppliers for services (wages and salaries); cash payments for other operating expenses (rents and insurances), cash revenue for interest and dividends received

operating items operating revenue and expenses arise from an entity's ordinary operations. Ordinary operations are regarded as those activities that are carried on regularly from one period to the next to achieve the objectives of the entity

operating lease a lease that is accounted for by recognising the lease payments as expenses only during the periods in which they are paid. No record is kept of the leased asset or the lease liability in the financial statements. Most appropriate for short-term cancellable leases

operating plans activity and resource requirements necessary to achieve set objectives

operating profit the difference between the firm's operating revenue and its operating expenses

operating statement *see* profit and loss statement

opportunity cost the contribution forgone from the next best alternative by devoting scarce resources to a particular alternative

ordinary shares the usual type of shares issued by a company, having full voting rights at ordinary or special meetings of shareholders and with no fixed dividend entitlement. *See also* shares

overapplied overhead the amount by which the overhead applied to jobs or projects during the period exceeds the actual overhead costs incurred

overdraft a bank account that can be 'overdrawn' up to an agreed amount (a bank loan)

overhead costs *see* indirect costs

owners' equity owners' interest in the entity or owners' claim on the entity. *See also* capital

paid-up capital the amount by which a company's issued capital has been paid

par value the face value of the share when the company is registered, where the total registered or authorised capital of the company equals the par value of its shares multiplied by the number of shares. Par value has been abolished by the Company Law Review Act

partnership the relation that exists between persons carrying on a business in common with a view to profit. Each of the partners is under a joint and several liability for all debts of the partnership. If bankruptcy occurs, the creditors of the partnership may lay claim to the personal assets of the partners

payback method a method of evaluating capital investment projects based on calculating the time period required for the net cash inflows associated with a project to recoup the initial investment

periodic inventory method a method of recording transactions involving stock, where stock purchased is recorded in an expense account. The cost of each sale is not recorded at the time of sale but derived at the end of the period; using a physical stocktake

perpetual inventory method a method of recording transactions involving stock where stock movements are shown in the stock control account asset (at cost price)

post-implementation audit an evaluation 6–12 months after the completion of a project implementation to assess the accuracy of all data used in pre-implementation analyses, whether what was implemented meets requirements, or whether improvement is possible in both what was implemented and in future project evaluations

preference shares a separate class of shares from ordinary shares, usually carrying a fixed rate of dividend, which may be cumulative if unpaid in the past. Preference shareholders have priority over ordinary shareholders for payment of dividends and repayment of capital in the event of liquidation and they usually carry no voting rights

prepayment cash flow occurs before revenue is earned or expense incurred

present value the comparable present value of a future cash flow determined by taking account of the time value of money

principle in relation to a framework for design, statements which are logical arguments from the assumptions on which they are based, i.e. IF (a certain assumption), THEN (a certain principle follows)

production budget the production plan for the budget period such that sales and inventory requirements will be met

production units depreciation a method of calculating depreciation based on an asset's pattern of use

profit *see* net profit

profit and loss appropriation statement *see* retained profit or loss

profit and loss statement a statement to determine net profit/loss or surplus/deficit by subtracting expenses from revenue for the period. *See also* operating statement, statement of surplus or deficit, income statement

profit and loss statement or operating statement reports as profit (or loss) the difference between the revenue earned and the expenses incurred during a given period

profit centre an organisational unit (e.g. a department) for which the unit manager is held responsible for the costs and revenues of the unit

proprietary companies these are generally small, privately owned companies. There may be one but no more than 50 owners. Transfer of ownership shares is generally restricted and cannot advertise directly to the public for funding, either via share capital or loans

prospectus an accompaniment to an offer by a company to the public to subscribe to an issue of shares or debentures, designed to inform potential subscribers about the financial position and activities of the company and the reason for the current issue

public companies a legally incorporated entity having at least five shareholders, but no restriction on the maximum number of shareholders. Public companies can advertise directly to the public for funding, whether via issues of share capital or loan capital

public sector refers to federal and state governments, local councils and all associated structures that they own or control such as departments, statutory authorities, boards and commissions

Public Sector Accounting Standards Board (PSASB) created by the Australian Accounting Research Foundation (AARF). Under the AARF's constitution, the PSASB has responsibilities for developing accounting standards (known as AAS standards) for the public sector and not-for-profit entities in the private sector. In contrast to AASB standards, AAS standards are generally not legally enforceable on public sector entities

purchase returns and allowances reductions in the invoiced price of goods purchased are usually given because goods have been returned by the buyer. The buyer receives a credit note. The reductions are usually accumulated by the buyer in a temporary expense contra account called purchases returns and allowances

realisation the conversion of an asset into cash or a claim to cash

recognition criteria the criteria set down in conceptual frameworks (such as the IASC *Framework*) determining when an asset, liability, revenue or expense should be brought to account or reported in the financial statements

recoverable amount in relation to an asset, the net amount that is expected to be recovered through the cash inflows and outflows arising from its continued use and subsequent disposal

recurrent grant a regular grant from the government to a public sector entity to enable its operating activities to occur. It is treated as revenue

reducing balance depreciation a method of calculating depreciation based on book value

registered capital the total of capital a company is authorised to raise, by issuing a stated number of shares (ordinary, preference or deferred) at their par value. Abolished by the Company Law Review Act

regression analysis a statistical method used to show the relationship between variables, e.g. to estimate the variable and fixed behavioural functions of cost items

relevant costs future costs that differ between decision alternatives

relevant information information has the quality of relevance when it influences, or has the capacity to influence, the economic decisions of users by helping them evaluate past, present or future events, or by confirming or correcting their past evaluations

relevant range the range of activity over which the specific function of the behaviour of a cost item remains valid

reliability information has the quality of reliability when it is free from material error and bias and can be depended on by users to represent faithfully that which it purports to represent

reporting entity an entity which is required to prepare general purpose financial reports and comply with accounting standards

required rate of return the minimum rate of return from a capital investment project deemed acceptable. *See also* discount rate, cost of capital

research involves the search for new knowledge that might lead to the development of a new product or process or that will significantly improve existing products or processes

reserves part of the proprietorship of a company but not part of paid-up capital. Revenue reserves result from the retention of profits while capital reserves result from the issue of shares at a premium and from the revaluation of assets

residual value *see* scrap value

responsibility accounting a system whereby the managers of organisational units are held responsible or accountable for the activities, operations and performance of their units

responsibility centre an organisational unit for which the unit manager is held responsible or accountable

retained profit or loss an account that represents the owners' claims on the entity's assets that result from profits that have not been paid out previously to owners in the form of dividends

return on investment (ROI) profit divided by investment

revaluation (of assets) revaluation relates to the process of restating non-current assets in the financial statements to some market appraised value. Increments above the original book value or carrying amount of non-current assets is credited to an asset revaluation reserve, which is displayed under owners' equity

revenue cash or claims to cash earned through provision of goods or services to customers, or grants from government to enable entity to supply services

revenue receivable a revenue earned but cash not received by balance date. *See also* accrued revenue

revenue centre an organisational unit (e.g. a department) for which the unit manager is held responsible for the revenues generated by the unit and the internal costs of the unit, but the revenue and costs cannot be compared to assess profit generation success

risk the degree of variability of returns from an investment

sales returns and allowances reductions in the invoiced price of goods sold are usually given because goods have been returned to the seller. The reductions are given by the seller by issuing a credit note. The reductions are usually accumulated by the seller in a temporary revenue contra account called sales returns and allowances (returns inwards)

scrap value the value of an asset when it is sold after being used by the entity for its useful life. *See also* residual value

segment reports usually disclose the sales, segment result and segment assets for each identifiable segment

self control the personal direction of energies to the task at hand in the absence of interaction with or pressure from others

semi-variable cost a cost item that comprises elements of both fixed and variable cost behaviour

share a specified amount of the capital of a company is represented by a share, which may also bear the right to vote at shareholder meetings and receive dividends. *See also* ordinary shares, preference shares, deferred shares

share premium the amount by which the dollar amount, at which the share is issued, exceeds the par value of the share. Such amounts are recorded in a share premium account. Abolished by the Company Law Review Act

social control *see* group control

sole proprietorship a business enterprise in which all the resources and debts belong to one individual

source documents documents which provide original evidence of a transaction, e.g. involves invoices, receipts, cheque butts

special purpose financial reports prepared for users who are able to command reports tailored specifically to suit their purposes and which are prepared according to agreed time-lines or on demand

standard costs predetermined costs of direct materials and direct labour based on present efficiency targets of acquisition and use and usually expressed as a per unit of output

statement of cash flows a report which summarises the cash movements for a period and also indicates the cash balance at the end of the period

statement of receipts and payments the statement which shows the inflows and outflows of cash and the change to the opening cash balance

statement of surplus or deficit *see* profit and loss statement

stewardship the responsibility given to some else (managers) by the owners of property to protect and utilise the assets for the owners' benefit

stock *see* inventory

stock exchange in Australia the Australian Stock Exchange (ASX) is a not-for profit, private sector body comprising over 100 stockbroker corporations and partnerships. The conduct of the ASX is governed by the Corporations Law

straight-line depreciation a method of allocating the cost of a depreciable asset by charging equal amounts of the asset's use to each period

strategic plan long-term plans made to achieve goals

substance over form this implies that transactions should be presented in accordance with their substance and economic reality and not merely their legal form

sundry creditors these are liabilities for various payments outstanding and are usually recognised at the end of the accounting period. They are similar to accounts payable

sunk costs costs that have been incurred or committed in the past and which cannot be changed by future decisions

surplus *see* net profit

SWOT analysis appraisal of internal strengths and weaknesses and external opportunities and threats

system a series of steps or procedures to be carried out in a particular sequence in order to achieve a desired objective

time value of money a cash sum available at the present time is worth more than an equivalent sum available at a future date because of the ability to invest and earn interest on the immediately available sum. May also be expressed as the preference to receive money earlier rather than later and pay money later rather than earlier

trial balance a list of ledger account balances on a particular date to check the accuracy of the ledger recording

unappropriated profits *see* retained profit or loss

unbilled revenue *see* accrued revenue

underapplied overhead the amount by which the overhead applied to jobs or projects during the period is less than the actual overhead costs incurred

understandability that quality of financial information which exists when users of that information are able to comprehend its meaning

users (of financial reports) users of financial reports include investors, employees, lenders, suppliers and trade creditors, customers, governments and the public. Users rely on financial reports in order to make and evaluate economic decisions relating to the allocation of scarce resources

unsecured notes financial instruments similar to debentures, except that they are not secured and are often for shorter periods

value in exchange the value an item has for exchanging for cash, some other resource or for the cancellation of a debt. It is generally its market price

value in use the value an item has for being used to generate other resources which have either some value in exchange or value in use

variable cost a cost that varies proportionally with changes in the level of activity

wasting asset asset whose benefits expire over time and/or as it is used

withdrawals resources taken from the entity by the owner. *See also* drawings

working capital available short-term funding, approximating net current assets (i.e. current assets less current liabilities)

work-in-progress account the record of direct materials, direct labour and overhead costs incurred in producing goods or working on projects that are not yet completed

worksheet a multi-column recording device commonly used by accountants to gather and organise information for the preparation of financial statements

zero-based budgeting an approach to budgeting which stipulates that the costs associated with an ongoing project and activity need to be justified and approved at the beginning of each budgeting period as if the project or activity were being proposed for the first time

Index